EDMUND MORRIS was born in Kenya a[...] Wales School, Nairobi and Rhodes Univers[...] He worked as an advertising copywriter in [...]ing to the United States in 1968. His biography *The Rise of Theodore Roosevelt* won the Pulitzer Prize and American Book Award in 1980. In 1985 he was appointed Ronald Reagan's authorized biographer. He has written extensively on travel and the arts for such publications as the *New Yorker*, *New York Times* and *Harper's*, and is a music critic for the *Washington Post*. The second volume of his Roosevelt biography, *Theodore Rex,* is currently under way, and will be followed by a third. Edmund Morris lives in New York and Washington D.C. with his wife and fellow biographer, Sylvia Jukes Morris.

'*Dutch* has reaffirmed Morris's reputation as a gifted writer.... with an elegant postmodern literary style.' ALBERT SCARDINO, *New Statesman*

'Morris displays enviable, incisive writing skills.'

LIONEL BARBER, *Financial Times*

'A narrative whose abundance of colourful anecdotes leaves it in no need of artistic embellishment.... Even as his memory dissolves, Reagan is on the way to becoming one of the most remembered presidents in history; and Morris's book is certain to fuel the growing nostalgia for a figure who, while credited with precipitating the downfall of an 'evil empire' remains a delicious enigma.'

MATTHEW CAMPBELL, *Sunday Times*

'An unprecedented insight into the presidential life.' *Sunday Herald*

From the American reviews:

'As Morris accompanied the President to meetings in the Oval Office, summits with Mikhail Gorbachev and political events around America, he must have realized that his experience would give unusual depth and richness to his overall portrait of Reagan. Nor was he wrong.... [he] gets the Big Picture triumphantly right.' JOHN O'SULLIVAN, *National Review*

'Morris can write beautifully, especially when limning action or sense impressions; his account of the 1981 attempt on Reagan's life, for example, is a marvel of muscular description.' HENDRIK HERTZBERG, *New Yorker*

'The perspectives with regard to Reagan are neither damaged nor diminished by his technique. Indeed, they are enhanced.... The book is well-written, copiously documented, and a delight to read.'

THOMAS V. DIBACCO, *Orlando Sentinel*

'Morris is a master prose stylist and leaves the reader in awe of his powers.... *Dutch* is a major work, one that approaches Reagan's persona as closely as may be possible.' JAY STRAFFORD, *Richmond Times-Dispatch*

'*Dutch* contains astonishing observations and insights, wonderful stories and incomparable story-telling.' TERRY GOLWAY, *New York Observer*

'As you read on – and such is the force and fascination of Morris's narrative that you can't help reading on – you begin to see the benefits of his highly unorthodox technique.... I can think of few conventional political biographies that bring their subject's pasts so richly alive.'

CHRISTOPHER LEHMANN-HAUPT, *New York Times*

A Memoir of
Ronald Reagan

DUTCH

Edmund Morris

HarperCollins*Publishers*

Publisher's Note
This is an authorized biography and a work of extensive scholarship.
All the words (written or spoken) of Ronald Reagan, all his recounted thoughts and
acts, and indeed those of every historical character in the text, are matters of fact
and of record. Full documentation is available in the Notes, and the contributions
of other writers or interlocutors indicated under 'Acknowledgements'.

HarperCollins*Publishers*
77–85 Fulham Palace Road, Hammersmith, London W6 8JB

www.**fire**and**water**.com

This paperback edition 2000
1 3 5 7 9 8 6 4 2

First published in Great Britain by
HarperCollins*Publishers* 1999

Copyright © Edmund Morris 1999

Edmund Morris asserts the moral right to
be identified as the author of this work

ISBN 0 00 710262 3

Printed in Great Britain by Clays Ltd, St Ives plc

Portions of Chapter 7 and of the Epilogue appeared in different form in
The New Yorker. The central portion of Chapter 27 has been adapted from an
article in *Time*, 19 August 1996.

Grateful acknowledgement is made to the following for permission to
reprint previously published material:

Commentary: Excerpts from 'A Guide to Reagan Country,' by James Q. Wilson
(*Commentary*, May 1967), and excerpts from 'Bitburg: Who Forgot What,' by Midge
Decter (*Commentary*, August 1985). All rights reserved. Printed by permission.
Editions Gallimard: Eight lines from 'LiArtiste et son temps' (in French) from
Actuelles II: Chroniques 1948-1953 by Albert Camus. Copyright © Editions
Gallimard. Reprinted by permission.
Estate of James Baldwin: Excerpts from 'Notes for a Hypothetical Novel,' by James
Baldwin, collected in *Nobody Knows My Name*, published by Vintage Books.
Copyright © 1961 by James Baldwin. Copyright renewed. Used by arrangement
with the Estate of James Baldwin.
Penguin Putnam Inc.: Excerpt from *Where's the Rest of Me?*, by Ronald Reagan.
Copyright © 1965 by Ronald Reagan and Richard G. Hubler. Reprinted by
permission of Dutton, a division of Penguin Putnam Inc.
Simon and Schuster: Excerpts from *An American Life* by Ronald Reagan. Copyright
© 1990 by Ronald W. Reagan. Reprinted by permission of Simon and Schuster.
Warner Bros. And the Estate of Roy Chanslor: Excerpts from the script of the film
'Inside Story' (released under the title *Love is on the Air*), which was based on the
story 'Hi Nellie,' by Roy Chanslor. Used by permission of Warner Bros. and the
Estate of Roy Chanslor.
A.P. Watt Ltd. on behalf of Michael Yeats. Twelve lines from 'An Irish Airman
Foresees His Death,' by W. B. Yeats. Reprinted by permission of A.P. Watt Ltd.
on behalf of Michael Yeats.
A.P. Watt Ltd. on behalf of The National Trust: Eight lines from 'Cities, Thrones
and Powers,' by Rudyard Kipling. Reprinted by permission of A.P. Watt Ltd. on
behalf of The National Trust.

PUBLISHER'S NOTE

The publication of the original hardback edition of Edmund Morris's *Dutch: A Memoir of Ronald Reagan* in the fall of 1999 caused one of the biggest literary sensations in years. Even before *The New York Times,* in a front-page scoop, trumpeted advance details of its method, the book had become the subject of intense anticipation. Fourteen years in the making, it was the first biography ever authorized by a sitting President and, even more remarkably, had been written under conditions of complete interpretive freedom.

Little was known of Edmund Morris, whose Pulitzer Prize–winning biography *The Rise of Theodore Roosevelt* had attracted Ronald Reagan's attention in 1981, except that he was a naturalized American citizen, born in Kenya in 1940, and married to the biographer Sylvia Jukes Morris. It was assumed that Reagan had chosen Morris because of the liveliness and impressive scholarship of his Roosevelt volume, and because he was, like most immigrants, likely to be politically conservative.

The author himself had assured Random House in the fall of 1985 that he was a writer, not an ideologue. "I want to make literature out of

Ronald Reagan," he said, emphasizing that what drew him was the complexity of the President's character and the improbable—yet, in retrospect, logical—sequence of roles that Reagan had played to rise, in a long life, from provincial ordinariness to the height of world power.

Morris's statement was taken seriously by his editor, Robert Loomis. But until that ambition was finally realized, little inkling of *Dutch*'s revolutionary nature seeped outside of Random House. As the years passed, and no book appeared (it was originally scheduled for publication in 1991), speculations mounted that Morris was in biographical difficulty, and was thinking of abandoning his project. He admitted to a closed circle of fellow historians at the University of Virginia that Ronald Reagan posed a formidable challenge to scholarship:

> Ronald Reagan is a man of benign remoteness and no psychological curiosity, either about himself or others. He considers his life to have been unremarkable. He gives nothing of himself to intimates (if one can use such a noun in such a phrase), believing that he has no self to give. In the White House he wrote hundreds of personal letters, and obediently kept an eight-year diary, but the handwritten sentences, while graceful and grammatical (never an erasure, never a flaw of spelling or punctuation!), are about as revelatory of the man behind them as the calligraphy of a copyist.

This admission, unaccompanied by any hint that Morris had found a creative solution to the problem, leaked into the press and caused a flurry of comment. Particular attention was paid to a section of text Morris had shared with the historians, which compared Reagan's advance ("an ever-thrusting, ever-deepening mass of chill purpose") to that of a glacier:

> Possessed of no inner warmth, with no apparent interest save in its own growth, it directed itself toward whatever declivities lay in its path. Inevitably, as the glacier grew, it collected rocks before it, and used them to flatten obstructions; when the rocks were worn smooth they rode up onto the glacier's back, briefly enjoying high sunny views, then tumbled off to become part of the surrounding countryside. They lie where they fell, some cracked, some crumbled . . . lateral moraine. And the glacier sped slowly on.

The passage suggested to headline-writers that Morris—if he ever completed his book—was not likely to be as admiring a biographer as Reagan loyalists might wish. Yet Reagan himself sympathetically wrote the author, "Believe me, I understand a problem we both have. Our friends (???) in the media delight in giving our remarks a twist that changes the meaning to suit their prejudices."

More years passed. Only Loomis was privy to the fact that Morris had had an epiphany of sorts, almost literally stumbling on a new way to write biography. He had visited Reagan's alma mater, Eureka College, in the fall of 1992, regretting that he could not share the life of his subject, or at least have been able to witness the young "Dutch" Reagan walking those same lawns in the fall of 1928.

An acorn cracked under his shoe, Morris told Loomis, and at that moment he realized that he "had, in a sense, been there" in Reagan's freshman year. After years of interviews and close scrutiny of diaries, letters, and old photographs, all biographers become *doppelgängers* of their subjects, vicariously living the very lives they tell. Why not make himself an actual, if imaginary, character in the story—in order to bring an extra sharpness of observation to events unquestionably authentic? Simply put, why not write a "memoir" of Ronald Reagan?

"After all," Morris wrote, "I actually was the President's *doppelgänger* from November 1985, shortly before the Geneva summit. I shadowed him in the White House, followed him when he traveled, freely interviewed him, and have been given access to his papers and diaries."

This closeness, however, was preceded by seventy-four years during which the author was unavoidably not present at Reagan's side. Morris believed that such an imbalance of viewpoints was bound to cause interpretive problems.

> One might compare my task to that of a film editor who has to integrate a few hundred close-focus frames with twenty thousand feet of gauzy long shots. But biography is sometimes freer than film to rise to such challenges . . . *providing the end result is honest and fully documented.*
>
> Reagan considers his life (quite wrongly) to have been unremarkable. He gives nothing of himself in private, believing that he has no self to give.
>
> Any orthodox quest for the real "Dutch," then, is bound to be an exercise in frustration. Hence the dullness of so many of the books written about him, their inability to capture his peculiar magic. Since Reagan has been primarily a phenomenon of the American imagination—a mythical apotheosis of the best and the worst in us—he can be re-created only by an extension of biographical technique.

And so the voluminous manuscript of *Dutch: A Memoir of Ronald Reagan* began to pile up, chapter by chapter, in the editor's office. Seen by none except a few senior executives, and then only in part, it remained closely embargoed through 1998, when the author at last announced that it was ready for publication.

Random House duly put *Dutch* at the head of its fall list for that year, only to have Morris withdraw the manuscript for further rewriting.

Continuing rumors of writer's block belied pretty good evidence, in the author's own words, that he was increasingly inspired by the professed "glacier" of yesteryear. Morris, relaxing his code of silence, had published two Reagan-related essays in *The New Yorker* that in turn reported on the former President's submission to Alzheimer's disease and the efforts of the Ronald Reagan Library to "edit" his life story. Seen in retrospect, these articles, and a third, humorous one in *Forbes FYI* on the longueurs of biographical research, amounted to advance notices that *Dutch,* when it at last appeared, would be an unusual book—scholarly, affectionate, yet uncompromisingly frank.

————

Dutch: A Memoir of Ronald Reagan was again announced for publication on September 30, 1999. But the expectations of fourteen years, plus the provocation of the embargo, proved too much for reporters. Doreen Carvajal of *The New York Times* managed to glimpse enough of the book's text to print the following bombshell on September 18, headlined WRITER AS CHARACTER IN REAGAN BIOGRAPHY.

> [*Dutch*] is days away from publication. . . . But in the meantime its publisher, Random House, is guarding copies zealously, partly for fear of a controversy about Mr. Morris's writing style, which employs an unconventional technique that disturbs historians and former Reagan officials who have heard about it.
>
> Simply put, Mr. Morris has invented a character: himself. For literary purposes, the author, 59, has essentially transformed his own life . . . revised his age, birthplace, identity and résumé to become a Zeligesque narrator who is a Reagan contemporary, glimpsing the future President on a Dixon High School football field; bumping into him beneath the elms of his Illinois alma mater, Eureka College; reporting for duty to Lieutenant Reagan at the Army Air Force's first motion picture unit.

Ms. Carvajal went on to quote the reactions, pro and con, of professional historians, from the "I think it will create . . . surprise and some chagrin" of Alan Brinkley at Columbia University to the "It is no different from the practice of those biographers who purport to see the world from the perspective of their subjects" of Stanford University's Hayden White. Over the next ten days—a period in which Random House managed to keep all but a handful of copies from being begged, borrowed, or stolen by newshounds—*Dutch* became the number one subject of cultural conversation on both sides of the Atlantic. "I thought this was pretty smart," Victoria Glendinning remarked on BBC *Newsnight,* and she praised the book's "real scholarship."

Richard Holmes, sitting next to her, agreed. "Morris is a serious biographer. The references are very exact. . . . The material, the quotes, are perfectly genuine. I think the importance of fact, of hard fact, in the end is absolutely crucial, but you *need* this play of ideas, this play of form."

In the United States, initial comments were much more negative. Even before *Newsweek* ran its advance excerpts on September 27, the television talk shows were dominated by outraged Reaganauts complaining that Morris had written a snobbish and untrustworthy portrait of one of the great Presidents in history. They particularly protested his reported conclusion that Reagan was "an airhead" (for the actual passage, see p. 579), and that the assassination attempt of March 30, 1981, had had a permanent, debilitating effect. Their choler was in no way moderated when four of Reagan's former aides—Michael Deaver, Edwin Meese III, David Gergen, and Lyn Nofziger—admitted, even as they attacked the book on *Larry King Live,* that none had actually read it yet.

The syndicated columnists Maureen Dowd and George Will, also showing scant acquaintance with the text, weighed in with vituperative advance notices, respectively accusing Morris of being "barking mad" in the use of his autobiographical device, and "dishonorable" in alleged manipulation of historical facts. Some of Will's accusations were particularly damaging:

The conversation in the green tunic [with Dr. John Hutton, about Reagan's 1985 colonoscopy] is make-believe. . . . Conscious distortion in history is necessarily dishonest. Morris's majoritarian epistemology [*sic*] is a license to fabricate, and an invitation to the sort of self-glorification Morris practices. . . . [He] enjoyed, to a degree unprecedented in the annals of presidential biographies, the cooperation—access to the subject and his papers—implicit in an agreement to write an authorized biography, meaning not an uncritical study but one given every opportunity for an accurate rendering of reality. What he produced is an act of bad faith.

With several hundred thousand copies of *Dutch* waiting to be un-
boxed in bookstores across the country, and sixteen million television
viewers primed by *60 Minutes'* documentary, aired on September 26,
Random House braced for the influential first review on publication
day in *The New York Times*. Written by Christopher Lehmann-Haupt,
it proved to be an unqualified rave:

> As you read on—and such is the force and fascination of Mr. Mor-
> ris's narrative that you can't help reading on—you begin to see the
> benefits of his highly unorthodox technique. . . . Is *Dutch* then finally
> flawed by Mr. Morris's technique? To judge from the book's extensive
> notes, it in no way distorts the record of Mr. Reagan's life, only the
> viewpoint from which it is told. It's difficult to approve the technique
> in theory; in less skilled hands it will doubtless prove a disaster. But
> it certainly suceeds in this case.

Sanctioned thus by "the newspaper of record," and further promoted by saturation television coverage, *Dutch* made its debut at number two on the *New York Times* bestseller list after only three days of
sales. Edmund Morris appeared on the same talk shows as his early
critics and addressed their claims that he had perverted the standards
of honest biography. In an open letter to George Will, he further de-
fended the scholarship that underlies *Dutch*'s high style:

> Pages 537–538, drawn to your attention by Nancy Reagan, describe
> the colonoscopy that was conducted on the President in July 1985,
> climaxing in the shock discovery of a malignant tumor. The imagery
> of this passage derives directly from the eyewitness testimony of Dr.
> John Hutton, who later became the White House Physician, and who
> has for fourteen years been my most generous source of medical in-
> formation about Ronald Reagan. Verbally, on occasions without
> number, he has told me about the "white, necrotic ridge" that loomed
> up ahead of the scope, beyond an undulating, plain-like foreground.
> The quoted phrase also appears in Dr. Hutton's diary, which he al-
> lowed me to read *in toto,* during many days of research in his office at
> the Uniformed Services University of the Health Sciences in Bethesda,
> Maryland.
>   You accuse me of fabricating a conversation with Dr. Hutton in
> which, gesturing and grimacing in his green surgical tunic, he referred
> to this white ridge and dramatically compared it to his first view of the
> Rockies, on a flight across the Great Plains many years ago. I did not
> fabricate a word of this transcribed conversation, which is docu-

mented on page 818, along with references to other, almost identical interviews (Dr. Hutton tends to repeat himself), and the notes that you yourself mention. I am a close observer of visual detail, and every movement of the doctor's hands, as he described the advancing scope, is imprinted in my memory, as are his facial expressions.

You say that Dr. Hutton "never wore" a green surgical tunic when he talked to me. He most certainly did. Our conversation took place just after he had been participating in a lecture-demonstration, in the university operating theater, of the impact of bullets on flesh (a subject in which Dr. Hutton is an expert), and his tunic was not only green, but spattered with blood. Medical universities are robust institutions, not subject to civilian restraints, and I thought it best not to enquire further into what he had been doing.

In the weeks following, *Dutch* fell victim to a proliferation of negative reviews. Written for the most part by political reporters, they found the book to be lacking in its coverage of Reagan's presidential campaigns, not to mention many economic, social, and foreign-policy issues. Its literary virtuosity annoyed them (although some confessed that they admired Morris's narrative skills) to the point of near abuse. "Strip away Morris's pretentious bric-a-brac, and what would be left is still a grossly inadequate biography," Robert Novak wrote in *The Weekly Standard.*

Perhaps the most important of these politically oriented reviews was that of Hendrik Hertzberg in *The New Yorker.*

In *Dutch: A Memoir* there is almost nothing about electoral politics, nothing at all about ideological politics, and not a word about political economy. About international politics there is narrative, some of it very strong, but no analysis. . . . Morris has told us more than we knew before about "Reagan's own humanity" and about "the quality of his personality." But it is fair to ask the question: So what?

A smaller segment of critical opinion was voiced by academe. The dismay of history professors, whose whole structure of scholarly procedure is challenged by *Dutch*'s innovations (particularly the imaginary footnotes the imaginary author occasionally permits himself), reached almost comical proportions. Professor Douglas Brinkley of the University of New Orleans published a three-column newspaper attack on the book, then announced that he was "looking forward to reading it." Professor Larry Sabato of the University of Virginia compared Morris's work, sight unseen, to that of a controversial show of British avant-garde art at the Brooklyn Museum, and called it "dung biography." Joseph Ellis, the Pulitzer Prize–winning biographer of Thomas Jefferson, was assigned to review *Dutch* by *The Washington Post Book World* and concluded on first reading that it was one of the greatest biographies he had ever come across. Only when he realized that the book's author was not, in fact, a Chicago-born octogenarian and former classmate of Ronald Reagan did he change his mind, somewhat ambivalently:

> [Morris's] book is not just a riveting read. It takes as its model what is generally regarded as the greatest biography in the English language, James Boswell's *Life of Samuel Johnson.* . . . As I turned the pages of *Dutch*—and it is an absolute page-turner—I marveled. . . .
>
> Morris does a splendid job of describing the most crucial and controversial chapter in Reagan's life. These were the postwar years, when he underwent a political conversion. . . .
>
> Morris lets this story play out gradually, poignantly, and without a trace of political prejudice for or against the conservative conclusions Reagan reached. . . .
>
> The debate that this predestined bestseller by now has provoked is not about Reagan's political legacy but about Morris's biographical methods. Does the stylistic briliance of *Dutch* justify Morris's scholarly shenanigans? . . .
>
> What Morris has done, in my opinion, is a scandal and a travesty.

Joan Didion conceded in *The New York Review of Books* that Morris's most daring experiment, the creation of a fictional son to articulate the feelings of student radicals in the 1960s, had produced "in many ways the most interesting character in the book." But she felt that inventiveness had compromised historical accuracy.

A minority of critics, most of them literary rather than political in their predilections, tried to affect the growing consensus that *Dutch* irresponsibly mixed fact and fiction. "A reader who surrenders to Morris's . . . blend of scholarship and imagination will be led through a riveting story to a transcendent conclusion with a surprise twist," Steven R. Weisman remarked in *The New York Times Book Review.* "*Dutch* never fails to evoke the power and mystery of its subject." Perhaps the most significant comment was that of Michael Pakenham in the Baltimore *Sun:*

> Edmund Morris, after 14 years, has produced a compelling, richly informative, conceptually courageous book that constitutes a relentless

pursuit of the truth. Arguably, it is the most insightful book in print about Ronald Reagan and the meaning of his presidency, and it may well remain so for many years. . . .

As far as Reagan and history go, [the biographer] is presented entirely as an *observer*—except for one dramatic, highly effective ornament at the book's end. He does not alter the course of Reagan's life—political or personal. He is a mirror, a lens, a prism, a device through which Morris chooses to examine Reagan in full context.

A main effect is to make the book more confiding, more conversational—certainly more swiftly moving and enthralling. Occasionally, that narrator became, to me, a clutter. . . . But never did that voice, for me anyway, intrude on the events or attitudes of Reagan's or history's doings.

I tried rewriting in my mind, again and again, passages where that narrator's voice is particularly present—where recognizing that he is a fiction is necessary to comprehend what is being read. In each case, my conclusion was that—yes, of course—the same material could have been written in an orthodox narrative manner, and if it were, however brilliantly executed, it would be far less interesting and illuminating.

———

Barring a few factual and typographical corrections, and the excision of one overwrought phrase in the Epilogue that Edmund Morris ruefully ascribes to "finishing fatigue," this HarperCollins edition of *Dutch: A Memoir of Ronald Reagan* is the identical text that shook the world of publishing in 1999. The author remains confident that his scholarship will survive the test of time, while the book's stylistic originality will inspire other biographers to experiment with "the endless reflections and refractions of human memory."

All that *Dutch* asks of a first-time reader is that he or she be willing to accept, in its early pages, the presence of a fictional narrator. Every biographical fact recorded, every one of Ronald Reagan's words and thoughts and acts, are all the fruit of hard historical research. Only the *means* Edmund Morris employs (deliberately varied throughout the book, to emphasize the fragmentary nature of Reagan's career) go beyond those of orthodox nonfiction. Yet close analysis of the notes will show that even the most apparently imaginary episodes are nothing more than imaginative in execution. They merely tell the truth in ways altogether new.

For example, Morris was criticized by Charles Krauthammer in *The Washington Post* for "imagining Reagan's thoughts while making his first movie." The thoughts referred to (see Chapter 9) are taken from the young actor's own written account of the production, while those of "Andy McCaine," the role he was playing, derive directly from the shooting script of *Love Is on the Air.*

Again, the nightmarish events of 1947, when Reagan nearly died of pneumonia while losing a newborn child (and soon afterward, the love of his first wife, Jane Wyman), are presented by Morris in film-scenario form. This is not so much a creative indulgence as a faithful reflection of the way Reagan himself remembered—and wrote about—the events of that traumatic year.

Elsewhere, throughout this long and polyglot book, cinematic devices abound, as do images of reflection and refraction (see the President's reaction to an Oval Office monitor on p. 647), audio montage (see the chorus of post-Reykjavík comment on pp. 600–602), and space technology. In every case, such passages present authentic material in Reaganesque fashion, illuminating our understanding of the strange and compulsive workings of the central character's mind. "Unless I can convey the extent to which RR lived in his own imagination," Morris wrote Loomis in 1994, "this biography will have failed in its task."

Whether *Dutch: A Memoir of Ronald Reagan* indeed fails, as the initial critics suggested, or whether it succeeds as brilliantly as many readers (judging from the mail pouring into the publisher's offices) seem to feel, only time will tell. HarperCollins, committed to publishing books that are likely to survive as classics, is proud to reissue it with confidence that it will soon attain that status.

CONTENTS

In Memoriam

CHRISTINE REAGAN

June 26, 1947

*Pause you who read this, and think for a moment
of the long chain of iron or gold, of thorns or flowers,
that would never have bound you, but for the formation
of the first link on one memorable day.*

—CHARLES DICKENS

Prologue

"For heaven's sakes!"

He holds the speckled leaf in his hand, caressing its green patches with his sharp, scarred thumb. The Oval Office is so silent I hope that the dry whisper of that caress will register on my tape recorder. "Direct from Lowell Park," I say. "Remember that big oak tree you used to sit under, when you were a lifeguard?"

He tilts his head at me, mildly amused but wary. Most public yet most private of men, he does not welcome undue familiarity with his past. I have never forgotten the blue anger that came into his eyes (no aquamarine flash like Jimmy Carter's, but a sort of dark flicker, like the inner flame of a candle) when I boasted that I had tracked down his first fiancée. "Oh, you found out about her, huh." It was a statement rather than a question—Ronald Reagan hardly ever used the interrogative form—signaling, for all its tone of polite interest, his resentment at being surprised, and his disinclination to hear another word about the preacher's daughter he once wanted to marry.

I should have kept my research to myself. Yet for sheer pleasure at having tracked down former intimates, I could never resist beginning an interview with, "Guess what—Glen Claussen's still alive. He gave me this photograph of you singing barbershop quartet!" or, "Joy Hodges says, 'Love to Dutch.'" I would pause for a reaction, but—unless you call a practiced chuckle reactive—always in vain. Perhaps his youthful readings in Calvin Coolidge taught him not to encourage interlocutors. *It only winds them up for twenty minutes more.* Even as a teenager, he had taken no personal interest in people. They were, and remained, a faceless audience to his perpetual performance.

Of course, if I said something like, "Mr. President, your old friend Pee Wee seems to be dying," he would bow his head in appropriate sorrow—checking, meanwhile, the schedule lying crisp before him:

> 1:30 PM   *Personal Staff Time*
> 2:00 PM   *Pre–News Conference Briefing*
> 3:30 PM   *Taping Session*

Perhaps because today's show-and-tell has vegetal rather than human associations, his moment of wariness passes. "That was in front of the little bath house," he says, speaking more to the leaf than to me. He is back under his favorite oak, sixty summers ago, his hot damp swimsuit unlooped from his shoulders and dropped to his taut stomach, leaving behind a pale ghost of itself. The river has "closed" for lunch, and he is eating a hamburger and reading Edgar Rice Burroughs. *At about the age of one thousand years, they go voluntarily upon their last strange pilgrimage down the river Iss, which leads no living Martian knows whither and from whose bosom no Martian has ever returned.*

That hard, splendid body, those bruising arms and knees, the prickle of wet wool are so manifest that I can feel them—as one skinny-dipper did on August 2, 1928, in the nocturnal rescue that gave "Dutch" Reagan his first newspaper headline. PULLED FROM THE JAWS OF DEATH. A sudden empathy with the drowning boy (who gave his name as James Raider) makes me want to retch, as if the Rock River's brackish waters are in my nose and throat, and my consciousness, too, swirling.

"Mr. President, when you—"

I am in such a frenzy that I have forgotten he is still addressing himself to the leaf. Our voices collide; his soft husk arrests my stammer. "There was a walkway," Reagan says. "And then a square on the end with a slide on it, and a diving board, and uh, a low-level thing along one side. . . ." He glances at me smiling, head cocked. The gray-blue eyes go from gloss to semigloss, and he returns the leaf. "Well, I'll be darned." We are back in the present.

I know now I'll never tell him. No wonder Ronald Reagan embraced the Strategic Defense Initiative—cosmic deflection is his game! *Research memo: look for the notion of a space-shield in Burroughs science fiction. Doesn't* Princess of Mars *have a dome of bombproof glass, five feet thick?*

Half an hour later, I emerge from the Oval Office, asking myself for the hundredth time, "How much does Dutch really know?"

There was no sign of recognition when I first saw him in the White House, at a state dinner in August 1981. Nor did he know me (although he pretended to) when I sat next to him fourteen months later, at a lunch with members of the Theodore Roosevelt Association. He again showed no sign of familiarity on Saint Valentine's Day 1983, when Senator Mark Hatfield invited a group of biographers to dine with the Reagans in Georgetown. I was not surprised. The President met an average of eighty people a day; he must long since have stopped relating handshakes to faces.

He certainly lit up, though, when Hatfield introduced me as the author of *The Rise of Theodore Roosevelt.* "Oh!" he breathed, warmly resting his left hand on my right hand engulfed in his other hand, "I read that. And Nancy was reading your wife's book about, uh—"

"Edith Kermit Roosevelt, sir."

"Yes. Those first few months in the White House, we would lay in bed and read 'em side by side!" He waited for me to express appreciation, then winked and turned to Frank Freidel. Happiness suffused my heart.

I watched Frank melting under similar treatment, then Daniel J. Boorstin and George Nash and the rest of our company. The President had a perfectly prepared quip for each man, a beam of sexless affection for each woman. We were all seduced, with the exception of Arthur S. Link, Ph.D., George Harding Davis '86 Professor of American History at Princeton University. Reagan grasped his disapproving Democratic hand. "Well, hello—" Link bent stiffly forward, craggy and crabbed, bowed by the erudition of forty-two consecutive volumes of *The Papers of Woodrow Wilson.* His detestation of the Gipper was legendary in academe. Some of us had taken bets that Arthur would not show up. But show he had, in the teeth of a snowstorm, out of courtesy to Senator Hatfield.

For a moment, his silver crew cut bristled inches from Reagan's chin. I braced for an upward jerk and thud. But then he straightened and

"He sensed Link's stiffness, and was figuring how to deal with it."
Ronald Reagan and Arthur Link, February 14, 1983.

tried to smile—a mirthless iguana gape. Reagan, nodding kindly, moved on to the butler.

Something about the back of the President's neck, as he ordered a vodka and orange, told me he sensed Link's stiffness, and was figuring how to deal with it. He had been the same at college, at Warner Bros., in the Army, on the road for GE in the Fifties: always the Actor, determined at all costs to captivate every person in the room. Compared with some of the more formidable dyspeptics he had beguiled—Eamon De Valera, Charles de Gaulle, and Chiang Kai-shek, to name but three—Link was easy meat.

It took him no more than twenty minutes, once we had sat down at Mrs. Hatfield's round table, ornamented with bulbous red plastic hearts. I noticed he kept beaming at Arthur. Rubicund from his cocktail, big, broad, lustrous with power, he exuded what Walter Pater called the "charm of an exquisite character, felt in some way to be inseparable from his person." The iguana began to cackle in spite of itself at the flow of his jokes. Who could help laugh, when Reagan himself laughed so irresistibly?

Arthur, being something of an expert on *sequitur*, must have noticed how each joke adapted to the conversation, how quickly and lightly the words spooled out, every punch line dropping like a fly on the stream. Joke-telling requires a special kind of intelligence, as anyone knows who has tried to write one out: a few syllables too many, a vital phrase misstated, and the humor dies. Reagan lacked wit—he was too cautious to risk repartee—and many of his jokes were hoary, but one could only marvel at their apparent spontaneity.

He grew serious when the conversation turned to a President's responsibility to endow posterity with personal documents. Whatever we recommended for the record, he said, he would do faithfully. But he doubted that details about himself *as a man* would interest anybody, now or in the future. "I still look over my shoulder when I'm, you know, walking out of the White House and the Marines are saluting and all, and I say, 'Who—me?' "

This was too much for Arthur, who by now was gazing at Reagan misty-eyed. "Mr. President!" he roared, almost sobbing with adoration. "*Six hundred years from now,* historians will still be fascinated by your manuscripts!" (I had a vision of scholarly lasers, programmed for Freudian clues, scanning Dutch's diaries without so much as a beep.) Arthur, rambling on, would not be stopped until he had begged the President and Mrs. Reagan to preserve their *billets-doux.* "Imagine what would have happened if Mrs. Wilson had burned those wonderful love letters Woodrow wrote her. How little we would know of his passionate humanity!"

There was nothing to do but let rapture run its course. Reagan sat listening, content at having prevailed once again over a potential enemy. The rest of us twirled our wineglasses and wondered what kind of ideological hangover Arthur was going to have in the morning.

Throughout the seventy minutes we stayed at the table, I was aware of Mrs. Reagan's stare, as a scuba diver in dark water senses two large, pale, accompanying jellyfish. I braced myself to glance at her: she gave a thin return of smile before looking away.

"And then along came Nancy Davis," said Reagan, "and saved my soul."

He was talking about 1949, his *annus horribilis,* when in the space of a few months he had found himself alone, aging, divorced, unemployed, upstaged in his last picture, and on crutches, nursing a shattered leg. There was a respectful silence while he gazed at his savior. Her eyes glittered with tears, perfectly on cue.

Hokey, yes, but I could not help being moved. The President's adoration of this brittle little woman warmed the room to such an extent that Mrs. Hatfield, draining her champagne, launched into a monologue on the subject of Love that had us all checking our watches. Only Reagan, with his bear's appetite for honeyed sentiment, seemed sorry when her speech, and with it the evening, came to an end.

"I'm going to ask only one favor from you scholars in exchange for this dinner," Senator Hatfield said after the Reagans had left. "Each of you must send me an account of what you've heard and seen tonight."

I wrote some pages from an imaginary *History of the United States in the Late Twentieth Century.* Its general tone was whimsical, aside from this mention of a proposal by the Librarian of Congress:

> . . . that Reagan appoint to his staff a historian trained to sense the long-term significance of events. Presidents, Dr. Boorstin remarked, are often unaware that their most cherished "achievements" might be judged insignificant by posterity, while others, hardly noticed at the time, blossom later to major importance. If the drama of the moment—a gala for the doomed Sadat, a visit to the Berlin Wall—can be captured by an official photographer, then why not also by an official chronicler? "As Chairman of the Senate Appropriations Committee," Hatfield interrupted with a grin, "I'll see you get the necessary funds."

After quoting Arthur Link's outburst about the "passionate humanity" of Woodrow Wilson, I concluded:

> Implicit in that remark was the suggestion that Reagan's own humanity, unchronicled, might fade faster than any other feature of his Presidency; that in the end what chiefly survives, or *should* survive, of any Chief Executive is the quality of his personality. Presidents, whatever their political symbolism, represent the national character of their era, and if we do not understand our leaders as people, we can never understand ourselves as Americans.

It was not until some time afterward that I learned that the real purpose of the Hatfield dinner had been to set *me* up as Reagan's "chronicler." So that was why Mrs. Reagan had stared so hard over her *volaille de poulet aux champignons.* That was why Richard Darman, the Administration's resident intellectual, had invited me to the White House for a follow-up discussion. Presumably, I was expected to offer my pen to the Reagan Revolution.

I didn't. I was at work on another volume of the life of Theodore Roosevelt, and had reason enough to keep my distance. *Ironia ironiarum,* that I of all people should be charged with rescuing the old Lifeguard from the chill current of history!

☯

Nine years later, however, I found myself literally escorting him back to his origins in Tampico, Illinois. He was President no longer, and had been seized by a sudden, senescent desire to visit, for the first time since 1911, what was now grandly called the Ronald Reagan Birthplace Museum. I walked down Main Street with him and Nancy, feeling transcendentally strange. An odd, Dantesque reversal of roles had occurred, as if I were now the leader rather than the led.

"Mr. President," I said, "you don't have to pretend you remember this place. You were only three months old when your parents checked out of number 111."

"Yes. We went to live over the store where my father worked. H. C. Pitney's General Store."

"No, that was in 1919, when you returned here from Monmouth. In May 1911, the *Tampico Tornado* reported that your parents had moved with their new baby to the Burden house, south of the depot."

I pointed down the one-block street, beyond the little crowd restrained by a police car, and across the tracks. "You can't see it because of the wheat elevator, but it's the house of your first memories."

"Are we going to visit?"

"I think they want us to go to church first, sir, and then go through the museum here."

Docile as ever, he nodded. I did not add that the current occupants of the white, double-story house had no desire to welcome him. Judging by the number of major appliances on the stoop, they were not Reagan Republicans.

Sunday-morning sunbeams streamed through the windows of the Christian Church. He sat immediately in front of me while the organ fluted "What a Friend We Have in Jesus," and Whiteside County's Disciples of Christ—a corn-fed lot—squeezed themselves into adjoining pews. I leaned forward and said, "Just think, Mr. President, if your father had gotten you baptized in Saint Mary's, we'd be attending eleven o'clock mass."

He chuckled and whispered conspiratorially, "Bells and smells."

We sang number 270 in the hymnal. It occurred to me that I had never heard him sing, apart from his execrable rendering of "They Fly Through the Air with the Greatest of Ease" in *International Squadron* (1942). So I leaned forward and was surprised by the sweetness of his breathy light baritone. Unlike most public worshipers, he sang without a trace of self-consciousness, quietly, almost to himself.

> There is a place of full release,
> A place full of joy and peace . . .

As so often before, I marveled at the dense lie of his hair, thick and shining as an otter's. Why is it old men and small boys always look so vulnerable from behind? Today, he seemed to belong to both categories. There was something engagingly innocent about the way he clutched his wife's hand throughout the prayers and sermon, and about his glance at her for approval when the preacher asked him to speak. Innocent, yet also strange: I had not seen him so dependent before. For the first time, I wondered if there was something wrong with him.

He spoke well enough, in his patented hesitant husk: "My brother and I were started off in the Christian Church by our mother, here in Tampico. I'm afraid I can't . . . uh, tell if this was the same building we—"

I nodded violently at him, over Nancy's coiffure, but he did not see me.

"Reason is, that was about seventy years ago. But I can't describe the feeling of being back here in my birthplace. Really, there are no words."

These were his standard clichés to express emotion required of him, but I looked around and saw many eyes fill with tears. Reagan checked too: the old actor counting the house. Satisfied, he ambled back to his pew, and we sang "That Old Rugged Cross."

After the service, we adjourned to the Birthplace, which was cordoned off for privacy. A voluble and energetic little lady led the returning pilgrim upstairs. I crowded close behind, not wanting to miss a moment of this *recherche du temps perdu.*

Only when it happened—a door thrown open, a threshold crossed, two windows full of sun, and then another, darker threshold—did I realize that none of us had anticipated its impact. "This, Mr. President," the little lady said, pointing matter-of-factly at a bed, "is where you were born."

Sixty years of public life had taught Ronald Reagan how to react. But these words were so sudden, the room so small, and the bed in its cramped corner so lumpishly *there,* that if a reproduction of Courbet's *Origin of the World* had hung over the headboard, he could not have been more shocked. I heard him suck in his breath. He swiveled on his heel, almost treading me down, and began to tell jokes.

❡

Later, over lunch at the "Dutch Diner" down the street (named, oddly enough, not after Ronald Reagan, but after the Mennonite women who run it), a delayed reaction set in. He showed no interest in what I tried to tell him about the events of eighty years ago in Tampico. Instead, he took refuge in his own stories about Hollywood, stories we had all heard a hundred times, except now he left out whole sections without noticing, while Nancy picked at her salad, her face a mask.

Listening to him, I asked myself who of us, forced so brutally to confront the nothingness from which we have sprung, would not have turned away as he did, knowing it to be indistinguishable from—indeed, identical with—the nothingness that looms ahead?

❡

"Don't blame me, this was Mike Deaver's idea," said Robert Tuttle, White House director of personnel, when I assumed the dread title of Authorized Biographer. "We were playing tennis one day, and I told Mike, 'What the President needs is an in-house historian.' He said, 'Don't worry, it's already done.' "

"Except it wasn't, Bob. I said no after the Hatfield dinner. I'm not a historian."

"Well, *we* thought you were. Couldn't understand why you hesitated so long."

"Two and a half years!"

If he thought of me as "in-house" help, well, let him. It had taken all that time, and the cheep of a bird four thousand miles away, before I suddenly wanted to write Dutch's strange story—and such of mine as might help illuminate it. I could not tell Tuttle the reason for my hesitation, nor Deaver nor Darman nor Boorstin nor Hatfield. No more could I tell the President himself, when I stood in the Oval Office and gagged on the fetid waters of memory and desire.

❡

Memory. Desire. What is this mysterious yearning of biographer for subject, so akin to a *coup de foudre* in its insistence? Yet so fundamentally different from love in its detachment? Dutch has intrigued me, on and off, most of my life, but until 1985 I never thought of being his bard. Even now, as we approach the end of our aloof intimacy, we are two bodies from remote systems, one a mere chip of rock, one huge—history cannot deny Ronald Reagan's *mass*!—asteroids whose trajectories briefly interlocked. Yet still I feel that gravitational drag, the product as much of disproportion as convergence. Before we recede to our respective darknesses, I must allow these floating fragments, these dusts of myself, to sparkle in his waning light.

DUTCH

1

The Land of Lost Things

I T WAS A BIRD at Bergen-Belsen that did it, that wet May morning in
1985 when Ronald Reagan stepped out of the *Dokumentenhaus,* his
face racked by what he had just seen. Precisely then, as he glanced over
the mass graves toward the monument where he was to speak, a skylark
sang out. I felt my heart constrict. Something about the way Dutch
looked against the gray sky, and the way the bird sounded through the
medium of my television set, made me wish passionately that I was
there. I knew then what I could not have believed two and a half years
before, nor even begun to imagine the first time I saw him mount a public platform (skinny, bespectacled, center-parted, rigid with excitement,
his lips wreathing ungracefully to the right).

Reagan stood within reach of presidential greatness. Time and
again—never more courageously than this day—he had struggled
against circumstance and bent it to his will. But for his reluctance to
boast, he might already be considered great, on the achievements of his
first term alone: an overnight resurgence of American patriotism and
positivity; a rethinking of old attitudes toward the government as pro-
vider; an assertion of popular rights on the federal shop floor, and on
the federal bench; a declaration of moral war upon the Soviet Union,

plus perfect willingness to bankrupt it by force of military spending; a rebalancing of executive power against the legislative; and a transferal of "compassion" from welfare to the womb. More impressive than all these, perhaps, had been his knightly display of valor after he lost half his blood supply on March 30, 1981. History admires the wise, but it elevates the brave.

Greatness, however, requires that leaders who change their times be seen to change themselves, or at least to embody great ideals. Abraham Lincoln not only suffered for the Union as much as any soldier in blue, he embodied in his nature the antagonisms and interdependence of North and South. Theodore Roosevelt both invoked and personified "the young giant of the West." Franklin Roosevelt's triumph over adversity was personal as well as political. To my mind, Ronald Reagan did not have these epic dimensions. I knew that his life story was as interesting and as prototypically American as Lincoln's or either Roosevelt's. Yet there was a slabby, alabaster-like quality to his character that put me off. I could see whorls and crystals beneath the gloss, without being able to probe them.

At times, I wondered if he was not simply a polished presence—like those chrome busts that Noguchi sculpted in the Jazz Age, reflecting only outside personalities. Was that James Baker's calculating gaze I glimpsed in the President's right eye? Did his mouth just flash with Ed Meese's pink pout?

Not until Reagan confronted the green mounds of Bergen-Belsen, and realized what dread fertilizer enriched their heather covering, did the alabaster become flesh, and terror and pity—emotions that Hazlitt says are concomitant with tragedy—stir in my breast. I feared the anger that he would unleash by going on to Bitburg, and disbelieved his assumption that, after forty years, he could reconcile the Holocaust's killers and its slain. He was deaf to the skylark; but it irresistibly summoned me.

I felt myself at the beginning of a journey into his past, a journey planned by mysterious agents—as a child, carried asleep aboard a midnight train, becomes conscious of enormous, purposeful movement in the dark, of acceleration backward rather than forward, away from the probes of light that penetrate and flicker around the walls of his new, gently rocking room.

Perhaps the journey had already begun. My reluctance to tell Ronald Reagan's life had begun to waver several weeks before the Bitburg crisis, at a private dinner on March 22, upstairs at the White House. The subject of biography had not been raised over the tall white freesias and tall white candles—indistinguishably merging while Reagan droned on about Hollywood, and I drank too much of Richard Nixon's excellent leftover Cabernet. But Michael Deaver was there, matching me glass for glass, and he had glared a message through the fragrant flames: *You blew it at the Hatfields', buddy. This is your last chance.*

Riding home afterward, in the luxury of a limousine, I discussed the idea with my wife. "I don't know if I can afford to pass up this opportunity," I said. "But it means putting TR aside for a few years."

The car cruised up Pennsylvania Avenue. A fine drizzle was falling. Ahead of us the Capitol wavered whitely, like some Tennysonian vision. *Clothed in white samite, mystic, wonderful.* Never had Washington looked so beautiful, so full of promise.

"There's one good reason to do it, apart from the money," I said, "and that is, I've known Dutch longer than anybody realizes. He least of all! Damned if I can figure him out, though. Is he a political genius, or a bore? Judging by tonight's performance, I rather suspect the latter."

"He managed to bore quite a few people into voting for him."

"Yes. Perhaps I'm the bore. Always looking for something that's not there."

So again I suppressed the idea, until the President flew to Germany five weeks later, and I idly turned on CNN and found myself mesmerized by the call of a *Lerche* over the Lüneburger Heide.

That bird called not only around the curve of the world separating me from Reagan in his agony, but back and back through all our years. Primarily, I suppose, it sang of loss. Loss, the biographer's torment: longing for treasures unrecoverable, hardly assuaged by the recovery of trifles—an oar or a floating hat, after everything else has gone over the weir. Private loss, too. So many other "last chances." Budding opportunities unblown, breasts not cupped in my hand, scripts unfilmed and books unfinished, a marriage in ashes, a boy gone underground. Loss of youth, of middle age, of Time itself. Sydney Ann. Gavin. Father. And before them all, before everybody who ever lived, young and beautiful and wise, Bess—lost, too!—singing Schubert in our big music room on Lake Shore Drive in the spring of 1919.

Horch! Horch! die Lerch' im Ätherblau!
Und Phöbus, neu erweckt . . .

Even as a child accustomed to my mother's effortless command of languages (she had studied *lieder* in Dresden and *bel canto* in Milan, not to mention the dialectical folksongs of her native England), I remember marveling that any foreign lyricist could so uglify Shakespeare's "Hark! Hark! the Lark."

At my urgent request, she sang it in the original, pointing out however that "These are *not* the words that Schubert set. He couldn't read English. What sounds ugly to you sounded poetic to him. *Ätherblau,* for instance. Now there's a lovely word, except to gross little American boys."

"What's *Ätherblau*?" I asked.

"Use you ears! *Ether. Blue.* And your eyes, too. Look through that window—what do you see?"

"Lake Michigan," I said resentfully. But Bess kept her temper.

"See how its dark horizon *etherizes* into the pale *blue* of the sky? *Ätherblau!*"

In countless conversations like this, combining the aesthetic and the practical, my mother made me aware of the music of words and the phonology of music. Which is to say, I suppose, that she made me a writer, although it took most of a lifetime to complete the process. More subtly, as when she pointed out that Schubert's Shakespeare was not *our* Shakespeare, she prepared me for the perception, essential to all authorized biographers, that the "original" person we think we are seeing and hearing is but a refracted image (bent, wavering, prismatic perhaps, but never quite still or solid) of someone who perceives us with equal mystification. *My* Dutch is not Nancy's Ronnie—nor Jane's, for that matter—and certainly not the "I, Ronald Wilson Reagan" our common original had in mind when he took his first oath as President of the United States.

Amateur Freudians, discovering that one of my mother's star roles during her ten years (1905–1915) on the Chicago operatic stage was the Woodbird in Wagner's *Siegfried,* would no doubt say that it was she, not Dutch, who called to me from Bergen-Belsen and thus impelled the writing of this book. Well, if they really want to psychoanalyze the matter, I may as well add that Father was Jewish—or as Bess delicately preferred to put it, "had German blood in his veins."

Her scruple, oddly enough, originated with him. Not once in his short, fierce life did Arthur Morris raise the subject with me. Like many other well-born, Yale-educated Jews of the time, he was an Episcopalian convert and a Roosevelt Republican. I do not think he even considered himself a Jew, having decided, with Henry James, that being American was "complex fate" enough. Compulsively, he dedicated himself to philanthropy and politics.

He and my uncle Ira (U.S. Minister to Sweden, 1914–1923) allowed their brother Edward to run the family firm. Morris & Co. was then Chicago's leading cattle feeder, with a thirty-acre plant at Racine and Twenty-third. It had been founded by Grandfather Nelson, a Bavarian immigrant who died in 1907, unable to understand why his two younger sons should prefer to spend money rather than make it, and yearn resectively for the worlds of government and diplomacy.

Had Grandfather known that Arthur Morris was even then preparing to marry a *shikse* opera singer ("Annette Dowling, the Kentish Skylark"), he probably would have expired sooner. As it was, they were wed three days after the old tycoon's demise. Father never went near Packingtown again, and within a year or two Uncle Edward resignedly bought him and Ira out.

Father never talked about his income—only, with satisfaction, about the amount he gave away. At any rate, he was a wealthy man. My earliest memories are of a tall and splendid peach-colored house, whose rooms smelled alternately of Montecristos and attar of roses, depending on which parent dominated them. It stood just off the corner of Lake Shore Drive and Bellevue Place, and shimmered most of the day with light from the lake. Nanny was German, the maids Irish, and the cook French—or so we thought, until he absentmindedly referred to *pain perdu* as "French toast," and had to confess he hailed from Schenectady. His readings in Escoffier, however, were revelatory. About the time young Dutch, ninety miles west, was discovering the delights of macaroni and cheese, I was developing a precocious taste for *quenelles d'huîtres à la reine.*

☯

Every spring we would relocate to "the Cottage," a huge farmhouse at Aurora, about forty miles west of the city (bringing me closer yet to that unguessed-at country boy in north-central Illinois). As part of the settlement from Morris & Co., Father had retained control of a small subsidiary, the Aurora Model Dairy, simply as a base from which to indulge his fascination with local politics. Dairying did not interest him at all. He drove into Aurora every day to work *pro bono* as commissioner-at-large and treasurer of the Aurora Republican Party—leaving Bess to run the farm, which she did badly but with great enjoyment.

I remember how his nostrils flared when he took me in one morning and showed me Town Hall squatting dully on its midstream island.

"This is a holy place, my boy," he said, gesturing reverently. "Here the G.O.P. was born." I assumed he was referring to some municipal organization and looked about in despair. Please God, why didn't Father prefer City Hall in Chicago? I did not understand that Cook County politics—let alone those of the state and nation—were too diffuse to engage him. He took a watchmaker's delight in the close, the intricate, the small, the tensely sprung; he liked to feel power ticking in his hand.

☯

Pleasant as the Cottage was for a month or two, it began to feel like a prison when the awnings dropped and the dog days came. I hoped when I turned six that school would enforce our early return to the city, but Bess hired a governess who drove out every day in a pretty little roadster, like Nancy Drew, and read me the comics page of the *Chicago Tribune.* Father ran annually for Mayor of Aurora. I prayed for his defeat, because I knew that victory would root him ever more firmly in the country, away from our charmed life on Lake Shore Drive.

Father lost as often as he ran, but by steadily diminishing margins. I can still see him striding hitch-heeled down Broadway to the campaign office, the tails of his black jacket billowing behind him, while Republican voters tipped their hats and Democrats crossed the street. Every first Monday in November, Bess joined him on the hustings—rather bold for a woman in those days—and they patrolled the street together, handing out his campaign flower (dark, scentless roses, specially grown for him in Oregon) and posing arm in arm for the flashlight cameras. I stood by them once—a furrow-faced little boy peering out of page three of the Aurora *Beacon-News,* November 4, 1919—and had my retinas pierced with such painful star bursts of magnesium as to blind me permanently to the charms of public life.

The time was coming, that furrowed frown makes plain, when the peach-colored house would have to be sold to a developer. To this day, I cannot look at a photograph of it. A few years ago, I came across a perspective drawing of 18 Lake Shore Drive in an old Rand McNally guide, and its disembodied, black-and-white starkness made the nostalgia bearable. Loss of detail, of texture and nuance, is what breaks the heart.

In my second childhood, as in my first, I choose to dream that Father's house still stands in "The Land of Lost Things"—that vast yet well-stocked territory roamed by historians, biographers, and other refugees from reality.

Reagan has often been accused of roaming there too. On the contrary, he was always happier in the Here and Now. His tendency to reminisce ("When we were Governor of California . . .") was not a looking back so much as an eager application of history to today and tomorrow. That swivel away from his birth bed in 1992 was entirely characteristic, as was his innocent delight—just before cognition began to fade—in the mechanics of the hillside crypt that awaits him and Nancy in Southern California.

"There's a few feet of rail in there, ready for when they open that steel door and slide me in. Then they'll seal the door, but you know, *temporarily,* until—uh, she joins me. Then we'll lie there, just the two of us, and look at the sea together."

It is characteristic of him to believe that the sea can be seen through steel, and after death.

But I digress—or rather, I neglect the larger digression from Ronald Reagan that this chapter necessarily undertakes. I am attempting, you see, to get myself out of his biographical way, before it develops its own improbable, burgeoning momentum.

Bess once teased me by saying that on the night of my conception she had lain back, like any decent Edwardian woman, "and thought of England." Perhaps that, and Father's burning Americanism, explains why my star has tended to center over the mid-Atlantic, although it has at times shone as far east as the Kentish Downs and as far west as Santa Barbara.

My birth, on August 9, 1912, more or less coincided with the archaeological furor over Piltdown Man, while other scientists were finding that genes could be lined up along a chromosome. Who knows, the latter discovery may prove as fraudulent as the former. The past is delusion, the future illusion; one locates one's center where one can. (Or in cases like Reagan's, where one wishes.)

Where, I wonder, was Father's? Bess maintained that the worst thing that ever happened to him was being blackballed by the Chicago Club. Maybe his staunch Republicanism, his desperate giving of money to Christian charities, were attempts to buy respectability in a Gentile world. In that case, the mayoralty of Aurora, which Father eventually won, and held until death, was a triumph of sorts.

Arthur Morris was stiff, dark, and bristling, a driving piston of a man who spoke in snapped-off sentences, as if his larynx were a pressure valve. I wish I had inherited half his head of steam. His verbal ejaculations were so forceful and so few, in contrast to my own childish garrulousness, that I could never coax him into a relaxed conversation; halfway through some tentative opener, I would literally feel on my face the plosives of his eager reply.

"Father, Uncle Ira wants to take me to Maywood Field—"

"See the airplane show [*puff!*], yes, yes. Now, Arthur, promise [*puff!*] you won't go near any propeller [*puff! puff!*]. Chop you to pieces, my boy!" And with "pieces" my forelock would lift.

He always addressed me by my first name, despite Bess's insistence on calling me by my second. Arthur, of course, is a name hallowed by Christians, but to me it has always sounded Jewish, and after Father's death in 1923 I buried the name with him. *Morte d'Arthur.* This gesture of denial did not come back to haunt me until three quarters of a century later, when I visited Bergen-Belsen and walked with no sense of strangeness among my father's people, and felt the breeze fanning the heath, as his breath once fanned my hair.

The Rainbow
on the Roof

"**W**HAT ARE THE FIRST MEMORIES you have of your father, Mr. President?"

"I . . . Jack . . . I can remember dimly my father coming home from the store, and giving me a kiss, and he had stubble and I cried. He was very upset," said Reagan, looking very upset. "And I've often regretted that, because now I know he must have been kind of hurt, when—when I backed away."

In my notes, I underscored the last three words, thinking of "the little bit of a fat Dutchman," as Jack called him, recoiling from the hot, prickly breath of affection. In one way or another, Jack's younger son has been rejecting intimacy ever since. I wish I had a dollar for each of the friends and family members who complained to me that Dutch never let them "get anywhere near."

The President stopped talking and sighed. John Edward Reagan—shoe salesman, lapsed Catholic, wanderer, and binge drinker—has always loomed large in his memory: once, indeed, with hallucinatory force. That was at Jack's funeral service in 1941, when Dutch admitted to feeling greater despair than ever before in his life. Was it remorse for "backing away" so many other times, in childhood and adolescence? And as an adult, embarrassing Jack with charity? If so, the voice that sounded suddenly in his ears—kiss-close at last!—was consolatory. "I'm OK." Dutch turned to his mother: "Jack is OK, and where he is he's very happy."

It was natural to turn at such a moment to Nelle Wilson Reagan (1883–1962) and equally natural to find her beside him, in church. Somehow, that is where one always sees the old lady: stiffly erect under a stained-glass window, a floppy Bible in her lap, hard features thrusting, gray-blue eyes furrowed on her favorite son. "God, what an old battle-ax," one of my sources recalls. Yet those who invoke Nelle's memory (most worshipfully, Dutch himself) speak of her as a saint capable of healing the sick. Family members go so far as to accord her divine powers. "Nelle," they say at times of crisis, "will take care of us." Pieties like these, usually accompanied by a soulful glance upward, frustrate research. I went to Tampico in the late summer of 1986, determined to prove, or disprove, the "battle-ax" theory at all costs.

In the Ronald Reagan Birthplace Museum, I met a scholarly gentleman with one arm and (he assured me) three university degrees. His reverence for Nelle was such that the mere sight of her handwriting made tears run down his face.

"I didn't know her personally," said Paul Nicely, founder and proprietor of the Museum. "But I guess I've talked to every Wilson and Reagan in Whiteside County and gone through their scrapbooks and letters, and lemme tell you, Nelle was a saint."

"A saint with regard to Jack?"

Mr. Nicely pretended not to hear the question.

I suggested that it could not have been easy for her, as a pious Protestant, to live with a Catholic who never went to mass, yet insisted on baptizing their first son, Neil, in Saint Mary's Church.

Mr. Nicely stared at me. He looked as if he was about to weep again. I said hastily, "Or maybe she felt Jack could have been a stronger father? He tended to be too kind of buddy-buddy with the boys. You know, 'Dutch' instead of 'Ronald' and 'Moon' instead of 'Neil.' She never used those nicknames . . ."

I let my voice trail off, because Mr. Nicely was not dumb. He knew that *I* knew overfamiliarity was hardly the problem between Jack and Dutch. Something Neil said replayed in my head: "I guess I'm still the son of my father, while Dutch was always Nelle's boy."

Yet a studio photograph lying on Mr. Nicely's table revealed an almost complete physical identity between young Jack and the President of the United States. Their twinship was less a matter of the same deep chest, level brows, and thick, centrally parted hair (bulking flamboyantly on the left) than of a shared statuesqueness: legs solidly anchored, big shoulders thrown back, arms held rather than hung, and faces determined to stay cheerful. But were they indeed statues, Jack would have to be carved shorter—five feet ten and a half inches to his son's six feet one.

In the flesh, Jack was rather darker and duller (Dutch remembers him as "swarthy"), but there is no question that he was handsome when young, too handsome by far for Tampico, which was then, as now, a home for the homely. He made the most of his darkness with snowy shirts, spotless collars and ties, and (a particular fetish) the best and brightest of city shoes. "I want," his eyes tell the Tampico photographer, "the hell out of this dump."

Mr. Nicely, shuffling photographs awkwardly with his one hand, tossed over a snapshot he found in an old scrapbook. "You can keep that—it's a copy." It shows the Reagan family on the dive deck at Coon Creek, and it glows with happy sexuality. Nelle, full-breasted and laughing in a loose black swimsuit, sits with her legs apart, feet dangling into the water; Jack, standing waist deep, has thrust his head between her thighs. Behind them, and somehow apart, is the future lifeguard of Lowell Park, streaming wet and looking blue about the lips, as small boys do when they have swum too much, and are pining for jelly sandwiches.

"I think he was a hell of a guy," Mr. Nicely said, looking at the man grinning in the water. "Great sense of humor."

But I could not take my eyes off Nelle's breasts. Here was a young woman full of the milk of life, relaxedly half-naked in public. How to reconcile this earth mother with the shrunken old Bible-thumper who would not undress until she had shut the bedroom door, *and gotten into a closet?* Her forehead was not yet marked by the frown she took to the grave—that slight peaking of the forehead which makes Dutch's smile so enchantingly quizzical.

I guess the frown began to etch itself when Jack's ambitions took Nelle away from here, to larger towns with more opportunities for advancement—and dissipation. Mr. Nicely thinks Jack had a great future in Tampico, where, in addition to being clothes manager and buyer at the Pitney Store, he was at various times councilman, assistant fire chief, finance chairman of Saint Mary's (a job he seems to have taken in lieu of worship), baseball-team manager, a Knight of Columbus, and an enthusiastic amateur actor.

"Blackface comedian," said Mr. Nicely. "Jack liked to disguise himself."

That figured, I thought. The alcoholic and his mask.

Mr. Nicely led me past a table littered with review clips and souvenirs of Tampico entertainments in the early years of the century. "Here's one of my first pictures. In the background is the theater." The postcard trembled as he tilted it toward the light. Outside, the sun was setting: a blond nimbus glowed along his arm.

"I wish I had a camcorder," I said, "to follow you around."

Ronald Reagan Birthplace—Afternoon

EM   (*off*) Tell me some more about Jack Reagan's personality.

NICELY   Well, the guy was an extremely popular man; a productive person; perhaps a little more, uh, Chicago in him than local natives . . . with more gloss. . . . Extremely good-looking . . . extremely well dressed. A lot of people ask me if he was on the police records—no!

EM   I'm sorry to say he shows up on the blotter in Chicago.

NICELY   (*weeping*) There is a complete void of negative input here . . .

As he sobs, CAMERA PANS around front bedroom of Birthplace, overlooking Main Street. It HOLDS on a short, broad, cross-patched oak bed with heavily lathed and fluted posts. To one side stands a little wooden table and porcelain lamp. Two sickly religious prints hang on the wall.

NARRATOR   In this bed, at 4:16 A.M. on February 6, 1911, Ronald Wilson Reagan was born, feet first, after twenty-four hours' labor. Even in the womb, it seems, he plotted his entrance with dramatic effect. He weighed ten pounds. Perhaps it was this amplitude of flesh, and the *durchkomponierte* quality of his crying, that made Jack Reagan compare him to a "Dutchman." For the next twenty-six years, the boy would be known as "Dutch"—and "Dutch" he has remained to all who knew him in his midwestern days.

(*INSERT: a zodiac card*)

Should the second of his wives be watching this documentary, she will be interested to know that at the moment of his birth, Mars was in 4° Capricorn conjunction, the Ascendant in the First House, the Sun was in 16° of

Aquarius in the Second House, trine the Midheaven, and square the Moon in Taurus at the end of the Fourth House.

During the last sentence, a long, pianissimo D-natural is heard on violins: the first notes of the sunrise sequence from Haydn's Creation. *It increases in volume and begins to mount the scale as CAMERA begins a SLOW ZOOM toward the bedroom's west-facing window. Dutch's cot stands beneath it.*

NARRATOR	Was he already myopic, as he kicked in this cot and tried to focus on these luminous rectangles? Was his first field of vision similar to his last: a foreground buttressed with familiar shapes, each small, female, strong-jawed, authoritative—
NELLE REAGAN	(*firmly*) Ronald!
MARGARET CLEAVER	(*austerely*) Dutch!
JANE WYMAN	(*impatiently*) Ronnie!
NANCY REAGAN	(*snappishly*) Ronnie!
NARRATOR	—a middle distance wavering with taller, blurrier figures—
MAUREEN REAGAN	(*plaintively*) Dad?
MICHAEL REAGAN	(*plaintively*) Dad?
PATTI DAVIS	(*plaintively*) Dad?
RON REAGAN	(*plaintively*) Dad? (*The rising fanfare drowns them out*)
NARRATOR	—and, in farthest perspective, where the land rises to meet the sky, an intense concentration of light, a hint of towers and rooftops, a Shining. . .

Now his voice, too, is overwhelmed as the fanfare reaches its climax. CAMERA PASSES prismatically through the window, and Main Street, sunk in shadow, opens up below.

I stood on the opposite sidewalk, watching Mr. Nicely and his wife shut up shop for the night, waiting for the aureoles to fade from my eyes. I wished I had been here to see the radiance that descended, about this time of day, on the eve of Dutch's ultimate triumph. Two arcs of colored light shafted out of a dark sky onto the Birthplace's roof, pointing precisely at the spot where Nelle had labored so long to bring him forth. An amateur photographer caught the effect and sent a print to the President-elect.

Dutch delightedly pasted it into the scrapbook he keeps of his youth. *On Nov. 3, 1980,* he wrote in his careful, crabbed hand, *this double rainbow appeared in Tampico Ill. The rainbow appears to end on top of the First National Bank, where Ronald Reagan was born. The next day Mr. Reagan was elected Pres. of the U.S.A.*

Now only a bar of conventional, late-afternoon light sliced through the buildings behind me and irradiated number 111's flat, redbrick facade. I glanced at the upper windows and understood why the Reagans, recently married and newly come to town in 1906, placed their bed there, in the warmest of five small rooms. It must have been a pleasant place for Nelle to catch the sun's last rays (a gold nimbus glowing around her piled-up hair) before starting Jack's supper in the cold, dark kitchen. I half expected her to emerge with a water pail, but the Birthplace's doorknob did not turn, and its bricks suddenly lost their color. I checked my watch and made a note: *7:01 P.M.—sunset in Tampico.*

About this time, eighty years before, Jack used to come home from work, walking with cheerful, straight-spined dispatch, as his son would one day do from the Oval Office. There was no tavern to detain him: Tampico had already voted itself dry. Even now, the only beacon of refreshment I could see was a neon BUDWEISER sign about fifty yards away. It fitfully irradiated the hood of an old Volkswagen. Otherwise, Main Street, just one block long, was bare of cars.

I retraced Jack's imagined steps, hoping against hope that a porcelain roller advertising WHAT YOU BUY WE STAND BY might still gleam at 120–122 South Main, over the door of H. C. Pitney's General Store. Of course it did not, but the foursquare structure survives as a bleary bar. Here Jack arrived on March 23, 1906, as senior salesman in charge of the clothing and shoe department. With him he brought his twenty-two-year-old wife, the former Nelle Clyde Wilson. They had married sixteen months before in their hometown of Fulton, Illinois. Tampico was a village in comparison to that Mississippi port; still, Mr. Pitney's establishment was the biggest for miles around, and Jack looked forward to managing it whenever the boss went off to look after his other interests in neighboring counties.

At twenty-three, Jack was already a seasoned retailer, having clerked some eight years in a dry-goods shop and lived part of his boyhood with the family of a department-store owner. Nelle was a seamstress by trade, but the splendor of Jack's new position and Tampico's low cost of living temporarily freed her from any present need to work. For the next two and a half years, she could enjoy the last indulgences of youth before the arrival of her first son, John Neil Reagan, on September 16, 1908.

It is easy to guess what she and Mr. Pitney found attractive in Jack. He had the three qualities of a born salesman: optimism, courage, and what Dutch describes as "burning ambition." One would never have guessed, from Jack's urban manners and sartorial grace, that he came from a family of rural Irish immigrants. He was that rare type, the instinctive gentleman, born with a Jeffersonian repugnance toward any kind of social tyranny. This appealed to Nelle's own moral fervor (she was baptized a Disciple of Christ in 1910) and helped her forgive him, when he came back from Chicago smelling of drink and other women.

Alcohol was Jack's cross: perhaps symbolically, he was lying in a cruciform position the first time Dutch saw him drunk. The O'Regans of Ballyporeen had been famous for their liquor consumption—perhaps not in Ireland, where such fame is hard to come by, but certainly in Illinois, after three of them settled there in the 1850s and found that corn could be turned into products other than flour. Jack, tutored by an elder brother who drank himself mad, developed an early thirst for corn whiskey. Tampico aggravated this by banning liquor the year after his arrival. He then had to drink secretly, or go to Chicago on "buying trips" as often as possible. The big city loomed more and more to his percept as an Irish-green garden of refreshment.

Only one of the Reagan boys inherited their father's alcoholism. Both, however, laid claim to his copious blarney. Neil cherished the memory of Jack standing outside H. C. Pitney's "with a new story for everyone who came along," laughing uproariously in the sun. Dutch praised him as "the best raconteur I ever knew, especially when it came to the smoking-car sort of stories." In imitation or emulation, both sons cultivated a perpetual, maddening joviality, rambling on in their soft, peatsmoky voices.

The waters that closed over Nelle's head on Easter Sunday 1910 did not wash away sin so much as bathe her in a new spiritual glow. There is no evidence of her being dissentient before that date. She had accepted a Catholic wedding to Jack, a Catholic baptism for Neil, and even tolerated Jack's relapse into post-Catholic apathy. Now she emerged from the font (actually the Hennepin Canal, just outside of town) glowing with a new sense of mission—and, as if in earnest of her own rebirth, proceeded to conceive another son.

The question of little Dutch's Christianity did not immediately arise. Her new faith frowned on child baptism, and Jack had no problem with letting the boy choose his own salvation after reaching the age of awareness. So Ronald Reagan began life unshriven. God, to his infant consciousness, was Nelle: a small, auburn-haired woman, narrow of lip and strong of jaw, bending over him and singing in what he insists was "a very nice soprano."

☯

Tampico's eight streetlights crackled on. I pulled out some ancient travel notes and read that this was the hometown of "Admiral J. M. Reeves, Commander of the U.S. Fleet." So much for famous local sons in 1936!

As I stood irresolute, wondering whether to call it a day, the Budweiser sign went out. Two tall men emerged from the bar, folded themselves into the Volkswagen, and drove away. Now I truly was alone. The shop fronts were so quiet that I could hear cornstalks rustling to south and west. A similar peace, I supposed, prevailed as little Dutch's ears began to function in the early months of 1911. About the loudest commotion he heard was when some cart horses took fright at the creamery and bolted down Main Street, curdling the dust with sixty gallons of spilled buttermilk.

Possibly it was this alarming increase in traffic noise that persuaded the Reagans to move in mid-May to a house across the railroad tracks, some three hundred yards from the center of town. If so, they moved in vain. That summer Vern Glassburn went and bought a Hup runabout, and Jay Russell got him a new Buick, and O. D. Olssen sprung for an even newer Ford, and their combined backfires made every day sound like the Fourth of July. Jack, dreaming always of greener grass, tried to persuade Mr. Pitney that an automobile would sharpen his image as one of the best sales representatives in Whiteside County. Blarney prevailed; on June 27, 1913, the *Tampico Tornado* announced that Mr. J. E. Reagan had purchased a Model T.

Less than a month later, Jack was returning from Rock Island with a full payload of goods and family when he crashed the car into a stump, overturning it. Little Dutch was imprisoned inside the crumpled roof, and acquired the beginnings of a lifelong claustrophobia.

☯

Remembering what Mr. Nicely had said about Tampico's former entertainment industry, I surveyed the north side of Main Street to see what was left of former pleasure palaces. According to my notes, that boarded-up facade at number 119 must have been the "Grand Theater" (seating capacity, 20), while a rubble-strewn lot at number 104 once comprised the ground-floor "Electric Theater" and upstairs "Burden's Opera House." In this cube of empty air, a lifetime ago, Jack and Nelle used to tread the boards before audiences seated on folding chairs, while Dutch burbled in his baby carriage by the footlights.

The Reagans were evidently Tampico's reigning theatrical couple when the tiny town was at its population peak of 1,276 souls. They starred in three full-length plays at the Opera House in 1913 alone. On April 19, the attraction was *A Woman's Honor,* and their performances as Gregory Grimes and Olive/Sally (Nelle specialized in double parts) brought a trainload of people from as far away as Yorktown and Hoopole. In the admiring syntax of the Sterling *Gazette,* "A pin dropped could not be heard in the entire house." Seven weeks later, with temperatures rising in the cornfields, they played what sounds like a bodice-ripper, adapted to their own identities. Jack was "John Rider, young Master of the Maples," and Nelle was "Nell, the Dust of the Earth."

Summer was too hot for indoor entertainments, so the manager of the Electric Theater roped off Main Street every Wednesday and Saturday and showed open-air movies, with incidental music provided by the school band. On Thanksgiving Night 1913, the Opera House reopened with what seems to have been the highlight of Nelle's acting career. She starred in the title role of *Millie the Quadroon; or, Out of Bondage,* a five-act "play of antebellum trueness" by Lizzie May Elwyn. Every square foot of sitting and standing room, according to the *Gazette,* was packed as Mrs. Reagan rose to the "many difficult climaxes" of a multiple part that required her to be, successively, a genteel Northern matron, a French nun in green glasses, and a Southern field hand. Jack, corked and carmined and rolling his eyes, hammed it up as an escaped slave, but the triumph was clearly Nelle's. Insatiable for applause, she even sang a musical *entr'acte.*

Dutch has no conscious memories of this evening or, indeed, any other limelit nights prior to his family's first departure from Tampico. By the time Jack returned to town, and Mr. Pitney's service, the local

"The Reagans were evidently Tampico's reigning theatrical couple."
Jack and Nelle Reagan with Neil and Ronald, 1914.

dramatic society had disbanded and Nelle's extravagant histrionics were finding their outlet in religion. One can only guess how much Dutch absorbed, subconsciously, of her performance as Millie. Now that he has reverted to the equivalent of infancy, does Nelle pace again across some dim proscenium in his brain, her face ghastly with fuller's earth, her young body showing through cotton-field tatters, raising the rafters with maternal passion?

> *Oh, that I could die! But no—I must not leave my children; that woman shall not triumph. As the tigress fights for her young, so will I fight for mine!*

☯

I was back early next morning, in brilliant September sunshine, and breakfasted at the Dutch Diner. Styrofoam cup in one hand and cane in the other, I crossed the tracks into Railroad Park. Tampico's grain elevator was white enough to dazzle, so I swiveled and stared across the grass at 104 West Glassburn Street. This was the house Jack rented through December 1914. Two stories high, many-windowed, with a white-columned portico, modern plumbing, and spacious plot, it was the grandest residence the Reagans ever knew as a family.

Dutch, who was nearly four when they left, claims to remember nothing of the house. I wonder, though, if it is not the source of his most recurrent dream, which he told me about in the White House:

Q. All through my life, at certain times, I've dreamed about this tall house, very gracious, with white columns and all, and big rooms and high ceilings, which was for sale, or to let, at a very modest rent. And in the dream I would walk through it and was sure it would be mine, but it never *was,* you know. But the strange thing is, since we came here, I've never dreamed about that house!

A. Perhaps because you're living in it.

His only conscious memories that predate Chicago, apart from Jack's stubbly kiss, are violent ones. He is trapped in the overturned Ford as Nelle calls his name. He is soaring frighteningly high in a swing, and slipping out at the apogee, and hurtling down again as the rope burns his hands. He is crawling with Neil between the wheels of a stationary train, to beg some ice to suck; then the wheels behind them start to turn, slicing across their line of retreat, and next thing they know, a hysterical Nelle is upon them with flailing hands.

As infant traumas go, these were not particularly serious. Dutch's developing psyche remained unaffected by the ultimate violence: poverty. Jack might never earn enough to save, but the Reagans would never count themselves poor, here or anywhere else.

I strolled a couple of hundred yards along South Main, toward the end of town. There was no movement anywhere, except for a languid lifting of dead leaves in the breeze. Three pairs of freshly laundered blue overalls dragged on a line, too damp to sway. I went beyond the last house, about as far into the fields as a four-year-old boy might have gone before his mother ran after him.

All around me to every point of the compass the corn stretched dry and silent, innumerable stalks cut parallel to the horizon. Was there, in fact, a horizon, or had perspective itself gotten bored with the endless retreat, and allowed the sky to cut in? This fertile desert, this universe of sameness, closed off outside experience like a wall. Chicago seemed a thousand miles away, the rest of the world a million. For the first time, I understood the immense insularity of Dutch's personality. No long-distance wires found him here, no radio waves enmeshed him. Long before Jack jerked him away to the big city—and other towns—the child was already sheathed in a strange calm. This paralysis of sensibility was what steadied his heart when he walked coatless down those steps in Geneva to introduce himself to Mikhail Gorbachev. And when the Soviet leader nervously looked up at him, there was nothing in Reagan's eyes but this blank blue sky.

Jack's lust for wider horizons burgeoned in the years 1913 and 1914. The Model T, patched up, drove in ever-widening circles to Coleta, where Nelle's sister Jennie had a farm, to Quincy and Clinton on combined business and pleasure, to Iowa on vacation (a round trip of five hundred miles, through hub-deep drifts of dust), to Fulton and Sterling (where little Dutch caught his first view of the greensliding Rock River), then back to Clinton on yet another buying trip for Mr. Pitney.

Only when snow choked the roads did they revert to bobsled rides (the wind whipping Dutch's fat cheeks till he felt they would burst with blood). At first thaw, the restless Reagans were on wheels again, whirling westward and eastward, until they found themselves deposited, as if by centrifugal force, on Chicago's South Side in the new year of 1915.

3

A Dark Form Half Hidden in the Snow

R ONALD REAGAN came upon me one day in Air Force One, as I sat gazing through a porthole at the fields and forests of his father's *Wanderjahre*. We were en route to Chicago up the left bank of the Illinois River.

"Why aren't you writing?" he asked. It was his standard joke whenever he saw me without a pen in my hand.

"I'm contemplating your murky origins, Mr. President." I drew an imaginary arc in the distance, on a course roughly parallel to our own. "Somewhere out there in that haze are all the towns you lived in as a boy. Monmouth. Galesburg. Tampico. Dixon—"

He leaned past me, giving off a whiff of Royal Briar cologne, and peered down at the green-gold checkerboard, shaking his glossy head. "Darned if I know where we are." I noticed with amusement that he wore his velour flying pants. The presidential trousers were hanging straight and carefully brushed in his private compartment.

"We're about ninety miles southwest of O'Hare," I told him. "After we land, I'm going to go look for that apartment your father rented in

1915—if the building still stands. Neil says it was on Fifty-seventh, a couple of blocks off of Cottage Grove."

He seemed surprised that I did not want to ride in the motorcade to Rosemont Exposition Center, where he was scheduled to grip-and-grin with a crowd of party contributors, but confirmed the address.

Two hours later, I found myself standing outside the corner apartment house at 832 East Fifty-seventh Street in Hyde Park. Clouds of plaster dust were drifting out of a curlicued, cast-iron bay, one floor above the sidewalk. My notes identified it as the very window little Dutch once stood in, watching fire engines come down the street. From inside came the sound of mighty mallet blows, punctuated by a Polish conversation. Some developer must have found out that this was the home of the only President ever to live in Chicago. I got myself admitted by sign language, and sat on a stepladder in the largest of five small rooms, surrounded by opalescent dust. White bars of afternoon sunshine slanted in, irradiating the laborers as if their movements were being choreographed by some celestial projectionist.

Here Jack and Nelle Reagan had settled on or about January 2, 1915. Their younger son succumbed almost at once to big-city bacilli. He was not yet four. "I remember getting bronchial pneumonia. . . . My mother said I nearly died. Some neighbor came over and brought this set of lead soldiers, and I divided 'em into formations and played with 'em while I was recuperating in bed."

Jack was working ten hours a day uptown at the Fair Store, while Nelle took in needlework to supplement the family income. Curiously content to be left alone, Dutch deployed his lead soldiers until the weather warmed and he was well enough to follow Neil into the streets. The neighborhood was run-down Irish, and consequently well supplied with saloons to slake their father's thirst. Neil remembers bringing Jack butter-greased pails slopping over with "backdoor beer." As much of the Reagan pay packet as could be saved Nelle spent on liver, beef bones, and vegetables. The liver was fried for Sunday dinner, and on Monday night its remnants were combined with the bones "into a sort of stew" that thinned to potato-carrot-and-oatmeal gruel, and finally to soup as the week progressed.

Dutch, a dreamy, mild-mannered child, remained oblivious to the high cost of alcoholism. He did not understand why he and Neil, on baseball afternoons, were festooned around the neck with sacks of freshly-popped corn and told to "go sell it down in the amusement park." Nelle's violent reaction when they wastefully filled the apartment with gas one day only amused him, and he was philosophical about Jack's decision, after only eight months at the Fair Store, to "accept" a retail position in Galesburg, about a hundred and forty miles west. At four, he could hardly comprehend that his father had been arrested for public drunkenness.

Not for another seven years would he stand transfixed, like young Parzival, by evidence of mortality in the snow, and feel his first pangs of grief and betrayal. Even after that, he would retain a certain worldly innocence through adulthood, making at least one bookish observer wonder if he were not indeed *der reine Tor*, the Innocent Fool of medieval legend.

☯

Parzival. Perceval. *Pierce-vale*—"the way of dedication, of the Heart," John Matthews writes in *The Grail*. All his life, Ronald Reagan has ridden a long road dissolving, at the limit of sight, into something scintillant yet ethereal. His vagueness about that vision is the typical mythopoesis of Fools or mystics.

Possibly Dutch's youthful glimmer of the divine was small-scale, a desire just to shine at whatever he did. Yet qualities of brightness, elevation, fortification, and encirclement, common to Parzivalian metaphor, are combined in the one adult vison he admitted to, that of the "Shining City on a Hill." However derivative of Saint Matthew and John Bunyan, it is a haunting image, and nobody who researches his pilgrimage can fail to feel the compulsion it exerts on him.

Standing in the white glow of the old Reagan apartment, I mused that if Dutch were here now, he would be gazing out the sunny window, looking for more fire engines. Here was I with my back to it, casting a lank shadow across the room. What would I not give for Father's Benz to arrive outside, and whisk me eighty blocks north, seventy years back, to the peach-colored house!

In 1915, the South Side was as far below the limits of my universe as Lake Shore Drive had been above Dutch's. Possibly—just possibly—Father drove us down Cottage Grove on some roundabout route to Aurora, in which case I might have glimpsed a boy one and a half years older than me, with popcorn round his neck. *Quien sabe?* At any rate, we drew no closer to each other for another eleven years. Father was already involved in local politics, so we would have gotten back to Chicago after the mayoral election. By then the Reagans had left for Galesburg.

Nelle was no doubt relieved to move to that famously temperate town. While Jack took a job in the shoe department of Galesburg's largest store, she installed her sons in a temporary bungalow, and registered Neil in first grade at Silas Willard School. Then husband and wife looked for a larger house.

They found one at 1219 North Kellogg, about ten minutes' walk from downtown. Its dormered facade was deliciously dappled, on clear mornings, by a maple tree that stood between it and the sun. Hundreds of other maples spread their foliage along nearby dark redbrick streets. Dutch felt the neighborhood belonged in a Currier & Ives transparency, "a picture of bright-colored peace."

One day in the attic of his new home, he came upon a forgotten collection of butterflies and birds' eggs. For some reason, the fragility of these specimens made him feel he was breathing mountain air. Suddenly he knew what dawn in the desert looked like.

Sense and sensibility merged even more magically when Nelle lay beside him in bed, reading aloud. He watched the strange black ciphers streaming past her forefinger and arranging themselves into words on the page, like iron filings on a tapped drumskin. Their shapes became sounds, first in his ear, then in his mind. Soon he did not need her voice to hear what he saw.

On July 31, 1916, Jack noticed him on the parlor floor with the Galesburg *Evening Mail,* and teased, "Read me something." Dutch obliged. Soon a group of hastily summoned neighbors was listening to the Great Communicator's first public announcement:

FIVE STATES FEEL FORCE
OF POWDER BLAST
Property Loss Millions
As Result Of Explosion And Fire
On Black Tom Island

This ability at age five and a half to listen visually, or read aurally, was early evidence of his famed "photographic" memory. I think it also explains his later tendency to accept as black-and-white fact anything he was forcefully and dramatically told.

I remember visiting Galesburg as a young writer working for the WPA, and being repulsed by its downtown smell of dung and urine. "More horses and mules marketed here than anywhere else in nation," my field notes read. God knows what the place must have smelt like in the months following April 6, 1917, when Congress declared war on Germany and frantically began to requisition horseflesh.

In September of that year, Dutch was registered, like Neil before him, in first grade at the Willard School. He turned out to be an extraordinarily bright pupil, with perfect marks in spelling and arithmetic, scoring a 97 percent average in his final report of March 1, 1918. But by then his father's furtive binges again made it advisable for the Reagans to move on. Jack got another shoe salesman's job and rented another maple-dappled house on another redbrick street, seventeen miles down the Burlington road.

Their new address was 218 South Seventh in Monmouth. Something about Dutch—was it his air of gentle abstraction?—excited the hostility of neighborhood urchins, who harassed him on sight. He seemed braced for further punishment when he registered for second grade at Central School on September 9. Here, too, he would shine academically, and be promoted to third grade ahead of his classmates, despite a month's traumatic distraction.

"Spanish flu" reached Monmouth along with the first consignment of New York apples, and on October 13 the city's health officer closed all schools, churches, libraries, and dance halls. A column in the *Daily Review,* gloomily headlined MORTUARY, listed the mounting toll; shoppers crossed the streets to avoid one another.

Thanks to its quick precautions, Monmouth escaped the fatalities of neighboring Canton, which was burying a score of victims a day. But Nelle Reagan sickened seriously. Jack burned altar candles while Dutch and Neil waited in terror for the family doctor to confirm that their mother was dying. Instead, he prescribed rotten cheese. Whether or not this amounted, as Dutch later surmised, to primitive penicillin, Herzeleide recovered, and Parzival was saved from grief.

Pandemic gave way to pandemonium in the small hours of November 11. An unscheduled train from Chicago screamed through town, its whistle jammed wide open. Within minutes the streets of Monmouth were ablaze with lights and exploding with crackers and gunfire. Night gave way to a morning red with bonfires, as burghers and farmers, many already drunk, celebrated the Armistice.

That was when the peach-colored house began to close its shutters to us. Father's vote-getting efforts for Charles Evans Hughes had made him the darling—and chief bankroller—of the Aurora Republican Party. He remained a guarantor of the Chicago Opera Association, but Bess's career never recovered from that company's wartime boycott of Wagner. Peace found her resigned to private life, and management of the Aurora Model Dairy.

☯

It also saw the return of the roving Reagans to Tampico, eighty miles west of us. Once again, walls of corn shut Dutch off from the outside world. His scare of the previous fall made him aware "that other powers existed besides my mother and father." As yet he was not sure what these powers were; only that Jack and Nelle seemed to have different ways of dealing with them. The former—reinstated by H. C. Pitney with a flat over the store, a manager's title, and vague promises of profit sharing—would absent himself for days at a time. Nelle sought increasing solace in religion. Neil ran with boys of his own age.

Dutch, alone again, developed a pensive mannerism, as if he were miming Rodin's *Thinker*. Photographs taken of him seated on the railings at the Tampico Stock Meet, or posing with his fourth-grade classmates in September, show a withdrawn, wistful little boy, head cocked to one side, left hand supporting his chin. For all his air of hurt, he clearly does not invite anyone's arm around his shoulders.

He allowed himself to be semi-adopted by an elderly couple who lived next door. They gave him an allowance of ten cents a week, plus cookies and chocolate every afternoon, and made no emotional demands. As he wrote in a grateful passage of autobiography:

> The best part was that I was allowed to dream. Many the day I spent deep in a huge rocker in the mystic atmosphere of Aunt Emma's living room with its horsehair-stuffed gargoyles of furniture, its shawls and antimacassars, globes of glass over birds and flowers, books and strange odors; many the day I remained hidden in a corner downstairs in Uncle Jim's jewelry shop with its curious relics, faint lights from gold and silver and bronze, lulled by the erratic ticking of a dozen clocks.

He recalls reading "the Sermon on the Mount, King Solomon and the Ants by Whittier, Alfred the Great, and the History of the United Netherlands" at Tampico's white-steepled grade school. The eccentric list was probably determined by availability of texts, rather than any policy of eclecticism in the fourth grade. At any rate, the Sermon gave him a "city set upon a hill" to ponder, and King Alfred's carbonization of an ovenful of cakes alerted him to the dangers of too much executive withdrawal.

☯

While Dutch settled down to his third school in three years, I, effete child of privilege, had yet to enter my first. Bess undertook to teach me the rudiments, but warned that Father would send me to "some nice private academy" as soon as I could read and write.

In a special New Year's treat to explain the downfall of Icarus, she took me to the 1920 Chicago Aeronautical Exposition. Half stoned with the fumes of fresh dope, I wandered among fuselages glossed to a drumlike stiffness, and twanged the lyres of biplanes and triplanes. At the stroke of noon, three silver blimps rose silently and slowly until they crowded the Coliseum's ceiling. It was the first aeronautical motion I had ever seen, and dreams of levitation obsessed me for months afterward.

Since the war's end, awareness of a new, earth-liberated age had permeated even the corn country. Nelle Reagan published an aeronautical poem in the *Tampico Tornado,* hoping to lure local children to Sunday school. "We wish we could give you a flying machine," she wrote, "to travel about as you wished à la Wright." She felt sure they'd "come sailing right over," and "at the door of the classroom would light."

Indefatigable in her efforts to inspire everyone with her love of God—waxing as that for Jack waned—she shrewdly mixed proselytizing and entertainment. After Dutch's ninth birthday, she decided that he was reading and memorizing well enough to join her "in recitation" at the Church of Christ. Early in May 1920, he made his dramatic debut, declaiming a piece entitled "About Mother."

Dutch remembers this first platform appearance, along with later ones ("usually as the thing in the sheet"), more in terms of duty than pleasure. His self-discovery as an actor was still some years off. For the moment there were normal boyish things to do, like playing tag in Tampico's stockyard pens, picking strawberries for pay, barbecuing wienies down by the Blow Out, and hiking down the railroad to swim in the deep, dark, slimy-walled canal.

For a dime apiece, on Monday or Tuesday evenings, he and Neil could worship "America's Sweetheart" on the screen of the Opera

House. When the narrow auditorium began to stifle in mid-June, Mr. Burden rigged a white board outside on the sidewalk, set up a few dozen folding chairs opposite, and projected his four-reelers right across Main Street. Now they could watch Tom Mix riding off into a black-and-white sunset, while the real thing flamed unheeded beyond the fields.

That Fourth of July, the old Civil War cannon in Railroad Park belched and thundered, adding extra clouds to a lowering sky. There was more 'nuff roasted chicken and corn as evening came on, accompanied by a fireworks display, courtesy Mr. J. E. Reagan of the Tampico Ladder Company, climaxing in his patented special effect, "a tin can blown 30 ft. in the air by a giant 'cracker.' " Then ladies and gentlemen in aprons and overalls hoed down until the black sky broke, and everybody rushed for home.

Jack more or less ran the H. C. Pitney store now, since his boss was going blind. But the shared profits he had been promised were not in evidence. Business was bad throughout the rural Midwest. The Armistice had caused mass cancellation of government contracts, yet nothing could stop the flow of produce from America's overstimulated farms. Agricultural prices were plummeting. Jack's customers spent their reduced income on feed and fertilizer rather than on new suits and shoes. He raffled off a Model T, hoping to attract a cash-happy crowd. Bidders came from far and wide, but those who lost departed with a pleased sense of having saved money, and his stock stayed on the shelf.

At thirty-seven Jack was still young enough to be restless. He longed to live once more in a town where crickets were not the loudest noise at night, where shoppers had money and some sense of style, where there were at least a few Democrats, and where he might seek refuge from the scourge of Prohibition.

One small city beckoned twenty-five miles northeast of Tampico, in the Rock River Valley. It was industrial rather than agricultural, and, having an Irish-Catholic minority, was well sluiced with speakeasies. Jack suggested to Mr. Pitney that they relocate their partnership there. They should open a small, sophisticated shoe shop. He—J. E. Reagan, qualified "practipedist" and X-ray fittings expert—would manage it alone, in exchange for equity that would amount, over the years, to full purchase.

The proposal was persuasive. On September 9, 1920, the *Tampico*

Tornado announced that Messrs. Pitney and Reagan were "closing out," and moving with their families to Dixon.

I sit now staring at a photocopy of Jack's final "Clearing Sale" advertisement, seeing in its sacrificial prices and querulous subheads ("*This Is No Con Talk . . . Buy All You Want, For We Shall Have No More*") signs of the coming Depression. He may have foreseen, as he calculated his clearance, a continued deflation of farm prices against inflation elsewhere in the economy. But he could hardly guess that millions of speculative enterprises, such as the one he was about to embark on, would soar to fantastic heights of overcapitalization during the next decade, until their contrary dynamics, like backdraft and bushfire, ignited the conflagration that scorched us all.

Once again Dutch and I began to move toward each other. Our separation narrowed to a mere forty miles after Father's shock decision to enroll me as a boarder in Saint Alban's School in Sycamore, a pretty little town about an hour west of Aurora by train.

"Headmaster says you're a bit young, so you'll be coming home on weekends for the first year or so. It's Episcopal, and expensive," Father said (popping the *p*s, his mustache discernibly lifting). "You'd better not to disgrace us, my boy."

Around the same time Jack, aided by his sons, began to ferry shoe stock to Dixon in the Model T. At the end of November he rented a three-bedroom house on the south side of the Rock River. His last ferry consignment, on December 12, included Nelle, Dutch, a pile of household effects, and a cat named Guinevere.

Sycamore was and remains pretty, although its charms were lost on me during three resentful years there. Recently I went back for the first time since leaving, and found the streets paved and a few new buildings put up on the outskirts. Otherwise things were much the same. Golden afternoon light sliced across Somonauk Street, at exactly the same angle as when Paul Rae and I ran downtown to Smoke Schulz's for taffy apples, a lifetime ago. Well, Paul's lifetime anyway. I knew that Saint Alban's was long gone, yet I half-hoped that some structural part of it might still be standing. No, it had been replaced by a Victorian house that I remembered from across the street. Perhaps the flatbed truck responsible for the house's transposition also took away my school.

As often since beginning my pilgrimage into Dutch's past, I felt myself to be a traveler in Looking-Glass Land. North-central Illinois tends to Carrollian illusion, with its chessboard flatness, equivalence of light and shade, and landmarks elusive (like Ronald Reagan!) of direct approach. One's disorientation is bad enough at high noon in midsummer, when any way might be west. But on late October evenings, when the light comes in mistily from somewhere over Colorado, all definition fades, including that between space and time. Drive out of town, kill your motor, and you're back in the days of President Harding. The cornstalks stand as ragged, the windmills spin as slow as they did then. Even the old Lincoln Highway, five miles off and glimmering in the twilight, looks newly metaled. A pervasive ambiguity circulates, like cold Canadian air, unsettling to most people, wholly delicious to writers.

Were I to script a documentary called, say, *The Ronald Reagan Story,* I would extend this ambiguity through the winter solstice, and begin the Dixon sequence with a frame full of falling snow. The camera would start a slow advance through the flakes, moving forward and downward, with a sense of imminent arrival. Music: something icy and evanescent, like the first eighteen bars of Webern's Piano Variations. Then I'd have Dutch read from his own autobiography:

REAGAN   (*quietly, nostalgically*) It was ninety miles from Chicago, ten times as big as Tampico, with the Rock River running down the middle.

Vague dark verticals approach amid the snowfall, on either side of the screen; they pass by, pair by pair, and we realize we are crossing a bridge. Ahead huddle the shapes of waterfront warehouses, and an empty white avenue rising (at an angle exaggerated by the telephoto lens) toward an arch of surpassing ugliness. We dimly make out the legend on the arch's facade: D-I-X-O-N.

REAGAN   A small town of ten thousand—to me it was a city. (*The muted trumpet from Copland's "Quiet City" plays*) It was to be home to me . . . until I was twenty-one. All of us have to have a place we go back to; Dixon is that one for me.

NARRATOR   Ronald Reagan put down his first roots here at age ten, having moved house seven times in the previous nine years. (*The Dixon High School Choir begins to sing "Dixon, Queen of the Valley"*) There would be five further moves before he grew up, but none of them beyond the city limits of Dixon.

BARKER   Dixon—City of Opportunity on the Hudson of the West!

NARRATOR   Here a future President learned how to study and play
            football and save lives. Here, on a snowy day much like
            this, he was prematurely called upon to act like a man,
            and achieved the beginnings of wisdom.

CHOIR   (*singing with infinite tenderness the Innocent Fool motif
            from* Parsifal)
            *Durch Mitleid wissend,
            Der reine Tor!*

*During the previous narration, the camera has been carrying out a se-
ries of dissolves through the white, deserted streets of Dixon. It rests
now, without commentary, upon the porch of a small, two-story, wood-
shingled house, banked about with snow. After a few moments, it
moves on downtown toward a squat little church. The snowfall thins.*

NARRATOR   Here too, young Ronald would discover religion and sex.
            He was fated to fall in love with the daughter of his
            Christian Church pastor, the Reverend Ben H. Cleaver.
            Her name was Margaret, and she was the first girl he ever
            kissed.

REAGAN   (*coldly*) Oh, you found out about her, huh.

NARRATOR   From Dixon High School, Ronald and Margaret would
            go forth to college and come back engaged to marry.
            During his years of early fame as "Dutch" Reagan,
            sportscaster of Davenport and Des Moines, he returned
            to Dixon time and again on vacation. Not until he be-
            came an even more famous film star—

CHOIR   (*fortissimo*) I'm goin' Hol–ly–wood!

NARRATOR   —did his home ties loosen. Yet we hear of him revisiting
            Dixon once a decade for the rest of his life.

CHOIR   (*softly*) Blest be the tie that binds
            Our hearts in Christian love . . .

*As the choir continues to sing, camera rises and pans over Dixon,
making use of the snowfall to stress its utter ordinariness. Cut to a
narrow, glass-fronted commercial property, untenanted.*

BARKER   Watch—this—space!

NARRATOR   In January and Febuary 1921, this store at 94 South
            Galena was as empty as it is now. (*Wind sends a spray of
            ice across the glass.*) But on March 17, the Dixon *Evening
            Telegraph* climaxed a series of teaser ads with the follow-
            ing proclamation:

BARKER   We wish to announce to the people of Dixon that on Sat-
             urday, March 19, 1921, we will open a new and up-to-
             date shoe store. Stock and Fixtures All New!
REAGAN   (*proudly*) Pitney & Reagan.
BARKER   Young in Name—Old in Experience!

*Camera cuts again to the enigmatic little house with snow banked
about it. Music: a reprise of the Innocent Fool motif from* Parsifal,
played wordlessly on woodwinds.

NARRATOR   (*over*) Meanwhile, the Reagans settled into this house at
             816 South Hennepin Avenue, not far from the Fashion
             Boot Shop. Neil and Ronnie—or "Moon" and "Dutch,"
             as everybody but Nelle called them—completed their in-
             terrupted grades at different South Side schools. Neil
             went to South Central, while Ronald went to the old
             "Red Brick School" (*we see a speckled photograph of a
             quaint, spindly, Victorian structure, no longer standing*),
             just five football kicks from home.
REAGAN   Don't get me wrong, my memories are pretty happy and I
             enjoy closing my eyes now and then for a rerun or
             two . . .

*His voice-over sounds strangely fast-paced, until we realize he is not
reading his memoirs any more, but talking to the American people on
one of his innumerable radio broadcasts from the 1970s. He is trying
to make the spoiled children of today understand that there were certain things a shoe salesman's son took for granted fifty years before, in
a small city bleak beyond modern comprehension:*

             The cold early morning journey to the basement to shake
             the grate, uncover the embers, and shovel in coal. Dress-
             ing in the shivering cold while you waited for the house to
             warm. As for pollution, every chimney in town belching
             black smoke and soot every day from fall till summer. . . .
             Also, that night-time walk through the snow to that little
             wooden building out back—a journey repeated in the
             morning. Summer brought the flies incubated in those
             outhouses—of which there was one for every home and
             store and public building.
NARRATOR   Ronald Reagan, born two and a half years after Neil, was
             now only a year behind him academically. The two boys
             had little in common except a love of sport. Ronald en-

joyed rough-and-tumbles with street kids, but, unlike
Neil, he also liked the organized environment of the
YMCA. (*Camera shows a grim, symmetrical structure
fronting on Galena.*) Despite his small size, he qualified
for a basketball team called the "June Bugs." It was in
this role, on the very day that his father's shop opened for
business, that he got his first media mention.

We cut to a team listing on the sports page of the Telegraph, *March
19, 1921. Camera zooms in on the name, "Regan, R."*

REAGAN   It's Reagan, not Regan.

BARKER   (*in rapid, sportscaster style*) This coming Tuesday night,
            March 22, 1921, the Junior Bs basketball tournament be-
            gins at the Dixon Y. June Bugs to play the Bull Frogs—

REAGAN   We won, 1–0 on 22!

BARKER   —followed by Polly Wogs vs. (*pronounced "viss"*) Mud
            Turtles, and Grasshoppers vs. Spiders.

NARRATOR   Week after week, the June Bugs kept winning. But so did
            those pesky Spiders and Turtles. There had to be a double
            playoff. On April 23, Bugs beat Spiders. Three days later,
            after a game fought through the final second—(*rapturous
            cheering drowns out his voice*)

BARKER   (*shouting over the tumult*) June Bugs are Junior B champi-
            ons! "Dutch" Regan wins his first lovely, lollapalooza let-
            ter!!

REAGAN   (*wearily*) It's Reagan, not Regan.

No doubt my scenario would be criticized for its photographic colorlessness. But Dutch has always—unconsciously, no doubt—remembered his Dixon childhood in monochrome. He talks about coal smoke,
snow and frost, the Rock River hard as glass, black-and-white movies,
his father's shop full of marked-down black shoes. When he does remember color, it's the dead color of falling leaves, which, like D. H.
Lawrence, he associates with "pain."

These images, however, are objective rather than depressive. Nothing,
not even Jack's binges and Nelle's despair, seems to have affected his
preternatural, lifelong calm. Young Dutch was an equable boy, content
with his own company at home, but just as happy with other kids out of
doors. One admires his joyous physicality: "Football was a matter of life
and death." He loved to skate downriver for miles against the wind, then
spread his coat for the sheer pleasure of letting the wind blow him back.

Puberty brought two epiphanies that cry out for video treatment.

First Epiphany. It is the winter of Ronald Reagan's eleventh year, 1921–1922. We see a shot of the Galena Avenue bridge connecting Dixon North Side with Dixon South Side. Not today's concrete bridge, but an old iron structure (those dark verticals we glimpsed through the snow at the beginning of this documentary). The sound track is full of weird static—pips and whoops and whistles and occasional loud crackles.

NARRATOR   (*as interviewer*) Mr. President, do you remember that radio crystal set you had in Dixon?

REAGAN   That was the set of a neighbor. . . . my brother and I and a couple of other kids walked all around town trying to find if we could hear something. And finally we went down by the river, and something was coming! (*Splintery fragments of music*) We passed the headphones around and heard this orchestra playing, coming out of the air!

The music bursts out in full force. It is a historic aircheck of a symphony orchestra playing The Skaters' Waltz. *During the pause that follows the last chord, we hear Reagan's voice.*

REAGAN   (*reverently*) Let me tell you, that was a miracle.

ANNOUNCER   This is KDKA Pittsburgh—KDKA Pittsburgh. (*Time signal*)

REAGAN   We were actually hearing this. . . . Can you imagine our sense of wonder?

NARRATOR   To understand the impact of radio broadcasting upon an isolated, introspective, midwestern boy in the early 1920s, we must remember that until that miraculous moment under the bridge, young Dutch's idea of transmitted sound was something via a telegraph or telephone cable. Now, through some magic trembling of the ether, what was distant and strange became near and familiar; the invisible became the audible.

REAGAN   (*over*) You know—none of the developments that came after, talkies and television and so forth, were ever such a revelation as that day I first scratched that crystal with a wire whisker, under the bridge at Dixon.

Atmospheric whoops and whistles resume with full force, then fade out.

"Again we see the little Dixon house with snow banked about it."
Ronald Reagan's boyhood home, 816 South Hennepin Avenue, Dixon

Second Epiphany. Again we see the little Dixon house with snow banked about it. Only now, night has fallen and the weather is blustering up another storm. Camera advances on the porch.

BARKER   Watch—this—space!

An evergreen shrub to the left of the front steps tosses and strains in the wind, casting nervous shadows in the light of a street lamp.

NARRATOR   For several years, going back to Galesburg days, Ronald
              Reagan had known that his parents had a secret problem.

REAGAN   Sometimes, my father simply disappeared and didn't
              come home for days, and sometimes when he did return,
              my brother and I would hear some pretty fiery argu-
              ments. (*The evergreen shivers violently*)

NARRATOR   That was before Prohibition. Now the whole country was
              dry, so if Jack still drank, he had to do so secretly. Dixon
              lay along one of the main bootleg routes out of Chicago

and was heavily policed. One evening shortly after his eleventh birthday in February 1922, young Ronald came home from a basketball game at the YMCA (*camera is close to the porch now*) . . .

REAGAN   My mother was gone on one of her sewing jobs, and I expected the house to be empty.

The wind, gusting hard, whips the evergreen almost double, and for a moment or two we see a dark cruciform shape—is it a man or just a trough of shadow?—on the snowy boards of the porch, near the door.

REAGAN   It was Jack lying in the snow, his arms outstretched, flat on his back. He was drunk, dead to the world. I stood over him for a minute or two. . . . I felt myself fill with grief for my father. (*Softly, we begin to hear the Innocent Fool motif from* Parsifal) Seeing his arms spread out as if he were crucified—as indeed he was—his hair soaked with melting snow, snoring as he breathed, I could feel no resentment against him.

CHOIR   *Durch Mitleid wissend,*
Der reine Tor!

REAGAN   I bent over him, smelling the sharp odor of whiskey from the speakeasy. I got a fistful of his overcoat. Opening the door, I managed to drag him inside and get him to bed.

NARRATOR   So, like Parzival taking responsibility for the dead swan, young Ronald had his first intimation of mortality— which is to say, the vulnerability of all flesh to demonic forces. He put his father away and said nothing about the incident to his mother. (*Close-up of Reagan at eleven—an impassive, rather coarse-faced boy in a beanie*) She, in turn, said nothing to him. Midwestern to her hard core, she knew better than to address a painful issue directly. (*Close-up of Nelle at thirty-nine, her face furrowed*) What she did, in the most casual way possible, was to put a consolatory book into his hand. (*CHOIR sings the Dresden Amen from* Parsifal) It was neither Bible nor *Pilgrim's Progress,* but a novel. Sometime that Lenten season, Ronald read it, and it changed his life.

CHOIR   (*for the third time*)
Durch Mitleid wissend,
Der reine Tor!

Fade out.

Reading *That Printer of Udell's* was a religious experience for Dutch. He once told me, shyly, that the novel made him "a practical Christian." I checked the Library of Congress card catalog and found it to be one of a prodigious number of titles by Harold Bell Wright.

Within an hour I had a crumbling copy in my hands. To turn its coarse-fibered pages was to enter a world of small-town religiosity that radio and television have long since rendered extinct. Wright sold more than ten million copies of books like these, mainly to rural and small-town Americans like Nelle Reagan. They are now close to unreadable. Yet, since Dutch had been so profoundly moved by *That Printer of Udell's,* I found myself absorbedly reading it "through" his pre-adolescent eyes.

The novel is subtitled *A Story of the Middle West.* It opens with a prologue depicting the alcoholic prostration of a man who lies on the floor of a rude cabin, under the scared eyes of his son. ("He's full ergin . . . Don't stir him, Maw.") "Maw" can hardly stir herself; she is dying of poverty and a broken heart. Before her final agony, she asks God to "take ker" of her beloved little Dick.

The narrative proper begins sixteen years later. Dick Falkner, now a tall young man, arrives outside a midwestern industrial town. He is penniless, tired of wandering, and full of grim ambition. It is dawn in early March; the city lies wreathed in morning mist. Sun begins to shine down on the misty rooftops, and a new lightness surges in his heart.

He begins to walk the streets, looking for work. "I'm a printer by trade," he tells people. But the city's job market is tight. After days of resisting saloon ads promising FREE LUNCH WITH BEER, Dick wanders into a luminescent church. He's an agnostic, but is sure that "Christians won't let me starve." Won't they just! Meanwhile, "The city rumble[s] on with its business and its pleasure, its merriment and crime."

Dick is finally hired by the publisher George Udell, and becomes his printer and right-hand man. Enter Amy Goodrich, the daughter of a prosperous burgher. She is dark-haired, with wide brown eyes, and smiles a lot. Dick is instantly smitten: "If there is one girl in this world for me . . ."

Alone in his poor room, he fantasizes Amy laughing at his anecdotes, listening gravely to his "plans and ambitions." But how can he impress himself on her? A sympathetic, fatherly Christian, "Uncle" Bobby Wicks, nudges him in the direction of social involvement.

Worshipers at the church that once spurned him do not recognize the tall, handsome, newly tailored youth who walks down the aisle a few Sundays later. Here is an obvious leader. Surely not "that printer of Udell's?" Dick can think only of wide-eyed Amy. She, in turn, is interested enough to engineer an introduction to him in the church hall afterward.

He strikes her as amusing, if rather long-winded. But when Dick jumps up to make an impromptu speech, she is dazzled by his eloquence. He admits to some showbiz experience. They strike up a romance. Amy's parents are doubtful, until Uncle Bobby reassures them: "He may surprise you some day."

Church elders appoint Dick night manager of their reading room, hoping he will charm the city's youth away from saloons. He does so by treating everybody "in the same kindly, courteous manner," although he still insists he is not a practicing Christian. Amy, lovesick, prays for him. (She is given to teary upward glances.)

Winter settles over the city. There are no homes for the homeless. One night in a downtown doorway, Dick comes upon (we may imagine Dutch's emotions on reading this passage) "a dark form half hidden in the snow." It turns out to be the body of an anonymous vagrant. Dick blames "spasmodic, haphazard, sentimental" local welfare policies. As far as he can see, only the "shiftless and idle" are getting help, rather than the needy. "I have a plan."

Dick's great moment comes when he announces this plan, in the climactic central chapter of *That Printer of Udell's*. He attends a meeting of the reform-minded Young People's Society. Its agenda includes moral revival of the city. He takes the floor. Something about his handsome bigness and unassuming dignity makes the audience listen with respect. As he talks, he discovers that he is a natural political orator, with a gift for balanced truisms. To help the undeserving, he says, is to humiliate those in real difficulty, "by placing a premium rather than a penalty on crime."

Dick proposes that the city's wealthy class should endow a dormitory-*cum*-lumberyard that will offer free shelter in exchange for full-time work. Recipients must quit as soon as they are re-equipped for society. In the meantime, they will collect the city's daily accumulation of scrap wood, process it, and sell it for kindling. This will soon make the institution profitable.

Economics, evidently, is not our hero's strong point. He says with a smile that twenty cents should be enough to feed a man a day. "It is possible, of course, to live on less." The smile disarms Dick's audience. He hears nothing but admiring applause.

After this hortatory climax, the story goes into some melodramatic diversions that I won't describe, except to note that Amy suffers considerably before she gets her man. Ultimately, Dick's scheme is adopted and becomes a showpiece example of the power of private citizens to solve their own community problems. He emerges as the town's leading young spokesman. His gift of eloquent address, combined with genial manners and a penchant for brown suits, make him the throb of many feminine hearts.

Amy, however, remains his muse. He agrees to become a Disciple of Christ, and marries her. *That Printer of Udell's* ends with the people of the city voting to send Mr. Richard Falkner to "a field of wider usefulness." Our last glimpse shows Dick kneeling in prayer before leaving with his wide-eyed wife for Washington, D.C.

It is tempting to read more into a long-forgotten novel than Ronald Reagan probably did as a boy. The dark figure in the snow, for example, Amy's adoring stare, the brown suits, the prefiguring of Governor Reagan's welfare reform, are surely more coincidental than prophetic. If Dick and Dutch were refugees from alcoholic menace and would-be improvers of men, so have been countless other compensatory characters in history. Yet I cannot help feeling that the book's larger themes of self-indulgence versus Practical Christianity, of institutional apathy yielding to passion, of oratory as a tool and private values as public policy, unmistakably nurtured the embryo President, like fresh salts in the womb. He closed *That Printer of Udell's* and went to his mother and said, "I want to be like that man."

Nelle Reagan saw that he was thirsting for grace. But he was not yet twelve; her faith forbade her to force the sacraments on him. A few days later, he came back to her and said, "I want to declare my faith and be baptized."

Such was his fervor that he persuaded Neil—an apathetic Catholic— to join him in total immersion. On June 21, 1922, the two boys were welcomed at the First Christian Church, along with about two dozen other youths, and plunged into its chilly waters of Rebirth. "Arise," intoned the minister as they emerged. "Arise and walk in newness of faith."

The building had tall, south-facing stained-glass windows ornamented with wheat sheaves of green and pale gold. They were designed to let in as much of the abundant sunshine of the plains as possible, and dazzle the eyes of true believers.

They even dazzled me, although I was but a proxy member of the congregation. I bunched my brows against the brightness, trying to make out Dutch's skinny, dripping, swimsuited body. Was that him, walking toward me in spread of rays? No—this silhouetted form was too squat, too muscular, too dry in heavy white clothes. It paused, hitched what looked like a mallet over its shoulder, and said, "*Musimy zamkniete.*"

I stared at it stupidly. Some Disciple, I supposed, speaking in tongues.

"*Musimy zamkniete,*" the man with the mallet repeated. "Please— fife o'clock. Ve must go now."

Not tongues. Polish! I realized I was still standing in Dutch's old apartment, amid still-lit plaster dust. Leaving the Poles to lock up, I limped downstairs and out into the warm Chicago evening. If I could get to the airport in time, I might be able to catch a ride home on Air Force One.

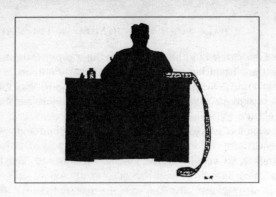

4

A World Elsewhere

O N SEPTEMBER 23, 1923, I was sitting in chemistry class at Saint Alban's when a Western Union telegram man entered and handed a wire to the teacher. As Dr. Jahn read it, amid silence so intense we could hear our bunsen burners hissing, I knew with certainty that Father was dead. He had not been well all summer. I had noticed a new habit of sudden deep sighs, accompanied by a rising pass of the left hand under the left suspender, as if to calm some sort of hysteria in his chest.

When I asked Bess what, exactly, killed Father, she said in a rough voice, "Read Robert Louis Stevenson's last book, *Weir of Hermiston*. See how it ends. That's what fetched him."

I got a copy out of the Sycamore libarary only to find that *Weir* was a fragment—albeit a magnificent one. The last half-sentence read:

> It seemed unprovoked, a wilful convulsion of brute nature

That sudden white space is as powerful an image of death as any I know. There, one fall day, was Father, with his billowing coattails and bristling mustache, and there, the next, he wasn't.

Arthur Morris, true to his impatient form, died intestate; Bess had no idea how much of our wealth could be protected from the numerous charities waving pledges at her. Evidently the family lawyers were pessimistic, because in November she wrote to say that we would be selling the townhouse.

So the color of peach, too, blanched from our lives, and my ache for Father was sharpened by nostalgia for the lost graces of Lake Shore Drive. Indeed, the pain became so physical that I had to cinch my belt tight for relief. Hunched wasp-waisted over my school desk, I drew hundreds of imaginary aircraft, engines of release from the snows of De Kalb County. There were monoplanes of prodigious wingspan (one not unlike the Rutan Voyager, which would circle the earth during Dutch's presidency), transparent zeppelins trailing guy ropes like bluebottles, hedgehopping autogiros, finny rockets, and squads of stubby triplanes. One afternoon, through some chance spurt of ink, I drew a pilot whose goggled gaze was curiously soothing. I let him hang free in space, and printed over the whir of his propeller,

DAVE DARE, DOGFIGHTER

and then wrote my own name above the horizon at the foot of the page.

The composition of this novel absorbed me through the rest of the winter. As Dave Dare dogfought his way to glory, I was able to loosen my belt, notch by notch.

I might have advanced by two and a half years my first encounter with Ronald Reagan, had I accepted an invitation to spend the summer of 1924 in Grand Detour, a village on the Rock River, just upstream from Dixon.

Grand Detour was the home of Paul Rae, a plump pink boy whose gift for drawing greatly exceeded mine. (He already specialized in the savage caricatures that would win him tabloid fame in the Thirties.) Although he became my best friend, there was something giggly about him that made me initially wary. So I chose instead to visit my uncle Ira at his country place in Massachusetts, an enclave of would-be WASP privilege as remote from Dutch's ken, I suppose, as the Azores.

His ideal of social exclusivity was the Dixon Country Club, which lay just north of town (and just beyond the Dixon Home for the Feeble-Minded). He was allowed to caddy there occasionally, and thus made his first acquaintance with golf-playing Republicans.

Sometime that summer, he discovered that the world was intricate, and that most of its beauty lay in its intricacy. Too blind to track even the blur of a softball, he had never been able to understand how his friends managed to pick, out of invisible air, points of ricochet so precise that ash wood and leather would collide with the most satisfying sound in sport. He philosophically accepted his failure at bat, just as he accepted the preference of girls for coarse, clever Neil. This last did not bother him at thirteen; his only obsession was football. Its points of impact were easier to see, its struggles more man-to-man. He did not have to identify whom he tackled, as long as the target mass was the right color.

Then one day, driving out of Dixon with Nelle, he idly picked up and put on her spectacles. The richness of landscape, the detail of townscape, the discovery of depth of field: one would expect such revelations to transform his perceptions, as they had the teenage Theodore Roosevelt's. But distance remained his preferred stance *vis-à-vis* other human beings, and large blocks of essentials his way of organizing information.

He did not need spectacles to luxuriate in the lemon-yellow light that spilled through the stained-glass windows of the Dixon Public Library, a Romanesque stone building just five blocks from his house on Hennepin Avenue. Most days after school he would stop by and browse in its four-thousand-volume collection.

His tastes were those of any middlebrow, midwestern boy, although he was one of the library's more enthusiastic young patrons, averaging two withdrawals a week. I asked him once what his favorites were. "Oh! I was a voracious reader." He cited *Tom Sawyer* and *Huckleberry Finn,* the Westerns of Zane Grey, Rover Boys adventure stories, and every science-fiction title he could get his hands on. With a fine discrimination, he also enjoyed *Tom Brown at Oxford* and *Frank Merriwell at Yale.*

I was expecting to go back to Saint Alban's in September 1924 when Uncle Ira said ominously, "Your mother wants me to have a little talk with you."

Bess had at last won control of Father's estate. Although depleted by his compulsive philanthropy, it was still sizable enough for her to sell the Aurora Model Dairy at a loss, buy a house on Dearborn Parkway in Chicago, and establish a trust fund for my education. Uncle Ira drummed his fingers and said, "Arthur, you're being sent to school overseas."

He must have been disconcerted by the joy this news evoked. *Overseas*—most thrilling, most transporting of words! Unlike most twelve-year-old boys, who tend to be homebodies, I dreamed of "a world elsewhere." My uncle flipped a prospectus across the desk and explained that Bess wanted me to have the kind of English classical tutoring her brothers had had in Canterbury. But there was no need to persuade me: I was already entranced by the prospectus's cover, which showed schoolboys in short black gowns walking across a courtyard in the shadow of a great cathedral tower. The title read SCHOLA REGIA CANTUARIENSIS, and below, in smaller print, appeared the mysterious legend, *This Place by Royal Henry Sett Apart.*

The King's School was to be my home, save for summer vacations stateside, for the next three and a half years. Bess had grown up in its precincts; that and her family connections got me in as the only "colonial" on the register. Or so the Head said, when I arrived, still sick from the transatlantic steamer, and interviewed him in his study overlooking Green Court. (Twilight darkening the lime trees; jackdaws wheeling; a faint whiff of piss from the old stone *necessarium.*)

In retrospect, I think Dr. Latter was desperate for dollars. While King's was probably the oldest private school in Britain, it was also one of the poorest. Some of its best masters and many of its brightest graduates had been lost in the Great War; it was therefore suffering both in morale and alumni support. I knew little of this in my time there, which was—how to put it?—transforming.

By the new year of 1925, I had been battered into an awkward approximation of an English schoolboy. Oddly enough, I welcomed the transformation: my vowels lengthened, as did my hair; I grew to enjoy the sharp embrace of the King's collar and the feel of my surplice floating as I ran from lesson to lesson. I eagerly, even passionately, learned the liturgy of "Cath," as we called the great church that dominated our lives. Lingering in the nave after evensong, I breathed the pure, cool perfume of a culture that had been ancient when Chicago was but a clutch of wigwams.

As Bess intended, the King's School endowed me with a kind of education that was then already out of fashion in America—classical, lettered, and gentlemanly—while its continuity with the remote past comforted my midwestern hunger for history. (A friend showed me how to outline my splayed fingers with a penknife on the Cloister's black stones, among similar handprints five centuries old.)

Nervously jerky and unathletic, I admired the effortless coordination of "bloods" on the rugby field, and tried to emulate their elegant sloth as they lounged down the Norman Staircase between classes. Or I dogged the steps of senior masters, whose chalky gowns and long tweed jackets draped over leather-buttoned cardigans and Oxford bags (twenty-one inches swirling around each argylled ankle) gave them a sort of multilayered motion, like jousting-horses, as they cantered across Mint Yard to tea. My ear rejoiced in the precise diction of deacons who equinunciated every syllable in words like *clerestory* and *prebendary*. But my lazy American tongue could not help lengthening the vowels.

Above all, I rejoiced in the perpetual proximity of Cath. Snug after lights-out in my curtained dormitory cubicle, I would curl close to the frozen window and gaze at "Bell Harry," towering huge and pale against the stars. Every quarter hour, its booming voice piled harmonic over harmonic and chime upon chime. As midnight approached, it seemed to toll continuously, until the very welkin (a word I discovered in Palgrave's *Golden Treasury*) rang in sympathy. Microscopic shards of ice shook off the panes. Bell Harry blurred, and I slept.

In an effort to impress Alec McDonald, the school's only veteran fighter pilot, I began a new novel in June. It was called *Rocketship X-50,* and I begged his opinion of the opening chapters. All he would say was, "If you're so keen on rockets, maybe you should sign up for the special party I'm taking to the R.A.F. display at Hendon on the twenty-seventh."

Ronald Reagan once claimed to be able to project stereoscopes of childhood at will, running them back and forth in memory "exactly as we used to do in the parlor." My own mental carousel carries at least that rapturous day in similar detail. A smoky press of charabancs, taxis, roadsters, and gargle-horned limousines around the grass expanse of Hendon Field. Poplars feathering a gray, scuddy sky. In the middle distance, wavering through blue exhaust fumes, a clutch of pedimented hangars. Nearer, two restless marquees strain at their pegs, surrounded by a flotsam of cloth caps and homburgs, bowlers, silk bonnets, some optimistic straw boaters, and the top hats of foreign dignitaries. (Mr. McDonald, sourly: "Plenty of Japs and dagos. Our future enemies, I shouldn't wonder.")

Overhead, lazily humming, little biplanes wheel and spin. O the alliterative beauty of English plane names! Gloster Grebes, Hawker Herons, Supermarine Seagulls and Fairey Flycatchers, even an ancient Sopwith Snipe, tumble in the stiff breeze, pap-pap-papping one another with blank cartridges (one eject perforates the hat brim of a man in the next box and knocks off his pince-nez), dropping "bombs" of flour that coat spectators with their downwind dust. Pale parachutes burst like dissolving aspirins and float down from a meniscus of silvery cloud . . .

☯

Where, I wonder now, was Ronald Reagan on June 27, 1925? What if (the passage of seventy-four years allows a certain measure of daft speculation) I had hijacked a dirigible and floated westward while time stood still? What bird's-eye view might I have gotten of Dutch's little world, under that same June sun?

Not quite the same sun, perhaps: its light would have been hotter and harsher. And the hour (whatever the Hendon clock might say) still early—a few minutes before nine. Dixon is not yet busy. From where I hover, about a hundred and fifty feet above the Galena Avenue bridge, I can hear crickets chirping in Assembly Park, and feel the heat beginning to rise from South Side's tin roofs and auto hoods. Flags loll at half-mast; some Rotarian must have died. I know without looking that there is a poultry-packing plant somewhere to windward. Occasionally the breeze shifts, bringing fresher air from the gardens and a large petunia nursery, and a pleasant caramel aroma from the Borden Condensed Milk cannery, about a mile downstream.

Dixon eschews the squareness of most midwestern towns, whose plats dully conform to latitude and longitude. Instead, it aligns itself with the Rock River, which approaches khaki-green from the northeast, and bends here to the right, as if feeling the distant pull of the Mississippi. The angle inclines a few degrees south of true west, paralleled by River Street's bright narrow-grade. Galena Avenue, vertical axis of the city, points in the same direction as my compass, i.e., not quite north.

A white-streaming weir and gray stone walls restrain the turbulent river. It splits Dixon socially as well as geographically. Jack Reagan and his family have been living for almost a year on the higher-income North Side. There are fewer commercial buildings on that bank, and more trees—particularly east of Galena, where managers and factory owners have their big houses. Pleached elms at 321 East Fellows shade the dignified residence of Jack's controlling partner, Mr. Pitney.

Downtown is mainly South Side. The Fashion Boot Shop (that tile-roof box with a garish awning at 94 South Galena) has not yet generated enough profits to allow Jack to luxuriate in the leafy environs of Assembly Park. He is renting a house at 318 West Everett—close enough to the Illinois Central tracks to taste soot and hear the "gasping, panting roar" (Dutch's phrase) of freight trains. One is approaching right now: I can see its drifting plume about ten miles north of town.

Looking down at Jack's ugly little two-story rental, the fourth in a gray-white row, I feel a surge of sympathy for him. He moved here in

Ronald Reagan's World
1911–1933

order to qualify his boys for Dixon High School North Side (a gabled brick-and-stone cube facing the river). Poor shoe dog, he has a long daily walk to work now, with the sun in his eyes in the morning and again coming home. He sacrificed over seven hundred square feet of living space when he quit Hennepin Avenue. Yet he sees less of his favorite son than before: Neil, in a gesture of educational independence, has chosen to remain at DHS South Side. Dutch is a one-year veteran of the more prestigious school.

So the Rock River has begun to carve a cultural gulf between brother and brother. Between father and mother too, I'd guess: Jack is temperamentally a South Side man. He still likes to loaf with the blue-collar Irish Catholics—firemen, pool hustlers, City Hall hacks—who can be seen most times outside the ladder-company headquarters at 115 West Second Street, playing pinochle and discussing the whereabouts of the latest Canadian stash through furtive veils of cigarette smoke.

Emerging now on the right bank—it is ten o'clock, a convenient hour to shop at Sproul's North Side Cash Grocery—is the middle-class meritocracy to which Nelle and Dutch aspire: polite boys who walk on the streetward side of girls and carry their bags of fruit; serious, straw-hatted businessmen with applications pending at the Dixon Country Club; Protestant matrons looking forward to a nice Saturday "dinner" at the temperance hotel in Assembly Park, where details of the new chautauqua season have just been posted.

The sun climbs high, and more and more of Dixon's rail grid dazzles as I frown down, wishing I had brought dark goggles with me. There must be at least six train or trolley tracks warping up, and another four or five woofing across, this hard sampler. Its geometry permits no ambiguous corners, no sanctuaries of mystery or romance, no eccentricities of behavior or imagination. I can understand Dutch's wry remark that his fellow citizens would have looked askance at him had he ever confessed the full extent of his youthful fantasies.

Might that be his scrawny figure running along the sidewalk, desperately looking up at me? Why does he throw his arms out in seeming supplication? Even as I stare down, the boy leaps and makes a convulsive contraction of his whole body, as though something has socked him in the stomach. Then he lands, straightens, and mimes a casual throw. A football fantasy! Perfectly acceptable by Dixon standards. But he better not pretend he's Richard III.

Not that that's likely. At fourteen, young Reagan has yet to act in a play at school. Recently, however, his mother persuaded him to deliver a recitation at one of her "readings." The applause stirred vague longings in his breast—if not for the theater, then for some life transcending the local and the present. He draws well enough to see himself "earning a living as an artist." Alternatively, he dreams of living in the wild with wolves, or joining his good friend Frank Merriwell at Yale, or following his *alter ego* Dick Falkner to Washington. Or perhaps he is a Warlord of Mars, and is about to deploy that planet's Strategic Defense Initiative against my dirigible:

> A great fleet of Zodangan battleships rose from the camps of the besiegers without the city, and advanced to meet us. . . . Our green Martian warriors had opened fire on them almost as they left the ground. With their uncanny marksmanship they raked the oncoming fleet with volley after volley.

It is time for me to beat a hasty retreat back to Hendon.

That running boy, catching that imaginary ball, still leaps and contracts in memory. "It wasn't play-acting," one contemporary spectator recalls, "it was reality, even to the facial expressions and grunts."

If so, then how much more real, and painful, it must have been for Dutch to hear, in the fall, that he was too slight to make the scrub at Dixon High. Purple and white varsity jerseys glowed in the window of Vaile & O'Malley's Menswear, but they were cut for "men" more massive than his 125 pounds. Had he been baptized a Catholic like Neil, he could not have more passionately perceived those colors as representing cardinal privilege and grace. "I just had to wear one of those purple and white jerseys."

The best he could hope for was to try for captain of the school's B team, in the hope that by his junior year he could tilt the scales in his favor.

I have searched the Canterbury and Dixon calendars of the mid-Twenties, and find only one other date when God, or whoever it is really authorizes biographies, might say that Dutch and I were in any kind of spiritual harmony. That was on Easter Day 1926, when as a surprise gift to Bess, I celebrated my first mass as a confirmed member of Christ's Church congregation. The service was conducted by no less a dignitary than the Archbishop of Canterbury himself.

Bell Harry was booming as we marched house by house through the cloister in our white surplices. Cath—Walter Pater's "place of memories out of reach"—loomed ahead of us, its stained glass coruscating. We entered to a burst of Handel. The Archbishop, still vested in the deep purple silks of Lent, took his throne. Then, with a booming of deep diapasons, the organ and entire assembly broke into Old Hundred: "*O God, our help in ages past . . .*"

Just about then, if my time-zone calculations are correct, Ronald "Dutch" Reagan was leading Dixon's annual Sunrise Prayer Meeting of the Disciples of Christ. He was assisted by Miss Frances Smice. With the sun behind him, and Nelle's eyes on his face, he stood in the middle of the Hennepin Avenue Bridge and improvised a long prayer in praise of the resurrected Lord. The Rock River—dark bluish-red upstream, radiant in the middle distance where it spilled over the hydroelectric turbines—ran under his feet and carried a vague reflection of some thirty or forty worshipers down toward the railroad bridge.

> *Arise and shine, thy light is come!*
> *Arise, arise and shine!*
> *With love's adorning, shine forth as the morning.*
> *Arise, arise and shine!*

Their voices floated over the water, more strained than full-throated. It was still only forty-eight degrees. To left and right, South Side and North Side, Dixon's flat facades were achieving a harsh definition, as if painted by Edward Hopper—block after block bathed in light or sunk in shadow.

From where Dutch stood he could see the big stores along First Street, and the Fashion Boot Shop on the cold side of Galena Avenue, the tall drab hotel where Lincoln once slept, the brown, vitrified-brick power station, the triple gables of his school and the squat towers of his church, gas stations with glass cylinders drained, taverns permanently padlocked, and a general dull glinting of steel roofs and iron drums. After the risen Lord had blessed all this, the Disciples dispersed for breakfast. But Dutch's devotions were not over. He had a Sunday-school class for young boys at nine-thirty, followed by a full program of worship at ten-forty-five. There would be some of his favorite hymns: "Rock of Ages," "The Old Rugged Cross." At the climax of the service, he would partake of a Eucharist of white unleavened bread and the Christian Women's Missionary Society's sacramental specialty, purple grape juice in cans.

That summer, Dutch worked as a laborer. Aside from his brief spells as a caddy at the country club, it was his first paid employment. For ten hours a day, six days a week, he cleared sites for a Dixon residential contractor, mainly swinging a pick at obstinate blue clay. He hated the work so much that once, when a whistle blast signaled noon halfway through his pick stroke, he simply let go and strolled away, leaving the tool to thud where it might.

Deaf and distracted six decades later, Ronald Reagan could still hear in his head that remembered whistle, down by the cannery.

> My father came to pick me up for dinner [*sic*], and he was so amazed to see me drop that pick in midair he just stood there with his mouth open. The foreman said to him, "That kid of yours can get less dirt on a shovel than any human being I've ever known." (*Chuckle*)

Surveying, which he was taught to do by the same company, suited him better. Rodman Reagan held the measure by which others more technically versed than he calculated the constructive possibilities of the mound he stood on. It was excellent training for a future President.

Of more immediate consequence, his summer in the open air added precious pounds to his slender physique and qualified him at last for the varsity.

Bess rented a lakeside house at Ravinia in August. All I remember of that vacation is a shuddering weakness when I found one night I could not get out of my bath. For days afterward bedroom, beach, and *Ätherblau* rotated around me nauseatingly.

As poliomyelitis attacks go, mine soon went, taking with it no more than a quarter inch of my left leg. I began a lifelong regimen of therapeutic swimming, and within six weeks was walking—although not as well as I walked before. Doctors delayed my return to the King's School through Thanksgiving.

"Paul Rae's mother telephoned to ask if you were well enough to go to Grand Detour for the Armistice weekend," Bess said one day in early November. "Are you?"

And that is how I first encountered Dutch.

Grand Detour (pop. 225) was an imposing name for about seventy old homes clustered around a horseshoe curve of the Rock River. If one of the village's languid crows could be persuaded to fly directly south, it would find Dixon just five miles away; by car or water the distance is about double. Mrs. Rae was the widow of an executive in the local John Deere corporation. Her life centered around her two children. Mary, the elder, was away at Eureka College, in midstate. Paul, having prepped out of Saint Alban's, now attended a private school "downtown," as everybody referred to Dixon.

On the Thursday morning of Paul's fifteenth birthday, November 11, 1926, Mrs. Rae drove us in to a matinée showing of a W. C. Fields movie. The weather was blustery and cold. Ice jostled in the river to the right of State 2. On the bottomlands opposite, bare oaks stood out like fossilized fish bones.

"That's Lowell Park," Paul said, pointing. "You can swim there in the summer."

Ahead, at the crest of Dixon South Side, loomed Nachusa Tavern, apparently not painted since Lincoln's departure. Turning onto Galena Avenue, we passed under a white arch festooned with Armistice Day crepe and rolled down toward River Street. A few dozen shabby storefronts—one of them must have been Jack's Fashion Boot Shop—rolled by to right and left.

"We'll get out at the foot of the bridge, Mother."

"Now remember, you're not to do much walking. And take a streetcar to the game. I'll pick you up there at five."

"Game?" I said, shivering as she drove away.

"Yeah, her idea of a special treat." Paul grimaced. It had been our shared lack of interest in football that drew us together at Saint Alban's.

"What game?"

"Dixon High versus Amboy."

We luxuriated for two hours in black bioscopic warmth, and for another hour more over milk shakes. When, reluctantly, we crossed the bridge and walked down the stone embankment toward DHS North Side, we heard a band playing.

"Damn, the game hasn't begun yet."

The football field's upper bleachers were heavy with bodies, so we took two low front seats. Almost immediately rain began to fall, rinsing away the afternoon's last colors. If any of the purple and white jerseys Dutch coveted were in evidence, I do not recall them—or, for that matter, Amboy's combination. Yet I can still see some action in close-focus clarity, and even hear a few crackly bursts of sound track.

The shimmering window blind in my study replays an intricate choreography of running youths, heads and ears cramped inside leather helmets, shoulders hulking out of all proportion to their bodies. Dixon was the heavier team, so the rain favored them. They regularly carried the ball for first downs, scoring at will throughout the second quarter. For whatever reason one picks out a shape among shapes, I began to notice the movements of their right guard. Lighter than his fellows, he ran tirelessly and tackled with wild determination. At half-time, the Dixon team trooped past our bench to towel off. I kept my eyes on the guard as he strolled toward me.

I saw—I registered—I calibrated—a square-cut youth of nearly sixteen, about five feet ten inches tall and one hundred and sixty pounds in weight. He was not yet grown to proportion (his legs lacked heft and his chest was shallow) but his shoulders were broad and he walked with extraordinary grace. There was none of the arms-out swagger that jocks affect, no sense either of hurry or hesitation, just flowing, forward, lynx-like momentum. His face irked me. It had an adolescent coarseness and an air of studied jollity, as if he knew he was being watched. When he waved at a cheering fan and grinned, his upper lip pulled to the right. His eyes had the rubbed, overstrained look of somebody used to glasses. I sensed that he was reacting to sound rather than sight.

"Who's this fellow?" I whispered. Paul shrugged. The square-cut youth and I briefly exchanged glances. I had an odd sensation of blueness and blindness. A million miles away, a factory siren wailed. His purposeful body moved on, exuding liniment. I dropped the candy wrapper I had been holding—and as I reached for it, his wet sleeve brushed my hand.

"His name's Dutch Reagan," the boy next to Paul said, leaning over. "Didn't make the first four games, but when we got licked 34–0 by Sterling, Coach fired the regular guard and took on *him*."

"Here's Mother," rejoiced Paul. "Let's say you're too tired for the second half."

"But I'm not tired." He stared at me.

"Dutch," the youth predicted, "gonna win his letter for sheer grit."

One effect of polio, as many victims have discovered to their consolation, is that physical debility greatly increases mental activity. When I returned to Canterbury, I became passionate for music and mathematics and rewrote my novel *Rocketship X-50*. Now my hero had a limp and a girlfriend and a new name, so I changed its title to *Jim Raider, Rocketeer.*

The memory of last year's attack faded. I actually rather liked my angular gait, because it was an excuse to shirk sports and construct model planes that flitted uncertainly among the limes of Green Court.

Doctors decided that I should spend the summer of 1927 swimming and exercising at an English spa. Bess came over and rented rooms in Harrogate. Desperate with boredom, I began to write letters to Paul and found to my joy that he was an arch and gossipy correspondent.

On July 27 he wrote, "Hydrotherapy my a--s. You're ashamed to expose your Limey whiteness over here at Lowell Park Beach. Regan [*sic*], that leatherhead you admired last year, is our new lifeguard. He's pulling sweet young things out of the water, 12 hours a day, 7 days a week—whether they want him to or not."

At first the misspelled name meant nothing to me. But then "Dutch" attached itself to it, and I remembered Dixon High vs. Amboy. I also recalled Paul pointing out the oak meadow at Lowell Park. References to the half-forgotten footballer began to proliferate, as Paul developed what King's School boys would call a "case" on Dutch—albeit one expressed in terms of envious sarcasm.

I learned that Regan/Reagan was something of a river rat, having swum and paddled and skated most of the distance between Dixon and Grand Detour. He had taken a lifesaving course at the South Side YMCA, and been certified for competence by the Red Cross. That meant, apparently, that he was able to "undress in deep water" and swim a hundred yards at top speed; to surface-dive eight feet down and recover no fewer than four heavy objects; to execute, repeatedly, four

"He was able . . . to execute, repeatedly, four carries."
Illustration from Ronald Reagan's Red Cross lifesaving manual, 1925.

carries ("Head, Cross Chest, Tired Swimmer's, and Arm-Lock"), to demonstrate "Double Grips" and "Strangle Holds," left and right and front and back; and, last, to perform one and a half minutes of "Prone Pressure Resuscitation."

These impressive qualifications, Paul wrote, had persuaded Mr. and Mrs. Graybill, the managers of Lowell Park Beach, to hire Dutch at a salary of fifteen dollars a week, plus all the hamburgers, onions, pickles, and root beer he could consume at the food stand. He had authority over all who came to swim or sunbathe, and the additional responsibility of keeping the Dixon sluice gate "free of drowned bodies."

What thoughts ran through Dutch's head on placid forenoons, when the river was an unbroken swell through his clip-on shades—only to be disturbed by the first busload of day-trippers bursting out of the forest? As it happens, we know. He doodled some "Meditations of a Lifeguard" and published them in his high school yearbook. Paul sent me a copy, superscribed "Mark Twain—move over."

> On they come, hoards [sic] of swimmers, bathers, sleepers, or what have you! A mob of water-seeking humans intent on giving the beach guard something to worry about.
>
> A "frail and forty" maiden out to enjoy the rippling waves, and to cling tightly to the lifeline, as she squeals and giggles. . . .
>
> An answer to love's sweet young dream—a proud little sweetheart dragging her manly catch down to the river's edge. . . .
>
> A Sunday School class, from the picnic up the park, swarms over the lifeboats and raft, and keeps on swarming as long as anything remains to be swarmed over. . . . Like a low accompaniment to their shreiks [sic] and howls, the lifeguard paints the ether a hazy blue, by the use of lurid, vivid, flaming adjectives. . . .
>
> Now in this motley crew there must be one ray of hope. There is, she's walking onto the dock now. She trips gracefully over to the edge of the crowded pier, and settles like a butterfly. The lifeguard strolls by, turns and strolls by again. . . . Somewhere, celestial music plays the haunting tune recognizable as "The End of A Perfect Day."

The lepidopterous girl was perhaps only fancy. Dutch was (according to Paul) going steady with a very earthbound young woman indeed. Margaret "Mugs" Cleaver was definitely not the type to laze away the Lord's time at Lowell Park—whose sands she equated with those of Sodom and Gomorrah.

Darkly pretty, short, terse, and tough, she dominated her class at North Side High School. She was ambitious without push, cultured, and charitably inclined. She spoke, wrote, acted, and debated with easy skill. An admirable young woman, even by Paul's account—except that she lacked humor. I would have thought that off-putting to Dutch, who, judging by his prose style, fancied himself a wit. Even Neil, a South Side punk if ever there was one, was scared of her.

Paul regaled me through the following winter with gossip about the Lifeguard and Miss Cleaver. Although I did not share his fascination with Dutch (who sounded pretty dull to me), the details of American high school life were so different from my own as to be positively exotic.

By the end of 1927, I was hearing that Dutch—taller and broader now, a DHS squad regular—was Dixon's "Model Boy," just as Margaret Cleaver was its most brilliant girl. Ladies at the Christian Church Missionary Society were predicting their engagement in about four years' time. He had been elected president of the North Side student body; she was president of the senior class. They were officers of the school Dramatic Society, cozily acting opposite each other in a play called *You and I.* Under her sophisticated influence, Dutch had been heard trying to speak French. She was writing most of the news articles for next spring's *Dixonian;* he was its art director.

When I saw the volume half a century later, I found to my fascination that Dutch had laid it out in the style of a silent-movie storyboard. The various sections were given such title cards as "Directors," "Cast," "Stage," and "Filming." Even more remarkably, he had illustrated each of these cards with silhouette drawings *of himself* as an authority figure. Reels of transparent film roll through his masterful hands. He calls orders through a megaphone. He sits behind his desk, solitary and darkly directorial. To this day, when I show this last silhouette to veterans of Ronald Reagan's White House, they gasp with recognition. The resemblance to the man in the Oval Office is almost occult.

"He drew it," I tell them, "when he was sixteen."

In the spring term of 1928 I fell in with a bad lot—two overbred louts who taught me how to drink sweet sherry and sing ribald songs in a cellar under the King's School Almonry. The casual perfection of their manners and the euphony of their vowels made me long to be like them, while I fought the dizziness their oval cigarettes (Balkan Sobranies) induced. One night in early May, the sherry ascended me to the brain, and I burst from the cellar like plump Jack from the laundry basket, roaring across Mint Yard:

> *The sexual desires of the camel*
> *Are greater than anyone thinks:*
> *Which explains why one night in the desert*
> *He attempted to bugger the Sphinx . . .*

A week later, I was sailing back across the Atlantic, to a modified welcome from Bess. "You *stupid* boy, to be turfed out only two months before Higher Cert. What *am* I to do with you?"

☯

Under the circumstances, it was a relief to be invited by the Raes to spend six weeks of the summer in Grand Detour. I arrived around noon one day in late July, and Paul lost no time in taking me to Lowell Park, an easy bike ride from his house.

We pedaled south along a sandy road hedged with corn taller than we were, under a scudding buttermilk sky. Then the Dixon Country Club golf course opened out to our right, and on our left the land dropped suddenly into a dense wood. Diamond glints pricked its shadows, betraying the presence, far below, of the river. We had to freewheel down through nearly a mile of trees (a sign en route warned, PARK CLOSES AT SUNSET) before we saw the water, a great luminous mass, about two hundred yards wide, sliding past a long meadow. The grass there was worn rather than mown, carbuncled with stumps. Three little buildings fronted on it: a bath house, an ice hut, and a food stand blue with hamburger smoke.

A line of oaks shaded the narrow beach, but I gathered from the restlessness of some old people sitting beneath them that they sheltered mostly mosquitoes. The most desirable place to sunbathe seemed to be a big raft anchored about ten yards from shore, jostling with damp teenagers. It bore a rough log derrick, on top of which swayed an empty chair. Whoever sat that high could gaze upriver and downriver (where a pier and rope of floating oil drums kept small children from being swept away), as well as at the east bank, a lushly forested *rive gauche*.

I wondered where the famous Lifeguard was, and why nobody was swimming. Paul explained that the river was "closed for lunch." He pointed along the beach and there, walking toward us, was Dutch Reagan, spectacles on his nose and a library book in his hand.

He was deeply tan, and at least four inches taller than when I had last seen him. His chest was bigger, his legs stronger and straighter. He wore a full-length black swimsuit, with LIFE GUARD stenciled across the front. Apparently he had just been for a dip, because the fabric steamed in the sun. He yelled a warning at some urchins leaning over the platform rails, sat down under an oak tree, took off his glasses, and opened his book. I craned my neck to look at the title: *A Princess of Mars*, by Edgar Rice Burroughs. He began to read. The day was hot and still. Presently he shrugged off the top of his damp suit. The loops fell away, leaving behind pale ghosts of themselves. Midges sang.

☯

When the one o'clock whistle went, followed by delighted yells and belly flops, Dutch remounted his chair, and I joined the splashing throng beyond the raft. Polio therapy had made me a strong swimmer, but I soon found why Lowell Park needed a lifeguard. Its sandy shore gave way to a few yards of mud before sloping precipitously to depths where hidden currents swirled among slimy fingers. Depending on the amount of rain upcountry, the surface tow could be strong.

In the days that followed, I saw Dutch training for the annual cross-river championship—which he later won in two minutes, eleven seconds. He was a specialist in the "Australian crawl," as we called it in those days, employing both the flutter and the trudgen kick. His long arms and easy coordination made his stroke look slow, but the glass-green water slid past him with minimal splash, and he pulled ahead of competitors with no apparent effort. Swimming had appealed to him from childhood (that little wet boy at Coon Creek, blue-lipped under the hot sun) as one of the few sports he could indulge in without spectacles. Its coordination of grace with power suited the natural economy of his movements. He enjoyed the feeling of going somewhere purposefully and rhythmically, with nothing to distract him en route.

Watching him—indeed, trying to imitate him—helped me understand at least partly the massive privacy of his personality. The swimmer enjoys a loneliness greater, yet oddly more comforting, than that of the long-distance runner. One tunnels along in a shroud of silvery bubbles, insulated from any sight or sound other than vague perspectives of water, and the muted thunder of one's own arm strokes and breathing. Others may swim alongside for a while, but their individuality tends to refract away, through the bubbles and the blur. Often I have marveled at Reagan's cool, unhurried progress through crises of politics and personnel, and thought to myself, *He sees the world as a swimmer sees it.*

In the late afternoons, when the sun dipped behind the bluff and a line of green gloom advanced across the park, we left him to the mosquitoes and pushed our bicycles up a shortcut trail to River Road. The climb was hard on my leg, and Paul always found an excuse to dawdle at a viewpoint that showed the whole of Dutch's little world, from the purple bend below Grand Detour to the dark water descending on Dixon. Memory (a snapshot album rather than a videotape) holds the Lifeguard at middle distance, gazing over the heads of his charges at the far shore suffused in sunshine.

We usually went to the country club on our way home, because Paul, like Dutch in the past, had a caddying job there, and was required to put in a few hours on the links. I would sit on the groundsman's porch and scribble at my novel, or, after the last party of the day had teed off, fly model airplanes on the green. Some of Paul's clients were so good as to sneak us the odd "sundowner" in a Coke bottle, which we would guzzle on the way home, along with peppermints to hide the guilty fumes.

On August 3, 1928, we were wildly excited to see "Life Guard Ronald 'Dutch' Reagan" mentioned on the front page of the Dixon *Evening Telegraph,* under an eighteen-point banner headline:

PULLED FROM THE JAWS OF DEATH

At nine-thirty the previous evening, reportedly, Dutch and Mr. Graybill had been closing up the bath house at Lowell Park when they heard a man splashing in deep water. The swimmer, whose name was given as James Raider, had failed to respond to orders, whereupon Dutch dived in and sought him out in inky darkness. He found a desperate person who had already "gone down once." There had been "quite a struggle" before Reagan, "making his twenty-fifth rescue," had brought the drowning man to shore. Mr. Raider had responded to artificial respiration and been escorted from the park. No charges were filed against him.

The story haunted me then, and haunts me now. Indeed, how can I forget it, knowing what I know? Black night, black water; Dutch flinging off his glasses, plunging into a limbo whose dynamics were as fluid as anything in Einstein's theory of relativity. No fixed point of departure (he dived off a bobbing platform); no fixable point of distress; only the memory of a sound somewhere, a sound no longer audible as he swam. He could not head straight there, anyway; the swift current forced him to project a curving parabola, whose cusp must intersect with that of the drowning man, already curving downstream. And having miraculously found him, grappled him, punched him out of his panic, taken him into an armlock, the Lifeguard had to *reverse* this physics of rescue, and swim back doubly encumbered, upstream whence he came, so that chaos could be brought to ground, death cheated, and Prone Pressure Resuscitation performed to Mr. Graybill's satisfaction.

I clipped the story from the newspaper and stuck it in my scrapbook. Yellowed and crumbling now, it survives as Dutch's first claim to fame, the earliest item of Reaganiana I possess.

Paul's sister Mary, now a Eureka College sophomore whose bare legs, emanating from short summer skirts, made me groan with desire, was unsympathetic about my expulsion from the King's School. "If you didn't graduate in England, you won't qualify for any of the Chicago universities. Or even U.I., at sixteen. Why don't you try Eureka? They'll accept just about anybody."

"So I see," I said. She threw a grape at me.

"It's very . . . small. Liberal arts. Just don't tell 'em you're Catholic, is all."

"*Anglo*-Catholic isn't *Roman* Catholic."

Paul rolled his eyes. He was going there himself in September. "Eureka is run by the Disciples of Christ."

"Not so you'd notice," Mary protested.

Anywhere her legs went, mine were bound to follow. And Bess did not object, when I broached the idea. "If what Paul says is true, at least you'll stay away from liquor."

I had no way of knowing that Mugs Cleaver was also headed toward Eureka College—not to mention her faithful friend from DHS North Side. And so *Das Ewig-Weibliche zieht uns hinan.*

5

Chimes at Midnight

T HE FIRST GIRL I embraced at Eureka—if you call an awkward
handshake and a bow an embrace—turned out to be Dutch's
sweetheart. She was small and dark and dour. "Margaret Cleaver,"
she said, withdrawing her hand after an absolute minimum of contact. Yet she did not redirect her gaze, which was disconcertingly
steady. She merely waited for the non-dance movement that brought
us together—a circle of forty-three girls rotating within a circle of
forty-seven boys—to reverse the process. The Victrola struck up, and
we notched away from each other in clockwork rhythm. When, sixty
years later, we meshed again, I had the same feeling of cold force.

It was Grind Night, September 21, 1928. After six days of registra-
tion, recitations, and searching for digs (Paul and I shared a room over
Haecker's Oyster Restaurant, in the village), the class of '32 socialized
for the first time in the gymnasium. We "gentlemen" were togged up in
short-lapeled, razor-creased three-piecers, with watch chains and spit-
polished shoes, and self-consciously wore the plump green caps that
were to identify us as frosh through Thanksgiving. Bow ties were big
that year, I remember, and none bigger than Dutch's. He seemed to

flash more foulard than anybody else, although his owlish horn-rims and rah-rah manner dulled the general effect.

Maybe he watched while Miss Cleaver and I exchanged stares (his devotion to "Mugs" was already a campus joke), but I was so overwhelmed by the parade of female flesh around me that I was hardly aware of him. Eight years of boarding school had denied me the casual familiarity most American boys enjoyed with the opposite sex; the very word *co-ed* was erotic. Under bunched balloons and phalli of colored concertina paper, girl after girl extended soft fingers and enveloped me in cheap perfume. Few were as reserved as Margaret. "Where'dja get that *ducky* accent?" They were, perhaps, shorter of leg and sturdier around the ribs than their Chicago sisters; Eureka was as provincial a school as any west of the Wabash. But by the same token, they had "It," a healthy, small-town sexuality that in no way conflicted with Christian virtues. In the parlance of the day, these were girls who would neck, maybe french a bit on the second or third date, but not frig. Even that modified promise made my libido throb like a plucked bass string.

How delicious they were in their loose, short, low-belt dresses and breasty blouses, bob cuts swinging at dimple level, bare necks warm with beads! I can still make a litany of the ugly names they volunteered in their high, flat voices: Thelma Harshbarger, Lora Weddle, Evelyn Van Buskirk, Hannah Hollembeak, Lola Lampe. At least two were classy as well as sexy: gorgeous, gray-eyed Sally Fleming, with her endless scarf and white silk stockings, and Gladys Vissering, an exquisite junior in Delta Zeta, water-curled, level-browed, smiling with celestial square teeth. . . . Incongruous among all these flowers of the Caucasus, yet accepted with utter naturalness as far as I could see, were three or four . . . well, in my diary I wrote "negresses."

After every "gentleman" had met every "lady," from graduate students down to the youngest scrub, we sat in rows and were preached to by representatives of the YWCA, YMCA, and college administration. The last to rise was President Bert Wilson himself, a pale, stiff, dried trout of a man whom Paul immediately dubbed "President Coolidge." He made so many references to the advisability of regular attendance at "chapel," that I realized the Disciples of Christ expected a dividend of devotion from their affiliated college.

When, in another age, I searched out Ronald Reagan's origins in Tampico (about seventy miles north-northwest of Eureka, as the buz-

zard flies), I stood where perspectives of corn intersected from all directions and felt, as never before, his fixed flat centeredness. Jack's wanderlust fortunes had disturbed that still centripetus, and even after
"settling" in Dixon, Dutch was shifted from school to school and house
to house. No wonder that when he came to Eureka and saw its nine
buildings standing no taller than the elms, ivy-hung, village-ringed,
midstate in the middle of the Midwest, he had a rapturous sense of
homecoming. For the rest of his life he would insist there was no love-
lier college in the United States, and even after he let the silks of Notre
Dame and Oxford fall on his shoulders, he made plain that the only degree he ever cared for was his B.A., Eureka 1932.

"Midstate in the middle of the Midwest."
Eureka College in the early twentieth century.

I confess I became fond of the place too. But lovely it was not, with
its ill-matched Gothic steeples and Georgian pediments floating above
a clutch of blocky fronts and too-tall windows. When the trees dropped
their leaves in October, the redbrick edges of "Mem Hall," "Admin,"
and "Chapel" were exposed, still raw-looking after half a century of
unpolluted breezes. Pritchard Gymnasium, a science hall, two women's
residences, and a central heating plant added their own discordant
notes. Thankfully for the eye, twenty acres of wide lawns and gravel
walks separated them. That was about all there was, apart from the little town adjoining (pop. 1,500), the enormous sky, blackbirds cawing,
and a whiff of dung in the air. (Eureka's endowment included four
local farms.)

But I forget the fairest of all sights to Dutch's four eager eyes—the football field on the edge of campus. I followed him there on a fresh-man tour. It was austere to a degree: rust-brown grass, some creaky, three-level bleachers set against a background of dry cornstalks, a tem-porary-looking shed with a huge padlock on the door ("only the squad gets keys"), goalposts crooked and splitting. We were allowed to ven-ture a few yards into the end zone, still hard with summer heat. Dutch's reverent tread (last year's caked lime whitely dusting his shoes) made plain that this was holy ground to him.

Paul snickered at his polite attempts to win the attention of "Coach Mac."

Ralph McKinzie was an austere, flinty little Okie, so obsessed with football that he could barely understand ordinary conversation. He had once been Eureka's premium jock, a household name for hundreds of miles. But as coach he betrayed the effects of being tackled too often, and wearing too light a helmet. He had spent most of the last two seasons puzzling out the mechanics of a string of defeats. Eureka was too strapped to hire anybody brighter. His pick of players was law, and he found Dutch wanting in speed and weight. (Also in modesty: a McKinzie intimate told me, "Coach didn't like the way Reagan claimed to be the star of Dixon High.") On List Day, "Reagan, D." had to be content with Team Five. He won a reserve place on the squad by dint of fanatic training. Even so, Mac kept him benched for the entire season.

This disappointment was one of the most humiliating Ronald Rea-gan ever suffered. When at the age of sixty-five he was denied his party's nomination for the Presidency, his reaction was to remember the day he posed in an unlettered jersey with members of the Eureka "E" Tribe.

I saw little of Dutch in class; he was majoring in sociology and minor-ing in economics, while I took mathematics and music. But since only ninety freshmen ranged "'neath the elms" (a coy Eurekism one quickly tired of), Paul and I were constantly bumping into him—which is to say, bypassing him: his unique, fluid walk enabled him to negotiate strange shoals as easily as an eel. It was impossible not to see him com-ing, with his floppy center part and jazz-style clothes, modeled on the *Chicago Tribune*'s comic strip, "Harold Teen." I recall in particular a pale tan sport coat worn over a loud turtleneck sweater.

Manifestly a loner, Dutch was never alone. There was something at-tractive about the simplicity of his enthusiasms—Eddie Cantor, the Olympics, last night's social, next week's game—and his urgent desire to tell us what we already knew. Although his manner was egalitarian and friendly, the only opinions he seemed to value were those of authority figures: senior faculty, varsity players, and society officers. He was already, irredeemably, a frat man, Mugs having gotten her sister's boyfriend to pledge him to Tau Kappa Epsilon. Even in those dim distant days, people did things for Dutch.

Paul and I took a stroll to the Teke house on Burton Street and were amused at its yellow-brick tackiness. We got into the parlor on some pretext. A group of seniors hunched around a whistling radio, ignoring us. Their big caps were propped against the mantel clock like a row of dead prairie dogs. The sofa sagged, bits of thrown bread stuck to the cedar paneling, and there was a effluvium of pipe smoke and stashed booze. Dutch was nowhere to be seen. He may have been lounging on his dormer bed in the attic, known as "Grand Central" because of its crowded conditions and nightlong pinochle games.

"Would you believe," Paul shuddered, "that *twenty-three* greeks live in that slum? One bathroom! They must have to pee in rings."

I was introduced to Dutch several times, and each was the first as far as he was concerned. Paul asked if he recognized us from the beach at Lowell Park, whereupon he tapped his glasses and shook his head, smiling.

Had I any knowledge of American sports, I might have become one of his colleagues as a reporter for the Eureka *Pegasus,* the school's weekly newspaper. He was assigned to cover football; I was put to work as a proofreader. Typescripts came in unsigned, but Reagan's prose was always recognizable for its *Boys' Own* colloquialisms—"still and all," "college young sheiks"—and irritating jocularity: "Reading this dumb stuff is not compulsory." For me, unfortunately, it was.

Margaret Cleaver was one of the few girls who did not live on campus. She stayed a few doors away from Dutch in the Christian Church parsonage. They would come up Main Street together, talking intensely, planning their day like a pair of aspirant pols—which is what they were. They volunteered by reflex, expressed concerns about the election of Herbert Hoover, and never missed a student meeting. Mugs was generally considered the stronger of the two, "young Miss Brains" to his "Mr. Congeniality." He smoothed her bristling desire to control people, teasing her when necessary, but paying serious attention to everything she said. At seventeen going on eighteen, he seemed, as someone put it, "inclined to buy something."

" 'Young Miss Brains' to his 'Mr. Congeniality.' "
Margaret Cleaver at twenty-one.

She was elected vice president of our class. Dutch wisely refrained from running for office until he had earned some athletic prestige. He was secure enough in his manliness to wash dishes at Lida's Wood, the older of the two female dormitories. Watching him thaw out the water pipes with a blowtorch one icy morning, I realized with a surge of pity that he was broke. That pale sport coat made do long after the last of Indian summer, and when it finally gave way to a wrong-size overcoat, he lost much of his flash.

In later life, when Ronald Reagan was rich enough not to know how rich he was, he told me with pride that "lifeguard money paid for half of my college education, and dishwashing the other half." Actually, he jobbed for board and had a 50 percent tuition scholarship from the school. When the Depression hit, he also got a student loan—but I'm getting ahead of my story. The fact is that in the waning days of 1928, he was not sure he'd be able to afford his degree.

The actor in him was recognized quickly by Alpha Epsilon Sigma, Eureka's dramatic fraternity. They accepted him after hearing him read a number of character sketches from various scripts. An opportunity for him to show his worth onstage arose more suddenly than anyone expected.

☯

Eureka was self-conscious about being smaller than the average high school. When the whole student body did a conga through town before the Homecoming game, there were only two hundred and twenty-seven of us. Faculty appointments numbered in the teens. Professors did crossover duty to widen the curriculum and earn themselves extra dollars. The alacrity with which the admissions office accepted me at sixteen suggested that enrollment was down dangerously for the academic year 1928–1929.

President Wilson had been worrying about Eureka's financial prospects for years. (Pre-echoes of the Great Crash were heard, like approaching thunder, long before Black Tuesday in the rural Midwest.) Not only were classes getting smaller, but so were contributions, as farm prices sank. Wilson appealed over the heads of his board of trustees to the Disciples of Christ. But those austere grape-juice sippers (was it from them that Mugs got her tight smile?) believed, like the church elders in *That Printer of Udell's,* that a man in trouble should shift for himself. So Wilson told board members over the Homecoming weekend that he had decided on a drastic reorganization of the college.

Just how drastic, we found out on November 16, when the trustees agreed almost to halve the number of Eureka's fifteen departments, combining such related subjects as English and rhetoric, and mathematics and physics. This would result in some loss of faculty, but we were assured that our studies would not suffer. On the administrative side, they proposed to divide the office of Dean and Registrar, massively occupied by three-hundred-pound Dr. Samuel G. Harrod. This particular change caused an outcry. Harrod was one of those jolly, rumpled, bearish types invariably described as "lovable." I thought him a conniving lardbottom, ambitious for Wilson's job, but his popularity on campus was great, and the prevailing sentiment in bull sessions around town was that he was a martyr to maladministration.

Among student liberals enraged by the plan, Dutch Reagan stood out for his righteous passion. He was getting his first (and by no means last) lesson in deficit crisis management, and loudly endorsed calls for Wilson's resignation. Most of these were issued by the leader of the TKE fraternity, Leslie Pierce. I do not recall Dutch aiding Pierce in any active way—he was, after all, a freshman of only nine weeks' standing—but he impressed seniors as a mouth to watch.

On November 20, a student committee met with representatives of the board and presented a declaration, with over one hundred and forty-three signatures, "that complete student, alumni, and church support would be found lacking until President Wilson resigned."

Paul and I were in the minority that declined to sign. We could not understand why Wilson's proposals had been so quickly flipped and refocused into a character attack on him. Then we learned that Les Pierce was very thick with Sam Harrod. They had been agitating against Wilson for three years.

To us, the "Dump Bert" movement looked like a faculty plot. A diversity of departments compensated, in academic eyes, for Eureka's embarrassing smallness, and helped secularize its clerical reputation. Profs valued what they called their "autonomy"—and, of course, their extra teaching fees.

Battle lines were therefore drawn between the campus and the church, with hapless Bert in the middle. It was hard to like him, with his fishy stare and domineering manner, but he was the only negotiant who made any sense. The tone of his published response to the student petition was unemotional. He addressed himself more to the trustees than to us:

> The problem is a far greater one than the question of whether I am to continue as president or whether any or all of the present faculty are to be retained. . . . The real question is, "Can Eureka, a small church college in a small town, survive at all in the face of the present trend of education and civilization?"
>
> Eureka . . . now looks to the Christian churches [Disciples of Christ] in Illinois for its support in money and students. Yet the churches for eighty years, while giving it moral support, have never given in a large way to Eureka's endowment. . . . It is a pretty general rule that unendowed private colleges die.

He proceeded to list figures showing that Eureka had raised little more than half a million dollars in its lifetime. Thus hampered, it had to compete with twenty-six other private or normal colleges in Illinois alone, as well as the state university. Most of these rivals, located in larger communities, offered a more tempting range of student jobs and amenities. Eureka was simply too strapped, and too bucolic, to remain unchanged in changing times.

The tide of plains civilization, Wilson wrote sadly, was ebbing from rural areas. According to the U.S. Census Bureau, less than a third of the population still lived on farmland. America was on its way to town, and Eureka was "off the main highway." Smaller in 1928 than in 1880, the college could hardly house, let alone instruct, a profitable number of students. Yet the faculty were infatuated with "curriculum spread." That was a luxury affordable only by major universities:

> My administration has been hampered from the very beginning because of this spreading out process. . . . Now that the issue has been clearly faced and action taken, the inevitable revolt has come. If blame and criticism come in large or small degree, it had to center on some personality. There can be no escape from that. . . .
>
> I am, therefore, handing to you . . . my resignation as president of Eureka College.

I remember reading these words in a rush edition of the Peoria *Journal,* hawked among us as we huddled under blankets at the Dad's Day football game. The news came almost as light relief, for Coach Mac was masterminding yet another shutout at the hands of Illinois College. "What's 'spreading out process' mean?" asked Mary Rae, her thigh warm against mine.

All along the bleachers, newspapers flapped in the raw breeze. Dutch read his copy down on the bench, where he sat reporting the game for *Pegasus.* As I gazed down, he turned his head and surveyed us with an expression of triumph. He looked as though he was counting the house.

Why, I wonder, does he recall the score that afternoon (Illinois 17, Eureka 0) as a win for us, clinched with "a drop kick of better than fifty yards"? He describes the newsboys, the serried pages, the afternoon's distracted mood accurately enough. I guess because Dad's Day kicked off, as it were, the most exciting week of his life so far. Denied his jersey, he was at least permitted to run with movers and shakers, to grasp (if only for a few minutes) the greasy leather of power, to hear, swelling around him, the cheers he craved.

The trustees declined to accept Wilson's resignation. It took six suspenseful days for them to reach a formal vote on the matter. During the interim, Dutch could not have gotten much sleep, for his attic at TKE became the hotbed of student unrest. "Harrod Headquarters," Paul called it, and we posted a mocking sign on the porch at dead of night: FRATS FOR FATS. Les Pierce commandeered the *Pegasus* hektograph machine for the dissemination of agitprop, and the words *student strike* were bandied about with increasing boldness. There were even threats of violence upon the trustees when they attended their special emergency meeting on November 27.

Since the outcome of the meeting was more or less given, word went out that we should all be prepared for a strike vote in the Chapel afterward. The "secret" summons (leaked to every newspaper within reportorial radius) was to be a tolling of the old campus bell, which we must obey whatever the hour. When bedtime came that night and the board remained in session, we left our underwear on beneath our pajamas and cracked our casements to the freezing night.

I was awakened shortly before midnight not by the bell, but by a voice yelling one block away on Burton Street, "Is Dutch Reagan there?" The chimes followed almost immediately. We grabbed our overcoats and joined the throng of students clobbering in unlaced boots up College Street to the Chapel.

At this point, alas, memory (hampered by drowsiness) begins to fragment. The chimes; the chilly auditorium; mist forming on the high, mullioned windows; nighties frothing out of fur coats; the little stage with its side organ, low-arched and springy, sonorous and bleakly lit; Dutch stepping forward, skinny, center-parted, rigid with excitement, his lips wreathing ungracefully to the right—such details endure—*but what did Reagan say?* I can't remember. No one can. All I scribbled in my diary (and by the way, not one of the newspapers next day bothered to mention his speech): "We all have to band together and make things work." The truth is, he was about the last of a wearying slate of speakers.

The student committee chairman, Les Pierce, set a democratic tone at the outset, to soothe nervous dissenters. "This committee has never advocated a walkout, and does not now." But the oratory soon became confrontational. A resolution was offered: *We, the students of Eureka College, on the twenty-seventh* (Paul jumped up in correction: "Twenty-eighth!") *day of November, 1928, declare an immediate strike, pending the acceptance of President Wilson's resignation by the board of trustees.* Then boy after raucous boy, and one shrill girl, laid ashes on poor

Bert's head. Members of the faculty slipped quietly in and listened with approval.

I sat mute, the youngest person there, afraid of exposing my plummy vowels to the mob. Tubby Müller, a Teke pledge I admired, had the guts to get up and confess that since the Disciples of Christ were paying half his tuition, he could not honorably strike their college. He was shouted down.

So what did Reagan say? In later life, he supposed that he had reviewed the impact of the cutbacks on Eureka's "academic reputation," and found fault with Wilson for not considering other ways of saving money. What he definitely did remember, though, was our "thunderous" applause.

Sure, we applauded—hell, even Tubby got a few claps. But Dutch, ecstatic, heard an ovation loud enough to warm his blood:

> I discovered that night that an audience has a feel to it and, in the parlance of the theater, that audience and I were together. When I came to actually presenting the motion [*sic*] there was no need for parliamentary procedure: they came to their feet with a roar—even the faculty members present voted by acclamation. It was heady wine.

Maybe he did formally present the motion, after two hours of debate. And the vote indeed was by acclamation. The bare-walled, uncarpeted room resonated with an extraordinary amount of noise.

So let Dutch get drunk on it, in retrospect. His first standing ovation! Thespians have to remember all productions in terms of their own performances; they're constituted that way. I hesitate, though, to say that he discovered himself as an Actor that night. He had done so the first time he spoke with a voice not his own, at high school theatricals, and noticed how it made people look at him and listen to him. As an Orator, then? It was certainly his first experience of a platform, as opposed to the stage. But what about the organ, the mullions, the fact we were assembled "in Chapel"? A Preacher, perhaps? Yet he spoke to the resolution, he addressed the chair, he was subject to rules of order—how about Politician? No, even at seventeen Ronald Reagan was something more than that.

Everybody won—with the exception of Fats Harrod, who ultimately lost out both as registrar and would-be president. Bert Wilson insisted on resigning and left town with such alacrity that we realized he had a better job lined up. Les and Dutch got their strike—if you can call an extended Thanksgiving vacation a strike; we goofed off through December 7. That hardly achieved anything, though; only a handful of students really objected to the reorganization plan. In fact, our strike ended with a pledge of respect to the board that stopped just short of an apology. The trustees strengthened their power over the faculty by putting their own president in charge until such time as they could find another Bert Wilson. And the faculty, while having to accept a few token firings, did not suffer greatly, either in salaries or "autonomy."

Two weeks after the strike ended, so did my first and only term of college. I did not realize it at the time, as I left Eureka on the Chicago-bound "Christmas Special" (cotton balls and tinsel in every compartment), along with dozens of other raucously excited students. But I recall being distressed by the coziness of the carols we sang ("Deck the halls with boughs of holl-ee!"), in contrast to the pure polyphony of Tallis and Taverner in Cath. Then some cheerleader type yelled, "Alma Mater, everybody!" Back over the dry fields went our windblown voices, in harmonies more lusty than reverent:

> When we leave thy halls forever,
> Never to return,
> Still within our hearts fond memories
> Steadily will burn.

Although I must admit the lingering drawl of that last word—surely the most beautiful in American phonetics—moved me then, as, indeed, the whole song does now (I choked on hearing it again, when Dutch and I returned to Eureka for the sixtieth reunion of our class), there was a heartiness to the ritual that alienated me. Spotty snob that I was, I assumed that the majority of these hicks would be taking out the feed on Christmas morning, while Bess and I drove to Uncle Ira's for champagne and eggs Benedict.

Uncle Ira compounded my disillusionment by announcing on New Year's Eve that the probate court sorting out Father's estate had sanctioned an extra legacy of $3,000 to me "to complete my education." I waited until Bess's attention was distracted, then asked him in an urgent whisper if the word *education* could be applied to flying school. He looked at me for a long time before saying slowly, "I guess so."

6

Air and Water

I DID NOT SEE Ronald Reagan again for another four years. That is to say, I did not see him *as himself.* There was one strange glimpse of him as a Greek shepherd boy, which I'll describe below. In the meantime, Paul, an indefatigable correspondent, kept me abreast of Dutch's dogged doings. I would have preferred to hear more about Mary Rae, but Paul's obsession with the Lifeguard of Lowell Beach was not unamusing.

Eureka, February 28, 1929

... Our four-eyed friend is getting increasingly rah-rah. After freezing his bum on the squad bench last semester, he's now leading the yells at basketball! Tried out first of course (his face in a cage), but even with glasses on he was too slow. Coach Mac gave him the thumbs-down after a couple of fumbles. So Dutch has settled for a white sweater & jumped up and down pretty good against Bradley Tech last Tuesday eve. Ernie Higdon allows, "He's a whale of a good cheerleader."

Between you & me I think the lad's under a lot of strain. Wants to be a jock but can't, & I heard him grumble he can't make head or tail of Prof. Gray's [economics] lectures. "If only I had Mugs's brains!"

Eureka, May 26, 1929

Lilac time—why don't you drive down & teach Sis something about the stars? She went to the Teke formal last night—35 couples, red bulbs & Mrs. Turmail looked the other way when they spooned. Dutch didn't lay a finger (she sez). Eyes only for Mugs, who believe it or not has gotten pretty, in a fierce sort of way.

When Mary Rae died in 1972, I helped Paul go through her stuff, and we found a scrapbook of dance programs and invitations covering the social events she attended during four years at Eureka College. There must have been over a hundred of them, all designed differently and decorated by hand. They coruscated on the page like stuck butterflies, specimens of an age when the mating game, even as played between boys and girls in a hayseed school, was beautified and ritualized to the point of religious ceremony. The programs were satin-tasseled or stitched with silk thread; some bound in white leatherette and Greek-stamped; others in gilt hessian, and dangling dice or pared moons. The invitations (carefully marked "Accepted" or "Regretted") were cut out like ivy leaves or accordions or pumpkins or movie frames glittering with silver dust.

One of the simplest cards, green-inked with a corner shamrock, was the work of a hand I instantly recognized:

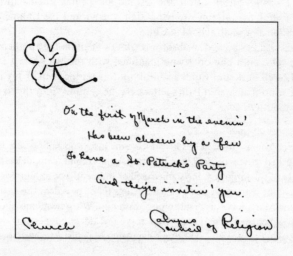

"Do look at the C doing double duty," Paul giggled, "like something in a shrimp salad! Wasn't he *just* the kind of sap to toast the patron saint of alcoholics with Pepsi? Meanwhile, up north in some bootleg vomitorium, Pa Reagan was doing what the Irish do best."

"I remember you writing me about those dropped *g*'s," I said.

Grand Detour, Ill., August 15, 1929

. . . How's the barnstormin', ace? Loopin' any loops? Excuse the apostrophes—caught the habit from Dutch. He thinks it's sporty. Feel kind of sorry for the big lug. His father's "Fashion Boot Shop" is all boarded up in downtown Dixon. Sad sight. Old Man Pitney must have lost a bundle.

Dutch is back at Lowell Beach, threatenin' not to return to Eureka. Says Coach Mac doesn't want him and that he has no future in football.

So now he's gone and borrowed a white canoe from Haney Glessner & pretends it's a scull. Swears he'll get a full rowing scholarship to U. Wisconsin. My guess is money's the problem with Jack out of work. Clodhopper brother Moon pounding sand down at the cement factory. Ma Reagan pretty desperate.

Why don't you fly one of them Jennies over here for dinner one day? Missya *beaucoup*.

The suggestion was a tease. I was then only in my second week at Parks Air College in East Saint Louis, having been told I had to wait until I was seventeen before they would accept me. But I had made good use of the interim, studying flight theory and the rudiments of navigation at a small school in Chicago.

These studies proved so absorbing (not to mention the apotheosis of going solo, on a day otherwise identified with the Wall Street crash) that Lowell Park and Eureka shrank to dots on the map of my interests. I seldom answered Paul's letters, but he continued loyally to write every month or so.

October 22, 1929

. . . Young "Ronald," as his adoring ma insists on calling him, has returned to school, snapping pigskin for the second team, defection to U. Wisc. forgotten. Says "the smell of liniment" got to him. More likely the astringent scent of Miss Mugs (class president this year). Anna Mae says M. is "real snippy" with him. When he moans about being benched, she says, "Well if you're no good perhaps you shouldn't play at all." The other day Anna Mae just *happened* to see a note from Dutch on Mugs's dressing table: "I always come back to you like a beaten dog—someday maybe I won't."

Meantime, he's hung his pin on her. The future Mrs. Dutch!

. . . P.S. Did you know Moon Reagan is now a pledge at Teke? Dutch persuaded him to quit the cement factory. Intriguing reversal: elder sibling is now "younger," waiting on Junior at table. Dutch paddled Moon's ass so hard at hazing that blood blisters popped out. Moon swears revenge next semester. I'll keep you posted.

On the reverse of the attached envelope, I note that Paul has blocked a huge "E"—the college letter—and scrawled beneath it, D. R. JUST MADE THE SQUAD.

When I raised the subject of brotherly hazing with Dutch, on the eve of our anniversary return to Eureka, he responded placidly, "No, I never beat him. I—we just used to say, 'Assume the angle,' and I'd pretend to whack him."

He did not entirely convince me, since Neil remembered no pretence at all about the impact of the paddle. I suspect that Reagan family relations were deteriorating in late 1929, following the collapse of Jack's business and the loss of Neil's cement factory earnings. Nor did the situation improve when Jack was hired in January 1930 by the Red Wing Shoe Company. His new job paid well, at $260 a month, but it entailed plentiful travel, with consequent opportunity to do "what the Irish do best." He began to spend large blocks of time in Springfield, where his operations were based, and in due course acquired an expensive local girlfriend. (I asked Margaret Cleaver Gordon about this affair, many years later, and she bristled with righteous disapproval: "I *won't* be quoted on that!")

Nelle stayed in Dixon, supplementing Jack's irregular checks with job work as a seamstress and becoming more and more obsessed with religion. By the spring of 1930, it was an open secret that the Reagans might divorce.

I was "winged and ready to fly" then, as I proudly wrote Paul Rae, having completed my course and won a full transport pilot's license at the quite legal age of seventeen. The only problem was, "Jobs are as scarce as June bugs right now, and Chicago being the airway hub doesn't exactly reduce competition."

Along with other aspirant flyboys, I haunted Municipal Airport, where nine airlines had hangars, in the hope that some envied captain might have a heart attack right on the ramp, enabling me to snatch his papers and rush for the personnel office. Since such emergencies were few, I whiled away the days scratching out short stories, and splurged the last few dollars of my education fund on a night course in radio copywriting at Northwestern University.

It was there, on April 10, 1930, that I was transfixed by the sight of Dutch's name on a cast list posted outside Swift Hall. The Drama Department's Fifth Annual Theater Tournament was under way, and the "Eureka Players" were scheduled to present Edna St. Vincent Millay's avant-garde verse drama *Aria da Capo* the following afternoon. Dutch was billed as "Thyrsis, a Shepherd Boy." I could not resist buying a ticket in order to regale Paul with witty criticisms of what would doubtless be the tournament's least-attended event.

To my surprise, both play and performance proved to be revelatory—and, I realize now, prophetic of Ronald Reagan's future presidency. To this day, whenever I hear the name "Thyrsis," I can see young Dutch in rough Greek cloth, leaning enraptured over a bowl of water and saying:

> The pool is very clear. I see
> A shepherd standing on the brink, with a red cloak
> About him, and a black weed in his hand . . .
> 'Tis I.

The curtain rose, however, not on a Hellenic pastoral setting, but a harlequinade. Margaret Cleaver, smudge-eyed and self-conscious as Columbine in a strawberry tutu, was dining with a skullcapped youth I did not recognize, at a table draped with black and white polka dots. Similarly patterned cushions lay tossed about the otherwise bare stage. At first, their dialogue was almost unendurably fey:

COLUMBINE   Pierrot, a macaroon! I cannot live
            Without a macaroon!
PIERROT   My only love,
            You are so intense! . . . Is it Tuesday, Columbine?
            I'll kiss you if it's Tuesday.

Miss Millay was satirizing both socialites and socialists (parlor pinks who disdained black-and-white reality). But how on earth was somebody called Thyrsis going to insinuate himself into this *commedia dell'arte*?

As it happened, by the ancient device of a play within the play.

Cothurnus, Masque of Tragedy, appeared and sent the exquisites scurrying. He then proceeded to act as stage manager, summoning Dutch and Enos Cole (of Eureka football fame) to begin their dialogue as two not over-bright Greek shepherds.

Dutch padded on barefoot in his red wrap, looking mildly annoyed at being called before he was ready. (This expression was what the script required. But how often, in later years, was I to see that same frown, when aides altered the President's schedule!) His voice floated out:

THYRSIS   Sir, we are not in the fancy
            To play the play. We had thought to play it later.
CORYDON   Besides, this is a setting for a farce.
            Our scene requires a wall: we cannot build
            A wall of tissue-paper!

Cothurnus, backstage, was inexorable. The two youths resignedly moved the table to one side and sprawled on the cushions, facing each other. Dutch stared into space for a moment, then said with complete naturalness:

        How gently in the silence, Corydon,
        Our sheep go up the bank. They crop a grass
        That's yellow where the sun is out, and black
        Where the clouds drag their shadows. Have you noticed
        How steadily, yet with what a slanting eye
        They graze?

The beauty of the poetry made me catch my breath. It was accentuated, rather than compromised, by his unstudied delivery.

Prompted by Cothurnus, Thyrsis remembered he was supposed to build a wall with Corydon. They joined in weaving a chain of colored crepe-paper ribbons down center stage. Then they flopped down on either side of the chain and surveyed the divided landscape. Corydon realized too late that Thyrsis had a strategic advantage, in the form of a large drinking bowl that he had abstracted when they were moving the table.

CORYDON   Oh, Thyrsis, just a minute!—all the water
            Is on your side of the wall, and the sheep are thirsty.
            I hadn't thought of that.
THYRSIS   Oh, hadn't you?

Dutch handled the line lightly enough to fill the auditorium with laughter. But the dispute over the wall became acrimonious, with Corydon protesting that sheep on whichever side were "all of one flock," and Thyrsis alternately scoffing and blustering. Both shepherds showed signs of real fear as their quarrel took on a life of its own and began to control them, rather than they it.

CORYDON   Oh, Thyrsis, now for the first time I see
                This wall is actually a wall, a thing
                Come up between us, shutting me away
                From you . . . I do not know you any more!
THYRSIS   No, don't say that! . . . How did it start?
CORYDON   I do not know . . . I do not know . . . I think
                I am afraid of you!—You are a stranger!

They stepped back and lay down as if exhausted. Then Corydon triumphantly discovered that jewels had been buried on his side of the wall. A water-for-jewels treaty was proposed, only to be abandoned for lack of goodwill. Thyrsis, furious, began to scrabble at his own ground, but turned up only black and bitter weeds:

THYRSIS   I wonder what
                The root of this black weed would do to a man
                If he should taste it. . . . I have seen a sheep die
                With half the stalk still drooling from its mouth.

Uncertain what to do with this lethal discovery, he sipped meditatively from his bowl of water until Corydon, mad with thirst, revived the notion of a jewel swap. Thyrsis sprinkled some black root choppings into the bowl and extended it over the wall. At the same time, Corydon reached across with a rope of *faux* jewels. He put his lips to the water and hung the rope around Thyrsis's neck.

THYRSIS   I'll hold the bowl
                Until you've drunk all.
CORYDON   Then hold it steady . . .
THYRSIS   Stop pulling
                The string so tight!
CORYDON   Why, that's not tight at all. . . . How's this?
THYRSIS   You're . . . strangling me!
CORYDON   I believe
                You've poisoned me . . .
THYRSIS   *Corydon!*

And with a gargled scream, Dutch died. Corydon had a moment before his own final convulsion to discover that the wall they had fought over was a vestigial thing, easily shredded and sundered.

I was so engrossed in this little allegory (which President Reagan would one day re-enact with Mikhail Gorbachev) that I jumped when

Cothurnus reappeared and shut his promptbook with a bang. He drew the table back to center stage, and kicked the bodies beneath it. Then Columbine and Pierrot danced back in to resume their dinner. They were momentarily disconcerted at what lay on the floor. "We can't sit down and eat with two dead bodies!" Cothurnus, bored, suggested, "Pull down the table-cloth."

They did so, and with both corpses out of sight, the stage looked just as it had forty minutes before. "Pierrot," Mugs trilled, "a macaroon— I cannot *live* without a macaroon!" As they segued into an exact recap of their opening dialogue, the curtain slowly fell.

All I remember about the ensuing ovation is Dutch bowing and smiling as only a recently strangled actor can smile. I ducked out and stood for a while on the steps of Swift Hall, looking out over Lake Michigan in a vain effort to shake Miss Millay's spell. The water was light toward the shore, darker in the east, where evening was already coming on. No *Ätherblau* in this spring weather. The horizon was a hard Greek blue, sharp as any stage edge. It seemed farther away than I had ever seen it, fraught with some immense tragedy that hung just beyond its drop.

As a result of his performance in *Aria da Capo*, Ronald Reagan was named one of the six best actors in the Theater Tournament. Professor Garret Leverton, director of Northwestern's School of Speech, told him that he should make acting his career. I heard this interesting news from Paul, who had seen the play in rehearsal at Eureka, and agreed with me that Dutch had distinguished himself. "He *was* good. Role of course made for him: impulsive oaf, not too smart, not too subtle. No I take that back—for once in his life he managed to impart a nuance or two."

I could not stop thinking about the play for weeks afterward. "The deepest irony of *Aria*," I gloomily wrote Paul, "is that its two homicides amount to suicides. I guess Miss Millay was thinking of the last war when she wrote it, but what scares the hell out of me is the *da capo* element, the cyclical sense that Columbine and Pierre [*sic*] are eating macaroons again as if there are no bodies in Flanders field, while all the time jewels are being hoarded and bitter roots burrowing and a new wall going up, no longer between nations of East and West, but also the worlds of Rich and Poor. Look at Germany—Reds already bringing down the govt. And right here in Chicago tomorrow noon, Fr. Coughlin has recruited *eighteen* veterans to protect him while he hurls the curse of Christ at communism."

Paul declined to be intimidated, and sent a cheerful postcard to say that Dutch's new thespian eminence had already been put to practical use:

Eureka, May 27, 1930

Coach Mac has put him in charge of "entertaining," i.e., selling Eureka to, this year's crop of high school heavies. With absolutely no embarrassment, Dutch grabs a broomstick and pretends to be announcing a game on the radio. Kids came out goggling, as if they'd just seen the Devils beat Notre D.

This short screed proved to be more anticipatory of what lay just ahead for Dutch than my own of Doomsday.

By Dutch's own testimony, the semester just ending was one of happy fulfillment. "That sophomore year, everything seemed to brighten all across my life." Not only was he now officially a blood, and a young actor of promise, but one of the "A" girls on campus wore his pin, and his elder brother was forced to be respectful.

When I interviewed Neil Reagan in old age, I was struck both by his resemblance to Dutch (same dense hair, and distant gaze and silky voice) and by a fundamental difference that seemed to reduce right down to molecular structure. Physically, spiritually, he was a monochrome copy of a color original. I see from one of Paul's letters that the difference was even more marked in youth:

Eureka, June 1, 1930

. . . You ask about Moon Reagan. Black Irishman, just like Jack. Catholic. "Saint Nelle" rebaptized him a Disciple along with Dutch, but no sooner did he start going out with some South Side colleen that [*sic*] he reverted to Rome. Guess to spite Ma, whom he can't stand. Smarter than his brother. Noisy; a bruiser. Cynic. Fancies himself as a wit, but his jokes mean to hurt. Handsome in a brutish sort of way, great dancer. Gals go for him, tho' he's scared of sex I think. Teases 'em until they cry & roars with laughter. Spits through his teeth. Desperate for attention.

The letter concluded with one of Paul's annual invitations to spend July or August in Grand Detour ("Come bathe in the cool Rock River—Dutch'll see you don't drown"). But I had gotten a maintenance job at Chicago Municipal Airport, which I hoped might sprout wings. Every night I laundered the concrete with power scrubbers and helped roll the carbon runway. The crisp smack of those cinders under Tri-Motor tires lingers in my ears as a sensuous sound, extinct as the cry of the passenger pigeon.

I was semi-rewarded in September with a slot as copywriter in the public relations office of National Air Transport. The understanding was that I would be put on the reserve roster for whenever an assistant pilot got sick.

Actually the job was quite interesting. I wrote articles for *N.A.T. Bulletin Board* ("Pleasant Trip, Says Texas Oil Man"), and the copy chief let me sign a typewriter out on weekends. "Don't laugh," I wrote Paul, "but I've begun a novel. It's called *Ailerons.*"

For the next year, I learned that copywriting was easy, fiction difficult, and that assistant pilots were among the healthiest specimens on the planet. Meanwhile, regular letters arrived from Paul with snippets of news about Dutch. Here follows a fragmentary selection:

Eureka, September 23, 1930

If you ever need to crash-land in these here parts, head for our new football field. Replaces that ol' dust bowl. The squad say it's like velvet to tackle on. Only surface scars so far dug by the elegant chin of Dutch R, with a few bone crushers riding him. At 170 lbs. he's easy meat. Mac has put a big freshman, Franklin Burghardt, next to him, I guess to draw fire (B. is a naygur).

Eureka, October 15, 1930

Does yr. masterpiece have a title yet? Liked that chapter you sent me, esp. the part about flying through the Lindy Light. Perhaps a few too many technical words, dear boy. How many readers know what a *yaw* is? But a distinct improvement, methinks, on *Jim Raider, Rocketeer*!

Talking of titles, it's "Senator Reagan" now, if you please. The Lowbrow Lad is elected to College Senate, which once more modestly called itself the student council. . . . As befits his new dignity, he's given up dishwashing & now gets paid to teach swimming in that dank little *pissoir* under Pritchard. When dry, he also acts as pres. of the Booster Club, so if you need any help in public relations, give him a call.

Eureka, Apr. 5, 1931

. . . Dutch is in mourning for Knute [Rockne, dead in an air crash]. So is every other thickneck on campus, but our boy is so red-eyed you'd think the Rock did it just to spite him. Good thing *you* weren't at the controls, ace.

Eureka, May 21, 1931

. . . Mary heard from Mugs that Dutch is unlikely to make it to Princeton's Institute of Advanced Study. His grades this year: 2 Ds (one in the Life of Christ!), 5 Cs, coupla Bs in Sociology & English Composition. Moon got straight As & won't let him forget it . . .

Grand Detour, July 25, 1931

. . . Dutch is back on the front page of the *Evening Telegraph*! He just made his 50th rescue at Lowell & has beefed out quite some. I saw him on a horse the other day (no saddle), trying to figure out which end did what. Most of the time he just sits in the sun and fries his brain, playing *Ramona* on a portable Victrola till we all beg for mercy. If he works up much more of a tan, Coach Mac won't be able to tell the difference between him & Burghardt . . .

Great news about your first hop to Cleveland. More fun than writing copy I should think. Must we call you "Cap'n" now?

Eureka, September 24, 1931

. . . Our friend is talking miserably of becoming a "janitor" this semester, if he don't get a student loan. Says his savings are down to $30 after forking out tuition through New Year's—hardly enough to buy books. Well, I know how Dutch feels. School can't help him, although he's the pres. Senior Class!! Eureka's going to be on the dole itself pretty soon, as old Coolidge warned in '28. Looks like we'll be graduating just in time.

Ronald Reagan has always been honest about money, and he was not exaggerating his privations in late 1931. When he became President of the United States at $200,000 a year, a retired executive of the Henry Strong Educational Foundation found this loan application of half a century before and sent it to him as a reminder of leaner times.

RECEIPTS	AMOUNT	EXPENSES	AMOUNT
Savings on hand	*$30*	Tuition and fees	*$90*
Earnings during school year	*$175*	Board	*$198*
Gifts (parents—friends)	*$50*	Room	*$90*
Loans	—	Books	*$25*
Loans from College	—	Organizations	*$36*
		Laundry	*$3*
Need to borrow	*$200*	Miscellaneous	*$50*
TOTAL	*$455*	TOTAL	*$492*

This budget shows a deficit of $37 which amt. will be paid in the summer following graduation as arrangements can be made with the college to defer payment of certain bills.

State briefly your past history and tell us what your plans are for the future:

I graduated from Dixon High School in '28. During my four years I was active in athletics and dramatics and spent three of my vacations working. The first one as a laborer, the other two life guarding at local beaches.

I have worked every vacation since entering college as life guard at Lowell Park and have worked during school earning my board each year, the first two years washing dishes and last year as swimming instructor.

I have no definite plans for the future outside of trying to get a position in some business probably as salesman. I have made several contacts in my summer work and have several offers of help which I am counting on when I graduate.

> *Ronald Wilson Reagan*

At the foot of this document, an unknown hand notes that the applicant has been granted $115—seventy-five dollars less than he requested, but enough, one hopes, to reduce his janitorial chores.

Oct. 18, 1931

. . . Dutch, bless his football boots, is finally a name to reckon with, or would be, if local reporters didn't keep spelling it *Regan.* He'll never be a grid flash like Bud "Corydon" Cole, but they also serve who only block & tackle. Devils 13–6 against Western Teachers Sat. before last!! Mac's still trying to puzzle out what we did right for a change. First three quarters they had us corralled at 6–0, then Bud started running like he had a pepper in his pants, & touched down back of their mud puddle. They rallied after that & pushed us back to the 35 stripe. Still tied at 20 secs. to go, whereupon Bud inserted another chili and next thing Teachers know, he's 65 yds. into their defense and galloping in all directions, like that lord of Leacock's. Then *slam.* Somebody converted, I guess, but we were already on the field mobbing Bud. *Pegasus* has nominated him for President of the U.S.

I print the above narrative, even though it barely mentions Dutch, because, for whatever reason, all the moves of that fourth quarter (even his own inability to keep up with and block for Cole) registered on his 16-mm. memory. He would "replay" them soon enough, to greater glory.

"A slow, half-blind, yet fanatically dedicated player."
Ronald Reagan as right guard for the Eureka Red Devils, ca. 1931.

From what Paul and others have told me of Ronald Reagan, right guard, he remained a slow, half-blind, yet fanatically dedicated player through the end of his last season. He prayed before every game, then walked onto the grid scared enough to piss himself. His bladder eased as soon as play began, and for the next hour he would hurl himself at bigger bodies without flinching. I have his proud scribble on an obituary of "Titan Tony" Blazine, a Hall of Famer who used to bruise for Illinois Wesleyan in those days and weighed two hundred and fifty-two pounds stripped: "*I played opposite him—60 mins. in '31.*" At the sixtieth reunion of the Class of '32, Pauline Husted Ford reminded him of that game, and told him tenderly, "When you came off the field, there were tears running down your cheeks."

A final football anecdote, which I admit neither Paul nor I found touching at the time:

Eureka, Oct. 22, 1931

Latest campus scandal: Dutch "kissing up" (Mary's phrase) to the sons of Ham. He now plays between *two* naygurs—Burghardt and Jim Rattan. Last Fri. eve the squad arrived at La Salle hotel for the Elmhurst game, mine host took one look into the bus & said "no" to gentlemen ob' color. Not to their face [*sic*], but Dutch followed Mac into the lobby & cottoned on, so to speak, PDQ. Mac was ready to sleep the whole team in the bus, but Dutch whispers that Dixon is not far away. "I'll take the two of them home . . . no problem." So Mac slips him the cab fare, and his parents welcome them like Amos 'n' Andy. Dutch v. pleased with himself—thinks naygurs dumb enough to believe it was just a case of "no room at the inn."

Burghardt, who lived just long enough to see Ronald Reagan inaugurated as President, confirmed this story in every particular. "I just don't think he was conscious of race at all." However, the Parzivalian paradox applied: a youth unaware of evil must also be unaware of evil's effects. Burghardt was willing to grant that "the hotel [incident] was his first experience of that sort," but could not conceal his irritation when Reagan, in debate with Jimmy Carter, asserted that in the Twenties and Thirties America "didn't even know it had a racial problem."

To that extent, *der reine Tor* remained a stranger to pity.

☯

The same could not be said of Jack Reagan, who was a "compassionate" Democrat long before the cliché lost its meaning. Perhaps because of his own frailties, he had a fierce reaction to injustice. The only pages of Dutch's memoirs that mention him in terms other than tolerance are those describing his refusal to let Moon and Dutch see *Birth of a Nation* (on the grounds that it glorified the Ku Klux Klan) and his refusal to stop in a hotel that discriminated against Jews. It was in character for him to let Dutch bring blacks home to stay in a town that was mostly white, Protestant, and nativistically Republican.

Jack's presence at home that night, October 16, 1931, indicates that he was no longer estranged from his wife. After more than a year of living two hundred miles apart, they had rented an apartment at 107 Monroe Avenue, on Dixon's South Side. Here, over the next six years, they would weather out the Depression and adjust to separation from their sons. It was by no means a period of security, according to Paul:

> *Eureka, Jan. 4, 1932*
> . . . Dutch came south after the holidays looking kind of gray round the edges. Told Mugs his Dad got fired by Red Wing, just when Ma Reagan thought they were back in the $. 'Twas the night before Christmas, too. Or so Dutch says, with a tear in his manly eye.

When Paul, pressed, relayed some of the Dickensian details—Christmas Eve, a tiny living room, a special-delivery envelope, a slip of blue paper, Jack bowing his head and muttering, "Well, it's a hell of a Christmas present"—I wrote back *à la* Oscar Wilde, "One needs a heart of stone to read such stuff without laughing."

Within days I was punished for this by a letter to similar effect from Professor John T. Frederick of Northwestern University, attached to the manuscript of my novel. It hurt so much that I mentally begged Dutch's pardon—and Jack's, too. For when I was fired myself by N.A.T. in February, I understood for the first time the double meaning of the word *depression*. If a young man-about-town still living at home could feel such fear, at a time when "fear itself" was spreading like yellow fever among the lower-middle classes, then I did not envy the insomnia of an unemployed shoe salesman with a bad heart and booze problem.

> *Eureka, June 8, 1932*
> . . . Too bad you didn't make it down to Commencement yesterday. Glorious weather. There wasn't much ivy left for Mary & Harry once we'd finished twining Dutch & Mugs—"No. 1 couple on campus." Our boy all flashed out in a sharkskin suit, she actually laughing for a change. Like a dark violet opening up. Rev. Cleaver acted as though he wanted to give her away right then and there. "Reagan's a lucky fellow," I heard Fats Harrod say.

After all these years of mocking Dutch's marbles, I'm *humiliated* to report he scored "much above average" in all studies, as far as Admin. is concerned. An A in Public Speaking, no surprise, 4 Bs (B+ Senior Econ.), only one C in Philos. . . . Mugs, of course, is *magna cum laude.*

Dutch has bet five of the fellows in Teke that he will be earning $5,000 (!!!!!) in 5 years. Meantime he's too broke to buy a class ring @ $30. Ma Reagan took a lien on his last fifty behind Jack's back. I don't think Mugs'll marry him till he gets a job. A while back he talked of American Bell Co., but that little dream seems to have died.

Let you in on a secret—I sent a portfolio to Art Students League (N.Y. City) and they say they'll take me this fall, if I can bite Pop for enough $. Gonna need moral support—how about coming to stay when you're through at N.U.?

So it was that, newly certified as a "graduate" of Professor Frederick's course in creative writing, I returned to Grand Detour for the first time since the summer of '24. August heat, plus Mrs. Rae's dismay over her son's "bozart" tendencies, drove us most afternoons to Lowell Beach. There, seven days a week, the Lifeguard still lazed. Were it not for his disconcerting tallness when he loped into the water to cool off (waist-deep in splashing children, horn-rims held aloft), four years might not have passed. On the few occasions Dutch nodded or grinned at us, it was with complete lack of recognition.

"There's only two ways to get him to notice you," Paul sniffed. "Grow tits, or drown."

One day, after an unusually shrill commotion at the river's edge, we saw Dutch rowing to shore with a retching girl huddled in his canoe. He allowed friends to help her out while he fetched an ax from behind the bath house. Then he walked upstream to where a black old log lay half hidden in grass, above the waterline, and began hacking at it.

"Seventy-three," said Paul.

"What?"

"Notches. Every time he saves a life, he blazes that log. That's all you are, all anyone is to him. He actually said once to some kid, 'You're just another notch on the log.' "

After Labor Day, when I was back home in Chicago, I got a postcard from Grand Detour, unsigned:

SEVENTY-SEVEN!!

7

The Indifferent Figure in the Sand

A Review

IT IS SAD, but not surprising, that the youthful literary effusions of Ronald Reagan remain unpublished. Mr. Reagan never pretended to be a writer, nor had he the least holographic vanity. Until he became President, he took pride in being the author of most of his speeches, but aides had to prevent him from throwing away the manuscripts once they were carded or typed. The only book he ever wanted to write was his middle-aged memoir, *Where's the Rest of Me?* (1965). Even that text, eloquent and frank to begin with, shows signs of creeping collaboration (he co-wrote it with Richard G. Hubler), and its overall didactic tone both cloys and annoys. *An American Life* (1990) is a ghostwritten work, undertaken at the behest of Mrs. Reagan, and may be safely described as the most boring book of its kind since Herbert Hoover's *Challenge to Liberty*.

Had Mr. Reagan not risen to world power, the few browning manuscripts of his late teens and early twenties—essays, fantasies, and some patently autobiographical short stories—would doubtless crumble unread. Archivists at the Reagan Presidential Library, who store so meticulously every last lunch voucher of the White House Interagency Low

Income Opportunity Advisory Board, seem unaware of their significance. The present reviewer found them in a tin trunk of items considered unworthy of display or preservation. There, wedged between tricolor elephants, meerschaum pipes, the pedigree of Armand Hammer, and other junk, lay a half-open envelope full of folded, faded, closely handwritten pages. One glance at a fat sheaf entitled "Moral Victory: A Football Story by 'Dutch' Reagan" was enough to warrant photocopying the whole cache for scholarly perusal.

There are seventeen pieces in all (see below), the earliest dating from November 1925, when Mr. Reagan was a Dixon High School sophomore, and the last written during his final semester at Eureka College. His handwriting at fourteen has the same patient punctiliousness (no abbreviations, few erasures, and generally flawless spelling) that characterizes the personal letters he wrote every Wednesday afternoon as President. But it inclines, with Spencerian symmetry, to the right:

Only the occasional involuntary straightening of a *d* shows that the penman is forcing himself to write with his right hand, which is what midwestern orthodoxy required of southpaw schoolboys in the mid-1920s. The script becomes shapely after the acquisition of a new fountain pen in 1927.

By the summer of 1928, however, Mr. Reagan's left-handed undertow begins to hoist the masts of his perpendiculars upright, like a canvas anchor drifting contrary to the wind. Four years later, he has reached the choppy equipoise that will sustain him for the rest of his life:

A *catalogue raisonné* of the Reagan juvenilia follows. As the present reviewer read through them, he was overcome by a most unprofessional feeling of tenderness. These seventeen pieces create a poignant portrait of an ardent, if dreamy young man. Although not quite literature, the best of them are not quite anything else. Even the blandest yield tiny explosions of personality, like specks of undissolved saffron.

> CHIROGRAPHICAL NOTE: *The collection totals sixty-nine pages of lined rough and exercise-book stock, letter size, holographed on recto, in many cases signed and dated on verso. A grocery flier, perhaps part of a protective wrapper intended for the whole, is attached to Item §16, and reads as follows: ">>FREE<< with the Purchase of SAWYER's SALTINE CRACKERS—Made with Milk—You'll Prefer Them." Aside from §7, a French* leçon, *all items are original compositions. Italicized titles and dates replace lacunae and are supplied for reference purposes only.*

§1. "Halloween"   Nov. 6, 1925
School paper. 1 p., ink, sgd., inscr. "Theme, English II" on v. Doodle (pencil): profile of a bald, pedagogical person with walrus mustache and flowing cravat.

A short, atmospheric sketch of Dixon City in thrall to mischievous masked urchins. Porch furniture and buggy wheels dangle from telephone poles, while the night resounds with noise effects characteristic of a boy who has grown up with severe myopia. "Laughter, running feet, and muffled shouts . . . then at twelve o'clock, a gasping panting roar awakened the town. . . . The freight due from the north was vainly trying to get over a hundred foot stretch of greased track."

§2. "School Spirit"   Nov. 4, 1927
School paper. 2 pp., ink, sgd., inscr. "English IV, Theme IV," on v. Marked by teacher, "94."

Sixteen-year-old Reagan castigates fellow students who, "beneath a cloak of attempted sophistication," mock him and his teammates for "choking up when the old school song booms across the field." Only those who have dug in their cleats and held the liniment-reeking line know what "love and loyalty" is like. The essay is so conformist that somebody has written across it, in an adult hand, *I wonder what change will come in your standards of value—8 years from now?*

§3. "Yale Comes Through"   Nov. 17, 1927
School paper. 4 pp., ink, sgd., inscr. "English IV, Theme VI" on v. Marked by teacher, "94."

Two Yale students foil a plot to immobilize the United States Treasury with poison gas. Cynics might see this short story as a portent of Reaganomics, but young Dutch is obviously only having fun. Its climax is interesting. When the plotters are run to ground, they protest that they are working on a film scenario. Our hero sends "the would be author" sprawling with a single punch. At least *he* knows the difference between imagination and reality.

§4.   "Sweet Young Things"   Dec. 6, 1927
School paper. 2 pp., ink, sgd., inscr. "English IV, Theme VIII" on v. Marked by teacher, "90—Late."

Sex raises its bob-curled head in this riverside sketch, the first of several set in Lowell Park. The author admits to being distracted from thoughts of football when young Clara Bow look-alikes undulate past him. But the nearest he gets to gripping female flesh is when a girl with "the build of a varsity tackle" goes under in midstream, and nearly takes him with her.

§5.   "Old Mother Hubbard"   1927
School paper. 2 pp., ink, unsgd., n.d., marked by teacher, "95."

Summer's young lifeguard turns right guard in early fall, and redirects his lust toward the "sweetheart" of the Dixon High School squad, "a headless, heartless body clothed in leather and rough canvas." He takes a palpable delight in hurling his lightness against her heaviness, even when she recoils and "sandpapers" the side of his face.

§6.   "This Younger Generation"   ca. 1928
School paper. 2 pp., unsgd., ink, n.d., both leaves torn, marked by teacher, "96."

A lame attempt to be funny about teenage rowdiness in the Dixon Family Theater. Reagan identifies not with actors onstage but with the Mayor in his box, surrounded by "aristocrats of the highest order."

§7.   "*Il Savait Écrire en Français*"   ca. spring 1928
2 pp., unsgd., n.d., marked by teacher, "B–." Doodle: embellishment around "B–."

Reagan renders the above words into English correctly but with little hope they will ever apply to him. ("I am suffering from French Condition," he lamented in a letter written around this time.) The language of Corneille and Camus—a name he would one day, as President, publicly rhyme with "famous"—did not compare, in his ears, with that of Edgar Rice Burroughs and Zane Grey. Even so, his only extended piece of

French translation (source unidentified), reads like an outtake from *L'Étranger*:

> One heard only the scraping of the pens on the paper. The shadows of the yard had grown. The clock in the church struck noon. Something choked him. "It is ended. Go away."

§8. "Over Emphasis"   ca. summer 1929
Short story, unfinished. 4 pp., pencil and ink, sgd., n.d.

Another Lowell Park piece, full of unconscious narcissism, written by someone who is now a college student. Tall, lithe Jerry Evans dozes on his strip of beach, "brown arms shading his eyes against the glare of the mid morning sun." He becomes aware of the proximity of "a slim young creature in a tight black suit"—which is to say, *she* attracts his attention by diving and splashing vigorously. Without lifting his head more than necessary, he admires her "over his broad chest and down his long brown legs." He considers making a move, but falls asleep again. (At this point in the manuscript, the author practices a new signature.) His aloofness maddens pretty Aline:

> She climbed up to the high diving tower and cast a hopeless look at him. . . . From this height the letters on his black suit were visible. LIFE GUARD, the title held infinite possibilities of approach.

Casting herself into deep water, she pretends to be in difficulties, and screams. Jerry is awake and swimming the instant he hits the river:

> As he reached her she redoubled her struggles and grabbed at him wildly. Her wrist was seized and she was roughly jerked around with both her arms pinned behind her and he ~~she was~~ towed her to shore . . . "You're alright now Miss. What was the trouble? Just drinking too much water?" "Oh no," she replied innocently, "I just wanted to see if you were awake."

Jerry ducks her twice and is supine again, dozing, by the time she stops spluttering. "Tears of helpless anger filled her eyes as she glared at the indifferent figure in the sand."

§9. "Bus Burke, Lifeguard"   1929
Short story, unfinished. 2 pp., pencil, unsgd., n.d. Fragile: water stain on p. 2.

A similar *mise-en-scène* to the previous story, only now there are two girls splashing and giggling and wondering why "six feet of glorious tanned male youth should be so obviously uninterested in their perfor-

"LIFE GUARD, the title held infinite possibilities of approach."
Ronald Reagan at Lowell Park Beach, ca. 1932.

mance." It is the end of summer, and the end of the day on the Rock River. Bus has things other than sex on his mind.

> [He was] intent on studying the evening-reddened sky, he was interested in the purple shadowed bend of the river, the trees still gleaming gold on the far shore and the peaceful park at the end of the dock.
>
> Bus had received a blunt letter that morning. . . . It had spoken of prospects, kickers, and had expressed a desire that he, Burke, would be back in September prepared to play football. The short "Sincerely, Mac" was characteristic of the sharp-tongued coach.

Here the fragment ends, as if young Dutch's ecstasy at being chosen by Coach McKinzie for the Eureka squad is beyond his powers of expression.

§10. "Squall"   Feb. 24, 1930
Essay. 2 pp., ink, sgd., marked "College" in author's holograph.

A beautifully written description of a canoeist's encounter with rough weather on the Rock River. He sees wind sweeping down the valley toward him as he paddles upstream:

> It bends the trees on either shore like a hand pulled across the bristles of a hairbrush. Close it comes, the sullen water shakes its back like a bear awakening from a nap. Oily rollers appear; swifter, higher, higher they climb,—white crests break at the peak of each swell. . . .
>
> Then like an avenging pack the wind is upon you.

Prose connoisseurs will note three original similes in just four sentences—not bad for a sophomore who has just turned eighteen. As a pre-presidential document, "Squall" resembles, and compares favorably with, Theodore Roosevelt's essay "Sou'-Sou' Southerly," preserved in the Library of Congress. Both pieces celebrate youth and strength in the face of elemental opposition. The same wild exhilaration in Roosevelt's "As the great waves struck, she would stand almost still, and then rushing forward, bury herself in the greenish masses of water" is apparent in Reagan's "The stern drops from under you—then up it comes on the crest and you surge forward borne on the very wave that has just defeated you." One detects in such language the physical forcefulness that drove both men to become political leaders, even though one may regret the loss of their early lyrical sensibilities.

§11. "The Stadium"   Feb. 23, 1931
Essay. 2 pp., ink, sgd.

Reagan's best piece of writing. It is worth reproducing in its entirety, not simply as proof of his imaginative "reach," but also because it hauntingly foreshadows his post-college career.

The two tiered walls with their great hanging balconies rise massive and empty above the drifted snow. High up on the west stand the windows of the press box gleam black and empty. The benches cushioned with soft whiteness stretch in long rows broken by the yawning mouths of the exits.

This is the temple of the great Goddess Youth, where for three months her devotees run the gamut of human emotions. Here the worshippers rise in frenzied victory or go down in bitter defeat. The clear sky receives their chants of acclaim, their disapproving cries, their anthems of loyalty.

On the level sward between these temple walls boys tear their hearts out for an ideal. They toil, strain and sweat, batter and are battered, snarling ~~at their~~ with primitive savagery at the opponent whose hand they will soon clasp in friendly congratulations. In short, they live life. Life with its triumphs and defeats, its jeers and praise. All the mingled brutality and kindliness of an adult society is met in this short season by these young gladiators.

One begins to feel this in the brooding loneliness of the stadium. Perhaps the ~~patient~~ eager Goddess does not see the snow and lifelessness of her temple. Perhaps she sees the stands fill with the screaming crowd, the white-clad cheerleaders, the toiling men locked in combat. As she watches, a graceful figure breaks from the tangle and skirts around and down the field—twisting and dodging toward the goal. The crowd rises to its feet and a great roar swells forth. Up in the press box, typewriters bang, a radio announcer barks into the microphone, "He's loose, loose—five—ten—twenty—and—he is over."

The dream fades—the swift figure is a curling wraith of snow borne along and cheered by the mournful howl of the wind. The crowd is merely the fluttering, eddying snow in the stands.

One sees now though, that the stadium is never empty, for the ghosts of past heroes play great games over and over for the Goddess who holds sway for them, as well as she does over the living crowds.

§12.   "Killed in Action: A Short Short Story"   May 7, 1931
5 pp., ink, sgd., marked "Adv. Comp." in author's holograph.

An anti-war piece. Its documentary details of trench life clearly owe much to R. C. Sherriff's play *Journey's End*. There is also a note of tragic irony, probably instilled by his performance in Edna St. Vincent Millay's verse satire *Aria da Capo,* just weeks before he wrote this story. Even the subtitle is a bitter joke. Reagan begins with a flashback from a comfortable club room to a shell hole on the Western Front in 1918. Two doughboys, James Edwards and David Bering, brace themselves in freezing rain for a mass attack by the Germans. The former's voice rings querulously: "What in God's name have any of us got against those Heinies? Not a thing. We're heroes now, but . . . when the fracas is over we'll be tramps."

Bering has a naive faith in the justice of the war. He looks forward to a quick victory, Harvard, and the thanks of a grateful nation. "There's a girl in my home town and—well, we've planned things together." Edwards, more pessimistic, silently curses "a world so ordered that once every generation it must be bathed in the blood of youth like this one."

Both youths are wounded in the ensuing battle, and Bering saves Edwards's life before succumbing to gas. After the Armistice, they lose track of each other. Now—thirteen years later—Edwards stares again at the newspaper item that prompted his reverie:

> *A tramp, David Bering, met his death today beneath the wheels of a fast Santa Fe freight. Bering, an ex-serviceman, had been gassed in the war and was bumming his way to the Speedway veterans hospital for treatments. He attempted to board the moving train and lost his footing. He was thrown under the wheels when he fell. . . . No relatives or friends have claimed the body. He will be buried in the potter's field.*

When historians finally grant Ronald Reagan a sincere pacifism, they might trace at least some of it back to "Killed in Action."

§13. "November 11, 1918"   1931
Short story, unfinished. 1 p., pencil, unsgd., n.d., self-rejected by author with a large "X." Fragile.

Another anti-war piece, set in "the St. Jouvin sector," where men exist "only to kill and be killed." Little more than a sketch, it frustratingly introduces, then abandons, Reagan's most intriguing *alter ego:*

> Out in a machine gun nest Corporal James Howard of the 77th sat, his blood shot eyes staring, heedless of the growling heavens and trembling earth. One year ago he would have been dreaming of home, of a campus where he had been Professor of Eng. literature.

§14. "Rock Redux: A Tale of the Supernatural"   1932
Unfinished short story. 5 pp., pencil, unsgd., n.d. Doodles: 3 cannons, 1 movie camera (p. 3), 1 head of handsome youth (p. 4), 1 floating

geometric figure (p. 5). Pp. 4 and 5 disfigured with cryptic Greek refer-
ences, e.g., "Athens (sent away) Dyonisius" and "Lystra (stoned)."
Fragile—leaves breaking along fold line.

Four clubmen sit around a fire, discussing the occult. They invoke phantom ships, werewolves, and the Angel of the Marne before one of them begins to reminisce about the days "when old Rocky Burke was coach at New Domain." There follows a story in which the ghosts of Knute Rockne and George Gipp intermingle to stranger effect than Reagan could possibly have intended. Switching protagonists, he seems to be half dreaming, half prophesying his own performance as "the Gipper" in a movie not to be filmed by Warner Bros. for another eight years.

> I was in school then—varsity manager. Big Punk Evans was only assistant coach. He worshipped Rock—you see Rock had taken him to New Domain to play football. . . .
>
> Well the night Rock died [of pneumonia] he sent for Punk. I was with him . . . it was a strange feeling to see the old man stretched out there so pale and helpless looking. He called Punk over to the bed and took his hand. "Well, Punk old boy," he said, and he was smiling. "I guess it's up to you now. Make 'em play the game. And if some-time the boys are going down, tell them I'm on the bench asking for a score." That was all, he was gone and for the first time in 8 years Punk was alone. He went down on his knees by the bed and sobbed like a baby.

§15.   "Night of the Rose-Colored Bulbs, Or, Too Much Gin for Him"   1932

6 pp., pencil, unsgd., n.d. Doodle: searchlight on p. 6. Fragile—
leaves stained, some flaking at corners.

The only item in this collection that deals directly with two subjects of profound concern to the young Ronald Reagan: acting and alcohol. One might expect his attitude to the latter to be censorious, in view of Jack Reagan's well-known drinking problem, but on the contrary he describes a student booze-up with relish. The story begins (as do most of his imaginative pieces) with an excellent expository sentence: "James Harris of the McNeal Theatrical Co. folded the manuscript in his hand and beamed his professional smile at the Haycraft talent arrayed before him."

Harris belongs to a species now extinct: the traveling theatrical director who is hired by small-town dramatic societies to produce plays at short notice. His cast at Haycraft is untalented, with the exception of Bill Dennis, "a tall, curly haired young man" on loan from the local college dramatic society. Dennis—calm, pipe-smoking, irresistibly attractive—operates in his own time and space. He shows up at rehearsals when he feels like it, strikes his matches on no-smoking signs, and deflects all of Harris's reproaches with affable jokes. Onstage, however, he performs "with practised ease." The director feels unaccountably inferior to him, and is overjoyed when Dennis says, "C'mon down to the [frat] house and meet the boys." Then Harris—a timid soul—begins to worry about being drawn into an evening of depravity: "Walking through the chill fall night he learned that his companion . . . liked Gin, but would drink anything if Gin could not be had."

As it turns out, "the boys" merely engage in some companionable hands of bridge. Harris returns to his lodgings, pleased to have been accepted as their equal, and particularly smitten with Dennis. He wonders if he is too old, at twenty-five, to become a college man himself. "It would be nice . . . to be lazily indifferent, to go hatless, to cut classes."

Dennis, evidently, is another version of Reagan's "indifferent figure in the sand." Time and again in these stories, a tall, genial, good-looking boy goes about his business (or lies comfortably, doing nothing), untouched by and unconcerned with the agitation of others. He is sexy without being sexual, kind yet calculating, decent, dutiful, gentle—and massively self-centered.

Aside from a few obviously fictional props, like his "Spirit of Yale" flivver and liking for strong liquor, he is to all outward percept the future fortieth President of the United States. What makes these stories revelatory is Ronald Reagan's willingness to give us the inner perception too: to confess to his ache for—what, exactly? In time he will talk with magnificent vagueness of shining cities, of stardom, of songs that fill the unknowing air, of *das ewig Weibliche* who is "the rest of me." Right now he can evoke only the mundane desires of a small-town college boy—athletic prowess, a steady girlfriend, peer popularity. It is the intensity of these desires that impresses the reader.

Indeed, Reagan's protagonists seem preoccupied to the point of catatonia. Alone or in company, they are forever drifting off. The words *dream, dreamed, dreaming* reappear constantly. Lifeguards muse future glory, coaches hallucinate, soldiers and veterans slip into time out of mind.

James Harris is not the hero of "Rose-Colored Bulbs," but he, too, dreams, after being welcomed at the frat house, of "someday joining this important clan." His friendship with debonair Dennis deepens over the next two weeks. There is no further mention of liquor until the evening of the dress rehearsal. As usual, the leading man is late. While

Harris "hastily slap[s] greasepaint on the handsome face before him," Dennis says, "The boys are having a house dance tonight and I've got us a couple of dates and some gin for company."

Later, "two slim young ladies" join them.

> Dennis had a Marjory something or other who was very cool and very blonde and talked from the corner of her scarlet mouth. Jim had a vivid brunette who looked an innocent thirteen and said, "Oh you are an actor—how *thrrr*illing—Call me Peg."
>
> It was only a short walk to the Delta house, but Jim would have walked right by it, so expectant was he of seeing a flood of lights and hearing loud music. As they entered the front door he searched desperately for a visible light and was finally rewarded by seeing one or two rose colored bulbs in out of [the] way corners.
>
> In the next half hour he learned how much Peg liked tall young men who were play directors, and how little one danced at a house dance.

Later, the quartet visit a dimly lit "confectionery" for sandwiches and soda.

> Suddenly from under the table a square bottle appeared. Peg cooed like a happy child as she grasped the treasure. Jim hardly realized he was drinking, so amazed was he at the reception given the licquor [*sic*] by the girls. The bottle went once around and was replaced. . . . Jim helplessly felt his tongue thickening and realized he was going to have to refuse the next one. He was spared disgrace however for Dennis killed the last Indian and said, "That's all." The girls howled with disappointment.
>
> Sometime later he sat in the Delta house and heard his companion say, "Now we can have a drink—those d--n women will get drunk on you if you don't match 'em—so I saved some for us." Like a man seeing his doom Jim saw the bottles shining in the lamp light ~~but he was game~~ like executioner's knives.

The ambivalence between erasure and superscript is striking. Reagan's final image would occur only to the child of an alcoholic. All his life he preserved the strange ability to nurse a beer or two through long evenings with hard-drinking friends, laughing and singing as loudly as they, showing no moral disdain and patiently driving them home after they passed out. With his background, he might be expected to shrink from such behavior, or to yield to it. Instead, he looked upon license as something he was quite strong enough to control.

James Harris's sad saga culminates in a hangover so bruising that he sleeps right through the following day, and wakes too late to be in the audience on opening night. "He saw himself jobless and disgraced," Reagan writes, with an authorial memorandum: *insert thoughts.* At the end of the evening, Bill Dennis appears, masterful and imperturbable as ever, still wearing play clothes. He waves aside the director's distress. "Oh, I went down and got those dames made up and we put it on. . . . Nothing to it."

Bacchus has no choice but to admit the superiority of Apollo and take the next train out of town.

§16.   "Moral Victory: A Football Story by 'Dutch' Reagan"
1932
   20 pp., ink, n.d. Leaves fragile, some in advanced state of rot.

Reagan's longest piece of fiction. On the final sheet, he notes with obvious satisfaction, "Between 3500 and 4000 words." Apart from another drinking episode, the narrative is as focused and forceful as its hero, star guard Stan Hensal. Charmless, even dour in contrast to the other self-portraits in these stories, Stan represents the private side of Reagan's public character—a force both masculine and austere, darkly, doggedly driving.

He is introduced to the reader in the course of a freezing college-football game that is going badly—as usual—for the purple-clad home team. Hampered by a college scholarship policy that favors "picolo [*sic*] players" over athletes, Stan is weary of pulling more than his own weight, and bruised and dispirited by several seasons of defeat. He plays now out of habit, rather than competitive spirit. Reagan's prose is dense with cold, hard images: battered water buckets, raw shins, wind stabbing through blankets, boots scrabbling in lime, shoulders thudding into groins. Stan hurls himself against charge after offensive charge until he has no strength left:

> Tired arms gave way and he went down clinging to the legs going over him. Cleats dug into his back something struck his aching ribs driving the breath from his body and his face was pressed into the cold mud. . . .

As the game proceeds from bad to worse, Stan begins to long for male comforts. "How nice it would be to feel the hot shower covering him with warmth, steaming the pain from his body. . . . [the manager] would massage tight muscles until he was drowsy."

Notwithstanding the jostle of "gleaming bodies" in the gym room afterward, there is no hint of homoeroticism in Reagan's imagery. On the contrary, Stan wants to breathe no more communal steam, accept no more sympathetic backslaps. He is tired of hearing the college president harrumph that every hard-fought defeat is a "moral victory."

Impulsively, Stan goes to the coach's office and turns in his suit. "I haven't got any more time to waste." He has a momentary pang on seeing the old man slump with despair, but stubbornly wheels and walks out.

The bus carrying the victorious Reds is just pulling away from the gym, "its lights gleaming in the early twilight." Stan bitterly imagines the welcome awaiting it at home, and what cheers would greet him if he were aboard. Instead, he has to trudge back to his frat house and make the best of yet another defeat.

Bypassing the radio-loud lounge when he gets there, he ducks upstairs to his room. He sinks into an armchair, glad to be alone. Then without explanation this passage occurs:

> A weakness amounting almost to nausea gripped him. He rose and walked over to his room mates desk, stood undecided for a second then jerked open a drawer. In rapid succession he rummaged every pigeon hole and drawer, but his search was unrewarded. He turned away and his eyes fell on a familiar overcoat thrown carelessly over a chair.
>
> Of course it would be in the coat he had worn at the game. He picked up the coat and drew a squat flat bottle from the inside pocket. There was barely a swallow left, but he tilted the bottle and drained it.

Carson, the team manager, comes in to urge him to reconsider. Stan, his face a dull red, will not be moved, even when Carson accuses him of lacking "stuff." The dinner gong sounds below. Stan descends furiously and tries to adjust to the company of men who talk rather than play football. He sits listening morosely, aware that the "overpowering rage" that made him quit is redirecting itself against them.

After a few minutes, he can stand it no longer. His chair scrapes back, and he quits the room. Carson accosts him at the foot of the stairs. "Where you goin', Stan?"

"Well I was going to eat but . . . I'm going to see the old man,—I hear he's looking for a tackle."

As he strides off into the night, the grinning manager is already calling ahead. "Hello—Coach? This is Carson. . . . Stan's on his way down. . . . Maybe we can just call it another moral victory."

§17.   "The Return of Jerry Dale, Senior"   1932
Autobiographical sketch, unfinished. 6 pp., pencil, unsgd., n.d. Doodle: giant bomb at top of head of p. 1, partially obliterating first version of opening paragraph. Fragile: p. 1 dog-eared but text legible.

This last, most autobiographical item in the Reagan juvenilia describes the return of "Jerry Dale" to Eureka as a football stalwart and president of the College Senate. Modesty—for the author here limns an exceptionally attractive specimen of Illinois youth—persuades him not to use the first-person singular, but all other details are documentary, down to the name of his girlfriend.

Jerry alights at midtown from the Central West bus, a brown gladstone in his hand. The grip is emblazoned with a maroon pennant proclaiming the proud legend E-U-R-E-K-A. Even without this identification, admirers in the bus and on the street (flooded with late warm September sunshine) would still recognize him as a college man: the elegant rise and fall of his black suit jacket as he shrugs it snugly around shoulders and neck, the decisive way he snaps the brim of his felt hat and steps onto the sidewalk, his athletic grace and cheerful expression—no wonder a toothless news vendor smiles at him, while a woman en route to Peoria "wonder[s] idly what such a nice young man could be doing in this town."

Palpable here, as in most of these pieces, is our hero's intense delight in being looked at. The stare of any eyes—male or female, old or young—is as sensuous as the sun on his back. He strides into the residential district under still-green trees, swinging his grip, so preternaturally self-aware that he fantasizes a whole trio of *doppelgängers:*

Like characters from a book he saw himself with three companions on this walk. Himself as he had made this trip for the first, second, third and now the last times [*sic*]. At the extreme right as number one he was tall a bit awkward and looking some way too new in his clothes. The next two figures each minus a few more rough edges and finally Jerry Dale—Senior—Campus leader smooth in his shark skin suit, neat blue tie, and narrow brim hat.

He liked this vision, liked to think of himself as [a] polished, typical college man, something apart from and above that gawky freshman he had been. Not that he was vain. He had confidence was self assured but free from obnoxious conceit . . .

Leaving that protestation to speak for itself, we move from the outer to the inner man, and follow the secret rush of Jerry's emotions:

Now like a bird in swift flight his mind left him self [*sic*] and sped down the avenue as though to keep pace with his thoughts. [It] took him around the corner into the elm shaded depths of Burton Avenue past the Theta Chi house and up to the wide Kappa Tau porch. ~~Then dispensing with greetings he saw himself before a white private house.~~

Lord, it was great to be back. Never knew he missed it so much . . . Margaret? She'd be at home reading. He'd clean up and walk in on her. No he should call first. He'd wait until she said hello and then he would say, "This is the President."

The presidency referred to is only that of the student senate, but all scholars must feel a *frisson* when they see that quoted phrase. A few lines later, the story peters out with Jerry's return to his frat house. Needless to say, the "fellows" are overjoyed to see him coming up the steps, followed by his three younger selves, and by Jerry Evans, and Bus Burke, and David Bering, and Corporal Howard of the Seventy-seventh, and debonair Bill Dennis, and dogged Stan Hensal, and all the other tall young men who fought the swells and rescued the swimmers and gazed at the trees gleaming gold on the far shore of the Rock River, in the last days of American innocence.

8

Long Blue Shadows

THE PRESIDENT OF THE UNITED STATES glared at me and hissed through his teeth, "My God, so that's it! You think I don't *care!*" He leaned forward, voice rising: "You bloody little swine, you think I don't care—the only one who knew, who really understood!"

For a moment he seemed about to punch me, then shook his head and chuckled. "I can see the whole scene, Stanhope in the dugout, and, uh—"

"Lieutenant Raleigh?"

"—reacting in shock."

I wasn't sure which production of *Journey's End* Dutch was talking about. The one Margaret Cleaver and her parents took him to in Chicago in November 1929? Or that at Eureka a few seasons later, featuring his own transfiguration as Captain Stanhope? Probably he was doing a memory mix of the general impact of R. C. Sherriff's play, and the more particular pleasure of hurling a boozy tirade at the heads of his peers, in his best college performance since *Aria da Capo*. For years after he graduated, midwestern talent scouts monitored the Eureka Players, in the hope of discovering "another Ronald Reagan."

With such promise and the powerful encouragement of Garret Leverton, he might well have made it into the Chicago repertory theater.

Yet a curious caution discouraged him from trying, and, indeed, from his even more secret dream of heading for Hollywood. As he pointed out in later life, any small-town youth with stagy pretensions in north-central Illinois, circa 1932, was treated as a deviant. "I didn't want to have a net thrown over me. Secretly, I was crazy about acting."

Besides, he did not want to add to his mother's sense of insecurity. Neil was still in college, and Jack only just off the dole, having been hired as an investigator in the Dixon office of the Illinois Emergency Relief Commission. There was Margaret Cleaver to consider as well. That no-nonsense young woman had no wish to go down the aisle with Macbeth. Last, he had a student loan to pay off.

One of the most complacent of Ronald Reagan's autobiographical myths is that he experienced at first hand the agony of the Dust Bowl years. Actually, he had money to earn the moment he left school. His old job at Lowell Park was available: all cash and no expenses. September would eventually come, of course, and with it the first chill breath of adult worry, but even then and beyond he could be sure of a full belly and a room in his parents' apartment. He honored his loan installments promptly, and confirmed in writing that he could afford to.

Those of us who swam beneath Dutch's placid stare were aware that he fancied himself as a sports announcer. He had perfected what Paul wittily called his "broom shtick" to the point that he could narrate whole games on request. Small kids on the raft laughed and formed cheering sections. I thought these games were imaginary, but Paul insisted they were accurate renditions of Little Nineteen Conference encounters that Dutch had either played in or reported.

"Moon says that's how he passed all his examinations. Never crammed worth a damn. Just photographed everything in his head the night before."

Most people hold at least some snapshots in the album of memory, images flat and foursquare, stuck down hard. But the mind capable of recording complex movements that flow into other movements and can be accelerated or slowed or zoomed in on is indeed unusual. Dutch no more thought about his playback equipment (phonographic as well as photographic: he recorded aurally, too) than any machine ponders method. Insofar as he has admitted to thinking of anything in the dog days of 1932, it had wistfully to do with acting—a dream that he lacked the daring to pursue yet, more and more, hated to lose sight of. "I realized dramatics was the only way I'd ever be happy."

Conscious of his elevated status on top of the lifeguard stand, he often felt himself to be in the middle of a performance. "I was the only

one up there. . . . It was like a stage. Everyone had to look up at me."
When he was alone except for a friend or two, on late afternoons, he did
scenes from the dozen-odd plays in his repertoire, playing several parts
at once: Shaw's *Apple Cart,* Molière's *Le malade imaginaire,* Shakespeare's *Taming of the Shrew,* Chekhov's *The Marriage Proposal,* and
Yeats's *Land of Heart's Desire*—ending, no doubt, with "You bloody
little swine . . . !" Paul and I were never privy to these moments of self-
expression. I will always regret that chance did not permit me to skulk
somewhere in the shadows and watch Dutch do his one-man shows,
while the sunset burned like limelight on the trees behind him, and doubled their fire in the river.

☯

On September 14, 1932, Mrs. Rae, resigned to her son's plan to study
art in the East, held a farewell lunch for him at the Nachusa Tavern in
Dixon. Paul saucily invited Dutch, along with other members of the
class of '32, but got a polite note of regret saying that Mr. Reagan
would be out of town on business.

This turned out to be true. Paul's former French teacher came (I got
the feeling that they had more than a fondness for Verlaine in common)
and said that Dutch had been seen in Eureka the evening before. He
was hitchhiking on to Chicago, where he hoped to "get into radio," and
had stopped by for a bittersweet parting from Margaret Cleaver. She
was herself headed for a teaching job in Cropsey. Although they were
now formally engaged, she would not marry him until he had found
steady employment.

During lunch, the magic word *radio* triggered a round of speculation
as to what chance Dutch stood of getting into the most glamorous field
imaginable, outside of movies.

"About a snowball's," I ventured, drawing in my vast expertise as a
part-time student of radio copywriting. "You have to be *summa cum
laude* just to work the elevators at CBS or NBC."

"Well *he's* confident enough," said Paul's friend. "He bet the fellows
at Teke that five years from now he'll be making five thousand." There
was a roar of amused disbelief around the table. That was about two
thousand more than the average doctor's salary.

That Reagan was gifted in the gab department nobody doubted. "I
think he was born wanting to solve all the problems of the world," remarked a senior named McClellan. "He's always so *excited* about
everything, so idealistic—always saying what *ought* to be." Apparently,

his latest passion—shades of *Aria da Capo!*—was pacifism. He had deeply shocked his father by saying that he would not bear arms in defense of the United States.

℮

The story of how Ronald Reagan impressed the program director of WOC Davenport enough to be tried out—and eventually hired—as a sportscaster became part of his personal oral history, repeated so often and so identically you could use it to time eggs. Any interviewer rash enough to drop one of its trigger words—*hitchhiking, arthritis, thump, bastard, cane, red light*—might as well shelve all further questions. I have at least three versions on tape, and each sounds like a dub of the other.

RR   I started out hitchhiking again . . . and down there, in Davenport, Iowa, was a radio station, and I don't know how many I'd been in by that time, and I went in, and this wonderful old man, Pete MacArthur, all crippled up with rheumatoid arthritis, told me that, that, uh, they had just hired an announcer the day before. And on the way out, just more to myself than anything else, I said: "How the hell do you get to be a sports announcer if you can't even get a job at a radio station?" And—did I tell you this story before?

EM   Uh, you *did*, once, but—

RR   (*disappointed*) Well—

EM   (*weakly*) I'm pleased to hear it again!

RR   Well, I heard this *thumping* coming down the hall, where I had just come, and I heard this voice, and he was saying, "Hold up, you big—" and a profane term—

EM   Big what?

RR   "You big bastard." And here it was: *him,* coming on these two canes, down the hall . . . he said, "What was that you said about sports announcing?" And I said, "Well, I—that's what I'd like to *be.*" And he said, "Well, do you know anything about football?" And I said, "I played it eight years." And he said, "Come with me." And he led me in, to a studio, and stood me in front of a mike, and said: "When that red light comes on, *you* start to imagining a football game broadcasting, and I'll be in the other room listening." And that was when I did a re-creation of the last quarter of the game we'd played the year before [Eureka vs. Western Teachers] and he came in and told me: "Be here Saturday, you're broadcasting the Iowa-Minnesota football game."

Actually, the Minnesota meet was the fourth and last of his test assignments. The first was Iowa vs. Bradley on October 1, 1932. Nor did Dutch hitchhike to Davenport, as he had to Chicago; his father sympathetically lent him the family Oldsmobile. All men have their stories, tumbled like stones in the current of telling, until they are polished into something less (or more) than autobiography. Yet this one is undoubtedly true in essence, if not in particular. And given Dutch's accuracy of auditory recall (see later in this chapter), one can even hear the words that began the audition, words practiced over many broomsticks and happily recited for the next sixty years:

> *A chill wind is blowing in through the end of the stadium, and long blue shadows are settling over the field. Western still leads, six to nothing, as Eureka—defending the south goal—puts the ball into play on their own twenty-yard line.*

The long blue shadows were an imaginative touch, since I remember that Eureka's low bleachers cast about as much gloom as a picket fence. But the chill wind was good. Dutch instinctively understood that action which cannot be seen or sensed by the listener will not long hold attention. "Radio," he wrote, in a nice phrase, "was theater of the mind."

Dawn on the day of the Bradley game found Dutch on the Dixon-Davenport bus, with emotions of joy and terror easy to guess. He drove on west from WOC with MacArthur, a staff announcer, and two engineers. By lunchtime, he was perched in the press box of Memorial Stadium, Iowa City, trying to digest a hot dog and watching the huge space beneath him fill up. He had hardly been in a grandstand before, let alone a press box. His excitement was so great, he felt he was vibrating.

The announcer, reading from handouts, did the pre-game fill. Then Dutch heard him say, "And now to begin the play-by-play, here is Ronald Reagan."

So it was as "Ronald" and not "Dutch" that he began his radio career. Later, when his voice became familiar to WOC's little audience of football fans, he reverted to the monosyllable we all knew him by. " 'Dutch' Reagan sounded like a sporty name. I remember sitting there in a discussion, and they were trying to come up with a name. They went through five or six . . . and, well—I got to keep my own name!"

The Hawkeyes scored first with a fifty-seven-yard charge by Bill Ash, so we can be sure that Bud Cole's even longer sprint the year before against Western was rerun for the occasion. Dutch did well enough to finish the game, and returned home ecstatic via Eureka: "Big news! I'm pretty sure I got a job."

🕑

What he got was three more freelance assignments, at ten dollars a game plus bus fare. Both the Davenport *Democrat and Leader* and the Dixon *Evening Telegraph* praised his "crisp" command of narrative and "quick tongue" that "seemed to be as fast as the plays." Peter MacArthur must have given him some hope for the new year, because he made no further effort to seek work. That was no winter to be going anywhere one didn't have to go. Chicago's usual brutal cold (the lake-ward edge of every telephone pole sheeted with ice; sparks cascading from the El as trains clattered over frozen couplings) seemed to bite more deeply because of the strange clarity of the air. Most of the big steel mills had shut down, and those of us living in privileged precincts were shamed into rationing our firewood.

Had I been twenty-one, I would have voted with Dutch for Franklin Roosevelt. The Governor simply seemed more likely than President Hoover to arrest the scattering of federal money that kept recharging the Depression like dry ice on rain clouds. Ronald Reagan has been mocked for protesting, "I didn't leave the Democratic Party—it left me." But he was correct in stating that in 1932 Roosevelt advertised himself as a stalwart of individualism, states' rights, rural values, and reduced government. So much for patrician promises.

In the new year of 1933 I desperately sought, and won, an unglamorous job as patrol pilot for Barnouw Operational Signals Systems, operating out of Stinson Field. The work involved flying a little Waco biplane up and down the strings of beacons that lit the night-mail routes radiating from Chicago—particularly the Cleveland run—and finding some place to drop an electrical engineer off when one wasn't blinking.

A few times we flew over Dixon, its pinprick lights stippling the frozen bend of the Rock River. Even the grimmest of cities looks magical at night. I would rather not think what it must have been like down there for Dutch that January. He has admitted that the weeks of waiting for a call from Davenport marked "the low point of my life." However, it enabled him to update the rudimentary notions of welfare he had gotten at age eleven from *That Printer of Udell's*. His father, who worked directly with Lee County's "Supervisor of the Poor," came home every night with a folder of claims to juggle against the short register of public jobs available: street sweeping, wood chopping, rake work. Many of the indigent names he dropped over dinner were those of family friends.

Through Jack, Dutch soon began to feel the encroachment of the federal relief agency (IERA) over the state relief commission (IERC). In later life he persuaded himself that the "welfare workers" arriving in town with metal desks and card cabinets represented the Roosevelt New Deal. On the contrary, they represented President Hoover and the previous summer's Emergency Relief and Construction Act. Ronald Reagan's first experience of "Democratic do-goodism" was actually visited on Dixon by a Republican Administration.

The relief he personally looked for came just before his twenty-second birthday, when WOC Davenport informed him that he had been appointed a staff announcer at one hundred dollars a month, effective February 10, 1933.

Even as he crossed the Mississippi, deposited his bags in Davenport's YMCA, and headed up Brady Street to WOC, Ronald Reagan was mentally moving farther west—across the invisible Rockies to California and Hollywood. "I was afraid to say I wanted to be a movie actor. . . . But I did think . . . 'Well, maybe *radio . . .* maybe by way of *that,* someday . . .'"

For the time being, he was confronted by a hillside compound fully as fantastic as any lot in Greater Los Angeles. The "World of Chiropractic," a college and treatment center surmounted with a five-thousand-watt transmitter mast, was emblazoned with wall legends that ranged from the cryptic (SLIPPING AND CHECKING—WHAT'S WRONG WITH ME) to the sonorous: THE HIGHEST MERIT WE ASCRIBE TO MOSES, PLATO AND MILTON IS THAT THEY SET AT NAUGHT BOOKS AND TRADITIONS.

Two imposing street doors offered entry respectively to the chiropractic school and radio station. Both were owned by the author of the texts outside, Colonel Bartlett Joshua Palmer, a globe-trotting millionaire whose other businesses included a cowboy lounge, an insane asylum, and the Davenport *Democrat.*

A tiny elevator cranked Dutch up to WOC's rooftop studio, a white-gabled longhouse apparently airlifted from Holland. It sat on a field of yellow tiles, and bore on its south gable a portrait of Krishna, discharging blue waves of enlightenment.

Dutch was no expert on Hindu color-coding, but Colonel Palmer seemed to infer a common *karma* between these rays and the blue velvet drapes that swathed the longhouse's interior. Lustrously fringed and tasseled, they hung heavily from ceiling to floor, absorbing every vibration of downstairs sound. Here, at the micropulsating heart of the Central Broadcasting Company (WOC Davenport and its sister station WHO Des Moines), two studios conjoined. The larger, for musical performances, had lacquered teak-log furniture, and two equally glossy teak saplings, from whose lopped boughs hung brass birdcages, an ear of corn, a fire extinguisher, and a mirror. The announcer's room beyond was decorated more austerely, except for a ceiling of more teak logs, dangling with stuffed animal parts: a bear's paw with claws extended, peacock plumes, a raccoon's tail, and various other *disjuncta membra* from four continents.

In this musty company, under the beady stare of twenty or thirty glass eyes, Ronald Reagan began to read radio scripts.

☯

In his first days before the microphone, he variously did duty as a record spinner, reporter, weatherman, network feeder ("This is WOC

"From whose lopped boughs hung brass birdcages."
Radio Station WOC, ca. 1933.

Davenport, Where the West Begins and the Tall Corn Grows"), and product plugger, hustling everything from fertilizer to the pamphlets and patent medicines of Palmer Chiropractic College. Nobody at the station seemed to have any interest in training him. Even when he mis-spoke, the control room maintained a distracted silence.

He did not realize that he had been hired as a stopgap, at a time of great insecurity for Colonel Palmer's employees. In the spring of 1933, WHO Des Moines was due to switch to an enormous new fifty-thousand-watt transmitter, capable of reaching every state in the union. This monolith would use up all the signal power available to Central Broadcasting under current state restrictions. Until that quota could be increased, Palmer had no choice but to merge his two stations. WOC executives from Peter MacArthur on down were bracing for no-tices of dismissal.

Dutch innocently assumed he was doing well. After two weeks of camping out at the YMCA, he received his first compensation—in cash—and moved to an apartment in the majestic old Vale House down by the Mississippi. Affluence, or what seemed like affluence to the son of a shoe salesman, stared him in the face. Every morning as he walked up the hill to work, he spared a dime for the first hobo he saw. In larger charity, he sent ten percent of his earnings to help Neil finish college. "I am at present announcing sustaining and commercial pro-grams from the Davenport studios of WOC-WHO," he boasted to the Henry Strong Educational Foundation on March 29. Then, with shocking suddenness, he was informed that he was being terminated.

Apparently, he had neglected to mention on the air that a program of organ music came courtesy of a mortuary downtown. Its directors were outraged, and demanded another announcer.

Dutch was saved by MacArthur, who told him that the Des Moines station was looking for a freelance barker to cover the Drake Univer-sity Relays on April 29 and 30. "Do you know about track?" He knew enough, at any event, to cover the huge meet satisfactorily, and in early May found himself rehired and transferred full-time to WHO.

His new title, Sports Director, was one he had long dreamed of. And it came with more money. (Over the next three years, his salary would rise to $3,900 a year, not far short of his goal of five thousand in five.) WHO's state-of-the-art studios were blessedly free of stuffed fauna; one room was so grand that it had a public observation gallery. Thanks to the station's new transmitter, Dutch had the agreeable prospect of addressing himself to millions of new listeners, some as far away as Mexico and New Zealand. Best of all, he could count on the continued fatherly presence of Peter MacArthur, who had also been transferred.

Here, over the next three years, he mastered the essentials of radio announcing, with the exception of sight-reading, a process that bothered him well into middle age. The natural equipment of a sportscaster he already had: lucidity, enthusiasm, an eye for visual detail, and a mouth that moved as fast as his mind. *Fast* is not a word most Americans today would use in remembering him, but the young Ronald Reagan could out-talk Bugs Bunny.

His voice was a light and sunny baritone that carried well on the air. As one of the minority whom it did not please—I found it less sunny than quicksilvery, running over the surface of everything without penetration—I churlishly tuned him out on the infrequent occasions I heard him. (He once wavecrashed an NBC recital by Rosa Ponselle with "*It's a hippity-hop to the left!*") Yet there was an indefinable something in the Reagan delivery that "spoke" to Dust Bowl brats like little Hughie Sidey, the future presidential correspondent of *Time*: "Life was hard for us, and the Depression seemed endless, but he managed to give us the feeling that things wouldn't always be that way, that they would get better."

Dutch also improved his rhetorical style in Des Moines. He joined the Advertising Club, a premier city showcase for outside speakers, and listened avidly to presentations at its "gridiron" lunches. Just how avidly, I discovered half a century later when I asked if any particular speaker stuck in his memory. There followed several bizarre minutes, during which the President of the United States temporarily became a corn-belt barnaby, convulsing fellow burghers with what passed, in 1933, as humor:

RR   I can remember the whole routine, word for word.

EM   Really?

RR   He began talking about uh, "Boffo Toilet Paper, Inc., made from thirty percent of the mighty spruce!" (*chuckles*) Sometime, when I'm not using up all of your time, I'll tell you about it.

EM   No, go on!

Reagan looks down at the carpet. His eyes glaze, his voice becomes high-pitched, and he begins to speak rapidly.

RR   Well, he said: "In the dark days after the Civil War, it became increasingly apparent to a number of civic-minded citizens that part of the hardship of pioneer life was due to the paper being used from the mail-order catalog. And so, Boffo was founded. And Boffo has grown to this day. It comes in seven pastel shades. Shades of brown are omitted; shades of red were discontinued when the secretary of the President, after she used 'scarlet number seven,' turned around, screamed, 'Thank God!' and fainted. You've heard about the Harvard Classics, and the shelf of books of learning for fifteen minutes a day toward a college education. Boffo does a college course, printed on every roll. . . . And then we also have the 'Boffo Thrillers,' with a detective story and a climax guaranteed to do away with compound cathartics. In the deluxe issue, Boffo comes a quarter-inch wider, which reduces the possibility of a social error. And it is wrapped in moisture-proof cellophane, about which I shall say more. We also have the 'Boffo Sweetheart' number, with hearts intertwined for the honeymooning couples, and for table decoration for appropriate holidays. As to the wrapping of our Boffo Tissue in moisture-proof cellophane, that was the result from the disaster I'd like tell you about. We received word that our toilet paper had arrived, soiled in transit—"

EM   Oh, *no.*

RR   "—and we had wired that a fifty percent discount would take care of the matter. But I took the night train because of my curiosity on how our tissue would become soiled in transit. Early in the morning, as I stepped down from the train, we were surprised to see all the citizens from Yazoo step down the railroad tracks, as if all the demons of hell had been set loose, plunking themselves into the icy water of the pond. They were soon followed by all, until everybody was either running, plunging into the icy waters of the pond, or sliding up and down the cinders on their keisters. And then, we discovered the cause—spilled in transit, by a leaky barrel of turpentine." (*Shakes with laughter*)

EM   Mr. President, I can't believe you heard that only once!

RR   (*reverting to normal voice*) Yes, just at that luncheon.

I quote the above at length not merely for the surreal subliminality of its associations (climax/catharsis, issue/tissue, Missy Le Hand/ Mississippi Delta) but to illustrate how receptive Ronald Reagan was in his early twenties, sensitive as silver salts to the images that came at him—and about as judgmental.

Aside from Chicago, Des Moines was the largest and dirtiest city he had ever seen, with three theaters, twenty-two motion picture houses, forty-seven hotels, and about as many insurance companies. The prevailing local hue was brown. Two tawny rivers intersected downtown, humidly ensuring that brown factory particulates, mixed with gypsum dust, rose and fell within the metropolitan area. Brown-uniformed personnel from Camp Dodge and Fort Des Moines rode down Central Avenue in brown trucks.

Dutch gazed happily about him and chose a brown-paneled apartment in a converted mansion at 330 Center Street. The neighborhood had seen better days, but this building's stonework was solid, there were plenty of family restaurants, and he had only six blocks to walk to work. He found a tailor who told him that dun shades flattered his coloring, and began to affect a briar pipe and brown tweed sport coat— progenitor of the infamous brown suits he would wear as President.

Large as Des Moines was, it had a pleasing air of isolation. Over a hundred and fifty miles of rolling hills (lofty to a plainsman's eyes) separated Dutch from Davenport and Dixon, thrillingly emphasizing the fact that he was now a grown man, building his own career "in the solar plexus of the country."

I came to know those Iowan hills myself in the summer of 1933, and learned, under the tutelage of a short, fey, freckled little genius, something of what art historians now contemptuously call the Regionalist vision. As a result, I was later able to deduce the extraordinary correlationship between it and Ronald Reagan's own way of looking at the world.

Paul Rae, home on vacation from New York, persuaded me to spend three weeks with him at Grant Wood's art colony in Stone City. "So what if you can't paint? Maybe he'll teach you how to write!" I don't know if it did, but any hack who aspires to a sense of form should be so lucky as to watch a real artist at work.

Wood was then at the threshold of his brief fame as "the chief philosopher and greatest teacher of representational U.S. art." Before the decade was out, he would incur the disfavor of modernist critics and die at the age of fifty, *passé* as Sherwood Anderson. I confess I cannot read *Winesburg, Ohio* any more, but Wood's paintings still fill an old airhog's soul with rapture. The greatest of them—*Stone City, Midnight Ride of Paul Revere, The Birthplace of Herbert Hoover,* and, above all, *Spring Turning*—share the exalted viewpoint one gets just after takeoff: figures and houses reduced to toys, the land diminishing yet acquiring a territorial hugeness, shadows sharpening in parallel while contours coalesce.

Dutch probably never studied a Wood composition, other than the inevitable cartoons of him standing with a pitchfork beside Nancy. Yet he could have walked out of one as a boy, and looked forward to retiring from the White House to another. For what was Rancho del Cielo (every pole measured out by himself, every last madroña tree pruned to his satisfaction) but *July Fifteenth* transported to California? The yellow light in Wood's farmhouse windows is the same light he used to read by in the Dixon Public Library; Herbert Hoover's birthplace is as remote as his own; that horseman crossing the Wapsipinicon is him; these brown-eyed girls are the kind he married. Here is his idolized mother, the comical chickens of his barnyard stories, the self-made businessmen and athletes and civil engineers he admired. Less figuratively, here are suppressed melancholy and anger, faith in parables, love of gesture, hygiene, and order, and an intense, all-pervading solitariness.

In one of the stranger juxtapositions of a biographer's life, I once found myself sitting beneath Wood's *Dinner for Threshers* in company with Mikhail and Raisa Gorbachev. They were visiting their old friend Dwayne Andreas, chairman of Archer Daniels Midland. Gorbachev was rumbling on about fodder supply lines in Stavropol while Raisa Maksimovna took a disdainful survey of Andreas's art collection. Her expression softened at the sight of the picture above my head.

"Who has painted dat?"

"It's by a great artist who lived not far from here in the nineteen-thirties, named Grant Wood. He is almost forgotten now." I tried to explain Regionalism, but her English was not up to it, and she interrupted me, her eyes still on the painting.

"Is very—very *American*," she allowed.

After returning to Chicago from Stone City, I dully continued to fly for Barnouw and wrote freelance copy and brochures, mostly for aviation-related industries. The following summer Paul Rae went to Europe and wrote from Paris that he had bumped into Margaret Cleaver "of all people." She had clammed up when he asked after her fiancé:

> Couldn't help noticing THE RING was missing!! Question is, who dumped *whom*? Whatever the case, Miss Mugs sure has gotten over her grief. Looking as cute as a Fragonard. Not half as fierce as she

used to be at college. (Actually *blushing* and exchanging glances with a good-looking Virginia boy she's got in tow.) Dutch better find himself another nurse.

I misunderstood that last sentence, thinking it referred to Mugs. Actually Paul was talking about a nurse who had been held up beneath Dutch's bedroom window in Des Moines. A warm Sunday night; the time about eleven o'clock; suddenly the sound of a man snarling something, and a young woman's voice, high and panicky: "Take everything I've got but let me go." Reagan leaps out of bed, seizes his latest acquisition, a .45 automatic (unloaded), and in the glow of a street lamp outside sees one of the girls from Broadlawns General Hospital with her hands in the air. The man menacing her is stooping to pick up her bag, when a light baritone that carries well on the air rings out: *"Leave her alone or I'll shoot you right between the shoulders!"*

Dutch modestly never mentioned this rescue until he was interviewed as President on the right to bear arms. He received a nostalgic letter of thanks from the former nurse, now living in retirement. She recalled that after scaring off her attacker, he had emerged calm and handsome in his robe and slippers, and escorted her back to Broadlawns.

A slight story, but what interests me is that Dutch, comfortable as he was in the world of Grant Wood, felt equally at home in the more threatening one of Edward Hopper.

When I repeated Paul's "Who dumped whom?" to the old Margaret Cleaver Gordon (sitting black-eyed and upright in her Richmond mansion, the very picture of genteel Southern rectitude), she declined comment but said that "I didn't want to bring up my children in Hollywood." Even in 1934, radio was secondary to Dutch's "obsession" with the silvery world of movies. "He had an inability to distinguish between fact and fancy."

Her lips unpursed, and she smiled in spite of herself. *Still pretty,* I scribbled.

"I don't want to say anything negative about Dutch. He was a nice man."

I asked if he had been distressed to get his ring back after seven years of intimacy.

Her eyes darted defensively to the fire. The clock ticked. "Why, yes. He was very sad."

I saw that same defensive look on Reagan's face at our Eureka reunion some years later. Tubby Müller regretted the fact that Mugs wasn't there, whereupon Dutch flinched and said in an involuntary *sequitur,* "You know, when she—we broke up, I was kinda floored, and whatsisname, our old high school drama teacher, wrote and said, *Take this and bear with it.*"

Not having any other choice, that's what he did, learning in his twenty-fourth summer that an aloof nature is no protection against hurt.

☯

A streamlined V-8 Lafayette convertible coupé helped lighten Dutch's mood. It was sheen-sprayed a metallic beige, in contrast to the black, black, and dusty black of most Depression-era cars. He knew he looked good stepping out of it in his brown clothes, with his hat pushed back. If his growing circle of friends and fans noticed this complacency, they forgave him, because otherwise he lacked interest in himself. It did not occur to him that anyone should want to see where and how he lived. The inquisitive few who looked him up came away with an impression of utter ordinariness.

When I asked him about these first friends of his maturity, I was struck by how easily he recalled them, in contrast to his usual indifference to names and faces. They were "Pete" and "Don" and "Moon" and "Cy" and "Jeanne" and "Joy": comfortable, mnemonic monosyllables, unless you counted "Pee Wee" as two. Since he never again enjoyed such a council of familiars, we might consider a few of them, to see how they related to him physically and professionally.

"Pete" was Peter MacArthur, Dutch's most tireless promoter at WHO. MacArthur assigned the young man to cover no fewer than one hundred and fifty baseball games in the 1934 season alone, and persuaded General Mills to sponsor him as a "telegraph commentator" on home games of the Chicago Cubs and White Sox. (Hastily typed slips shoved across the microphone table; dry codes flowering into vivid and voluble descriptions; redheaded kids leaping to catch fly balls, and enough long blue shadows to fill the Intermontane Gap.)

"Don" was Donald Reid, the horseman who encouraged Reagan to start riding at Fort Des Moines, headquarters of the U.S. 14th Cavalry Regiment. Hitherto Dutch's only equestrian experience had been bareback plods around Lowell Park. Now he got his leg round a thoroughbred, and loved the feeling of nervous control. Another friend suggested that he sign up with the Cavalry Reserve for the best training any rider could wish for. So on March 18, 1935, "Ronald W. Reagan,

Civilian" enrolled at 322d Cavalry HQ, Des Moines, and began to take extension courses toward a commission in the Army.

"Moon" was of course Neil Reagan, who had gotten bored with working for the government in Dixon and decided to check out Des Moines, from the vantage point of Dutch's apartment. His Catholic conservatism put some strain on their relationship, as did signs of an ongoing copycat tendency. One night at WHO, Dutch made the mistake of offering him the mike. Neil proceeded to show that he was equally articulate about sports, and read commercials rather better. Central Broadcasting promptly hired him as a Saturday-night score announcer. Happily for Cain, WOC got its signal back, and Abel was transferred to Davenport. He continued to visit Des Moines frequently, though, having fallen in love with a local girl, Miss Bess Hoffman (silent, bespectacled, expressionless as a Sears mannequin). They would soon marry.

"Cy" Griffith owned an inn on the western, woodsy edge of town. Even after Repeal, the smoky, illicit taste of Cy's "spiked ale"—slugs of grade A straight liquor fed into beer under the table—drew a nightly crowd of young revelers. Dutch liked to drive out there after signing off the air. He would pretend to get drunk with Ed Morley, Will Scott, and Pee Wee Williams, and sing "Baby Won't You Please Come Home" around a big horse tank full of ice and floating strung bottles.

Jeanne Tesdell was a Drake University senior, tall, beautiful, and horse-loving. When Dutch met her in the new year of 1936, he was dating dozens of the prettiest girls in Des Moines. But he showed an immediate interest, and began to pay court. Miss Tesdell was not entirely sure that his intentions were romantic. He kept delaying their excursions in order to lecture her father on the virtues of the Agricultural Adjustment Act. She wondered if Dutch might not be—well, just a teeny bit boring.

Finally and most formidably, there was the singer Joy Hodges: strong-jawed, dance-bandy, brittle-bright. A former WHO child artiste, she was one of the few "Desmoineselles" who had actually made it to Hollywood. So far, her career in pictures amounted to a couple of songs in *Follow the Fleet,* but RKO was talking to her agent, and in the meantime she had a regular gig at the Biltmore Bowl with Jimmy ("such a *darling!*") Grier.

These connections made Miss Hodges a star of extreme glamour to Dutch, when she stopped by the station on one of her regular visits home. She was happy to be interviewed by him, and found him not unattractive. ("Too bad about the thick glasses.") But she grew wary when he kept on quizzing her long after the red light went out.

"Kinda *personal* questions, too!" she told me in old age, laughing at the memory. "Where was I stayin'—with my *folks,* where else? Did I like horses? I'm a *prairie gal,* for gosh sakes! Next thing I know, he's got me to agree to a riding date in the morning. I change my mind overnight, and pretend to be out when he rings our bell. He just keeps on ringing, ringing, ringing. I thought he'd *never* go away! Ring, ring. I had to go stand in a closet and *cover my ears.* Well *finally* he stopped, but honey, you can't *believe* that *purposefulness!* And d'ja know, later on, when he and I became such *dear* friends, he *never once* mentioned how I'd stood him up! Like it never happened. That's why I've always known Dutch can't be hurt. It's water off a duck's back."

Ronald Reagan at twenty-five was recognizably the mature man of later years, no longer the local lad of Lowell Park and McKinzie Field. Yet to Joy Hodges, Dutch still reeked of the provinces—"the Ioways," in Hollywood parlance. His brown-and-white summer shoes and houndstooth tux, the pipe, the pushed-back hat, the second helpings of macaroni and cheese were straight out of *Collier's* magazine. He claimed to have read Sinclair Lewis; did he realize that Babbitt was breathing down his own close-clipped neck?

Apparently, yes. In February 1936, Dutch asked Joe Maland, WHO's station manager, to let him follow the Chicago Cubs to their spring training on Santa Catalina Island, California. By an uncanny coincidence, the resort they were headed for happened to be a playground of Hollywood producers.

There was much besides sheer sass to recommend this proposal to Mr. Maland. The gimmick of live commentary from Santa Catalina would increase listenership during a slack time in the broadcasting year, and cement WHO's relationship with one of the hottest teams in baseball. What was more, Reagan had begun to write a weekly sports column in the Des Moines *Dispatch.* His print reports, filed on location, would provide excellent additional publicity.

Dutch clinched the matter by offering to trade vacation time. He was rewarded with a through ticket to Los Angeles on the Southern Pacific Railroad.

Reaching San Francisco on the twenty-eighth, he changed to the Golden State Limited and swayed south through parkland and farmland already green with new life. What looked like snow on the Coast Ranges was actually almond blossom. Disorienting though this hibernal fecundity was to a midwesterner (he had just endured the worst winter in Iowan history), the Pacific Ocean was even more so. How laughable, compared to these endless beaches, was that little strip of sand at Lowell Park!

The farther south he got, the hotter the light and the whiter the foam. This was *February*? This was *America*—these blue-trunked trees, these tiled and whitewashed houses, almost obscenely brilliant with bougainvillea? By the time his train reached Los Angeles, the thermometer had risen to an incredible eighty-two degrees. He congratulated himself on having left his brown clothes behind in favor of a new "dago" wardrobe: linen suits, white sport coat, and white buckskin shoes.

Frustratingly, Union Passenger Terminal (with its trolley services to Hollywood) was but a stop on his continuing journey to the *embarcadero* to Santa Catalina. Eschewing a five-dollar flight by "amphibian" seaplane, he bought a ticket on the Avalon ferry. It wallowed out to sea from a shore already strange (Japanese and Portuguese fishing villages, oil derricks, and royal palms casually coexisting), and stranger still as Los Angeles became a purple-gray smudge on the horizon. Dutch was being detached from the only continent he had ever known, and for an unsettling quarter hour there was no evidence that anything lay beyond the hard blue line ahead.

Avalon in 1936 was one of the loveliest places in the world, and not only to eyes dulled by twenty-five years of living in the Midwest. Its perfect crescent bay, encapsulated by wild hills, was a mirror to villas and silvery olive trees, except when yachts (or ferry boats) broke up the reflection. Flowers bloomed twelve months a year, fountains that never froze splashed and sparkled, and the breeze carried a hint of wet seashells.

In a grove just outside town, eucalyptus trees screened off a green baseball diamond. Here mourning doves cooed, interrupted by the occasional mighty swat of Chuck Klein hitting a homer. Dutch lost no time in joining other Cubs on the bench:

Q. Say, Andy, what's the thing you have to guard against most in these spring campaigns—sore arms, charley horses, or bad feet?

A. None of these—of course we get a few bad arms, especially among the young ones who are trying to earn a glance by showing great form. . . .

Q. Any casualties in the crew?

A. Only Woody English who has a sore spot on his shoulder and an ingrown nail giving him some trouble. . . .

Q. Excuse me Andy, I want to see Charlie Root over here. Say, Charlie, I noticed today you kept refusing Stephenson's signs. Did that mean he was calling them wrong?

Palpable, in his attempt at league lingo and eager use of nicknames, was Dutch's delight in being able to "walk with heroes"—if not as an equal, at least as an intimate. His first love was still college football, but three years of covering baseball for WOC and WHO had given him a good press-box knowledge of America's Pastime. Now, three weeks of daily contact with the Cubs—smelling their sweat, swigging from the same pop bottles, joining them after dinner in their little village under the pepper trees—ripened that knowledge into empathy. In James T. Farrell's marvelous phrase, Dutch tasted "the salty pleasure of the white moment."

❦

The nearest he got to Hollywood, poor hick, was the Biltmore Bowl, where Joy Hodges wasn't *quite* sure if she remembered him. So he returned to Des Moines on March 22, put away his white shoes and neon dreams, and set about proving to the guys at Cy's that he could "ballcast" as good as Harry Hartman. Radio critics were quick to notice a new expertise in his delivery:

> Dutch Reagan's trip to California this winter to visit the Cubs and White Sox and to become personally acquainted with the players was a very good idea, whoever thought of it.
>
> The popular sports announcer's vivid play-by-play descriptions of the Chicago baseball games, all the more phenomenal because they are taken from telegraphic reports, are even more colorful than they were last season because of his intimate knowledge of the personalities of the players themselves.

Intimate or not, it was his reflex reactions to wire-service codes that kept WHO's audience from switching to announcers who were actually *in* the press box at Wrigley Field.

REAGAN (*noticing through studio window that telegraph operator, headphones on, has begun to type something*) Lon Warnecke has the sign, he's coming out of the windup, here's the pitch. (*Operator hands him a slip reading "S2C"*) It's a called

strike breaking over the inside corner, making it two strikes
on Augie Galan. Hartnett returns the ball to Lon Warnecke, Warnecke is dusting his hands in the resin . . .

If WHO's telegraph receiver failed at such a moment, Dutch could
keep the resin dust hovering long enough to defeat gravity. But he was
rarely more than half a pitch behind the actual play when the slips kept
coming.

He seemed determined to emulate Damon Runyon as a coiner of
original slang. His *Dispatch* columns dissolved into a kind of Dada
prosody wherein the hard geometrics of movement were obscured by
a fog of metaphor so dense that it was difficult, sometimes, to figure
which sport he was writing about. From the grapefruit circuit to Viking
schools, under suns that spotted and stars that splattered, men with
potato mashers big as wagon tongues bent 'em past the war clubs. Gas
house gangsters paid more attention to their sandpaper collars than to
their duke handling. And speaking of dukes, was that Max Schmeling's
dream of a white right crossing Joe Louis's black left, like the moon
over the mountain? 'Way down slap alley, a trombone went *waw.*

The balmy air was full of skeeters. Any more haze around those
smoke balls, and old Mose would be sent back to the bulrushes. Far
across the Atlantic, Adolf stuck his fuzzy lip through the Olympic stadium gate. *Eins, Zwei, und Spiel!* Around the corner, a tambourine
thumped. Here was his stack up for the next few days. Broad jump: the
black thunderbolt, Jesse Owens. Hundred meters: Owens. Two hundred
meters: just put down Owens again. Who did you like in the series?
Ever smell a burning goat?

He didn't seem to be riding the rods on the same train of thought. It
was hard to reconcile September's ninety-degree heat with the squeal of
the tackling dummy and the distant bark of a coach. As the sun sank
back of the poplars, he heard the green-melon "ping" of leather on
leather. High spiral punts went shimmying. The light grew pale.

October. Mm, frosty air, topcoat weather. Hysteria of Homecoming.
Chic dolls in fur "bennies" and chrysanthemums. Streets resplendent in
maroon and gold. Great horseshoe stadium banked high with humans.
Combined bands playing as the flag rose through the swirling sky.

It was a glorious saga, right through the last November day.

Ronald Reagan was more content with himself that fall than he had yet
been in his largely untroubled life. His health was superb, his girlfriend

beautiful, his swell clothes fit, and he had more money than he could modestly spend, even after contributing ten percent to "the Lord," helping out Jack and Nelle, and trading his '34 Lafayette for a brand-new Nash convertible.

A *Sporting News* poll rated him the fourth-most popular baseball commentator not working in a major league area—qualified fame, perhaps, but better than unqualified obscurity. Thanks to flattering photographs (with glasses off) in the *Dispatch* and regular performances (with hat on) in WHO's observation studio, he was beginning to generate beefcake copy. "Dutch has nothing to be ashamed of in any physical fashion," a gossip columnist gushed. "He is over six feet tall with the proverbial Greek-god physique: broad-shouldered, slim-waisted and a face that would make Venus look twice. . . . Watch him; he's stream-lined."

The year did not end, however, without some drag on his progress. His father was becoming something of a burden, having suffered a heart attack and been laid off by the Works Progress Administration. Clearly ailing at only forty-three, Jack Reagan would never work full-time again. Then Jeanne Tesdell's affection suddenly cooled.

It was not that the landslide re-election of Franklin D. Roosevelt had made Dutch more of a New Deal drone than he already was. It was, rather, the same note of "Hollywood" that had repelled Margaret Cleaver, his tendency to behave as though he were on-screen, his every word and gesture addressed to some imaginary audience. When Jeanne danced in his arms she felt his pleasure, not in her as a woman, but in themselves as a tall and handsome couple, whom everybody else on the floor was ogling. She declined to play opposite him any longer.

"He's a people pleaser," she told me long afterward. "Always was."

"Happy nineteen thirty-seven!" Dutch declaimed into WHO's black-and-silver microphone as the new year dawned. His determined cheerfulness matched that of the Roosevelt Administration, anxious to reassure voters that the Great Depression was over. That promise turned out to be illusory, but for Dutch personally, kinder fates seemed to be conspiring, pointing him again in the direction of Hollywood. From the moment Joe Maland approved another trip to Santa Catalina with the Cubs, Ronald Reagan the would-be actor began to step out and distance himself from Dutch Reagan the sportscaster, like those ghost figures, half tone and half negative, that photographers conjure out of corpses.

"Watch him; he's stream-lined."
Ronald Reagan in 1936.

On Friday, March 12, he arrived in Los Angeles in a dark maelstrom of wind and hail. There was no question of crossing over to Catalina in such weather, so he checked into the Biltmore and took a bus to Republic Productions, where a WHO band happened to be playing. Its manager got him admitted to the studio and introduced him to a casting director. When Dutch stepped back into the storm, he had an invitation to return at his convenience and do a "reading."

All this happened so fast that he was unable for the rest of his life to remember much of what happened inside Republic's gates—only that "there in the studio the dream re-awakened." It was the dream that had possessed him more than seven years before, when he first saw *Journey's End:* of being "carried into a new world" where things really mattered, of wanting, "more than anything else in life," to speak words that were not his words, in a voice not his own.

That night, at the Biltmore Bowl, he sent a note backstage to Joy Hodges, asking her to join him between floor shows. Either she had softened some, or he had gotten more persuasive, but they ended up swapping confidences over drinks. "I have visions of becoming an actor," Dutch said shyly. "What I really want is a screen test."

Miss Hodges was touched by his ardor and willingness to forget the day she had stood him up. Moreover, she could see, when he took off his dark horn-rims for her, that he was some hunk of horsemeat. "I think I might be able to fix something," she said. "Just don't ever put those glasses on again, as long as you live."

☯

Tossed about the sky in a seaplane the next day, Dutch doubted he would live long enough to reach Avalon. He had never flown before, and childhood claustrophobia, combined with the sight of whitecaps rising and sinking beneath him, made him regret that he had invested in a return ticket.

The feeling of imminence Joy Hodges had planted in his mind lasted throughout the twelve days he spent with the Cubs on Santa Catalina. *Variety* reported his presence there, as though to remind him he was no longer obscure. Hollywood's elite came out to celebrate Saint Patrick's Day at the Avalon Casino and breathed the same air he breathed. Olivia de Havilland let him hold her exquisite hand for a second or two. She noticed him, the way a woman notices, and would remember him, the way a woman remembers, when they were both old: "this charming young man . . . full of good nature and affability and grace."

His distraction from baseball training was so obvious that Charlie Grimm, manager of the Cubs, voiced loud displeasure. "How could I tell him," Reagan wrote in later life, "that somewhere within myself was the knowledge I would no longer be a sports announcer?"

He spent most of the pre-exhibition period riding mountain ponies and boating and getting rid of his Iowa pallor. In the process, he fell in love with Southern California—its heady mix of seasons, fragrance and fire, Greece and Mexico, salt and chaparral, and (most addictive of all) its bracing lack of melancholy.

No sooner had he returned to the mainland on Thursday, March 27, than Joy Hodges informed him that her agent, George Ward, would see him the following morning at ten o'clock. Blindly unspectacled, Dutch walked in at the appointed hour and loomed over Ward to such an extent that the headhunter had to tilt his chair back.

"Joy said you would level with me. Should I go back to Des Moines and forget this, or what?"

The Easter weekend was about to begin, but Ward responded by arranging an immediate audition with Max Arnow, the proverbially peevish casting director of Warner Bros.

Arnow's first words, when they got to Burbank, were disconcerting. "Stand up against that door. Are those your own shoulders?" Dutch began to realize that to talent management, all actors are but beef. Or wind instruments.

"Let me hear your voice," Arnow said.

Dutch obliged.

"Is that *your* voice?"

"It's the only one I've got."

Arnow gave him some pages of a script by Philip Barry and told him to memorize them over the weekend. He said to Ward, "We'll shoot a test—"

Here biography must intrude on autobiography and protest that Arnow cannot have said "Wednesday," as Ronald Reagan remembers. It must have been "Tuesday," for reasons so pedantic I will relegate them to a footnote. What's relevant is that he replied, "I've got to get back to my job in Des Moines."

Whether he was being dutiful, as he pretends, or more likely pushing his luck (that fatal insolence, equally composed of adrenaline and testosterone, that surges up in young men at moments of uncontrollable excitement), Arnow agreed to advance the test by twenty-four hours.

Weak with stage fright on Monday morning, he reported to Warner Bros. to be made up. A stylist asked, in tones that were evidently studio policy, "Where the hell did you get that haircut?" She did what she could with his center part and pompadour, then abandoned him to the cameras. Painted, glossed, irradiated, unable to see much farther than he could reach, Dutch at least had the comfort of an Iowan assistant— the actress Helen Valkis.

Their scene together was so brief that he felt a sharp sense of anticlimax. Depression set in after he boarded his train back to Des Moines.

He regretted having treated Max Arnow so condescendingly. "What a damn fool you were," he told himself, and doggedly began to write his next baseball column.

> *GOLDEN STATE LIMITED*—That dateline tells the story. Another training season swings into the sleeper jump exhibition tour and we must pack a lot of memories into a safe corner. . . .

❁

Dutch was back at work on Friday morning, April 2, when a telegram came from George Ward. WARNERS OFFER CONTRACT SEVEN YEARS, ONE YEAR'S OPTIONS, STARTING AT $200 A WEEK.

❁

"You'd better get me out of here soon," a dazed Dutch wrote George Ward. The consequences of celebrity were beginning to sink in: "I average sixteen insurance salesmen and three car peddlers a day, not to mention a couple of guys anxious to help me invest the money we hope we'll get."

He was not certain of wealth, because his contract carried the usual Hollywood three-month probationary period. Even so, two hundred dollars a week was double what he had sworn five years ago to be earning this summer. He ordered a new white sport coat, and promised grandly to look after anybody who wanted to follow him, from his parents to his singing partners at Cy's.

Some practical matters had to be taken care of before he quit town. He wrote two final columns for the *Dispatch,* signed an agreement with the *Sunday Register* for a series of articles about Hollywood, and went to Chicago to address the first-ever convention of radio sports announcers. For as long as possible, he kept covering Cubs and Sox games. "See, I am very vain about my sports 'telling.' "

Somehow, he found time to complete his Army Extension courses, at an overall average of 94 percent. A Medical Corps examiner found him to be a perfect physical specimen, except for 20-200 myopia in both eyes. This disability did not stop Dutch from satisfactorily drilling a war-strength mounted platoon at Fort Des Moines. On April 29, 1937, he was accepted into the Reserve Corps as a second lieutenant with a double "Excellent" rating for character and military efficiency.

Three weeks later, after a last loud evening at Cy's, he loaded up his Nash convertible and headed west toward the Rockies.

9

Inside
Story

Dutch had the last ten days of May 1937 to get to Los Angeles. But he was filled with such excitement that he vowed to do the journey in three. On Saturday the twenty-second he drove six hundred and fifty miles, before night-stopping in Cheyenne, Wyoming. Next day he drove six hundred miles to Nephi, Utah, on the edge of the Great Basin. Finally he drove six hundred and sixty miles, until desert and sierra gave way to orange groves and the long Santa Monica highway, at the end of which the sun was setting, red with fatigue.

When the redness faded, he was showered and changed and trying to keep his eyes open in the Biltmore Bowl. He wanted to thank Joy Hodges for services rendered, but had to wait until she finished the first half of her floor show. In the event, it was she who came to him, shook him awake, and sent him upstairs to bed.

With all the vibration in his bones, he slept badly. He felt disembodied the following morning. Yet he could not resist putting on his white sport coat and driving over the Verdugo Hills to Warner Bros.

The giant studio lay like a compressed and teeming city on the far side of the Los Angeles River, geographically separated from Hollywood. In practical fact, it *was* a city, walled and gated. It had its own police department and fire company and power plant and hospital and school, not to mention four cinemas, thirty miles of streets, a working railroad, and a rather dusty-looking quay, whence a seventeenth-century galleon seemed about to sail for San Bernardino. There was even a local radio station: two transmitter towers loomed up, weirdly reminiscent of those in Davenport and Des Moines.

Dutch was not, of course, a stranger, having come through the gates twice already, in company with George Ward. But he had been too overawed then to get more than a general impression of hugeness and efficiency. (Omnipresent armed guards, and a grim-looking executive complex, suggested a government intolerant of dissent.) Now he was free to stroll and speculate, as far as his tired mind would allow, which parts of the city were real, and which not.

A charming, old-world sleepiness hung over its residential streets, unpaved and posted with an eight m.p.h. speed limit. Some were tree-lined like Hennepin Avenue in Dixon. Others were more exotic to Dutch's eyes, with wrought-iron *jalousies* and tiled fountains; others still, ending in cobbled squares and *hôtels de commerce*, looked positively French. On close inspection, many beckoning interiors proved to be no thicker than paint on glass. These "fronts" backed only on air; these "roofs" stopped no rain.

In contrast, the city's industrial area was throbbing and three-dimensional. Harsh concrete alleys separated nineteen hangar-sized warehouses. Yet they stored the stuff of dreams: oases on wheels, Tudor thrones, summer snowbanks, jewels and ingots, dance floors slick as glass. Fragmentary though much of this stuff was, it at least had solid substance, as did the men and women who hurried from building to building in Chinese silks and tutus and zoot suits, dodging smuts from the downtown incinerator.

The paradox of the city's ultimate product, Dutch came to understand, was that it was never actually possessed by the millions of people who paid for it. All they got in exchange for their money was a *look* at the way things were in these warehouses. So the look had to be as tactile, as weighty, as reassuring as possible. If the ingots picked up too easily, if the galleon betrayed any hint of mechanized movement, their resentment would be extreme.

Here, for Thyrsis, lay the absolute contrast between the theater of his past and the cinema of his future. In *Aria da Capo*, he had built a "wall" of paper ribbon onstage, while the audience watched sympathetically; had he struggled with real, dusty stones, we would have suspended our belief. Now, whatever walls he built, so to speak, must be stone before they became ribbon—celluloid ribbon, the tissue of illusion. Nor could he expect to hear a murmur of sympathy when he next died of strangulation. He could only imagine the feelings of viewers hidden behind the camera's cold glass eye.

"Where in hell did you get that coat?" Max Arnow wanted to know.

After enduring several other sartorial insults from the casting director, Dutch was permitted to view his screen test. He had once horsed around in his swimsuit for somebody's home-movie camera, so he was not unprepared for what he saw. But to *hear* himself, too, to move into a close-up of his own features—so familiar yet so strange, the reverse of what he was used to in the mirror—was deeply depressing.

"Why did you hire me?" he asked.

"You'll be okay," Arnow said. "I hope."

There was enough menace in the qualification for Dutch to infer that if he wanted to succeed in this no-nonsense city, he must make as positive an impression as possible. That meant showing up daily—even though he was not yet on the Warners payroll—and moving to the Hollywood Plaza Hotel, so as to be instantly available if needed.

On May 25, Arnow rewarded him with a script to read.

Already he felt that he was moving and talking in a production "that might have been called *The Remaking of Dutch Reagan.*" He worked with a dialogue director to loosen his radio man's habit of talking chin up and stiff-necked. Scissors whacked expertly at his clothes and his hair, sculpting them to a sleeker look. *Ave atque vale,* Harold Teen! Cameramen complained that his neck was too short for his shoulders, so James Cagney's shirtmaker was called in to carve the deep V collar, more breastwork than fillet, that he would wear for the rest of his life. Finally, cosmeticians submitted him to a three-hundred-and-sixty-degree examination as scientific, in its way, as that of the Army doctors who had recently probed his every orifice.

The sensation of being appraised as an object rather than as a subject was not unpleasant to somebody basically shy. Dutch absorbed a variety of other scrutinies—directorial, commercial, and (in the case of Errol Flynn) warily competitive. A photographer from the public relations department followed him day and night, blazing away at every "opportunity" until he could not be sure whether he was posing, or being posed. He was introduced to so many stars—Ann Sheridan, Dick Powell, Anita Louise, Leslie Howard, Joan Blondell, Olivia de Havilland again—as to feel quasi-stellar himself. At the same time, these divinities *behaved* so ordinarily, as they speared their salads in the commissary or wandered half-dressed into the makeup salons (de Havilland slathered enchantingly with cold cream, unabashed by his bare chest), that his own ordinariness was comforted. She and he, he and they, were all of one flesh. And what flesh!

For some reason, the press office seemed keen to advertise his radio connections. Every Hawkeye on the lot was rounded up to be photographed with the former voice of WHO. The three singing Lane sisters allowed as how they had gotten their first break on his station. Arrangements were made for him to "date" Margaret Lindsay, Dubuque's favorite pin-up girl.

Dutch obligingly played the straight man in each two-shot. He rebelled only once, when Max Arnow and a group of publicists peered at him, trying to decide what his screen name should be. He could almost hear their unspoken question, "What name does he *look* like?" Four years before, another group of executives had debated what he *sounded* like. Nobody asked his opinion, so he ventured it.

"May I point out that I have a lot of name recognition in a large part of the country, particularly in the Middle West, where I've been broadcasting sports."

"Dutch Reagan?" somebody scoffed. "You can't put Dutch Reagan on a marquee."

Several ungraceful alternatives were proposed. Just in time, he remembered what was on his birth certificate. "How about Ronald? . . . Ronald Reagan?"

There was a cautious murmur of approval. "*Ronald* Reagan . . . Ronald *Reagan* . . ." Not only were the rhythmic syllables alliterative, they balanced out typographically at six letters to six—ideal for display purposes. "Hey, that's not bad," Arnow said.

Nevertheless, when he reported officially for work on Wednesday, June 2, everybody started calling him "Andy" or "Mr. McCaine." He was directed to KDTS, the city's broadcast station. So that was what the publicists meant when they said he would be "practically continuing his actual radio experience" here! Well, at least it was something to do.

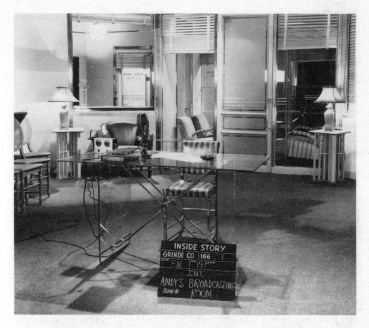

"KDTS was certainly a dazzling improvement on WHO."
Set for Inside Story *(release title:* Love Is on the Air*), 1937.*

Many young contract players sat around for months waiting to be cast in their first picture.

And KDTS, with its sleek cream-and-chrome reception room, was certainly a dazzling improvement on WHO. The adjoining studio was spacious and softly lit and featured an almost-invisible glass broadcasting table, on which microphone and time chimes seemed to float suspended. Down the corridor, a new office awaited him, with "Mr. McCaine" elegantly stenciled on its ground-glass door.

Stepping through a wall of light, he met the station chief, J. D. Harrington, and four or five staffers. He recognized one darkly pretty young woman from his last visit to Los Angeles: her father happened to be vice president of the Chicago White Sox, and he had tried in vain to get her to come and hear him narrate the Cubs-Sox Easter game. Although she was tactful enough not to mention this rejection, a gleam in her green eyes betokened future teasing.

He could have sworn her name was June, but here she answered to "Jo." She worked behind another ground-glass door ("Miss Hopkins") as producer of the KDTS children's program. Well, she was just a gal.

He was the station's top announcer, with a male assistant to help him round up city news!

☯

For all the state-of-the-art facilities at KDTS, there was something unsettling about the way its clocks and calendars moved backward as well as forward. Lit cigarettes stayed the same length. The blinds in Jo's office were drawn against the sun, while J. D.'s disclosed night vistas of the glittering city. News events were reported before they happened. And sackfuls of listener mail addressed to "Andy McCaine" awaited his attention, although he had yet to make his first broadcast.

Perhaps all this dream-like dislocation explained his constant, illogical notion *that he had worked here before:* that J. D. had once hired him, then fired him to placate some angry sponsor. It was his ancient humiliation at the hands of B. J. Palmer duplicated, right down to the detail of an employer who liked to hide behind a pair of initials. Had he come all the way from Iowa to find himself once again a toy of radio management?

Anger boiled in him as the wall of light (his own term for a downfalling radiance that periodically bathed his face and clothes, sealing off all outward consciousness) intensified. Station KDTS dissolved like Alice's looking-glass, and was replaced by the law office of Grant McKenzie, talent attorney. Three hundred and eighty-three leatherbound books frowned down, their spines fretted with shadow. There was a moment of dead silence. Then he lunged forward across the Persian carpet. He plucked his contract off McKenzie's desk and waved it at him.

"You mean I have to go back and work for that crummy outfit after they bounced me?"

The lawyer, smiling, said, "But you refused to bounce, and they notified me they wanted you back."

"Doing what? They've already turned my time over to Goulden."

Eddie Goulden was his rival in the KDTS newsroom.

"What do you care?" McKenzie taunted. "You collect maybe just for sweeping the dust out."

"I wouldn't go back for that dough," he shouted. "It's not enough to buy peanuts."

He paced the room, snorting, then grabbed McKenzie's telephone.

"Get me J. D. Harrington at KDTS . . . Hillcrest eight nine hundred."

"You better let me do the talking," McKenzie said, as he recradled it.

"You had your say—on paper." He resumed his pacing. "I'll handle this my way."

"Sure. But your salary's not peanuts, either."

The phone rang, and he jumped to answer. "All right, J. D., the lollipops are all yours. . . . I quit."

No response came from the receiver, so he blustered afresh. "I'm through! Any station in town will give Andy McCaine a job."

Again he heard nothing. He held the mouthpiece against his chest and gave McKenzie a nasty look. "How about it: you're the great legal mind. He says I can't work for anybody else."

"Sure. Not while you're under contract to him."

For a moment he was tempted to break the phone over McKenzie's head. Then he controlled himself and said resignedly into it, "Very well, Mr. Harrington. . . . I'll be in at noon tomorrow."

A warm glow swept over him, dispelling nervousness. By now he was completely surrounded by the wall of light. As from a far distance, he heard a man's voice call out. He saw no faces, and did not miss them. He liked the wall's feeling of privacy. It was soothing and secure, and he was sorry when it faded.

☯

At "noon" on Thursday—or nine, according to his inner clock—he was irradiated again and casually smoking one of the boss's cigarettes. His anger of the morning before had mellowed. He knew Harrington needed him, just as he knew that he would end up kissing that green-eyed girl down the corridor. So he merely shrugged when J. D. cautioned him against indulging his old habit of editorializing on the air.

By now he was recovering all sorts of memories: how Roy Copelin, a popular, reformist business leader, had vanished with $250,000 in cooperative creamery funds; how "Nicey" Ferguson, the city's chief racketeer, and E. E. Nichols, its biggest retail tycoon, had been suspiciously quick to call it a case of fugitive embezzlement; how he, Motormouth Andy McCaine, had publicly challenged this claim, and promised to broadcast the "inside story" of their role in the affair . . . no wonder Mr. Nichols had leaned on J. D. to get him fired!

Even now, the station owner made it clear that he was not going to be reinstated as a reporter. He was reassigned to—hot darn it—the daily *Kiddies' Hour*! While Jo Hopkins, she of the dangerous green eyes, had been *promoted over his head*!!

She teased him with open arms as "*Uncle Andy.*" Those arms, and the access they offered to small high breasts and pearl-like teeth, were hard to bypass, but he moved on with a dirty look and slammed the door behind him.

He lost his temper a lot in the days that followed, often shouting the same words over and over. Anyone could see he was under great strain. Things kept coming at him: leads indicating that Copelin might have been murdered; cruel orders to read commercials at 6 A.M.; his idle assistant's feet plunking down on his desk ("Put those webs back in the stream of consciousness," he snarled); Jo's constant put-downs; colleagues criticizing his "hokey, rapid-fire" microphone style; a sudden demand, from *very* far beyond the wall of light, for one day's service in naval uniform; six-day work weeks, nine or ten hours a day; it was a wonder he did not crack.

Other young people evidently did in this hard-driving city, judging from a headline in its principal newspaper:

JANE WYMAN HOSPITALIZED FOR NERVOUS BREAKDOWN

However, he not only endured but triumphed. He transformed his show into a junior news magazine, addressed pre-teens without condescension, and covered their bike races in the best sportscaster style. After a few weeks, the program had become so popular that E. E. Nichols moved adroitly to sponsor it. "He's bought himself a hit program," Harrington crowed. "At the same time he's insured himself against your meddling again in politics by tying you to the kids' hour."

Another explosion.

Past and present, fact and fantasy, night and day, love and enmity, good and evil—all the familiar antitheses he had known since childhood dissolved and resolved into just two states of being, "INT." and "EXT." The former was characterized by the brightness and sense of ensconcement that he had felt on his first day, punctured by disconcerting puffs of face powder. The other was more open and glaring, subject to wind and heat and always the same box lunch: half a chicken, a cream-cheese-and-jelly sandwich, a piece of fruit, cake, candy, and coffee.

"EXT." also tended to be crowded with children. One street-smart urchin, named Mouse, hinted that if he visited a certain tenement building, he might learn something to his advantage. In the shabby lobby he saw scribbled above the pay phone: "530 Lakehurst." The address electrified him: Mrs. Copelin had jotted it down when her husband called to report a "business engagement" just prior to disappearing.

Mouse said that the pay-phone scribble had been made by his brother Danny—something to do with "a little see-ment job" at Nicey Ferguson's country house. Danny had vanished too.

A radio man's natural instinct was to jump into a Buick and head straight for Lakehurst Road. But irresistibly, at this moment, Jo Hopkins asked if he would take her to dinner. At the swankiest joint in town, no less: Nicey Ferguson's 7-11 Club!

Here, to the beat of a six-piece combo (gold leaves above the white piano, shimmering at every cymbal stroke), Jo surprised him by sliding into his arms and burying her face in the hollow of his shoulder. *He loved it.* But before he could kiss her, the little tease collapsed in detumescent giggles. Foiled again!

Suddenly she was gone.

The clock twirled, and he sat down in a different suit. An ashtray before him filled with butts. He worried that if Jo came back, she might expose herself to danger. For tonight was the night that the city's long-smoldering crime war was gonna break out. If not right now, then later at 530 Lakehurst. How could he be so sure about *that*? Because in either dream or foresight he felt he knew the place already. He had seen the FOR SALE sign outside, admired its white portico and tall columns, toured its twenty rooms. And its garage, too, with that coffin-sized patch of new cement. . . .

Band still playing. Open mike. Broadcast live on KDTS. To h--l with slow foxtrots, he had news! Xylophone chime. Thanks, pal! Here's that inside story, folks. Roy Copelin murdered by the mob. Was about to blow the whistle on this burg's political ring. Those "embezzled" funds a camouflage. Suspiciously similar disappearance of Danny Malone, laborer. Danny's kid brother has squealed—

Caramba! Here's Jo coming upstairs with Mouse! If Nicey Ferguson lays eyes on that brat . . . Hustle 'em both back into the street. Pitch-dark outside: eighteen thousand square yards of heavy black canvas, stretched from roof to roof. Give her car keys. "Pile into my heap, and step on it!"

There go Nicey and a bunch of mobsters. Two long black sedans accelerating out of town. To 530 Lakehurst, where else? Call KDTS. Pick me up pronto in bulletproof truck! Tell cops! Where's that shortwave portable I asked Jo to hide? In this black doorway, maybe—

"Looking for someone?"

Like some fragrant night violet, she appeared *ex tenebris.* All my life, baby, but is the kid safe? Here comes my truck. Busted his heart to drive away. Pretend not to see her jumping up behind, snuggling between sacks of his fan mail. Best bulletproofing in the world!

Ventura Boulevard. Make that "Lakehurst." White mansion through the trees. Sedans parked outside. Cop cars concealed. Hope this transmitter works good. Wait for total darkness.

Quiet now. Sounds of digging inside the garage. Body-shaped bundle loaded into the first sedan, along with blocks of cement. Alarm in the house as cops storm the sedan. Air full of lead. Thank H----n for these mail sacks. Hey, what's this soft shape touching me?

As the fusillade crackled overhead, he pushed Jo gently down and sensed that she did not mind being pushed. A phrase he had read somewhere described the look in those green eyes: "mocking sweetness." But no time to kiss her. A police whistle shrilled from the ambushed sedan, where cops had unwrapped the bundle. "That means it's Copelin. We start broadcasting!"

He lay with her beside him, talking rapidly into the portable. He heard the police chief bemoan the lack of a loud-hailer, and shouted sarcastically, "You got five. How many more do you want?" Bewildered stares. "In your cars . . . the radios."

O, airhog ecstasy! All the cop drivers spun their dash dials to KDTS, maxed the volume, blasted his baritone out into the night air. Over bullets and trees, rattling the windows of the great white house (incandescent now, as headlights and floodlights focused on it) and reverberating through every speaker in the distant city, floated the aural apotheosis of Andy McCaine: "*RIGHT NOW I CAN HEAR MY OWN VOICE COMING BACK TO ME FROM THE POLICE-CAR RADIOS WHICH CAPTAIN LANG HAS CONVERTED INTO A PUBLIC-ADDRESS SYSTEM.*"

He yielded the mike to Lang, who issued a two-minute ultimatum. Nicey Ferguson & Co. desperately tried to escape. Tommy guns tore the air, and the battle culminated in a Wagnerian pyrocone as Andy set fire to his own fan mail and tossed it into the yard. "They won't shoot *this* light out!" Bedazzled, the crooks surrendered.

"And the hero of this story," Jo announced, seizing the mike herself, "is your radio commentator, Andy McCaine, who proved he can think as fast as he can talk."

Driving back to Burbank at 5 A.M., Dutch watched the sun rise over the orange groves, in exact reverse of the image that had greeted him four weeks before. Now, as then, he was bleary with tiredness. Except for a steak break, he had just worked sixteen and a half straight hours. But whereas that first sun had set, so to speak, on his midwestern past, this orb was crescent with Californian promise.

"Boy, when it comes up over the rim of mountains that hedge in Hollywood on the east, with the misty clouds radiating all the colors of the rainbow, it's something to write home about."

10

Love Is
on the Air

I spent most of the spring and summer of 1937 cruising the buggy backroads of Illinois in a battered Willys Overland. This was something of a comedown for the former Barnouw hedgehopper, but I did not much care if I never saw another row of beacons, and besides, flattered myself that I was on the verge of literary fame as an employee of the Federal Writers Project—about which more later.

Like any young Chicagoan away from home, I listened to Cubs and White Sox games on whatever signal my car antenna picked up. Only slowly did I realize that Dutch had left WHO Des Moines. His move to California may have made headlines across the Mississippi, but I was unaware of it until Paul Rae (now working as a roving sketcher for the *Greenwich Villager*) sent me a wire copy of an AP dispatch, dated August 19, 1937:

DUTCH IS HIT IN FIRST FILM

Critics Agree That He's "New Find"

Hollywood, Cal.—Ronald Reagan has made a hit in his first motion picture, previewed at Warner Bros. Beverly Hills theater.

Critics united in hailing him as a "new find" and predicted a bright future in pictures for the young man who but recently was a radio sports news commentator in Des Moines.

"Best" Performance

In reviewing LOVE IS ON THE AIR, the *Hollywood Reporter,* leading trade paper in the industry, said:

"It presents a new leading man, Ronald Reagan, who is a natural, giving one of the best picture performances Hollywood has offered in many a day."

"Completely at Home."

"Reagan was completely at home in the role of Andy, a radio news broadcaster, but demonstrated an ability which will not confine him to radio-announcer roles."

Reagan is at present on vacation, but is slated for another film assignment soon.

Across the bottom of this carbon, Paul wrote in ink still blue: *Send to Ripley's "Believe It or Not"!!!!*

☯

My youthful interest in Dutch had waned, but his emergence as a "leading man" was news indeed. While awaiting the release of *Love Is on the Air,* I began to clip and save reports of his burgeoning career. Two more B pictures, *Sergeant Murphy* and *Accidents Will Happen,* were already in the can; he had also played small parts in an A picture, *Submarine D-1,* and a musical, *Hollywood Hotel.* There was a photograph of him escorting Joy Hodges to a preview of Busby Berkeley's *Varsity Show,* which he had "emceed" for radio listeners in his mellifluous, microgenic voice. "What price Dutch's broomstick now?" I wrote Paul, sending the cutting on.

Another article reported that Reagan, confident of having his contract validated, had persuaded his parents to come out and live near him in Los Angeles. There were some hokey paragraphs about Jack and Nelle seeing *Love* en route, which I now find quite touching:

A little lady sat in a theater in Des Moines on Thursday and with lace-trimmed handkerchief poked at tears that coursed down her lined cheeks.

"That's my boy," she whispered. "That's my Dutch."

At her side a gentleman with iron gray hair sat bolt upright in his chair, folded his hands under his chin, and blinked his eyes very fast.

" 'That's just the way he is at home.' "
Nelle and Jack Reagan with their screen-actor son, 1937.

"He doesn't change. He'll always be the same," he said gruffly. It was the first time Mr. and Mrs. John Reagan, of Dixon, Ill., had seen their son Ronald (Dutch) Reagan, former Des Moines radio announcer, on the screen. . . .

"That's just the way he is at home," said Mrs. Reagan as Dutch flashed a quick smile. "He's no Robert Taylor, he's just himself."

After the show was over they walked out arm in arm.

For some reason, *Love Is on the Air* never came to Chicago, although it did reach New York. Paul went to see it and sent a dry postcard: "They shoulda called it *Love Is on the Cutting Room Floor.* All Dutch does is make whoopee with a microphone. He finally gets to kiss June Travis, but you never saw such a fast fadeout!! Maybe she bribed the cameraman."

As things turned out, I did not see *Love* for another fifty years. By then Andy McCaine was President of the United States. I found a pristine print in the Library of Congress and ran it through a Moviola.

[*Screening Notes, October 13, 1987*]

Out of a dark sky, Warner Bros. logo looms, then presents "RONALD REAGAN." Top billing in his first flick: not bad.

Am surprised by my emotions when Dutch appears on-screen: young, muscular, perfectly spruced in dark pin-striped double-breaster, chasing down his "inside story." Poignant to see this reverse child of himself, so young, so tightly tense.

Cut to studio scene of RR waiting, smoking. Gazes at announcer with the same grave trust I have seen so often in White House. Blows last puff over shoulder, stubs out cigarette, leans forward full of youth & eagerness. Focuses, frowns, hitches himself to mike. Wears his watch on inside wrist: old script reader's habit. Out comes the voice. Rapid, more tenor than baritone, full of air, lacking its later peach-fuzz husk.

Noticeable throughout is the extreme, almost convulsive, mobility of Dutch's mouth. He must have worked at controlling it in later movies. Desperate to project every syllable, lest any word of dialogue (sample: "Put those webs back into the stream of consciousness") be lost. I switch to manual control & swing the reels back & forth, watching his lips undulate like willow leaves afloat on ripples. Will these, ultimately, I wonder, be all we remember of him?

Signing on with the Federal Writers Project had been easy, given the Chicago office's self-image as a relief agency for intellectuals. All that one needed to do was confirm that one had tried and failed to sell manuscripts to commercial publishers, and I certainly had proof of that. The salary—ninety-six dollars a month—was less than half of what my flying job paid. But the work was delightful. Along with about fifty other hacks, I had to write a thousand words a week for what eventually became *Illinois: A Descriptive and Historical Guide* (Chicago, 1939). This quota, batted out on coarse canary-yellow paper, was attainable in two days, or at most three. No questions were asked as to what we were working on the rest of the time, it being tacitly understood that everybody had a separate muse.

As one of the few staffers with a car, I took every opportunity to head out of town on "field trips." Although I missed the suspended solitude of flight, I found the flat country agreeable, and enjoyed the intermittent delusion that I was stationary, rotating the whole world under my wheels. Travel copy came easily, at least the noun-rich stuff my supervisor liked. I would pull the Willys over and scribble, *Gravel dumps, fruit stands, market gardens, switch tracks, smokestacks, barbecue huts, and patches of farmland flank the highway.* There was plenty of time, over supper in jerkwater hotels, to scribble short stories and poetry.

With the completion of the Illinois Guide in June 1938, my pleasure in being a federal writer diminished. Saturation with the landscape and lore of the corn country had purged me of the last of Grant Wood's Regionalism. Wood himself was already being purged by eastern academe. Not only did he find Nature beautiful—clear proof of his sentimentality—he also depicted loneliness and isolation, and must therefore be an enemy of the people. Any art that did not express social outrage, worker solidarity, class struggle, equalization of wealth, and other Marxian clichés was dismissed as reactionary. "I have to draw people as cubes nowadays," Paul Rae wrote, only half jokingly. "Builder blocks of the welfare state."

The Spanish Civil War, that ideological earthquake, cracked open a fundamental fault in the American political landscape. On the one side were those of us who, averting our eyes from what was going on in the Deep South, believed the United States to be democracy perfected—a polity so pure that it should not be corrupted by foreign squabbles. Across the fault stood the internationalists, including (to my subsequent astonishment) Ronald Reagan. These ardent souls believed that fascism anywhere posed a threat to free people everywhere.

I sided, in a vague way, with the America-Firsters. Somebody angrily remarked that too many hours airborne had made me a political lightweight. This was very likely true. I could not distinguish any moral difference between communism and fascism; both looked to me like enslavement of the soul. And since communism was the nearer threat—as close, in fact, as the desks of my immediate neighbors at the Illinois Project—I did not see why American boys had to go to Spain to fight for freedom. There were plenty of would-be totalitarians back home.

I wrote an impassioned poem on the subject, and submitted it to *American Stuff,* an anthology of creative writings by FWP members. The Communist-controlled editorial board rejected it for rightism.

Either that, or because it was written as a fugue, in quadruple lines intended to be read simultaneously.

My discovery of musical form in August 1938 was not unrelated to my discovery of Sydney Ann Brown, first violist of the Los Angeles Philharmonic. She came to play the Hindemith Concerto at the Ravinia Festival, and was wished upon Bess (as visiting soloists often were) as a house guest. I had the honor of escorting her around town that weekend and driving her to the arena on Sunday night.

From a front-row seat, I watched Miss Brown make her entrance, tall, languid, auburn-haired, loose-limbed in her white dress. There was something sensuous about the way she held her big fiddle at the neck, as lightly as if it were a violin. When she raised it to her chin after the initial *tutti* and filled the air with a plangent alto sonority, I became as physically aware of her as if she were in my arms. She played as if drunk, while the white dress flowed around her legs with the grace of a négligée.

It was one of those moments when the ground shifts beneath one's shoes. Afterward, I asked her to marry me.

She considered the question gravely. "I'm not going to quit the Philharmonic."

"Of course not."

"So what will *you* do?"

"Transfer to the California Writers Project, I guess."

I didn't, though. The news of Dutch's incredible good fortune had filled me with a wild desire to turn *Ailerons* into a script I could sell to one of the Hollywood studios. I was twenty-six years old and in love. With Bess talking of retiring to Santa Barbara, Paul Rae settled in Manhattan, and the midwestern literary scene moribund, there was little to keep me in Chicago. I left it on September 23, 1938, and stayed away until Dutch himself brought me back, forty-eight years later, on Air Force One.

11

On the Beach with Ronnie and Jane

*T*hrough salt-bleared eyes, I see them stroll across the sand. It is my first glimpse of him in the flesh in more than eight years. This mature Dutch—"Ronnie," she calls him—is tall and sparely straight, constructed in flats, a mobile Mondrian. Wide shoulders jut perpendicular to the columnar neck, long swimmer's arms hang at right angles to the sea, long legs rise and fall like slow pistons. Even his pectorals are flat and square: he has no bulges in him, of brawn or brain. He looks hard and clean—yesterday's lifeguard mutated into today's expert body-surfer. His thick, fine hair, slicked with something expensive, flashes blue as Clark Kent's. Except this guy would never change clothes in a phone booth; he is much too cautious, too conscious of his dignity.

Hence the graceful extension of his slim tanned fingers as he touches Jane's elbow without holding it, proclaiming rather than possessing. She, too, is slender, but her body is all curves to his corners. How Grant Wood would revel in her roundness! Huge eyes, with irises like half-sucked, dark-chocolate pralines; forehead and cheekbones making a perfect oval, intersecting with the sideways arch of her eyebrow and the spiral of blond, pinned hair around the whorl of her ear. The head be-

"An ingenue . . . seasoned in her sexuality."
Jane Wyman around the time she first met Ronald Reagan.

*neath these contours, gleaming with oil and sweat, is an almost regular
sphere; it centers on a child's snub nose. Her pouting lips are shaped for
kissing. The lower one invites a gentle bite, like a grape at the point of
bursting. She is taller than I would have guessed from* Brother Rat—
*about five foot five, with lean calves and a lovely line from thigh to ass.
But her hands are large and cruel.*

*Smiling their Pepsodent smiles, they tread the beach carefully, leav-
ing behind the prints of their beautiful . . .*

The manuscript, on MGM stationery, ends like that. I was scribbling so much, those first joyful weeks in Santa Monica, that few things got finished. Sydney Ann seemed reluctant to grant me her hand, but she granted enough else to make me appreciate why Mozart coveted the viola above all instruments. And, incredibly, I already had a screenplay assignment. A friend of hers who worked in the music department at Metro had shown *Ailerons* to Sam Marx, the legendary story editor turned producer, and he was impressed enough to option it. ("Although you're gonna have to do something about that wing-walk sequence— biplanes are as dead as dodos.")

So on October 15, 1938, I got my first freelance writing fee: a check for one thousand dollars, bearing the imprint of Louis B. Mayer.

e

It was inevitable that I should see Dutch and his cutie down by the pier sooner or later. Lifeguards like to strut their stuff, and Jack Warner, a swimsuit man himself (his squat Polish peasant body solid enough to shrug off a beach buggy), saw to it that the shapeliest of his young talent exposed themselves regularly to seaside photographers. "Aren't they beautiful?" he would leer. "No wonder they screw each other."

Dutch was not yet a one-girl guy. He was seen squiring dishy Lana Turner around town, and joked that he "wasn't acting" in her company. He also dated Margaret Lindsay, Mary Jane Crane, and the exquisite Anita Louise. How much sex he was getting was a matter of speculation. Sydney Ann was friendly with a starlet named Lucile Fairbanks and we heard from her and her boyfriend Owen Crump, a writer at Warners, that Dutch was regarded as the studio's porch warmer, more gab than grab, and no threat to any virgin.

Yet his local cavalry commanding officer asserted that Lieutenant Reagan was a "greater 'swordsman' " than Errol Flynn—a remark I gathered was meant metaphorically. If so, Dutch was shy about communicating it. We guffawed over a magazine spread of suggestive "swimming lesson" cheesecakes that showed him intertwining limbs with a buxom starlet (RONALD REAGAN SHOWS SUSAN HAYWARD THE PROPER POSITION). Their couplings reminded me of nothing so much as Greek sculpture: a cold choreography of elbows, knees, and clenched buttocks. Dutch exuded no hint of musk. His skin shone with clean health, his eyes with clean thoughts.

Warners publicists sought to pair him off with somebody more midwestern than Miss Hayward, an ingenue equally curvy yet tougher, more seasoned in her sexuality. Twenty-one-year-old Jane Wyman not only looked the part (that button nose was definitely trans-Mississippi), she was eager to play it. In *her* case, however, a considerable degree of "acting" was necessary.

Not that she didn't find Reagan attractive: she had been unable to repress a squeal of delight when she first saw him. Her challenge was to hide the fact that although she was six years his junior, she was far ahead of him in adult experience, both professional and emotional. She had come to Hollywood when he was still in high school. His idea of trauma was being benched by Coach McKinzie; Jane had a couple of previous husbands to keep quiet about, and dark memories of being given away in childhood.

She had been born Sarah Jane Mayfield in Saint Joseph, Missouri, on January 5, 1917. Her father had decamped for San Francisco when she was five years old, and her mother, desperate for money, made what seems to have been an unofficial "adoption" deal with some middle-aged neighbors. So little Miss Mayfield became "Jane Fulks," and, after Mrs. Fulks was widowed in 1928, moved with her to Southern California. She attended Los Angeles High School under that name, and, when barely sixteen, married a young salesman named Ernest Wyman. The marriage did not last more than a year or two. Meanwhile, Jane sang and hoofed her way onto the sets of various Fox and Paramount musicals, winning a Warner Bros. contract on May 6, 1936.

Her nervous breakdown around the time she first laid eyes on Ronald Reagan might have had something to do with the fact that she was about to become Mrs. Myron T. Futterman. But Jane was not the type to let another marriage get in her way. Within three months, the wealthy Mr. Futterman (who had something to do with the rag trade) was history. When I first saw Jane on the sand with Dutch, she was suing for divorce.

I gathered that their affair was older than Warners would allow—officially, they were supposed to have met on the set of *Brother Rat* in July 1938. Whatever the case, there was no question about their mutual attraction. He saw the small, fine bones, the easy smile, and wide-eyed brown gaze that had always been his ideal of female beauty. And Jane?

An undated interview clip preserved in the State Historical Society of Wisconsin gives a hint of what, besides simple desire, drew her to Ronald Reagan in 1938, and transformed her. She admitted to being unable to "trust or confide" in anyone until she met him:

Marrying Ronnie worked a miracle for me. It changed a dull, suspicious, anxious woman [into] someone at ease. . . . I was drawn to
him at once. . . . He was such a sunny person . . . genuinely and
spontaneously *nice.*

℮

So far this chapter has been largely about sex. How could it not be? We
were all of us, actors and writers and musicians and dancers, so young,
healthy, and hedonistic in one of the most sensual cities since Sodom. I
do not mean that we banged away with anything like the public gross-
ness now considered the norm in, say, Bismarck, N.D. Ours was a generation that believed in closed bedroom doors and discreet allusions. In
any case, our sensuality went beyond sex into a general celebration of
the life physical. We exercised hard (in the surf, I was as lithe as the next
man) and later, driving off to cocktails somewhere in loose pale clothes,
we felt proud of our lean, tanned bodies.

Eros, to us, was a pantheistic god, indistinguishable from Narcissus.
Los Angeles's Hellenic light and white houses, its mild air and ozone,
its perpetual efflorescence and cooing of doves, its pristine pools, the
sweetness of its fruits and flowers, its ocean—half a world of water—
washing the air with morning mist and daily pounding the beaches
cleaner and finer. God, how good we felt there!

"Make that good-*looking,*" one of my friends from that time
amends, with a sad jangle of oversized earrings. (To me, she will always
be a sleek teenage half-Turk, "Bubbles" Schinasi, but she answers now
to Mrs. Arthur Hornblow, Jr.) "And *predatory.* When Clark Gable or
Errol or Ty Power came into the room, you could just feel the heat
waves shimmering."

"What about Reagan?"

"Oh no, *never* Ronnie."

"Why? He was as attractive as any of those guys."

"Yes, but female desire is attuned to male desire. Clark, Errol, obviously were crazy about women. Ronnie just—wasn't. I don't think he
ever looked at Ann Sheridan, and she was *luscious.*"

Perhaps not. He certainly admired a lot of other girls, though, and
was admired right back. I remember a class of Los Angeles art students
voting his "the most nearly perfect male body" in Hollywood, and at
least two women told me that his voice was irresistible, particularly the
way he had of "breathing around words." I also recall him sitting on
the sand with a bunch of guys ogling some pouter pigeon—it may have

"So young, so healthy, so hedonistic."
Jane Wyman and Ronald Reagan, ca. 1938.

been Jane—as she breasted her way into the sea. He must have been under orders not to wear spectacles in public, because he peered painfully at the retreating figure. Then he jabbed at the sides of his eyes, pulling the flesh tight, and stared long and hard through sloed slits. The effect was of almost oriental lechery.

☯

Brother Rat was a "cadet pic" set in the Virginia Military Institute. It starred Wayne Morris, Priscilla Lane, and a cocky newcomer from New York named Eddie Albert. (Wayne was another of the heat-seeking sexual predators Bubbles might have mentioned: she ended up marrying him.) Dutch and Jane got lower billing, but the plot was so well integrated that they played to co-equal effect, and enjoyed the first real hit of their careers. It was his tenth picture in just over a year, her twenty-fifth in two.

Watching *Brother Rat*, I could see that hard work agreed with Dutch. He looked virile and handsome in his dress whites, towering over Eddie, and might have loomed as the romantic lead, had Wayne not been even bigger and handsomer. But in the movie as in real life, Jane had eyes only for "Ronnie."

Discreetly, he downplayed his own regard for her. Jane was still, in his view, a married woman, and until she was actually divorced from Mr. Futterman, he thought it best to act cool.

So the heat waves shimmered in one direction only. Jane was so gorgeous in what was supposed to be a plain-girl-in-glasses role that no frumpery of clothes or hairstyle could justify her on-screen neglect. Dutch was dull in contrast, I thought—humorless, overly forceful, irritable behind his simulated high spirits. That infallible sign of a bad actor, the inability to listen, was apparent in the on-again, off-again animation of his dialogues. Even when Jane was flirting with him, you could sense his impatience as he waited with his next line.

Yet there was one moment when his hands and eyes betrayed a proprietary interest. "Does this happen all the time when a girl doesn't wear glasses?" she asked after their first kiss in the boys' dormitory. She had taken off her horn-rims and had that vulnerable look. Dutch gazed at her with sudden tenderness, holding the hand that held the spectacles. "Practically all the time," he breathed.

Jane's hand dropped slowly (the camera tracking it) and tossed the spectacles onto a bed before rising again to embrace him. For those few seconds, the screen pulsated with—well, heat waves.

Bubbles now says that Dutch was "crazy" about Jane Wyman from the start, but I think she's thinking of the year they got married. Others remember Jane as "the aggressor, the intent pursuer" in 1938. The eroticism of that dorm-room scene derived from the avid way she gave herself to him. Whatever he gave back did not satisfy her. I heard that on the set of *Brother Rat,* she indulged a macabre hobby of modeling her fellow actors in clay, then sticking pins into their eyes or disfiguring them with melanomic lumps.

☯

Dutch, meanwhile, passed the time in his favorite fashion: talking. Hitherto the Reagan *spiel* had been sports; now, with a minimum wage established and Munich looming, it was economics and world politics. His hortatory manner, as if he alone knew who Jan Masaryk was, caused Wayne Morris to nickname him "teacher." Impervious to sarcasm, Dutch lectured on:

He found a ready listener in Eddie Albert. The young actor had a serious interest in politics, and like Dutch, tended toward the far left of New Deal theory. His Mexican wife, Margo, went them both one better, acting as Hollywood agent of La Rasa Party while pursuing an independent, activist, political agenda. Eddie today is evasive about just how far left she traveled, but if Margo was not a Communist in 1938, neither was La Pasionara. Thereby hangs a tale, confided to me fifty-two years later:

ASTOR HALL, NEW YORK PUBLIC LIBRARY.

Black-tie reception honoring 200 "Literary Lions." SFX: buzz of billionaires; a distant, ineffectual fanfare of trumpets. Camera follows as Author, bemedaled, searches for his seat in lineup of honorees.

EM   (*to lone Lion, already couchant in the F–J section*) Wrong part of the alphabet, but do you mind if I join you for a while? There's not a living soul in K–O.

LION   Be my guest. (*Inspects Author's name tag*) Are you the guy that wrote that Teddy Roosevelt bio?

EM   Yes.

LION   I'm Howard Fast. (*They shake hands*) What are you working on now?

EM   An authorized biography of Ronald Reagan.

FAST   You know about him trying to become a Communist, of course.

EM   I beg your pardon?

FAST   Happened after he got to Hollywood. Reagan got carried away by stories of the Communist Party helping the dispossessed, the unemployed, and the homeless. Some of his friends, people he respected, were Party members. So he turned to them. Said he wanted to become a Communist.

EM   (*guffawing*) Ronald Reagan? Oh, please. That can't possibly be true.

FAST   Ask anyone in the Party—it's common knowledge. I was a member myself, you know, for fifteen years. Got a memoir coming out soon, called *Being Red.*

EM   (*incredulous*) Reagan asked some Communist friends—

FAST   Not asked, told 'em. Said he was determined to join. They discussed it with the local Party leader, who asked around, and word came back that Reagan was a flake.

EM   Who was this leader?

FAST   (*hesitating*) Well, I don't know if I should say. He's dead now. A well-known screenwriter, a playwright, a historian. . . . Anyway, they said that Reagan couldn't be trusted with any political opinion for more than twenty minutes. So the decision was taken to prevent him joining, but to use him as a friend of the Party.

EM   Reagan a fellow traveler! I just don't—

FAST   The task of talking him out of it was given to Eddie Albert. They were buddies, you know. Eddie sat up all night persuading Reagan he'd be of more use to the Party outside than inside. Don't believe me, huh?

EM   (*floundering*) It just doesn't seem—

FAST   Like it or not, Reagan wanted to join. Ask Eddie. Or Margo. No, not Margo—she died too, I think.

EM   I will, but Eddie's cagey.

FAST   Better still, talk to Cy Gomberg. Do you know him?

EM   No.

FAST   One of the best memories in the industry. Ask Cy. He'll tell you all about it. (*Another fanfare*)

EM   Guess I better take my seat.

Camera holds without following as he walks down the row of chairs. Amid the general crowd noise, we hear him musing in voice-over.

EM   Dutch a Red—God, could it be true?

FADE

Cy Gomberg turned out to have one of the worst memories in the industry as far as this particular subject was concerned. And Eddie Albert caged up as expected, although he did reluctantly concede that "there were conversations of the kind you mention." Barbara Poe Levee, a close friend of the Albert family, said that Fast's story was quite true. Only it was Margo, not Eddie, who talked Dutch out of joining, thus saving his future presidential career. When I pressed her as to what authority Margo had to speak on behalf of the CPUSA, Mrs. Levee succumbed, like Cy, to a violent attack of amnesia.

The Red Question is still the sorest subject in Hollywood discourse, at least among those of us whose memories extend back beyond the Committee. Rage, regrets, guilt, disillusionment, terror, contempt: all the negative emotions rush to reflex the moment one asks, *Were you? Did she? Was he? When? Who?* Dutch's own protective reflexes, always abnormally fast, operated so swiftly when I asked him the Question point-blank one day that the pupils of his eyes (I fixed on them) did not contract. His face remained smooth and his expression was one of polite puzzlement. "Why, no. Good Lord, no."

As I write these words today, Lenin's *Sotsialisticheskie Revolutzie* is (as Ronald Reagan would say) on the ash heap of history. From some distant corner of consciousness comes the echo of a voice—Buddy Holly's?—singing, *It just doesn't matter any more.* So what if Dutch, young and ardent in 1938, thrilled to the message of Marx for a few experimental months? Minds colder and clearer than his fortunately saw that he was not socialist material. With Jane's encouragement, he entered a political arena that suited him better: the Screen Actors Guild.

He was not an aggressive unionist. His own studio struck him as a strict but fair employer, renewing his contract annually without question and generously hiring his father to handle his fan mail. Just as Jack Reagan rejoiced in the continuing paternalism of the New Deal, Ronald Reagan was sure that Warner Bros. had his best interests at heart. He never complained about the parts he was handed, even ones so patently unsuitable as that of a boozy dilettante in *Dark Victory.* Had it not given him the privilege of playing against Bette Davis?

Moreover, SAG (as the guild was always called) did not encourage young firebrand recruits. Unlike the Writers Guild, it was a conservative union with many millionaire members. Its starry board was dominated by the likes of George Montgomery, James Cagney, Joan Crawford, and Boris Karloff. They tilted instinctively away from confrontation and toward a negotiatory partnership with Hollywood's powerful crafts union, the IA (International Alliance of Theatrical Stage Employees). That partnership was somewhat strained in the winter of 1938–1939, for the IA was mob-dominated and attempting to poach SAG's poorer members, the extras. But until some purer alliance arose to represent Hollywood's blue-collar community, screen actors had little choice but to live with the *status quo*.

e

In the spring of 1939 I got two jobs, which I hoped would impress Sydney Ann's father enough to allow us to get married. Sam Marx hired me as a reader at MGM (sixteen dollars a day plus office and typewriter), on the tacit understanding that I could use the facilities, after hours, to complete my adaptation of *Ailerons*. I also became a weekend instructor at Mines Field, under the government's Civilian Pilots Training Scheme. The deteriorating situation in Europe had caused a surge in license applications. It was good to fly again, and hone my stick skills in Southern California's thermal-prone skies.

One of my first students was Philip Dunne. I had heard about him around the lot at MGM, where he had earned a reputation as a screenwriter's screenwriter. Just married to the exquisite ingenue Amanda Duff, he was now senior scribe at Twentieth Century–Fox. Unbeknown to me, I had his former office. I was working there one wet morning when a tall, beaming, sandy-haired man looked in the door. "Hullo. Philip Dunne. Just visiting my old lair. Did they ever fix the fan?"

He was four years my senior, with a faint Harvard drawl. I asked if he was related to the great satirist Finley Peter Dunne, whose *Mr. Dooley* books I had collected in Chicago.

"He was my father. Nobody seems to understand dialect humor these days, alas. So you're from 'Mr. Dooley's' hometown?"

Thus began a lifelong friendship, based as much on mutual need as on opposition of character. I taught Phil to fly; he taught me to body-surf. And over the years, as Ronald Reagan became more and more an object of wonder in Hollywood, we joined in laughing at the dreadful movies, and debating the political implications.

e

Sydney Ann and I were married on August 26, 1939. Britain's declaration of war with Germany eight days later cast an instant pall over our honeymoon. *Ailerons*—that paean to barnstorming days—now had about as much chance of making it to the screen as *Mein Kampf.* We came back from Yosemite, settled into Jeb Brown's *pied-à-terre* in Santa Monica (he was a wealthy citrus rancher in Bernardino County), and I tried to sell MGM a script about the Spanish Civil War. But the studio was more interested in readying *Gone With the Wind* for release. Meanwhile, Ronald Reagan began to shoot a new, cautionary spy thriller, *The Enemy Within.*

Crossing the ramp at Mines Field with Philip Dunne one chilly November evening, I was transfixed by the extraordinary sight of Dutch, pink with embarrassment, being serenaded by a trio of rubes. He was escorting Jane (dark-haired now) toward a chartered TWA DC-2, and press cameras were flashing.

"Isn't that Ronnie Reagan?" Phil asked. "Don't tell me she's made an honest man of him."

"Not officially," I said. "They just got engaged."

"Louella Parsons is taking them on her cross-country tour," an eavesdropping reporter advised. "Stars of tomorrow. What was that about 'not officially'?"

Phil grabbed my arm and pulled me away. "Watch your mouth in this town."

"Well, he's moved to the same address and as a divorcée Jane's hardly *virgo intacta.*"

"Ronnie may be, though," said Dunne. "My friends at SAG say he's a bit of a Boy Scout. But maturing fast. Comes to all the meetings."

Phil approved of that sort of thing. He was an active member of the Writers Guild, and had just founded the Motion Picture Democratic Committee.

A few days later, my mother wrote from Santa Barbara, where the Parsons Show (actually a publicity junket for Louella herself) had tried out en route to San Francisco, "Saw your old friend Dutch Reagan with Luella [*sic*] and his not-so-plain Jane. He's a bit too oilyslick for my taste—she looks hard. Pretty though."

It took half a century, but I was eventually told how Jane made an honest man out of Dutch. My informant was her successor:

PATIO RESTAURANT OF BEL-AIR HOTEL, LOS ANGELES—DAY.

SFX: a quiet splash of fountains, a murmuration of dowagers, clinking of heavy silver on Villeroy & Boch plates. Down by the pond, below the little cupola where Patti Davis got married, a swan stretches his wings and gapes, silently roaring. Author is buying lunch—if Bibb lettuce and Pellegrino water counts as such—for a Former First Lady.

EM   (*recounting biographical gossip*) . . . so when Clare found out about Harry and Jeanne, she threatened suicide and—

FFL   (*interrupting, her eyes hard as the V&B*) That's just what Jane did to Ronnie.

EM   Excuse me?

FFL   Said she would kill herself if he didn't marry her.

EM   (*reaching furtively for his notebook*) You've got to be kidding. (*She stares at him*) No, you're not.

FFL   Ronnie, of course, didn't . . . uh . . . want to marry, he was too . . . much too young, he was, uh, just playing around. So she sent him a suicide note and swallowed a whole, uh, lot of pills, and got herself taken to the hospital.

EM   Good God.

FFL   As soon as he got the note, he rushed . . . rushed down there, while they were, uh, pumping her out, and said, "Of course I'll marry you!" You know how soft . . . softhearted he is.

EM   Good God.

FFL   (*bitterly*) She knew which of his buttons to press.

Second wives are, of course, notorious prosecution witnesses. When I told Mrs. Reagan's story to Joy Hodges, she refused to believe it. "Dutch was so *crazy* about her, and Janey about him." But I thought of the "nervous breakdown" story in *Variety,* after Dutch's arrival at Warner Bros., and the abrupt split with Mr. Futterman, and the large cruel hands, and investigated Jane's studio work records. Sure enough, a memo dated October 4, 1939, had Wyman hospitalized with a sudden "stomach disorder." I spoke to some more people. The Hollywood oral historian Douglas Bell said he had heard Jane tried to kill herself over Reagan, but knew no details; Owen Crump was evasive; and Eddie Albert growled, "I think I'd better not get into that." Finally, I turned to Sam Marx, the ultimate authority on pre-war Hollywood.

At eighty-four, my old mentor was at work on a book about the Paul Bern murder case, and had useful contacts in the Los Angeles Police Department. He made a few calls on my behalf, without result.

"There are no records of a medical emergency involving Jane Wyman at the time you say. I'd be surprised if there were."

"Well, she *was* taken violently ill just as she and Ronnie began to shoot *Brother Rat and a Baby*. And they did get engaged in the hospital."

"Hollywood Receiving Hospital?"

"The file doesn't say. Why?"

"There was a young doctor there, known as 'stomach pumper to the stars.' "

"Why would you be surprised if there were a police report?"

"Because as I know from the Bern-Harlow case, studios were very good at keeping that sort of thing secret. Warners would have had several cops on the take, ready to go in and erase records. Then again, Nancy might be lying."

"When she reacts as quickly as that?"

Marx fell into one of his close-lidded ruminations. "Well, all I can say is, Ronnie got lucky. Janey was a nice young lady."

Louella Parsons used similar language in her gossip column on November 1, 1939, reporting that "two of Hollywood's very nicest young people" had fallen in love. They had plighted their troth with a fifty-two-carat amethyst ring, Wayne and Bubbles Morris were going to give them an engagement party, and "they will be married as soon as they return from a personal appearance tour with me later this month."

It was Ronald Reagan's peculiar luck that the most powerful movie columnist in America happened to hail from Dixon, Illinois. Miss Parsons therefore doted on him as her personal boy-next-door, and thought he and Jane had stacks of style. With her network of informers, I do not see how she could have avoided hearing about their little hospital drama, but the fact that Dutch had behaved so decently was reason enough not to mention it. Besides, she needed them to add romantic interest to her road show, opening in San Francisco on November 15.

"La Louella" was a frustrated actress, lacking such useful qualifications as looks and talent. She promised to showcase the gifts of six other young "comers," including Joy Hodges and Susan Hayward, but she meant to focus the spotlight on herself as stage mother to "Ronnie and Janey." Poor Nelle Reagan, now living in genteel retirement with Jack in West Hollywood, could hardly compete.

"I hope my Ronald has made the right choice," Nelle wrote worriedly to a friend in Dixon. "I was in hopes he would fall in love with some sweet girl who is not in the movies."

❡

I am not sure if the TWA plane Phil and I saw Dutch board was the one that took Miss Parsons and her company East on November 22, but I do know that he vowed never to fly again after a snowstorm tossed them about on descent into Chicago. It was his claustrophobic experience in the amphibian to Santa Catalina repeated, but with zero visibility and vomiting co-passengers. One can only hope he was not sitting next to Louella, who was famously incontinent (Paul Rae dubbed her "Miss Pee"). At any rate, Ronald Reagan remained earthbound for the next twenty-five years.

He was more pleasantly shaken, in Philadelphia, Pittsburgh, Baltimore, and New York, by the avid grasping of female fans. They tore at his clothes, beat on his hotel-room door, stole his socks, and ecstatically screamed his name. It was his first experience of erotic hysteria, and he was almost as surprised as *Motion Picture* magazine, which published a profile of him entitled, "What! No Sex Appeal?"

Onstage and off, Jane Wyman played the demure role required of her. She was smart enough not to upstage Miss Parsons, who could with the flick of an adjective make or break the career of any performer. Every skit, every serenade redounded to the columnist's dowdy glory. Paul caught up with the show in New York, and wrote me shortly before Christmas:

> Dutch is emcee for Miss Pee, introducing her so fulsomely you'd think she pays his salary. On she comes, white & wobbling, & after he kisses her, it takes a while for the dent in her cheek to fade. Jane simpers at *extreme* Stage R. while Joy Hodges & Junie Preisser suck up enough to makeya groan. The only gal with any "balls" is little Susie Hayward, who sasses Louella right back. Joy does a good torch job on "Day In, Day Out" while Dutch listens with that attentive look that says, "Wonder how the Black Hawks are doing." Climax of show: Miss Pee dictates tomorrow's column *right there onstage* without so much as a pause for breath, doncha wish *you* had such a polished style . . . ?

❡

Paul's contempt for Louella Parsons is ironic in that he was on the way to becoming a professional gossip himself. He had begun to attach acerbic paragraphs to his caricatures in the *Greenwich Villager,* to the distress of the paper's legal department and the delight of thousands of readers. Within a year he would have his own syndicated column, "Rae's Round-Up," covering the entertainment scene on both coasts. It was never any competition for Parsons or Hedda Hopper (its acid content was too high), but it brought him a modest income. At my urging, he came west and settled in Studio City, whence he lampooned with glee the *lumpenproletariat* of Tinseltown—Dutch naturally being a favorite target. But I always felt that his heart was in the Village, where he maintained a walk-up, and I think a friend, for the rest of his divided life.

On December 27, 1939, the Parsons Players arrived in Washington, D.C., for a six-day engagement and checked into the New Willard Hotel. Only Louella had seen the nation's capital before, and her younger charges were transfixed by the sight of snow etching out its grand design. In an eerie "trailer" of future politicking, Ronald Reagan found himself being hosted by representatives of Washington's three major newspapers. Flashbulbs popped as he engaged Casey Jones, managing editor of the *Post,* in a long discussion of the situation in Finland.

If Jane had ever heard of Finland, she probably thought it was an aquarium. She cheerfully told reporters, "I'm not very bright" and confessed that some of Ronnie's conversation went over her head. Yet she admired his deeper nature. When he escorted her to Mount Vernon early on New Year's Eve (trees tinkling with ice, the Potomac a sheet of silvery steel), she noticed that he stared long and reverently at George Washington's desk. Secretly, she ordered a replica for his study.

After their long train journey back to Los Angeles, Louella's two "lovebirds" chose January 26, 1940, as their nuptial date. Warner Bros. publicists were swift to announce that when they got back from their honeymoon, "they'll be husband and wife for the first time in . . . *Angel from Texas.*" Miss Parsons allowed as how her own husband (a dipsomanical doctor whose name nobody would ever remember) would give

Jane away, and that the reception would be held *chez* Parsons. Jane asked Bubbles Morris to be her bridesmaid, while Dutch rounded up Will Scott, one of his old barbershop-quartet buddies from Des Moines, as best man.

Paul Rae was hugely amused to hear that the wedding was going to be held at the "Wee Kirk o' the Heather," in Forest Lawn Memorial Park. "Will Dutch-boy wear a kilt, d'ye ken, and will Jane arrive in a hearse?" He may have touched on something, because Forest Lawn was where a distraught Jane had buried her first father-in-law, only fourteen months before.

Bubbles was economical with her adjectives when she described the ceremony to me. "It was *awful*. Janey's *awful* sister was maid of honor—just like a stork! And Ronnie's *awful* brother, such an ignoramus, and his *awful* wife. And his father and mother—God, what an old battle-ax."

"Anybody there who wasn't awful?"

"Jane. Beautiful beyond dreams. In the palest blue imaginable, sky blue covered with wash after wash of white on white—"

"*Ätherblau!*" I said. But women describing clothes are deaf to interruptions.

"—huge skirt, smocked and quilted bodice buttoned up to the chin. Little sable muff, pale blue hat trimmed with the same fur. . . . Of course, it all came from the studio."

When the newlyweds got back from Palm Springs early in February, Dutch headed straight for Santa Monica. It was not the chilly sea that drew him. For some reason, he seemed to want to practice running and throwing a football; I guess he thought the sand would build up his leg muscles. Sydney Ann and I saw him there one day with some friends yelling at him. They were trying to control his habit of sticking out his tongue when he threw.

"Why shouldn't he, if he wants to?" my wife said pettishly. She was five months pregnant and going through the irritable stage.

It dawned on me. "He must be prepping a movie."

Actually, he was rehearsing for a screen test, the most momentous of his career. Nine days before marrying, he had been electrified by an announcement in *Variety* that Warners would soon shoot "The Life of Knute Rockne," with Pat O'Brien in the title role. He had been talking up the idea of a Rockne movie ever since arriving on the Warners lot—even offered to script it for free. There was no indication who would play George Gipp, Notre Dame's legendary doomed halfback, but the casting notes for that character could have been lifted from one of Dutch Reagan's autobiographical college stories:

> [Teammates] respected him for his ability, but none of them ever got very close to him personally. . . . He had a great ability to relax, which was the secret of his success.

It was inconceivable to Dutch that anybody other than himself should get the part. When the executive producer, Bryan Foy, opined that he was too skinny, he said, "Would it impress you to know that the Gipper weighed about five pounds less than what I weigh right now?"

Foy shrugged, but Hal Wallis, head of production, ruled that Ronald Reagan could compete with Dennis Morgan and Donald Woods in a football-field test on February 28. Three more tests—one six hours long—were necessary before Foy finally said yes.

With a sense that the ghostly boots of George Gipp were propelling him to new, possibly starry heights, Dutch prepared to start shooting on April 11, 1940.

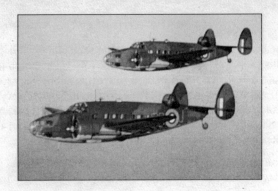

12

A Lonely Impulse
of Delight

W HILE RONALD REAGAN, alias George Gipp, was kicking himself to fame (and trying to keep his tongue in), the only boots I could think of were those advancing on Paris, and the only tongue a lispy one warning us, via BBC shortwave on May 20, 1940, that London was next in line. "After this battle for France abates its force, there will come the battle . . . for all that Britain is, and all that Britain means." Had Sydney Ann not been in the last stage of her pregnancy, I might have visited the British Consulate and offered myself, game leg and all, in His Majesty's service.

President Roosevelt's response to the crisis in Europe was to call for the immediate production of fifty thousand new military aircraft a year—more than the nation's factories had turned out in the thirty-six years since Kitty Hawk. Charles Lindbergh huffed that the President was "asking for war," but a majority of the country disagreed. When little Gavin was born on the twenty-seventh, the assembly lines at Lockheed and Douglas were already bristling with warbirds. *Gawain, that didst the black falcon follow.*

Dutch, whose location work on the Loyola University football field

was hampered by a noisy increase in airplane traffic, well understood
the belligerent drift of events. Not only was he better informed than
most screen actors (as the *Washington Post* editor had found out), but
he was a young, childless officer in the United States Cavalry Reserve.
If war came, he could be sure of a prompt telegram from Uncle Sam.

Warner Bros., itself the most politically aware of the major studios,
moved to put Lieutenant Reagan into uniform right away—any uniform that would capitalize on the military straightness of his stance,
and his well-scrubbed ardor (what Paul Rae called his "Lifebuoyish-
ness"). Within twenty-four hours of wrapping *Knute Rockne: All-
American* on June 4, Dutch was cast as General George Armstrong
Custer in *Santa Fe Trail.*

In mid-July, before either of these pictures opened, Phil Dunne sent
me a press release showing Reagan improbably togged in pilot's cover-
alls. He was about to open in *Murder in the Air,* a B movie aimed at the
Saturday-afternoon kiddie market. "I thought your friend didn't like to
fly," Phil scribbled. "Shall we see how he handles a whip stall?"

We went to see it in a cinema full of shrieking boys. Apparently, it
was the fourth of a series of low-budget thrillers featuring Dutch as
"Brass Bancroft," flying agent of the United States Secret Service. He
heroically pursued a Lindbergh-like pacifist bent on preserving American neutrality, and Public Enemy Number One, a saboteur who bore
the *mitteleuropäisch* name of Swenko. We cheered along with the rest of
the audience when Dutch, airlifting an enormous, sky-splitting photon
machine, liquidated both foes of freedom. *"All right, Hayden—focus
that Inertia Projector on 'em and let 'em have it!"*

"Ronald Ray-Gun," Phil mouthed in my ear, as the din reached its
height.

I am sorry to say that neither of us, in our mirth, perceived what
records have since made clear: that Warner Bros. was using Dutch for
propaganda purposes. As the imaginary hero of a kid flick, he could
subvert U.S. neutrality restraints (which forbade mature movies from
suggesting, for example, that the Axis powers were involved in terrorism) and teach patriotic children the value of domestic vigilance.

Emerging into the lobby, we must have missed the counter where
"Junior Secret Service Club" cards signed by "Ronald Reagan, Chief"
were issued to youths willing to look out for foreign agents. Still less did
we divine that the Inertia Projector (that light both lethal and benign,
silently purifying the American sky) might one day figure in the strategic defense thinking of Ronald Reagan, Commander in Chief.

No, about all I remember of that midsummer afternoon is the shrill enthusiasm of our fellow moviegoers. Most of them had seen Dutch's previous fly-spy features, as had countless brats across the country. At least one boy, ten-year-old Jerry Parr of Miami, Florida, vowed that he, too, would become a Secret Service agent like Brass Bancroft, "dauntless in the face of danger . . . fearless in the face of death!" Readers interested in young Parr's subsequent career should check his name in the index.

Four days after the premiere of *Knute,* an article in the *Los Angeles Times* greatly interested the Warner Bros. story department:

FLYERS' UNIT AIDS BRITAIN

American Pilots Form
Eagle Squadron Like
Lafayette Escadrille

LONDON, Oct. 8. (U. P.)—An all-American fighter command, the Eagle Squadron, formed in the tradition of the famed Lafayette Escadrille of the World War, will soon take the air with the Royal Air Force, Air Minister Sir Archibald Sinclair announced today.

The Eagle Squadron is composed entirely of qualified American pilots who have volunteered for combat service with the British forces and will become a regular unit of the Royal Air Force as soon as its "shakedown" is completed.

The cinematic potential of such a subject was obvious. Soon, treatments variously entitled "Eagle Squadron," "So Fly the Valiant," and "Flight Patrol" were circulating through the studio for possible development. The last-named—an ingenious reworking of *Ceiling Zero* (1935)—emerged as the favorite, and Bryan Foy took an option to produce it. Ronald Reagan was mentioned as the likely action lead. "Can't wait to see Dutch in a toothbrush mustache," Paul sniggered.

Needless to say, the *Times* article also inspired other studios, not to mention just about every local pilot who ever fantasized about getting his hands on the spade grip of a Spitfire. Which of us did not dream of thumbing that red firing tit, and blasting ME-109s out of the sky? Who did not secretly envy the nine Californians already recruited as Eagles? Who said Britain's battle was not our battle? In Los Angeles County, center of the air industry, stepped-up production galvanized both the economy and popular hostility to fascism. On my CPTS instructional trips up the coast, I could see waspish little AT-6s swarming along North American's flight line in Inglewood, while shiny Douglas DC-3s mutated into brown C-47s on the flats of El Segundo. Further inland, at the big Lockheed plant at Burbank, hundreds of dull, rubber-sprayed Hudsons awaited delivery to RAF Coastal Command. An ominous new haze, translucent yet acrid, suffused the metropolitan area. Sometimes I swooped through it, and found its scorched-steel, acetylenic reek curiously thrilling. It was my first whiff of war.

Shortly before Christmas, Warner Bros. seized on another help-the-RAF piece in the *Times*. It reported that a Los Angeles pilot named Jimmie Mattern had agreed to fly a free Hudson to London, courtesy of Lockheed's labor force.

Even as studio synopsists tried to work Mattern's story into that of *Flight Patrol* (what if the pilot-hero were to apply for RAF wings?), I was excitedly batting out a script on spec. Here was an unbelievable opportunity to combine my knowledge of flying and Anglo-American social relations into a scenario that Bryan Foy might option, and Dutch want to play!

Already I saw my title, "Tumult in the Clouds," streaming out of a bank of radiant cumulus, to the sound of the latter's silvery voice reading Yeats:

> *Nor law, nor duty bade me fight,*
> *Nor public men, nor cheering crowds,*
> *A lonely impulse of delight*
> *Drove to this tumult in the clouds.*

Then, over the rumble of an approaching bomber, more clouds would reveal the words, *Starring RONALD REAGAN* . . .

The alliterative trochees floated at center frame, as no doubt they did in Dutch's own dreams. I confess that vision makes my heart lurch to this day. The Hudson never quite seen (merely a dark bulk racing through the shreds, or casting its portly shadow on the sea), and further credits scrolling—one the most personal of all! And then to dissolve to a windsock with an RAF rondel on it, as Reagan came bellying in to land, his reflection on the wet runway rising to meet him. . . .

Creative desire, like sexual desire, burgeons careless of denial. One assumes that one's inspirations are unique, only to find again and again that they're not. No sooner had I shown my draft to Sam Marx than he shook his head and said, "Every shop in town's working on that idea. Think of something new, for Chrissake."

Sam, however, was an MGM man, majestically unaware of the willingness of less scrupulous studios to buy freelance scripts cheap and, on occasion, under the table in defiance of Screen Writers Guild regulations.

Ronald Reagan ranked as Warners' top feature player when the studio published its official list at the end of 1940. A mere space break separated him from the astral regions where Cagney, Bogart, and other actors famous enough to be known by their surnames hung in lone splendor. Commentators predicted he would join them very soon, if not for *Knute Rockne,* then probably for *Santa Fe Trail,* just released. They were right. Early in the new year, Warners elevated him. Paul and I gaped at the announcement on the front pages of both *Variety* and *The Hollywood Reporter.* We doubted, though, that Dutch would ever be just "Reagan." So much for our foresight.

His stardom only increased my hopes of selling Bryan Foy an Eagles screenplay. Owen Crump (married now to Lucile Fairbanks, and one of Jack's favorite screenwriters) said that I might have a chance if *Flight Patrol* ever needed a "technical revise."

Dutch's new dignity was compounded by fatherhood. He had been so sure that Jane would present him with a son and heir that he had a mock military birth notice to that effect already set in type. Instead, she produced a five-and-a-half-pound girl on the eve of her own twenty-fourth birthday. "Gee!" he complained, "such a little homely red thing." The birth notice went out only slightly amended:

— This is the announcement we were going to send —

HEADQUARTERS
FORT REAGAN

1326 LONDONDERRY VIEW
HOLLYWOOD, CALIFORNIA

SUBJECT: EXTENDED ACTIVE DUTY

1. GENERAL RONALD REAGAN, JR., HAVING PASSED FINAL TYPE PHYSICAL EXAMINATION, IS AVAILABLE FOR ACTIVE DUTY.

2. GENERAL REAGAN WILL ASSUME COMMAND OF THE POST

3. EFFECTIVE JANUARY 4, 1941.

FOR THE EXECUTIVES:

A. STORK

AIRCORPS MEDICAL DIV.
BUT IT'S HARDLY APPROPRIATE FOR . . .

MAUREEN ELIZABETH REAGAN

IS IT?

Thus was a superintelligent young person excluded, not for the last time, from the world of male esteem.

Dutch's lame attempt at Aircorpspeak suggests that he had begun to prep the part of "Pilot Officer Jimmy Grant" in *Flight Patrol.* Besides having to learn how to talk and gesticulate like an airman, there were other characteristics for him to master. Grant was an intriguingly complex creation, as I had to acknowledge when Owen showed me the draft script.

Written by Barry Trivers (*South of Suez, Big Broadcast of 1937*), it told the story of a driven, disreputable test pilot, loose with both money and girls, who takes advantage of the Hudson delivery program in order to escape Los Angeles, just minutes ahead of a paternity suit. Doubtful about returning home after collecting his fee, he is persuaded to join an RAF volunteer squadron. In Kent, as in California, Grant makes free with other men's women, while his recklessness on sorties over France renders him *pilotus non gratus* at Fighter Command. Contrite after causing the death of a comrade, he usurps a dangerous assignment, executes it brilliantly, and is killed on his way back across the Channel.

The hard outline of this story moved me. But Trivers, bewilderingly, had written it as light comedy. The dialogue had an incessant, labored jokiness. I flicked through the script with rising hopes: anything this dumb would surely end up in Jack Warner's wastepaper basket.

"Just get me a rewrite," I begged Owen, "and I'll give you the best RAF script you ever saw."

"Well, Jack did say it needs work."

Owen persuaded Bryan Foy that *Flight Patrol* would benefit from the attentions of a scribe who understood both aeronautics and British English. Foy was less convinced by these qualifications than by my willingness to work at $150 per screen minute, well below the Writers Guild rate. On February 1 the assignment was mine. I had just thirty days to deliver.

With a sense that Heaven's gates were opening—*Ätherblau,* at last!—I dispatched my wife and son to Brown Orchards and wrote and wrote. I scrubbed the Hudson idea, the womanizing, and the purgative finale and sketched a scenario whose melodramatics now strike me as drearier than Trivers's attempts to make light of war. *An impoverished writer-flier, unhappily married in Los Angeles, hears that RAF recruiters are in town, looking for volunteer pilots. . . .*

Well, to cut a dumb script short, if Dutch had ever acted it, he would have found himself betraying the RAF by talking too much in a London nightclub, and causing the obliteration of his squadron in a surprise enemy attack on the eve of an important mission. *Camera lifts in silence to a high, long hold on dozens of bodies and burning Spitfires. We hear the voice of Jimmy Grant declaiming Yeats's bitter last lines: "A waste of breath the years behind / In balance with this life, this death."*

Certain that I had created the modern equivalent of *Battleship Potemkin,* I delivered it to Warners on deadline. Owen Crump, coldly angry, called next day. "Foy's bringing in Ken Gamet to help Barry rewrite his original script PDQ. If you want to see a dime of your fee, you better be available as technical consultant."

Ronald Reagan was duly announced for the part of Jimmy Grant, his first top-billing role in an A picture. *Flight Patrol's* eclectic cast included James Stephenson as squadron leader, a luscious French ingenue, Olympe Bradna, as Jimmy's main squeeze, and a hack comic, Cliff Edwards, to supply the sort of slapstick interludes that amused Jack Warner.

At 9 A.M. on Monday, March 24, 1941, I obeyed a call to attend the first day of shooting at Alhambra Airport.

I had not seen Dutch in the flesh since that day on the sand at Santa Monica thirteen months before, and my impression was that he had coarsened. Perhaps it was his test-pilot suit, but the flat-chested, narrow-hipped spareness seemed to be gone. At thirty, his face had lost the curves of youth and not yet acquired the planes of middle age. It was stiffer, with dents where the dimples used to be and frown lines that did not quite smooth when he laughed. He had the cured look of a man who sunbathed too much. I noticed that he wore heavy glasses all the time now, except when he was called before the camera, and that he was hard of hearing. (A sound engineer told me he had blown his right eardrum in the shootout scene in *Code of the Secret Service.*)

"There's something disturbingly mechanical about RR's grin," I wrote in a diary I kept of the production. "It beams too often on and too little off, like a malfunctioning traffic light." As the week proceeded, however—we were shooting hangar and ramp sequences—I realized that the fake jollity was Jimmy Grant's, not his. Dutch was a better actor than I took him for. His verbal memory was so good that he had actually to work against it, to stem the glibness of total recall. When the director, Lothar Mendes, huddled with him on points of action or interpretation, he was all serious attention. Professional to a fault, he always showed up on time and was just as prompt in departing.

The frown lines were caused by simple fatigue. *Flight Patrol* was his twenty-seventh picture in forty-two months of pretty constant work, six days a week. Since the *première* of *Knute,* he had shot a loan-out Western, *The Bad Man,* for MGM, returned to Warner Bros. in the new year as a classical pianist in *Million Dollar Baby,* gone back to MGM for twelve days of retakes in late February, then plunged immediately into preparation for this, his most demanding role yet. Even as he zipped himself into Jimmy Grant's overalls, the casting department at Burbank was considering him for a supporting lead in *Kings Row,* a major picture scheduled to roll on April 21. "Reagan will be used solid every day until he finishes *Flight Patrol,*" Hal Wallis advised the head office, "so he will have to be tested at night."

Not having been on a Warners set before, I was impressed at how hard Mendes worked both cast and crew. For eleven days, he presided with Teutonic thoroughness over the script's early scenes, including one that called for Jimmy to make a near-sonic vertical dive from thirty thousand feet. Dutch never left the ground (his actual aerobatics were left to Special Effects), but he climbed in and out of a disguised Ryan trainer with the right degree of nonchalance, and, when he hit maximum G, dribbled chocolate syrup to great effect. The dive took all day to shoot, by which time he had ingested enough syrup to retch with enthusiasm. How he got the stuff to come out of his nose as well I would rather not speculate. And he screamed so convincingly as he "blacked out" that for the first and last time in his acting career Ronald Reagan actually made my flesh creep.

The weather in the Valley grew unseasonably hot. Swimsuited children hung on the airport fence, shrilling for "Ronnie's" autograph. He must have endured agonies of discomfort under the sun-arcs in his padded helmet, thirty-pound leather flying suit, and knee-high, sheepskin-lined boots. Yet he had the gift (envied by Errol Flynn) of never breaking into a sweat. When required to do so, he would placidly allow a makeup man to slap glycerol on his cheeks.

Bryan Foy replaced Mendes with Lewis Seiler on April 4, in an effort to speed up production. Over the next month and a half, Dutch was on set or on location, word perfect and camera ready, for 323½ hours, shooting as many as twelve scenes a day. There were countless rewrites and retakes: Jack Warner seemed terrified of plagiarism suits from Universal or Fox, who were respectively making *Eagle Squadron* and *A Yank in the RAF*. Our script got so fat with blue-page inserts it began to look like a pharmaceutical catalog. *Kings Row,* now officially Reagan's next picture, was postponed again and again.

On May 1, because of my presumed Spitfire expertise, I was ordered to attend a dogfight scene, and nearly saw the course of history altered.

Dutch, silk-scarfed, was bravely flying a fuselage from stage right to stage left, pursued by imaginary Messerschmitts. Seiler interrupted the shooting to ask me, by messenger, whether a Spit's cockpit canopy could be winched back at such a moment, because Reagan had to "hold something out the window." Mystified, I advised that Spitfire pilots generally slid their tops back by hand. After some tinkering, P/O Grant was re-encased in Plexiglas, and pneumatic tubes began to toss the fuselage about. Dutch (what agonies of claustrophobia he must have been feeling!) plied his joystick in directions that, had he been truly airborne, would have sent him into an inverted spin. He remembered to look over his shoulder at the MEs, reacted on cue, then, to my complete disbelief, produced an oil-soaked mop and set fire to it. The Plexiglas swam with smoke, and his goggled face disappeared.

"Shouldn't he—uh, the canopy?" I asked the nearest grip. But my voice was drowned by an alarmed shout of "Fire!" Technicians mobbed the still-bucking fuselage and pulled Reagan free, as dense fumes billowed and the sound technician's needles spun to the convulsions of his coughing. He was rushed to the studio hospital, and stayed away sick for two days.

Investigation disclosed that he had been innocently obeying instructions to feed a false trail of flame into his slipstream, fooling the FWs into thinking he was *kaputt*—so that he could pulverize them as they peeled off. A more fatuous air tactic would be hard to conceive.

The publicity department announced that Reagan's canopy had jammed when he tried to slide it back. Seiler obstinately reshot the scene, and *Flight Patrol* was declared "finished," barring stills and an extra take or two, on May 6, 1941.

Just twelve days later, at one-thirty in the morning, Jack Reagan was walking round the head of his bed, when he suddenly jerked upright, raised his hands imploringly, and fell dead. After a lifetime of alcoholic binges and "one match" chain-smoking, he had succumbed to coronary thrombosis at fifty-seven.

Dutch happened to be on the other coast of the United States, at a Warner Bros. event in Atlantic City. Nelle reached him by phone and lovingly advised that he should not think of flying back to Los Angeles. She and other family members would attend to all the unpleasant details of certification, embalming, and encasement. So he had plenty of time to brace himself before attending the funeral service at Saint Victor's Catholic Church, where he suffered the acute but brief attack of despair recorded earlier in this book.

Morally, as far as he was concerned, John Edward Reagan had "died" two decades before, on the snowy porch of the family house in Dixon. Then as now, an insult to the brain had thrown Jack back, arms outstretched, "as if he were crucified." Then as now, Dutch felt tenderness, mixed with more selfish sorrow. Now as not then, his father was able to console him.

From somewhere *in excelsis* a cheerful, black-Irish ghost whispered, "I'm OK."

☯

As a final chore before being paid by Warners, I was asked to supervise the return of Jimmy Grant's Hudson bomber (actually an ancient Electra, rendered warlike with water-soluble paints) to Lockheed, which had leased it to us for the duration. Paul Mantz, the great stunt pilot, was to do the actual hop from Van Nuys to Burbank; my job was to complete the necessary paperwork.

"Paul is generally too pissed to sign on the dotted line," Owen Crump explained with a grin.

Mantz was already up front, gunning both engines, when I got to Metropolitan Airport. I went forward to introduce myself, got an indifferent handshake, and settled deferentially into the seat beside him. Anyone who cared about flying in those days worshiped Mantz as the greatest stick man in the business. He could fly under bridges a horse would balk at, hook handkerchiefs off the roof of a hangar, or spin a corpulent Tri-Motor through fifteen perfect turns.

Beyond virtuosity, though, was the art that concealed the art, the unshowy ease with which he transformed speed into apparent stillness.

"The greatest stick man in the business."
Paul Mantz, ca. 1941.

Pissed or sober, he took that Electra off the ground as if we somehow remained at rest, while the world dropped gently away. The heavy ship seemed to hang in a weightless, bumpless empyrean more ether than air. I doubt that we were aloft more than twenty minutes, yet that flight stays in my memory as an elevation in the purest sense, neither beginning nor ending nor rising nor falling. Time and space canceled themselves out, and nothing brought me all things.

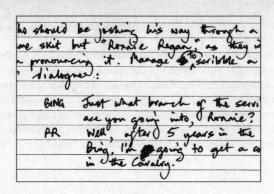

he should be joshing his way through a
one skit but "Ronnie Regan" as they'r
~ pronouncing it. Manage to scribble a
~ dialogue:

    BING   Just what branch of the servi
            are you going into, Ronnie?
    RR   Well, after 5 years in the
            Bing, I'm going to get a co
            in the Cavalry.

13

The End of
the Beginning

FLIGHT PATROL was scheduled for release in the fall of 1941 under
the new title of *International Squadron.*

An exhausted Reagan got the last three weeks of May "off," which in
studio parlance meant time at home to learn two more upcoming parts.
One was the tragic role of Drake McHugh in *Kings Row* and the
other a comedy turn as a reporter in *Nine Lives Are Not Enough.* He
was encouraged to accept the latter lead with a promise that Jane would
play opposite him. But in the shadow-world of movies, nothing is constant or concrete. By June 1, Jane had been replaced by Joan Perry and
Dutch was back in uniform as Jimmy Grant—the production department having decided to reshoot all his Electra scenes in a genuine Hudson. When these reshoots collided with the opening scenes of *Nine
Lives,* he was obliged to be a pilot on Monday and a press man on Tuesday. He wrapped the quickie in twenty-one days, getting measured
meanwhile for an elegant wardrobe of suits appropriate to high life on
Kings Row, somewhere around the turn of the century.

Screen actors are adept at moving from one production to another—sometimes between different productions shot simultaneously on neighboring sound stages. Hence, I suppose, the fabled shortness of Dutch's later attention span, which an exasperated aide would compare to that of a fruit fly. Both the fable and the simile strike me as unjust: he was generally a serious, even dogged study. Yet Ronald Reagan remained all his life an actor, a man of exits and entrances, whether the "production" that engaged him was as short as a conversation or as long as the Presidency. When he stepped onto the set, he knew exactly what to do and how to fill the space allotted him. And when he left it, it was with the word *CUT* sounding in his ears. On to the next cast of characters!

I remember greeting him one morning, having entertained him at home the night before. Not only did he fail to mention our dinner, it was obvious from his smiling yet distant demeanor that he did not recall it.

To those readers who will seize on this as evidence of incipient dementia in the White House, I reply: *You do not understand that actors remember forward, not backward.* Yesterday's take is in the can; today is already rolling: tomorrow's lines must be got by heart.

Writers are different. Their stock in trade is past experience (particularly past rejections!), and their whole instinct is to turn it to literary account—make art out of life, as the cliché goes. In my case in the summer of 1941, I went further and sought to make life imitate art. I did what Jimmy Grant *alias* Ronald Reagan had done: ferried a Hudson to Great Britain, and volunteered for service with the RAF. The eighteen months I spent with the Eagles as liaison officer and squadron historian remain so dreamlike in their dislocated vividness (and so oddly black-and-white, with jump cuts and reel changes) that at times I wonder if my recollection of them is not merely an old man's memory of a young man's movie.

Yet here, jammed into drawersful of Reaganiana, are the letters I exchanged with Sydney Ann and Owen Crump and Paul Rae and Philip Dunne, the long article Paul sent me about Dutch's return to Dixon, review clips of *International Squadron* and *Kings Row,* RAF and USAAF cablegrams, radio air checks, and my own 1941–1942 diary: inescapable, unarguable, documents of war overseas, and what passed for war at home.

Since most of these items refer to Ronald Reagan (one can sense that we all, even patrician Phil, were more interested in him than we cared to admit), I have made the following edited selection of them, with bits of linking commentary, as a sort of group portrait of Dutch at the end of his youth—patchily rendered, perhaps, but at least unglossed by later fame.

☯

"Looks like Reagan will lose only one leg," Owen Crump wrote me at OTU Tern Hill, Shropshire, on July 30, 1941. I presumed this had something to do with Dutch's new movie, but Owen did not elaborate. The tone of his letter was coldly disapproving of my defection. "Sydney Ann called Lucile in the small hours to say she'd seen you off on the train. Sounded v. calm, said it was 'something you had to do.' Excuse me asking, but who's going to play father to little Gavin?"

I checked a copy of Henry Bellamann's *Kings Row* out of the Shrewsbury Public Library and read it with the fascination that small-town fiction, full of furtive grapplings, induced in the days before *Peyton Place*. Round about p. 461, I began to hear Dutch's voice whenever Drake spoke, and from then on could not help seeing him too. How was Regular Ron going to handle the skinny-dipping scene, key to Drake's unstated (and unconsummated) homosexual relationship with Parris?

Several lurid chapters later, Dutch/Drake lost his legs. This explained Owen's cryptic remark, if not Hal Wallis's desire to save one of them. However, the book's remarkably economical dialogue could be applied to paraplegia of any sort:

RANDY   Drake! Drake!
DRAKE   Randy!
RANDY   Yes, I'm here, Drake. I'm here with you.
DRAKE   Randy!
RANDY   Yes, dear, I'm here.
DRAKE   Randy—where—where's the rest of me?

Remembering Dutch's delight in being strangled in *Aria da Capo*, I felt sure he would want to lose as many legs as possible.

When I wrote to Owen Crump, informing him that the RAF did not consider me fighter-pilot material, he was mollified and replied: "Well liaison work is just as important I should think. Way things are going here, I'll soon be in uniform myself. Went to military school as a kid—and you can be sure Uncle Sam knows that."

Paul Rae informed me, in the first of many waspishly entertaining letters, that Warners was planning "a big junket" for the movie I still thought of as *Flight Patrol*:

Wanted you to be the first to know. Dutch-boy's new pic *International Squadron* (why title change?) is going to preem GUESS

WHERE? Doleful Dixon!! I *suppose* there are less appropriate places to open a flick about Limey flyboys, but right now can't think of one. Bob William of Warners P.R. wants me to write local-boy-makes-good story. Well it's a chance for a visit with the folks in Grand Detour.

Only thing I'm not looking forward to: they are threatening to combine the preem with a tribute to the dread Miss Pee. Did you know she's also from Dixon? Once Louella gets her mouth near a mike, Dutch may as well go fishing. What fun if he loses his Irish & takes a swing at the old pisspot!! After all, she *did* make him marry Janey.

Who by the way, won't be accompanying Dutch north. My guess is, poor gal needs some relief from his monologues on world affairs. He chews the fat all day on Lend-Lease and such. Did you know he's losing both his legs in *Kings Row*?

Try not to lose yours, & come back soon. Missya *beaucoup*. —*Paul*

P.S.—Reagan just sold a story, "The Cavalry Rides Again," to Warners. As if they don't produce enough horseshit already.

I am sorry to say that after searching through the Warner Bros. papers, I have not been able to find Dutch's scenario. When I asked him about the plot he couldn't remember, but allowed with a grin, "I'm sure the good guys won."

☯

Paul's letter whetted my appetite for his column on Dutch's triumphal return home. Instead of the expected short clipping, what I got, weeks later, was the carbon of a long and ambitious typescript. I doubt that it was syndicated entire, but posterity is glad to have the details:

WELCOME HOME "DUTCH"

Ronald Reagan, Star of "International Squadron,"
Returns to Dixon, the Town Louella Made Famous
By Paul C. Rae

Dixon, Ill., Sept. 15—Ronald "Dutch" REAGAN revisited his youthful haunts on the Rock River this weekend. If beauty-starved Dixonians were looking forward to ogling his curvaceous wife, they were doomed to disappointment. Instead of an eyeful of Jane WYMAN, they got an earful of Louella PARSONS.

Miss P. also hails from Dixon, & when she heard that INTERNATIONAL SQUADRON, Reagan's new starrer from Warner Bros., was preeming here tonight, a whole flight of Messerschmidts [*sic*] couldn't keep her away.

Such is the power of La Louella's pen, Bob HOPE, Joe E. BROWN, George MONTGOMERY, Bebe DANIELS, and Ben LYON also showed up to kiss her skirt—as did the city fathers. But ordinary folks seemed more interested in their local lad. They held placards reading, "WELCOME HOME DUTCH."

Nelle REAGAN, the star's 56-year-old mother, looked pleased.

Seventy-seven Grateful Swimmers

For this reporter, the most moving event was a tribute to Reagan that didn't make the official schedule. Yesterday afternoon he revisited Lowell Park, a few miles north of town, where he once worked six summers as a lifeguard. The old log on which he notched his 77 documented rescues has washed away. But a delegation of men and women who owe their lives to "Dutch" was on hand to present him a clock bearing the simple message, "From 77 Grateful People." Afterward Reagan said that he's going to write a story of his lifeguard days entitled, "I Knew Them Better in Five Minutes Than Their Mothers Did in a Lifetime." He hopes to sell it—where else?—to the movies.

Mr. Nice Guy

This reporter was a classmate of "Dutch" Reagan at Eureka College, and can confirm that he's as swell a guy now as he was back in '28. Bigger and broader (watch them strawberry shortcakes, mister) and certainly richer (he just inked a fat new seven-year contract) but still a decent, unassuming fellow, the kind you'd trust with your wife. Hell, I'd even trust him with Louella Parsons. Maybe success has made him a touch slick. He courteously asked former buddies how they'd been doing since he left town in '33, but at the first sign of a hard-luck story, "Dutch" was ready with a joke and a handshake. Knows how to keep the fans coming—and going. "This fellow must be running for Congress!" marveled Jerry COLONNA.

Reagan doesn't want anybody's shadow across the sunny landscape of his life.

Back in Tinseltown, talk is that the 30-year-old star, currently #7 on the Warner talent roster, is headed much higher. He may even displace that inseparable duo, Errol FLYNN and Johnnie WALKER. Reagan is shooting his final scenes in KINGS ROW (biggest weepie to come out of Burbank in years) and reveling in raves for his newspaper thriller, NINE LIVES ARE NOT ENOUGH. Next? Frank

Capra wants him for ARSENIC AND OLD LACE, and then he's due to play WILL ROGERS in another big-bucks Warners blowout.

Just one pesky problem, though . . . before I blab, let's move into CLOSE-UP.

Déjà Vu, And The Same To You

Reagan is six feet one, weighs about 170 lbs., has smoky blue eyes that he hides behind horn-rims when no camera's clicking.

Loves to talk, hates to listen. Is a good all-round athlete. Okay, so he exaggerates his college football prowess—thinks he could be a writer—but don't we all? Likes company, including his own. Also horses, lilacs, sleep, box lunches (sign of a midwestern boy), rainstorms (another sign), golf. Drives his battered brown convertible with the top down. Dislikes rocking chairs, tennis, tomatoes, traffic noise. Signs autographs with his right hand, shoots with his left, combs his hair the wrong way. Puffs pipes. Keeps his shoes on while he undresses, don't ask me why. Has a memory like film—detail, no depth. Maintains a scrapbook of flattering news clips ("my Ego Elevator").

Has a pretty little daughter. Remind him some time, won't you? Seems to enjoy nightspots (married to Jane, he'd better) but can nurse a beer longer'n anybody since Carrie NATION. Yet he's just as happy to sneak off to the Screen Actors Guild and put in a long evening. Interested in politics is our boy Ron—but not so interested he wants to quit show business. Ask Dick POWELL and friends. They tried in vain to get him to run for Congress on the Republican ticket last fall. They forgot one tiny detail: Reagan's a passionate New Dealer.

Is a fan of Bing Crosby, and by logical extension, macaroni and cheese. For all his 100-watt grin and storehouse of jokes borrowed from George BURNS and Jack BENNY, he's basically "Mr. Norm," a serious, hardworking, uncomplaining fellow. Jack WARNER gave him a roll of bills for his willingness to work overtime on KINGS ROW. Spies tell me Ronnie's invested this wad in a new house he's building in the Hollywood Hills. If the design looks familiar, that's because you saw it last winter in THIS THING CALLED LOVE, starring Rosalind RUSSELL. Ronnie and Jane liked Roz's layout so much they borrowed the plans from Columbia.

Oh, I Almost Forgot

That pesky problem I mentioned, which could spin THE RONALD REAGAN STORY right off its reel: Uncle SAM wants him. Warner Bros. won't comment, but Ronnie holds a commission in the U.S. Cavalry Reserve, which puts him in the top priority for call-up. Rumor is, he's already gotten his trotting orders. WATCH THIS SPACE!

I read Paul's carbon at the American Eagle Club in London. It arrived in tandem with another letter from Owen Crump, surprisingly good-humored considering his terse, tough personality:

> ... You asked about Ronnie Reagan's legs. Hal feels that amputating both of 'em will make audience wonder if maybe the doctor sawed off something else as well. But Sam Wood has raised such Cain they've left the scene intact. A joke went round the lot—Hal's real concern was to prep Ronnie for another property we're developing, *One Foot in Heaven*.
>
> *K. R.* should wrap any day now. Production dept. thought it would never get done, because we had such trouble with the Hays Office. They wanted all the sex (and homo-sex) out, all incest, insanity, etc., even the mercy killing. Sam somehow managed to put a picture together. I hear it's quite good. Should be, at $750,000.
>
> Feel sympathetic toward RR these days. He got back from his Dixon junket to find himself on Adj. Gen.'s Priority List. He's set to start *Jook Girl* [*sic*] next week—head office is worried as hell. So is Janey. Here's her [*sic*] and Ronnie with nearly $1 million in new contracts, and if *K. R.* is a solid sock, he will be able to choose his own scripts. But this induction business could jinx all that. He doesn't stand a chance of deferment if we go to war.
>
> I enclose some early reviews of *International Squadron*. As you see, they're mixed. *Our best, Owen.*

Most critics seemed to feel that Ronald Reagan had done what he could to save a mediocre movie. It was "regrettable," said the New York *Herald Tribune*, "that his script constantly forces him to be . . . a little too unaware of the great events and thoughts around him."

RAF Station Eglinton N. Ireland October 21, 1941
Dear Paul:—Excuse long delay in replying to your v. interesting article about Dutch's return to Dixon. I thought you treated Dutch quite sympathetically. . . .
Did he remember you from college? Not without specs, I'll bet. Even with, he looked right through me at Alhambra Airport. The

title of his fantasy lifeguard story gave me pause. Guess what he means is, people who are about to drown will reveal all the essential elements of their character, noble or ignoble. Hence the embarrassed truculence of rescuees: they have been found out.

I still have the news clip of Dutch's midnight rescue back in '28. Maybe Dutch would like it for his "Ego Elevator"??

Don't know if I told you this last time, but HQ found out I was a scribe & suggested I keep a sort of diary of the three Eagle Squadrons, as I commute from one to another. Maybe even publish it, "when this show is over." Have begun doodling a few entries, less narrative than thematic. Psychology of volunteer fighter pilots is intriguing. For all their camaraderie in mess & pub, not to mention tight teamwork in the air, there's a definite lack of warmth among them. Men at war learn to cast a cold eye (Yeats) on life & death, but such coldness is brought about by an effort of will: it's an achievement. Coolness on the other hand is an endowment. You get the weird feeling these guys are not as upset as they should be, when somebody "goes west." They feel no loss, because they're complete unto themselves. Remind you of anyone you've profiled lately?

Regards, E.

International Squadron opened in London on November 2, 1941, at the Warner Theatre in Leicester Square. I went to see it, along with practically every Eagle who could get a pass out of North Weald, and reported to Owen Crump the next day.

Audience laughter (unscripted) began with the first title frame misquoting Churchill & rose to a roar when that dinky little test prototype appeared onscreen, "flying" bravely by means of an all-too-obvious wire. Real planes changed identity from shot to shot so often (Jimmy Grant's new Hudson mutates into Paul Mantz's old Electra somewhere over Labrador) that we began to take bets whether what went up would ever come down.

Reagan, believe it or not, gets the British equivalent of a rave in this morning's *Times.* Here's the review in its terse entirety: *That bravery without discourse may be too much of a good thing in modern war is obvious, and it is almost equally obvious that a film hero possessing this kind of bravery must atone for the harm he has done. This Mr. Ronald Reagan brings off very excitingly.*

I think they're using *discourse* in the archaic sense of rationality. Jimmy Grant certainly rambles on beyond reason, but that's because most of his dialogue is written for laughs. RR is smart enough to

sense this, & as the critic says, acts like a man doomed by his own ir-
rationality. Such a decent, driven performance, ruined by a corny
script & hasty direction. *Regards, E.*

P.S. What saddens me is the pic's flip inability to understand that
what we Eagles—even those of us who "also serve"—are doing here
is deadly serious.

When the news of Pearl Harbor hit Britain, early in the evening of December 7, 1941, I was sitting with a bunch of Eagles in a sour snug on
the outskirts of Londonderry, Northern Ireland. A crowding blackness
is what I remember of those first seconds of shock: black night outside,
black rain on the window, glasses of black Guinness halfway to our
lips. I guess the tonelessness of the BBC announcer's voice, as though
he was giving some football results, slowed down our reaction, because
we sat silent at first. Here it was: war around the whole world. And here
were we, wearing the uniforms of a foreign government, marooned on
the wrong side of a black ocean.

Into my ears another voice breathed—silvery, sympathetic, well
trained in microphone technique—the unmistakable tones of Dutch
alias Jimmy Grant declaiming Yeats:

> *I balanced all, brought all to mind,*
> *The years to come seemed waste of breath,*
> *A waste of breath the years behind*
> *In balance with this life, this death.*

Paul Rae sent an urgent air letter asking for anecdotes about the impact of the news in Britain.

SatEvePost is interested in a "Where Were You?" piece ... I've
quizzed a lot of people here, including Dutch, who confesses that he
was asleep. Well whaddya expect on Sunday morning, at the crack of
noon? Typically, it was his brother who called him: nothing Moon
enjoys more than scaring the shit out of people. Dutch, equally typically (ain't it marvellous how emergencies establish people's priorities?), called Lew Wasserman [his agent] for career advice. Lew, in
turn, listened quietly, then hung up on him—whether in shock or
sudden grief for a client demonstrably headed for military service, we
will never know.

Another buddy of yours I spoke to was Philip Dunne. Said that he
& Amanda were flying in to Mines Field in their Luscom Silvaire
when they got a radio flash that Nip was on his way & all private

planes should return to base PDQ. How 'bout *you,* migrant bird?
Time you flapped Stateside again—*Affec., Paul*

P.S. Pearl couldn't have come at a worse time for Dutch ("rapidly
developing into a first-rate actor"—*L.A. Times*!!). *Kings Row* preems
Jan. 8. Poor sap's just prepping *another* RAF movie, *In the Shadow of
Their Wings.* What happened to defending Uncle Sam?

That last line echoed, because strange to say, not a single Eagle had
yet applied for transfer to the U.S. Air Corps. We could not quite believe that America the Beautiful had become America the Vulnerable.
Being half English, I had some reason to be ambivalent. But all of us
felt a queer kind of protectiveness to Britain, so small, so visibly battered, so obviously threatened with extinction.

A few weeks into the new year, I heard again from Paul Rae:

. . . Our classmate, believe it or not, has managed to get himself
declared legally blind, or as near as dammit @ "7\200 bilateral." This
info. courtesy of a naughty clerk at Warners head office, is headed
STRAIGHT for my next column. There's no doubt the rest of the
world is a blur to the poor guy. Defect correctible with specs, but still
disqualifies him for "extended active duty." [Roy] Obringer is fighting
to exempt him even from "limited service."

Has *Kings Row* reached England yet? Huge hit here, but don't
bother unless you enjoy watching coffee perk. Never seen so many
folks brewing up on screen! Could have used some myself to keep
awake. Dutch too nervous, straining at charm—the effort makes him
seem over-rehearsed. And he don't respond to the other actors.

Legless or not, he's getting almost as many fan letters as Errol
Flynn these days. Bette Davis wants his strong brown arms around
her in *Now, Voyager,* but she's gonna have to fight Annie Sheridan,
who's cast with him in *Casablanca.*

You wouldn't recognize your old *ciudad.* Ack-ack guns ringing
Mines Field, fake fields & villages sprouting on top of the Douglas
plant in Santa Monica, Sunset Strip as drab as an Amish buggy
trail—no neon, no Camel puffs—& all around town, after dark,
autos furtively feeling their way, with blue pinprick lights. . . .
Affec.—Paul

I was interested to hear that Dutch was so myopic. Vision pre-
scripted at "7\200" meant that a Japanese tank identifiable by normal

eyes at two hundred feet would advance within seven feet of him before he could figure whether it was friend or foe.

On April 3 Owen Crump sent a postcard of the White House, inscribed with annoying caginess, "Something I'm not at liberty to tell you about yet is going to involve Jack and yours truly directly in the war effort. We may both take a leave of absence from the studio."

A subsequent letter from Paul retailed the dope behind Owen's pomposity:

Buzz at "Bros." is that Jack Warner is going to be a Colonel!!! He flew off to Washington last month, *shvitzing* self-importance like a toad, to wheedle commissions out of Gen. Arnold for himself and Crump. Jack told Hap that what the Air Corps needed was "a very effective propaganda department" to stimulate recruitment by means of movies. What could be better than a special military production unit at Warners, headed by himself in full uniform? Cited as exemplars of the studio's patriotic idealism Dutch-boy's two RAF movies. Undertook to produce at least 6 big pics and 18 to 26 shorts a year—all inspirational & educational & instructional. Col. Jack's peroration must have brought tears to the CG's eyes: He allowed that no one in Hollywood dislikes him, "*outside of four or five thousand enemies!*"

Looks like he'll get what he wants—recruitment is a big problem for the Air Corps, and movies will help. Your taciturn friend O. Crump is already at work, writing an Air Corps quickie called *Winning Your Wings* for the Colonel-elect. I'll bet that when the unit's officially activated, Crump will be left to do all the exec. work, while squat Jack hops off to the golf links at Hillcrest.

Dutch's disqualification for active duty didn't stop the Cavalry from nabbing him anyway. Same job as you—liaison officer. He galloped out of town six days ago with enough bran in his saddlebag to get him as far as Fort Mason. Appropriately, Hal was just about to cast him as Buffalo Bill!!! Damn—I was looking forward to seeing our lad in a goatee.

"Button Nose" is by no means pleased. Ronnie's the *first* Hollywood actor with a child to be called, & as a working gal, Jane doesn't see why she should be the one left holding Baby Maureen. Financially, the suspension of his contract is a blow: they've only just moved into their "dream" house (9137 Cordell). Dutch kinda disconsolate: "I'm afraid *Kings Row* will come along only once in my life."—*Affec., Paul*

War Diary, April 30, 1942 [*North Weald*]

Still here with No. 121. Damp blustery spring weather. Shifting pools of iridescence on the runway. Routine ops. During the hour or so the boys were up, a smell of sheep on the east wind.

After lunch I escort a party of blotchy schoolboys round the hangars. "Please sir have you killed any Germans sir?" Then interview P/Os Daley & Skinner, who jointly splashed a JU-52 last week. Cannot face another mess dinner of cauliflower cheese & red dog, so cadge lorry ride into London. Sky clears as we bump down the Edgware Road. Citrus-yellow twilight. City looking sad, stripped: park gates & railings torn up for munitions. I go to see Phil Dunne's movie *How Green Was My Valley* at the Odeon. Magnificent, if sentimental. Depressed. I should feel joy for a friend whose gifts have been so splendidly realized, but feel only envy.

Dinner *solus* Eagle Club. Postcard from S.A., reminding me G. turns two on the 27th. Urges me to take home leave. Easier said than done, half a world away. John Mooney in the bar: no hope in hell that HQ would grant transatlantic (let alone transcontinental) furlough. Likely to be a belligerent spring for all sqs.

Mike Duff lifts me back to the 'drome. To officers' lounge for a nightcap—bunch of guys listening to *Kraft Music Hall* on shortwave. Who should be joshing his way through a lame skit with Bing Crosby & Mary Martin but "Ronnie Regan," as they insist on pronouncing it. Manage to scribble a bit of dialogue:

BC   Just what branch of the service are you going into, Ronnie?

RR   Well, after five years in the Reserve, Bing, I'm going to get a commission in the Cavalry.

MM   Oh, that's wonderful! You know, I think they should give every man in the army a commission.

RR   How could they give every man in the army a commission!

MM   Oh, it wouldn't have to be much. Just a little something—say thirty cents a Jap.

RR   Too many guys willing to do it for free!

Sometime in the late spring I heard from Paul that Dutch had gotten "tired of being used as a showpiece" by starstruck Cavalry brass in San Francisco.

At least that's the official reason. But he told George O'Malley, our mutual friend from Dixon days, that he felt "guilty" at seeing recruits shorter & scrawnier than his six-foot self marching up the gangplank at the Port of Embarkation. So he's applied for a transfer to Col. Warner's nascent film unit, headquartered guess where—Burbank!!

The anniversary of what Paul called my "defection" came and went, and I had my first acute attack of homesickness. We heard rumors that RAF and USAAF representatives were discussing incorporating the three Eagle Squadrons into the Eighth Air Force by autumn. But nothing definite came down from HQ, and we continued our dreary moves from field to field, sending out patrol after patrol after patrol. As a non-fighter, I never flew on any of these, but was allowed a Miles Master for liaison work, and so had liberty to spin across the annoyingly neat Southern Counties. "A shortage of sierras," my diary complains.

☯

One day I got this official-looking missive from Owen Crump:

ARMY AIR FORCES
First Motion Picture Unit
4000 West Olive Street
Burbank, California
July 4, 1942

Dear E.: I guess the letterhead says it. Call me Captain now. "Sir" would be okay too. Excuse long silence, but I've been helping Jack Warner (Lt. Col.) organize this unit. The above address will change effective Jul. 15—we'll be taking over the old Vitagraph studio at 1708 Talmadge. I'm writing to ask if you'd consider joining us.

Last Feb. 24 the Adj. General issued a directive proposing a motion picture unit, tabbed exclusively to the air force, right here in the heart of the industry. Its purpose initially is to aid recruitment, ultimately to make a whole range of training, P.R., documentary, combat camera films etc., using the best talent in town. Hap's all for it, in fact I think it was his idea. Jack flew to Washington to offer his services, came back a colonel, called me into his office, and said "Crump, you're going into the Army." My first urgent assgmt: to write the recruitment pic., *Winning Your Wings.* We made it in just 18 days! Lt. Jimmy Stewart starred. It's been a hell of a success—kiwis signing up by the thousand. Now my job is to bring the FMPU to start-up strength: 62 officers, 206 enlisted men.

Surprise: Ronnie Reagan (2/Lt.) arrived June 8 to help out. He actually saluted me. Still wearing his fly-slicer's uniform. I appointed him personnel officer, whereupon Jack sent him off to Vegas to do *Rear Gunner* (a sort of *Wings* for turreteers). So who's left to write all the letters? Me.

I've gotten a number of enlistment pledges, but mainly lensers and older directors and producers. Actors tend to be more leery, Ronnie promises to work on them when he's through shooting. Other than landing Eddie Gilbert, I'm pretty desperate for writers, esp. those who have a knowledge of aviation. Could be a break for you—work with top people, see your scripts produced, etc. We could swing a transfer through Hap's office. What say? *Best, Owen*

The idea of serving in a unit with Dutch as PO made me strangely shy, and I put off replying while I brooded about it.

War Diary, August 17, 1942. [*Biggin Hill*]
First time I've ever been wanted as a writer. Good career move, Owen thinks.

Funny how events shape themselves, with Eagles due to be absorbed into the Eighth Air Force any day now. I'm tempted, & yet, & yet—*Dutch.* Might have to be vetted by him—an intimacy I don't much relish. Work is bound to be dull. . . .

Atmosphere here not conducive to decision-making (squadrons nervous about Wednesday's big show over Dieppe). So after breakfast I fly to Hawkinge, chock Guinevere & ride a bike along the coast. White Cliffs nearly deserted—odd for midsummer. Haze over the Channel. To my amazement, I am privy to my first dogfight. A clash of sound rather than sight, the sky blindingly white-blue. I hear everything, see nothing until a small piece of airframe (theirs? ours?) slants through the blur & hisses into the dark sea.

The combat lasts about as long as a two-part Bach fugue, which it sonically resembles: alto & soprano pursuing each other in a grotesque counterpoint. *Fuga:* flight. But I cannot tell who is fugitive, who the attacker: Merlin or Daimler-Benz? Now one, now the other is in the ascendant. They try all the academic tricks: imitation, inversion, doublings back. At last there is a truly ominous unison, *molto crescendo,* which seems to herald a climax, but the fugue does not finish: the voices simply separate & fade away. Am left standing there with a feeling of confused irresolution.

☯

Eight weeks later, with nothing yet decided, I received another letter from Owen, via USAAF rush mail. He brusquely repeated his offer of a writing job, and there was a veiled threat in the next sentence: "Apparently, your units are now part of the Eighth Air Force." This was true enough: we had all, with conflicting emotions, just changed our uniforms from blue to olive brown. Owen continued urgently:

Please consider this offer and reply soon, because plenty of writers are calling and my quota is not large. Irving Wallace, Norm Krasna, Jerry Chodorov the playwright, Richard Baer producer of *Citizen Kane,* know any of them? Also Bernard Vorhaus, director, Roy Seawright, best special-effects man in town, Ted McCord camera whiz, and others. I intend the FMPU to be the absolute tops in talent and production capability—"about $200 million worth of talent on the hoof," as 2/Lt. Reagan jokes. Ronnie's helping bring in actors and producers. After a spell working in P.R. for Jack he came aboard as personnel officer effective Sept. 28.

Owen added with satisfaction that the FMPU had quit the Vitagraph lot for a much more sophisticated $3 million facility in Culver City. "It's at 8822 W. Washington Blvd., which you may remember as Hal Roach's studio—5 sound stages, theater, special FX building, open-air pool etc. Hal has leased to us at a nominal rate. Already wags are calling it 'Fort Roach.' " There was a casual postscript: "I'm now promoted to major and exec. officer, as Col. Warner will retire from active dy. effective Nov. 7, to be succeeded as C. O. by Maj. Paul Mantz."

My hero of the lighter-than-air Electra! From that moment on, repatriation and reassignment were mere matters of time.

War Diary, November 10, 1942 [*Great Sampford AFB*]
[Ultimatum cable pinned to page]: QUOTA NEARLY FULL STOP IMPERATIVE REPLY BY 2400 PCT TOMORROW STOP CAN ARRANGE TRANSPORTATION TRANSFER PAPERS THIS END STOP REQUIRE YOU REPORT FORT MAC-ARTHUR LOSANGELES NO LATER JAN FOUR 1943 END CRUMP O MAJOR EO FMPU AAF

I go to the mess this evening to brood about the above, & the radio broadcasts a triumphant speech by Churchill at the Lord Mayor's luncheon today. "Now this isp not the end. It isp not even the beginning of the end. But it isp, perhapsp, the end of the beginning." And with that last phrase I suddenly find myself lightened, chastened, purged of doubt.

☯

Before sailing for home, I had a long-postponed pilgrimage to make. It was prompted by the Prime Minister's announcement that at 9 A.M. on Sunday, November 15, all England's church bells—silent since the Blitz—might ring again, in celebration of El Alamein. I decided to go and hear Bell Harry.

Early that morning I put on my brown Yank uniform, hoping it would brace me against too much Pateresque nostalgia, tanked up the Miles Master at Great Sampford, and crabbed south, following the old Kent Road. I landed again at Hawkinge and hitched a ride to Canterbury, arriving shortly after eight. So I had plenty of time to revisit the King's School—which to my chagrin was boarded up and padlocked. A groundsman informed me that classes had relocated to Cornwall "for the duration." I strolled under the limes and arches, accompanied by a few inquisitive jackdaws, discovering with surprise that my memories of long ago were more sweet than bitter.

I became so absorbed that I forgot my purpose in coming, and the enormous tintinnabulation that filled the air at ten o'clock nearly made me pass out. Pigeons and starlings boiled into the sky; a plywood window filler, which I happened to be leaning against, vibrated down my spine like a drum. For the next hour invisible ringers leaped and plunged, saluting the End of the Beginning, and it seemed to me, as I stood there drunk with the joyful noise, that there would never be such music again.

14

Celluloid
Commandos

WHAT WITH CHRISTMAS LEAVE at Brown Orchards, and that annual
wake over the corpse of wasted time known as New Year's, I did
not report for induction at Fort MacArthur until January 4, 1943.

My fish-white body was the subject of much Angeleno mirth, when
I presented it to the medics for inspection, and I instantly became
known as "Moon-Tan." I dreaded that the nickname might precede me
to Fort Roach, where it was bound to attract the jocular attention of
Personnel Officer Ronald Reagan.

When I drove to Culver City on the twentieth, San Bernardino's sun
had at least re-Americanized my face and arms. It was not yet eight in
the morning, but I had the top down, and could feel the shadows of
passing palm trees as I cruised down West Washington Boulevard.
Sprinklers tossed their plumes over garden walls to rinse the sidewalks:
the air smelled deliciously of damp dust. An even sweeter smell came
over the windscreen when Helms Olympic Bakery ("Daily To Your
Door") loomed up ahead, all ports open, ready to release a fleet of
busy, fragrant little trucks. As before in boyhood, transferring from the
Old World to the New, I marveled at my country's careless prodigality,
its benign, perpetual hustle.

Railroad tracks sliced across the blacktop a few hundred yards further on, then the white columns of Hal Roach's old house rose across a sweep of lawn. Military barbed wire enmeshed both it and the nine-acre spread of studio beyond. A large sign emblazoned with the spread star of the Army Air Forces read FIRST MOTION PICTURE UNIT. I counted five large, shabby sound stages, plus a sprawl of lesser buildings. No doubt the smallest and hottest of these would be the writers' department.

The MP at the post gate shook his head over the flimsy I presented him, ordering me to report to the Personnel Officer at 0815. Lieutenant Reagan, he said, was conscientious about reporting for duty at 0900, and even more conscientious about leaving at 1700. Forty years on, the President of the United States would maintain the same compulsive routine.

I parked in the boulevard while a succession of more privileged cars swung into the gateway. Some were long and shiny, with Beverly Hills dealer plates. At the stroke of nine the MP beckoned me.

"Okay. That was your Loot in the La Salle. P/O is down there, in front of Stage One." Like all policemen, he pointed with his chin. "Second floor, first door after the fire extinguisher."

I walked over to the indicated building—a rough clapboard structure with running balconies—and stood for a moment looking down Fort Roach's main drag, dividing the sound stages. Hydrants leaked brilliantly onto its ancient cobbles. An invisible band saw screamed, spicing the air with cedar. There were few soldiers about; distant rhythmic tramping sounds suggested that most of the unit was at drill.

Bracing myself, I mounted the stairs to Dutch's office. The door was open, yet barred by an insect screen. With nothing to knock, I drummed my knuckles on the fire extinguisher. A voice—not his—bade me enter, and I was confronted by a clerical-looking sergeant.

As I handed over my transfer orders, I became aware of Ronald Reagan dominating a desk in the corner of the office. Over the years, I've often tried to find words for that quiet, palpable mass, at once majestic and unthreatening. It's not simply an aggregate of height and breadth. Many other actors I've known—George Montgomery and Charles Heston, for example—have been bigger men than Dutch, yet they lack his way of crowding one's horizon.

The mass, this morning, was so inert that I hoped he and Jane had been out on the town last night, and that drowsiness might cut our interview short. Glancing furtively, I saw he was absorbed in a thick typescript. I did a double take at the bars on his chest. They were bright silver and measured a full six inches across, the most extraordinary set of military hardware I had ever seen. Evidently he had been promoted to first lieutenant, and was not shy of advertising the fact.

The sergeant told me to sign and date some forms, "then take the whole folder over to the lieutenant." I braced myself, half crossed the room, and thumped to attention. The moment had come.

A more pompous man than Dutch would have waited before lifting his gaze, but he closed the typescript at once and smiled at me. A sudden brackish taste filled my mouth.

I saluted RAF style. He returned the gesture with an exaggerated snap that might have been different, but definitely wasn't "GI." His eyes, unspectacled, were strangely bright and staring. They did not refocus when I stepped forward to hand over my documents, but seemed to be fixed on an image I had left a few yards behind me, like a hermit crab's shell.

(Half a lifetime later, I would discover that Reagan, in early 1943, had been painfully adapting to a pair of newfangled contact lenses. They covered his entire eye, with a bulge over the iris, and had to be yanked out with a suction cup.)

Whatever the case, I felt *persona non cognita*, and gratefully relaxed when he said, "At ease." As he studied the sergeant's covering memo, I made out the title of the document he had put aside. It read:

THIS IS THE ARMY

There was no mention of Eureka College in my 201 tag file, but one entry made him pause, with a waggish glance at the sergeant. It had to do with my two years' readership at MGM.

"This is really a Warner Bros. outfit, you know," he said, and waited for us both to laugh.

He picked up a pen, then laid it down. "Any questions?"

"No, sir."

Dutch wrote in capitals, "*JANUARY 20—1943*" on the dateline of my pay book, then added his careful, characterless signature. As if this were not already legible enough, he clarified it in capitals too: *RONALD REAGAN 1st LT. AC, P. O.*

"Thank you, sir."

"Well—" He stood up and offered his hand. "Good luck!"

It was a precisely calibrated shake, neither languid nor too long. I stepped back, saluted, and marched out. As I passed by the window on my way downstairs, I noticed that Lieutenant Reagan was already re-absorbed in his typescript.

The first person I saw on regaining *terra firma* was Clark Gable, look-ing thinner than I imagined him, but handsome beyond reason in a major's uniform. He was walking out of the administration building with another officer, and to my amazement seemed to know me.

"Owen," I said. "I thought it was you-know-who."

Crump grinned, used to the confusion. "Obviously I don't mind, but it's tough on Clark."

Captain Gable might well have been flattered. Owen was one of those elegantly spare men born to wear a uniform. His tunic fit to creaseless perfection, not because he could afford Dutch's kind of tai-loring, but because his chest and shoulders were regular Army issue.

He introduced me to the officer at his side. "Paul, I think you gentle-men met when we were shooting *International Squadron.*"

Had Major Mantz been in flying overalls, I would have recognized him as the short stocky man who shook my hand so indifferently in the cockpit of that never-to-be-forgotten Electra, some twenty months be-fore. He returned my salute no less casually now.

I could see that he was already tired of the job of Commanding Of-ficer. If Owen was the model soldier (and Dutch the soldier model!), Mantz was an undisciplined flyboy, impatient of earthly restraint. That furrowed, where's-magnetic-north look, the cockpit slouch, feet sprad-dling at an angle suited only for rudder bars: everything about him protested the grounding Colonel Warner had forced upon him. I sensed his yearning to be back where he belonged.

[War Diary, Jan. 20, 1943]

Tour of "Fort Roach." *C'est magnifique, mais ce n'est pas la guerre.* Nearly 800 professional illusionists going about their business, as purposefully as they chased phantoms across the screen in peace-time—directors, cameramen, artists, writers, actors. An almost Latin contempt for Army codes of dress & deportment (Dutch seems to be the base dandy). I salute a bemedaled colonel, who promptly re-sponds with one finger. It's Eddie Foy in costume. Distinctions of rank sabotaged further by the socialism inherent in movie making—FMPU already a major studio, producing 8 pics per month. Owen vows to "militarize" it by spring.

After lunch he deposits me in the Writers' Dept—"home base of the Flying Typers." A 2-story, tin-roof, right-angle shack crammed with metal desks, 1920s-style Underwoods. I'm supposed to report to Capt. Vorhaus. Nobody about except (furiously tapping away) a sleek, pointy-faced porcupine of a man with pencils, red & blue, protruding from behind each ear: Irving Wallace.

Vorhaus drifts in. Vague manner, yet quick, lucid mind. "Crump says you're an aviation writer." "Well, hardly, sir—" But he is already scribbling an assignment sheet. "As you can imagine, we're short of men with your special skills, so I'm teaming you up with Sgt. Wald. Script on 'Use of Multiple Flotation Equipment.' Report back tomorrow."

☯

Forty-nine years later, when Captain Vorhaus had achieved a special kind of fame in Britain—mild, autumnal, in no way comparable to the wordwide blaze of Lieutenant Reagan's—I sat doodling notes about him in the restaurant of the Bel-Air Hotel in Los Angeles, waiting for Nancy Reagan to join me for lunch.

NR   (*arriving noiselessly in a cloud of Giorgio*) I hope that's the last chapter of Ronnie's biography you're writing.

EM   (*rising to kiss her*) Actually, it's notes about his best buddy from Army days. Bernard Vorhaus.

NR   Who? His best friend was Bill Holden.

EM   Not until much later. Ronnie never talked to you about Bernie Vorhaus?

NR   (*warily*) I don't believe so. (*To waiter*) Uh, Perrier?

EM   Writer-director. Very left-wing. He was blacklisted afterward. (*Stares closely at her, but she does not register.*) But there was a period, from about '43 to '44, when he and Ronnie talked a lot of politics, and appeared on political platforms together.

NR   Vorhaus. No, I can't say—

EM   (*carefully*) Well, somebody fingered him at some point and he got out of this country just ahead of the Feds. Kind of a tragedy, because he was a truly gifted director before the war. Taught the young David Lean how to cut. There's been an Edinburgh Festival retrospective—

NR   (*bored*) What did he direct?

EM   Low-budget thrillers, believe it or not. *The Ghost Camera—*
      Dusty Ermine . . . ah . . . (*losing her*) Wanna hear a limerick on
      his name?

NR   No!!

*She laughs richly. It is one of her charms, this easy, practiced response
to clumsy male humor. Camera holds on the two of them, she sitting
back, smiling, shaking her head (the coiffed curls do not budge), he
reaching for his wine.*

☯

[*War Diary, Jan. 21, 1943*]
  This morning I find a desk for me jammed opposite that of Malvin
Wald. Vaguely recall seeing him in commissary at MGM before the
war. Shy, kind, scholarly; jerky speech. Brother Jerry Wald, who co-
wrote *Brother Rat.* "Because of that, I'm one of the few writers Reagan recognizes."
  Dutch, apparently, has quite a temper. A few weeks ago Mal was
authorized to produce the scratch track of a short on mechanized
targets. Who should the narrator be but RR. "When I gave him instructions, he bristled & said, 'Look, son, I don't need a kid like you
to teach me how to read the English language.' "

Wald and I were halfway through our flotation script when Captain
Vorhaus re-assigned me to a technical revise of *Recognition of the Japanese Zero Fighter.* This top-priority project, starring Lieutenant Reagan and directed by Vorhaus himself, was spurred by an alarming
number of friendly-fire downings of P-40s in the Pacific. Dutch had already wrapped his role as a U.S. flier who nearly shoots down a colleague's plane after misidentifying it. (He was predictably effective in
scenes calling for puzzled, long-distance focusing.)
  To me, his dialogue with other officers had the correct yet somehow
unauthentic tone that lawyers detect in courtroom scenarios. The most
I could do was change one or two inaccuracies in the voice-over commentary.
  Script problems apart, *Zero* was a flawless little picture, a pioneering
example of the training film as art. Vorhaus managed to get a pristine
captured T-02, freighted posthaste from the Philippines, for the air-to-
air shots. Some lucky shortass (Mantz was too fat and I was too tall to
fit into the tiny cockpit) got to tumble it in the hot sky over the San

Gabriel Mountains. There it still spins on the screen, the most maneu-
verable fighter ever made, soaring and spinning with wings that alternately flash silver or darken, in parabolas as symmetrical as those of
Yin and Yang.

Ironically, Ronald Reagan's performance in the lead role cramped his
future career as a Unit actor. After viewing *Zero,* Owen Crump decided
that he was too famous a "face" for instructional purposes. "We're in
service to save lives, not entertain," he reminded us, and cut an order
banning "stars" from FMPU productions. Dutch was allowed one
more role—a small one—in *Land and Live in the Desert,* but after that
he never shot another frame for us. We saw much more of B actors such
as Arthur Kennedy, Van Heflin, George Montgomery, Lee J. Cobb, and
a boozy, irresistibly charming boy named William Holden.

Dutch was a remote, bureaucratic figure to the "above-the-line guys,"
as we writers, artists, and actors vaingloriously styled ourselves. As Personnel Officer, he seemed quite happy to stay on his side of the base, fil-
ing medical and disciplinary reports and affixing his patient signature
to pay dockets, furlough papers, and insurance-policy renewals. On
slow sunny afternoons, he could often be seen chatting to back-lot
types outside his office building. Unlike most FMPU officers, he was
democratic and showed no condescension to his beer-bellied audience.
Carpenters, grips, sound technicians, and warehousemen clustered
adoringly at the foot of the wooden stairs while Dutch, grinning and
graceful, towered a level or two above them, his thin lips wreathing.
Usually, he waved a talking point of some kind—a magazine or a newspaper—in his hand. I stood one day on the fringe of the crowd and
noted the experience afterward:

[*War Diary, Feb. 19, 1943*]
Dutch has discovered *Reader's Digest.* Reveres it as the sum of all
human wisdom, monthly added to. Its indiscriminate accumulation
of facts, whether sterile or significant, its braying religiosity, its vir-
ginal jokes & muscular Christianity arouse his simple wonder that
the world can be so ordered & decent, so endlessly interesting. Irv
Wallace says he's showing off—memorizes each month's issue before
it hits the PX newsstand.

The guys listen enchanted, while I stare in fascination at Dutch's
forehead. I have not noticed before how low it is, how heavy & con-
fining the thick fine thatch above. One gets the uneasy feeling that

only the smoothest, most processed grain can be blown into that shallow loft, & that once it reaches capacity it will compact & atrophy into something harder than bone.

I wish I had transcribed a sample of his spiel as I did many bits of dialogue at Fort Roach (still fantasizing a screenwriter career), but the truth is, Dutch was a bit of a drone. Neither then nor ever did he have a gift of phrase or quirk of view or original humor—let alone any insight, any indication that he *thought* about the things he took in—such as to make one reach for one's notebook. When he did say something memorable or simply funny, you could be pretty sure it was something he had read.

Rather than quote him, I quoted guys like Arnold Laven, a script clerk, talking about Jane Wyman's big round eyes:

It's 1938, I'm nineteen, I'm working in publicity at Warners, sorting photographers' proofs. Suddenly here's the pinup of all time. It's Jane, just an ingenue, and she's lying back sunbathing in this little swimsuit. With this *amazingly* gorgeous figure. What gets me is, she's got two white cotton pads on her eyes. Just big enough and round enough to cover them. They kinda detached her from her personality, like she was nothing but body. Lying there all warm with sun. I been dreaming of her ever since.

The first time I saw Jane at Fort Roach was when she came to watch Dutch play basketball—a new sport for him, made possible by his contact lenses. She had softened and darkened since I last saw her, peroxided and flat bellied, on the beach at Santa Monica. I thought she looked attractively tired, with a smudge under each wide eye. She sat with one trousered leg ankled on the opposite knee; her left hand patted it (how casually those we desire caress the parts we desire!), and her blood-red fingernails occasionally wandered to fidget with a little, white, peek-toe shoe. Dutch went to sit with her at halftime. They smiled a lot. But I noticed that he never really looked at her, only at us looking at them.

That night the Officers went down to the Enlisted Men, 66–24. No better than a good high school player, Lieutenant Reagan lacked the speed and toughness of his yardbird opponents. Yet there was an easy grace to his running, and his long shots (one swished through the hoop from at least twenty-five feet away) had the propulsion of a throwing arm that was totally relaxed in preparation and follow-through. He was top scorer for the Officers, with twelve points in the game.

"He never really looked at her, only at us looking at them."
Lieutenant Reagan and Jane Wyman at Fort Roach, January 1943.

On February 23, 1943, "the Colonel," as Jack Warner now insisted on being called, arranged for Dutch to be temporarily detached from service and returned to Burbank, where Irving Berlin's propaganda musical *This Is the Army* was in production. A joint patriotic venture of Warner Bros. and the War Department, it had already won extraordinary success as a stage show. Its profits were earmarked for Army Emergency Relief. We were amused to hear that our Personnel Officer had been cast as a writer, and was walking around the set with a thoughtful frown and a pencil behind his ear.

The word from Warners was that he was as garrulous there as at Fort Roach. Notwithstanding the poetical pencil, he had become an obsessive supporter of President Roosevelt's leftward swing, and his lunchtime dialogues with the conservative actor George Murphy verged on oratory.

"If that son of a bitch doesn't stop making speeches," Alan Hale complained, "he'll end up in the White House."

In my opinion, Dutch's politicization at thirty-two (if we discount his early doctrinaire Democratism and Red flush as *folies de jeunesse*) was stimulated by his recruitment into the Hollywood Democratic Committee. This radical, pro-FDR activist group was, I should emphasize, Communist-organized but not Communist-controlled. Despite its name, it was more interested in preserving a pro-Stalin government in Washington than in subverting movie production in Southern California.

I was not aware of any Communists at Fort Roach, although there were several gentlemen of the extreme left, including Bernard Vorhaus, who called themselves "progressives," a term I subsequently learned was the Party's code word for true believers. Bernie—a sweet, ardent, addled intellectual—was by far the most political guy on the base. Nobody more perfectly illustrated the theory of Whittaker Chambers, that Communism appeals to the brain rather than the heart. In particular, to the disorganized brain: Bernie's thoughts were so scattered, like iron filings, that he needed a magnetic field to bring them together. When he was writing or directing he became so abstracted that he had to be diverted from walking in front of trucks. At times when he was not creatively engaged, he was drawn to the constant, if weaker, polarity of Moscow.

Dutch and Bernie had a political intimacy in 1943 that I can compare only to that of Ronald Reagan and William P. Clark, Jr., in 1982–1983. Unlike that later relationship, it was founded on argument rather than mutual philosophy—an argument they, for the moment, clearly enjoyed. They even took to pooling rides in the La Salle. An undated scrawl in my diary for that spring reads: "Bernie V. says Dutch R. knows more about politics than any other actor in Hollywood."

☯

By April 1943, Major Crump's reorganization of the FMPU—or "Celluloid Commandos," as we were sarcastically called—was complete, and he was rewarded with a colonelcy. (Of course, Paul Mantz had to get one, too.) The post roster now numbered nearly a thousand men. In addition to the administrative staff, combat camera crews, and a flight echelon, there were separate departments for Animation, Art, Camera, Casting, Construction, Directors, Editorial, Film Editorial, Intelligence, Liaison, Personnel, Public Relations, Quartermaster, Signal, Sound, Special Effects, Stenography, Transportation, Wardrobe, and (last, in studio priorities) Writing.

The genius of Owen's plan was to establish a vertical agglomeration of the creative parts of this structure into one Production Department, while deluding Washington into thinking it was pure, horizontal Army. Each producer was responsible for as many as five projects in various stages of development.

We saw even less of Dutch under the new system, although he, as a member of Owen's "Executive Council," saw more of everything we produced. His responsibility was to comment on nuances of acting and editing. Owen told me that he was "always full of opinions," which he would articulate to the last syllable, even if they had already been voiced by somebody else.

[*War Diary, June 26, 1943*]
First anniversary of the FMPU. To the post at 7 P.M. for "Beer Bash" on Stage Five. Actually, a v. elegant affair: palm trees, South Seas cyclorama, 40-piece band, Dinah Shore. Feel spare in dress uniform without Sydney Ann (says she has to "teach tomorrow"). And tomorrow & tomorrow.

A thousand guys, most with dates. Girls wearing flowers or lace in their hair. Air sweet with Coty, Chanel. Paul & Terry Mantz, the former smashed as usual. Owen & Lucile: 2 slinky leopards. Irv & his disturbingly pretty wife Sylvia.

The most beautiful couple however Dutch & Jane. Together yet somehow separate. He uncreased, affably sober, monitoring some imaginary lens. She large-eyed, luscious, attentive to whoever addresses her. Loves to dance. Smiles over Dutch's broad back when she sees me staring. Am tempted (3 whiskeys) to cut in, but Jack Klock beats me to it. Dutch couldn't care less. "Go ahead."

Jack gets Jane to jitterbug. Now the whole room's watching. She scintillates in tightly tailored, sequined suit, her shoulders & boy's hips spangling, a black pillbox floating on her blonde curls. "Lookit that $5000 throat," Mal Wald groans. A big diamond trembles in the soft hollow of her neck, sending winks & flashes into our eyes. "She'll be a star one day," says Mal.

"Twinkling pretty good already," I say.

That midsummer eve in the middle of the war was the last night we all shared Dutch's happy certainty that hostilities would be over soon. Good news flashes came from the Mediterranean and South Pacific theaters, yet every retreat, every bitter surrender by Wogs or Wops or Jerries or Japs seemed to require incremental expenditures of blood and time. At home, wildcat strikes cramped war production. We did not need slide rules to figure out that at this rate most of us would be middle-aged or worse before we got out of the Army.

Professional doggedness set in as Owen Crump drove us to higher and higher levels of efficiency. Often we had fifty projects going at once, many of them super-secret. I had no clearance, but could divine through osmosis that a recent B-24 raid in Romania had been the worst disaster in the history of the Army Air Forces. Dutch (promoted now to Captain) and Bernie Vorhaus hastily canceled a pep talk on air power they were about to deliver jointly at community centers around town.

Our work sheets suggested desperate revisions of strategy and tactics at Command Headquarters in Washington. First there was a proliferation of #1 priority instructionals aimed at improving precision-bombing runs. I worked on a mysterious and beautiful little film about condensation trails, which I took to be a portent of high-altitude raids on Japan. Then Vorhaus brought me down to earth as technical consultant on a three-reeler, *Tactical Use of the CG 4A Glider.* Given the glider's performance specs, I concluded that an invasion, probably of Europe, was being planned.

So 1943's bright summer darkened toward a winter of uncertainties. Further gloom spread across the post when Colonel Mantz, boozy but beloved, returned to private life with what was rumored to be a "blue discharge." It related to some procurement scandal in the PX. Crump continued as acting CO until Colonel Roy M. Jones, another titular pilot, took over in mid-December. The latter's first official act was to appoint Captain Ronald Reagan Post Adjutant.

One might have expected Dutch to relish his new position. Since he now processed all classified orders, he was the best-informed officer at Fort Roach. He also wielded an influence far above his rank, on the principle that the man who controls the paper flow in a bureaucracy controls the executive branch. Yet an odd querulousness began to affect his demeanor around this time, combined with flare-ups of what I can describe only as moral passion. We heard that he had "almost gotten into a fist-fight" with somebody who made antisemitic remarks at a party in Beverly Hills.

"Ronnie's kinda sensitive about discrimination," Captain Bill Orr told me, repeating a recent conversation with the Adjutant. "He says, 'Bill, do you belong to Lakeside Country Club?' He knows perfectly

"He was the best-informed officer at Fort Roach."
Ronald Reagan in 1944 with Owen Crump (cigar) and fellow officers.

well I do, because he belongs there himself. I say, 'Yeah—good place to catch the eye of directors.' "

Bill was a handsome and ambitious actor, who would one day marry Jack Warner's daughter.

"He says, 'Ever see any Jews there?' I say, 'Jews? I dunno, why?' 'Well,' says Ronnie, 'it's restricted.' 'Restricted, how?,' I say. 'No Jews,' he says. 'I don't like that. We should give up our memberships.' 'Now *wait a minute*,' I say, 'my mother and sister love that place!' "

The record shows that Ronald Reagan did indeed resign from Lakeside, whereas Orr did not. Not only that, Dutch subsequently and ostentatiously joined Hillcrest Club, the favored locale of Beverly Hills Jews. I asked him in the White House if Jack Reagan's antidiscriminatory ghost had impelled this action, and he said no. "It just seemed the right thing to do."

Not all his behavior was righteous, though, during this period of strain. "Funny thing about Ronnie," Vorhaus said to me after a night out with him. "He kept telling dirty jokes in front of the women."

I was surprised: this didn't sound like Dutch. "Double entendres?"

"Single entendres. Gross stuff. He seemed to want to shock them. Finally one dame says, 'What's the problem, Ronnie, don't you fuck too good?' "

One day in early October one of our military policemen showed me a snapshot of Captain Reagan in costume at MGM, where he was again on DS, shooting an inspirational quickie called *For God and Country.* He wore a Catholic chaplain's white tropical cassock. I must say it suited him: there has always been something of the missionary about Dutch. "A really down-to-earth guy—fabulous," the cop remarked. But what struck me was the wistfulness of Dutch's smile.

Thanks to the wild success of *This Is the Army,* following on last year's *Kings Row,* he was now, incredibly, the top box-office draw in Hollywood, rating nine percentage points above James Cagney. Yet there was nothing he could do about it. At thirty-two going on thirty-three, Ronald Reagan had "peaked" as a film star.

Which might explain the furrowed eyes, the what-am-I-doing-here look. I have seen that same look on the faces of many screen actors between takes. It betrays their chronic loss of identity, re-emphasized every time the rush of Light and Speed and Action is "cut" from them. The spots snap off, the reels stop rolling. For an hour or an afternoon your poor player has to suffer the ordinary light of day, and the strains of unscripted dialogue. He does so with a sense of unreality, because to the actor, only artifice is actual. He yearns to be back where he belongs: On Set.

Maybe I'm reading too much into an old snapshot. Lieutenant Eddie Albert got the impression that what ailed Dutch was lack of warfare. While *For God and Country* was being cut at MGM, Albert was fighting with the Marines at Tarawa in a battle so savage he still gags to talk about it. "I got airlifted back to California," he says, "and dunno why, Ronnie was the first person I went to see. I had something for him." The something was a *netsuke,* tugged off the uniform of a dead Japanese. "I handed it over and explained what it was, and he was appreciative—but I've never forgotten the way he looked. Like I'd humiliated him."

When I asked Dutch about this incident in 1987, he interrupted me halfway through Eddie's surname. "Now, there was a soldier," he said reverently. "A Marine, you know. He fought in that—that great battle, and then he went back for more." An envious chuckle. "I was legally blind. Lucky to have been allowed to do what I did."

I don't want to give the impression that Dutch was a sad sack in the Army. In fact, he was consistently the best-tempered man on the lot, and, that strange hint of sexual frustration aside (which I would not mention if Hetty Vorhaus had not confirmed it), impressed us with his perfect manners. As a liaison officer for the Eagles I had had ample experience of what passed for manners in Britain, and found his to be entirely devoid of superciliousness or condescension. When business had to be transacted, he was quick, efficient, courteous. During sport he observed every rule without seeming to be a martinet, and on the rare occasions he drank with us, he could cuss with the best.

It's not generally known that his acting powers included an excellent ability to clown. Veterans of the FMPU still talk about "Ronnie's pissing mime," played against the mahogany panels of the Adjutant's office, wordless and economical of gesture, save for suggestive manipulations of his necktie.

First, he would imitate the Little Boy with bursting bladder, hoisting himself high on tiptoe. Then the furtive Adolescent, a copy of *Esquire* in hand, making vague masturbatory motions. Next came Mr. Regular Fella, who unzipped, peed, zipped, washed, and exited whistling. The Pansy followed, mincing up to the wall and ogling to left and right, while taking as much time as possible *in flagrante.* He was elbowed aside by the Athlete, who unfurled a prodigious member (here Dutch would use the full length of his tie) and hosed the mahogany with such force that he staggered in recoil. Then the wobbly Drunk, spraying everybody in sight. Finally and pathetically, the Old Man doddered in, fumbling at his fly buttons—oh but here it became cruel.

Did Dutch, I wonder, realize that he was making a ribald parody of the seven ages of man? Probably: he's not unlettered. What struck me about the performance, aside from the fact that it was extremely funny (one could laugh at such things in 1944), was his ability to go through vulgar motions and yet remain unvulgar himself. Only at the end of his sketch was grace compromised. He went all the way, as an actor must, but compassion cramped his movements, and as the laughter got louder and harsher, he began to hurry. I liked him for that.

Of all the productions of the First Motion Picture Unit, the most ambitious was Project 152, an immense, Q-classified series that Ronald Reagan narrated as Briefing Officer. I got special clearance to research it, if not to see the actual scripts. It occupied all of our best talents through the last year of the war. So sensitive was 152 that cleared project personnel were forbidden to discuss it even with one another, except in the confines of specialized "cells" of two to ten men each.

Our first indication that something extraordinary was on the schedule came on August 27, when Dutch was seen walking rapidly to the post gate, accompanied by three MPs. They fell in round a scared-looking warrant officer, whom we recognized as Jack Glass of Special Effects. He had been mysteriously missing for a week. He carried a large briefcase that—as they hustled him off to be debriefed—was seen to be chained to his person.

Glass, the aptly named optical cameraman who spent most of his time polishing, gimbaling, and weighting expensive lenses, had been summoned to Washington on the strength of his work on a series of Norden Bomb Sight instructionals. He had been asked by Colonel William J. Keighley, Chief of Motion Picture Services, HQAAF, if we could "make a relief model of Japan so real it'd fool even a Nipper pilot." His particular advice had been sought on whether such a model could then be photographed with a slowly moving camera for training films, "in such a way that when we send in our B-29s, every guy on board's gonna swear he's been there before."

For several weeks after that first delivery of air-surveillance shots, further consignments of Q-classified material flooded in from HQAAF, always under guard. But it turned out to be ludicrously outdated. Some maps went back to the 1920s.

It was plain to us researchers, as we swung into action on August 30, 1944, that we were going to have to amass our own intelligence, at high speed, if Project 152 Phase One was to meet its forty-day deadline. Colonel Keighley's formal directive was uncompromising: Special Effects must "reconstruct Japan in complete detail," on a scale of one foot to a mile. Every hill, every pond, every clump of trees and field of grain; every building, bridge, harbor, power line, road, and cemetery; everything a crow could see of Japanese civilization had to be duplicated. This prodigious task would call upon all of Hollywood's power of illusion.

We began by establishing Japan's own hard topographical foundation, rendered in the form of relief maps from the Los Angeles Public Library. These maps were traced by the Animation Cell onto plastic transparencies, then projected, from a floating Bell Optikon, onto a vast virgin baseboard that covered most of the north floor of Sound Stage Five. (Outside, twenty-four hours a day, military police and federal agents prowled.) Carpenters built up the contours, stratum by stratum, into hills and mountains, filling each step with clay, then sanding and sizing them smooth. A naked newborn land curved under their godlike hands. Perhaps their subtlest achievement, with the help of the Art Cell, was a saucerlike upcurve of the far terrain beyond the target area that simulated the actual distortion of perspective. This enabled us to contain our model within the sound stage's four walls. Had Colonel Keighley's directive been followed to the letter, we would have had to construct a hangar over the whole of Fort Roach.

Dutch clearly looked forward to narrating the Ota run, which, if successful, threatened to flower into at least thirty different films. He was fascinated by our Lilliputian landscape, vegetating and urbanizing itself in Sound Stage Five, and stopped by often to watch Special Effects at work. I remember his quietness as he stood at the edge of the plat, a folder of documents in one hand, both arms hanging motionless from his broad, sheen-shirted shoulders.

Our modelers, too busy to salute him, carefully trod the spray-painted hills in burlap socks, reconnaissance photographs in hand, bestrewing tiny trees, farms, villages, and toothpick temples. They stuck green crumbled latex onto the rainy side of mountains and draped lamb's-wool mists across the carpet-pile reeds of enamel lakes. Downstage, Tokyo's malignant mass spread daily wider. Every house, every brothel and factory and fisherman's shack was carved out of balsa cubelets or ply or plaster. Whole neighborhoods were gerrymandered on sheets of glue-soaked netting and laced with silken power lines. No props were too eccentric if they served a visual purpose. Dry ice-cream toppings sprinkled along city streets gave an excellent effect of traffic. I saw Roy Seawright plucking his eyebrows to make a wrought-iron bow-bridge. Some SOB filched my last Turkish cigarette from England, and wove several perfect, if pungent, haystacks.

Next came the artists. They lay prone on low suspended platforms, with trays of pigment and number-nine brushes, daubing rooftops and shop fronts until their eyes watered and their chests wheezed. ("Land of the Rising Fumes," one of them called the model.) Every one of the thousands of ripples lapping Yokusa Naval Base received its individual fleck of sunlight. Patches of flowering weeds spread along piano-wire railroads, and industrial dumps leached yellow poison into watercolor streams. I thought the artists painted with an overbright clarity until I realized that they were deliberately not painting shadows: the Lighting Cell had undertaken to cast real ones once principal photography began.

Our cameramen and their boys, meanwhile, constructed an immense wheeled deck that straddled the whole model at a height proportionate to that of a B-29 overflying at thirty thousand feet. It was motorized to truck forward on soft rubber tires at an equally reciprocal speed. I must admit that I lay on that deck many times, bravely piloting my own Super Fort at an altitude of ninety-seven inches, airspeed 6.66 feet per minute. When, forty-two years later, I flew with President Reagan to the Tokyo economic summit, I looked down on Japan with distinct feelings of *déjà vu.*

"Been here before?" my seat neighbor asked.

"Yes," I said. "Sort of."

I can still hear Dutch intoning the Ota script under his breath, check-ing his timing, the day Bob Creamer's camera platform began its first slow roll over our finished model. And not just in memory either. I have fragments of that narration, re-recorded on August 18, 1988. Ronald Reagan never read a cue line that didn't engrave itself permanently on his vinyl mind. "My voice was pointing out the targets and all," the Commander in Chief whispered, more to himself than me. "My voice said, 'Bombs away!' "

Tiny sticks of TNT exploded silently in the depths below the Oval Office.

I wish I could say that the love (there is no other word) we lavished

on our model, and the miraculous verisimilitude of our films, had a signal effect on the course of the war in Japan. The truth is, all our "runs"
were keyed to a strategy of high-altitude precision bombing, and that
strategy proved ineffective in winter rains and mist. Captain Reagan
dropped his imaginary bombs in vain.

We did what we could to compensate. We re-shot each run through
veils of dry ice fumes, and when recce photographs disclosed certain
areas of damage, the carpenters conscientiously vandalized their hand-
iwork, and we shot yet again. Dutch narrated himself hoarse on audio,
while couriers set up a regular shuttle of reels back and forth between
Culver City and Saipan, until General Curtis E. LeMay, admitting failure, reverted to prehistoric tactics of fire and surprise. He sent in three
hundred stripped, incendiary-crammed Twenty-nines on March 9,
1945, and inflicted upon Tokyo what remains to this day the greatest
holocaust in military history—more lethal than Hiroshima and Nagasaki combined. Four weeks later, they were still dragging corpses out
of the ash.

☯

[*War Diary, March 18, 1945*]

Today, WB announces that Dutch & Jane wish to "share their
good fortune" with somebody less fortunate, & are adopting a baby
boy. This cutesey Special Order comes out of the Adj.'s Office:

[*stapled to page*]

HEAVENLY HQ

MICHAEL EDWARD REAGAN IS RELIEVED FROM ASSIGNMENT AND DUTY
WITH PRESENT STATION AND IS ASSIGNED TO THE REAGAN BASE UNIT,
9137 CORDELL DRIVE, HOLLYWOOD, CALIFORNIA. DUTY ASSIGNMENT,
"SON AND BROTHER." RATIONS AND QUARTERS WILL BE PROVIDED.
TRAVEL BY STORK AUTHORIZED.

☯

By the time President Roosevelt died on April 12, 1945, I was no longer
at Fort Roach. Our latest CO, Colonel J. K. McDuffie, had appointed
me liaison officer to an FMPU historical unit touring U.S. air bases in
Britain.

I heard from one of my Project 152 colleagues that Captain Reagan
had taken the news flash from Warm Springs particularly hard:

That weekend I had to stay over at the base, and Ronnie was Duty Officer. Saturday afternoon the whole place was empty. I saw him coming down Main Street, past Stage 2, with his head down and slowly shaking. He seemed really stricken, like he had a migraine. When he looked at me I saw he was in despair. "Oh sergeant, I don't know what's going to happen to this country."

An even more sobering letter from Malvin Wald reached me on V-E Day. I read it in London, to a triumphant blare of sirens and voices singing in Trafalgar Square. Reports had already reached Britain of the atrocities at Bergen-Belsen, but I hadn't pondered the details, and was in no hurry to. Now Mal told me that an FMPU combat-camera unit, headed by Owen Crump, had entered Ohrdruf and Buchenwald just ahead of Eisenhower, and seen things human eyes should not have to see. Their lenses, at any rate, remained cold. The raw color footage was flown back to Fort Roach for cutting, preparatory to screening at the Pentagon, and Dutch as Adjutant had arranged a "preview of it" for all cleared personnel:

> In the projection room Col. McDuffie took the seat of honor and next to him were Bob Carson and Ronnie Reagan. I was up front with a few other enlisted men. Together Bill [Graf]'s footage took us on a journey out of reality, into hell.
>
> We saw gaunt emaciated living skeletons, wandering around like lost souls in some kind of purgatory. Some of them stood naked and shit where they stood. We saw a skull complete with face sliced in half like a melon (so the camp doctor could study the special conformation of the Jewish brain). If my grandfather from Krakow hadn't emigrated here ninety years ago, that might have been mine. We saw stacks of cured and flattened human skins. The commandant's wife had selected inmates with colorful tatoos [sic] to be killed and flayed for lamp shades. I guess these were the rejects. Somebody told Bill Graf that she liked skins with large nipples, because of the pleasing aureole effect when light shone through them. We saw—I don't want to tell you what else we saw. It makes me want to puke, even now. When the lights went on, I felt chilled to the bone as if I were in an ice house. I feared I was going to freeze and smother at the same time. I had trouble swallowing and desperately needed water and warmth. I rushed out into the sunlight and looked around to make certain I was not dying in Germany but was here alive, in Culver City.
>
> The others shuffled out of the projection room more slowly, like men who had seen ghosts. Reagan was strangely silent, buried in

thought. It was if [*sic*] we had attended a mass funeral, and that in some way we were the ones that had died.

Graf subsequently collected some of the most graphic of his footage into a production called *Lest We Forget*. I managed to avoid this terrible testament for nearly half a century, and thus never guessed the true depth of Dutch's "strange silence" that day. Having seen it at last—and been sick for days afterward—I heard from Dutch's sons Ron and Michael (the adoptee heralded above) that each of them was made to sit through *Lest We Forget* when they turned fourteen. "Dad seemed to regard it as an essential rite of manhood."

I wish I'd known that on May 5, 1985, when I saw him emerging gray-faced from the induction center at Bergen-Belsen, and persuaded myself he'd never really "understood."

Our historical unit remained in Britain through the summer, conscientiously recording life on the great bases even after Japan surrendered and our notes became academic. I applied to Dutch's office for early release, on the basis of previous credits as an American Eagle, but heard nothing from him. Mal wrote to say that the Adjutant was in virtual command now, since most of our senior officers had scrambled to get out. "Can't figure why he hasn't been promoted. But you know Ronnie—never complains."

By the end of August, Captain Reagan was gone too—relieved from active duty pending demobilization. My recall in late September was signed by Dutch's deputy. I was ordered to proceed directly to Fort MacArthur on arrival in Los Angeles, there to receive my termination papers. So I did not go back to Fort Roach—not then, not for another half lifetime. When I finally did, it was with Owen Crump, ramrod straight at eighty-eight, still the sentimental Exec of the First Motion Picture Unit.

"You won't like what you see," he warned, as we cruised down West Washington Boulevard. "And what you see you won't recognize." He was wrong on at least some counts. The same lank palm shadows stroked our windscreen, and—*mirabile dictu!*—Helms Olympic Bakery loomed up unchanged. Its ports were closed, however, and it released no busy, fragrant little trucks. Three hundred yards farther on, the same old railroad tracks sliced across the blacktop, but their steel was dull, and weeds grew thickly between the sleepers. No sweep of lawn lay ahead, no white-columned administration building stood aloof, no barbed wire protected the shabby splendors of the Eighteenth U.S. Air Force Base. Where once we worked with love and passion to perfect the model that filled the frames that trained the pilots that dropped the bombs that destroyed the empire that Nipper built, four festooned lots proclaimed the logotypes of Culver City Mazda, Culver City Nissan, Culver City Honda, and Culver City Mitsubishi.

15

The Regeneration
of the World

LAKE ARROWHEAD glimmers in the San Bernardino Mountains sixty miles east of Los Angeles, like mercury in a cupped hand. It spreads among narrow forested valleys, almost but not quite flooding its namesake village at five thousand feet above sea level. Incense cedars spice the air, and the surrounding "Rim of the World" creates a pleasant feeling of isolation. Sails bend across the bright water. There is a white beach (where, narrowing my eyes, I can still see a small, dark, five-year-old boy playing) and a pier where you can rent a speedboat by the hour or by the week.

Today the little lake is rendered almost inaccessible by freeway gridlock. Half a century ago, Ronald Reagan, fresh from the army, had no trouble driving out from Hollywood in a couple of hours. He had a generous new Warner Bros. contract in his pocket, guaranteeing him $150,000 annually for the next seven years, and comforting instructions from the boss: "Just relax until we find a good property for you."

He had decided to do his relaxing at Lake Arrowhead that September because Jane was there, shooting *The Yearling* on loan to MGM. She, Maureen, and little Michael welcomed him in a summer house just vacated by a wealthy Angeleno. Other members of the Metro company, including Gregory Peck and June Lockhart, had similar quarters nearby, on secluded estates with private docks. They visited one another by water, and dined at home rather than have to deal with vacationers in the village.

Reagan was thus spared the immediate reality of post-war economic dislocation, which was more apparent in resorts like Lake Arrowhead than in flatland cities still flush with wartime spending. I went up there with Gavin (it was less than twenty miles from Brown Orchards) and was reminded of Depression days. Gas rationing had killed the village's economy. Its *faux*-Norman arcades were splintered and sagging, service was slow in the only hotel, and the steepled pavilion, where big bands used to play, had become a bleary cafeteria. The lakeside square was a drab sea of military uniforms. Men without women came here to get drunk, await discharge, and adjust to the anticlimax of peace.

At thirty-four, Ronald Reagan was by his own standard "well fixed," with a beautiful wife, two pretty children, and more than one and a half million dollars coming in before he next had to worry about the future. Aside from his myopia and a few allergies, he was in superb physical shape; if the reports of Army doctors were to be believed, he had grown taller in the service, to six foot one and a half. One might say he was almost anesthetized by good fortune—that, in proletarian parlance, "he didn't know that he didn't know." Or as he afterward put it himself, "I was the calm vacant center of the hurricane."

There was indeed a hurricane brewing in American society in the early fall of 1945, close enough to shiver the waters of Lake Arrowhead. Like all such disturbances, it was caused by unsettled conditions, hard to analyze at first. Those of us who had to make do on less than six figures were conscious only of vague loss and gloom. Say what you like about the pre-war decade, it had been a time of clear alternatives. You worked or you starved. Industrial monopoly was bad, individual enterprise good. One kind of girl "did"; the better kind didn't. You loved the New Deal, or you hated Roosevelt's patronizing guts so much you spun the dial on his fireside chats. "Negroes" minded their manners, or picked cotton.

This social equipoise was now disintegrating. Black GIs, returning stateside from French whorehouses, furtively ogled your wife. Every business page in the *Los Angeles Times* seemed to bring news of corporate retrenchments or strikes by swelling, truculent unions. Inflation threatened personal savings, and jobs were scarcer than before Pearl Harbor. Marxists preached that man was a perfectible animal, but the evidence from Buchenwald and Bergen-Belsen was that he was an animal only.

Creative intellects sensed that something fundamental had fallen apart. Jackson Pollock's meaningless explosions illustrated without explaining the nihilism of Hiroshima. Scribes began creating anti-heroes with names like Yossarian and Kowalski. Those of us who sought answers in religion and music had to take into account the pusillanimity of the Pope and the terrible beauty of Furtwängler's Wagner. What finally did it for me was the news that Project 152, that thing of intricate loveliness on the floor of Sound Stage Five, had been destroyed. Trivial as that might have been in comparison with the destruction of Dresden, I felt as if youth had finally died.

Reagan admitted to being bored and restless at Lake Arrowhead when Jane was working. He began to make a model of the U.S.S. *America.* The soothing busyness of his hands (looping and spooling, pinning and painting, stretching sixteen tight little tarpaulins over sixteen miniature lifeboats) encouraged a rare spell of introspection.

He had plenty to brood about. Age, for one thing: he could not help noticing how much publicity Warner Bros. was giving young actors like Robert Hutton and Zachary Scott, while he was so unctuously told to "relax." Image, for another: Max Arnow seemed to be seeking a sedate part for him, while his fellow veterans Wayne Morris and Gig Young had already been cast in heroic, back-from-the-war roles.

Jane, moreover, was showing unmistakable signs of moving ahead of him professionally. All the time he had been in uniform, she had worked hard at being a good "Warners girl." In reward, Jack Warner had lent her out for two parts that any ingenue would kill for. The first was that of the enabling girlfriend in Billy Wilder's *The Lost Weekend* (just about to be released, to rave advance reviews). The second was her current, much larger role, Ma Baxter in *The Yearling*—the most ambitious Technicolor extravaganza since *Gone With the Wind.* Dutch now found himself living with a pallid, empty-eyed, washed-out woman who seemed to be nursing some secret grief.

He told me that Jane *in medias res* "would come through the door, thinking about her part, and not even notice I was in the room." I detected a note of envy in his voice. Ronald Reagan the performer never had that kind of possession—although he flattered himself that he got into the skins of George Gipp and Drake McHugh. His basic lack of interest in character, his bland, blind, hail-Everyman equableness denied him the leap of belief that constitutes real acting. This did not make him, generically speaking, any less a thespian than Jane. But it did mean that he would never achieve catharsis, as long as he confined his act to Hollywood.

"All I wanted to do," Reagan has written of his sojourn at Lake Arrowhead, "was to rest up awhile, make love to my wife, and come up refreshed to a better job in an ideal world." He added sadly, "As it came out, I was disappointed in all these postwar ambitions."

At the time he was less disillusioned than lacking any immediate sense of personal or political direction. He still glowed with the "near-hopeless, hemophilic" liberalism of his late identification with Franklin D. Roosevelt, and thought he could best express it through a new, *echt*-Rooseveltian organization, the American Veterans Committee. Even before leaving Fort Roach, he had signed up as chairman of the AVC's Hollywood membership board.

I still have the ugly little pamphlet he sent each veteran of the FMPU. It is replete with cartoon soldiers and half-naked cuties brandishing glasses of champagne. "NOW . . . WHAT DO YOU WANT?" the headline screams. According to the body copy, what we wanted more than cuties and carousing were jobs, houses, and security for our children. These entitlements were best assured by joining the AVC, which unlike other vets' groups did not dwell nostalgically on the glories of armed service. It looked forward to "a system of private enterprise in which business, labor, agriculture, and government work together to provide full employment and full production for the nation."

"Let me tell you, I was impressed with Reagan," the AVC's founder told me many years later. Gilbert A. Harrison was then the retired editor of *The New Republic,* and a fellow biographer. "We had some big names on our national planning committee—FDR Jr., John Hersey, Michael Straight—but Ronnie wasn't about to be pushed into joining. I've never known a man ask such careful, probing questions before agreeing, after long thought, to give us his support. It was as if *he* were recruiting *me.*"

The support, once given, was total. Harrison said that what Dutch liked about the AVC was, first, its determination that the bad old days of isolationism and relief would never return, and second, "my idea of expanding the Committee into an international lobby under the aegis of the United Nations, working to contain the A-bomb."

Both men were gratified to see the national enrollment rate rise to twenty-five hundred a week. Dwight D. Eisenhower signed on, as did such other celebrated vets as Bill Mauldin and Audie Murphy. Reagan was personally responsible for at least two hundred new members.

☯

For me too, the fall of 1945 was a season of marital reassessment. Sydney Ann had undergone a strange personality change after the birth of our son, and become increasingly *innig,* as her favorite composer Schumann would say. She lost interest in concertizing, resigned from the Los Angeles Philharmonic, and during my service in Britain more or less resettled with Gavin on her father's citrus ranch. I had grown used to commuting there every weekend from Fort Roach.

Now Redlands University, flush with new students under the GI Bill, offered her an assistant professorship in the music department. To my distress, she abandoned her daily viola practice (those surges of dark-gold sound that made me feel we still had something to share) for drink and endless ruminations about academic affairs. We no longer spoke of the possibility of her coming back to town. It was tacitly agreed that we would live as weekend man and wife. I got to keep the Santa Monica apartment.

☯

Shortly before dawn on Friday, October 5, I was awakened there by a call from Philip Dunne. "There's going to be big trouble at Warners. I only just heard. It's something we should see."

He was talking about a strike by set decorators, which had been simmering since the spring. All I knew was that a plug-ugly former painter, Herbert K. Sorrell, had called the strike against all major studios in defiance of wartime industrial regulations—gambling, apparently, on its becoming post-war Hollywood's first major labor victory. Sorrell, a rumored Communist, had managed to affiliate both decorators and cartoonists with his own painters' union, and was now president of what he grandly called the Conference of Studio Unions.

"Wear shoes you can run in," said Dunne. "I'll stop by at five."

The urgency in his soft voice was galvanizing. He was just back in Los Angeles after two years working for the Office of War Information.

Now more than ever, he was the best-connected writer in town, with a circle of acquaintance that ran all the way from East Coast high society to Southern California's grubbiest labor locals. If Phil said that "big trouble" was in the offing and worth seeing, one would be foolish not to be on hand at the time appointed, with a thermos of hot coffee.

"I'm glad you thought of that," he said, accelerating along the deserted Strip with Irish disdain for red lights. "And you'll be glad I thought of these." He gave me a lapel badge reading *SWG OBSERVER.*

I protested that I was not a Writers Guild member.

"Better be one today, unless you want Jack Warner's goons to think you belong to the CSU. Or worse still, have Herb's conclude you're a scab."

He proceeded to explain, as we drove on east (the black ripple of the Verdugo Hills paling and furring), that the CSU "posed a real threat" to the IA, or International Alliance of Theatrical Stage Employees— the crafts union preferred by producers and actors.

"Not to mention the Mafia," Phil added. "Although Roy Brewer's begun to clean the IA up. The bad old days of Willie Bioff are over. But it's still a company union, and Roy and Jack are very thick."

I asked why he had used the word "goons."

"Because both sides are spoiling for a fight, and they've recruited professional spoilers. Last night Herb told the CSU to—and I quote— 'pick out one studio and hammer it good.' The rank and file were pretty clear which studio he had in mind."

Warner Bros. was the biggest motion picture production center in the world, so Sorrell, I surmised, must be a rash man—or a stooge backed by secret powers with plenty of roubles.

"I'm afraid what we're going to see this morning," Phil said gloomily, "is the start of a general assault on the Four Freedoms, now that Roosevelt's gone. You yawn. But of course—you voted for Dewey."

We swung north over the hills, and I struggled to pay attention as his soft voice droned on about seventy-seven set decorators wanting to transfer from IA Local 44 to CSU Local 1421. Or was it forty-four from Local 77? Phil assured me that the issue of the current strike was one of the most lethal in labor politics: "jurisdiction." Just as empires went to war over scraps of territory, so did unions (in this case, two union coalitions) fight for the right to affiliate the smallest band of brothers.

"What's at stake is the entire post-war power structure in Hollywood. You see, the studio bosses believe that if these decorators get away with it, other IA unions might wander off the plantation too. That would spell the end of paternalistic management."

I could understand why the prospect of such a diaspora would traumatize Jack Warner, or for that matter Phil's boss, Darryl F. Zanuck. Hollywood's block of craft workers was huge, anti-centrist, politically unstable—everything that the monolithic and authoritarian Association of Motion Picture Producers was not.

"Jack's a very nervous guy," Phil said, "when he thinks there are Reds under his bed. Just how nervous, I think we're about to see."

"Is Herb Sorrell definitely Red?" I wanted to know.

"I suspect he was once, but he isn't now. He's a decent sort, in my opinion. Smart, too—that's why he's chosen to hit the bricks in Burbank. Warners is way beyond Los Angeles police control. No Red Squad here. No 'Red' Heinz."

Reds. Red bricks. Lieutenant "Red" Heinz—the LAPD's most notorious Commie-basher. We were all beginning to talk red, see red wherever we looked. Even Phil, mildest of men, flushed angrily whenever he described the defection of Communists from his pre-war anti-fascist alliance. His long pink fingers would pluck agitatedly at the drape of his trousers, and his freckled face turn the color of a coho salmon.

Day was breaking over Cahuenga Peak as we crested the pass and descended toward Burbank. Warner Bros. lay brooding in foothill shadow, its broad frontage along Olive Avenue still pricked with streetlights. We could make out a dark mass of men milling outside the big west gate. "I think we'd better park this side of the river," said Phil. Leaving his little Crosley out of sight, we strolled as casually as possible over the bridge and up the opposite sidewalk to where a smaller crowd of observers and press stood smoking and checking their watches. It was about five to six. Just then, a dark-blue Lincoln came down the avenue and headed straight for the studio gate.

I had lived three decades and been through a war without yet seeing mass violence. It erupted now, with amazing rapidity, even as we walked the last hundred yards, and my first reaction was surprise at the absence of uproar. Almost silently, the Lincoln came to a halt amid the mass of men, hesitated, then rolled over on its left side like a small, obedient elephant. There were no shouts, just a few muted cheers as a picketer in a veteran's uniform reached through the passenger door. He seemed apologetic. Hurrying, we saw why: the man he helped out was a studio police officer. But three hundred determined faces warned the cop against any forceful reaction.

Clearly this incident was but a prelude. We stationed ourselves outside a juke joint across from the gate. The streetlights flicked off. "Clock-punching time," said a reporter, checking his watch. As he spoke, a black coupé and a big pale Plymouth cruised north on Olive and, swerving in front of the felled Lincoln, tried to enter the studio at about ten miles an hour. They, too, were quietly met, lifted, and laid on their sides, at angles designed to block any further approach to the gate.

There ensued some hours of gathering tension, of which I remember little except hunger unappeased by thermos coffee. A CSU sound truck blared Earl Robinson's lugubrious labor songs.

Our side of the boulevard became almost as populous as the other, as a swelling crowd of IA workers got ready to cross the picket line. By noon, there were at least two thousand rival unionists facing off in brilliant sunshine. The overturned cars remained on their sides, grotesquely stable amid minor skirmishes. As if responding to a secret signal, two large squads of Glendale and Los Angeles police arrived from opposite directions. So much for Sorrell's theory that Warner Bros. would be left alone by outside cops.

Suddenly, two jets of water burst from inside the gateway, with such hissing force that several picketers were knocked over. One jet slammed against the coupé's chassis, almost rolling it onto its roof. Now the suppressed bedlam broke out. Yells and pitched bottles greeted IA members as they surged across the boulevard. A Los Angeles squad car switched on its siren and accelerated up Olive Avenue, tires screaming. Four or five bystanders were buffeted aside as it slid to a halt in front of us. The ensuing *mêlée* was Keystonian. Cops jumped out, nightsticks flailing, only to be blasted by the same indiscriminate hoses, while the sound truck's loudspeakers blared over and over: "*STAND FAST AGAINST THE WARNER BROTHERS BRAND OF LIBERAL-ISM!*" The slick street surface reflected all this mayhem upside down, to such ludicrous effect that I found myself laughing, until Phil said, "Here comes somebody who doesn't think it's funny."

A big man with squint eyes and a boxer's nose was striding up our side of the street, accompanied by several bodyguards. They wore white union armbands, which gave them an oddly wounded look. Flashbulbs popped. A female reporter called out, "Mr. Sorrell . . ." but the big man ignored her. He faced directly into the spray and began to walk toward the gate, hunching his shoulders, planting his feet purposefully as the jets combined their fire. He advanced like a Highland caber tosser, bent against the water column that threatened to collapse his chest. Some shining canisters bounced down from the studio roof and lay smoking on the wet blacktop before him. A photographer said, "Jesus, are those grenades?"

We all scattered. Sorrell stood pressed against the spray, staring stupidly at the canisters. Then he seemed to lose all sense of direction. He put his fists to his eyes, as though weeping, and staggered at an angle toward the tree where I had taken cover. I saw a woman with a black eye embrace him and heard her say, "Herb, don't cry. We will give them hell before we get through."

Then something intensely cruel and stinging struck my own eyes, and I could do nothing but choke and run. Where Phil went I neither knew nor cared. Tear gas does that to you. So does the *ssss-THOK* of tire chains whipping around heads, leaving neat tiaras of blood, and the sound of nightsticks breaking bones, and the surgical glint and swish of hacked-open tin cans.

☯

In an early demonstration of his genius for being above the fray, Ronald Reagan remained at Lake Arrowhead through the nineteen days of violence that followed Burbank's Black Friday—violence bloody enough to shut down Warner Bros. production. It ended in a Pyrrhic victory for the CSU, which had its right to affiliate reaffirmed by both the National Labor Relations Board and the American Federation of Labor. However, as will be seen, the AFL's arbitration award was worded clumsily enough to guarantee even worse violence in 1946.

Phil and I have often joked about witnessing the first pitched battle of Hollywood's Cold War, while "Ronnie sat in the clouds building toy ships." Reagan has always been defensive about the slowness of his reaction to events down below:

> What I heard and read in the papers placed me on the side of the strikers. I was then and continue to be a strong believer in the rights of unions, as well as in the rights of individuals. I think we have the right as free men to refuse any work for just grievances: the strike is an unalienable weapon of any citizen. I knew little and cared less about the rumors about Communists.

That last disingenuous claim does not jibe with his pre-war interest in the Party, his political intimacy with Bernard Vorhaus, nor his avid scrutiny of *Reader's Digest*, which was already warning of Soviet expansionism and infiltration. Reagan knew what the Reds were up to in the fall of 1945. He simply thought there were more immediate threats to America's stability, and wanted to fight those. It is hard to question the sincerity of:

> The results of my weeks of freedom crystallized a determination in my mind. I would work with the tools I had: my thoughts, my speaking abilities, my reputation as an actor. I would try to bring about the regeneration of the world.

His earlier bewilderment after President Roosevelt's death ("Oh sergeant, I don't know what's going to happen to this country") had cleared to a perception of problems that the New Deal had largely ignored. Chief among these, he decided, were neo-fascism and race prejudice.

They lay dead ahead of the ship of state, pale shoals in a newly calm sea. Happy portent, that the model in his hands should be named *America*! Less happy was the consciousness of how intricate she was, and how fragile, for all her mass and streamlined design. Somewhere on her gleaming decks surely, maybe even on her bridge one day, was a navigational role for him.

Ronald Reagan used to claim that as soon as he came down from his mountain, he set about "blindly and busily joining" every liberal orga-

"Somewhere on her gleaming decks . . . was a navigational role for him."
Ronald Reagan's model of SS America, *1945.*

nization he could find. In fact, he devoted himself to only three, all of which he belonged to already: the AVC, SAG, and a reconstituted version, still in the process of formation, of the Hollywood Democratic Committee.

He was content at first with boardroom and back-room work, not venturing any public political opinion until December 8, when he appeared at the Santa Ana Municipal Bowl and made a short but strangely moving speech. The occasion was "United America Day," held to protest some ugly outbreaks of hostility in California against returning Nisei veterans. General Joseph W. Stilwell had made a personal pilgrimage to Santa Ana to honor the memory of a dead, slant-eyed American hero, Staff Sergeant Kazuo Masuda.

Ranked about "Vinegar Joe" on the dais were the Masuda family, fresh from wartime internment, and a variegated party representing at least nine subcategories of the national census. Ronald Reagan, wearing uniform for the last time, handsomely projected a Caucasian rosiness that no depth of suntan could darken.

The general spoke first, and barked a fierce eulogy in praise of GIs of whatever ancestry who were willing to make "a fair exchange" of life in defense of freedom. When Reagan's turn came, he simply thanked Mr. and Mrs. Masuda for their son's sacrifice. Then, looking out over the half-empty arena, he declared, "The blood that has soaked into the sands of the beaches is all one color. America stands unique in the world—a country not founded on race, but on a way and an ideal. Not in spite of, but because of our polyglot background, we have had all the strength in the world. That is the American way."

These four sentences, which launched him on his career as articulator of public hurts, were all he said, and all that needed to be heard. He never surpassed them in sincerity.

On January 17, 1946, Jane Wyman wrapped her role in *The Yearling.* Meanwhile, Warner Bros. informed her husband that *Stallion Road,* the "good property" that Jack Warner had finally found for him, was being downgraded from Technicolor to black and white, and would not start production until spring.

Gracious as always, Reagan showed neither envy nor chagrin. Not that *Stallion Road* was much to look forward to, being the story of a young horse doctor dying of anthrax. At least he had further time to help "save the world." Action seemed more urgent than ever, as unemployment lines lengthened across the nation, strikes paralyzed General Motors, General Electric, and Big Steel, and ugly camps for homeless veterans sprouted on the manicured lawns of UCLA.

To begin with, he wrote an article for *AVC Bulletin* expanding on the theme he had sounded at Santa Ana. His piece, published on February 15, noted that Gerald L. K. Smith was preaching hatred of Jews and Catholics, and that one new veterans' organization accepted only white Gentiles with firearms. "Native fascism" might yet bring about the downfall of democracy:

> One of the reasons I inflicted myself upon you as a guest colum-nist is because I believe this is a great menace, and is closely aligned with part of the present attack on labor and price controls. It is the obvious hope of home-grown fascists that runaway inflation with its resultant depression and army of unemployed would give the hate-mongers the fertile field necessary to realize their dream of a strong-man government in America. . . . World War III, for your son and mine, would then be a certainty. . . .
>
> I think the AVC can be a key organization in the preservation of democracy for which 300,000 Americans died, and because I have at-tacked the extreme right does not mean I am ignorant of the menace of the complete left. They, too, want to force something unwanted on the American people, and the fact that many of them go along with those of us who are liberal means nothing because they are only hitching a ride as far as we go, hoping that they can use us as a vehi-cle for their own program.

Ronald Reagan thus publicly endorsed the AVC's draft constitution, which was "liberal" enough to satisfy a Swede. It called among other things for peaceful coexistence with the Soviet Union, cession of Amer-ican nuclear power to the United Nations, full employment and a min-imum wage, comprehensive national health and education programs, protection of strikers from compulsory arbitration, abolition of all dis-criminatory laws, minority rights to sue for slander, and federal en-forcement of civil liberties.

Not content with his column in the *Bulletin,* he went further on Feb-ruary 26 and allowed his name to appear in the Communist *People's Daily World.* A group called the Los Angeles Committee for a Demo-cratic Far Eastern Policy included him in an advertisement that de-manded the abandonment of Chiang Kai-shek, and the "liberation" of British and Dutch Indonesia. Beady eyes took note of Ronald Reagan's new affiliations, and began to assemble a file on him.

It was during these same early months of 1946 that some of the nation's most powerful institutions, including the Justice Department, the FBI, both chambers of Congress, and the conservative press, began to close ranks against what Attorney General Tom Clark called "a sinister and deep-seated plot" to subvert the United States Constitution. The alleged conspiracy by "Communists, ideologists, and small groups of radicals" included the coordination of strikes to cripple free enterprise, agitprop inserts in radio and movie scripts, attempts to foment racial unrest, infiltration of government departments, and the alienation of youth by socialist professors.

Ronald Reagan, dreaming his "liberal" dreams, failed to see any Communist conspiracy at home or abroad. He was deaf to the "Red Reports" of California State Senator John B. Tenney, a purse-mouthed paranoiac obsessed with campus Marxism, and paid no attention to the dire, almost daily alarums of Westbrook Pegler's newspaper column. At a time when I was transfixed by Albert Maltz's attempt to humanize Marxist literary theory (the squabbling of political intellectuals has a curious dry entertainment value, like sex among iguanas), Dutch was preaching the values of home equity to little old ladies in Santa Monica.

Not until April 26, when he attended the AVC's state convention in Los Angeles, did he notice with amazement that a tiny, well-organized minority of Communists manipulated the entire proceedings. "They even succeeded in having the words 'Private Enterprise' struck from the paragraph reaffirming our support of the Statement of Principles!" he wrote to Charles Bolté, chairman of the National Planning Committee.

> I will defend to the death the right of Communists or anyone else to belong to the AVC but . . . I think we will add strength to the entire liberal cause if we publicly re-affirm our belief in our present *form* of govt. and our belief that our present *ills* can be cured within the framework of democracy.

He confessed that he did not like to be identified with the AVC's most radical chapter, but felt he could not responsibly resign merely "because about *six* known party members are beginning to bed down there." And he was prepared to take the consequences: "I am still being called a Red in certain Hollywood circles."

The word *still* is significant. It suggests that Reagan had known for some time that his liberalism was a liability. For a few more weeks he remained bravely loyal to his Hollywood chapter. Lacking parliamentary guile, he found himself at a loss to combat the tactics of the Communists and their allies, the "progressives." They tricked him by relocating one meeting to a hall so small that the minority, crowding in early, made itself a *de facto* majority. Introducing the guest speaker at a luncheon conference, he was embarrassed to hear a recital of Stalinist tenets that were instantly adopted and passed. By June 14, when delegates flew to Des Moines to attend the AVC's first national convention, the entire Los Angeles area council was under Communist control.

Bolté urged Reagan to come to Des Moines as a moderating influence, but *Stallion Road*'s production schedule prevented him. I often wonder what might have happened to Dutch had he gone. The convention turned out to be a brutal ideological confrontation, ending in defeat for the Red insurgency, but destroying the AVC's sense of solidarity. At very least, the experience would have accelerated what Dutch afterward called "the slow awakening of my faculties."

Nevertheless, awaken they did, to a world so unredeemed as to call into question everything Roosevelt and Churchill had stood for. The Pentagon admitted that it had incinerated countless innocents at Hiroshima and Nagasaki. Fascism was recrudescent in Spain. Socialism threatened the exquisite civilizations of Italy and France. Stalin invaded Iran and demanded a military presence in Turkey. Britain's Raj seemed determined to self-destruct. Sheeted men rode rampant through the streets of American cities. Throughout the industrialized West, strike after violent strike paralyzed what was supposed to be peace.

Modern Screen noticed "a touch of desperation" in Dutch's current behavior, as if he was struggling toward some new reality beyond film, beyond the shibboleths of liberal politics. The public role he had pondered in the mountains was not yet mastered. He wore the necessary costume—boxy suit, studious spectacles—awkwardly, and when he addressed his favorite subject, totalitarianism, he sounded out-of-date, almost quaint: "Wars are never over for the German High Command." For all his earnestness, he still thought of hinself as an actor, as some Democratic operatives discovered when they asked him to run for Congress. "Heck, no, I couldn't do that—I'd be the subject of criticism as a politician."

In short, Ronald Reagan was going through an identity crisis. After almost a year out of the Army, he could not bring himself to order a letterhead. "My personal conversion to civilian life isn't quite complete," he admitted, on a sheet that bore the crossed-out imprint JANE WYMAN.

Then, on July 2, he attended his first meeting as an executive coun-
cilor of the Hollywood Independent Citizens Committee of the Arts,
Sciences, and Professions, improbably known as HICCASP.

☯

He joked that the name sounded "like the cough of a dying man," but
he took HICCASP seriously as the logical peacetime successor to the
HDC. Its membership was stellar, its finances flush, and its benevolence
embraced everything from support of the United Nations to the rights
of rehearsal pianists. If Communists constituted an appreciable minority of members, that was only to be expected in an organization that
sought to represent all of Hollywood and a good chunk of Southern
California.

"Lots of people here I didn't think I'd see," he whispered to Dore
Schary, a producer for David O. Selznick. There were sixty-two men
and women in the room. They represented the cream, or in some cases
the curds, of Hollywood activist society. Among them Reagan recognized James Roosevelt, eldest son of the late President and HICCASP's
chief political strategist; Olivia de Havilland, its prettiest spokeswoman; Dr. Linus Pauling, representing the sciences; Artie Shaw of big
band fame; John Cromwell the director, Howard J. Green the composer, and several socialistic scribes, including Ring Lardner, Jr., John
Howard Lawson, and—natty, owlish, chronically constipated—Dalton
Trumbo.

Ideologically, it was as broad a spectrum of opinion as could be
squeezed into a Beverly Hills salon. Dutch saw himself as just left of
center, nearer the cagey equivocations of a Roosevelt than the outright
radicalism of a Lawson. He had hardly settled into his seat before he
sniffed a conspiracy to manipulate the proceedings in order to provoke
a capitalist/Communist showdown, like that which had nearly wrecked
the AVC.

This time, however, the spoilers were moderates. Cromwell presented
for "open discussion" some allegations by members that their organization was being "controlled by the left." Roosevelt at once unfolded
his full six feet four inches and called upon the Executive Council to
issue a resolution in favor of democratic principles. For a start, it might
endorse the Preamble to the AVC Constitution, as recently adopted in
Des Moines.

The room at once erupted in angry debate. Reagan, boggling, heard
Artie Shaw declare that if constitutions were to be endorsed, that of the

Communist Party was "a lot more democratic" than the Bill of Rights. One of the scribes (he forgot who) jumped up to shout, "If United States imperialism leads to war between us and Russia, I will be on the side of Russia." Insults were leveled at the Truman Administration's "imperialist policy," and one leftish lady became so excited that she was carried out with a purported heart attack.

Olivia de Havilland and several other non-Communists spoke in support of Roosevelt's resolution, which specifically promoted private enterprise. When Reagan added his own voice, he was bombarded with hissy epithets by friends of the common man. "Fascist!" "Witch hunter!" "Capitalist scum!" Lawson was particularly vituperative, behind a long, accusatory finger. But moderates had a majority.

In the sour anticlimax that followed adoption of the resolution, both victors and losers agreed HICCASP needed a more explicit statement of its "policies and program." With its huge membership and inchoate ideology, part New Deal, part post-Yalta, it had grown into a sort of Spruce Goose of good intentions, too ill-balanced and fragile to stay airborne without ideological trim. It should address itself in particular to the coming congressional campaign, the first in fourteen years likely to be dominated by the Republican Party. Reagan found himself appointed, along with Roosevelt, Pauling, Trumbo, and Lawson, to a seven-man committee that would draft such a statement and report back to the Executive Council.

Three nights later, this disparate group huddled and squabbled in Roosevelt's house. Reagan struck the others as detached, even bored, although it was he who came up with a text that they all agreed to consider.

Still a procedural *naif,* he did not sense the secret stresses to the left and right of him. The ambitious Roosevelt, worried by HICCASP's eclecticism, was actually looking for an excuse to resign, in order to become chairman of the Democratic State Committee. Trumbo and Lawson, in turn, were disconcerted by the political opportunity Roosevelt's departure would present. If they objected to the democratic tone of the draft statement, they could be sure that Roosevelt would resign. This would strengthen their power within HICCASP, yet at the same time they would be seen as provocateurs of the son of Stalin's greatest ally.

Reagan's quietness during the committee debate possibly reflected shock at the way the Communists reacted when he suggested that the final statement, when approved, should go to all members of HICCASP for ratification. Lawson snapped that the rank and file was not "politically intelligent enough" to vote on anything so fundamental as a set of principles. For many years, Dutch would recall the sound of that phrase, with its unmistakable, shivery overtone of totalitarianism.

A consensus was eventually obtained by the insertion of enough borrowed boilerplate to swell the statement to fifteen paragraphs. In went the Four Freedoms and Tripartite Declaration of 1940. Thus amended, the statement was accepted on July 10 and recommended for publication in HICCASP's next brochure.

Reagan did not notice that the Tripartite Declaration artfully papered over his original clause condemning Communism. Only when James Roosevelt resigned anyway, followed closely by Olivia de Havilland, did he realize that the Spruce Goose's veer to port could not be corrected. On July 23, he strapped on his own parachute.

But he did not jump—not for several more months, when it was plain that there was going to be a crash. In subsequent accounts, he has said that he resigned "by telegram" the same night as Miss de Havilland did. The wire has never been found, nor is the resignation noted in any surviving minutes. On the contrary, we find Ronald Reagan nominated to HICCASP's new Standing Committee on Labor more than a month after his fellow liberals left.

Is he merely misremembering? A simple truth lies behind his talk of resignation telegrams—truth he felt it prudent to conceal. Reagan remained at HICCASP at least through October 1946, in what Miss de Havilland delicately refers to as the capacity of "an observer."

16

Star Power
A Dialogue

FOUR DECADES after Ronald Reagan's disillusionment, I came across a letter he had written about it, to Hugh Hefner, of all people. It was patriotically dated July 4, 1960, and appeared to have been prompted by Hefner's decision to allow the long-blacklisted Dalton Trumbo to write for *Playboy*.

Hot anger drove Dutch's pen across six large sheets. Perhaps I should say cold anger, because the sentences were lucid, unmarked by the slightest erasure or second thought, to a degree unusual by even his holographic standards. The letter impressed me so much that I drove out early one evening to Philip Dunne's place in Malibu and read it aloud to him and Amanda. They sat in their Eames chairs, silhouetted against the violet sea, listening to the passions of the past.

> *I question whether I can write in a way that will make sense to you. . . .*
> *Because so much doubt has been cast on "anti-communists", inspired by*
> *the radicalism of extremists who saw "Reds" under every "cause", I feel I*
> *should reveal where I have stood and now stand.*

"Stage left, moving to stage right," Phil twinkled. Amanda shushed him.

Following World War II my interest in liberalism and my fear of "neo-fascism" led to my serving on the board of directors of an organization later exposed as a "Communist Front," namely the "Hollywood Independent Citizens Comm. of the Arts, Sciences, & Professions." Incidentally, Mr. Trumbo was also on that board [with] John Howard Lawson and a number of others who have since attained some fame for their refusal to answer questions. . . .

How can I put down in less than book form the countless hours of meetings, the honest attempts at compromise, the trying to meet dishonesty, lies and cheating with conduct bound by rules of fair play? How can I make you understand that my feeling now is not prejudice born of this struggle but is realization supported by incontrovertible evidence that the American communist is in truth a member of a "Russian American Bund" owing his first allegiance to a foreign power?

Phil shifted his long legs uncomfortably. "Strong stuff, that. And just not true. Even Reds like Trumbo loved the United States."

"Reagan calls them 'swimming-pool Communists.' "

" 'Bathtub Communist' would be a better description of Dalton. He wrote best when he was literally steamed, up to his tits in hot water and scribbling on a pad in the soap tray. Now there was a *real* pinko!"

"What Reagan's saying is, he realized in July 1946 that the extreme left of liberalism is as undemocratic as the far right of fascism."

"Keep on reading. I'm intrigued to note that our President was once able to express himself in English."

I, like you, will defend the right of any American to openly practise & preach any political philosophy from monarchy to anarchy. But this is not the case with regard to the communist. He is bound by party discipline to deny that he is a communist so that he can by subversion and stealth impose on an unwilling people the rule of the International Communist Party, which is in fact the govt. of Soviet Russia. I say to you that any man still or now a member of the "party" was a man who looked upon the death of American soldiers in Korea as a victory for his side. For proof . . .

"Excuse me interrupting, but you can't possibly defend that remark. That's sheer bigotry."

"I don't defend it. Reagan was not a tolerant man in 1960."

"Was he ever?"

I hesitated, aware of Dunne's ironic stare. "He's *personally* tolerant to a fault. He finds it almost impossible to dislike people, although I grant you that's because he's not interested in anybody as an individual. He was *politically* tolerant, I think, right through the end of the World War II. He loved arguing politics with Bernie Vorhaus, and Bernie was as red as a jar of borscht. But then, as Joseph Heller would say, something happened."

"What? Did desperate Dalton try to recruit him into the Russian-American Bund?"

"No, but in '46 both the AVC and HICCASP went pink on him. Then in the fall the labor situation in Hollywood broke down again. Things got really ugly, and Reagan became a Red-baiter almost overnight." I continued to read.

> For proof of this I refer you to some of the ex-communists who fled the party at that time & for that reason, including some of Mr. Trumbo's companions of the "Unfriendly 10"—

"Wait a moment," Phil said. "Before he sounds off about the Hollywood Ten—where was Jane Wyman in all of this?"

"Well, there was a party that fall where Ronnie lectured everybody in the room about Communism, and Jane whispered to a friend, 'I'm so bored with him, I'll either kill him or kill myself.' "

"Ah," said Dunne. His cheeks twitched mockingly beneath their high bones. "Now we know why he started to pack that shoulder holster."

"Ronnie went armed? Whatever for?" Amanda asked.

"He received an anonymous threat after the CSU went out on strike again," I said. "On September 24, when he was shooting *Night unto Night* for Owen Crump. Gets called to the phone, and this voice says, 'There's a group being formed to deal with you. They're going to fix you so you'll never act again.' Meaning acid in his face."

The former exquisite ingenue winced. "Kind of call that gets an actor's attention."

"Even so, he didn't take it seriously until studio police licensed him a loaded .32 Smith & Wesson."

"I hope Ronnie doesn't imagine Trumbo made the call," Phil said. "Dalton was intellectually mean, but physically harmless."

"No. He's convinced it was one of Herb Sorrell's goons."

"You're going to have to help me. I got distracted by congressional politics after our expedition up Olive Avenue. Another CSU lockout, wasn't it, in September '46?"

"Frankly, Phil, the whole craft-union situation in Hollywood those years was so Byzantine, only Reagan's kind of intelligence could sort it out."

"*Intelligence?*"

"The trouble with you Harvard snobs," I said, laughing in spite of myself, "is that you measure IQ in terms of culture."

"No—in terms of curiosity and retention, neither of which Ronnie has. All he wants to know is what's on TV tonight."

"Mock him if you will, but I've never known anybody with such an ability to reduce a situation to its simple essence. And simple is not necessarily simplistic. Isn't this the most complex country on earth? We need somebody in the White House who can divine our common—"

"*Divine?*" Dunne pounced on the pomposity. "Are you imputing mystical ability to a man who thinks Rimbaud is Sly Stallone?"

"I mean a President who *feels* what power is, and doesn't have to compute it from poll figures."

"So what did Ronnie 'divine' after the acid threat?"

"That a clear and present danger threatened the entire movie industry. Which was your opinion too in 1946. Although you say you weren't paying much attention." I pulled a photocopied article from my briefcase. "Here's Philip Dunne writing in the July issue of *The Screen Writer*—a magazine edited by one Dalton Trumbo."

Tilting the sheet toward the setting sun, I read: " 'We must be awake to the fact that this is not true peace, but only an uneasy truce. Tomorrow, next week, next month, another crisis may burst upon us, as suddenly and as devastatingly as the last one did.' "

"Now I know how poor Ronnie feels when you zap him with essays he wrote in college. But that was an accurate prophecy. The 'uneasy truce,' as I recall, was a temporary victory for Herb Sorrell."

"Accent on *temporary*." I attempted a Dutch-style simplification. "Herb thought he had won big—won his decorators, won the right to affiliate any IA union, won more money and more job security. But the uneasiness you felt—the danger that Reagan saw—was that it wasn't a victory really, more like a weak internal arbitration by the AFL."

"Ah, yes. Three labor leaders, wasn't it? The 'Three Wise Men'?"

"Right. Who came from the East and settled the jurisdiction, just before Christmas. Their names were Doherty, Knight, and Birthright."

Dunne shook with silent amusement. "Ronnie probably remembers them as Gold, Frankincense, and Myrrh."

"What he remembers is that the language of their directive was vague—vague enough for Jack Warner and the other studio heads to stall for six months on a contract that would allow major IA unions to switch to the CSU. Like Big Bill Hutcheson's carpenters."

"Now *there* was a labor force to reckon with," Dunne said admiringly. "Three million mallet-swingers across the country, all willing to crack skulls in behalf of any brother. Solidarity in sawdust."

"By then Reagan was on SAG's special strike committee, and even he agreed with Big Bill that the Three Wise Men should issue a 'clarification' of their December directive."

"Oh—I'd forgotten. The infamous Clarification."

"It *tried* to clarify two words in the original directive, 'construction' and 'erection.' "

"Was it the last word Ronnie didn't understand?"

We laughed and laughed. Amanda rose. "I think I'll go and start dinner."

☯

Since sunset, the Pacific had dulled to blue-black. Its southern edge stained the sky's translucent bowl, like ink rinsing from a fountain pen. "*Ätherblau!*" I said.

We sat for a while in deepening dark. It was Dunne's lifelong habit to end the day thus, ignoring lamps until his features were invisible, and talking so softly I had to lean forward to hear him.

"Excuse me, Phil?"

"If memory serves, the Clarification clarified nothing."

"Well, the Wise Men ruled, and I quote, on August 16: 'The word *erection* is construed to mean assemblage.' That differentiated it from 'construction,' or the actual building of constituent parts of a set. It was a decent compromise that permitted the studios to hire both CSU carpenters and IA grips. Again, Sorrell thought he'd won."

☯

Amanda called us in to eat. I saw with a pang how old Phil looked as he bent his long body forward to spear, tremulously, a minute portion of fish.

"If I remember rightly," he said, "the producers were deliberately plotting with Roy Brewer and the IA to ignore the Clarification and break the CSU. Meanwhile, your amiable friend Ronnie was persuading the Screen Actors Guild to cross Herb's picket lines."

"It wasn't quite that conspiratorial. Roy and the producers maybe, but on September 11 Reagan did try to talk Herb Sorrell out of another strike. Shortly after that, he got the threat to fix his face."

"Herb was protesting 'hot sets,' wasn't he? Wonderful phrase."

"Meaning?" Amanda asked.

"The producers," I told her, " 'created an incident' by ordering CSU workers to touch up some sets the IA had built in defiance of the Clarification. So out they all walked and began overturning cars. Just like old times! Except now it wasn't hose water that was splashing around. It was sulphuric acid."

"September you say," said Phil, musing. "That was when we were launching our congressional campaign, and word went around Democratic headquarters that Ronald Reagan had suddenly swung to the right. And had become the man to watch."

"Yes, he was up for election as third vice-president. And by the way, the very next morning after his nomination, a vicious attack on his war record was published in the *Hollywood Reporter*. Eddie Albert and Bill Holden came to his defense, but that plus the acid, and the gun, would make any man angry."

"Leaving aside for the moment," Dunne purred, "your interesting correlation of conservatism and anger, let me say that I never blamed the actors for crossing the CSU lines. All the unions involved belonged to the AFL. SAG simply declined to take sides in a jurisdictional dispute between co-equals. We stayed clear ourselves in the Writers Guild— although Dalton said we would fry in fascist hell for our cowardice."

"Oh, Dalton was such a phony," said Amanda. "He would dye only half of his mustache—anything to get attention. Was crossing the line difficult for Ronnie?"

"All he will admit is that it was dangerous. The actors were driven through studio gates in Tanner buses with all windows closed, and told to crouch out of sight. Those days are branded on his brain. He says the buses left from different points every day for security. One morning, he showed up late for pickup, and to quote his punch line, 'The bus was still burning when I got there.' "

I helped Amanda carry plates through. When I returned, Phil was staring absentmindedly at Dutch's letter, which lay where I had left it.

"I just thought of something," I said. "Reagan's real emergence as the future president of SAG, and you might even say the future President of the United States, was on October 30, 1946, when he delivered the keynote address at a mass meeting of SAG in Hollywood Legion Stadium. It must have been a *déjà vu* experience for him."

"How so?"

"I'll bet he felt he was reliving the circumstances of his first speech at college. That was also an emergency meeting held at night, and the agenda was strike policy. On both occasions, he had to articulate something he'd only just begun to comprehend. He'd been a freshman student in 1928; he was a freshman board member now."

"Articulation without comprehension," Dunne murmured. "That about sums him up."

"No it does not," I said, irritated. "Give the guy credit for *fifty years* of articulating his own thoughts, before he ever got to the White House. You should see his speech manuscripts, every paragraph figured out, every word written by hand—"

Phil apologetically pushed his chair back. "*Touché.* I withdraw my wisecrack. You were telling me about the keynote address . . ."

"He took great trouble over it, studying the whole history of Hollywood labor reform going back to 1913. He wanted to prove that SAG had never involved itself in craft-union disputes. And he'd rehearsed it in the best way possible, by gate-crashing a gathering of radical actors at Ida Lupino's a few days before. They all booed and hissed him, as Trumbo and Lawson had at Jimmy Roosevelt's."

"I'm not surprised."

"Now, just as he's getting used to the feel of a rod under his arm, he steps to the podium of the stadium, and sees three thousand other faces staring up at him. Practically every star in the industry is there, from Dietrich and Sinatra to Bogart and Bergman. Pretty 'heady wine,' as he would say."

"Did he repeat his remarks at Ida's?"

"Yes. Only this time he went on for an hour and a half. At least, it seemed that long to Adolphe Menjou."

Amanda Dunne reappeared with a coffee tray and headed toward the now pitch-dark sitting room. Her husband hurried ahead to give her light. As I reconfigured myself to the Eames sofa—an awkward task—I wondered if I should read them any more of Dutch's letter. But flicking forward to page five, I saw the sentence *Hollywood has no blacklist,* and decided not to. Phil wore a pacemaker, and such a statement, even if it was twenty-six years old, was enough to raise his blood pressure dangerously. I reverted to Hollywood Legion Stadium.

"Would you be interested in what the President said when I asked him about that speech in our last interview?"

Phil sighed. "By an uncanny coincidence, I suppose, you happen to have the tape cued in your cassette recorder."

Dutch's unmistakable silvery baritone floated into the darkness.

RR   After I made that speech—everyone was out there, booing and yelling, and, well [*chuckle*], about half a dozen of the huskiest

guys you've ever seen just stepped up to me and I thought,
"Whoa, whaa—?" And they said, "We'll take you to your car—"
They were Teamsters. They said they had just heard some
threats, and they'd see to it that I got to my car all right.

I pressed STOP. Phil said, "Is that all you're going to play?"

"Well, he goes on and on about typical Party floor tactics, like the
'diamond formation' and those delaying motions designed to bore
everybody but the faithful into going home before the final vote. It
didn't happen that night, though. He says he'd finally learned to beat
Commies at their own game. There's a bit near the end that might interest you. I'll fast-forward."

RR   . . . and so I said, "The meeting is adjourned!" (*Laughing*)
EM   You know, sir, Robert Stack says that after the mass meeting you
      all went to Trader Vic's, and he told you, "You have an obligation
      to do something for this country." And you said, "Tell you what,
      when I run for President, you can vote for me."
RR   I might have. I don't recall.

"Notice the sudden loss of warmth in his tone," I said, pressing the
PAUSE button this time. "He doesn't like any questions to do with ambition. Always insists that he 'had to be dragged kicking and screaming'
into office."

"Actors hate to audition. They want casting directors to call up and
beg for their services."

"Exactly. Listen to this—"

EM   Mr. President, didn't you consider running for public office in
      1946?
RR   You know, Bob Cummings used to say this all the time, right in
      front of me, "One of these days I'm going to vote for you to be
      President," and I'd laugh it off and so forth, but he did keep say-
      ing it! And I have to say, *never* in my *wildest* dreams did I ever
      consider seeking public office . . .

I faded his voice out and snapped the machine off. There was a long
silence. "Nice night outside, Phil, if you want to do any stargazing."

He made no move. "You've managed to achieve the impossible," he
said slowly. "You've got me more interested in Ronald Reagan than in
searching for Jupiter."

"*Searching for Jupiter.* I might just call my book that!"

"How so?"

"Well, it's an attempt to fix on a large, diffuse, amorphous object with a huge gravitational force."

Phil pondered the metaphor.

"I assume the mass meeting was a whopping victory for your friend?"

"More for Robert Montgomery and Franchot Tone, actually. They were his seniors on the SAG Board, and his speech was their basic policy. He did carry one smart resolution that the vote be conducted by mail, since actors were so vulnerable to physical reprisal. The result was 2,748 to 509 in favor of continued neutrality."

"Well, bully for Ronnie," said Phil, standing up and stretching. "Let's go out and relate him to the larger scheme of things."

☯

Malibu's December air was as clear as any telescopist could wish. The dark bulge of Phil's hill, sloping to ravine and beach, screened off lower lights, and the mountains behind us the rising moon. Above, the zodiac prickled. I gazed at it and felt the usual—what? Fallings from us, vanishings.

Dunne coughed a little as he adjusted his big Celestron. He was then in his seventy-seventh year. I watched him hunch over the diagonal viewer, and thought of the days we used to body-surf together at the foot of this dark hill.

"Polar axis set," he said in a satisfied voice. "And now, by Jove—"

"Phil, is it true that the star of Bethlehem was a supernova?"

He glanced at me quizzically. "Still thinking about Ronnie's Three Wise Men, aren't you. Well, that was Kepler's theory. Most astronomers these days say the Star might have been a triple conjunction of Jupiter with Saturn and Mars, about 7 B.C."

"So Jesus was born seven years before the Birth of Christ."

"An interesting theological conundrum, don't you think?" He consulted a pocket planisphere by penlight. "I can't show you a triple, but this very night Jupiter happens to be in double conjunction with Mars."

Swinging the scope southwest, he began to track through Aquarius. "Didn't Ronnie go to Chicago to plead with the Wise Men one more time?"

"Yes. There was an AFL convention on. He and a bunch—perhaps I should say constellation!—of other stars went there to get a new slant on the Clarification. Which was itself a slant, of course. By adding slant to slant—"

"More or less what I'm attempting here," Dunne muttered into his viewer.

"—they hoped the industry would end up the same way it was before, when actors and producers and the IA co-operated for mutual profit. Really the whole thing was a publicity junket directed against the CSU. They even hired a P.R. firm. Reagan takes Jane, plus his new buddy Robert Taylor, and Gene Kelly and Walter Pidgeon and Alexis Smith and June Allyson. The two Georges, Montgomery and Murphy, go along, too."

"George Murphy alone must have raised the delegation's IQ level a full ninety points."

"They crowd around the Three Wise Men—who are of course dazzled by all this star power—and say, with the fake friendliness that actors do so well, *About that Clarification.* And Jane leans forward, squeezing her breasts together ever so slightly—"

"Now, now," Phil said, wagging his free forefinger at me, "you can't possibly have researched that."

"All right, I withdraw the cleavage, but there's got to be an explanation for the fact that both sides differ completely in their accounts of what happened next. According to Reagan, the Wise Men admitted that the Clarification had been 'a mistake.' But he hokes his account up with melodramatic details: Big Bill Hutcheson roaring with rage, Herb Sorrell swearing to become Hollywood's labor czar, and the president of the AFL bursting into tears."

"Actors," said Dunne, "should never be allowed to write their own scenarios."

"However, the rest of the delegation confirmed what Ronnie said about the Wise Men backing down."

"But they didn't back down. I remember very well that they testified under oath, and to Reagan's face, that they stood by every syllable of the Clarification."

"Right. That's why Reagan suggested that the only way to resolve things was to arrange a conference call between all parties concerned and the Wise Men . . ."

Phil's sudden silence and stillness indicated that he had found his double conjunction.

"Can I see?" I asked.

He stepped aside and let me gaze into the viewer. I stared at a dim orb and a smaller, reddish aureole about half a degree away. Dunne advised me to take off my spectacles, whereupon the two planets merged into a pale smudge that contracted and glimmered when I tried to focus on it.

"It doesn't exactly make me want to load up a camel."

"If Saturn was there, too, you might. Let me find something more to your taste." He reclaimed the scope and began to crank it toward Andromeda, almost directly overhead. "A conference call, you say? No doubt Ronnie did all the talking."

"No, he claims to have listened so hard he got a sore ear. But bumbling Mr. Birthright just made matters worse. The conference call, like all conference calls, proved only that people hear what they want to hear. By the time Birthright sent a telegram to correct something he'd said, the Wise Men had reclarified themselves . . ."

"I hope you don't think I'm following any of this," said Phil.

". . . into a state of complete obfuscation." I was laughing so much that I could hardly continue. "Ronnie is trying to finish *Night unto Night* by day and throw light on the strike after dark. He's convinced that the Wise Men are out to communize the unions on behalf of Hutcheson and Sorrell—not to mention Marx and Engels! What with the AVC preaching 'socialism,' and HICCASP pushing 'progressivism,' and Dalton Trumbo vowing to die in Red Army uniform, and goons burning his bus . . ."

"Keep your voice down. I think Amanda's gone to bed."

"I just wanted to emphasize how many factors conspired all at once to turn him into an anti-Communist, just as anti-Communists were sweeping into Congress."

"Richard Milhous Nixon among them."

"Know what Reagan said after the election, to a crowd of vets? *'I am no longer neutral.'* "

"And no longer 'tolerant,' either."

"I think he went through his final conservative catharsis when he reported back to the membership of SAG on December 19. He knew himself now to be a figure big enough to generate real passions. Throughout his speech there was this *yoink, yoink, yoink* of heavy boots on the roof. Alexander Knox says Reagan spoke so fast that he seemed to be talking out of both sides of his mouth at once. Some liberals, including Alex and Katie Hepburn and Edward G. Robinson, tried to interrupt him, but when they rose, down the aisles came a troop of IA goons slapping bicycle chains against the chair legs, causing such a row that the resolution never got off the floor."

"*Yoink yoink. Slap slap.* Quite a noisy evening."

"I'm not sure I believe Alex's bit about the chains. But I do believe what SAG's executive secretary told me, that nobody watching could doubt that Ronald Reagan was going to take charge of the Guild, and run it for years. All this crap about him turning to the right after marrying Nancy—he became a rock-ribbed anticommunist then and there."

"And a power politician too, I think," Dunne observed. "Righteousness is one thing, but the instinct for power is another. I'll bet he sniffed power that night, and found it sweeter than all the perfumes of Araby. He knew that the actors, not the producers or those IA bullies, were in a position to break the CSU, simply by ignoring it. Which is what happened."

"Reagan's phrase is, 'the CSU dissolved like sugar in hot water.' "

"A typically benign image. He's always careful to hide his own aggression. The CSU didn't melt, it was crushed to powder. Poor old Herb ended up as he began—a painter. I may not admire Ronnie's IQ as much as you do, but I've never doubted his political skills. He's always known exactly when and how to shape things to his advantage."

Dunne tightened a knob and stood away from the Celestron. "Here, take a peep. I need to get a sweater."

To my delight, he had fixed on a spiral galaxy. It floated with infinite softness, a frozen silver centrifuge, its millions of stars spilling outward, rarefying till they were indistinguishable from the general sparkle of space. Not for several minutes did I figure out Phil's sly purpose. He was showing me how in cosmogony, as in psychology, the freak convergence of forces creates a centralized whirl. Momentum enters a field of expansion—nuclear particles seeking release, a man's desire to embrace something larger than himself—and the result is all whipping concentration, wherein every particle has purpose, and mass builds out of dust.

"It's M31 in Andromeda," Phil said through an open window. "Conspiracy theory writ large. Do you want to watch the eleven o'clock news?"

I was already too enraptured to reply. As in a dream when one finds oneself overcoming ignorance and effortlessly conducting an orchestra, I roamed from constellation to constellation by the simple process of aiming the Celestron at Polaris, then tracking it south along the lines of right ascension until I found something diamantine amid the rhinestone scatter. At first, I was puzzled by the fact that Cassiopeia's brooch flashed a *W*, rather than the *M* plotted on Phil's planisphere. But biographers get used to receiving images backward. I learned to handle the telescope as one does an interviewee: as nothing more or less than a construct of mirrors. Whether from instrument or man, what glints out is merely the inverse of what glinted in, years or light-years before.

Pisces presented some of its best suns for inspection. None compared to the Andromeda galaxy for beauty or drama. Thinking still of that great spiral as symbolic of 1946 and the coalescence of Dutch's political personality, I wondered whether winching the scope one "hour" higher, spatially speaking, might locate a star field just as representative of his situation one decade later.

Not that I could remember, offhand, what Reagan was doing in 1956. But at once a telling configuration swam into sight: the double cluster below Perseus that blazes red, white, and blue. Ah, yes! Days of almost binary intimacy with a new wife, of flag-waving prominence as president of the Motion Picture Industry Council. Another winch through space-time scrolled Aries and Cetus. At a level co-ordinate with 1966, I looked in vain for something meteoric, suggestive of his rise to the Governorship of California. Aries Beta shone in approximately the correct ascension, but it was not a star of the first magnitude. Well, neither was Dutch when he arrived in Sacramento.

I tilted the Celestron again, almost vertically past the hot, slow blink of Algol. Another hour of ascension, another decade of life. At 3′30″ r.a., just before +50 declination, I saw Mirfak glowing full and lambent in a field of lesser lights. Dutch effortlessly dominating the 1976 Republican convention!

I probed the zenith for confirmation of my feeling that he had reached *his* zenith, as President, during the year just ending. At first only blackness, lightened with the merest dusting of stars, yawned at the ascension relative to 1986. Were the heavens so up-to-the-minute that they knew Dutch, right now, this moment, was ill and depressed, broken by the Iran scandal, a shadow of what he had been only months ago?

Aware that what had begun as an idle optical game was approaching astrological foolishness, I nevertheless gave the Celestron's knobs one last twirl, southward down the meridian. And there I came upon the display, the heavenly confirmation I sought. Taurus's improbably dense brilliance, between orange Aldebaran and the Hyades, burst from the viewfinder like some vast enlargement of the fireworks over New York Harbor last July 4, the Statue of Liberty's one hundredth birthday, as Dutch sat irradiated on the flight deck of the *John F. Kennedy* . . .

"Having fun?" Phil stood over me, thickly sweatered. "Aren't you frozen?"

I explained what I had been doing. "Well, I'm glad I interrupted," he said. "Or else you'd have gone on to find signs of what the future holds for your friend and gotten very depressed."

"Why so?"

"Because," Phil said with relish, "his presidency's heading into a black hole."

As we walked round the house to my car, I said, "Wait a minute. The date today is—?"

"December 19. Or was, until midnight."

"Well, what do you know."

"Know what?"

"It was forty years ago, Phil. Forty years exactly that he stood up at that second mass meeting and decided he'd had it with stardom, it was politics from now on."

17

Down the Divide

Four Short Scenarios

I T IS ONE OF Hollywood's most hackneyed narrative tricks: the dissolve from day into night. Then a hazy montage of images, double-exposed upon the feverish, tossing body of our hero. But what if the dissolve is real, the images true, our hero the man, not the actor? What if the screenwriter charged with rendering such a scenario tells it as *Reagan* has told it in memoirs and monologues, even to the extent of plagiarizing Reaganesque figures of speech? "Hazy montage," for example. And "cocooned in blankets." And "down the divide." Would that not make it authentic as well as cinematic, a suspenseful episode of *The Ronald Reagan Story*?

   Dutch very nearly died in June 1947 from acute viral pneumonia. As he lay fighting for life, so did another person, almost as primary as himself, flesh of his flesh yet lacking his strength. For her, the struggle was unequal. For him, recovery was a gift. But although his fever gave way to "blessed sweat," and the haze eventually dispersed, he could not shake the feeling that he remained in a state of dream—indeed, much of the time, a nightmare, whose shades would not entirely lift for another sixteen months. And even when he woke, at the end of November

1948, he found himself in a place so distant, so strange, so fogbound, he might as well have regressed to delirium.

We need not extend our scenario that far ahead. The first half-year is nightmarish enough, and packed with enough drama to script three other linked shorts—linked, perhaps, in the manner of those portmanteau movies popular in Europe in the Fifties. Any director wishing to shoot the following material should apply to Reagan's lawyers for permission, since these are his memories, not mine. All I have done is to suggest a few camera angles and sound effects, and to insert some amplifying details from other sources. I recommend black-and-white photography with soft-focus effects in Part I ("Fever"), deep-field detail of domestic objects in Part II ("Silence"), a grainy newsreel look to Part III ("Testimony"), and handheld, documentary-style tracking shots in Part IV ("But Mary Doesn't Love John").

I: FEVER

This short documentary begins in real time, at about 10 P.M. on June 17, 1947. We get an establishing shot of the Carthay Circle Theater on San Vincente Boulevard, Los Angeles. Searchlights play above its high tower, signaling a Warner Bros. première. The show has just ended: limousines wait in line, their black hoods gleaming. We hear the sound of violent coughing. Camera zooms in on RONALD REAGAN, convulsed as he steps out into the night air. He looks bewildered, as though someone has just stabbed him in the chest. He can't remember ever hurting this much.

Dissolve to the back of JANE WYMAN's head as she places a call, early next morning, to Warner Bros. production department. She reports that "Ronnie" is running a temperature of one hundred and two. He cannot come in to work on his current movie, That Hagen Girl, *with SHIRLEY TEMPLE.*

WYMAN is a fine actress (she was nominated for an Oscar this year for her performance in The Yearling*), and she is able to convey with voice alone the message that her husband, sick as he is, doesn't mind staying away from a picture he detests. But she is not acting anymore when she turns to face the camera. We see the face of a woman six months pregnant, who suspects something is not quite right in her womb.*

Cut to a private ward in Cedars of Lebanon Hospital, late the following day. We hear a doctor telling WYMAN that REAGAN's strain of pneumonia is so rare as to be beyond the power of "miracle" drugs.

Dissolve to a hazy montage in which five days and nights merge.

WYMAN maintains a worried vigil at REAGAN's bedside. He alternately shivers with chills and burns with fever. At one point, he asks to be cocooned in blankets and fed hot tea through a glass tube. He is harking back to memories of his mother doing this to him when he was a sick child.

Midnight—when? Probably June 25, but REAGAN's not keeping track. His fever has reached one hundred and four. The haze becomes hallucinatory. He sees a street lamp, a lonely stretch of sidewalk. There is a sense of danger in the darkness. Enter HUMPHREY BO-GART in a trench coat. The two men converse in furtive, broken sentences. They sound as if they are trying out lines. Is REAGAN remembering the time he was cast to play in Casablanca*? He mutters something. Camera goes into close-up on his lips: "Big Casino, bet or throw it."*

His lips and face are dry. So is his wrapped body. He strains to sweat—the blessed sweat that ends fevers. Where is WYMAN? The darkness deepens.

Exhausted, he tells a NURSE that he does not have the strength to go on breathing. Her silhouetted form leans over him, coaxing him to inhale. "Now let it out," she says. "Come on now, breathe in once more." Over and over she makes him obey. He does so out of instinctive courtesy. At last, the sweat comes and washes him back down the divide he's been climbing.

Crosscut to the maternity ward at Queen of Angels Hospital, two and a half miles away. It is 11:26 A.M. on June 26, 1947. WYMAN has just given premature birth to a baby girl. Another nightmare montage begins, as doctors try to save the baby's life. But at 8:45 P.M., she succumbs to cardiac arrest.

Cameraman: I ask you not to focus too closely on WYMAN's face when she hears her daughter is dead. Remember we are dealing with those quaint, pre-television days when privacy of emotion was respected.

Dissolve to the ambulance taking REAGAN home from the hospital. He is seventeen pounds lighter and hardly able to lift an arm without gasping. But he cannot get enough of the world streaming past his window—even the most ordinary things seem transfigured to new, strange beauty.

Director: As with the cameraman above, I beg you to keep a respectful distance when REAGAN and WYMAN cremate their daughter six days later. Enough, after they have gone home, to do an insert of the certificate they hold:

REAGAN, CHRISTINE
PLACE OF DEATH: *Los Angeles*
NAME OF HOSPITAL: *Queen of Angels*
LENGTH OF STAY: *9 hrs., 11 min.*
BIRTHDATE OF DECEASED: *June 26, 1947*

And no music when you fade.

II. SILENCE

Again, no music as the interior of the REAGAN house is disclosed about two weeks later. Silence has become characteristic of the place as husband and wife deal with their grief in separate ways: WYMAN mute, inconsolable, REAGAN almost perpetually absent as he finishes That Hagen Girl *and spends the rest of his waking hours at SAG headquarters.*

He has been president of the Guild since March 10, specifically elected for his negotiatory skills. The CSU strike is still crippling movie output; a new actor's contract has to be arranged with producers; ominous hearings "regarding the Communist Infiltration of the Motion Picture Industry" are being scheduled by the House Un-American Activities Committee (HUAC). There has already been a preliminary hearing in Hollywood by a subcommittee of the Committee, and REAGAN is bracing to appear before another in August.

The work fascinates him; he is good at it, enjoys the minutiae, the research, the rules of order, the sour coffee, the long, unpaid hours, the ugly building on Hollywood Boulevard, the camaraderie of WILLIAM HOLDEN (his new best friend), GENE KELLY, and GEORGE MURPHY. Above all, REAGAN exults in the responsibility of being head of Hollywood's major trade association at a time when good labor relations are of as much import to national security as a strong foreign policy. (His election coincided almost exactly with the annunciation of the Truman Doctrine in Washington.)

There was a time when WYMAN enjoyed Guild business, too—but no more. It has gotten too political, too grandiose for her taste. So, for that matter, has her husband. Even before last month's catastrophe, she had begun to retreat from him. They have been seen quarreling in public. She cannot take much more of his compulsion to "talk up" the left, right, and center of every political issue under the California sun. It was bad enough back in the days when he bored her and ANN SHERIDAN with imaginary baseball games, all nine innings' worth, play by play by play. Not to mention his habit of reading the newspaper aloud at break-

fast (does it never occur to him that she might have thoughts of her own?), starting at the top left of the front page and proceeding with commentary, column by inexorable column, until she . . .

Director: I suggest a flashback here. Show WYMAN rising from the breakfast table, quietly leaving the kitchen, picking up her purse, and letting herself out the front door, while REAGAN reads on and on.

Or if you don't like flashbacks and want to stay with her in the still house, in real time, continue to shoot as follows:

Camera holds on WYMAN gazing at her husband's George Washington desk, stuffed with scribbled papers. Fade in sound track of REAGAN in full political cry:

RR Ibelievetheonlylogicalwaytosaveourcountryfromallextremistsis-
toremoveconditionsthatsupplyfuelforthetotalitarianfire . . .

The tireless voice loudens then diminishes, like a wild-goose leader dragging a skein northward. As silence refills the house, pan around other tokens of their seven years of marriage—his presentation clock from "77 Grateful People," her Toby jug collection, the two ceramic whiskey-keg lamps with miniature spigots, MAUREEN's teddy bear, MICHAEL's little life jacket. Outside, the pool inert in July heat, the cypress trees motionless, carved-looking against the sky. Nowhere any feeling of wind, of sap rising.

The clock chimes. Enough of this! She must work to save herself from inner emptiness, just as he is working to ward off exterior political threat. The clock's chimes continue, becoming deeper and more gong-like, as we dissolve to . . .

. . . a hearing room in downtown Los Angeles. REAGAN is testifying before a special House subcommittee chaired by Representative CARROLL D. KEARNS. (Director: Make this sequence extremely brief, because we do not want to spoil the drama of his more important testimony to HUAC, below. Also, he is discussing last year's craft-union disputes, about which enough has already been said.) Perhaps one line of dialogue will suffice:

RR When the August Clarification arrived and the ultimatum was delivered to the producers, and it looked like we were threatened
with a strike again . . . we said, "Here we go again."

He will use a similar colloquialism to much greater effect one day.
Cut back to the REAGAN house in the Hollywood Hills. Late summer afternoon. Silence is still the note here, but it has become a busy si-

lence, full of implications and inferences. WYMAN, her ears plugged with wax, is studying the lip and hand movements of a deaf and dumb Mexican girl. Her expression is alive with excitement. Camera watches as she imitates the girl. It swoops down and focuses on a script between them: the title page reads Johnny Belinda.

When REAGAN comes home tonight, he will get the uneasy feeling that WYMAN cannot hear what he is saying. As Labor Day approaches and the script becomes a shooting script, she will start wearing earplugs full-time, in order to be alone with the sound of her own breathing and swallowing.

I'm tempted to suggest a neat—perhaps too neat?—crosscut at this point from that Johnny Belinda *title page to the label on a bottle of Johnnie Walker. Then a hand tilts the bottle, and camera pulls back to show WYMAN pouring herself a double on location. Well, what else is there to do, nights, in this godforsaken corner of Northern California?*

Our scenario now becomes a film within a film. Which is to say, daily rushes from Johnny Belinda *(JEAN NEGULESCO, directing) are seen "beneath" shots of a speeding convertible as REAGAN, deeply worried about his wife's mental state, drives north to visit her at Fort Bragg. Camera shows her in character: brown hair cut unflatteringly short, the pudge of her recent pregnancy coarsening her features, farm clothes hiding her body.*

More to the point is that these rushes show a thirty-year-old actress coming into full possession of her gifts. We see REAGAN watching with the crew as she works, adjusting to the fact that she has moved beyond him. Never in his own acting career—not even when he imagined himself to be the Gipper, or when he bewailed the loss of his legs—has he managed to subsume himself so utterly in a part. Nor will he, as long as he remains in pictures.

Between takes, he notices WYMAN's unconcealed attraction to her co-star, LEW AYRES. Director: have REAGAN listen stone-faced (while the rest of the company chuckles) to his wife saying with absolute assurance, "No matter what they do, the Oscar is mine this year." Dissolve.

Last scene of this segment: he is back in Los Angeles, sitting unrecognized at a sneak preview of That Hagen Girl. *On-screen, RONALD REAGAN, looking decidedly fortyish after his bout of pneumonia, is saying to the schoolgirl SHIRLEY TEMPLE, "I love you." The entire audience cries, "Oh, no!" Go into a close-up of his cringing face, then do a slow fade as the theater empties, leaving him huddled in the darkness.*

III. TESTIMONY

A shock cut, with flashbulbs exploding, to HUAC's jam-packed hearing room in the Old House Office Building, Washington, D.C. The place buzzes with anticipation. It is Thursday, October 23, 1947. Jaded political correspondents, Congressmen, policemen, and pages are agog at the prospect of seeing some of Hollywood's most glamorous stars testify on this, the fourth day of hearings by the full Committee.

We are still in the "friendly" phase of HUAC's investigation (inquisition, if you prefer) into subversive activities by Hollywood writers, directors, and actors. Since Monday, obsequious informers have been assuring Chairman J. PARNELL THOMAS that they have long been aware of "ideological termites" in their midst, chewing at the foundations of freedom. The tone of the proceedings was set by JACK WARNER, who named twelve names without being asked. Already, the Committee has a Red harvest of seventy-five.

Today's roster of "friendly" witnesses includes RONALD REAGAN. Director: before presenting his testimony, sample the performances—no other word will do—of some of his screen colleagues. Like most actors, they are ill at ease with their own personalities (GARY COOPER comes over as disconcertingly effeminate, giggling and writhing and blowing little puffs of air onto his fingernails). That does not mean, of course, that they do not play up to the newsreel cameras and microphones. The foppish ADOLPHE MENJOU uses his cigarette as a prop. "This is a foul philosophy, this Communistic thing," he allows, preparing to inhale. "I would move to the state of Texas if it ever came here, because I think the Texans would kill it on sight!" He drags deeply as the audience enjoys this sparkling sally. Little asterisks of smoke punctuate his speech as he disdainfully continues: "Any m✲n who is a decent Am✲rican and believes in the Constit✲tion of the United St✲tes . . ." (Cut here before he coughs.) Next, ROBERT TAYLOR, double-breasted, brilliantined enough to send spangles of light around the room (his real name, appropriately, is Spangler A. Brugh): "If I had my way about it, they'd be sent back to Russia, or some other unpleasant place" (Applause).

Let the crowd sound fade as you dissolve again, this time to a wall clock that reads ten minutes past eleven. Pan downwards into the chamber. REAGAN's tall body stands up. A long, drawn-out, feminine "Ooooooh!" arises as he wends his way Indian-like through a forest of tables and chairs. He wears a light tan suit, white shirt, and blue knit tie. His step seems unhurried, yet he reaches the testimony table with amazing speed. He grins affably and stands as the oath is read to him. "I do," he says, with a duck of the head that will one day endear him to millions. Then he sits down and slides on his spectacles.

No greater contrast could be imagined to the preenings of his predecessors. He is all business, unself-conscious, totally relaxed. From time to time, as he replies to questions from the high table, he takes up an empty paper cup and stares into it, concentrating his thoughts.

Q. As president of the Screen Actors Guild, and as an active member, have you at any time observed or noted within the organization a clique of either Communists or fascists who were attempting to exert influence or pressure on the organization?

A. Well, sir, my testimony must be very similar to that of Mr. Murphy and Mr. Montgomery. There has been a small group within the Screen Actors Guild which has consistently opposed the policy of the Guild Board and officers of the Guild, as evidenced by their vote on various issues. That small clique referred has been suspected of more or less following the tactics that we associate with the Communist Party.

Director: When he looks up from the paper cup and exchanges glances with members of the Committee, zoom into the Cyclopean stare of freshman Representative RICHARD M. NIXON, Republican of California.

Q. Would you refer to them as a disruptive influence within the Guild?

A. I would say that at times they have attempted to be a disruptive influence.

Q. You have no knowledge yourself as to whether or not any of them are members of the Communist Party?

A. No, sir, I have no investigative force or anything, and I do not know.

Director: No well-intentioned person, Communist or conservative, can object to this mild testimony. But documentarians are not required to be nice. Here's a great opportunity to fade REAGAN's voice under as you cut to the beating slugs of an FBI typewriter and show the following classified sentence:

The investigative report sets out information obtained from T-10 (Ronald Reagan, President of the Screen Actors Guild) who said that meetings of the

Guild were attended by a clique of individuals
headed by—

*Legal problems at this point. You'll have to annoy your viewers by
making the shadow of the typist's pipe, or his fat, out-of-focus thumbs,
obscure the name as it smacks out. Any cryptologist who knows something of SAG history will be smart enough to count the smacks and
figure that "Anne Revere" would fit, before the typist hits a comma and
follows up with a few other names—*

—who invariably followed the Communist Party line
at Guild meetings.

*Back in the hearing room, REAGAN's public testimony is continu-
ing. He tells a long story about how he was tricked into letting his name
be used by the promoters of a Paul Robeson concert, purportedly to
raise funds for a multi-racial hospital. As reported in the newspapers,
the concert had nothing to do with the hospital, but everything to do
with celebrating two roseate rhetoricians "and remnants of the Abraham Lincoln Brigade."*

*Were he not so honestly upset by this, one might be tempted to play
his distress for laughs. Further courteous questions are asked by the
Committee counsel, ROBERT E. STRIPLING, and REAGAN answers them in kind. (The days of angry, gavel-pounding interrogation
of nineteen "unfriendly" witnesses have yet to come.) Let REAGAN
conclude with what even PHILIP DUNNE allows afterward is "a fine
statement of civil-libertarian principles." He points out that the Communist Party has not yet been outlawed:*

I believe that—as Thomas Jefferson put it—if all the American
people knew all of the facts they will never make a mistake.

Whether that party should be outlawed, I agree with the gentlemen preceding me that that is a matter for the government to decide. As a citizen I would hesitate, or not like, to see any political
party outlawed on the basis of its political ideology. We have spent
a hundred and seventy years in this country on the basis that democracy is strong enough to stand up and fight against the in-
roads of any ideology. . . .

I detest, I abhor their philosophy, but I detest more than that
their tactics, which are those of the fifth column and are dishonest. But at the same time, I never, as a citizen, want to see our
country become urged, by either fear or resentment of this group,

[to] compromise with any of our democratic principles. . . . I still think that democracy can do it.

Hold on his Indian retreat, the thanks of the Committee ringing in his ears, then slow fade.

IV. BUT MARY DOESN'T LOVE JOHN

This very short short could be connected to the last by means of a rapid sequence of newspaper headlines, datelined from October 24 to December 5, 1947. They successively report that the Committee has zeroed in on the "unfriendly Nineteen," then on the "unfriendly Eleven," and finally (after Bertolt Brecht absconds to Europe) the "Hollywood Ten": Dalton Trumbo, John Howard Lawson, Adrian Scott, Ring Lardner, Jr., Albert Maltz, Alvah Bessie, Lester Cole, Herbert Biberman, Samuel Ornitz, and Edward Dmytryk. All are cited for contempt of Congress, having refused to say whether or not they belong to the Communist Party.

The sound track should be noisy, mixing LAWSON's contemptuous shout, "This Committee is on trial here" with the constant banging of THOMAS's gavel, the barking of newscasters, and clashing choruses of the "Internationale" and "America the Beautiful." Briefly, at the height of this noise, we glimpse a headline reading REAGAN, WYMAN SET TO STAR IN "JOHN LOVES MARY." Then zoom to another headline, accompanied by the loudest bang of all—a thunderclap, no less:

Camera holds on it as the thunder rumbles to silence.

Now the screen divides, and we get a split two-shot of the principals reacting in their different ways. WYMAN (on a shopping trip to New York) is saying furiously to JOY HODGES, "If he's gonna be President, he's gonna do it without me." REAGAN, returning home from Washington to an empty house, is for once in his life speechless. He registers disbelief at first, then bewilderment, then—like any son of Illinois whose wheat elevator has exploded—a querulous certainty that the damage can be fixed.

In the immeasurable distance, singing begins again. We cannot distinguish the tune at first, because REAGAN's own voice, heard in soliloquy, is rehearsing what to say to the press: "I love Jane, and I know she loves me. I don't know what this is all about, and I don't know why Jane has done it. For my part, I hope to live with her for the rest of my life."

Slow dissolve to a scene of revelry somewhere in Beverly Hills. Handsome couples are drinking and dancing to the radio music of GUY LOMBARDO. Midnight strikes, and the distant chorus swells to a strain we at last recognize:

> Should auld acquaintance be forgot,
> And never brought to mind . . .

Camera is passing quickly through the revelers as they laugh and hug and kiss. Ahead of it strides a sixtyish woman. She goes out onto the patio, where we see our hero standing alone, his face contorted. She puts her arms around him. He cries on her shoulder.

> We'll drink a cup of kindness yet,
> For sake of auld lang syne!

The lens swings up into the black sky of 1948.

18

Red or Palest Pink

A Letter

629 Idaho Ave., Santa Monica, Calif. October 20, 1948

My dear Jacob—The friendliness of your salutation—on BBC stationery, no less!—tempts me to address you as "Alaric," but schoolboy habits die hard.

I've rather lost touch with your journalistic exploits. My mother was a great subscriber to English newspapers before the war & she used regularly to send me clips of your Reuters dispatches. Called them "perversely brilliant"—i.e., didn't agree with them! She died last year, an unreconstructed Tory.

I had no idea you'd gone to Moscow for the *Express* and presume you're happy to be back home—although I hear life's bleak in Britain under Attlee.

Now as to your request: sorry to disappoint you, but I have no inside knowledge of the Hollywood blacklist. Had a few odd jobs, options etc. with MGM and Warners in '38 to '41, and was a member of the First Motion Picture Unit USAAF '43 to '45, but never really got into "the industry" as it's called. Am now doing what I'm best at,

I guess—writing freelance ad copy. Wife (musician) and I go our separate ways. *Ça vous amuse, la vie?*

Hence, am by no means privy to the professional paranoia rampant here since last November's "Waldorf Conference" of the Motion Pic. Producers' Assoc. (MPPA). The producers insist they are not "blacklisting" the Hollywood Ten—just don't think names like Trumbo and Lardner are good "box office" any more! Fact remains that their list extends to actors, broadcasters, lensers, talent of any description. Whoever joined a Red or palest pink organization, no matter how far back, can't get work. But all this you surely know.

Happily, I can recommend one "insider" whom you might be able to interview next month in London. And that is Ronald Reagan, Pres. of the Screen Actors Guild. In the last ten months, he's become the most prominent anti-Communist in town—respected because he doesn't seem to have any malice, only a great deal of moral passion, rational rather than visceral. He's an intriguing paradox *vis-à-vis* the blacklist: principled against it to begin with, but now reluctantly for, on the grounds that self-censorship is preferable to outside Govt. policing. A year ago he was one of the few "friendly" witnesses to distinguish himself at the HUAC hearings. Made a calm statement to the effect that democracy's best defense is democracy. And he grilled the producers like frankfurters when they got back from the Waldorf Conference. Could they *prove* anybody was a Red, if he or she denied it? Was innocent membership in a Communist "front" more, or less culpable than venal membership in a patriotic organization? Etc., etc. The frankfurters sizzled until Louis B. Mayer popped with rage & said producers knew a Commie when they saw one.

Reagan's reaction was to go back to his guild & in effect throw down a moral gauntlet—something you're not supposed to do in this town. Proposed a statement saying that the SAG board would not join producers in blacklisting talent & usurping the powers of Constitutional law. They would sign personal affidavits of loyalty to the U.S. government, but not deny Communists the right to belong to SAG. It was a free union in a free country.

All very courageous, but actors are an insecure lot, & he couldn't get a majority in favor. By the end of the year, SAG had capitulated to the producers, & now Reagan doesn't sound much different from old Mayer. I guess that makes him a politician—quick to jump aboard a bandwagon.

Strike the last sentence. He's in charge of "Hollywood for Harry Truman," which looks to be less of a bandwagon than a slowly derailing train.

Reason I'm telling you all this is, Reagan will be heading your way immediately after Dewey's election. Never been out of the country before! He and Patricia Neal are starring in one of those transatlantic production deals aimed at getting frozen dollars out of Britain. It's called *The Hasty Heart,* a war flick I think. RR is scheduled to spend the whole winter at the Savoy with nothing much to do at night, having been made a miserable *divorcé* by J. Wyman. (Watch out for her in *Johnny Belinda*—opened recently to amazing reviews.)

He's a good-natured guy, always available to the press. Loves to talk. My advice is to look for him in the bar, flash your BBC card, & he'll tell you all you want to know. And then some.

Best wishes in your new job.

Yrs. ever,

E.

P.S.—Since writing the above I've talked to my MGM buddy Sam Marx & he tells me that Warner Bros. wants to get RR out of the country because he's "on the verge of emotional collapse" over his divorce. JW accused him of extreme mental cruelty & is going around town saying, in language unfit for this typewriter, that he was a bore in bed. So treat him gently!

19

This Dismal Wilderness

RONALD REAGAN STRODE DOWN the gangway of the *Britannic* on November 28, 1948, and found the Merseyside docks busy with nervous activity. The word *fog* was on a thousand chapped lips, although Liverpool—what he could see of it beyond Princes Dock— seemed fairly clear, bathed in weak mid-morning light. Evidently, the nationwide pea-souper his captain had raced to beat and which departing passengers on the *Parthia* were now hurrying to escape, had yet to blanket this part of Britain.

The light filtering through the reception hall's high windows and open doorways—did this frigid country have no heat?—was strange to American eyes, used to the definitions cast by a fixable sun. England's luminosity seemed to emanate from no single source; it seeped from low-lying clouds in a sort of opalescent, fine-falling mist that drained the world of color. Maybe that explained the underexposed quality of the faces he saw all about him, beneath brims of working-class tweed or stiff official black: a smoothly porous pallor, transparent to the beat of blood, and permanently damp-looking—so different from the dry tan that glossed his own features that he might have been born of another race.

In a way, he had been. This English light and English skin, these laughable accents, this omnipresent smell, equally composed of coal soot, cow dung, diesel fumes, milky-white disinfectant, and blue Woodbine smoke, all breathed *foreign* at him. For the first time in his life, he knew himself to be strange. Whatever his reaction, of delight or dismay, it was (the smooth faces assured him) of little interest to a society that had been centuries old when Tampico was but a wave in the grass.

He was clear of customs in time for the one o'clock Boat Train from Riverside Station. As it carried him through the outskirts of Liverpool, still clear of fog, he was able to see more of English urban life than he would for another six days. Even that was not much: the streets of identical black brick houses were suffused with Sunday calm, while hordes of housewives, unseen, sweated "dinner" out of coal stoves.

The train swung southeast and, rocking on ancient rails, accelerated toward London. Dark came with depressing swiftness—dark already thickened with the first acrid curlings of fog. Reagan's sensitive sinuses recoiled; the air was so charged with bituminous particles he wondered it did not ignite.

South of Birmingham, the train barreled through gloom unpricked by electric light. He was surprised to see no neon signs, no fluorescent shop fronts in passing towns. Only an occasional necklace of gas lamps swept by—dull pearls whipped out of sight, as if England was embarrassed to wear them on her bosom. Evidently, the worst visibility emergency in years was not going to alter the Labour government's power-saving policies. As the blackness turned to yellowish whiteness and the train's speed slowed to an eventual halt, Reagan felt stirrings of his old claustrophobia. Jack's Model T was back on its roof, crumpled blindingly about him as Nelle called and called his name.

He awoke the next morning in a luxurious hotel bedroom whose velvet-draped picture window opened on nothing but swirling vapor. The cloud outside gave off a remote, irregular tinkling of bells. When these chimes coincided with river noises—slaps, creaks, and low splashy rumbles—Reagan understood that boats and barges were passing close by, and that his room, as the Warner travel agent had promised, did in a technical sense "overlook" the Thames.

He was not, however, as alone as he had been the day before. The Savoy was full of American actors and producers. Patricia Neal (who had replaced Jane as his romantic partner in *John Loves Mary* and was now to be his nurse in *The Hasty Heart*) was staying in a suite adjacent to his own: local gossip columnists were sure to get a rise out of that. Alan and Sue Ladd, Michael O'Shea and Virginia Mayo, Joan Caulfield, and Billy De Wolfe were also within reach of his house phone. They had been invited across the Atlantic to attend tonight's Royal Command Performance of *Scott of the Antarctic;* they were jolly and rested and rich and knew their way around London, even in the fog. Tonight at dinner, they would be receptive to his jokes, and afterward, one or the other would give him a limousine ride to the Empire Theatre.

Cheered by this prospect, Reagan could read with disinterest the bleak news items that had become daily fare for Britons in the waning days of 1948, as winter, and King George VI's frailty, and nationalization, and rationing ("What's rationing?" he wanted to know) bit to the bone of public morale. A Westminster Bank economist estimated that since 1946 Clement Attlee's government had forced the private sector to save about one and a half billion pounds—then used the money to finance an equivalent amount of deficit spending. The National Coal Board was reported to be producing more paper than anthracite. Britain's breakfasters faced a reduction in their bacon allowance to one ounce a week. There was a nationwide shortage of fresh fruit; tobacco supplies were down, excise up, beer thinner, spirits dearer. Judging by the laxative advertisements on every other page, half the country was constipated.

Stories of Communist aggression and left-wing appeasement filled enough columns to tighten Reagan's lips. The British Minister of War had risen to speak at a recent public meeting and—shades of Hollywood Legion Stadium!—been shouted down by a gang of toughs in red ties until violence cleared the hall. Sir Stafford Cripps, Chancellor of the Exchequer, had waived currency-export restrictions so that British socialists might subsidize a radical newspaper in Paris, yet refused to allow contributions to a French memorial for the Allied war dead. Further afield, Red Army troops had reinforced their blockade of West Berlin; the Hungarian government was denuding its border with Austria, in order to shoot would-be refugees; Communist guerrillas continued to pour across Greece's Balkan frontier; Chinese Communist forces were closing in on Nanking; and, back home, a submarine sprouting what looked like a Russian periscope had been seen prowling off Corpus Christi, Texas.

The only positive news, in Reagan's view, was that the Five Powers were negotiating a North Atlantic treaty alliance, and that General Charles de Gaulle was rumbling in retirement against the new Marshall

Plan. Reagan disliked it, too. Why should an "overgenerous" United States pay for the restructuring of Europe?

☯

During the next week, Ronald Reagan and Patricia Neal dutifully went "sight-seeing" *à deux,* although the fog remained so thick that they saw little more than two beams of yellow light swimming in front of their Rolls-Royce. As a result, they were not much "seen" themselves, to the distress of studio publicists, who hoped that rumors of a romance might arouse interest in *The Hasty Heart.* Visibility, however, was hardly the problem. The popular nose for sexual chemistry is acute, and these two tall, splendid American animals with adjoining suites gave off no whiff of musk.

Reagan tried to kiss Pat once, more out of duty than desire, and she fended him off easily: "Oh, Ronnie, no!" She was neither the first nor the last woman to find him more attractive than desirable. Joy Hodges once told me a similar story, and said that Dutch *en s'excitant* gave her a curious urge to giggle. Pat was touched by the despair behind his incessant, nervous jocularity. Pining secretly for Gary Cooper, she sensed that he, too, was pining, if not for Jane . . .

"For what, Mr. President?" I asked forty years later.

There was a long silence as he tried to escape the question. "I think the thing that I missed most was not, uh, somebody loving me. I missed not having someone to love."

I wrote the words down and followed them with a spiral curlicue useful to biographers, meaning, *He feels the opposite of what he says.*

☯

Reagan admits frankly—or used to, before another marriage made him defensive—that Jane's divorce action left him dead inside for several years. The worst thing a woman can do to an actor is to announce, in public, that he bores her. What Jane said in private may have been more brutally specific, but again, actors are not like you or me: they hurt worse onstage than they do in the bedroom. Because the stage is where they really live. When Jane put on her tangerine shirtwaist and went to court with reporters and photographers in tow, she was in effect making a grand exit from a production Dutch thought he dominated, leaving him with no cue, no lines memorized, before an audience of millions—picture-goers encouraged by her to yawn at him.

The fact that he had recently discovered himself to be more politician than performer only compounded the humiliation. In finding him dull, Jane also dismissed what he passionately believed. At the same time, she complained that he never gave her credit for her own political views. This would remain true through the day I asked him, as President, whether she had been a Republican or Democrat. "I don't think I ever heard her say."

Finally, there was the simple fact that Jane had eclipsed him professionally. While he languished in a foreign fog, her name was up in lights across America, and rising on everybody's Oscar list as a favorite for Best Actress of 1948.

At 7:00 A.M. on December 16, a small black limousine (why were all cars black in Britain?) came to pick Reagan up for the first day of shooting at Elstree Studios. It might have been the first night, for all he could see as he cruised northwest up the Edgware Road into Hertfordshire. At these latitudes, with the winter solstice looming, the sun's scheduled workday was shorter than his own.

Elstree—a dark jumble of gray and white hangars—liked to call itself "Britain's Hollywood." The resemblance was more wishful than actual. About a dozen local studios owned or rented its various sound stages, most of which were dark when Reagan came through the gates. Evidently, the post-war production slump was as bad here as at home. His destination, at any rate, showed signs of life. It was the largest studio on the lot, freshly renovated and painted with the imposing legend ASSOCIATED BRITISH PICTURE CORPORATION.

Aside from Pat Neal and Vincent Sherman, the director, there were no other Americans on the set of *The Hasty Heart*—a frigid compound spread with sand and bristling with bamboo huts. The largest of these *bashas* was mounted on a turntable. It simulated a Burmese army hospital, and was open-sided to allow circulation of tropical breezes, or the English equivalent. Here Reagan was to spend the next three months, in light pajamas and loose shirts.

Technicians and fellow actors crunched to and fro, speaking what he calculated to be at least fifty provincial tongues. The thickest accent of all was the Highland burr of Richard Todd, a truculent-looking former paratrooper cast to play "Lachlan Maclachlan" opposite Reagan's "Yank." It was something of a relief when Todd, over lunch, reverted to his normal cultured English. Neither Reagan nor Neal (playing

"Sister Parker") took Todd seriously as an actor, for this was only his second movie role. But it soon became apparent that the young actor's gamecock fierceness was calibrated perfectly to desentimentalize the role of a corporal doomed by kidney failure—and indeed, to steal the movie from them both.

Incapable of jealousy, tall, smiling, and courtly, Reagan went out of his way to be friendly to Todd. He even insisted that they commute together in his Rolls.

"Ronnie couldn't have been nicer to a total unknown," Todd told me in 1987, plump and sherry-red with success. As the big car whispered north through the dark of early morning, and south through the dark of early night, Reagan had talked endlessly about agriculture, sports, acting, union politics, and strategic and military affairs.

Like Eddie Albert before him, Todd felt Reagan was "a frustrated soldier," wistful for raw battle experience and the clarifying morality that survival teaches. He compensated by expounding on "what he thought should happen in the post-war world." It was clear that he did not understand the complexities of European recovery, with coalitions and minority governments and multi-power conferences weaving a new tapestry of welfare states—except that he noticed a number of Red threads running from east to west, and heartily disliked the pattern. Aware of his emotional frailty, Todd made no attempt to correct him on points of socialist theory.

When Reagan turned his attention to matters at home, the younger man's tolerance changed quickly to respect. "I have never met an American who so profoundly believed in the greatness of his nation."

Pat Neal, at twenty-two, was more interested in affairs of the heart than those of state. She could see that Reagan was still painfully in love with his wife. Jane's rejection seemed to have unmanned him: "He told me how sad it was—that somebody had fixed him up with another woman, but the desire just wasn't there."

Although she felt no more than mild sympathy for him, they were inevitably in each other's company. British union regulations closed the Elstree Studios from Friday evening to Monday morning. So, as winter deepened and darkened, they made many dogged forays out of town: to Brighton, where the gray sea lashed the gray pebbles, and gray gulls mewed, to dour country pubs and dance halls. Neal enjoyed foxtrotting with Reagan. His tall grace comforted her five feet eight inches.

There was a bland bigness about him, and an assurance, for all his current hurt, that he would recover.

Old, crippled, sentimental, and vague, she leaned on my arm a few years ago at the Carlyle Grill in New York and said, "You know, I remember Ronnie writing something extraordinary about himself that winter. It was in a book of drawings—captionless cartoons—that my friend Hamish Thomson showed us. We were supposed to autograph the ones that resembled ourselves. He wrote beneath his, *I want to be the biggest man in the world.*"

In Miss Neal's subsequent memoirs, Reagan went further and wanted to be "President of the United States." I wrote Mr. Thomson for confirmation and got back a copy of the cartoon. It was both surreal and scary: a sort of baboon in a Grecian robe, standing half-asleep (or comatose with concentration?) in front of a blackboard covered with geometrical projections. One glance at the spare brushwork—bristles almost dry of ink, lightly dragged across the paper—identified it as the work of William Steig, *The New Yorker*'s famed inscrutabilist. But what had Dutch identified with? There was nothing here of bigness or future leadership. Nor could I figure out the meaning of his superscript, which was nothing like what Pat remembered.

Then I noticed that she had also been wrong about there being no captions. The cartoon indeed had something printed on the blank page opposite, presumably rejecting the thoughts of the simian philosopher: WHOEVER WANTS THE ANSWER MUST COME TO ME. And Dutch had added his own empathetic qualifier: *It May Not Be Right, But I'll Have It.*

So maybe Pat was correct, after all, in detecting the note of leadership-to-be. For what distinguishes the executive persona is self-confidence and absolute philosophical certainty.

A much less cryptic document survives as evidence of Reagan's mood in December 1948. It is a determinedly humorous letter addressed "To the Finder—Please see that this letter reaches J. L. Warner—Burbank, Calif." Poor wiseass, he hadn't much to be jovial about that Christmas. Most of British industry, including the Elstree studio, shut down for three days. Pat Neal went off to stay with the Gene Kellys in Paris, Richard Todd left town with his fiancée, and the Savoy emptied out.

> Dear J. L.
>
> I am putting this letter in a bottle & throwing it on the tide with the hope that some how it may reach you. Perhaps my report of life here in this dismal wilderness will be of help to future expeditions.
>
> You will recall with what light hearts we set out such a long time ago—optimistic about our ability to find and thaw the "Frozen Dollar." If we could have known then what lay ahead (*lay*—there's a word I no longer experience or understand) . . .
>
> The natives [of Britain] speak a strange jargon similar in many ways to our own language but different enough to cause some confusion. For example, to be "knocked up" here refers in no way to those delights for which "Leander swam the Hellespont"—it merely means to be awakened from a sound sleep. . . .
>
> Mentioning a pain in my "fanny," (which is easy to get here) I was distressed to learn that even this standard American term has an opposite meaning. If I had what they call "a fanny" I could be Queen of England.

There followed a few labored jokes about foxhunting and British cooking—"What they do to the food we did to the American Indian"—before he concluded:

> My strength is failing now . . . Cheerio! (That is a native word meaning good bye—it is spoken without moving the upper lip—while looking down the nose.)
>
> RONNIE
>
> P.S. Due to the fuel shortage we are keeping the fire alive with "Frozen Dollars" (yours).

It would have taken more than Warner's peasant sensibility to feel the loneliness behind the desperate jocularity.

On the first shooting day of 1949, Ronald Reagan performed the most demanding monologue he had ever learned:

KIWI   Get away!

AUSSIE   You didn't!

YANK   Well, I can still do it. (*Closing his eyes*) Genesis, Exodus, Leviticus, Numbers, Deuteronomy, Joshua, Judges, Ruth, Samuel, Kings, Chronicles, Ezra, Nehemiah, Esther, Job, Psalms, Proverbs, Ecclesiastes, Solomon, Isaiah, Jeremiah, Lamentations . . .

He had to repeat the books of the Old Testament nine times before Sherman printed it, but not on account of any groove jumps in his shellac memory. Seven takes were interrupted by flickering arcs or cracks of *basha* bamboo. These last were a constant hazard on set, because the sound stage was drafty enough to serve as a set for *King Lear.* Although the great fog was gone, lesser mists drifted in whenever Sherman needed to simulate the noonday sun, only to disperse magically if the script called for dawn vapor. On such occasions, the crew trundled out a "fog machine," but its workings were as haphazard as everything else at Elstree.

Reagan, who took pride in his own clockwork reliability, could not believe Britain's "incredible inefficiency." The country seemed designed around frustration and discomfort, from its clanky coins jamming call boxes to its refrigerated toilet seats and its omnipresent posted rules and regulations.

He vented some of his spleen on Vincent Sherman. The director, a liberal Democrat who had known him since the war, was surprised by his new conservatism. They had some long arguments over the Labour government's so-called Welfare State. As far as Reagan could see, nobody was well, and everybody fared badly. If this was socialism—stoppages, six-hour hospital queues, mile after mile of slate-roofed council houses—what price the New Deal?

Both men were destined to live long, and look back on their winter in Britain as a time of serious engagement. Sherman had to admit "that on some issues, especially regarding the Soviet Union, he was more correct than I was." Reagan wrote that he arrived, in 1949, at the "third plateau" of his political journey. First had come his disillusionment with the federal bureaucracy as an adjutant in the Army. Then there had been his revelation at Jimmy Roosevelt's that Communists were enemies of the Constitution. And now, having seen what happened when the economic order was forcibly turned upside down—civil servants becoming civil masters—"I shed the last ideas I'd ever had about government ownership of anything."

On January 6, 1949, Jack Warner replied to Reagan's letter. He had been predictably amused by its sexual innuendos and jokes about Anglo-English. "One of their expressions which [always] struck me as being very peculiar is 'keep your pecker up'!"

Wet week followed wet week, and the interminable little movie dropped foot by foot into Sherman's patient cans. One creaky *basha* board was enough to cause half a day's delay, as technicians debated whether tracking the creak to its source was properly a function of management or of labor.

Would color never return to the world? Through the black branches of chestnut trees, black cars beetled along the Victoria Embankment, sending sprays of puddle water into the gray river. Reagan had lost his own healthy glow, after two and a half months of malnutritive British meals. He did not trust the "steaks" in most London restaurants. There was no guarantee that they had not flexed, originally, between the poles of brewers' drays.

Pallor did not suit him. It accentuated his newfound care lines—an unflattering frown kept showing up in the daily rushes at Elstree. His skin yearned for the dry kiss of sunshine, and his bones for warmth. "Reagan does not look at all well," Jack Warner, Jr., reported to Steve Trilling on February 23. Then at last, daffodils blazed in Hyde Park. March had come. Sherman announced that *The Hasty Heart* would be finished, barring retakes, within two weeks.

Arthur Abeles, assistant managing director of Warner Bros. (U.K.), was taken aback when Ronald Reagan appeared suddenly in his office and said, "You want to go to the south of France?" Reagan explained that he had a long weekend free of retakes before his scheduled departure for the United States on March 24.

Abeles was agreeable, providing his wife came along. On March 19 they set off *à trois* for Dover. The car was no sooner loaded onto the ferry than Mrs. Abeles discovered she had forgotten her passport. She had no choice but to return home for it and follow by train while the two men continued south. Items of her silk underwear, delicately permeating their luggage, raised official eyebrows at Calais, but they were permitted to proceed with a murmured *"très joli."*

The rest of their journey to the Riviera was uneventful, except for several side trips in search of a tourist attraction called Poids Lourds. They failed to find it, although it was well signposted. During those long hours on the road, Abeles became aware of a "desolate" sadness in his traveling companion. He asked if there was any chance that Jane Wyman might relent on her decision. Reagan shook his head. "It seems like a lost cause," he said with eyes brimming. "There's nothing I can do."

Mrs. Abeles was waiting for them in Monte Carlo, where Reagan had a run of luck at the Casino.

On March 23, he was back at Elstree, considerably richer, his mood noticeably improved. He breezed through his retakes, and bade a cheerful good-bye to the rest of the cast. No doubt spring weather and the prospect of a first-class cabin on the *Queen Mary* had something to do with this recovery, but another reason might have been the pearly prettiness of Margaret Abeles. After seventy-two hours in his proximity, she sensed that Ronnie's "pecker" was at last on the rise.

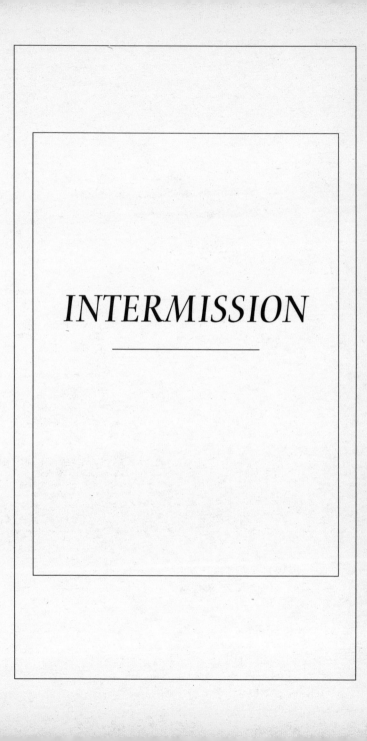

INTERMISSION

20

And Then
Along Came
Nancy

EVEN BEFORE *The Hasty Heart* opened in the fall of 1949, rumors were going around Hollywood that Ronald Reagan's career was on the skids. God seemed to agree, breaking the poor sap's right thigh so badly in a charity baseball game that he spent seven weeks immobilized in hospital. That gave him plenty of time to brood about Jane Wyman's Best Actress Academy Award for *Johnny Belinda*.

Released on aluminum crutches, he elected to stay away from the preview of his latest movie on October 11. This was probably just as well, because clanking painfully along in a bunched-up suit, his spectacles awry, he was by no means a glamorous sight. And Richard Todd, as expected, stole the show with insolent ease.

I am not sure if it was this preview or a later press screening that Paul Rae took me to, but I do remember us both being struck by the parallel between the cinematic Reagan being discharged from his *basha* into the arms of no one, and Dutch in real life having to deal with the same situation. We reacted with simultaneous shock during the following farewell scene between him and Pat Neal:

REAGAN   (*helping her with a heavy box of medicine*) Who's going to
         carry things for you when I'm gone?
NEAL   (*unconcerned*) I have no idea.
REAGAN   You'll find somebody. (*They face each other*)
NEAL   Yes, I suppose I will.

At that moment, a whiplash expression cracked across Dutch's face so quickly that it was gone by the time Paul ejaculated, "Did you see *that*?" We watched for further evidence of inner torment, but Dutch performed to the end with his usual insouciance, and afterward we were at a loss to say what, exactly, we had glimpsed. But the memory of that flash frame embedded itself, like the sliver of mirror in Andersen's fairy tale.

No question about it, 1949 was Ronald Reagan's *annus horribilis.* He was so helpless on crutches that Jane, shooting Hitchcock's *Stage Fright* in London, told him to stay in her new house, which was fully staffed. (They were both intermittently aware that their children lived there, too.) Reagan was still disabled when she got back, so he moved in with Nelle until such time as he could graduate to walking sticks and return to his bachelor apartment.

He began to fret for lack of work. The Screen Actors Guild occupied him only one night a week, and the Motion Picture Industry Council, which had elected him chairman *in absentia,* had not yet geared up to its self-appointed task of helping Hollywood Reds rehabilitate themselves. Now, if ever, he needed the support structure of his studio contract. Unfortunately, he and Lew Wasserman had renegotiated it just before his accident in order to win him the greatest possible independence—in exchange for a 50 percent reduction in guaranteed salary. All he could look to from Warners now was one $75,000 picture a year. And freelance "gimp" roles were few and far between. He calculated he was already down $160,000 in lost work and hospital charges.

Like Charles Ryder in *Brideshead Revisited,* Reagan found himself homeless, middle-aged, and loveless as his thirty-ninth year waned. Or, to quote a book he was more likely to have read, there was this passage in *Kings Row* about his paraplegic *alter ego,* written by Parris to Randy:

> The first thing that you must realize about him is that he is all at once living in another world, totally different from the one he has always known and inhabited. A different world, but he has only the old equipment that he had and used. . . .

The repairs to the body can so often be made in a short period of time. The injury to the mind, the *self,* to the deeply buried ego, to what is called the *psyche*—this takes longer. And that injury is more severe probably in Drake's case than it would be with an ordinary person. These psychic injuries strike at his pride, his self-respect, his independence and self-reliance, at his initiative, and at every phase of what is the real life of the personality. We shall have to save all of these if we are to save Drake.

Over the years, Reagan has belabored Drake's great cry, "Where's the rest of me?" to the point of cliché. I do not doubt, though, that he heard its overtone of castration more keenly in late 1949 than when he first shouted it on camera. All the qualities cut from Drake seemed to have been cut from him, too. Jane's surgical stroke (her decree became absolute while he lay trussed in hospital) called into doubt his sexuality, his acting ability, his political power. He had gotten used—too used— to bourgeois comforts: the chintzy house, the double paycheck, the button nose, the taut, available body (so delicious on free afternoons, when they were both fresh from the shower). Now his life was reduced to a clanking emptiness.

He was not, however, short of a date on Saturday night. Lame or not, Ronald Reagan was still one of Hollywood's prime eligibles. Nor was his professional situation as bleak as he might think. Jerry Wald wanted him to co-star, limp and all, with Ginger Rogers in *Storm Warning,* and Wasserman had struck a $375,000 deal with Universal for five pictures over five years. With stock income and bonuses, he could easily clear $200,000 a year through 1954. Yet he ached for another Jane. The young writer Doris Lilly sensed this replicative wistfulness, and decided not to encourage it.

"I just can't get it right," Reagan said, staring at her with an air of wounded innocence. "I'm no good alone."

She knew she was being proposed to, and the perplexity of his look touched her, but

what I knew for sure was that he didn't love me and I didn't love him. . . . I could have had him if I wanted him. If I was willing to make the big moves, push, be there, encourage him, never leave him alone for a moment, he would never leave me if I made him think he would be wrong to do so. Those soft, vulnerable eyes were staring into mine. I couldn't do it. . . . I would only bring him more misery later on. I let the moment go.

And then, to quote his later grateful words, "along came Nancy Davis and saved my soul."

☯

The name "Nancy Davis" may have crossed Reagan's gaze on October 28, 1949, when the *Hollywood Reporter* published a list of two hundred and eight co-signers of an *amicus curiae* Supreme Court brief filed in behalf of John Howard Lawson and Dalton Trumbo. But there were names of greater political weight to distract him. And that particular Nancy, being married, was unlikely to save his soul.

Quite another Nancy Davis happened to be working at MGM—a recently arrived ingenue—and she was decidedly not the type to sign bleeding-heart briefs. Sam Marx told me he had taken one look at her and decided to keep his distance. "A tough little broad with a jaw like Mammy Yokum. Ambitious as all get out. Doctor's brat—Smith College, Lake Shore Drive. One of Dore Schary's social obligations."

According to Sam, she had been hired not for talent or beauty, but because Dore Schary wanted to repay her father for medical favors. Nancy says that Schary had "a little crush" on her. I don't know; Dore was a cold fish. But they certainly had ambition in common. He wanted to be the first Jewish President of the United States, and Nancy—well, look what she got! How she engineered her first date with Dutch on November 15 is a matter of debate. Her story—and his—is that it was indeed the *Hollywood Reporter* list that brought them together. But Jill Schary Robinson swears Nancy and Ronnie were separate guests at a dinner party in her mother's house, weeks before the list was published. And there is a mid-October note in the SAG archives to the effect that Nancy Davis had informed the president, Ronald Reagan, of her "desire to run for the Board" in next month's annual election.

Well, so what if she made the first couple of moves? They are entitled to cite the list as a secondary, if not prime factor in their early relationship. Conservative Miss Davis was so worried about SAG confusing her with liberal Mrs. Davis that she got an MGM director, Mervyn LeRoy, to call Dutch and hint that her distress over imagined Communist associations would be greatly soothed by a dinner invitation.

Subtlety has never been Nancy's forte, but the fact remains that when Dutch rang the bell of her apartment that November night, leaning heavily on two canes, the door opened on a future beyond their combined powers of belief.

So there she stood in her black-and-white dress: exactly the right outfit for what was, after all, a professional appointment with the head of her union. Unlike Jane, who liked noisy bracelets and was quite capable of wearing patent-leather boots to the golf course, Miss Davis had a sense of style, her clothes always expensive, cut a cautious half-season behind the latest line, nicely mediating between *nouveau riche* vulgarity and upper-class dowd.

But Dutch, blind to fashion as to art, saw only, beneath the brunette hair and smooth brow, the wide-spaced brown eyes (actually hazel, he decided) that had always mesmerized him. Patient eyes, promising him the narcotic of endless attention. Nelle's eyes; Margaret's; Jane's, until the loss of Christine darkened them. Black pupils charmingly displaying duplicates of himself. Eyes a lifeguard might drown in.

One day, he would decorate his study with an oil painting of this face, done in such loving close-up that each eye was the size of an *oeuf en gelée.* Even so, he did not love the face at first sight, or persuaded himself that he did not.

Years later, he admitted that bells must have rung as they studied each other. "It was just that I had buried the part of me where such things happened so deep, I couldn't hear them."

ᕮ

The traditional privilege of being divorced, handsome, rich, and heterosexual is that you can make up for all the cheerleaders who rejected you in high school. Add to that a Cadillac convertible, and the celebrity quotient of being a star in a town with more pert breasts per square mile than anywhere outside of Bali, and it is no wonder that Errol ("In Like") Flynn congratulated Dutch on joining the ranks of Hollywood *roués.*

"Be happy, old sport. . . . Think of the parties, think of the *girls.* Do what I do."

A "girl" Nancy Davis wasn't. At twenty-eight, she already looked older than Jane, and her figure—five feet four inches of pile-driver purpose—was more suited to table-hopping than couch football. She was not averse to sex, as Dutch would discover. But for the next two years, he seemed keen to follow Flynn's advice.

My research cards show him stepping out with at least sixteen different young and beautiful actresses, from Doris Day and Rhonda Fleming to the peachy and not-yet-legal Piper Laurie. God knows how many more there were or how many came back to spend the night with him in his hillside apartment, with its celestial view of the sparkling city. He was always shy about speaking of such matters when I interviewed him as an old man, and to tell the truth, I didn't think it was my biographical business.

He did admit, once, to sleeping with so many girls that the morning came when he did not know who one of them was. I'll discreetly leave it at that.

☯

Dutch's "cocker spaniels," as he strangely dubbed them, tend to remember two things about him. One was his wounded quality, which at times verged on the masochistic: he would even visit the sets of Jane's pictures to watch her act, while she studiously avoided his gaze. The other thing was his torrential talkativeness. He seemed unable to understand that this, more than anything, had brought about his divorce. Political platitudes, committee chat, today's headlines, tomorrow's weather, *Reader's Digest* jokes poured from him in an unceasing stream, as his thin grin curled sideways and his gray-blue eyes begged for audience reaction. The mere word *Budapest* was enough to get him going on how the Reds broke Cardinal Mindszenty. "It really wasn't conversation, it was rather talking at you," Doris Day recalled. "I remember telling him that he should be touring the country making speeches."

Only one pair of ears, one set of wide-spaced eyes, could withstand this relentless spiel. Nancy Davis was a born receiver. Since childhood, she had been listening to the jocular (and frequently obscene) stories of her mother, a sometime trouper and one of Chicago's most Herculean gossips. These were admixed with the ongoing *viva voce* medical memoirs of her stepfather, Dr. Loyal Davis, a neurosurgeon of surpassing self-satisfaction. Even as a stage actress, which Nancy had briefly been on Broadway before coming to MGM, her gift was to vibrate like a membrane to the sonority of other speakers. Unlike them, she never seemed desperate to orate herself. She was, in other words, free of narcissism, that endemic plague of the *genus thespianus egotisticus.*

Nancy's chief charm was, and would always remain, a delightful laugh, never too prompt, as it so often is with society women, never forced, never condescending. Reagan was an occasional guest at the fast Jewish table in the Warners commissary, where Jack Benny and

Norman Krasna and the Epstein brothers tried daily to outrace one another's *niftiks.* Although he never matched their speed or verbal brilliance, he memorized such jokes as he could understand, in the sure knowledge that one person, at least, would crack up at his retelling. Again and again and again.

What did *she* want? Just Dutch, I think. In all the repetitive accounts of their courtship, her listening and laughing, her careful cultivation of his political side (she ran repeatedly, and with eventual success, for election to the SAG Board), amid all Kitty Kelley's innuendos about her sleeping her way to extensions of her MGM contract, one misses the simple conjecture that Nancy Davis was crazy about Ronald Reagan. "She's out for her own little self," Sam Marx sneered. I stopped believing that years ago. From the start, I think, she loved Dutch to the exclusion of any other man she had met and anyone else she would ever know, their own children included. As I write these words, he is drifting beyond all comprehension of who she is and what she has done for him. Cool to her at the start, warm, even adoring when she suited his larger purpose, he is cold to her at the end.

Meanwhile, she loves him still.

21

The Unexplored Mystery of Ploughed Ground

THE POST-WAR AIRLINE BOOM caused a boom in aviation advertising, and my ability to write technical copy brought freelance contracts with several Los Angeles agencies. One of them, McCann-Erickson, was headed by none other than Dutch's bullying brother, J. Neil Reagan.

Shelving dreams of Cinemascope glory, I wrote trade ads for Lockheed, brochures for Douglas, radio scripts for Pan Am. The money was good and the work easy, leaving me with plenty of time to indulge a hobby that had become a consuming interest, the collection of twentieth-century presidential manuscripts. It had begun before the war, when I saw a letter Theodore Roosevelt had written to Philip Dunne's father. A biographical seed was sown, I guess, for later flowering.

Preoccupied with these mundane pursuits, not to mention the to-and-fro responsibilities of a separated husband and father, I went to very few of Dutch's later movies. I remember only the one he made with Nancy Davis, *Hellcats of the Navy,* a turkey so many-feathered it practically squawked off the screen. Like most people, I lost interest in him as an actor, and assumed he would soon retire to a little stud farm he owned in Northridge and become a full-time breeder of racehorses.

It was impossible, though, to forget about him, because of his prominence as president of SAG and chairman of the Motion Picture Industry Council (MPIC). Movie actors often affect an interest in politics, usually when they're "between parts" and are going through character withdrawal. But Dutch's drive to orate, to change, to administer was nothing if not serious. On February 8, 1950, he attained *gravitas,* as the word is understood west of Cal Tech. That night, six hundred members of the Friars Club, representing Hollywood's élite, honored him in black tie at the Beverly Hills Hotel. The atmosphere was so respectful that the Friars dispensed with their traditional "roast." With Jane Wyman smiling at him from a side table, a succession of speakers praised him for the "stature and dignity" he had conferred upon the industry. Al Jolson sang "Sonny Boy" and said that he hoped that Al Jolson, Jr., would grow up "to be the kind of man Ronnie is." Cecil B. DeMille reminisced about the bad old days of pre-Reagan Tinseltown, Pat O'Brien hailed him as George Gipp reincarnate, and Ed Wynn injected some heavy humor with a speech punningly confusing "Ronnie Reagan" with the Irish tenor Phil Regan. (The fact that it worked shows how consistently Dutch's surname was mispronounced, even then.)

Paul Rae, who attended, said that he found the evening to be "more of a wake than a fest." The word *television* kept recurring in speeches at the podium, as if everyone sensed that a new entertainment age was dawning. George Burns had done a curious turn in which—forgetting about Dutch—he said he would try to adapt to the small screen. "I don't want to die with a silly expression on my puss, wondering if I could have made it."

Somber or not, the Friars ceremony was evidence that Ronald Reagan, still only thirty-nine, was being saluted for his future as well as his past.

Why such early adulation for a man I still thought of as a pleasant, if purposeful, mediocrity? I'm sure it was because his genial optimism stood in such contrast to contemporary *angst.*

"The only difference between an optimist and a pessimist," Clare Boothe Luce used to say, "is that a pessimist is usually better informed." Foreboding amounted to a fashionable posture in Los Angeles in the Fifties. We dreaded not only the westward creep of a television culture emanating from New York, but the worldwide spread of a repellent ideology promulgated in Moscow. HUAC had not stopped it; it was still here, undermining the state.

Paranoia and concealment became the American norm. Persuaders went into hiding. Nervous Brahmins formed the Committee on the Present Danger. The Bomb haunted Gavin's dreams. A flock of geese, homing in on the White House, blipped defense radar screens and caused a war scare. Ranch houses hunkered down. Jazz suppressed melody. Design became dun and dreary. Or "Dunne-dreary," as I joshed Phil when he filled his house with uncomfortable Eames furniture.

The corporation took control and the phrase *organization man* entered the language. Even J. Edgar Hoover's FBI dubbed itself "the Firm." MCA, Reagan's talent agency, reconstituted itself as an entertainment conglomerate, while its executives began to imitate the IBM "uniform" of charcoal suits and thin black ties.

Corporatism begat monolithism. Ayn Rand's *übermensch* novels sold by the millions, mainly to short businessmen. Everything got bigger: Big Business, Big Brothers of America, Big Labor, Big Government, Big Tits. Beyond bigness, greatness beckoned. The University of Chicago put out its series of Great Books of the Western World, most of them apparently written by Will and Ariel Durant, and followed up with its Great Ideas program to further improve the American mind. (Dutch improved *his* by going to see *The Great Caruso.*) Was this a great country, or what? Well, it wouldn't be for much longer if it didn't do something about the Great Conspiracy that was threatening its institutions! Before the decade was out, Capitalism and Communism would clash head-on in the Great Kitchen Debate.

It's easy enough to smile at the Fifties now. But it certainly was an age of fear and distrust—at home between black and white and left and right, abroad between East and West. Gavin's nuclear nightmares ("I saw God's face burning, filling the whole sky, and he looked just like a Chinaman!") were an amalgam of images he'd studied on the little screen of my TV: Mao Tse-tung, evil genius of the Korean War, and the mushrooming fireball over Eniwetok Atoll. God knows I dreamed of the Yellow Peril myself, not to mention the Red Menace, recrudescent as another round of HUAC hearings loomed.

The onset of that second inquisition happened to coincide all but exactly with Dutch's testimonial banquet. Less than twenty-four hours after the Friars went home, Senator Joseph McCarthy stood up before an audience in West Virginia and announced that he had in his hand "a list of two hundred and five . . . members of the Communist Party . . . working and shaping policy in the State Department." The rush to name, to punish or purge, was on.

Reagan reacted cautiously at first. Even though he was now earning serious money again, and dating a doctor's daughter, he still considered himself a liberal Democrat. This was true only in the sense that he stood just left of center on the boards of SAG and the MPIC, both of them conservative organizations. He did, however, campaign energetically in behalf of Helen Gahagan Douglas for the Senate in 1950, heedless of the "Pink Lady" taunts of her opponent, Richard Nixon.

"We appreciate your friend's help," Phil Dunne said wearily over the phone in late October. He was calling from Douglas headquarters. "But I wish," he went on, "that he'd stop sounding off about Commies at Council meetings. He's playing right into Nixon's hands."

"Well, you sound off about them yourself."

"Yes, but I'm not six foot something of movie-star muscle in a silk bow tie. He's a hard man, is Ronnie. People listen to him."

It was the first time I had heard anyone use the word *hard* in connection with Reagan. But Phil was an astute observer, and I began to sense hardness—indeed, something locomotive-like in Dutch's political progress, under a slowly mounting head of steam.

Now in his fourth year as president of SAG, he headed all negotiations with producer groups, often into the small hours of the morning. At membership meetings and press conferences, he could be verbose, but when he got a pen in his hand, his language was to the point. Here is Reagan on January 22, 1951, writing about the confusion over who was "Red" or not:

> Suppose we quit using the words Communist and Communism. . . . Substitute "pro-Russian" for the word Communist and watch the confusion disappear. . . . Democracy does guarantee the right of every man to think as he pleases, to speak freely and to advocate his beliefs. Democracy also provides defense against those who would deliver our nation into the hands of a foreign despot. Call them pro-Russian and take away the screen. If we must fight, make the enemy be properly uniformed.

I was so taken with this article that I added it to the scrapbook file I'd started back in 1928, when Dutch pulled off his midnight rescue at Lowell Park.

Looking at it now, I'm less impressed. On the surface, it reads like an invocation of one of the basic principles of the Bill of Rights: that freedom of speech is the best defense against sedition. Yet what disturbs a modern devotee of the First Amendment is evidence that Ronald Reagan "properly informed" against his own professional colleagues (if not in 1951, then certainly in 1947 and 1948) as FBI source T-10. The evidence, obtained under the Freedom of Information Act, was published in the San Jose *Mercury News* after his re-election to the Presidency. Although it is fragmentary (all language not pertaining directly to him has been blotted out by the Bureau's overworked staff of graffiti artists), it is specific.

I taxed him on the subject one day, and he retreated behind such a fog bank of circumlocution that there was no way to pursue him without shipwreck. I'll print something of what he said, but here first is what he *did*. His behavior was, as Richard Gid Powers would say, not without honor.

In 1943, Captain Ronald Reagan willingly answered FBI questions about the party at which he "almost came to blows" with a drunken antisemite (my guess: Errol Flynn). In September 1946, when he was under threat of an acid attack, he was recruited as informer T-10 by three Bureau representatives. On April 10, 1947, Ronald Reagan and Jane Wyman were "at home" with an agent (she co-operating with extreme reluctance) and together named at least six SAG members whom they suspected of being Communists. T-10 told the story of his HICCASP showdown with Dalton Trumbo and John Howard Lawson. On December 19, 1947, clearly despondent amid the ruins of his marriage, he complained about the prosecutorial tone of HUAC's recent hearings and said that the unfriendly witnesses "would have condemned themselves in the eyes of the public more efficiently" had they been allowed to air all the fatuities of their ideology. He also felt it was the business of Congress, and not *ad hoc* industry groups, to prosecute Communism. "Do they expect us to constitute ourselves as a little FBI of our own?" Finally, on February 10, 1948, he named or repeated about five names as representing the leader and members of a "clique . . . who invariably followed the Communist line" at SAG meetings.

Here's the nearest he ever got to naming names with me, when I asked him in 1987:

RR   I remember very well, there was this director who was suspect.
You looked at the record, you knew who was a Communist. . . .
Several of us asked this director to have dinner with us in one of the Hollywood cafés, and we said, "This is ridiculous. Tell us,

when you did such and such—some charity—who persuaded you to do that?" And he named a writer. And then he said, "Why, that son of a bitch!" because we were able to prove to him that this writer was a part of a Communist organization.

EM   Who was the writer?

RR   (*pretending not to hear*) This is what they would do . . . an old technique—

EM   Who was the director?

RR   I hate to say it now—it was . . . oh, Lord . . . still directing—the man with the beard—

EM   John Huston?

RR   Yes.

Again, not dishonorable—indeed, a protective gesture, no matter how clumsy, toward a creative original worth protecting. But those blotted-out names still float like flash marks in my eyes when I stand looking at the clean stone wall in Simi Valley where his own name will be carved.

☯

Let just three interrelated stories evoke the bitter flavor of those days. On March 13, 1951, Gale Sondergaard, a veteran Academy Award–winning actress, informed the SAG board of directors that she had been served a subpoena to appear before HUAC. If asked to name names, she absolutely would not, even though "by the next day I may have arrived at the end of my career as an actress." She intended to take the Fifth Amendment, and asked her union to support her. The board should denounce the Committee's "attacks, insinuations, and sneers," and make "a public declaration that it will not tolerate any industry blacklist against any of its members."

Miss Sondergaard's letter was published in *Daily Variety* and caused wild excitement at both ends of the political spectrum. With guts and superb timing, she had dared Ronald Reagan and his fellow directors to accept the reality of an actors' blacklist, or to deny there was one in the face of her own self-sacrifice.

One might have admired her courage more had she not been married to Herbert Biberman, one of the original Hollywood Ten, and had her letter not been such an obvious political trap. Reagan's reaction was predictable, given what he had himself written about "cynical" Reds hiding behind the Constitution. At an emergency session of the board, he said that Miss Sondergaard wanted SAG to condone and help conceal everything she had ever done politically. And he did not see how HUAC could be condemned for the tone of a round of hearings yet to begin. The lady's appeal must be rejected.

His board agreed, and on March 20 John Dales, SAG's executive secretary, published an impatient answer to Miss Sondergaard in the *Hollywood Reporter.*

> The Guild Board believes that all participants in the international Communist Party conspiracy against our nation should be exposed for what they are—enemies of our country and of our form of government.
>
> It is not the province of the Guild Board to decide what is the best method of carrying out this aim. It is our hope that the current House Committee hearings will help to do so, in an objective and intelligent manner. . . .
>
> The Guild as a labor union will fight against any secret blacklist. . . . On the other hand, if any actor by his own actions outside of union activities has so offended American public opinion that he has made himself unsaleable at the box office, the Guild cannot and would not want to force any employer to hire him.

Or her. John Dales, a mild dull man, told me long afterward that he regretted the tone of this letter and implied that it was forced on him by Dutch. Revisionism is a perquisite of old age. At any rate, Miss Sondergaard did not enter a movie studio again for twenty years.

The Anne Revere affair, in contrast, was moral rather than political. Reagan came off badly: cool, uncaring. Miss Revere, whom he knew from HICCASP days, was an Academy Award–winning actress, an admitted former Communist, and a board member of SAG. As quiet and scrupulous as Miss Sondergaard was pushy, she now heard that the Committee was after her.

It was typical of Anne Revere's dignity that she did not beg the help of her fellow directors. Reagan had to raise the matter himself at a board meeting on May 28, 1951.

"You know," he hinted, "anybody that's got a problem, all they have to do is come to us."

There was a silence, then she said, "I have a problem. What's your suggestion?"

"It's so simple. All you've got to do is just name a couple of names that have already been named."

"That's it," Miss Revere said. "I can't climb up on somebody's neck." She resigned at once, and did not act again in Hollywood for eighteen years.

After she left town, Paul Rae printed a sardonic couplet in his column:

> Listen, my children, and ye shall hear
> Of the career suicide of Anne Revere.

My third bitter little story grows directly out of the first two. Dutch hated the idea of government vigilantism, and had what he thought was a simple scheme to prevent it. The second round of Committee hearings had brought forth such unctuous confessions and self-purgings from men such as Larry Parks, Sterling Hayden, and Edward ("I was a bad Communist") Dmytryk that he proposed the creation of a permanent MPIC forum to encourage other repentant Reds to come forward. They would volunteer their past *petits moments d'embarras*, find out what was being "said about them" in Washington, beg forgiveness, swear loyalty to the flag, and have certificates of corrective information issued to prospective employers. The forum, to be known as the Patriotic Services Committee, would be empowered to hear confessions and keep records, but not punish wrongdoing.

Dutch had personally helped "rehabilitate" Dmytryk, and one can only assume that the experience of watching a man struggle for grace had satisfied the old Sunday-school teacher in him. But leave it to scribes to stir up dissent—the Screen Writers Guild (urgently lobbied by Philip Dunne) used its veto power on the MPIC to kill Dutch's proposal.

Phil explained to me that his guild disliked the whole idea of a central repository of names and confessions. It could only grow and develop an appetite for more information. "And information is power." He'd already heard that the ultra-conservative American Legion was talking about giving the MPIC a list of all *its* lists, compiled from posts all over the country.

"There seems to be a new breed around town," Dutch declared angrily. "The anti-anti-Communists . . . their minds need reconditioning."

☯

Nancy Davis, meanwhile, had become Ronald Reagan's steadiest date. She reached the height, if that's the right word, of her brief movie career in *The Next Voice You Hear,* which had her name up in lights outside Radio City Music Hall in New York. Paul Rae saw it and reviewed it in his column. He trashed its sentimentality, but he was kind to her as "a capable and steady-eyed young actress." In particular he praised the beauty of her low and cultivated voice, quoting Shakespeare on the subject.

Commentators who like to *chercher la femme* behind every strong leader try to blame Reagan's rightward shift on Nancy. But it had demonstrably occurred five years before he met her. In any case she was not a political person, unless you call social climbing a form of politics. (Which I guess it is: the cultivation of facilitators, the private plotting and public self-display, the distribution and retrieval of chits.)

Nor did Miss Davis have his undivided attention before the end of 1951. Dutch was still, to her intense chagrin, carrying a torch, and there were rumors of him and Jane remarrying. They dined out occasionally, appeared at each other's celebrations, and maintained a dignified silence about their divorce. When Laurence Beilenson, one of Dutch's lawyers in *Reagan v. Reagan,* was in his nineties, he told me he had never known litigants so free of rancor.

What torments of jealousy their reunions inflicted on Nancy can be imagined. I remember a magazine picture of Jane showing up radiant at the 1951 Photoplay Awards, followed by Dutch in earnest horn-rims and Nancy, his nominal date, looking like a matron of honor. When I saw the picture again in one of the Reagan scrapbooks, Jane's image had been savagely torn off.

Matronliness, at any event, prevailed. On March 4, 1952, Dutch and Nancy were married at The Little Brown Church in the Valley, with only two witnesses present, and seven and a half months later they confirmed the birth of their first child, Patricia Ann Reagan.

In November, Ronald Reagan stepped down as president of the Screen Actors Guild, just as Dwight D. Eisenhower was elected President of the United States. Were fate not to bring them together years later, this clockwork coincidence would be hardly worth noting. Significant, too, is the fact that Reagan was one of the millions of Democrats who voted for Ike.

He did not do so without pangs of liberal guilt. "I must confess my enthusiasm cooled a little as the campaign progressed," he wrote an old friend in Eureka. "[Eisenhower] did not grow in stature, and frankly I thought Stevenson did." Dutch was even franker in his opinion of the Vice President–elect:

> Pray as I am praying for the health and long life of Eisenhower because the thought of Nixon in the White House is almost as bad as

that of "Uncle Joe." Let me as a Californian tell you that Nixon is a
hand picked errand boy with a pleasing facade and naught but
emptiness behind. He has been subsidized by a small clique of oil
and real estate pirates, he is *less than honest* and he is an ambitious
opportunist completely undeserving of the high honor paid him.

By the new year of 1953, he began to feel the first chill winds of insecurity. At Warner Bros., he was regarded as yesterday's talent. From
time to time on the advertising-agency circuit, I heard that Dutch was
thinking of a job in television. An announcer at KTTV said that a little old lady had brought Ronald Reagan into the studio to see how he
looked behind a sculpted news desk.

"His *mother*?"

"Yes. Dynamic old devil—strong—like a ramrod. Hair as dark as
his. She did most of the talking. Seemed to be worried about him."

I reported this item to Paul, for inclusion in his column. He rolled his
eyes. "People aren't interested in Dutch-boy anymore."

Then, during the holiday season, when I was subbing for a radio
writer at McCann-Erickson, the control man came in with a manuscript. "You know this guy, don't you?"

Even upside down, I recognized Dutch's dogged handwriting. "Creative director wants to know what you think of it," the man said, and
went off.

I leafed through fourteen sheets of rough gray notepaper, each let-
terheaded "YEARLING ROW." Perhaps I should say "horseheaded,"
because the awkward block capitals were flanked dexter and sinister by
profiles of two sable stallions, regardant. The name alone was enough
to identify it as Ronald Reagan's new ranch in Agoura. (Odd that wife
number two should tolerate an address so clearly inspired by wife number one.) Attached was a memo: "Maybe we should consider this proposal seriously, RR being Mr. Reagan's brother."

I settled down with the document, wishing Paul Rae were with me so
I could read it aloud and hear his reaction.

  The foregoing article was written to give some hint of the flavor of
Yearling Row, our ranch in the Malibu Hills. The few incidents related are true.

  It is our idea that a radio series could be built based on the personal incidents as well as the ranch happenings of a Hollywood couple, an Actor and Actress who go into ranching.

  Not only is the unusual Husband and Wife situation enhanced by
a motion picture background, but it is played in a setting boasting its

own glamor and adventure, a thoroughbred horse farm. Remember too that we ride them as well as raise them because in addition to racing stock Yearling Row is the home of fine hunters and jumpers. One has been featured in several pictures of mine.

I flicked down a few paragraphs in search of something more personal. Yup, there it was, halfway down page two—a pretty clear hint that Dutch was hard up:

In the spangled world of show business where money comes, not often but in chunks, the uncertainties of a feast or famine existence have added to the dream a sort of "being practical for the future" tinge . . . thanks to the U.S. dept. of Internal Revenue whose legal take can amount to as much as 91% of an actors salary.

If I had known what a passionate tax reformer he was to become, I guess I would have taken notice of this early assault upon Uncle Sam. But my attention was diverted by another personal hint—that Dutch had become uxorious:

The rest of "we" is my wife Nancy Davis and she must certainly stem from pioneer stock. I know of no other way to explain her courage in being willing to trade the familiarity of curb stones for the unexplored mystery of ploughed ground. Reared in Chicago, educated at Smith and in Hollywood via Broadway she brought to the land a love of beauty, a complete rejection of anything that crawled, flew or slithered and an unexplainable conviction that my ideas made sense. This latter quality I am hoping will survive the familiarity of the forthcoming years of marital experience.

There followed a guarded description of Yearling Row: three hundred and fifty acres of mountain and valley high above Malibu, yet only a "hop-skip-and-a-Cadillac" from Tinseltown. Its mortgage was crippling, its chaparral rampant, its well water bitter as hemlock (despite fifteen thousand dollars sunk into new pumps). Fifty expensive and greedy steers had contracted pinkeye and were now worth about half of what he had paid for them. A "grand old mare" had gotten tangled up in barbed wire, bloodily enough to have to be shot ("I couldn't ask someone else to do my job, so I loaded up the rifle"). And— Dutch's idea of irony—a phone call from Hollywood had just come in, saying that he had been rejected for an outdoor-picture role "because the producer didn't think I was the ranch type."

I had to inform McCann-Erickson that I didn't think Dutch was the
radio type, either.

> At least three pp. of the narrative material he offers us are devoted
> to hydraulics. Possibly this might appeal to Agri-Flo, Inc., should you
> approach them for sponsorship, but I don't see many listeners, aside
> from the 874 licensed plumbers in L.A. County, holding their breath
> over pipeline problems. Mr. Reagan seems to think that his film-star
> status is enough to guarantee widespread interest. In that regard, we
> should note that Warner Bros. were happy to let him go last year
> (after sixteen years contract service), and that even his fan club has
> gone out of business.
>
> The point has been made that Mr. Reagan is the brother of JNR.
> I would suggest the most tactful way to spare them both embarrass-
> ment would be for somebody in the New York office to write and say
> that McCann-E. is concerned with a possible conflict of interest.

Having thus helped materially to impoverish a future President of the
United States (*mea culpa,* Dutch!), I went back to freelance work and
heard nothing more about Yearling Row—either the ranch or the series.

Thirteen months later, on February 15, 1954, Paul ran the following
item in his column:

> RONALD REAGAN, former prexy of SAG, has signed up as
> emcee for a variety act in Vegas. He opens tonite at the Last Frontier
> Hotel with THE CONTINENTALS, four slapstick minstrels in the
> Marx Bros. tradish. Ronnie won't dance (though he swings a mean
> shoe, says DORIS DAY). He'll crack a few Irish jokes, do his
> patented Kraut beer-garden routine (*Vas vils du haben?*), horse
> around with the guys, and yell "Fire!" if the show bombs. Club date
> is for two weeks only.
>
> It's a long way down for Reagan from his box-office glory of 11
> years ago—for a while there, before UNCLE SAM doused his glims,
> he was Hollywood's No. 1 draw. How quickly we forget! But that's
> showbiz, and Ronnie has always been a trouper.
>
> Big-eyed NANCY DAVIS will be in the Ramona Room to cheer
> her hubby on. Or up, as the case may be.

My scrapbook of Paul's clips preserves this rather shamefaced se-
quel, dated March 5:

"From there . . . he's gonna watch the sun go down on Hollywood's golden years."
Reagan riding in the Malibu hills, ca. 1955.

RONALD REAGAN has nixed an offer from HERMAN HOVER to extend his fortnighter in Vegas. Show was a sellout smash, with regular standing O's for Reagan as raconteur and graceful fall guy.

Hover tried to tempt him with more big bucks, plus offers from the Waldorf in New York and other glitterspots, but Rancher Ron, 43, is hanging up his straw hat and cane. Says he has critturs to feed at "Yearling Row," his retreat in the Malibu hills.

From there, we guess, he's gonna watch the sun go down on Hollywood's golden years—while TV's cool moon rises in the east.

22

Remember
Old Ma Reagan

A Studio Interview, 1954

S HE HAS ALREADY BEGUN TO SING "Beautiful, Beautiful Brown
Eyes," in a surprisingly sweet and steady soprano, before the studio engineer is quite ready to record. Gene Sterling, her partner in amateur duets, strums a guitar, his reedy tenor belting out the melody while she holds the descant.

Listening through earphones as the fragile tape unwinds from reel to reel, I fight to stay clearheaded and contemporary, to identify elements of Dutch's diction in hers. But the sound of Nelle singing that hokey old hit makes the past surge up like wine to the head.

Nothing, aside from the primal scents we all carry in memory, is more evocative of other days, other lives, than trapped voices. Just one refrain, and I am back in 1954, humming along with her. She seems to have had a personal reason for choosing this particular song, coyly substituting a new line into the refrain:

> *Nellie, I love you my darlin' . . .*

Nothing here of Dutch, unless it is the grace with which she approaches her final cadence, lungs still full of breath, and sustains the last note for three full beats. Maybe she taught him how to time his punch lines and benedictions. More likely, she didn't need to. A sense of meter, as Bess used to say, comes with mother's milk.

The sound level changes, and suddenly we are into the formal interview, which appears to have gone out from a Los Angeles radio station. Somebody named Neil Morrow introduces her in the unctuous tones mikesters deem appropriate for little old ladies:

MORROW   She's so famous and so talented and everyone just loves her
          for the many, many—
NELLE   (*interrupting*) Now dear, dear, dear.
MORROW   —good works she does. It's all very true.
NELLE   (*laughing heartily*) No-o. I'm afraid it isn't. I'm afraid I'm a
          has-been.

Aha: first evidence of Dutch in that "No-o." Jovial self-deprecation; the monosyllable enunciated as a complete sentence. One can see her lips pursing around it, the same way his used to. And does she also, perhaps, tilt her head winningly to the right? She knows that she is being patronized, but does not mind; is content, for the moment, to let Morrow handle things.

Dismayingly, he feeds her a cue she is not ready for. "I understand this is also for the Children's Hospital. . . . Is that right, Mrs. Reagan?"

Bewildered at the podium, the President of the United States stands wordless, waiting for aides to prompt him. Three seconds of dead air ensue. Sterling comes to the rescue: "The Olive View Sanitarium and the USO Shows." She recovers quickly—"Oh yes, yes"—and laughs with relief when Morrow soothes, "I can see where Mrs. Reagan's famous son gets his talent now."

He tells her that he recently had the pleasure of interviewing "Ronnie" in Las Vegas. "And his wife Nancy Davis—such a lovely couple." Nelle's response is short and cool. "Oh."

I sense the quick annoyance that egocentrics betray the moment attention is diverted from themselves. *Who's this interview about, anyway?* Dutch used to react in just the same way, although he hid it better. Sterling backs Morrow up: "Such a handsome couple." It is time for her to take control.

NELLE   They tell me that Ronald, that he looks so much like me—
          and I would call him handsome—it's like you just called
          me handsome—

MORROW   Well, you're much prettier, naturally—

NELLE   (*interrupting*) Well, of course, of course! Yes, indeed!

MORROW   All the boys at USO in Hollywood say that, too.

NELLE   Yes. Well, why wouldn't they love old Ma Reagan? (*Catching herself*) She's seventy . . . those soldier boys, they make such a fuss over me that I just think, oh dear, they must think I'm about eighteen or twenty years old! (*She stops and waits for confirmation*)

STERLING   Oh, why certainly you *act* like you're eighteen years old.

More hearty laughter. She is in excellent humor again, ready for the moment she knows is coming. Morrow gives it to her. "Would you like to say something, ah, for the folks . . . ?"

If I thought I recognized some filial inflections in her last speech, all doubt is swept aside now. Nelle affects the same shy surprise that Dutch did as President, when offered the privilege of the floor. "Oh, to my friends up in Dixon?" Her voice is soft and tentative.

STERLING   Uh huh.

NELLE   (*still questioning*) And all around, wherever they might possibly get a chance to hear this here—if you're making a record of it? (*She needs no further encouragement and segues rapidly into her memorized remarks, speaking with confident briskness*) Oh yes, my dears, I've been so wanting to have a record made, so that I could talk to you and tell you how much I love you, and how I hope that my son Ronald will let me go back, because at the age of seventy, you're never quite sure just when your time is up. And I must see you all (*emphatic ritardando*) just—once—again. So God bless you, I love you, and don't you ever forget old Ma Reagan, will you. Old Nelle Reagan.

No we won't, Ma, not as long as we remember Ronald, dub off your master, reel off your reel.

ê

VALEDICTORY

Three years after this interview, Nelle Reagan, afflicted with severe arteriosclerosis and taking what comfort she could in the church, began to confuse her younger son with his father. "His heart is bad like mine. . . . I am sorry that Ronald has to suffer for he isn't old like me."

In 1958, the family removed her to a nursing room in Santa Monica. "Don't worry," a staff member assured Nancy Reagan, "after twenty-four hours here, she'll never remember she was anywhere else."

If so, Nelle's final awareness of her environment must have been like Ronald's first: a narrow bed, close walls, one window full of light. She spent her last years clutching a teddy bear, and died of a cerebral hemorrhage on July 25, 1962, aged seventy-nine. Like Jack Reagan before her, she was buried without a headstone.

23

Ladies and Gentlemen of the California Fertilizer Association

A Speech

THE PAST IS A SCREEN on which memory projects movies. I view the Thirties in a nostalgic Technicolor glow, and the Forties as richly *noir,* full of guys in low-brimmed hats stepping into dark doorways, or fleeing their shadows as they race down wet cobbled streets. (Blacklisted Bernie Vorhaus got out of the country just ahead of the Feds.) My vision of the Fifties is grayer and more diffuse, cramped within a smaller, round-cornered frame. The sweeping saga *Pax Atomica,* reformatted to fit your TV!

Images of my son and depressive wife flash onto it—her features blurring, then snowed out altogether on December 22, 1955. *Fein Liebchen, gute Nacht!* Dissolve to a series of other portraits in no particular order: John Foster Dulles in a yachtsman's duffel, Roger Bannister breasting a thin white ribbon, Dominguín swirling a *verónica,* Ike momentarily dropping his grin for a "sneer of cold command," Phil Dunne scriptwriting in his Malibu garden, the sun gilding his pale hair. And again and again, every Sunday night it seemed, Ronald Reagan walking wide-shouldered onto the set of *General Electric Theater* and saying, "Progress is our most important product."

I can't say I cared for him in his new guise of corporate spokesman for GE (too glib, too reverential) even though I was a whore of Madison Avenue myself. Indeed, I used to watch the marvelous educational commercials on Dutch's show with envy, wishing that they could be farmed out to freelance writers. To "script a spot" on the nation's top-rated weekend program was to win the respect of account executives in New York, where I wanted to relocate, away from Sydney Ann's memory and Gavin's adolescent *angst,* away from the demoralized and shrunken picture industry.

Dutch, who has always had a sense of current historical change, was aware of television's ascendancy long before he married Nancy and invested his savings in Yearling Row. All those nervous jokes about the new medium at the Friars Club had not prevented him from making his small-screen debut on CBS's *Nash Airflyte Theatre* before the Fifties had fairly begun.

Then, on July 23, 1952, exercising all the powers he had acquired in five years as president of the Screen Actors Guild, he signed a "blanket waiver" that allowed his own talent agency, MCA, to operate as a television producer. This *carte blanche,* exclusively granted, went against SAG's whole history of insisting that agents stay out of production. Now MCA could hire its own actors and shoot its own shows, uncontrolled by any studio.

One did not have to be a cynic to note that Lew Wasserman, the president of MCA, would be a principal beneficiary of the deal, and was likely to reward a client who had been so generous. Even I, believing Dutch to be incorrupt, was rendered thoughtful by Paul Rae's captionless cartoon the day after the waiver was signed. It showed "Ron and Lew," identically clad in black suits and thin black ties, doing a jubilant soft-shoe at the "Revue Club"—Revue being the name of MCA's new production subsidiary.

(I thought of that cartoon many years later, when Wasserman, rich beyond computation, came to the White House and was welcomed by President Reagan in the East Wing: "Lew, did you ever think, when you were a theater usher in Cleveland and I was a lifeguard in Illinois, that we might end up here?" And they strolled, still dark-suited, into the Oval Office together.)

Despite the burrowings of several determined conspiracists, no evidence of Ronald Reagan profiting personally from the waiver has ever been found. Indeed his fellow board members, some of whom were not MCA clients, gave him unanimous authority to sign. The determining factor, Wasserman told me many years later (cadaverous, bony, nail-polished, tensely rictal atop his black glass tower in Universal City) was *film.* Television technology in 1952 was poised uncertainly between "live" production—easy, cheap, blooper-prone—and filming, which was more expensive but editable. Wasserman figured that the latter alternative would be more profitable in the long run, because producers could guarantee advertisers a consistent product. But Hollywood studios were loath to waste good celluloid on "commercial trash."

It was this obstructionism that had caused Wasserman (desperate to begin filming thirty-two episodes of *Kit Carson* for Coca-Cola) to ask for the waiver. Reagan responded positively in behalf of SAG's film-trained majority. Otherwise, he feared that SAG would lose out to AFTRA (the American Federation of Television and Radio Artists), whose members were already flocking in droves to "live" studios in the East. His duty as president was surely to agree to any deal that would increase the diminishing number of film roles available on the West Coast.

So Kit Carson rode again, SAG's index of tapped players went up, and Coca-Cola moved nearer to its marketing dream of one Coke per person per hour, everywhere in America every day. Ronald Reagan, in the meantime, was reincarnated as "Mr. Progress."

He has been maligned over the years by former liberal colleagues for selling his soul to GE. Actually, all he did in the spring of 1954 was allow MCA to lease his voice and body to the New York advertising agency Batten, Barton, Durstine & Osborn. BBD&O in turn offered him to GE as the "program supervisor" of a new Sunday-night series: thirteen half-hour dramas, to be produced by Revue. As an added—perhaps clinching—inducement, the agency stated that Mr. Reagan, a gifted speaker, would be available for personal appearances at GE facilities across the country during non-production periods. He could be relied on to improve plant morale and do useful public-relations work within the larger "GE community."

General Electric Theater made its debut on September 26, 1954. It proved instantly popular, topping *I Love Lucy* as early as November. "I am seen by more people in one week," Reagan boasted, "than I am in a full year in movie theaters." The realization seemed to make him nervous at first. I watched the show's pioneering "Christmas Special" in color, and found him not quite comfortable as host, with a hand-washing habit reminiscent of Mr. Jaggers in *Great Expectations*. But Dutch was always a quick study, and by the spring of 1955 had established himself as one of the most relaxed and attractive hosts on the air.

BBD&O paid him well, on a rapidly sliding scale starting at $125,000 per annum, but drove him hard. A clause in his five-year contract required him to travel—shades of Jack Reagan!—for GE at least sixteen weeks of the year. Much of that time was devoted to sitting and sleeping in trains, since he still refused to fly. He was encouraged to say what he liked wherever he went, as long as he promoted the general idea of free enterprise, and the clean appeal of electricity. After two initial eight-week trips, his later itineraries were mercifully reduced to seven weeks each, and then to six.

Even so, the routine remained punishing. Already, by the summer of 1955, Reagan calculated that he had met a hundred thousand GE workers in 185 facilities across the country. (Or was it the same worker a hundred thousand times? The great corporation was so uniform in dress and image design it might have been managed by Mao Tse-tung.) "A typical day," he wrote, "would include a press conference, noon and evening banquets, high school or college campus appearances, and anywhere from six to fourteen meetings with industry employees." His final estimate, after eight years of corporate spokesmanship, was that two of them had been spent on the road. "I was on my feet in front of a 'mike' for about 250,000 minutes."

This hortatory chore, which most actors would have found intolerable, perversely appealed to Reagan more than did the klieg-lit glamour of the show itself. The fact that he found it delightful—indeed, deeply satisfying to his didactic urges—proved that he had at last become more politician than actor. He now sought to instruct as well as entertain, using all the histrionic skills he had acquired since Nelle taught him dialect humor as a child.

And he succeeded brilliantly, with standing ovations wherever he went. A 1958 survey found him to be one of the most recognized men in the country. Thus was amply fulfilled a fantasy he had indulged twenty-one years before, on first hearing that Hollywood wanted him: "Hmmm! Suppose some day Reagan will be greeting America as some Guest at plenty of bucks per syllable?"

As television became more and more the daily drug of American domestic life, it institutionalized itself, and freelance hacks such as I had to be content with less and less glamorous assignments. My business reverted almost entirely to print: airline brochures, corporate reports, the occasional radio script for a menswear store. In final humiliation, I was "awarded" a contract to sweeten the malodorous image of the California Fertilizer Association.

My first assignment was to record and publicize the Association's annual convention in Los Angeles on November 10, 1958. The guest speaker was—"But *of course,*" Paul groaned—none other than the Lifeguard of Lowell Park, in the latest of his bewildering transformations.

So here I was, taking my place on a plywood chair in the Ambassador Hotel Ballroom, with a long afternoon to go before drinks, bracing for the usually depressing experience of hearing an actor talk in his own voice. Almost in spite of myself, I quickly became fascinated by Dutch's own fascination with what he was saying, and by the hypnosis I felt all around me—that slow-breathing, slack-jawed attention orators thirst for.

My notes are mainly atmospheric and visual, because I had a tape recorder, and as long as its needle kept flickering, could let a stenographer worry about how to handle the amazing speed of his delivery.

He started off with four well-paced jokes, each funnier than the last. My needle went into the red zone for half a minute after he told one about a minister friend who arrived to preach at a rural church and found only a single worshiper in attendance. The minister came down the aisle to ask whether, in the circumstances, a sermon was called for:

> And the fellow said, "Well, I wouldn't know about that sort of thing, but [*rapidly*] I do know this, if I loaded up a truckful of hay and took it out on the prairie and only one cow showed up [*half breath*], I'd feed her." [*Laughter*] Well! Bill [*laughter*], Bill figured this was a cue, so he got back in the pulpit and an hour and a half later said "Amen." And he went down and said, "Well, my friend . . . what did you think?" and the fellow says, "Well, like I told you, I don't know about that sort of thing, but [*extremely rapidly*] I do know this, if I loaded up a truckful of hay and took it out on the prairie and only one cow showed up, I sure as hell wouldn't give her the whole load."

Crapmeisters crack up, I scribbled. *Guy next to me purple in face.*

Dutch let the laughter roll like a breaking wave, then said half apologetically, before it dissipated, "You know, any speaker at any kind of affair always tries to establish some relationship between himself and the audience." They were still laughing; the relationship was his to consummate. He did so quickly. "There are certain critics of a hostile nature to my business who would say that there's probably a similarity of product that would make my being here—"

This time the wave drowned him out, and he knew he could talk as long as he liked.

There was little humor to follow, except for occasional flashes of sarcasm. He segued into a demographic description of Hollywood's movie community, with statistics that proved it was more God-fearing, good-neighborly, monogamous, and anti-Communist than the national average.

> Seventy percent of our people are married, more than seventy percent of those to their first husband or wife. . . . We lead the nation in proportionate numbers in church membership and attendance, and we have the lowest crime rate of any industrial or professional group in the world, not excluding the clergy.

His voice got harder as he described the present dereliction of his beloved "three-billion-dollar" industry. Racked by the uncertainties of freelance contracts, paralyzed by antitrust restrictions at home, crowded by protectionist powers abroad, Hollywood picture producers were now "prey to government interference and harassment at every level, and its twin evil, taxation."

Actors, too, were suffering, with surtax rates of 91 percent. The surtax applied to all top-bracket earners, but only actors were forced to pay double income tax if they worked part of the year overseas. Reagan thought he detected a lingering Puritan disapproval of the playing profession in such discriminations.

Then he began to complain about the unfairness of a State Department exchange program that permitted "Russians" to re-edit Hollywood movies into anti-American propaganda. "But even more serious than this, in the field of government interference, is the field of political censorship." I thought he was veering dangerously far from the interests of manure merchants, yet there was no coughing or shifting; the corrugated necks in front of me did not swivel. They sat there in their shiny-trousered suits, nodding at his certainties, enraged by his rage. And I understood that he had chosen his audience well.

These men worked, literally, at the grass roots of the American economy. Their business was growth, the force that through the green fuse drove the flower. Any idea of restraint—whether of free enterprise or free speech or worship or water—was abhorrent to them. Parched, they eagerly drank in what Dutch had to say. It amounted (I realize now) to his basic domestic-policy message for the next twenty-two years. If they didn't all vote for him quadrennially from '66 until he finally stopped running, then they must have died, or been bribed by Democrats.

Which brings me to a circled item in my notes: *RR anti-govt. but studiously non-partisan. Rep. or Dem? Maybe just MGF.* (Sloan Wilson's Man in the Gray Flannel Suit, the classic decent, anti-authoritarian businessman.)

Dutch went on at surprising length about the First Amendment. I would not have expected a corporate spokesman and learner of scripts to question the right of "experts" to control expression. He noted that in the last session of Congress, no fewer than five bills "would have put non-defense departments and bureaus of the government under the security provisions, and would have made it a felony to report [their] doings."

Political censorship, he said, was concerned more with power than morals. "It gets into the very dangerous area of thought control." What worried him was that Americans were getting used to it, that a whole generation of young people was being taught "to accept that someone can tell them what they can read, and what they can hear from a speaking platform, and what they can think, and what they can say." I could hear an applause line coming. "Freedom," Dutch declaimed, "is never more than one generation from extinction."

I kept on listening because he was dancing all over the ring now. The words *government* and *taxation* burst from his lips so often that they lost their meaning, and became mere rhythmic jabs whose force depended on frequency. Mixed in with the blows were countless statistics, flying too fast to concentrate on, stinging us like sweat until we could only retreat before his relentless advance. "Thirty-four percent of your phone bill is taxed, and twenty-seven percent of your gas and oil, and more than twenty-five percent of your automobile . . ."

Aware that we needed some light relief, Dutch treated us to a bit more entertainment. He said that the complexity of the U.S. tax code had forced the government to issue "a simplified form ten-forty." Not so simple, though, that the 1040 didn't need a separate book of instructions to explain it. "I was very interested in reading one sentence I would like to quote to you."

There followed a two-hundred-and-twelve-word convolution that sounded like a parody of *Finnegans Wake.* He read it *accelerando,* with only the slightest pauses for breath, and well before he was through he had us laughing and groaning. It was a virtuoso performance, akin to his recitation of the books of the Old Testament in *The Hasty Heart.*

But then he turned serious again, pointing out that a government capable of this kind of verbal terrorism reserved the right to penalize, years later, any honest citizen confused by it. As for supertax payers like himself, its progressive scales threatened "propertyless uniformity and collectivism."

The last word got our attention.

If I had to choose one word to describe the salient characteristic of the revolution of our times, the word would be *collectivism*—the tendency to center the power of all initiative in one central government. One central authority and its organs. And the weapon, the revolutionary agent that has brought this about has been the tax machine. . . .

[Today's] entire system of taxation was spawned more than a hundred years ago by Karl Marx, who listed it as the prime essential of a socialist state.

Unquestionably, GE had chosen its spokesman well. "Mr. Progress" managed to make Washington sound worse than competitive against private enterprise, even predatory: "When you ask the government for help, you wind up with a partner." He went on at such length about the "outright socialization of the medical profession" that I wrote in my notes, *Dr. Loyal Davis??*

Dutch was by now in the state of fine frenzy that signals peroration, but seemed unable to stop. I let the tape roll and jotted the remainder of his speech in word clumps:

- *average citizen "abs. helpless"—concentration of power "v. essence of totalitarianism"*
- *either we run govt. or govt. runs us—Burke: "all that's nec. for evil is for good men to do nothing."*
- *must have courage, when calling for govt. cuts, to accept them in our own communities.*
- *"No govt. in hist. has ever voluntarily reduced self in size"*

- *stats stats stats stats—sign of budding politician.*
- *"most moments of world's freedom" have occurred here in "last best hope of man on earth"*
- *"late in the P.M. of day of decision"*
- *RR looks tired stepping off podium—45 mins.—applause loud.*

History has long forgotten Ronald Reagan's address to the California Fertilizer Association on November 10, 1958. He spoke, after all, to thousands of similar audiences across the length and breadth of the United States during the eight years he was the voice of GE. Some of these speeches might have been better; most, I should think, were similar, given his Dictaphone memory. At any rate, this was the only one I heard.

By all accounts, the reaction wherever he went was enthusiastic. He himself wrote Vice President Richard Nixon in 1959 that the pent-up passion of ordinary Americans "amazed" him: "I am convinced there is a ground swell of economic conservatism building up which could reverse the entire tide of present day 'statism.' " Within five years, the swell would elevate Barry Goldwater to the Republican presidential nomination, even if it was not high enough—yet—to flood the tax-and-spenders out of Washington.

Party historians like to refer to Dutch's nationwide telecast on behalf of Goldwater on October 27, 1964, as "The Speech," always with a cap *T,* as though it was the *Urtext* of his subsequent political career. But every time I watch that admittedly dazzling performance, I remember the day I saw him expound much the same message, with less skill but more raw force, in a ballroom on Wilshire Boulevard, forty years ago.

24

Dark Days

Early in 1959, I heard that Gavin, a University of California freshman at Berkeley, was interesting himself in campus politics, so I sent him my tape of Dutch's Fertilizer Association speech.

"As you know," I wrote, "RR & I went to college together v. briefly in '28. We weren't friends, but I've always been intrigued by how far he's gotten on the strength of good looks and gab—what your profs. doubtless call Rhetoric. I thought you'd like to hear this, recorded a couple of months ago. Shows what can happen when 'a second-class intellect' is combined with extraordinary powers of persuasion."

Gavin being a passionate student of the New Deal, I knew he would recognize the quoted phrase as something applied by Justice Oliver Wendell Holmes, Jr., to Franklin D. Roosevelt in 1932. I added a postscript: "RR was not yet 18 when he first addressed our student body. You better hurry up!!"

An answer came by return of mail, jabbed out on a postcard of Berkeley girls in bobby sox:

Dear Dad—Thanks for the tape, I think. 5 mins. about as much as I could stand. Persuasion my ass. That's Big Bully Business talking. At

least Reagan's honest enough to admit that he and the fertilizer industry (all beholden to Calif. landowning class) share the same philosophy: *excreta tauri vincit omnia*—G.

P.S. Read Mills, ch. 4.

C. Wright Mills had published *The Power Elite* only three years before, yet already it had attained such classic status that the single word
"Mills" telegraphed familiarity with one of the seminal sociological
works of the mid-century. Of course, I had not read it, so I guiltily re-
paired to the Santa Monica Public Library and spent a morning looking at my country through the eyes of a seer.

Mills turned out to be a maverick, mechanistic, leather-jacketed Columbia University philosopher, forty-two years old, respected by colleagues for his brutally unsentimental analyses of the American
Dream. There was something draughtsman-like about the clarity with
which he delineated, chapter by chapter, a post-war corporate society
as structured as the lost world of the Astors. Where once the "400"
ruled, a new interlocking élite of "the warlords, the corporation chief-
tains, [and] the political directorate" now controlled everything, from
the cloister to the Bomb.

What seized my attention was this sentence: "Mingling with them, in
curious ways which we shall explore, are those professional celebrities
who live by being continually displayed but are never, so long as they
remain celebrities, displayed enough."

As far as I know, this was the first time that the word *celebrity*, now
vulgarized beyond meaning, was used by a serious scholar to discuss that
media phenomenon, the person famous for being famous. Mills did not
add, as he might have, that such fame tends to grow at a compound rate.
The very "continualness" of television display (Dutch walking wide-
shouldered onto the set of *General Electric Theater* every Sunday night)
meant that even modest familiarity could be parlayed, over the course of
a few seasons, into power that could be felt on Wall Street and in Washington. For what was power, in an age of channeled perceptions, but
public esteem—and what better measure of it than viewer ratings? In
1929, the chairman of General Electric had been considered too important to run for President of the United States. Thirty years later, that
same executive could not match his own spokesman in recognizability
and glamour. Ralph Cordiner was known, at most, to a few thousand
Americans. Ronald Reagan was "Mr. Progress," the intimate of millions.

I flipped to the chapter Gavin had recommended, and understood
why my son hadn't needed to listen to the tape I sent him. He had
"heard" Ronald Reagan already, in the pages of *The Power Elite:*

[Celebrity] is carried to the point where a chattering radio and television entertainer becomes the hunting chum of leading industrial executives, cabinet members, and the higher military. It does not seem to matter what the man is the very best at; so long as he has won out in competition over all others, he is celebrated [and] mingles freely with other champions to populate the world of the celebrity.

This world is at once the pinnacle of the prestige system and a big-scale business. As a business, the networks of mass communication, publicity, and entertainment are not only the means whereby celebrities are celebrated; they also select and create celebrities for a profit. . . .

Horatio Alger dies hard, but in due course will not those Americans who are celebrated come to coincide more clearly with those who are the most powerful? . . .

Here are the names and faces and voices that are always before you. . . . Now they are news, later they will be history. . . . Here is the money talking in its husky, silky voice of cash, power, celebrity.

When Gavin came home that summer and joyously threw himself into the Santa Monica surf (he was a born beach boy, with his long straight limbs and swarthy complexion, luxuriating in the hottest sunshine), I was able to tell him that whatever Mills said, the voice of "Mr. Progress" might soon be silenced.

I'd heard on the advertising agency grapevine that BBD&O executives were nervous about the increasingly anti-Washington tone of Dutch's speeches. Insofar as General Electric employed *them*, they felt responsible for any embarrassment he might cause their client. His latest target was the Tennessee Valley Authority, which he scornfully cited as a New Deal program that drained the U.S. Treasury better than it did its own basin. He seemed not to know, or care, that GE had a major bid in for TVA generators—some fifty million dollars' worth. BBD&O did not feel, in the circumstances, that he should be offered another five-year contract as company spokesman.

Gavin's response was to wave a brown finger at me and intone, "Horatio Alger dies hard."

He was right: I did not realize that Dutch had become a skilled corporate tactician.

When somebody at GE headquarters in Schenectady advised BBD&O, "Call off Ronald Reagan or we're not going to get our generators," Dutch countered by telephoning Ralph Cordiner directly. "I understand you have a problem and that it concerns me."

The chairman, disarmed, replied: "It's my problem and I've taken it on."

Dutch was properly appreciative. "Mr. Cordiner, what would you say if I said that I could make my speech just as effectively without mentioning TVA?"

Another government agency was duly substituted, and he was retained at a substantial increase in salary, along with a 25 percent stake in all future *General Electric Theater* shows. And in flattering evidence that his former colleagues had not forgotten him, he was brought back on November 16 for a record sixth term as president of the Screen Actors Guild.

"Well, hooray for Horatio," Gavin drawled when I called him with the news.

The full irony of Ronald Reagan's return to the halls of labor did not occur to me until I read in *Variety* that SAG had specifically charged him with responsibility to negotiate a new general contract with the major studios. Strictly speaking, his investment stake in *General Electric Theater* should have been a disqualification, but I suppose the rank and file persuaded themselves that he was still spending a lot of time in front of the camera. They were a desperate constituency, what with a continuing paucity of film roles and the absolute refusal of Hollywood producers to grant them any residual rights in the sales of their old performances to television. If any man could symbolically bestride the chasm looming in the industry on January 31, 1960, it was Dutch the actor-producer.

Whether he did so to the benefit of his former colleagues (they were forced to go out on strike for five weeks, eventually conceding all pre-1960 performance rights to the producers, in exchange for a $2.26 million pension- and welfare-fund kickoff) has become a matter of debate. Wheelchair wisdom at the Motion Picture Country Home still has it that "Reagan traded away our residuals." Bitterness over the deal was at least a contributing factor in SAG's decision, twenty-one years later, to deny him its lifetime achievement award.

I will only remark the historical fact that when Dutch announced his strike-settlement package to a mass meeting of the membership on April 18, 1960, he received a standing ovation and a landslide approval vote of 6,399 to 259.

Just over a month later, on May 27, Gavin turned twenty. He was now a huge dark young man, whose height would have been intimidating had it not been mitigated by elegance of bone and a sort of stooped, scholarly gentleness. He was majoring in French literature and philosophy, and since the death of Albert Camus had taken exaggeratedly to black sweaters and Gauloise cigarettes. His favorite phrase was *la tristesse au fond de tout,* but, being sunny by nature, he never managed to sigh it with the right degree of world-weariness.

I hoped he might become a writer, but his mind was too binary: he loved the either-or of logic and the black-and-white progressions of chess. This made him a difficult person to talk politics with, because he saw everything so clearly—too clearly—in terms of right or wrong.

A compulsive precisionist, Gavin insisted that 1960 was not the beginning of the Sixties so much as the end of the Fifties. But if there was anything Fifties-ish about a summer that saw the disgrace of Dwight D. Eisenhower over the U-2 affair, and the nomination of John F. Kennedy for President of the United States, it escaped my notice.

For Ronald Reagan, Kennedy's acceptance speech at the Democratic National Convention was nothing less than "a frightening call to arms." Its scariness had nothing to do with Communism or race relations, but with Kennedy's obvious relish for government programs. "Unfortunately he is a powerful speaker with an appeal to the emotions," Dutch wrote to the Republican nominee, Vice President Richard Nixon.

> He leaves little doubt that his idea of the "challenging new world" is one in which the Federal Govt. will grow bigger & do more & of course spend more. . . .
>
> I have been speaking on this subject in more than thirty-eight states to audiences of Democrats & Republicans. Invariably the reaction is a standing ovation—not for me but for the views expressed. I am convinced that America is economically conservative and for that reason I think that some one should force the Democrats to publish the "retail price" for this great new wave of "public service" they promise. I don't pose as an infallible pundit but I have a strong feeling that the twenty million *non voters* in this country just might be conservatives who have cynically concluded the two parties offer no choice between them where fiscal stability is concerned. . . . A Republican bucking the give away trend might re-create some voters who have been staying home.

One last thought—shouldn't someone tag Mr. Kennedy's *bold new imaginative program* with its proper age? Under the tousled boyish hair cut it is still old Karl Marx—first launched a century ago.

Nixon made no comment on this interesting historical parallel, but annotated the letter to his staff: "Use him as speaker whenever possible. He *used* to be a liberal!"

☯

It is strange, almost four decades later, to read such things with absolutely no memory of "Ronnie" and "Dick" campaigning together in 1960. The former certainly did his oratorical bit (two hundred platform appearances, by one calculation) and had the Kennedy television phenomenon not been so interesting, I guess I would have paid some attention to their relationship. The only two-shot that stays in my mind is that of the famous debate, Nixon dark of jowl and desperate, his eyes getting closer and closer together until I thought they would implode. "Apollo v. Cyclops," I wrote in my diary.

Which goes to show that 1960 was the first cosmetic election. In the end, we voted pretty. For better or for worse, film was now a factor in politics—and this was good news for Dutch.

☯

"For I have thought thee fair, and found thee bright,
Who art black as hell, and dark as night."

Gavin scrawled this slight misquotation across the back of an envelope I received from him just before the election. I supposed he, too, was thinking about Apollo v. Cyclops, but found inside his transcript of a lecture given by one James Baldwin at San Francisco State College on October 22. The name meant nothing to me, so Gavin attached an explanatory note: "A sweet, sibilant little Negro, or so he seemed till he began his 'rap.' Such *anger* you cannot believe. I felt the bottom drop out of my complacent world. Yours mine Mom's. Moved to rage & tears."

There's no point in reprinting the lecture, because Baldwin included it in a subsequent book of essays, *Nobody Knows My Name*. I did not react in the way Gavin hoped I might. Baldwin, I thought, went on much too long about how tough things were for an "artistic Negro" in the ghetto. What else was new?

What *was* new, what Gavin heard and what I wouldn't hear, was this:

It seems to me that the myth, the illusion, that this is a free country . . . is disastrous. Let me point out to you that freedom is not something that anybody can be given; freedom is something people take and people are as free as they want to be.

And this, pitched directly at "Mr. Progress":

Without having anything whatever against Cadillacs, refrigerators or all the paraphernalia of American life, I yet suspect that there is something much more important and much more real which produces the Cadillac, refrigerator, atom bomb . . . and that is the person. A country is only as good [and] strong as the people who make it up and the country turns into what the people want it to become.

And finally this:

Now, this country is going to be transformed. It will not be transformed by an act of God, but by all of us, by you and me. . . . We made the world we're living in and we have to make it over.

Now *there* was the "call to arms" that should have frightened Ronnie and Dick in 1960—Jack, too! But the hour was too soon for any white man over the age of twenty to worry. About what? Some frail little fag shaking his fist at a literary symposium, traditional retreat of the powerless? Too soon for *us,* too late already for Baldwin, who eventually gave up and headed back to France. In retrospect, though, that fist was the first of millions, stronger, blacker, higher (my son's brown one among them), climaxing in Tommie Smith's sky-punch at the Mexico City Olympics: *le geste fuck-you,* semaphore of the Sixties.

Besides his Cadillac and his refrigerator and his ranch and his steers, Dutch had one other considerable asset to tabulate as he braced for the tax paragraphs of Kennedy's inaugural address on January 20, 1961. It was "the House of the Future," which a grateful employer had built for him and Nancy at 1669 San Onofre Drive, Pacific Palisades, and equipped with enough General Electric gadgetry to trip every fuse box in the neighborhood. From the zebra-skinned black-slate foyer to the sunken living room and shelves gleaming with Boehm birds, from triple carport to climate changer to pool to patio (wet-cemented with a pair of hearts, marked "NDR-RR"), it fairly shouted *nouveau-riche* values.

Also a sense of arrival: each glass-fronted room overlooked the sea, and backed on the rest of America. Inevitably "seen on TV," the House of the Future represented everything James Baldwin wanted to fire-bomb.

Dutch had to think of his children as well. The youngest was a son and heir, Ronald Prescott Reagan, just two years and seven months old. Patti was eight years and a bit; Michael, a high school junior, nearly sixteen; and Maureen just twenty, a college dropout living, with difficulty, in Washington, D.C.

They found in him a responsible, but at the same time disengaged father. He did not grudge them the best private schools, as long as their mothers decided where to send them. In the case of Jane, who was now an ardent Catholic convert, that had meant Loyola for Michael and Marymount for Maureen. Patti and Ron were between them destined for John Thomas Dye in Bel-Air, Orme School in Arizona, Webb, Harvard High, and Yale.

However, he did not seem bothered by Maureen's failure to graduate, any more than he was by her obvious need for money. In his tranquil view, a privilege forfeited did not admit of compensatory entitlement. None of his children, as it happened, would get a degree. Nor would any provide him with descendants. Whether these derelictions caused him the slightest regret is one of the imponderables buried in the alabaster depths of Ronald Reagan. We may ponder an anecdote Michael tells:

> I was real proud when Dad came to my high school commence-ment. He was the guest of honor and chief speaker, and I was in the group that posed with him in our caps and gowns. After the picture he introduced himself to all of us and came up to me and said, "Hi, my name's Ronald Reagan. What's yours?" He was looking right into my face.
>
> I took my cap off and said, "Dad, it's *me*. Your son. Mike."

In one respect, at least, Ronald and Nancy Reagan were model parents, and that was at family photo opportunities. Paul Rae cherished one group portrait of the GE years, in which accents of Nancy's favorite color, red, were distributed with the symmetry of a kaleidoscope. He had clipped it from some glossy magazine and giggled that he might donate it one day to the National Museum of American Kitsch. "Will you *please* note that Dutch's cravat and sox—the little girl's ribbon and rosette—the bowl—the cushions—even the *poppy* in the *picture,* all *exactly* match Mommie's nail polish?"

I gazed at it reverently. It indeed was a monument to the departing

"Paul Rae cherished one group portrait of the GE years."
Ronald Reagan and his second family, 1958.

Age of Eisenhower, right down to the jewel-like brilliancy of Dutch's two-tones, hedged around with shag. But I was more arrested by the interplay of three expressions floating out of frame: Nancy serenely happy, almost beautiful, Dutch doing his left-to-right Film Star Grin #2, Patti's small face dull with discontent.

As "Karl Marx" settled into the White House and his commissars of entitlement, oozing compassion from every pore, looked for ways to redistribute the national wealth, GE executives began to wonder how much longer they could tolerate Ronald Reagan's anti-Washington rhetoric. Nineteen sixty-one was a year of almost constant humiliation for the new Administration, what with Yuri Gagarin becoming the first man in space, Fidel Castro mockingly proclaiming a Communist state after the Bay of Pigs, and Nikita Khrushchev making a patsy of Kennedy at the Vienna summit in June. Although Reagan was patriotic enough not to criticize the President personally—yet—it was clear whom he meant by "well-meaning and misguided people" prepared "to drink the bitter cup of capitulation in Laos." Neither did he zip his mouth on the subject of domestic policies, finding just as much "socialism" in current bills before Congress as on that "Soviet beachhead ninety miles offshore."

All this was before the two most dangerous developments of the year: the rise of the Berlin Wall in mid-August and Khrushchev's detonation, two weeks later, of a fifty-eight-megaton bomb. Something seemed to snap inside Reagan. In his next major speech, given at Huntington Memorial Hospital in Pasadena on January 4, 1962, he directly accused Kennedy and a presidential aide, "Professor" Arthur M. Schlesinger, Jr., of policies that could lead to social "slavery." These included welfare statism at home, aid to pro-Communist governments abroad, boondoggling in Vietnam, and a general leftward retreat before "the roughnecks of the Kremlin."

It was the TVA story all over again, except that now the stakes were much higher for General Electric. Several company executives were under federal indictment for price-fixing, and a prosecutor appointed by Attorney General Robert Kennedy was about to grill dozens of witnesses, including Reagan, before a grand jury inquiring into the SAG-MCA "blanket waiver" of 1952.

Clearly, GE was going to have to get rid of its spokesman, or risk enduring warfare with Washington. Yet the Millsian paradox applied:

Reagan was by now too much of a celebrity to fire outright. According to one head-office calculation, only former President Eisenhower had more prestige on the lecture circuit. There was also the delicate question of keeping him loyal while he testified.

He did so on February 5, so secretly that I was unaware of it until Paul Rae printed an enigmatic filler in his column: "RONALD REAGAN is back before the cameras at Revue after his recent attack of selective amnesia. Teleplay, to be broadcast on *General Electric Theater* March 25, is called 'My Dark Days.' Odd title for a power company production. Are the folks at GE preparing to kill Ron's solo spotlight?"

Shortly after that, more rumors reached me from BBD&O in New York. "Reagan has become a liability to GE," I wrote Gavin. "They may have to close down the show in order to fire him."

When things happened, they happened quickly. BBD&O executives consulted with Ralph Cordiner, then telephoned Reagan, who was traveling, and gave him the bad news. His response was to head straight for New York and demand an audience with the agency chief, Charles Brower.

A quarter of a century later, I asked Brower's widow about Dutch's dismissal. "Mrs. Brower, the President absolutely denies this story. He says that he got a call from Schenectady asking him to confine himself to plugging company products, and when he refused, GE canceled the show."

"Well, the call came from the Parker Polo Club in the Waldorf," the old lady said precisely. "It was made by Tom Dillon, and he told Mr. Reagan that GE didn't want him anymore."

"The President says Ralph Cordiner had nothing to do with it, he had already retired as chairman."

She gazed across the park of her retirement home in New Jersey. The sun had set behind a thick stand of trees, and wheelchairs were rolling in for supper. "No, Mr. Cordiner was still there."

"The President also denies that he cried."

"My husband came home and asked me to take a walk with him after dinner. He was feeling bad. He needed to talk about how Mr. Reagan begged him, *What can I do, Charley? I can't act anymore, I can't do anything else. How can I support my family?*"

"But the tears?"

"That's what my husband told me. He cried."

☯

The Reagans spent Easter, as they usually did, with Dr. and Mrs. Loyal Davis in Arizona. A friend there noticed that Dutch was uncharacteristically subdued, riding off alone every morning with his head hung in thought. He talked of getting back into studio screen acting and of writing a memoir. The first pages of *Where's the Rest of Me?* might have been sketched out on this vacation. He was to work at the book, without much enthusiasm, for more than a year, and would need the services of a collaborator to finish it.

There was also politics to ponder. Even before his ouster from GE, some conservative California Republicans had asked him to run against Senator Thomas Kuchel in the spring primary. He had begged off, pleading lack of interest and lack of funds, as well as the small matter of being still a registered Democrat. Yet he agreed to chair the campaign of another challenger, Loyd Wright, and also support Richard Nixon for Governor.

The strangeness of these commitments (Wright, seven years before, had represented Jane Wyman against him in their divorce suit) merely concealed the fact that he was a Republican in all but name. Indeed, he had delayed switching in 1960 only as a favor to Nixon, who had asked him to hold off in order to draw as many conservative votes as possible away from Kennedy. Now he was free to identify himself with the kind of rich Republicans he had gotten to know since marrying Nancy: hard, tanned men who wintered in Scottsdale, talked mostly in digits, and ornamented their dens with Steuben glass eagles.

Yet he hesitated, confessing in *Sunset* magazine, "Like any actor, I keep thinking that the big part is still ahead." He was desperate to get back into pictures, and Hollywood's executive élite was largely Democratic. As long as his anti-Communist political philosophy was reconcilable with that of, say, Dean Acheson, he might still be considered *persona grata* by casting directors. But only established stars, such as Robert Taylor or John Wayne, could formally embrace the GOP without prejudice to their careers. So for the time being, he tried to be all things to all men. In this, he was assisted by his ambitious wife.

Philip and Amanda Dunne, who moved in the highest circles of Los Angeles society, reported with disapproval that the Reagans had begun to appear—always a little overdressed, ill at ease with cultural chat, but determinedly, smilingly *there*—on patios hitherto denied them.

"I think I offended your friend the other day," Phil confided, with absolutely no sign of regret. "He was wearing this tie embroidered 'Ron-

nie,' so I said, 'Why don't you put your phone number on it, too—you'd
get a lot more business.' "

Dutch was, in fact, getting no business at all. He did not seem to understand that Lew Wasserman, to whom he still instinctively turned as
an agent, was now CEO of one of Hollywood's biggest production
conglomerates—MCA/Revue/Universal—and under pressure from the
Justice Department to get out of the talent business altogether. As long
as Reagan remained under contract to Revue, Wasserman was prepared to send his résumé around, but the eight-by-ten photographs attached to it showed a fiftyish actor of no particular glamour. There was
a humiliating lack of response.

"You've been around this business long enough to know that I can't
force someone on a producer if he doesn't want to use him," Wasserman said.

Dutch took this bad news almost as hard as he had his firing by
BBD&O. He was convinced that Wasserman—an ardent Kennedy
Democrat—had dropped him because of his politics. "It was a real
parting of friendship," he told me years later. "I—uh—I felt that I had
been betrayed, and I guess Lew felt that he was doing what he had to
do, and we just went our separate ways."

Gavin did not reply to my note about Dutch's demise. He was taking
his final examinations at Berkeley (A.B. in Philosophy and French). I
went north in early May to see him graduate *summa cum laude* and
took him to lunch afterward at the Top of the Mark.

"Appropriate, don't you think?" I said.

A waitress came to clear the extra places from our table. Gavin asked
her to leave one of them, and for the first time in years we talked without rancor about Sydney Ann. I told him how I had driven her around
Chicago in '38, looking for a showing of *Love Is on the Air,* how the rain
had brought out her scent of lemon verbena, and how her body had
moved as she played Hindemith in a loose white dress.

"Why, Dad," Gavin grinned, refilling my glass, "you're a dirty old
man."

A few weeks later, he was off to Port Huron, Michigan, for something
he vaguely referred to as "strategy talks" with a group of young activists.

He called from there on June 15 to say in a voice hoarse with excitement that he was going on to New York with "Tom" to help "put out a statement."

"Tom who? Statement about what?"

"Oh, you know, generational values. It's only a draft. Guy called Tom Hayden. Bit of a windbag, but man, can he push a pen. Brilliant."

"You're helping him write it?"

"Well, we put in our two cents worth. Now he just has to polish. Then we publish."

"Who's *we*, Gavin?"

"Students for a Democratic Society. Listen, I gotta crash. Haven't slept in two days."

Something in his tone made me ask, "Is this some kind of Communist group?"

"Cool it, Dad. There were one or two of 'em here, but they got kicked out."

When I next heard from him, it was characteristically on the back of a bulky envelope, postmarked August 9—my fiftieth birthday. Gavin had an eccentric habit of communicating in this public manner, while enclosing material too abstruse to read:

> *Dad, hi*—Here's our manifesto at last. Don't "look uncomfortably" on it. Hayden, Haber, Harrington the purest people I've ever met. *Hommes engagés.* Back as soon as I can scrub off this mimeo ink. Love—*G.*

Malraux's phrase touched me tenderly. Gavin was a Camus groupie, and affected the collar-up, tired-eyed, droopy-cigarette look required of all French intellectuals. He said that after a spell of foreign-exchange study in Algeria, he would like to do a dissertation on "black existentialism."

His enclosure, gift-wrapped, was a smeary fifty-page mimeograph entitled THE PORT HURON STATEMENT OF THE STUDENTS FOR A DEMOCRATIC SOCIETY. The last phrase was typographically arranged to emphasize the initial capitals *S D S.* I heaved a dutiful sigh and opened it. The first paragraphs of Hayden's introduction were not without eloquence:

> We are people of this generation, bred in at least modest comfort, housed now in universities, looking uncomfortably to the world we inherit.
>
> When we were kids the United States was the wealthiest and strongest country in the world; the only one with the atom bomb, the

least scarred by modern war, an initiator of the United Nations. . . . Freedom and equality for each individual, government of, by, and for the people—these American values we found good, principles by which we could live as men.

Below, however, the dread words *social, economic, mankind,* and *agenda* proliferated like flies. Gavin anticipated my move to skip. Something long and silk-smooth unfolded from the top of page two: a riband of Japanese paper, lightly gummed, and covered with his script:

SUMMARY FOR BRAIN-DEAD PARENTALS
WHO PRETEND TO READ BUT WON'T

- 2 great evils that pervert the peace & power we are supposed to thank you for: *racial bigotry & the enclosing fact of the Cold War*
- Other evils: *superfluous abundance* amid world starvation & *supertechnology* mass-producing modern organization man ("Mr. Progress"!)
- We look at our country today, what do we see? Politically, no major diff. between the two big parties. Paranoia about Communism abroad, blindness to fascism at home, partic. in Deep South
- On the personal level, *the felt powerlessness of ordinary people.* Glorification of the group. *Isolation of the individual*
- (And this directed at you Dad!) *The serious poet burns for a place to work; the never-serious poets work at the advertising agencies*

I must say, that one hurt. But what did these callow visionaries propose to do, if and when they got power? Gavin was ready for me:

- We commit to a new social experiment, based on man's *unfulfilled capacities for reason, freedom & love*
- Our laboratory: the University. We will no longer permit it to act as whore to the corporate & military élite who pay for its R & D
- Big business must be broken up, subjected to community control. Public sector expanded at cost of private. *We seek the establishment of a democracy based on* <u>*individual participation*</u>

I flicked through the Statement's text proper, and found it to be fairly predictable, with long sections headlined "Poverty," "Military-Industrial Politics," "Automation," "The Stance of Labor," "The Individual in the Warfare State," and "The Economy." They said nothing that one hadn't heard already from C. Wright Mills and I. F. Stone—the obvious gurus of this New Left.

There were periodic denunciations of "the Communist system," but they struck me as oddly stilted. Time and again, Hayden and his colleagues emphasized their "basic opposition" to socialism, then spoiled the effect with conditional clauses. One line, about the "least desirable" economic developments being those "in the form of private enterprise," could have been phoned in by Fidel Castro. I got the feeling there had been more than just "one or two" Marxists at Port Huron.

Perhaps I should have noticed a total lack of interest in feminist issues, but I didn't. On the whole, the Statement breathed the pleasant fragrance of extreme youth. Some of the things it said were more prophetic than I realized at the time. For example, there was this pre-echo of an argument Ronald Reagan would have to answer one day, at Geneva and Reykjavík: "The 'counter-force' theory of aiming strategic nuclear weapons at military installations . . . [will] generate a perpetual arms race [and] make outer space a region for militarization."

Over and again, Students for a Democratic Society pledged to make the University a crucible of change. From ivied halls and lawns would flow new waves of activism, argument, provocation, and fraternal love. Gavin underscored Hayden's peroration: *If we appear to seek the unattainable, as has been said, then let it be known that we do so to avoid the unimaginable.*

For Ronald Reagan, too, the late summer of '62 was one of maturing ideology. Despairing of his acting career, he finally registered as a Republican and began to campaign for John Rousselot, a far-right Congressman running for re-election. He was unembarrassed when Rousselot was revealed to be national public-relations director for the John Birch Society, a private organization of extreme social paranoia.

Race riots at the University of Mississippi on September 30, followed within weeks by the Cuban missile crisis, made this paranoia seem almost reasonable. Convinced that World War III was about to break out, I tried to get Gavin to take his Peace Corps assignment in advance of the elections. But having just qualified for the vote, he was determined to exercise it. "I'm glad you think Algeria offers more security, Dad!"

Together we watched Reagan's election-eve endorsement of Nixon for Governor. Or so it was billed. The paid-for minutes flowed by—

"No one's paid *me*," said Dutch—the glossy head kept nodding, and somehow Nixon's name kept being postponed:

> My ideas, my words are my own. I'd like to talk to you about what I think is at stake. . . . We've come to one of those infrequent moments in history when there is a change; when we're choosing between two party philosophies, and a wide ideological gulf separates the policies of the two parties.

"This guy," Gavin said acutely, "isn't talking about the country, he's talking about himself."

For twenty-eight minutes we were given Dutch's views, mostly apocalyptic, on planned economics, one-world socialism, government growth, subsidized agriculture, and welfare abuse. Somehow, he managed to relate feed grain to federal penitentiaries, Robert Frost to Nikita Khrushchev, and Babe Ruth's batting record to light taxes. When, at last, he got around to mentioning Nixon, it was with a left-handed obliqueness that the Babe would have admired:

> Can you possibly believe that a man like Dwight David Eisenhower . . . whose love of country is beyond question, could have been closely associated with Richard Nixon, as he was for eight years, and now recommend him for high office, as he is doing, if he did not believe him worthy to serve?

"Talk about your Brylcreemed rats deserting the sinking ship!" Gavin groaned. "I might just vote for Nixon out of sheer sympathy."

Hours after the defeated candidate's "last press conference," Gavin flew off to Algeria. Through a lobster-quadrille of fate, I would not see him again for almost seven years.

The assassination of President Kennedy in November 1963 afflicted me with a sudden desire to quit the crass and crazy netherlands of America and relocate to New York, or even London, if some agency could be persuaded to hire an aging adman with no television experience. I made some calls on the old flyboy network and heard that the UK office of Foote, Cone & Belding was looking for "an airline guy" for its British Overseas Airways account.

FBC hired me sight unseen—American copywriters were currently "hot" on Baker Street—and after a male-menopausal frenzy of deaccession in Santa Monica, I flew to London, rented a small flat in Belgravia and reported for work on September 23, 1964.

I thus missed most of Senator Barry Goldwater's doomed campaign to unseat President Lyndon B. Johnson. More to the point, I missed Gavin's return from Algeria to Berkeley (where he had been accepted by the Graduate School of Modern Languages), and his almost instant enlistment in the first great student uprising of the Sixties.

This was, of course, the Free Speech Movement, that sudden inexplicable surge of anti-authoritarianism which Ronald Reagan blamed for the dereliction of higher education in the years following. On October 1, 1964, Gavin described it to me in terms we could both relate to: "You know that feeling when a *really* big wave comes in & sucks up so much forewater you can see the sand beneath you, & there's no *way* you can't ride it in right through to the beach, with all the power of the Pacific boiling around your ass? Well that's how I felt here today."

"Here," I gathered, was Sproul Plaza, the university's main meeting place. I'd heard at least something of the demonstration there on BBC radio news—a girl named Joan (in my diary I spelled it "Byass") singing *The times they are a-changin'*, hundreds of young people applauding her, then some furious speaker hoarsely protesting the Berkeley administration's decision to ban political fund-raising and recruitment on campus.

"We set up ten more tables in defiance, & I sold my last copies of the Pt. Huron Statement," Gavin wrote proudly, in a letter apparently scribbled across someone's back.

About a quarter of noon, a cop car noses into the crowd, slow and quiet. Meanwhile 2 deans & some campus police come to the CORE table, where some of us are sitting. (Why do they *happen* to choose the one that wants justice for Negroes?) I stand up—asking for trouble, since I'm so tall. Bastards ignore me, arrest Jack Weinberg, drag him into the car. We crowd around. The driver guns his engine.

The wave builds. I feel it lifting me up, dark & angry yet exultant. I yell, "Sit down!" jump in front of the car & park myself. Next thing I know, the wave's spread out & the car with Jack inside is becalmed in a sea of sitting students. At least 1,000 of us. Mario Savio, one of my philos. buddies, carefully takes off his shoes & climbs up onto the car. Wiry, frizzy, burning kind of guy (spent the summer teaching poor Negro kids in Miss.), shaking like a filament on its last flare.

When Mario's hot he's super-articulate. He used Mills's machine metaphors to convey the image of us all being drawn into the cogs of

the "multiversity." If we don't pull free, we're going to be rolled out
the other end "with all our sharp edges worn off," our hearts & minds
stamped with orthodox thought patterns.

Now here we are one o'clock in the A.M. & Jack's still in the car.
Looks like being a long night.

I saw some press photographs of the sit-in. It looked pretty harmless
to me. One of the cops by the car was clearly laughing and joshing with
the students. However, Clark Kerr, president of the University of California, took it seriously enough to negotiate with Savio himself. Gavin
described him as "a small bald sleek geek, trying to oil us up with one
hand & shaft us with the other."

Kerr, not Savio, had coined the word "multiversity," in a book published the year before. It connoted a massively funded research institution working hand in hand with government and industry to advance
the power of the state, at cost to individual student education. One of
the supreme ironies of that divided time was that such a concept should
scare the ideological hell out of both the Free Speechers and Ronald
Reagan.

If the "wave" that Gavin felt rising in Sproul Plaza on October 1, 1964,
was that of the New Left, schooled on Mills rather than Marx and
more concerned with race than labor, then the almost simultaneous
wave that lifted Dutch to political prominence just before the election
represented all the force of a New Right, whose aspiration owed little
to party loyalty, and would only be swelled by rejection of Goldwater's
peculiarly Republican conservatism.

Even as faculty and student committees argued over the right of political "advocacy" at Berkeley, Reagan was asked to record an emergency television address in aid of the Goldwater campaign. The
brilliance of his performance, beamed nationwide on October 27,
transformed him overnight into a serious contender for the governorship of California.

So, at least, Gavin opined over five thousand miles of phone line.
"Dad, I take back what I said about that fertilizer speech. Not that he's
not still full of *merde,* but, man, can he work up an audience. The whole
country's talking about it. Including bakery ladies."

"The whole *country*?"

"Half an hour on NBC, prime time. The GOP went for broke, and did it *ever* pay off. Money's coming in so fast they don't know what to do except replay the speech, over and over on local stations. Too late to save Goldwater, I think."

"What did Reagan say? We've not heard about it here."

"Oh, you know, government in your pocket, better dead than Red."

"And you were impressed."

"No, I was *repulsed.* He's Babbitt, don't you think I rumble that? Quick, strong, funny—dangerous as hell."

"What's dangerous?"

"The fact that he uses humor to express hate. He smiles and beguiles. And he's got this *microphone* quality, like he's reading it from some invisible script—"

"Very true."

"He kids you and coaxes you, and suddenly you're hearing that intellectuals and poor people and black people are living off the rest of us—"

"He said all *that*?"

"Not in general. What he does, he chooses specific examples of welfare fraud or faculty politics and makes you laugh and groan so much, you don't pause to wonder if they're generally true or not."

"Gavin, what you say about him really bothers me. I just don't think it's fair."

"Of course it's not fair. It's accurate!"

That had me laughing, and I changed the subject. "Listen, with all this Free Speech stuff, are you spending any time in class?"

"Oh Dad, get lost."

"I hear Clark Kerr is saying you're a bunch of Communists."

"Oh *Dad—!*" And he rang off.

A few days after Johnson devastatingly defeated Goldwater, I got a circular parcel from Paul Rae. Inside, tied up with a big bow and labeled "LUV FROM THE NEXT GUV" was a kinescope copy of Dutch's NBC speech. It was unplayable on British equipment, but I managed to dub the audio and listened to it, wondering what Gavin found so repulsive. The only anti-intellectual remark was an excellent crack to the effect that while it would be cheaper to send problem children to Harvard than to enact a current bill for remedial education, "I'm not suggesting Harvard as the answer to juvenile delinquency." Nor did Dutch demonstrate any "hate" other than a healthy contempt for the Great

Society. He sounded much as he had when I recorded him in 1958, but stronger, terser. He ranged impressively over foreign and domestic policy, and his praise of Goldwater was generous, in contrast to the way he had coldly dismissed Nixon in 1962.

Nothing is more faded than old campaign rhetoric, so I won't belabor "The Speech" any more than to say it was (for all of Reagan's innocent protestations) clearly a proclamation of himself as Goldwater's successor. (We should remember that Nixon, in 1964, was by then as *passé* as Harold Stassen.) Paul's attached note offered some interesting background details:

> A GOP elder says this speech generated "the most amazing response I've ever seen in any political campaign." Dutch himself modestly allows, "I've never had [such] a mail reaction in all my years in show business." Calif. Secy State is calling on him to run for Governor in '66, and I even hear dark threats to make him *Pres. of U.S.* in '68!! If so, rent me a flat on your side of the Atlantic.
>
> Speech, wh. he grandly calls "A Time for Choosing," is not new. I guess you know he co-chaired Calif. Citizens for Goldwater? Delivered speech at big Ambassador Hotel fund-raiser last Aug., with such flair that Holmes Tuttle the car dealer grabbed him afterward & practically bullied him into auditioning for a bunch of fellow big-biz billionaires: Cy Rubel of Union Oil, Henry Salvatori of Western Geophysical. Rock-hard guys like that. They'd already written Goldwater off; looking around for "future" stock.
>
> They make him an offer: will pay all production costs if he will do a studio recording of The Speech, for broadcast on one of the major networks. Dutch says yes, but not in a studio, I want *a large room full of students.* A few weeks later, they book him into the biggest set they can find, round up some Young Americans for Freedom, & he proceeds to give the perf. of his life. Goldwater reviews the tape & says: "What the hell's wrong with that?"
>
> The rest is history. And so, unfortunately, is Barry.

On December 2, 1964, negotiations between the Free Speech Movement and Berkeley authorities ended in physical confrontation. Eight hundred radical students took over Sproul Hall to protest the university's calculatedly vague response to their demands for an "open forum" on campus. Their desperation was driven by signs that the

Movement was losing its momentum in the face of collusion and buck-passing between various bureaucracies at the state and local levels of academic government. By now, even BBC-TV realized that Berkeley was showcasing an issue of constitutional import, and bought some news feed. I sat in my Belgravia bedsit, with blue twilight in the window and the gas fire hissing, peering for a glimpse of Gavin.

Once or twice I thought I saw him in blurry crowd scenes, but the camera naturally favored Savio, who was calling for a student strike in a voice almost choked with urgency:

> There's a time when the operation of the machine becomes so odious, makes you so sick at heart, that you can't take part, you can't even tacitly take part. And you've got to put your bodies upon the gears and upon the wheels, upon the levers, upon all the apparatus, and you've got to make it stop. And you've got to indicate to the people who run it, to the people who own it, that unless you're free, the machine will be prevented from working at all.

I had seen it before, as Gavin was seeing it now: the student orator, skinny, rigid with excitement, his lips wreathing ungracefully as he tried to turn attention into action. For that matter, hadn't I heard Dutch expound exactly the same philosophy, give or take a few nuts and bolts, just days ago, in the FCB sound room? That "a time of choosing" had come between free will and the "weight" of social engineering?

If so, Savio had the satisfaction of even swifter response. A crowd singing "We Shall Overcome" followed him into Sproul. Subsequent news broadcasts reported that California Governor Edmund ("Pat") Brown had sent in over three hundred and fifty police officers to clear the building of young bodies. Although the Governor was a close friend of Clark Kerr, he apparently acted at the behest of a truculent deputy district attorney from Alameda County, Edwin Meese III. When, after twenty-eight hours, the final protester was dragged out, the Free Speech Movement had gained the support of an overwhelming majority of students and two hundred liberal professors.

President Kerr convened the university on December 7 and appealed for a democratic settlement whereby "persuasion" would transcend "force." Mario Savio tried to approach the podium. Eighteen thousand pairs of eyes watched fascinated as he was collared by campus police. After that, there was little the Academic Senate could do but vote 824 to 115 in favor of "complete political freedom" at Berkeley, plus amnesty for all FSM leaders. Gavin called me collect in the middle of the night to play "Blowin' in the Wind" at the highest reach of his harmonica.

Piper, pipe that song again! Sweet yet inevitably spending itself, it resounds across time as the very note of doomed youth.

By the time President Johnson delivered his 1965 State of the Union Address, to the most heavily Democratic Congress in thirty years, Goldwaterism had become a cause to giggle at across most of the country, like Pelmanism and Positive Thinking and Moral Rearmament and other cults that still advertised in the pages of *Reader's Digest.* Only in those spacious, mainly sun-baked enclaves where Holmes Tuttle and his friends holed up and teed up—Montecito and La Jolla, Palm Beach and Palm Springs, Scottsdale and Jupiter Island—was there no sound of mirth. Over margaritas and screwdrivers in dark, freezing desert restaurants, yesterday's Power Elite set about transforming itself into tomorrow's Silent Majority.

In my experience of such men, admiration for their patriotism and granite honesty has always been tempered by the alarm—no other word will do—that an endemic lack of humor inspires, not to mention a shoot-from-the-hip hostility toward intellectuals. Aesthetically blind, culturally retarded, vaccinated for life against such foreign frailties as criticality, irony, and (God forbid) satire, they view all threats to the Constitution—*their* Constitution—with the utmost seriousness. I would not want to be a Communist, or a pornographer, within range of the heavy guns they hang in their dens.

Nor would I want to be a fifty-three-year-old actor who perfectly articulated their philosophy and yet was "frightened"—Dutch's own word—by the extent of their political ambitions for him. He affected a lack of interest in high office, and for the rest of his life would insist that he yielded to Tuttle, Rubel, and Salvatori only out of a sense of civic duty. Insofar as he was still an actor, this reluctance was sincere. The choice, after all, was a fundamental one, between two years of training and campaigning against an entrenched opponent and the security of a television contract his brother Neil had wangled for him, as series host for *Death Valley Days.* Were he *only* an actor, he might have hearkened to Polonius and stayed true to himself. But Ronald Reagan was now—had been for years—primarily a politician. Nor was Hollywood necessarily a hindrance to a political career: his breakfast buddy from *This Is the Army* days, George Murphy, had just managed to win a seat in the U.S. Senate.

"If only I could think of it as a script that would run for four years," Dutch joked.

Holmes Tuttle thought of it more as the first part of a grand strategy. *He* saw eight years, not four, in Sacramento, followed by four years, maybe eight, in the White House. By 1985, with God's grace, Communism would be vanquished at home and abroad, the Republican Party reunited, and the word *conservative* might regain its old relevance to the Bill of Rights.

Tuttle personally pledged that should Reagan enter politics with this same strategy, he would never want for funds. Vainglorious as such a twenty-year investment might have sounded to anyone less trusting, Reagan accepted it. History shows that he repaid Tuttle in kind and in full, only four years late.

☯

Pivotal year of a pivotal decade, 1965 saw many transformations other than that of the Actor into the Politician. In quick succession, the Alabama riots and assassination of Malcolm X turned Negro nonviolence into Black anarchy. The dispatch of our first combat troops to Vietnam marked the end of popular support for the war, and turned President Johnson (who had won his landslide vote by obsessively promising *peace, peace, peace*) from domestic dove into foreign hawk. Assistant Secretary of Labor Daniel P. Moynihan announced the consummation of the New Deal, saying that all its great programs were in place, and predicted that future social spending would concentrate on the American family (as has indeed been the case, to the family's virtual destruction). And then, at the flash point of the year—*Burn, baby, burn!*—Watts blew up, and urban warfare became the annual dread of all cities with large "minority" populations.

All these swings from positive to negative occurred with terrifying rapidity. Reagan continued to pretend that his own transformation was tentative, that he would happily go back to private life if California Republicans found another candidate more likely to oust Governor Brown. My guess is that the sight of the entire state convention rising to applaud him on March 27 made him an instant political alcoholic. "Heady wine," indeed!

But he was not yet a declared candidate, and they would not consider his nomination for another year. That meant a summer and fall of precampaign campaigning: driving upstate and downstate (since he still would not fly) to party rallies, paying attention to what ordinary people had to say, trying to adjust his own big-business philosophy to theirs.

This was going to be difficult for him, for he had never been a good listener. The very qualities that made Reagan so compelling on the podium—loquacity, forcefulness, love of the spotlight—served him ill in conversation. Middle age made his genial egotism worse. By 1965, he was, in the words of Gore Vidal,

> far and away, Hollywood's most grinding bore—Chester Chatter-box, in fact. Ronnie never stopped talking, even though he never had anything to say except what he had just read in the *Reader's Digest,* which he studied the way that Jefferson did Montesquieu. He also told show-biz stories of the sort that overexcites civilians in awe of old movie stars, but causes other toilers in the industry to stampede.

Jane Wyman would doubtless agree. Holmes Tuttle (who in fact had first met Reagan through her) saw that the pre-candidate needed strict management. To that end, Spencer-Roberts, a hot new firm of campaign consultants, was asked to interview Reagan and report on his liabilities. Chester Chatterbox restrained himself, and Stuart Spencer and Bill Roberts signed one of the most portentous contracts in political history.

❡

Their first problem was an unusual one: the publication on April 23 of Reagan's eccentric personal memoir, *Where's the Rest of Me?* Like Theodore Roosevelt's *Autobiography* of 1913, it was a confused mix of sharp but selective personal recollections and long stretches of presentist political philosophy, unreadable by anybody of sound mind. Originally these stretches had bulked even longer, and the publisher, Duell, Sloan & Pearce, had brought in Richard G. Hubler to clarify and shorten Dutch's sprawling manuscript. Hubler (a former editorial colleague of Philip Dunne on *The Screen Writer*) left the personal passages largely alone, but elsewhere cut so ruthlessly that lacunae had to be bridged by ellipses.

Spencer-Roberts was less concerned about what was left out than what was still in. From Reagan's opening joke ("The story begins with the closeup of a bottom") to his concluding bromides ("The most important part of me wears a hat I treasure above all others—designed by Nancy and well smudged by sticky little fingers"), the book was a mine-field of potentially embarrassing quotes. Even the anti-Communist passages were so bellicose as to guarantee opposition from the new anti-war movement. And the overall talky tone, beguiling for a page or two, was as cloying as country music.

Since the book was already in distribution, it could not be stopped. Spencer-Roberts moved brilliantly to minimize its political effect. Thousands of copies were bought up and passed out to reporters with permission to quote them at length. As a result, *Where's the Rest of Me?* was quoted hardly at all.

☯

I dined once with the staff and trustees of the John F. Kennedy School of Government at Harvard, and was asked by my neighbor, one Gerald Blakely, if I knew what Ronald Reagan had learned from JFK.

"Certainly not!"

"Well, have you noticed how the President always conveys special regard for someone by touching them? The hand on the shoulder, or the double handclasp?"

"I have, and it's odd, because he doesn't much like being touched himself."

"But it works! When Reagan was just beginning to campaign for Governor—long before he announced—he and I happened to stay one night in the Fairmount Hotel in San Francisco on different floors. Didn't know each other, but he somehow found out that I had been a close friend of Kennedy's. Invited me to his suite to talk politics. I wasn't keen—thought he was just a dumb actor—but agreed to stop by. First he told me all about being President of the Screen Actors Guild, dealing with Communists and such, and I must admit I was fascinated. Then he says, 'Campaigning with the general public is gonna be a lot different than running for the SAG board.' The man was obviously looking for advice, so I told him about JFK's rationale for reaching out and touching people: 'You can touch two hundred in the time it takes you to shake hands with twenty.' That got him. He became obsessed with working the crowd Kennedy-style—kept asking questions like a scientist trying to figure something out. We stayed up till four in the morning. I came away amazed at his ambition. I thought he was terrific."

In asking so many questions and listening with such care, Reagan was not altering his essentially incurious nature. He was merely learning a new part, as actors do: working out the movements, looking for cues, trying to figure out the sensibilities of tomorrow's audience. As he cracked, "I've never played a governor before."

What he heard from the sort of Californians he met at country fairs amid summer chautauquas was a crescendo of complaints about "the mess at Berkeley." They feared that free (i.e., filthy) speech, Red propaganda, and drug-crazed behavior would seep like effluent from that campus, and through the whole university system, if drastic action was not imposed soon by Sacramento. Heads must roll, particularly the shiny bald one of President Kerr, for being too tolerant of dissent, or too weak to suppress it.

In their opinion, Governor Brown had acted commendably in breaking up the Sproul sit-in last fall, yet shown a failure of nerve in allowing seditionists to regroup and pervert the faculty. Brown was further perceived as being so much in love with his nine-campus "multiversity" that he could not bring himself to control its rampant demands on the state budget.

The perception was accurate, as Brown himself once admitted in an interview with me. "I never had a college education myself. Always felt intellectually inferior to faculty people, even some of those brilliant student leaders. That's why I was kinda . . . tender toward them, I guess."

An honest, engaging, backroom-boy Irish pol, he also said that he should have taken more notice of Reagan in '65, and sized him up as a serious challenger. "*Serious* is the word. I remember the first time I met him in '48—we were just two Democrats campaigning for Harry—and I said to him, 'Good to meet another Irish Catholic.' He said pleasantly, yet very deliberately, 'Mr. Brown, I'm of Irish descent, but my mother raised me as a Protestant.' I should have realized right then Reagan was a weightier man than me. More intense. I'm light."

There was nothing lightweight about the Brown campaign organization, though: a juggernaut loaded with patronage, well oiled with Democratic money, and confident of its third successive electoral win. Nor was the sixty-year-old Governor's personal modesty without guile. From his round, bespectacled head to the turnups of his shapeless suits, he looked utterly ordinary, yet beneath the turnups, expensive black cowboy boots peeped with an air of reptilian threat. His flaccid handshake and pompous bloopers (San Diego's Del Mar Bridge had been "my last erection") similarly concealed a ruthless power player. No Galway peasant ever dropped a hot potato faster than Pat Brown dispensed with people no longer useful to him. "He's a very tough guy," recalled one of his victims in the State Senate, ". . . as savage in political infighting as anybody I've ever met."

Spencer-Roberts noticed with some concern that, in a state where Democrats outnumbered Republicans three to two, Ronald Reagan had none of these qualities. He was about as contrary a foil to Brown as could be imagined. Even their shared Irishness was divided between luck on his side and hubris on the Governor's. I owe this perception to my chess-playing son, who wrote in the aftermath of the Watts riots and the Berkeley troop-train protests:

Every cop beaten or building looted & burned was a blow to
Brown's abilities to keep the peace. Every locomotive we sat down in
front of had his name on the embarkation order. And nobody can
forget him sending the squad into Sproul last fall. What scares the
merde out of me is, if we keep demonizing the Gov., we'll recast him
as the villain rather than the architect of the multiversity—with all its
faults still the glory of this state. He'll no longer be able to boast of it
as his best achievement, and likely bring about the election of your
Yahoo classmate, higher education's worst enemy.

Gavin added a helpful postscript: *Definition Yahoo: someone who
doesn't know what "Yahoo" means.*

On January 4, 1966, Ronald Reagan formally announced his candidacy
for the Governorship of California. Intrigued as I was by this latest
metamorphosis, I confess I paid the campaign no heed. For some
months now, I had been preoccupied with a young, apple-cheeked English high school teacher. Despite her pellucid accent and Anglo-
Catholic faith, she hankered engagingly for New York, where she had
recently lived and worked.

Since she is now the larger part of my life and guards her privacy
(except insofar as she is, in her own right, a published author), I will
venture her but little into this manuscript. But I should record this
early snatch of conversation between us. We were discussing Lyndon
Johnson's dwindling prospects for re-election. "Watch out for
Richard Nixon," Sylvia said.

"*Nixon?* He's politically dead."

"Well, I saw him at a party in the Plaza Hotel, not long after Pat
Brown beat him in '62. For a dead man, he was doing plenty of politicking. He courted just about every person in the room. I'm sure he's
still at it."

We were married on May 28, 1966, at All Saints' Church, Margaret
Street, London. Gavin, who turned twenty-six that same Whitsun
weekend, pleaded an urgent research trip to Algeria. I thought him a
little old for that kind of behavior. Paul Rae sent a congratulatory
telegram from Vietnam, where he was working on a book of war drawings. Phil Dunne wished us well on a sheet of yellow legal paper, and
ended his letter thus:

If your reason for quitting California and marrying a Brit is to
avoid the ludicrous spectacle of Ronald Reagan running for Gover-

nor, *mea culpa*. Last year, when I was casting *Blindfold* at Universal, Bob Arthur told me Ronnie was "dying" to play the bad guy—a Communist, no less! I refused even to consider the idea, on the grounds that Reagan was so irredeemably "nice" he couldn't frighten anybody.

More fool I. In recent weeks he's managed to scare half California with his daffy assertions that 15% of the state is on welfare (actually it's 5%), and that we are in danger of being crowded into the Pacific by rampant redwoods ("A tree is a tree—how many more do you need to look at?"). There was a bizarre episode in March when he attended a meeting of the Negro Republican League in Santa Monica with his primary challenger, George Christopher. A black businessman asked him what support he thought he was going to get from Negroes if he felt the Civil Rights Act was "a bad piece of legislation." He was still reeling from this when Christopher weighed in with some remark about the party's legacy of prejudice, whereupon Reagan stood and shouted, "I resent the implication that there is any bigotry in my nature"—and strode offstage in tears. (He also apparently cast aspersions on Christopher's parentage.) It was hours before his managers could coax him back to apologize for walking out.

Knowing actors as well as I do, I'm a little suspicious as to whether his emotion was genuine. What's clear is that he lacks judgment. Better for all of us if Christopher whips him on June 7. Yet the polls favor Ron. If he's nominated, will you forgive me? If he's elected, will we ever speak again? And if, in two years time, he . . .

My pen quails at the thought.

Primary day found my new wife and me on the Côte Blayais, among vineyards and lime groves, far beyond reach of the *International Herald-Tribune*. Not until we returned to London did we hear that Dutch had beaten Christopher by a margin of more than two to one.

Gavin's reaction to the news was frank horror, intensified by a post-primary poll that showed Pat Brown trailing by fifteen percentage points. Brown did little to lessen the gap by publicly praising Reagan's "infinitely superior" command of public relations, and for the first time his supporters began to wonder if the Governor (the only man alive to have defeated Richard Nixon) had lost his political smarts. He seemed determined to cast Reagan as a dangerous extremist beholden to the John Birch Society, rather than as the "nice guy" millions of Californians were now seeing in late-night reruns of *Kings Row*.

Reagan, in contrast, showed an early instinct for the right issues to focus on. One of these was "the morality gap at Berkeley," which he blamed on Clark Kerr's "appeasement of campus malcontents." Gavin furiously wrote to say that he was going to spend all of July and August campaigning against the Yahoo in radical publications.

> Dad, this is urgent. I just can't spare the time to come over & see you all, not thru the election anyway. Reagan has got to be stopped. Men who speak of morality but really mean thought control, who talk in parables that sound comforting but actually subtly reinforce prejudice, who allow buzz phrases like "our city streets are jungle paths after dark" to transmit a subliminal image of African savages, are using rhetoric to spread lies, & only words, hard words in black & white, will throw the lies back at them.

Dutch's call for campus morality sounded measured in contrast to this diatribe. He remarked that teachers were supposed to uphold those "family values" demanded by the American majority, and not side with an iconoclastic minority. "If scholars are to be recognized as having a right to press their particular value judgments, perhaps the time has come also for institutions of higher learning to assert themselves as positive forces in the battle for men's minds."

For the next few months, our chaste London letter box was profaned with protest mail from Berkeley. Gavin's envelope embellishments kept the postman *au courant* with Californian affairs, although I had to explain what was meant by JANE WYMAN WAS RIGHT.

Dutch once told me that he began campaigning in 1966 with an actor's usual feeling that all tours must end, sooner or later, with a return to private life. "In my mind, I had agreed to something that would only last until November . . . until I said, 'Wait a minute! If I win this damn thing I'm out of show business! I'm in politics!'" (Jovial laughter.)

I think he was always in earnest. Only sheer will would have made him conquer his thirty-year fear of airplanes, and consent to a series of stop-go flights in a battered white DC-3. He needed to cover the state from Tulelake to Twentynine Palms, because by early fall Brown had advanced from fifteen percentage points behind to only five.

But he proceeded to draw ahead again by working eighteen-hour days and using personal charm to combat Brown's major campaign document, *Ronald Reagan, Extremist Collaborator: An Exposé.* Its allegations filled twenty-nine pages of close print. Rather than answer them all, he simply deflected the major one: "Any members of the [John Birch] Society who support me will be buying my philosophy. I won't be buying theirs." The other charges fell away. When Brown abandoned all courtesy in a television commercial, saying, "I'm running against an actor, and you know who shot Lincoln, don't you?" Dutch allowed the bluster to speak for itself.

"Whatever you think of RR, he's got restraint," I wrote Gavin.

Unimpressed, Gavin reported that Dutch's every word and action were being programmed by Spencer-Roberts. "To be precise, by BASICO, a group of 31 behavioral scientists to whom he has been subcontracted like a robot in need of rewiring. 'The Organization Man' has become the Data Processor. Any moment now, look for perforated paragraphs to flick out of that slitty mouth."

This strange image derived from Gavin's new interest in computers. (Solid state circuitry suited his binary mind.) Its relevance did not fully strike me until twenty years later, when I came across a stack of Dutch's 1966 campaign speech cards. Pocket-sized, six inches by four, they were handwritten in tall, cramped capitals, the important words squeezed dry of vowels and unnecessary consonants, the unimportant ones reduced to a series of carefully counted dots:

The effect was indeed of data processing and perforation, except for the crookedness of Dutch's script and the lines he drew between his rhetorical periods, like a singer calculating breaths. Gavin must have seen him use such cards on the stump, although most people did not. Their smallness allowed Reagan to hold them in one hand and slip them out of sight when he was through. One droop of his eyelids was enough to "photograph" a whole card and keep him talking for several minutes with apparent spontaneity. Only ears as acute as my son's noticed that the measured rhythm of Dutch's diction did not correspond to the impulses of thought. What Reagan wrote as script, he memorized as sound; it was the reverse of the way he had learned to read, with Nelle's voice seeming to run out of her finger and form "funny black marks" on the page.

To that extent, the candidate was programmed, but Gavin overestimated BASICO's rhetorical input. Ronald Reagan remained his own main speechwriter at least through 1980. What he got from BASICO (more properly, the Behavior Sciences Corporation) was, however, invaluable: an ongoing crash course in California issues, position papers arguing both sides of every question, constant company on the trail, and frank analyses of his faults, such as a tendency to "overanswer" reporters and blow up when goaded. One or another of the corporation's officers was with Reagan every day to coach him. "Remember, this is a chess game."

Their counsel was necessary because he had "zero" knowledge of what went on in Sacramento. For a conservative candidate obsessed with states' rights, Reagan was surprisingly uninterested in local government. His mind turned to national and ideological subjects, rather than to the number of beds in California's mental-health hospitals or problems of pesticide runoff in the Tehachapi Mountains. "Damn," he said one day to Dr. Stanley Plog, "wouldn't this be fun if we were running for the Presidency?"

Like many later advisers, Dr. Plog found Reagan to be a conscientious crammer, open-minded on policy suggestions that were new to him but inflexible on those he had formulated himself. "I have worked in a variety of campaigns, and Reagan, unquestionably, has the most integrated political philosophy that I've seen in anyone. . . . Everything, for him, flows from the Constitution."

℮

When, one damp October afternoon along Piccadilly, I saw Dutch's face on the cover of *Time* magazine, I gazed at it with the same incredulity I had felt twenty-nine years before, when Paul Rae sent me that wire copy of an AP dispatch about "our friend's" metamorphosis as the hero of *Love Is on the Air*. How could anybody so boringly recognizable, the lowbrow lifeguard of teenage memory, apotheosize twice: first as film star, now as probable Governor and possible President, "the most magnetic crowd puller since John F. Kennedy"? For the first time, I empathized with Gavin's alarm. Not at *his* Reagan, sinister embodiment of all that was corporate and corrupt—but at *my* Dutch, my Thyrsis, my Adjutant, all of them good enough guys, but so ungreat they could not possibly handle power. Could they?

On November 8, 1966, a huge majority of Californians decided that they could. Ronald Reagan defeated Governor Brown by nearly a million votes, sweeping all but three of the state's fifty-eight counties, with enormous majorities in Los Angeles and the south. His total poll amounted to the full strength of the state Republican Party, plus almost four hundred thousand Democrat defections. Virtually every GOP candidate for state and local office rode to power on his coattails. Gavin called up, stoned, after Dutch's victory statement. "At least we beat his ass in Berkeley."

☯

The Governor-elect lost little time in announcing the first political target of his coming administration. "In all the sound and fury at Berkeley, one voice is missing," he told a specially called press conference at the Ambassador Hotel in Los Angeles. "And since it is the voice of those who built the university and pay the entire cost of its operation, I think it's time that voice was heard."

He was referring specifically to a new SDS strike in protest against U.S. Navy recruitment on campus. But reporters in the room (the same one where I heard him give his fertilizer speech) were aware that Reagan's transition team was planning to make a issue of the general right of "Cal" students to attend classes without radical interference. Nervous Regents, hoping to perpetuate the *entente cordiale* that had existed between the state and university administrations, had tried to arrange a meeting between Reagan and Clark Kerr. Ominously, Reagan had postponed that pleasure until after he was sworn in.

Naturally, I was sure that Gavin was one of the student strikers. He surprised me, however, by writing in the new year to say he had given up "campus politics" and would be devoting the next couple of years to "my diss. on Camus." I suppose I should have noticed his careful choice of adjective. By January 1967, most of Berkeley's revolutionary activity had shifted back downtown.

In the meantime, Reagan was making himself very clear, as post-landslide politicians are wont to do. "No one is compelled to attend the university. Those who do attend should accept and obey the prescribed rules, or pack up and get out."

25

Reagan Country

R ONALD REAGAN was sworn in as Governor of California on January 2, 1967, at two minutes past midnight, under the dome of the
State Capitol in Sacramento. No official reason was given for the ceremony's eccentric timing. Privately, Reagan said that he wanted to take
power as soon as possible, to prevent his predecessor from burdening
him with presumably corrupt appointments. But Pat Brown had already had two months of grace to exercise such patronage. Cynical observers suspected the possible involvement of Jeanne Dixon, Mrs.
Reagan's favorite astrologer.

"Well, George," said Reagan to Senator Murphy in the front row,
"here we are on the late show again."

*NOTE TO CAMERAMAN: As the small, invited audience (which
conspicuously excludes former Governor BROWN) roars with laughter, pull back upward into the rotunda, out through one of the great
portholes, then pan slowly around the little agricultural city that will be
REAGAN's home, five days a week, for the next eight years. Sacra-*

mento sleeps. It has seen thirty-two Governors come and go, and has plenty of time to adjust to this one.

Where have we seen a similar loop of river—just such a cannery and waterfront warehouses, the same dingy downtown, with its obligatory Woolworth's and Pick 'n' Pay and Chinese restaurant (camera takes special note of the signboard, "Frank Fat's"), and those Hopperesque facades sunk in shadow? Dixon? Davenport? Des Moines? From a certain elevation, at dead of night, all provincial cities look the same. They vary in details, but they share a common lack of luster; they do not glitter or throb.

Now tilt the camera down, so we can see the only thing that really shines around here, the gold cupola dome of the Golden State Capitol. (SFX: fade in the sound of REAGAN's amplified voice pledging to "bring to public office the teachings and precepts of the Prince of Peace." He is speaking ad lib.) The Capitol, built in 1861, is somewhat the worse for earthquakes, but its Roman Classical E-shaped layout is nobly proportioned and surrounded by forty acres of California flora. Unfortunately, all this symmetry is despoiled by a ghastly "East Wing": six floors of office and committee space added by the sort of modern architects who think a concrete box is the sum of all aesthetics. The ground floor of this box will be inherited by the new gubernatorial administration; REAGAN will occupy a suite on the southeastern corner.

Since the Governor is still speaking, we may as well zoom in there for an "establishing" shot. NANCY REAGAN has not yet had a chance to do anything about the torn-up rug and cigar burns that BROWN has left behind (along with an ingeniously postponed $350-million deficit). Her husband's office consists of a conference room, soon to be restyled "the cabinet room," and a private study, twenty by twenty. The latter chamber is dominated by a massive walnut desk, on which rests a single paper clip. Doors and walls are steel-framed to prevent the Governor from being crushed, in any seismic accident, by falling Senators and Assemblymen. Those second-floor legislators are going to weigh upon him enough as it is.

(Distant sounds of REAGAN's speech being applauded, and a choir breaking into "America the Beautiful")

One last shot before we pass out through the Governor's picture window, back into the night. Camera holds briefly on an elm in the Capitol park. Just that one solitary elm. A tree's a tree, how many more do you need to look at?

Dutch's first remark to his senior staff, when they joined him to take up state business on January 5, has become legendary: "What do we do now?"

It was not so much a *cri de coeur* as an announcement of executive attitude. Ever since his first recruitment as a student orator (the word EUREKA pleasingly embellished the Great Seal of California behind him), he had placed his talents in the hands of other people. Strike leaders, program managers, casting agents, directors, producers, colonels, friends: all had placed their scripts in front of him, and none had been disappointed. As far as he was concerned, the people of California had given him their mandate, and it was the job of his aides to reduce that mandate to a list of priorities.

Chief of these mostly young men (average age: thirty-one) was a hyperactive, hyperambitious Los Angeles lawyer named Philip M. Battaglia. The hard edge of his crew cut failed to strengthen the soft bow of his mouth, but nobody disputed Battaglia's brilliance, nor (for the moment) the appropriateness of his appointment as executive secretary to the Governor. This gave him authority over a staff of eighty-seven. Lyn Nofziger, press secretary, had a wounded face and looked like a used sleeping bag. Nobody, however, was quicker or funnier in political debate, or more brutal in defending Reagan's interests—as Battaglia was to find out. William P. Clark, Jr., cabinet secretary, was handsome, solitary, shy, a fifth-generation Californian, tough as a roll of rawhide. Caspar W. Weinberger of San Francisco was even tougher (horn to Clark's hide) and superbly qualified to handle the state's finances; but he had opposed Goldwater in '64 and must wait in the wings until party conservatives had forgiven him. Thomas C. Reed, appointments secretary, was so purely political that he could relocate at a moment's notice to Arkansas, or Africa, and instantly plug into the local power network. Vernon L. Sturgeon, legislative secretary, had just been redistricted out of the State Senate, so he had a useful network of contacts "upstairs." Finance director Gordon Paul Smith, a short and obsequious management consultant, represented a compromise choice to handle the largest state budget in the world.

That superlative was something for Reagan to consider, as he waited for Smith to tell him how the budget could be balanced at anything less than five billion dollars in fiscal 1967. Equally intimidating was the fact that California would be the world's sixth-ranked economy, were it not part of the United States. Reagan was now boss of a public corporation with one hundred and fifteen thousand employees, serving twenty million customers.

Their comforts, which they looked to him to extend, included the most income, cars, pleasure boats, parks, beaches, pools, patios, color televisions, and cats in the nation. Californians divorced more, drank more, smoked more, and, if the consumption in his own household was anything to go by, popped more pills than other Americans. This did not seem to affect their intellectual achievements: here lived the nation's greatest concentration of doctors and Nobel Prize winners—most of the latter in Berkeley. An astonishing 80 percent of young Californians went to college, and thanks to propagandists such as Clark Kerr, seemed to think that higher education was their right.

Reagan needed no help in addressing that presumption, at least. He looked forward to his first meeting with Kerr as a Regent *ex officio* of the University of California. In the meantime, he thought his words to student rebels might profitably be circulated around the executive wing. He had a bronze plaque engraved and mounted over his office door: OBSERVE THE RULES OR GET OUT.

So much for the "legend" of Governor Reagan's first days—days that Lyn Nofziger now admits were characterized by an almost total ignorance of Capitol procedure. "Only one member of his senior staff [Sturgeon] knew anything about how government really worked." At the time, I had to rely for most of my Californian information on Gavin. He wrote angrily to complain that the new administration was "white as Wonder bread," and seemed especially incensed by the appointment of "Ed Meese" as Dutch's clemency secretary. "The title is a perverse joke. Euphemism for chief cop. Meese was the pig who got Gov. Brown to break up our sit-in when we took over Sproul in '64."

What interested me was Gavin's use of the word *pig*. He was too fastidious to stoop to loose invective, so it must have some new, colloquial meaning that had not yet crossed the Atlantic. This was indeed the case. According to W. J. Rorabaugh's book *Berkeley at War,* black radicals in the Bay Area began using *pig* in 1967 to express the meaty ugliness and greed of white establishmentarians—in particular the Oakland police force, which Meese had dominated in his days as deputy district attorney. More subtly, to those with ancestral memories of Southern hog barbecues, *pig* suggested a rich readiness to be "slaughtered, roasted and eaten" by the community at large. Rorabaugh does not add that Meese had— still has—a pink, porcine joviality and manifest obsession with law enforcement, but I would bet those further connotations occurred to Gavin.

Clark Kerr's dismissal from the presidency of the University of California on January 20, 1967, made headlines even in Britain. Although Kerr forced the issue, and was let go by a 14–8 majority of the Board of Regents, liberals everywhere blamed the Governor. Reagan was seen as a Beverly Hillbilly bent on reshaping the world's finest university system into an approximation of contemporary Hollywood: eight competing lots that pinched every penny and turned out a homogenized product guaranteed not to offend popular taste. It was a variation of the old data-processing image leveled against Kerr himself three years before, except that now the threat to academic freedom was seen as coming from outside.

"I simply was conducting the meeting, and that was the decision of the Regents," Dutch told me when I asked him afterward about Kerr's ouster. "I went along with the group." Having studied a transcript of the proceedings, I can confirm that he said little and voted according to the promise of his campaign. But for the rest of his career in Sacramento and in Washington, this kind of "group" decision, intuitively reflecting the feelings rather than the instructions of the Chief Executive, would characterize his governing style. I can compare it only to the phenomenon of the conductor who beats time imperceptibly, often with eyes closed, before a band of players, few of whom even look up from their decks. Somehow, a concerted sound emerges.

One document—a drawing doodled during the meeting—survives as evidence of his true feelings about President Kerr. Lovingly shaded for extra curvature, it represents a horse's ass.

☯

Clark Kerr probably would not have asked for a vote to "clarify his status" had he not been placed in an intolerable position by Reagan's demand that the University of California reduce its 1967–1968 appropriation request by 15 percent. This was in line with a general "squeeze, cut, and trim" policy to be applied throughout the state government, in an effort to combat a looming deficit bequeathed by Governor Brown. But what particularly blew Kerr's mind (as Gavin would say) was a further proposal that Cal start charging tuition. The idea of giving students something for nothing was so sacred a tenet of the Great Society that Kerr did not know how he could fight for it unless the Regents supported him. Instead, they fired him.

This did not mean that they went along with the tuition idea. Since Regents are all-powerful in Californian educational policy, Dutch had to drop it. His revised five-billion-dollar state budget went through to the Legislature on March 27, and here the pen of a fiscal retard begins to quail. Suffice to say that Gordon Smith's desperate attempts to achieve an overall 10 percent cutback failed to alter the necessity of a one-billion-dollar tax increase—the largest in Californian history.

Executive authority, meanwhile, forced Reagan to deal with questions of madness, life, and death. He was not well equipped to do so, being by nature sentimental and unable to lock eyes with the black dog Despair. "Hello, everybody," he would say as he entered a cabinet meeting, "what do you have to offer to make me feel better?" Depersonalized numbers he could face—as when he coolly announced the layoff of four thousand state employees. But he left it to Battaglia to note that thirty-seven hundred of these would be dropped from just one department: Mental Hygiene.

There was such an immediate outcry (liberals and conservatives alike accused him of cruelty to psychotics) that he reduced the figure by a thousand. No amount of persuasion, however, would coax the Governor into any of the hospitals he had hit, and his reputation for niceness was damaged permanently.

Then there was the case of Aaron Mitchell, a black cop-killer on Death Row in San Quentin State Prison. Pat Brown had not hesitated to uphold Mitchell's conviction just weeks before Reagan took office. Since then, the Supreme Courts of state and nation had denied a stay of execution. On April 10, Edwin Meese told the Governor he must decide Mitchell's fate, after a final "mercy hearing" that afternoon.

It was one of those *moments critiques* when a leader has to act with absolute courage. Brown, an opponent of the death penalty, had not flinched. Reagan, who favored it, felt compelled to carry out the law, but could not face Aaron Mitchell's mother. He left Meese to explain that he was "not a lawyer" and flew to Los Angeles for an urgent engagement at the Academy Awards.

When Meese communicated the message to Mrs. Mitchell, she ran out of the gubernatorial suite sobbing, "Why, Jesus, why?" Her attorney followed her and said, as television cameras clustered around, "This man is protecting himself. . . . He's afraid. He's running for the Presidency."

I am quoting these words from a *Los Angeles Times* news clip sent to me by Gavin, with the last sentence heavily underlined. He enclosed another one headlined "REAGAN REFUSES TO GIVE CLEMENCY TO MURDERER," plus a letter whose bitterness amazed me:

1141½ Hearst Av Berkeley 11 Apr. 1967

Tough shit for your Hollywood friend. He hoped he'd get an Oscar for his new movie *Capitol Punishment*. But the first thing I saw when I got to San Quentin at dawn was a sign outside the gate: "RONALD REAGAN—NO ACADEMY AWARD FOR LEGAL MURDER."

Serve him right for giving away the ending at a press preview yesterday. Allowed as how the cop-killer had gone up "every legal avenue" & each time ended up on Death Row. Most heinous crime on the calendar—far worse than wasting a few thousand Vietnamese peasants. So: "hang down your head, Black Aaron, po' boy you gonna die." At 10:01 this A.M., to be accurate, in a chair last warmed by Caryl Chessman.

Cyanide pills in sulfuric acid. *Splosh!* Soothing silent fumes. All around the Bay, church bells tolling. First execution in Calif. since '63. *First in the whole fucking country this year.* We sang, "I really do believe," but I don't believe, Dad, not anymore, not in Reagan's Amerikkka.

That line of Dylan Thomas keeps banging in my brain, *After the first death, there is no other.*

Dutch assured me years later, when he had considerably more blood on his hands, that the night before Mitchell's execution was the worst of his governorship. He spent some of it praying with Rev. Donn Moomaw, a born-again former football star who had flown up from Los Angeles to counsel him. Meanwhile, candles flickered and hand-bells tinkled around his rented house on Forty-fifth Street, courtesy of the Sacramento Committee for Life. Nancy was enraged at the effect of the demonstration on eight-year-old Ron, but the Governor's only response was to wonder, mildly, why bells never rang "every time there is a murder."

He certainly heard nary a chime early in May, when something called the Therapeutic Abortion Bill began to take shape in the offices of Senator Anthony Beilenson (D.–Beverly Hills). It was not quite the first state measure to propose that pregnant women be allowed to terminate embryos prejudicial to their "physical or mental health." But its implications were more lethal—at least, to unborn babies—than bills already enacted by Colorado and North Carolina. Not only was California the nation's most populous state, and a particularly fecund one, but Beilenson also wanted to extend the power of abortion to women who had been raped or subjected to incest.

Reagan had to admit, rather unhappily, that he agreed with these proffers, in particular "the moral principle of self-defense." If one hundred thousand Californian women were desperate enough to undergo illegal abortions every year, he could at least make it safer for some of them. The metaphysical and religious consequences frightened him, however—not to mention Beilenson's suggestion that a deformed fetus was another good reason to call for the forceps. "This is not in my mind a clear-cut issue," he told reporters, refusing to say whether he would sign the bill. "I . . . I just can't give you a decision." He needed time to reflect and exchange views with Senator Beilenson. "It is a very profound and deep issue."

In the event, he got five weeks—about as long as it takes a zygote (that abstract speck of color floating in microspace) to become a functioning neurological entity (that pale, cross-hatched, preparturient child asleep in sonograms). Beilenson agreed to withdraw the "cripple clause," since Reagan did not see why symmetry should be a prerequisite of existence. Thus amended, the bill passed through the Legislature with enough votes to override any veto. As signing day drew near, the Governor went into an uncharacteristic funk. "Bill, I've got to know more—theologically, philosophically, medically," he told his cabinet secretary. Clark, a devout Roman Catholic, loaded his briefcase with patristic *idées reçues.* By the time the Therapeutic Abortion Act reached him on June 13, Reagan was quoting Saint Thomas Aquinas.

He signed it into law nevertheless, comforting himself that he had helped purge it of eugenics and that no abortions of any kind would be permitted without strict medical or legal review. Only as time went by and abortion became an extension of welfare, would he wish he had paid more heed to the bill's manipulative language. The very word "Therapeutic" was a medical euphemism, sanitizing essentially bloody procedures. Section 25954 defined "mental health" as something delicate enough to be at risk if a pregnant teenager went out and smashed a few windows. And in common with the more liberal laws it was to spawn at state and federal levels, the Act ignored the feelings of fathers.

Reagan was left with an undefinable sense of guilt after signing it. "If there is a question as to whether there is life or death," he awkwardly wrote one protester, "the doubt should be resolved in favor of life." Before the end of his first term as Governor, some eighty-two thousand souls would be debited to that signature, as against the seventy-seven he took credit for as a lifeguard.

The lesser figure, at least, he could do something about. On the

Fourth of July, he and Nancy held a staff garden party around the pool at their residence, to celebrate the end of the legislative season. As the adults talked and laughed over their flashing cocktails, a little black girl tumbled into the pool and quietly sank. Reagan threw off his jacket and was in the water before anybody else realized what had happened. He emerged with pompadour intact and set her, living, on the wet concrete.

☯

All this I learned later, since Gavin, like most young destructors, was more interested in pulling down pillars than pondering the rights of

"He . . . set her, living, on the wet concrete."
Ronald Reagan's seventy-eighth rescue, Sacramento, July 4, 1967.

women, let alone babies. He delightedly reported that some armed Black Panthers ("bad cats I dig in Oakland") had managed to bluster their way into the State Capitol. His only regret was that they had not gotten into the Executive Wing "and scared the shit out of Reagan."

In common with most people in Britain, I had not heard of the Panthers. But the incident made them notorious overnight, and Gavin's claim to have "introduced those guys to the works of Fanon" was deeply disturbing. I knew enough about Frantz Fanon, the most dangerous of all terror theorists, to think for the first time that maybe I should go home and check on what was happening to my son.

I now trace the occlusion of Gavin's personality (a slow sweep of shadow over what had once been sun-filled terrain) back to his discovery of Fanon's *Les Damnés de la terre* in Algeria, before it was translated into English as *The Wretched of the Earth* and became a basic text of the Panthers.

Worried as I was about Gavin's possible involvement with the likes of Huey Newton, I took comfort in evidence that he was still more scholar than saboteur. He wrote to say that he had decided to incorporate Fanon into his Ph.D. dissertation. It was now to be called "Locked into the Infernal Cycle: Camus, Fanon, and the Moral Ambiguities of Revolution." I could only hope he would concentrate on Camus and resist the Marxist blandishments of Sartre, that *nègre* in so many a scholarly woodpile.

"More power to your *plume,* son," I wrote in an early Christmas card. "Now how about doing something *really* radical and seeing in the new year with us?"

As it happened, 1968 was the last year we "saw in" on that side of the Atlantic. Four years of Labour government had so re-socialized the British economy as to reverse the law of supply and demand. What Reagan had blanched at two decades before—a public expenditure approaching 40 percent of GNP—had now passed 50 percent, so we were, in effect, enriching the state rather than ourselves. Sir Winston Churchill was dead, Evelyn Waugh, too: splendid, peevish, brandy-red Conservatives who had seen the sun set on Empire and not cared for the twilight that ensued. In their footsteps sidled Harold Wilson and his clones, little gray lager-sippers, constantly burping the word *technology.* Muzak polluted the pubs, provincial accents crassed out the Third Programme, and, in a final blow to English culture, *The Times* began to run news on its front page. When my wife discovered in March that the London school system actually rewarded teachers for working fewer hours, we agreed that America, whatever its current instability, was still—to quote undeclared presidential candidate Ronald Reagan—"the last best hope of man on earth." Now that President Johnson had pledged not to run again, there was a real chance of peace in Vietnam.

Pausing only to complete the last best opus of my career as a British copywriter (*The Heatrae Natural Gas Boiler: A User's Guide*), I resigned and wired my New York headhunter to find me a job "anywhere on Madison Avenue." We put our flat on the market and began to pack. I remember stashing some volumes of Thackeray as a BBC news flash announced that Martin Luther King, Jr., had been killed. Early next morning, Gavin called to say that Washington was in flames.

"And guess who's there getting his Brylcreem burned off! California's favorite son!"

For the next thirty years, Lyn Nofziger (shapeless, squinty, chuckling and wheezing over his Mickey Mouse tie) would tell the story of how he managed to launch Ronald Reagan's first presidential campaign on the worst day of urban rioting in American history. He and Tom Reed had been plotting this moment since 1966, despite repeated demurrals from Dutch ("Feels kinda premature, fellows, I just don't think I'm ready"), and they were dead serious about it. Hapless, podgy Phil Battaglia had long since been bullied back into private life for showing too much interest in a cute intern named Jack Kemp. Funds had been coaxed out of Tuttle and Salvatori, a network of paid or pledged operatives established nationwide, and a secret campaign office opened in San Francisco.

All that was lacking, as the primary season got under way, was a public gesture from the Governor that would give him *gravitas* and turn him overnight from a favorite son with eighty-six convention delegates into a major contender with three hundred or more. Such a gain could come only at the expense of Richard Nixon, whom Nofziger and Reed saw as a vulnerable front-runner, banking on many political IOUs but tagged with the image of a loser. They persuaded Reagan to speak on domestic issues before the National Women's Press Club on April 5. He must have been in the air at the same time I was packing, because when he arrived in Washington, Nofziger greeted him with, "We're going to have to go through with this, but we're not going to get any publicity. Somebody has shot Martin Luther King."

Reagan dutifully delivered his speech while the smoke of hundreds of burning shops drifted down the Mall and blotted out all but the tip of the Washington Monument. Nofziger madly escorted him on to a meeting with black militants, whence they were sprung, just in time, by police: "You'd better get out of here. The city's going up."

About half an hour later, the Governor of California was forced to emerge from his jammed limousine downtown and walk hastily back to his hotel, with Nofziger and Arthur Van Court, a security guard. He wore a borrowed pair of sunglasses, but could do nothing about his famous hair and Golden State tan. The sooty air was full of the sound of breaking glass and not-so-distant gunfire. Two black youths lounged menacingly against a wall, eyeing him as he approached. Nofziger and Van Court were struck by his absolute calm. One of the youths suddenly straightened and, before the guard could draw, stuck out his hand: "Guv'nor Reagan! Glad to see you!"

Or, depending on whom you talk to, he said to his friend, "Hey man, there's Ronald Reagan." Dutch, of course, is convinced that the youth asked for his autograph. At any rate, he dispensed with dark glasses for the rest of his walk and left Washington alive. As he flew back west, a hundred and twenty-nine other cities burned into the night.

My wife and I arrived in New York late on April 23, in the teeth of a torrential rainstorm. Gavin was supposed to meet us, but the weather delayed his plane from San Francisco, and he did not land at Kennedy until long after we had checked into a Manhattan hotel. He called in the middle of the night, awakening me from jet-lagged sleep.

"Dad, this won't work out. I'm booked on to Paris in seven hours. Gonna have to take a rain check, visit with you guys on my way back."

"Paris? What's so important in Paris that you can't—"

"Big things happening, man." He spoke to me as if I were an uncomprehending newspaper reporter. "The University's falling apart, de Gaulle's spoiling for social war, and SDS needs somebody on the scene who's hip in French. In any case, I gotta be there for my diss. The situation's pure Fanon."

So it was—not just in France, but around the world for the rest of that demented year. To be a student, it seemed, was to be totally alienated. I remembered Gavin's summary of the Port Huron Statement, warning that the University would be the crucible of change. Even as I shopped my portfolio of ads up and down Madison Avenue, SDS activists were trashing the Columbia campus. From Maine to California, other colleges rocked to the borrowed "pig" cry, *Up Against the Wall, Motherfucker!* In Paris, Prague, West Berlin, Rome, Mexico City, Tokyo, Dakar—even, incredibly, Moscow—yesterday's children took to the streets, stained their brains, copulated like rats, and screamed against the state. *Je marcuse,* I spit on society. Gavin approvingly sent us a graffito that he had copied from the wall of the Sorbonne: *The more I make love, the more I want to make revolution; the more I make revolution, the more I want to make love.*

With Johnson headed for retirement, Robert Kennedy blown away on June 5, and the leadership of neither party certain, there was no public figure formidable enough to serve as a general focus of hatred. Certainly not Ronald Reagan, whose managers were still unable to provoke him into an all-out candidacy. His rhetoric on the stump was confrontational: "The wind of the time is against us. The new social philosophy has all the answers . . . never mind a hand up: a handout is everyone's just due, and no need to work in the vast Federal plantation." But it simply reflected opinion, not a thought-out campaign strategy. Political journalists can smell ambivalence, so his appearances were under-reported, especially in New York.

Through July at least, I do not recall Dutch's face appearing at all on the enormous black-and-white TV that dominated our sublet apartment on the Upper East Side. My job hunting was not going well, and most nights I watched the news through a blur of self-concern.

The blur did not clear until Ogilvy & Mather, the Anglophile "long-copy" shop, came to my rescue at the end of the month. In sudden focus, as it were, I saw Dutch face the nation (literally, on the show of that name) on Sunday, August 4. It was the first time I had caught him "live" in six years, and I was surprised at how much he had aged, albeit attractively, in a windburned, Marlboro Man sort of way. The seams in his face were mainly laugh lines, radiating contentment from eyes and nose. A set of shorter ones compressed his mouth at serious moments. They were purposeful rather than petulant, the lip bite of an executive who had learned to measure his words. He was no longer the too-eager actor, trying to hold the camera by not pausing for breath. He calmly insisted that he was not running for the nomination against Nixon and Nelson Rockefeller. Nor was he interested in the No. 2 spot; he much preferred being Governor of the nation's No. 1 state.

It occurred to me, looking at him, that should Nixon win, as now seemed likely, and serve a couple of terms as President, Dutch would be sixty-five in 1976, the age most men retire. So he must be sincere about having no desire for federal office, now and probably ever.

O&M assigned me to its least "creative" account, International Business Machines. Visiting IBM's Austin, Texas, facility on my first research trip gained me *entrée* into a world about as far removed from Gavin's, or Daniel Cohn-Bendit's, as could be imagined. It was the very world they feared, where the crew cut and the slide rule, the white shirt and Bible and enormous, swaying, flat-hooded car were as omnipresent and indiscriminate as the hard light. Dustbowl dweebs: Dutch's guys.

Fifteen thousand of them working in the same glass box. They all wore their trousers too short and their shoes too wide. Their manners were better than any I had encountered in England. I was being briefed by three—or was it thirteen?—of them shortly before noon on August 5 when I observed a strange folk ritual in the parking lot outside: hundreds of secretaries fanning out among the cars, jumping into them, then hurrying back inside as exhaust fumes boiled. One of my briefers explained, "Air-conditioning."

Exactly five minutes later, we emerged and drove to lunch downtown in a freezing Fairlane. We ate steaks and strawberry shortcake, washed down with water. I asked them if they'd seen Dutch on *Face the Nation,* and they lit up like barbecue torches. "Oh, he's running all right. Tonight he'll declare he's no longer a favorite son and use that big ol' block of votes to hold out through the first ballot."

"Then what?"

"Land-wagon fever. Senator Dirksen says he's seen it before. Nixon's pledges will attrit."

I scribbled this remarkable verb on a napkin and said, "What about Rockefeller?"

There was a disapproving silence, then somebody hissed, "*Divorcé.*" He made it rhyme with Dorsey.

"Surely the party won't nominate a governor who's only had a year and a half in politics."

"Abraham Lincoln spent but one year in Congress before he got elected President," my host allowed, in tones that suggested recent emigration from Louisiana. "Not that that's much recommendation." The IBMers roared with laughter.

They were right about Reagan's opening tactic at the convention, if not the result. He indeed tossed his hat in, impulsively, believing that Nixon could not win on the first ballot. The move failed: he had been a "non-candidate" too long. Nevertheless, he came within eight votes of succeeding, by his own count. On August 8, he had the unenviable chore of stepping to the podium and calling for a unanimous declaration in behalf of "Richard Nixon as the next President of the United States."

Ever afterward he would remain embarrassed by his clumsiness at Miami, and be almost fanatically cagey about announcing when he would run, or not run, for anything. Still, as William Clark (Battaglia's replacement as chief of staff) noted, the experience was good for a man who had always come easily by success. It toughened him, carved a few more seams contrary to the laugh lines, made him warier of hustings hustlers like Nofziger. He learned to pay more attention to his own "feel" for the mood of American voters. In 1968, a majority of them wanted Richard Nixon, for good or, as things turned out, ill.

☯

At a biographical conference once, I told Tom Wolfe about my trip to Austin in '68, and he recommended that I read an essay called "Reagan Country," by James Q. Wilson. "It was published, I think, in *Commentary.* Wilson was the first writer to sense the power of Reagan's constituency as it spread out of Southern California and up through the West, completely changing our politics."

I located the article and, sure enough, there were my Austin friends—actually, Wilson's Long Beach and Inglewood friends of some years before, but, as Wolfe remarked, the species was spreading. "We must, I think, take Reaganism seriously," Wilson had written after Dutch's election to the governorship. "It will be with us for a long time under one guise or another. We will not take it seriously by trying to explain it away as if it were something sold at one of those [clichéd] orange-juice stands or preached from the pulpit at some cultist church."

Reagan Country, he went on, was neither small-town nor urban, but suburban, homogeneous communities of detached houses and lawns and pools linked, often over great distances, by cars that seemed to put no price on gas. The men and women who lived in these houses were middle-class but not highly paid, inclined toward a "fundamentalist Protestant individualism." Unlike ethnically varied Easterners and their cramped concept of *territory,* they shared "a strong, socially reinforced commitment to property." Their politics was "slightly populistic," exclusive of lobbyists and deal makers, conservative but nonpartisan—which meant that a Republican candidate like Reagan could effortlessly attract and hold large numbers of Southern Democratic votes. He had only to promise that he would not let government interfere with the phenomenon they put their faith in: free, developmental, future-oriented "growth."

Positive and trusting as they were, the residents of Reagan Country were strikingly discontent. "*The very virtues they have and practice are, in their eyes, conspicuously absent from society as a whole,*" Wilson wrote, using italics for emphasis. These people thought they saw a general "decay of values" every time they turned on the tube. They knew whom to blame: "a self-conscious intelligentsia with common ties to prestigious centers of liberal-arts education . . . especially in the East and Bay Area."

Reagan, their oracle, was able to trace and date the decay more precisely, back to "a captured police car and an imprisoned representative of the law at Berkeley."

☯

Gavin remained in Paris after the street riots that crippled France and very nearly brought down President de Gaulle's government. He became a comrade of "Danny the Red," and I am pretty sure his frontline dispatches to Berkeley activists influenced the copycat riots that broke out along Telegraph Avenue at the end of June. He then pleaded urgent work on Camus at the Sorbonne, and waited for my trip to Texas before flying back to Chicago. "I know you think I'm avoiding you, but 'It is the cause, my soul,' " he wrote. "We're planning a little 'offensive' against the Dem. National Convention in August."

So I watched, along with so many other helpless Americans *d'un certain âge,* as nightsticks bit into young skulls (Gavin's among them? Impossible to tell, with the blur of the blows and the blood and all that long flying hair) and the convention degenerated into a mass cockfight, with Mayor Daley, mad with rage and mortification, screaming at Senator Abraham Ribicoff (oh so audibly to any lip reader), "*Fuck you Jew son of a bitch you lousy motherfucker go home.*" Not to mention William F. Buckley, Jr., bridling on ABC at the superciliously delighted Gore Vidal and roaring, "Listen, you queer, if you call me a crypto-Nazi again I'll sock your goddamn face." And Hubert Horatio Humphrey being nominated and Ronald Reagan saying with a chuckle, "He's a modest man with a lot to be modest about."

Perhaps Dutch was right to be amused. The only alternative was to cry for American democracy. I wondered if maybe we should have stayed in England. The whole body politic seemed poisoned. And being representative in its manifestations, it subsequently elected a poisonous President.

With my help, I must confess. I'd always voted for Nixon in the past, and although the ever-narrowing gap between his eyes worried me, I believed his diplomatic skills would soon bring North Vietnam to the bargaining table. In November 1968, nobody could have guessed the ferocity of his desire to prove, once he had invested and re-invested this gift of power, that someone, somewhere, somehow was gonna bring him down.

A surprisingly cheerful letter from Gavin (his first since a telegram, "CHILL OUT I'M OKAY," after Chicago) arrived in early December, postmarked Death Valley Junction:

Dear Parentals—Believe it or not, I wuz actually tempted by your "invite" to spend Christmas in New York. But *hélas, non, j'ai une petite fillette ici,* name Suzi Cola, & we're putting in serious pool time at this motel. She's with Joe Chaikin's Open Theater. Dig?

Probably not. Well 2 make long story short, guess who got gassed with me in Windy City. None other than Michelangelo Antonioni. *Sì,* Mr. *L'Avventura* himself! In Chicago casting "unknowns" for his new movie, *Zabriskie Point.* Said I was too tall at first, but we hit it off, & I got him through a few doors (he wanted to rap with SDS). When he started shooting at Cal he hired me. $1000 a month: not bad bread. Computer work mainly: payroll, props, and a few scenes as an extra.

Between you & me, I think *ZP* will be a dog. Antonioni's a compositional genius (wait till you see us in the desert orgy!!), but he hasn't a clue what SDS is about.

"Wait till you see us in the desert orgy!!"
Scene from Antonioni's Zabriskie Point *(1969).*

On the other hand, neither does SDS anymore.

I should be back in Berkeley mid-Jan. Same address: 1141½ Hearst. Finish diss. by spring. It's in chess-game form: Black— Fanon, White—Camus. Black wins!

Love, G.

This letter delighted me, not just for its sunny spirits and lack of political cant (that enigmatic line about SDS notwithstanding). For the first time in our correspondence, my son had mentioned a girl. I felt he was shyly trying to tell me something.

☯

The new year brought four months of absolute silence from Gavin. I assumed he was working out the final moves of his "chess game" and left him undisturbed.

Lulled by this assumption, and the apolitical tone of his last letter, I read news of yet more disturbances at Berkeley in late January with feelings of bored *déjà vu.* Something called the Third World Liberation Front, a new militant movement consisting mainly of downtown blacks, struck the university and denied students access to classes. Local police were unable to quell the rioting that raged on and off campus. On February 5, Governor Reagan, angered by the Front's determination to "close this goddamn place down," declared a state of extreme emergency. "I have just one message for the dissidents outside the gate," he said. "Grow up."

After two years in power, he had won the grudging respect of Democrats in the Legislature and consolidated his authority as Chairman of the Board of Regents, while retaining his huge popularity among California voters. The appointment of Edwin Meese III as Reagan's third chief of staff (Clark had returned to private life) clearly signaled Reagan's intent to clean up, at last, "the mess at Berkeley."

When a preliminary infusion of California highway patrolmen failed to break up the rioting, Reagan told the Regents that radical protests had passed beyond the point of mere propaganda. Berkeley's huge majority of law-abiding students was being abused by "a revolutionary organization of professionals, for the purpose of destroying the nation's education system." He forced them to acknowledge the emergency, then sent in the National Guard.

I did not have time to be alarmed by this because the guardsmen moved so quickly and efficiently that Berkeley was numbed into a state of truce overnight. Reagan seemed to have struck a major blow for democracy, and conservatives applauded him. The truce lasted through early April, when the university moved to clear out and develop an ammoniacal, junk-strewn, weed-choked parking lot downtown.

The field was academic property, but it had lain fallow for a couple of years, and so become a hangout for Berkeley's growing population of hippie malcontents. They called it "People's Park," but it remained their exclusive preserve until Chancellor Roger Heyns announced that tractors were moving in to clear it. Radicals immediately declared the lot a battlefront between the forces of totalitarianism and freedom. "Who the hell does the chancellor think he is?" a Free Speech veteran wanted to know. "It is our park." Gavin's sometime newspaper, the *Berkeley Barb,* called for a horticultural takeover, with picks and shovels, on April 20. Abbie Hoffman and a few of his Chicago Yippies exulted that the coming confrontation would "suck Reagan into a fight."

Picks and shovels and at least one purloined tractor beat out the university's earthmovers, and by May 13 Heyns, nonplussed, informed his faculty, "We have been presented a park we hadn't planned or even asked for." The fact remained that property law (that gospel tenet of Reagan Country) was being challenged. If the state university did not move at once to assert its rights, then the state government certainly would, with consequences likely to make freethinkers sigh for the forbearance of Pat Brown's policemen, pussyfooting through Sproul Hall in '64.

"So what happens next?" the Chancellor asked rhetorically. "We will have to put up a fence." He ordered an announcement to that effect to be published in the Berkeley *Daily Gazette.*

I was in my office at O&M around noon on Thursday, May 15, when a mysterious phone call, full of long-distance atmospherics, reached me. "Gavin?" I asked, hearing nothing at first but what I took to be his breathing. Then there was the creak of a metal window thrust open and a sudden rhythmic roaring, *crescendo,* as of demonstrators coming up a street: "*No fucking fence! No fucking fence! No fucking fence!*" The chant reached a climax, then faded, and was cut off. I sat there with the receiver burring in my hand, possessed by a feeling of doom. Several times during the day I dialed Gavin's number, but his phone just rang and rang.

That night, we were waiting for the evening news when Philip Dunne called from Malibu. I had not heard from him for three years, except for the odd Christmas card. Age alienates. He wasted no time on pleasantries.

"Is that boy of yours still up at Berkeley? Gawain?"

"Gavin, Phil. You never could get his name right."

"Well, if I were you I'd find out if he's all right. It's urban warfare up there. Ed Meese has just ordered the sheriff's deputies to switch from bird to buckshot. We just heard a flash that a kid got it in the heart."

"Oh, Jesus."

Dunne was instantly contrite. "No, not your boy—the name was Rector, James Rector. Not even a student, I don't think. Sorry to shock you, but my girls say it's likely to get worse. Reagan's sending in the National Guard again tonight."

I was due in Rochester, Minnesota, next day for a weekend IBM symposium and could not fly on to San Francisco until Sunday evening. When I got to Berkeley on Monday, May 19, Telegraph Avenue looked and smelled like a bomb site, the sidewalks blackened and crunching underfoot with broken glass. There were sheets of razor-edged tin roofing lying on the asphalt, corners bent. A barefoot girl told me kids on the housetops had thrown them down, "hoping to slice some bacon." She said James Rector had been one, before he got shot.

"Is he all right?"

She looked at me expressionlessly and said, "Fuck you, sir, he's dead."

I found Gavin's little house on Hearst locked and silent. Neighbors said they hadn't seen him since "Bloody Thursday," a date already, apparently, enshrined in local legend. I stood for a moment in the street, irresolute, then something—the memory of that strange call perhaps—made me return to the porch and look under his doormat. An envelope, hand-checkered in black and white, lay crisp on the floor. He'd known I would come.

I sat on the steps and read the single sheet inside. It was an exquisitely calligraphed rendering of Camus, done in mirror translation:

Les tyrannies d'aujourd'hui	Today's tyrannies
se sont perfectionnées;	have perfected themselves:
Elles n'admettent plus	they do not tolerate
le silence, ni la neutralité.	silence or neutrality.
Il faut se prononcer,	One must proclaim oneself,
être pour ou contre.	For or against.
Bon, dans ce cas,	Well, in that case,
Je suis contre.	I am against.

All that day and through the following morning, I asked after Gavin. He was widely known but untracked. Was it my imagination, or were some of the replies deliberately vague? "He's a lone wolf, man, you never know where he's at." I was perplexed by the hatred in many young eyes, brought on, I suppose, by my IBM-friendly suit and briefcase.

Both town and campus were still dangerous with boots and bayonets. A tense peace prevailed, but the news of Rector's death was simmering, and I heard rumors of another "move against the pigs."

I was eating a late lunch in the sun on Sproul Plaza on Tuesday, debating what more to do, when to general disbelief a military helicopter thwacked its way over the bell tower, hovered a moment, then squatted over our heads, pissing what looked like a yellowish spray of heat haze. One whiff, and I was back on Olive Avenue outside Warner Bros. in the fall of '45. Except this gas was so acid and biting that I felt the skin in my nose blistering as I ran desperately, like everyone else, for Sather Gate. Our exit was blocked by goons with masks; by then, most of us were crying and vomiting.

Some cop, seeing me limp, took pity on me and helped me through. "C'mon, old fella, you don't want to be messed up in this." As I leaned on him, I took a look back at the plaza to where the helicopter still hovered. A few youths, their faces wrapped with towels, were throwing stones at it. Then there was a popping of buckshot, and they ran away from us. As far as I could see through my tears, one of them was immensely tall.

And that was the end of Gavin, apart from two communications. The first was a simple, unsigned telegram, dated June 23, 1969: GONE UNDERGROUND. The other, much bulkier, reached me from Oregon more than a year later when Ronald Reagan was campaigning for a second term as Governor. It was addressed in a round female hand and contained nothing but my son's political manuscripts, most notably the chess-game dissertation, complete to the last word: *noir.*

Gavin cannot have been the only Weatherman to "drop out"—awful phrase—as the Sixties became history. Hundreds of other old men, I'm sure, nurture querulous hopes that one day their graying sons will come back home from Sweden or Vancouver. But Gavin won't. Child of the south, beach boy, desert lover, he never took to northern light. Going underground, where there was no light at all, meant the same to him as to any ancient Greek.

And it was you, Dutch, who sent him there.

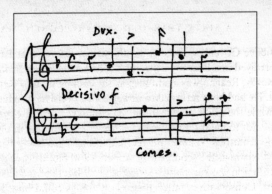

26

A Sixty-Year-Old Smiling Public Man

T HE GOVERNOR had just begun to take his second oath of office when a voice yelled, "*Fuck you, Ronald Reagan!*" and an orange came flying out of the gray sky. It would have splattered on the Capitol steps, had State Comptroller Houston Flournoy not expertly caught it.

"I take this obligation freely," said Reagan, pale with anger.

January 4, 1971, was a raw day in Sacramento, but his shoulders-back stiffness was perhaps not due entirely to the weather. Democrats now dominated both houses of the State Legislature; inevitably, as they consolidated their grip, he would find it more and more difficult to execute policy.

"I will well and faithfully discharge the duties upon which I am about to enter . . ."

In just over a month, he would be sixty. Although he looked only slightly craggier than the sleek fifty-five-year-old who had intoned these words before, he was resigned to the approach of his seventh decade. By 1973 or early 1974, he would be a spent force in Sacramento. Allowing for the distractions of next year's presidential election, he had but two legislative seasons left to prove himself a constructive Governor, rather than the negative force that Pat Brown had portrayed in a bruising little book called *Reagan and Reality.*

Ironically, Reagan was again seen as the coming man of Republican politics. He had been returned to power with a decisive, if reduced, majority while the GOP, elsewhere in the country, had lost eleven statehouses—not to mention two seats in the Senate and nine in the House of Representatives. Blame and recriminations were being heaped on Richard Nixon as the scourge of Cambodia and bloody oracle of Kent State. Inflation was rampant, as was the growth rate of the federal government. Conservatives failed to see how things could have been any worse with Hubert Humphrey in the White House. "If fortunes of leadership compel President Nixon to retire at the end of his first term," Sydney Kossen wrote in the *San Francisco Examiner,* "Reagan might loom as the party's next standard bearer."

Reagan was no fortune-teller. There is no evidence that he thought for more than three minutes in 1971 about running for the presidential nomination in 1972. Yet ever since People's Park he had been conscious of a darkening of the national mood. That orange dipping, tripping out of the sky came like a final, wistful reminder of the Age of Aquarius. "A blast from the past," as Gavin would say. Yesterday's hot passions were today's cold anger—against the war, the declining dollar, the incompatibilities of old and young and rich and poor. Most ominous of all, there seemed to be a dissipation of American energies now that the moon was no longer virgin.

Ronald Reagan's paradoxical appeal (given his happy nature) was to the prophets of darkness on the Republican right, who found him their most articulate representative, and to the bewildered centrists of either party—men and women at odds on many issues, yet united in their common belief that something positive needed to be done to restore the optimism that had died in Dallas on November 22, 1963.

The years ahead would see his slow transformation from state executive to statesman with just this reconciling ability. But he was too naively fatalistic to imagine such an apotheosis now, as he asked God to help him and dropped his hand. Faulty wiring muted his subsequent speech, a dogged call for reduced government, while Viet Cong flags rose and dipped mockingly. For fifteen minutes he tried to override hecklers shouting "Bullshit!," then stepped from the podium, purse-mouthed with frustration.

"They're like mosquitoes and flies," he muttered. "They're part of the world, and you have to put up with them, I guess."

The Governor's words read better now than they must have sounded then, given the cold, the heckling, and his hurry to finish. "It is almost a cliché to remark that we live in a time of accelerating change," he had begun. "Events once measured against a lifetime are compressed into a decade or even a year. Space and time and distance have been both stretched and shrunk, and yesterday is but a preview of tomorrow."

This relativistic preamble (had Dutch been browsing Thomas Mann? More likely Isaac Asimov) served to introduce his main theme: that the new dynamics of change were nowhere more apparent than in California's exploding welfare system. Relief money mandated by federal regulation was going out three times faster than tax money was coming in. Inflation threatened to compound the problem into "a Leviathan of unsupportable dimensions." There was no greater challenge to the state and the nation in 1971 than fighting a two-way neurosis sanctioned by the Sixties: that of government as supply and citizenship as demand.

"Here in California," Reagan warned, "nearly a million children are growing up in the stultifying atmosphere of programs that reward people for *not* working, programs that separate families and doom these children to repeat the cycle in their own adulthood."

☯

He had been wanting to take on the federal government's Aid to Families with Dependent Children program since long before the election. His disillusionment with AFDC, indeed, went back to the days when Jack Reagan, as a relief officer in Dixon, had found unemployed married men loath to take any job that paid less than welfare. It had been less a matter of laziness than law. Under the 1935 Social Security Act, a family on welfare was re-classified as "self-supporting" the moment Pop was hired, no matter what pittance he was paid. Poor men had the choice of staying on the rolls and losing their self-respect, or leaving home out of desperation so that Washington would continue to feed their dependents. Wives thus "abandoned" found it profitable to go on having babies—by whomever—in order to notch up the family income.

For a generation or so, social and sexual scruples had mitigated against too widespread an abuse of AFDC. It remained, through the 1950s, a program intended primarily to help widows. But with the return of Democratic liberalism in 1961, the New Deal idea of "benefits" as emergency help, to be applied for reluctantly and granted responsibly, became the Great Society concept of "entitlements." Reagan had especial contempt for government touts "boiling over with the milk of human kindness," whose job performance was appraised by the length of their lists. "They go out and actually recruit people to get on welfare," he complained. In case after case, by thousands and then by millions, the true head of household became Uncle Sam—cuckold *extraordinaire,* profligate begetter of bastards.

The Governor's prejudice against AFDC was practical as well as moral. He believed it discriminated against the destitute—those who were very old or very young or badly disabled—by encouraging the shiftless to promiscuity. At latest count, according to the little black box where he stored relevant statistics, fourteen million Americans were receiving welfare, an increase of about a quarter over the year before. California's case-growth rate was even greater, at forty thousand new cases a month.

For the sake of innocents born and unborn and the chastening of their parents, he announced that he would submit a program of welfare reform to the new Legislature.

"I want to know what each of you thinks of our chances of getting this thing through," Reagan said to senior staff members. Winter sunlight slanted into his office. As usual, he sat with his back to the park view outside, diffused through more than a ton of armored glass: shaven lawns, camellia shrubs, and a gnarled and ancient elm.

Before him lay eighty proposed policy changes, exhaustively researched by a gubernatorial task force. There was a brief silence. Somebody answered, "None."

Other voices chimed in. "We shouldn't try." "No way can you reform welfare in the state of California." "And with Moretti angling for your job . . ."

Robert "Macho Bob" Moretti, the new Speaker, was a young, ambitious Kennedy Democrat who had grown up on the wrong side of the tracks in Detroit. He had one of the more exotic degrees on the American academic calendar, a baccalaureate in accounting and philosophy. Reagan's aides doubted, however, that this would help him appreciate either the arithmetic or the logic of state welfare reform. As a child of the New Deal, Moretti was sure to lobby Washington for help instead.

There he could count on an unlikely ally. President Nixon shared Reagan's belief that welfare reform would be the great issue of the Seventies. However, Nixon sought not so much to abolish AFDC as to expand it into a vast Family Assistance Plan that would double the rolls overnight and guarantee a minimum income to every poor person in the country.

Reagan gazed around his sun-filled office, unmoved by the pessimism on every face. "Well, we're not going to get any reform unless we try." He confirmed Robert B. Carleson, the task force's most aggressive member, as his new Director of Social Welfare, and ordered the production of an executive "blue book" that would contain all but ten of the proposals on the table. As soon as the document was ready, he would present it personally to the new Legislature.

Nixon's 1971 State of the Union Address concentrated on welfare reform through revenue sharing, to the total exclusion of foreign policy. He was careful not to mention his Family Assistance Plan by name, having already tried and failed to push it through Congress. But the plan's essence—social support without social responsibility—was clear to the millions watching him speak. "Let us place a floor under the income of every family with children in America," Nixon said. "Let us provide the means by which more can help themselves."

His first caller at 1600 Pennsylvania Avenue next morning was Ronald Reagan. The two men exchanged grins for a White House photographer, then got down to one and a quarter hours of political brinkmanship.

For the most part, they discussed their different welfare philosophies. They had done so amicably before, but now they knew that the domestic ideology of the Republican Party was at stake. Nixon needed Reagan's cooperation in selling, or at least not sabotaging, the notion of relief through revenue sharing. What he absolutely did not need from his own home state was a set of competitive proposals that struck at the whole notion of federal relief. If by some miracle the Governor's blue book became law and revenue sharing failed, Nixon was quite paranoid enough to start worrying about a Reagan presidential insurgency.

Reagan himself was willing to go along with the President, for at least a month or so. Right now, California was extremely vulnerable to White House disciplinary measures. Nixon's Secretary of Health, Education, and Welfare, Elliot Richardson, had found the state to be noncompliant with federal law, in neglecting for years to index its share of AFDC payments to inflation. And Frank Carlucci, acting director of the Office of Economic Opportunity, was demanding that Governor

Reagan be penalized for hampering the operations of California Rural Legal Aid, a federally supported program cherished by the sort of liberals who gagged on non-union grapes.

But Nixon in turn did not want to alienate Reagan hard-liners. They might avenge any humiliation of their hero by bulldozing next year's convention. Even if they failed, he could hardly be re-elected without the help of a popular, silver-tongued Governor, able to sway the nation's largest bloc of electoral votes. Given the stakes, President and Governor had no choice but to accommodate each other.

Reagan coyly told the National Press Club that he liked Washington, "but I wouldn't want to live here." Asked if that meant he was declining to run for the Presidency in 1972, he said with a chuckle, "I thought I was pretty subtle about that." As for long-term ambitions, he believed he worked best without them. "It gives you a great sense of freedom and power."

There was no comment from the White House. But on January 30, Director Carlucci announced with a straight face that California Rural Legal Aid would be investigated, pending possible closure, on the strength of serious criticisms by Governor Reagan. And from Secretary Richardson came nothing but benign silence.

Reagan and Nixon proceeded to send their respective budgets to their respective legislatures, and in February both received parliamentary snubs from officials named Mills. On Capitol Hill, Representative Wilbur Mills, chairman of the House Ways and Means Committee, let the President know that his federal-relief proposals were going to have to look much more bipartisan (i.e., Democratic) if he wanted them to become law. And in Sacramento, James R. Mills, president *pro tem* of the State Senate, declined the Governor's request to make a personal presentation of his seventy-point program to a joint session of the Legislature.

The canonic nature of these sequences, extending, as it were, the duet begun by Reagan and Nixon in January, was such that echoes and answers, clashes and concord on the theme of welfare reform continued to sound through midsummer 1971. It was as neat a round as any by Bach, with the notes A, F, D, C predominant, a sense of steady forward movement, and neither voice rising over the other for long.

Nixon sent a revised Family Assistance bill to Congress, only to see it reincorporated as "House Resolution 1," an even more expensive measure aimed at centralizing most welfare in Washington. Reagan's blue book was received with equal coolness by the California Assembly on March 3. Speaker Moretti simply allowed the 179-page volume, stamped *Meeting the Challenge: A Responsible Program for Welfare and Medi-Cal Reform,* to gather legislative dust. He told Pat Brown he thought it "punitive and reckless in the extreme."

The Governor did not seem bothered by this recalcitrance. He had reacted to Senator Mills's discourtesy by going on state television and spelling out his seventy welfare reform proposals to a much larger audience than he would have gotten in the Assembly Chamber. Meanwhile, Robert Carleson had quietly initiated a series of administrative and regulatory reforms that were already reducing the rolls. Carleson promised benefit increases as soon as the reductions generated excess income. These ploys left Moretti with two unpalatable alternatives: he must at some point take the blue book seriously, or devise another welfare plan that offered more and cost less.

Reading *Meeting the Challenge* myself a quarter century later, I thought it less cruel than impersonal, in a dit-dit, corporate-software sort of way. Parallel categories (such as father and stepfather) were merged, payment schedules automated, loopholes plugged, and appropriations capped. Complex and conflicting rules were translated from HEWspeak into English. Some three hundred thousand cases were targeted for deletion from the state's welfare data bank, through the enforcement of tighter eligibility requirements. The money thus saved would amount to an $836 million levy on opportunists and spongers. Redistributed, it would raise the benefits of deserving recipients *and* balance the state budget, as required by law.

There was a lot of Loyal Davis in the blue book's hard-line humanitarianism. It insisted, for example, that the poor should not expect any more in free Medi-Cal benefits than ordinary taxpayers received under their own, paid insurance. But there was also more than a little of Harold Bell Wright. In words that could have been written, or at least typeset, by That Printer of Udell's, Reagan proposed "a public assistance work force" of able-bodied indigents who would labor for the common good until they were rehabilitated enough to look after themselves. Elsewhere, he darkly called for the state's two hundred and thirty thousand hit-and-run fathers to be pursued, prosecuted, and taught the responsibilities of family life—"the basic element in our society."

On March 27, he thought it prudent to make another public endorsement of Richard Nixon. He was rewarded with an invitation to visit the

Western White House for what Nixon termed "a summit meeting on welfare reform." The President's language conveyed a certain urgency, prompted by rumors that Democratic bill drafters in Ways and Means were stealing ideas from both their programs in order to draft the biggest relief boondoggle since the WPA. Nixon evidently hoped for a joint *communiqué* that would show he and the Governor of California were in agreement on the essentials of Family Assistance.

In canonic language, *dux* was seeking some sort of harmonious resolution with *comes*. But Reagan struck an angrily dissonant note on April 3, publishing a *New York Times* Op-Ed piece entitled WELFARE IS A CANCER. He stressed that his anger was not directed against those whom he called (in a grating catchphrase) "the truly needy," so much as against distant, impersonal federal functionaries, "building a bureaucratic empire on . . . misery" and treating all welfare recipients as demographic data, rather than "individuals, each with his [*sic*] own personal reason for dependency." One out of nine Americans already enjoyed some form of relief. Welfare for the sake of welfare was "a national moral and administrative disaster—a cancer that is destroying those it should succor and threatening society itself."

The delicacy with which Nixon approached the "welfare summit" the next morning was evident in the attendance of Caspar Weinberger as a diplomatic link between Washington and Sacramento. (The Governor's former finance director was now the President's Budget Director.) Secretary Richardson also sat in. During three hours of negotiations, Reagan was politely warned that he was still under notice of subsidy suspension in the AFDC matter. He, equally politely, argued that *Meeting the Challenge* was not against the spirit of Family Assistance.

Nixon emerged afterward long enough to tell the press that California was going to be given special permission to institute certain "experimental" reforms, in the hope that they might yield "valuable data" of use to the federal government. Dutch stood looking modestly down, his Brylcreem flashing blue under the noonday sun.

"The possibility of finally getting a handle on this entire welfare situation is at hand," he said, after Nixon ducked back inside.

❡

The sound of President and Governor in sudden *unisono* alarmed radicals. In California, the Welfare Rights Organization sued both men for conspiracy to violate the 1935 Social Security Act, and in Washington, twenty-one high-minded Congressmen introduced an entitlements bill that would allow half of all Americans to live and reproduce for free.

Alarm of a different kind began to spread among conservatives. They felt that Nixon was unleashing socialistic forces at home, while sending craven peace signals to Communists abroad. On April 12, Senator Robert J. Dole, chairman of the Republican National Committee, growled that he would not be surprised to see a Democrat elected in '72. Nixon helicoptered after him to Williamsburg, Virginia, where Republican governors were having their spring conference, and in a hastily written speech said that welfare should be judged "by the dignity it promotes and not by the dole it provides."

One marvels afresh at Tricky Dick's mastery of the rhetorical *gaffe*. He promptly surpassed himself: "Emptying bedpans—my mother used to do that—is not enjoyable work, but a lot of people do it, and there is as much dignity in that as there is in any other work to be done in this country—including my own."

Having added this psychologically interesting metaphor to the imagery of the American Presidency, he strained to present himself as a social conservative. He praised California for challenging the dependency ethic, and attacked welfare fraud with such Reaganesque fervor that even Dutch said "Amen."

☯

About this time, a stealth committee to re-elect the President, appropriately acronymed CREEP, opened for business on Pennsylvania Avenue. Several prominent liberal Republicans, meanwhile, announced that they were forming a nationwide "Dump Nixon" organization.

Reagan felt his own fortunes surging as non-Democratic voters, polled in mid-May, declared him to be their preferred alternative to the President in 1972. But when Young Americans for Freedom, always his most ardent supporters, volunteered a formal campaign, he responded with surprising vehemence. "I . . . must ask with all the urgency I can express that you desist."

The Governor's nervousness had less to do with concern for Nixon than worry about a news story that threatened to embarrass him just as he was trying to get the state Supreme Court to cut 27,500 freeloaders from the welfare rolls. He was reported by a student radio station to have paid no state income tax in 1971. Since this was true, all he could do was protest that he had paid over ninety thousand dollars since 1966, on a salary of $44,100. The law, he added, entitled him to seek relief for "once in a lifetime" business losses caused by the current recession.

It also unfortunately entitled public protestors to proclaim him, to his face on May 24, "California's Highest-Paid Welfare Recipient." *The New York Times* followed up with a well-researched article that identified his "business" as the Reagan Cattle Company, a high-depreciation tax shelter managed by Oppenheimer Industries. Although such operations were legal, the article strongly suggested insider trading. Oppenheimer—which specialized in paper losses for the rich—was run by a stepson of Jules Stein, founder of MCA, and Reagan's investment papers had been signed by his chief fund-raiser, William French Smith, now chairman of the University of California Board of Regents.

Irish luck saved him. The same day the *Times* ran its article—June 13, 1971—it also published the biggest scoop of the Vietnam era: Daniel Ellsberg's purloined "Pentagon Papers." Reagan, relegated to page 71, could only complain ungraciously to William F. Buckley, Jr., "Do you think not paying a tax you don't owe rates as many demerits as receiving stolen property and selling it for profit?"

Speaker Moretti joined in jokes in the Assembly about the Governor's personal tax burden being light enough for the "truly needy." But his good humor faded as he realized he was going to have to work with Reagan on welfare reform, or miss out altogether on what promised to be a major policy success. Since March, Director Carleson's pre-legislative stringencies had continued to decrease the rolls. With no revenue sharing flowing in yet from Washington, and a constitutional requirement that he have a draft state budget by June 30, Moretti had no choice but to blow the dust off Reagan's blue book. He descended to the Corner Office, walked in alone, and said, "Governor, I don't like you. And I know you don't like me, but we don't have to be in love to work together."

As a veteran negotiator, Reagan had been listening to variations on this cliché since at least 1947. He waited for the inevitable follow-up— "If you really want to do something about welfare reform, then let's sit down and do it."

Moretti was, as it happened, sitting down already, but Reagan simply said, "Okay." He recognized the Speaker to be a liberal of the best sort—rational, humane, and honorable—and was confident that his own similar qualities would project across the bargaining table. The task before them was, plainly, to rewrite the blue book in a way that would keep California both solvent and charitable. Common sense, as well as the law, required them to reconcile these conflicting priorities.

The two men embarked on a series of binary, plenary, and lower-level skirmishes that continued for the next month and a half. Moretti calculated that he personally spent "seventeen days and nights" of face time with Reagan, fighting him "line by line, statistic by statistic" until they were both exhausted. Obscenities went back and forth. Gradually, grudgingly, he came to respect the Governor for being hard on principle but flexible in details. Reagan often surprised him by yielding to fair argument, and once even agreed to renegotiate a point that Moretti regretted conceding. At other times, the Governor would flare with sudden anger: "By God, that's it. I'm through with this." Moretti replied with tantrums of his own but timed them carefully, since Reagan retained the ultimate weapon of a line-item veto.

Most of all, Moretti admired Reagan's honesty as a deal maker. The Governor never lied, and honored every commitment. Yet there was a vague, unreachable complacency in his manner that militated against any feelings of affection.

"I think he really believes his own attacks on welfare," Moretti told Pat Brown, after the last sub-clause had been initialed. "He is a guy who sees everything as all good or bad—no gray scale at all. He really became convinced that a handful of cheats represented all the people on welfare."

Brown asked if the Governor showed any "compassion" for welfare recipients.

"No. Nor for anyone else, either."

The California Welfare Reform Act finally became law on August 13, 1971. Reagan did not exaggerate when he called it "probably the most comprehensive" such initiative in American history. At least twenty-one states had tinkered with work/relief programs already, but their schemes were makeshift in comparison. California's great machine of a system was engineered to be smooth running, economical, and generously distributive. While fully compatible with AFDC (a reluctant concession on Reagan's part), it would save three hundred million dollars a year through sheer operational efficiency. Nor was it cruel to any but layabouts, illegal immigrants, and women whose pregnancies lasted longer than nine months.

Reagan got his cherished workforce, per agreement with Nixon, as well as stricter eligibility standards and an increase in the state's powers of monitoring and cross-checking applicants. He could truthfully boast in later years that "we reduced the rolls by more than three hundred thousand people, saved the taxpayers two billion dollars, and increased the grants to the truly deserving by an average of forty-three percent."

What was more, the Reform Act had an inspirational effect on welfare policy across the country. But Reagan would have to wait a quarter of a century before his basic dream, the repeal of AFDC, became a reality.

Moretti's reward in 1971 was less tangible. His role in the negotiations had been the negative, though vital, one of restraining a reformer more interested in policy than in people. I thought there was something, well, touching about the way he stood behind the Governor's chair at the signing ceremony and, when Dutch put nib to paper, gently rested both hands on his shoulders.

The ink on the new act was barely dry when Richard Nixon announced that his own welfare program, currently facing doom in the Senate, was being put on hold. He managed to represent this withdrawal as a strategic advance by linking it to the shock imposition of wage and price controls, which he said were necessary to revive America's ailing economy. "The time has come for a new economic policy for the United States."

And so the strange, catch-me canon President and Governor had been sounding for eight months ended with one voice on a triumphant *fermata,* the other modulating out from under. Both performers got what they wanted: Reagan, applause and the feeling that he had re-established his authority over the Legislature, Nixon, a rise in economic indicators that suggested that his bold action had helped turn the recession. Not to mention a truly stunning development on the foreign-policy front.

Nixon's announcement that the United States would soon establish relations with Communist China had come at the height of Reagan's duel with Moretti, and not until the Governor and President met again on August 20, ostensibly to compare notes on welfare reform, did the former realize that he was being sized up as a special envoy to Taiwan. Someone with impeccably pro-Nationalist credentials was needed to convince Chiang Kai-shek of the continuing goodwill of the United States.

His ambivalence over such a mission is evident in the manuscript of a speech he wrote a few days later, apparently for delivery to the Young Americans for Freedom, who were united in their horror of Chairman

Mao. Its densely written legal-size pages are worded so as neither to endorse nor reject Nixon's initiative. "[The President] has been blunt in
his declarations that we will not under any circumstances desert an old
friend and ally . . . give anything away, or betray our honor. If I am
wrong and that should be the result—time then for indignation and
righteous anger."

This was good enough for Nixon. On October 10, 1971, the Governor found himself appointed special presidential envoy, and dizzyingly
translocated to a throne room in Taiwan.

Chiang Kai-shek received him stiff with rage.

"Look, Generalissimo, I don't like this any more than you do," Reagan said, pocketing the formal *apologia* he was supposed to read aloud.
He rose from his low chair and ambled over to the throne. "But it had
to happen sooner or later, and we're a hell of a lot better off having
President Nixon do it instead of Hubert Horatio Humphrey."

The mandarin mask loosened. Flying home, Reagan found, as diplomats often do, that he had been converted by his own mission. Taiwan
was ironically more secure now than before, since "the People's Republic"—it would be a while before he pursed his lips around *that*
misnomer—would have to respect its sovereignty or compromise the
new *rapprochement*. By extension, a nervous Soviet Union must now
think twice about re-assigning any of its one hundred and forty divisions along the Chinese border. "One wonders how adventurous Russia might be tempted to be in Europe and the Middle East, if they
didn't have to keep that force there."

I watched him saying this to Clare Boothe Luce on *Firing Line* early
in the new year. To this day I can see in my mind's eye, clear as any
screen, Dutch's glossy head-tilt and quizzical frown, and her ironic
smile. They cynically struck me as a pair of political junks, trimming
from starboard to port as Nixon's new wind blew. Now, one has to admire their willingness to believe that Triangular Diplomacy might
make the world a safer place. Reagan's rambling rationale was and
would remain, "If we believe as conservatives in the idea that we can
have a peace—that the great Armageddon is not inevitable, the great
nuclear holocaust in which civilization disappears—then we have to be
prepared, be realistic about the changing face of the world, and do
something about this."

Which, of course, is what Nixon—tormented visionary!—had been
saying for at least four years. Three months after going to Peking in
February 1972, he returned in triumph from Moscow, with the first
arms-limitation treaty of the thermonuclear age.

If ever there was a resurgent political leader, it was Richard Nixon at that moment. Two historic foreign-policy initiatives, inflation reduced, GNP rising, incomes up, taxes down, and Democrats seemingly hell-bent on nominating George ("Let's give every American a thousand dollars") McGovern—the election was his to lose.

Reagan emerged as a potent campaigner for Nixon and Spiro Agnew in the West and Southwest. Unlike the Vice President, whose alliterative tirades were clearly the work of Eastern wordsmiths, he wrote his own speeches in language that was both epigrammatic and unpatronizing. "You've found in your political activism an affinity for the Republican Party," he praised young conservatives, "rejecting the albumen-brained social engineers who would set mass above man. . . . I marvel at the way you have obtained an education, yet remained steadfast in your beliefs, resisting the Zeitgeist—the wind of our times." Agnew's writers would have eschewed the last five helpful words.

Campaign camaraderie warmed between the gubernatorial office in Los Angeles and CREEP headquarters in Washington. Nixon appreciatively asked Reagan to undertake another roving embassy, this time to Europe in July, and afterward to serve as chairman *pro tem* of the Republican National Convention. A delegation headed by John Mitchell, Nixon's national chairman, came west at once to discuss pre-convention strategy.

On the morning of Thursday, June 18, the Governor's limousine rolled up at the Beverly Hills Hotel, to link up with Mitchell's. They were scheduled to proceed downtown in convoy. A CREEP aide was deputized to ride with Reagan, but just as he opened the car door, the voice of a White House staffer stopped him: "Bob, John said for you to come with us. We've got a problem."

"What kind of a problem?"

"A slight problem."

Reagan went on to the meeting alone. That evening, the networks reported that a party of political burglars had been arrested at Democratic National Committee Headquarters in the Watergate Hotel, Washington.

All the great names, as Gore Vidal might say, were on Special Envoy Reagan's list of European appointments between July 2 and 20, 1972:

Prime Minister Jens Otto Krag of Denmark, EEC Commissioner Sicco Mans Holt, NATO General Secretary Joseph Luns, Acting French Foreign Minister Jean de Lipkowski, Spanish Minister of Foreign Affairs Gregorio López Bravo, British Prime Minister Ted Heath, and various other dignitaries, including Pope Paul VI and three or four supermarket royals. A senile Francisco Franco, *caudillo* of Spain, was penciled in at the last minute, as was Ireland's blind, ninety-year-old President Eamon de Valera.

Afraid that he might be perceived to be junketing, Reagan left a handwritten account of his trip, emphasizing its official trappings (Air Force plane, State Department escort, and Secret Service protection) and serious purpose: to persuade NATO allies that President Nixon's recent negotiation of the Anti–Ballistic Missile Treaty did not imply a unilateral willingness to scale down Western Europe's defenses.

"This can't be 'Dutch' Reagan here," he told himself, as he was bowed into salon after gilded salon. "I should still be out on the dock at Lowell Park." He had become, in Yeats's words, a sixty-year-old smiling public man. Apart from learning niceties of protocol and *politesse,* he was getting some feel for the exercise of American power. Far ahead, down the perspective of his own years, he would reorder NATO's security more radically than Nixon ever did. The fact that he could do so with confidence owed much to the privilege of being chosen as a presidential envoy in 1972.

Ronald Reagan was not by nature appreciative (he merely accepted favors, as he did the mail), nor did he have much sense of historical irony, but he did take note of a gravestone epitaph in Ireland, and quoted it after inheriting Nixon's legacy, for better or worse:

> *Remember me as you pass by,*
> *For as you are so once was I,*
> *And as I am you soon will be,*
> *So be content to follow me.*

It was not until October 12, 1972, when the California campaign was well on the way to racking up a million-vote majority for Nixon and Agnew, that Reagan found himself touching on the subject already known as "Watergate." Two *Washington Post* reporters, apparently, had succeeded in following a trail of political espionage to the door of the White House. Richard Nixon was not named as a conspirator, but the Governor, at a press conference, spoke at curious length about the perils of presidential responsibility. His words would resonate for himself one day: "You go to bed at night with the knowledge that you've done your best to see and hope that these people that you've directly appointed meet the standards that you want them to meet. But there can be someone, while you're sleeping, doing something he shouldn't do, and it breaks over your head."

Nixon, however, remained uninundated through Election Day. On November 7, George McGovern was triumphantly elected President by the voters of Massachusetts.

ℰ

Postscript—I researched the above chapter in Dutch's presidential library, tranquilly situated above Simi Valley in the mountains northwest of Los Angeles. The largest archive of its kind, it is also the least patronized by serious scholars. Most of the days I spent in its vast oak-tabled reading room (in whose windows, sometimes, hummingbirds jerk and flash) were undisturbed by sight or sound of other human beings, with the exception of a clerk dozing at the service desk, and the head archivist sporadically visiting to ask, "Finding any goodies?"

Just as invariably, I would cite the dullest and largest document I could think of, sending him away satisfied while—alone again in my glassed-in carrel—I would pull another gray box toward me, wondering which of its miscellaneous folders might disgorge Dutch's Rosebud. Or

"The largest archive of its kind."
The Ronald Reagan Presidential Library, Simi Valley, California.

at least *something* like, say, a photograph of a tense, thin-lipped Governor raising his hand on the steps of the California State Capitol, unaware that an orange was zooming in from out of frame . . .

"MISC" is a sweet word to the archival researcher. It signals the point at which sterile process gives way to fertile chaos. Beyond number, beyond the alphabet and the calendar, lie what D. H. Lawrence called "the leavings of a life"—scraps, stubs, notes, doodles, rough drafts of letters and speeches, unidentified photographs, cryptic souvenirs. Like bits of shell along the shoreline, they wink their fragmentary messages, some sharp, some pearly, one or two possibly precious. One has to keep walking, watching for similar flashes, to infer—with luck—a whole shell from the general sand.

On my last afternoon of gubernatorial research I closed the box marked 1972 and pulled another trolleyload of papers toward me. It had been in a trunk of junk that I had found his early autobiographical stories. Might these boxes, covering the period 1973–1974, be equally revealing of his mature personality, as he declined to run again as Governor and monitored Richard Nixon's fall from power? I was not optimistic, but a biographer lives in hope.

There were a few dry Corner Office files, and as I finger-walked through them I heard Clare Boothe Luce drawl, "Politics is the refuge of second-class minds." One disgorged a stout booklet entitled *A Reasonable Program for Revenue Control and Tax Reduction, Submitted to the California Legislature by Governor Ronald Reagan, March 12, 1973.* Ah yes, the "proudest accomplishment" of Dutch's second term. Or so he boasted in advance, until Speaker Moretti threw it out of the Legislature. It was a fiscal construct, slightly simpler than Einstein's special theory of relativity, that required the state to limit the total revenue of taxes over the next fifteen years by means of a reverse-ratio annual rollback cross-referenced to the Consumer Price Index. That November, Reagan, confessing charmingly that he did not understand it himself, had referred the proposition to the people of California, who rejected it for similar reasons. I took one look at its fifteen-page appendix of tables and graphs and decided that I, too, would vote No on "Prop One."

Next came a packet of memo material from Dutch's young and sexy secretary, Helene von Damm. "Governor," she typed in vivid ribbon, "wouldn't it be nice if you had personal stationery for such letters? I could order some if you'd like me to." Somebody must have written him in hope of an autograph reply. His laconic superscript showed a perfect understanding of such correspondents: "*I think they like to get the official paper—RR.*"

Intrigued, I sorted out a batch of similar little sheets, each bearing the ghost of an ancient paper clip, each stained with bright blue question and dark blue answer, exchanges short or long, important or banal, sounding the *phon* and *antiphon* of executive decision-making. Mostly undated, they had been typed at odd moments, on quiet Mondays when "Boss" was out of town, or during biweekly Cabinet meetings, or hot Friday lunch hours while he and Bob Moretti chewed over policy at Wing Fat's. Dutch had replied at moments even odder, for he had an old-fashioned dread of wasted time. One wobbly superscript seemed to have been penned during a ride on Walter Annenberg's golf cart in Palm Springs.

A folder labeled "1973: Pictures and Letters from P.O.W.'s" caught my eye. I opened it and shook it out. A Vietnamese prison spoon tinkled onto the desk, followed by a Diên Biên cigarette pack (autographed to Nancy Reagan), a guest list headed "Governor's Private P.O.W. Reception," and a sheaf of unusually long thank-you letters. One, from a woman, was an effusive appreciation of "the 'welcome home'" the Governor had shown her husband, who had been brainwashed by the Viet Cong into believing that he "was not wanted by his own people."

Throughout his Sacramento years, Ronald Reagan had proclaimed the war a noble cause, and every returning serviceman, dead, alive, or drug addicted, a hero. He held prayer breakfasts for them, and celebratory receptions for as many as he could crowd around his hearth. (One was a Navy pilot on crutches named John McCain.) Dutch listened grimly to their stories of the real 'Nam, as he had once listened to Eddie Albert talk of Tarawa. His distress hardened to anger at Presidents Kennedy and Johnson for "dragging on a winless war," and at the failure of most Americans to honor its conscripts. This was a double theme that he was to pursue forcefully when he campaigned for the job of Commander in Chief.

A military couple wrote him, "You have our two votes for *any* office in the land."

I put the spoon and cigarette pack away with a good deal of tenderness, and pulled out, rather more roughly, a 1974 departmental chart printed on snowy paper. It was one of dozens compiled by Executive Secretary Edwin Meese III, one of those personally disorganized people who loves to organize everybody else. I could see that this particular chart was designed to free "Boss" from all but the essential duties of public office. Hadn't I registered it before, though—somehow "copied" every line and rectangle? Symmetrical clusters gridded east and west of a common, northbound highway, which tolerated them without touching, only to become a ring road in open country, around the largest oblong of all. . . . Stinson Field in 1933, headquarters of Barnouw Operational Signal Systems.

Whatever else the chart spoke for, its political purpose was plain. Ronald Reagan was already, in his last year in Sacramento, accepting every speaking invitation and television appearance he could wangle outside of California. This was long before the resignation of Richard Nixon, whom he obstinately supported until the "smoking gun" newsbreak of August 6. I leafed through a few of his itineraries, including one with the eye-catching instruction, "10:00 AM—Depart LAX for SEX." Beyond, like leaves muting the advance of a T-34 tank, there was a proliferation of letters, press statements, and speech drafts, all clearly written with candidacy in mind.

"Governor, you're looking at that Oval Office, aren't you?" a sassy Assemblyman challenged him one day. They were alone, and Reagan, caught by surprise, said "Yes."

Publicly, he continued to protest that he had no political ambitions beyond Sacramento. His predecessor devoutly hoped that was true. "As a human being and an American . . . I am chilled to the bone at the thought of Ronald Reagan one day becoming President of the United States."

Outside in the reading room, the noise of archival drawers being shut and reshut with deliberate loudness signaled the approach of closing time. I was re-boxing a final clutch of documents when a protruding page caught my eye with its wide margin and strange splotchy graphic. Plucked out and set upright, the graphic became an elegantly engraved tree, illustrating a poem by the Governor of California. It appeared to have been written on his last day in office. I got to the photocopy machine with seconds to spare, and copied it without having time to read it. When I did, later, I was appreciative, because Dutch had done me the favor of summarizing his governorship succinctly, in forty-five simple words:

Time

Budgets
Battles
Phone calls
Hassles.
Letters
Meetings
Luncheons
Speeches.

Politics and
Press Releases.
News conferences
Delegations
Plaques and
Presentations.
Travels
Briefings
Confrontations
Crises
Routines
Mediation.
Eight years pass swiftly.
But I look out the window.
The elm in the park looks just the same.

27

The Ripple
Effect

O N JANUARY 3, 1975, Ronald Reagan somewhat ruefully handed
the Governorship of California over to the son of his predecessor,
and returned to Pacific Palisades, insisting that he was now a private
citizen with no political ambitions. Only he could get away with such an
ingenuous statement. His actor's disinclination to rehearse past performances prevented him from acknowledging that he was—always had
been—ambitious enough to crack rocks.

For the better part of a decade, he had been the strongest man in a
state richer than most of the world's countries. When in the space of
five more short years he became the strongest man of all, he was
unjustly accused of living in the past. Few Presidents have been as
forward-looking. Of course, like most Americans, he tended to sentimentalize *temps perdu*. He enjoyed looking back on Tom Sawyer days
and Cocoanut Grove nights, on the "clean hatred" of college football
and the coy allusiveness of twin-bed movies. His political stories, too,
told and retold the lessons he learned in youth. Poor Nancy, the most
patient wife since Cosima Wagner, must be able to recite them all back-

ward in Swahili. But these anecdotes of Communists confounded and budgets balanced were allegorical in purpose, intended to show that what was possible once was still possible, that historic verities endured, that the world, in his favorite bromide from Tom Paine, could be started over again. And if any ironist pointed out to him that the stories invariably showed him to have prevailed against the bad guys, he would be taken aback and say with that self-deprecating head-shake and crimp of the mouth, "*No-o-o.* But you see . . ."

The record shows that ever since he was president of his high school, Ronald Reagan smilingly, honestly, affably got what he wanted. Life-saving athlete, college leader, successful broadcaster, No. 1 box-office star, top-rated soldier, sexual "swordsman," seven years as a popular and effective trade-union executive, celebrated corporate spokesman, excellent Governor: such a résumé spoke louder in 1975 than any protestations that all he wanted to do now was sink fence poles in the Santa Ynez Mountains.

Politely turning down an invitation from President Ford to become Secretary of Transportation, he began to develop a new property he had bought high above Santa Barbara. Right now, "Rancho del Cielo" consisted of little more than a flyblown adobe shack and about seven hundred acres of overgrown valley. But it had three of the things he most prized: elevation ("You feel you are on a cloud looking down at the world"), seclusion, and freedom to ride in any direction. It also promised years of hard labor, to make up for all the sedentary time he had spent in the Corner Office. His big body craved man-sized jobs: trees to clear, ponds to dredge, floors to lay, roofs to fix. He joked that he would not care if he never saw an executive desk again.

Yet he raised no objection when two of his most Washington-minded Sacramento aides, Michael Deaver and Peter Hannaford, opened a "public-relations agency" in Westwood, Los Angeles, with Ronald Reagan as their sole client. For at least a year they had been trying to get him to admit to a desire to relocate to 1600 Pennsylvania Avenue (Deaver went so far as to remind him of his recurring dream about living in a white house with tall columns), but Reagan was maddeningly evasive. They persuaded themselves that his failure to say "yes" was a refusal to say "no," and concentrated on selling his services as a freelance speaker, writer, and broadcaster.

One hundred radio stations and at least that many conservative newspapers were already lined up to carry regular current-affairs commentary by "former Governor Reagan." Deaver and Hannaford planned to spend six months expanding this core media constituency. Their gamble was that, given enough time, Reagan would talk himself into an open challenge to Gerald Ford for the Republican presidential nomination in '76.

Stunningly sooner than they could have dreamed—before January was out—a little old lady did the talking for them. She recognized Reagan on a commercial flight from San Francisco to Los Angeles and forcefully insisted, "You *gotta* run for President!" He brooded for a while, then turned to Deaver, who was sitting next to him. "Mike, I guess I really do have to run."

Deaver boggled as Reagan explained, with no apparent emotion, "I've always been the player on the bench. It's time for me to get into the game."

Around the same time, I decided to get out of it, and made a decision that, unforeseeably, set me up as Dutch's future biographer. Looking back, I can see now how one thing led to another, like the gathering roll of a raindrop down glass. But for most of 1975 (he kept his decision to run tacit until late November), I neither thought of him nor imagined he would ever re-enter public life.

Like most Americans, I had been transfixed by Richard Nixon's fall from grace the summer before. Amid all the fake sentimentality of the parting ceremonies, I heard one small note of real eloquence, and it moved me more than whatever Dark Dick was trying to say. Apropos of absolutely nothing, in his farewell address to the White House staff, Nixon began to quote Theodore Roosevelt: *"As a flower she grew, and as a fair young flower she died. . . ."*

I remembered reading those words somewhere, or hearing them from Malvin Wald, and vaguely connected them with Roosevelt's youth. Wasn't it to do with the death of his beautiful first wife, incredibly on the same night and in the same house that his mother died too? Hadn't he given up politics after that, and gone west to repair his soul, and become a ranchman?

Nixon maundered on, but without my further attention. A vast curiosity about the effect of that double bereavement took possession of me, and the Republican Roosevelt became my *idée fixe.* It occurred to me that TR had, at odd times in my life, drifted within cognitive reach, as a reflection will do on the inner surface of one's spectacles, leaping into sudden focus or dissolving, according to the angle of the light. There had been a childhood glimpse of him from my father's shoulders, outside some Chicago hotel in 1916: a friendly flash of teeth, a burly arm raised over a sea of wet black hats. And conversations with Phil Dunne before the war, about *his* father's closeness to the great man, and Malvin Wald (to my acute envy) producing his play about Teddy and Alice in 1946 . . .

Maybe I also remembered the intriguing fact that Ronald Reagan had told Mal, "I'd be interested in that part. I'd like to play a President." If so, I pushed it from my mind. Mostly I thought about TR, to the extent that I began to draft a teleplay about his pre-presidential career. The year 1976 was going to mark the Bicentennial of the United States; patriotic properties were already circulating around the story departments of the Big Three networks. What saga could possibly be more inspiring than that of the asthmatic East Coast snob who became a rancher in the Badlands of Dakota Territory, made a virile man of himself, found a new wife in his childhood sweetheart, then galloped on to the White House, by way of San Juan Hill? The drama would end with the assassination of President McKinley, and a desperate search for Vice President Theodore Roosevelt (played by Richard Dreyfuss), atop the highest mountain in New York State:

> The messenger comes running through the trees, clutching the yellow slip of a telegram. He takes off his cap, and hands the telegram to TR. As the Vice President begins to read it, other members of the party take off their caps too. FADE.

On my sixty-third birthday, I quit Madison Avenue for good, and plunged full-time into historical research.

The phenomenon of "Reagan Redux" naturally fascinated Paul Rae, who wrote at the end of March to say that Dutch's weekly column was being published in thirty-nine states. "Not in Arkansas, where they can't read, or Maine, where they won't. In fact only Mass., of all the chilblain states, carries him: Boston *Herald-Adv.* and would you believe, the Hyannisport Cape Cod *Standard Times*!! He'd better do something in New Hampshire if he wants to be Pres., and better learn how to push a pen, too: Seattle *Post-Intelligencer* just dropped him for

Pat Buchanan. Told Copley that RR's pieces 'failed to carry the punch we had expected.' "

This may have been because most, if not all, were the work of Peter Hannaford and Lyn Nofziger. Reagan preferred to devote his writing time to speeches and daily radio mini-scripts, each only three minutes long. He recorded the latter in batches of ten or fifteen with huge enjoyment, tapping away the countdowns with his foot and starting each one with a teaser: "To err is human—it takes a government computer to really louse things up. I'll be right back."

Nancy Reynolds, another Sacramento holdover and now Reagan's press secretary at Deaver & Hannaford, politely asked if he did not think it was a little *infra dig* for a former Governor to pitch for Saturday-afternoon slots on hayseed radio stations. "You don't understand the ripple effect, Nancy," he replied. "Only a coupla thousand might hear me one week in one signal area, but they'll get the tone if not the gist. Some of them are going to like it and talk about it, and next week I'm back with more, and more people will listen, and pretty soon all those ripples could build up into a mighty big wave."

Indeed they did, ultimately comprising three hundred and fifty radio stations, and reaching an audience of ten to fifteen million every time he spoke. One ripple bellied as far as the plains of North Dakota, and reached me, courtesy WDIX Dickinson, as I drove west from Bismarck toward the Badlands. Dutch was careful not to sound too much like a candidate. He talked about America's forgotten work ethic, and argued that restraints on free enterprise were part of the problem. The voice was deeper and huskier than it had been when I caught it forty years before, out of WHO Des Moines; but it still packed plenty of force—along with what Pat Brown, in a lovely phrase, called Reagan's "cool intensity."

I notice that the tone of my subsequent diary references to Dutch became wearily more respectful in 1975, as it dawned on me and millions of other Americans that he just might unseat Gerald Ford. When his total of stations reached two hundred and twenty-six, I wrote Paul, "What price Dutch's broomstick now?" and underlined the last word, since I had asked him the same question in 1937, after the premiere of *Love Is on the Air*.

Here again was "the hero of this story, Andy McCaine," proving that he could think as fast as he could talk.

☯

President Ford, suspicious of Ronald Reagan's future intentions, kept trying to distract him with appointments. He asked him to serve on the Rockefeller Commission investigating CIA domestic activities during the Watergate era, and offered him another Cabinet job, this time Secretary of Commerce. Reagan politely accepted the one honor, and not the other.

Nine years before, campaigning for the Governorship, he had sworn to observe what he called "the Eleventh Commandment," *Thou shalt not speak ill of any Republican.* Yet now he hesitated only six weeks before beginning to speak out in public against his own President and party leader. It was all the more surprising because Reagan has always had a midwestern disinclination to criticize people: his diaries perpetually insist that everybody he encounters is a good sort. Yet he never quite managed to conceal his distaste for Nixon's chosen successor.

When I asked why, he murmured something about wearing one of Ford's silly WIN ("Whip Inflation Now") buttons as a courtesy, only to have the President clumsily say, "What the hell are you still wearing that thing for?" But there was clearly something more. Pressed, Dutch went on, "I just didn't think he was—presidential quality." Pressed again, he explained, "The people never voted for him; he was *appointed* to that position for two years."

The last, I thought, was the real reason. Dutch was fundamentally a constructionist, a lover of order and sequence and tradition. It didn't matter how good or bad a Chief Executive Ford might have been; *he was unelected,* and therefore not "presidential."

When Young Americans for Freedom endorsed Reagan for President on March 23, an incredulous Ford heard from professional strategists that the Reagan threat was real. "Ron has wanted to be President for years," Stuart Spencer said. "He feels he was cheated out of his inheritance when Nixon left." Until Reagan declared, however, there was little Ford could do—except hire Spencer to run his own campaign, which he hastily did.

Early in April, the non-candidate made a bid for overseas notice by flying to London and addressing the Pilgrims' Society, a private transatlantic alliance of mostly conservative grandees, on East-West foreign policy. New currents were stirring in British politics, after the previous fall's decisive defeat of the managerial Tory leader, Edward

Heath. Although the vote had sentenced Britain to another spell of semi-socialistic Labour government, the Conservative Party was transforming itself along the same lines Reagan envisaged for the GOP: by making "so sharp" a break with statist thinking as to present voters at the next election with a clear choice between free-market economics or *status quo* socialism.

"*Status quo,*" Reagan liked to joke, "that's Latin for the mess we're in."

He would have preferred to talk about American domestic policy in London, but Deaver and Hannaford wanted him to widen his rhetorical base. Confessing ignorance of NATO and European affairs, he allowed his speech to be written for him by a pair of those earnest young think-tank Republicans who like to use the word *mankind* in conversation. The resultant text, delivered stiffly in black tie with none of his usual humor, amounted to a programmed rejection of détente. *The Times,* at least, was moved to call it "a strong attack on Western weakness" and "a criticism of Republican foreign policy appropriate to a presidential candidate."

Before leaving London, Reagan met for an hour and a half with Edward Heath's successor as Leader of the Opposition. By rights this person should have been Sir Keith Joseph, the brilliant and acerbic architect of the New Conservatism, but Sir Keith had madly embraced eugenics just as Heath fell, and Mrs. Margaret Thatcher was the beneficiary of their combined hubris. After only eight weeks in office, she gave little indication of being anything more than a precise, humorless housekeeper, to be replaced by someone more manly when another election loomed. Neither did Reagan strike her as a likely future President of the United States. In later life, they would both read more import into their first meeting than it merited. Still, they liked what they saw of each other: he the "sharp" decisiveness and directness, she the simple certainties and the fact—unignorable to her as a woman—that he was a big and remarkably attractive man.

Dutch once took me into his saddle room at Rancho del Cielo and showed me a poster of himself, as Clark Gable, carrying Maggie, as Vivien Leigh, upstairs for a night of wild abandon. "This is very funny," I said. "Why don't you hang it in the ranch?"

He shook his head. "No, because *she* might see it." For a moment I thought he was talking about Nancy. "Sometimes *she* visits with us, and I, uh, wouldn't want . . ."

To my amazement, the President was blushing.

Reagan returned home in 1975 at a time of no great glory to the United States. The Khmer Rouge genocide in Cambodia was under way, and by the end of April the last defenders of South Vietnam were scrambling to flee Saigon on—or under—any helicopter that could lift them. Live images of the rout were televised around the world, in a final proclamation of American impotence in Southeast Asia. President Ford impassively announced, a week later, that the nation was "no longer at war," but no amount of White House spin could alleviate a general sense of strategic disgrace.

Since Ford was not yet an announced candidate, this was an obvious moment for Ronald Reagan to declare that enough was enough, and volunteer his own leadership to the Republican Party. However, the 1976 convention was still over a year away. Something dramatic might happen next month or next spring to restore the President's popularity. Native caution told Reagan to continue sending out ripples.

And indeed, on May 12, something dramatic did happen. Khmer Rouge soldiers pirated the American merchantman *Mayaguez* and held its forty crew in Sihanoukville, effectively daring the United States to do something. Ford, enraged, responded with enough military force to spring an aircraft carrier, succeeded in his mission, and almost overnight turned himself into a popular hero.

On July 8, he confirmed that he would be a candidate for the Presidency in his own right.

☯

Ford's declaration had the paradoxical effect of solidifying an amorphous campaign organization, chaired by Senator Paul Laxalt of Nevada, which announced itself a week later as the "Citizens for Reagan Committee." Reagan himself retired behind veils of inscrutability. This suited the style of the committee's strategist, a cagey thirty-five-year-old Beltway insider named John Sears, who felt that Reagan would benefit by *seeming* reluctant to divide the Republican Party. For most of the rest of the year, while Sears and Laxalt built a network for 1976, their candidate in waiting could continue to do what he did best: beguile more and more Americans.

Ronald Reagan was now sixty-four. Eight years of intense engagement in the Governorship of California had distracted his staffers from noticing a growing remoteness in his manner. Now, those who stayed with him began to be ever so slightly chilled by it. While never unfriendly (he remained the most outwardly genial of men) he withheld more and more of himself, and no longer pretended to recognize lesser names or faces. One aide who had worked for him at close quarters for eight years complained to Peter Hannaford, "Every time I see the Governor, I have to remind him who I am."

I find this significant because the *suddenness* with which Dutch forgot, and the speed with which he adapted to any new player onstage, indicates that his lapses of memory had nothing to do with age. Maybe computer imagery is better here: he had only a limited supply of RAM, and he wiped it clean whenever he switched to a new application. Again I say—there never was a politician less interested in the past.

Another more worrying development was the rigidifying of his views. Once he had made an emotional commitment to this or that policy or story, no amount of disproof would cause him to alter his belief in it. Exhaustive research by Scripps-Howard reporters in the late Fifties had established that one of his favorite "Lenin" quotes ("The way to conquer capitalism is to debauch the currency") had actually been fabricated by John Maynard Keynes. Reagan stood corrected, but also stood by the quote, to the ultimate exasperation of Mikhail Gorbachev.

Michael Deaver had become aware of the aggression behind this stiffness as long ago as 1973, when the Governor had reacted with outrage to Vice President Agnew's enforced resignation. "It's terrible what happened to him," Reagan said, playing nervously with a bunch of keys.

"Jesus, Governor, the guy is a crook—he took money in envelopes!"

They were sitting face-to-face across the cabinet table in Sacramento. Reagan cursed, hauled back, and threw the keys straight into Deaver's chest.

What interests me about the anecdote is that Dutch had reasons other than sentimentality to react that way. He was under heavy pressure from Holmes Tuttle and other Nixon loyalists to offer himself as Agnew's replacement. They had been unable to shake him, though.

EM: (*in 1988*) Apparently, you just sat there listening to these passionate arguments go back and forth in the boardroom, and you eventually said, "No, I think not." Do you remember that meeting?

RR: Yes, I said I wasn't interested at all. I was Governor of California, and that's what I wanted to continue doing.

EM: Did it ever occur to you that by saying that, you made Gerald Ford President of the United States?

RR: (*curtly*) No.

One set of facts and figures that Reagan's campaign team wished he'd never committed himself to was put together by Jeffrey Bell, co-author of his Pilgrims' Society speech. It imaginatively postulated that if the federal government would only decentralize most of its arrogated powers, and transfer local authority back to the states, Congress would get a windfall of ninety billion dollars in cash savings, enough to balance the budget, put a down payment on the national debt, and reduce income taxes by nearly a quarter. Reagan seized upon the statistics with his usual credulity, carded them, and on September 26 presented them to the Executives Club of Chicago, along with a mass of other promises that amounted to the prospectus of his still unannounced campaign.

He was fortunate in addressing an audience so complacent that they took everything he said on trust. His "Ninety Billion Dollar Plan" therefore did not get much play in the press. But to his later acute embarrassment, a strategist working for President Ford picked up the numbers and filed them.

☯

Reagan finally decided to announce in Washington on November 15, and, two weeks before, summoned his wife and children to tell them. (It was the first and last time they all met to this purpose.) Only the rebellious Patti failed to show. Nancy was predictably supportive; Michael approved; Maureen was pessimistic. Seventeen-year-old Ron seemed more interested in moving on to a Halloween party.

Not until son and father went riding, just before the announcement, did the boy's real feelings surface. He detested the "nicotine-stained, wheezing, gray-toned amoral people" who had begun to pervade the pleasant house in Pacific Palisades, and thought that Reagan demeaned himself by listening to them.

"Do you really need it?" he asked, with all the querulousness of youth. "Can't you fulfill yourself some other way?"

Reagan replied at length, but his voice was pitched a little too far, and his sentences too well turned, for intimacy. "I can do a lot of things for America," he said, and proceeded to enumerate them for an imaginary camera. Ron realized that all chances of a decent dialogue with Dad were now past.

☯

I watched Dutch's announcement at the National Press Club on television, and was less struck by his speech—a routine complaint about Soviet imperialism and U.S. government greed—than by the fact that Nancy alone stood with him onstage. Paul Rae took note, too, and sent me the following letter:

> *Dear E:*—We've often discussed Dutch-boy's debt to four small, strong women, from Nelle & Mugs to Janey & Nancy. But have these parallels between the last pair ever occurred to you?
>
> Same size, same eyes, same job when he got to know 'em—each the toughest starlet on their respective lots. Both owed their big breaks to Merv LeRoy. Both had to shanghai the slow sap into marriage. Daughters of absentee fathers, whose names they refuse to speak; traded as kids; completely changed their own monikers. Both bruised, flinchy, pushy, short-fused, suspicious to the point of paranoia, neurotically tidy, *love* to give orders; formal, censorious, kid-whacking mothers. Both crazy about red, not to mention Ol' Blue Eyes. Neither can figure out the diff. between a pot & a pan, but they sure know a phone when they see one. Both convinced doom is around the corner—and in this case, Nancy may well be right.

A perceptive letter, so far as it goes. I could add later touches, such as the tendency of both women, in old age, to talk to themselves in the luxury of their mirrored bathrooms. However, the annals of biography are replete with "both" lists, mostly trivial. As Phil Dunne used to remind me, even Castor and Pollux are separated by light-years.

The Bicentennial year of 1976 opened with gloomy advice from my agent that she had been unable to sell my Theodore Roosevelt teleplay, "The Dude from New York," to the networks.

"How about writing a short 'popular' biography of Teddy?" she said. "You seem to have plenty of research material. I could get you a contract from Coward, McCann."

And with disconcerting quickness, she did. The contract amounted to little more than loose change, but it was a serious literary assignment—my first ever, vouchsafed to me at an age when most men are accepting the attrition of their gifts. With the permission of the National Park Service, I set up a desk in the defunct library of the Theodore Roosevelt Birthplace in downtown Manhattan. The speckled smell of old books, the life trapped in old photographs, the dead quiet of the oak-paneled room filled me with a strange content. I found a ream of smooth white certificate bond, discarded the top dust-covered sheet, and wrote at the top of the next, *January 6, 1976.*

When I went home that night and turned on the news, it reported that Ronald Reagan had arrived in Moultonboro, New Hampshire, to begin his first primary campaign.

☯

For a few weeks, I tried to keep up with Dutch's peregrinations around that grim little state, but New England campaigning is politics at its worst (all those dour people in parkas being coaxed into reluctant handshakes), and my thoughts kept reverting to the easy elegance of Theodore Roosevelt's Washington. I remember that reporters—primed by the Ford campaign—began badgering Dutch about the specifics of his Ninety Billion Dollar Plan. They asked if he realized that decentralization of federal programs would force New Hampshire to raise local taxes. He could not deny the figures they quoted, and looked increasingly unhappy. In early February, President Ford flew north to join the mocking chorus. "Dutch puzzlebrained in N.H.," my diary records.

I was in Washington on the twenty-fourth, interviewing Alice Roosevelt Longworth, and that evening in my hotel room heard with stupefaction that Ronald Reagan was leading Gerald Ford by fifteen hundred votes. Evidently the anti-congressional bias of his plan had appealed to GOP conservatives more than its peculiar math. But not quite enough, as next morning's final returns showed. Ford won by a shadow-thin margin of 1,317.

Campaign specialists generally agree that had Reagan not delivered that hasty speech in Chicago, five months before, he would have won in New Hampshire and gone on to win his party's nomination in 1976. People seemed to want him to succeed. The Ninety Billion Dollar Plan was but one of a series of rhetorical excesses, any of which would have crippled a less engaging candidate. His little black box of napkin notes and clippings from newspapers and magazines (undocumented, but many of them typographically traceable to the *Los Angeles Times, National Review,* and *Reader's Digest*) acted as a sort of information blender, from which poured a welfare queen with "eighty names, thirty addresses, and twelve Social Security cards," or the nude theaters subsidized by the federal government, or the heroic black mess attendant who had ended U.S. military segregation by shooting down Japanese planes at Pearl Harbor.

Reagan had an especial fondness for numbers with lots of zeros in them, the more groups of three the better. "I've been told that something like forty-two trillion rate decisions were given by the ICC in its eighty-five-year history," he said on national television, "and they are not even indexed." A reporter for *The Washington Post* worked out that this decision rate must have kept the commission extremely busy, at over fifty-six billion rulings an hour. But when he wrote a piece on Reagan's propensity for gaffes, he found that his editors would not run it, nor would others across the country. "They all said the same—'We don't believe Reagan's serious.' "

Speech audiences were equally forgiving. The candidate said things with such earnest intensity that they believed in *him* rather than in his information. And to the annoyance of pedants, some of his most fanciful-sounding stories turned out to be true. Dorie Miller, the black hero of Pearl Harbor, was, as Reagan precisely described, "a Negro sailor whose total duties involved kitchen-type duties," who had shot down four dive bombers with a borrowed machine gun. After passionate lobbying by civil-rights activists, Miller had been awarded the Navy Cross. If Reagan was, to quote Garry Wills, "remembering a movie," then it was the raw film of fact.

In other words, imagination, not mendacity, was the key to Dutch's mind. He believed both true and untrue things if they suited his moral purpose—and because he believed in belief.

When I heard that Dutch had again been beaten by Ford in Florida, and that his campaign was almost insolvent, I stopped reading about him, and returned to the more interesting politics of 1907. Biographical research is hallucinatory, especially when conducted in an absolutely silent library, heavily curtained off from the outside world. One feels one's clothing becoming thicker, with bulkier buttons and studs, and familiarity grows with—what is Truman Capote's phrase?—other voices, other rooms.

If I had spent the next few months uninterruptedly at work there, I would probably not have registered Dutch's surprise recovery in the North Carolina primary, nor his accelerating momentum after that. However, Alaric Jacob, who remembered my long-ago letter about Reagan the emerging politician, wrote from London with a surprise assignment:

"He seems to be unstoppable . . . after that big win in Texas."
The candidate and his team, 1976 (clockwise, from RR's left): John Sears,
Nancy Clark Reynolds, Jeffrey Bell, Paul Laxalt, Peter Hannaford,
Martin Anderson, Lyn Nofziger, Michael Deaver,
Richard Wirthlin, Nancy Reagan.

Dear E:

A colleague of mine edits a small journal of transatlantic concern,
The Anglo-American, & can offer a press ticket to the Rep. National
Convention and £100 if you would care to give us 2,500 wds. or so on
yr. friend Reagan. He seems to be unstoppable this side of the water,
after that big win in Texas. What a brilliant political ploy, to choose
a running mate now, before the proceedings have fairly begun! Or un-
fairly, as the case may be. . . .

Actually Reagan's "brilliant" choice (he had asked the liberal Senator Richard S. Schweiker of Pennsylvania to run with him on July 20) amounted to an acknowledgment that his delegate strength had peaked at a level insufficient to beat Ford on nomination day, August 19. John Sears was hoping at least to keep uncommitted delegates interested in Reagan as a vital alternative. I persuaded myself that a tax-deductible trip to Kansas City, site of the convention, might profitably be combined with a research tour of Rough Rider Country. Also, that any biographer of an American President must witness at least once the purgatory that produces a party nominee. And what if, *mirabile dictu,* the nominee was Dutch?

Exhausted on August 20, after three days of being reminded of my father's descriptions of the Chicago stockyards (acres of beefy jostling bodies, bullhorns sounding incessantly, a sour, cumulative, animal reek), I sat in a Missouri motel and typed up this report for Alaric:

THE PRESIDENT WHO NEVER WAS

Kansas City—Now that Gerald ("Jerry") Ford is the dutiful choice of the Republican Party to lead its fall campaign against Governor James Earl ("Jimmy") Carter, one senses a wistfulness among the departing delegates for Ronald Reagan, who but for a handful of disputed votes might have been the next President of the United States.

Few political punters give Mr. Ford—forever branded with his pardon of Richard Nixon—a chance of beating the Georgia Democrat, who has all the advantages of youth, health, born-again piety, and a ruthless tactical intelligence comparable to Harold Wilson's. Reagan, they say, could have done it. Older, slower, and seemingly gentler than Carter, he nevertheless exerts a bruising political will. Witness his decision to fight and win the North Carolina primary after five straight losses, when both his wife and campaign manager were begging him to withdraw.

In person, moreover, the former California Governor conveys such charisma and confidence as to beguile every voter he confronts. In recent memory, only John F. Kennedy has had Reagan's ability to cast a spell simply by walking onstage. Last night, President Ford learned that to his cost.

———

Twenty-four hours before, Reagan had lost the nomination squarely if not fairly to a President armed with all the White House's power of patronage. Gerald Ford's winning margin was narrow—only 117 votes—but it had come on the first ballot and was decisive enough to run a campaign on. At sixty-five, after two full terms as Governor of California, Ronald Reagan was apparently headed for retirement.

His "final service" to the Republican Party, apart from a reluctant promise to make some speeches for Ford in the fall, was to dictate the choice of Kansas Senator Robert Dole as the President's running mate. Then, in a bleak ballroom early Thursday morning, he delivered his valedictory to anguished staffers. "The individuals on the stage may change," he said, "but the cause is there, and the cause will prevail because it is right."

Apart from the theatrical metaphor, this was routine rhetoric for a defeated candidate. But the rest of Reagan's little speech was personally revealing. He three times repeated, "Don't get cynical," although everyone in the room knew that the nomination had been wrested from him by a naked, last-minute exercise of White House power. There was a touch of his trademark humor ("Someone once described backstage politics as a little bit like looking at civilization with its pants down"). He contained his own emotion almost to the end, breaking down only as he growled out his six final words:

"Don't give up your ideals. . . . Recognize that there are millions and millions of Americans out there who want what you want . . . *a shining city on a hill.*"

———

It was a striking image, one that nobody in the Reagan camp seems to have heard before. As far as this reporter can determine, it derives from Matthew 5:14 by way of John Bunyan.

All that remained for him to do after that was sit through Ford's acceptance speech and maybe wave from his high, glassed-in box when the President said something about party unity. "I'm at peace with myself," he told the eager NBC reporter Tom Brokaw, who invaded his box at prime time and nearly poked Nancy Reagan's eye out with a portable antenna. Brokaw asked if he would agree to appear on the platform with President Ford. A tranquil shake of the glossy head. "No, I have no desire to go down there."

If Reagan was unaware that the President's men wanted such a two-shot—indeed, wanted it so desperately that they kept Ford out of the hall until assured of it—then he was about the only innocent among five thousand delegates and press. Conversely, none but he knew how he would respond if called upon. The assurance had been given in his name by an aide pretty sure that the old actor would be unable to resist a cue from center stage.

Old actors, however, do not like to seem over-anxious to perform. For most of the evening's proceedings, Reagan slumped out of sight, paying little heed to the sound system but drinking copious draughts of water—a sure sign that he had oratory in mind. Ford delivered a tolerable speech, scripted for him in the plainest possible English. Then, sweating mightily as the hall applauded him, he began waving at the glass box in an attempt to get Reagan's attention. The Governor chose this moment to swivel at an angle of forty-five degrees and start signing autographs. "It's his night," he muttered. "I'm not going down there."

Ford was forced to yell over the thumping of the band, "Ron, will you come down and bring Nancy?" All eyes were focused now on the box, rather than the candidate, who prowled the stage gasping with frustration. It was his fault that Reagan was located so far away. The White House had been afraid that Mrs. Reagan (immaculate in cool white, with pearls) would generate more flashbulbs than Mrs. Ford.

A steady chant of "We want Ron" arose on the floor, in Ivesian cross-rhythm to the band's quickstep. Would he or wouldn't he descend? The box was too dark to show any signs of movement. John Chancellor, anchoring for NBC at a vantage point overlooking the floor, actually pulled out a pair of binoculars. "It's possible that Governor Reagan may be coming down. . . . He may be going down the hallway."

Indeed he was, ambling with Nancy through caverns measureless to man, content to let the suspense build. Ford kept seizing Dole's left hand and jiggling it overhead, miming joy, although both of them could sense that their moment of triumph had been perverted into one of anticipation. There was nothing they could do but keep grinning. Around them, Betty Ford, the three Ford children, Elizabeth Dole, and Nelson Rockefeller stretched their rictus muscles, too, until the stage, flashing with teeth, began to look like a tetanus ward.

At last Reagan appeared, tall, relaxed, improbably handsome, to a huge upsurge of applause. Ford led him to the podium. The applause refused to die, while the band swung saucily into "California Here I Come." Reagan shook with laughter as Ford stood frozen-faced, unable to command his own convention.

"I would be honored on your behalf," the President said when the music ended in a discord, "to ask my good friend, Governor Reagan, to say a few words."

———

Reagan approached the microphone with the sureness of a salmon returning to home waters. "Thank you very much. Mr. President, Mrs. Ford, Mr. Vice President, Mr. Vice President–to–be—"

The auditorium rumbled with laughter. He had already, with the utmost grace, emphasized the jarring presence onstage of both Nelson Rockefeller and Robert Dole—an old-style liberal now headed for retirement, and a new-style conservative indicative of the party's changing mood. In his next sentence he effortlessly reached toward a much larger constituency: "—those who are watching from a distance, all of those millions of Democrats and independents who I know are looking for a cause around which to rally, and which I believe we can give them."

As he continued with a few sentences of thanks for his reception, the bitterness and vulgarity of the last few days seemed to float out of Kemper Arena, along with a single white balloon riding the blue air. Ford visibly relaxed. But then Reagan, instead of stopping, launched into what was patently the acceptance speech he *would* have delivered, had a handful of Mississippi delegates not deserted him at the last moment.

"I believe the Republican Party has a platform that is a banner of bold, unmistakable colors, with no pale pastel shades," he said, and the crowd predictably erupted. There followed the first real hush of the convention, as Reagan went on to do what he did better than any candidate in memory: tell a story.

"Someone asked me to write a letter for a time capsule that is going to be opened in Los Angeles a hundred years from now, on our Tricentennial. It sounded like an easy assignment. They suggested I write something about the problems and issues of the day. I set out to do so, riding down the Coast in an automobile, looking at the blue Pacific out on one side and the Santa Ynez Mountains on the other, and I couldn't help but wonder if it was going to be that beautiful a hundred years from now. . . .

"And suddenly I thought to myself, if I write of the problems, they will be the domestic problems of which the President spoke here tonight, the challenges confronting us, the erosion of freedom that has taken place under Democrat rule in this country, the invasion of private rights, the controls and restrictions on the vitality of the great free economy that we enjoy. These are the challenges that we must meet."

Behind him Ford stood in gathering gloom, aware that his own speech had been but a warm-up for this one.

"And then again there is the challenge of which he spoke, that we live in a world in which the great powers have poised and aimed at each other horrible missiles of destruction, nuclear weapons, that can in a matter of minutes arrive at each other's country and destroy, virtually, the civilized world we live in.

"And suddenly it dawned on me, those who read this letter a hundred years from now will know whether those missiles were fired. They will know whether we met our challenge. Whether they can have the freedoms that we have known up until now will depend on what we do here.

"Will they look back with appreciation and say, 'Thank God for those people in 1976 who headed off that loss of freedom, who kept us now a hundred years later free, who kept our world from nuclear destruction'?"

By now, hundreds of faces across the floor were wet with tears. "This is our challenge; and this is why . . . we must go forth from here united, determined that what a great general said a few years ago is true: there is no substitute for victory, Mr. President."

The roar that followed this apparently spontaneous address (it had been memorized, one suspects, in Reagan's tape-recorder brain) dwarfed any heard so far at the convention. "Beautiful—just beautiful," Rockefeller was heard to say, as he seized the Governor's hand with professional respect. Only after Reagan glided offstage, accepting congratulations with his trademark shy duck of the head, did the realization sink in that he had not said a word in praise of President Ford.

Just as the stage had earlier seemed to be awaiting him, it was now permeated with a sense of his absence. Ford and Dole resumed their crazed hand-in-hand jiggle to the music of the band, but the Convention was demonstrably over, and none too happy with its choice.

Gerald Ford has been a decent President and is a worthy, if lackluster, nominee. History will remember him for the simple beauty of the words he spoke upon assuming office after the resignation of Richard Nixon: "My fellow Americans, our long national nightmare is over. Our Constitution works; our great Republic is a Government of laws and not of men." Ronald Reagan will probably never match those few terse sentences, the most eloquent inaugural remarks since Lincoln's in 1865.

His own rhetoric, as this Convention has made plain, is (despite Rockefeller's praise) neither beautiful nor especially original. There was a good deal of the Gettysburg Address in his invocation of the future, and his biggest applause line was lifted from Douglas MacArthur.

What distinguished it was the magic of its delivery, its precise application to the moment, and the sense that the speaker believed every word he said. Indeed, Ronald Reagan in private thinks and speaks exactly as he does in public, with absolute conviction that his plain pieties will prevail when a divided world has come to its senses.

Last night's demonstration for the Gipper was overlong and sentimental—but what is an American political convention, if not a chance to display our perennial tendency to slop over? Back of all the braying and blubbing, however, one could feel a sort of wistful nostalgia for the President Who Never Was. At sixty-five, Reagan is clearly too old to make a third try for the White House. He will make a few token speeches for Ford, then retire to his ranch above Santa Barbara.

So we are unlikely ever to know what, exactly, the Shining City meant to him. At least Ronald Reagan has held it in steady prospect, and the reason Americans are already starting to miss him is that they fear neither candidate in this election has any such vision.

On that elegiac note I once again took leave of Dutch as a subject of interest. Intermittent bulletins came my way, suggesting that he was indeed a spent force. Paul wrote on August 29 to say that he had glimpsed him outside his glass-fronted house in Pacific Palisades, and been shocked at "how old he looked all of a sudden—colorless too, like something vital had drained."

I recognized the symptoms: Dutch was not so much a retired pol as an actor at the end of a long run. We now know that he was already musing a return to the boards. To reporters, he would say only that he intended to campaign for President Ford, and to revive his syndicated column and radio commentaries. He gave *The New York Times* a hint that this would allow him to "stage a crusade if there's something I feel needs crusading [*sic*]." But with Jimmy Carter emerging as America's latest Christian warrior, the remark got little attention.

Early in September, Reagan told the last few veterans of his campaign team that he wanted all leftover funds—roughly a million dollars—to be plowed into "a political action committee" that would perpetrate his philosophy. Lyn Nofziger took charge of the new PAC and called it Citizens for the Republic. With that, Citizens for Reagan disbanded. Michael Deaver and Peter Hannaford returned to public relations, the policy expert Martin Anderson went back to academe, and Edwin Meese moved south to found a college of criminal justice in San Diego.

Only Richard Wirthlin, the pollster, saw portent in the fact that Reagan had so freely sacrificed a million dollars that Nancy Reagan (the fastest endorser of checks since Jacqueline Kennedy Onassis) could have deposited in the family account. Wirthlin's whole instinct was to weigh current words and behavior in terms of the political future. "I knew right then that Ronnie would run again."

❦

Jimmy Carter's presidency opened on a high note when he stepped out of his limousine on the slopes of Capitol Hill and walked down Pennsylvania Avenue with his pretty wife at his side, exulting in the cheers and sunshine. After all the armor-plated defensiveness of the Watergate era, a sense of openness and optimism seemed to be returning to American life. It was a wonderful moment, and since no others followed it, I did not hesitate when he asked me years later for advice on how to begin his "me-moirs."

"Without question, Mr. President, you should start with that walk you took on Inauguration Day . . ."

He heard me out, then said, "No. Ah'll begin with th' day when Ah triumphed over Scoop Jackson."

The Princeton parlor where I sat with six or seven other presidential historians went quiet as we tried to think what "triumph" Carter could possibly be thinking of. The *Florida primary* of March 9, 1976, was his greatest political moment? Evidently, because he sat there staring at us, his eyes flashing pale blue fire.

"I've seen them all, from Eisenhower to Reagan," my neighbor murmured to me, "and they all have one thing in common—they make the room seem bigger. But this guy makes the walls contract."

Contraction, or the state of self-withdrawal Germans describe as *innigkeit,* was indeed the characteristic of the Carter years, at least what I perceived of them as I labored to complete my Roosevelt book. An obsession with allegedly dwindling national resources; a smallness of outlook, from the cancellation of supersonic transports to the issuance of bills for White House hospitality; public lights dimmed, cardigans unbuttoned, hemorrhoids proclaimed, human rights called for, the Panama Canal forfeited; fifty-two American hostages taken hostage in

Iran; eight helicopters sent in to rescue them, in a demonstration of dragonfly wrath; and finally, a front-page image that burned itself, I should think, onto the retinas of every citizen who saw it: two bearded hostage-holders using the Stars and Stripes to carry garbage out of the U.S. Embassy in Tehran. The flag's heavy curve represented the nadir (*nadïr-es-semt,* as they say in Arabic) of American prestige in the post-Eisenhower era.

"I suppose you've heard the one about Theodore Roosevelt and Jimmy Carter," Henry Morgan said to me. The once-great radio satirist—shrunken, too!—was now doing a book-chat program out of somebody's basement on the West Side of Manhattan.

"No, I haven't."

"The President's working late one night when TR's ghost drifts into the Oval Office. Jimmy turns down *Das Rheingold,* jumps up, and offers him his chair. 'No,' says TR, 'you're the President now, I'm just haunting the place. How's it going?' he says. 'Not too good,' says Jimmy, 'th' Iranians have imprisoned fifty-two of our diplomatic personnel.' 'So you sent in the Marines, right?' says TR. 'Uh, no, but Ah registered a strong protest at th' United Nations.' TR says in a cold voice, 'Anything else?' 'Well, uh, th' Russians just invaded Afghanistan.' TR says, 'And of course you retaliated with every weapon in our arsenal.' Jimmy says, 'No, but Ah've withdrawn our ath-eletes from th' Olympic Games.' TR blows his top and shouts, '*The next thing you're going to tell me is you've given back the Panama Canal!*' "

It was during these years of bitter humor and malaise that Reagan rose again to the leadership of his party, and—seventeen days short of his seventieth birthday—to the leadership of the free world.

I elevated my own Chief Executive on March 29, 1979, which is to say I published an 863-page biography entitled *The Rise of Theodore Roosevelt.* It left TR as Vice President on a mountaintop in the Adirondacks, reading the telegram that told him William McKinley was dying. After a lifetime of failure, I knew I had achieved something fine—if only because of the fineness of the book's central character. It sold well if not spectacularly, and garnered a fair selection of awards, including one which a young neighbor celebrated as "the Wurlitzer Surprise."

Modesty would urge me to be circumspect about *Rise,* had Dutch not read it, causing one thing to lead to another over the next few years.

However, I also think that there were aspects to TR's character, and implications in the story, for which I could take no credit, since they addressed themselves to the national mood. Theodore Roosevelt was rightly perceived as representing everything that Jimmy Carter did not: optimism, expansionism ("like all Americans, I like big things"), hair-trigger reactions to any infringement of the national honor, and no particular sympathy for men who would not fight or women who would not breed. If bearish Teddy had run for President in 1980, he would doubtless have scared the hell out of most voters; but there is no question that Ronald Reagan subtly evoked a similar set of values. The kind of people who asked me at book seminars, "What would TR do about our hostages if he were in the White House today?" were the kind of people who voted for Dutch.

I was in Washington one night during the primary season, attending a Jefferson Lecture, and walked past 1600 Pennsylvania Avenue en route back to my hotel. On impulse I went to the railings and hung on them, as millions of others have done, inhaling the scent of mown grass and hyacinths and gazing at the classical facade glowing in the dark. It gave off waves of stability and tranquillity, the still center of world power: Jefferson's house, Lincoln's house, TR's and—who could begrudge it?—Jimmy Carter's too, by democratic right.

Then I went on to bed and woke to the news that at the very hour I had conducted my midnight vigil, the President had been frantically handling the failure of his helicopter-rescue attempt. Eight Americans were dead and two aircraft still smoldering in the salt wastes south of Tehran.

☯

So Dutch won. Declaring almost exactly four years after he last declared, and propelled by five years of cumulative rhetorical "ripples," including one that washed George Bush out of contention in New Hampshire ("I'm *paying* for this microphone, Mr. Breen!"), he engulfed the candidacies of eight other Republican contenders, and was nominated by a resurgent party on July 14, 1980. Magnanimous (or was he simply uncaring?) in victory, he offered the vice-presidential slot first to Gerald Ford, then to Bush, who accepted with alacrity.

From that moment on, as the hostage crisis worsened, there was an inevitability to Reagan's forward motion. The liberal press, incredulous that a man so old, so Western, so quaintly sure of himself could sweep this far, cited poll after poll to show that President Carter would hold him back. Yet Richard Wirthlin saw victory coming as early as mid-September, with no goodwill for Carter in the West, and plenty of it in the South for Reagan. The President began to run scared, all but accusing Reagan of hate-mongering and fealty to the Ku Klux Klan. This ill became a politician who had whored after Georgia's reactionary white vote in 1970, and in any case made no political sense, because anybody could see that Dutch simply could not understand racial animosity. ("There are none so color blind," I wrote Phil Dunne, "as those who will not see.")

Throughout the campaign, as Carter grimaced and whined, Dutch kept his dignity. He also managed to restrain his tendency toward gaffes, although there was one sublime riff about air pollution on October 8 that could have been written by Woody Allen. Apparently "ninety-two percent, ninety-three percent, pardon me" of America's "oxides of nitrogen" were caused by decaying vegetation, and this was good news for TB sufferers. What was more, the "sixteen permanent oil slicks" that had been floating off the coast of Santa Barbara "as long as the memory of man" acted as giant air scrubbers, purging the area of infectious diseases.

Stuart Spencer, back in Reagan harness, saw to it that such lapses were few. He gambled on Dutch's charm being able to withstand the President's mastery of fact in a debate on October 28, and succeeded beyond expectation. Carter attacked too fiercely to inspire voter confidence ("There you go again," said Dutch, with masterly lightness) and revealed the disconcerting fact that his twelve-year-old daughter, Amy, was one of his nuclear-policy advisers. When Dutch, at the end, ignored Carter altogether and simply asked the American people, "Are you happier today than when Mr. Carter became President of the United States?" I knew that he had won.

On November 3, eve of the election, a double rainbow appeared over his birthplace in Tampico. And by dark next day, Ronald Reagan was chosen as the next President of the United States by a flood of votes that just kept on rippling in, to a total of forty-four million. Jimmy Carter, ten points behind, got thirty-six million, and the third-party maverick John Anderson fewer than six million.

An announcer at WSDR Dixon sent Dutch a message: "The Rock River flows for you tonight, Mr. Ronald Reagan."

28

I,
Ronald Wilson
Reagan

RONALD REAGAN adjusted his white tie in the mirror, then, conscious of being watched, spun on his dance pumps, winked, and leaped into the air. His heels clicked. "I'm the President of the United States!" he said.

And so he was, happily and confirmedly, after an Inauguration Day that had realigned the American political landscape with a suddenness unmatched since Franklin Roosevelt's accession to power in 1933. Unlike his predecessors, he had seen no reason to take the oath of office behind the Capitol, in the shade, overlooking a dull parking lot. Instead, he staged the ceremony on the great building's front terrace, where he could feel the sun on his face (the gray sky broke and sent down a shaft of light as he began to speak). He directed his oratory down the sweep of its steps, the slope of its park, reverberantly onward and outward, through loudspeakers and monitors and transistors, along the expanding angles of Pennsylvania and Maryland Avenues and the grand axis of the Mall, crowded with thirty-two thousand people, across the Potomac and over the Blue Ridge Mountains, west, west, west.

Watching on television, I silently begged him to match, with his marvelous voice and command of gesture, the eloquence of the last great American inaugural, John F. Kennedy's in 1961. He did not even try. He spoke of his accession to power as "a commonplace occurrence" and, after perfunctory thanks to Jimmy Carter for "cooperation in the transition process," got straight into a survey of "the business of our nation." All the bromides of Economics 101 dropped like lead pennies: *sustained inflation, tax burden, mortgaging our future, live beyond our means, pay a higher price, runaway living costs.*

It was evident, as he proceeded, that he had written most of his speech, or at least drastically toned down the draft prepared for him by Ken Khachigian, a veteran of the Nixon White House. Not for Reagan the rhythmic alliterations of JFK, Nixon's "driving dream," or even the awkward eloquence of Gerald Ford. He spoke in plain language of the ever-growing power of an indifferent, centralized government, of runaway living costs and interest rates and a pervasive sense of national decline, worsened by foreign terrorism. These were trends he pledged to reverse, and quickly, starting right where he stood:

> It is my intention to curb the size and influence of the federal establishment and to demand recognition of the distinction between the powers granted to the federal government and those reserved to the states or to the people. All of us—[*Applause*] all of us need to be reminded that the federal government did not create the states; the states created the federal government.

Two recurring themes were apparent as his speech ran its plainsong course. One was a populism that addressed itself equally to "shopkeepers, clerks, cabbies, and truck drivers" and to the board of Archer Daniels Midland ("heroes [who] produce enough food to feed all of us and then the world beyond"). The other was a proud, almost agnostic activism straight out of *That Printer of Udell's*: "I do not believe in a fate that will fall on us no matter what we do. I do believe in a fate that will fall on us if we do nothing."

So much for domestic affairs. Reagan's paragraphs on foreign policy were worded so carefully, it was obvious that he did not want to jeopardize the Carter Administration's desperate last-minute negotiations to have the fifty-two American hostages in Iran released. But he did issue a warning that his own Administration would not be passive in the face of future terrorism from any quarter: "When action is required to preserve our national security, we will act."

Only at the end of his speech did the new President attempt any westward-ho rhetoric. "Standing here, one faces a magnificent vista . . ." But he looked no farther than Arlington National Cemetery, and segued into a sentimental story about a small-town boy who had joined the American Expeditionary Force in 1917 and, before being blown up, left behind a patriotic pledge: "I will work, I will save, I will sacrifice, I will endure, I will fight cheerfully and do my utmost, as if the issue of the whole struggle depended on me alone."

Whatever the cadence of these words may have owed to Tennyson, there was no mistaking the fervor of Reagan's delivery. As far as he was concerned, young Martin Treptow had left him a creed to live by.

The first Reagan Inaugural, then, was not so much an address to posterity as a conversation with ordinary Americans who could not afford to attend the most expensive exercises in presidential history. (The cost of hiring obligatory morning dress—pearl-gray vest, silk tie, and cutaway coat—acted as a further deterrent to clerks and cabbies.) But they could listen, and they could look at him towering over his drained little predecessor, noting above all the way that he *faced*. After all the self-doubt of the Seventies, Ronald Reagan gave his back to Islam and Communism and Malaise, and just about burst the tube of every television set in the country with his message that Independence was redeclared.

❦

What did he see that night in the mirror of the Washington Hilton Hotel holding room, just before he turned to face his family and clicked his newly presidential heels? More to the point, what did the mirror see?

A man just about to turn seventy, one inch taller than six feet, weighing about a hundred and eighty-five pounds stripped, broad as a surfboard and almost as hard, superbly balanced, glowing with health and handsome enough for a second career in the movies. Hair so dense and fine as to amount to a Marvel Comics helmet, slicked with Brylcreem and water to a blue-black sheen, diffusing any hint of gray. Teeth white, gums like a boy's (dentists even praise the clarity of his saliva), breath sweet, fingernails naturally shiny, unribbed, lucent as seashells. No fidgety mannerisms; an air of always being comfortable in his clothes. Rather fewer wrinkles, especially about the jowls, than photographers remember seeing a few years ago. Absolutely no makeup—just a clear and sanguineous complexion that blushes the moment he sips alcohol, or fears a woman has overhead one of his ribald jokes.

Since salubrity is an important aspect of American power—we do not like our leaders to look unhealthy, as Richard Nixon discovered—and since Reagan's physical impact is so potent, we might ponder its larger implications. This perfectly functioning body (weak eyes, deaf right ear, and a swelling prostate aside) moves, or rather glides, toward every obstacle with neither hesitation nor hurry. It is driven by a strange will consisting mainly of paradoxes: aggression without hostility, ego without vanity, superiority without snobbery, and that moral passion Reagan describes as "a clean hatred." Unlike Woodrow Wilson or Jimmy Carter, with their killer smiles and passion to preach, he has no contempt for the ungodly, nor does he have Theodore Roosevelt's bulldozer determination to move in a straight line. He advances by simply not noticing obstructions. Thus, when one deflects him, he assumes he has changed course voluntarily, and if it rolls out of his way, shows neither surprise nor gratitude.

Earlier today, for example, Iran relieved him of Carter's hostage problem before he had so much as come down from Capitol Hill. Were the fifty-two freed so soon after his speech for fear of him, or as a final taunt to Carter, or was the timing a mere matter of logistics? Whatever the truth, Reagan has the gift of luck.

He is also endowed with a happy nature, his optimism unquenchable, his smile enchantingly crooked, his laughter impossible to resist. If these attributes, together with all the others listed above, do not constitute grace, in the old sense of favors granted by God, then the word has no meaning. Even his rare explosions of anger are, in an odd way, benign, as when he silently and accurately hurled a bunch of keys at Mike Deaver's breastbone, or referred a disloyal California legislator to the baseball bat in his office: "I should have shoved it up your ass and broken it off." But such explosions only briefly disturb his equanimity, which otherwise surrounds him like a pool. He seems nerveless, incapable of fear, as when he once piled too many rocks into a trailer at Rancho del Cielo, and found his Jeep being dragged backward down a boulder-strewn escarpment: Sisyphus relaxedly steering in reverse, while all four wheels scrabbled for stability, and the engine screamed *nying-nying-nying*.

Considering that tonight is the most fulfilling of Ronald Reagan's life, he is surely entitled to indulge a moment's self-congratulation. Fewer than forty men have been able to look at themselves in the mirror and exult, *I'm the President of the United States!* (Jimmy Carter did so for the last time today, with no pleasure, only weariness.) And even fewer can have so looked forward to the Inaugural balls—on this particular evening, eight in succession. He loves to dance, and is very good at it.

Are there no flaws, then, in this image of a supremely happy person? What do the forty-two million Americans who tried to keep him out of the White House worry about? Well, for a start, his Daliesque ability to bend reality to his purposes. Inserting the story of the World War I soldier into his speech this morning had been his own obstinate idea, even when researchers found out that Martin Treptow was not buried at Arlington National Cemetery, but more than a thousand miles away in Bloomer, Wisconsin. Nobody who knows Reagan doubts that young Treptow lies forever in some Arlington of his mind.

The world that rotates inside his cerebellum is, if not beautiful, encouragingly rich and self-renewing. It is washed by seas whose natural "ozone" produces a healthful brown smog over coastal highways, and rinsed by rivers that purify themselves whenever they flow over gravel. Its rocks suppurate with so much untapped oil that Alaska "alone" has more petroleum reserves than Saudi Arabia. Americans should not feel guilty about pumping this bounty into their private cars; the automobile has "exactly the same" fuel-efficiency rating as the bus.

Reagan's world is not entirely without environmental problems. It glows with the "radioactivity" of coal burners (much more dangerous than nuclear plants), and is plagued by "deadly diseases spread by insects, because pesticides such as DDT have been prematurely outlawed." Acid rain, caused by an excess of trees, threatens much of the industrial northeast. Geopolitically, the globe presents many challenges. "Almost all" its heads of government, with the exception of Margaret Thatcher, are older than himself; China seems determined to reincorporate with Taiwan, although Reagan's personal preference would be to recognize them both; similarly, North and South Vietnam should never have been permitted to join, having been "separate nations for centuries." The Soviet Union, bent on invading the United States via Mexico (a strategem of "Nikolai" Lenin), is largely proof against retaliation, its vital industries throbbing away in "hardened" underground caverns; the economy of South America is a mess, particularly in Portuguese-speaking Bolivia; even the Last Best Hope of Man is under siege by the United Nations, which threatens to replace the Fourth, Fifth, and Fourteenth Amendments with covenants abolishing private property.

In fairness toward Ronald Reagan, even those most horrified by his encyclopedic ignorance must accept that a President-elect has for years been fielding hundreds, sometimes thousands, of questions a day, and often has to improvise policy, or call up anecdotes on the spot, when he is groggy with fatigue. What horrifies, though, is that Reagan says exactly the same things when he is fresh, and *after* he has been repeatedly corrected; his beliefs are as unerasable as the grooves of an LP. The only reliable way to recognize the approach of a Reagan untruism is to listen for signal phrases: *I have been told . . .* and, *As I've said many times . . .*

When he expresses views simply and declaratively, they should nevertheless be taken seriously, because they represent core philosophy. God wrote the Bible, and the Bible condones capital punishment. "Sodomy" is a sin. However, homosexuals have a Constitutional right to teach in public schools. Abortion is murder. Property is sacrosanct; so is privacy. Men may bear arms. Women are superior to men, therefore equal rights will downgrade them. Art should affirm moral values. Hard work is mandatory, boredom impermissible. Charity begins at home. Communism is evil because it saps the individual will. "When men fail to drive toward a goal or purpose, but only drift, the drift is always toward barbarism."

The hardening of his mind would seem to be the result of several factors beside the onset of old age. One is the big secret of top-level politics: that most of its duties are merely automatic, and that most "decisions" are a matter of initialing the recommendations of underlings. For a long time now, he has been doing things over: campaigning for the Governorship twice, traveling from town to town and delivering the same basic speech (with variations from his well-worn file of variations); spending two terms in Sacramento, each consisting of four budget battles, four legislative sessions, four summers, and four seasons of strategy. And there have been three campaigns for the Presidency, during which the towns and speeches and babies and barbecues streamed into the equivalent of a video loop. No wonder Reagan sometimes gives the impression of being incapable of surprise.

Two other noticeable characteristics of the new President's personality—hard to reconcile with his air of natural authority—are passivity in matters that do not interest him, and uxoriousness. After a lifetime of accepting direction (from his four strong women, his coach, his station, his studio, his C.O., his guild, his company, his campaign managers), Reagan is willing to share most power and responsibility. At home, he submits to management like a child.

Nancy Reagan's determination to keep him well fed, well rested, and undistracted by any hint of family problems (of which there are plenty) has profoundly indebted him to her:

> *My Dear First Lady . . .* I could offer you my heart but I'd have to get it back from you first. There just isn't any thing to get for some one who already has everything I can afford. . . . Perhaps I should

talk about what you've given me because that makes you the most blessed person in these here parts.

Your gift to me is uninsurable. No appraiser can put a value on it. How would he figure the market value of feeling a tingle of excitement and anticipation every time I start for home? Or the way I can't help but walk fast when I get there, hurrying for the first sight of you? Just waking up becomes a warm glow because you are there—just as the whole house is haunted when you aren't.

It's like fruit of the month on a lifetime subscription—a perpetual motion happiness machine. It starts off fresh and brand new every day shining up my whole world.

Thank you for loving me and seeing that I'm smart enough to stay very much in love with you. . . .

Your Husband.

*

To her credit, Nancy Reagan has never pretended fully to understand Ronald Reagan's aloof yet ardent nature. She claims only to love him back, and know him (insofar as he *can* be known) better than anyone else. This knowledge extends to his principal weakness, a tendency to trust everybody, which she compensates for by trusting nobody at all. There is a photograph of the Reagans being received by Pope Paul VI, in which it is clear that His Holiness better not mess with Ronnie.

In a town famous for its coldness—where one can be in mid-sentence at a cocktail party, only to find one's interlocutor striding away sans any apology at first sight of somebody more famous—Nancy will soon be feared by many as an operator *par excellence*. Although her famous father Dr. Loyal Davis ("I have his hands . . . surgeon's hands") is actually only her stepfather, she seems to have inherited his neurologist's conviction that all human behavior can be controlled, if necessary by cutting.

As yet, she has few people to protect Reagan from. The new Administration is being formed with spectacular speed and efficiency, and loyalty to last year's campaign promises is a condition of appointment. Liberals in Congress and the national press are in no hurry to challenge so popular a President, while Washington hostesses delight at the message winked by Nancy's beaded, white, one-shoulder Galanos gown: it is party time again on the Potomac. Not for her the dimmed lights and reluctant white wine of the Carter era, Rosalynn's dour discussions of mental health and human rights. Her compatibles are the fashionable wives of very rich men and amusing walkers like Truman Capote and

Jerry Zipkin, who keep her supplied with scuttlebutt from both coasts. She loves to lunch out, "gives good phone," and never tries to finish her husband's jokes. In a word, the Reagans look like fun.

And what of their children? They are a dissimilar group, divided between two mothers, united only by their starved love for Ronald Reagan. The President simultaneously dazzles and intimidates them with his celebrity, now amplified beyond imagining by the busyness of power: the dozens of guards, the platoons of policemen, the spangling cameras, and the fact that every face that stares at him seems to be wearing the same goggly smile. He was always a remote father (delicious though his company was, when available), and was made shy by their love when they tried to express it. What chance of requital now, as Dad becomes the father of all the people?

Ron Reagan is a decent and well-balanced youth, with all of his father's easy charm and none of his mystery. Although the beautifully proportioned body is recognizable to anyone who ever swam at Lowell Park Beach in the 1920s, the long Botticellian face is *sui generis*. A Yale dropout, Ron is one of the Joffrey Ballet Company's more promising young dancers. When he first announced, three years ago, that he intended to follow that career, his parents reacted with the usual speculation that he might be gay. But on returning home early from a campaign trip, they were confronted by very definite evidence that he was not. "He was using our room and our bed!" Twenty-two years old and recently married to a New York editor (also Italianate, though in the dark style of Piero della Francesca), Ron lives in bohemian austerity in a Greenwich Village walkup. His mother idolizes him to the point of possession, but a distinct counterclaim gleams in Doria Reagan's black eyes.

Patti Davis is twenty-eight now, a rangy, beautiful young woman whose long rope-veined arms and thin-tipped hands bear a disconcerting resemblance to the President's. In her case, the sameness is ironic, since she dropped the name of Patricia Ann Reagan some years ago, as a gesture of independence. There is double, even triple irony here: by doing so, she further distanced herself from her adored father, and identified herself with her unloved mother. Patti is an authentic product of the Age of Aquarius, sexually and pharmaceutically adventurous, limber from yoga, pro-abortion and anti-nuke, vegetarian, guitar-thumping, street-smart. Like all the Reagan children, she is perpetually short of money. She has not yet realized a modest talent for writing, and when she does, her only real subject will be herself.

Michael is the most starved child of all, not even flesh of Reagan's flesh, a thirty-five-year-old cauldron of secret shame (he was repeatedly molested by a camp counselor in childhood) and occasional uncontrollable anger, which he vents in smashed glass and telephone tirades. He used to be proud of his father's nickname for him, *schmuck,* until he looked the word up in a Yiddish dictionary. Among siblings noted for at least a veneer of sophistication, Michael is blue-collar in looks and manner, a racer of speedboats, a wrecker of cars, a shooter of small birds. Until the President understands why his son has such desperate feelings of defilement and sexual insecurity—and the day will come— he can only conclude, privately, that Michael is "a really disturbed young man." They communicate best in the male argot of jokes and sports chat. Michael's demeanor, while worshipful, distinctly suggests that he feels his father owes him something.

Maureen is the eldest and largest of the President's children, her brilliant smile and button nose reminding the world that there once was another Mrs. Reagan. The starvation, in Maureen's case—"I've never really *been* with him"—is compounded by frustration that she can emulate neither of her parents in their respective fields, although she abundantly shares their gifts. Had she Jane Wyman's graceful body, she might have made a career in show business, since she sings and acts well, memorizes like a VCR, and luxuriates in the spotlight. Had she Ronald Reagan's emotional discipline, she might be an assemblywoman somewhere. She is fascinated by politics, and is, if anything, a better speaker than he is, with an avid interest in every issue, and a near-Neapolitan fluency of gesture. But she has never been permitted to play much of a part in his political career, which has been managed by men who find her too temperamental by half. Childless at forty, she is preparing to marry for the third time.

The only grandchild that Ronald and Nancy Reagan have so far is Michael's two-and-a-half-year-old son, Cameron, a striped-sweater presence in this evening's formal family portrait. The photograph was taken in the Red Room, before the family fanned out to their various Inaugural balls, and it glows with a common desire to restore harmony. Even the less public figures—Neil Reagan and Bess, Nancy's half brother Richard and his wife and two children, Maureen's fiancé Dennis Revell, Michael's wife Colleen—exude bonhomie, as well they might in a house so beautiful, so hushed and safe, so appropriately perfumed with the scent of narcissus.

The President looks splendid, of course, towering over his sons and daughters with an air of entitlement, as if he has stood here for years. Yet his hands clearly want to reach forward and grasp the slender shoulders of his wife, who sits at center frame, in the ringed center of the carpet, at the center of this tall-columned house, at the focal point of Ronald Reagan's new universe.

Through the small hours, as Washington's new élite celebrated around town, a band of bums (not yet euphemized as "homeless") camped out in Lafayette Square, jeering the stretched limousines that cruised past 1600 Pennsylvania Avenue. The most vocal among them, unlovely, unkempt, yet somehow magnetic, was one "Mitch" Snyder, determined to remind the world that Reagan populism did not extend down to those Americans who lived, quite literally, at the grass roots.

"The inaugural was an emotional experience," the President wrote in his newly cracked, leather-bound private diary, "but then the very next day it was 'down to work.' "

January 21, 1981, was indeed no holiday: his Cabinet had to be sworn in at 9:30 A.M., while the rest of his bleary appointees had to commence the executive business of the United States, as if every desk and telephone had not been manned, twenty-four hours before, by Carter staffers.

Fortunately, the Reagan Administration was already the beneficiary of the most conscientious transition in White House history. An advance planning team headed by Edwin Meese III had set the agenda (item number one: a freeze on all federal hiring) by dividing four hundred experts into fifty different policy task forces. Work on Cabinet appointments had begun even before Reagan's nomination. After his election, he had made clear that he wanted a complete reform of the executive branch of government, not to mention a realignment of the judiciary, and a quick cementing of relations with the new Republican Senate leadership. He had insisted on a choice of three candidates for every major office at his disposal.

One appointment, at least, would have seemed a foregone conclusion: that of Meese as Chief of Staff. Not only had "Honest Ed" served Reagan in the same capacity in Sacramento, he had fought in all his campaigns and, over the course of thirteen years, become ideologically indistinguishable from him. Meese had the same genial courtliness, the same law-and-order conservativism and waterproof inability to absorb bad news. Yale-educated, a lucid and forceful public speaker, he could be relied on to articulate the President's beliefs better than any press secretary. What was more, he was a born bureaucrat, who doodled personnel charts the way electronical engineers plot circuitry.

For these reasons, Meese had emerged as the likely manager of the Reagan White House. But savvy observers doubted he would succeed in Washington. He was too unyielding, too doctrinaire, too professorial with reporters. Alarmingly, he liked sweet sherry. He laughed out of courtesy rather than amusement, while his unctuous manner did not conceal the fact that he was dismissive of women. At forty-nine, his plump, pink, freshly scrubbed look grated on Nancy Reagan, who disliked fat people. More serious, as far as the President-elect was concerned, was Meese's disorganized manner (so at odds with his love of procedure), and the way he treated his briefcase as a sort of portable document compactor.

Reagan, who could be ruthless when necessary, had devastated him by pointing at the box marked "Chief of Staff" on the chart and saying that it would be filled by the name of James A. Baker III, George Bush's former campaign manager. Meese was partly consoled with a new, free-floating box all to himself, labeled "Counselor to the President." It came with a guarantee of direct Oval Office access and, even more gratifying, a seat in the Cabinet.

Baker did not have the latter perquisite, but he managed to secure the second biggest office in the West Wing, plus control over every document intended for the President's eyes. Meese, used to dealing with Reagan *viva voce,* did not at first realize that paper, in ultra-procedural Washington, was power. A broken line marked *appointments and paper flow* was typed onto the chart between his box and Baker's, meaning he would never be able to get Reagan to hire anybody or sign anything unless he persuaded the Chief first.

It also meant—this deceptively delicate-looking string of dots, a mere fifty-three keyboard strokes—that the core conservatives who had groomed, supported, and financed Ronald Reagan's political career for the last seventeen years must now cede their influence to a sleek Washington strategist whose loyalty was unproven. Yet such men could not help being impressed by James Baker. He combined the poise of Princeton with, on calculated occasions, the *huevos*-grabbing aggression of a Houston oil lawyer. Fifty years old, he was handsome in a polished-brow, boardroom-portrait sort of way, matching both his ties and ideology to current fashion and rating "A" at the best Georgetown dinner parties. (One couldn't, somehow, imagine Honest Ed swapping Eurochat with Pamela Harriman.) He moved easily among editors and lawmakers, all of whom he cultivated with the skill of a born deal-maker. The former went away sluiced with judicious leaks, the latter, with legislative promises, and both rewarded Baker with little increments to his power. Personally, he was relaxed, witty, unchauvinistic, and about as self-revealing as a CIA agent. He rarely needed more than thirty seconds to make any point, talking in a steady Texas twang. The dowagers who dined him might have been surprised to know that he was just as comfortable chewing plug and talking trash with rough guys in rough country. In fact, Baker's need for frequent such expeditions was an indication of how much of his real personality was suppressed during the work week. Another indication was his temper. Provoked, he would redden and spout obscenities in his unpleasantly throaty voice, until he resembled one of the wild turkeys he hunted each fall. Predictably, he was a beer-out-of-the-can man.

The third member of Reagan's ruling troika was the most subtle and unpredictable. If Meese was policy-maker and Baker was manager, forty-one-year-old Michael Deaver was the complete servant, subsuming his whole life into that of his employer. "You know, I *am* Ronald Reagan. . . . Every morning after I get up I make believe I am him and ask what he should do and where he should go." He could accurately claim to have saved the Lifeguard's life, having once wrestled him into a Heimlich maneuver to dislodge peanuts from his windpipe. The experience only reinforced Deaver's sense of their mutual identity. His peculiar power as Deputy Chief of Staff derived from the fact that he was also the agent, comforter, and confidant of Mrs. Reagan. Her countless telephone calls did not faze him, and he was sharp and quick in undercutting people she disliked. She used him to transmit bad news on behalf of the President, which he did with a nonchalance ("Dan, about that embassy: chances of your getting it are pretty slim") that hurt more than deliberate cruelty. He was a virtuoso gossip and a dryly amusing joke-teller. Unlike Meese and Baker, Deaver had some aesthetic sense, primarily in the areas of fashion and flowers. He played cocktail piano, grew gingko trees, and drank fine California wines.

Deaver's casual style gave the impression he cared little about governance. On the contrary, he was an astute analyst, and quite capable of tantrums on points of policy. But his particular talent—evident in the reoriented Inaugural ceremony—was for the Hollywood-style *production* of power: statesmanship rendered as drama. This was why he had Reagan's particular respect, and why, of the troika members, he was the least dispensable.

As the new Administration cranked into action, strains gradually became apparent between its dogmatists and its pragmatists, or, to use their own wry distinction, between the Californians and the Washingtonians. Meese and two other Sacramento stalwarts, Defense Secretary

Caspar Weinberger and Assistant Secretary of State William P. Clark, Jr. (reluctantly descended from a seat on the California Supreme Court), had to contend with Baker and Deaver for policy control. A pair of astute, ill-dressed strategists joined in the struggle: on the right, Political Affairs Director Lyn Nofziger, and on the liberal left, Staff Secretary Richard Darman, arguably, and often demonstrably, the brightest young man in the White House.

David A. Stockman, Director of the Office of Management and Budget, was another such prodigy, tensely self-aware, professedly an "intellectual." Unmarried and monkish at thirty-four, he loved numbers so much that he actually read the federal budget line by line, the way Nofziger read Louis L'Amour. Nobody questioned his temporary preeminence as the Cabinet's most vital member. Even Secretary of State Alexander M. Haig, Jr., had to accept that foreign policy was of less concern, in January 1981, than the American economy's accelerating slide toward recession. The last posted prime rate had hit a terrifying 21.5 percent, President Carter had left behind a deficit of fifty-eight billion dollars, and the national debt was about to top a trillion. Emergency fiscal legislation had to be coaxed out of Congress, and Stockman, one of the House's most articulate tax reformers before taking over the OMB, presumably knew how to do that. As a reputed computational genius, he was the only man around who might manage to translate Reagan's quadruple campaign promise—a sharply lowered tax rate, a huge increase in defense spending, reduced inflation, and a stripped-down, balanced budget—into a formulation that made mathematical sense. And as a born-again economic conservative (who had once flirted with Marxism), he professed confidence that the free market would supply whatever corrective forces were necessary if the welfare state, by some miracle, began to dismantle itself under Ronald Reagan.

"This was the big night," Reagan wrote in his diary on February 18, 1981, after addressing a joint session of Congress for the first time. "I've seen Presidents over the years enter the House chamber without ever thinking I would one day be doing it. It was a thrill and something I'll long remember."

His platitudes did not begin to convey the drama of this appearance. After only twenty-nine days in office, he had announced a "Program for Economic Recovery," the most galvanizing executive initiative since Franklin D. Roosevelt's proclamation of the New Deal. Its budget-crushing scope (extended nine days later by further cuts that brought the total to nearly fifty-five billion dollars) was so ambitious, and its "supply-side" economic argument so peculiar, that there was a stunned quality to the bursts of applause that Reagan effortlessly drew from his audience. The feeling of Keynesian surrender was reinforced within forty-eight hours by a *Washington Post*–ABC poll that showed that two out of every three Americans wanted what the President wanted, whether his proposals made economic sense or not.

Reagan's program amounted to a full, $695 billion "white paper" federal budget for the fiscal year beginning in October. Its specific numbers—eighty-three major programs cut; only defense to be increased, by $7.2 billion; a 30 percent tax cut for individuals over the next three years—worried realists much less than its overall presumption that less revenue now would mean more revenue later, while poor people and artists suffered and the Pentagon became a second Fort Knox. Neglected, somehow, was the gnawing fact that the 15 percent of GNP currently spent on inherited domestic programs would have to be reduced to 9 percent, in order to offset rearmament and an impoverished Internal Revenue Service. Powerful Republicans on Capitol Hill could not see how such a budget could be translated into legislation. Representative Barber Conable publicly guaranteed that any bill to reduce taxes by a third would fail to pass. Senator Robert Dole condescendingly remarked that the President would be better advised to negotiate some more modest cuts with his own Finance Committee.

These announcements, however, were as pine trees before the avalanche of the Administration's will, backed as it was by a huge electoral mandate, concentrated to the exclusion of anything non-budgetary, and piling up so fast that Reagan was able to send his formal legislative proposals to Congress on March 10, 1981, just forty-nine days after taking office.

"Everywhere we look in the world, the cult of the state is dying," Reagan remarked to his first important foreign guest, Prime Minister Margaret Thatcher of Great Britain. Their reunion had been scheduled as a top priority so that liberals everywhere would understand that free-enterprise capitalism was back. Privately, Mrs. Thatcher had to confess that she wished she had been as bold as he in demanding "an entire package—all or nothing" from her own ministers. But the President was heartened by her determination to stand with him in what they both perceived would be a propaganda war against Soviet Communism, should Congress approve his mammoth defense budget.

Evidently, ordinary Americans did. Supportive mail poured into the White House in quantities that Reagan did not fail to mention in meetings with Congressional leaders. On March 13, he was surprised and moved to find that New Yorkers, of all people, cared about him enough to cheer his motorcade all the way from Wall Street to the Waldorf-Astoria. He had not yet gotten used to the ubiquity of applause wherever he went, and admitted in his diary that it humbled him. "This warmth and affection seems so genuine I get a lump in my throat. I pray constantly that I won't let them down."

Capitalizing to the full on his popular momentum, he personally lobbied hundreds of Congressmen and opinion-makers. They were seduced less by his arguments (he clearly had no command of budgetary detail) than by his extraordinary personal charm and humor. Whatever the occasion, no matter how tense the power play behind it, Reagan's jokes were always relevant to the conversation, perfectly timed and aimed. One of the most irresistible photographs ever to come out of the White House shows him, glass in hand, convulsing Walter Cronkite and Burton Benjamin, vice president of CBS News, outside the Oval Office on March 3. A group of senior aides stands around, laughing too, aware even as they do so that the Gipper has lined up another pair of useful allies.

For the rest of that month, while David Stockman frenziedly tried to keep his virgin budget from being raped by protectionists and pork merchants, Ronald Reagan continued to enjoy himself as President. The job suited him better than any he had ever had, with its flawless scheduling, variety of interests, frequent opportunities to perform, and sense of huge purpose. To see Ed Meese and Mike Deaver every morning, and hear Helene von Damm's guttural voice in his outer office ("I vill make sure President Rheagan gets your massage") was to be pleasantly reminded of Sacramento days. Gratifying, too, was the almost constant proximity of Nancy, her world of the East Wing and upper White House quarters contiguous to his own.

Like many aging men, he loved routine. At two or three minutes before 9 A.M., he would emerge from his private elevator in the Residence, impeccably dressed and giving off discreet waves of cologne. David Fischer, his personal aide, would be waiting to escort him along the colonnade, armed with the latest edition of his schedule and whatever verbal elaborations seemed necessary. As they rounded the corner of the Rose Garden, Reagan's attention would always divert to the window of Helene's office, on which he liked to tap good morning. Promptly at nine he would enter the Oval Office through its French door and find the troika waiting for him. This "Senior Staff time with the President"

"They were seduced . . . by his extraordinary personal charm and humor."
The President with (left to right) Walter Cronkite, James Brady,
Burton Benjamin (foreground), David Gergen, Edwin Meese,
George Bush, and James Baker, March 3, 1981.

lasted a quarter of an hour (Baker always on the alert to head off excessive input from Meese), and was followed by another quarter hour's briefing by National Security Adviser Richard Allen. The troika would generally stay in the room until Allen was through, then stay with the President if he needed them further. From ten to eleven he absorbed himself in paperwork sent to him by Darman. Then, according to the day of the week, he met with Congressional leaders or the National Security Council until the noon lunch hour.

"The President prefers to eat alone," cautioned a White House memo. He was denied that respite on Mondays, when senior staffers gathered to discuss "any 'hot' items that should be brought to [his] attention," and on Thursdays, when he entertained George Bush in his private dining room off the Oval Office. (I have no record of what they talked about early in the first Administration, but can attest that their later lunches were enlivened by uproariously obscene jokes.)

Except for the occasional hamburger, Reagan ate sparingly: usually just soup and crackers, and Jell-O for dessert, with iced tea. He sat at his table as he did at his desk, always with his coat on and his tie tight.

Although he was by no means a dandy, and had a weekend wardrobe that may best be described as cheerful, he believed that a President should look like a President, and not "dress down" the office of Jefferson and Lincoln.

At 2 P.M. on Tuesdays and Thursdays, an hour of "Cabinet time" was reserved, but not always used. Departmental heads unfamiliar with the President's executive style learned that he preferred them to work at their jobs, rather than intrude upon his own.

He always looked forward to Wednesday afternoons, those being classified as "Private Time" and generally assigned to the Residence. His eager retreat there at 2 P.M. (5 P.M. sharp on other weekdays), plus his well-known need for eight or nine hours sleep a night, gave rise to the myth that Ronald Reagan was a lazy man. This was true only in the sense that he lacked intellectual energy: he had long since abandoned inquiry for the reiteration of old certainties. But the journalists who joked about his clock-watching were unaware that he always took home whatever work he could not finish during the day. Faithfully, after dinner, he would read through the last page of every colored folder (red for Classified, green for Action Items, gray for Speeches and Statements, blue for Information), checking what he approved and adding terse marginalia until duty was done and he could go to bed. Richard Darman learned not to give the President more than one and a half hours of work a night, knowing that if he did, Reagan would be tired and withdrawn the following morning.

Like Eisenhower before him, Reagan let people think what they wanted to think about his habits, while he kept his motives to himself. He was aware that somehow, in spite of his alleged indolence, he had gotten himself the world's top job, and seemed to be handling it better, so far, than the workaholic Jimmy Carter. So he worked at his own steady speed, taking what rest he needed and exercising, as he had done all his life, with patient regularity.

That meant evening sessions with bars and weights and wheels before he showered for dinner. If he and Nancy were going out (which they loved to do: the Reagans were among Washington's most reliable accepters of elegant invitations), he would dab on more Brylcreem and slip into one of his custom-made dress suits. Otherwise, it was bushy hair and pajamas in front of the television set, and desk time afterward in his private study.

Entertainment remained an essential part of his life, and the blander the better. Most sitcoms were too slick for his taste; he preferred news programs and serious magazine shows like *60 Minutes*. But his soul really craved the kind of movies he used to act in himself, where sex was implicit, crime did not pay, and tall, strong men gave freckled kids fatherly advice. He and Nancy would watch two or three such pictures every weekend, always with popcorn.

Shyness, more than apathy, kept Reagan away from public worship. He had always considered prayer to be a private business, and did not care to be stared at while he sang hymns. Nor did he want his huge retinue of guards and advance men to disturb the peace of churches around town. Whatever spiritual counsel he needed he got from silent colloquies, usually at an open window, with "the Man Upstairs"—that being his usual coy substitute for the Holy Name. (Although he could cuss as well as James Baker in male company, he never blasphemed. Neither would he write profane words without the careful insertion of hyphens: *h--l, d--n, d---l.*)

His diaries avoided spiritual or metaphysical speculation, and on the rare occasions he alluded to the mortal dangers of high office, he did so as obliquely as possible. Thus, the following remark, written after his first visit to Ford's Theatre late that month: "There is a definite feeling when you see the flag-draped Presidential Box where Booth shot Lincoln."

On March 30, Ronald Reagan's schedule called for him to return to the hotel where, seventy days before, he had clicked his heels and saluted himself as President of the United States. He had a speech to deliver after lunch to the Building Trades Council of the AFL-CIO. Without knowing why—some instinct against offending blue-collar sensibilities, perhaps?—he took off his usual Corum gold watch, and exchanged it for one that was older and cheaper.

Helene von Damm saw him off at 1:45 P.M.—he gave her a cheerful thumbs-up—and returned sluggishly to her desk. For some reason, her alarm clock had gone off at four that morning, and she had not been able to get back to sleep. The whole West Wing seemed nervous, shrilling with other bells. A journalist had published its private telephone directory, and the normally hushed corridors were permeated with a sense of invasion.

Reagan's speech at the Washington Hilton was an uninspired appeal for support of his budget proposals. He got just enough applause to satisfy him, and left the hotel at 2:25 P.M., stepping through a side door into gray, damp afternoon light. The usual retinue accompanied him: his doctor, a senior aide (Michael Deaver), three or four Secret Service agents, and James Brady, Press Secretary to the President, a fuzzy bear of a man loping a yard or two behind. The usual motorcade awaited in the hotel's curveway, not more than thirteen feet ahead, engines humming; the usual little knot of press and onlookers stood to his left, restrained by the usual cops.

What was not usual was a fluttering, cracking noise in the crowd as he raised his arm to wave. Suddenly everyone around him was moving and swaying and falling. A force like a battering ram shoved him forward, and he found himself hurtling through the open door of the presidential limousine. (He thought he caught a glimpse, as he passed the window, of a blond bystander crouched in police-pistol style, spraying bullets: two zinged against the metal and bulletproof glass around him.) He hit his head on the doorjamb and fell onto the car's transmission hump, so violently that his upper back was almost paralyzed with pain. "Haul ass!" a voice in his ear shouted. "Let's get out of here!"

Now it was the car that was moving, accelerating down the slope of Connecticut Avenue back toward the White House. The way was clear, because the avenue was already cordoned off. In seconds they were traveling at sixty miles an hour. The rest of the motorcade followed, sirens screaming. Reagan realized that the heavy body lying on him was that of Jerry Parr, his White House security chief and a former member of Brass Bancroft's Junior Secret Service Club.

"Jerry, get off, I think you've broken one of my ribs," he managed to say, but then pain choked his voice, and blood began to cough from his lungs. He assumed, as did Parr, that he had spiked himself internally. Neither of them yet knew that six bullets fired in less than two seconds had hit four people outside the Hilton; that James Brady was on the sidewalk with a shattered skull; and that one of the bullets was now lying within an inch of Reagan's heart. It was a .22 "Devastator," designed to explode on impact. Missing flesh at first, the slug had hit his car's armored right-rear panel and forged itself into a tiny, high-speed circular saw blade, spinning into his chest with such surgical precision that Parr, feeling him all over, detected no sign of entry.

"Rawhide not hurt," Parr radioed to an agent in the car behind, using the President's code name. He was deliberately lying, to mislead eavesdroppers on the Secret Service frequency. "Let's hustle," he added, hoping that his colleague would sense that Rawhide was, on the contrary, hurt quite badly. The blood Parr saw, bright and frothy, frightened him enough to redirect the motorcade along Seventeenth Street,

then west to George Washington University Hospital. It plunged
through uncontrolled traffic, miraculously reaching the clinic in just
three and a half minutes. By general medical consent, Parr's decision to
divert saved the life of the President of the United States.

Reagan, ashen-faced, was by now having difficulty breathing. He
made himself get out and walk toward the emergency-room door. Parr
offered no help, sensing that it was important to him to cover the fifteen
yards alone. Just inside, out of public sight, the President's knees buck-
led and his eyes rolled up.

He remained conscious enough to feel himself being caught up, carried, laid on a cart, and stripped. His lungs could not take in enough
air; he was afraid of suffocating. A voice cried, "Let's get some oxygen
into him." He could not move under the mask they clamped on his face.
His vision tunneled: all he could see above the mask's bulge was a white
tiled ceiling. He did not know that he was losing blood internally, at
such a rate that his systolic pressure dropped by half. Yet his obstinate
heart continued to beat, lowering the pressure still further, until his
brain was at the point of drought.

By now it was clear that one intravenous line was not going to be
enough to save his life: packed red-blood cells and fluid would have to
be sloshed into him through three more venous lines that were not so
much conduits as canals. Only when a nurse lifted his left arm to insert
one did the neat slit on the side of his chest manifest itself. "Oh-oh, he's
been shot."

She remembered this as a thought rather than a remark, yet Reagan
somehow absorbed it and, half dead, half enraged, remembered the
crouching, shooting figure he had glimpsed through the car door.

I focused on that tiled ceiling and prayed. But I realized I couldn't
ask for God's help while at the same time I felt hatred for the mixed
up young man who had shot me. Isn't that the meaning of the lost
sheep? We are all God's children and therefore equally beloved by
him. I began to pray for his soul and that he would find his way back
into the fold.

I opened my eyes to find Nancy there. I pray I'll never face a day
when she isn't there. In all the ways God has blessed me, giving her to
me is the greatest and beyond anything I can ever hope to deserve.

℮

Earlier, when the white phone rang on the emergency-room desk,
signifying a White House "extreme response" alert, a voice had said,

without elaboration, "The Presidential motorcade is en route to your facility." Reagan's car had arrived so quickly that the sound of beepers paging senior staff physicians mixed with the wail of sirens outside. Trauma teams had one fully equipped bay ready for the President, while another was set up for James Brady, coming separately by ambulance. Yet another awaited Timothy McCarthy, a Secret Service agent shot in the chest. Walkie-talkie messages advised that the blond bystander's fourth victim, a Washington policeman, was being treated elsewhere for a bullet to the spine.

All of this urgency built up into a sort of audiovisual montage around Reagan, more multilayered than he could register. Compounding it was a huge influx of agents from the White House and the FBI, many of them waving guns. Jerry Parr blocked off a protective "perimeter" around the emergency area, while waves of panic and grief eddied outward into the drizzle. The Department of Defense sent out a worldwide advisory, raising crisis readiness one notch. Live footage of the shootings began to play on television. Michael Deaver, who had nearly been shot himself, tried to calm James Baker on the phone ("It looks like the President has been nicked"), but came close to fainting when he saw Brady being wheeled by, open-headed.

In the West Wing of the White House, Richard Darman watched Baker take Deaver's call, saw his pen scratch out *P hit/fighting,* and noted the time: 2:40 P.M. Elsewhere, staff huddled round monitors, weeping. They did not yet know that the President was wounded, but Helene von Damm saw enough of James Brady's blood and brains to retire to a bathroom, where she vomited fit to rupture herself. All across the country, citizens sat dumb with shock in front of their television sets, staring at the loop-like replays of Ronald Reagan waving, suddenly losing his smile, and being hustled offscreen.

Most chilling of all was the random accuracy of John Hinckley, Jr.'s bullets. Four men mown down in less than two seconds by a person impossible to see either before or after the chattering explosions; rain; ricochets; a mad scrimmage; yet within all the chaos, an accidental geometry so precise as to bring Reagan to the edge of death. *Let A–B, passing between plane 1 and parabola 2, intersect with L–M at (x)* . . . We had no idea how close the President actually came to dying that afternoon. His blood loss of 3.7 quarts—well over half his total supply—was at first given as only 2.5 quarts, and not adjusted upward for another two days.

Joseph Giordano, head of the ER trauma team, inserted a chest tube to relieve the pressure in Reagan's pleural cavity. But blood continued to gush. An X-ray showed the Devastator floating palely behind the heart shadow. Or was it actually *in* it? At first, not even Dr. Benjamin Aaron, the hospital's senior thoracic surgeon, could tell. He inferred, however, that the bullet had been deflected by a rib and "expressed" through some major vascular structure. It would have to be removed to stop the bleeding, which was now a steady and lethal 300 cc. per quarter hour. That meant an immediate thoracotomy. After fifty minutes in the trauma unit, the President was wheeled to Operating Room 2, Nancy holding his hand.

Notwithstanding his failure to remember the ensuing hours, he was already coming back from the edge, with systolic pressure reverted to 120 and, incredibly, his wit intact. The little jokes Ronald Reagan perpetrated, through blood-caked lips, before lapsing into unconsciousness have become part of American legend: "Honey, I forgot to duck," "Who's minding the store?" and—to a solemn company costumed in surgical greens—"Please tell me you're Republicans."

It was entirely in his actor's character that the third and best of these cracks was delivered as he entered a theater.

The operation, beginning at 3:24 P.M., was not easy. "It took me forty minutes to get through that chest," Dr. Aaron told Deaver. "I have never in my life seen a chest like that on a man his age." Another quarter hour was spent feeling for the bullet, which lay so deep in lung tissue that it had to be tracked with a catheter and squeezed out like a tiddleywink. Bleeding soon stopped. The President's chest was closed at 5:20 P.M. He had "sailed through" surgery, the hospital announced, and was an "excellent physical specimen."

Reagan's recovery, unlike that of the brain-damaged Brady, was instantaneous. (News of the other victims was kept from him, to avoid complicating his emotions.) Regaining consciousness at 7:30, he was unable to continue joking aloud, because tubes crammed his nose and throat. So he reverted to weak scribbles on pink paper:

> *I am aren't alive aren't I? [sic]*
> *Did they get the guy?*
> *I'd like to do this scene again—starting at the hotel*

and,

> *Winston Churchill said that there is no more exhilarating feeling than being shot at without result.*

He was able to speak again when Meese, Baker, and Deaver visited him the following morning, March 31—"I should have known I wasn't going to avoid a staff meeting"—and he signed a bill they had brought, to demonstrate that he still was President of the United States. Four nights after the operation, however, Reagan developed a mysterious fever, and on April 4 began to bring up fresh blood. Renewed terror spread through the West Wing: his doctors could not diagnose what was wrong. He proceeded to heal himself, with the help of broad-spectrum antibiotics, over the course of the next week. On April 11, the President was well enough to walk out of the hospital on his wife's arm, with Jerry Parr again behind him, as nurses clapped and cried. The entire White House staff was waiting for him in the Rose Garden, under light spring rain. Seeing them, he lifted his left arm in the same gesture that had incited John W. Hinckley, Jr., twelve days before, to shoot him.

"I know it's going to be a long recovery," he wrote on his first evening back in the White House. "Whatever happens now I owe my life to God and will try to serve him every way I can."

A few days later, I wrote a letter to *The New York Times*:

> Analysts drawing parallels between the recent attack on President Reagan and those on nine of his predecessors have not yet mentioned its even more remarkable similarity to the attempted assassination of Theodore Roosevelt in 1912.
>
> The former President, campaigning for a third term in the White House, emerged from his Milwaukee hotel and waved genially at the crowd as he prepared to enter his automobile. Just then a blond, pudgy, dull-eyed person elbowed out into the open and shot TR point-blank in the chest.
>
> The bullet entered just below the nipple, ricocheted off a rib, and stopped within inches of his heart. Aides and policemen wrestled the attacker to the sidewalk, and TR, not at first realizing he had been hit, was driven off at high speed. He insisted on making a scheduled address downtown before walking unaided, with bloody shirtfront, into Emergency Hospital.
>
> Despite momentary faintness, he reassured his wife that the wound was "trivial" and joked with physicians on the operating table. Subsequent bulletins praised his "placid" nerves and "magnificent physical condition."

If nothing else, such a precedent should reassure us that psychotics know no time frame, and that if our best and bravest men continue to lead us, this Republic will somehow prevail.

During the days that followed, Reagan was buoyed by a predictable landslide of get-well mail, and the White House correspondence office, making a selection to send over to him, paid particular attention to postcards addressing him as "Dutch." These were sure to be from the kind of people he needed to hear from at present. I would guess that this misspelled one, in an elderly woman's trembly handwriting, spoke to him as encouragingly as any other:

> *Dear Mr. President Duch Reagan* . . . I met you in the 20s in Lowell Park Ill. Do you remember the good times we had in the 20s—you were 17 years old then and every one cald you *Duch*. . . . Please please get well soon. We need you to save the Country—remember all the lifes you saved in Lowell Park.

"The kind of people he needed to hear from at present."
Dixon, Illinois, wishes the President well.

29

Back into
the Iron Vest

A IDES CONDITIONED to thinking of Ronald Reagan as ageless were
dismayed to find him definitely a septuagenarian when they went
to visit him in mid-April 1981. Apart from the debilitating effects of
surgery and fever, he had traded half of his own fresh blood for the
staler, cooler contributions of strangers—a major physiological insult
from which he would never entirely recover. His face seemed to have
collapsed, his eyes were melancholy, his hearing noticeably worse.
Chest "splints" stabbed him when he tried to take deep breaths. A
strange respirational device lay at his elbow.

On Good Friday, April 17, he suddenly expressed a desire to "talk to
a minister." Michael Deaver, a former seminary candidate, sensed that
this was not an occasion to phone for the usual hearty Baptist. Reagan
was obviously perplexed at having been "spared." He needed to have
the mystery of earthly salvation spelled out to him at the highest spiritual level. Deaver called the Archdiocese of New York and asked if
there was any chance that Terence Cardinal Cooke could make a quick
shuttle trip to Washington. "The President wants very much to spend
some time with him."

The upshot—less of a visit than a visitation—ended with the President telling the Cardinal, upstairs in the White House: "I have decided that whatever time I have left is left for Him."

☯

Which meant, among other things, a coming to terms with Evil. Not the accidental evil (actually a perverted search for love) of John Hinckley's assault, but that institutional murder of all liberties known as Soviet Communism. Reagan had hated it for thirty-five years, on the simple grounds that it was not accidental but ideological: a doctrine perfected by a cynical minority to enslave—i.e., enforce labor from, and deny self-determination to—a terrorized majority. Almost as much, he hated the reciprocal doctrine of détente, by which the Western world allowed the enslavement to continue, in the callow hope that Soviet Communism might contain itself. Demonstrably, since the invasion of Czechoslovakia in 1968, General Secretary Leonid Brezhnev had flouted that understanding, crushing patriots under his tanks, threatening to do the same with pro-democracy trade unionists in Poland, aiding Marxist insurrections in Angola, North Africa, and Nicaragua, and "liberating" Afghanistan from its own citizens—all the while arming Cuba and treating three successive American Presidents to black-browed tirades against American "imperialism."

Ronald Reagan had just as demonstrably, over the same period, made plain his intent not to be the fourth President so cowed. He had always believed (like George Washington and Theodore Roosevelt before him) that the surest way to negotiate peace was to build up a massive military endowment. In 1968, he had inveighed against Lyndon Johnson's policy of "appeasement," and later called for a "threat of force" at the Paris peace talks. As early as 1976 he had confidently asserted that the Soviet Union would never be able to afford an accelerated arms race. "The Russians know they can't match us industrially or technologically." His only complaint after losing to Gerald Ford had been that he could not now sit across a summit table from Brezhnev and refuse to make any arms-limitation concessions. "I sure would like to have said *nyet* to him." In 1978, he had echoed Alexander Solzhenitsyn's apocalyptic warning that the West was losing its moral courage.

Anti-Communism had been a major theme of Reagan's 1980 campaign against Jimmy Carter (who since kissing Brezhnev in 1979 had suffered agonies of unrequited brotherly love). And this year Reagan had waited no longer than his first press conference before assuring reporters that the days of polite East-West dialogue were over:

> So far, détente's been a one-way street the Soviet Union has used to pursue its own aims. . . . I know of no leader of the Soviet Union since the revolution, and including the present leadership, that has not more than once repeated . . . that their goal must be the promotion of world revolution and a one-world Socialist or Communist state. . . .
>
> The only morality they recognize is what will further their cause, meaning they reserve unto themselves the right to commit any crime: to lie, to cheat, in order to attain that. . . . I think when you do business with them, even at a détente, you keep that in mind.

"How is he going to do business with us?" the bewildered Soviet Ambassador asked Secretary of State Haig. After nearly twenty years in Washington, Anatoly Dobrynin had never heard such language from the White House. He wondered if Reagan's "extremely hostile" remarks were intended to set the tone for future relations with Moscow.

"I'll ask the President," said Haig.

That exchange had occurred in January, only nine days after the Inauguration, and Reagan's private reply to Dobrynin, conveyed by Haig, had been as unequivocal as his public statement: there was "a new realism" in Washington regarding Soviet interventionism, and until the Red Army stopped massing along vulnerable borders (most recently and threateningly, around Poland), Moscow could expect "more of the same."

Now it was spring, and a very different President sat in the White House solarium on April 18, soaking up sun, looking out at the Mall and monuments through windows boxed with daffodils. Lent was at an end; the White House lawns were being readied for tomorrow's eggrolling. As in 1947, when he had nearly died of pneumonia, he rejoiced in the beauty of the world. Except now he was more aware of its fragility. Even before he had been shot, his thoughts had turned, suddenly and apropos of nothing, to the "madness" of MAD, or Mutually Assured Destruction—Robert McNamara's quaint assumption that Armageddon could be prevented by the threat of Armageddon.

He wondered how to begin a dialogue with Leonid Brezhnev, who, according to intelligence reports, was almost as weak as himself, ailing with arteriosclerosis, and possessed perhaps with similar thoughts of mortality. The Russian leader was not a stranger to him. They had met once before, during his Governorship. A June day in 1973; the Western

White House at San Clemente . . . Reagan's old urge to write possessed him, and he got out a yellow pad. The result, proudly clipped to his diary that night (and carefully detached from it by later hands) was a draft letter to Brezhnev, asserting that all human beings had certain basic beliefs, and should be allowed to exercise them. "Don't know whether I'll send it," he wrote alongside, "but enjoyed putting some thoughts down on paper."

With that, he resigned it to the editorship of "the striped pants set" in the State Department. So far he was not impressed with Al Haig's vast bureaucracy, least of all with Haig himself as bureaucrat-in-chief. The handsome, high-maintenance general was forever demanding more, or clearer, paper authority over paper threats from elsewhere in the Administration. Apparently that mild paranoia also extended to yellow paper stamped with the presidential seal. But gratifyingly, the revised draft that came back on April 22 preserved most of his original language. Reagan wrote it out again in longhand:

> *Mr. President* . . . I am reminded of our meeting in San Clemente a decade or so ago. I was Governor of California at the time and you were concluding a series of meetings with President Nixon. . . .
>
> When we met I asked you if you were aware that the hopes and aspirations of millions and millions of people throughout the world were dependent on the decisions that would be reached in your meetings.
>
> You took my hand in both of yours and assured me that you were aware of that and that you were dedicated with all your heart and mind to fulfilling those hopes and dreams.
>
> The people of the world still share that hope. . . . They want the dignity of having some control over their individual destiny. They want to work at the craft or trade of their own choosing and to be fairly rewarded. They want to raise their families in peace without harming anyone or suffering harm themselves. Government exists for their convenience, not the other way around. If they are incapable, as some would have us believe, of self-government, then where among them do we find people who are capable of governing others?

This much, at least, State was prepared to tolerate. But Haig, still a military man who disbelieved in unilateral concessions, objected to the sudden goodwill gesture of the letter's final paragraph:

> In the spirit of helping the people of both our nations, I have lifted the grain embargo [imposed by Carter as a sanction against the So-

viet invasion of Afghanistan]. Perhaps this decision . . . will lead to
the meaningful and constructive dialogue which will assist us in fulfilling our joint obligation to find lasting peace.

It seemed to the Secretary that there was a contradiction in this, Reagan's first major diplomatic gesture. Haig acknowledged that lifting the
embargo was "inevitable," given the already severe plight of midwestern farmers (as always, the first to hurt in a recession) and the willingness of other countries to sell grain to Moscow. But he had hoped to
extract some concessions from Moscow, particularly in regard to
Poland, as a fee for opening the American breadbasket.

Reagan heard him out, then ordered him to send the handwritten letter as revised. To soothe Haig, he permitted State to cover it with a
more formal presidential message blustering against "the USSR's un-
remitting and comprehensive military buildup over the past fifteen
years," and postponing any consideration of a superpower summit "to
a later day." He left it to Brezhnev to figure out which letter more truly
conveyed his personal feelings.

The strange device that lay at the recovering President's elbow was a
"Respirex," prescribed to improve his breathing. Rumors went around
that he had been seen sucking at it for extra oxygen. Actually, it was a
pneumatic rig, familiar to pilots, built around a Ping-Pong ball that had
to be kept aloft with breath power. Day after day, he blew into it until
he was dizzy, and sac by sac his damaged lung reinflated. He pushed
himself to do his usual stretching and lifting exercises, and as strength
began to flow back, his power of concentration increased. By April 24,
he was well enough to walk to the West Wing and chair a full Cabinet
meeting. And four days later, live on prime time, he made the most dramatic presidential appearance in Congress since Franklin Roosevelt's
return from Yalta.

The millions watching saw a large and splendid man, literally death-
defying, appear at the threshold of the House as the doorkeeper roared
the traditional "The President of the United States!" All members rose
as required, but their respect on this occasion verged on reverence—
and also signaled a near-helpless capitulation to the message they knew
he was bringing.

"I walked in to an unbelievable ovation that went on for several minutes," he wrote afterward. His speech—a call for one hundred percent
support for his Program for Economic Recovery—was interrupted by

fourteen bursts of applause and three standing ovations. "In the 3rd of these suddenly about 40 Democrats stood and applauded. Maybe we are going to make it. It took a lot of courage for them to do that, and it sent a tingle down my spine."

Not forty but sixty-three Democrats subsequently joined the solid Republican minority, sending Reagan's budget to the Senate with a vote of 253–176. If not quite the total support he had dreamed of, it was a huge victory, and the first official register of his legislative power. As Speaker Tip O'Neill philosophically reminded reporters, Congress was ultimately responsible to the American people, "and the will of the people is to go along with the President."

A May victory, however, is but a skirmish in the two-battle campaign which Congress fights every spring and early summer in exercise of its power to tax and spend. The Administration, overconfident, tried to restructure Social Security—which was clearly spending itself into bankruptcy—and discovered within days that "the will of the people" did not extend so far as to mandate cutting the benefits of retirees. Meanwhile, negotiations on the specifics of budget cuts and tax reduction proceeded with increasing urgency.

After projections, maneuverings, floatings, and retrofirings of almost astronautical complexity, the House on June 29 sent into orbit a final, Rube Goldberg budget so patchily put together that the digits 255-4844, being the telephone number of a young woman in the Congressional Budget Office, were clearly visible among its other figurations.

I tend to remember that particular day in terms of space because I spent it in Dallas, addressing a symposium of teenage achievers along with Commander Alan Shepard of Apollo 14. We were but two of an eclectic list of speakers that also included Tim McCarthy, the Secret Service hero who had interposed his body between the President and John Hinckley's spray of bullets. Another member of our panel was a Harvard astronomer, and over lunch he, Shepard, and I discussed the mysteries of gravitational force fields reordering the cosmos. I cannot say I understood my companions much better than I did David Stockman, explicating something called "Gramm-Latta II" on the nightly news, but at least their conversation related somewhat to flying, and was conducted in English, a language not spoken in the Office of Management and Budget.

The following evening at the symposium's awards dinner, I was seated in alphabetical order between McCarthy and a distinguished-looking person of color named Samuel R. Pierce, Jr., who allowed without visible rancor that he was the only black man in the Reagan Administration. I had heard—as who had not?—the famous story of Dutch greeting him as "Mr. Mayor" and having to be told that Pierce was in fact his Secretary of Housing and Urban Development. Throughout dinner, these celebrated neighbors of mine were pressed for autographs by the teenagers, while I sat undisturbed, musing on the evanescence of literary fame. *The Rise of Theodore Roosevelt* was already more than two years old, a *succès d'estime* but no best-seller, nearly forgotten amid a rush of newer titles.

I asked McCarthy (who got the evening's biggest round of applause when he accepted his award) how Dutch was, and like all security men he was curtly circumspect. "President's just fine, sir. Wish we could say the same of Jim Brady."

"Is he not doing well?"

"Jim's, uh, got a long ways to go," was all McCarthy would say.

That night I lay insomniac, thinking of Brady's fuzzy head lying on the sidewalk like a broken breadfruit as Dutch's limousine sped away. Some lines by Lionel Johnson nudged at memory—

> *Go from me: I am one of those who fall.*
> *What! hath no cold wind swept your heart at all,*
> *In my sad company? Before the end,*
> *Go from me, dear my friend.*

For two years I had managed, thanks to the distraction of my book and the modest publicity it had generated—library lectures, reviews, reader letters—to avoid any emotional involvement in Dutch's apotheosis as President of the United States. Sure, I had wept to see him come back from the dead. But again, who had not? Theodore Roosevelt still loomed as a much more impressive and fascinating figure, good for at least two more volumes: more than enough to round out my late-blooming literary life. However, my extraordinary seating that evening between two of Ronald Reagan's appointees, and a series of other oddly connective experiences recently, gave me momentary pause.

Was it mere coincidence that he had chosen to quote Theodore Roosevelt during his address to Congress? ("The American people are slow to wrath, but when their wrath is kindled, it burns like a consuming flame.") Then there had been a private lunch with his predecessor in New York. Jimmy Carter mentioned Dutch only once in our discussion—a follow-up to some of the narrative suggestions I had given him at Princeton—but I had been chilled by the amount of contempt he could pack into the single word *Reagan*. Next, my wife had signed a contract to write a biography of Clare Boothe Luce, now serving as a member of the President's Foreign Intelligence Advisory Board. Through Mrs. Luce, we had gotten to know Dr. Daniel J. Boorstin, the Librarian of Congress, a forceful advocate of a historian's presence in the White House. Most recently, out of the proverbial blue, had come two invitations to meet the Reagans in person: at a Georgetown lunch for Nancy on July 15, and a state dinner on August 5, honoring President Sadat of Egypt.

Dawn in Dallas finally blanched away my visions of the fallen Brady. I drifted off to sleep, but not before wondering whether some sort of convergence, along the lines of yesterday's astrophysical conversation, was drawing me willy-nilly back toward Dutch.

Diary, Jul. 15, 1981

Lunch with Lucky & Archie Roosevelt & several Georgetown ladies, all tense with excitement at meeting "Rainbow," as the Secret Service refer to Mrs. Reagan.

She comes up the stairs, a small woman perfectly dressed in purple and white. Large-pupiled brown eyes; calm unforced smile. Perhaps a bit *too* calm? Well-bred in a Smith College, Colony Club, Biltmore Circle sort of way. "You must talk to my father, Dr. Loyal Davis," she says to Sylvia, on being introduced. "He was involved in trying to save Henry Luce's life in 1967."

NR is a delightful listener, easy to talk to. Seems a person of no pretensions, other than her frank enjoyment of her husband's power wealth & prestige. Clearly enjoys talking to non-political people, but rarely ventures opinions of her own. When she does they are specious, broken by long, cagey pauses. She tells me that "Ronnie" has read *Rise*. "He's *so* interested in other Presidents." As for Sylvia's last book, "I identify with Edith Roosevelt—she valued her privacy but, uh, certainly knew how to *entertain.*"

Dutch, meanwhile, was preparing for his first major foreign conference—the annual "G7" economic summit, or as the French preferred to call it, "la réunion du Club des pays riches." Actually, he had to fly no farther than Ottawa, since Prime Minister Pierre Elliott Trudeau of

Canada was this year's host. He knew Trudeau and Chancellor Helmut Schmidt of Germany slightly, and Margaret Thatcher somewhat better, but Giovanni Spadolini and Zenko Suzuki, prime ministers respectively of Italy and Japan, were little more than awkward names in his briefing book. As for the nondescript new President of France, whom even Mrs. Thatcher mistook for a doorman, all Reagan cared to know that he was a socialist. But at the opening dinner meeting at Chateau Montebello on July 19, François Mitterrand made everyone round the table realize that a formidable, and staunchly anti-Communistic, statesman was in charge of the world's third nuclear power. Mitterrand's habitually sour expression, which suggested that he was in the habit of sipping neat lime juice, masked a dry, deadly humor and considerable private sensuality, noticeable to anyone who watched him eat. He had by far the fastest mind in the room—less superficial than Trudeau's, more flexible than Mrs. Thatcher's—and he was the only person there equally capable of discussing high interest rates, theology, viticulture, or the drawings of Henry Moore.

As such, he was taken aback by Reagan's intellectual emptiness. Mitterrand came from a country where for centuries conversation had been disciplined and refined into a form of music. The exposition of themes and counterthemes, their development and variation and resolution, were as natural to him as breathing; it was how men and women *d'une certaine éducation* expressed themselves and understood one another. He stared in disbelief when Reagan, sitting beside him, pulled out a pack of typed "talking points" and read from them in a measured voice. There was no doubting the charm of the voice—*chaude, douce, enveloppante, heureuse,* a French aide noted—but it seemed to proceed from some inner recording mechanism, located none too high in the big body.

Mrs. Thatcher tactfully suggested a "free-wheeling discussion," whereupon Reagan, unembarrassed, put away his cards and began to tell stories about his youth as an anti-Communist in California. He recalled a Jesuit priest who had been "trained in Moscow," then sent to Hollywood for the express purpose of infiltrating one of the unions.

"You don't think," Mitterrand suggested, smirking, "that was a huge, rather risky investment for such a trivial posting [*un poste finalement secondaire*]?"

Reagan, sarcasm-proof, was quite sure it had not been.

The following afternoon, during a long discussion of North-South aid, he launched into such a long riff about the necessity to get Mexicans thinking in terms of water hoses rather than watering cans that Suzuki fell asleep and Mrs. Thatcher took out her powder puff. Afterward Mitterrand took Trudeau aside in amazement. "What planet is he living on?"

Trudeau made no attempt to conceal his contempt for Reagan. But Mitterrand, fascinated, studied the President quietly and decided that he liked him, with reservations. "This is a man without ideas and without culture," he told Schmidt. "A sort of liberal, for sure, but beneath the surface you find someone who isn't stupid, who has great good sense and profoundly good intentions. What he does not perceive with his intelligence, he feels by nature."

Of course none of these confidential details came out at the time. I recall only an amusing group portrait of the Big Seven in one of the newsweeklies, photographed a little too soon: Schmidt was hiking up his trousers, Mrs. Thatcher adjusting her hair, Spadolini talking to an aide, while in the middle Dutch stood elegant, posed, and smiling, preternaturally aware that a shutter was already snapping.

For all that, he seemed to collapse on Air Force One back to Washington. His longtime observer and biographer, Lou Cannon, found him "exhausted nearly to the point of incoherence," unable to remember anything about the summit except Mitterrand's hostility to Communism. Sixteen weeks after his near-death experience, Ronald Reagan was not yet the man he had been, and Cannon wondered if he indeed ever would be.

℮

On August 5, my wife and I came down from New York to attend the state dinner. We traveled by train. The President, buoyed by Congress's recent enactment of his tax cut, had just fired more than twelve thousand air-traffic controllers for striking the government in defiance of law. It was an ironic reversal for a former labor leader who prided himself on having led the first strike in the history of the Screen Actors Guild. But as he said, in a remark widely quoted, "Dammit, the law is the law."

The taxi driver taking us to our hotel allowed that the strike and the firings had nearly paralyzed his business. "I'm an old union guy, and lemme tell you, this President don't look like no friend of po' people and black people. But I gotta say, I'm with Reagan on this one. Them controllers took an oath not to strike. He done what he had to do."

Years later, reading Dutch's diaries, I discovered that at the very hour of this conversation, he was informing President Sadat in the Oval Office of his intent to send American warships over the "line" Libya sought to draw in international waters, at 32°30′N across the Gulf of Sidra. He quoted Sadat's "almost shouted" reaction: "*Magnificent!*"

That evening, we approached the same railings I had clung to, fifteen months before, when the White House was remote and unattainable. Now, at the mere flash of a photo ID, its gate swung open. We joined other perfumed couples strolling toward the diplomatic entrance, and the exquisite building grew against the violet sky. I had written in my Roosevelt book of the freedom every American citizen enjoyed to do just this, on days the President chose to be at home; but old records had not begun to convey how good it felt to be received in the heart of democracy, by tradition and by right.

The sounds of a string trio, with harp, floated out as we approached. "Is that Henry Kissinger in front of us?" my wife wanted to know. A naval aide, all starched whites and gold, offered her his arm, and led us past flashing cameras upstairs into the East Room. Here, inevitably, we were announced as "Mr. and Mrs. Edwin Morris" before being abandoned to the wine waiters. Dutch was nowhere to be seen; the great room had not yet filled up. But another Edwin took pity on us. "I'm Ed Meese, counselor to the President," he said. "I guess you know why you're here."

"Not really."

"Because of your books. We politicians do read, you know, heh heh." Meese laughed engagingly, and I revised what I had heard about him. He seemed a sweet, unassuming man, incorruptible, a touch naive. Dutch without the mystery.

"By the way," he confided, "when you meet the President tonight he'll probably tell you we just decided to name our new nuclear aircraft carrier the *Theodore Roosevelt.*"

Guests were being announced thick and fast now. "Senator and Mrs. Howard Baker." "Secretary of State Alexander M. Haig." (A bull-like advance parting the crowd, as if he had just returned from Pamplona.) "Mr. David Stockman." (More like a whippet, pointy-nosed, nervous and trembling.) "Vice President and Mrs. Bush." I was surprised at Bush's bigness and *vigor di vita:* this was not the rumored wimp whom Dutch secretly despised. At last, to a drum roll: "The President of the United States and Mrs. Reagan; President of the Arab Republic of Egypt Anwar el-Sadat and Mrs. Sadat." The Marine band thumped out "Hail to the Chief" and in came Dutch, looking not much older than he had been when I last laid eyes on him, at the Republican National Convention in Kansas City, five years before.

Aides marshaled us into a single-file line as the official party stood in reception formation at the door. A small, darkly intent man crossed the room and tapped me on the shoulder. "Cap Weinberger. Secretary of

Defense. Reviewed your book in the *San Francisco Chronicle.* When you meet the President, he'll probably tell you—" And I heard again about the aircraft carrier.

Dutch loomed up, red-cheeked and twinkling. His handshake was warm and prolonged, but as he launched into his memorized couple of sentences, I felt that the husky voice was pitched just a little louder than it needed to be. He wanted others along the line to hear what he was saying. "Well, now, I want you to be the first to know. We had a meeting this morning about naval appropriations, and we've decided to call our new nuclear carrier—" I tried to register the appropriate surprise and pleasure, but by then he had already turned his attention to my wife.

Meanwhile Nancy was greeting me. "Did Ronnie tell you? Did he?"

President Sadat was very dark and Mrs. Sadat very pale. We moved on down the long corridor to the Executive Dining Room and took our places at Weinberger's table.

I spent the next hour and a half between a female theologian who talked entirely of patristics and a Palm Beach socialite so stiff with jewelry she could hardly lift her wineglass. We ate cold, fresh Columbia River salmon with *sauce verte,* roast quail and wild rice, salad, Brie, and peach mousse. The chardonnays and cabernet sauvignons, all Californian, were excellent. "People don't realize that Ronald Reagan is a real wine buff," Weinberger said. "He and Deaver can talk vintages all night."

I checked Dutch's consumption, but he emptied only half of one of his glasses, and when he stood up to make the toast, contented himself with a mere sip of champagne. His speech was formulaic, except for a gentle jibe at Sadat for being in a cinema on July 22, 1952, when other Egyptian Army officers were bringing off the *coup d'état* that toppled King Farouk. "You wouldn't by chance remember who was in that movie, would you?"

He tossed it off so lightly, with a grin at his guest, that even as we laughed I marveled at his improvisatory gift. Not for another fifteen years, going through his papers, did I notice how carefully he worked at such moments of apparent spontaneity, turning what had been a speechwriter's leaden draft into easy humor:

~~Similarly, I understand that~~ President Sadat, ~~who~~ I know you

struggled many years, ~~playing~~ and played a prominent role in creating

the organization which brought independence to ~~his~~ your country,

~~had taken his family to the movies~~ and then on the night the revolution

began, WERE IN A THEATRE WATCHING A MOVIE WITH YOUR FAMILY. YOU WOULDNT I ~~sure hope it wasn't one of my movies.~~ BY CHANCE REMEMBER WHO WAS IN THAT MOVIE WOULD YOU?

Sadat laughed along with us, his teeth flashing Nubian-white beneath the swart mustache. There were no jokes, however, when he made his return of toast—a long, grim speech reminding the President of his moral duty to recognize the Palestinian Arabs.

The next day, Reagan flew west on vacation. Two items of official business awaited him at Rancho del Cielo: his budget and tax bills, finally ready for signature. Richard Darman, aware that the bills would begin to accumulate darkening deficits the moment Reagan signed them, was sardonically amused to see fog cottoning the valley at the appointed hour, 10:30 A.M., August 13. What had begun eight months before as a radiance of pure numbers in David Stockman's calculator brain had been dulled by so many political IOUs that nobody really knew just how many billions of debit the President was about to visit on the Treasury.

There was no doubt, however, that Reagan and his economic aides had brought about the largest spending-control bill, and the largest tax reduction, in American history. Their budget was revolutionary in that it reversed—or, more properly, inversed—an economic theory dating back to the first days of the New Deal. Hallowed by Franklin Roosevelt, intellectualized by John Maynard Keynes, trumpeted by John Kenneth Galbraith, and codified by the social engineers of the Sixties and Seventies, the theory called for high, progressive tax rates, manipulative government spending, welfare-state "entitlements" centering around Social Security and Medicare/Medicaid, plus forcible downward redistribution of wealth and capital. "Reaganomics"—to use an unavoidable new catchphrase—questioned the wisdom of all these tenets, with the exception of Social Security, by now clearly too much of an article of American faith even to be debated.

Reporters and cameramen gathering for this morning's misty signing ceremony did not know that Stockman was now saying, to the President's face, that Reaganomics was bad math. The equation OMB had been charged with in January (taxes down, defense up, no inflation, no deficit) was simply unworkable, in the face of Congress's rewriting of the spending bill and Secretary Weinberger's absolute refusal to slow the arms buildup—not to mention a standing $300 billion and counting in annual entitlements. Among all the millions of numbers that had been processed through Stockman's computers, the latest was the most depressing: a fiscal 1982 deficit of $60 billion, which recession would only worsen.

There the two bills lay, at any rate, and here in blue jeans came the President to sign them with twenty-four different pens. Stroke by stroke in the mist, Reagan reduced the income-tax burden on individual Americans by almost a third, or $280 billion over the next three years, and saved them a further $130 billion in federal spending. Darman watched with the beginnings of guilt for having let him get so far and presumably understand so little of the negative consequences of what he was doing: farm foreclosures, shut hospitals, dirty schools, dirty air.

Many years later, Darman would list no fewer than ten reasons for the legitimization of Reaganomics, ranging from a disillusionment with tax-and-spend liberalism to brilliant White House liaison work and Congressional confusion. Implicit in his list, but not emphasized enough, was the major cause, surely: the President's own absolute refusal to hear any arguments against deficit spending, no matter how logical or cautionary. Caspar Weinberger was widely perceived as the most stubborn man in the Administration, about as movable as Mount McKinley on questions to do with rearmament. Yet that very immovability enabled tacticians to figure out ways of bypassing him. Reagan was not immovable so much as incommunicable. Instead of countering every argument with a Weinbergian "Nope," he listened but would not hear, or looked at figures and did not see. It was not obstinacy so much as an inability to comprehend the reason that challenges faith. Weinberger denied out of brute conviction; Reagan said "Well..." and shook his head and smiled because he *believed* the way a child believes— ardently and absolutely. He believed in Reaganomics; therefore Reaganomics had to be. God had saved him from death; therefore God wanted him to do the things he had vowed to do.

And so he committed the American economy to eight years of self-compounding deficits, and a trillion-dollar shortfall, greater than the entire debt of the past two centuries. Yet—such is the mad logic of economics—he also initiated the greatest sustained peacetime boom since the founding of the Republic. Since 1982, the general profile of the Dow Jones Industrial Average (plateau-like in the late Sixties and Seventies) has risen like the flank of a mountain whose summit has yet to be seen. As I write in 1998, the zero annual deficit Stockman predicted for 1984 has finally been achieved. Liberals say that corrective taxes are responsible. Moderates praise the Federal Reserve. Conservatives credit the free economy, and note that Reaganism, if not Reaganomics, still determines the political argument. Was it not Reagan *redux* who told Congress in 1996 that "the era of Big Government is over"?

I can only note that what Dutch believed has largely come to be. Across America and Europe, and in huge areas of the world where commerce was once state-controlled, his philosophy of hard work and earned reward has made Marxism a memory. If he had laid down his last pen on August 13, 1981, and said to the press, "Ten years from now, you fellows, there are going to be stock markets in Moscow and Shanghai," guffaws would have filled the valley. But who can doubt that somewhere deep down (as he leaned back in his chair, put one high-heeled boot on the table, and mugged for the cameras), Dutch *believed*?

The photograph that appeared on the front page of *The New York Times* next morning, of a denim-clad President laughing at his boot and his bills, was, I would guess, so foreign to Russian sensibilities that the Kremlin merely tossed it. Moscow was more impressed by a less publicized photograph—of the leader of the air-traffic controllers' union being taken to prison in chains. That, as the Sovietologist Richard Pipes remarked, was the kind of image totalitarians understood. It showed that the President was no mere cowboy, but a sheriff capable of swift hard action.

Had the KGB been able to see Reagan's annotations on memoranda from labor advocates in Congress, pleading for consideration of the union's "legitimate" demands, they would have been even more impressed. Secretary Weinberger could not have more firmly scrawled "Nope," "No," "Can't do," and "No way" in reply. Opposite one warning of "injury to innocent third parties," he wrote serenely, "Innocent 3rd parties are happy." It was a remark that pretty well applied to himself, in the recuperative summer of 1981.

"Magnificent" though the prospect of U.S. Navy exercises in the Gulf of Sidra might have seemed to Anwar el-Sadat, the Libyan leader Colonel Muammar al-Qaddafi was not so pleased. He had succeeded in frightening off Jimmy Carter the year before, and would clearly lose face in the Arab world if he allowed Ronald Reagan to bully him back. No sooner had two advance carrier-based F-14s approached the Libyan coast on August 19 than Qaddafi sent two Soviet-built SU-22s to challenge them. There was a brief armed flurry, and the SU-22s were pulverized by a brace of heat-seeking Sidewinders.

Reagan heard about the encounter from Edwin Meese at 4:28 A.M., Pacific Coast Time, ascertained that no American lives had been lost, and with characteristic equanimity returned to his pillow. Unfortunately, what should have been an upbeat news story became an embarrassment, when reporters found out that Meese had been in full possession of the facts at 11:05 the previous evening, Pacific Coast Time, and thus could have woken the Commander in Chief a good deal earlier. His delay in doing so (while Secretary Weinberger continued to phone in frequent advisories about further U.S. crossings of the Libyan "line") gave the obvious impression that the Administration's number-one priority was to see that Ronald Reagan got plenty of rest.

Within twenty-four hours both counselor and President were being lampooned for irresponsibility. Nobody seemed to remember that McGeorge Bundy had made an exactly similar calculation not to disturb President Kennedy's "badly needed" sleep when a U-2 confirmed the presence of offensive missiles in Cuba. Meese's reputation as an able staff man was badly damaged, and the ascendancy of Baker and Deaver can be dated from that moment. Reagan became "Ron Van Winkle," the laziest President since Calvin Coolidge, proverbially nodding off at Cabinet meetings. Johnny Carson cracked, "There are only two reasons you wake up Ronald Reagan. One is World War III. The other is if *Hellcats of the Navy* is on the late show."

Perhaps the funniest comment on the Gulf of Sidra incident was made by the President himself. Across the top of a letter from a little boy inquiring what he would do in the event of another surprise attack by "Lesbian aircraft," he wrote, "How do we answer this without getting in trouble with an organized minority?"

On September 3, 1981, Reagan returned to Washington and noted resignedly in his diary, "Back into the iron vest." He was referring to the heavy, hated sheath of webbing that the Secret Service now made him wear on public occasions. But "iron vest" could just as well have been a metaphor for the constricting economic arguments in which David Stockman and Caspar Weinberger enmeshed him, as they fought each other over defense expenditures.

The Budget Director urgently felt that corrective measures should be taken before the recession—now palpable everywhere—drove the deficit to $100 billion or more. Stockman no longer made any pretense of believing that balance could be achieved by 1984, or even by 1986, without new economies. Weinberger was equally frank in saying that the deficit was Stockman's problem. *His* only concern was defense, in

view of continuing intelligence about a three-to-one Soviet strategic superiority. If there was to be any debate over budget priorities, he was
for warships first, bookkeeping later.

Reagan agreed. "Defense is not a budget issue. You spend what you
need." He reminded Stockman that he had campaigned on the theme
of restored national security. His election had signaled to the Soviet
Union that this theme would become policy, and Congress's approval
of his first budget made it official. "There must be no perception by
anyone in the world that we're backing down one inch on the defense
buildup."

Just for a start, he announced on October 2 that the United States intended to rearm with a hundred B-1 bombers, a hundred MX multiple-
warhead intercontinental ballistic missiles, a second generation of
Trident submarines with doubled strategic capability, and a new, radar-
invisible "stealth" warplane.

Given this determination, Stockman asked for something less than
an "inch" in public-relations terms: an almost unnoticeable trimming
of the stupendous five-year, $1.46 trillion appropriation he had
promised Weinberger in the first days of the Administration. If the Secretary would only agree to a mere 2.5 percent reduction in the growth
rate of the defense budget, that would yield $32 billion in savings by
1986. Weinberger, however, regarded the promise as a contract. Stockman soon discovered that getting him to cede any money back would
be about as easy as rescinding the Louisiana Purchase.

The cheerful, garrulous Defense Secretary was a formidable infighter
by virtue of Harvard smarts, lawyerly reasoning, long political memory, and a high moral seriousness. Not only had he once served as Reagan's finance director in Sacramento, he had held Stockman's own job
under Nixon, as well as those of Federal Trade Commissioner and Secretary of Health, Education, and Welfare. At Cabinet meetings, he was
able to argue knowledgeably, and at clock-stopping length, against
every item Stockman raised.

Reagan, meanwhile, would sit doodling various parts of horses. He
hated open dissension. "Why don't you fellas get together," he said on
September 9. "See if you can work it out in this area in-between."
There was, of course, no "area," at least on Weinberger's side. It was his
oblique way of overriding Stockman. But the young man, unschooled
in Reagan's executive style, kept on coming with money-saving ideas for
the Pentagon.

Staffers ranged along the wall of the Cabinet Room would watch
with delight as Stockman hiked his chair forward, exhaled a dragon

breath of cigarette smoke, and launched into a fiscal construct that he had sat up all night memorizing. Invariably, after the first two or three points, the President would be reminded of something that had happened in Hollywood in 1947. For as many minutes as remained of the meeting, the anecdote would proceed, climaxing with a punch line just before Reagan's next appointment. Amid general laughter, he would head for the door, leaving Stockman behind, gray-faced and incredulous. "How can he *do* that to me?"

One of the Budget Director's less inspired proposals for reducing the defense budget was to save three billion dollars by canceling the new nuclear aircraft carrier *Theodore Roosevelt*. He thus showed an incomprehension of the value of huge, salutory military symbols, and was ignored. Secretary Weinberger scratched his initials on the ship's first weld in Newport News, Virginia, on October 31, 1981. The act served notice that the modern United States Navy, created by TR in the first decade of the century, was being rebuilt to reach its maximum strength in the last.

Notwithstanding Reagan's and Weinberger's defensiveness on defense, the White House troika took serious note of what Stockman was saying about the consequences of military deficit spending. They could hardly do otherwise, with Treasury receipts collapsing, and unemployment around 10 percent.

There had been a noticeable decline in the President's popularity since the Libyan shootdown. Polls and media commentary showed a tendency to regard the Administration as a club for rich white men, notwithstanding his widely praised appointment of Sandra Day O'Connor to the Supreme Court. Lavish refurbishment of the White House and Oval Office by Nancy Reagan (albeit paid for mostly with private funds), contrasted ill on the nightly news with images of welfare lines in the South Bronx and tents along the Santa Monica Palisades. Agony letters in the Presidential Correspondence Office showed an increasing tendency to blame Reagan for the recession.

Separately and together, the troika lobbied a reluctant President to make Weinberger accept a $20 billion cut, and cooperate with Congress on a 1982–1983 budget less fanciful than the last, even if it included some "revenue enhancement"—an ingenious euphemism for new taxes.

"We are going through a period of difficult and painful readjustment," Reagan told the nation at the height of the negotiations. Stockman eventually got $13 billion, plus advice that House Republican leaders were cool to his idea of remedial legislation.

Then, at 6:32 P.M. on November 10—a day made gloomy by advice from the President's Council of Economic Advisers that the depth of the recession was likely to reach 4 or 5 percent "negative real growth"— the White House was hit with its worst publicity of the year. Late workers in the West Wing, half-listening to *CBS Evening News,* heard Lesley Stahl pronounce the name of David Stockman, along with the words *embarrassing* and *explosive.*

Ms. Stahl proceeded to report that the nation's budget chief had been repeatedly telling a Washington journalist, William Greider, that Reaganomics would not work. In conversations apparently recorded for "posterity"—i.e., next month's issue of the *Atlantic*—Stockman had called the President's tax cut "a Trojan horse" full of treasure for the rich.

It was an unfortunate metaphor to say the least, with its associations of hollowness and woodenness and danger to the state. Nobody doubted that Reagan would fire Stockman at once—"He's outta here," said Deaver—except for the fair-minded James Baker. After reading an advance copy of the *Atlantic* article, the Chief of Staff concluded that it was accurate in its account of how politics had been allowed to pervert the purity of Reagan's original reform plan. Stockman was still allegedly the best fiscal brain in Washington; who else could better manage the deficit? The upshot was an Oval Office lunch, arranged by Baker, at which Stockman masochistically abased himself.

"Dave," Reagan said, "how do you explain this? You have hurt me. Why?"

Their respective accounts of the conversation that followed, with Stockman unable to eat and Reagan's eyes shining with aggrieved tears, suggest a fair degree of histrionics on either side. At any rate, the Budget Director did not resign for another three and a half years, by which time the annual deficit stood at $223 billion.

If Stockman and other chart-wielding advocates of "mid-course correction" sensed a polite impatience in Reagan's manner in the fall of 1981, they were not mistaken. His mind tended toward dispensation (witness the satisfied cross-outs on his daily schedule), and as far as he was concerned, the Program for Economic Recovery was in place. Nuclear-weapons policy preoccupied him now. Even before Weinberger signed the *Theodore Roosevelt*'s keel, he had secretly approved National Security Directive 13 "—what I'm told may be the most momentous decision any Pres. has had to make."

The directive authorized a menu of nuclear-war plans for him to choose from in the event of strategic attack. These plans, each one lethal enough to erase memories of World War II, were collectively acronymed SIOP (Single Integrated Operational Plan), and the power to initiate them resided in a small plastic card that Reagan carried in his pocket. The codes on the card spoke to codes readable only at Offutt Air Force Base in Nebraska. Offutt's computers, in turn, had been programmed with secret mathematical formulas. Thus the fate of millions if not billions of people depended on the ability of a few military operators, underground in the Great Plains, to type without dropping a digit. Their keystrokes assigned missiles to targets around the world (Kiev alone rated forty warheads), and mapped the deployment of nuclear bombers, ships, and submarines. While doing so, they must at all costs keep these engines of death from bumping into one another.

It was SIOP; it was BSNP gone MAD; it was a world bristling with ICBMs and MIRVed SLBMs and SRAMs. Yet none of these acronyms of arms control had managed to keep Anwar el-Sadat from being machine-gunned to death on October 6, or headed off what looked to be, within weeks, the imposition of martial law in Poland. Now Reagan had three new letters to learn, courtesy of Paul Nitze, leader of his delegation to the theater nuclear-forces negotiations in Geneva: INF, for Intermediate-range Nuclear Forces.

Apparently these were not to be called Euromissiles anymore, because West Germany and France disliked the implication that they were not a part of United States global strategy. Overshadowing everything else in the current balance of power was the menace posed to Western Europe and China by the Soviet Union's arsenal of SS-20 missiles—technically INFs, but capable of traveling three thousand miles and "inserting" three warheads apiece. President Carter had reluctantly agreed to provide West Germany with a retaliatory INF of Pershing II missiles. Nitze's hope was that both menaces could be talked away in Geneva.

That was Reagan's, too, although Weinberger (an ardent disciple of Theodore Roosevelt) wanted to deploy the big sticks before speaking softly. For once, the President listened to his Secretary of State, who counseled the opposite. Haig felt that it would be in the interest of the

United States to push for bilateral arms reduction, since an anti-nuclear "peace" movement was burgeoning alarmingly in all the European NATO countries.

With some misgivings, Reagan went even further and, on November 18, 1981, proposed a "zero-zero option"—total elimination of INFs on either side of the East-West frontier. He was aware that the option amounted to a major shift in U.S. defense policy, and was collectively opposed by most arms-control experts at home and abroad, not to mention his own State Department. However, it at least amounted to a peacable gesture toward the Soviet Union, while buying Weinberger more buildup time.

His sober speech, flawlessly delivered at the National Press Club, was relayed around the world to an estimated two hundred million viewers. Among them was Chancellor Schmidt of West Germany, who called to say that he was meeting with Brezhnev in a few days, and wondered if the President would like to suggest any topics of conversation.

"Tell him I really mean it about the SS-20s," Reagan said.

On December 13, Brezhnev replied by forcing his puppet government in Poland to impose martial law.

By the time Ronald Reagan held his first White House dinner for the diplomatic corps, on February 13, 1982, the Kremlin was convinced that he was "a dangerous confrontational figure" whose "deeply disturbing" animus against all things Russian had created a "solid front of hostility" among Politburo leaders. The phrases are those of Anatoly Dobrynin, the Soviet Union's veteran Ambassador to the United States. Dobrynin did not say them out loud, during a brief moment alone with the President, but he did warn him that U.S.-Soviet relations were "at their lowest point since World War II."

Reagan did not seem intimidated, or even particularly concerned. He had already heard back from Schmidt that Brezhnev was querulous about him, to the point of fearing war, and from Haig that Andrei Gromyko, the Soviet Foreign Minister, was exceedingly "nervous." Doubtless both men were wondering what he was going to do about Poland, where thousands of Solidarity members had been arrested in their beds, and every major crossroads turned into a military checkpoint. Actually that he had decided to do nothing, beyond discussing possible sanctions and quarantines with U.S. allies in Europe. But fear was a powerful incentive at the bargaining table, and he thought the INF talks in Geneva might benefit from a little Russian insecurity. "The plain truth is, we can't—alone—hurt the Soviets that much."

A sense of philosophical certainty and willingness to ride out coming storms pervaded Reagan's current diary entries. It was as if the steady worsening of the recession, paralleled by the growing perception of him overseas as a nuclear warrior, pervasely calmed him. If so, his calm was bolstered by a new, wholly compatible presence in the White House, that of William P. Clark. As of the new year, Clark—generally known as "the Judge"—had become his National Security Adviser, replacing Richard Allen, who had resigned because of temperamental differences with Haig.

Clark's appointment protected Reagan from the volatile Secretary. Haig had gotten to like and respect Clark as Deputy Secretary of State, and assumed that he now had a friend rather than an adversary in the National Security Office. Clark, a fellow Catholic, shared Haig's deep contempt for Communism and agreed that the Church was in danger of suppression in Poland—not to mention El Salvador, Nicaragua, and Cuba—which in the Secretary's robust opinion should be paved over and turned into "a fucking parking lot."

Unlike Haig, however, Clark was neither a diplomat nor a politician. Both those professions require a certain glibness, whereas Clark made almost an art form of taciturnity. In his youth, he had spent a year in a seminary that permitted only two hours of speech a day. At forty-eight, he could get by on considerably less. Tall, handsome, expressionless, and slow-moving in black alligator boots, he stood out among conservative Washingtonians like the proverbial Stranger come to town, his pinstripe suits too well cut, his gold-rimmed half-moons too thin for Beltway comfort. He lacked the usual nondescript wife, being married to an elegant, articulate, former Czech-Jewish refugee. The only secret he did not mind sharing was that he looked forward to returning to California as soon the President could do without him, because he was by nature a ranchman, happiest when riding out alone over his vast estate in San Luis Obispo County.

Ironically, it was that side of the Judge's character that appealed to the proprietor of Rancho del Cielo. When Reagan snuck out on Wednesday for a couple of hours in the saddle at Quantico or Camp David, Clark often rode along. The relationship went both ways, and extended far back. Veterans of Sacramento days remembered seeing "that 'the son I never had' look passing from Reagan to Bill" and joked about a genetic resemblance in the way they walked. Robert Moretti, recording an oral history in California, was sure that their old teamwork would flourish again. "Clark takes a studious, intelligent approach . . . right now I think he is probably the best thing that ever happened in the White House during the Reagan Administration."

Editorial opinion echoed this view during the first few weeks of Clark's tenure. He restored morale and efficiency in the National Security Council, firing and hiring as objectively as if he were improving stock at Clark Ranch. He brought in as his deputy Robert C. "Bud" McFarlane, a stiff-faced strategy specialist who had impressed him at State. He proved adept at containing Haig and cajoling Weinberger. But rumors of empire-building began to circulate as Clark swiftly replaced Edwin Meese as the most powerful man in the West Wing. His year in the plush parlors at State did not seem to have compromised his austere purposefulness. He neither leaked nor courted personal publicity—a recipe for image attrition in a town that requires press collusion. He had insisted on direct access to the President as a prerequisite of his appointment, and to the alarm of Michael Deaver took immediate advantage of it. "You can't just *walk* in," Deaver protested, when Clark strode through the door of the Oval Office unannounced.

Clark looked down on Deaver from his superior height and said with disdain, "Mike, if it wasn't for me, you wouldn't be here."

This was true enough, but only to those whose memories went back to early days in Sacramento. Deaver bided his time.

Instead of boring Reagan with long, Haig-like sermons on world events (the Secretary of State liked to call himself the "vicar" of U.S. foreign policy), Clark wrote concise PDBs—President's Daily Briefings—and saw to it that plenty of CIA and Defense Department documentaries were delivered to the White House. He personalized the international situation, with gratifying results. Reagan, whose concerns tended to be ideological, actually began asking human questions: "What are they saying about the Pope in Warsaw this morning? Did Jaruzelski have a good night's sleep?"

One face that kept showing up in Soviet leadership profiles was the ascetic, disdainful countenance of Yuri Andropov, sixty-seven years old and longtime chairman of the KGB. Even in a land where public officials were apparently forbidden to smile, Andropov's "sneer of cold command" was chilling. He made William Casey, Director of the CIA, look like a loose-mouthed, absentminded incompetent—an image that Casey assiduously cultivated. Andropov's health was rumored to be delicate, yet on April 10 it was he, not Brezhnev, who delivered the Lenin's Birthday address, traditionally a keynote of Soviet policy.

As Secretary-designate of the Central Committee, Andropov was already the second most powerful person in the Kremlin, and Brezhnev's likely successor. This made him the prime addressee of Reagan's second major arms-control statement, scheduled for May 9.

By happy coincidence, that was both Mother's Day and the sixtieth anniversary of Reagan's graduation, so the White House announced that he would give his big speech at his *alma mater* in Eureka, Illinois. I anticipated the event with some emotion, and considered attending in order to have the queer sensation of seeing Dutch step once again onto that little stage with its side organ, where he had first tasted the "heady wine" of applause back in 1928. But an advance team decided that the Chapel was too small; he would speak in the Ronald Reagan Physical Education Center.

"Why don't they call it the *Dutch* Reagan Center?" Paul Rae groused on one of the last of our rare evenings out. Shabby and increasingly reclusive since the retirement of his column, he was battling a series of mysterious, degenerative ailments. He would not survive the summer. I suppose I should have related his passing to a number of similar deaths that had attracted attention in San Francisco four months before, but I didn't. Few people did in mid-1982.

I am aware that these paragraphs are being pushed away from SALT and START toward the most dread acronym in late-twentieth-century style. However, that is the way it was with AIDS, in public awareness as well as pathology, at the dawn of the Reagan Era. First a slow insinuation, met with strong resistance; then further insinuation, and weaker resistance; then a full-scale invasion, turning resistance to terror; finally, a capitulation that amounted to bewilderment. One had read about the progression of *la peste* in Camus, even accepted it as a metaphor for the fall of France in 1940. But one could not begin to apprehend that this new virus might be traceable back to that same year, nor that it would soon become so real a plague—the only completely lethal one in history—that to treat it symbolically would be to trivialize it.

Reagan (we may as well follow through with his own education in the matter) would remain unconcerned by AIDS at least until the death of Rock Hudson in 1985, which shocked him into asking one of his doctors a few shyly clumsy questions: "It's a virus, like measles? But it doesn't go away?" My research cards have him finding it a fit subject for humor as late as December 1986, and five months after that waxing biblical in his opinion that "maybe the Lord brought down this plague" because "illicit sex is against the Ten Commandments."

To be fair to him, he made no moral distinction between homosexuality, heterosexuality out of wedlock, or abortion on demand. All three were abhorred by God, in his opinion. The best that could be said about the first "sin" was that its consequence was, perhaps, a caution against the other two:

> I think people were happier and better off when there wasn't the tremendous plague of single motherhood cases or abortions—the thousands and thousands and thousands that take place regularly now and, uh, whether it's going to take such a tragic thing as that disease . . . that horrible disease to return us to a sense of values that were very much a part of our generation.

Better even than Nancy Reagan, Judge Clark understood the fundamentally childlike, bipolar quality of the President's mind, its tendency to see all moral questions in terms of opposites. Like a magnet among iron filings, it either concentrated acceptable facts in a tight cluster, or repelled them and kept itself clean. I suspect that Clark was responsible for the apparent balance of the Eureka Commencement address, which proposed a mutual 30 percent reduction of land-based international nuclear warheads, down to about five thousand each, and a superpower summit as early as June. "And when we sit down . . . I will tell President Brezhnev . . . that his government and his people have nothing to fear from the United States," Reagan said, to long applause.

The speech seemed to signal a new peaceable intent on his part, with its call for strategic arms *reduction* talks (START) in place of mere arms *limitation* agreements (SALT). But Andropov's analysts quickly noted that Reagan's language was disingenuous. His qualifier "land-based" applied to almost all of their ICBMs, but not to the many American ones housed in submarines; he was in effect proposing a strategic *im*balance, which would give the United States three missiles for every two the Soviet Union deployed, and twelve warheads for every four. Nor, ominously, had he said anything about continuing to observe the restraints of the unratified SALT II treaty. On May 12, Andropov sent the Politburo a furious memo, co-signed by Gromyko and Defense Minister Dmitri Ustinov, accusing Reagan of warmongering and wanting to bomb détente. The President's speech had been "saturated with gross, unadulterated hostility toward the Soviet Union"; his obvious long-term intent was to destroy Communism.

Within a matter of days, the Andropov memo was internally confirmed as official Soviet policy. Not by one syllable did Gromyko betray the panic running through the Kremlin. He instructed his diplomats to say that the idea of a summit was acceptable, providing President Reagan ventured something less "one-sided" than START. Clark, meanwhile, conquered his usual taciturnity long enough to deliver a militant address at Georgetown University.

The United States, Clark said, meant to shape foreign policy only on the basis of strategic strength. Conventional forces were being built up and made more battle-ready around the world—he listed a range of theaters that amounted to an encirclement of the Soviet bloc—but the core of American "defense" was nuclear. The Reagan Administration intended "to modernize the manned bomber force, increase the accuracy and payload of our submarine-launched ballistic missiles, add sea-launched cruise missiles . . . and deploy new, larger, more accurate land-based ballistic missiles." He added that the first purpose of such a strategy was to buttress an international order dedicated to American institutions and principles. In language broad enough to condone any degree of interference in the affairs of other countries, he said that the United States "must be prepared to respond vigorously to opportunities as they arise and to create opportunities where none existed before."

I quote deliberately from a report of Clark's speech made by the Soviet press agency, TASS, on May 21, 1982, to show how his language sounded in Marxist-Leninist ears. He proudly showed me the dispatch after the collapse of Communism, as proof that he had helped contribute to history. But even then, ten years later, he did not know how telling a moment he had chosen to convince the Politburo that American imperialism was on the rise worldwide, just as that of the Soviet Union was faltering.

The statistics of decline were economic rather than military, and held in such neurotic secrecy that key budget figures were not even discussed in the Walnut Room of the Politburo. Andropov and his brilliant protégé on the Central Committee, Agriculture Secretary Mikhail Gorbachev, were among the few Soviet leaders who knew how catastrophic the situation was. At the beginning of a decade in which Western technological innovation was clearly on a roll—particularly in the area of computer science—Mother Russia could not even feed herself. Her mismanaged farmlands were eroding, reverting to weed, or simply turning sterile under a rain of harsh herbicides. Vast industrial schemes were carving up the countryside and poisoning the rivers, then failing for lack of an efficient transportation network. Nuclear-power stations throbbed wastefully and dangerously. Urban industry was still cranking along on plant built in the age of Stalin. The Aral Sea, freshwater jewel of the southern republics, was becoming a disk of bitter salt.

Three days after Judge Clark's speech, Leonid Brezhnev reported to the Central Committee on a "food program" designed by Gorbachev that amounted to a desperate effort to reform at least the agricultural sector of the economy. His slurred presentation gave no indication that he understood, much less endorsed, what he was reading. He had a dying man's resistance to frightening facts. "Is it really that bad?" he would say when forced to confront one, and weep with perplexity.

Although Clark, Haig, Casey, Jeane Kirkpatrick, and the other conservatives who dominated Reagan's foreign-policy apparatus were on tenterhooks for most of 1982 about Soviet intentions in Poland, they had to relax as time went by and Red Army divisions showed no signs of belligerence in that theater. Haig sensibly theorized that it was not in Moscow's interest to invade yet another satellite state. (Indeed, if he could have bugged Politburo meetings, he would have heard Brezhnev saying "Poland is not Czechoslovakia or Afghanistan.") Apart from the huge cost of such a move, it would alienate the pro-Soviet "freeze" movement in Western Europe, which Soviet propagandists were counting on to stop the deployment of American INFs.

So Reagan contented himself with a secret directive, NSDD-32, that authorized Western counterpropaganda inside Poland, along with a range of economic sanctions and covert activities to keep the spirit of Solidarity alive until Jaruzelski's regime bankrupted itself. Early in June, he flew to Europe for the 1982 "economic summit," shrugging off advice to be equivocal about START. "To h--l with it. It's time we tell them this is our chance to bring the Soviets into the real world and for them to take a stand with us."

His principal statement to this effect, delivered before members of the British Parliament on June 8, was a strained attempt at grand rhetoric ("Must civilization perish in a hail of fiery atoms?"), celebrated by Cold Warriors as "the Westminster Address." Its climactic image of Marxism-Leninism relegated to "the ash heap of history" had unfortunate overtones on a day that saw scores of British troops incinerated in the Falklands. Reagan's listeners were aware that his Administration was divided in its policy toward the eccentric war that Britain was waging against Argentina to retain control of a few sheep-splattered islands in the South Atlantic. Their consequent forebearance, and the "speechwriterly" tone of the Address, prevented it from being quite the "triumph" Prime Minister Margaret Thatcher claimed it to be. Yet it reads now as prophetic in its confidence that Poland would become the crucible of Soviet ideology. Reagan also saw that Communism's struggle against capitalism would be resolved by market, not military forces.

"In an ironic sense Karl Marx was right," he said, reading the words off an invisible prompt screen. (Mrs. Thatcher marveled at his memory.) "We are witnessing today a great revolutionary crisis, a crisis where the demands of the economic order are colliding directly with those of the political order. But the crisis is happening not in the free, non-Marxist West but in the home of Marxism-Leninism, the Soviet Union."

Two days later, Reagan paid a quick visit to Berlin, and drove to Checkpoint Charlie—the primary point of collision—for his first view of Communism. He stepped out of his limousine to see it better. To left and right stretched the Wall: gray, slabby, pocked, barbed, spiked with gun towers, echoing somewhere down its double-layered length with the yowls of guard dogs, sliced through by a single boomed road that disclosed streetscapes totally lacking in color—unless darker grays, gray-green trees, and gray-brown apartment blocks were to be considered additions to the spectrum. East German soldiers with submachine guns stood in little knots around the guardhouses, looking expressionlessly back at him.

A reporter asked the President what he thought of what he saw. He gestured at the Wall and said succinctly, "It's as ugly as the idea behind it."

On midsummer days at Lowell Park, when the river was especially crowded, young Dutch Reagan used to comfort himself with the old lifeguards' saw, "Every beach has only one or two danger spots, and ninety percent of his work will be done there." So far in his Presidency, the most troublesome currents had swirled around Poland; now a sudden whirlpool developed around Lebanon.

He had known for at least a year that Menachem Begin, the waspishly aggressive little Prime Minister of Israel, was spoiling for war in the Middle East. Last June 7, Begin had scared him badly ("I swear I believe Armageddon is here") by bombing a nuclear reactor just outside of Baghdad. As if in some crazed anniversary celebration, Begin accomplished a full-scale invasion of the southern part of Lebanon, in order to rid the area of Palestinian terrorists and Syrian "deterrent" forces. By the time Reagan got back to Washington on June 11, Beirut was under siege. Meanwhile, American-built Israeli warplanes were carving Soviet-built Syrian ones out of the sky, in a display of technical superiority not entirely to the distress of Caspar Weinberger.

So began the bloodiest foreign entanglement of Ronald Reagan's years in office, culminating sixteen months later in his worst humiliation as President. Lebanon had been a racial and religious "killing ground," in Weinberger's phrase, since the mid-1970s, but until now its murderousness had not extended far beyond its borders. In fact, it seemed to be dying from the outside in. With Syria and Israel crowding it between them, it had degenerated into so many warring cells—Maronite, Greek, and Roman Catholic Christians; Druse, Sunni, and Shiite Muslims; Palestinians, terrorist groups, and warlord gangs—as to evoke the image of metastasis.

Israel's declaration of a temporary cease-fire on June 12 more or less coincided with the resignation of its best friend in the Reagan Cabinet. One cannot date precisely the moment when Reagan lost confidence in Alexander Haig, who was in the habit of threatening to step down at slights to his dignity. (Weinberger, Clark, and Michael Deaver vied with one another to provide them.)

"It's amazing how sound he can be on complex international matters, but how utterly paranoid with regard to the people he must work with," Reagan wrote after authorizing Clark to search in strictest confidence for a new Secretary of State.

Clark's first choice was Caspar Weinberger. The Defense Secretary was, oddly for a man so devoted to rearmament, much less of a hawk than Haig, believing that force should be used only as a last resort, when American interests were directly threatened. Even then, there should be a clear public majority in support of offensive action. He held no brief for Israel, and did not think that United States should support piracy. Reagan liked the idea of "bringing Cap across the river," but changed his mind after discussing it with Nancy. Accurately or not, Weinberger was *seen* as warlike, and Clark knew better than to argue with Hollywood people about perception. So he called George P. Shultz.

Superficially, Shultz had some points of resemblance with Weinberger, having also served President Nixon in three capacities (Secretary of Labor, Director of OMB, Secretary of the Treasury) and held a high executive position at Bechtel. But he had as many differences, and they were fundamental. His background was academic and he had little intimacy, political or otherwise, with Ronald Reagan. Indeed, it was difficult to tell from Shultz's dull demeanor and careful record, not to mention a face as blank as a slot machine's, what he felt about anything. One inserted one's coin and waited for the spools to spin.

Clark asked what he felt about the current Lebanese situation. After the usual whirring pause, Shultz said that he disapproved of Israel's violent behavior. "Arabs are people, too." That confirmed him, in the Judge's mind, as a strong potential Secretary of State, one prepared to challenge the sentimentalities of the most powerful lobby in the country.

"Watch out for him," Nixon warned. "He'll become part of your Administration, and after a while he'll be disloyal."

Reagan did not think so. He liked what he had seen of Shultz's qualities—solidity, strength, taciturnity—in contrast to Haig's perpetual *Sturm und Drang.* On June 25, he summoned the Secretary, received him standing, and handed over a note. "Dear Al," it began. "It is with the most profound regret that I accept your letter of resignation." While Haig was still reeling—he had not written one—Reagan asked him to continue serving until his successor could be confirmed by the Senate.

Haig spent the next couple of hours tearfully drafting the requested letter. "I don't want to do it, I want to stay." And when he finally finished it, he found that Reagan had already announced the appointment of George Shultz as sixtieth Secretary of State.

Thus, a tight little toggle-circuit of yeas and nays, threats and consequences, doubts and resolutions led to the deaths, sixteen months later, of two hundred and forty-one American servicemen in Beirut.

Secretary of State Weinberger would not have endorsed U.S. participation in the first multinational force (MNF) that was quickly deployed in Lebanon in July 1982. He opposed it as Secretary of Defense, along with the Joint Chiefs of Staff, but was overruled by Reagan, who was repulsed by Israeli use of cluster bombs to clear Beirut of obstructions, such as Palestinian women and children. Weinberger did not see why peacekeeping in Lebanon could not be accomplished by United Nations troops, whether or not Menachem Begin liked the idea. However, he acknowledged the MNF's effectiveness in bringing about the diaspora of the Palestine Liberation Organization, hitherto headquartered in Beirut. Its job was accomplished by September 1, when Reagan proposed a peace plan offering the Palestinians some form of autonomy on the West Bank, under the aegis of King Hussein of Jordan. This plan was the first substantial fruit of George Shultz's tenure at the State Department. Weinberger was pleased to see that both the Secretary and the President seemed to agree that "the plight of the Palestinians" was the fundamental issue in Middle Eastern diplomacy. Somewhere, Anwar el-Sadat's dark ghost was surely smiling.

What Weinberger certainly would have fought, with all his famous tenacity, was the creation of a *second* MNF, only fifteen days after the disbandment of the first. Its ostensible purpose was to separate Syrian forces to the north of Beirut and Israeli forces occupying the city itself, pending withdrawal of both from Lebanon. Weinberger saw that MNF II would be drawn into a "spiraling panic" following the massacre in Beirut, on September 16–17, of seven hundred Palestinian refugees by Lebanese Christian militiamen. (Israeli forces had stood by and even helpfully sent up flares.) Once again, he and the Joint Chiefs of Staff advised against American involvement in tribal warfare, unless the United States could see some clear advantage to its interests. And once again they were overruled by Reagan and Shultz, with the encouragement of Robert McFarlane, who had emerged as the NSC's leading interventionist. On September 29, U.S. Marines returned to Beirut and were posted to the airport with instructions to keep it open.

Whereas George Shultz's attitude to Lebanon was that of restrained belligerence leading to diplomacy, Ronald Reagan's was biblical. At least, I've always felt that when he planted the Stars and Stripes there in 1982, he was identifying with Ezekiel's great-winged eagle, "which had divers colors, came unto Lebanon, and took the highest branch of the cedar." But William Clark scoffs at such oracular conceits. A devout man himself, he insists that the President's protectiveness toward Israel was compassionate rather than religious, and based on a sensible reading of history. The little Jewish state—that artificially created land, a ghetto among nations—had been menaced for decades by outside terror. Its recent discovery that Iraq was on the verge of a nuclear capability could only have confirmed the neurosis of a Menachem Begin that somewhere, always, someone was building an oven for the Jews.

Clark further believes that Reagan suffered, in his quiet way, from moral guilt. "I've always felt that he overreacted to the Holocaust—its horrors left such a mark on him that he let his emotions flow into almost any issue involving Israel. As if he were compensating." This did not mean that the President forgave Begin and Ariel Sharon, the Israeli Defense Minister, for encouraging the carnage there. Revealingly, at the height of Israel's bombardment of Beirut, he had invoked race memory in a furious telephone call to Begin:

> I told him that it had to stop or our entire future relationship was endangered. I used the word holocaust deliberately & said the symbol of his [*sic*] was becoming a picture of a 7 month old baby with its arms blown off.

Robert McFarlane, listening, was astonished at the vehemence and rapidity of his speech. So, apparently, was Begin, who called back within minutes to say that the attack had been stopped.

Reagan has been derided for later telling another Israeli Prime Minister, Yitzhak Shamir, that he had personally witnessed the opening of the first German concentration camps in April 1945. The White House went to elaborate lengths to imply that Shamir had a language problem—that the President was referring only to the live color footage that he had screened for the benefit of First Motion Picture Unit personnel, days after the liberation of Ohrdruf. I have already told *that* little story. But as both Lou Cannon and Michael Korda have demonstrated, Reagan revived his "I was there" fantasy on at least two other occasions, to auditors who understood English as well as he did.

George Shultz, on the other hand, got the FMPU version from him in every detail. So who is telling the truth? Everybody, I'd say—including Dutch, who has never tried to conceal the fact that to him, seeing is believing, that raw film is the same as raw experience. Of course he was "there" at Buchenwald with Owen Crump and the combat camera crew. Do we not speak of being *transported* by great drama, *moved* to pity? What matters, surely, is that one of history's worst truths registered upon Ronald Reagan half a century ago, with a primacy that affected him the rest of his life. The new computer age will determine whether such virtual perception is authentic or not.

☯

All the above discussion of imagination is by way of background to an isolated diary entry Reagan wrote on September 14, 1982. After noting that President-elect Bashir Gemayel of Lebanon had been bombed to death that morning, he added, "Dr. [Edward] Teller came in. He's pushing an exciting idea that nuclear weapons can be used in connection with Lasers to be non-destructive except as used to intercept and destroy enemy missiles far above the earth."

❦

For the rest of 1982, news from both home and abroad was mostly depressing for the President, his Administration, and his party. It was all very well for Reagan to tease Paul Nitze, as he left for another round of INF talks in Geneva, "Just tell the Soviets that you're working for one tough son of a bitch," but the veteran ambassador found that openings negotiated during the summer had been closed on instructions from Moscow. The Kremlin was not prepared to tolerate "even a single Pershing II or ground-launched cruise missile" on European soil. At home, the stricken economy remained resistant to reform. Republican Congressional candidates had to pretend that a parcel of "revenue enhancements," signed by the President to calm nervous markets, was not the largest corporate tax increase in history. In October, unemployment rose to its highest level since 1940, and protest mail poured into the White House. Some of it was from children: "Dear Pres. Ronald Reagan, Is the U.S.A. broke?"

Speaker Tip O'Neill, whose Boston Irish joviality had never quite concealed a basic contempt for Reaganomics, began to treat the President like a fiscal retard. Even the free-market economist George Stigler personally accused him of courting a "depression." Michael Deaver came into the Oval Office to find Reagan seeking solace in the society of his dog, a galumphing and not entirely urbanized black Bouvier named Lucky. "One of these days that dog's going to piss on your desk," Deaver remarked.

"Why not?" said Reagan mildly. "Everybody else does."

On October 27 I returned to the White House for a lunch in memory of Theodore Roosevelt. It was TR's birthday, and a large delegation of Rooseveltians was on hand to present his 1906 Nobel Peace Prize for permanent display in the Roosevelt Room. I found myself sitting close to Dutch.

He was dressed, appropriately enough for the times, in a black suit that drained his face of color, but after two or three sips of wine he became as ruddy as a Hals burgher. For ten minutes he talked nonstop to the table in general (it was large and round), mostly banalities about the forthcoming election. I noticed that his lobster bisque, untouched, was beginning to skin, and decided to interrupt, so he could spoon it up.

"Mr. President, you might be interested to know that TR faced a midterm situation in 1902 very like the one you're in now."

He didn't like the *you* and *you're*. But on the other hand he obviously like his soup, so I went on while he ate.

"A Republican party divided over the issue of tax reform; a President committed to a conservative program, yet realizing that reforms are crucial; a comfortable majority in the Senate, which is in danger of being lost; vital governorships like New York poised to go either way; an Administration accused of arms buildup and lack of sympathy for working men . . ."

At every negative verb—*divided, lost, accused*—I saw his face stiffen further, so jumped to what I should have started with: "Well, TR decided to take a last-minute swing through the country, made the most of his personal charm, talked plain English, grinned a lot, and made deals with every politician he met. The result was a reduced Senate majority, but still enough to govern with. His program was endorsed, with two more years to give it time to work, and from that point on, things got better, his power grew, and he galloped on to a big victory in 1904."

Galloped gave Dutch the cue he needed to break free of me. "You know," he said to my companions, "once you throw your leg over a thoroughbred, you're spoiled for life."

When he stood up afterward to address the room, he did not fail to remind us that a great aircraft carrier named after Theodore Roosevelt was under construction at Newport News.

Six nights later, the election more or less emulated the precedent of 1902. Reagan, if not Reaganomics, was safe for another couple of years. His conservative coalition in the House was preserved—just—and he maintained an eight-seat majority in the Senate. Seven Republican statehouses were posted for new occupancy.

In public, the President maintained his usual cheerfulness, but in private he was subdued, even grim. "We came here to change things, not to follow opinion polls." And when, on November 10, he heard that Leonid Brezhnev had died, he adamantly refused to go to Moscow in a show of respect that he did not feel.

The final blow of a bitter year was the decision of the House of Representatives on December 7 to reject a centerpiece of his arms-buildup program—the MX missile in "dense pack" deployment—with fifty Republicans defecting. "We had rabbits when we needed tigers," Reagan wrote.

The accession to power in the Soviet Union of Yuri Andropov coincided with a subtle but fundamental change in Ronald Reagan's strategic thinking.

As long as Brezhnev had remained alive, he had been able to remember the two hairy hands enclosing his own at San Clemente, and persuade himself that in an emergency, he could pick up the red phone and talk to a Russian who was at least semihuman. But everything he heard about Andropov was ominous. According to George Shultz, who had gone over for the state funeral, the new *gensek* was wasted with diabetes and kidney disease, yet projected a malevolent intelligence that had no trace of Brezhnev's sentimentality. Shultz sensed a cold "capacity for brutality."

Reagan had to ponder this information at the same time as the Joint Chiefs of Staff sought guidance on what to do about Congress's rejection of the MX. Meeting privately with them before Christmas, he mused aloud, "What if we began to move away from our total reliance on offense . . . toward a greater reliance on defense?"

His executive style was so elliptical (long anecdotal reminiscences serving for "No," tranquil silences conveying "Yes") that the Chiefs were never quite sure whether they were being consulted or commanded. "Did we just get instructions to take a hard look at missile defense?" their chairman, General John Vessey, asked Judge Clark afterward.

"Yes," said Clark.

The National Security Adviser authorized his deputy, Robert McFarlane, and his military aide, Rear Admiral John Poindexter, to work with Dr. Edward Teller and Admiral James Watkins, Chief of Naval Operations, on the technological implications. Missile defense— or "strategic defense," as McFarlane preferred to call it—was both an old and new idea, going back to the anti-ballistic dreams of the early Sixties, and necessarily looking forward now, in the early Eighties, as far as computer science could project.

Meanwhile, at the very end of the year in Moscow, a pale Andropov was warning Mikhail Gorbachev, "Act as if you had to shoulder all the responsibility one day. I mean it."

30

Huge Cloudy Symbols of a High Romance

NINETEEN-EIGHTY-THREE AND -FOUR were Ronald Reagan's defining years as President of the United States, beginning with his
approval rating at a nadir of 35 percent—the lowest such midterm figure in forty years—and ending with a landslide re-election, Communism confounded, Western Europe fortified, the national economy
thundering, and a general feeling of resurgent patriotism and optimism.

At first, in his State of the Union address to Congress on January 25,
1983, he seemed to be abandoning the conservative economic philosophy that had brought him to power. He called for bipartisan, emergency action to save Social Security from bankruptcy, even if that
meant increased taxes. He cited Franklin Roosevelt's belief that "the
great public is interested more in government than in politics," to the
dismay of libertarians who remembered his old mantra, *government
isn't the solution, government is the problem.* And to the sound of revolving corpses in Orange County cemeteries, he smoothly added: "Because we must ensure reduction and eventual elimination of deficits
over the next several years, I will propose a stand-by tax—" at which
the revolving noise drowned out further details.

Only those veteran observers who remembered his perfect willing-ness to compromise, when necessary, as president of the Screen Actors Guild and Governor of California were reassured that Reagan knew what he was doing. And Michael Deaver, interested only in how Rea-gan was perceived, shrugged at the sight of Senator Moynihan and other Democrats leaping to their feet to applaud the President mock-ingly. Republicans were forced to leap to their feet, too, or look like in-grates. Irony did not transmit over network television; a standing ovation was a standing ovation. Trust Reagan, too, to turn it to his ad-vantage! "And here all that time," he told the Democrats, when their cheers began to subside, "I thought you were reading the paper."

☯

On February 11, the President heard back from the Joint Chiefs of Staff regarding his strategic defense initiative. *His*—how easily the pos-sessive flows from one's pen, as from Reagan's: "It was my idea to begin with." And from his lips: "My dream . . . my dream." Well, not quite: the original dreamer-up of a shield in space had been one Nicholas C. Christofilos, a colleague of Edward Teller's at Livermore Research Laboratory in California. In 1957, Dr. Christofilos had postulated that exo-atmospheric nuclear explosions might sow a stardust of magne-tized electrons thick enough to sandpaper incoming missiles out of ex-istence.

What Reagan meant by *my dream* (and let us note, he rarely took credit for anything) was *my initiative*. It was he—not Teller, not his pol-icy advisers—who elected to make strategic defense a metaphor of na-tional resolve in 1983. He had been interested in lethal rays at least since his days as Brass Bancroft, when he deployed the photon-spitting Inertia Projector at airborne enemies of the state. Long before that, in-deed, he could remember the warring empyrean of his favorite boy-hood novel, Edgar Rice Burroughs's *Princess of Mars*. I keep a copy on my desk: just to flick through it is to encounter five-foot-thick polished glass domes over cities, heaven-filling salvos, impregnable walls of car-borundum, forts, and "manufactories" that only one man with a key can enter. The book's last chapter is particularly imaginative, domi-nated by the magnificent symbol of a civilization dying for lack of air.

So much for the science-fiction quotient. But Reagan also had a seri-ous, if amateurish, interest in strategic defense. He had visited Liver-more in his first year as Governor, and been briefed by Dr. Teller on experiments involving gamma-ray missile interceptions. And on July

31, 1979, he had paid a similar visit to NORAD (North American Air Defense Command) in Colorado's Cheyenne Mountain, where he learned for the first time how vulnerable America was to intercontinental attack. Not to mention NORAD itself: an official there had admitted that a single Soviet SS-18, aimed at the vault facility's steel door, "would blow us away."

At that time, the Soviet Union had more than three hundred such monster missiles to fire. Less than two and a half years later, as Reagan and Caspar Weinberger sat down to lunch with the Joint Chiefs in the Cabinet Room, the total had risen to four hundred and thirteen. Meanwhile, the nation's discontinued anti-ballistic missile defense facility, at Grand Forks, North Dakota, was reverting to prairie. Nothing but a few fragile windows, and Thomas Jefferson's Rose Garden colonnade, protected the high command of the United States from an incoming missile.

The Chiefs were familiar with the new year's most frightening fact: the total number of nuclear weapons in the world had now passed sixty thousand, enough for more than a million Hiroshimas. Admiral Watkins was particularly worried by what he had heard from Dr. Teller about Soviet superiority in this area. As a devout Catholic, he also believed in the moral imperative of defense, and said so in words that made the President light up.

"We should protect the American people, not avenge them," Watkins said.

"Exactly," said Reagan, memorizing the line for his diary that night.

He asked the Chiefs for their individual opinions, and all five endorsed a strategic defense program. But they were vague as to how comprehensive it should be, how much it would cost, and how it should operate.

"Well, I would like very much to pursue this," the President said. He seemed unusually excited.

"None of us believed that he would seize on it with such passion," McFarlane says now. "I was a little alarmed at his urgency." Had McFarlane understood the compulsions of an essentially imaginative mind, he would have been less surprised. When I met with Dutch three nights later (at the Valentine's Day dinner described in the prologue to this book), his continuing emotional high was obvious.

Yet, even as the Chiefs researched new ways to "protect," Reagan began work on a speech sure to provoke the Soviet Union. He was shortly due to address the National Association of Evangelicals, and needed a text that would cater to their especial worldview—as opposed to that of the National Conference of Catholic Bishops. His assigned speechwriter was a fiercely conservative, thirtyish Yale graduate and Pulitzer Prize winner named Anthony R. Dolan.

I am reluctant to suggest that anyone other than Dolan coined the phrase *Evil Empire*. However, two foreigners with direct experience of totalitarianism had touched on it before, in ways that seem to have gotten Reagan's attention. One was Alexander Solzhenitsyn, who told the AFL-CIO in 1975 that the Soviet Union was "the concentration of World Evil." The other was Alexandre de Maranches, the chief of French intelligence who flew all the way to Los Angeles in December 1980 to warn Reagan against "*l'empire du mal.*"

With Arnaud de Borchgrave, *Newsweek*'s foreign correspondent, translating, Maranches had prophesied, "You are the American President who will lead the free world to final victory over Communism. . . . But first, the Red Army must be forced to retreat from Afghanistan. Shoulder-fired anti-aircraft missiles are the key."

Whether or not Reagan understood the last (absolutely accurate) tactical detail, anticipating his eventual issuance of Stinger missiles to the Afghan rebels by five and a half years, de Borchgrave is convinced that the phrase *l'empire du mal* sank in. De Maranches had used it again and again: "Once their fighter bombers and fighter tanks can no longer fly . . . the evil empire will begin to disintegrate."

What really matters more than phrasemaking in oratory is force and timing of utterance. The facts are that Reagan met with Dolan, Dolan wrote the speech, Reagan lightly rewrote it and delivered it at Orlando, Florida, on March 8, 1983. The evangelicals came to their feet.

Ironically, for an address now remembered as a political statement, it was a lay sermon from start to finish. It dealt with questions of morality in public life, and discussed public matters only in relation to that theme. Reagan said that his Administration believed, as the Founding Fathers did, that America's inalienable rights were not accidental, but God-given. "Now I don't have to tell you that this puts us in opposition to, or at least out of step with, a prevailing attitude of many who have turned to a modern-day secularism."

The most disturbing evidence of this attitude in government was Washington's funding of clinics that provided "birth control drugs and devices to underage girls without the knowledge of their parents." Sex itself was being secularized. "Are we to believe that something so sacred can be looked upon as a purely physical thing with no potential for emotional and psychological harm?" Apparently, yes, for that cynicism extended to the womb:

"Abortion on demand" now takes the lives of up to one and a half million unborn children a year. Human life legislation ending this tragedy will someday pass the Congress—and you and I must never rest until it does. Unless and until it can be proven that the unborn child is not a living entity, then its right to life, liberty and the pursuit of happiness must be protected.

Only after noting that the United States was the most religious society on earth, purging itself of racism and class prejudice largely through faith, did he address his "final point," the phenomenon of Marxist-Leninist leaders sacrificing morality to the revolution.

I think the refusal of many influential people to accept this elementary fact of Soviet doctrine illustrates an historical reluctance to see totalitarian powers for what they are. We saw this phenomenon in the 1930s; we see it too often today. . . . Let us pray for the salvation of all those who live in that totalitarian darkness . . . the focus of evil in the modern world.

And in a peroration addressed to the proponents of a nuclear freeze (who prominently included his own daughter Patti) he invoked *l'empire du mal*. "I urge you to beware the temptation . . . to ignore the facts of history and the aggressive impulses of an evil empire, to simply call the arms race a giant misunderstanding and thereby remove yourself [*sic*] from the struggle between right and wrong, good and evil."

The reaction to Reagan's speech was extraordinary, not only for intensity but for the diametric opposition of conservatives who loved it and liberals who took it to be a declaration of rhetorical war. And that was just within the boundaries of the United States, where evangelical language was at least understood. In a much-quoted remark, Henry Steele Commager called it "the worst presidential speech in American history," because of its "gross appeal to religious prejudice." In Europe, the President was variously perceived as the archetypal American *naïf,* an old actor moving from script to script, and a binary-minded simpleton who thought all issues could be reduced to check boxes marked YES or NO. The consensus of critics was that he had expressed coarse and confrontational sentiments that were bound to increase East-West tensions.

In an official response circulated by TASS, Yuri Andropov accused the President of being deliberately "provocative" and obsessed by a "bellicose, lunatic anti-Communism." KGB agents were instructed to make a slogan of the phrase *Reagan eto voina* [Reagan means war]. Ironically, little attention was paid to Soviet domestic opinion. Not for years would evidence begin to gather that the word *evil* had penetrated the Russian soul as surely as the cadmium poisoning Russian beets. It was a word, however unspoken, guiltily familiar to every *apparatchik:* the Party had, after all, killed more innocents than any despotism in history. Those with long memories could look right back to Lenin's Cheka and see the "focus" that Reagan spoke of already irising in at the end of 1917.

Western travelers who happened to be well connected and in Moscow at the time of the President's speech remember a feeling of instant shock. "Within twenty-four hours," one of them told me, "I was hearing of the reaction spreading through society—of self-disgust and self-acknowledgment."

"Other Presidents have bad-mouthed Soviet Communism."

"Yes, but never so directly, and in such plain language."

Reagan waited just fifteen days before following up, on March 23, with a second major statement that added fear—the dark, Dostoyevskian variant, verging on paranoia, that periodically clouds Russian perceptions—to shame. Again he segued into the statement as a sort of afterword to the main text of his speech, which was billed as a routine television address to the American people on Soviet global strategy. But this time the statement was an announcement so determinedly radical that George Shultz, unconsulted until two days before, listened in a resentful fury:

> Let me share with you a vision of the future which offers hope. It is that we embark on a program to counter the awesome Soviet missile threat *with measures that are defensive.* Let us turn to the very strengths in technology that spawned our great industrial base and that have given us the quality of life we enjoy today.
>
> What if free people could live secure in the knowledge that their security did not rest upon the threat of instant U.S. retaliation to deter a Soviet attack—*that we could intercept and destroy strategic ballistic missiles before they reached our own soil or that of our allies?*
>
> I know this is a formidable, technical task, one that may not be accomplished before the end of this century. Yet current technology has attained a level of sophistication where it's reasonable for us to begin this effort. . . .

My fellow Americans, tonight we're launching an effort which holds the promise of changing the course of human history.

Shultz's rage was compounded with discomfiture at having to watch this proclamation of the Strategic Defense Initiative on a big screen in the East Room of the White House, at dinner with several dozen senior scientists and former and present Cabinet officers. "I know all of you are here on very short notice and at some inconvenience," Reagan had said in welcome, casually conveying their irrelevance as policy-makers. "Bud McFarlane and Jay Keyworth will be along in a moment to provide you with more details and answer any questions you may have."

Dr. George A. "Jay" Keyworth II was the President's Science Adviser, a boyish, thatch-haired, torrentially talkative nuclear physicist, in thrall to Edward Teller. Even he had been kept out of the SDI "loop" until March 19, when McFarlane presented him with an ill-typed draft of Reagan's "vision of the future" and asked if it was scientifically realizable. Keyworth thought so, and was asked to help edit the draft. He was not permitted to consult with anyone else except the National Security Adviser. Only when the text was pretty well final would George Shultz be allowed to boggle at it.

The Secretary of State was well equipped for boggling, being by nature baggy of eye, suspicious of surprise, and thin of skin. On four days out of five Shultz was a delightful person, as genial and reliable as Haig had been touchy and incendiary. His lumbering, fullback forcefulness, coupled with courtesy of manner, made him a natural negotiator, the embodiment of American resolve, as many foreign ministers had already discovered. Only on the odd day, when his vanity was bruised (often by some slight so minor as to be imperceptible), did the Secretary suddenly become a stone-faced sulk, ignoring all comers and giving off waves of gloom. "If you want to know the true meaning of silence," a State Department aide told me, "you should be alone in the elevator with George when he's on a bummer."

A veteran of a thousand gray-suited executive meetings, Shultz liked things "aboveboard," "on the table," "moved and seconded," and "agreed to"—comfortable, cautious, corporate phrases. Any threat to received wisdom was "way out of line"; his idea of daring individuality was a quorum. He particularly mistrusted the Lone Ranger in the NSC, who seemed able to communicate with the President by smoke signal, with little regard for European insecurities. (Was it a coincidence that Clark and McFarlane were rushing the Strategic Defense Initiative through while NATO met for a nuclear conference in Lisbon?) And to be lectured in strategy by a slide-ruler like Jay Keyworth, in a room crowded with other dumbfounded dignitaries, was an affront to Schultz's status as the President's senior adviser.

☯

As described by Keyworth—as "dreamed" by Reagan—the Initiative was an invisible, multilayered hemisphere of security, hugely floating in space over North America. It would require a godlike ruling intelligence ("battle computing") to coordinate millions of actions and reactions, milliseconds apart, probably without assistance from below. Strategic missiles, soaring up from whatever evil empire dared to deploy them, would alert a miniature galaxy of sensors, mirrors, and command centers in high orbit, whereupon X-ray lasers, particle beams, chemical rockets, and rail guns firing "smart rocks" would pulverize the missiles en route, reducing them and their warheads to clouds of radiant chaff. Since much of the system would function at the speed of light—indeed, *be* light—tens of thousands of such interceptions could be accomplished in the thirty-odd minutes it would take for a missile fleet to arrive from, say, the Ukraine.

The whole concept was so heaven-filling, so imponderably complex (necessitating, for a start, some forty to a hundred million lines of programming, and enough money to buy another navy), as to pass beyond physics into metaphysics, and thence into metaphor. In which case Dutch's "vision of the future" was as old as it was new, dating back at least to the night in 1818 when John Keats stood on the shore of the world and saw "huge, cloudy symbols of a high romance" drifting among the stars.

To the more earthbound perception of a George Shultz, the SDI was a cosmic joke. Only a "lunatic" like Keyworth could have perpetrated it on the President. Even the Joint Chiefs were upset about the surprise announcement and its likely effect upon their uniformed colleagues in Europe. "This paragraph is a revolution in our strategic doctrine," Shultz had told Reagan, when finally permitted to see a draft of the speech.

What particularly bothered the Secretary was a clause in the Anti–Ballistic Missile Treaty, which was sure now to become the most vexed talking point in arms-control talks with the Soviet Union:

> Each Party undertakes not to develop, test, or deploy ABM systems or components which are sea-based, air-based, *space-based,* or mobile land-based.

Shultz had been even more disturbed by the President's obvious reluctance to change a word of the speech draft. He had tried to make Reagan understand that some powers were bound to feel that strategic defense was "destabilizing." Might the Soviets, for example, not see an armed *and* attack-proof United States as more dangerous than it was already?

"I can see the moral ground you want to stake out," Shultz said, "but I don't want to see you put something forward so powerfully, only to find technical flaws or major doctrinal weaknesses."

The Secretary's memoirs are typically mute here as to what Reagan said in reply. Very likely he just sat and listened. As Martin Anderson once remarked, his obstinacy was absorbent: he accepted criticism, but never reflected it back. One could not tell whether it had in fact sunk in. At any rate, Shultz got half of what he wanted—presidential lip-service to the ABM Treaty and the efficacy of deterrence, a disclaimer of any aggressive intent in space, and one strong paragraph confirming that the United States still regarded Western Europe's security as identical with its own.

In exchange, he had to listen to the rest of the speech as written, including one sentence that was neither Keyworth nor Clark nor McFarlane but pure Ronald Reagan:

> I call upon the scientific community in our country, those who gave us nuclear weapons, to turn their great talents now to the cause of mankind and world peace; to give us the means of rendering these nuclear weapons impotent and obsolete.

After the television lights faded in the Oval Office, the President rejoined his guests for coffee. He felt good about the speech, and luxuriated in every polite compliment. "They all praised it to the sky," he wrote later, "and seemed to think it would be a source of debate for some time to come."

So it was, in the sense that the Emancipation Proclamation had given Northerners and Southerners something to discuss in 1862. On Capitol Hill, Senator Edward Kennedy made the inevitable comparison to *Star Wars.* Fiscal experts quailed at the SDI's probable cost. Diplomats feared that a new age of American isolationism was dawning. NATO ministers wondered if the President's promise to deploy a European INF still held good.

Most scientists reacted with disbelief to Reagan's assertion that "current technology" was sophisticated enough to make space defense feasible. There was, for a start, the problem of compound deterioration inherent in laser physics. A pencil-thin beam might melt missile sheathing at a few hundred yards, if it was sharp and bright enough; but reflected into space—even *within* space—it would thicken and coarsen and cool. To keep an X-ray laser thin over a distance of three to four thousand kilometers would require such Vesuvian reserves of energy that only a "nuclear event" could trigger it. In other words, space would have to be radioactivated in order to prevent the destruction of God's Own Country.

This hardly assuaged the fears of freezeniks (whom Reagan referred to in his diary as "that whole d--n gang"). They pointed out that rads might well sift down into the upper atmosphere. A signwriter outside the White House ominously demonstrated that "Ronald Wilson Reagan" could be anagrammed as INSANE ANGLO WARLORD.

The phrase more or less summarized Moscow's official reaction. Yuri Andropov came out of dialysis to issue a furious denunciation of strategic defense as "a bid to disarm the Soviet Union" by denying it a retaliatory capability. He warned that the Reagan Administration was "continuing to tread an extremely dangerous path," and asking for nuclear war. "This is not just irresponsible, it is insane."

During all the above uproar, I was a fellow at the Woodrow Wilson International Center for Scholars in Washington, working on my second Roosevelt volume and attending the various "colloquia" that comfort the loneliness of long-distance academics. Most of my colleagues were specialists in foreign, economic, or political studies, and hence took little notice of me. My dinner with the President at Senator Hatfield's caused a brief flurry of interest. I was asked to speak of it in the refectory one day, but when I quoted Dutch's line, "Along came Nancy Davis and saved my soul," they rolled their eyes and returned to the exchange of abstract nouns.

Ronald Reagan was not then, and still is not now, generally admired among the professoriat. Memories die hard of some of his philistine pronouncements as Governor ("The State of California has no business subsidizing intellectual curiosity"), not to mention his suggestion that university libraries could save money by trashing all old editions. The Ivy League has never forgiven him for not caring a damn, as President, what Harvard or Yale thought about anything. The only scholars who took him at seriously at the Wilson Center were its director, James Billington, a Russian expert who will figure later on in this book as Librarian of Congress, and Arnold Kramish, a veteran of the Manhattan Project. I regret not cultivating the latter gentleman, who thought Reagan's SDI speech had been a historic pronouncement. He wrote a *Washington Post* Op-Ed piece to that effect, which was posted on the Center bulletin board for nobody to read:

> In 1941, the consequences of the discovery of nuclear fission three years earlier were demonstrated four years later. In 1983, the hoped-for benefits of discoveries of the previous two decades may or may not be decades ahead. The President did not promise more.
>
> What he did turn toward is a goal, not a certainty, to try to erase the specter of nuclear retaliation and annihilation from the animus of the populations of the world. It is a bold and risky course, but why should anyone be faulted for any conceptual attempt to resolve these burning issues? How is it that . . . eminent scientists, betraying the scientific spirit of free enquiry, should dictate that humankind should not even *think* of ways to improve its condition? Where are the scientists of yesterday who were great through the virtue that they recognized that they were merely part of the human condition, sought to improve it, but knew their fallibilities?

☯

Reagan followed his speech with an immediate directive authorizing the Pentagon to study the technological and political implications of space-based defense. Secretary Weinberger set up a new Strategic Defense Initiative Organization unit under his own command, to protect it from interference by the Joint Chiefs of Staff. All the Pentagon's funds allocated to ABM research and development were now diverted to this new power center, which was placed under the direction of Lieutenant General James Abrahamson, a veteran administrator of the space-shuttle program.

The President signed one more appeal for the protection of innocents from incoming missiles—an article entitled "Abortion and the Conscience of the Nation" in the spring issue of *The Human Life Review*—then, as cherry blossoms thickened along the Mall, braced himself for a seasonal restlessness among his senior staff. Not only pollen but party politics had begun to charge the air. Four Democrats had already declared themselves candidates for the Presidency in 1984, with former Vice President Walter Mondale a clear front-runner. In less than a year, the primary season would be under way.

Reagan meant to delay any decision about running for a second term until the last possible moment. He knew that as soon as he declared he would become more candidate than President, liable to lobbyists and fund-raisers. Loath to sacrifice any power, he kept his true ambitions secret even from his diary. This enigmatic attitude was frustrating to his aides, who needed to think about their own futures.

The person most interested was the one who stood to gain the least from another Reagan campaign. George Bush was convinced that the President would announce in June or July. Sounding slightly bitter, he told Ambassador Dobrynin that if through some trick of fate he himself became the nominee, he doubted Reagan would be a strong supporter. "The best I can expect is his benevolent neutrality."

Dobrynin remarked that the President's extreme anti-Communism might be a hindrance to his re-election. "Well, he's hard, very hard indeed," Bush agreed.

☯

A sudden disaster in Lebanon, early on April 18, took everyone's mind off campaign politics. The President was awakened early with the news that a van bomb outside the U.S. embassy in Beirut had killed scores of people, including five Marines. "First word is that the Iranian Shiites did it—d--n them." The toll rose to sixty-three, with the CIA's top Middle East expert among seventeen American dead. Reagan allowed himself a rare flash of anger in his diary. "Lord, forgive me for the hatred I feel for the humans who can do such a cruel and cowardly deed."

At Andrews Air Force Base on April 23, he discovered for the first time what it felt like to salute a row of coffins, and look into the eyes of Americans whom he had personally bereaved. "All I could do was grip their hands—I was too choked up to speak."

Nevertheless, speak he had to, and he delivered a eulogy that struck me (watching with a vindictive crowd in the Wilson Center library) as unfeeling and tasteless in its promise that "more great accomplishments" lay ahead for those who were to remain in Lebanon. *Mea culpa,* Dutch—I should have known that such a speech would have been tuned by every spinmeister in the White House. Too bad they didn't let you articulate the thoughts you drafted yourself, in your patented shorthand:

TODAY . . . FAMLYs . . . THS. HONORD DEAD . . .
GALLNT AMs UNDRSTOOD . . . DANGR . . .
WNT WILLNGLY . . . BEIRUT . . .
DASTARDLY DEED—UNPARALLELD COWARDICE
AFLICTD MNKND LOOKS . . . US . . . HELP . . .
COWARDLY, SKULKING BARBARIANS

This was a juncture at which Caspar Weinberger's philosophy of foreign entanglement (that it be absolutely in the national interest, and
even then subject to constant review) would have seemed to apply. But
George Shultz, hastily decamping for the Middle East, worked out an
"agreement" whereby Israel and Syria would leave Lebanon within
twelve weeks, in exchange for mutual guarantees of security. The agreement lasted about as long as he took to get home. As Weinberger sarcastically noted, it had the slight flaw of giving the Syrians (who were
reported to have been involved in the embassy bombing) veto power
over any of its provisions; indeed, when the twelve weeks were up,
Beirut was as beleaguered as ever.

By then Reagan had handed over micromanagement of Middle
Eastern politics to Robert McFarlane, and persuaded himself, in his
best Innocent Fool manner, that the embassy bombing had been an isolated terrorist incident. He was all too willing to let the desperately ambitious McFarlane try for another accord in Lebanon, while he and
William Clark monitored two other cauldrons of doctrinal violence,
much closer to home.

Throughout his Presidency so far, Reagan had avoided making any
scripted public statement about El Salvador and Nicaragua. Both countries, however, worried him a great deal, if only because he was forever
being harangued about them by conservative advisers. First Alexander
Haig and now Judge Clark, with the assistance of such other Castro-
watchers as William Casey and Jeane Kirkpatrick, were convinced that
the future of democracy in Central America depended on his firm goodwill and ability to wrest aid from Congress. In El Salvador, the pro-
American government needed money, supplies, and "military advice" to
avoid defeat at the hands of Marxist guerrillas—and not too many
questions asked about the death squads who meted out "justice" there.
In Nicaragua, a reverse situation applied. The ruling Sandinista government was pro-Soviet, while its would-be overthrowers, or *contrarevolu-
cionarios,* again looked for help to the "colossus of the north."

Reagan liked the last phrase, being unconscious of its irony. Yet he was not so police-minded as to want to send troops to either country. Quite aside from the fact that both were jungly enough to prompt cautionary memories of Vietnam, his sense of fairness reminded him that the United States had had a role, in 1979, in setting up the Sandinistas, to free Nicaragua from the corrupt dictatorship of Anastasio Somoza. And El Salvador's current "democratic" regime was so reactionary as to make Somoza's look benign.

Neither of these considerations bothered Kirkpatrick, Clark, or Casey. They were only concerned with north-of-the-border security, and felt it to be threatened by a documented flow of Soviet arms and propaganda from Cuba into Nicaragua, and thence via guerrilla trails into El Salvador. Clark darkly reported that Castro's agents had also arranged an alliance between the Marxist-oriented governments of Grenada and Suriname—the latter a former Dutch colony which threatened to become the first Communist state on the South American mainland.

On the other side of the President's NSPG (National Security Planning Group) table, ideologically speaking, were Shultz, Weinberger, Deaver, and Baker. None had much knowledge of Central American affairs, but they knew enough to be uncomfortable with a secret "finding" that Reagan had given the CIA on December 1, 1981, in favor of covert aid to the Nicaraguan *contras*. Initially set at twenty million dollars, to allow Argentina to train a Honduras-based guerrilla band, this commitment had now, in 1983, escalated to twenty-six million dollars in support of an army of nearly eight thousand insurgents, including not a few nostalgic *Somocistas*.

Shultz agreed that the evidence of Communist mischief in Central America was "alarming," but was characteristically hopeful for a diplomatic solution. Weinberger approved covert activities only insofar as they lessened the chance of direct intervention. Deaver and Baker were concerned with possible political damage (what if the *contras* perpetrated a Beirut-style massacre?), but went along because they feared a frustrated President might resort to military force. Haig, Casey, and Clark had long since convinced Reagan that "all of Central America is targeted for a Communist takeover."

Congressional opinion about *contra* aid was equally divided, with the Republican-controlled Senate generally in favor, and the Democrat-controlled House showing signs of making it a campaign issue in 1984. Representative Edward P. Boland, who chaired the House Intelligence Committee, had already gotten a unanimous vote prohibiting the CIA from using taxpayer money "for the purpose of overthrowing the Government of Nicaragua." Now came a letter to the President, signed by thirty House members, which warned him that Casey's agency might be breaking the law south of the border. If so, all *contra* aid, covert and overt, was in danger.

"Congress," Reagan fumed in his diary, "has eroded away much of the Const. authority of the Presidency in foreign affairs . . . they can't and don't have the information the Pres. has & they are really lousing things up." He decided that the time had come to defend his Central American policy in the forum that had served him so well twice before: a joint session of Congress. Obviously, he could not say much about what the CIA and NSC were up to, but at least he might be able to communicate a sense of crisis to his real target audience, the American people.

As was his habit with important speeches, Reagan drafted his proposed remarks himself, in page after legal page of reasoned prose. He began by remarking that the Soviet presence in Central America was real enough to feel. "El Salvador is nearer Texas than Texas is to Mass. Nicaragua is closer to Miami, New Orleans, Houston, San Antonio, Los Angeles & Denver than these cities are to Wash. where we are gathered tonight." But strategy, not geography, was the issue: Soviet colonization of the Caribbean basin put Gulf ports and the Panama Canal at risk. "It is well to remember that in 1942 a handful of Hitler's submarines sank more tonnage there than in all of the Atlantic Ocean."

He recounted the known facts. Cuba had air and submarine bases that extended regular hospitality to Soviet nuclear forces. "The tiny island of Grenada" was building a Soviet-style air base with Cuban help; when completed, it would provide a direct link in the supply of matériel to Nicaragua and El Salvador. There were thirty-seven new military bases in Nicaragua, serving a 25,000-man army equipped with the most sophisticated weapons roubles could buy. This fighting machine was strengthened by 50,000 militia and trained by "eight thousand quote-unquote Cuban advisers." Hundreds more strangely interested observers were on hand from the Soviet Union, East Germany, Libya, and the Palestine Liberation Organization. "We," Reagan noted in a cramped insertion, "have 55 mil. trainers in El Salvador." Meanwhile, throughout Central America, "the people's plight remains the same; hopeless, helpless and hungry."

Reagan permitted no major changes to his draft, except for the addition of several pages of policyspeak to satisfy Shultz, and a request for six hundred million dollars in overt aid. (The only reference to *covert* aid was a comment that the government in Managua should not be protected from "the anger of its own people.") Baker, Deaver, and Meese approved the speech for delivery on April 27, 1983. They did not think that the President would get all the money he wanted, but hoped for enough standing ovations to erase memories of his sad trip to Andrews Air Force Base.

☯

Unfortunately, the law of diminishing returns applies as much to Congressional appearances as anything else. Having only just invoked Armageddon in space, Reagan was hard put to relocate it in El Salvador, and convince skeptical Democrats that the Evil Empire was colonizing the Lesser Antilles. His reception was merely courteous, and the heaviest applause line came when he said he had "no thought of sending American combat troops" into Central America.

On May 3, members of the House Intelligence Committee, voting along partisan lines, banned all covert operations in Nicaragua. Their colleagues in the Senate temporarily restored funding, but warned the President that he would have to make a better case for the *contras,* or risk a permanent cutoff in September. Public opinion settled solidly against the Administration's Central American policy. Reagan, not used to being rejected after a major rhetorical effort, was reduced to semi-coherence when a delegation of print journalists pressed him on *contra* aid. One of them was Lou Cannon, who detected the same signs of exhaustion he had seen two years before, after Ottawa. Cannon's resultant story in *The Washington Post* did much to encourage rumors that the President, now in his seventy-third year, might not run again.

A feeling of declining morale affected the West Wing. Until recently, Reagan had seemed godlike in his ability to convince both Congress and the American people of the righteousness of his beliefs. But the long recession, the tragedy in Beirut, and proliferating evidence of tyranny in El Salvador indicated that he was not infallible. While he still engendered strong feelings of personal affection, his political support was noticeably divided, now, between the old Californian conservatives who wanted to "let Reagan be Reagan" and the Washingtonian pragmatists who felt that only James Baker could protect him from the new opposition in Congress.

On May 16, stalwarts of the former group gathered in the State Dining Room to witness the swearing-in of Helene von Damm as Ambassador to Austria. Judge Clark administered the oath while Reagan looked on benignly, and sealed her elevation with a kiss that had all the aspects of a benediction. This metamorphosis of the young immigrant who had trekked across the country to volunteer for his first gubernatorial campaign was looked at askance by the State Department. Austrian experts there feared—correctly, it turned out—that Ms. von Damm's Tyrolean tones would offend the notoriously snobby Viennese. Nor was Nancy Reagan able to attend. To the President, however, the idea of Cinderella returning to her "native land" in a pumpkin coach emblazoned with the Stars and Stripes was "heartwarming."

With the departure of bright, brash Helene, an extra shadow occluded Judge Clark's brow. She had always personified to him—and to Meese and Deaver—the spirit of those early days in Sacramento when they had all been young and intoxicated with political success, cooperating smoothly in an administration free of rancor. Even though Clark was now at the apogee of his reluctant career in politics, he hated Washington for what it had done to them all—Reagan, slowed, aged; Weinberger, hardened; Meese, embattled; Deaver (another conspicuous absentee from the swearing-in), slicked and sly. As for himself, he had become so obsessed with the Communist threat that he felt unable to resign and go home as long as the President was surrounded with soothsayers like Baker and Shultz. What if they brought back the bad old days of détente?

On May 27 at Williamsburg, Virginia, the President hosted the annual G7 economic summit. It was his third such event, and he was relaxed enough about it to dispense with the briefing book that Baker prepared for him. "Enough already," he told himself, and watched *The Sound of Music* with Nancy.

The subsequent proceedings found Reagan in such "radiant" form—the adjective is Margaret Thatcher's—as to belie recent doubts about his physical and mental condition. He basked in the admiration of his guests, who had to admit that the American economy had performed astonishingly in recent months, while their own were still in recession. Figures such as a dizzy ten-point drop in inflation (from 13.5 percent in the last year of the Carter Administration to 3.2 percent now) could not be ignored, nor the resolve with which Reagan had cut taxes and forced up military spending. Even if due credit were given to Paul Volcker, chairman of the U.S. Federal Reserve, for keeping interest rates punitively high since 1980, Europeans could no longer joke about the illogicality of *Reaganomiques*.

"Tell us about the American miracle," said an enormous, jolly German, who seemed to have replaced Helmut Schmidt as Chancellor of West Germany, but fortunately had the same first name.

Reagan ranged over his old philosophy of reduced government and deregulated private enterprise. Then, switching to the future tense, he began to talk about his intent to deploy cruise and Pershing missiles in Europe, as soon as Chancellor Kohl obtained a formal vote of approval in the Bundestag. That could come as early as November. Neither François Mitterrand nor Pierre Trudeau of Canada objected to the sudden change of subject. Next morning, however, they jibbed at signing a statement that endorsed both deployment and negotiations toward "*l'option zéro.*" Trudeau was clearly afraid of provoking the Kremlin at a time when Yuri Andropov was threatening to increase Warsaw Pact nuclear forces.

For the first time in three conferences, they found themselves dealing with an angry, fist-thumping Ronald Reagan. He tossed his briefing book down on the green leather table and lectured them for twenty minutes, delaying lunch. Afterward, Mrs. Thatcher weighed in. "I thought at one point," Reagan wrote in his diary, "Margaret was going to order Pierre to go stand in a corner." Against such fervor—buttressed by that of Kohl, Amintore Fanfani of Italy, and Yasuhiro Nakasone of Japan—Mitterrand and Trudeau were powerless, and the summit ended with a communiqué that fairly purred agreement.

"Except," Mrs. Thatcher mourned, "for a little misty language on the subject of exchange rate coordination."

Much as she adored her "Ronnie," she had often worried about his lack of interest in detail. It was incomprehensible to her that financial tables, which she crunched like cornflakes, did not fascinate him. But she had to admit that this time

he had plainly done his homework. He had all the facts and figures at his fingertips. He steered the discussions with great skill and aplomb. He managed to get all he wanted from the summit, while allowing everyone to feel that they had got at least some of what *they* wanted, and he did all this with an immense geniality.

Had she known that he had "done his homework" in the Tyrolean Alps with Julie Andrews, she might have been even more impressed. Or worried.

☯

On the same night the Big Seven toasted themselves in Williamsburg, a spreading flotsam of steak and lobster scraps marked the entry into Lebanese waters of yet another consignment of U.S. Marines. The fantail dump, ordered by an officer, pretty well symbolized the feelings of all those aboard: they were celebrating their last night of freedom as American soldiers, and had contempt for the part of the world they were required to defend.

As one of them would shortly scrawl on the wall of a squalid bar in Beirut: "Don't send me to hell. I've already served my time in Lebanon."

The failure of Shultz's withdrawal agreement had committed the Reagan Administration to maintaining its lightly armed "peacekeeping" garrison at Beirut International Airport, isolated from other MNF emplacements, while factional fighting raged all around and occasional shells whistled down from the Chouf Mountains, reminding the Marines of their vulnerability. It was a situation beyond the comprehension of the average grunt: American boys trained to fight, yet forbidden to respond to hostile fire, guarding the gateway to a country that could not be governed, awaiting the departure of invaders who had every selfish reason to stay. But as Weinberger sourly observed, military stalemates are cherished by diplomats, who see them as mandating more and more negotiation, and attracting the notice of jurors for the Nobel Peace Prize.

The Secretary of Defense argued for much of June that the objectives of the MNF could not be achieved. Unless Reagan decided actually to go to war in Lebanon, then the Marines could do nothing but draw the fire of any force that wanted to hit the "bull's-eye" of their four-story barracks. They should be recalled before they came home in body bags. The Joint Chiefs of Staff concurred. Shultz, however, insisted that his agreement needed time to work, while Reagan allowed Casey and Clark to persuade him, once again, that Central America was more immediately dangerous—and more directly related to Soviet imperial ambitions.

"We're losing it if we don't do something drastic," the President wrote, after a particularly apocalyptic briefing. El Salvador was bleeding to death, while Congress dribbled out "about ¼ of what we ask for. . . . If the Soviets win in Central Am. we lose in Geneva and every place else."

At this moment of pessimism, a letter arrived from Yuri Andropov. It was, of all things, a Fourth of July message, calling for peaceable relations and "elimination of the nuclear threat" that overhung East and

West. Behind the stiff language, Reagan sensed a pleading tone, and was moved to draft another of his yellow-legal-pad, man-to-man notes, in the hope that Andropov might prove more receptive than Brezhnev. Again he had to deal with the resistance of his advisers. William Clark was shocked at the following scribbles: *If we can agree on mutual, verifiable reductions in the no. of nuclear weapons we both hold, could this not be a first step toward elimination of all such weapons? What a blessing this would be for all the people we both rep.*

Defense experts on the National Security Council agreed that such language might cause Soviet negotiators in Geneva to "up the ante" in opposition to INF deployment. Reagan accepted their scruples. The edited version of his letter was consequently formulaic. Dated and dispatched on July 11, it effectually ended any chance of a *rapprochement* with Andropov, if indeed there had been one.

It also marked Clark's last negative achievement as the naysayer of NSC. George Shultz and Michael Deaver were now seriously afraid of what they saw as his appeal to "Reagan's dark side," and tried to bring about his demise. On July 25, Shultz demanded, and got, a showdown meeting in the Oval Office, with Clark, Baker, Meese, and Bush in attendance. "The process for managing foreign policy has gone completely off the track," Shultz informed the President. After a year of hard work in the State Department, he did not care to have his diplomacy undercut, nor did he appreciate being left out of the national-security loop when reporters, or second-level staffers, were included. He cited a *New York Times* story that the Administration had decided on a blockade of Nicaragua without him, and his discovery that Robert McFarlane had just returned from the Middle East in a Jacuzzi-equipped 707, courtesy of King Fahd of Saudi Arabia, after negotiating directly with Syria on Lebanon.

"There is no way I can do my job as Secretary of State when secret missions like this take place without my knowledge," Shultz said, working himself into a rubicund rage. He declined to be "an errand boy" any longer, and suggested that Reagan might be better served by someone with more taste for intrigue. "Bill Clark seems to want the job, because he is trying to run everything. There is also Jeane Kirkpatrick. Or Henry Kissinger."

The President listened silently, as was his wont when confronted by strong emotion. He had a deep distaste for staff squabbles, yet here was Shultz forcing him to take sides, and a circle of expectant eyes staring at him. All of them knew something, none everything of what he knew. Shultz did not know that one of his own suggested successors

(Kissinger) was the author of the blockade plan. Clark had no clue that Reagan felt the loss of Shultz would be a "disaster" for the Administration. Bush, Meese, even the acutely political Baker were still unsure if there was going to be (in Reagan's cagey language), "a Presidential campaign involving me."

Reagan, looking pained, told Shultz that he wanted him to stay. But he did not issue the guarantee of exclusivity that Shultz craved, and the Secretary left his presence, like many supplicants before and since, unsatisfied and insecure.

Shultz's self-confidence was hardly bolstered, a week later, when he saw his rival on the cover of *Time* magazine. Clark was surrounded by a map of Central and North America, under a banner reading THE BIG STICK APPROACH. Seven pages of text inside proclaimed him as the gray eminence of American foreign policy. There was a sidebar article devoted to Shultz, entitled DISAPPEARING ACT AT FOGGY BOTTOM, and splattered with disparaging phrases: "influence continues to wane . . . 'too passive' . . . too reticent to take control."

The cover story's real damage, however, was accomplished by a large photograph showing the President, seated, uncharacteristically dwarfed by Clark standing on his left and Ambassador Kirkpatrick on his right. The latter looked as though she had just demanded the defoliation of El Salvador, while Clark had the veiled smile of a ventriloquist talking through his dummy. There followed a profile of Clark, headlined THE MAN WITH THE PRESIDENT'S EAR, and written by a bright young scribe named Maureen Dowd. It emphasized Clark's early ignorance in foreign policy, and featured the following paragraph, guaranteed to make Nancy Reagan lunge for the telephone:

> His management ability, infighting skills and close ties to Reagan have made him, in the judgment of many, the second most powerful man in the White House. Clark has encouraged the President to follow his raw, conservative instincts rather than the more pragmatic and politically savvy agendas suggested by White House Chief of Staff James Baker. This uncritical "let Reagan be Reagan" approach has resulted in a harder line and some political embarrassments.

The worst of these embarrassments, according to yet another article, was a recent vote by the full House of Representatives to shut off covert aid to the *contras*. It had been provoked by news that the Administra-

"Uncharacteristically dwarfed by Clark on his left
and Ambassador Kirkpatrick on his right."
*The President with his two chief Central American policy advisers,
August 1983.*

tion was preparing an NSC-authorized joint military exercise with Honduras along three of Nicaragua's four borders, including mock bombing runs and the deployment of nineteen warships. Democrats were described as "whooping and cheering" at Reagan's humiliation.

Shultz did not have much time to nurse his own bruises before Nancy Reagan called to say that Clark "ought to be fired." He did not have Ronnie's "best interests at heart." The Secretary cautiously agreed with her, and put down the phone with the feeling that foreign-policy-making would soon revert to Foggy Bottom, where it belonged.

August came to the District of Columbia: hard, hot days smelling of burnt rubber along the Mall, and barbecue smoke in the suburbs. Congress and senior members of the Administration left town—Reagan and Clark to their respective ranches, Bush to Kennebunkport, Shultz to his farm in Massachusetts. They did not get much relief. For week after week, across the country, temperatures soared to historic highs. Hundreds of people died of heat. Dry, stalled air over the Plains states aroused fears of another Dust Bowl. On Capitol Hill, where I had taken an apartment, half the population seemed to have gone fishing, and dead cicadas crunched underfoot like nuts.

Is it just in hindsight that I remember that month as being full of menace, its fetidness presaging something, as the weather around volcanoes is said to do, before they erupt? My diary is blank, and so, I note, is Dutch's, for the first time since he started to keep it in 1981: nothing from August 12 until he had an excellent reason to resume it just before Labor Day.

One's sense of an unnatural stasis everywhere embraced the political stalemate in Lebanon. The Israelis could not retreat from their positions, because the Syrians would not; the Lebanese government cowered undercover in Beirut; the U.S. Marines sweltered on the flats of the airport. Between these various redoubts, in valleys and villages and slums, nineteen armed sects and factions fought with ancient hatred while Robert McFarlane, importantly styling himself "President Reagan's Personal Representative in the Middle East," shuttled back and forth, vainly trying to reactivate the idea of a bilateral withdrawal.

Feelings of paralysis also emanated from Moscow, where Yuri Andropov, or what looked like a talking waxwork of him, announced that the Soviet Union was imposing a "unilateral moratorium" on the deployment of anti-satellite weapons.

In Jerusalem, another ailing leader, Menachem Begin, announced his retirement as Prime Minister. He was depressed by Israel's near bankruptcy (the occupation of South Lebanon was costing a million dollars a day) and the seeming impossibility of a settlement. The belligerents around Beirut increased their aggression. So many shells landed on the airport that the Marines finally received orders to hit back. On August 28, they pounded a Druse battery in the Chouf. Two of them were promptly killed by return mortar fire.

A hastily recruited crisis management team, headed by the Vice President and staffed by Shultz, Weinberger, and Casey, convened in Washington to review the War Powers Act of 1973. When I went out for a *Washington Post* on the last morning of the month, the machine at the corner of Second and East Capitol had sold out. Clouds to the northwest promised rain at last, and cool Canadian air.

It was about 9 A.M. local time, I guess, that I got my quarter back and went to look for another newspaper machine. Dutch, vacationing at

Rancho del Cielo, would have been good for another two hours in bed. And Korean Air Lines Flight KE007 was lifting off, in pre-dawn darkness, from Anchorage, Alaska, swinging west toward Seoul with two hundred and sixty-nine aboard.

For whatever reason—or non-reason—a normal organism becomes malignant, the 747 did not swing quite far enough, and settled on a course infinitesimally out of true. Degree built on degree as it headed out across the Bering Sea, dragging the darkness with it. By the time the President sat down to breakfast, KE007 had already attracted the alarmed attention of Soviet radar operators. It crossed the International Date Line into September, and entered forbidden airspace over the Kamchatka Peninsula at 5:33 A.M., Soviet Far Eastern Time. Four MiG-23s rose to pursue it, but ludicrously ran out of fuel before they could get within interception range.

KE007 left the peninsula behind and flew for another fifty minutes on automatic pilot, straight toward the prodigiously fortified Soviet naval base of Vladivostok. Only its cockpit and navigation lights glowed; most passengers were still asleep. Six MiG-23s and SU-15s scrambled as the long shape overflew Sakhalin Island, and at 6:26 A.M., they sent it spiraling into the Tatar Strait.

The first CRITIC ("critical intelligence") of an incident, probably military, and a lost plane, possibly civilian, reached Reagan at Rancho del Cielo about eight hours later. Judge Clark called him from San Luis Obispo and reported that the lost plane appeared to be a Korean airliner, "forced down or shot down by the Soviets."

(Two low-roofed haciendas in the California hills; two tall men on the phone; black trees, black herds under the early stars; for them, September had still not dawned.)

"Bill," Reagan said, "let's pray that it's not true."

Not until he was ready for bed did Clark call again, this time with definite evidence that KE007 had been downed by Soviet missile fire. A National Security Agency surveillance station in northern Japan had actually recorded an SU-15 pilot's satisfied shout of "*Yolki palki!*" as he fired his rocket at the 747—presumably on orders—followed by a confirmatory "The target is destroyed."

Edwin Meese came up to Rancho del Cielo at seven the next morning to brief Reagan on the solidifying story, which George Shultz was just about to announce in Washington. The Secretary's subsequent performance was impressive: anger controlled yet visibly seething, fact following fact. He reported the probable loss of all aboard KE007, including sixty-one Americans. "The Soviet plane was, we know, in

constant contact with its ground control. . . . The United States reacts
with revulsion to this attack."

Reagan allowed Moscow's initial explanation (that the 747 had
crashed of its own accord, after being warned off with tracer shells) to
wither in a firestorm of public disbelief. He returned to Washington on
Friday, September 2, and found the city depopulated for the Labor Day
weekend. This suited his purposes: he did not want to be pushed into
an overreaction by too many vengeful advisers. Senator Howard Baker
of Tennessee suggested he demand "reparations" from the Soviet government, and got a terse, "Remember, Howard, I'm President, and
you're not."

Not until Monday evening, September 5, did he deliver a personal
commentary on "what can only be called the Korean Air Line massacre" from the Oval Office. His anger was cold in contrast to Shultz's,
and his words contemptuous even by the standards of the Evil Empire
address. Like many viewers, I assumed they were the work of some
young turk of a speechwriter. Would that we could have seen the President scribbling them himself just a few hours earlier, seated in a damp
swimsuit, too driven to get up and change:

> Make no mistake about it—this attack was not just against our-
> selves or the Republic of Korea; this was the Soviet U. against the
> world, and the moral precepts which guide human relations among
> people everywhere. It was an act of barbarism born of a society
> which wantonly disregards individual rights, the value of human life
> & seeks constantly to expand & dominate other nations.
>
> They deny the deed but in their conflicting and dishonest protes-
> tations they reveal that—yes, shooting down a plane, even one with
> hundreds of innocent men, women, children & babies is a part of
> their normal procedure.

"We shouldn't be surprised by such inhuman brutality," he said
on television. "Memories come back of Czechoslovakia, Hungary,
Poland, the gassing of villages in Afghanistan." If the perpetrators of
the crime thought they could intimidate free people anywhere, they
were mistaken: "From every corner of the globe the word is defiance in
the face of this unspeakable act and defiance of the system which excuses it and tries to cover it up."

The President's every word seemed to express our collective outrage.
But then he adopted a milder tone and announced two or three ineffectual gestures of reproach, such as reaffirmation of an already exist-

ing ban on U.S. flights by Aeroflot. This apparent weakness was puzzling. Richard Viguerie, publisher of *Conservative Digest,* accused him of being a "Teddy Roosevelt in reverse"—speaking loudly and carrying a very small stick—while Elizabeth Drew, writing in *The New Yorker,* noted that President Carter had taken stronger action following the Soviet invasion of Afghanistan. The White House said nothing about hate mail received, but years later I discovered some defensive draft replies in Dutch's handwriting: *No one is more frustrated than I am. . . . Send their diplomats home? They would send ours home. And believe me this is no time for us to be without eyes and ears in Moscow.*

We now know that the KE007 crisis was more fraught with danger than anybody in the West realized at the time. Contrary to Kremlin denials, the airliner's black boxes were found by Soviet divers, and proved that it had been a civilian plane, easily divertible. Other long-secret Soviet records show that the pilot who destroyed it did so by direct order of a four-star general, and in conformity with a new border-security law that gave defense forces absolutely no tolerance for "intruder planes," whatever their shape or speed. The border law's ultimate author, and the addressee of all this official evidence, "Comrade Yu. V. Andropov."

Reagan, then, was operating under a supersensible instinct when he reminded Senator Baker that there are some situations only a head of state can handle. He somehow knew that his opposite number was responsible for what had happened, and that a strong speech of condemnation was all the response necessary. No number of diplomats expelled or negotiants recalled could alter the enormous news that two hundred and sixty-nine mostly sleeping people had been killed, without warning, for flying over a corner of the Evil Empire. The atrocity spoke for itself, as did Marshal Nikolai Ogarkov's insistence that KE007 had been a "deliberate, thoroughly planned intelligence operation." What happened to a Korean airliner could happen to a Norwegian cruise ship, or a round-the-world balloonist; it was a threat all human beings could relate to.

"This is not purely them versus us," Reagan told his critics. "It is the Soviet Union against the world, and we intend to keep it that way."

Presidents, being but flesh, live serially in real time, move from sleep to action and back to sleep again, from place to place and event to event. Yet their business is non-linear: any ordinary day may inflict upon them legislative humiliations, leukemic children, honorary degrees, national-security decisions, natural disasters, and emergency phone calls in Polish. In Reagan's case, he tried to impose at least a semblance of linkage upon his schedule by means of a descending chain of arrows, all pointing down the page to "home & Mother."

This compulsive *sequitur* was tested through the next fourteen weeks—by far the most stressful of his Presidency—to such an extent that we can only be thankful "Mother" was there to hold him together. Reagan was, after all, an old man, with scar tissue near his heart and steadily atrophying powers of concentration. Crisis complicated crisis until there seemed to be no fixed point in his universe but the strong-jawed profile beside him in bed, as he lay silently reciting his mantra against insomnia, "The Shooting of Dan McGrew."

To the dismay of White House pragmatists, he remained "hard, very hard" in all essential policy matters until the year was almost out. Only then did he show signs of having been been changed by the realization that he had helped bring the world close to war in 1983. For what was Andropov's increased alert along Soviet borders but a reaction to Ronald Reagan's military buildup, and deliberately provocative rhetoric? And what were El Salvador, Nicaragua, and Lebanon but markers against the Empire's further spread?

The trouble with markers (as he had learned in boyhood, reading *The Adventures of Tom Sawyer*) is that they tend to stiffen opposition on either side. Not only that, they imply that any dispute can be settled bilaterally—whereas certain strategic situations may be many-sided, if not sometimes polymorphous. Nowhere was this more true than in Lebanon. Israel the aggressor was now in shamed retreat, the PLO reappearing, the Syrians acting like Soviets one week and like Iranians the next, while the "peacekeeping" presence of the MNF was prolonging the civil war. Even as Reagan protested against the shootdown of KE007, two more American Marines were reported killed in Beirut.

"We have to show the flag for those Marines," he told himself, trying to control angry fantasies of F-14s "blowing hell" out of Druse emplacements in the Chouf. He now had two thousand extra troops stationed offshore in a carrier and other vessels, and had ordered the battleship *New Jersey,* which had been exercising in the Caribbean as a threat to the Sandinistas, north into the Mediterranean to intimidate the Syrians.

As François Mitterrand, his staunch ally in Lebanon, had observed more than two years before, Reagan was a man of finer instincts than intelligence. His brain, resistant to detail, quailed at making sense of a

"There seemed to be no fixed point in his universe but the strong-jawed profile beside him."
Nancy Reagan on vacation with her husband in Barbados, 1982.

world situation more convoluted than it had been since the early Sixties. Here were George Shultz and Gromyko barely able to speak to each other for anger, President de la Madrid of Mexico warning that U.S. interference might soon touch off "a conflagration" in Central America, mad Muammar Qaddafi destabilizing North Africa, Israel leaderless, Beirut reverting to anarchy, Chile and the Philippines rioting, and the Pope wondering if the world was not moving into "a new prewar phase." William Clark soothingly suggested that Reagan not run for a second term.

"You've done what you set out to do," the Judge said, citing tax cuts and budget reform, almost a year of steady economic growth, a revitalized military, Communism disgraced, and nuclear terror confounded by the SDI. Another few months of "standing tall" should restore the arms balance in Europe and very likely influence the rise of a less dangerous Soviet leader than the dying Andropov. Then Reagan could hand over his party leadership to some such trustworthy conservative as Paul Laxalt, and prepare for a dignified retirement from politics.

The President listened with courteous inattention. He took his main counsel from Shultz these days—insofar as he took anybody's. Everything Shultz told him (not to mention David Stockman, apocalyptic as usual about next year's budget) emphasized that the promises of 1980 were by no means fulfilled. There was also the slightly important fact that he enjoyed his job. "Well, thanks, Bill," he said. "I'll think about that."

On Friday, September 16, Reagan authorized a new secret directive in favor of aid to the *contras*. It replaced the vague language of his original "finding" with more specific orders to the CIA to

> provide support, equipment and training assistance to Nicaraguan paramilitary groups as a means to induce the Sandinistas and Cubans and their allies to cease their support for insurgencies in the region; to hamper Cuban/Nicaraguan arms trafficking; to divert Nicaragua's resources and energies from support to Central American guerrilla movements; and to bring the Sandinistas into meaningful negotiations . . . with their neighbors on peace in the region.

Then he was off to Camp David for the weekend. As usual, he and Nancy took no guests. Less usually, he needed her political counsel. She had not been privy to his earlier decisions to run for office; but now, since the only alternative to running was retirement, he felt they should discuss soberly the prospects of a second term.

"I think we're agreed," he wrote on Sunday night, "that I'll have a go at it."

Even so, he put off informing his nascent campaign team (again under the management of Senator Laxalt and Stuart Spencer) for several more weeks, and made clear that he would not announce publicly until the New Year.

As fall approached, the feeling of a clash coming somewhere in the world tumbled in the air like drums. "If there is still a world . . ." the normally equable Elizabeth Drew wrote in *The New Yorker,* after reporting that Congress would allow Reagan sixty days of unrestrained military action in Lebanon. On September 28, Yuri Andropov issued another diatribe against Reagan's "militarist psychosis" and "extreme adventurism." The statement was remarkable for its hopeless tone: "If anyone had any illusions about the possibility of an evolution for the better in the policy of the present Administration, recent events have dispelled them once and for all." State Department semanticists noted the last four words.

Reagan's cheerful opinion was that "the Russians" had finally accepted the fact that they could no longer afford to keep pace with his arms buildup. If not, he was prepared to spend twice as much, if necessary, to force them to terms. And by *terms* he meant the total abolition of nuclear weapons. He was so resolute in this intent at a bipartisan meeting of Congressional leaders on October 6 that they gave him a standing ovation in the Roosevelt Room.

Even his optimism, however, quailed when he saw an advance print of *The Day After,* a seven-million-dollar ABC movie about nuclear winter. The image of Jason Robards walking through the radioactive ashes of Lawrence, Kansas, left him dazed, and he entered into his diary the first and only admission I have been able to find in his papers, that he was "greatly depressed."

The declaration on October 12 of Marxist martial law in Grenada did not altogether surprise him. Earlier in the year, a strange greeting card had come his way, showing a split fruit hanging in the garden of the Grenadian Prime Minister, Maurice Bishop. Loquat-gold on the outside, it had plumped open through internal pressure, revealing a bright red seed with a black heart.

Now Bishop was under arrest, not radical enough, apparently, for his Leninist deposers. The situation was pre-revolutionary, just the kind of Cuban-inspired coup Clark had been warning against. But someone other than the Judge would have to monitor it. Weary of the unceasing hostility of Deaver, Shultz, and Nancy Reagan, Clark chose this moment to resign as National Security Adviser.

A White House power struggle of Lebanese intricacy ensued. It was triggered by the coincidental resignation of Secretary of the Interior James A. Watt, who needed to return to private life after offering reporters extremely specific proof that he was an Equal Opportunity Employer. Clark applied for Watt's job, and got it. James Baker, rejoicing in the fall of another Californian conservative (only Meese remained, hidden behind a mounting pile of papers), at once maneuvered to take over the NSC. He was ambitious for foreign-policy experience, and Michael Deaver was equally keen to succeed him as Chief of Staff. Their combined intent was to break up the troika and—while ever more papers were earmarked for Ed's urgent attention—realign the White House as a pragmatic institution, anxious to conciliate both Congress and the Kremlin as election year '84 loomed.

Reagan distractedly approved the job switches on the morning of Friday, October 14. Another Marine had been killed in Beirut, and he was still fighting the depression caused by *The Day After.* But he made the mistake of saying to Clark, as they walked to their last NSPG meeting together, "I've got your successor already chosen."

"Who is it?"

"Jim Baker, and Mike will be Chief of Staff."

Clark, who kept a Colt .45 on permanent display over his desk, lost no time in rounding up a posse. He passed notes to Meese, Weinberger, and Casey as they sat in the Situation Room, and at the end of the meeting—which Baker and Deaver inexplicably did not attend—Reagan found himself corralled in Clark's office. One by one, the four hard-liners told him what they thought of his double decision. With Pershings ready for installation in Western Europe, and the Soviet Union threatening to emplace Russian missiles in Syria, this was the wrong time to put a deal-maker in charge of national security. As for Deaver, whose attention span had been in recession since Inauguration Day, he could not begin to manage the executive business of the United States.

"Mike," Reagan said on returning to the Oval Office, "I've got bad news for you."

Deaver was bruised to the bone. Baker, tougher and more philosophical, shrugged off the President's assurance that the NSC job was still "on hold." Actually, it was. Reagan spent the weekend fielding passionate calls from moderates in favor of Baker and conservatives in favor of Jeane Kirkpatrick. By Sunday evening, he saw the necessity of a compromise candidate, somebody bland enough not to threaten anybody. "I lean toward Bud McFarlane."

The appointment was announced the next day, along with the killing of yet another Marine in Beirut. Just over three years later, when McFarlane had enmeshed the Administration in scandal and both he and Deaver were out on the street, the latter said to me, grinning humorlessly: "I've been thinking. If Jim and I had gone to that meeting, none of this would have happened. Iran wouldn't have happened."

☯

If there was such a thing as a strategic satellite, capable of tracking political cyclones the way NASA does the weather, it would have shown three areas of accelerating turbulence across the globe in the week following McFarlane's promotion. Those around Grenada and Beirut became whirlwinds simultaneously, while conditions between Geneva and Bonn remained threatening but unsettled. As far as Reagan was concerned, his daily national-security briefings became an exercise in storm control.

Radio Free Grenada went off the air on Wednesday, October 19. When service resumed some hours later, it spoke in the name of a Cuban-trained military junta. Maurice Bishop was reported executed by a firing squad, along with five supporters. A twenty-four-hour curfew was imposed, effectively jailing everybody on the island. While other East Caribbean governments appealed in vain for help from Britain and France—old colonial dependencies die hard—crisis groups at the State Department and White House debated what to do about six hundred American students who happened to be registered at the little island's medical school.

At least through Thursday afternoon, the crisis groups relieved Reagan of any immediate policy-making. Their problem was how to deal with a revolutionary government that seemed unwilling to constitute itself. William Casey argued eloquently in favor of an invasion of Grenada: "Hey, fuck, let's dump these bastards." McFarlane and his new deputy, Admiral John Poindexter, initiated themselves with sleepless hours of rescue-mission contingency planning, but nobody at the NSC worked with more fanatical energy than the deputy director for political-military affairs, Lieutenant Colonel Oliver North.

It was North who pointed out that a shipload of Beirut-bound Marines had left Norfolk, Virginia, on October 20, and was still close enough to the Caribbean to turn south and consummate Director

Casey's objective. That evening, over the objections of the Joint Chiefs of Staff, Reagan signed an order diverting the flotilla, but restraining it to a mere cautionary presence in the general area of Grenada.

Ludicrously yet unavoidably—since any sudden change in the President's schedule might trigger an invasion scare in the press—Reagan left for Augusta, Georgia, on Friday to participate in the annual four-player "George Shultz Invitational Golf Tournament." He was accompanied by Shultz and his fellow contestants, Treasury Secretary Donald Regan and Senator Nicholas Brady of New Jersey. The usual presidential retinue flew along, including McFarlane.

At a quarter to three the next morning, Saturday, October 22, McFarlane was advised by phone that six East Caribbean states had formally requested American assistance in restoring democracy to Grenada. If the Cuban-fomented revolution there was allowed to succeed, then they feared for their own freedoms.

Reagan, asleep in Dwight Eisenhower's old cottage, was awakened by McFarlane and Shultz a few minutes later. He joined them in robe and pajamas, and agreed with their opinion that the situation had passed the limits of tolerance. "There's no way we could say no to this request." Less than an hour later, having listened to tactical cautions from the Vice President, Secretary of Defense, and Chairman of the Joint Chiefs of Staff in Washington, he asked McFarlane how soon "an outright invasion" of Grenada could be mounted. McFarlane said forty-eight hours.

"Do it," Reagan ordered.

He delegated immediate planning responsibilities to Bush's Special Situations Group, and emphasized the prime purpose of evacuating the students. Zero hour was set for Monday night or Tuesday morning, under conditions of total secrecy.

Shultz and McFarlane approvingly noted his quickness and decisiveness. "Should we go back to Washington?" the Secretary asked.

"No, it would give the story away."

Much later on, President and partners managed a truncated golf game. It was brought to an end by the kind of half-comic incident that Shakespeare uses to presage tragedy. Just as they were teeing off at the sixteenth hole, a gunman drove a pickup truck through the course gate and took five people hostage in the pro shop, where he fired off a warning shot and demanded to speak to Reagan. Within minutes, a Secret Service helicopter was throbbing over the links as an armored car rescued the presidential foursome. When last seen, Reagan was cooperatively trying to telephone the gunman.

The man proved to be confused, and the hostages were released.

There was no evidence of any organized plot. But could Dutch, I wonder, *conceivably* have gone to bed that night and not revisited, for at least one drowsy moment, its vestiges: the crazed loner, the breached barrier, the trapped human beings, the bang, the smoke?

If so, there was a pathetic inevitability to the call that again broke his sleep in the small hours, this time at 2:27 on Sunday morning, October 23. McFarlane and Shultz had further news. A grinning suicide bomber had driven a yellow truck full of explosives through the guard gate of the Marine headquarters at Beirut International Airport, and reduced the whole building to rubble. More than a hundred soldiers were dead, at first count; hundreds more were still being searched for. The only clue as to the possible motive of the terrorist was that almost simultaneously, downtown, there had been a sudden diaspora of personnel from the Iranian embassy.

The President looked his age as he tried to absorb this information, McFarlane thought: a deflated septuagenarian asking childlike questions. "How could this happen? How bad is it? Who did it?"

☯

The next few days were ones during which Reagan, in John Kennedy's phrase, earned his salary. From the moment Air Force One returned to Washington early on Sunday morning, he was involved in post-tragedy and pre-invasion meetings. He had to weigh a rapidly increasing death toll in Lebanon against the danger, in Grenada, of a Carter-style rescue fiasco. What if the shadowy soldiers who held the island massacred medical students? His presidency could not survive the loss of six hundred innocents, on top of the lives already chargeable to him in Beirut.

That total was finally drawn at two hundred and forty-one, making the barracks bombing the worst surprise attack on a U.S. military installation since Pearl Harbor. Adding on six Marines killed earlier, and the sixty-three people blown up in the American embassy, Ronald Reagan's "peacekeeping" policy in the Middle East had already resulted in three hundred and ten deaths. Yuri Andropov's responsibility for the two hundred and sixty-nine passengers aboard KE007 was light in comparison.

At least he could commiserate on Monday morning with François Mitterrand, whose MNF headquarters in West Beirut had been struck almost simultaneously by another suicide bomber. Fifty-eight French were dead. Mitterrand had already, in a display of *l'audace* inconceivable under the American system of government, made a flying visit to

Lebanon disguised as "Monsieur Morland," to give himself a sense of the situation. What he saw depressed him deeply.

"There is no counterattack possible," he said, when Reagan asked if Iranian and Syrian Shiites could be blamed for the bombings. "There are Soviet officers in uniform twenty kilometers from Beirut. Attack Syria, and you attack Moscow."

Both leaders were aware, as they talked, that two million Europeans had demonstrated over the weekend against Pershing missiles. Mitterrand urged Reagan to delay deployment until June 1984. Otherwise, it might fatally coincide with the current "conflagration" in the Middle East. "It would bring about what the Russians are looking for in Lebanon, an accumulation of causes for world war."

Reagan said nothing about his anti-Soviet intentions in the eastern Caribbean, now definitely set for that night. But since Grenada was still a member of the British Commonwealth, he had to share them with Margaret Thatcher. She cabled back in a temper. "This action will be seen as intervention by a western country in the internal affairs of a small independent nation, however unattractive its regime." In tones hardly less cautionary than Mitterrand's, she warned that her Parliament might reconsider the siting of cruise missiles in Britain. "I cannot conceal that I am deeply disturbed by your latest communication."

Twenty minutes later, she followed up on the hot line. It was 8:10 P.M., Washington time, and the President was upstairs in the White House, halfway through briefing leaders of Congress about his intent. They could hear her stentorian complaints. "We are already at zero," Reagan said.

The invasion was, in fact, already under way, with landings scheduled for first light Tuesday morning. Reagan put down the phone and resumed his meeting, looking only slightly disturbed. By all accounts, the deflated old man of forty hours before had recovered his tone and exuded absolute determination. He had absorbed the full horror of Beirut, right down to details of bulldozers scooping up brains and breakfast food, endured renewed Shultz-Weinberger disputes about past and present policy (the Defense Secretary felt that the invasion was being rushed), and heard from the U.S. Ambassador in Moscow that the Geneva arms-control negotiations seemed doomed. Two of his closest allies had just signaled profound doubts about him.

Yet he spoke as if success in Grenada was assured. The Speaker of the House, Tip O'Neill, wondered if he was not trying to compensate for yesterday's disaster. Then Reagan launched into a sudden anecdote about Marines and GIs quitting the reliberated Philippines in 1946. A quarter of a million joyous islanders had seen them off, waving American flags and pelting them with flowers.

"God save us all," O'Neill thought. "This really *is* about Lebanon."

Of course it was not; the one crisis had preceded the other. Yet Reagan being Reagan, there was no moral difference between the American eagle descending on the cedars of Lebanon, or upon the nutmeg trees of Grenada. In both cases, the protection of Christians from dark forces was involved, as was the perpetuation of American ideals.

"Operation Urgent Fury" was an embarrassingly clumsy success. The world's ranking superpower, hampered by old tourist maps and incompatible radio frequencies, needed two full days to overcome the resistance of an island not much bigger than Washington, D.C. State-of-the-art helicopters were brought down by World War II vintage ack-ack guns. Democracy was restored, and some damp Cuban documents impounded, along with 24,768 signal flares—clear evidence of incendiary Red activity. Nineteen U.S. servicemen were killed, but all the students were rescued, and returned to kiss home soil. American television viewers, Reagan included, wept at the sight. Margaret Thatcher and her compatriots were less moved. "Sodding Yanks," Philip Larkin complained, "breaking and entering British territory."

On November 22, 1983, West Germany voted finally in favor of INF deployment. The first missiles arrived on the Continent the following day. A scrawl on a wall in Paris pretty well expressed the opinions of Europeans: *Mieux un Pershing dans votre jardin qu'un soldat russe sur votre femme*—"Better a Pershing in your garden than a Russian soldier on your wife." Simultaneously, in Geneva, the Soviet delegation walked out of the negotiations. For the foreseeable future, INF arms control was dead.

Yuri Andropov issued a statement accusing the United States of "a crusade against socialism," retired to Moscow's Kuntsevo Hospital, and was never seen in public again.

In Lebanon, world war did not break out. But neither was peace kept, nor honor assuaged. The MNF remained, largely due to the insistence of Shultz, who pushed for retaliation over Weinberger's contemptuous dismissal of "eye-for-an-eye" warfare. Reagan sided with his Secretary of Defense until December 3, when an F-14 was fired upon over the Bekaa Valley. But the only punishment he could bring himself to agree to was a limited strike against Syrian emplacements around Baalbek—hardly the kind of "disproportionate" retaliation Jeane Kirkpatrick afterward celebrated as a hallmark of his anti-terrorism policy.

Two days before Christmas, a Pentagon commission of inquiry into the Beirut barracks bombing humiliated Shultz, and embarrassed Reagan, by concluding that the dead Marines had been victims of a myopic Middle Eastern policy. The commission called for "a more vigorous and demanding approach to pursuing diplomatic alternatives" in Lebanon. After that, U.S. withdrawal was just a matter of time—as much time as Reagan might need to accept that there were some places in the world that did not want a *pax Americana*.

Or as the President himself remarked, in a year-end letter to William F. Buckley, Jr., "Bill, the Middle East is a complicated place—well not really a place, it's more a state of mind."

He reflected on this, and added sadly, "A disordered mind."

Nineteen eighty-four turned out to be a disappointment to the followers of George Orwell, and an almost unalloyed triumph for Ronald Reagan. He declared on January 25 that he would run for a second term as President, again in company with George Bush. The only Orwellian character on the international scene, Yuri Andropov, died on February 9, and with him died the Evil Empire—not that many Westerners realized it at the time. His successor Konstantin Chernenko, all cheekbones and scowl, looked fairly typical in the usual parade of astrakhan hats atop Lenin's Tomb; and even his obvious ill health—the wheezing and disorientation, the slow shuffle, the inability to stand up without help—seemed to signal a sort of sickly continuity with *genseks* of the past. Sovietologists were mildly surprised that Andropov's chosen heir, the young and formidable Gorbachev, had not prevailed in Politburo voting. But from the point of view of the United States and Western Europe, it was probably just as well to have another near-corpse in the Kremlin, while Warsaw Pact states got used to the installation of INFs, warhead by warhead by warhead.

Reagan presented himself, in his State of the Union Address and campaign commercials, as a sort of sun, glowing with good news and good intentions, banishing memories of the recession and last year's stand against the forces of darkness. In the cloying slogan of his video scriptwriters, it was "Morning Again in America." One could use phrases like *love of country* and *right to life* without embarrassment any more. The national economy was not just expanding, it was exploding. The national "home" imitated this dynamic in slo-mo, as foyers opened up, ceilings soared, dens engulfed sitting rooms, and bathrooms revived the marble industry. Personal computers multiplied. Malls splotched the landscape like extrusions of magma, hardening overnight.

On the night of the Fourth of July, I was working in my Washington apartment when the irresistible sound of fireworks over the Mall drew me to the Capitol terrace. I stood near where Dutch had taken his oath of office and, as I watched the rockets rise and fall, thought of his ingenious suggestion that the old political dynamic of Left v. Right should be refigured:

> Isn't our choice really one of up or down? Down through statism, the welfare state, more and more government largesse, accompanied always by more government authority, less individual liberty and ultimately totalitarianism, always advanced as for our own good. The alternative is the dream conceived by our Founding Fathers, up to the ultimate in individual freedom, consistent with an orderly society.
>
> We don't celebrate Dependence Day on the Fourth of July. We celebrate *In*dependence Day.

After a while, I found myself looking less at the coruscations overhead, but at the young faces crowded around me. There was an extraordinary general feeling of happiness and hope, and when at some point a band struck up and we all sang "The Star-Spangled Banner" (music that five years before might have provoked them to Bronx cheers and obscenities), I was struck by their unselfconscious ardor.

"He can't lose," I thought.

Poor decent, dull Walter Mondale realized that when he debated the President in Kansas City on October 21, and was famously rolled after trying to raise the age issue. "I am not going to exploit, for political purposes, my opponent's youth and inexperience," Reagan promised, erasing in a few deft seconds the impression he had made, in an earlier debate, of total befuddlement. Even Mondale had to laugh.

"He's won," I decided.

Post-debate polls gave Reagan an unbeatable lead for the rest of the campaign. Americans favored him because for four years he'd kept, or fought to keep, all his campaign promises. He had cut taxes, harnessed government, revived the economy, freed the entrepreneur, and cursed the ungodly. The ship of state was realigned, empowered, larger, prouder—and for those reasons less considerate of people who sailed steerage, or of powers that got in its way.

Such at least was my impression when I went down to Newport News on October 27 and watched the launching of the *Theodore Roosevelt*. The enormous $2.7 billion carrier, about as long as a prone Empire State Building, fluttered at every extremity with red, white, and blue. But no amount of bunting could diminish its frightening, battle-gray mass: the flight deck, four and a half acres in area, shut out much of the sky. It was a symbol of national resolve, as both the Secretary of the Navy, John F. Lehman, Jr., and Senator John Warner of Virginia made plain. They reminded the crowd (pointillistically flashing with Reagan-Bush buttons) that "President Jimmy Carter and Vice President Mondale" had tried to stop the *Roosevelt*'s construction. Caspar Weinberger, dwarfed under the arch of the bow, told us that "a decade of neglect" had vitiated U.S. sea power. Not so this decade: America was back. Mrs. Lehman smashed a champagne bottle against the hull, the band played "Anchors Aweigh," a skein of balloons went up, and four F-14s cut over them, making the air shake. *Tremble, you sons of Soviet bitches!* their exhausts seemed to say.

Where, I kept wondering, was Dutch?

31

Physicians
of Memory

S NOW—POLAR SNOW, driven by arctic wind and rattling against every north-facing surface in Washington—blurred the shape of the White House at three minutes to noon on Sunday, January 20, 1985. The thermometer stood at nine degrees above zero. Traffic lights, their timers frozen, stared vainly up the empty length of Connecticut Avenue, whose alignment with the wind made it a howling tunnel aimed directly at Lafayette Square. Snow granulated to the caliber and hardness of steel filings whipped through the White House's railings and whitened the backs of photographers huddled like hoboes beneath the North Portico. They breathed on their lenses and prayed that the President would emerge as soon after twelve as possible. All they wanted was a quick shot for the evening news—with luck, a shot of this snow slamming right into his face—to justify their painful vigil.

Inside the vestibule, Ronald Reagan stood on the Grand Staircase and raised his right hand at the request of Chief Justice Warren Burger. The Twentieth Amendment to the Constitution required him to do so at this hour and on this day. Time enough for pageantry tomorrow, when he would take the oath again, more publicly, on Capitol Hill. He laid his free hand on Nelle Reagan's Scotch-taped, indexed Bible, narrow fingertips caressing, as hers had, the words of II Chronicles 7:14: *If my people, which are called by my name, shall humble themselves, and pray, and seek my face, and turn from their wicked ways; then will I hear from heaven, and will forgive their sin, and will heal their land.*

"Repeat after me," rumbled Justice Burger.

As the President courteously allowed himself to be led through a text he had memorized at a glance four years ago, he felt Nancy Reagan's counter-pressure supporting the weight of the Bible and the weight of his hand. She stood looking at him throughout the oath, her face blank with pleasure. The eyes of three of his four children were on him, too, and those of Vice President Bush, and the senior White House staff, and twelve of the thirteen officers of his Cabinet. Ninety-four other dignitaries and favored friends sat on narrow gilt chairs, sweating as television lights irradiated their winter clothes. In the East Room, champagne lay ready to pop, and silver salvers sizzled with *pasta carbonara.*

"So help me God," Reagan ended. He bent to kiss his wife.

When, moments afterward, he stepped out onto the portico coatless, the ferocity of the wind took him by surprise. His pompadour rose in comic-book shock, his spine stiffened, and he rocked back on his heels with an audible gasp. The photographers got their shot. As always, Dutch delivered.

Later, it grew too cold even for snow. The "Dixon Dutchesses," thirty-five pom-pom girls from Reagan's old high school, practiced for the inaugural parade until their thighs cramped. Bandsmen lacquered the mouthpieces of trombones and cornets with nail polish, but got lip-stuck anyway. When an overnight temperature drop below zero was forecast, plus continued wind through Monday morning, three doctors informed the Inaugural Committee that in such conditions flesh would freeze in minutes. They cited the case of President William Henry Harrison, who had been killed by inaugural weather far warmer than this, and strongly advised that Reagan move tomorrow's outdoor ceremony into the Rotunda of the Capitol. Not only that, he should also cancel the parade.

When told, the President expressed only two concerns: "Where are all the kids going to go?" and "Where will the television cameras be?" Reassured that the Dutchesses would be able to strut in an indoor arena, and that the Rotunda was video-friendly, he consented.

The cold spread all over the Eastern states and down into the Deep South. Shreveport, Louisiana, shivered under a shroud of unaccustomed white. Frozen grapefruit hung in Florida groves. It was the kind of cold that thrills children and possesses the aged with thoughts of death. I lay insomniac in my apartment one block from the Capitol, hearing the constant crack of flag cables as the gale slapped them against their poles.

☯

Inauguration Day dawned clear but bitter, with twenty-eight degrees of frost. The air was coughingly dry, evanescent as acetone. Pennsylvania Avenue's bleachers were deserted except for a few parka-plump out-of-towners, clumped like walruses in their determination to see Dutch drive up the Hill. At Fifth and K, half a dozen shelter residents who thought the parade was still "on" clustered around a fire barrel. They hoped to be hired by the city for trash removal. Then one of them switched on his transistor radio and learned about the cancellation. Eyes tearing, he uncorked a bottle of whiskey. "Here's to Ronald Reagan," he said. "May the hell he has caused us freeze over."

The walruses were rewarded at 11:13 A.M., when fifty-four processional vehicles swept up Pennsylvania Avenue in a fine spray of dust and salt. First came six snarling motorcycles of the District of Columbia Police, a Capitol Police squad car, with all signals flashing, and a White House staff sedan; then an identical pair of long, low, flag-fluttering limousines, one of which (yes, but *which*?) was carrying the President; the Secret Service's open "war wagon," heavy with weaponry; an open Secret Service control car close behind with the nuclear "football"; a support station, medically equipped; a telecommunications vehicle; a second pair of long, low limousines, this time flying the Vice President's colors; an extra control car; four VIP cars packed with inaugural dignitaries; three press vans; a tail car; and finally a rearguard of motorcycle police in the early stages of carbon-monoxide poisoning.

I got to the steps of the Dirksen Building in time to see the first police headlights crest the Hill, followed by hood after gleaming hood as the motorcade swerved onto the Capitol grounds. The majesty of mass movement wrought its usual spell. Like or loathe Ronald Reagan, his sheer sovereignty emanated from the roar and swish. I caught a dim glimpse of him waving. Then his Lincoln passed under the Senate porte-cochère, and I hurried home with aching ears to watch the Inauguration on television.

Reagan's Second Inaugural—his last largely self-written oration—was projected in husky, intimate tones designed to fill the Rotunda without echoes. Perhaps because of its *sotto voce* delivery and the small size of the applauding audience (fewer than a thousand were present, at least half of them Democrats), it did not succeed. I noticed quite a few flared nostrils, suggestive of suppressed yawns.

To me, the speech had an awkward eloquence. It was patently an old man's oration, tired-sounding in places, softening often into sentimentalities. Yet in back of the softness there bulged a sort of calcified, obstinate urgency.

> Four years ago I spoke to you of a new beginning, and we have accomplished that. But in another sense, our new beginning is a continuation of that beginning created two centuries ago when, for the first time in history, government, the people said, was not our master. It is our servant; its only power that [which] we, the people, allow it to have.
>
> That system has never failed us. But for a time we failed the system . . .

He recited his familiar litany of authority usurped by the federal government, of taxes and regulation slowing the national machine. By controlling such abuses, his administration had seen inflation drop dramatically and employment figures rise in proportion: "We are creating a nation once again vibrant, robust and alive."

Ahead lay four more years of opportunity to restate America's traditional values of "faith, family, work and neighborhood," to continue rebuilding its defenses, and to redirect history "away from totalitarian darkness."

Twenty-five straight months of economic growth, the President went on, proved his tenet "that freedom and incentives unleash the drive and entrepreneurial genius that are at the core of human progress." But deficit spending (for which he took no blame) might cramp that drive even as it gathered force. To combat it, he would ask Congress to hold program spending at current levels for another full year.

After a couple of perfunctory paragraphs on race relations, Reagan switched to foreign policy. Surprisingly, he made no fanfare of a new agreement, just reached by George Shultz and Andrei Gromyko in Geneva, that made possible the first substantive arms-control talks in fourteen months. It was as though their negotiations had skirted the real issue:

We're not just discussing limits on a further increase of nuclear weapons. We seek, instead, to reduce their number. *We seek the total elimination, one day, of nuclear weapons from the face of the earth.*

In peroration, he invoked the very item that had brought Shultz and Gromyko together (after initially drawing them apart): his cherished Strategic Defense Initiative, now under intensive research and development. "It wouldn't kill people, it would destroy weapons. It wouldn't militarize space, it would help demilitarize the arsenal on earth. It would render nuclear weapons obsolete."

He concluded with three enigmatic images that must have taxed the resources of the KGB reference library. The first was "My friends, we live in a world that's lit by lightning." This was followed by "History is a ribbon, always uncurling." And last:

> A settler pushes west and sings a song, and the song echoes out forever and fills the unknowing air.
>
> It is the American sound: it is hopeful, big-hearted, idealistic— daring, decent, and fair. . . . We sing it still. We raise our voices to the God who is the author of this most tender music.

Insofar as the images could be analyzed, I thought them revelatory of Dutch the fatalist, Dutch the farseeing, Dutch the melodious knight.

Over sole mousse and champagne in Statuary Hall afterward, Tip O'Neill told Reagan privately he was "very conscious" of the size of the recent presidential vote. "In my fifty years in public life, I've never seen a man more popular than you are with the American people."

Had the Speaker been in government since 1800, he still would not have witnessed such an electoral-vote landslide. Reagan had swept every state but Walter Mondale's own Minnesota, and even there, the popular majority could barely have filled a football stadium. Every age group in the national franchise had voted four more years for the oldest President in history. Now Wall Street seemed to be agreeing with O'Neill. Stocks soared all day, buoyed by reports of a 7.6 percent GNP growth rate in 1984, with inflation running at less than half that figure. The Dow Jones average rose thirty-four points, the largest increase since 1981. Statisticians had to look back a further thirty years, to 1951, for economic news as good.

A spirit of *bonhomie* spread through the nation's capital as the day wore on, although the sunshine remained frigid and public spaces empty. Mitch Snyder, the street people's advocate, boggled at a cornucopia of sushi, Westphalian ham, crab sandwiches, quiches, and French *gâteaux* pouring into his shelter, courtesy of various oversupplied reception committees.

That evening, Reagan attended eleven Inaugural Balls. He noted with amusement that whenever he and Nancy stepped out to dance, bands played slow music in deference to his great age. He did not get to bed until midnight, by which time the temperature had sunk to single digits again, and Washington, sheathed in ice, gleamed like one of the "alabaster cities" he had hymned at the pre-Inaugural service at Saint John's.

☯

Around the curve of the world, as he slept, other white-clad cities awoke and went to work. Geneva prepared for an invasion of *internationaux* when the new arms talks began in early March. Moscow's spade-wielding *babushki* renewed their assault on the heaviest winter precipitation any of them could remember. To them a deep snow was *chorosh dlia chlieb,* "good for bread." And in East Berlin, just beyond the concrete slabs and barbed wire and gun towers that deterred West German immigration, a historic steeple shook to the sound of dynamite. Germans of all faiths mourned as the Lutheran Church of Reconciliation collapsed into its own icy yard. When the white fog cleared, DDR border guards had what they had long wanted: "an open field of fire" all the way to the Wall.

There is something in the Teutonic soul that craves *Schlusstrich,* the decisive drawing of a line, or the building of a wall, between opposites: *Gute* and *Ubel, Mann* and *Natur, Ganger* and *Doppelgänger, Demokratie* and *Totalitarismus.* The line, once established, is paradoxically satisfying to the national love of precision, and painful to a more mystical sense of universal harmony, which is the legacy of German Romanticism. Chancellor Kohl had actually cried in the Oval Office when he spoke of his handshake with François Mitterrand over the graves of Verdun in 1984. He longed for a similar gesture from the President of the United States. As a result, Reagan now found himself invited across the *Schluss* of Nazi memory.

The Chancellor's idea, expressed with careful vagueness, was that they should make a joint pilgrimage to some site of German sacrifice. By a fluke of protocol, Kohl was due to host this year's economic summit in Bonn, just before the fortieth anniversary of V-E Day. President Reagan should extend his stay to a formal state visit, and help make the anniversary a symbol of both quietus and commencement.

The proposal was perfectly calculated to appeal to Reagan's Christian notions of forgiveness and rebirth. Kohl, he realized, had been a mere schoolboy when Patton crossed the Rhine. Most Germans by now had no direct memory of World War II; it was time that "the hatred stopped and peace and friendship began."

Unfortunately it was also time, in the view of his own State Department, to commemorate the fortieth anniversary of the liberation of the concentration camps. At least one West German periodical, *Der Spiegel,* was already speculating that Ronald Reagan would insist on touring Dachau.

Reagan was quite sure he would not. The days when he had forced both the ignorant and the innocent—including his own sons—to confront the evidence of the camps were long gone. He had no inclination to look at any more pictures of stacked human skins. Nazism was an aberration, a nightmare never to be dreamed again; Soviet Communism had replaced it as civilization's principal scourge. Together, he and Kohl faced a nervous totalitarian power, infinitely more lethal than the Third Reich. In earnest of that threat, and in gratitude for West Germany's loyal alliance since 1945—not to mention its willingness to deploy Pershing II missiles in 1983—he felt he "owed Helmut one" in 1985.

The President's State of the Union Address, delivered in the House chamber two weeks later on his seventy-fourth birthday, was an oratorical triumph that had senior Democrats shaking their heads in admiration. Substantively, it was hardly more particular than the recent Inaugural, but in style it was inimitable, from his first deferential entrance (as if surprised at the prolonged applause) to his final "Let us begin." Even the by-now-predictable moment of introduction to "an American hero" in the gallery was charged with drama, for not one but two heroes arose, both women. One was young, a former Vietnamese refugee wearing the dress gray of West Point; the other was old and black, foster mother to nearly a thousand drug-addicted babies. With a sweep of his long left arm, he conferred upon them the grace that was his by gift and theirs by right. They stood smiling as roar built on roar. Reagan, placidly straightening his speech cards, was at last what he had never been on stage or screen, a great actor.

Watching on CBS, I thought of Shakespeare's lines about those who, moving others, are themselves as stone, and how they rightly inherit heaven's graces.

A changing roster of appointees crowded around to congratulate the President as he left the Senate floor. Gone was William P. Clark, to ranchland retirement in California; gone too were Terrel Bell and James Edwards. In their places as Secretaries of the Interior, Education, and Energy stood Donald P. Hodel, William J. Bennett, and John S. Herrington. James Baker discharged new dignity as Secretary of the Treasury, and Donald T. Regan showed more muscle as White House Chief of Staff. Reagan beamed at them indiscriminately, as he had agreed to their job swap with indifference. Their loyalties were the same; his purpose held.

On television, the Democratic leadership could field no single spokesman to answer him. Instead, several second-string party representatives debated how to deal with the Reagan Revolution. Their conversation was somber, lightened only by an aside from the moderator, Governor Bill Clinton of Arkansas: "By the way, Mr. President— Happy Birthday tonight."

Michael Deaver had one service left to perform before he, too, left the Administration: to finalize the details of Reagan's state visit to West Germany. In mid-February, he took a "survey trip" to see what site Chancellor Kohl had in mind for the joint pilgrimage. He found himself being escorted around a little military *Ehrefriedhof* at Bitburg, on the Eifel plateau. Snow blanketed the graves and their stone markers, which lay flush with the earth and betrayed vague, stubby shapes of crosses. More out of form than curiosity, he asked, "Will any of these graves embarrass my President?"

Kohl's protocol chief reacted defensively. "You think maybe Mengele is buried there?"

That evening in Munich, Deaver discussed the advantages of the Bitburg site with his aides. It was small, but because of that, presumably innocuous: the Nazis would have interred their major killers elsewhere. There was an eponymous U.S. air base nearby; after thirty-three years of fraternization and intermarriage, the area was about as Americanized as any in the Federal Republic. Both Reagan and Kohl—who as a boy in 1945 had been rescued from near starvation by U.S. food trucks—would feel comfortable there.

A veteran advance man worried about the cemetery's snowy inscrutability. "It's important we get a register." Deaver said the State Department would check into that. Then, moving on quickly as was his wont, he began to explain why the idea of Reagan visiting Dachau was unacceptable. "Too emotional. Too gruesome."

Somebody remarked that Jerry Ford had been able to stand Auschwitz, where the very dust still smelled of bones. But Deaver shook his head. "You don't understand what it would do to Ronald Reagan."

e

On Friday, March 8, the President saw his new arms-control negotiating team, headed by Max Kampelman, off to Geneva. He was in an elated mood, having gone "round for round" the day before with an aggressive member of the Soviet Politburo, Vladimir Shcherbitsky. "I think he'll go home knowing that we are ready for negotiations," he wrote in his diary, "but we d--n well aren't going to let our guard down or hold still while they continue to build up their defensive forces."

Shcherbitsky's aggression betrayed a sensitivity to intelligence, which the CIA was freely circulating, that Konstantin Chernenko was suffering from terminal emphysema. Absent from public view for seven months, the old party plotter had recently failed to deliver his annual Supreme Soviet election speech. There were rumors that he had also suffered a stroke and might not outlast the winter.

Reagan, in contrast, had enjoyed almost unalloyed health since his escape from assassination four years before. He was due this very day to undergo a routine examination at Bethesda Naval Hospital. Preliminary soundings indicated that his peripheral vascular system "was that of a young man." During the course of the afternoon, a series of specialists stared into his eyes with slit lamps, hammered his joints, ausculated his massive chest, spirometered his lungs, and cardiographed his heart rhythms. (After eighteen minutes on the treadmill, his blood pressure rose to a bounding, boyish 130/74.) Then five of them, plus a nurse and Secret Service guards, congregated for the afternoon's main entertainment. A flexible sigmoidoscope was passed through the presidential colon, snaking and coiling until Reagan politely asked if they were looking for his larynx. An hour later, he was dressed and helicoptering to Camp David, looking forward with a faster's appetite to dinner.

He did not know that the snake had microscopically bitten him inside. Even as he wrote in his diary, "I'm so healthy I had a hard time not acting smug," a polyp specimen was being subjected to biopsy.

Winter's white covering was at last wearing thin on the Eifel plateau. One by one, the flat markers of Bitburg cemetery came wetly into view, for anyone who had eyes to see.

Years later, in another sodden season, I walked among them, pondering the inscrutability of names, the chiseled fixedness of dates. *Ogefr. Christian Brandt* ✝*22.4.12* ☒*6.1.45. Ofeldw. Walter Wagner* ✝*1.2.15* ☒*24.1.45.* One stone read simply, *Ein Deutscher Soldat.*

There came to me Philip Larkin's image of thaw, coined when these graves were still fresh: *all the dingy hospital of snow / Dies back to ditches.* As ever in spring, tiny tributaries were going about their business, responding to forces men could not control:

> *Here, busy with resurrection, sovereign waters*
> *Confer among the roots, causing to fall*
> *From patient memory forestfuls of grief.*

The President returned from Camp David only to be awakened, at four on Monday morning, with news of Chernenko's death. It confirmed his sardonic conviction that the leadership of the Soviet Union was moribund. Since he had been elected President, Kosygin, Suslov, Brezhnev, Pelshe, Andropov, Ustinov, and now this latest *apparatchik* had passed on to the Great Collective. "How can I be expected to make peace with them, if they keep dying on me?"

When he got to his desk, George Shultz was waiting to urge attendance at the state funeral, in the hope of improving East-West relations. But Reagan was no more disposed to mourn Chernenko than any of his predecessors. He agreed, however, to drive to the Soviet embassy and sign the condolence book, joking that it would be his third such trip. Before leaving, he noted without comment in his diary: "Gorbachev has been named head man in the Soviet Union."

This story shared space on the evening news with a bulletin that physicians had found an "inflammatory pseudopolyp" in Ronald Reagan's colon. The growth seemed to be benign, but there were signs of occult blood, which would necessitate careful monitoring for a while.

To guard against false alarms, the President would be put on a soft diet recommended by the American Cancer Society. At once, his popular image was transformed from that of Chernenko's healthy, younger adversary to that of an ailing elder statesman, easy meat for the fifty-four-year-old Mikhail Gorbachev. The networks all but signed off with menacing music from *Peter and the Wolf.*

With his usual disdain for medical information, Reagan joked about the diet, saying that he looked forward to it on account of its ban on broccoli. Within a few days, his hemoccults were negative, and the cancer scare faded.

☯

The real pathophobia affecting world affairs in March 1985 lay not between Gorbachev and Reagan, but between Gorbachev and the decrepit empire he had inherited.

Few Americans—let alone that archive of obsolete information, the Central Intelligence Agency—realized just how decrepit the Soviet Union really was. Gorbachev's own privately researched information showed that its gross national product was half that of the U.S., while its economic development was lagging "ten to fifteen years behind the capitalist countries." This "exceptionally grave situation" was worsened by a new strategic inferiority, brought about by the Reagan Administration's arms buildup. All signs pointed to "further weakening of the USSR's international position, and its decline into a second-rate power."

Unlike any previous Soviet leader, the new *gensek* had no memories of the Revolution, and no defensive attitude to the policies of the past. Nor had he any respect for such Kremlin traditions as isolationism and conformity. His idea of a vacation destination was France or Italy, rather than dour Black Sea resorts. His closest intellectual companion, Yegor Yakovlev, was a diplomat who had spent nine years in Canada. Incredibly, Gorbachev also had an American friend—Dwayne Andreas, chairman of Archer Daniels Midland—who had once splashed in the Rock River under Dutch Reagan's watchful eye.

Sleek, forceful, twitching with nervous energy, Gorbachev stood out at Chernenko's funeral. He had the mysterious power of a Nureyev or a Nijinsky to draw attention even when doing nothing. Yet Reagan, watching on television, seemed much more interested in Lidiya Chernenko. Far from being the usual portly *babushka* with chapped cheekbones, she was a sweet-faced woman whose behavior struck him as innately pious. He became obsessed with the notion that an "underground religion" was rising like a water table beneath the surface of Soviet society, and asked his national security adviser if Gorbachev, too, might be a closet Christian. McFarlane, startled, pointed out that love of God did not normally go with love of Lenin. But Reagan clung to his conviction.

Addressing the White House press corps on March 21, he said casually that he did not feel "rebuffed" by Gorbachev's failure to respond—so far—to a letter he had sent proposing a summit meeting in the United States. "The man has only been in office a few days." Then followed this change of subject:

Q. Mr. President, could you tell us [about] your decision not to visit a concentration-camp site when you make your trip to Germany commemorating V-E Day?

A. Yes. I'll tell you. I feel very strongly that this time, in commemorating the end of that great war, that instead of re-awakening the memories and so forth, and the passions of the time, that maybe we should observe this day as the day when, forty years ago, peace began.

The following evening, I met Dutch again for the first time in two years. The occasion was the inscrutable private dinner, upstairs in the White House, mentioned on p. 4. Assured now of his incuriosity, I was able to enjoy him unreservedly, to bask in his peculiar bland glow, not unlike that of the white candles that translucently separated us. *Il se trouvait,* as the French say, *bien dans sa peau,* he filled his own skin with grace. For perhaps the hundredth time that day, the eight thousandth time that year, he heard how well he was looking, and beamed with pleasure.

"My blood pressure," he boasted, "is lower now than it was this time last year." He lustily spooned up the curlicues of cream on his lobster bisque. "How about your weight?" Michael Deaver grinned. But Dutch seemed to have his hearing aid on low. I silently admired his hair, in what Zippy the Pinhead called "all its sh-shimmering glory." With the actor's awareness of scrutiny, he apologized for not slicking it with the usual Brylcreem, and said he had just washed it.

"I always take a shower after exercising. I have two machines in my dressing room." Like all Presidents, he had gotten into the habit of building his sentences around the personal pronoun. "You know, I never would have guessed as a young man that when I was seventy, I would start puttin' another two inches on my chest!" He waited to be asked his current measurement. *"Forty-four inches!"* After the required reaction, he informed us that new muscle was four times as heavy as old flab. "My weight's up to a hundred ninety-two."

So he had heard Deaver's question after all, and figured out a dignified response at his leisure.

I tried to get his opinion of Gorbachev, whereupon he effortlessly changed the subject to other leaders. "That German feller—the other Helmut, uh . . ."

"Schmidt," Deaver supplied, in the midst of a huddle with Nancy.

"Well, at Ottawa he kept sniffin' snuff off of his wrist like *this.*" Dutch mimed an effeminate lift of the forearm, and shook his head quizzically. "Maggie had to teach him how to behave."

Perhaps because there were so few of us, he spoke of his predecessor with candid contempt. "Even wanted the *help* to call him 'Jimmy.' And after he left here, he was the only President to become a nobody."

Dutch said that Eisenhower and FDR and Coolidge were the Presidents he most admired. He asked if I had noticed the view of "another great man" from the Yellow Sitting Room. "I'll show it to you when we go through for coffee."

We followed a sad aroma of decaf across the hall. Dutch stood pursing his thin lips over a cup and saucer that had floated into his hands and pointed with nose and eyes along the oval room's axis. "My favorite view," he said. I peered over his shoulder, through rain-swept glass, out across the Ellipse, and saw a floodlit dome trembling above its own reflection in the Tidal Basin. Between two pale crescents, a dark giant brooded. "Thomas Jefferson," Dutch breathed into his steam. "I look at him from here, and he looks at me."

The evening's professional purpose remained tacit through ten o'clock, when Deaver gave the signal to go. But as we took our leave, I got the definite feeling that the Reagans were, biographically speaking, making themselves available. Next morning, I sent Dutch a copy of Margaret Leech's *In the Days of McKinley,* inscribed "Hoping this brings back happy memories of the 19th Century," and felt the first faint stirring of literary lust.

April came, and with it Easter, and the first cold white explosions of magnolia on Capitol Hill. Then on Thursday, April 11, the White House released the President's itinerary for his upcoming state visit to West Germany, confirming that on May 5 he and Chancellor Kohl would lay wreaths together at Bitburg military cemetery, in a ceremony of remembrance and reconciliation. All Jewish hell broke loose.

It happened to be the height of Passover week. Throughout the Diaspora, Jews were preparing for the twenty-first of Nisan, the holy seventh night commemorating the transit of their ancestors across the Red Sea. For a tormented few, today was more personally the fortieth anniversary of deliverance from Buchenwald. At least one of these survivors, Elie Wiesel, looked back on April 11, 1945, as the specific day he had been scheduled for execution. By whatever inscrutable fate draws *Schluss* between life and death, the soldiers who came for him had worn American and not German uniforms.

Now chairman of the U.S. Holocaust Memorial Council, Wiesel tried and failed to make moral sense of Reagan's announcement. "I cannot believe that the President whom I have seen crying at a Holocaust remembrance ceremony would visit a German military cemetery and refuse to visit Dachau," he said in a public statement. Incompetent aides must be responsible for this paradox and for the timing of its announcement, so crassly insensitive to the feelings of Jews. "Rarely have I known such outrage."

Wiesel said that since both Friday and Saturday were holy days, he would wait until Monday to summon his council into emergency session. Almost simultaneously, news came in that the *deutsche Soldaten* in Bitburg's graves included forty-nine members of Hitler's Waffen SS. Had the body of Heinrich Himmler made it a round fifty, Reagan could not have been more humiliated. The White House hastily advised that the President's German itinerary was "under review."

As I browsed the story in the Sunday papers, it seemed to me that the clash over Bitburg was no mere stroke of cymbals. It was a fundamental collision between faiths, rendered all the more deafening, this year, by Passover's commencement on Good Friday. To understand one another, Christians and Jews must answer a question that went back at least to the Constantine era: whether or not their two most solemn festivals were in spiritual essence different, or one and the same.

To Dutch, Easter—the defining event of Christianity—signified optimism and "newness of faith." His whole religious instinct was to tiptoe as quickly and sentimentally as possible past Calvary, with its ugly associations of blood, thorns, and vinegar, to the auroral Sunday of Resurrection. Pristine in his memory, like some lovingly laminated

Hallmark card, was a picture of himself on Easter Day 1926, leading Dixon's Disciples of Christ in dawn prayers.

To Jews generally, if not Wiesel himself (after Buchenwald, he might be excused any belief at all), Passover—the defining event of Judaism—was also a feast of transcendence. If Jesus had escaped the tomb and risen into Heaven, had their ancestors not escaped the spiritual death of slavery and gone on to find the Promised Land?

But as the bittersweet menu of *seder* made plain, Jewish folk memory was weighted with thirteen more centuries of discrimination than any Gentile could complain about. I felt it was to Christian credit that as late as A.D. 325 at least some ecumenists had tried to make the synchrony of Easter and Passover an article of faith: to attest that the fate of Christ was, like the fate of the Jews, tragic rather than triumphant. The Council of Nicaea had ended *that* pretty heresy, of course, fixing Easter as a celebration of life over death, a day of sun rather than a night of the moon. From then on, the spiritual paths of Reagan's and Wiesel's ancestors had diverged.

It wishfully seemed to me (drowsing rather than browsing now, on a bench in the Capitol park) that Christians and Jews still had enough in common to achieve the "conference" liberals on both sides called for. Why, then, did Dutch's dilemma make me feel so sad? Perhaps because somewhere among the magnolias a dove was cooing, in measured tones that seemed oddly consonant with the endless minor cadences of Judaic psalmody. It was music Theodore Roosevelt had found expressive "more than any other sound in nature . . . of gentle, hopeless, neverending grief."

White House staffers who hoped that Chancellor Kohl would retract his Bitburg invitation were confronted by a surprise obstacle: the President himself. "There is no way I'll back down and run for cover," he wrote in his diary. There were hints from Bonn that a compromise location might be found, but "I still think that we were right. Yes, the German soldiers were the enemy and part of the whole Nazi hate era. What is wrong with saying 'Let's never be enemies again'? Would Helmut be wrong if he visited Arlington Cemetery on one of his U.S. visits?"

The ethical parallels between Arlington and Bitburg did not occur to members of Elie Wiesel's Holocaust Memorial Council when it met in New York City on Monday. Nor were they particularly sympathetic to West German feelings of alienation since World War II; they knew what forty years in the wilderness felt like. Reagan appointees to a man, they were forced to reconsider their previously held opinion that the President was the best friend Jews had ever had in the White House. Unable to bring themselves to censure him, they deferred action on a motion of mass resignation. It was hoped that he would change his mind before Yom Hashoa, the national Day of Holocaust Remembrance.

They reckoned without Helmut Kohl, who while they were still debating subjected Reagan to a cable of pathological length. The Chancellor stated that his government could not survive the humiliation of a presidential snub. He revived the idea of a visit to a concentration camp or synagogue, and said that it could perhaps be made on the same day they went to Bitburg.

Reagan was both persuaded and relieved. "Helmut may well have solved our problem re. the Holocaust." He dispatched Deaver at once to inspect Dachau, along with some other sites holy to Jews, and announced that he would lay a wreath in one of them on the same day he visited the military cemetery.

To nobody's surprise but his own, this gesture was widely interpreted as cynical. Fifty-three United States Senators called upon the President to stay away from Bitburg, while Nancy Reagan added her private objections. Interdenominational protests came in from all over the country. "Dear Mr. President," wrote five-year-old Chelsea Clinton of Little Rock, Arkansas, "I have seen *The Sound of Music.* The Nazis don't look like very nice people. Please don't go to their cematary [*sic*]."

As always when confronted by passions he did not share, Reagan grew defensive and obstinate. "I think that there's nothing wrong with visiting that cemetery," he blurted to a lunch group of reporters on the eve of Yom Hashoa. "Those young men are victims of Nazism also, even though they were fighting in the German uniform, drafted into service. . . . They were victims, just as surely as the victims in the concentration camp."

In my diary for that night I find:

> Dutch informed the world today that there is no moral difference between Bitburg's corpses in SS uniform and the naked dead of Auschwitz and Ohrdruf. More now than in 1969 he seems to me *der reine Tor*: unconsciously cruel in his innocence, blind to the significance of blood in the snow, too dumb to ask the Question that will give him Pity and make him Wise. Courtly, beautiful, brave, and blundering, he has agreed to visit a sick land whose king is inca-

pacitated by the wound of Memory, whose knights will never re-gain their grace, until a Stranger bereft of guile or guilt can be made to understand them. *Nun endet Sorg' und Leid!* But: here's the awful fact he does not yet comprehend (and unless he asks the Question, never will): the Grail they keep in their castle, which they daily raise to heaven in despairing hope of absolution, is full of Jewish blood.

Reagan had sanguinary reflections of his own after watching the eve-ning news. He scrawled angrily, "The press . . . really are sucking blood and finding every person of Jewish faith they can who will denounce me."

In another ironic congruence, he was scheduled next morning to award the Congressional Medal of Freedom to the most eloquent Jew in America. Elie Wiesel visited his office at 10:20 A.M., preparatory to a nationally televised ceremony in the Roosevelt Room. Soft-spoken, marble-pale, the writer gave off waves of sepulchral distress. "Well— welcome!" said Reagan, towering over him, not even trying to pro-nounce his name.

Outside in the Rose Garden, it was over eighty degrees, and the thorns were in green bud. Wiesel's manner was subdued and weary throughout the twenty-minute audience. His beseeching stare never left the President's face. But Reagan gazed back, impervious.

"Mr. President," Wiesel said, "you know we are your friends, yes?"

There was a wary pause. "Yes. What I've been hoping for some days is, you know I'm yours."

"We are here to give you some understanding why certain words hurt us, and certain decisions. It's not that we've changed our friendship for you, or our admiration for you."

"Well, I think we're all the victims right now of a lack of under-standing, and let me make clear what has taken place. I have to say that I've always believed that forgiveness is divine, but I don't think I'm ever going to be able to forgive the press for this." Wiesel sensed the begin-ning of a monologue, and ran despairing fingers through his hair. "This entire situation came about as a result of Helmut Kohl's really sincere desire to make the observance of this end-of-the-war day, instead of one of shootin' fireworks and so forth, make it certify that we've ended that war in peace and friendship . . ."

He rambled on for seven minutes, recalling what he had said publicly in March, but giving several new and obviously contrived reasons not to go to Dachau. A German "individual" had suggested he do so, in order to embarrass Chancellor Kohl. . . . Dachau, being "sort of re-built," was not suitable for an authentic ceremony of remembrance. . . . But happily, a compromise site had been found.

"We have selected now, as a result of Mike [Deaver]'s being there, Belsen-Bergen."

Wiesel leaned forward in annoyance, not so much at the President's verbal slip as at his air of pleased decisiveness. "It was *my* suggestion," he said.

"What?"

"Bergen-Belsen."

Reagan, uninterested, went on talking. He said he just put the phone down after a conversation with Kohl, who was "quite dismayed by what has arisen." The Chancellor had known nothing of the SS graves in Bitburg. In any case, most of the bones in those graves apparently belonged to teenagers conscripted in the last desperate days of the Bat-tle of the Bulge. That was what he had meant when he called them "vic-tims."

Wiesel gave up any hope of a private *rapprochement* before they went next door to face the television cameras. The President had not asked him a single question about the "hurt" he had expressed a quarter of an hour ago. When Reagan noted, smiling, that Germans did not seem to mind when *their* leaders visited Arlington to honor American war dead, Wiesel sat aghast and silent.

During the ceremony in the Roosevelt Room, Wiesel listened impas-sively as the President praised him for being the bard and prophet of six million murdered Jews, "among them one million children." Then, stooping slightly, he approached the lectern and became possessed with what I can describe only as rabbinical fervor. Gesticulating and keen-ing, his face contorted with urgency, he reminded Reagan that the Holocaust had come about because of the ignorance or the apathy of "the leaders of the free world." (An oil portrait of FDR stared serenely into space above both their heads.) "You spoke of Jewish children, Mr. President," Wiesel said.

> One million Jewish children perished. If I spent my entire life recit-ing their names, I would die before finishing the task. Mr. President, I have seen children—I have seen them being thrown in the flames alive. Words, they die on my lips.

Reagan's own lips began to tighten. Under the television lights, Wiesel's waving right arm threw shadows across his face.

> I have learned, I have learned, I have learned . . . that the Holocaust was a uniquely Jewish event, albeit with universal implication. Not all victims were Jews. But all Jews were victims. I have learned the danger of indifference, the crime of indifference. For the opposite of love, I have learned, is not hate, but indifference.

His rhythmic repetitions filled the too-small chamber, which had been substituted for the East Room when staffers realized that he was not going to celebrate the President. By now, many watchers were weeping.

> I am convinced, as you have told us earlier when we spoke, that you were not aware of the presence of SS graves in the Bitburg cemetery. Of course you didn't know. But now we all are aware.
>
> May I, Mr. President, if it's possible at all, implore you—to do something else, to find a way, to find another way, another site. That place, Mr. President, is not your place.

It was the first time Reagan had ever been lectured in front of the American people. His eyes flicked sideways, and he blinked with disbelief. George Bush, who less than an hour before had been obsequiously praising the President for standing by Kohl, ran nervous fingers over his razor burn. But Wiesel was not finished:

> Your place is with the victims of the SS. The issue here is not politics, but good and evil, and we must never confuse them. For I have seen the SS at work, and I have seen their victims—they were my friends, they were my parents.

If the President had been at all doubtful before, this *drasha* convinced him. Massively angry, he announced afterward, "The final word has been spoken as far as I'm concerned. I think it is morally right to do what I'm doing, and I'm not going to change my mind about that." He left no doubt as to Whom he took orders from. "All of those in that cemetery have long since met the Supreme Judge of right and wrong, and whatever punishment or justice as was needed has been rendered by One who is above us all." Forty years ago, he said, he had been one of the first security-cleared officers to view raw film footage of the liberation of Buchenwald. He had kept some of that footage to show to friends who disbelieved the Holocaust. For himself, he could not forget, and never would.

When a bushfire like Bitburg flares after a long news drought, the American press becomes pyromaniacal. So avidly did correspondents fan the flames for the rest of the month that they were deaf to the soft, match-strike sound of a new word, declaimed by Mikhail Gorbachev at a plenum of the Central Committee of the Communist Party on April 23: *perestroika*. Philologically, its formatives *pere*, re-, and *stroika*, constructing, were as old as the Russian language, but politically they combined to incendiary effect.

Just how incendiary, the next six years of Soviet history would show. For the time being, it was enough that the General Secretary himself should admit in public to a need for "sweeping changes in the area of labor and the material and spiritual conditions of life." In the words of his Second Secretary, Yegor Ligachev, there was "a revolution knock-ing at the country's doors," a revolution neither ideological nor mili-tary, but scientific.

Since at least the time of Brezhnev, Soviet realists had been aware that the West was computerizing itself at a rate that threatened to ad-vance the millennium, while Russian shopkeepers in central Moscow were still using the abacus. Foreign technological supremacy, moreover, was being achieved at no cost to parity in arms and space. East of the Finland Station, the opposite equation applied: it was the *expense* of parity that kept Mother Russia poor, and prevented her from compet-ing in the technological race. When one factored in the coefficient that computers improved themselves at a compound rather than a simple rate, the arithmetic grew truly frightening. By the turn of the century, if Soviet sciences continued to lag, Moscow's world power might prove to have been as transitory as that of Manueline Lisbon.

It was not surprising, therefore, that Gorbachev accompanied his call for *perestroika* at home with proposals for a temporary freeze on the deployment of intermediate-range missiles in Europe. He was will-ing to discuss extending the freeze in November—a clear hint that he would agree to a summit that month.

Reagan got the impression that the General Secretary was dissem-bling. Such peaceable protestations ill became a leader who refused to apologize for the killing of a U.S. Army major in East Germany just days before. The major, an accredited liaison officer at Potsdam, had been shot and allowed to bleed to death while Soviet soldiers stood by, refusing first aid. "The American people see this as a tragedy through the eyes of the widow and an eight-year-old child," he wrote Gor-bachev on April 27. "Consequently it will remain a penetrating and en-during problem until it is properly resolved." In view of this and other "recent events," such as the Kremlin's openhanded welcome of Nicaragua President Daniel Ortega, he declined to observe any INF freeze. As for a personal meeting between the two of them, he added coldly, "I assume you will get back in touch with me when you are ready to discuss time and place."

❷

Once it became clear that Reagan intended to visit Bitburg "no matter how much the bastards scream," Michael Deaver called Kenneth Khachigian, a veteran speechwriter from the first Administration, and said that their old friend was faced with the crisis of his career. Elie Wiesel's reproof was being replayed constantly on television, and a majority of both houses of Congress was condemning the President. Even the American Legion had registered a strong protest. In Britain, Prime Minister Thatcher issued a statement describing the Reagan itinerary as "deeply offensive and insulting to the memory of the victims [and] to all who fought in the last war to destroy the Nazi tyranny."

Reagan, Deaver felt, could redeem himself now only through oratory. He asked Khachigian to compose the eulogy the President would deliver at Bergen-Belsen.

The saturnine Southern Californian flew to Washington and was shown into the Oval Office late on Friday, April 26. He remembered from Nixon days what a wounded President looked like, and found himself looking at another.

"How can they *think* that?" Reagan kept saying of critics accusing him of anti-Semitism. "Don't they *understand*?"

He stressed the themes he wanted to sound on May 5. First, that the full reality of the Holocaust was comprehensible only to its victims. "No one of the rest of us can completely understand [their] true feelings. . . . They have a memory beyond anything we can recognize or imagine." Second, that those unafflicted were in sympathy bound to ensure that history must not repeat itself. He uttered the words *Never again* with such feeling that Khachigian decided to use them, confident in Reagan's ability to transcend cliché.

"*Out of these ashes came something good,*" the President dictated. He talked about war and the seeds of war, noting that those planted after V-E Day had borne mostly peaceful fruit. Next week's Big Seven conference would show that, with the exception of Great Britain, the United States had "no stronger allies" than Germany and Japan. "I find myself thinking. . . . 'But we killed these people. Are *we* holding a grudge?'"

For twenty-five minutes, Khachigian sat scribbling in amazement. Normally, Reagan needed to be coaxed into the mood of a speech by staff tossing phrases at him; today, he was impatient of interruption. Only when the Oval Office clock struck five did the interview end, with a Monday deadline for a first draft.

Khachigian felt he already had an opening, *No one of us can understand,* and an ending, *Never again.* Between these two negatives he needed a Reaganesque positive, some atmospheric metaphor of reconciliation and renewal. He asked White House researchers to comb through travel guides and the Talmud, but his imagination remained locked until an advance man returning from Bergen-Belsen mentioned casually that the local countryside, the Lüneburger Heide, was "greening" with spring. Words, or the feel of words, began to come.

Yet the eulogy remained fragmentary through Sunday morning, when Khachigian attended a service at Arlington National Cemetery for his Armenian forebears, massacred by the Turks seventy years before. A sudden sense of ethnic suffering possessed him, and he hurried back to his hotel to write. *"Chancellor Kohl . . ."*

". . . and honored guests," Ronald Reagan said hoarsely to a small audience of German and American dignitaries. They sat facing him on six rows of damp folding chairs, their backs to a thousand-acre field edged with spruce and white birch. Its heathery surface, dull green under the dull North German sky, rose flatly over long, low earthen barrows, unmarked except for tablets that recorded the number of bodies buried in each. HIER RUHEN 3500 TOTE. HIER RUHEN 5000 TOTE. Two hundred meters away from where he stood, a squat little Jewish memorial proclaimed, EARTH CONCEAL NOT THE BLOOD SHED ON THEE.

The President's raincoated shoulders rose with a big intake of breath. He looked down at his cards. "This painful walk into the past has done much more than remind us of the war that consumed the European continent. What we have seen . . ." He left out Khachigian's next phrase, *and what we feel.* Nancy Reagan sat staring at him with eyes huger than usual. Half an hour before, they had stood clutching each other in the *Dokumentenhaus* at the entrance to the field, forcing themselves to look at blowups of white, stork-limbed, tangled corpses.

> What we have seen makes unforgettably clear that no one of the rest of us can fully understand the enormity of the feelings carried by the victims of these camps. The survivors carry a memory beyond

anything that we can comprehend. The awful evil started by one man . . .

Khachigian had written *Adolf Hitler,* but Reagan, with his strange distaste for proper names, chose not to acknowledge the Führer directly. One man among men had "victimized all the world," while concentrating with unique brutality on places like Bergen-Belsen. His voice began to tremble.

> Here lie people—Jews—whose death was inflicted for no other reason than their very existence. . . . Here death ruled.

He was listened to in absolute silence. His every sigh was audible in the misty air, as was the surrounding rustle of the woods. Unnecessary loudspeakers brayed his words across the emptiness of the Bergen field. Not so much as a cornerstone broke the smoothness of grass and heather: the camp had proved so pestilential on liberation that British soldiers had burned it to the ground. Reagan swung with relief into Khachigian's paragraphs of affirmation:

> We are here because humanity refuses to accept that freedom or the spirit of man can ever be extinguished. We are here to commemorate that life triumphed over the tragedy and the death of the Holocaust—overcame the suffering, the sickness, the testing, and, yes, the gassings. . . .
>
> Out of the ashes—hope, and from all the pain, promise.
>
> So much of this is symbolized today by the fact that most of the leadership of free Germany is represented here. . . . Chancellor Kohl, you and your countrymen have made real the renewal that had to happen. . . .
>
> As we flew here from Hannover, over the greening farms and the emerging springtime of the lovely German countryside (*sigh*), I reflected that there must have been a time when the prisoners at Bergen-Belsen and those of every other camp must have felt that the springtime was gone forever from their lives . . . all these children of God, under bleak and lifeless mounds, the plainness of which does not even hint at the unspeakable acts that created them.
>
> Here they lie. Never to hope. Never to pray. Never to love. Never to heal. Never to laugh. Never to cry.

He began to lose control. Did the ghost of Christine Reagan hang in that damp air? His voice growled on each verb, and he fought tears throughout a peroration on the camp's most famous victim, Anne

"His voice growled on each verb."
The President speaks at Bergen-Belsen, May 5, 1985.

Frank. But the only line that stopped him was one of hers: "In spite of everything I still believe that people are really good at heart." The rawness of his delivery was threatened ultimately by sentimental evocations of hearts and angels and glistening hopes. But he held himself stiffly to the end, and Leonard Bernstein could not have better timed his agogic beat before "*Never again.*"

There was no applause. He shuffled his cards, tried and failed to find a pocket to put them in. The wet breeze whipped his coat. Then, with eyes still downcast, he stepped off the monument, leaving a wreath of green ferns behind him. The silence lasted until he found his seat.

As literature, Ronald Reagan's Bergen-Belsen eulogy fell short of the *Challenger* tribute and his final telecast as President. As oratory, it did not begin to compare with the eloquence of Charles de Gaulle returning to Paris, or Cardinal Wojtyla revisiting Auschwitz as Pope. Even Elie Wiesel's simple statement in the Roosevelt Room outclassed it. The essential difference, the curse of American good fortune, was that what he merely felt, they actually knew.

To his credit, he emphasized on that granite platform that he was neither a witness to the Holocaust nor its oracle. He merely reported the little he could understand, and showed himself to be chastened. His agony—such as it was, brief as it was—transmitted itself, via television, into millions of human hearts. One commentator fatuously remarked that he "seemed to be moved," prompting Tom Shales—always the most perceptive critic of the President in performance—to write in *The Washington Post,* "When are they going to realize that with Ronald Reagan, 'seemed' and 'was' are one and the same?"

Two hours after quitting the Lüneburger Heide, President and Chancellor made an anti-climactic visit to Bitburg. In eight wordless minutes, they perambulated the tiny cemetery, fingered rather than laid wreaths on the Wehrmacht memorial, allowed Generals Matthew Ridgway and Johannes Steinhoff to shake hands in their stead, then left without looking at any graves. Kohl used a large handkerchief to brush tears from his face.

That evening, a purified Parzival allowed himself to be entertained at the Augustusburg castle outside Bonn. Handsome and happy in white tie and tails, he mounted the marble staircase with his wife at his side. She too wore white, glittering on white. "Mr. President, how do you assess the day's events, sir?" Reagan considered the question. "It's been a wonderful day!" He strode on into a radiant banqueting hall illuminated by thousands of ivory candles and decorated with green "trees" of spring flowers. Before he and his host rose to speak, the castle rang with trumpets.

While Reagan accepted President Richard von Weizsäcker's hospitality at Schloss Augustusburg, Mikhail Gorbachev accused certain unnamed Americans of "paying respects to the Third Reich." As a result, Reagan paid none to the Red Army when he commemorated V-E Day at Strasbourg on May 8. His speech before the European Parliament, a listing of U.S. terms for reduced bilateral tensions, was so dogged that conservative members seemed tempted to follow radicals trooping out of the chamber. Gorbachev used his own anniversary oration to declare that the United States was positioning itself at the "forward edge of the war menace."

"Handsome and happy in white tie and tails . . . she too wore white."
*President and Mrs. von Weizsäcker of West Germany entertain the Reagans,
May 5, 1985.*

Reagan, flying on to Madrid and Lisbon, professed to be unalarmed
by the Soviet leader's apparent hostility. "What's new about that?" he
asked, blinking placidly in the Portuguese sunshine. "It's just their way
of doing things."

When the President returned to the Oval Office on May 13, he found no
reply from Gorbachev to his last terse letter. But the next day in Vienna, Andrei Gromyko drew George Shultz aside after a six-hour discussion that had covered every aspect of international relations, with
the exception of a meeting between their leaders.

"What about the summit?"

"What about it?"

Gromyko said that President Reagan would be welcome in Moscow in November. Shultz assured him General Secretary Gorbachev would get an equally warm reception in Washington. Gromyko thought that perhaps a neutral venue might be found in a third country. Shultz pounced.

"Are you suggesting Geneva?"

"If you say Geneva, I'll have to say Helsinki."

Shultz returned importantly to Washington, only to find the President cool to the idea of meeting Gorbachev anywhere in 1985. Reagan felt that the United States should play "play hard to get." This plunged Shultz into one of his sudden slumps. He said he was tired and wished to step down as Secretary of State. Reagan reacted with little more than a mild expression of sympathy. Disconcerted, Shultz came back a few days later with a detailed "scenario" for a November summit in Geneva.

Reagan allowed himself to be persuaded by it, and advance teams for both sides swung into action.

June 1985 taxed the President with multiple problems of national security, each capable of triggering a confrontation with the Soviet Union. He began the month distressed by news that another American had been captured by "those d--n barbarians" in Beirut. That brought the current Middle Eastern hostage total to six, and he contemplated an air strike against "the bastardly Hezbollah" if any U.S. citizen died at their hands.

Congress chose this moment to ask him for a statement of intent with regard to the unratified SALT II Treaty, due to expire in December. Legally, he was not bound by it, but as Robert McFarlane explained, his only decent choice was to continue observing the treaty on a voluntary basis. He could be as "narrow" or as "broad" in that observance as he liked, narrowness implying an extension of détente, and breadth permitting research and development of the SDI.

Reagan tried to balance a personal lack of faith in the treaty—which he felt the Soviets kept violating with impunity—against George Shultz's fear that any move toward a "broad" interpretation would endanger the summit. Although Congress had given him until June 10 to respond, he made up his mind four days early, during a campaign trip in Air Force One. Something about the cheering of fresh-faced Texas teenagers made him decide to "go the extra mile" in their behalf. "We will continue to practice restraint on the building of nuclear weapons.

That restraint will keep us generally within the frame work of SALT II but . . . only as long as the Soviets abide by [similar] restraints."

Meanwhile, a seventh American hostage was taken in Beirut.

Mikhail Gorbachev was not fooled by Reagan's announced treaty policy. He correctly saw neither "narrow" nor "broad" distinctions, only an ambiguity that placed no "restraint" on the SDI at all. On July 12, Reagan received a letter from the General Secretary that stopped just short of diplomatic abuse. Gorbachev's proper nouns and acronyms were the standard argot of European arms control, but his images and qualifiers, separated out, were near-poetic in their truculence:

> The United States crossed a dangerous threshold,
> Sought to sharply tilt
> The fine-tuned balance;
> We too are deploying.
> We see an attempt to gain
> Virtual monopoly.
> Seriously undermining,
> Sharply destabilizing,
> Dangerous.
> Things have gone too far.
> Have one's pie;
> Eat it too.
> Unseemly attempts—
> Mortal sins—
> Imaginary Soviet violations—
> Why mince words?
> Cast aspersions—
> Sow mistrust—
> Artificial pretext—
> Accelerated and uncontrolled
> Arms
> Race.
> All this became evident to us
> Long ago.

The Middle East reverted to type on June 14, when a pair of Arabs hijacked TWA Flight 847 out of Athens and forced it to commute crazily between Algiers and Beirut. They discovered a U.S. Navy petty officer, Robert Stethem, on board, shot him through the brain, and held thirty-nine other Americans and crew members hostage when the plane finally came to rest at Beirut Airport. Reporters and cameramen, excited by the sight of Stethem's body hitting the ramp like a sack of *couscous,* courted the hijackers for news bites ("Do you have a message for President Reagan?") and photo opportunities, including one where the TWA pilot had to sit with a hijacker's gun jammed against his skull. When the price of freedom for the hostages became clear—release by Israel of over seven hundred Shiite political prisoners—network producers downplayed the fact that such a release had already been planned, and made it difficult for Prime Minister Peres to proceed without seeming to yield to coercion.

Talking heads around the world assured Reagan that his only choice was to appeal publicly to the Israelis, who would then hand over the prisoners as a diplomatic favor. The idea made his moral gorge rise; "This of course means that we—not they—would be violating our policy of not negotiating with terrorists."

So wrote the man of principle. Then the politician wondered if a private appeal to Peres might bring about the same result. The crisis dragged on for two weeks, while other terrorist groups murdered Marines in El Salvador, blew up an Air India flight with 329 aboard, and bloodily bombed Frankfurt and Tokyo airports. Reagan, weary and confounded, pining for his ranch, drifted slowly into *impotentia Carteris,* power paralyzed by Christian conscience.

The unlikely rescuers of President, Prime Minister, hostages, and prisoners were Hafez al-Assad of Syria and an obscure Iranian cleric named Hashemi Rafsanjani. If Reagan registered the latter name, he did not think it worthy of record in his diary. In time, he would register it well enough.

"Both the President and Nancy will be writing their own books," Michael Deaver warned me, when I told him, over breakfast at the Four Seasons, that I would like, after all, to become Dutch's biographer. "That going to be a problem?"

I said I thought not.

"And I'm no longer in their employ, you realize that. I can get you into the White House, but after that you're on your own."

"Any chance of a seat on Air Force One to Geneva?"

"You'll have to take that up with Don Regan," Deaver said, signaling for the check.

I called the Chief of Staff after the Fourth of July weekend and was told he would be in touch. For forty-eight hours, the phone hung on its hook like a dead bat. Then I understood why. Dutch's deputy press secretary, Larry Speakes, announced that the President would return to Bethesda Naval Hospital for intestinal surgery on Friday, July 10. The operation, a "polypectomy," was not urgent, but had been deemed advisable after last March's discovery of a benign growth in his colon. Naval physicians intended to combine it with a full colonoscopy to make sure no other polyps lurked unseen in the cecum.

I sensed this was no time to push my own invasive intent, and awaited the results of the colonoscopy with foreboding. No White House protestation could alter the fact that Neil Reagan, flesh of Dutch's flesh and bone of his bone, had had a positive-testing colonectomy just one week before this news release.

At lunchtime on Friday, I parked my car near the Ellipse and stood with tourists at the south fence of the White House garden, waiting to see Marine One take off. It batted over us shortly before two, wheeled, and headed for the northern suburbs.

Years later, one of the passengers on board, White House Physician Dr. John Hutton, remembered the flight as mutating into another, infinitely mysterious and frightening. He transferred at Bethesda via a draped security corridor (Dutch's sport-shirted back moving calmly before him) into a gloomy departure lounge crowded with other medics. Here the President hugged his wife good-bye, changed into pajamas, took sedation, and retired behind private curtains. The room darkened further, and somebody put an optical instrument in Hutton's hands.

He found himself suspended—like the observer of some glass-nosed, silently advancing bomber—over a glistening plain. With Commander Edward L. Cattau, the Navy's chief gastroenterologist, both flying and navigating, Hutton was free to search the landscape as it undulated beneath. Other crew members manned other turrets. Shortly into the mission, a low, fibroid outcrop appeared and grew under the glass. Cattau recognized it and steered onward without reducing altitude. The bomber changed course, banking steeply. There was another steady advance, followed by another veer and bank. The landscape, though still smooth, was changing; it seemed increasingly remote and unfamiliar to Hutton, with shadows dark as bruises.

"And then we were there."

"Where, John?"

"At the end of the cecum." He leaned toward me in his green surgi-cal tunic, grimacing. "Just when we thought we were through, this *enormous* mass loomed up in the scope. I couldn't say anything. Neither could Ed. We just stared. Funny, all I could think of was my first flight to the West Coast, crossing the flat part of Colorado, and . . ."

His hands spread and curved like a pilot's. "Suddenly, I saw the dark face of the Rockies, surging up to the snow line. This white, necrotic ridge."

"What does white signify?"

"Carcinoma. Unmistakable. Tumors get like that when they've been left too long. They degenerate and outgrow their own blood supply. We still said nothing—the President would hear us if we talked. We just quietly biopsied that mountain four times, and fulgurated the other polyp on the way back."

"And you?"

"I stood there weak at the knees, thinking, *Why me? How am I going to tell him?*"

Block headlines the next morning shouted the discovery of "a large precancerous growth" in Ronald Reagan's colon, located exactly where his brother's had been. Biopsy results were due later in the day, but there would be no delay in performing a formal right hemicolectomy through the abdominal wall. The President was expected to be under the knife by noon.

At that hour, I walked in ninety-degree sunshine to Saint Peter's Catholic Church on Capitol Hill. I was surprised to find the pale stone building empty. Unventilated and uncooled, it glowed with hot dappled outside light. I sat fanning myself with a leaflet, gazing up at the roman capitals chiseled to right and left of the apse: CHRIST HAS DIED. CHRIST HAS RISEN. In between hung the most familiar image in Western iconog-raphy. Yet it shocked me with the disagreeable strangeness of *déjà vu.* Where, not long ago, had I seen this identical emaciated body, these white arms stretched so far as to crack the rib cage? And why did it have such blasphemous associations with Dutch?

Only when I tilted my head forty-five degrees did I remember. *Ja, ja!* That stark single corpse, hugely enlarged on the wall of the *Doku-mentenhaus* at Bergen-Belsen. King of the Jews. And Dutch looking at it for as long as he could, his face furtive with disgust.

Less willingly then than now, he had subjected himself to emergency treatment—allowed "physicians of memory" to do what they would with him for the general good. For that agony, and for the agony beyond agony of Elie Wiesel, and whatever pain Dutch was suffering now, and for the general good, I prayed until the church's heat became unbearable.

On the way out I lit a candle for him. Its flame stood straight in the motionless air, as if cut from foil.

32

Almost
Air Force One

"I'M NOT going to charge up San Juan Hill for you," said Dutch.
He leaned back smiling, and I sensed from a slight abstraction in
his gaze that he was memorizing the wisecrack for diary purposes. I returned his smile. "That won't be necessary, Mr. President."

The Oval Office was full of soft, diffuse, early November light. He
wore one of his favorite suits, a ghastly gray-brown glen check, formally buttoned, and a Countess Mara tie. An inch of crisp cotton pro-
truded from his breast pocket, two inches from each cuff. Just below his
sternum lay a gold lug of not quite *nouveau riche* proportions. The
patina on his laceless, handmade Oberles must have been at least
twenty years old. He was still the shoe salesman's son, unable to toss
anything that still flexed and shone.

His face was paler than I recalled it, pinkening only along the right
side of the nose, where he had recently undergone cryotherapy. Skin
cancer hardly compared to intestinal cancer on the malignancy index,
of course. Still, two basal-cell carcinomas since July's successful
colonectomy served as further evidence that the President was but flesh.

A reminder to us, if not to him: as far as *he* was concerned, the tumor in his cecum had been something alien and accidental. "I had something inside of me that had cancer in it, and it was removed." Facial irruptions, in contrast, struck him as no more than funny. At the height of the recent *Achille Lauro* crisis he had delayed taking an emergency call from the Secretary of Defense while he admired his outraged nose in the bulge of a chrome towel dispenser. "I look like W. C. Fields."

Pallor and healing scar apart, Dutch appeared well. His broad torso filled the curve of his chair, and his brilliantined hair was dense and dark. I searched for signs of Grecian Formula, but saw only an even foresting of silver shafts among the brown. Our eyes met. He extended his left hand toward a pair of half-moon spectacles, and I tasted the same brackish effluvium that filled my mouth, long ago, during our interview at Fort Roach. But all he did was gently switch them back and forth across his desk. Two reflected lunettes moved in tandem, and I relaxed.

"Thank you for seeing me this morning, Mr. President. I thought that, after so many months of negotiating with other people, I should at least give you a chance to say no!"

He laughed. "Like the fella who's last to find out his wife's been cheatin' on him. Well, I'm certainly the husband in this case."

It was true that Nancy had been his most active agent, with Michael Deaver acting as go-between. The President did not seem to care whether he was chronicled or not.

"As I wrote to Mrs. Reagan, sir, events like Bitburg throw up a huge amount of journalistic debris—"

"Of what?"

I remembered he was half deaf, and repeated the phrase, leaning forward as far as his silver water pitcher allowed. "It tends to settle and stratify. Next thing you know, it becomes the bedrock of history."

"History!" Dutch breathed, suddenly animated. "That reminds me, now . . ." He popped on the spectacles, pulled open a drawer, and began to riffle some papers. I waited with my writing arm awkwardly propped along the side of his desk. Under my fingers, aged to the color of old honey, lay the timbers of HMS *Resolute*. How Theodore Roosevelt had revered this oak! Beneath the lacquer it was coarse-grained from Arctic exposure, pores pitted, microscopic bladders sunken, medullary rays obscured. A discreet shim raised the desk three inches higher than in TR's day. This had less to do, I thought, with presidential height than presidential bearing. TR had been a huncher over, a scrawler upon, a devourer of documents. Reagan leaned toward them with aloof dignity, straight-spined, links not quite touching the leather as he read.

He addressed himself thus to two yellow legal sheets, laboriously filled with his own handwriting. "Those media fellows, you know, they said I got my facts wrong when I said about the New Deal borrowing some of its ideas from the Fascists and all. But I know! I was *around* in '32! I was out looking for a job! So, I wrote this—uh . . ."

He began to read a historical argument, convincing at least to himself. *"It is a matter of record that Franklin D. Roosevelt's liberal Cabinet officers admired Mussolini for putting together a government-controlled or Fascist-directed economy. Secretary Ickes wrote a book that expressed his desire for Fascism in America—but he called it modified Communism . . ."*

This was news to me, and, indeed, to Ickes experts. The President continued to read for several minutes, beaming at his own addled scholarship. Somewhere in the thicket of declarative sentences a fact or two lurked, like lost golf balls. It was true that New Deal technocrats had been impressed by the mechanistic efficiency of Mussolini's reforms, and that some of them were wise to the similarities between Fascism and Communism. But to Reagan, every golf ball signified the proximity of a fairway, every *objet trouvé* was part of a grand design—God's, or his own, or something conjured up by "those media fellows."

When he was through he looked at me, tapped the manuscript meaningfully, and refiled it. "I wanted to release that," he said, "but the press office here . . ." He chuckled and shook his head. "A little too strong for them."

I congratulated Dutch on the recent release of one of the Beirut hostages, Reverend Benjamin Weir. "Six more to go," he said, declining any credit. He said that he was looking forward to meeting Gorbachev at the Geneva summit, now only two weeks away. If he was concerned about the General Secretary's onslaught on George Shultz earlier this very morning in Moscow, he showed no sign. I tried to elicit some words of excitement or trepidation, but might as well have asked him about his next haircut. He glanced at the clock and began to talk about Hollywood. In time, I would learn this was his way of winding down a conversation.

"Somebody in the story department approved a script, uh, *Mission to Moscow,* without lookin' too closely at what was written between the lines, agitprop and so forth . . ."

At intervals I glanced furtively around the beautiful bone-white room, asking myself as every Oval Office visitor does in so many words, *Is this me, here? Is that really him?* Within those encapsulate walls, one has the sensation—illusory yet irresistible—that while the rest of the world might be spinning dangerously, here at the center, all is stability and certainty.

Here, too, a classic tolerance obtains for whatever bourgeois values Presidents may temporarily inflict. I noted the great slab of acrylic sheeting under Dutch's casters, protecting a carpet of Bel-Air beige splotched with blue rosettes, the too-heavy drapes and potted bamboo blocking his garden view, the inevitable spread eagles, goiter-sized paperweights, and corporate mottoes ("THERE IS NO LIMIT TO WHAT YOU CAN DO IF YOU DON'T MIND WHO GETS THE CREDIT") gilt-lettered on bronze. There were twelve miniature saddles and enough bucking Remingtons to round up every half calf on the bookshelves. A rear window table was stacked with silver-framed photographs of Reagan children and grandchildren, arranged so that visitors could see them, while he could not.

Mission to Moscow was just about to preem at the Hollywood Gaumont when Jim Kuhn, the President's young personal aide, came in to end the interview. My half hour was up. "Gee, and you didn't get to ask all your questions," said Dutch, looking apologetic. "Well—"

"See you in Geneva, sir. And with respect—break a leg."

He laughed softly and stood up as I left. Before the door closed I caught a glimpse of him, bespectacled again, writing on another sheet of yellow legal paper. Something about his intent stillness suggested that he had already forgotten who I was, if indeed he ever knew.

Is this, I wonder, what he wrote? It is clearly the manuscript of a President who has had about as much pre-summit advice as he can take from obstructionists and accommodationists, and wishes to work out his own strategy, undistracted by their squawkings and cooings. Years later, I found it among his papers.

> I believe Gorbachev is a highly intelligent leader, totally dedicated to traditional Soviet goals. He will be a formidable negotiator and will try to make Soviet foreign and military policy more effective.

He is (as are all Soviet General Secretaries) dependent on the Soviet Communist hierarchy and will be out to prove to them his strength and dedication to Soviet traditional goals.

If he really wants an arms control agreement, it will only be because he wants to reduce the burden of defense spending that is stagnating the Soviet economy. This could contribute to his opposition to our SDI. He doesn't want to face the cost of competing with us. But another major reason is because the USSR's military planning differs from ours. They basically think aggressively, in terms of targets. We generalize and plan in a kind of defensive pattern—how must we be able to cope with various contingencies worldwide. On the other hand, our recent PFIAB study makes it plain the Soviets are planning a war.

The President's Foreign Intelligence Advisory Board, dominated by such aging conspiracists as Henry Kissinger and Clare Boothe Luce, was a prime target for KGB disinformation in 1985. Reagan did not challenge their findings in his memo, but he coolly observed that the best way to postpone such a war was to up the technological ante. "Any new move on our part, such as SDI, forces them to revamp, and change their plan at great cost."

Gorbachev, in his opinion, was primarily a propagandist, and was determined to alienate America's European allies. "That means making us look like the threat . . . while he appears to be a reasonable man of peace, out to reduce the tensions between us." Nevertheless, Reagan felt it was worth playing such a role at Geneva, rather than compromise "the long-term interest of the United States." He himself would count the summit a success "if we fail to arrive at an arms control agreement because I stubbornly held out for what I believed was right for the country."

☯

Two days later, in the Roosevelt Room, I sat opposite TR (graying over lightly painted lapels, looking wistful for lost power) and listened while Robert McFarlane gave senior staff an account of Shultz's recent meeting with Gorbachev in Moscow. "Those reports of him bullying us," the National Security Adviser said defensively, "just aren't true. He's not bad news, he's good news from the negotiating point of view. Yes, he's aggressive, but for the first time the Soviets have a leader who listens. Absorbs. Takes notes and asks deep questions. That doesn't necessarily mean he's well briefed."

Behind McFarlane a fire burned brightly, yet somehow failed to infuse the cold gray clay of his personality. Donald Regan, farthest away from the flames, sat burnished and ruddy, as if he had drawn their heat. "*A 'sudden' face,*" I noted, "*that even in repose seems about to explode, in amusement or anger.*" He glared down the polished length of the table with the air of a man who disliked equivocation.

"Systematically," McFarlane continued, "we are dealing with a system that doesn't always get word to the boss. Gorbachev seems not to understand our mature SDI policy. He is convinced that we are a militarily obsessed nation—despite the fact that we spend only four percent of our GNP on defense. George told him that, but I don't think he believed it. Now as regards Geneva, the following information is secret."

I remembered Clare Luce telling me, "Bud needs secrecy the way other men need sex."

"Our advice to the President will be to regard Mr. Gorbachev as a realist, a leader conscious of his country's strengths and vulnerabilities. Mr. Reagan's policy is also one of realism *vis-à-vis* the Soviet Union. He knows, as every Politburo member knows, that the stresses they face on their side are very, very grave now. And they, whether they admit it or not, appreciate the enormity of the American revolution wrought by Ronald Reagan. Gorbachev can compare for himself the shambles the President inherited in 1980 with what he has now: a solid economy, a strong military, a landslide mandate, and the full backing of our allies. That's why I came away convinced that this will be a very, very useful meeting between two strong leaders. It could be very, very historic."

Fire could not crack the clay, but fervor might. MacFarlane's straining for superlatives belied the monotony of his voice and face. Just above him on the mantelpiece, the gold disk of the first American Nobel Peace Prize—TR's again—glistened like a thought bubble. None of us, of course, were aware of what he was up to in Iran. But I got the feeling that if Geneva turned out to be very, very historic in ways Bud didn't bargain for, he, and not Donald Regan, would be the likely one to explode.

Accompanying Dutch to Geneva, let alone seeing him break a leg there, was not as easy as I thought it would be in the heady aftermath of being appointed his biographer. The President's favor, once granted, has to be administered by others, and these "assigns," from the Chief of Staff on down, are not necessarily as accommodating as he. Nobody who has not watched army ants swarm can imagine the frenzy with which White House staffers nip and sting for precedence when there is a summit trip in the offing. Proximity to the leader is all. Those who crowd closest, and stay alongside the longest, reflect the most of his mighty-mandibled glory. Right now my urgent need was to get a place—any place—in the delegation scheduled to leave Washington on Saturday, November 16.

"Air Force One?" Donald Regan snapped when I broached the subject with him. "Every seat was spoken for weeks ago. Why don't you hop on the press plane?"

"Because I can't fly with reporters, don't you see. I'm supposed to be—"

"In the loop?" Urgency aside, I liked the sarcastic way he pronounced this cliché. Here was no Beltway bureaucrat, but a Boston Irish slugger, not entirely smoothed by Harvard, who had learned enough about life and death on Iwo Jima not to be bothered by any subsequent vanities. "There's just no space," he said. "I'm sorry, but you'll have to fly commercial."

The obvious thing to do was appeal to Dutch, but instinct warned me not to tax his vast indifference. A President absorbed in preparation for one of the most momentous missions of the Cold War could not care less whether a scribe flew or swam. And in terms of delegate importance, I ranked somewhere between a speech researcher and a copy typist. That is in fact where I ended up, near the rear toilets of AF 26000, Dutch's backup Boeing 707. For this and an unlimited supply of matches with the Executive seal on them, I had to pay the White House Military Office "first class plus a dollar," that being the rate at which the government persuades itself it is not competing with commercial airlines.

"The dollar I can afford," I said to the researcher, an enchantingly braced young blonde named Kim Timmons. "It's the other eighteen hundred that hurts."

"But as the President's biographer," she lisped, puzzled, "aren't you . . . shouldn't the White House—"

"No, I'm an independent writer. Mustn't indulge any government freebies. Like that phone, for example."

Across the aisle, one of the copy typists, giggling, had placed a call home via the White House operator. "Honey," I heard her say, "it's almost Air Force One. If the President was aboard, it *would* be."

Kim mused, "I never heard of anyone paying to fly with him before. You should be on the manifest as his guest."

I explained the Schlesinger Syndrome, whereby poor Arthur was

compromised, biographically speaking, by being a salaried member of
the Kennedy Administration. She looked solemn, as young people do
when spoken to about times before they were born.

Our conversation languished, and I began to write my diary. Kim interrupted only once, between pages, to ask, "Does the President get to
read your book when you write it?"

"To his credit," I said, "and, more surprisingly, to Mrs. Reagan's, neither of them has raised the subject of text approval. I hope they never
do."

"Why?"

"I'd have to say no."

"Do you *like* the President?"

"I'm not sure," I said truthfully. "Here comes dinner."

❡

[*Diary Extract, Saturday, November 16, 1985*]

Aboard AF 26000 en route Geneva—12:13 P.M. About three degrees east of the Labrador fjords, not that one can see much from 40
thou. in sub-Arctic haze. Gray sky, gray air, a consciousness of gray
sea beneath. Pale glow beyond port wing probably Greenland: ice so
densely packed it breathes its own miasma. Have had ice on the brain
from constant repetitions of the phrases *cold war, nuclear freeze* in
background reading for this trip. Also V[arlam] Shalamov's image of
totalitarianism as "permafrost of the soul." Quoted it in a letter to
Mrs. Reagan, who seems more nervous about having tea with Raisa
G. than Dutch is about meeting the General Secretary.

Everyone else on the delegation (300 of us) is nervous too. For a
decade & a half the Soviet Union has been led by ailing ideologues
too old, or too medicated, to contemplate the prospect of a nuclear
confrontation with the United States. Gorbachev may be no less of
an ideologue, but he's a lot younger, & from what one hears of the
Nov. 5 meeting with Shultz he has trouble controlling himself. Hyperactive; blindingly fast; a table banger. That splash of turkey blood
all over his forehead is disconcerting. There is a neurological rumor
to the effect he might have von Hippel-Lindow's Syndrome. Apparently birthmarks that big are often mimicked inside the cerebellum
by a duplicate vascular mass which can engorge at times of stress &
cause bizarre behavior, even seizures. What might happen next Tuesday, when he butts up against the President's brutal geniality? "It will

be a case," jokes Dutch, "of irresistible force meeting an immovable object."

Later—Lunch so-so, wine standard Air Force issue. My young companion (daughter of lobbyist Bill Timmons) charming. Like all young Republican girls in the Administration, she is blonde, beautifully mannered, & called Kim. When Dutch ambles over to the old Executive Office Building, for some reception or other, they emerge like chrysalizing butterflies, flutteringly competing for his attention: "Ooh, look this *wayyy,* Mr. President! We love you, sir!" Tagging behind him the other day, I felt the waves of adoration & to my amazement had to choke down a sob. Must beware *lues Boswelliana.* He, of course, while smilingly acknowledging every squeal, remains as neutral as bakelite.

Their futures in his hands next week & to round out the cliché, those of Gorbachev's grandchildren too. Why then such trepidation, given such mutual responsibility? I guess because when summiteers (ghastly word) have to choose between love & ideology, they will always choose the latter. Dutch is in his way more of an ideologue than Gorbachev—who at least acknowledges the derelictions of his own system. Perhaps that's what we all privately fear: not godless Communism but Practical Christianity, that blind belief in belief which Dutch acquired at age eleven, & has never so much as questioned since.

Later still: Dropped off to sleep—cabin lights dimmed. God knows what o'clock it is out there in the dark, but we've less than an hour & a half to go. Air Force One, which departed Andrews AFB 35 minutes before we did, must be on its final approach to Geneva. Dutch gazing out of his porthole at the looming Alps. Is he really nerveless, or does he at least sense the apprehension all around the world? McFarlane & Regan affected hearty optimism at the pre-brief Thursday, but you could smell their fear. Will Gorbachev turn out to be yet another reincarnation of that Russian folk character, Mr. Bear-Squash-You-All-Flat?

Mark Helprin writes about *Höhenlust,* fear of peaks that goes with compulsion to attain them. There's plenty of this paradox in the history of U.S./Soviet diplomacy. Having prepped all the previous summits *seriatim,* I'm scared myself. A sort of cold cordillera, more ice than rock, stretching back forty years. Practically every hopeful ascent followed by the inevitable glacis toward disappointment, or extreme danger. Glacis. Stasis. Locked molecules of mistrust.

Seat-belt lights flashing. Kim uncurls from her blue-eyed drowse like some Fragonard nymph. For a second or two she focuses on me with non-recognition. Now she is staring fascinatedly at this moving pen. "Have you been writing *all the time*?"

10:25 P.M. Captain announces that Air Force One has just touched down ahead of us at Cointrin Airport, amid light flurries of snow. Everybody in the cabin claps softly, to wish Dutch luck.

33

One on One

"A LITTLE PROBLEM getting to sleep," the President complained in his diary for Saturday, November 16, 1985. It was not for want of comfort, since he and Nancy were plushly ensconced at Maison de Saussure, Prince Karim Aga Khan's lakeside villa. The chimes of Geneva, sounding distantly across the water, protested in vain that the hour was midnight. His own obstinately ticking circadian clock assured him it was time for the six o'clock news at Camp David.

Some deep need for order and spacing, whether of appointments, allergy pills, meals, or madroña trees, always caused him to react with silent outrage when the White House advance team ordered him to adjust his watch. Loss of daylight traveling east was bad enough; loss of time itself on the way back added insult to injury. Reagan's every facility focused on getting the universe back in sync with himself as soon as possible. His arms-control advisers, even now testing their room phones at the Hotel Inter-Continental for suspicious echoes, would have felt easier about him as a negotiant had he studied their position papers as carefully as he had Dr. Smith's rules for the conquest of jet lag.

Before retiring, he paid equal heed to some house-sitting instructions left behind by his host's young son, Hussain. The boy's bedroom—made over to him as a study for the duration—contained an aquarium of tropical fish whose habits were as regular as his own. Perhaps with a certain amount of fellow feeling, he pinched and sprinkled two portions of fish food.

Around ten o'clock the next morning, I was awakened in my less palatial quarters downtown by the sound of the same church bells summoning the faithful to prayer. *Les cloches de Genève* . . . I recognized with delight the motif from Liszt's piano piece of that name, a minor third falling to a major, mingled with the general clamor. Pushing aside the Ramada Inn's orange draperies, I looked out at a hard, gray, charmless city. One hundred and fifty years before, almost to the day, Liszt had commiserated with George Sand about the blighting effect of Calvinism on what had once been an exuberantly French Catholic *ville de lac.*

Since then, Geneva had only gotten grimmer, as generations of *internationaux*—those expressionless types you see leaning forward to blot the signatures of statesmen—kept the canton's paper mills busy and cluttered every restaurant in town with their enormous briefcases. How many protocols, conventions, communiqués, pacts, *temperamenta,* treaties, and codes had been sweated out here, most of them to protect or placate "obliterated grandeurs, fallen majesties, snuffed-out powers!" Liszt again.

The President, meanwhile, was breakfasting with Nancy and likewise noting the grayness of the weather. But their view of Lac Léman, blue-green under lowering mist, was lovely enough to suggest a walk in the grounds after lunch. By nature as well as staff design, Dutch was unconscious of the barbed wire and motion detectors that ringed him, the offshore patrol boats and inland armored cars, the anti-aircraft gun pits dug into Prince Karim's landscaping, and the nervous, hidden binoculars that focused and refocused every time he looked out the french doors.

Nancy, equally by nature, could think of little else, and her blood temperature—about that of a newt—curtailed their walk to four min-

utes. But later that afternoon, he persuaded her to join him in a tour of
the facilities at Villa Fleur d'Eau, further down the lakeside, where the
summit was to begin on Tuesday. A fire was burning in its tiny parlor,
and she sank luxuriously into one of the two armchairs angled against
the glow. "Why, Mr. Gorbachev!" said Dutch from the seat opposite. "I
had no idea you were so pretty!"

Diary, November 17, 1985—A mostly private day for the President
and NR, which I am not permitted to despoil. He makes just one
quick trip to Fleur d'Eau, in order to prepare for a "spontaneous" invitation he will deliver to Gorbachev at some point in the summit.
Soviet advance men have been working for weeks with our own, to
ensure that the *gensek* reacts with similar impulsiveness. No Japanese
imperial marriage proposal was ever planned as carefully, down to
the last smile and bow. If Gorby has any sense of humor, he'll wait
for Dutch's moment of inspiration, and then say *nyet*.

I walk up to the Inter-Continental, where most of the delegation is
quartered, and am intrigued to see that one "retail" establishment, at
least, defies this city's Sunday gloom. It is a lamp and chandelier
shop two blocks from the hotel, blazing brilliantly although the door
appears locked. There are three little men inside, heavily cheekboned,
smoking and staring at me through the plate glass. When I come
back toward midnight, they are still there, and their smoke has
formed a nimbus round the higher bulbs. I am carrying a copy of
Dutch's summit schedule under my arm—184 pp. of meticulous timings, maps, and diagrams, stamped on the cover with his presidential
seal. Instinct warns me to hold it to my chest as I walk by, and I feel
them watching my back until I am out of their circle of light. For
some reason, the experience makes me feel deathly sad.

The President, still out of sync, slept fitfully that night. Denied the
eight ("nine if I can get them") hours he needed, he awoke gloomy and
noted that Monday's weather was cold and dark. He breakfasted late,
dressed in a suit as gray as the trees outside his window (slender wands
of birches, their last leaves whipping in the lake wind) and at eleven
o'clock strolled without enthusiasm to Villa Pometta, Prince Karim's
guest house. Here his advisers and his overawed biographer awaited
him in rococo armchairs.

"Didn't get enough sleep," he complained, and sank into a gilt sofa. Throughout the ensuing briefing he stared at his shoes under the glass cocktail table, looking up only when he heard something that challenged him. I got the impression of a man too polite to say that he thought the distinctions Paul Nitze drew between mobile MIRVed ICBMs (worth banning because of the stabilizing effect of a reduced target-to-warhead ratio) and mobile unMIRVed ICBMs (worth preserving because they would permit a Midgetman RV system to counteract deployment of the SS-25) might just as well differentiate two cans of spinach.

He nodded, at any rate, when the veteran diplomat advised that the growing perception of "a new arms race," fostered by the SDI, "favors the Soviets and not us." Gorbachev had scored a propaganda coup well in advance of the summit by proposing a 50 percent cut in offensive strategic weapons. He might well push for a second by getting Reagan to accept, or consider, the notion of an INF treaty that would force France and Britain to defend themselves. Nothing would delight Western radicals more than to have the United States resume its pre-war isolationist role.

Reagan stirred angrily. "We can't start treating our friends as if they were possible enemies. The alliance is aimed at one enemy and one enemy alone: the Soviet Union."

His irritation lasted through a follow-up by Robert McFarlane, who urged him to hold Gorbachev to a strict interpretation of the SALT I Treaty. It was plain that he resented having to make a pledge to that effect himself. "I don't see why we should break up Poseidons when we know what they're doing . . . taking older submarines and enlarging 'em and filling 'em with 'missiles.' "

"They've done more breaking up than we have," George Shultz purred. I wondered how he knew.

Nitze changed the subject to the SDI. Gorbachev would certainly demand concessions—"nothing you can agree to"—and try to persuade him that the ABM Treaty's allowance for future innovations in defense technology did not justify the heaven-filling scenario the President had sketched in 1983.

Reagan shook his head. "That won't happen."

From arms control, the meeting moved on to discuss other likely subjects of contention between himself and the General Secretary, starting with Afghanistan. He was urged to protest Soviet "extra-border" aggression there, but proved surprisingly reluctant. I got the feeling that he regarded it as an inherited embarrassment for Gorbachev, as Vietnam had been for Richard Nixon. "We know they've had their tail kicked by the Afghans for the last six years—can't we offer them a way to get out with grace?"

There was a short silence. I looked at my watch. Twelve minutes to noon: Gorbachev's plane would be touching down at Cointrin about now.

When discussion resumed, it concerned that most droning of subjects, the Middle East, and Dutch's eyes reverted to his shoes. *Somber, saving himself,* I scribbled. At last Jim Kuhn came in to rescue him. He stood up with alacrity and headed out the door. But his advisers followed, determined to continue boring him through lunch.

"Lord," he wrote later, "I hope I'm ready and not overtrained."

☯

Tuesday, November 19, dawned bitingly cold. The lake lay dull and dented, like old pewter. At nine o'clock I took a ride out along the Route de Lausanne with Pat Buchanan and found the President's motorcade already forming in a reticulated sequence of black hoods and blue exhaust fumes. It looked long enough to reach Fleur d'Eau without leaving Maison de Saussure.

Reagan was closeted upstairs in the Villa Pometta for a final, secret session with his advisers. "How's he bearing up?" I asked the first of them to emerge, Assistant Secretary of Defense Richard Perle. "Sons of bitches are trying to get him to grant Gorby all sorts of concessions," he muttered. "At one point he asked, 'You don't want me to give back Wrangel's Island, do you?' "

I joined nervous staff members in the vestibule, waiting for Dutch's scheduled appearance at 9:40. "Please God," I heard a female voice whisper behind me, "don't let him wear that fuck-awful brown suit." Precisely on time, he materialized at the top of the stairs, clad from head to foot in dark navy—what the French call *bleu minuit*—a white silk scarf at his throat. Buchanan exulted, "He looks like a million bucks!"

The stairway was spiral and designed for eighteenth-century Savoyards a good deal shorter than Reagan. Across its curved overhang some wag had taped a sign: JERRY FORD SAYS WATCH YOUR HEAD, MR. PRESIDENT. He caught sight of it while descending and began to laugh. We found ourselves applauding as he passed between us. At the door he called over his shoulder, "Jerry, watch this!" and still laughing, strode across the gravel to his limousine. Little puffs of mirth hung on the air behind him. Palpably, there spread through the rest of us a confidence

that the world's future was safe in the hands of a man who could laugh
so easily at such a time, with such things to do.

Then we dashed for our various vehicles.

Shortly before ten o'clock at Fleur d'Eau, an electric sense of Gorbachev's approach ran through the delegation. It found its terminal in
Reagan, waiting just inside the front door. The thrill seemed extra-
sensory, but was in fact flashed by urgent twitterings in the earplugs of
advance men and Secret Service agents. "He's two minutes away, Mr.
President." A distant wail of sirens grew louder, then cut off. "Sir, he's
coming through the gate." The door swung open. For a moment, Reagan looked out on an emptiness of stone steps, gravel, mist-hung trees
and fields. He sucked in a huge lungful of air—actor's training—and
stepped out onto the patio.

"Don't be nervous!" Sam Donaldson's shout was addressed, I
thought, more to the watching world than to Reagan, who stood imperturbable. Despite three degrees of frost, he wore no overcoat. There
was not a hint of tremble at the cuffs of his suit. Silence fell. Then a
long, black, prismatically polished Zil flatnosed its way around the corner of the villa.

My vantage point—with the White House television crew inside the
curve of the steps—was so close that I could hear the great car's brakes
squeak as it ground to a halt. It did so a few yards short of a line perpendicular to the President. In Moscow, no doubt, there would be jokes
about the driver being shot. A big KGB man got out and opened the
rear right door.

The forty-eight seconds that followed replay in my mind in extreme
slow motion, as if each frame were too fraught with drama to roll any
faster. Similarly, the sounds I remember are dry and distinct, although
they must have been part of a larger web: the first crunch of Gorbachev's shoes on the gravel, the answering swish of Reagan's on li-
chened stone, the surgical sound of a hundred camera shutters slicing
the light, and a mysterious roar that gathered overhead as the two leaders drew near. It was, of course, the pass of some military jet, but so intent was I on the business at hand that I subconsciously equated it with
blood thundering through Gorbachev's birthmark.

Not that anyone could see that famous stigma at first. He emerged
from the Zil wearing the traditional homburg of the *nomenklatura*. Its
low rim and the mass of his unbuttoned overcoat (widening as he

raised both hands to adjust a loose scarf) made him look shorter than his actual five feet nine. The President, descending tall and tailored in the near foreground, took advantage of the laws of perspective to dominate their encounter. He moved—insofar as I was conscious of him moving at all—with typical smoothness, the steps seeming to melt beneath him, while Gorbachev strained forward, clutching at coat and scarf.

I see them now closing with the static momentum of spacecraft. Reagan's elegant silhouette, still stairborne, begins to blot out the oncoming tangle of clothes. Gorbachev's left hand rises a third time, reaching for his hat, then disappears, along with the rest of him, as the blue bulk reaches center foreground. Reagan pivots on polished heels, arms straight yet relaxed. As he does so, the bare splotched head appears over his shoulderline. I am reminded of one of those full moons you see in puppet shows, pale and tightly beaming. The smile fades. Contrary to expectations, Gorbachev looks scared.

His right hand moves forward in greeting, and for a moment Reagan's left seems to be aimed at parrying it. But their trajectories are different, and do not intersect. Instead, Reagan's right sweeps around in a beautiful arc, neither cramped nor exaggerated. Just as flesh touches flesh, that higher left hand reaches the thick folds above Gorbachev's elbow, so he is both welcomed and caressed simultaneously. He breaks into another smile, broad and relieved this time.

He looks into Reagan's eyes and sees—what? All *we* can see is the back of the presidential pompadour, glossy and impenetrable. The roar in the sky drowns out their initial exchange—perhaps mercifully, since neither man can understand the other. Reagan points twice, with easy authority, at the steps, and inch by inch those two figures, ill-matched in shape and size yet already companionable, move across the screen of memory and ascend out of frame.

Many years later, I asked Gorbachev the question that tantalized me that morning: what he saw when he looked up into Ronald Reagan's eyes.

"Sunshine and clear sky. We shook hands like friends. He said something, I don't know what. But at once I felt him to be a very authentic human being."

"Authentic? What word is that in Russian?" I asked the interpreter. He was startled to be addressed directly, and shot Gorbachev a nervous look.

"*Lichnost.* It is a very difficult word to translate because it means 'personality' in English. Or 'figure,' but in the dignified Italian sense, *figura.* But in Russian its meaning is much bigger than in these languages: a *lichnost* is someone of great strength of character who rings true, all the way through to his body and soul. He is authentic, he has—"

"*Kalibr,*" said Gorbachev, who had been listening intently. He is so intuitive that he can follow dialogue without vocabulary.

"I know what *kalibr* is, Mr. President," I said. "We have the same word in our language."

☯

Inside Fleur d'Eau that frigid morning, Gorbachev divested himself quickly of his overcoat. He had recovered his aplomb by the time the press was allowed to photograph him and Reagan at the beginning of their "one on one." They sat in a small blue parlor, enduring two of the minor penalties of power: flash after flash branding the retinas, and silly questions lobbed in defiance of access rules. Amid the glare and the noise, Gorbachev stared amazed at *Playboy*'s official representative, a horse-faced youth in red hightop Reeboks, blue jeans, and shirt the color of borscht. Whether or not he knew that this boy (steadily returning his gaze) was Ronald Reagan, Jr., he need look no further for evidence of Western libertinism at its most depraved. The battle of eyes lasted so long that I, looking from an angle only slightly less acute than young Ron's, received almost the full force of Gorbachev's personality. I will carry that face forever: the fathomless brown eyes, which seemed to hold all the grief and guilt of Mother Russia, the clamped mouth and jaw tense with energy, the transforming glow of a large intelligence, and—who could help ogling?—the livid birthmark. I tried to visualize the duplicate neurologists inferred, spreading across the brain. Interestingly, it was Gorbachev, and not young Ron, who looked away at last.

He listened with the same apparent contempt to a question about his rumored iron bite. Yet hardly had the translation begun than his body was contorting with merriment, and he said over ebullient chuckles, "As of now, I'm still using my own teeth." Reagan, deaf as usual in any confined, crowded space, sat bemused. I wrote in my notes, *G. the fastest reactor I've ever seen. R's only hope*—but then agents cleared the room. My last impression, before the doors closed, was of President and *gensek* removing to chairs nearer the fireplace and of Gorbachev saying, as they settled down, "Well! A fire is always a symbol of life."

With no more than ten minutes scheduled for the one on one, there was little attempt at fraternization between U.S. and Soviet negotiators, who sat around in the main salon, waiting to be introduced formally at the plenary session. Another fire flickered here, but it failed to warm the cold white light pouring in through high french windows. Outside, a Swiss flag snapped stiff against a backdrop of snow-dusted hills. Notwithstanding our confidence earlier in the day that Reagan would be able to handle Gorbachev alone, the image of his sudden discomfiture in the parlor lingered. A palpable concern floated that maybe, behind those closed doors, he was being savaged.

Throughout the house, and in every house in this land of clocks, the minutes ticked away. Ten, then twenty; thirty; forty-five . . . incredibly, an *hour*? Around the sixty-five-minute mark, Jim Kuhn murmured, "Should I go in and break it up?" Secretary Shultz's overreaction betrayed, I think, his own worry: "Look, if you're dumb enough to do that, you don't deserve your job."

The clocks chimed eleven-fifteen, then ticked some more. Their rhythm reminded me mnemonically of a passage in Bertrand Russell's *ABC of Relativity*, read an eternity ago, on the beach at Lowell Park:

> If we choose one out of a number of equally good clocks, we may find that the universe is progressing as fast as the most optimistic American thinks it is; if we choose another equally good clock, we may find that the universe is going as slow as the most melancholy Slav could imagine. Thus optimism and pessimism are neither true nor false, but depend on the choice of clocks.

Who, I wondered, had lost count of time in there: the optimistic American, or the melancholy Slav?

When I asked Dutch afterward what he and Gorbachev talked about, he winked and said, "Jet lag." To Donald Regan, he was more forthcoming, saying he had begun the conversation with a reference to their similar backgrounds (Dixon being transformed for the purpose into "a small farm town") and historic responsibilities. "Here you and I are, two men in a room, probably the only men in the world who could bring about World War III." Alternatively, they could "bring about peace to the world."

He followed by remarking, "Mr. General Secretary, we don't mistrust each other because we are armed, we are armed because we mistrust each other." In the days and years to come, Gorbachev was to endure countless repetitions of this and other Reaganian bromides, always intoned with exactly the same emphasis, rhythm, and air of pleased discovery. Today, however, he felt not so much patronized as flattered by the President's determination to deal with him on equal terms. Reagan went out of his way to call the Soviet Union a "superpower," showed no disdain for its policies, and added that Russians had every right to disapprove of the American way of life. At the same time, he spoke frankly of "competition" rather than "cooperation" in their relations, within a desired framework of trust. To *lichnost* and *kalibr,* Gorbachev mentally added the word *ravnovesiie,* balance.

For the rest of the *tête-à-tête,* Reagan had the novel experience of being crowded out by a talker more voluble than himself. Speaking with torrential energy, the General Secretary said that the "mistrust" he mentioned could be allayed only by "great will at the top." This meant they should ignore the advice of obstructionist advisers and look afresh at the "central issue" confronting them. It was *voina i mir,* war and peace.

Perhaps Dutch the determinist, thinking vaguely of Tolstoy, misremembered this phrase when he repeated it to us afterward. War *and* peace was not an "issue," it was a condition, the double estate of man. War *or* peace—*voina ili mir*—was a moral choice, rendered dread by Hiroshima, that only man could debate, and only heads of state decide. The General Secretary certainly seemed to want such action, insisting that they must "end the arms race" and "create an impetus—an impetus toward—"

Reagan, oscillating his hearing aide between Gorbachev's excited Russian and the interpreter's toneless English, was not sure what kind of impetus was supposed to go where. But he heard enough simple words—such as *peace, different, simple, young, old*—to listen with interest, and was touched when Gorbachev apologized for "going on so long."

The only proposal he did not like, and was determined to answer before they went into plenary session, was that East and West should "take a political approach" to resolving conflicts in the Third World. This sounded to him like an argument for interventionism. The United States, Reagan said firmly, "was for self-determination" rather than "Marxist ideas of social revolution" applied from outside.

Gorbachev replied that his country did not "export" revolution. Before Reagan could react, he did an expert segue to the subject of California's next major earthquake. Clearly, he had been well briefed on the

President's weakness for doomsaying. Soviet seismologists, he said, were predicting 7 to 7.5 Richter-scale tremors in Reagan's home state "within the next three years."

From then until they got up to go, Reagan ranged happily up and down the Pacific fault lines from Mount Saint Helens to Nevada el Ruiz.

&

Finally they came through to the main salon, looking pleased with themselves. But the euphoria of intimacy often dies when leaders ready to do bilateral business realize they will have to do so in plenary session. Reagan's smile faded to purse-mouthed impatience as they posed for yet more photographs at the head of the negotiating table. Gorbachev kept grinning, but jabbed at the polished wood with stiff, frustrated fingers. A German reporter called out, "Your meeting has gone on much longer than planned. Why?" Their replies nicely illustrated the difference between the democratic and autocratic mind. "Because whoever was scheduling didn't allow enough time," said Reagan. "The duration of this or that meeting," Gorbachev bristled, "is determined by the President and General Secretary. Themselves!"

With that, they parted, exposing a gold clock whose hands stood at 11:25. The television kliegs faded, and ordinary light refilled the room. Reagan seated himself at center table with his back to the lake, allowing Gorbachev the privilege of its vaporous views. To the left and right of each man, six aides symmetrically spaced themselves. George Shultz looked across at Eduard Shevardnadze. Donald Regan faced Georgy Kornienko, First Deputy Foreign Minister; Ambassador Arthur Hartman his opposite number, Anatoly Dobrynin; and Robert McFarlane Gorbachev's closest adviser, Aleksandr Yakovlev. On the fringes, Jack Matlock, chief Soviet specialist at the National Security Council, and Assistant Secretary of State Rozanne Ridgway confronted Gorbachev's nuclear expert, Anatoly Aleksandrov, and Kremlin spokesman Leonid Zamyatin. All except Matlock and Dobrynin donned earphones for simultaneous translation. Reagan, as host, asked Gorbachev if he would like to begin, and switched off his hearing aid. For the next thirty-five minutes, the dead amplifier lay like a stopple in his nearly deaf right ear, while the other was filled with the toneless voice of an offstage interpreter. Hearing that voice rather than his guest's, he remained unmoved by a performance that Gorbachev had prepared with great care.

The General Secretary started quietly, even graciously, giving Reagan credit for initiating the first U.S.–Soviet summit meeting in nearly seven years. "This is your idea, Mr. President: talking *to* each other and not *about* each other." The more talking the better, to build trust and encourage the exchanges—commercial, cultural, touristic—that demilitarized the rivalry of superpowers. Recent history showed how noncommunication at the top caused mistrust to spread through all levels. "We are going back now: our relations are at their lowest point."

Reagan was interested to hear that this was the fault of "U.S. think tanks" and "the U.S. ruling class," which had given him certain "illusions" about international Communism. One was that "you should push Soviets to gain your foreign policy—which is to obtain superiority in the military area." Another was that Moscow had designs on Western Europe. "We are not at war with each other, and let's pray God we never will be."

Unless his hearing aid deceived him, Reagan had just heard a heathen invoke the Lord of Hosts. On Western lips such a reference might pass unnoticed, but no Marxist-Leninist, surely, would use it without deliberation. Was some subtle signal being sent forth, a fish sketched in air? If so, Gorbachev hastened to cover up. He redoubled his attack on American alarmists. *Gushing out words at this point,* Donald Regan noted.

"You want to reduce nuclear arms, we share that goal. You want equal security, we favor that. You want exchanges of people, we share that goal. You want people to choose their own way, we share that." The General Secretary spoke for half an hour. Analysis of his monologue reveals a subtext of economic pleading beneath the standard rhetoric of arms control. Apart from one boast that the Soviet Union could pay its own way, he all but begged for Western aid. There were wistful references to the commercial and technological "weight" of the United States, and to the prosperity of West Germany and Japan, who "spend so little on armaments." The moral imperative of arms control was surely to re-allocate funds from offensive to peaceful purposes, by mutual agreement, for mutual benefit.

Again and again, Gorbachev used the words *voina i mir.* "This afternoon we will discuss specific questions of war and peace. . . . We came to Geneva seeking how to bring about peace."

The hands on the gold clock now stood at noon. Reagan had enough time before lunch to echo Gorbachev's generalities, and maybe invoke the same peaceable God. But he responded with words that stopped just short of provocation. "Let me tell you why we mistrust you and are suspicious of you." The veteran Kornienko stared at him with narrowed eyes. Not since Richard Nixon's vice-presidential days had a General Secretary been addressed in such language.

Reagan accused the Soviet Union of turning on its ally, the United States, at the end of World War II. It had taken cynical advantage of the pace of American demobilization ("We reduced from twelve million to one and a half million men almost overnight"). It had rejected Washington's arms-control initiatives and snubbed an offer to share A-bomb technology. It had developed its own nuclear weapons and deployed them to such an extent that now, in 1985, it bristled with more warheads than ever before. Meanwhile, the United States' capability had diminished to pre-1969 levels. Not anymore, though: "We are rebuilding."

He saw sinister links between Moscow's arms strategy and its extra-border activities. "Your government has talked of one Communist world, fomenting revolution everywhere. . . . You have an expansionist policy. You are in Cuba, only ninety miles from our shore. In Angola, Afghanistan, Ethiopia. I'm citing these not to be antagonistic, but to show you why we're suspicious. . . . I've told you as frankly as I can that we fear you." The summit should focus, he felt, not on arms control *per se* but on the madness of MAD, which led to nuclear stockpiling. Once *that* neurosis was taken care of, "the mountains of weapons to which you refer can shrink."

It was almost twelve-fifteen, and they were due to go into recess. Reagan chose this moment to make a proposal he knew would anger Gorbachev, who, unable to reply, would have to brood on it for the next two and a quarter hours. "I have made an argument—to share with you our anti-missile shield. We don't know if it is possible, but we are optimistic. You've been researching such a system also. . . . If either one of us comes up with a solution, let's share it, make it available to everyone. Remove all fear of a nuclear strike."

Everyone? No idea could have seemed more addled, to Soviet perceptions, than a universal defense against the ultimate offense, unless the President's "shield" was, like the *testudo* of Marcus Aurelius, the sort of defense that kills. Yet here he was insisting, "It's not a weapon, it's a system . . . a worthy dream."

Reagan rose to escort Gorbachev back outside. This time they coated up together. I was waiting again in the curve of the steps with the White House television unit. My impression was that the General Secretary would just as soon have seen himself off. His large eyes looked bruised and bewildered as Dutch bade him farewell. Perhaps he was rehearsing what he would tell his comrades at the Soviet mission: "This man is a real dinosaur."

☯

Dinosaurs have, if nothing else, an air of oncoming massiveness, and Gorbachev did not make the common mistake of assuming this one had a pea-sized brain. At lunch in Maison de Saussure, Reagan contentedly chewed lake fish and repeated to his advisers, word for word, what he had told the General Secretary about volcanic/tectonic activity along the West Coast. He ranged back as far as the sixth century A.D. before the impatient Kenneth Adelman, fearing an excursion into Pliocene times, hazarded that Gorbachev was the kind of man who might walk out of a summit if toyed with too much. Someone else asked the President what he would do if the famous "iron teeth" showed.

He pushed back his chair with a lovelorn expression. "I'll say, 'Mike, what about all those nice things you said to me this morning?' "

☯

Before the second plenary started at two-thirty-five, I stood in the grand salon chatting with Ron Reagan. His tall athleticism reminded me of the young Dutch, but his soft handshake and eyes were Nancy's. We became so engrossed in our conversation that we did not notice that the President had entered through the far door.

"The literary set!" Dutch called out, pointing at us and laughing. His entourage smiled primly.

"Uh-oh," I murmured to Ron, "I'm in danger of losing my objectivity here."

"That can happen. He represents the good things."

"Like what?"

"Kindness. Honesty. Decency."

"You really do believe that, don't you. It's not because—"

"He's my father?"

"And President of the United States."

He shook his head, and held up a finger and thumb, millimeters apart. "I love my dad, but our relationship is about this deep."

The big Zil reappeared unexpectedly outside. Dutch went to meet it, and Ron and I were pushed into the blue parlor by an urgent little Russian whose face was oddly familiar to me. We found ourselves alone with him behind a not-quite-shut door. Through it came the noise of summiteers taking their chairs and unzipping briefcases. Incredibly, the little Russian did not seem to notice that he had left the door ajar. His sleeve had brushed the stamens of some lilies in the salon, and he was inspecting the resultant brown stain.

"Spy dust!" I whispered to Ron, winking. Our friend reacted violently, slapping the pollen and blowing at it. Then he stepped out onto the patio to consult with some KGB colleagues. Again, I wondered where I knew him from.

Dutch's voice, calm and silvery, floated in from the salon. "Well, as discussed this morning, you, uh, have the floor—" Maddeningly, an unseen hand clicked the door shut.

There arose on the other side, low-pitched at first, then resonating dully through the blue-and-gilt panels, a baritonal monody, as Slavic in sound and timbre as any *melodya* in Russian music. It reminded me of nothing so much as the slow movement of Rachmaninoff's Cello Sonata, which I had heard performed unforgettably by Mstislav Rostropovich and Vladimir Horowitz at Carnegie Hall nine years before. Something about that encounter, and this, caused all the accumulated *uma* of the Motherland to pour forth—aggrieved melancholy, passion, foreboding—in a flood that Russian scholars acknowledge cannot be stopped once it starts.

Gorbachev's voice rose to such a volume that we were emboldened to crack the door open again. Lacking Russian, neither of us were much the wiser, but we heard him now in full sonic splendor. It was a beautiful voice, unhurried, unhesitant, prodigal in its cumulative effect. Among the few words I understood—*mir, voennyi, Weinberger*—was one repetitive acronym, *S.O.I.,* "S.D.I."

We were joined, from the patio, by a young man wearing a White House badge but no other identification. The little Russian followed him in expressionlessly.

"Don't know about you," Ron murmured, "but I feel spooked."

Spook or not, our compatriot was an obliging fellow who listened knowingly at the crack, and summarized what Gorbachev was saying.

"He's going on about parity—says we've increased our SNCs three times since 1960—"

"SNCs?"

"Strategic nuclear charges—they're monitoring us to keep up—but want mutual reduction—says we're ahead of them in computers—first time I've ever heard a Soviet admit *that.*"

The little Russian grew agitated at the sight of me scribbling and tapped me on the shoulder.

"He wants to check your badges."

I twisted my lapel at him. He peered, then peremptorily put his hand over my pen. *"Nyet, nyet."*

It was one of those moments when a man with his wits about him will tell another man to go jump in a lake. We were, after all, on our own diplomatic territory, and Léman's gray waters were available for me to jerk a thumb at. But I confusedly put the pen away. The young American left the room, hissing at him, "You're on my shit list, buddy."

Next door, Gorbachev seemed to be saying something similar to Reagan.

☯

Actually, as surviving notes reveal, he stayed within the bounds of *politesse*. Yet there was no mistaking the threat in his violoncello voice when after forty-six minutes it rose to a climax:

> Weinberger says if the Soviet Union has a space-based ABM system, it would be terrible for the United States. What are we to feel if you have it? This is mistrust. . . . The SDI is a terrible arms race—a race in space. We would have to take steps to smash your shield, like a porcelain plate!

I crouched as close to the crack as I could, and squinted through, hoping to see how Dutch was taking this. All I could glimpse was a sliver of french door behind him. I was about to stand up when one of the panes flickered, and I caught a mirror-perfect image of Gorbachev leaning forward to gesticulate. His face was pale against the gathering gloom outside, his birthmark an angry blotch. He wore a strange half grin, like those characters in Tolstoy who keep smiling under the stress of contrary emotions. Then his reflection slid off the glass as he sat back and abruptly stopped talking.

Reagan responded in a husky, confiding voice that did nothing to mute his obstinacy. "It's just what I said this morning: we don't trust each other." He began to tell a story of Russian perfidy in World War II as perceived from the vantage point of Fort Roach. Our bombers, wishing to fly deep into Germany, had been denied refueling and rearmament privileges at Soviet airfields, forcing them to make shorter sorties from Britain, at great loss of men and matériel.

I winced at the majestic perversity of his memory. He was referring to air support for the Warsaw Uprising, news of which reached us at

Culver City in late August 1944. For a week or two, it was all over the base that British and American arms-dropping efforts were being stymied by the Reds. But landing rights had been granted after negotiation. Even if Dutch had forgotten that, I thought he might have had the grace to acknowledge that the Red Army spilled a lot more blood to win the war than we ever did.

However, he was President of the United States, I merely his querulous scribe. Jimmy Carter, no doubt, would have made some such unctuous remark. Mightn't the truth be, though, that we Yanks—most fortunate and therefore most foolish of innocents—have no right to sentimentalize what we cannot comprehend? "The Great Patriotic War" is the fundamental trauma of twentieth-century Russian memory: a mark from birth, a blotch on the brain. Perhaps Dutch, *der reine Tor,* was wise (or dottily inspired) to reveal his lack of education, evoking from Gorbachev neither rage nor contempt, but something akin to tenderness.

The General Secretary listened with equanimity (*twiddling thumbs— literally,* Donald Regan noted) as Reagan rebutted his rebuttal, itemizing all the disappointments of the Cold War. Tiring after about fifteen minutes, Reagan got lost in a Chinese fable about warriors fighting with "an impenetrable shield" and "a spear that will penetrate anything." Gorbachev's voice was gentle when he interrupted and suggested that "weapons" floating in space, whether shields or spears, were in fact military.

"No, I don't agree," said Reagan coldly. There was a short silence.

"It looks like a dead end," Gorbachev said.

After another uneasy pause, the President cleared his throat. "At this point, I have a question. Why don't we, just the two of us—"

Something beeped inside my little Russian's raincoat, galvanizing him. He grabbed his hat and rushed outside, leaving the patio door open. The noise of his departure drowned whatever it was Dutch was saying.

"Let's go," said Ron, zipping up his parka. "Dad's taking Gorby for a walk."

"Walk—where?"

"The pool house."

I hurried after him, boggling. "Is this the spontaneous invitation?"

"Well, it was supposed to be a quote surprise, unquote. But, of course, our guys had to tell their guys."

The air coming up from the lake was cold enough to make us cough as we waited for the two leaders to emerge in their overcoats. When they did, they coughed too. Reagan led the way down a flinty path to the water's edge. His breath and Gorbachev's intermixed whitely, as did that of the rest of us—interpreters, medics, personal aides, Secret Service agents, photographers. My little Russian had his hat on now, and, looking at him as he puffed along behind the *gensek,* I recognized him at last. He had been one of that trio of squat smokers in the chandelier shop on Sunday night.

I managed to jostle close enough to hear Gorbachev say he had enjoyed some of the President's movies, "particularly the one where you lost your legs."

"Why thank you," said Dutch, flushing with pleasure. "And by the way, will you tell, uh, Arbatov that they weren't all B movies. That one, *Kings Row,* has been voted one of the ten best pictures of all time."

Drake McHugh's amputatory agonies lasted all the way down the slope. Gorbachev interrupted once to ask, "What is it like—to see yourself so young on the screen?"

"You've set me up for a great one-liner," said Dutch. He spaced it out for the interpreter: "Like-meeting-a-son-you-never-knew-you-had."

Laughing, they stepped through glass doors into the pool-house parlor. We watched them shrug off their coats and settle down in front of a blazing fire. Reagan handed Gorbachev one copy of a set of arms-control proposals drafted by Paul Nitze. They sat reading like a pair of clubmen, with such absorption that a flying coal, ejected by the fire, sailed over their heads and sizzled unnoticed on the floor.

The proposals, written in the form of guidelines for the START negotiating teams, called for a 50 percent reduction in intercontinental offensive systems. Gorbachev read without comment until he came to a subsection on space defenses, which Reagan was determined to include in the overall package. It allowed the United States and Soviet Union to research and develop any anti–ballistic missile system consistent with the 1972 treaty.

I saw the General Secretary look up from his copy with a weary expression. He said something vehement, and Dutch shook his head regretfully. The fire between them continued to blaze, but the room seemed to have lost some of its glow.

☯

For the next fifty-five minutes, we stood around the pool house, stamping our frozen feet. "Where's the rest of me?" an advance man groaned. Even the Russians, who were presumably used to extreme cold, turned blue and crimped, like ornamental cabbages. A low mist hung over the lake, and *les cloches de Genève* sounded at quarter-hour intervals, with inexpressible sadness. "I have the feeling things aren't going too well in there," I said to Ron. He was about to reply when the glass doors opened to the sound of Gorbachev's rich, deep chuckle. He and Dutch came out beaming and rosy from the fire. They marched companionably up the hill, and the rest of us scrabbled as before in their wake. I caught up in time to hear Dutch say, "So you want to continue these talks."

The homburg, bobbing along beside him, nodded vigorously.

"Well, Mr. General Secretary, I'd like to invite you and Mrs. Gorbachev to visit us in Washington next year." By now they had reached the driveway and were stopped, facing each other. To my surprise, Gorbachev went quite pale as he improvised his answer. The big Zil, responding to some unheard signal, came creeping up.

"Yes, after that you must come to Moscow," Gorbachev's interpreter droned. "But there is still tonight for talking, and tomorrow too!"

They locked hands and eyes with a sudden affection that had in it elements of relief. I have rarely witnessed such mutuality. Nobody moved. Dutch said, "Till tonight, then." They parted, and the Zil's door closed with a bulletproof thud.

e

Debriefing the President afterward, Shultz, McFarlane, and Regan were so exhilarated by his news of two more summits that they failed to register alarm at what had evidently been a high-risk encounter in the pool house. Gorbachev had set the tone by declaring that the Soviet Union would not reduce strategic offensive arms unless the United States halted its deployment of "space weapons." Reagan had rejected the last word and repeated his offer to share research into a mutual "shield." Gorbachev suggested that a President capable of embracing both "broad" and "narrow" interpretations of the ABM Treaty should perhaps clarify what he meant by *research*. There was the kind that confined itself to the laboratory, and that which involved the actual construction of prototypes.

The General Secretary's sarcasm was clearly intended to make Reagan reveal himself as either a Shultzian accommodationist or a Weinbergian cold warrior. He did not hesitate, careless of Soviet sensibilities: "The laboratory theory of the ABM Treaty isn't enough."

Gorbachev took this to mean that Reagan wanted to test "a first-strike capability" in space. Were Russians seriously to believe that American scientists would share such test data? Even if they did, and both sides deployed their respective systems, who could keep track of all the floating hardware but God? The prospect was not reassuring because "God provides information very selectively and rarely."

Reagan repeated these strange words to his debriefers as further evidence of closet Christianity. It did not occur to him that Gorbachev might have been dropping the Holy Name to beguile him. But he was clear-eyed in detecting, or suspecting, fear of the Politburo in his opponent's negotiating style. "Gorbachev has a political problem. [He] doesn't know how to back down on [the] SDI."

He listened to a summary of the rather dogged discussions that had gone on in the villa during his absence. George Shultz did not tell him about Kornienko's rage over the landing-rights story ("Your President was totally *wrong*"). Long experience had taught the Secretary one might as well re-carve Mount Rushmore as seek to change one of Reagan's *idées fixes*. Nor did anyone communicate Secret Service reports, already humming over the drop from Maison de Saussure, that Nancy and Raisa Gorbachev, meeting for tea, were engaged in a major battle of hormones. So it was a contented President who left Fleur d'Eau (winking conspiratorially at Ron and me on the way out) and told his chief of staff that he was looking forward to dinner and another day's debate with the General Secretary. "You could almost get to like the guy. I keep telling myself I mustn't do it, because he could turn."

And turn Gorbachev did next morning. From the moment of Reagan's arrival at the Soviet Mission—a bleak white box that looked as if it had previously stored chemicals—Gorbachev made clear that yesterday's friendliness was on hold. The two principals met alone, inconclusively, on the subject of human rights (Gorbachev snapping that Soviet Jews were better off than American women and blacks) before joining their teams in a long, brown-draped hall, flooded with the shadowless light favored by totalitarians.

Reagan himself was in a restless mood, having drunk more caffeine at breakfast than was good for his bladder. He was further irritated by last-minute advice from Secretary Shultz to avoid ideological debate on Afghanistan and Nicaragua and coax Gorbachev into some statistical concessions on arms control.

No sooner had he re-tabled Paul Nitze's proposal for a 50 percent reduction in strategic offensive systems than the General Secretary demanded a simultaneous scaling back of American defense plans. "You feel that SDI is consistent—we find this amazing. It is a weapon in space, a destabilizer."

They were back to the impasse of yesterday afternoon. Only this time neither man controlled his anger. The session was plenary, but they paid so little attention to aides they might still have been one-on-one. They accused each other of "delusions" and "fantasies." At one point, the President, refusing to be interrupted, extended his left arm, fingers splayed: George Gipp booming a rogue lineman. Gorbachev quoted Soviet scientific estimates that put the cost of the SDI as high as one trillion dollars and asked if Americans had "money to burn." Reagan felt that freedom from fear was worth it. "My dream (*loudly and firmly*) is to prevent these missiles from raining down on innocent people."

"You dream of peace," said Gorbachev, even louder, "but realities are not so."

As they got angrier, their imagery became more primitive, regressing from the "gas masks" of World War I to the "bows and arrows" of Agincourt and the "firebird" of Russian myth. By noon, they were eye to eye across the table, all others forgotten.

MG: Why don't you believe us when we say we will not use weapons against you?
RR: Why won't you believe that all I want is a shield?
MG: Please answer me—what is your answer?
RR: I am answering—with a question for *you.*
MG: Answer my simple question, Mr. President.

This the President could not or would not do. He disliked being outmaneuvered, and Gorbachev was acute enough to see the danger of pinning him down. "I am too heated and emotional not to show you my sincerity. I beg you to stop this arms race before it gets started." But Reagan remained inflexible, taking personal credit for the SDI and reminding Gorbachev that the Soviet Union ("Don't let us kid around") had its own treaty-violating defense system, the Krasnoyarsk radar. For perhaps the twentieth time, he asked, "Wouldn't you like to share?"

At this they simply sat staring at each other in silence. The room froze for what seemed, to Shultz, like thirty seconds. Then Gorbachev tossed his pencil onto the table and said, "I regret you cannot see it our way."

Diary, November 20, 1985—November 21, I guess I should type, since the *cloches* have long since tolled midnight. As medieval criers

would report, all's well. The summit's over—bar some formal joint
statement that's being bashed out right now by second-tier staffers
down at the International Conference Center. There was a brief explosion of rage by Shultz earlier tonight, as the Gorbachevs were getting ready to leave Maison de Saussure after dinner: Soviet team
apparently obstructive over para 38 sub-para 4 clause 3(c) of phraseology, meaningless to anyone but a diplomatic glossarian. Gorbachev calmly ordered Kornienko to break the block & shook hands
with Dutch for the thirteenth time in two days. They seem unable to
stop touching each other & exchanging long looks, brown eyes into
blue.

What is it, this clutching *vis-à-vis,* almost sexual in its eagerness?
Were it not so friendly, one might consider it querulous, a reach for
reassurance that they are not in fact at sword's point. Or shield to
shield. This morning's session (which degenerated into just such medieval language) brought them to the point of open hostility. Had
Gorbachev walked out then, as Khrushchev probably would have
done . . . well, he didn't. Came back after lunch as if nothing had
happened, & they spent most of the afternoon swapping stories in
yet another one on one. That pencil drop was *le moment critique.* If
summitry be a war of nerves, Dutch won by default.

When the plenary ended at five-twenty, they went on to a reception
hosted by the Swiss at Le Reposoir. I attended hoping I might meet
Gorbachev, but the room was so jammed with desperate diplomats
that I took a rain check. Nowhere to "hold" but outside in the freezing dark. A kindly chauffeur offered me sanctuary. As a result, I have
the intoxicating pleasure of riding back to Saussure in a presidential
motorcade. After one's first fool urge to restrain the driver—hey, that
was a *red light!*—one abandons oneself to its inexorable momentum.
My Mercedes is the fourth of five behind Dutch's big black Cadillac,
which is in turn preceded by a twin decoy, a gray lead, an advance car,
a control vehicle, a communications car, & another limousine bearing the Secretary of State. Behind us come two press cars & an ambulance, & the whole procession is both preceded & succeeded by
Swiss police cars & motorcycle fleets, winking their lights & wailing
an *ostinato* of falling fourths. Reminds me of those haunting cornet
calls on the sound track of *Patton.* Snowflakes fall. All the way along
the Lausanne road, Swiss soldiers stand at the ready, their backs to
us, Swedish tommy guns cradled in their arms. Onlookers jump &
shout. Their faces, whipping by, are white with cold, but rapturous.
They have seen the passage of power, caught Dutch's grin and wave:

> *Your benedictive fingers beating*
> *Like a gull's wing in the storm.*

The fourths die as we sweep into the grounds at Saussure. While the Reagans change for dinner, the rest of us have a *kaffeeklatsch* in Villa Pometta. Theories are offered as to the extraordinary "chemistry" between the principals. A saturnine youth from the CIA ascribes it to RR's humor. "He cracked Gorby up this afternoon about Moscow being just as democratic as Washington—anyone there can do what Americans do at home—stand up & yell, 'President Reagan is an incompetent SOB!' "

When I hear the Soviet motorcade coming—half an hour late, at 8:28—I hurry out & join the press pool by the steps of the mansion. Its Palladian facade is exquisitely illuminated. A few snowflakes are falling, sprinkling & scintillating as they hit the floodlight beams. Cameramen peer anxiously at the black sky & blow the flakes from their lenses. Four bare poplars stand like feathers in the frozen air.

Gorbachev's speed-cops are polite enough to kill their klaxons as they come down the Rue Creux de Genthod. As a result, the motorcade, slowing to about ten miles an hour, approaches in virtual silence. Antonioni would be hard-pressed to match the beauty of this dark advancement upon the gate. First (diffused by the black grille & our own vaporous exhalations) a dancing blue light that grows & pulsates like a will-o'-the-wisp, materializing into a wobbly-wheeled police motorcycle. Others follow as the gate swings open, then comes the larger hulks of advance vehicles & finally the vast Zil, its red wing flags glowing as they come within klieg range. Meanwhile, the night is filled with soft roulades of harp music. I turn in the direction of the sound & see that Dutch & Nancy, glittering gold, are standing in the villa's open doorway.

The Zil (whose brakes appear to have been fixed) sighs to a halt. I get my first, & with luck last, view of Raisa Gorbachev: eyes small & hard as kopecks, a killer smile, earrings jiggling. Nancy examines her from coiffure to stilettos with leisurely contempt.

"Gott help us," an Austrian reporter mutters, "should vimmin deploy nuclear veapons."

As they line up to be photographed, Mike Wallace's boy from NBC asks when the blackout will be lifted. "The news is so good—" Dutch says, but the rest of his sentence is drowned by a cataract of shutters. They go inside.

We stand around, reluctant to disperse. Why? No activity is visible through the heavily curtained windows.

"Zhust think," the Austrian breathes, "of the in-*kredible* power at that table tonight. *Total* vorld control between the two of them!"

6:15 A.M.—Still here at the Inter-Continental, sleepless, at one of the last functioning Displaywriters. Had a scoop after typing the above—a kindly WHTV lenser asked if I would like to see the raw videotape of "last night's toasts" at Maison de Saussure. RR & G. so verbose, & the nuances between them so fascinating, that I may as well transcribe it scenario-style:

RR   (*massively calm, starched cuffs resting on freesia-stacked table*) We've come to the end of the meetings. I said, and I'm sure others did, that this summit was a beginning, not an end.

He pauses, and his invisible interpreter, squatting on the floor between him and Raisa, translates for the benefit of Gorbachev, immediately opposite.

And whatever we failed to agree on, one important decision was that we would continue meeting like this.

INTERPRETER   Vyso ravno, bylo odno vazhnoe reshenie prinyato chto my budyem prodolzhat'.

His hands, white as the freesias, flutter out of concealment, speaking another language altogether.

RR   And each one of us has accepted the invitation of the other to visit our two countries. . . . I consider that, while we have made some gains and arrived at some mutual decisions (*Raisa, who understands English, casts a disdainful look at the ceiling*), we have also not closed the door on anything, and we will continue to meet. One of the early leaders of the revolution that gave birth to our country—Tom Paine—said, "We have it in our power to start the world over again." (*He enunciates this slowly, with grandfatherly conviction. His eyes never leave Gorbachev's face.*)
I think some of that (*nodding*) has been present in what we have been doing. Because the problems we've attempted to solve are the things that have plagued mankind with sorrow and tragedy. I believe that we have started something here.

Around the cramped table, they all sit listening: Gorbachev huge-eyed, motionless, Nancy ditto, Raisa showing the President the nape of her neck, Don Regan sending McFarlane a silent up-yours from his seat at G.'s elbow, Kornienko slit-eyed and dangerous, Shevardnadze staring into space, Shultz doing his usual imitation of a Toby jug.

> I choose to believe that there was something present in these meetings—a will and a desire on both sides to find answers that would benefit not only the people of the world but also (*head rearing*) the unborn. So my toast, Mr. General Secretary, Mrs. Gorbachev (*turning and twinkling at her*), and guests here, my toast to all those. And it is to the devout prayer (*he husks devoutly*) that we can deliver to them something better than what has been known in the past.

He reaches a long arm for his champagne flute. Crystal clinks all around, and he drinks deeply and appreciatively. Then a strange thing happens. The little room breaks into applause.

GORBACHEV   (*waiting for silence*) Ya prinimayu fekel'.
INTERPRETER   I take up the relay.

He means *baton.* The General Secretary goes on even longer than Dutch, but the interpretation is so stilted (at one point, our man has to correct his man) that there seems no point in transcribing it. His beseeching gaze and agitated finger movements betray the true result of this summit. On Dutch's scorecard, it's Immovable Object 1, Irresistible Force 0.

7:05 A.M.—For the first time since our arrival, Geneva's blue-gray mists have risen to show the Alps across the lake, snow-streaked & colorless. White House workers are dismantling the offices here on the twelfth floor, unplugging computers, shredding papers. The air smells of sweat & rotting apple cores. A plump stenog., bleary from typing all night, hands me the text of this morning's "joint statement." It is emblazoned, HOLD UNTIL 10 A.M. What's to hold? The "agreements" it registers on cultural exchanges, North Pacific air-safety precautions, nuclear risk–reduction centers, & consulate swaps are trivial compared to the disagreements it tries to mask: over human rights, regional mischief, SALT II observance, & above all, the SDI. There are the usual pieties about strategic arms reductions, "appropriately applied," and the need for an INF agreement, but there is also this—Dutch's—litany: *A nuclear war cannot be won and must never be fought.* After forty years of lethal buildup, leaders of East & West have agreed to curb the race for nuclear supremacy.

After the joint signing ceremony and champagne reception (at which Gorbachev, wanting to make statistical history, elbowed Reagan into *two* more one on ones), the President flew to Brussels and reported to NATO leaders that he was now in dialogue with a strong but peaceable Soviet leader. It was nearly six o'clock before he broke free of their congratulations and headed back to Air Force One. Sleepless across the Atlantic, he prowled the aisle in velour pants, proclaiming the wonders of time regained. He shamefacedly confirmed the death of one of young Hussain Aga Khan's goldfish, despite his conscientious feeding. An urgent search of Geneva pet shops had yielded two identical replacements, who were now happily swimming at Saussure. Any normal head of state would have decamped without further notice, but Dutch had felt impelled to leave behind a note explaining the mysteries of death and transfiguration:

Dear Friends

I put the white half dome in the tank according to the directions and fed them with 2 good pinches morning and night from the big food container.—Now and then I added some of the colored flakes. . . .

On Tuesday I found one of your fish dead in the bottom of the tank. I don't know what could have happened, but I added 2 new ones (same kind). I hope this was alright.

Thanks for letting us live in your lovely home.

RONALD REAGAN

The workday begun at 8 A.M. Swiss time ended nineteen hours later with the President descending onto a helipad behind the U.S. Capitol. Inside, both houses of Congress waited in joint session. He told them ("Maybe it's the old broadcaster in me, but I decided to file my report directly to you") what he felt he had achieved in Geneva, on behalf of the American people, and basked in overwhelming applause.

Next morning he slept late and awoke to the sunshine of an 81 percent approval rating. His only significant business of the day was a meeting with Robert McFarlane about the hostages in Beirut. "We have an undercover thing going," Dutch wrote in his diary, "which could get them sprung momentarily."

34

Explosions

IF THERE WAS ANY MOMENT when Ronald Reagan could be said to have arrived at the climax of his power and popularity, it was when he pressed a button at 9:39 P.M. on the eve of Independence Day 1986, and, choking back tears, watched a laser beam slice across New York Harbor and immolate the Statue of Liberty. Hundreds of thousands of spectators around the bay, and an estimated one billion television viewers worldwide, watched along with him.

Lady Liberty's apotheosis was not instant. At first, only her stone pedestal glowed red, while the dark copper mass above continued to brood against the encircling glitter of shoreline and skyscrapers. Then the glow climbed and whitened until all color burned away and the entire statue incandesced, as if carved from magnesium.

"That's two thousand kilowatts you lookin' at," said the inevitable statistician behind me in the VIP bleachers on Governors Island.

More to the point, I thought, was a perhaps unintended allegory between the lighting and Dutch's own presidential progress to this point. First the blood staining his shirtfront and the red ink of his defense buildup, then the dark years of the recession and the Evil Empire, followed by surging prosperity and brightening hopes! Oldest of Presidents, he had just scored an unprecedented 86 percent approval rating among young Americans, and his legislative potency had returned, just eight days ago, with a big vote in the House to renew *contra* aid.

☯

An hour and a half earlier, I had caught Dutch in the middle of a huge, sunset-facing yawn. We were in a holding pavilion out of sight of the crowd, and he was going through his usual pre-event withdrawal.

"Going to be a long night, Mr. President."

The yawn dissolved into laughter. "And an early morning too," he said.

President Mitterrand of France, who was due to accompany him onstage in celebration of the Statue's centennial, had begged to be excused for a quick *pipi.* It struck me that Dutch, who also had prostate problems, would never have allowed himself to be caught short at such a time. A hundred and twenty trumpeters were already sounding John Williams's "Liberty Fanfare." Nancy Reagan looked at me wide-eyed, clearly hoping for a remark that would save her from having to *entrer en conversation* with Madame Mitterrand.

The last of the sunset was catching her white silk dress, and I could manage nothing more intelligent than, "You look good in that light."

"Thank you," she said. "But I'm not looking forward to the wind."

A breeze from New Jersey, surprisingly cold for midsummer, was lifting the flaps of the tent, and there were two and a half hours of ceremonies ahead. She had nothing to protect her but a thin red cardigan. I looked at the white dress, and her blue hands, and thought cruelly, *She matches the bunting.*

"Mr. President, how was your reunion with Mr. Mitterrand?" I asked.

He was checking his watch, and for a moment or two seemed not to understand the question.

"Oh—uh. Yes. Good. It went well." Nancy reached up and adjusted his forelock.

Advance men around us whispered frantically into their wrist mikes. The two biggest no-no's in the Reagan White House were to let the President's schedule slide, and to allow his wife to get cold. But until Mitterrand zipped up, there was little anyone could do. I thought of Napoleon's long halts leaning against a tree, waiting for his bladder to relax.

"I hear he's on his way to meet Gorbachev," I said.

Mitterrand returned, rescuing Dutch from having to answer this. Now it was the turn of French aides to talk to their wrists. The band outside promptly struck up a *marche militaire*. We waited for "Ruffles and Flourishes," then followed the Mitterrands to the Presidential boxes.

I detached myself from the rear of Dutch's retinue and hurried off in order to avoid a "musical tribute" to Franco-American ideals, presented by Kenny Rogers, Andy Williams, and Mireille Mathieu. Mitterrand's amplified voice pursued me across the fresh-laid turf: he must have been prevailed upon to speak first. The wind, gusting hard, blew most of his French away, but not a final, despairing attempt to sound ebullient in English: *"'Appy berthday, U-nited States! 'Appy berthday, Mees Liber'arty!"*

Most of the island's military buildings were dark under the emerald sky. White tents pitched for the ceremonies inflated and deflated like aspirating whales. Elizabeth Taylor emerged from one of them in a neck brace. She gave me a sour look, and headed for the grandstand on wobbly heels.

Dutch was not due to speak for another half hour, so I was able to find a way through the trees to a viewpoint that encompassed the shimmering sweep of the bay. It was quilled from east to west with the masts of hundreds of "tall ships" rocking silently at anchor. Earlier in the day, they had hoisted the flags of thirty nations and paraded under full sail for the two Presidents, along with forty thousand smaller boats and a massive display of U.S. naval equipment. To my disappointment, the *Theodore Roosevelt* was nowhere to be seen, but tomorrow night a nuclear carrier almost as enormous, the *John F. Kennedy,* would make its deck available to Dutch for the biggest display of fireworks in the history of the world.

Or so the literature said.

I flattered myself that writer's instinct, the urge to be on the periphery of things—to see and hear from different angles—had brought me to this remove, and favored me with a sight more beautiful than anything David Wolper, the producer of tonight's show, and his "Liberty Weekend" team could conceive: Lower Manhattan stockpiled and stackpiled, each glass box a galaxy. But to be honest, I was fleeing Ronald Reagan out of a sense of failure. Things were not going well for the Official Biographer.

It was not that Dutch had cooled to the idea of me dogging his footsteps and scribbling down everything he thought and said. As he joked to the Alfalfa Club, "Frankly, I hadn't given it much thought until the other night, Nancy sneezed in her sleep and I heard Edmund say *Gesundheit.*" For seven months now I had been interviewing him, following him halfway around the world, lunching with his wife, sitting in on senior meetings in the Roosevelt Room, and trying to understand why the future of mankind depended on something called Gramm-Rudman. I had made friends with Mike Deaver, Don Regan, George Shultz, and Cap Weinberger. The scholarly Senator Hatfield had sold me his townhouse near the Library of Congress, and its ground floor was already an archive bulging with Reaganiana. Young Kim Timmons, she of the blue eyes and enchanting brace, played occasional hooky from the White House speechwriting department to help me build a chronology, and I was about to hire a full-time assistant. Yet the magic of Geneva had faded. Dutch remained a mystery to me, and worse still—dare I entertain such heresy, in the hushed and reverent precincts of his office?—an apparent airhead.

"What you see is what you get," several of the above-named intimates had warned me, when I asked about his hidden depths. Nevertheless, I could not believe how little one indeed "got," and how shallow those depths appeared to be. It was not that Ronald Reagan bored everybody with political *idées reçues,* as he had forty years before. At seventy-five, he was disconcertingly taciturn much of the time, conducting meetings with only the barest of introductory remarks (which he would read from typed cards in a manner I can describe only as docile). When he was asked direct questions he would refer again to his cards, and if there was nothing there to help him, he would smile, shrug, and let Shultz or Regan answer in his stead. Sometimes a stray phrase would remind him of a joke or an anecdote—the former usually funny and pointed, the latter tending to wander into regions of total irrelevance. After an awkward pause, Regan would then have to bring the meeting back to order. What amazed me was Dutch's lack of embarrassment about being thus helped out, and his imperviousness to the contempt rising on the faces of Congressional opponents such as Representative James Wright of Texas, and Senator Ernest F. Hollings of South Carolina, who sometimes seemed to be looking around the room for a spittoon.

Beyond amazement, I was distressed by the relentless banality, not to say incoherence, of the President's replies in interviews:

EM: In Tokyo, on that Monday morning, was it you who took the initiative for the State Department on terrorism, or someone else?

RR: The first question we were faced with, was "Why didn't you mention it in the statement?" And she was supportive and . . . they
accepted it, and it was put then, and we broke for lunch at the
teahouse, and as we passed, the questions there, evidently someone had seen the statement and we had added things to it, and
Sam Donaldson yelled, came to me, "Why didn't you mention
Qaddafi and Libya?" And [*chuckle*] I was surrounded by the rest
of them! And I said, "Sam, if you haven't seen it, find a copy." It
was a very pleasant walk to the teahouse!

What was really frustrating was his tendency to blank out on events
closed to me. I could not figure if he was being tar baby or fox.
Notwithstanding my extraordinary access to him as a person—
extraordinary in the sense that no independent writer had gotten that
close to a President before—it was not access to high affairs of state.
Reagan's White House Counsel, the affable but inflexible Peter J. Wallison, had ruled that my non-governmental presence, at meetings dealing with national security and other vital policy, would breach
executive privilege, and invite unwelcome subpoenas from Congress.

No defender of the Constitution can argue Wallison's point. I guess
I could have begged a token job in the Administration, but that would
have gone against another necessary separation of powers: non-
collusion between biographer and subject.

At times of sad self-analysis (brought on, for example, by the sight
of tall ships rocking), I had to admit that penetrating the polished
doors would have left me little the wiser. Thanks to Watergate and its
assault on executive privilege, not to mention its sanctification of
leaks, the real business of the White House, when policy was decided
and actions initiated, was done in one-on-ones or two-on-twos between Reagan, Regan, Shultz, and a few others, sometimes in the
Oval Office, but as often as not outside of it, on the South Lawn, or
amid the din of Marine One, or even in private bathrooms with the
faucets running. The executive sessions I did manage to attend might
as well have been conducted in Serbo-Croatian, for all I understood of
them. I recollect a Cabinet meeting at which Clayton K. Yeutter, the
new U.S. Trade Representative, made a presentation of such dryness
as to violate the District of Columbia fire code. My only consolation
was the discovery that Dutch, too, had little interest in Multifiber
Agreements. I could tell by his especial calm, and exaggerated nods
whenever Yeutter paused for breath, that he was on horseback somewhere.

Since the President's biweekly receptions with leaders of Congress were not "privileged," I was allowed to sit in, or rather stand at a small lectern in the corner of the Cabinet Room. It made a convenient ledge to scribble on, but until the Congressmen got used to my graybearded presence, I tried to hunch down as much as possible and not look at Dutch. One day, while Wright was criticizing his policy in Central America, I felt his gaze, and made a conscious effort to ignore it. But it continued to play on me like a mild searchlight. Other gazes increased the candlepower; my pen began to waver; Wright's voice took on an edge of irritation; helpless, I looked up at last, and Dutch triumphantly winked at me.

Was he using me to make a point to the Speaker, that he'd heard enough, and wasn't going to change his mind about helping the *contras*? I thought so at the time. Now, knowing him better, understanding that he saw much more than he seemed to see, I wonder if he hadn't felt my growing biographical unhappiness, those early months of 1986, and sent me a sympathetic signal: *Relax.*

For Dutch, behind his apparent disengagement, was capable of great subtlety and sweetness. The perfectly paced jokes, the easy, apt quips scribbled on the bottoms of thousands of photographs, and above all the clarity of his diaries and letters and speech drafts, all testify to the fact that he retained a useful intelligence throughout two terms as President, and for three years thereafter.

What set in after his cancer operation was, I think, a program of conservation of mental resources. Like an aging mainframe computer, he found himself with only a limited amount of random-access memory to accomplish a lengthening menu of tasks. He had an idea that those of the least personal interest to him—Third World initiatives, environmental reform, support for the arts, data delivery to pesky biographers, and such like—would get done anyway, whether or not he cooperated. So he saved his RAM for the tasks he really cared about: rescue of the hostages in Lebanon, *contra* aid, strategic defense, abolition of nuclear weapons, moral warfare against Communism, and continued restoration of the national spirit.

He also deleted all data that threatened to encumber him. Hence his absolute refusal to believe that he had ever had cancer: only the excised polyp had "developed a few cancer cells." Hence his certainty that he had never wanted to join the Communist Party. And hence the five low-energy monosyllables that I got when I asked him about his reunion with Mitterrand. That chore was over and done with; he had a major statue to light.

The grandstand area was quiet now, and flickering as Dutch and company watched the induction, simulcast from Ellis Island, of two hundred and fifty new citizens by Chief Justice Warren Burger. I resisted the spectacle because that of New York across the water was so hypnotic I could not move.

It hung before me twinkling and trembling, as Paris once did in Henry James's imagination, "a jewel brilliant and hard . . . and what seemed all surface one moment seemed all depth the next." Dutch's presidency, I thought, was much the same: seemingly static and glittering, yet permeated with a sense of movement, of busy goings-on in dark corners.

At least, I think I thought that. My notes say simply:

Manhatt./HJ "jewel"—RR Admin.—static glitter / dark deeds?

By the summer of 1986, I had had but two vague indications that something was not right in the Reagan White House. Maybe *expressions* would be a better word, since each of them was simply a matter of the way a man looked. On the first occasion—about three weeks after we got back from Geneva—I had come across Robert McFarlane standing in black tie outside the men's room at the Shoreham Hotel. The corridor was thronged with members of the Administration seeking relief from a presidential reception upstairs. Jovial, pre-Christmas banter filled the air, but nobody addressed a word to McFarlane. I stopped short, transfixed by the abject misery on his face.

He had recently resigned as National Security Adviser, citing bone-weariness and family constraints, and the President had appointed his deputy, Admiral John Poindexter, to succeed him. I had heard that Washington was a brutal town, but could not believe the suddenness with which yesterday's man of power—and putative next Secretary of Defense—was now being ignored by guys reaching for their zippers.

Was it only callousness that made them pass him by? McFarlane had stepped down voluntarily, lavishly praised by Dutch. No, I think it is the nature of most men to recoil from what a writer cannot resist: the sight of primary human emotion. Hardly knowing him, I went to shake his hand and mumble something awkward about "a loss to the Administration."

McFarlane was polite, but the face at close quarters was so frightening that I went back upstairs wondering what his real reason for resignation had been. Christmas was not the right time for such an obvious depressive to be out of work.

The other expression that gave me pause was Pat Buchanan's. I liked the White House Communications Director, whose broad shoulders and skinny shanks, seen from behind at staff meetings, reminded me of Babe Ruth—another free-swinging street mauler rendered harmless by humor. I was asking him about the President's *contra*-aid policy. He assured me that Nicaragua and Suriname were but stages in the Soviet subversion of all Latin America; Marxist Angola and Mozambique similarly menaced South Africa. Then, in the midst of explaining how these two subcontinental pincers could choke off the oil routes to the United States, he suddenly said, "Have you talked to Ollie?"

"Who?"

"Ollie North. Down in NSC."

"No, what about?"

Buchanan sat silent for five or six seconds, staring at me with a quizzical look that slowly turned to disdain. I sensed that I had been weighed in some balance, and found too light.

"Nothing," he said. But there was something.

Liberty Weekend's opening festivities went on so long after the Statue was lit that I left the Reagans and Mitterrands to shiver in their boxes, and took a ferry to Manhattan and bed. I was already dozing in my West Side apartment when I heard Dutch's big helicopter beating up the Hudson to the Rockefeller estate in Pocantico Hills.

The Fourth dawned warmer and calmer. Reagan came downriver again to meet up with Mitterrand and review "Operation Sail," one of those interminable pageants that are the penalty of power. At noon, the two Presidents adjourned to a closed "bilateral luncheon" of caviar soup, crab soufflé, "Lady Liberty" sorbet, and petits fours. Had I been permitted to attend, I would have found Dutch in his best anti-nuclear form, and boasting to the French President that he had given Gorbachev two choices in Geneva: arms reduction, or a renewed arms race that the Soviet Union simply could not afford.

When he dropped back into my ken, some eight hours later, the night air was balmy, and his landing pad—the flight deck of USS *John F. Kennedy,* cleared for VIP seating—spectacularly at rest midharbor. The Statue now loomed large, but not so close as to infringe upon a bar of reflected gold, sent straight our way from the New Jersey horizon, and lying almost still on the placid water.

Marine One and its backup helicopter, Nighthawk Two, settled forward, over the bow. Dutch emerged with Nancy (in red), flashed his fly-slicer salute and strode down an avenue of dipping flags, escorted by Secretary Weinberger. Flashbulbs scintillated all over the ship, even from the crow's nest. "Making up for his non-appearance at Newport News in '84," I thought. It was obvious, in hindsight, why he had forgone that heaven-made photo opportunity: his re-election was assured, and the world had heard quite enough about the Reagan arms buildup. Here he came now, grinning and nodding at the *Kennedy's* crew (their young faces wearing the same ardent look I had noticed on the Mall, exactly two years before), looking about as dangerous as Jack Benny. There was no possible way this benign, grandfatherly man could ever have sent Marines into Beirut. Or the National Guard into Berkeley.

A bugle blowing "Taps" reproved my cynicism. The whole bay seemed to go quiet as the sun wobbled and spread along the horizon. Then, in one of those quintessentially American moments when hokeyness and heritage and pageantry combine to transcendental effect, drums began to vamp, and an invisible chorus half-chanted, half-whispered Ronald Reagan's favorite text:

> *We the people of the U-nited States,*
> *In order to form a more purr-fect Union . . .*

There was no way, after this, that he could deliver a Fourth of July speech half as powerful. His oratory had gotten noticeably duller in recent months. Donald Regan's chairman-of-the-board management style has been rightly blamed for the attrition of such talented writers as Ken Khachigian, Bently T. Elliott, and Peggy Noonan, but as surviving speech drafts show, the President's own editorial energy was petering out. He was inclined simply to declaim what "the fellers" typed up for him, and improvise quick cuts if—as tonight—his audience did not respond.

We were waiting for the fireworks, of course. Dutch called for them shortly before ten o'clock, feeling, I should imagine, as excited as Mr. J. E. Reagan of the Tampico Ladder Company in the summer of 1920. For the next half hour, forty thousand shells lifted off Liberty Island

and a necklace of barges around the Battery—Red Illuminations, White Fires, and Blue Feather Fountains; efflorescent Peonies and Chrysanthemums; shredding Silks and Silvery Swallows; Flitters, Crossed Comets, and swirling Suns. The air thudded until the rotors of Marine One began to sway gently up and down.

I was seated a few rows behind the Reagans and the Weinbergers, among a plump encroachment of military women. The view was not good, so I asked an MP if I could go forward.

"Long as you don't push that big bird overboard," he said, peering at my White House badge.

With the incredulous sense of freedom that strikes all wanderers inside the cordon of presidential security, I strolled down the *Kennedy*'s "steel beach" and sat on its very lip, under the helicopter's drooping blades. Every burst of light in the sky was mirrored right beneath me in the water. New York periodically flashed and glared, shadowless. I glanced back to see if Dutch was aware that a Shining City was close at hand, but he had eyes only for the Statue of Liberty. I wondered if he was remembering the time he first looked at her, thirty-seven years ago, a desolate bachelor on his way back from Britain. He had gotten up at four A.M., just to make sure he saw it at first light.

The thudding became almost insupportably loud. Since there was no shortage of candlepower, I pulled out my notebook and jotted: *1986 a yr. of explosions.*

Which was true, both physically and politically. Four cataclysmic events all demanded Reagan's urgent attention. No wonder he was uninterested in multifibers. First, the blowup of the space shuttle *Challenger* on January 28. (I had been reminded of it by a shell burst whipping and plunging.) Then the bombing of a GI-frequented discotheque in Berlin on April 5, followed by our retaliatory raid on Libya, nine days later. And finally, just in time for May Day, the explosion of a Soviet nuclear reactor at Chernobyl.

Dutch had articulated the nation's sorrow over the shuttle tragedy so movingly, in words scripted for him by Peggy Noonan, that for a few minutes he seemed to be speaking with all our voices. "The future doesn't belong to the faint-hearted. It belongs to the brave." We had been expecting him to address us on the State of the Union that very night. Nobody watching, except the few who had watched him behind closed doors earlier in the day, talking what Tip O'Neill accurately called "crap" about welfare abusers, could have believed that the President was anything other than a wise, all-knowing father figure. Even O'Neill wept, admitting that in the space of a few hours he had seen the worst and best of Ronald Reagan. "He may not be much of a debater, but with a prepared text he's the best public speaker I've ever seen. . . . I'm beginning to think that in this respect he dwarfs both Roosevelt and Kennedy."

Two U.S. citizens had been killed, and at least fifty wounded, in the explosion at Disco LaBelle in West Berlin. The President instantly suspected "that villain Qaddafi" as the authority responsible. Ever since the Gulf of Sidra naval clash of August 1981, he and Qaddafi had been approaching a final showdown. As a result of at least seventeen Libyan-sponsored international terrorist incidents in 1984 and 1985, their two countries had now severed diplomatic relations. There had been another Gulf of Sidra clash just before the disco bombing, and when intelligence confirmed Reagan's suspicion about the latter, he felt he had provocation to strike back numbingly.

With no help from François Mitterrand, who declined to make French airspace a medium of "maladroit" American revenge, the President sent thirty USAF F-111s round the corner of Western Europe on April 14, and hit Benghazi and Tripoli in the middle of the Libyan night. The strikes were supposed to be "surgical," aimed at military, administrative, and terrorist targets, but they killed mainly civilians— including an infant girl, identified as Qaddafi's adopted daughter.

When I asked Dutch how he felt about this death of a child by fire, he winced and said, "I'm kind of sorry you don't want to talk about Dixon."

The raid, however, was a huge popular success among Americans, and helped assuage a gathering sense of hopelessness regarding our hostages in Lebanon. If anyone could "spring" them, it would be this moralistic President, with his iron intolerance of terrorism. At Tokyo, three weeks later, even Mitterrand had joined in signing a tough new communiqué condemning "its blatant and cynical use as an instrument of government policy."

I wish I could say that the sight of Liberty Weekend's most elaborate effect—an eighteen-inch Japanese shell named the Kamuro, settling down over the whole bay like a many-tendriled willow—coincided with the thought of Chernobyl, but such spectacles make the mind go blank with pleasure. Only now do photographs of it remind me that on April

28, 1986, en route to Tokyo, we heard reports of a mysterious fall of radioactivity, descending willow-like all over Scandinavia. The Kremlin vaguely announced that "an accident" had "damaged" a reactor in the Chernobyl power plant, and that "measures" were being taken "to eliminate the consequences." Not for another twenty-four hours did Reagan receive confirmation that the fall, now drifting slowly around the world, had been precipitated by a total meltdown four days before. Mikhail Gorbachev remained silent throughout our five days in Japan, and for another week afterward. His commitment to *glasnost*— transparency, free speech—did not yet extend, apparently, to acknowledging the worst nuclear accident in history.

"*Chernobyl* means 'Armageddon' in the Ukrainian Bible, you know," Dutch told me when we got back to the United States. This sounded too good to be true. But the details unofficially seeping out of the Soviet Union were apocalyptic enough. Thirty-two people had already died; one hundred and thirty-three thousand were being moved out of the "dead zone" around Pripyat. Nobody could guess how many of these refugees, including unborn babies, had been irradiated. The tonnage of lethal particles released equaled ten Hiroshimas.

Dutch's theological citation was not entirely fanciful. *Chernobyl* turned out to be Ukrainian for *Wormwood,* a name that Revelation 8:10–11 applies to the great star that descended from heaven, "burning as it were a lamp," and doused itself in a third of the Earth's rivers and fountains, whereupon "many men died of the waters, because they were made bitter."

When Gorbachev finally did speak, on May 14, he admitted that "Chernobyl represents a lesson that cannot be avoided." But his tone was unapologetic, and his expression a strange combination of truculence and confusion. He complained that the West was trying to make "anti-Soviet propaganda" out of the catastrophe, while drawing attention to its cautionary significance himself. Chernobyl in any case needed neither propaganda nor pointing, as the product of a system no longer capable of maintaining a safe energy industry (the reactor core had exploded after triply exceeding its allowable heat limit), a clean environment, or an efficient communications system. It was the catalyst of true *glasnost,* the precipitator of breakaway movements in the Ukraine and Byelorussia, the first meltdown of Soviet Communism.

A final flight of Silver Tail Twice Blooming Kamuros descended on the *John F. Kennedy,* and darkness returned amid a wailing of sirens. I rejoined the crowd amidships while Dutch and his wife said farewell to their hosts. Marine One lifted them off the deck, hovered a moment, then headed north. Almost at once, the armada of lights around us began to stream slowly into the Narrows.

35

The Beginning
of the End

The witness of the body. Alfred North Whitehead's phrase comes to mind as I read two diary entries written by Ronald Reagan at the end of July 1986. The first entry records the release of Father Lawrence Jenco, one of the original Beirut hostages. "A delayed step in a plan we've been working on for months," the President writes guardedly. "It gives us hope the rest of the plan will take place."

The next entry records a passage of blood in his urine that same evening. "[Dr. Smith] thinks it is an inflamed prostate."

He had been distracted by cancer the first time he ever heard of any hostage-release "plan," almost exactly a year before. Now that the plan, his cherished "undercover thing," was at last bearing fruit, he did not need the possibility of a second tumor. Smith's warning to that effect—pending a more detailed examination by specialists from the Mayo Clinic—visibly depressed him. He feared he might be perceived as "falling apart," and, almost in anger, approved yet another secret attempt to spring some hostages.

Nancy Reagan swung into instant protective action. She was aware that if the word *cancer* was breathed to the press again in connection with her husband, his reputation for agelessness and indestructibility would be destroyed. Dr. John Hutton, soon to succeed Smith as White House Physician, was ordered to tell his uniformed colleagues in Bethesda that if they "leaked one word" about the President's illness, "they would never set foot in the Naval Hospital again."

The results of the Mayo team's examination, on August 8, happily indicated no tumors, and no more blood. I flew with Dutch to Illinois four days later, on the trip described in Chapter 3 of this book, and marveled at his apple-cheeked joviality. After we parted in mid-month for our separate vacations, I found a little crystal set, vintage 1922, in a junk shop, and sent it to him on the West Coast: "This will help you keep in touch with world events while you are away." Days passed, then he called from the ranch in mock distress. "I'm having trouble getting Radio Moscow."

It was a typically physical three weeks for him, with plenty of riding in the morning and madroña-felling after lunch. The body exulted, and he actually noticed a slight improvement in his hearing. But there is a diary entry to do with the mind that sounds a quiet, distant gong-stroke. Helicoptering to Los Angeles on August 26, he looked down on the hills and valleys he had roamed for forty years, and was disturbed to find that he "couldn't remember their names."

Blood or no blood, Reagan's prostate continued to trouble him. It was becoming chronically distended, and his doctors recommended surgery before it hardened. But he had serious business to conduct when he returned to the White House. The Republican majority in the Senate was threatened in the upcoming elections, and Gorbachev, angered by a lack of diplomatic progress since Geneva, seemed to be looking for excuses not to come to Washington for another summit. A tetchy Soviet-American quarrel over mutually held "spies"—in our case, a real KGB agent, in theirs, a virtually kidnapped *U.S. News and World Report* journalist, Nicholas S. Daniloff—dragged on so long that when Eduard Shevardnadze arrived, importantly bearing a letter from Gorbachev, Reagan received him without shaking hands, ignored the letter, and subjected him to a long, unsmiling lecture on the subject of fake arrest.

The letter, when he came to read it afterward, was no less confrontational. It ranged as far back as KE007 and Afghanistan, citing them as enduring grievances, and accused the President of the United States of using Daniloff as a "hostile" propaganda tool against the Soviet Union. But it had a surprise ending, couched in exaggeratedly casual language:

> An idea has come to my mind to suggest to you, Mr. President, that, in the very near future . . . we have a quick one-on-one meeting, let us say in Iceland or in London, maybe just for one day, to engage in a strictly confidential, private, and frank discussion (possibly with only our foreign ministers present). The discussion—which would not be a detailed one, for its purpose and significance would be to demonstrate political will—would result in instructions to our respective agencies to draft agreements on two or three very specific questions, which you and I could sign during my visit to the United States.

So the summit was still on! Reagan, suddenly forgetting his pique about Daniloff, liked the idea of a preliminary meeting. "I opt for Iceland."

The "spies" were swapped, the venue agreed upon, and a formal announcement issued on September 30, in such haste that I had literally to run after the President as he ambled into the press room. "I am pleased to announce that General Secretary Gorbachev and I will meet October 11 and 12 in Reykjavík, Iceland. . . . It will take place in the context of preparations for the General Secretary's visit to the United States."

It is always moving, indeed sometimes tear-jerking, to see a professional performer mutate from stroll-down-the-corridor ordinariness to step-onstage mastery. One thinks of the waddle of ballet dancers suddenly purifying into arabesques, or the juggler putting down his lunch and filling the air with weightless objects. I watched Dutch do what only he could do, and remembered him going through this same transformation so many times: on the little stage at Eureka, climbing into his Ryan monoplane on the Alhambra ramp, wowing the California Fertilizer Association, shaming the '76 Republican Convention, gracefully choreographing Gorbachev up the steps of Fleur d'Eau. It was hard not to admire him profoundly. Then he stepped down from the lectern, caught my eye, and said with the klieg lights still shining on him, "Oh—about that water hole. It was on the Stedmans' farm."

We had been talking, two weeks before, about Tampico.

Icelanders, who live over lava and have been bathing in sulfurous hot water for a thousand years, are accustomed to volcanic disturbances of their peace—sudden hurricanes of ash, new land masses rising black and seething from the sea. But even they were hard put to accommodate the eruption of advance men, intelligence agents, Greenpeaceniks, and media representatives that transformed Reykjavík, over the next ten days, into the world's most significant city.

An exhausted Steingrimur Hermannsson, the Prime Minister, expected some words of appreciation when he welcomed Reagan formally to Reykjavík on the morning of Friday, October 10. But he got nothing except a mild, vacant stare. Hermannsson remarked politely that Iceland would be very grateful, in return for its hospitality, if the danger of nuclear shipping in the Northern Atlantic was addressed at some point over the weekend. His people worried that their pristine environment might be destroyed by an accident not of their own making.

Reagan did not react, so Hermannsson tried a direct approach.

"What do you hope to get out of this meeting with General Secretary Gorbachev, Mr. President?"

"Oh!" Reagan said, suddenly coming to life. He pulled some cards from his pocket and began to read from them. "I'm very happy to be able to tell you, Mr. Prime Minister, that Icelandair will be granted landing rights in Boston."

Gorbachev, whom Hermannsson received a few hours later, was all business and snapping, smiling energy. "We hope this will be an important step to end hostility and rivalry between the two superpowers. And you Icelanders—what do *you* hope for?"

Night fell over the elemental landscape around Reykjavík. In electing to meet here rather than in London, Reagan had unwittingly chosen a theater of epic symbolism. Iceland after dark, in October rain, is the world stripped to its essentials, geography reduced to geometry. No trees; no visible vegetation; only black and carbuncled lava, spreading on the one hand toward black sea, and on the other toward dead, distant volcanoes. The all-pervading sense is always of ice and more ice massing in the interior, forcing its way seaward down every available fjord, plus fire and more fire building under the ice. These opposites are so ancient, and unresolved, that Icelanders (like summiteers) tend to see everything in terms of polarity. Common ground is dangerous ground, liable to freeze or erupt without warning.

"The elemental landscape around Reykjavík."
Thingvellir, birthplace of parliamentary democracy.

Religiously and politically, even tectonically, Iceland is what François Mitterrand would have called an *affrontement,* a place more of struggle than confluence. Here, about halfway between Washington and Moscow, the North American and Eurasian land plates grind together and ream apart, in a rift clearly visible northeast of Reykjavík. At Thingvellir, on the very lip of the rift, the world's first parliamentary republic established itself against the rule of the gods in A.D. 930, but its *modus operandi* was so violent that legislative debates were often settled with swordplay. Now Reagan and Gorbachev were returning, more than a thousand years later, to argue essentially the same issues that had divided those early Christian and pagan chiefs: treaties versus weaponry, democracy versus totalitarianism, human rights versus tribal values.

At least, that was Gorbachev's intent, for all his talk of a "quick" meeting of not-quite summit stature. From the moment that he sat down opposite Reagan at 10:44 A.M. on Saturday, October 11, it was clear that he wanted a major agreement. He was in no mood to be beguiled by charm, then blocked by sheer obstinacy, as he had been at Geneva. The thickness of the briefcase that he brought with him suggested that he had spent a busy summer preparing for this engagement—or, as Reagan might justifiably call it, "this trap."

The two men faced each other down the length of a pale, rectangular table, inlaid with chilly copper, in the study of Höfdi House, a small mansion overlooking Faxaflói Bay. Rain hissed against the windowpanes, admitting a weak white light that blanched both their faces. Had they been ironists, they might have teased each other as to who had the more depressing view: Reagan, of gray water and glistening oil tanks, Gorbachev, of gray water and a distant, dirty glacier.

But there were to be no jokes this weekend, none of the yearning looks and handclasps that had drawn them together at Fleur d'Eau in Geneva.

Gorbachev spoke first, announcing that he had a mass of "new" arms-control proposals. He noticed at once, as Prime Minister Hermannsson had the day before, that he was dealing with a man abstracted to the point of catatonia. Reagan kept staring out of the window, his big body inert.

When the President's turn to reply came, he fiddled with his cards in obvious confusion, and dropped some on the floor. Gorbachev helped him out. "Well, we are talking about specific problems, so let us invite our foreign ministers in to join the talks."

A six-on-six plenary ensued, attended by Shultz, Shevardnadze, and two note takers, but Reagan's torpor continued all morning. By his own account, he was trying to figure why Gorbachev was speaking with such strange urgency. Had Chernobyl—for all its radioactivity, less lethal than a single nuclear warhead—shocked the General Secretary into an awareness of what *ten* warheads in just *one* missile could do?

Shultz, too, was unprepared for the Soviet negotiatory onslaught. Gorbachev's cello voice poured forth roulade after roulade. Strategic weapons should be reduced by a total of 50 percent, as Reagan had himself proposed in the past, but across the board in all classes—intercontinental ballistic missiles, submarine-launched ballistic missiles, and nuclear-bomber deliveries. There should be a total elimination of Soviet and American intermediate-range missiles in Europe. Moreover, there should be a freeze on short-range missiles, and a ban on all future nuclear tests.

"What it really amounts to," Gorbachev said, "is your own zero-option proposal of 1981."

This was not true, because the General Secretary had said nothing about the Soviet INF arsenal in Central Asia. But he was clearly in an urgent mood to disarm. He might have mentioned that he had made a zero-option proposal himself, less than two months after Geneva, and gotten little from the Reagan Administration in return but coolness and obstructionism. On January 15, 1986, he had called for a complete, worldwide ban on nuclear weapons by the turn of the century, beginning with an INF-reduction plan much like the "new" one he now brought to Reykjavík. On February 25, he had presented his nuclear disarmament plan to the Twenty-seventh Communist

Party Congress, along with some of the most heretical foreign-policy reform proposals in Soviet history: a switch from military intimidation to diplomatic persuasion, a one-world security program rather than the *yin* and *yang* of superpower rivalry, respect for the goodwill of ordinary Americans, and an end to "confrontation between capitalism and socialism." On May 23, he had told a convocation of all Soviet ambassadors that their primary job must henceforth be the pursuit of peace. But none of these initiatives seemed to have made any impress on the President of the United States, whom Gorbachev presumed was still beholden to "the American military-industrial complex."

Disillusionment—Gorbachev's own, and Reagan's gathering annoyance at being suckered into a conversation full of arms-control algebra—hung in the air between the two leaders. Only a quick acceptance "in principle" of the 50 percent option by Shultz prevented them from getting into a too-soon squabble. A summit meeting, like any other political or business negotiation, needs hope in its early and late stages. If hope dies early, there is no chance of endurance through the crucial central stage; and if hope is not resurgent toward the end, suddenly everything is detumescence and despair. "There's *nothing* worse," an international executive once told me, "than to have a deal go sour just when you can smell its perfume. You both want to go out and kill yourselves."

Still talking, Gorbachev suggested a way in which SDI research might be made compatible, in his opinion, with the ABM Treaty. If the United States would pledge to observe the Treaty "strictly and in full" for ten years, the Soviet Union would tolerate space-defense research in "laboratories, *but not outside of them.*"

This was a major concession, given his total opposition in Geneva. Reagan began to revive. He reminded Gorbachev, affably but firmly, that a perfected SDI, shared by both sides, would obviate ballistic missiles, and render the Treaty moot.

℮

Lunch fueled the President's recovery. He was cheered by the excitement of his senior advisers, who clearly did not think he had been tricked. "This is the best Soviet proposal we have received in twenty-five years," said the normally phlegmatic Paul Nitze.

When Reagan faced Gorbachev again at 3:30, he had a return-monologue privilege, and indulged it for an hour. Shevardnadze's note taker was impressed enough to perpetrate the following delightfully mixed metaphors:

> Suddenly he flare up, crisp, engaged. When you touch raw nerve, Reagan's flare will fill the room. He feel something close to his heart, he is like lion! When lion see antelope on the horizon, he is not interested, he go to sleep. Ten feet away, too much, leave it. Eight feet, *the lion suddenly comes to life!!*

A more prosaic interpretation would be that the lion now had a detailed set of talking points, typed out for him during lunch. But his subject matter—the need to develop and deploy a shield against ballistic missiles—was something that always animated him. He tried to overcome Gorbachev's hostility toward it.

"I don't understand. Why is this such a big problem? First of all, we know you've been researching on this same subject for twenty years."

The General Secretary sat stone-faced, and Reagan felt that he had scored. ("When you tag them with something that's really true, they don't deny it," he told me afterward. "They just don't react, as if you haven't said it.") He declared that the United States was willing to research in tandem, and test in the presence of Soviet observers. He would even sign a two-way treaty to that effect. "Whatever both of us come up with, we'll share. And if ours is first in the program that is practical, then we'll agree to wipe out our nuclear missiles, we'll eliminate them."

When Dutch repeated these words to me, his face took on a look of such goofy benevolence, like a priest proposing an ecumenical picnic, that I do not wonder Gorbachev erupted.

"You will take the arms race into space, and could be tempted to launch a first strike from space. . . . I do not believe that you will share SDI."

It was back to Geneva and the tossed pencil. For the next hour and a quarter, Reagan and Gorbachev argued arms control and human rights, with no agreement except to refer all issues to overnight working groups. Then they went out into the drizzle, parted with stiff smiles, and retired to their respective quarters—the little American embassy on Laufásvegur, and a Russian cruise ship lying in the choppy harbor. All through the night, lights burned upstairs in Höfdi House, while whitecaps moved uneasily across the bay.

☯

I was not a member of the United States delegation to Reykjavík in 1986—Don Regan bumped me for lack of space—so the details above, from the hissing rain to the stone face and whitecaps, are Dutch's and Gorbachev's and other men's memories, not mine. I did, however, make a later pilgrimage to Iceland, and enjoyed the scribe's traditional advantage of being able to recollect emotions in tranquillity.

The black night of October 11–12, 1986, was hard to conceive, in late-summer sunshine so clean and strong it glowed like limelight. Exquisite girls with hair the color of cotton grass bumped pleasantly into me along Reykjavík's narrow sidewalks. I went down to the harbor and sat on a bollard near where Gorbachev had slept in his luxury stateroom. Jellyfish pulsated in the bright water, like animated condoms. Höfdi House stood about a mile away, white-shingled, isolated from the busy spread of the city: little more than a memorial, now, to one of the most desperate nights of negotiation in arms-control history. Fifty percent is an easy fraction for any mind to grasp, but when the differential is applied to "unequal end points" (Soviet and U.S. warhead arsenals being disproportionate to begin with, category by category) only the mind of a Paul Nitze, or a Sergei Akhromeyev, can comprehend every numerical nuance.

I tried to imagine the seventy-nine-year-old Nitze emerging into the drizzly light of early Sunday morning, exhausted but triumphant ("I haven't had so much fun in years"), and driving over to the Hótel Holt to report a general agreement to Shultz: "The last sentence on sea-launched cruise missiles took an hour and a half." That was fairly easy. But how to feel what Dutch felt, eight hours later, when he sat reading the summit's final protocol, and heard Gorbachev say, "Wait a minute, why do you have just missiles in there?"

By then it had gotten dark again, and rain was still falling. Downstairs in the basement, members of the Soviet secret-service detail were watching *Tom and Jerry* on Icelandic TV. Cat v. Mouse, above and below!

Reagan shot an unbelieving look at Shultz, and said to Gorbachev, "Well, what are *you* talking about?"

He wondered if what he held in his hand—a U.S. redraft of a Soviet redraft of a U.S. zero-ballistics proposal, itself a redraft of Gorbachev's roulades the day before—had lost something in translation, or transit. But the General Secretary was staring straight at him.

"All nuclear weapons," Gorbachev said. "Bombers, everything else."

Reagan again exchanged glances with Shultz and said, "Well, that's all right with us, all nuclear weapons."

The tension in the room was tremendous. Their respective airplanes had been on hold since noon. It had been a battering day of back-and-forth negotiation, with both principals and support teams (waiting equally tensely upstairs) aware that Höfdi House was on the brink of becoming the most momentous Cold War site since Yalta. As matters now stood, the two superpowers had agreed in principle to ten years of strict observance of the ABM Treaty, at the end of which period they were to have dismantled all their strategic offensive arms, and all the INFs in Europe. British and French systems were no longer to be counted as part of the European balance. After 1996, either side could, if it wanted, deploy a strategic defense system, although the Soviets could not see why it was necessary. As a bonus, Gorbachev had even offered to scale down the Warsaw Pact's huge conventional-arms superiority over NATO. Reagan thought to himself, *We have negotiated the most massive weapons reductions in history.*

But now, smiling, Gorbachev demanded something in return. "This all depends, of course, on you giving up SDI."

Reagan had been bracing for this ultimatum for more than twenty-four hours. What the General Secretary meant, in Soviet treaty parlance, was, "The testing of in-space components of anti-ballistic missile defense is prohibited, *except research and testing conducted in laboratories.*" Leonid Brezhnev might just as well have demanded that Project Apollo be confined to Moon Crest, Pennsylvania.

"I've said again and again the SDI wasn't a bargaining chip," Reagan said, annoyed by the smile. "If you are willing to abolish nuclear weapons, why are you so anxious to get rid of a defense against nuclear weapons?"

Gorbachev kept smiling and repeating the word *laboratory,* while the President got angrier and angrier. Both of them realized that their rush toward a zero option in Europe had been cowardly rather than courageous—a desperate feint to postpone the unresolved issue dividing them. What Reagan saw as a shared defense, protecting them both from nuclear attack by "another Hitler," Gorbachev saw as a disguised offensive capability, convertible into a first-strike engine of war.

Like most men when disaster looms, they became alternately truculent and querulous (*Reagan:* "A meeting in Iceland in ten years: I'll be so old you won't recognize me. I'll say, 'Mikhail?' You'll say, 'Ron?' " *Gorbachev:* "I may not be living after these ten."). They summed up their positions again and again, while the clock ticked toward six-thirty and Shultz and Shevardnadze sat dumb with disappointment.

"It's 'laboratory' or nothing," Gorbachev said at last. He reached for his briefcase.

There was a long silence. Reagan slid a note over to Shultz: *Am I wrong?* The Secretary whispered, "No, you're right."

"The meeting is over," Reagan said. He stood up. "Let's go, George, we're leaving."

Gorbachev—incredibly, still trying to look amused—accompanied him out of the study, while the hall staircase drummed to the shoes of hastily descending aides. Everybody could see from Reagan's clamped lips (and Shultz's utter dejection) that disaster had struck. They got into their raincoats under the chandelier.

"You planned from the start to come here and put me in this situation!" Reagan said.

"There's still time, Mr. President. We could go back inside to the bargaining table."

"I think not."

They strode out into a wet glare of television lights. Reagan headed straight for his car.

"Mr. President," Gorbachev said, no longer smiling, "you have missed the unique chance of going down in history as a great president who paved the way for nuclear disarmament."

"That applies to both of us."

"I don't know what else I could have done."

"You could have said yes," Reagan said. He lowered himself onto the Cadillac seat and, red with rage, told his chief of staff as the motorcade began to move, "Goddammit, we were *that* close to an agreement."

When Steingrimur Hermannsson bade farewell to Gorbachev at Keflavík Airport, shortly before midnight, sleet was blowing across the ramp and threatening their shared umbrella. But the General Secretary—unlike Reagan, who had departed earlier, too angry to speak—was in no hurry to get away.

"Mr. Prime Minister, I can understand your disappointment," he said, holding on to his homburg. "The Americans did not take seriously the question of nuclear disarmament. But there will be more coming out of this meeting than anyone realizes. For the first time in forty years, both great powers tried to eliminate all nuclear weapons. This is the beginning of the end of the Cold War."

After the Cold War was indeed over—rather sooner than Gorbachev expected—I found myself in the study where he and Dutch had tried to disarm the world. Höfdi House was silent except for the murmurings of a television set somewhere. Perhaps the curator was watching *Tom and Jerry*?

Buttery, glossy Danish maple glowed slightly blue with refractions from the bay outside. I stood looking at the little rectangular table, and did the things biographers do when they are alone with something primary. I sniffed, stroked wood, I stared out the window from Gorby's angle, then from Dutch's, and then, emboldened, sat down in the presidential chair. As I did so I felt—well, a chill. Maybe it was just the copper under my forearms.

Höfdi is supposed to be haunted. For me it was, in the sense that I could "hear" the voices of the principals who wrangled here, and of the secondaries who sat listening to them, alternately thrilled and aghast at what was happening—or what nearly happened—and the continuing cacophony of comment that makes Reykjavík a *locus classicus* of Cold War debate to this day:

RONALD REAGAN	We came so close. It's just such a shame.
KENNETH ADELMAN	(*disgustedly*) Arms control . . . more high-level talent chasing fewer results than any other human endeavor.
RONALD REAGAN	(*places thumb and index finger a half inch apart*) We were *that* close to an agreement.
MARGARET THATCHER	I'm flabbergasted!
RONALD REAGAN	Laboratory, laboratory, laboratory . . . One lousy word!
GEORGE SHULTZ	(*lips trembling*) We are deeply disappointed.
TIP O'NEILL	We're all deeply disappointed. No American should walk away from a fight.
ROBERT DOLE	Mr. President, saying "No" was an act of statesmanship.
JOHN POINDEXTER	(*puffing pipe smoke, confidentially*) George let the President down.
ALEXANDER HAIG	(*sourly*) The most serious misjudgment by a President since World War II.
MARGARET THATCHER	Reagan is clinging to the SDI as a means to avoid war! He's dreaming!
MALCOLM WALLOP	(*to Reagan, reprovingly*) Heads of state ought not to engage in detailed negotiations . . .

KENNETH ADELMAN	. . . in an area so laden with technicalities, yet significant enough to affect the national security for decades.
MARGARET THATCHER	New arms can always break through this so-called shield.
ROBERT KARL MANOFF	(*reverently*) The Reykjavík summit meeting has shown Americans that President Reagan is a man of greater vision than many of us expected, bolder and more foresighted than most of those who oppose his policy.
BIOGRAPHER	(*aside*) Who's Robert Karl Manoff?
RESEARCH ASSISTANT	(*whispering*) Co-director of New York University's Center for War, Peace, and the News Media.
DONALD REGAN	We said to the Soviets, "We will do away with all nuclear weapons—"
KENNETH ADELMAN	Everybody's got it wrong! It was *Gorbachev,* not Reagan, who wanted all strategic weapons banned in ten years. We never went beyond the word *ballistic.*
RONALD REAGAN	(*drafting his report to the American people*) "They proposed a ten-year period . . ."
JOHN POINDEXTER	(*altering the President's text*) "We proposed a ten-year period . . ."
WILLIAM CROWE	(*on behalf of the Joint Chiefs of Staff*) Mr. President, we've concluded that the proposal to eliminate all ballistic missiles in ten years' time would pose high risks to the security of the nation.
MALCOLM WALLOP	Mr. President, SDI must be moved from the vision as expressed to the reality that exists.
TIP O'NEILL	Mr. President, I have probably the most scientific constituency in the world, and over fifty percent of them disbelieve that SDI is possible.
RONALD REAGAN	Tip, I don't have respect for those scientists you mention.
BARNEY OLDFIELD	(*USAF, Ret.*) Whether it works, celestially speaking, is nowhere near as important as what it does cerebrally—
RONALD REAGAN	(*angrily bursting out*) How the devil can we sit around here and question the validity of the SDI when *they're* so desperate to get rid of it?

SERGEI AKHROMEYEV	This was a great moral breakthrough in our relations.
MIKHAIL GORBACHEV	(*on television in a Moscow bar*) After Reykjavík, it is clear to everyone that SDI is a symbol of obstruction to the cause of peace, the epitome of militarist schemes and—(*The barman changes channels*)
JAMES BILLINGTON	(*to the barman*) You switch your General Secretary off? Surely this is important to you?
BAR PATRON	We Russians have only two questions. One, will there be war? Two, will we have more food? The answer to both is clearly "Nyet."
RONALD REAGAN	You just don't know how broken-down their economic system is.
ROBERT MCNAMARA	We must rid ourselves of the idea that the Soviet economy may collapse.
MARGARET THATCHER	(*yielding to despair*) Everything, now, is turning to the advantage of the Russians, all round the world!
A FRENCH VOICE	My reflection on all this is that you should not allow two men to negotiate on a Saturday night in a haunted house.
POLLSTER	How well has President Reagan handled relations with the Soviet Union?
AMERICAN PEOPLE	(*all together*) Approve! Disapprove! Don't know! (*Fade out*)

An analysis of this chorus by New York Times/CBS News computers reveals 72 percent in favor, 20 percent against, and 8 percent undecided.

☯

On October 22, 1986, the President signed a tax-reform bill on the South Lawn of the White House, before thousands of applauding supporters, and was puzzled to notice that *Reagan* came out of his pen before *Ronald*.

Tiredness—or whatever else had begun to ail him—notwithstanding, he had to embark now on the last campaign of his political career, in behalf of a raft of Republican members of Congress facing difficult re-elections in November. A public-relations blitz engineered by his communications director, Pat Buchanan, had persuaded many Americans that Reykjavík was the greatest diplomatic triumph since the Louisiana Purchase, and that the Tax Reform Act was proof that Reaganomics still worked, with minor adjustments.

Private polls, however, indicated some doubts among voters as to whether the GOP deserved continued control over the Senate. The very words "Reagan's last campaign" had a valedictory ring, as if to remind party strategists that come November 4, they could no longer rely on him to seduce the electorate. An elegiac note, hitherto absent from commentary on the President, began to affect Op-Ed pages, hardly to the comfort of Vice President Bush and Senator Howard Baker.

"To most Americans," wrote the veteran reporter Chalmers M. Roberts, "all the potential '88 candidates in both parties look like pygmies compared with the political giant currently astride the White House. . . . I've covered, or watched them all, from Franklin D. Roosevelt on, and Reagan and FDR are twins when it comes to the mastery of politics—and political manipulation. No one else in this century came even near, with the possible exception of Teddy Roosevelt."

Came. The slip into the past tense was significant. With over two years of power still due him, Ronald Reagan was already being written off as an active force in government.

He campaigned across the country with his usual detached enjoyment, and was particularly pleased when Admiral Poindexter informed him, forty-eight hours before Election Day, that David Jacobsen, one of the five remaining Beirut hostages, had been released. Reagan accepted this happy coincidence as proof that "all things happen for the best"—his mother's favorite bromide. For a while it seemed that Poindexter might be able to supply another hostage, but Americans went to vote on Tuesday without such an added inducement. By late evening, two things were clear: that the Democratic Party had regained control of the Senate, and that the news media were avidly interested in a story, just published by the Lebanese weekly *Al-Shiraa,* that Robert C. "Bud" McFarlane had recently visited Iran in an airman's uniform, with two planeloads of military hardware, and a message from the President of the United States.

In due course, *recently* was corrected to May 1986, and the two planeloads shrank to a single pallet of spare parts for Hawk missile batteries, apparently purchased by Iran from Israel to use against Iraq. But the other facts about McFarlane's journey to the heart of darkness were too specific to ignore, especially when two of his traveling companions were identified as employees of the Reagan National Security Council: Lieutenant Colonel Oliver North and Howard J. Teicher. They were accompanied by two CIA operatives, one of whom spoke Farsi. The complete roster suggested that Admiral Poindexter and William J. Casey must have authorized the trip, if not Ronald Reagan himself. Such august names, and the staring fact that Reagan's former National Security Adviser was doing some kind of military business with a terrorist state, aroused an instant moral uproar, louder than anything heard since Bitburg.

As with Bitburg, the President lost no time in taking a defiantly righteous stance, declaring on November 6 that the stories about McFarlane's trip had "no foundation." The United States had no mercenary interest in Iran, whose responsibility for the kidnapping and murder of American hostages in Lebanon was a matter of international notoriety. "We will never pay off terrorists, because that only encourages more of it."

But what was *it*? More terrorism, or more trade? And what price moral resolution, when the price of David Jacobsen turned out to be five hundred TOW antitank missiles, delivered just five days before his release? Even if the TOWs were (like the Hawks) obsolescent equipment that Israel no longer needed, the U.S. Treasury seemed to have been defrauded. Congress, after all, had supplied the missiles to Israel in the first place as aid, not merchandise. While Reagan denied that there was any secret arms-for-hostages deal, five hundred brand-new TOWs were en route to Israel via a CIA proprietary airline, courtesy of the American taxpayer.

The "Iran Initiative," so called by McFarlane (perhaps in the hope that it would attain the prestige of the Strategic Defense Initiative), has been pretty universally accepted as a violation of American and moral law. Ronald Reagan authorized it almost sixteen months before its consequences broke upon him. He did so in a moment of weakness, as he lay recovering from cancer surgery in Bethesda Naval Hospital:

Thursday July 18, 1985
    What a morning—the Dr. took the metal clips out of my incision—what an improvement that made . . . he told me he'd take the feeding tubes out before lunch and he did. Such a feeling of freedom. . . .

Nancy and I had lunch, I find that I can only eat a few mouthfuls. A lot of cards and messages to look at. Then around 4:30 P.M. a wave out of the window to the press and down to X-Ray.

Bud came by—it seems 2 members of the Iranian govt. want to establish talks with us. I'm sending Bud to meet them in a neutral country.

Gorbachev has passed the word he'd like to establish a private channel of communications. . . .

I watched a TV press round table on their handling of my "illness." I detected an effort on the part of some . . . to use the term— "The President *has* cancer." My Dr's said use of the present tense is a mis-statement. The President *had* cancer—it has been removed.

Let us in fairness consider this diary entry of a half-deaf man who has, only five days before, been hacked open from pubis to breastbone, and, seventy-two hours before, received about the most terrifying news that doctors can deliver: a positive biopsy. He has been awake since 5:15 A.M., and is trying without much success to get his shocked and shortened intestinal system back into action. At 10:22 A.M. (the diary's paragraph arrangement is misleading), an expressionless little man comes in and drones something about wanting to meet with some reform-minded Iranians. Even Donald Regan, who monitors the briefing, hears nothing but a "general" mention of hostages still in captivity. If there is any implication that McFarlane's foreign contacts might be "helpful," one day, in springing them, it is vague enough not to alarm the famously reactive Chief of Staff. Reagan, like Regan, hears nothing about hostages worth recording. He hears only the encouraging words *want* and *talks* and *neutral* applied to two Iranian "government" officials, together with what sounds like a request for travel. He says yes, and the little man is gone by 10:45.

The rest of the day is occupied with medical matters—with "the withness of the body." Dr. Steven Rosenberg, who gave the President his cancer confirmation on Monday, may say privately that Ronald Reagan is in the "top one percentile" of patients exhibiting self-control at *le moment critique*. But major surgery is an insult to both body and mind, no matter how strong the former or how determined the latter. The primary instinct of every cell and circuit is to recuperate. Hence the characteristic abstraction of convalescents. They are otherwise engaged; they take in only a minimum of what the healthy try to tell them.

Reagan's July 18 diary entry is terse, but historically important. It was written *at the time,* whereas his and McFarlane's and Regan's later versions of the conversation (ten, by one count) vary. Did McFarlane indeed tell him that representatives of the Israeli Prime Minister, Shimon Peres, had relayed a message from representatives of Iran's Speaker of Parliament, Hashemi Rafsanjani, to the effect that certain "authoritative" Iranians wanted to "develop a dialogue with the West"? And did McFarlane add that his Iranian contacts were confident that they could "achieve the release of the seven Americans now held hostage in Lebanon"? Again, did McFarlane drop the name of Manucher Ghorbanifar as a classic Middle Eastern volunteer middleman, who naturally felt that the Iranians should "show some gain" in any hostage transaction?

One can almost hear, in a quiet corner of the Vier Jahreszeiten Hotel in Hamburg, the soft rubbing of Manucher Ghorbanifar's finger and thumb as he talked of a few hundred TOWs "from Israel" to spring the first hostage. Ghorbanifar was a Persian carpet dealer, a former secret policeman to the Shah, a rumored Israeli spy . . . but he flourishes in other books. The question this one asks is, did *Ronald Reagan* hear any such soft rubbing, in his hospital room on July 18, 1985? McFarlane insists that he did:

> The President was sitting up in his hospital bed, in good spirits and listening attentively, although he still looked a little weak. . . . I told him of the new twist in the Iranian matter, the request for the TOWs. His face seemed to fall and he pursed his lips.
>
> "What do you think?" he asked me.
>
> I went over the pros and cons. . . . I said: "Arms will be essential to any ultimate effort to change the government, but at this point, I don't think we know enough about the people we're dealing with to take that risk."
>
> Reagan thought for a few seconds. Then he nodded. "We can't do it," he said.

This—taken from McFarlane's 1994 memoir *Special Trust*—is so contrary to some of his earlier accounts, not to mention those of Donald Regan ("There is nothing in my notes or in my memory to suggest that the idea of swapping arms for hostages was mentioned") as to recall Clare Boothe Luce's crack about all biography being alibiography. Here we have the President being brought up to date on a "matter" that McFarlane says was first presented to him, in detail, at least a week before his operation, in the Oval Office. Except that McFarlane, testifying in 1987, transferred the Oval Office briefing to the hospital, complete with presidential comments ("Gee, that sounds pretty good"). Here, again, we have McFarlane alternately laid-back ("There was nothing to report that could not wait") and so desperate for an audience ("I've just got to see the President") that Nancy Reagan fended him off until her husband had at least been unhooked from the IV. And such discrepancies are mild in comparison with others that proliferated when the full details of the Iran Initiative began to emerge sixteen months later.

Since I am writing Dutch's personal story, and not correlating the millions of impressions of the hundreds of witnesses whose testimony fills more than fifty thousand pages of documents with titles such as *Testimony at Joint Hearings Before the House Select Committee to Investigate Covert Arms Transactions with Iran and the Senate Select Committee on Secret Military Assistance to Iran and the Nicaraguan Opposition,* I will convey his experience of the next few months—the nadir of his Presidency—as briefly as possible, in terms of the way he heard and saw and spoke.

Admittedly, he did not speak with much clarity when I interviewed him on November 18. All the world knew by then that the United States had been secretly sending military supplies to Iran, in order to bring about the release of three hostages (Benjamin Weir, Lawrence Jenco, and David Jacobsen), who had been replaced with three more (Frank H. Reed, Joseph Cicippio, and Edward A. Tracy). Reagan had decided on a basic response to all critical inquiries—"We have not dealt directly with terrorists, no bargaining, no ransom"—and then gone out and said so publicly. Congress, unconvinced, was threatening to investigate. Reagan's own counsel, Peter Wallison, found that Israel's sale of American arms to a terrorist nation had been in violation of the Arms Export Control Act. Attorney General Meese insisted that it had not. George Shultz and Caspar Weinberger claimed to have opposed the Initiative from the start, although not enough, apparently, to turn in their limousines. Jacobsen, paraded in the Rose Garden like a *yeti* brought down from the Himalayas, was warning that the press frenzy might endanger the lives of the other hostages. Robert McFarlane, enjoying his renewed celebrity, was denying on the talk shows that he had tried to seduce Tehran officials with a chocolate cake. (Actually, he had: the cake, baked in Tel Aviv, had not been a success, since he had delivered it during the fast of Ramadan.) Admiral Poindexter had retreated behind a fog bank of pipe smoke, impossible to penetrate. Outside of the White House, the name of Oliver North was not yet known.

Conversation in the Oval Office,
November 18, 1986

The following conversation is reproduced at length as a testament to the President's mental and emotional state before his disastrous press conference of November 19, 1986.

EM: Do you wish you had stuck to breeding horses?

RR: No. These last couple of weeks I've had difficulty controlling my temper, which I think is a wise thing to do. But I've never seen such a concerted campaign of dishonesty with results that can be tragic for some people as has been going on here. And I'm just amazed at the lengths that they've gone, and the phony staging, even. One network-news broadcast in the evening—and while Mr. Rather was talking—it was the pictures they were using. But they weren't even using the pictures about what they were talking about. For example, he was talking about weapons and so forth, but they had on the screen F-14s flying and zooming and so forth. And then: cut to a man, obviously an Iranian, throwing rifles into an open-back truck, piled high with these AK-47s—the Russian rifle—but all of this, if pictures speak a thousand words, and people are going to go away with the impression that these were the weapons we were dealing in.

EM: I was at the American Book Award ceremony last night, and George Will was the speaker. . . . He was on the subject that the news these days requires visual images. You can't photograph and show on the news a peace initiative that took six months [*sic*]. But you can show a picture of an F-14. And they'll always go for the image, rather than a long story that requires time and space.

RR: It's been quite a two weeks! And I imagine tomorrow night will be kind of exciting, with the press conference. The hell of it is, I am still bound to a certain extent on how specific I can answer because of—well, oh, Terry Waite explained it last night on television . . . hostages fear for their lives. I remember when I was on the Rockefeller Commission . . . (*Long anecdote about open debate compromising covert sources*)

EM: Mr. President, the Chief [Donald Regan] was telling us at lunch about what David Jacobsen told you, that they tortured him, that they strung him up and lashed him out "from his feet down to his nuts." Is there anything more you can remember Jacobsen saying?

RR: Well, no, (*distressed*) he told about that, but at the same time, he
      told us that these people, the guards, were actually people, and
      he said that actually they could be pretty friendly at times. . . .

EM: Sir, are you also feeling angry at the Iranians in the sense that,
      out of the goodwill of your heart, you wanted to make a gesture
      toward them, and you expected, I presume, a fairly clean ex-
      change. [But] you found yourself forced into a continuous barter
      arrangement—

RR: Well, no, that didn't bother me. We weren't going to—the thing
      was so simple and, of course, the first hostage did come, from a
      hostile—from a side we were avoiding in Iran. (*He begins to
      flounder*) But we told them that we could not do this as long as
      Iran was sponsoring terrorism. And they told our people that
      even Khomeini had written a piece disavowing support for ter-
      rorism, that they were not terrorists. . . . They wanted some evi-
      dence they could use on their own associates, of our good faith.
      So this was the arms thing. But when they told us that, we said,
      "Well, look, we want a little more than just your word for it, that
      you're through with terrorism, and there's some pretty good evi-
      dence to that effect. But what about the hostages?" Well, the
      truth is, Iran cannot order the Hezbollah to give up those
      hostages. But we *do* know that . . . the Hezbollah does not feel
      hostility toward Iran and yes, there is a way they can be ap-
      pealed to by Iran and would want to be of help. So, when we
      said this they succeeded in getting three out. And we have every
      reason to believe that the other two [*sic*] would be home by now,
      if it hadn't been—(*he hesitates*)

EM: For all this—

RR: (*sadly*)—what was made public.

EM: Mr. President, I'm kind of interested to know what made you
      take this Initiative. Was it something in your heart, was it com-
      passion towards families of these hostages, and if so, what made
      you tip over the brink?

RR: (*clears throat unhappily*) Well, this was a two-track thing, and we
      have been exploring every channel we could to find a way to get
      at freeing these hostages. But the other thing was very much on
      our minds for quite some time. . . . Suddenly, like a door had
      been open, and we began to explore in this direction . . . it was
      evident that the kidnappers [had], however tenuous it might be,
      a tie with Iran, that opportunity was offered. But to say "a deal
      involving some kind of ransom" is utterly ridiculous. (*He is*

thinking of some sarcastic words by former President Carter on television this morning, and becomes vehement) What if . . . in all our searching, it was never off of my mind: you see, you say, "What's in my heart?" Yes, I campaigned on this thing about terrorism, and I still mean it, but what I also campaigned, and I said a number of times, "I have a belief: if there is any excuse for a government, the kind we have in this country, it is [this]—any place in the world, even the least among us as citizens, a person is being unjustly denied his God-given Constitutional rights— life, liberty, and the pursuit of happiness—it is the responsibility of the government to go to his aid. . . . I feel, as strongly as anyone in the world, you cannot ransom with a kidnapper. You just make that a thriving business. But you *do* explore how you can get them back. Now that doesn't rule out if you can do it by force. (*Long, wistful anecdote about the effectiveness of Italian anti-terrorist commandos*) I don't care how much Mr. Carter wants to snipe at me as he did on TV this morning on this one. But there's a great difference when you've hostages that are being held by a government . . . and if he wants to talk about ransom—how the hell did we did get *them* back? We ransomed them—grant you, it was their money, but it was money we had frozen, since the overturn of the Shah, hundreds of millions of dollars—we said, "We'll give your money back . . ." (*He is unable to continue for anger*)

EM: I'm just wondering if there was a little personal pressure on you, that made you decide to go that final inch. Was it simply strategic, [or] had you met with the families?

RR: Oh, I had met with the families the time the hostages were taken, and tried to keep them apprised of what we were doing, and yet, in many instances, we couldn't say specifically, "We're talking to a man who is going to do this or that." And I can't tell you how many heartbreaking calls we had, where sometimes people we had counted on couldn't come through, couldn't deliver. . . . We thought we were going to have some action and then! (*snaps fingers*) It just blew up. . . .

EM: Do you mind if I ask a pretty tough one?

RR: All right.

EM: We have stated as fact that we gave them 261,000 pounds of arms—that's the content of one plane—in exchange, and simultaneously gotten three hostages back. Now, a cynical Arab fundamentalist mind might say, Well, that works out to 87,000 pounds per hostage. So in the future, whenever we need another 87,000 pounds of arms, we kidnap another American. I'm wondering whether you ever felt you might have set a precedent—whereby other hostages might become the victims of your compassion for these three.

RR: No. And there again, this is where I say, the *press* has cost us so much. *They're* the ones—just as they're still insisting that we traded Daniloff for the spy, when we didn't. (*This is true enough: what he had done was trade the spy for Daniloff. Reagan fulminates on about the press, as all Presidents have done before him, and gradually reverts to Topic A.*) . . . What if you found a fella over there that came to us with a plan of rescue and said, "I can rescue the hostages, I can get them out, but there's going to be a cost associated that's more than I can do, and it's gonna cost me *x* amount of money to spring 'em." Now, are you paying ransom? Or are you *hiring* someone to get your hostages out for you? And I think of this thing that we did was kind of in that framework. Our payoff was to people who believed that they could do something we couldn't. . . . But nothing was given to them or offered to them. What would you do? So . . . (*He runs dry*)

The President's essential decency, passion ("What's in my heart?"), obstinacy, and moral astigmatism are all apparent in this interview—as is his tendency to put a film frame round everything, and believe the best of barbarians, as long as they do not hail from the Evil Empire. He can no more comprehend that he has broken the law of the land (a specific embargo against selling arms to Iran) than he can accept a positive biopsy. By changing the word *has* to *had,* he rids himself of disease; by *hiring* intermediaries rather than *paying* them, he retains his honor; by so intensely *feeling* the injustice of hostage-taking, he makes hostage-trading respectable.

Nothing, not even a forced admission to the contrary on national television, will ever shake his certainty that he did the right thing by Benjamin Weir, Father Jenco, and David Jacobsen, at an eventual cost of $3.1 million each, and permanent damage to his own reputation.

The obfuscation began next day, at a "pre-brief" (White House dress rehearsal) for Reagan's evening press conference. He was capable of white lies when he thought his mother's ghost would approve—primarily to avoid hurting people or breaching confidences—and whoppers if he had read them in conservative magazines, but, as both pre-brief and press conference showed, he was terrible at concealing what he knew to be true.

I attended the former meeting, to the extreme consternation of Peter Wallison, and found Dutch querulously dependent on Admiral Poindexter for basic facts. (Regan, his normal prompter, was out of town.) He fumbled the first "question" about Iran's terrorist record—"What answer have we got on that?"—and could not manage the details of the next, about the specifics of the arms transfer.

"Not quite accurate, Mr. President," Poindexter said calmly. "I recommend you say all shipments out of the United States or by third parties could be placed in one aircraft."

It would have to have been a prodigious aircraft, given the fact that Iran had received, in aggregate, 2,004 TOWs, eighteen Hawks, and more than two hundred Hawk spare parts. But few of us knew that on November 19, 1986, and if Dutch did—having authorized all the shipments—he was very willing to forget. Poindexter also made sure that the word *Israel* slipped his memory. If asked whether the United States had authorized the Peres government to ship arms to Iran—"arms we ourselves provided, bought, and paid for"—the President should talk only vaguely of "a third country."

Dutch did not like this. He kept trying to say *third country,* but his mental phonograph replayed it as *Israel.* "Perhaps," he said unhappily, "I will just say I won't answer questions on how the arms were delivered."

He did better when asked about the possible illegality of his authorizations under the Arms Export Control Act, which required him to report foreign military sales to Congress. "I am granted certain rights and waivers as President. . . . I felt it was in the interests of the national security to go forward with this initiative. . . . I was within my rights to notify Congress at a time that I should choose." Now Wallison looked unhappy, feeling that he had given "the right answer to the wrong question." Dutch agreed to say only that he had relied throughout on the counsel of Attorney General Meese.

The atmosphere in the White House theater, already apprehensive, became near-desperate when he guessed that the total value of the shipments might be "one billion dollars" ("*Much* less, Mr. President!" Poindexter groaned. "Don't get into specifics!"), and stated that CIA representatives were "not engaged" in the Initiative ("Yes, sir, they *were!*").

It was the nearest I had ever seen the Admiral to a display of open agitation. Normally, he preserved a dimpled, polished-pink, mandarin cheerfulness, about as penetrable as jade. But now his brow wreathed in alarm, as did Wallison's. If the President went public with this CIA denial, after copious White House confirmations, it would fuel the rumors already circulating that Ronald Reagan was out to lunch.

I ducked out early, not liking the way Wallison was eyeing my notebook. Dutch's stricken face as he listened to another question haunted me out the East Wing gate. I knew he was struggling with his own revulsion at having to say what he did not mean, and remember what he did not know.

Predictably, he floundered at the press conference that night, avoiding the *I* word with such obvious clumsiness that viewers actually sympathized with him. The White House was forced to issue a presidential clarification twenty minutes after he stepped down from the podium.

"They were out for blood," he wrote in his diary, but took comfort in the flattery of a few sympathetic aides. "Our gang seems to feel 'I done good.'"

More than ever, in Reagan's seventy-sixth year, the prime member of his "gang" was Nancy. Although he relied on Donald Regan for hour-to-hour executive support, greatly enjoying the Chief's Boston-Irish, son-of-a-cop, jovially bruising personality, he showed an increasing need to be mothered at the end of every working day, striding long-legged down the Rose Garden colonnade at the stroke of five, and climbing into his pajamas the moment he had exercised and showered. Peter Wallison was disconcerted to find both of them *en déshabillé* upstairs one evening shortly after six, the President robed and slippered like a small boy waiting on Oreo cookies. Wallison had a codicil to their will for them to sign, and observed how Nancy "hovered over him all the time."

Her power inside the Reagan White House has been exaggerated politically and underestimated psychologically. And her much-celebrated "humanization" of Dutch's prejudice against the Soviet Union is hard to prove. She certainly managed to make Andrei Gromyko smile—a major diplomatic achievement—when he visited the Oval Office in 1984, and promised that she would whisper "peace" in her husband's ear every night. If so, it was his deaf right ear, because he made clear at Reykjavík that he still believed Moscow was bent on world domination.

Insofar as Nancy did launch West Wing offensives, using her preferred cruise missile, the telephone, she aimed at three principal targets: Donald Regan, White House Physician John Hutton, and the President's young aide, Jim Kuhn. Hutton and Kuhn were born to serve, and, adoring Reagan without reserve, obeyed her every instruction. Between them, in their masculine way, they mothered him, too, watching over his health and schedule all day, until she took over for the night shift.

Regan was another proposition. *His* kind of masculinity, toughened by Harvard, the Marine Corps, and Merrill Lynch, responded ill to the incessant demands of a woman who seemed to think that Ronald Reagan was a child of the zodiac. As the Chief famously revealed after returning to private life, Nancy had fallen under the influence of a San Francisco female astrologer, always cited as "my Friend," and for years had insisted that the President's movements be coordinated with those of the planets.

Michael Deaver had proved a discreet functionary in this respect during Reagan's first term. As a Californian (now waxing prosperous as the best-connected lobbyist in town), Deaver was star-friendly, and always seemed faintly amused that reporters had never guessed why he so frequently rescheduled presidential appointments. "D'ja ever ask NR about astrology?" he grinned at me one day, and changed the subject when I asked why.

Regan, an impatient, no-nonsense multimillionaire, had at first discounted, then deplored, Nancy's need to consult her Friend on the timing of events as important as Bergen-Belsen and Reykjavík. But like everybody else who served at the pleasure of the President, he needed to please her, too, and learned to tolerate her ditsiness. It was disconcerting, because she was in most respects not a fool. His problem in dealing with her day by day lay in having to reconcile the street smarts and sound instincts with the conversation-stoppers, such as the prediction of "dire events" in the last two months of 1986. Only now, her Friend seemed to have got it right. And events became direr.

Attorney General Meese came to see the Chief on the morning of Monday, November 24, to say that, after reviewing documents to do with the Iran Initiative not yet shredded by Admiral Poindexter and Colonel North, he had found evidence of what looked like "a diversion of funds" to the *contras.*

I knew something had gone seriously wrong when I was barred from the President's regular "issues lunch" with senior staff. At three that afternoon, I waylaid Pat Buchanan and asked what had been discussed.

"Oh, a new set of economic figures the President is taken with."

"But what about Iran?"

"Nothing. Hardly touched on it."

I found this hard to believe, and stared at him. He looked back as he had done once before, long and searchingly.

"The music's stopped playing," he said.

☯

If we are to believe Donald Regan, a man of generally accepted honesty, the blood drained from the President's face when Meese told him at 4:30 P.M. that some of the money paid by Iran for TOW missiles had been siphoned off from Israel by Colonel North and funneled, through a Swiss bank account, to the *contras*. Reagan looked drawn and stern, as he had when he heard that the space shuttle had blown up. But now he wore an expression the Chief had never seen before, and could not adequately describe.

It was the reaction, in Regan's opinion, of a complete innocent, unable to say much more than, "Get to the bottom of this, Ed," and, "What does John Poindexter say about this?"

Or it was the reaction, a cynic might say, of someone who had been found out. Guilt drains blood just as fast as shock. Typing these words at 3:39 A.M. on a cold morning eight years later, I am no wiser than Regan was then, or Dutch in his desuetude now. Granted, his diary for November 24, 1986, summarizes what Meese had just told him, and adds: "North didn't tell me about this. Worst of all, John Poindexter found out about it and didn't tell me." But the tone of the whole entry is oddly stiff and sequential, as if he is copying out a briefing paper supplied by Meese.

Only the Admiral knows whether Ronald Reagan knowingly authorized the transfer of illegal funds from illegal mercenaries in the Middle East to another set of illegal mercenaries in Central America. Maybe "Ollie" knows, but by proclaiming himself to Congress as a liar, Colonel North has forfeited any claim to the truth. My guess is that the answer will forever be swathed in pipe smoke.

My suspicion, for what it's worth, is that Dutch did authorize the transfer, not having the smallest comprehension of the laws he was subverting—the Arms Export Control Act (which even Poindexter had never heard of) and the second Boland Amendment, barring secret funding of *contra* operations in Nicaragua. Ronald Reagan's character by 1986 had become so lacking in curiosity, and his life as President so repetitive (except for great moments such as Reykjavík, which called on all his faculties), that when I went in to interview him I was often reminded of that MP's snapshot taken at Metro in '43: the furrowed eyes, the what-am-I-doing-here look of a screen actor between takes.

At times like this, a National Security Adviser could truthfully tell him that there was another "undercover thing going" to the benefit of "the freedom fighters," and that an eyes-only, unquotable annex to Boland II granted him full power to authorize it as Commander in Chief. He would be uncapping his fountain pen halfway through the speech, and asking where to sign. That's the way he was. Six years before, Mitterrand's man had elegantly summed him up: "Formidable will, based on mediocre understanding of the facts. As often in politics, ignorance sustains strength."

Ignorance also deals the occasional devastating blow, all the worse because naïveté does not expect it. In 1939, when he was making *Secret Service of the Air,* Reagan had made the mistake of stepping in front of a studio wind tunnel in his flying kit. His parachute began to unravel, and he was dragged with bruising force across the props department railroad track, finally ending up against the studio's wire fence.

Now he felt a similar unraveling and yanking, as a cold wind of reality tore the silk from his shoulders. The word *impeachment* was heard on Capitol Hill. Nancy Reagan, weeping, demanded that he fire Donald Regan. George Shultz furiously threatened to resign in protest against both the Iran Initiative and the Contra Diversion. William Casey, who appeared to have been involved in both, suffered a brain seizure. The President's record, post-Reykjavík approval rating dropped precipitously, to 46 percent. He suffered the humiliation of having to appoint a three-man board of inquiry, headed by former Senator John Tower, to look into the doings of his own Administration. Meanwhile, the Senate and House of Representatives set up a joint investigative committee, and the U.S. Court of Appeals gave Judge Lawrence Walsh of Oklahoma unlimited prosecutorial power, not only over the twin scandals, but over the whole question of *contra* aid. And Mike Deaver visited the Residence at dead of night to recommend that Reagan hire a "criminal practice" attorney.

In mid-December, Reagan's doctors announced, with unavoidably ironic overtones, that the President would have to undergo a prostate-gland surgery early in the new year. And as Christmas approached, for the first time in thirty-four years, his own wife stopped speaking to him.

36

Album Leaves,
1987–1988

"President Regan"

Nancy (privately) on last month's story that Dutch told her to "get off his God-damned back": "Ronnie *never* says 'God damn.' " How's that for a resounding denial?

The person, the issue, the item coming between Dutch & NR this winter is Don Regan. Their estrangement a matter of mutual sulks for a day or two, but Regan remains a continuing problem. Although it's clear that McF. & Poindexter & North deceived him, the imperious & hot-headed Chief looms as an ideal scapegoat. He's the second most powerful man in town; smart & rich & hard-working, with a tendency to boast. His true spiritual home would appear to be Wall Street rather than Washington.

Best of all, he's indispensable. During his two years in the Corner Office, Regan has concentrated all the power that Clark, Baker, Meese, & Deaver used to share, while simultaneously relieving Dutch of any need to settle policy squabbles. Nancy was worried about this even when things were going well for her husband. She recognizes (although she wd. *never* admit) that Dutch's fatal tendency toward passivity has become more marked, now that the achievements of his first term are in place, & the momentum of his second halted by scandal. He needs to be kept engaged; Regan's quickness & capability are simply too convenient for him.

Also—what she particularly dislikes—the Chief seems to have supplanted the Judge as presidential *alter ego*. Gales of common-Irish laughter come out of the Oval Office whenever the two men spend time alone. Unlike Clark, who had never had the temerity to speak for RR (indeed, hardly spoke at all), Regan participates so freely in Cabinet meetings & press encounters that jokes are going around Georgetown to the effect that it's now OK to mispronounce the phrase "President Reagan." When Frank Carlucci visited the Oval Office recently as a candidate to succeed Poindexter as Nat. Security Adviser, he asked RR four questions, and Regan answered every one.

Nancy & her private advisers (Deaver, Bob Strauss, Stu Spencer, Judge Clark, & others) feel the Pt.'s very dependency on Regan will make firing him look like a decisive & painful necessity—the act of a Chief Executive determined to clean house, etc. But, as when she tried to get Dutch to fire Bill Clark in '83, he's lapsed into quiet obstinacy. Feels that "Don" is honorable & loyal & has done nothing to warrant dismissal.—*Author's Notes, January 3, 1987*

The Patient Did Exceptionally Well

The prostate surgery was scheduled for 8:30 A.M. on January 5. The procedure was carried out by Drs. Utz and R. Beahrs without difficulty. . . . Early specimens were taken from the prostate using a Thompson resectoscope and these were studied after cryostat (fresh frozen section) preparation. They showed nodular prostatic hypertrophy with some inflammatory reaction, but no evidence of cancer. . . . The operation took 50 minutes. Blood loss was 350 cc and 23½ grams of tissue were removed. The patient did exceptionally well without discomfort and remained awake and alert during the operation. . . .

It was suggested that the President delay his State of the Union address, scheduled for January 20, but he did not delay. Two weeks after the prostatectomy, he presented the address in style, as he had all previous talks.—*Oliver H. Beahrs, "The Medical History of President Ronald Reagan."*

Word Salad

Bill Casey—the most coveted witness in upcoming Cong. hearings—reverting to subcortical savagery after op. for brain tumor. Half of the lesion remains in what Dr. Hutton calls "area where ape resides." Mumbling obscenities, imprecations—"word salad." Functional vocabulary down to 100: basically an expressive aphasic. Bob Woodward has been trying to get to see him in guise of "old family friend." Should be a great interview. RR, no lover of *The Washington Post* these days, incensed at news. "Those bastards."—*Author's Notes, January 1987*

Rare Rage

DEAVER   (*upstairs in the White House, acc. by Stuart Spencer*) Mr. President, I just have to tell you, and Stu here agrees, that you ought to think seriously about firing Don Regan.

REAGAN   (*slamming down pen in rare rage*) Listen, I'm *not* going to sacrifice anybody's ass to save *my* ass.

DEAVER   It's not a question of anybody's ass. You were elected to serve the country—it's the country you should worry about.

(*Silence. Deaver waits for Spencer to back him up. Reagan glares. The silence becomes intolerable. They leave.*)

SPENCER   (*in the elevator*) Jesus Christ, Mike.

—*Author's Notes, February 1987*

It's a Wonderful Life

Nadir—so far—of the Admin. Physician's office warned to be on the lookout for bizarre behavior. Shultz & Weinberger fighting like old Rottweilers, out of sheer habit. The Chief red-eyed, dangerous: "If She [*hissing the word as if about to say* Shi'ite] doesn't let the President come out and say something about all this mess pretty soon, she can kiss off any chance of restoring his reputation."

Landscape littered with moribund Reaganites. Casey dying. Bud McFarlane found nearly dead in bed with his wife Feb. 9, rattling with at least 20 Valium pills, 2 hours before due to testify Tower Board. Rushed to Bethesda, pumped out. Remains catatonically depressed. But getting the attention he's always craved. Somebody sent him a videotape: *It's a Wonderful Life.* Mike Deaver, recovering alcoholic, no longer *persona grata* at White House, goes to visit him. Two more bits of moraine, tumbled off RR's ongoing glacier.

RR himself showing signs of depression, failing to read even summaries of important work papers, constantly watching TV & movies. Tower Board frustrated by his almost complete inability to remember anything. New York joke: *What did the President forget, and when did he forget it?* Drs. worried by occasional double heartbeats.—*Author's Notes, February 1–20, 1987*

That Does It

A long walk with Nancy . . . It was a cold but beautiful day. Press reported that Don R. had told the staff that Nancy was responsible for the appointment of Jack Koehler [as White House Communications Director, replacing Pat Buchanan]. That does it—I guess Mon. will be the showdown day. Nancy has never met J. K. and certainly had nothing to do with his appt.—*Ronald Reagan Diary, shakily written in the presidential helicopter, February 22, 1987*

"A Thousand Hours at the Top"

Suggested title among West Wing wags, after Koehler's resignation, Feb. 25, upon reports that he belonged to a Nazi youth party as a boy. Rumor is that Koehler's appointment had been particularly requested by Nancy Reagan.—*Author's Notes, February 27, 1987*

Thank You God

Lunch with the V.P.—he met with Don R. and for the 1st time the side of him he hadn't seen—the outburst of temper. Finally he snarled he'd be out of here Mon. or Tues. . . .

[*Upstairs in the White House, after hearing from Paul Laxalt that Senator Howard Baker would make an excellent Chief of Staff*] It's not a bad idea. He thinks Howard is looking for a graceful way of getting out of running for Pres. V.P. just came up—another meeting with Don. This time totally different. He says he'll hand in his resignation 1st thing Mon. morning. My prayers have really been answered.

And this answer continued. I called [Baker]. . . . I asked him to take the job. Paul was right—he accepted immediately & is coming to Wash. tomorrow. Now I'll go on reading the [Tower Board] 'Report' til [*sic*] I fall asleep. Thank you God.—*Ronald Reagan Diary, February 26, 1987*

Intense Compassion

The NSC system will not work unless the President makes it work. . . .
By his actions, by his leadership, the President therefore determines the
quality of its performance. . . .

By his own account, as evidenced in his diary notes, and as conveyed
to the Board by his principal advisors, President Reagan was deeply
committed to securing the release of the hostages. It was this intense
compassion for the hostages that appeared to motivate his steadfast
support of the Iran Initiative, even in the face of opposition from his
Secretaries of State & Defense. . . .

Nevertheless, with such a complex, high-risk operation and so much
at stake, the President should have ensured that the NSC system did not
fail him.—*Tower Board Report, February 1987*

Arms for Hostages: A Balance Sheet

More dismal news for Dutch. Not only is he being accused of hostage
trading, but of dumb bargaining too. Whatever his culpability (if any)
in the Contra Diversion, his balance sheet for the Iran Initiative works
out as follows:

DATE	TRANSACTION	CREDIT/DEBIT
• *Sept. 15, 1985*	408 TOWs begat Rev. Benjamin Weir	+1
• *Feb. 17, 27, 1986*	1,000 TOWs begat no hostages	0
• *Apr. 14, 1986*	Hostage Peter Kilburn murdered	−1
• *July 26, 1986*	A pallet of TOW parts and a chocolate cake begat Rev. L. Jenco	+1
• *Aug. 3, 1986*	Twelve more pallets fail to beget further hostages: Reed, Cicippio, Tracy soon seized	−3
• *Oct. 28, 1986*	500 TOWs begat Jacobsen	+1
• *Jan. 24, 1987*	Alan Steen, Jesse Turner, Robt. Polhill seized	−3
Total	*3 returned, 6 taken, 1 killed* Net debit:	−4
Other expenses	Cost of military hardware (cake gratis)	$31 million
	RR's moral reputation	Incalculable

—*Author's Notes, February 27, 1987*

"Baker and his aides . . . check RR's behavior literally from all angles."
Lunch in the Cabinet Room, March 2, 1987.

Horror Stories

James Cannon, the courteous, slow-voiced Southerner who is helping
Sen. Howard Baker rescue Dutch from the Slough of Despond, says
that despite Don Regan's paroxysm of fury on Friday afternoon—
I saw the Chief leave at 4:15 after sending in his precipitous resignation:
his face was the color of fresh liver—they had a "most civilized" transition meeting next morning. Regan may be choleric, but he's a gentleman.

However, when Don was gone, leaving his gray guys behind to handle the details, Jim heard such horror stories about the President's recent performance (or non-performance) of official duties that he wrote
an emergency transition paper, suggesting that the new team observe
RR carefully all day on Monday [March 2], with a view to invoking
Twenty-fifth Amendment Sec. 4 (Presidential Disability) if he proved
to be "disoriented."—*Author's Notes, February–March 1987*

Waves of Benign Power

Before lunch in the Cabinet Room of the White House today, Baker &
his aides position their chairs so that they can check RR's behavior literally from all angles. In walks the depressed, somnolent, prostatically
challenged President, moving with his usual fluid grace, tall, beaming,

apple-cheeked, amethyst-eyed, tailored, giving off waves of benign power. Even before they sit down they realize that "the Gipper is back." He cracks Tennessee jokes for Baker's benefit, reminisces about Sacramento days, easily monitors the conversation, and ambles off precisely on the hour, with his usual deft exit line. The Twenty-fifth Amendment is shelved.—*Author's Notes, March 2, 1987*

Right Back Where I Started From

[*A spring afternoon in the garden of the Singleton Residence, Beverly Hills, California. Ronald Reagan receives his new Library Foundation, and their checkbooks*] To the sound of a Viennese quartet scraping out "California, Here I Come," he stands pale, aloof, twinkling, in blazer and slacks as his basic backers hobble by—austere, cadaverous Holmes Tuttle; austere, cadaverous Lew Wasserman (frequently hitching up a lanky leg, to activate some hardening artery); Armand Hammer in orthopedic shoes, rolling great chameleon eyes; Aaron Spelling struggling to breathe in his mummy-tight suit; Paul Laxalt, soft-palmed, syrup-smiling, confiding to everyone that he will announce for the Presidency in ten days' time; Judge Clark, dull-eyed and grim in alligator boots (I notice with surprise that he is taller even than Dutch). When Clark takes Nancy's hand, she looks at him with such contempt I brace for the sound of a slap. What has he ever done, except fail to flatter her? (Gore Vidal's line: "There is a lot of rage in this little lady.") He saunters on across the silky lawn, unconcerned.

Yellow-striped marquee; prodigal heaps of food and Belgian chocolates, which the men wolf but the women disdain. They are all homely enough to be on the cover of *Town & Country,* hard-haired and Chanel-suited, their faces smallpox-stiff (tiny silvery scars under the skin). They bare their perfect teeth and shift their little patent-leather pumps, impatient to be photographed with the President. He stands patiently gripping and grinning, posing and passing them on, and I think, *This is what your life's going to be like every day, Dutch, twenty-one months from now.*

Muffie [Brandon] tells me that NR wants the Ronald Reagan Library to be her palace, her backdrop, where she will receive the traveling greats of the world, whence she will fly for long stays in their parks and playgrounds: Ascot; Fontainebleau; Estoril; Majorca; Balmoral. . . . *Quelle folie.* Aristocrats move on. Dutch, at least, understands the transitoriness of power.

Later, as the chocolates melt and the champagne bottles give up their bubbles to the lazy air, he gets up to speak. The usual catchphrases: "Old friends . . . absence makes the heart grow fonder . . . this Saturday afternoon, with all the golf clubs open . . . as Henry VIII said to each of his wives, I won't keep you long."—*Author's Diary, April 19, 1987*

God Aids Them as Aids Themselves

"Issues lunch" in the Cabinet Room. RR's eyes turn flinty and his jaw sets when the subject of AIDS comes up—as it does too often these days for his comfort. (On April 1, he agreed after considerable prodding to declare it Public Health Enemy No. 1.) "Why is this disease any different from any other disease?"

His hearing aid whistles, and he fiddles with it painfully.

"I saw a TV show on AIDS in Africa the other day—they spread it there like the common cold."

However, he waves aside a domestic-policy memo on the subject of compulsory sequestration of AIDS patients as too draconian and too expensive. "No, not unless the problem gets to be really important."

Howard Baker is relieved. "If it ever got out that this Administration is considering quarantine . . . !"

Vice President Bush approvingly quotes Phyllis Schlafly: "This is the only virus that has come down the road with civil rights."—*Author's Notes, May 4, 1987*

Something There Is That Doesn't Love a Wall

[*Berlin, June 11*] An extraordinary sight on the eve of RR's appearance before the Brandenburg Gate: workers erecting another wall in front of the Wall. Specifically, a screen of bullet-proof Plexiglas to prevent the Pres. getting shot by an annoyed border guard tomorrow, when he challenges Gorby to erase the *Schluss* between E. & W. Berlin. Screen is sufficiently large to disclose ample backdrop of Gate, graffiti-splotched Wall, booms, border stones, electrified fence, and beyond, the sooty splendors of the "German Democratic Republic." . . .

[*June 12*] "Mr. Gorbachev, tear down this wall!" declaims Dutch, trying hard to look infuriated, but succeeding only in an expression of mild petulance. The occasion too staged, the crowd too small and well-primed, to make for genuine drama. One braces for a flash of prompt lights to either side of him: *APPLAUSE.*

What a rhetorical opportunity missed. He could have read Robert Frost's poem on the subject, "Something there is that doesn't love a wall," to simple & shattering effect. Or even Edna St. Vincent Millay's lines, which he surely holds in memory, floating over that chain of paper ribbons, woven by him and Bud Cole onstage, fifty-six years ago:

> *Only now for the first time I see*
> *This wall is actually a wall, a thing*
> *Come up between us, shutting me away*
> *From you . . . I do not know you any more.*

—Author's Notes, June 1987

An American Hero

Arthur Liman, Counsel for the Senate Committee, is getting nowhere with Ollie North. He sits nid-nodding at him in the hearing room, jowls wobbling like unset blancmange, husky voice wet. One can sense he is clearly frustrated by the ramrod-straight aggressiveness of that most dangerous of democratic creatures, the military man given control over policy.

"Yes, Senator, I lied!"

Ollie has let it be known that RR called him up and praised him as an "American hero." Hard to believe: flattery is foreign to Dutch. Unless somebody wrote it out and put it in front of him to read. . . . He would declaim *Dred Scott* if asked to.

Arthur is a gentleman. He tried to get his hands on my notes, etc., and when I said I would not give them up, "on the grounds of freedom of intellectual property," he suppressed a smile at my constitutional ignorance and said, "Look, if I wanted I could get your ass up here in minutes. But I'm not going to because it would be a lousy precedent, and an infringement on the idea of a writer in the White House."

Privately, he says he is impressed with RR's diaries—such entries as Peter Wallison has let him see. "I'm amazed at the clarity of his executive thinking, his modesty and lack of emotion. Not at all what I expected."—*Author's Notes, July 10–27, 1987*

The Day Is Brighter

[John Poindexter] has flatly denied ever telling me about the extra funds & their diversion to Contras. This was the bomb shell I've been waiting for 7 months. The day is brighter. . . .

My problem now is that John & Ollie were dropped by me from NSC because they had not told me of the extra money or the diversion. . . . Now it seems that Ollie did tell John with the expectation that John would tell me. I don't see though how I can do anything until they close down this investigation.—*Ronald Reagan Diary, July 15–16, 1987*

The Shadows of His Cap

[*Rancho del Cielo, Aug. 13, 1987*] The P. greeted her—what a warm embrace—you would think it had been a month or more since they had seen each other. They stood by themselves by the helicopter, kissed, hugged, and kissed again. Then when she saw the sun creep below the shadows of his cap, she put her hand up to shield his healing nose from its rays.—*John Hutton Diary, August 13, 1987*

A Book I Should Write

George Scharfenberger & Mort Janklow re a book I should write after I leave the W.H. I agreed.—*Ronald Reagan Diary, August 27, 1987*

A Weird and Sleazy Brew

I've just been reading Richard Secord's remarks in *Playboy,* indicating that he thought Ronnie wasn't quite up to understanding the geopolitical significance of the "opening" to Iran. My, my, now we have arms dealers passing judgment on the intellectual capacities of Presidents. . . . What a weird and sleazy brew the times have mixed for us, with the skim milk everywhere rising to the top!—*Philip Dunne to Author, August 30, 1987*

I Could Really Spin Them Off

[*September 26, 1987*]
   Dear Edmund:
   I can't find the verse you sent in any of the [Robert] Service poems in my book which may not be complete. I have a newer book at the ranch, I'll try there. . . .
   In my early boyhood—very early—I found my mother's little, leather bound book of Service poems. I became a fan. I read them over and over again.
   Much later in life I discovered that I could come close to reciting 2 of his poems—"Dan McGrew" & "Cremation of Sam McGee." . . . I could really spin them off. I hadn't realized back when I was reading his

works that these 2 had stuck in my mind until my Governor days. Then somewhat later I found myself using them to put me to sleep. . . .

Sincerely,

RR

Coming Apart

NR has breast cancer.

John Hutton braced himself to tell RR after the Cab. meeting Oct. 5—"Mr. President, I'm afraid I have rather bad news regarding the First Lady's mammogram." Says never before realized the power of Dutch's denial. Listened at desk, pen in hand, then softly & stonily: "Well, you're doctors, & I'm confident you'll be able to take care of it." End of interview.

John repairs perplexed to residence: "Mrs. Reagan, the President's too stunned to say anything." Stays with her until RR arrives, carrying work. Awkward greetings; no mention of the news. Exit Hutton, even more perplexed.

Next day, RR stops by his office: "John, I handled it very badly. Just couldn't talk about it, somehow."

Only following morning, at Bethesda Naval, after RR has been given confirmation of the pathology, & is sitting dumb with dismay in a private room, does he "come apart"—when Nurse Paula Trivet is sent in to comfort him. She holds him in her arms & he sobs like a child.

She won't speak of what happened in there, & says she never will.— *Author's Notes, October 1987*

Not Just a Little Wiggle

Mastectomy apparently successful. The stock market crashes today, but RR, purged of worry by his wife's clean bill of health, strides in beaming like a boy. His bubbling *joie de vivre* affects gloom in room. His only comment on Wall Street's nervousness: "Maybe they should change their symbol from a bear to a chicken noodle."

Chairman of the CEA [Council of Economic Advisers] tries to make him understand the seriousness of the situation. "Mr. President," he booms in a stentorian voice, "this is not just a little wiggle in the market that we can ignore. This is *a very serious condition.*" RR tries to look solemn, but this is difficult to do when one's mouth is full of jelly beans and one's interlocutor goes by the name of Beryl Sprinkel. He takes refuge in genial reminiscence. "Didn't we do better before there was a Federal Reserve?"—*Author's Notes, October 19, 1987*

High, Nervous Featherings

NR's spirits, weighed down by recent loss of her mother, very low. She's always been lachrymose—"cries when we send out the laundry," says RR—but weeping jags now alarm East Wing staffers.

I have managed to establish the actual date of the night they met in 1949, and since the anniversary of it is upcoming—Nov. 15—think it might cheer her up if we gave them dinner on that date, and then surprised them with it. They love to go out; I could invite a bunch of writers and solicit impressions. . . . Discuss it with his & her social secretaries, enjoining secrecy. Within twenty-four hours, "The President and Mrs. Reagan will be delighted." So will Design Cuisine, Inc. . . .

[On the fifteenth] we find ourselves with the townhouse wired for instant communication with every red phone in the world, a Secret Service sniper on the roof, twelve other security personnel hidden in various rooms, and a bunch of literati in formal dress (Gay & Nan Talese; Robert K. Massie; Anthony Haden-Guest; Marion Elizabeth Rodgers; Kenneth & Valerie Lynn), all peering fascinatedly out the bay window as Dutch and Nancy approach. The convoy three blocks long, vanguarded by motorcycle cops, scintillant with blue and gold lights. Every street from Twelfth Northwest to Fourth Southeast empty of traffic; the park opposite crowded with press; champagne chilling, the round table dense with flowers and silver—while the air inside and out vibrates with the high, nervous featherings of a helicopter.

"Nancy," I say, after we have all been introduced, "I know you're a Perrier person, but this is one night I hope you'll accept champagne."

"Why?" she asks, as a butler waits.

"I'll tell you why when you've got the champagne in your hand."

She shakes her earrings. "No, Perrier please."

Dutch accepts a flute of Veuve Clicquot and gracefully plays right into my hand. "You know, honey," he tells her, "the night we went out on our first date, we drank two bottles of champagne between us!"

"Well, Mr. President, you've really set me up. The reason for this celebration is, I've found out the exact date of that evening. It was thirty-eight years ago today, and here's the proof." I pull a card from my pocket and read an item from Hedda Hopper's column in the New York *Daily News,* November 20, 1949:

RONNIE REAGAN and NANCY DAVIS, pretty Metro player and daughter of a famous Chicago surgeon, acted as though they cared at Ciro's the night SOPHIE TUCKER . . . received a plaque as the first woman of show business.

"According to the *Hollywood Reporter*," I say, "Sophie got that award on the fifteenth, which means that tonight"—I raise my glass—"is the anniversary of your first date. Congratulations!"

We all drink and applaud, and Dutch responds with some joke. After the laughter, I ask Nancy (trying not to look at the stiffness of her left shoulder, and the carefully shaped padding beneath) if she remembers what she was wearing. She answers without hesitation.

"Yes. A black dress with a white collar."

I note this on the card. "Great! Now we can make this evening tax-deductible."—*Author's Diary, November 7, 15, 1987*

Round Table Roundup

As Senator Hatfield did after his Valentine's Day dinner in '83, I asked our guests the other night to write their impressions of RR on paper. Sample quotes:

[*Robert K. Massie*] Somehow, he was both there—very much there—and not there at the same time. I was surprised by his affability and vigor. He is an extremely nice fellow and the reports I've read or heard about his "senility" are absurd. . . . What bothered me about Reagan was his lack of curiosity as to what we did and what we thought about the world. There was a kind of impenetrable curtain hanging between us and the President. . . . But I must say—and perhaps it is the invisible crown all Presidents wear—that he seemed to dwarf all of the twelve men currently scrambling round the country, trying to take his place.

[*Kenneth and Valerie Lynn*] If we were utterly beguiled by the President's surface charm, we were conscious of inner depletions, of the sort which afflict a great many people who hold public office for considerable periods of time. Intellectually, Reagan struck us as a man who had been living off capital for so long that he had finally exhausted his resources.

[*Gay Talese*] Mrs. Reagan did surprise me in that she talked when *He* was talking. . . . Is this a sign of her independence? Does it bother him? Does he hear it, care? . . . Speaking of hearing, I thought his two hearing aids were beautifully designed—very deeply implanted in the lobes, and skin-colored to match his own pigment.

[*Marion Elizabeth Rodgers*] His mouth closed in the tiny tight gesture I have seen him use for reporters. "Honey—" And then it was time to leave. The President shook our hands, but there was not a flicker of recognition. . . . I realized we had not been individual Americans around the candlelit table. We were simply dinner guests, who had been entertained.—*Author's Correspondence File, November 15–28, 1987*

An Epochal Event

[*Monday, Dec. 7*] Gorbachev arrives in Washington to sign INF Treaty. Privately begs Shultz to cut tomorrow's one-on-one short. Clearly dreading a third repetition of all Dutch's anti-Soviet jokes.

[*Tuesday, Dec. 8*] Welcoming ceremony on South Lawn. A Corot morning: silver-gray sky, bare trees silver-gray in TV lights; scent of wood smoke & freshly mown grass. A Marine flagbearer near me disdainfully holds Soviet flag erect. Military affairs officer: "First time in history. President's orders."

RR's speech not partic. friendly. "Our people should have been better friends by now." He keeps trying to engage G.'s eyes; G. studiously stares straight ahead; RR keeps on pausing, peering; eventually G. gives him an exasperated nod.

Morning plenary: G. on masterful, aggressive form, hardly bothering to refer to dense handwritten notes. (Powell—"Knew his goddamn facts, right down to the millimeter measurement of our binary shells.") Dutch bemused, as he was the first morning at Reykjavík. When G. fires a question at him, he has to turn to Shultz.

After lunch they sign INF Treaty in East Room. Dutch trots out *trust but verify* once too often for G., who replies with an irritated smile, "You repeat that at every meeting."

Still, the Treaty is an epochal event—as G. says, "It will be inscribed in the history books." For the first time in Cold War, U.S. & USSR have committed to reducing their respective nuclear arsenals. 1,846 Soviet & 846 U.S. missiles to be trashed within next three years, under mutual supervision.

P.M. plenary: Pres. sinks into postprandial torpor, while G., on a post-treaty high, launches into another monologue. Speaks with astonishing, even touching, frankness about flaws & problems of current Soviet state. RR (*interrupting*): "Reminds me of the one about our two educational systems. Here, you ask a college graduate what he's gonna do, he says: 'Haven't decided yet.' In Russia, kids say, 'We haven't been told.' " G., clearly cut to the quick, does not even attempt to smile.

RR remorseful afterward. "I wasn't very good this afternoon, was I?"

[*Wednesday, Dec. 9*] Pres., having briefed & rebriefed himself overnight, in much better form today. Rejuvenated, aggressive, humorous. Demands "a date certain" for Soviet withdrawal from Afghanistan. G (*defensive*): "When you stop helping the *mujahadeen.*" RR: "SDI is essential to our goal of total nuclear disarmament." G (*stung*): "Go ahead—build it—we can do the same, 100 times cheaper." RR: "Oh, so you *are* working at strategic defense." G: "I didn't say that!"

[*Thursday, Dec. 10*] Drizzly departure ceremony. But Pres. & *gensek* affectionate again, as at Geneva. Just before coming out in front of cameras, they embrace, slapping each other's backs.

This evening I go down to watch Dutch report on the summit from the O.O. Afterward (as still photographers kneel and flash) he relaxes by reciting Robert Service:

> *In the long, long night, by the lone firelight, while the*
> > *huskies, round in a ring,*
> *Howled out their woes to the homeless snows . . .*

—*Author's Notes, December 1987*

Scoop

Something badly wrong at W.H., and I can't figure out why. I keep getting excluded from meetings, or politely "disinvited" halfway through them whenever RR gets too talkative. Also he seems to be holding back in interviews with me. Howard Baker's team has never quite adjusted to the presence of a scribe in its resolutely political precincts; they are all careful, cagey Washingtonians, afraid to be quoted if you ask them the time. I call Jim Cannon, who's close to Baker, & he advises me tonight, "It's Mrs. Reagan."

"*Nancy?* She was always very high on the idea of an in-house biographer."

"Well, apparently she's worried you're going to scoop the President. Before he publishes his own memoirs."

Incensed, I take it up with him at our next interview. "Mr. President, I've heard on the grapevine that Mrs. Reagan is afraid I'm going to scoop you. That's *never* been our understanding. It'll take years to do my book, and if you want I'll guarantee in writing not to come out first—"

He laughs embarrassedly. "Well, she keeps saying, 'Don't tell him too much.' "

I am so angry I go up to the Residence & confront her in her red den. Blank-eyed, fake bewilderment. "Oh but I never—I—uh, I *never* have anything to do with, with West Wing meetings. I don't know who could have told you that. . . ."

An hour later a nervous Jim Kuhn calls to confirm her protestation of innocence. "Yeah, Jim, right, right."

Access, thank God, has improved since then.—*Author's Diary, December 14–17, 1987*

A Totally Ruined Man

Mike Deaver has been convicted of lying to Congress, and a Federal grand jury, about his post-Administration lobbying activities. He is a totally ruined man: aside from a possible fifteen-year prison term, he is afflicted by kidney stones, alcoholism, bankruptcy, unemployability, and now the apparent hostility of the Reagans, to whom he gave the twenty best years of his life. Neither of them has called him since he got into legal difficulties.—*Author's Diary, December 18, 1987*

"Our Weather Has Been Quite Strange"

I go to the White House for my regular interview. "Well, hello, hello!" says Dutch, radiating cheerfulness like a big, blue-suited beacon.

"You're in a good mood today, Mr. President."

"I'm *always* in a good mood!" Which is true enough.

We talk mainly about religion. I have been reading a book about his Armageddon complex, and, when I mention the subject, am rewarded by an animated speech, full of jovial doom, that lasts the rest of the half hour. "For several years, you know, our weather has been quite strange," he muses, unaware that the same adjective might be applied to himself.

Howard Baker and Colin Powell arrive, impatient for their own thirty minutes.

"We're having a cozy chat about Armageddon," I say. They stand grinning nervously as he continues.

"When it comes, the man who comes down *from the wrong side,* into the war, is the man, according to the prophecies, named Gog, from Meshech, which is the ancient name of Moscow—"

"I tell you, Mr. President," says Baker, eying my tape recorder, "I wish you'd quit talking about that. You upset me!"

"But on the *other* side," says Dutch inexorably, "are ten kings from

Europe. Well, the European conference, now, is ten nations. And then from the West, comes a young nation, under the sign of an eagle! Now, this was all there, written long before there was any country in the West like ours. These are some of the prophecies."

"Gog's on his way," I warn the National Security Adviser, *sotto voce,* on the way out.—*Author's Diary, February 9, 1988.*

The Ark in the Egg

[*Moscow, USSR, late May 1988*] The perfume of lilacs in Red Square. Moscow oviform, membrane within protective membrane, formed through the centuries: the Kremlin buffered by the Old City buffered by Russia buffered by the other republics buffered by the Warsaw Pact; onion domes shaped like breasts. Everything feminine, inscrutable. "The Motherland"—nurturing, vulnerable; the Church's other layers of ritual & sacrament protecting the inner ark, the golden egg. For the first time I understand their historic fear of rape.

[*Sunday, May 29*] Pres. meets with Gorbachev today for an initial one-on-one in the Kremlin. After forty minutes he emerges, unable to remember a single word of what they said to each other. Not a good omen. . . . Gorbachev not partic. pleased. Dislikes RR's dogged insistence on calling him "Mikhail." Tolerated it at the Washington summit, but here considers it *lèse-majesté.* If Pres. had any real concern for Russian manners, he would essay the occasional "Mikhail Sergeyevich," as Gorby squeezes out the odd, reluctant "Ron." Fortunately nothing diplomatically substantial expected at this summit. Suspect Gorbachev's real reason for inviting RR here is to show him the real "human" face of Communism.

Some face! Walking across the bridge tonight & up the far bank of the river, I peer through the windows of ill-lit apartment buildings (even the yellow moon is dull) and am reminded of Tolstoy's plaint about the misery of Russian features: "Few . . . are not disfigured by alcohol, nicotine, or syphilis." Bodies—even the bodies of young girls— are goitered, bent, bunioned: I've not seen so many cripples outside of Africa. *This* is the Moscow Dutch should be seeing, not the gilt & beeswaxed splendors of the Kremlin: this third-world city of dirt streets & weeviled garbage heaps. He should be breathing this universal reek of kerosene & boiled artichokes, & noting the extraordinary languor with which people just sit & stare & drink & sew, or doze alone under the dusty trees. Gnats moan; dogs howl. One has the feeling of a society beaten into utter submission.

I take a taxi back to the Hotel Mezhdurodnoya. The driver kills his engine at every red light, to save gas.

[*Monday, May 30*] RR & Gorbachev getting on much better. Gorby up to his usual trick of dropping the Holy Name at every opportunity: "God willing, we are going to make permanent peace. . . . We'll all be praying for peace." Dutch eats it up with a spoon. However, he causes something of a theological *frisson* when he addresses Metropolitan & senior priests at the Daniloff Monastery this P.M.—spiritual heart of Russian Orthodox Church. Praises the reliberalization of worship under Gorbachev (bearded nods & smiles all around the chamber). Trusts that similar freedoms will soon be extended to suppressed Catholic Church of the Ukraine (beards, electrified, billow & bristle).

Jim Billington [Librarian of Congress, Russian scholar, and a member of the U.S. delegation] contentedly accepts responsibility for advising this deliberate provocation in RR's speech. "Good thing to remind those bastards that their predecessors collaborated with Stalin in driving the Ukrainians to pray in the woods."

Dutch oblivious, of course. Bows out with winks & smiles.

[*Tuesday, May 31*] Lunch with RR at the House of Writers—HQ of *apparatchik* state scribes. Best food in Moscow. Yevtushenko in beautiful white linen suit; Tom Wolfe should be so elegant. *Glasnost* or no *glasnost,* Communism rewards its collaborators.

Endless speeches on the glories of Marxist artistic expression. Dutch, roseate with vodka, nods off. Who can blame him?

I sit with Felix Kuznetsnov, director of the Gorky Institute, and Sergei Baruzdin, editor in chief of *Druzhba Narodov.*

SB	I hear you are writing a biography of President Reagan.
EM	Yes.
FK	We will arrange to have it translated and published in the Soviet Union.
EM	Why, thank you!
SB	And what is more, I will give it an excellent review.
EM	That is most generous—
FK	(*agitated*) Who is this man behind the velvet rope, staring at us with such malevolence?
EM	Oh, don't worry about him. That's Sam Donaldson of ABC.
FK	What is he? What does he do?
EM	He's a thorn in the President's flesh. (*this phrase requires explaining*)
SB	Ah, but in Russian, we say it better. He would be a splinter in the President's ass. (*guffaws*)

"They give him a standing ovation that beats against Lenin's carved colossus like waves of an imminent storm."
Ronald Reagan addresses the students of Moscow State University, May 31, 1988.

After lunch I copy the phrase out & send it to Dutch to use next time Sam starts bellowing at him.

We go on to Moscow State University, where the Pres. gives his best speech since Bergen-Belsen, written by Josh Gilder and Tony Dolan. Here in this huge, cold marbled hall are a thousand or so children of the *nomenklatura*—notably lacking in goiters & gloom, born & bred in the exclusive precincts of Lenin Hills: Gorbachev's heirs. They are fresh-faced & well-dressed & have that palpable hunger for new information characteristic of all intelligent youth. I am touched by the nods and smiles and careful note-taking whenever Dutch says something in praise of basic human freedoms. Alas, he tires during the Q&A session afterwards, and rambles off into an embarrassing defense of U.S. government policy toward Indians, but the amazing thing is that these children understand what is happening: that he is old and somewhat naive and the dupe of some of his own sentimentalities. They know he is talking nonsense, but they forgive him *because they know that his heart is good.* And they give him a standing ovation that beats against Lenin's carved colossus like waves of an imminent storm.—*Author's Notes and Diary, May 1988*

A Vote for Zippy

[*Election Day 1988*] Dutch sits this day out in the Residence—slightly wistful, one suspects, because the torch is passing to Bush—so I go around for our last interview of the year. Next month, well before Christmas, he and NR will be off to LA to establish residence in the new house the friends have bought for them.

He is quiet and sad and has nothing of any interest to say on any question. After half an hour I get up to go, and try to cheer him by saying I have to go up to New York to vote. "Not meaning any disloyalty to the Republican Party, Mr. President, but I'm going to vote for Zippy."

"Who the hell's Zippy?"

"I thought you read all the comic pages! Zippy's the pinhead in the muu-muu who's running to succeed you!"

"Oh, yeah. I could never understand that one. The one I read every day is *Mary Worth.*"—*Author's Notes, November 4, 1988*

Miming Masturbation

Lunch with RR and the VP (difficult to think of Bush as Pres.-elect). Their regular Thursday Mexican meal in the little dining room off the

O.O. Cheese soup the color of concrete, chili, chips. Bush slurps and crunches with gusto as Pres. looks on.

RR   My weight's up a tad. Four pounds here I gotta get rid of.

GB   (*reaching for sauce bottle*) You're not a Tabasco man, are you?

RR   No.

GB   Love the stuff. (*splatters his plate so vigorously the Filipino waiter steps out of range*)

RR   Well, that campaign of yours. We missed a number of these lunches.

GB   Got clobbered in Iowa. (*crunch*) Tough state. But got the other Plains states. (*crunch*)

RR   Iowa is a peculiar state. It's tough.

GB   My newspaper image out there is real bad. (*crunch*) Dunno why—

RR   When I was out there as a young man, the Des Moines *Register* was rock-solid conservative. It's owned by a family, you know.

GB   (*crunch*) Cowles.

RR   No, it's family-owned. (*Bush decides not to contest the point*) Now, with the new generation in charge, they've just gone the other way!

GB   Same with the Chandlers and *L.A. Times.* Buffy still alive?

RR   Don't know.

GB   Now I hear there's a tie-up between the *Times* and *The Washington Post.*

RR   (*uninterested*) There is?

The ensuing conversation, affable but impersonal, is remarkable for a complete avoidance by either party of any form of address. Otherwise it is intellectually indistinguishable from millions of masculine chats in executive dining rooms across the country. It covers all the usual subjects: sports (mainly baseball), horses (competitive anecdotes about randy stallions), broadcast news, tax policy, & jokes about sex (uproarious laughter).

A soft sunbeam, which at noon illuminated a pot of red begonias, moves steadily around the little room and warms Dutch's back as he tells one about the father, anxious for a new form of birth control, who is advised by his doctor to practice "hand sex." Among my enduring memories will be the sight of the leader of the Free World miming masturbation with his thumb over the top of a Tabasco bottle.—*Author's Diary, December 17, 1988.*

"It's Too Late"

We go to dine with Bob and Donna Tuttle. The guest of honor is old Holmes Tuttle, who twenty-four years ago heard Dutch make "The Speech" in Los Angeles and dedicated the rest of his life, and much of his considerable fortune, to making Ronald Reagan Governor and President of the United States. A proud man, tall, hard, austere, incorruptible.

"In all these years," he tells me, "I've never asked but one thing of Ronnie. And that was for my wife and I to spend but one night in the Lincoln Bedroom." He hesitates.

"And?" I ask, guessing what is coming.

"He said, 'Of course you can stay, Holmes, I'll see to it.' But I guess it slipped his mind. Or hers."

"Did you remind them?"

"Two, three times. Always the same reply, 'We'll see to it.' Eight years go by. Then, just a few weeks ago, after the election, suddenly we got an invitation."

He takes a swig of his drink, his hand shaking with anger.

"I said no thanks. It's too late."—*Author's Diary, December 19, 1988*

"Not a Word of Thanks"

[*Christmas Eve 1988*] I go round to the President-elect's house to interview him. Barbara sits in, knitting dangerously *à la* Madame Defarge. They clearly have something to get off their collective chest about their eight years as "the help," but Bush's preppy politeness keeps moderating her fury.

"Gotta tellya, I really love that guy, he's such a terrific fellow. Only one thing kinda bothered me, whichistersay, just *never* been able to understand—guy never seemed to *need* anybody."

"Except Nancy," says BB, needles *accelerando*.

"Off to Camp David every weekend, never took their *kids* with 'em! Bar and me," the VP allows, "we'd go *crazy* if we found ourselves up there without a whole bunch of family runnin' around."

"Anything else about the President bother you?"

"Listen, he was a prince of a feller, I'd never say anything against him. Nancy neither . . ." There is a pause as the Bushes exchange glances. "Well, sometimes," he says reluctantly, "I kinda wished they'd shown—y'know, a little appreciation. Didn't seem to want us upstairs in the White House."

"We would always thank them for their gifts," BB says pointedly.

"Guess they didn't always thank us," he goes on. "Gave him, oh such a *neat* present for his seventy-fifth birthday, took a whole lot of trouble customizing it to the right measurements, borrowed his boots so it would stand up real pretty—"

He notices my perplexity and stands up, a huge, hurt, lovable, distressingly ordinary man. "Lemme show you. We had a duplicate made."

He escorts me to a bathroom upstairs, outside of which stands the single most terrifying piece of kitsch I have ever seen. It would not be out of place at Auschwitz. There, standing booted and spurred, are *Dutch's feet and lower legs,* supporting, like some flattened dwarfish torso, an embroidered seat, with the presidential seal *au centre*.

While I marvel, as so often before, at the aesthetic perversity of well-born WASPs, Bush shakes his head and says in the same hurt voice, "Not a word of thanks."—*Author's Diary, December 24, 1988*

The Glacier

As the old year dies, I feel a sudden urge to revisit Tampico. Why, I don't know—perhaps, subconsciously, I'm hoping that some bitter cold will shock me into a clearer understanding of Dutch's personality. If so, naive hope dies as I drive into town and find it even more deserted than two years ago. Main Street is black with frozen mud. Dry snow blown in from the north stings my cheeks like sand. A sign on the door of number 111 reads, in characters more querulous than hopeful: *FOR TOURS CALL 438-6395.* I step into the mud to take a last photograph of the Birthplace. Plastic weathersheeting blears its windows like cataracts; it has the sad look of a shrine where people no longer worship. Apparently the University of Northern Illinois is interested in some of its contents, but cannot afford to purchase them.

A few doors down, at the Dutch Diner, I order some restorative coffee and ask about Mr. and Mrs. Nicely. Apparently neither of them is well. "Paul's had a coupla strokes," my waitress says, "and Helen's too old to run the museum alone. Guess they gonna have to look for somebody." She gives a sigh and whispers with dour disapproval, "I heard he put two hundred thousand of his own money in that place, and Reagan never even came to visit."

I have some blackberry pie with my second cup and tell her that Theodore Roosevelt, too, had a strange lack of interest in his birthplace. "Maybe it's something to do with the drive to be President. Men like that don't like to look back."

The word *drive* makes her peer over my shoulder at the weather.

"Lotsa stuff comin' down," she says. "If you wanna get to a motel, you better hit the highway." I rise to her warning and go out again into the cold. The snowflakes are thicker now; I stand for a moment amid wisps of caffeinated steam, watching them purify Main Street. I think of the terrible last lines of Joyce's "The Dead," and wonder if Tampico—ghosting even now, before my eyes—will long survive its famous son.

Before driving on to Sterling I retrace my steps of two and a half years before and stand again in the fields. Snow blankets the corn stumps. There is nothing to see but whiteness, nothing to feel but wind. No birds sing. I turn and gaze back at the little town, a few dull lights in the charged air. Were it not for Jack's wanderlust, I reflect, Dutch might have grown up in this place, might still be here, perhaps one of those seamed and silent retirees in the diner, champing on fruit pie with toothless jaws.

Yet even as the thought arises, I reject it as unworthy of him. For whatever reason, there was born here, far from the mattering world, an ambition as huge as it was inexorable. Out of Tampico's ice there grew, crystal by crystal, the glacier that is Ronald Reagan: an ever-thrusting, ever-deepening mass of chill purpose. Possessed of no inner warmth, with no apparent interest save in its own growth, it directed itself toward whatever declivities lay in its path. Inevitably, as the glacier grew, it collected rocks before it, and used them to flatten obstructions; when the rocks were worn smooth they rode up onto the glacier's back, briefly enjoying high sunny views, then tumbled off to become part of the surrounding countryside. They lie where they fell, some cracked, some crumbled: Dutch's lateral moraine. And the glacier sped slowly on.

In that sense, I suppose, one could say that the story of Reagan's life is a study in American topography. Thirteen hundred miles southeast of Tampico this winter day, the glacier has at last stopped growing. The nation's climate is changing; so is that of the world. New suns, new seasons, are due. Yet when all the ice is gone, when fresh green covers the last raw earth and some future skylark sings heedlessly over the Ronald Reagan National Monument, men will still ponder Dutch's improbable progress, and write on their cards, *How big he was! How far he came! And how deep the valley he carved!*

—*Author's Diary, December 31, 1988*

37

The Shining City

I T WAS THE EVE of my last interview with Ronald Reagan as President. I drove through drifting drizzle to the new Canadian embassy at the foot of Capitol Hill, where Allan and Sondra Gotlieb were bidding good-bye to half a thousand close friends. "I don't envy you your assignment," Allan said as I wished him well. "You're going to have to find the key to the most enigmatic character of modern times, and I think you'll end up echoing what Samuel Johnson said to Oliver Goldsmith: 'The more you explain it, the less you will understand it.'"

Dutch greeted me on Monday, January 9, with his left hand wrapped incongruously in an open-top plastic bag. I recognized it to be one of the bleary Zip-Locs he kept acorns in, to feed to the White House squirrels. Inside, his fourth finger was linted and splinted from an operation for Dupuytren's contracture.

"The doctors let you wear that? Isn't it kind of unsanitary?"

"Well, you see, I have to keep the fluff off of my suit."

All through our subsequent conversation he sat enduring this humid envelope. I suspected the finger was troubling him, but he pretended otherwise.

"Mr. President," I began, "I want to thank you for all the hours you have spent with me over the last three years. And also for letting me watch you perform here and abroad at the summit meetings. Those were truly"—what were they, in truth?—"life-enhancing times." He twinkled uninterestedly.

"I'm sure you're getting tired," I said, "of being asked what the seminal moments of your presidency have been—"

"What the whaa—?"

"Seminal." For some reason, the blankness of his face transported me back to Dixon, Illinois: to a cold, hard place, absolutely resentful of bearded intrusion. "I'm trying to think of another adjective. . . . I mean those moments when you really felt that you were making a difference in the world, that you were here for a reason, doing something that only you could have done."

"Well, I think, I have to say, that one of them had to do with the tax program." My heart sank, and I mentally deducted ten minutes from the time remaining. The mellifluous voice ran on. *Silver water flowing over peach fuzz,* I doodled on my notepad. *Or one of Clementi's slow mvmnts.—molto express.—no melody worth a damn.* Nothing for it but to await the final cadence.

"And as it went on," Dutch said at last, "suddenly we were into this economic recovery, that we are now in, for the, uh, seventy-fourth month."

"Right. That is more exciting to you than the knowledge, when you first met Gorbachev, that you had struck up something strong—that some dramatic re-alignment was possible between you?"

"Well, that too of course . . . there again, to see the results beginning to show. When I called the Soviet Union an 'evil empire,' I meant it!"

And you did, too, I thought, regretting my previous sarcasm. The most vilified presidential utterance in modern times, the truest, and most . . . seminal! Those two words, which translate so unmistakably into Russian (*imperiya zla*), convinced Yuri Andropov more than any number of bombs that the United States was morally ready to fight the century's ultimate war.

"But then this man hadn't taken office yet," Dutch went on, with his usual indifference as to whether foreign leaders have names or not. "I told him, right out, one thing: 'An arms race you can't win.' "

I remembered how apprehensive we had all been that icy morning in

Geneva, before the President descended laughing after breakfast, and crossed the driveway with little chuckles of mist trailing over his shoulder. "Were you scared of Gorbachev when you left the Villa Pometta for that first meeting with him?"

"No." Dutch seemed amused. "I can't say I was scared of him, no."

"Have you ever been scared during your presidency? I mean, genuinely frightened."

"Well, I don't know if I would called it 'frightened.' "

He paused for a moment, and adjusted the bag around his hurt hand. I felt a wave of tenderness. "The most difficult thing to do in this position, that I've done several times, is to order young Americans into action, knowing the risks. That isn't fear, it's just . . . something that has to be done. I've never," he went on, "lost in my mind a conversation I had with Lyndon Johnson while I was still governor. Nixon was having the first state dinner ever held outside Washington, in California. It was in honor of the outgoing President of Mexico. LBJ and his wife, and Nancy and I, were at the head table. And Nancy took advantage of it to ask him [Johnson] some questions—"

Trust Dutch not to ask questions himself!

"—like, what is it like now to be out of office, and so forth. And he made a remark that I never forgot. . . . 'When Richard Nixon took the oath,' he said, 'I had the greatest burden lifted from me that I ever carried in my life.' He said, 'There was never a day that went by that I wasn't scared that I might be the man who started World War III.' Well, how *can* you be scared?"

Dutch spoke with unusual vehemence. His mouth curled with contempt for a predecessor with so much self-doubt. "As if that's something that comes on you, and you don't have anything to do with it! If such a war became necessary, through no choice of our own (in our country, we've never started the wars), you . . . you have to accept that. That's part of what this job is all about! How could he have sat there, living in fear that somehow he might trigger a war?"

At this point, the President noticed a small shadow, perhaps reflected on the curve of my spectacles, in the shape of a Caribbean island, and remembered that he had "triggered" something in Grenada. "But that was never a war. That was a request at about three in the morning."

Noted, as they say in *The New Yorker*.

"Here it was, a Commonwealth of the United Kingdom, being taken over and made into a Communist state, and the papers and things would see on the paper confirmed that this was the Soviet intention, that Grenada would be the first."

His syntax might be crumbling like the breastworks of Saint George's, but not the fervor of his convictions. "Right," I said soothingly.

"I didn't see that as getting us into a third World War or anything."

"Is your lack of fear, your confidence, based on the knowledge of America's military power? Or is it your belief in the essential goodness of man?"

He evaded either alternative, but was willing to take credit for making military men and women feel good about themselves for the first time in twenty years. "When I was Governor they felt they were kind of pariahs!"

"I'm going to embarrass you, Mr. President," I said, changing the subject. "I'm going to give you a couple of quotes that relate to Ronald Reagan, the first directly, the other indirectly. I'd be interested to see how you respond. Last night, the outgoing Canadian Ambassador said to me soberly that you were the most enigmatic character of modern times"—And I recited the words of Oliver Goldsmith given at the beginning of this chapter.

Dutch looked shocked. "That's me? I think I'm an open book!"

Dreading the second quote, he maundered on for five minutes with another *catalogue mal raisonné* of his tax policy. When he finally paused for breath—"I think I've told you a story like that, haven't I?"—I nodded and said, "Mr. President, the other comment I've got about you is indirect, because it was originally made about Lord Melbourne, Queen Victoria's first Prime Minister." The Dixon look came into his face again, and he glanced at the clock. We were five minutes into overtime. "It's from the biography by Lord David Cecil."

Trying to keep his attention, I explained that the passage reminded me of his own repeated claims that he had had to be "dragged kicking and screaming" into politics. Then I read it aloud, as he sucked in a series of huge, deep sighs:

> If circumstances should happen to push him into a position of power, he was perfectly ready to take it on; for men and their affairs inspired him with far too little respect for him to shrink from assuming responsibility for them. But, on the other hand, he did not think it worth while stirring a finger to mould circumstances to his will. Smiling, indolent and inscrutable he lay, a pawn in the hands of fortune.

"Does that sound like Ronald Reagan to you?"

He hadn't registered a word after my own "kicking and screaming."

The phrase, instantly spinning his anecdotal rolodex, had already directed him to November 9, 1966. "If I heard you correctly," Dutch said with relief, "the morning after the vote was in, the first question was, was I going to be a favorite-son candidate for President? And I said . . ."

I let my Sony do the listening. Fortunately I had several photocopied pages of Cecil's biography in my folder, and read them with surreptitious enjoyment while Dutch retraced his steps to the '68 Republican Convention. The great clock ticked on and on. I was amazed that Jim Kuhn had not come in to end our interview on schedule. Probably—generous young fellow!—he was compensating me for foreshortened sessions in the past.

Dutch continued until the recorder signaled its cassette was full. I took advantage of the change of tape to tease him about not kicking and screaming very loudly in 1976.

"The only reason for doing that in '76," he said, lips very thin, "was, I was never too high on Gerald Ford. I didn't think that he had done anything very impressive here."

"However," I suggested, "he did help pull this nation together after Nixon's resignation. His finest moment was when he came out of the house and said, 'My fellow Americans, our long national nightmare is over. Our Constitution works.' "

The President lapsed into contemptuous silence, then suddenly began to weave his head. He swatted the air with his good hand.

"Is a bug after you?"

"It's a gnat! Down South they call 'em 'no-see-ums.' "

Emulating the bug, I tried a surprise attack. "What about the homeless? Do you think you could have done anything for them?"

"Well, the damn thing is, it's been so exaggerated. *Millions*," he snorted. "There aren't millions. Real research reveals probably three hundred thousand or less, nationwide. And a lot of those are the type of people that have made that choice. For example, more than forty percent of them are retarded, mentally deficient people—that is a result of the Civil Liberties Union."

Noted, once more. He spoke with genuine concern about the irresponsibility that had exposed these unfortunates to urban predators and the elements. But with the quick anger that is often a sign of physical pain—he plucked constantly at the now hot-looking plastic bag—he launched into a diatribe against those "refugees" from areas of low employment who learn how to massage liberal neuroses. "Look at the girl in New York who went to court after Koch had ordered her to get off the street and be put in a shelter. She went to court, and actually fought, under her Constitutional rights, to go on living in that card-board box on the street, where she shit in the gutter, and peed in it, and so forth."

He tried to recall who "—oh, what's his name? He's very big on tele-vision—" was currently making political capital out of such rights.

"Mitch Snyder."

"This," Dutch hissed, "is the world's biggest phony. I understand he makes pretty good money in his speaking engagements."

I started to say something, not in disagreement, but that printer of Udell's was back on the public platform of a distant, dreamed-of city, lecturing an audience of Practical Christians: "There's a lot of unused shelter space in Washington, public shelter space, and in addition to that a lot of people that are really waiting to get in a home, and so forth, to go to private shelters, like churches, and so forth, and be taken care of . . ." His voice tailed off, and I felt—I shared—the exhaustion of great age. *RR,* I scribbled, *is the tiredest man I have ever seen.*

"I don't know what more you can do," Dutch whispered.

"Did it ever occur to you, Mr. President," I said as gently as I could, "that your own father might have become a hobo?"

He did not flinch. "Yes. If it wasn't for his wife and two kids—"

"I'm sorry to bother you," said Jim Kuhn, entering noiselessly, "but I told Dr. Hutton to be ready at four-fifteen to look at that paw there."

"Having any pain?" I asked as I stood up.

He shook his glossy head and looked at me without smiling. I knew he was having plenty.

A few minutes later, as I stood in the outer office chatting with Kathy Osborne, Dutch's secretary, it occurred to me I should have taken leave of him as President more formally. Other farewells would preoccupy his time in the days ahead. So I waited until he came through to deposit his last mail of the day on Kathy's desk.

"I forgot to say good-bye, Mr. President."

Not expecting him to be in the least bit moved, I was unmoved my-self. "I hope I'll be able to see you from time to time in L.A.," I said, "but not too often, because you'll probably charge for interviews now."

He chuckled. "No, yours will be free."

I took his hand. "Well, good-bye, sir—"

He put his other, bagged hand over mine, interrupting me. "I always feel that I go on so long you don't have a chance to ask me all your questions."

"Not this time," I said. "Except maybe one."

"What was that?"

"Do you believe in evil? Have you ever met a purely evil person?"

"Well, no person. But I believe evil exists."

"As in 'evil empire'?"

"Yes." He let go of my hand. "It was evil, until he—until this one man made all the difference."

"So you do believe in the power of human goodness."

"Of course!" he said, contact lenses twinkling. "That's what it's all about."

The twinkle slid off as he turned to speak to Kathy, and with it slid my reflection from his eyes, and all consciousness of me from his brain.

Diary, Wednesday, January 11—At eight-thirty this evening I go down to the White House to hear the President's last speech. It is a poignant occasion, all of us sitting in the glaring, gutted Oval Office (stripped of its comforts in order to look "comfortable" on television), aware that we are watching the end of a historic relationship with the American people.

His presence in the room makes itself felt, at 8:45, by an indraft of cold air from the Rose Garden and a sudden drop in the sound level of our conversation. Dutch looks, as usual, larger than life in dark blue. He crosses surefootedly to his desk, moving among the cable coils like a panther in deep jungle. This is the kind of thing he does best; his eyes, like Jeeves's after a fish dinner, "shine with the light of pure intelligence." He sits down and at once begins to stare at the monitor, waiting for his image—his real self—to pop up: "Ah! There he is!"

His pleased smile fades into a look of practiced geniality as, still staring, he recomposes the image to his liking. Does he glimpse, I wonder, a boy's face, a flash of a red cloak in that clear pool? Someone puts a glass of hot water, wrapped in a white napkin, into his hand. He takes a purposeful sip, evidently the first of many, and begins to read through the speech (Peggy Noonan, tense, black-smocked, follows the movement of his eyes, knowing just what paragraph of which page he is absorbing). He is a million miles away from us, conscious of nothing but the white pages before him and the glass at his elbow. At regular intervals he reaches for it (eyes never straying from the paper) and drinks, steam waving around his nose and cheeks, pinkening them. He begins to declaim the speech *mezza voce,* miniature expressions playing across his face, rather too rapidly for ordinary communication. In the VCR of his mind, he is operating at fast-forward. Thus, the twenty-minute speech is rehearsed in ten minutes. He has five minutes left to visit with us and finish his hot water.

"Nobody noticed this desk is darker," he says, making conversation, and drumming on the timbers of HMS *Resolute.* "It's just been restored." He catches sight of me and winks. "Hey, Edmund." He has hardly ever addressed me by name. I wink back, trying to restrain a surge of adoration, reminding myself that we are all audience to his perpetual performance.

"Two minutes to the President!" the producer calls out, and the room goes silent. Dutch finishes his glass, and it is whisked away. The silence becomes more silent as the seconds tick by—literally, inside the grandfather clock just behind me. I have a sense of this quietness spreading out through the french door (still draftily ajar) and enveloping the whole country. But he spoils it by pulling out a spotless handkerchief and trumpeting with surprising energy. The effect is Hiroshimic. He is purposefully deflating tension, and there is a mischievous glint in his eye as he tucks the handkerchief away. Both hands on the typescript; eyes on the monitor. "Please God," I say in my head, "let his nose fade." Amazingly, it does. "One minute, Mr. President." Now the silence is as brittle as ice. It is too much for him: he must break it again. "Have I time to make a phone call?" Laughter. "Thirty seconds." Suddenly we have lost him; his head bows, he stares into the dark leather of his desk, his body seems to shrink. "What the hell's he doing?" Peggy Noonan hisses, terrified. "Praying?" "Just concentrating his faculties," I hazard. What do I know? Maybe he's reciting Robert W. Service. "Ten—nine—eight . . ." Dutch emerges from the abyss, sees Peggy distraught, winks and smiles at her. "Five—four . . ." He mushrooms before our eyes, shoulders rising, head rearing into position, the big chest filling with air, the irrigated throat preparing to vibrate. "Two—one . . ." There is no "zero," just a chop of the hand in front of the camera, and that movement "cuts" him off from us, his support system, the White House staff agog before the great set in the Roosevelt Room, Nancy Reagan statue-still and staring upstairs in the Residence. For a splinter of a second, he is the loneliest person I have ever seen. Then his lips part, and out comes a big, husky, extraordinarily beautiful syllable: "MY." By the time he gets to "fellow Americans," the lonely man is once again President of all the people.

My fellow Americans, this is the thirty-fourth time I'll speak to you from the Oval Office, and the last. We have been together eight years now, and soon it will be time for me to go.

"These leaves, your lips," I think as I watch them caress Peggy's expertly varied monosyllables. It is a long speech, a sentimental recapitulation of the "great triumphs" he has presided over. Chief of them are the recovery of the economy, and of national morale. He advocates "an informed patriotism" based on "more attention to American history and a greater emphasis on civic ritual." His peroration is initially thrilling:

I've spoken of the Shining City all my political life, but I don't know if I ever quite communicated what I saw when I said it . . .

Alas, he now proceeds to communicate too damn much by half, or I should say Peggy's script does, penetrating the City's luminiferous radiance with such precision of lens and infrared filter as to expose all sorts of mundane detail—beacons and granite ridges, walls with doors, and ports humming with commerce and creativity—that vaporizes the essence of his vision: its splendid, its cloudy, its Parsivalian vagueness.

It is a relief when he returns to simple rhythms:

My friends, we did it. . . . We made the City freer, and we left her in good hands. All in all not bad, not bad at all. And so, goodbye. God bless you, and God bless the United States of America.

Afterward, as the still photographers rush in to click and genuflect, he sits half smiling, miming speech with his lips, tilting his head to accommodate their cameras. Anybody else putting on this charade would look silly, in view of the drama we have already witnessed, but Reagan's poise is such that he remains somehow majestic. Is not the height of professionalism, I ask myself, attention to the lowliest detail?

The technicians awkwardly proffer champagne to celebrate their thirty-four sessions with him. He sips and listens, smiling, hearing nothing, then gives a little wave and lets Jim Kuhn take him off into the night.

☯

Thursday the nineteenth was Dutch's last workday in the Oval Office. I went down to the White House after lunch and hung around on the off chance something might happen. Lachrymose "lowlifes," disappointed of tenure by the incoming administration, were clearing their offices and commiserating. At three-thirty, the senior staff was summoned to a final joint audience with the President and Vice President before tomorrow's ceremonies. There were about sixty of us in the Roosevelt Room, almost suffocated by heat and communal emotion. When Dutch came in, pale in his brown suit, he looked oddly diminished by his six-foot-three-inch heir. It was Bush's meeting. "I came by to say thank you," he said, in his flat voice, "for the last eight years. Believe me, I wouldn't be President—" (*But you're not!* we mutely chorused) "—if it hadn't been for my, uh, teacher here." Reagan gave the obligatory duck of the head.

"We all feel richer for what he has done," Bush continued. "In all the eight years I've been here, I've never heard him say anything about the loneliness of his job. I remember an article Lloyd Cutler wrote during the Carter years, saying that the job had become too much for any man, and maybe it was time for a parliamentary system in the United States. Well, that was before Ronald Reagan came along."

He stepped aside for the President, who said in mock gratitude, "You know, in eight years, George never once took my pulse!" The room rang with laughter. Dutch grew serious. "Nancy and I couldn't have done it without the—without the help of—" He gestured with his splint, reluctant to name him again—"of the man standing beside me. This is a bittersweet time, this leave-taking. A lot of pangs go with it." His voice husked.

e

At 4:15 I went and sat with Kathy Osborne, wanting to see Dutch leave the Oval Office for the last time. It was quiet in the little antechamber; Kathy had done most of her packing, and her file drawers, freshly vacuumed, awaited another woman's paraphernalia. The President's door was closed; every now and again, protectively, she went to the spy hole to check on him. "Who's he with, Kathy?"

"No one."

At 4:55 the President came out. He glanced past me unseeing and said to nobody in particular, "Well, I gotta go up and pack." As he stepped to the french door, he noticed Kathy's distraught face and winked at her. A blast of air, and he was gone.

I went out onto the colonnade and watched him cross to the Residence with Jim Kuhn at his side. He walked quickly, head down, listening to something Jim was saying about tomorrow's schedule. He did not give the Rose Garden a glance; they moved like men with business still to do.

After the swing doors of the conservatory had swung shut behind them, I stood taking my last look at the garden.

It was an almost springlike evening, and the grass and dormant plants gave off an exquisite chill fragrance. The metropolitan freeways, invisible beyond the grounds, rumbled distantly, but here all was silence. I heard the puzzled cheep of a starling wondering whether to sing or not. Yellow diamonds flashed through the dark trees beyond the South Lawn: the sun was setting over Virginia, duplicating itself, hundreds of times over, in the windows of the Department of Commerce. I gazed up at the family corner of the Residence, caught in its last rays. Hoban's white moldings glowed with unreal purity, as if rendered by Maxfield Parrish. Over the roof shot the high soundless silverfish of a vapor trail, streaming southwest in the exact direction Dutch would take tomorrow. Something surprised the starlings; they scattered across the sky and vanished, like grains of pepper blown across a tablecloth. From down Pennsylvania Avenue came the sound of the Old Post Office clock chiming five. To all intents and purposes, the Presidency of Ronald Reagan was at its close.

On my way back through the West Wing, I stopped by the Roosevelt Room, where I had attended my first staff meeting three years and two months before. It was clean, glowing, empty, with twenty-six deep leather chairs awaiting twenty-six new occupants, and twenty-six fresh White House pads with sharp pencils tucked into them. I stood there for a while, hearing again Donald Regan's tirades and those frequent deep roars of collegial male laughter, brought to an end by the Iran Initiative. I straightened the portrait of Theodore Roosevelt, then went out via the Northwest Gate and surrendered my pass.

Inauguration Day dawned dry but blustery, with intermittent sun that gave way to gray sky as noon approached. Notwithstanding yesterday's finality, I found myself going back to the White House to watch the motorcade leave. In the West Wing basement, I ran into Colin Powell, magnificently uniformed. "You missed the President's farewell to the Oval Office," he said.

"But I was there when he left last night," I protested.

"Yeah, well, we realized that nobody had photographed his exit, so we brought him back this morning to pretend a little for the record."

"In that case, I'm glad I wasn't around."

He seemed put out, as if he had wanted to tell me something, so I said, "Anyway, what happened?"

"Well, to add some meaning to it, I thought I'd give him his last national-security briefing. He was standing at that empty desk, looking rather spare, so I went up to him and said, kind of formally, 'Mr. President, the world is quiet today.'"

We looked at each other for a moment. "That was nice of you, General," I said. "That was a nice thing to say."

"And true, too."

"Then what?"

"Then he did what he was told—you know, tapping the empty desk and stuff, while the cameras rolled, and going to the door and looking back sentimentally, one more time."

"Oh, please."

"But you know what I was thinking while all that went on? This was the conclusion of a big dramatic production. Here we were, his senior staffers, all of us who directed him and scripted him and made him up and gave him his cues. And here were the cameramen, the sound guys, the light holders and the grips. And there, all alone against the backdrop of the Oval Office, was Ronald Reagan shooting his last take."

❡

From the driveway came a revving of police motorcycle engines. I went out and stood by the North Portico. Nancy Reagan, her face stiff and staring, was escorted past me on the way to her limousine. I blew her a kiss, feeling absolutely no emotion. The great procession got under way, reticulating itself slowly around the corner of Fifteenth Street. When the last flashing light had disappeared from sight, I took a military bus to Andrews Air Force Base, getting there just in time to see the swearing in of George Bush on television. Chief Justice Rehnquist introduced him to the audience as "the President of the United States," and I felt, like a tiny drop of ice in my stomach, the transfer of power away from Ronald Reagan.

About forty-five minutes later he and Nancy arrived by helicopter, and he reviewed his last honor guard, stepping as always in sync with his escort. The wind whipping across the ramp drove his trousers against his shins, making him look—how shall I say?—suddenly aged. Of all his Cabinet officers, only John Herrington was there to see him off. No Shultz. No Powell. No Carlucci. As the joke cards said, "He's history." But there was a large crowd of ordinary Americans and their children—among them a crying West Wing secretary, whom I cuddled. "I just had to see him through," she said, her face red as bacon in the wind.

Dutch mounted the stairs of AF 27000—as of noon, no longer Air Force One—waved, and at that moment, with entire predictability, the sun flooded out of the cloud cover, bathing us all in its pallid warmth. Trust the Actor to go out with a spotlight on him!

Epilogue

Four years later Ronald Reagan returned to the White House, at the reluctant invitation of President Bush, to receive the Medal of Freedom before William Jefferson Clinton took office. I attended, along with five hundred other former appointees and associates wistful for their days of glory. Even Don Regan and John Poindexter showed up. The latter had the gray transparency of someone sucked dry by legal process, as did Cap Weinberger. Bush himself looked disillusioned, and a touch resentful as he led Dutch into the East Room. He must have known that the event's main purpose was to bring together, once more, veterans of what would always be remembered as the Reagan Era. "Just think," sniffled Kathy Osborne, "the next time we'll all see each other will be under the rotunda of the Capitol!"

When Dutch—eighty-one years old now—stepped to the podium to give a short speech of thanks, his voice was rough and his delivery slow. But he still personified *la notion de l'état,* and the room was hushed with respect for him. "God bless," he concluded, for perhaps the millionth time in his life, "the United States of America." He said it so reverently that I wondered if, for all his uxorial protestations, love for country was not Ronald Reagan's one and only passion.

Afterward, in the receiving line, he took my hand and nodded with patent lack of recognition. His eyes were dulled by the confusion that had been lowering upon him since our trip to Tampico, eight months before. Or so I thought. "Still dressing up for the camera, Mr. President?" I said, nodding at the brilliant bauble around his neck. "Oh—yes, heh heh"—and he shifted his attention to the next in line.

Well, it had to happen, I told myself as I moved on to the champagne table. *Dutch finally stopped recognizing me.*

Yet the following afternoon, Fred Ryan, his retirement chief of staff, called from Los Angeles to say that Reagan had remarked, flying home, "I saw Edmund in the reception line this morning. And you know what? I think he's waiting for me to die before he publishes his book." So yet again I had to brood, *How much does Dutch know?* Even in his dotage, he had seen something in my gaze that I did not want to acknowledge.

☯

Less than a month later he gave his first public evidence of cognitive frailty. I attended his eighty-second birthday celebration at the Ronald Reagan Presidential Library in Simi Valley, along with several hundred other guests, including Margaret Thatcher, and we all froze when he toasted her twice, at length, and in exactly the same words. There was nothing we could do but give her two standing ovations, and not look too closely at Nancy Reagan's stricken face, while Dutch stood obliviously smiling.

After that, I visited with him as often as I could, whenever I went to Los Angeles on research. He no longer traveled if he could help it, exhibiting distinct signs of panic at any itinerary that ranged farther afield than Santa Barbara. On April 2, I went to his big suite of offices—at the top of the highest glass tower on the Avenue of the Stars, at the crest of Century City—and found him sitting alone at his desk, bent over what I assumed to be work. But it was only the comic strips from the *Los Angeles Times,* neatly cut out for his enjoyment. I asked him if he had any important events coming up, and he floundered a bit until he found his schedule. "Here, let me show you this." The following day, Saturday, he had to open an exhibition of presidential memorabilia, "From Washington to Clinton," at the Ronald Reagan Library. On Monday morning he would host a reception for Prime Minister Brian Mulroney of Canada. Thereafter the schedule consisted, soothingly, of nothing but the word *RANCH,* for page after page after page.

"Will you be coming to the opening?" he asked, and without listening to my answer pointed at a framed photograph he had shown me several times before. It showed the five surviving Presidents standing shoulder to shoulder at the dedication of his Library in 1990, flashing their usual ceremonial smiles: Bush's aimless, Reagan's carefully rehearsed, Carter's not so much a grin as an exposure of teeth too large for his lips, Gerald Ford's mirthless, Nixon's an impatient cut-this-crap snarl.

"Guess who's the oldest man there," Dutch said.

His lunch was wheeled in, and he walked toward it eagerly, forgetting me. I took my leave of him—"See you tomorrow, Mr. President"—as he shook out his starched napkin and sat down to eat without another word. This struck me as strange, but nothing like as strange as his eerie willingness to sit there alone, silently spooning up soup, in full view of anybody who happened to be outside.

At five the next afternoon I drove out to the Library—a long, low, Mission-style building overlooking the Pacific from its own hilltop—and heard that he and Nancy were "holding" in their private parlor upstairs. I went up to see them and found her lying on the sofa, looking small and weary, while Dutch stood with his back to the picture window.

"I hear you're coming to New York for a round of ladies' lunches, Nancy," I said.

"Shoosh," she whispered, "he doesn't know yet."

He watched us incuriously, detached by his deafness. The setting sun silhouetted him and set his pompadour on fire. His shoulders were still lifeguard-broad, and his legs straight and strong. But when we went down to the ribbon cutting, I noticed how bowed his back had become. He seemed to clutch his wife's hand for guidance now, rather than mere companionship.

At the end of that month I participated in Hofstra University's Ronald Reagan Presidential Conference, which was attended by numerous scholars from the former Soviet Union. *The former:* what unimaginable dissolution and destruction, as of a comet sideswiping half the planet, lay behind that innocuous phrase! Here were we presenting our papers and arguing the finer points of economic and diplomatic theory, as sedately as if forty million Russians had not died, and half the world's potential economy not been immobilized, under the most brutal tyranny in human history—before one man (as Dutch would say) had the courage to say to another man, in front of all his cheekboned stalwarts, *Let me tell you why we mistrust you and are suspicious of you.* The same man, indeed, who in 1983 had simply and accurately equated totalitarianism with Evil.

The proceedings opened with much pageantry and four formal addresses by Mike Wallace, Ralph Bledsoe, myself, and Edwin Meese, in that order. We wore enough silk to festoon the royal court of Morocco, and respectively reviewed Ronald Reagan's personality, presidential policies, rhetorical imagery, and west-of-the-Hudson conservatism.

After lunch, the plenary assembly broke into smaller panels, each debating specialized areas of study. Wandering from one room to another, I thought how amused Dutch would be to find himself analyzed under such pompous rubrics as "Hazardous Waste, Regulatory Reform, and the Reagan Revolution: The Ironies of an Activist Approach to Deactivating Bureaucracy." Even though he was more interested in comics than Communism nowadays, I found myself writing a report for him. I felt he should be made aware, however dimly, that his historical image was beginning to take shape, and that its mass looked large:

> I attended a discussion of your use of the Cabinet, in which the principal speaker noted that Ronald Reagan, unlike his recent predecessors, really did decentralize power from the White House to the departments. . . . Then there was a panel on "Reagan and the Conservatives." Marty Anderson gave a review of your economic reforms, insofar as they still affect the 1990s, and a prof. called Andrew Busch said that as President you amounted to a combination of Jefferson and Hamilton, with the former strain predominating ("wise and frugal government," etc.). He said that unlike Jefferson you were not a rewriter of your own previous policies. . . .
>
> Frank Fahrenkopf told an interesting anecdote about Zbigniew Brzezinski being asked, at a recent public meeting in Berlin, when the Cold War was won. "This may surprise you," said Zbig, "but I think it was won at Reykjavík."

A forum followed in which the veteran journalist Lou Cannon—for thirty years Dutch's most dispassionate chronicler—nicely called him "a mirror of the American people" and praised his anti-nuclear and pro-Israel stances. But Cannon also leveled many economic criticisms, and made the alarming accusation that "if all Reagan's budgets had been passed as written, we would still have 92 percent of the deficit."

Two presidential professors said grudgingly that Dutch had been right to stand firm in the PATCO strike. One of them, Henry F. Graff of Columbia University, got a big laugh when he remarked, "If Carter had done it, there would have been a crash the next week." The other, Herbert S. Parmet of Queensborough College, felt that Reagan's most significant achievement, politically speaking, had been to capture the loyalty of blue-collar Democrats. He doubted that future Republican candidates would manage to do the same.

> After dinner the first night [I wrote Dutch], a huge forum discussed your U.S.-Soviet relations. Ken Adelman commanded the pro-Reagan forces splendidly, stating what became a theme of the entire conference—namely, that it was your obduracy over the SDI that caused that brittle monolith to collapse, and brought about "fundamental world change." A German historian named Ullmann argued that on the contrary, the USSR collapsed because of its own economic despair, and would have done so anyway, no matter who was President of the United States. He said this nation had squandered its own technological advantage, and challenged us to name a single U.S. manufacturer of U.S. laptop computers. He seemed disconcerted when a fellow panelist presented him with a list of several.
>
> Jack Matlock, one of the stars of the conference (lucid, erudite, impassioned, yet controlled), talked of Russian puzzlement at the reluctance of American intellectuals to give you any diplomatic credit. He emphasized that the Soviet Union remained a threat to this country through the mid-eighties, and quoted Marshal Yazov telling him, "Until Chernobyl, I was convinced we could fight a nuclear war with the United States and win."

Another former American envoy, Arnold A. Saltzman, said he "didn't believe that SDI helped the peace process one minute." Computers, not "imaginary lasers" had won the Cold War: the Soviets had felt themselves increasingly isolated from the Western technological revolution. Gorbachev had personally told him that a generation was growing up there who felt starved of the consumer benefits young Westerners took for granted.

The most inflammatory language of the evening came from Genrikh A. Trofimenko, a former Brezhnev adviser and U.S. expert at the Soviet Academy of Sciences, now lecturing at Columbia. "Ronald Reagan was tackling world gangsters of the first order of magnitude," he screeched. "Ninety-nine percent of Russian people believe that you won the Cold War because of your President's insistence on SDI. Yet the greatest flimflam man of all time, Mikhail Gorbachev, was made the Nobel Peace Prize laureate."

Don Oberdorfer, the diplomatic correspondent of *The Washington Post,* spoke honestly of his own misapprehensions of Ronald Reagan as a nuclear warrior in the early 1980s. He confessed that reviewing the facts of that decade, for his new book *The Turn,* had taught him that journalism is only "the first rough draft of history."

There was a predictably contentious session on international terrorism the following day, April 23. With some trepidation, I included it in my report to Dutch:

> Professor Yonah Alexander of George Washington University reviewed the "bloody record" of some eight hundred terrorist acts directed against U.S. interests from 1981 to 1989. You certainly had to contend with a lot of painful emergencies. While praising your Administration's role in containing terrorism and in increasing public awareness of its unacceptability, he said that the Iran Initiative fatally damaged your plausibility as a President who promised not to deal with hostage takers. I am afraid this is the pretty universal view of thinking men (although Michael Ledeen and Constantine Menges came valiantly to your defense), and it is something you are going to have to live with.

There was a rather repetitive debate on Reagan defense policy, in which speaker after speaker again sounded the themes of the SDI and Reykjavík as crucial to the downfall of Communism. Kenneth Adelman pointed out that Reagan's vaunted military buildup had never been more than 7 percent of the U.S. gross national product—as opposed to an estimated Soviet level of 25 percent, or even Mr. Trofimenko's incredible suggestion of "nearly 50 percent."

The most sincere tribute to Dutch's leadership came during this session, when Paul Nitze was finally prevailed upon to get up and say something. Small and silver-haired, he spoke so quietly that many attendees missed the import of his remark, but I noted it down because he was a lifelong Democrat who had served every President since Truman. "The first time I met Ronald Reagan I admired him," he said, "and when I went to work for him I admired him more and more. . . . I ended up thinking he was a great man."

There was an unintentionally comic foreign-policy conference, keynoted by Stephen Ambrose of the University of New Orleans, keeper of the Nixon flame. He gave what he called "an overview" of Dutch's diplomatic record, and said that it consisted largely of "screwups." Having listed them at length, however, he had to conclude, "Not in half a century has a President handed over a foreign policy to his successor in such good shape." There was some laughter, and Ambrose said defensively, "Maybe Reagan was just lucky."

"Lucky like a fox," somebody behind me muttered.

A professor from the University of Virginia named Whittle Johnston gave an erudite and moving analysis of the Westminster Address (which he compared to the Bill of Rights and Franklin Roosevelt's "Four Freedoms" declaration as a basic document of U.S. policy). *En passant,* he had a good one-liner to the effect that "Eisenhower had the military-industrial complex to contend with; Reagan had the academic-media complex."

Few other conferees said anything worth recording, with the exception of James C. Miller III, Reagan's second Budget Director, who recalled a historic exchange between the President of the United States and a Southern governor exasperated by conservationist legislation:

GOVERNOR   Mist' Presiden', Ah want ter know why a b'ar needs more fresh air than a yumin bein'.

REAGAN   (*thoughtfully*) Well, Governor, have you ever smelled a bear?

Needless to say, I made sure to include that one in my letter to Dutch.

For most of the rest of the year I worked steadily at his biography. Brian Mulroney—out of office now, and settled in Montreal—called to boast that of all the G7 Western leaders, "I was the one Ronnie felt closest to. . . . Often, the others would come to me to try and gauge what he was thinking, how he'd react to this and that."

"How did *they* react to him?"

"With increasing respect. He had a simple but very definite power. Mitterrand said to me, 'You know, Brian, I like your friend Ronnie. *Mais il est dans ses pensées un théocrate.*' "

It takes a secular voluptuary to recognize Practical Christianity. No matter how cornball Dutch's regular references to "the Man Upstairs," he really did dream of a godly government staffed by semi-clerical believers, practicing universal charity and exercising retribution on the wicked. Mulroney, rambling on, ventured his own epigram: "If Reagan's beliefs were few, and stripped of sophistication, they were also stripped of sophistry."

This comment applied pretty well to the four leather-bound volumes of Dutch's presidential diary, which I read in the conference room at Fox Plaza while he sat next door puzzling out the perils of Mary Worth. I calculated the document's total length at about half a million words, handwritten every night (or sometimes, when the script was especially trembly, during spare time aboard his helicopter). On one level it was boring enough to glaze the eyes, with its daily, dogged listing of events already printed in his schedule. Not one sentence, not even the odd stray phrase, was colored with original observation. But on another level Dutch's diary was coldly impressive, the work of a man who knew exactly what he believed and wanted and was not interested in anyone else's dreams. Policy decisions were entered tersely, often without explanation and always without doubt. Presidents and prime ministers, Nobel laureates, monks, hunks, farmers, princes, and refugees visited the Oval Office, saying nothing memorable, educating him in no way, leaving behind them no fragrance of personality. It was the same at the Residence and Camp David. His children came and went (their departures carefully noted). Movies were shown, always enjoyable; every smile was happy, every little girl cute, and at all social events "a good time was had by all." The only idiosyncracy, apart from his fascination with jet lag, was an extreme conscientiousness in tabulating the number of times his speeches were interrupted by applause.

Oddly enough, though, the diary lacked vanity. Those bursts of applause merely monitored his ongoing performance; he noted them with as little self-satisfaction as a runner timing laps. A speech interrupted only three times was a speech that had to be worked on some more; standing ovations before he began meant less than those following his traditional snapper, "God bless America." He never praised himself, or crowed after victories, or took undue credit. (The reverse of those statements also applied.) Nowhere did I detect that manipulative "posterity" note so often evident in Theodore Roosevelt's diaries.

One further fact struck me. The diary—all eight years of it—was uniform in style and cognitive content from beginning to end. There was no hint of mental deterioration beyond occasional repetitions and non sequiturs; and if those were suggestive of early dementia, many diarists including myself would have reason to worry.

On December 20, 1993, I flew to San Luis Obispo to interview the only man who ever got within a furlong of intimacy with Dutch, his fellow lone ranger, William P. Clark. He greeted me in a dusty Mercedes, and we drove to his law office in Paso Robles.

I found the Judge (as Clark is still generally known) much aged since his departure from the White House eight years before, driven west by Nancy's unflagging jealousy. She had always been rendered insecure by her husband's pleasure in the society of a man who never said anything. She did not understand one of the strangest things about the Great Communicator: that on horseback in male company, or working with "the fellows" around the ranch, he expressed himself mainly in mono-syllables and grunts. When Ron and Bill went riding, indeed, their mounts contributed most of the sound effects.

Today Clark revealed himself to be, like many taciturn men, a cy-clone of private emotions. Age and illness—he was losing his sight from Lyme disease—unlocked his lips to such an extent that I was re-minded of a similar interview with Lew Wasserman, some years before. Alas, however, he was no more successful than Lew in articulating Dutch's "cool intensity"—the long-ago phrase of Pat Brown's that had kept coming into my head as I read the diary.

The *Leitmotiv* of his reminiscences was that Dutch was a substitute for his adored father, a "cattleman and law-enforcement officer" who never had thanked him for any favor. "Didn't have to. I knew he was grateful. Ronald Reagan was the same. Whenever he came into the room, as Governor or President, he didn't need to say anything, I could tell what he wanted. Just like when my dad brought stock into the cor-ral: I never had to ask him which gate I should open."

I gathered from this that he had not heard from Dutch in recent years. "Not directly, no. But a friend of mine at the Cowboy Hall of Fame called up a few months ago and said that he's, uh, kind of con-fused these days. Asked him, 'Now Ronnie, what about Bill Clark? Why don't you see him anymore?' And there was a little tear in his eye, and all he could do was shake his head and say, 'Ah, Bill and I go a long way back.' "

At this Clark put his hands to his eyes and wept. It was some time before he regained control of himself. After lunch, he showed me a Catholic chapel he was building at his ranch, then flew me back to San Luis Obispo in his private Bird Dog, over winter-brown grasslands.

When Richard Nixon died on April 22, 1994, I was at Fox Plaza going through Dutch's scrapbooks. Word came down the corridor that the arrival of the coffin at El Toro was being shown live on CNN, and I went to the crowded press office to watch. After a moment or two I was taken aback to realize that the large brown presence in a side chair was Dutch. He watched the screen with extraordinary attention, quiet and sad and motionless, long legs stretched out and pale fingertips joined. I noticed that his staff, mainly young women, had gotten into the habit of talking over his head, as if he were no longer there.

Nancy told me afterward that Nixon's demise had brought home to him the full import of his oft-repeated remark about being the oldest living ex-President. And it showed the next day at Yorba Linda, when the five in his wall photograph were visibly reduced to four. Dutch listened to the eulogies and execrable music with a strained, deaf man's look, his mouth slightly open. Probably he had turned off his hearing aid. But he did not miss the tearing sweep across the sky of six F-16s, the inexorable slow rhythm of cannon shots, and, most beautiful of all, the geometry by which Old Glory was folded, triangle upon triangle, in white-gloved hands.

That summer, doctors at the Mayo Clinic confirmed what they had provisionally diagnosed a year before, and what everyone watching the Nixon funeral could plainly see: that Ronald Reagan was in the preliminary stages of degenerative cognitive dementia. He knew himself that something was badly wrong—had known it, I suspect, ever since a riding accident in July 1989 had inflicted a massive contusion on his brain. But now the degeneration had passed beyond trauma, and his last public decision must be when and how to announce it. "On a good day, I oughta let them know."

Discussing the news privately with young Ron—of all Dutch's children, the only one to inherit his peculiar grace—I said that I had found a reproduction of Leonardo da Vinci's *Codex Leicester* in a tin trunk at the Reagan Library, and been struck by a page of jottings on the occlusion of the moon. Delightfully wrongheaded, they speculated that the moon's light was reflected onto it by the earth, and that it grew dim only when it receded. "I've always felt there was something lunar about your father. The closer he got to us, the more he glowed, but since he turned away and drifted off, he's slowly lost his luster."

Dutch delayed his announcement through the beginning of November, by which time action became necessary because the San Diego

Union-Tribune was said to be working on a story. Family, friends, doctors, and aides urged him to write the text himself, in his own hand, so that the world would see the words were his own. Sullen at first, then resigned, he shut himself in his study and wrote the following valedictory on two sheets of thick paper, embossed with his presidential seal:

RONALD REAGAN

Nov. 5, 1994

My Fellow Americans,

I have recently been told that I am one of the millions of Americans who will be afflicted with Alzheimer's Disease.

Upon learning this news, Nancy & I had to decide whether as private citizens we would keep this a private matter or whether we would make this news known in a public way.

In the past Nancy suffered from breast cancer and I had my cancer surgeries. We found through our open disclosures we were able to raise public awareness. We were happy that as a result many more people underwent testing. They were treated in early stages and able to return to normal, healthy lives.

So now, we feel it is important to share it with you. In opening our hearts, we hope this might promote greater awareness of this condition. Perhaps it will encourage a clearer understanding of the individuals and families who are affected by it.

At the moment I feel just fine. I intend to live the remainder of the years God gives me on this earth doing the things I have always done. I will continue to share life's journey with my beloved Nancy and my family. I plan to enjoy the great outdoors and stay in touch with my friends and supporters.

Unfortunately, as Alzheimer's Disease progresses, the family often bears a heavy burden. I only wish there was some way I could spare Nancy from this painful experience. When the time comes I am confident that with your help she will face it with faith and courage.

In closing let me thank you, the American people for giving me the great honor of allowing me to serve as your President. When the Lord calls me home, ~~whenever that~~ whenever that may be, I will leave with the greatest love for this country of ours and eternal optimism for its future.

I now begin the journey that will lead me into the sunset of my life. I know that for America there will always be a a bright dawn ahead.

Thank you my friends. May God always bless you.

Sincerely,

Ronald Reagan

The letter was reproduced in facsimile on November 6, in newspapers around the world. My wife and I read it as we walked home from our newsstand in Washington, and for the first time in my life I felt love for Ronald Reagan, and overpowering sadness.

Later, I called Nancy Reagan to say, or try to say, the inadequate things that come to mind when a tragedy of this dimension strikes. "I don't know if this is of any comfort to you, but Max Kampelman wants to give him a prize on behalf of the U.S. Institute of Peace, whether he understands it or not."

"Well, that's very nice of Max. Uh, we'll see."

"How *is* he, Nancy?"

Unguarded for once, she said that Dutch's deterioration over the last six months had been dramatic, with the final letting-go coming immediately after finishing his letter. "After all that's happened to him—the assassination attempt, the cancer, the riding accident—I just can't believe this. It's worse than anything. I'm a doctor's daughter, I can handle anything medical, but not . . . this." She sobbed into the receiver.

In Los Angeles on December 9, 1994, I braced myself and went to see Dutch in his skyscraper suite. When I entered his office, he was sitting in the same quiet pose he always assumed during "personal time" at the White House: glossy head tilted forward, jacket sleeves half on his desk, white cuffs protruding exactly one inch, his black Parker lying ready on its own polished leather reflection. He rose with his usual air of gentle surprise, but I got the feeling that if I had come in through the window he would have reacted no differently. As I made desperate small talk, he held on to the edge of his desk.

"Mr. President, those lead soldiers make a great display with all your books! Like when you were sick with pneumonia in 1915, and played with armies on the counterpane?" He smiled faintly, not remembering, and I noticed something unimaginable before: a patch of silvery stubble on his chin. It glowed incandescently as a sunbeam slanted across his face.

"Uh, the fellow who made them, he—uh, came . . ."

"Came here and presented them to you?"

"Yes. He—we—we had to make space, uh—for them. Move those trees." Mystified, I followed his gaze, and saw only a set of *Papers of the Presidents: Ronald Reagan,* relegated to the shelf beneath the soldiers. Well, if Keats could liken stacked volumes to garners of grain, I guessed Dutch could call his collected works trees, if he wanted. They did after all bear fruit, in a dry sort of way. And how he had always loved to prune speech drafts and proclamations, just as he pruned the live oaks and madroñas at Rancho del Cielo! "See?" he used to say, after having buzz-sawed another grove to Woodian geometry, "see where the light comes through?"

Courteous as ever, he took me to see something framed on the far wall. I expected it to be the Five Presidents picture, but a pleasant riverside watercolor study presented itself. I recognized every curve of the oak trees and the long grassy slope of the meadow.

"This," Dutch breathed, "is where I was a lifeguard for seven [sic] summers. I saved seventy-seven lives. And you know, none of 'em ever thanked me!"

It was his only unhesitant speech during our short interview, a confidence exchanged between strangers. He had long since stopped recognizing me; now I no longer recognized him. For all the intimate familiarity of that face and body, and the soft husk of his voice, I did not feel his presence beside me, only his absence.

☯

I freed myself as soon as I could, and before going downstairs asked his secretary if I could see the original manuscript of the Alzheimer's letter. She brought it to me in the conference room. I sat staring at its crabbed script and enormous margin (so evocative of the blizzard whitening his mind), and above all at the mystery of that black and scary erasure, concealing God knows what. Reading it again, I realized that I held in my hands a masterly piece of writing. It had the simplicity of genius, or at least the simplicity of a fundamentally religious nature accepting the inevitable.

I now begin the journey that will lead me into the sunset of my life . . .

And as if on cue, Dutch wandered in, not seeing me, going from entrance door to exit door. A young woman ran after him. "No, Mr. President, you don't want to walk that way!" Shortly afterward, I saw him being escorted to the elevator for his limousine ride home, surrounded by bored-looking Secret Service agents.

I did not visit him again. Biographical instinct warned me against the danger of too much sympathy for a man now frail, once so formidable. As Dutch had once held off all competitors for his favor—*Don't ever crowd Ronald Reagan,* Bill Clark used to warn—I must now retreat from him, closet myself with books and cards and paper, and finish the Life he had so casually authorized me to write, nine years before.

Two pilgrimages became necessary, at times when no amount of study could compensate for the actuality of experience. The first was to Bitburg and Bergen-Belsen. I had never seen a German military cemetery before, much less a concentration camp, and felt that I would not understand Dutch until I did.

The sky was neither gray nor lowering (a qualifier he liked to use) over the Eifel plateau this spring, as it had been the day he and Chancellor Kohl took their stiff march past the stones of *Ogefr.* Christian Brandt, *Ofeldw.* Walter Wagner, and many unknown *deutsche Soldaten* who might or might not have been members of the SS. But there had been much recent rain (as a gardener informed me, pronouncing the word *Regen* exactly like Dutch's surname), following weeks of thaw, and the grass around the flat markers was muddy enough to recall the grim colorlessness, the dull determination of the ceremony here on May 5, 1985. How Dutch had lit up when duty was done, and he could move on to a hero's welcome at the U.S. Air Force base just outside town! "*Vielen Dank!*"

I left the little graveyard and drove north toward the Lüneburger Heide. It was a long journey, and the Bergen road, running through woodland, was barred with late-afternoon shadows by the time I reached the Belsen turnoff. This was the way Dutch's reluctant motorcade had come, a decade ago; ahead was the *Dokumentenhaus* he was forced to endure; and all around (when I stopped in the memorial parking lot and turned off my engine) was the same subdued twittering of birds.

Like him, I went through the induction area with all deliberate speed, pausing no longer than he had before the white cruciform blowup, a copy of which I had already studied *ad nauseam* at home. I wanted, before the memorial grounds closed, to walk out into the great green clearing where he had spoken and where—somewhere—Anne Frank lay buried.

I walked through the gate, past a sign reading RESPECT THE PLACE OF THE DEAD, hearing again in memory a protestor's cry, "*Mr. President, you have come here: do not go to Bitburg!*" There was no one about; nothing to see either, except grass and distant trees, the heather-covered barrows, the little Jewish tower, and the larger formal obelisk where Dutch had delivered his speech. The platform beckoned me; I approached it, searched out his spot, and, feeling slightly foolish, stood there trying to see Belsen field with his eyes.

But again I saw no one, nothing, *nichts*. The whole purged space gave off an overwhelming sense of absence, of departed souls. It was the most awful yet beautiful landscape I had ever seen. And when, walking back past the long graves, I stopped at the Jewish memorial and saw its frieze of lopped-off trees (some much shorter than others), I thought of my father and Gavin, and Dutch and Anne Frank, and found myself crying.

Driving on north in the twilight, I turned on the car radio just in time to hear the concluding "Chorus Mysticus" of Liszt's *Faust* Symphony. Hushed male voices sang the almost untranslatable words of Goethe:

> *What's gone before*
> *Is but cast back at us;*
> *Our hoped-for more*

> *Is now a fact to us;*
> *When poor words fail*
> *We yet see light;*
> *The all-Female*
> *Lifts up our sight.*

Ronald Reagan, God knows, never had much time for poetry or music, but I like to think that sublime chorus would have resonated with him, had he been coaxed to listen to it before he lost his mind. It compressed just about all of his simple philosophy: that permanent truths apply, that prayers are answered, that the common man is wise, and that life with a loving *Ewig-weibliche* is the nearest thing to Heaven.

Nancy Reagan, God knows further, is no Gretchen. Yet Dutch is lucky to have been loved by her so passionately and exclusively for nearly fifty years. His children would argue that her monomania cramped his emotions and made him overly dependent on her. Less querulous observers might counter that by freeing him of family cares, she enabled him to father the Reagan Revolution.

At any rate, the doctor's daughter has made his "long good-bye" as comforting as possible. At the time of writing, hers is the only face he still recognizes. He still has his slow, unstoppable energy. He will rake leaves from the pool for hours, not understanding that they are being surreptitiously replenished by his Secret Service men. Perplexities crowd upon him. Why do these printed shapes beneath his moving finger not form themselves into words, as they used to when Nelle read to him? Who is this big brown-suited man in the television documentary, saluting and smiling? Why does the light go dim when clouds drift together? Why are "the fellows" so uncooperative at three in the morning, when he dresses for an urgent appointment? Why do magnolia blossoms, pristine on the tree, darken when they fall? And what is this pale ceramic object on the sandy floor of his fish tank at Fox Plaza? A miniature white house, with tall classical columns, hauntingly familiar. He takes it home, clenched wet in his fist: "This is . . . something to do with me. . . . I'm not sure what."

My second pilgrimage was made on August 2, 1998, when most of this book was already in galleys. I drove south from Grand Detour, Illinois, along the river road that Paul Rae and I used to take on our bicycles, seventy years ago. Lowell Park was as luxuriant as ever, as I graveled down through greenglowing trees. The last time I had come this way was in 1986, when I picked that leaf for the President, too preoccupied with research to feel much emotion. Now fear—"blind, unreasoning fear," as FDR would say, fear of the past more than the future—filled me at the sight of water below.

Youth's remembered meadow was not, as I had hoped, bare of contemporary revelers. Some youths in John Deere caps were lounging around a park bench with beers and a boom box, and a woman in a white speedboat was blaring back and forth across the river. A posted sign read: NO SWIMMING BY ORDER OF DIXON DEPARTMENT OF HEALTH. I parked near the oak where I once watched Dutch reading Edgar Rice Burroughs, switched off, and rolled my window down. But a rotting pike lay nearby, so I rolled it up again and sat sweating in the late afternoon heat.

After an hour or so, the meadow began to fill up with dark, although the river stayed light. To my relief, the woman in the speedboat throttled down.

"Maxine, let's go!" one of the boys on the bench yelled. She cruised in to shore, and they helped her drag the boat onto a trailer. Then they drove away, leaving their beer cans behind them. The great sheet of water in front of me calmed. Its swells became waves, and the waves broke into ripples that still caught the sun: a million quicksilver hyphens, alternately deleting and reinserting themselves.

I got out and, bypassing the fish, stepped beyond Dutch's tree. It was so quiet that I could hear the bones in my neck creak. A mosquito whined and stung. Breaking off a fern, I fanned it away.

From across the water came a lowing of cows. They had been drinking on the opposite bank, where the sun lay gold upon their backs—it was just about to sink in the high woods behind me—and now a dairyman was driving them back to pasture. They ambled uphill, udders swinging, and disappeared from view, like the herd in Gray's *Elegy Written in a Country Churchyard*. Pulling out a notebook, I attempted the elegiac mode myself:

> *Here where tangled grasses sop each wave,*
> *And midges moan and sting on autumn air,*
> *The oak that gave you shade still bends its boughs*
> *And drops its last where once you splashed to save . . .*

But then arthritis cramped inspiration.

It was a good thing Dutch was not there, or I might have blurted what I wanted to write, my confession to him at last: that the drunken youth he pulled ashore here in the dark, exactly seventy years ago, had been me. How smart of that boy, after one and a half minutes of Prone Pressure Resuscitation, to identify himself as the hero of *Jim Raider, Rocketeer*! Raucous "James Raider" had downed several slugs of illegal bourbon an hour or two before, in the garage at Dixon Country Club, where his best friend caddied. Had it not been for Dutch's acute ears, sharpened by years of myopia, my splashing might have gone unheard.

Paul, bless his epicene loyalty, never shared the story with anyone. "You'll tell Dutch, of course," he had said in 1985, when the news of my appointment was made public. "Of course," I said. But then Paul died, and I never got around to it. Perhaps Dutch, most inscrutable of men, knew. Perhaps not. In either case, he was now beyond caring. Who was I but one of seventy-seven? I heard his husky chuckle. *You're just another notch on the log.*

Even with the realization, I felt bound to testify, in prose if not speech, that I owed these last seven decades to Dutch. He had given me fresh opportunity to buy and sell, love and lose, fail and prevail. He had given me this familiar brackish taste in my mouth, and I should not gag on it, because it evoked the thick and teeming water of life.

Some day, I hoped, America might acknowledge her similar debt to the old Lifeguard who rescued her in a time of poisonous despair and, in Joseph Grucci's words, carried her "breastward out of peril."

To my right, the quicksilver hyphens were winking out, going to their downriver doom. Upstream, the last rays of the sun shone. I looked at the coming water, and felt, as I guess Dutch does too, the silent onrush of death.

APPENDIX

Three Poems

1. These Leaves Your Lips
To R.R.

These leaves your lips will sink as rot they must
Too logged at length to ride the up and down
Of us who mingling mixed our brackish beads
And bore you up, and washed you of your dust.

Yet still you leach your steeps of green and brown
Your resins rinse, your cold carotene bleeds
Into our depths, in pure return of trust.
We fear our glass will darken when you drown.

2. Bergen-Belsen
18.v.95

Hier Ruhen 5000 Tote. *Whatever's said*
Or written of this place, must leave unsaid
The unsayable, grant the comprehending dead
Relief from specious script or sound.

This green ground,
These bitter flowers,
Nullify articulate powers,
Paralyze the heart, till some
Trite yet fundamental questions come.
Who was here? Whence, and why? If they lie
Transubstantiated, then do I
Profane them when I pluck this heather,
Without so much as wondering whether
Its roots might bind two souls together?

3. Old Moon

Where once the full quicksilver flowed
A bright intelligence through your chasms,
Bare slopes of black and gray obtrude,
No longer nudged by fluid prisms,
And what remains of linking light
Now runs with soot at edge of night.

The vast and silent swing of spheres
Tilts you from us by degrees,
Minutes run off into years,
Crater cupfuls spill and freeze,
Disintegrate the Other Side,
Where madness, life, and death collide.

ACKNOWLEDGMENTS

This biography was written with the help, and on some pages the actual literary collaboration, of four of the author's oldest Hollywood friends: Philip Dunne, Sam Marx, Owen Crump, and Malvin Wald. Only the last-named survives. To him, thanks, and to the others, *ave atque vale*.

The author also expresses his gratitude toward the following co-contributors:

Benjamin Aaron; Arthur Abeles; Morris Abram; Kenneth and Carol Adelman; William Adler; Eddie Albert; Richard Allen; Martin Anderson; Dwayne Andreas; Edward Anhalt; Terry Arthur; William T. Bagley; Howard Baker; James Baker; Malcolm Baldridge; Thomas Barron; Antony Beaumont; Jim Beaver; Lynne Beer; Laurence Beilenson; Douglas Bell; Conrad Berger; Mimi Berlin; Robert Bernstein; Seweryn Bialer; James Billington; Gerald Blakely; Ralph Bledsoe; Herbert Block; Paul Boertlein; Pat Boone; Daniel and Ruth Boorstin; Georges Borchardt; Valerie Borchardt; Arnaud de Borchgrave; Tom Bostelle; Ralph Bower; L. Thompson Bowles; Steve Branch; Henry Brandon; Elizabeth Brower; Brock Brower; Charles Brower; Edmund G. "Pat" Brown; Bobby Brown; Tina Brown; Vernon Brown; B. Bruce-Briggs; Christopher Buckley; William F. Buckley, Jr.; Jeanne Burington; Richard and Gahl Burt; George Bush; Patrick Butler; Mabel Cabot; Michael Cahill; Philip D. Caine; Lou Cannon; James Cannon; Robert B. Carleson; David Carliner; Frank Carlucci; Jimmy Carter; Colleen Cattrell; Karen Chapel; Bruce Chapman; Lynne Cheney; Richard Cheney; William P. Clark, Jr.; Glen Claussen;

Ty Cobb; Claudette Colbert; John F. Collier; Ned Comstock; Sienna Craig; Elvin Crawford; Bob Creamer; Kenneth Crews; Greg Cumming; Walter and Isabel Cutler; John Dales; Helene von Damm; Richard Darman; Patti Davis; Doris Day; Amanda Deaver; Michael and Carolyn Deaver; Christopher DeMuth; Regina Drew Dentore; Armand Deutsch; Nancy Dickerson; Timothy Dickinson; Joan Didion; Guenter Diehl; Bruce J. Dierenfield; Anthony R. Dolan; Walter Doniger; Sheila Dowling; Betsy Drake; Joanne Drake; Benjamin Dreyer; Laurie Dunlap; Amanda Dunne; Dominick Dunne; William Dye; Thomas Edmonds; Ruth G. Edwards; Frank Eggert; R. G. Elliott; William Emerson; Harold Evans; Frank Fahrenkopf; Frank Fat; Wayne Federman; Jack Ferguson; Edwin Feulner; Fred Fielding; David Fisher; Michael Flynn; Marion Foster; Milton Friedman; Alfred Friendly, Jr.; Craig Fuller; John Gable; Hugh Gregory Gallagher; Leonard Garment; John Garrard; Patricia Gayman; David Gerson; Tom Gibson; Josh Gilder; Jack Glass; Barry Goldwater; Mikhail Gorbachev; Margaret Gordon; Allan and Sondra Gotlieb; June Masuda Goto; William N. Graf; C. Boyden Gray; Victoria Gray; Nancye Green; Richard Hafner; Robert Alan Handy; Peter Hannaford; Andrea Harris; Gilbert Harrison; Sam Harrod III; Mark Hatfield; George Hearne; Gloria Hébert; Richard and Cynthia Helms; Amy Henderson; Paul Hendrickson; William Henkel; Steingrimmur Hermansson; John Herrington; Charlton Heston; Christopher Hicks; Jerome Himmelstein; Charles D. Hobbs; Joy Hodges; Leonora Hornblow; James Hooley; Herman Hover; Austin Hoyt; Fred Hummel; John Hutton; Fred Iklé; Alaric Jacob; Vivia Jayne; James Jenkins; George Johnson; Robert Johnson; Victor Johnson; Whittle Johnston; Marilyn Jones; Jean Kinney Jones; Ingvi-Hrafn Jonsson; Clark Judge; Fred Kaiser; Robert Kaiser; Howard Kaminsky; Max Kampelman; Joseph Kanon; Irving Kaplan; Jascha Kessler; Ralph Keyes; George A. Keyworth; Kenneth Khachigian; R.I.M. King; Carol Kirk; Lane and Irina Kirkland; Jeane Kirkpatrick; Sidney Kirkpatrick; Sven Kraemer; James Kuhn; Jayne Lambert; Rene Laursen; Arnold Laven; Helen Lawton; Paul Laxalt; Irving Lazar; Ronald Lehman; Jules Levy; Daniel Lewis; Marvin Liebman; Doris Lilly; Arthur Liman; Phillip Linderman; Sol Linowitz; Neil Livingston; Mark Locher; June Lockhart; Carol Logue; Pruda Lood; Robert Loomis; Mary Lovell; Clare Boothe Luce; Henry Luce III; Kevin Lynch; R. Dale Marin; Woody Mark; James Marlas; Robert K. Massie; Jack Matlock; Chris Matthews; Madeleine Matz; Bill Mauldin; Roslyn Mazer; Msgr. James F. McCarthy; William R. McClellan; Stephen McConnell; Lloyd and Amy McElhiney; Robert C. McFarlane; Kathy McLane; Nell Mecklenburg; Harry Medved; David Meeker; Edwin Meese III; Timothy Mennel; Burgess Meredith; Carolyn Mesic; Bob Metzger; Adam Meyerson; Chester L. Migden; Johnathan Miller; M. A. Buster Miller; Morton Mintz; Margaret Moreau; John Mosley; Sandy Muir; Lola and Wilfred Müller; Brian Mulroney; Ken Murray; Arthur Nadas; Tanya Nadas; George Nash; Patricia Neal; Donald Neltnor; Howard Nemerov; Paul and Helen Nicely; Paul Nitze; Lyn Nofziger; Peggy Noonan; Herbert Northrup; George O'Malley; David Olson; William Orr; Gregory Orr; Kathy Osborne; Marc Pachter; Pavel Palazchenko; Charles Palm; Tom Pantages; Arthur Park; Herbert S. Parmet; Landon Parvin; Cherl Pence; Jami Phelps; Rev. Canon A.C.J. Phillips; William Phillips; Tony Phipps; Paul Pollak; Colin Powell; Stuart Proffitt; George Putnam; Willis Pyle; Robert Raison; J. Neil Reagan; Maureen Reagan; Michael Reagan; Nancy Reagan; Ron and Doria Reagan; Ronald Wilson Reagan; Donald Regan; Nancy Clark

Reynolds; Kurt Ritter; Peter Robinson; Olin Robison; John Robson; Marion E. Rodgers; Joseph Rodota; Thomas Roeser; Selwa Roosevelt; Harold Rosenthal; Mitchell Rosenthal; Norman Ross; Stanley Rubin; Daniel Ruge; Frederick J. Ryan; Brian Sajko; Martin Salditch; Jan Saunders; Elaine Sawyer; James Schlesinger; Robert J. Schmuhl; Lynda Schuler; Bunny Seawright; Norman Shaifer; Jill Robinson Shaw; Walter Sheldon; Richard Shenkman; Vincent Sherman; Walter E. Shotwell; George Shultz; Paul Slansky; John Sloan; William and Jean French Smith; Kathy Smith; Richard Norton Smith; John Snelling; Pete Souza; Bernice Spears; Robert Stack; S. Frederick Starr; George Steffes; Johannes Steinhoff; James Strock; Teri Swanson; Gay Talese; Mae Tally; Serge Tarasenko; Michael Teague; Margaret Thatcher; Rich Thomas; Dennis Thomas; Hamish Thomson; Kim Timmons; Richard Todd; Molly Sturges Tuthill; Holmes Tuttle; Robert Tuttle; R. Emmett Tyrrell; Steve Umin; Chase Untermeyer; Arthur Van Court; Frank Van Riper; Sam Vaughan; Steve Vaughn; Bernard Vorhaus; Ralph Wagner; Don Walker; Diana Walker; John Wallach; e. robert wallach; Peter J. Wallison; George Ward; Richard Warren; Wilcomb Washburn; Lew Wasserman; Richard Webb; Jack Weber; John Weicker; Caspar Weinberger; Bill Whittington; Charles and Mary Wick; Glenda Wiese; Arthur and Meta Wilde; Mari Maseng Will; Robert William; Mr. and Mrs. H. J. Williams; Garry Wills; William A. Wilson; Richard Wirthlin; Rabbi Mitchell Wohlberg; MacDonald Wood; Joseph Wright; Efrem Zimbalist, Jr.; Tom Zinnen; Benedict K. Zobrist.

BIBLIOGRAPHY

The following published works are cited frequently in the Notes in short-title form. All other published sources are cited in passing.

Abrams, Herbert L. *"The President Has Been Shot": Confusion, Disability, and the 25th Amendment in the Aftermath of the Attempted Assassination of Ronald Reagan* (New York, 1992).

Adelman, Kenneth. *The Great Universal Embrace* (New York, 1989).

Aitken, Jonathan. *Nixon: A Life* (Washington, D.C., 1993).

Anderson, Martin. *Revolution: The Reagan Legacy* (Stanford, Cal., 1990).

Andrew, Christopher and Oleg Gordievsky. *Comrade Kryuchkov's Instructions: Top Secret Files on KGB Foreign Operations* (Stanford, Cal., 1991).

Attali, Jacques. *Verbatim I: Chronique des Années 1981–1986* (Paris, 1993).

———. *Verbatim II: Chronique des Années 1986–1988* (Paris, 1995, pocket edition).

Barrett, Laurence I. *Gambling with History: Reagan in the White House* (updated paperback edition, New York, 1984).

Beahrs, Oliver H. "The Medical History of President Ronald Reagan," *Journal of the American College of Surgeons,* Vol. 178 (Jan. 1994).

Brown, Edmund G. ("Pat"). *Reagan and Reality: The Two Californias* (New York, 1970).

Brownstein, Ronald. *The Power and the Glitter: The Hollywood-Washington Connection* (New York, 1990).

Burke, Vincent J., and Vee Burke. *Nixon's Good Deed: Welfare Reform* (New York, 1974)..

Cannon, Lou. *President Reagan: The Role of a Lifetime* (New York, 1991).

———. *Reagan* (New York, 1982).

———. *Ronnie & Jesse: A Political Odyssey* (New York, 1969).

Ceplair, Larry, and Steven Englund. *The Inquisition In Hollywood: Politics in the Film Community, 1930–1960* (Berkeley, Cal., 1983).

Darman, Richard. *Who's in Control?: Polar Politics and the Sensible Center* (New York, 1996).

Davis, Patti. *The Way I See It* (New York, 1992).

Deaver, Michael. *Behind the Scenes* (New York, 1987).

Dobrynin, Anatoly. *In Confidence: Moscow's Ambassador to America's Six Cold War Presidents, 1962–1986* (New York, 1995).

Draper, Theodore. *A Very Thin Line: the Iran-contra Affairs* (New York, 1991).

Dunne, George H. *Hollywood Labor Dispute: A Study in Immorality* (Los Angeles, 1952).

Dunne, Philip. *Take Two* (New York, 1980).

Edwards, Anne. *Early Reagan* (New York, 1987).

Erickson, Paul D. *Reagan Speaks: The Making of an American Myth* (New York, 1985).

Gentry, Curt. *The Last Days of the Late, Great State of California* (New York, 1968).

Goines, David Lance. *The Free Speech Movement: Coming of Age in the 1960s* (Berkeley, Cal., 1993).

Gorbachev, Mikhail. *Memoirs* (New York, 1996).

Green, Mark, and Gail MacColl. *Reagan's Reign of Error: The Instant Nostalgia Edition* (New York, 1983, 1987).

Haig, Alexander M., Jr. *Caveat: Realism, Reagan, and Foreign Policy* (New York, 1984).

Halsell, Grace. *Prophecy and Politics: Militant Evangelists on the Road to Nuclear War* (Westport, Conn., 1986).

Hamilton, Gary G., and Nicole W. Biggart. *Governor Reagan, Governor Brown: A Sociology of Executive Power* (New York, 1984).

Hannaford, Peter. *The Reagans: A Political Portrait* (New York, 1983).

Hartman, Geoffrey, ed. *Bitburg in Moral and Political Perspective* (Bloomington, Ind., 1986).

Johnson, Paul. *Modern Times: The World from the Twenties to the Eighties* (New York, 1983).

Kornbluh, Peter, and Malcom Byrne, eds. *The Iran-Contra Scandal: The Declassified History* (New York, 1993).

Ligachev, Yegor. *Inside Gorbachev's Kremlin: The Memoirs of Yegor Ligachev* (New York, 1993).

Mayer, Jane, and Doyle McManus. *Landslide: The Unmaking of the President, 1984–1985* (Boston, 1988).

McClelland, Doug. *Hollywood on Ronald Reagan* (Winchester, Mass., 1983).

McFarlane, Robert C. *Special Trust* (New York, 1994).

Medvedev, Roy, and Giulietto Chiesa. *Time of Change: An Insider's View of Russia's Transformation* (New York, 1989).

Miller, James. *Democracy in the Streets: From Port Huron to the Siege of Chicago* (New York, 1987).

Moldea, Dan E. *Dark Victory: Ronald Reagan, MCA and the Mob* (New York, 1986).

Navasky, Victor. *Naming Names* (New York, 1980/1991).

Nitze, Paul. *From Hiroshima to Glasnost* (New York, 1989).

Nofziger, Lyn. *Nofziger* (Washington, 1992).

O'Neill, Tip, and William Novak. *Man of the House: The Life and Political Memoirs of Speaker Tip O'Neill* (New York, 1987).

Oberdorfer, Don. *The Turn: From the Cold War to a New Era—The United States and the Soviet Union, 1983–1990* (New York, 1991).

Powers, Richard Gid. *Not Without Honor: The History of American Anticommunism* (New York, 1995).

Quirk, Lawrence J. *Jane Wyman: The Actress and the Woman* (New York, 1986).

Reagan, Maureen. *First Father, First Daughter* (Boston, 1989).

Reagan, Michael. *On the Outside Looking In* (New York, 1988).

Reagan, Ronald. *An American Life* (New York, 1990).

Reagan, Ronald, with Richard G. Hubler. *Where's the Rest of Me? The Autobiography of Ronald Reagan* (New York, 1965, 1981).

Reagan, Ronald. *Abortion and the Conscience of the Nation,* with afterwords by C. Everett Koop and Malcolm Muggeridge (Nashville, 1983).

Regan, Donald. *For the Record: From Wall Street to Washington* (New York, 1988).

Ritter, Kurt, and David Henry. *Ronald Reagan: The Great Communicator* (Westport, Conn., 1992).

Rorabaugh, W. J. *Berkeley at War: The 1960s* (New York, 1989).

Severo, Richard, and Lewis Milford. *The Wages of War: When America's Soldiers Came Home* (New York 1989).

Shultz, George. *Turmoil and Triumph: My Years as Secretary of State* (New York, 1993).

Smith, Hedrick. *The Power Game: How Washington Works* (New York, 1988).

Speakes, Larry. *Speaking Out: The Reagan Presidency from Inside the White House* (New York, 1988).

St. Vincent Millay, Edna. "Aria da Capo: A Play in One Act," in *The Chapbook* (London) 14 (August 1919).

Stockman, David. *The Triumph of Politics: How the Reagan Revolution Failed* (New York, 1986).

Strober, Deborah Hart, and Gerald S., eds. *Reagan: The Man and His Presidency* (Boston, 1998).

Thatcher, Margaret. *The Downing Street Years* (New York, 1993).

Vaughn, Stephen. *Ronald Reagan in Hollywood* (New York, 1994).

Von Damm, Helene. *At Reagan's Side* (New York, 1989).

Weinberger, Caspar W. *Fighting for Peace: Seven Critical Years in the Pentagon* (New York, 1990).

Wills, Garry. *Reagan's America: Innocents at Home* (New York, 1987).

Witcover, Jules. *The Pursuit of the Presidency 1972–1976* (New York, 1977).

Woodward, Bob. *Veil: The Secret Wars of the CIA* (New York, 1987).

NOTES

Archival Sources

AC	Author's Collection, Washington, D.C.
BOL	Bolling Air Force Base Research Library, Washington, D.C.
CHS	Chicago Historical Society, Chicago, Ill.
CLA	William P. Clark III Papers, privately held.
DEA	Michael and Carolyn Deaver Papers, privately held.
FWP/LC	Federal Writers Project Papers, Library of Congress, Washington, D.C.
FWP/NA	Federal Writers Project Papers, National Archives, Washington, D.C.
HAR	Sam Harrod III Papers, privately held.
HER	Margaret Herrick Library, Academy of Motion Picture Arts and Sciences, Beverly Hills, Calif.
HOP	Hedda Hopper Collection, HER.
ISHL	Illinois State Historical Library.
JHP	John Hutton Papers, privately held.
JLWP	Jack L. Warner Papers, Cinema-Television Library, University of Southern California, Los Angeles.
KEY	Ralph Keyes Papers, privately held.
LAW	Helen Lawton Papers, privately held.
LC	Library of Congress, Washington, D.C.

MGMP	Metro-Goldwyn-Mayer Papers, Cinema-Television Library, University of Southern California, Los Angeles.
NA	National Archives, Washington, D.C.
NIC	Paul Nicely Collection, RR Birthplace Museum, Tampico, Ill.
NPRC	National Public Records Center, St. Louis, Mo.
NYPL	New York Public Library, New York, N.Y.
NYPL/pa	New York Public Library for the Performing Arts, New York, N.Y.
OCP	Owen Crump Papers, privately held.
RAA	Steven S. Raab and Shaun Thomas Reagania Collection, privately held.
REG	Donald T. Regan Papers, Library of Congress, Washington, D.C.
RNL	Richard Nixon Presidential Library, Yorba Linda, Calif.
RRH	Ronald Reagan Gubernatorial Papers, Hoover Institution, Stanford University, Stanford, Calif.
RRL	Ronald Reagan Presidential Library, Simi Valley, Calif.
RRL/av	RRL, Audio-Visual Collection.
RRL/oh	RRL, Oral History.
RRL/pp	RRL, Personal Papers of Ronald Reagan.
RRL/pp/hw	RRL, Personal Papers of Ronald Reagan, Handwriting File.
RRP	Ronald Reagan Papers, privately held.
SAGA	Screen Actors Guild Archives, Los Angeles, Calif.
SAL	Martin Salditch Collection, privately held.
SCLSS	Southern California Library for Social Studies, Los Angeles, Calif.
SHSW	State Historical Society of Wisconsin, Madison, Wisc.
SLA	Paul Slansky Collection, privately held.
UCB	University of California at Berkeley.
WBC	Warner Bros. Collection, Cinema-Television Library, University of Southern California, Los Angeles.
WGBH	WGBH Public Television Archives, Boston, Mass.
WHCA	White House Communications Agency videotapes, in RRL/av.
WHTV	White House Television videotapes, in RRL/av.

References

Boldface phrases below mark the beginning of a cited sentence or paragraph, or, on rare occasions, a string of paragraphs whose common sourcing is clear. The author has included translations of some foreign phrases, plus explanations of buried quotations and allusions not common to Reagan scholarship. The following abbreviations apply:

EM	Author
GM	Gavin Morris
JR	Jack Reagan
JW	Jane Wyman
NR	Nancy Reagan
PR	Paul Rae
RR	Ronald Reagan
ms., ts.	manuscript, typescript

n.d.   no date on original
qu.   quoting, quoted
trans.   translated by

Epigraph

PAGE
   xix   Charles Dickens, *Great Expectations,* 11.

Prologue

xxi   **"For heaven's sakes!"**   RR interview, Sept. 17, 1986; EM Diary, Sept. 17, 1986.

xxi   **He tilts his head**   Ibid.

xxii   *It only winds them up*   Calvin Coolidge to Bernard Baruch, qu. in Bill Adler, ed., *Presidential Wit from Washington to Johnson* (New York, 1966), 120.

xxii   **Of course**   The Schedule of President Ronald Reagan, Nov. 18, 1986, RRL.

xxii   **He is back**   RR with Richard G. Hubler, *Where's the Rest of Me? The Autobiography of Ronald Reagan* (New York, 1965, 1981), 21; Edgar Rice Burroughs, *A Princess of Mars* (Garden City, N.Y., 1917, 1970), 20. The author's text of RR's memoir is the E. P. Dutton reprint issued by Karz Publishers in 1981.

xxii   PULLED FROM THE JAWS   Dixon *Evening Telegraph,* Aug. 3, 1928.

xxiii   *Research memo*   Burroughs, *A Princess of Mars,* 123.

xxiii   **Half an hour**   EM Diary, Sept. 17, 1986.

xxiii   **He certainly lit up**   Except where otherwise indicated, this account of the Hatfield Valentine's Day dinner is based on EM Diary, Feb. 14, 1983. See also Hugh Sidey, "Taking Notes for History," *Time,* Feb. 28, 1983. Scholars on the guest list included Daniel J. Boorstin, Librarian of Congress; Frank Freidel, biographer (*Franklin D. Roosevelt*); Sylvia Jukes Morris, biographer (*Edith Kermit Roosevelt: Portrait of a First Lady*); George H. Nash (*The Life of Herbert Hoover*); Arthur S. Link (*Woodrow Wilson: A Biography*); and the author (*The Rise of Theodore Roosevelt*). Hatfield himself is an academic historian and expert on Herbert Hoover.

xxiii   **His detestation**   Link, who died in 1998, went on to publish nineteen more volumes of Wilson's papers, for a final total of sixty-nine. This freed him to return to the project closest to his heart, a biography of Wilson in eight projected volumes. The last three were never written. *The New York Times,* Mar. 29, 1998.

xxiv   **"charm of an exquisite"**   Walter Pater, *Emerald Uthwart* (Folcroft, Pa., 1973), 41.

xxv   **Joke-telling requires**   RR once told his Attorney General that he had been awed, in his early Hollywood days, by the speed and precision of studio comedians who would congregate in Chasen's restaurant to practice their jokes on one another. He worked doggedly to emulate their techniques and build up a competitive repertoire. Edwin Meese interview, June 26, 1988.

xxv   **billets-doux**   Love letters.

xxv   **annus horribilis**   See below, Ch. 20, "And Then Along Came Nancy."

xxvi   **that Reagan appoint**   EM to Mark O. Hatfield, Feb. 18, 1983, AC. The Senator was joking.

xxvi   **It was not until**   Michael Deaver interview, May 27, 1985.

xxvii   **Nine years later**   The following account is based on EM Diary and notes of RR's return to Tampico, May 10, 1992.

xxvii   **Sunday-morning sunbeams**   Some of the musical episodes from this church service are preserved in the audiobook version of *Dutch: A Memoir of Ronald Reagan* (New York, 1999).

xxviii   **Sixty years**   Gustave Courbet's *Origine du monde* (Brooklyn Museum, New York City) is a famous but long-suppressed painting of the female genitalia.

xxix   **the events of eighty years**   See below, Ch. 2, "The Rainbow on the Roof."

xxix   **"Don't blame me"**   Robert Tuttle interview, Jan. 13, 1986.

xxix   **coup de foudre**   Stroke of lightning = fall in love.

1: The Land of Lost Things

3   **It was a bird**   EM Diary, May 5, 1985; WHCA and WHTV video coverage in RRL/av; and "Bitburg," a compilation of commercial- and cable-television coverage assembled by Paul Slansky, Apr.–May 1985, SLA.

4   **At times, I**   See, e.g., Noguchi's portrait of Buckminster Fuller in the Fuller Institute, Los Angeles, Calif.

4   **Not until Reagan**   The Bitburg crisis of 1985 is the subject of Ch. 31 below, "Physicians of Memory."

4   **Perhaps the journey**   EM Diary, Mar. 22, 1985.

5   *Clothed in white*   Alfred, Lord Tennyson, *Idylls of the King*, 1. 267.

5   **So again**   Lüneburger Heide, the heather-covered plain in northern Germany surrounding Bergen-Belsen. *Lerche* = lark.

6   **Amateur Freudians**   Annette ("Bess") Dowling (1881–1947). British-born lyric soprano, a pupil of Nellie Melba. She joined the Dresden Staatsoper in 1901 and became a specialist in the German repertory. Her debut recital in Wigmore Hall on Oct. 22, 1903, was attended by the American impresario H. Holt Marsden, who, impressed by her interpretations of the work of Richard Strauss, brought her to the United States as a touring artist in 1904. She settled in Chicago and in Mar. 1905 scored a sensation as the First Flower Maiden in *Parsifal*. It was at this time that she attracted the eye and lavish spending of Arthur Morris. The Chicago Opera was given over to visiting productions in those days, and Dowling sang only guest roles until 1910, when Mary Garden took over the ill-fated Chicago Grand Opera Company. Motherhood removed Miss Dowling from the stage for the next several years. After a

group of wealthy businessmen, including Arthur and Ira Morris, formed the Chicago Opera Association in the spring of 1915, she was offered the *jugendlich* role of Elisabeth in *Tannhäuser.* The opera played three times in the 1915–1916 season. Then war hysteria forced German opera off the Auditorium boards, and she never sang professionally again. Retiring at thirty-five, she spent the rest of her life teaching. See Edward Moore, *Forty Years of Opera in Chicago* (New York, 1930, 1977), and "A Short History of Grand Opera in Chicago," ms. in FWP/LC.

6   **Her scruple, oddly**   Frederic Cople Jaher, *Urban Establishment: Upper Strata in Boston, New York, Charleston, Chicago, and Los Angeles* (New York, 1982), 1492.

7   **He and my uncle**   Ira Nelson Morris (1875–1942), diplomat, art collector, chronically unpublished author; Edward Morris (1866–1913), businessman, married the packing heiress Helen Swift, 1889; Nelson Morris (1840–1907), German immigrant, founder of the packing business Morris & Co. For more on the Morris dynasty, see Ira N. Morris, *Heritage from My Father* (New York, 1923, 1947); "Packers Are People," *Field Illustrated* 28 (1918), and Edward N. Wentworth, *A Biographical Catalog of the Portrait Gallery of the Saddle and Sirloin Club* (Chicago, 1920).

7   **Had Grandfather known**   Arthur Morris and Annette "Bess" Dowling married on Sept. 30, 1907. After Arthur and Ira quit the firm, Morris & Co. went on to become, briefly, the greatest cattle export business in the world. See Ira Morris, *Heritage,* 30, 54, 252–53; Wentworth, *A Biographical Catalog,* 184. For the company's subsequent history, see Bertram B. Fowler, *Men, Meat and Miracles* (New York, 1952), 92–101.

7   **About the time**   The author entertained RR at dinner in 1987 and made a joke to the effect that while other guests were to be served *ris de veau à l'estragon, sauce champignons sauvages,* he, as head of state, would be treated to an especially elaborate preparation: "macaroni and cheese." The President's eyes lit up with such joy that the joke backfired. EM Diary, Nov. 15, 1987.

8   **I remember how**   There was some truth in Arthur Morris's claim. Although the initial resolution to form a new anti-slavery party took place in New York City on Feb. 28, 1854, the first formal state organization of the GOP took place in the First Congregational Church in Aurora, Ill., on Sept. 20, 1854. Franklin L. Burdette, *The Republican Party: A Short History,* 2d ed. (New York, 1972), 41; Vernon Derry, *The Aurora Story* (Aurora, Ill., 1976), 32.

9   **"There's a few feet"**   RR interview, May 9, 1992; Edmund Morris, "A Celebration of Reagan," *The New Yorker,* Feb. 16, 1998.

2: The Rainbow on the Roof

11   **"I . . . Jack"**   RR interview, Sept. 16, 1986.

11   **"a fat Dutchman"**   RR, *Where's the Rest of Me?,* 3.

12   **"I'm OK"**   Maureen Reagan, *First Father, First Daughter* (Boston, 1989), 61.

12   **It was natural**   Leonora Hornblow interview, Jan. 25, 1989; "His

Mother Was Nelle Reagan," *Bread of Life,* May 30, 1981; Maureen Reagan interview, Feb. 23, 1991. Except where otherwise indicated, the following account of a research visit to Tampico is based on EM Notes, Sept. 8 and 9, 1986.

12   **"I didn't know"**   Paul Nicely, a former Tampico High School teacher and founder-curator of the RR Birthplace Museum, is the author's principal source of non-documentary material for RR's wandering childhood in north-central Illinois, 1911–1920. A passionate local historian, Nicely spent most of the 1980s interviewing Reagan and Wilson family descendants in Whiteside County, plus their surviving neighbors and friends from Tampico days. His eccentric "Researching Reagan" notes in the *Tampico Tornado,* Feb. 18, 1981, and later, contain much colorful local detail.

12   **"I guess I'm"**   Neil Reagan interview, Mar. 7, 1987.

13   **a shared statuesqueness**   RR's height was officially confirmed at 6′ 1″ when he became Governor of California in 1967. According to his White House doctors, he remained that height throughout his Presidency, and began to shorten only in retirement, as age and illness stooped him. The calibrations recorded by various military physicians in his U.S. Army personal file incredibly assert that RR grew by almost two inches between the ages of twenty-six and thirty-four. They measured him at 71″ in 1937, 71½″ in 1941, 72″ in 1942, and 72¾″ in 1945. RR "201" file, NPRC.

13   **In the flesh**   RR interview, Sept. 17, 1986; family photographs in Birthplace Museum; Paul Nicely interview, Sept. 9, 1986.

13   **But I could not**   "Friends Remember Nelle Reagan," *Los Angeles Times,* May 10, 1981.

14   **I'm sorry to say**   Thomas F. Roeser to EM, Jan. 7, 1987, AC.

14   **In this bed**   RR birth certificate, RRL/pp; *Tampico Tornado,* Feb. 10, 1911; RR, *Where's the Rest of Me?,* 3. The aftereffect of RR's birth upon Nelle was a prolapsed womb and advice from her doctor that she was unable to have any more children. Paul Nicely interview, Sep. 8, 1986.

14   **Should the second**   Astrological details: Vivia Jane to Tanya Nadas, Sept. 19, 1990, AC.

16   **the scrapbook he keeps**   Now in RRL/pp.

16   **Tampico had already**   Paul Nicely interview, Sept. 7, 1986.

16   **I retraced**   EM Notes, Sept. 8, 1986; Garry Wills, *Reagan's America: Innocents at Home* (New York, 1987), 17; John E. Reagan Employment Record, 1936, NA. According to *Federal Census of Whiteside Co., Ill.,* 1910, JR and Nelle were both twenty-six (census taken June 15). The Mormon Church's "Genealogical Record of Ronald Reagan" (RRL) has JR born July 13, 1883, and Nelle born July 24, 1883. However, Nelle's belated birth record, filed in 1943, says July 18, 1882. When she married JR on Nov. 7, 1904, she claimed to be two years younger than he. Wills, *Reagan's America,* chapters 1 and 2 contain detailed background material on both Reagans.

17   **It is easy**   RR, *Where's the Rest of Me?,* 7, 8; Neil Reagan interview, Jan. 31, 1990.

17   **Alcohol was Jack's**   See below, Ch. 3, "A Dark Form Half Hidden in the Snow." Donal Begley, *Presented to Honorable Ronald Reagan . . . on Be-*

half of the People of Ballyporeen, etc., specially printed genealogy, Burke's Peerage, London, June 1984, RRL; Wills, *Reagan's America,* 16; Neil Reagan interview, Jan. 31, 1990.

17   **Only one of**   Neil Reagan interview, Jan. 31, 1990; RR, *Where's the Rest of Me?,* 9.

17   **The waters that**   Wills, *Reagan's America,* 17; Paul Nicely interview, Sept. 8, 1986.

18   **"a very nice soprano"**   RR interview, Sept. 17, 1986.

18   **ancient travel notes**   WPA mss., Federal Writers Project, Illinois Guide Field reports (1936), ISHL.

18   **About the loudest**   *Tampico Tornado,* May 19, 1911.

18   **Possibly it was**   Ibid.; see also the issue of June 19, 1913.

18   **Less than a month**   Paul Nicely interview, Sept. 9, 1990; RR interview, Dec. 22, 1986; *Tampico Tornado,* June 17, July 16, Aug. 7, Oct. 13, 1913.

19   **In this cube**   Neil Reagan Oral History, RRL/oh; Paul Nicely interview, Sept. 9, 1986: "The [Reagans'] baby-sitter . . . could remember Nelle struggling to get the baby up the stairs, and she would put him at the edge of the stage, by the footlights, so that she could watch [him] while she practiced."

19   **The Reagans were**   Sterling *Gazette,* Dec. 8, 1913; Lizzie Mae Elwyn, *Millie the Quadroon; or, Out of Bondage* (Clyde, Ohio, 1888).

21   **Nelle's extravagant histrionics**   "She recited classic speeches in tragic tones, wept as she flung herself into . . . melodramas." RR, *Where's the Rest of Me?,* 15. Paul Nicely interview, Sept. 9, 1986.

21   *Oh, that I!*   Elwyn, *Millie,* II.i.

21   **I was back**   EM Notes, Sept. 8 and 9, 1986, AC. The Glassburn house comprised approx. 2,000 sq. ft., according to a Sanborn Fire Insurance map, *Tampico, Ill., December 1910,* LC.

21   **All through my**   RR interview, Apr. 29, 1987. See also Ronald Reagan, *An American Life* (New York, 1990), 245.

21   **His only conscious**   RR interview, Sept. 16, 1986; Neil Reagan interview, Mar. 27, 1987; RR autobiographical questionnaire filled out for the Knights of Mark Twain, Sept. 2, 1971, RRL.

22   **blank blue sky**   See below, p. 556. With the exception of coastal Delaware and Louisiana, Illinois is the flattest state in the Union.

22   **Jack's lust**   Sterling *Evening Gazette,* Sept. 9, 1913; *Tampico Tornado* miscellaneous clips, RR Birthplace Museum; RR, *Where's the Rest of Me?,* 23; Paul Nicely interview, Sept. 6, 1986, recalls the move as being "late 1914, or the second of January, 1915." Dixon *Evening Telegraph,* Feb. 4, 1984, says that at the time of the announcement on Jan. 7, 1915, JR was on a return visit to Tampico, and had already been employed by the Fair Store.

3: A Dark Form Half Hidden in the Snow

24   **Ronald Reagan came**   This presidential trip to Illinois occurred on Aug. 12, 1986.

PAGE

24   **He leaned past me**   EM Notes, Aug. 12, 1986. RR's cologne was specially made for him in Bermuda. RRL/pp.

25   **He seemed surprised**   The Schedule of President Ronald Reagan, Aug.
12, 1986, RRL; EM Notes, Aug. 12, 1986; RR interview, Sept. 17, 1986.

25   **White bars of**   RR interview, Apr. 8, 1992. RR recalled the apartment's
streaming sunlight in a *Modern Screen* interview, Mar. 1943.

25   **Here Jack and Nelle**   RR interview, Sept. 17, 1986.

25   **Jack was working**   Neil Reagan interview, Mar. 7, 1987. Q. "Why
greased with butter?" A. "To prevent foaming, stupid!"

25   **The liver was**   Ibid; RR, *An American Life,* 24.

25   **Dutch, a dreamy**   Neil Reagan interview, Mar. 7, 1987; Thomas F.
Roeser to EM, Jan. 7, 1987, AC.

26   **Parzival. Perceval.**   John Matthews, *The Grail: Quest for the Eternal*
(London, 1981), 62.

26   **Possibly Dutch's**   The Gospel According to Saint Matthew 5:14; John
Bunyan, *Pilgrim's Progress,* concluding pages of Part One.

26   **By then the Reagans**   In Dec. 1915, Neil's Galesburg school record
showed that he had already completed four months in first grade. Silas
Willard School Records, School District no. 205, Galesburg, Ill.

27   **One day in the**   RR, *Where's the Rest of Me?,* 11.

27   **Sense and sensibility**   RR interview, Apr. 8, 1992; RR, *Where's the Rest
of Me?,* 12; RR, *An American Life,* 12.

27   **On July 31**   Galesburg *Evening Mail,* July 31, 1916. Both RR (*Where's
the Rest of Me?,* 12) and Neil Reagan (Oral History, RRL/oh), also cite
headlines to do with an anarchist bombing in San Francisco. But that
event occurred at 1:30 P.M. on Saturday, July 22, 1916, too late for inclusion in either the Galesburg *Evening Mail* or the Galesburg *Republican-
Register,* neither of which was published on Sundays.

27   **I remember visiting**   WPA mss., Federal Writers Project, Illinois Guide
Field reports (1936), ISHL.

28   **In September of**   RR's actual percentages were: Reading, 95; Spelling,
100; Arithmetic, 100; Language, 93. Silas Willard School Records,
1917–1918, School District no. 205, Galesburg, Ill.

28   **But by then**   Anne Edwards, *Early Reagan* (New York, 1987), 38, states
without a citation that JR had been fired for drinking. This is not unlikely. RR, in *An American Life,* 25, remembers becoming aware in
Galesburg of "a mysterious source of conflict" between his parents. See
below.

28   **Their new address**   Wills, *Reagan's America,* 390; classmate Gertrude
Crockett, interview in Edwards, *Early Reagan,* 38–39. Monmouth Public
Schools Boy's Permanent Record, 1918–1919, rates RR as an A student
in second grade, and a B after promotion to third on Jan. 6, 1919. According to Edwards, *Early Reagan,* 39, RR's teacher in the latter class
was amazed at his ability to memorize dates, names, and mathematical
tables.

28   **"Spanish flu"**   Monmouth *Daily Review,* Oct. 9, 13, 18, and 19, 1918;
Edwin O. Jordan, *Epidemic Influenza* (Chicago, 1927), 119, 127.

PAGE

28   **Thanks to its** Monmouth *Daily Review,* Oct. 24, 1918. RR recalled
waking up every day "with a weight dragging at the pit of [my] stomach." RR interview, *Modern Screen,* Mar. 1943. See also RR, *Where's the
Rest of Me?,* 13; Edwards, *Early Reagan,* 39. If Nelle's attack was typical, she collapsed with extreme suddenness, turned a dusky plum-red,
ran a temperature as high as 104 degrees, and lay utterly prostrated for
four days, the last two being the most critical (Jordan, *Epidemic Influenza,* 260–61).

28   **Pandemic gave way** Monmouth *Daily Review,* Nov. 12, 1918 (5 A.M.
Extra, ISHL); RR interview, Aug. 12, 1986.

29   **It also saw** RR completed his promotion to third grade in Monmouth
on June 6, 1919, and the Sterling *Evening Gazette* announced the return
of the Reagans to Tampico on Aug. 25, 1919. For "the outside world" of
this time, see William Klingaman, *1919: The Year Our World Began*
(New York, 1987).

29   **His scare of** RR, *Where's the Rest of Me?,* 13; RR to the Mayor of
Tampico, Jan. 12, 1976, RRL; Paul Nicely interview, Sept. 9, 1990; Neil
Reagan interview, Mar. 7, 1987.

29   **Dutch, alone again** RR's initial solitariness in Tampico moderated after
he began to attend school in the fall of 1919; he even became the leader
of a local gang. See Edwards, *Early Reagan,* 41–42.

29   **The best part** RR, *Where's the Rest of Me?,* 15.

29   **He recalls reading** RR radio address, n.d. [1976], transcript in AC;
"President Reagan's School Records, 1920," Tampico Historical Society.
RR scored A's in reading, arithmetic, and deportment, and B's in everything else (spelling, language, penmanship, physiology/hygiene, geography, music, and drawing). He missed only one day of school, was never
"tardy," and was rated "Excellent" overall.

30   **Since the war's** *Tampico Tornado,* Nov. 18, 1920.

30   **Indefatigable in her** Ibid., Dec. 12, 1920. Helen Nicely (interview, Sept.
9, 1986) recalls "a coolness growing between Jack and Nelle," apparent
to her as a child who was much in their house.

30   **Dutch remembers this** RR, *Where's the Rest of Me?,* 15; RR on "Conversations with the Presidents," broadcast on ABC, Sept. 16, 1988; RR
to Mrs. Fred A. Eckstrand, Nov. 15, 1947 (NIC); Paul Nicely interview,
Sept. 8, 1986.

31   **That Fourth of July** Neil Reagan Oral History, RRL/oh; Sterling
Evening Gazette, July 10, 1920; RR superscript on Anthony Dolan,
Fourth of July memo, Apr. 7, 1981, RRL/pp/hw; Wayne Bastian, *White-
side County* (Morrison, Ill., 1968), 437.

31   **Business was bad** Sterling *Evening Gazette,* July 24, 1920; George Soule,
Prosperity Decade: From War to Depression, 1917–1929 (New York,
1947), 78; Paul Nicely interview, Sept. 8, 1986.

31   **At thirty-seven** To be a Democrat like JR at this time in a small town in
the grain belt was to court unpopularity. President Wilson's wartime manipulation of wheat price controls had led to a complete rout of the
party in the Midwest in the congressional elections of 1918. David

Kennedy, *Over Here: The First World War and American Society* (New York, 1980), 243–44.

31   **One small city** RR, *An American Life,* 26; *Tampico Tornado,* July 24, Sept. 2, 9, and Dec. 9, 1920; Sterling *Evening Gazette,* Sept. 9, 1920.

32   **I sit now staring** *Tampico Tornado,* Sept. 2, 1920.

32   **Around the same** Paul and Helen Nicely interview, Sept. 9, 1990; *Tampico Tornado,* Dec. 16, 1920.

32   **Sycamore was and** Sycamore's downtown residential district is listed in the National Register of Historic Places as being "close to the popular American image of the ideal small town." EM Notes, Sept. 4, 1986; Carol Logue of Sycamore Public Library to author, Aug. 28, 1990.

33   **It was ninety miles** RR, *Where's the Rest of Me?,* 17.

33   **A small town** Ibid. Dixon's population was actually only 8,191 in the 1920 Census. RR is thinking of the 1930 Census, which registers a rise to 10,570.

33   **Dixon—City of** The shouts of the Barker are taken from JR's teaser ads in the Dixon *Evening Telegraph* between Mar. 3 and 17, 1921.

34   ***Durch Mitleid*** "Made wise through pity, the Pure Fool!" *Leitmotiv* from Richard Wagner's *Parsifal.*

34   *a small, two-story* Now the Ronald Reagan Boyhood Home. For descriptive articles, see *Good Housekeeping,* Aug. 1984, and David Badger, *The Badger Collection Featuring Dixon of Illinois,* ISHL.

34   **He was fated to fall** RR, *An American Life,* 40–41, 75. For a detailed analysis of the relationship between RR and Rev. Cleaver (a morally constant figure in contrast to the binge-prone JR), see Stephen Vaughn, *Ronald Reagan in Hollywood* (New York, 1994), 8–16.

35   **We wish to** Dixon *Evening Telegraph,* Mar. 17 and 25, 1921. The Fashion Boot Shop did not open at a propitious time as far as the local economy was concerned. Dixon had been hit badly by the previous year's price crash—one of the most violent in U.S. history—and its surrounding farmland was rife with foreclosures in early 1921. See ibid., Jan. 13, and Feb. 4 and 7, 1921.

35   **"Red Brick School"** Esther Barton, RR's former fifth-grade teacher here, wrote him on Feb. 2, 1982, and awarded him an "A+" for his first State of the Union speech. RRL/pp.

35   **Don't get me wrong** RR radio script, "The Bad Old Days," ca. 1975–1976, RRL/pp/hw.

36   **"Dutch" Regan wins** The exploits of the June Bugs are chronicled in the Dixon *Evening Telegraph,* Mar. 19–Apr. 17, 1921.

36   **When he does remember** RR: *pain with the coloring of the falling leaves in the autumn* (*Where's the Rest of Me?,* 18); D. H. Lawrence: *as autumn deepens and darkens / I feel the pain of falling leaves.* "Shadows," *Last Poems,* ed. W. E. Williams (London, 1965), 133.

36   **"Football was a"** RR, *Where's the Rest of Me?,* 17–18.

37   **That was the set** RR interview, Sept. 17, 1986; see Harry Dice, "Radio Crystal Sets," *Cedar Co. Historical Review* (Iowa), July 1978.

37   **Let me tell you** RR, "Hail to the Medium," *Broadcasting,* Sept. 8, 1986; RR interview, Sept. 17, 1986. KDKA began the world's first regularly

scheduled radio broadcasts on Nov. 2, 1920. But RR could not have heard it before the very end of the following year. On Dec. 14, 1921, the Dixon *Evening Telegraph,* noting the presence of many young amateur radio operators in the city, announced that they would "very shortly" be able to benefit from the local installation of a "high power wireless telephone plant." Dixonians would probably soon be able to "hear the Chicago Grand Opera . . . without leaving home." RR states, puzzlingly, in *Where's the Rest of Me?,* 17, that his radio epiphany took place "in a room," whereas in several interviews with the author and in an address to the students of Eureka College in 1984 (*Time,* Feb. 20, 1984) he said it occurred "one Sunday afternoon . . . down by the river" and "under the bridge" in Dixon. The author has also interviewed Mrs. Howard Hall, the widow of the boy who built RR's borrowed crystal rectifier, and she corroborates these later memories.

37 **You know—none** RR interview, Aug. 18, 1988.

38 **Watch—this—space!** JR teaser ad, Dixon *Evening Telegraph,* Mar. 3 1921.

38 **For several years** RR, *An American Life,* 25–26.

38 **That was before** The Dixon *Evening Telegraph* ran countless front-page stories of booze-busting and still-bashing in the early 1920s. See, e.g., Jan. 3 and 4, Sept. 23, 1921.

39 **My mother was gone** RR, in both autobiographies and several conversations with the author, was specific that the following revelation occurred when he was "eleven"—i.e., after Feb. 6 and before the last snows of Mar. 1922. In a superscript on tear sheets from a *Saturday Evening Post* profile of Nelle (May/June 1985) he again confirms his age and says he had been "playing basketball" at "night." RRL/pp/hw. Margaret Cleaver Gordon, RR's former fiancée, confirmed to the author that the incident could not have occurred the following winter, since it definitely predated her arrival in Dixon in Sept. 1922. Interview, Jan. 27, 1988.

39 **It was Jack lying** RR, *An American Life,* 33; RR, *Where's the Rest of Me?,* 7–8. RR remembered JR saying to Nelle around this time, "If you ever smell a drop on me, lock me in. Lock me in the bedroom if you have to. Don't let me out." RR interview, Jan. 9, 1989.

40 **Reading *That Printer*** RR to Jean B. Wright, Mar. 13, 1984, RRL/pp/hw, copy in AC; RR interview, Sept. 17, 1986. Harold Bell Wright (1872–1944), was the son of an alcoholic and had grown up in poverty. After the enormous success of *That Printer of Udell's,* he went on to write many other inspirational novels based on the tenets of the Christian Church.

40 **The novel is** Wright, *That Printer,* 11–13.

40 **The narrative proper** Ibid., 14.

40 **He begins to walk** Ibid., 22–33.

40 **Dick is finally** Ibid., 40, 59.

40 **Alone in his poor** Ibid., 63.

40 **Worshipers at the** Ibid., 77–90.

41 **He strikes her as** Ibid., 91–98.

41 **Church elders appoint** Ibid., 101–7.

41   **Winter settles over**   Ibid., 110–17.

41   **Dick's great moment**   Ibid., 121–24.

41   **Economics, evidently**   Ibid., 125.

42   **Amy, however**   Ibid., 342–45.

42   **"I want to be like"**   RR interview, Sept. 17, 1986.

42   **Nelle Reagan saw**   Wills, *Reagan's America,* 21; RR to Jean Wright, Mar. 13, 1984.

42   **Such was his fervor**   RR to Rev. Adrian Rogers, qu. in Edwards, *Early Reagan,* 58. A neighbor recalls coming into the Reagan house that day and finding both brothers in swimming trunks. "Shh, we're going to get baptized—don't let Jack know." George O'Malley interview, Feb. 4, 1988. Neil soon reverted to Catholicism. But there never seems to have been any question in RR's mind that he wanted to worship with Nelle and the Disciples of Christ. RR interviewed by Myron C. Cole, pastor, July 1980, Dixon First Christian Church literature; Diary of Mrs. Howard Hall, June 21, 1922, copied by Marion Foster, privately held. See also "Ronald Reagan's Boyhood Church," brochure published by the First Christian Church of Dixon, ca. 1981. The church had been dedicated on June 18, 1922, just three days before RR's baptism.

4: A World Elsewhere

44   **I got a copy**   Robert Louis Stevenson, *Weir of Hermiston* (1896).

46   **Sometime that summer**   RR interview, Aug. 18, 1988; RR, *Where's the Rest of Me?,* 19.

46   **Then one day**   Ibid. The phrase *large blocks of essentials* is borrowed from Dorothy Caruso's description of her husband in *Enrico Caruso: His Life and Death* (New York, 1945), 58.

46   **His tastes were those**   Edwards, *Early Reagan,* 53; RR interview, Sept. 17, 1986.

47   **"a world elsewhere"**   Shakespeare, *Coriolanus,* 3.3.

47   **My uncle flipped**   King's School prospectus, 1924–25, copy in school archives, Canterbury, England.

47   **The King's School was**   Descriptive and atmospheric details in the following paragraphs are based on the author's own recollections of the King's School, supplemented by interviews with Alaric Jacob, Nov. 15, 1990; Peter Pollak, May 22, 1990; and Canon A.C.J. Phillips, May 22, 1990. See also Alaric Jacob, *Scenes From a Bourgeois Life* (London, 1949), 67–79, and David Edwards, *A History of the King's School, Canterbury* (London, 1957).

48   **Ronald Reagan once**   RR, *Where's the Rest of Me?,* 11. The following description of the Hendon Air Display of 1925 is based largely on illustrated accounts in *Flight,* June 25 and July 2, 1925, and in *The Aeroplane,* July 1, 1925.

49   **Dutch's little world**   The following description of Dixon is based on aerial photographs in NA, and by a Sanborn Fire Insurance map of the city so exquisitely detailed as even to indicate the number of shutters on each house. Atmospheric touches: EM Notes, Sept. 4, 1986.

49   **A white-streaming**   Photographs in RR Dixon Scrapbook, RRL/pp.

50   **Looking down at**   RR recalls 318 W. Everett as a step up, "a larger house on the north side" (*An American Life,* 29). In fact, it was so much smaller than the already small house on S. Hennepin that he and Neil had to sleep on the porch. RR entered DHS North Side on Sept. 3, 1924.

51   **So the Rock River**   Neil Reagan interview, May 7, 1987; RR, *An American Life,* 20.

51   **veils of cigarette smoke**   Q. "Jack smoked as well as boozed, Mr. President?" A. (*chuckling*) "I guess you could call him a one-match-a-day man." RR interview, May 10, 1992.

51   **the new chautauqua**   Dixon *Evening Telegraph,* June 25, 1925.

51   **Dixon's rail grid**   Dan Shiaras, "Riding the Milk Run to Sterling on the SD&EI," Dixon *Evening Telegraph* clipping, n.d. (ca. 1981), AC.

51   **Might that be**   Reminiscence "By One Who Knew Him," Dixon *Evening Telegraph,* Sept. 15, 1941; RR, *An American Life,* 30.

52   **A great fleet**   Burroughs, *A Princess of Mars,* 166.

52   **"It wasn't play-acting"**   "By One Who Knew Him."

52   **If so, then**   RR interview, Aug. 18, 1988; RR interviewed by Mark Shields, *The Washington Post,* Mar. 2, 1981.

53   **Bell Harry was**   Paul Pollak interview, May 21, 1990; un. news clipping, Mar. 29, 1926, King's School Archives, Canterbury.

53   **Just about then**   RR interview, Aug. 18, 1988; *Famous Gospel Hymns,* ed. D. B. Towner and E. O. Excell (Chicago, 1907). Heirloom Christian Church hymnal in possession of Marion Foster, Dixon, Ill.; Marion Foster interview, Aug. 20, 1991; photographs in Dixon Public Library.

54   **That summer, Dutch**   RR handwritten insert on speech draft, United Brotherhood of Carpenters, Aug. 15, 1981, RRL/pp/hw; RR, *Where's the Rest of Me?,* 20.

54   **Deaf and distracted**   RR interview, Aug. 18, 1988.

54   **Surveying, which**   RR, *An American Life,* 49.

54   **Grand Detour (pop. 225)**   Dan Shiaras, "Dixon Electric Trolley Line," Dixon *Evening Telegraph* clipping, n.d., c. 1981, AC.

55   **On the Thursday morning**   Dixon *Evening Telegraph,* Nov. 11 and 12, 1926; photographs in Dixon Public Library. The Fields movie was *So's Your Old Man.* Had the author read the local paper that Armistice Day, he would have come across a long poem by Nelle Reagan entitled "Lest We Forget." Its last lines had some applicability to the future career of her son: *But this we know, that you have won / For the world Democracy, / And doomed forever and alway / The cruel Autocracy.*

55   **The shimmering window**   The following account owes much to a detailed report in the Dixon *Evening Telegraph,* Nov. 12, 1926.

56   **I saw, I registered**   RR, *An American Life,* 40. See also the photograph of RR as schoolboy footballer in *Life,* Dec. 1980.

56   **exuding liniment**   Neuropsychologists note that the sense of smell is rooted in the most primal part of the brain—hence the unsurpassed power of certain fragrances to reawaken memory. RR frequently, both in his writings and *viva voce,* cited that of liniment as inseparable, in his

mind, from football and fall weather. See, e.g., his short story "School Spirit," RRL/pp (and below, Ch. 7); RR, *Where's the Rest of Me?*, 31: "The air . . . somehow kept smelling like liniment and football."

56 **"Dutch," the youth** This remark was evidently overheard by a DHS reporter. See *Dixonian* (1927), 84: " 'Dutch,' the lightest but fastest guard on the team, won his letter through sheer grit."

57 **Hydrotherapy my** PR to author, July 13, 1927; Wills, *Reagan's America,* 31. A confusion has arisen as to whether RR spent six or seven summers as lifeguard at Lowell Park. RR himself got in the habit of using the figure seven, as a consequence of having saved seventy-seven lives there. Actually, he served six summers from 1927 to 1932, after his first vacation job as a construction worker in 1926. RR to Henry Strong Educational Foundation, Sept. 14, 1931, RRL/pp.

57 **I learned that Regan** Helen Lawton interview, Sept. 6, 1986; *American National Red Cross Life Saving Methods* (Washington, D.C., 1925), 5.

58 **These impressive** The sluice gates frequently opened without warning, dragging weak swimmers downriver. RR, interview, July 15, 1993.

58 **What thoughts ran** RR interview, Feb. 27, 1991.

58 **On they come** *Dixonian,* 1928. See also Jim DuBois, "Dutch Reagan the Lifeguard," *U.S. Lifesaving,* 3.2 (summer 1981).

59 **Darkly pretty** RR, *An American Life,* 40; *Dixonian,* 1927, 1928, *passim;* Neil Reagan interview, Mar. 7, 1987. "Mugs," he told the author in old age, "spat tacks."

59 **By the end** Marion Foster interview, Aug. 20, 1991; *Dixonian* (1928).

60 **We pedaled south** The following description is based on old photographs collected by the author, WPA notes, ca. 1936, NA; EM Notes, Sept. 5, 1986; and Beatrice Howell Lanphier, "History of Lowell Park and the Dixon Park System," ts. in Dixon Public Library.

61 **He was deeply tan** Physical description based on home movies of the young RR taken at Lowell Park and preserved in RRL/av.

61 **When the one o'clock** The phrase "hidden currents swirled among slimy fingers" is RR's own.

62 **On August 3, 1928** This was RR's twenty-fifth rescue, according to the Dixon *Evening Telegraph.* Wills, *Reagan's America,* 31.

63 **"They'll accept just"** At a meeting of the Eureka board of trustees in July 1928, President Bert Wilson emphasized that the school's precarious financial position had created a desperate need for more freshmen. Harold Adams, *History of Eureka College* (Henry, Ill., 1982), 187–88.

63 *Das Ewig-Weibliche zeiht uns hinan* "The Eternal Feminine leads us on." From the "Chorus Mysticus" in the second part of Goethe's *Faust.*

5: Chimes at Midnight

64 **The first girl** Eureka *Pegasus,* Sept. 24, 1928; Margaret Cleaver Gordon interview, Jan. 27, 1988.

64 **It was Grind Night** *Eureka College Bulletin,* 1928–1929, Chapman A. Cottrell photo album; Eureka *Pegasus,* Sept. 24, 1928; Bill Major interviewed by Ralph Keyes, Jan. 23, 1967; KEY.

65   **Under bunched balloons**   Lola Lampe Müller Scrapbook, privately held; RR ms., Dec. 2, 1927; Neil Reagan interview, Mar. 7, 1987.

65   **How delicious they**   Wilfred Müller interview, May 10, 1992; Eureka yearbook, *Prism,* 1930; EM Diary, Sept. 21, 1928.

65   **After every "gentleman"**   William McClellan interview, May 26, 1991.

65   **When, in another age**   RR, *Where's the Rest of Me?,* 23–24. Specifically, Eureka lies nineteen miles east of Peoria, and one hundred forty miles south of Chicago. RR, improvised remarks at Eureka Reagan Fellows dinner, Washington, D.C., Sept. 23, 1986, WHTV, RRL/av.

66   **I confess I became**   *Eureka College Bulletin,* 1929; EM Notes; Adams, *History of Eureka, passim.* The Administration Building (1858) and Chapel (1869) are now National Historic Sites.

66   **But I forget**   EM Notes; photographs in Lola Lampe Müller Scrapbook, RR; *Where's the Rest of Me?,* 25.

67   **Ralph McKinzie was**   Eureka Class of '32 group interview, May 9, 1992; Wilfred Müller interview, May 10, 1992; Cannon, *Reagan,* 37; RR, *Where's the Rest of Me?,* 35, 25.

67   **This disappointment**   Nancy Clark Reynolds interview, June 30, 1985; Michael Deaver interview, Aug. 6, 1990. See Eureka yearbook, *Prism,* 1930. Howard Short, team manager, said, "He got battered all over the place in practice and never played a minute in a game," qu. in Gannett news clip, n.d. [1980].

67   **I saw little**   RR interview, Apr. 8, 1992. Carl Ed's comic strip about the adventures of a dandyish, football-fumbling, perpetually lovesick youth was popular in the fall of 1928. *Chicago Tribune,* Dec. 2, 1928. Photographs in RRL/pp; RR, *Where's the Rest of Me?,* 23; Adams, *History of Eureka,* 190.

68   **the Teke house**   Still standing at no. 635. Neil Reagan interview, Mar. 7, 1987; RR to Ward Quaal, Nov. 29, 1971, RRL; Chicago *Sun-Times,* Apr. 30, 1967; Rhonda Rothballer, "Reagan Slept There," Peoria *Journal Star,* Nov. 30, 1980.

68   *twenty-three* **greeks**   *Prism,* 1929.

68   **but Reagan's prose**   Eureka *Pegasus,* Oct. 1 and 8, 1928.

68   **Margaret Cleaver was**   Margaret Cleaver Gordon to author, May 13, 1994. Class of '32 group interview, May 9, 1992.

68   **She was elected**   Eureka *Pegasus,* Oct. 1, 1928; RR quoted in Chicago *Sun-Times,* Sept. 29, 1980; Olive Barker Howard to RR, Dec. 9, 1980, RRL/pp.

69   **In later life**   RR interview, Apr. 8, 1992. Eureka's annual fee, payable in advance, was $180 (*Eureka College Bulletin,* 1929). In *Where's the Rest of Me?,* 24, RR recalls having saved the respectable sum of $400 (lifeguarding paid him about $175 per summer), but much of this money went to help his mother in the difficult times ahead. As will be seen, he had to apply for a loan to get through his last two years at Eureka.

70   **The actor in him**   Eureka *Pegasus,* Nov. 12, 1928.

70   **Eureka was self**   Ibid., Nov. 26, 1928, stresses the urgent need for more "frosh"; ibid., Oct. 15, 1928.

70   **President Wilson had**   S. H. Goodnight, trustee, to Richard Dickinson, Nov. 24, 1928, Eureka College Papers. Actually, Wilson had communi-

cated this news to the board at its annual meeting in July, but it was kept from the student body. For more detail, see Wills, *Reagan's America,* 36–40, and Adams, *History of Eureka.*

70   **Just how drastic** Eureka *Pegasus,* Nov. 19, 1928; Ernest Higdon and Mary Reesman interviewed by Ralph Keyes, Jan. 23, 1967, KEY.

71   **Among student liberals** Wills, *Reagan's America,* 44, shows that the dump-Wilson movement had been developing for three years. The strike's other leader was Senior-class President Howard Short, who remembers RR as "brash, smart-alecky, . . . cocky. He had a sharp tongue and a good wit." Qu. in Gannett news clip, n.d. [1980].

71   **On November 20** Eureka *Pegasus,* Nov. 26, 1928.

71   **Then we learned** Class of '32 group interview, May 9, 1992. Previous to Bert Wilson's assumption of the presidency of Eureka in 1923, Harrod had served as acting president.

71   **The problem is** Eureka *Pegasus,* Nov. 26, 1928.

72   **I remember reading** Peoria *Journal,* Nov. 23, 1928; *Prism,* 1930, 58.

72   **All along the bleachers** RR, *Where's the Rest of Me?,* 27: "Looking back from the bench was like looking at a card stunt: every one was hidden by a newspaper."

72   **Why, I wonder** Ibid. He also records a punt by "Lump" Watts that rose "over eighty yards in the air," and "through some technical error . . . has been kept out of the national records." The nearest Watts came to this was to punt thirty-five yards in a game against Normal some weeks previously.

73   **The trustees declined** Adams, *History of Eureka,* 189; Wills, *Reagan's America,* 46–47; Burrus Dickinson, qu. in Des Moines *Register,* May 7, 1967.

73   **Since the outcome** Class of '32 group interview, May 9, 1992; RR, *Where's the Rest of Me?,* 28.

73   **I was awakened** Eureka *Pegasus,* Dec. 11, 1928; Wilfred Müller interview, May 10, 1992; Mrs. C. O. Patterson, among throng in 1928 ("Goodness, it was so exciting!"), Peoria *Journal-Star,* Mar. 8, 1981.

73   **At this point** EM Notes, Oct. 6, 1989. Anna Mae Hulett Roberts interview, May 9, 1992. Howard Short recalled that RR was chosen because "he was the loudest freshman there." Wilfred Müller interview, May 10, 1992. According to Margaret Cleaver Gordon, interview, Jan. 27, 1988, "his speech didn't make waves." The strike, however, was big enough news to be reported in *The New York Times,* Nov. 29, 1929.

73   **"This committee has"** Qu. in Eureka *Pegasus,* Dec. 11, 1928. To this was added a vague pledge of "loyal and whole-hearted support to a reorganization for the betterment of Eureka College."

74   *So what did* RR, *An American Life,* 48.

74   **I discovered** RR, *Where's the Rest of Me?,* 28–29.

74   **Maybe he did** Eureka *Pegasus,* Dec. 11, 1928; *Flight,* June 27, 1925.

74   **Everybody won** Adams, *History of Eureka,* 191; Eureka *Pegasus,* Dec. 11, 1928; RR, *Where's the Rest of Me?,* 30. The student committee also withdrew—too late—its demand that Wilson resign. Qu. in Wills, *Reagan's America,* 50.

75   ***When we leave***   Score and lyrics, AC. For a recording by the Eureka College Chorus, see the audiobook version of this biography (New York, 1999).

6: Air and Water

76   **Our four-eyed**   Wilfred Müller interview, May 10, 1992; RR, "Moral Victory," ms., RRL/pp (see next chapter); *Prism,* 1930; Ernest Higdon interviewed by Ralph Keyes, Jan. 23, 1967, KEY. "Red Devils" = Eureka basketball team.

76   **Between you & me**   Class of '32 group interview, May 9, 1992; Elmer Fischer qu. in Peoria *Journal-Star,* Nov. 30, 1980.

77   **Lilac time**   RR waxes nostalgic for Eureka's lilacs in a letter to Kip Hayden, Oct. 30, 1974, RRL/pp/hw.

77   **When Mary**   Mary Rae's scrapbook has been lost. A similar one is preserved by her classmate Lola Lampe Müller, in Long Point, Ill.

78   **Feel kind of sorry**   Wills, *Reagan's America,* 14. JR employment record, NA. The Fashion Boot Shop appears to have closed down early in 1929, a victim of the already roaring farm-states depression.

78   **Dutch is back**   RR to H. L. Glessner, ca. Nov. 9, 1982, RRL/pp; RR interview, Mar. 28, 1987. His idea was to work as a surveyor's rodman for a year, train on the Rock River, and attend Wisconsin in the fall of 1930. RR, *An American Life,* 49.

78   **Jack out of work**   Actually, JR, after a humiliating temporary job at the Dixon Home for the Feeble-Minded, was again employed as a shoe salesman. Dixon *Evening Telegraph,* Aug. 30, 1929.

78   **Young "Ronald"**   RR interview, Mar. 28, 1987; RR, *Where's the Rest of Me?,* 31; Anna Mae Hulett Roberts interview, May 9, 1992.

79   **Meantime, he's hung**   RR, *An American Life,* 51. "They were the one sure thing in campus—everyone knew they would get married if he got a job." William McClellan interview, May 26, 1991.

79   **P.S. Did you know**   Neil Reagan Oral History, RRL; TKE Scrapbook, RRP.

79   **On the reverse**   The block letter may have been a visual pun by PR. According to RR, a desperate practice tackle at mid-season earned him his promotion. "Never before or since did I throw such a block. I hit him [the assistant coach] solidly. It seemed as if [he] was in the air long enough for me to recite 'Mary had a little lamb.' " RR, *Where's the Rest of Me?,* 36; RR, *An American Life,* 52.

79   **"No, I never"**   RR interview, Apr. 8, 1992.

79   **He did not entirely**   Neil Reagan Oral History, RRL; JR employment record, NA; Margaret Cleaver Gordon interview, Jan. 27, 1988.

79   **Nelle stayed in**   JR employment record, NA; Marion Foster interview, Sept. 9, 1990.

79   **"winged and ready"**   EM to PR, Apr. 1, 1930, AC. Transport pilot recruiting was down, following the spectacular crash of a TAT airliner in Sept. 1929, just as the industry was gearing up for coast-to-coast service. Chicago *Herald and Examiner,* Apr. 13, 1930.

PAGE

80   **It was there**   Official Program, LAW; Lynn Miller Rein, *Northwestern School of Speech: A History* (Evanston, Ill., 1981), 232–34, 57.

80   **The pool is very**   Edna St. Vincent Millay, "Aria da Capo: A Play in One Act," in *The Chapbook* (London), no. 14 (Aug. 1919), 18.

80   **The curtain rose**   Production photographs in Eureka *Prism* (yearbook), 1931.

80   **Pierrot, a macaroon!**   Millay, "Aria," 3.

81   **Sir, we are not**   Ibid., 9.

81   **How gently in**   Ibid., 10.

81   **Oh, Thyrsis, just**   Ibid., 12.

82   **Oh, Thyrsis, now**   Ibid., 13–14.

82   **I wonder what**   Ibid., 14.

82   **I'll hold the bowl**   Ibid., 22.

83   **We can't sit**   Ibid., 24.

83   **All I remember**   "Dying is the only way to live in the theater." RR, *Where's the Rest of Me?,* 43. In the early 1930s, Edna St. Vincent Millay was at the height of her fame as a poet and dramatist. For contemporary critical reactions to the play, see *Critical Essays on Edna St. Vincent Millay,* William B. Thesing, ed. (New York, 1993).

83   **As a result of**   RR, *Where's the Rest of Me?,* 44; RR, *An American Life,* 58; Eureka *Prism,* 1930; PR to EM, Apr. 20, 1930, AC. With his usual romanticizing hindsight, RR remembers the Eureka production coming in second among twelve contestants. Actually, it ranked third of nine.

83   **I could not stop**   *Chicago Tribune,* Apr. 12, 1930. The "Priest of the Air" had received death threats as a result of his anti-Marxist radio broadcasts. In Germany, Chancellor Heinrich Brüning's fledgling government was on the point of collapse, caught between the rising contentions of Nazis and Communists.

84   **Coach Mac has**   RR described his stick technique as follows: "You listened to radio and you listened to the games, and pretty soon I was talking like that. I'd sit around with the fellas in the fraternity house, and I'd do it as if it were an imaginary game, and say to them [*voice quickening*]: 'The ball has snapped and so-and-so's going wide right; Cupsack is on tackle—reverses it—and he's into the secondary—' things like this. . . . It didn't come strange to me, [these were] things you heard on the radio [*chuckle*]." RR interview, Nov. 8, 1988. W. Franklin Burghardt recalled his performances in an interview with Henry Allen, "The Saga of Burgie and Dutch," *The Washington Post,* Mar. 7, 1981. Ralph McKinzie told the Chicago *Sun-Times,* Apr. 30, 1967, that RR used to lace his commentaries with humor: "He had us all in stitches."

84   **By Dutch's own**   RR, *Where's the Rest of Me?,* 32.

84   **You ask about**   William McClellan interview, May 26, 1991; Helen Lawton interview, Sept. 1986; Jean Kinney Jones interview, spring 1991; Wilfred Müller interview, May 10, 1992; George O'Malley interviewed by Marion Elizabeth Rogers, Feb. 4, 1988. Neil became a Catholic again in Apr. 1927, and for the rest of his life resented the fact that Nelle Reagan kept his original baptism a secret from him. McClellan (Neil Reagan's TKE roommate) remembers him as coldly intelligent and not unkindly,

"but his needling manner made you want to kill him. . . . Moon could bring Dutch to tears." Mutual friends interviewed by Ralph Keyes and the author agree that Neil was much the quicker of the two brothers, and the more powerful personality at Eureka.

84   **But I had gotten**   "Chicago Nation's Air Center for Mail and Passengers," Chicago *Daily News,* July 1, 1929; John Drury, *A Century of Progress: Authorized Guide to Chicago* (Chicago, 1933), 61.

85   **Actually the job**   *N.A.T. Bulletin Board,* June 1931; EM to PR, Sept. 18, 1930.

85   **the Lindy Light**   The Lindbergh Beacon, just dedicated atop Chicago's Palmolive Building, was the world's largest searchlight, with 2.2 million candlepower. It was the opening and closing symbol of the author's unpublished novel, *Ailerons.*

85   **Talking of titles**   RR to Henry Strong Educational Foundation, loan application form, Sept. 14, 1931, RRL/pp; *Prism,* vol. 32, 136.

85   **Dutch is in mourning**   Knute Rockne, the great football coach of Notre Dame, had been killed in a Fokker Tri-Motor crash five days before.

86   **Mary heard from**   RR to Henry Strong Educational Foundation, Sept. 14, 1931, RRL/pp. His junior-year grades were as follows: Principles of Sociology, B; Advanced Composition, B–; Europe since 1815, C+; Principles of Economics, C+; Immigration, C+; Intermediate French, C+ and C; Apostolic Age, C; English History, D; Life of Christ, D (RRL/pp).

86   **Moon got straight As**   William McClellan interview, May 26, 1992.

86   **Dutch is back**   Dixon *Evening Telegraph,* undated clipping, ca. July 1, 1931, Nelle Reagan Scrapbook, RRL/pp.; Edwards, *Early Reagan,* 65–66. The horse was used to haul cleaning equipment around Lowell Park. "Before I knew it I liked riding." RR to Rudolph Hines, Sept. 9, 1985, RRL/pp.

86   **Our friend is talking**   RR to Henry Strong Educational Foundation, Sept. 14, 1931, RRL/pp. Most of the Eureka student body was receiving aid of some kind in 1931–1932. See Adams, *History of Eureka,* 201.

86   **this loan application**   Copy in RRL/hp.

87   **Dutch, bless his**   *Western Courier* (Macomb, Ill.), Oct. 15, 1931. In an unidentified newspaper interview by Adam Street, "Never Call Him Ronald" (Nelle Reagan Scrapbook, RRL/pp, ca. Sept. 30, 1936), RR said that at Eureka he "never allowed anyone to call him Ronald." Nor did he ever "use quotation marks" about the name Dutch.

87   **Devils 13–16 against**   RR, *Where's the Rest of Me?,* 50; Eureka *Pegasus* and *Western Courier,* Oct. 15, 1931.

87   **I print the**   RR to Ron Cochran, May 12, 1980, RRL/pp; see below, pp. 111–12.

89   **From what Paul**   William McClellan interview, May 26, 1991; RR qu. in John Hutton Diary, Jan. 4, 1987, JHP.

89   **"I played opposite"**   News clipping, n.d., RRL/pp; EM Notes, May 9, 1992. "[Football] is the nearest thing to war without being lethal. It is the last thing left in civilization where two men can literally fling themselves at one another in combat and not be at war. It's a kind of clean hatred."

RR interviewed by Mark Shields, "Reagan on Athletics," *The Washington Post,* Mar. 7, 1981.

89   **Latest campus scandal**   RR has often told this story himself, although he misremembers the incident as occurring entirely in Dixon.

89   **Burghardt, who**   Allen, "The Saga of Burgie and Dutch." The two men became lifelong, if distant, friends. Burghardt expressed great affection for the President but said of his remark to Carter (Oct. 28, 1980), "It was the dumbest thing a person could say." See also Shields, "Reagan on Athletics."

89   **The same could not**   RR, *Where's the Rest of Me?,* 8–9.

90   **Dutch came south**   Ibid., 41.

90   **When Paul, pressed**   Ibid., 41; EM to PR, Jan. 31, 1932; RR interview, Dec. 22, 1986. Garry Wills, in *Reagan's America,* analyzes RR's "confused" chronology of his father's employment record, centering on the Christmas Eve incident. According to Wills (60–61), the blue slip must have arrived in 1932, not, as RR says, "that last year of mine in college." Wills reasons that RR's subsequent segue (*Where's the Rest of Me?,* 52) into details of New Deal programs that rescued Jack Reagan from unemployment in 1932 is deluded because the New Deal did not become operative until after Franklin Roosevelt's inauguration in 1933. This is true enough, but RR's chronology is more accurate than Wills thinks it is.

The Fashion Boot Shop was out of business at least by Aug. 13, 1929, because the Dixon *Evening Telegraph* has JR working for another local shoe store on that day. On Jan. 7, 1930, the same paper reports his employment by the Red Wing Company as a traveling salesman (Wills, *Reagan's America,* 14). In his employment record, NA, JR states that he worked for Red Wing throughout 1930 and 1931. RR relates the blue slip to JR's job as a traveler (*Where's the Rest of Me?,* 41; *An American Life,* 55; RR interview, Dec. 12, 1988). The author therefore goes by this chronology:

1920–1929 "Own retail shoe business" (JR employment record)

1930–1931 "Red Wing Shoe Co., Red Wing Minn." (ibid.)

Sept. 1931 JR still a "shoe salesman" (RR student-loan application, RRL/pp)

Dec. 24, 1931 JR fired

1932 JR unemployed through June, then employed by the IERC.

90   **Too bad you didn't**   Mary Rae had announced her engagement to one of the graduating seniors.

90   **"No. 1 couple"**   William McClellan interview, May 26, 1991; Harrod qu. in class of '32 interview, May 9, 1992. The ivy PR refers to is a traditional garland woven at Eureka graduation exercises, entwined in such a way that engaged couples are separated from the rest of the student body. Rev. Cleaver was by then living in Eureka, having become pastor of the local Christian Church in 1931. For a detailed analysis of the relationship between RR and Rev. Cleaver (who was something of a father to him), see Stephen Vaughn, *Ronald Reagan in Hollywood* (New York, 1994), 8–16. RR could congratulate himself on an exemplary college record, having scored well above the academic average, served three years

as a first-string football guard, three years as chief basketball cheer-leader, three years as the school's top swimmer, one year as swim coach, one year as a reporter on the Eureka *Pegasus,* and two years as feature editor of the yearbook, *Prism.* He had served two years as a member of the student Senate, and one year as its president. He was also at various times president of the Homecoming celebrations, and president of his class in 1931–1932.

91   **After all these years**   PR was mistaken in thinking these were RR's final grades. They in fact reflect his half-year standing of several months be-fore (Clara Bentley, Eureka registrar, to Henry Strong Educational Foundation, Feb. 1, 1932, RRL/pp). Ms. Bentley confirmed in a subse-quent letter to the Strong Foundation (June 16, 1932) that RR at gradu-ation was "much above average in ability and accomplishments." His final baccalaureate degree in social sciences and economics registered the following marks: Labor Problems, B; Investments, B; Senior Economics, B; Creative Writing, B–; Criminology, B; Principles of Education, C. Ibid.

91   **Dutch has bet**   As will be seen, RR fulfilled this extravagant promise with just over a month to spare.

91   **too broke to buy**   RR at Eureka Class of '32 reunion, May 9, 1992; RR, *An American Life,* 55; RR to A. J. Wilson, Feb. 3, 1932, RRL/pp. On Sept. 23, 1987, the President was "finally awarded" his class ring at a cer-emony in Washington. WHTV clip, RRL/av. RR remained a generous patron of his *alma mater* in later life (though not as generous as his brother, Neil). In 1947, he gave the college fifty thousand dollars to endow a "Reagan-Wyman School of Speech," and pledged to extend this gift to seventy-five thousand dollars over three years. He also "gave the college a forty-acre tract of land in the middle 1950s, and in three or four years he sold it and the college was given the profit." Sam Harrod inter-viewed by Ralph Keyes, Jan. 22, 1966, KEY. Because of RR's divorce from JW in 1948, the school of speech was never built.

91   **You're just another**   Or, as RR told the author on Jan. 27, 1991, "They were just figures in the water." He went on to say that he developed the habit of notching the log as a means of controlling his anger because of the invariable failure of any of his rescuees to thank him. In all his career, "only one man did, and he was blind" (ibid.). See also A. Beachcomber, "A Man, a Log, and a River," Dixon *Evening Telegraph,* Sept. 12, 1941; RR, *Where's the Rest of Me?,* 21.

7: The Indifferent Figure in the Sand

92   **Until he became**   To this day, the first page of RR's First Inaugural ex-ists only in xerographic copy (RRL/pp). RR vaguely recalled asking an old friend if she wanted the original as "a souvenir."

93   **His handwriting at**   Like many another excellent speller, Reagan has some orthographical blind spots. He invariably retains the *y* when plu-ralizing words such as *belly* and *mystery,* and has a quaint, adman's habit

of writing *nite* for *night*. White House aides snickered at his insistence on writing *burocrat* and *burocracy,* unaware that the President was being faithful to the Simplified Spelling reform movement of his youth.

93   **Only the occasional**   "As long as he could remember things seemed more natural with the left hand, but by convention he had learned to use his right. His dominant eye was his left." John Hutton Diary, Aug. 27, 1987, JHP. Other signs of RR's suppressed left-handedness: as an actor he shot and twirled his revolver in his left hand, and slapped and punched with it. He combed his hair from right to left and when accosted by photographers, always tended to wave with his left hand. Of all the forty presidential signatures reproduced in the anteroom of the Reagan Library Museum, RR's is the only one that slopes backward.

94   **§1. "Halloween"**   All mss. cited hereafter are on deposit at RRL.

95   **Reagan renders**   RR, open letter to Neil Reagan, *Dixonian,* 14 (1927), 111.

96   **"Tears of helpless"**   Katy Boyd, who was rescued four times as a child by RR and later became a Lowell Park lifeguard herself, recalls that "the girls were always sitting around mooning at him, but it was not a two-way street." Qu. in DuBois, "Dutch Reagan the Lifeguard."

98   **"Sou'-Sou' Southerly"**   The Roosevelt essay, written at age twenty-two, has been published in *Gray's Sporting Journal,* 13.3 (fall 1988).

101   **sobbed like a baby**   The great coach Knute Rockne had been killed the year before this story was written. (See p. 85.) George Gipp ("the Gipper") was an equally legendary halfback, trained by Rockne before dying prematurely of pneumonia in 1920. Sentimental tradition has it that Rockne used Gipp's dying words to inspire his players when they were facing defeat against Army in 1928. As Murray Sperber has shown recently in *Shake Down the Thunder: The Creation of Notre Dame Football* (New York, 1993), 284, the legend originates in a ghostwritten autobiographical article "by" Rockne in *Collier's,* Nov. 22, 1930. In old age RR was enraged by Sperber's documented revelations that the article was written by one John B. Kennedy and that neither Kennedy nor Rockne was present at Gipp's deathbed. "It's just not *true!*" For the relationships between fact, legend, and RR's 1940 movie *Knute Rockne: All-American,* see Wills, *Reagan's America,* 120–23.

101   **The story begins**   The ability to start well—to arrest attention while telegraphing a vital minimum of information—is a sure sign of literary talent. Young RR's openers indicate that he could have become, if not a writer of fiction, at least a good journalist. Here are a few other examples: "Mark had with an air of mystery and promise, insisted that I dine with him" (§4). "The morning sun pushed its feeble warmth through the cold mist that sought to hide a world of torn earth and blood" (§14). "Someone whose word was generally accepted advanced the statement, 'Any time three or four men get together, the conversation will eventually turn to either women or religion' " (§15). "Gears grated noisily as the huge bus crawled across the main corner of the little town and drew to a grumbling stop before the dingy news stand which served as depot to the Central West lines" (§17).

102   **tall, genial, good-looking boy**   RR lives, literarily speaking, in lofty company. The only short person in his entire *oeuvre* is the wax-mustached crook who plots to burgle the U.S. Treasury.

107   ~~white private house~~   The building described in this erased sentence is the Eureka Christian Church parsonage, where RR's fiancée lived. Margaret Cleaver Gordon to the author, May 13, 1994.

8: Long Blue Shadows

108   **The President of**   RR interview, June 12, 1986. See also RR, *Where's the Rest of Me?*, 29. RR's remembered version of the speech is slightly different from the original: *"My God! You bloody little swine! You think I don't care—you think you're the only soul that cares!"* R. C. Sherriff, *Journey's End* (New York, 1933), 3.2.

108   **I wasn't sure**   RR, *Where's the Rest of Me?*, 29. RR wrongly dates this as occurring in his freshman year. *Journey's End,* a worldwide sensation in 1929, opened at the Adelphi Theater in Chicago on Sept. 9, 1929 (*The New York Times,* Mar. 16, 1930). See also RR, *An American Life,* 57: "I was drawn to the stage that night as if it were a magnet, astonished by the magic of an ordinary man convincing an audience that he was someone else."

108   **Or that at Eureka**   Alma Steider, Eureka College librarian in the 1930s, interviewed by Ralph Keyes, Jan. 23, 1967. RR acted the part at Eureka on Apr. 8, 1932.

108   **With such promise**   See also RR, *An American Life:* "Hollywood and Broadway were at least as remote from Dixon as the moon was in 1932," 59. RR interview, Ann Marsters, Chicago *Record-Herald,* Oct. 4, 1939; see also RR, *Where's the Rest of Me?,* 44; JR employment record, NA.

109   **Those of us**   Katy Boyd, qu. in DuBois, "Dutch Reagan the Lifeguard."

109   **"Moon says"**   Neil Reagan interview, Mar. 7, 1987; see also Cannon, *Ronnie and Jesse: A Political Odyssey* (Garden City, N.Y., 1969), 8.

109   **"I realized dramatics"**   RR to James Masters, Apr. 25, 1968, RRL/pp.

109   **"I was the only"**   RR, qu. in Edwards, *Early Reagan,* 64; Beachcomber, "A Man, a Log, and a River." "He did it well. And the reason he did it well was because he had enough imagination to visualize how someone other than himself would react under a given set of circumstances."

110   **a bittersweet parting**   According to Margaret Cleaver Gordon (interview, Jan. 27, 1988), RR was not even able to give her a ring until the following summer, when he presented her with "a solitaire." See also RR, *Where's the Rest of Me?,* 45. After RR became President, he heard that Richard Bryan, a writer and member of the Authors Institute of America, remembered picking him up on the road to Chicago and treating him to dinner. The President wondered disingenuously "if he ever knew I finally did land in radio." RR to Hamilton Stewart, Mar. 28, 1983, RRL/pp. For his parting from Margaret Cleaver, see RR, *Where's the Rest of Me?,* 45: "How could we know it would truly be a farewell to the

romance of youth? . . . Our lovely and wholesome relationship did not survive growing up."

110 **"He bet the fellows"** RR, *Where's the Rest of Me?*, 45.

110 **That Reagan was** William McClellan interview, May 26, 1991; RR to GOP Congressional leaders, Sept. 15, 1987; EM Notes.

111 **I started out** RR interview, Feb. 9, 1988. For a video version of the entire story, see RR address to the Eureka Reagan Scholars Board in Washington, D.C., Sept. 23, 1986, WHTV, RRL/av.

112 *A chill wind* Des Moines *Register,* Oct. 2 and 23, 1932; RR, *Where's the Rest of Me?*, 50. For a presidential replay, see, e.g., RR to Hugh Sidey in *Time,* Jan. 5, 1981.

112 **Dutch instinctively** RR, *An American Life,* 59.

112 **The announcer, reading** *Where's the Rest of Me?*, 51.

112 **So it was as** RR interview, June 12, 1986.

112 **The Hawkeyes scored** *Chicago Tribune,* Oct. 2, 1932; RR, *Where's the Rest of Me?*, 52; William McClellan interview, May 26, 1991. McClellan was present in the TKE lodge the night RR stopped over.

113 **What he got was** RR, *Where's the Rest of Me?*, 52; newspaper accounts qu. in Vaughn, *Ronald Reagan in Hollywood,* 23, 248.

113 **But he was correct** John H. Garraty, *The Great Depression* (New York, 1986), 46, 82.

113 **In the new year** Chicago *Daily News,* July 1, 1929. Although radio beacons were fast supplanting these "landmark lights," pilots frustrated by poor reception, bent beams, and "false cones of silence" continued to rely on them for many years. See Richard Duncan, *Air Navigation and Meteorology,* 3d ed. (Chicago, 1936), 82.

113 **"the low point of"** RR, *An American Life,* 81.

113 **His father, who** RR interview, Nov. 4, 1987; RR, *Where's the Rest of Me?*, 52–53. See also RR, *An American Life,* 68–69.

114 **Through Jack, Dutch** RR fails (or forgets) to mention in his memoirs that JR's public employment began not with the *federal* government but with the *state* government (specifically, the Lee County branch of the IERC) in June 1932. JR's two-year gubernatorial appointment was as a "Work Relief Superintendent," so RR is correct in remembering him handing out workfare jobs in the year of FDR's election (RR, *Where's the Rest of Me?*, 53). The state's 1932 relief appropriation, voted that Feb., was drained so quickly by emergency applications that it all but ran out of funds at the end of July. The federal relief act of July 21, 1932, established a *new* IERC, effective immediately, and empowered it through FDR's inauguration in Mar. 1933. A nightmare of bureaucratic entanglements resulted, as Jack's office had to administer both state and federal programs. A summary of Jack Reagan's government jobs follows:

> *June 1932* [State] IERC Investigator of Relief Families, Lee County
> *July 1932* [Federal] *ditto*
> *Nov. 1933* CWA Certifying Officer
> *May 1934* CWA Work Relief Superintendent (promotion)
> *Sept. 1935* WPA County Technician
> *Jan. 1936* WPA Superintendent, Division of Labor Management, Lee County

From this it will be seen that JR's only period of joblessness in the Great Depression was the first five months of 1932. Sources: JR employment record, NA; Walter C. Hart, "Relief—As the Clients See It," M.A. diss., University of Chicago, School of Social Service Administration, 1936, copy in FWP/LC, 3; Frank D. Smith to H. E. Spencer, chairman Lee County ERC, Sept. 16, 1935, WPA Personnel Papers, NA.

114   **The relief he** RR, *An American Life,* 69; RR to A. J. Wilson, Mar. 25, 1933, RRL/pp; Dixon *Evening Telegraph,* Feb. 10, 1933. One hundred dollars a month was a generous starting salary in 1933, even by radio-station standards. RR's rent for rooms in the well-equipped Vale Apartments, down by the river, was eighteen dollars a month, and he could eat three times a day in the Palmer School cafeteria for $3.65. "You could get a made-to-measure suit with two pair of pants for $18.50," he wrote in *Where's the Rest of Me?,* 55. He could thus easily afford to pay ten dollars a month toward the cost of Neil Reagan's last year at college. Lou Cannon, *Reagan* (New York, 1982), 44.

114   **Even as he crossed** RR interview, Nov. 8, 1988. "His ambitions sort of crystallized—after radio, Hollywood." Margaret Cleaver Gordon interview, Jan. 23, 1988.

114   **For the time being** See "Bartlett Joshua Palmer," *National Cyclopaedia of American Biography,* vol. 47, 567; "50 Years of WOC," brochure, Feb. 18, 1972, in Putnam Museum, Davenport, Iowa. For a solemn portrait of Palmer, see Joseph E. Maynard, *Healing Hands: The Story of the Palmer Family, Discoverers and Developers of Chiropractic* (Freeport, N.Y., 1959). The book is rich with medical *aperçus* ("It would pay no one to drink his urine, from a nurturing standpoint") and contains a useful description of Palmer's proudest patent, the "electrococephaloneuro-mentimpograph." It also features the following affecting tribute to Pete MacArthur: "Eventually his entire body became solid bone from head to toe, even his jawbone. . . . But sickness didn't get Pete down. He still belonged to a quartet in Davenport that sang at noon Kiwanis meetings" (362, 82). See also Wills, *Reagan's America,* Ch. 11.

114   **A tiny elevator** Charles Freburg interview, June 23, 1990; RR, *Where's the Rest of Me?,* 47; picture postcards, ca. 1933, in AC.

114   **Dutch was no** Jean Kinney Jones interview, May 25, 1991; photographs, Davenport Chamber of Commerce. See Marlys Svendsen, *Davenport: A Pictorial History* (Davenport, Iowa, 1985), 147.

115   **In this musty company** RR, *An American Life,* 70. See also Wills, *Reagan's America,* 99. B. J. Palmer's interest in animals was by no means confined to dead specimens. He could sometimes be seen swaying over the crest of Brady Hill on a live elephant.

116   **He did not realize** B. J. Palmer had purchased WHO on New Year's Day 1930, but the formal merger of the two stations did not take place until Apr. 25, 1933. Ernest F. Andrews, Jr., "The Development of Amplitude Modulation Radio Broadcasting in Iowa," Ph.D. diss., University of Iowa, 1956, 549.

116   **Dutch innocently** B. J. Palmer had a policy, convenient for himself if not for his employees, of issuing no contracts and signing no salary checks. Wills, *Reagan's America,* 100, 104; RR to Henry Strong Educa-

PAGE

tional Foundation, Mar. 1929, 1933, RRL/pp; RR, *Where's the Rest of Me?*, 56.

116   **Apparently, he had**   RR, *Where's the Rest of Me?*, 56–58.

116   **WHO's state**   Colonel Palmer had invested nearly a quarter of a million dollars in re-equipping WHO "from the ground up." Its 532-foot antenna tower was the tallest structure in Iowa. Photographs and technical details in *WHO Barn Dance Frolic Souvenir Program,* 1936, ISHL.

117   **Here, over the**   "I just lack personality when I read." RR, *Where's the Rest of Me?*, 78–79. All his life, he found it easier to learn what he had to "read" by heart before going on the air. See comments by Burton Jewel and Ted Giesel below.

117   *Fast* **is not a word**   No aircheck exists to document RR's microphone style. However, there is ample evidence of the way he sounded in his first movie, *Love Is on the Air.* The script calls upon him to improvise sports commentary twice, at a junior "bike derby" and boxing match, and he does so with such energy and volubility that his voice has to be tuned down beneath the dialogue of other characters. Video copy, LC.

117   **"It's a hippity-hop"**   Favorite phrase of RR the sports broadcaster, recalled by a contemporary listener in *The Washington Post,* Sept. 30, 1980. Ponselle was singing Schubert's *Ave Maria.* Rosa Ponselle, *A Singer's Life* (New York, 1982), 267.

117   **"Life was hard"**   Hugh Sidey interview, Nov. 30, 1985.

117   **I can remember**   RR interview, June 28, 1988.

118   **I quote the above**   Marguerite ("Missy" LeHand) was the "secretary of the President" referred to in RR's monologue.

119   **Aside from Chicago**   *WPA Guide to Iowa* (Ames, Iowa, 1938, 1986), 227–29; Walter E. Shotwell interview, Oct. 4, 1989; RR interview, Dec. 22, 1986; random reading in Des Moines *Register,* Apr.–Sept. 1933. For a more recent description of the city, indicating that its blandness remains unchanged since RR's day ("Everyone is strangely serene"), see Bill Bryson, "Fat Girls in Des Moines," *Granta* 23 (spring 1988).

119   **Dutch gazed happily**   According to shoe shiner Mike Falbo, RR "always wore brown and white shoes" in summer. Interviewed by Walter Shotwell, Des Moines *Tribune,* Dec. 12, 1981.

119   **Large as Des Moines**   *WHO Family Album* (Des Moines, 1982), 2; RR, *Where's the Rest of Me?,* 58. The station's official call sign was now WHO-WOC, and remained so until the Davenport station regained its independence in the fall of 1934. RR's difficulty with the written word seems to have continued for many years. Burton B. Jewel, a Des Moines producer who hired him ca. 1935 to narrate a series of "Iowa News Flashes" taken from local newspapers, had to fire him because "he wouldn't follow the script." Des Moines *Tribune,* June 6, 1980. As late as Mar. 1945, Ted Giesel, making an anti-fraternization film with Frank Capra called *Your Job in Germany,* had to do the same, finding that RR's narrative tone lacked "understanding" as a narrator. Joseph McBride, *Frank Capra* (New York, 1982), 496.

119   **Wood was then**   "U.S. Scene," *Time,* Dec. 24, 1935. The first three Grant Wood paintings listed can be seen in, respectively, the Joslyn Art Mu-

seum, Omaha, the Metropolitan Museum of Art, New York City, and the Des Moines Art Center. *Spring Turning* is in private hands. See Wanda M. Corn, *Grant Wood: The Regionalist Vision* (New Haven, Conn., 1983) and James M. Dennis, *Grant Wood* (New York, 1975).

120   **In one of the**   EM Notes, Oct. 3, 1995. See also H. W. Janson, "The International Aspects of Regionalism," *College Art Journal* 1–2 (1941–1943), 113–14.

120   **Couldn't help noticing**   PR to EM, Aug. 21, 1934; RR, *An American Life,* 75. The "Virginia boy" was James Waddell Gordon, Jr., Margaret Cleaver's future husband. She married him on June 18, 1935.

121   **A warm Sunday night**   RR, qu. in *Sports Afield,* Feb. 1984; Des Moines *Register,* Jan. 28, 1984. RR's melodramatic shout is quoted by the nurse in question, Melba Lohmann King. He himself, in conversation with the author, recalled it simply as "Drop it—and get going." RR interview, Dec. 22, 1986; Ms. King to RR, Jan. 28, 1984, RRL/pp.

121   **A slight story**   Wills, *Reagan's America,* 110, notes that Ms. King does not recall seeing RR with a gun and therefore assumes the President was letting his imagination supply melodramatic details. It is a fact, however, that RR did acquire a 1934 Walther PPK .380 pocket-size police pistol early in his stay in Des Moines and kept it lovingly the rest of his life. He even toted it in his briefcase as President. "A man should be able to defend himself." RR qu. in John Hutton Diary, JHP.

121   **When I repeated**   Margaret Cleaver Gordon interview, Jan. 27, 1988. Mrs. Gordon was definite about returning the ring personally. RR, *An American Life,* 75, claims that she mailed it to him.

122   **I saw that same**   "Whatsisname" was B. J. Frazer. EM Notes, May 9, 1992. "Margaret's decision shattered me, not so much, I think, because she no longer loved me, but because I no longer had anyone to love." RR, *An American Life,* 75–76.

122   **A streamlined V-8**   RR had placed the order out of state as a favor to Margaret Cleaver: the dealer was her brother-in-law. It was a 1934 model (RR to Kathy Osborne, Apr. 17, 1984, RRL/pp/hw).

122   **He knew he looked**   RR to Monte Osburn, Mar. 29, 1982, RRL/pp/hw; Jeanne Tesdell Burington interview, Oct. 4, 1989; Jean Kinney Jones interview, May 25, 1991; Paul McGinn interview, Oct. 4, 1989; Walter E. Shotwell, "Dutch Reagan's Des Moines Days," Des Moines *Tribune,* June 6, 1980. Shotwell's article, based on extensive local research, is the best description of RR as a young sports broadcaster. The following paragraphs owe much to it, and to a day the author spent exploring Des Moines with Shotwell on Oct. 4, 1989.

122   **assigned the young man**   These commentaries, reaching listeners in seven or eight states, were in addition to RR's twice-daily "Teaberry Sports Reviews," Friday-night winner predictions, and Saturday-night summaries of results. McArthur biography in *WHO Barn Dance Frolic Souvenir Program, 1936;* RR, *Where's the Rest of Me?,* 48; Eureka *Pegasus,* Feb. 7, 1933; "Dutch Reagan Gives Sports Fans Daily Baseball Games," unidentified 1934 news clipping, Nelle Reagan Scrapbook, RRL/pp.

122　　**"Don" was**　RR, *An American Life,* 74–75; Shotwell, "Dutch Reagan's Des Moines Days"; RR "201" file, NPRC. His application for an appointment to the Officers' Reserve Corps is dated a month earlier (Feb. 27, 1935) and states that he is already a private in the Enlisted Reserve Corps Cavalry.

123　　**"Moon" was**　Dixon *Evening Telegraph,* Sept. 4, 1934; Davenport *Democrat,* Nov. 9, 1934; RR, *An American Life,* 72; Neil Reagan Oral History, RRL.

123　　**Happily for Cain**　Neil describes their fraternal relationship as affectionate but distant. "We didn't have what you would call great companionship . . . There was no thought of, you know, putting my arm around his shoulder." Neil Reagan Oral History, RRL; RR interview, Sept. 23, 1987.

123　　**"Cy" Griffith owned**　Shotwell, "Dutch Reagan's Des Moines Days." RR once described to the author, with relish, how the spiking was done: "You'd take out your flat bottle of alcohol and then you'd fill it up. . . . If you had a girl, you'd put her thumb over the bottle, and your thumb over hers—and you'd turn it upside down, and it'd almost blow your nose off!" Nothing remains of Cy's Moonlight Inn except its faded outdoor sign, now hung at the RR ranch in California. For more on RR's relations with Drake (the flagship school of the Disciples of Christ), see Wills, *Reagan's America,* 112–13.

123　　**He would pretend**　Glen Claussen and Pee Wee Williams interview, Aug. 31, 1987; David Dillon, "Sing a Song of Friendship," *ATØ Palm,* Sept. 2, 1982. Apparently the ensemble cut one record, now lost.

123　　**Jeanne Tesdell was**　Jeanne Tesdell Burington interview, Oct. 4, 1989; Shotwell, "Dutch Reagan's Des Moines Days".

123　　**Finally and most**　Joy Hodges interview, May 30, 1989.

124　　**Ronald Reagan at twenty-five**　Ibid. Myrtle Williams, who was something of a den mother to RR in Des Moines, takes credit for his lifelong love of macaroni and cheese.

124　　**Apparently, yes**　RR, *Where's the Rest of Me?,* 69; J. Maland biographical news clipping, ca. 1936, Nelle Reagan Scrapbook, RRL/pp.

124　　**There was much**　RR, *An American Life,* 77; RR to Ron Cochran, May 12, 1980, RRL. The Cubs came out of nowhere to make it to the 1935 World Series after a scorching twenty-one straight victories in Sept. RR had been associated with the team since his first days at WOC, when negotiations were begun to have him cover Cubs home games (and those of the White Sox) as "the sports announcer of the Atlas Special Brewing Co." Eureka *Pegasus,* Feb. 7, 1933.

124　　**What was more**　According to Wills, *Reagan's America,* 411, RR's column ("Around the World of Sports with Dutch Reagan") dates from June 2, 1935. The clips pasted into Nelle Reagan's Scrapbook (RRL/pp) seem to date from Jan. 1936.

124　　**Reaching San Francisco**　*Los Angeles Times* and Des Moines *Register,* Mar. 1, 1936. Three weeks before, a blizzard had immobilized all of Iowa. Temperatures plunged as low as −22° in Des Moines, −36° elsewhere. Even skunks froze.

125   **eighty-two degrees**   *Los Angeles Times,* Mar. 1, 1936. RR traveled to Santa Catalina as a sports broadcaster only twice, although he implied in his autobiographies that he went west with the Cubs at least three times. See, e.g., RR, *Where's the Rest of Me?,* 69–74. Both Edwards, *Early Reagan,* 152–57, and Wills, *Reagan's America,* 114, have him doing so only once, in 1937. The author has assembled all available points of reference, including numerous clips of RR's Des Moines *Dispatch* column, "Around the World of Sports with Dutch Reagan," in Nelle Reagan Scrapbook, RRL/pp, into a chronology too long and complex to print here. A reference copy has been deposited at RRL.

125   **Frustratingly, Union**   *The WPA Guide to California* (New York, 1939, 1984), 421–22; EM Notes, Mar. 7, 1987.

125   **Avalon in 1936**   Photographs in Avalon Historical Society; *WPA Guide to California,* 423–25; EM Notes, Mar. 7, 1987; Russell Fact Book, Avalon Casino Museum.

125   **In a grove**   Des Moines *Register,* Mar. 1, 1936.

125   **Say, Andy**   Andrew Lotshaw, Cubs trainer. Dialogue from RR, "Around the World of Sports," ca. Mar. 1, 1936, Nelle Reagan Scrapbook, RRL/pp.

126   **In James T. Farrell's**   *Extempore* quote by RR at White House Old Sportscasters Lunch, Oct. 20, 1986; David Voigt, *American Baseball* (1983), vol. 2, 240.

126   **The nearest he got**   Oral History interview, *Frontline,* PBS, Jan. 18, 1989; Unidentified news clipping, Nelle Reagan Scrapbook, RRL/pp.

126   **Intimate or not**   Edward C. Lambert, former WHO listener and broadcast executive, qu. in clip in Wilfred Müller Scrapbook, n.d.; RR, *Where's the Rest of Me?,* 65–66. The author has taken the liberty of replacing *pitcher* and *batter* with the names of Warnecke and Galan, whom RR mentions specifically on p. 67. In conversational reminiscence over the years, RR was just as likely to cite Dizzy Dean or Billy Jurges or both. For an amusing 1974 transcript, see Jules Witcover, *Marathon: The Pursuit of the Presidency, 1972–1976* (New York, 1977), 94.

127   **If WHO's telegraph**   RR, *Where's the Rest of Me?,* 65. This lag took into account the tapping of the press-box operator in Chicago and the typing of the studio telegrapher in Des Moines.

127   **He seemed determined**   The phraseology of this section derives entirely from clips of Ronald Reagan's column in the Des Moines *Dispatch,* Feb.–Nov. 1936, preserved in Nelle Reagan Scrapbook, RRL/pp. Some of his more obscure images need explaining. *Gas House gangsters:* Saint Louis Cardinals. *Moon over the mountain:* possibly derives from Max Baer's fight with Primo Carnera ("the Ambling Alp") in 1934. *Old Mose:* Robert Moses "Lefty" Grove, who was making a comeback in the 1936 season. *Bacon and beans:* the U.S. Olympic team had a pre-departure deficit of $150,000. *Goatskin underwear:* obscure, but RR had been using goat imagery ever since a wild goat–hunting expedition on Santa Catalina that March. *Adolf stuck his fuzzy lip:* Hitler opened the 1936 Olympic Games in Berlin. *Admiral Jack:* Jack Sharkey, world heavyweight champion, 1932. *Squeal of the gear:* tackling dummy. *Ebony eel:*

Ozzie Simmons, great ball carrier for the University of Iowa. *Maroon and gold:* colors of the University of Minnesota.

128   **brand-new Nash**   RR to Ralph Tipton, May 29, 1987, emphasizes that this Nash, "the one I drove to California," was different from his first, "a Nash [*sic*] Lafayette" (RRL/pp/hw).

128   **A *Sporting News* poll**   *Sporting News,* Oct. 15, 1936. RR's 4,710 write-in votes should be matched against 11,030 for the winner, Harry Johnson (KFAB, Lincoln, Neb.). Johnson was, moreover, one year his junior. However, it is interesting to see that they each had more fans than the great Red Barber (WSAI, Cincinnati) at 4,550. Harry Hartman of WCPO (Cincinnati) led among major-league commentators with 41,715.

128   **"Dutch has nothing"**   Adam Street, "Never Call Him Ronald," unidentified newsclip, ca. Oct. 1936, Nelle Reagan Scrapbook, RRL/pp.

128   **"He's a people pleaser"**   Jeanne Tesdell Burington interview, Feb. 24, 1991; see also Shotwell, "Dutch Reagan's Des Moines Days."

128   **"Happy nineteen-thirty-seven!"**   News clipping, n.d., in Wilfred Müller Scrapbook. RR's mike is now on permanent exhibition at RRL.

129   **On Friday, March 12**   *Los Angeles Times,* Mar. 13, 1937; RR, *Where's the Rest of Me?,* 71. Farther up the coast, Amelia Earhart was also deciding to put her immediate travel plans on hold.

130   **"there in the studio"**   RR to Kathy Osborne, superscript on Thomas Gibson memo, Jan. 28, 1986, RRL/pp/hw.

130   **"I have visions"**   Joy Hodges interview, May 30, 1989.

130   **"I think I might"**   Joy Hodges interview, Des Moines *Register,* Sept. 8, 1974; interview with author, May 30, 1989.

130   **Tossed about in**   RR called it a seaplane in his Des Moines *Dispatch* column, although it was actually an amphibian, the Douglas Dolphin. RR, "Around the World of Sports," n.d., 1937; Nelle Reagan Scrapbook, RRL/pp; WPA, *Los Angeles: A Guide to the City and Its Environs* (New York, 1947, 1951), 373.

130   **The feeling of imminence**   Catalina *Islander,* Mar. 18, 1937; Olivia de Havilland interview, *Frontline,* PBS, Jan. 18, 1989.

130   **"How could I tell?"**   RR, *Where's the Rest of Me?,* 71.

130   **He spent most**   RR, "Around the World of Sports," ca. Mar. 30, 1937, Nelle Reagan Scrapbook, RRL/pp.

131   **No sooner had**   George Ward interview, Hugh Sidey, *Time,* June 17, 1985, privately held, RR interview, Mar. 22, 1985.

131   **"Joy said you"**   RR, *Where's the Rest of Me?,* 72. Ward allegedly said, "Max, I have another Robert Taylor sitting in my office."

131   **Arnow's first words**   *Where's the Rest of Me?,* 73; *An American Life,* 79–80.

131   **"I've got to get"**   *An American Life,* 80.

131   **She did what she could**   RR heard her say something about a "bowl number seven." Qu. in Des Moines *Register,* June 27, 1937.

132   **"What a damn fool"**   RR, *An American Life,* 80; RR, "Around the World of Sports," Des Moines *Dispatch* news clipping, ca. Mar. 29, 1937, Nelle Reagan Scrapbook, RRL/pp. Dates in this section: see the author's "Chronology Raisonné of Ronald Reagan's First Visits to California," ts., RRL.

132   **Dutch was back**   RR wired back, "SIGN BEFORE THEY CHANGE THEIR MINDS." RR, *Where's the Rest of Me?,* 74; RR, *An American Life,* 81. RR's contract, a standard one for the time, in effect gave the studio a seven-year option on his services, renewable every six months at a graded raise in salary. His first chance to renegotiate terms would come after four years, by which time his salary would have risen from two hundred to six hundred dollars a week. "History of Ronald Reagan's Contracts with Warner Bros. Pictures, Inc.," ts., Sept. 24, 1951, WBC.

132   **"You'd better get me"**   RR to George Ward, Apr. 7, 1937, privately held.

132   **He was not certain**   "History of Ronald Reagan's Contracts," ts., Sept. 24, 1951, WBC; "Advance Feature" press release, Warner Bros. *Love Is on the Air* production file, WBC; Pee Wee Williams and Glen Claussen interview, Aug. 31, 1987.

132   **Some practical matters**   Jack D. Norman to RR, n.d. [1984], RRL/pp; Des Moines *Register,* Apr. 4, 1937; *Daily Variety,* Apr. 14, 1937; news clippings, Apr.–May 1937, Nelle Reagan Scrapbook, RRL/pp; RR to George Ward, Apr. 29, 1937, privately held.

132   **Somehow, he found**   RR "201" file documents, Apr.–May 1937. RR's official appointment letter was dated May 25, 1937. His course marks were as follows: Organization of the Army, 85; Organization of the Cavalry, 90; Administration, 91; Military Law, 76; Military Discipline, 96.6; Interior Guard Duty, 97; Map and Aerial Photograph Reading (I), 94.3, (II), 87.3; Military Sanitation and First Aid, 98.

132   **Three weeks later**   On May 21, 1937. Wills, *Reagan's America,* 114; RR to George Ward, Apr. 29, 1937, privately held; Pee Wee Williams and Glen Claussen interview, Aug. 31, 1987.

9: Inside Story

133   **Dutch had ten days**   RR, "Dutch Reagan's Own Story," part 1, Des Moines *Sunday Register,* June 13, 1937. See also RR, *Where's the Rest of Me?,* 76. The first source (hereafter cited as "Dutch's Story," with date of publication) comprises seventeen articles and covers the entire probationary period of RR's first contract. Although the articles were written with the cooperation of Warner Bros. publicists (who set up most of RR's encounters with fellow actors and assigned a photographer to dog his steps), the subjective experiences are genuine, and the prose style manifestly his. The author asked RR if anyone at the studio helped him write the pieces, as Garry Wills claims in *Reagan's America,* 114. He said, looking slightly hurt, "No, I wrote 'em, and I never got paid."

133   **When the redness**   "Dutch's Story," part 1, June 13, 1937.

133   **The giant studio**   The following description is based on "Dutch's Story," parts 1 and 7, June 13 and July 25, 1937; contemporary photographs in the "Sets" file of Warner Bros. Research Collection, Burbank, Calif.; EM Notes, Feb. 9, 1994; and "Warner Brothers," *Fortune,* Dec. 1937. The latter article describes the studio as being "neither in Hollywood nor of it . . . a moated feudal city, from which raids have occasionally been conducted . . . but which has not often been raided from without."

134   **Dutch was not**   See Edwards, *Early Reagan,* 163–64, for the near-paranoid security situation at Warner Bros. in the 1930s.

134   **In contrast, the city's**   See "Warner Bros." in Ethan Mordden, *The Hollywood Studios: House Style in the Golden Age of the Movies* (New York, 1988). This chapter is a good short study of the studio's "city" style in the 1930s.

134   **The paradox of**   Sam Marx, *Mayer and Thalberg: The Make-Believe Saints* (New York, 1975), 31.

134   **Here, for Thyrsis**   "The oldest rule of theater," RR wrote in 1986, "is that nothing done on stage or screen can match the audience's imagination." Superscript on Smithsonian News Service questionnaire, Feb. 11, 1986, RRL/pp/hw.

135   **"Where in hell"**   "Dutch's Story," parts 1 and 2, June 13 and 20, 1937.

135   **On May 25**   "Dutch's Story," part 2, June 20, 1937.

135   **Already he felt**   RR, *An American Life,* 81–83; "Dutch's Story," part 2, June 20, 1937, part 1, June 13, 1937; U.S. Cavalry Reserve medical certificate, Apr. 29, 1937, in RR "201" file, NPRC. For details of RR's makeup session with the Westmore brothers, see Edwards, *Early Reagan,* 167. Edwards's error-filled account of the subsequent shooting of RR's first movie should, however, be read with caution.

135   **The sensation of being**   "I loved the poking and the prodding." RR, *Where's the Rest of Me?,* 76. For RR and Flynn, see the photograph of them shaking hands in "Dutch's Story," part 1, June 13, 1937.

136   **He was introduced**   "Dutch's Story," parts 1–3, June 13, 20, and 27, 1937.

136   **Dutch obligingly**   RR, *An American Life,* 83. The weighting of the syllables in "*Ronald* Reagan" and the identification of Arnow were given by RR to the author in conversation on Mar. 22, 1985.

136   **Nevertheless, when he**   *Love Is on the Air* production and publicity files, WBC. The original title of this movie (itself based on a 1934 Warner Bros. production called *Hi, Nellie!*) was "Inside Story." RR, *Where's the Rest of Me?,* 76.

137   **And KDTS, with**   Set photographs, *Love Is on the Air* production file, WBC.

137   **Stepping through a**   "Dutch's Story," part 3, June 27, 1937; publicity brief for *Love Is on the Air,* ca. Aug. 1937, WBC; visual details from *Love Is on the Air,* video copy, LC. The image of the "wall of light" appears in "Dutch's Story," part 5, July 11, 1937.

138   **Anger boiled in him**   Set photograph, *Love Is on the Air* production file, WBC; video copy of original movie, LC.

138   **"You mean I have"**   "Inside Story," revised final script, May 29, 1937, Scenes 56–59, WBC; *Love Is on the Air* production file, WBC. Ellipses in the original ts. have been replaced here by em dashes to avoid any suggestion of deletion. The shots and sequences that follow are described in actual production order. Movie productions hardly ever follow the narrative order of the shooting script. The reader should also understand that "Inside Story" was radically revised, simplified, and reshot before being issued as *Love Is on the Air.* Thus many of the scenes described

here ended up on the cutting-room floor—including, sadly, the whole of RR's debut scene in the lawyer's office.

139   **A warm glow**   Except for the last remark, this paragraph is written almost entirely in RR's own words. See "Dutch's Story," parts 1 and 4, June 13 and July 4, 1937. He admits to having had acute stage fright before shooting started. However, as soon as the distant voice of director Nick Grinde called for action, "automatically, I snapped into my well-rehearsed role and forgot about . . . everything but the part."

139   **Even now, the**   "Inside Story," 77, 101–2.

140   **He lost his temper**   Ibid., 30–32, 83, 104–7, 60–66; *Love Is on the Air* production file, June 10, 1937; "Dutch's Story," part 6, July 18, 1937. The naval assignment, on June 15, 1937, was to *Submarine D-1*, a big-budget thriller that Lloyd Bacon was then filming in San Diego. On some directorial whim, RR was brought in to compete with Pat O'Brien and Wayne Morris in romantic pursuit of Doris Weston. "Dutch's Story," part 17, Oct. 3, 1937.

140   **JANE WYMAN HOSPITALIZED**   *Daily Variety,* June 23, 1937, 67.

140   **However, he not**   "Inside Story," 88–99, 118–29, 114.

140   **Past and present**   "Dutch's Story," part 5, July 11, 1937.

140   **"EXT." also tended**   "Inside Story," 12.

141   **Mouse said that**   Ibid., 13.

141   **A radio man's**   Ibid., 16, 107–8; *Submarine D-1* production file, WBC.

141   **Here, to the beat**   "Inside Story," 109. This scene has unfortunately been cut from the release print of *Love Is on the Air.*

141   **The clock twirled**   Ibid., 140–46; copy of *Love Is on the Air,* LC. The house was actually the Warner Bros. ranch at Calabasas.

141   **He had seen the**   "Inside Story," 140–46.

141   *Caramba!*   Ibid., 174; "Dutch's Story," part 5, July 11, 1937.

142   **"Looking for someone?"**   Ibid., 190–201; "Dutch's Story," part 6, July 18, 1937.

142   **Ventura Boulevard**   "Inside Story," 202; "Dutch's Story," part 6, July 18, 1937.

142   **Quiet now**   "Inside Story," 208.

142   **As the fusillade**   Ibid., 218, 215.

142   **He lay with her**   "Dutch's Story," part 6, July 18, 1937; "Inside Story," 218.

142   **O, airhog ecstasy!**   "Inside Story," 221–22. This whole ambush scene is much truncated in the release print of *Love Is on the Air.*

142   **"And the hero"**   "Inside Story," 235.

143   **"Boy, when it"**   "Dutch's Story," VI, July 18, 1938.

10: Love Is on the Air

144   **DUTCH IS HIT**   News clipping, AC. See also *Hollywood Reporter,* Aug. 19, 1937, and Des Moines *Register,* Aug. 22, 1937.

145   **Across the bottom**   PR to EM, Aug. 19, 1937, AC. Although *Love Is on the Air* (release title of "Inside Story") was dismissed as junk by critics

across the country, RR garnered some excellent notices in New York. "Young Reagan's debut takes on sensational proportions," wrote a female reviewer for the New York *Daily News,* adding that he "has poise, a voice, personality, and a face that the camera loves" (Oct. 14, 1937). The *New York Post* (Oct. 15, 1937) called his performance "good and honest" and said he made a "dashing" reporter. The New York *Journal* (Nov. 12, 1937) remarked that he "displays definite promise for more important vehicles."

145   **Two more B pictures** Dixon *Evening Telegraph,* Sept. 27, 1937; Des Moines *Sunday Register,* Sept. 5 and Oct. 3, 1937; EM to PR, Sept. 13, 1937, AC. RR's part in *Submarine D-1* was cut before release. He received no credit for his part (again a radio staffer!) in *Hollywood Hotel* but nevertheless caught the eye—and became a favorite—of the movie's guest celebrity, Louella Parsons. See later in this chapter for important consequences.

145   **A little lady** Unidentified news clipping, ca. Sept. 23, 1937, Nelle Reagan Scrapbook, RRL/pp. According to Marion Foster, daughter of Nelle's closest friend, the Reagans arrived in Hollywood on Sept. 25, 1937 (interview, Sept. 8, 1990). Jack Reagan had been unable to work for the WPA since suffering his debilitating heart attack in 1936. RR offered him light employment in Los Angeles as his personal secretary, principally to handle fan mail. Until RR bought his parents a house—the first non-rental home Jack had ever occupied—they lived at 1842 North Cherokee Avenue, not far from their son's own apartment in the Montecito Building on West Franklin Avenue.

146   **For some reason** PR to EM, Nov. 12, 1937, AC. This fast fadeout was more likely a matter of timing, because *Love* was edited down to sixty-one perfunctory minutes. RR admitted candidly that he had fallen for his leading lady, and boasted of a joyous morning of frenching it up for publicity shots. "The director said 'Action' and that's just what he got." June Travis's movie career never took off. She returned to Chicago a year or so after shooting *Love,* became the darling of the White Sox, and married a mail-order executive.

147   **Out of a dark** EM Notes, Oct. 13, 1987. By the time RR made *Flight Patrol* (*International Squadron*) in 1941, he had worked at his overarticulation enough to joke about it. *Flight Patrol* production file, WBC. Appendix, "These Leaves Your Lips."

147   **Signing on with** Subsequently famous members of the Chicago Project of the FWP included the novelists Saul Bellow, Richard Wright, and Nelson Algren. Note: the author is not the Edmund Morris who wrote the screenplay of Algren's *A Walk on the Wild Side* (1956). See Jerre Mangione, *The Dream and the Deal: The Federal Writer's Project 1935–1943* (University of Pennsylvania Press, 1983), 119–31.

11: On the Beach with Ronnie and Jane

150   ***Through salt-bleared*** Ms. fragment, written shortly after the opening of *Brother Rat* on Oct. 27, 1938, AC.

152   ***Ailerons* to Sam**   Sam Marx (1902–1992), a protégé of Irving Thalberg, was MGM's story editor from 1930 to 1937. A frustrated writer himself, he employed many would-be writers (including the young Lillian Hellman) as readers of literary properties. As a producer, Marx was involved in such classic pictures as *Grand Hotel, Mutiny on the Bounty,* and *Goodbye, Mr. Chips.* In his later years he became the most fabled of Hollywood raconteurs.

152   **"Aren't they beautiful?"**   Qu. by Pat Buttram in Gregory Orr, *Jack L. Warner.*

152   **Dutch was not**   RR, "Dutch Reagan's Own Story," part 13, Des Moines *Sunday Register,* Sept. 5, 1937; RR, *Where's the Rest of Me?,* 88; "RR Groups," drawer 3, WBC; Glen Claussen interview, Aug. 26, 1987.

152   **How much sex**   Owen Crump and Lucile Crump, interview, Sept. 26, 1992.

152   **Yet his local cavalry**   Howard Darrin qu. in B. Bruce Briggs to author, Feb. 15, 1989; "A Swimming Lesson from Hollywood," Chicago *Daily News,* July 23, 1938.

153   **Not that she didn't**   Jane Bryan Dart, former Warner Bros. starlet, qu. in Nancy Clark Reynolds interview, Dec. 26, 1986. She was standing in a trailer on the Warners lot when RR walked by and remembered how JW "wiggled with delight" at the sight of him. From that moment on, JW's acting coach William Demarest noted, "she was the aggressor, he the intent pursuer." Qu. in Lawrence J. Quirk, *Jane Wyman: The Actress and the Woman* (New York, 1986), 30–31.

153   **Her challenge was**   Jerry Asher, a mutual acquaintance, describes JW in 1938–1939 as "experienced, hard-boiled, intense, and passionate" and RR as "well, rather a square." Quirk, *Jane Wyman,* 42. "She was difficult—had a very short fuse—the toughest of all the Warners starlets. Pugnacious. Curt. Always took command." Robert William interview, Feb. 15, 1991.

153   **Jane had a couple**   RR hinted at JW's first marriage to the author in a rare moment of confidence in 1989. "What you have to look at [is] that there were a few husbands before me." RR interview, June 27, 1989. A wedding certificate on file in the California Department of Welfare Services confirms that Jane Fulks, daughter of Richard D. and Emma Reise Fulks (see following note), was married to Ernest Eugene Wyman on Apr. 8, 1933. Although JW claims in her own handwriting to be "19" at the time, she was actually little more than sixteen. According to an undated clipping in the Los Angeles *Examiner* morgue file at USC, JW was divorced from "Ernest F. [*sic*] Wyman" in 1935. Ernest F. Wyman was in fact her father-in-law. See note below.

153   **She had been born**   Edwards, *Early Reagan,* 188–89, cites the Jan. 5, 1917, Missouri birth certificate of Sarah Jane Mayfield, and points out that her parents, Manning J. Mayfield and Gladys Hope Mayfield, had been married less than eight months before, on May 17, 1916. Her new "mother," Emma Reise Fulks, further certified that she was born in 1917 upon registering her in first grade at the Noyes School, Saint Joseph, on Sept. 10, 1923. The Mayfield marriage had broken apart by Oct. 1921,

when Gladys Mayfield filed for divorce and herself decamped to Cleveland, Ohio. Manning Mayfield died the following year. In the light of JW's subsequent teenage first marriage, it is understandable that JW has always claimed to be two years older than she is, and refused to confirm persistent rumors that she was twice married before becoming Mrs. Ronald Reagan. See, e.g., Quirk, *Jane Wyman,* 16.

153   **So little Miss**   *Daily Variety,* June 2 and 30, 1937; Edwards, *Early Reagan,* 191–92. The latter source states that after Richard Fulks died in Mar. 1928, his wife, then sixty-two, moved with eleven-year-old Jane to Los Angeles to live with a daughter from a previous marriage, Elsie. (They had visited once before, in early 1922.) RR told the author in 1992 that the bond that developed subsequently between the two girls (who considered themselves sisters) was the fundamental link in JW's life.

153   **Her nervous breakdown**   See p. 140. According to the Los Angeles *Examiner* morgue file, USC, JW divorced Ernest Wyman in 1935, married Myron Futterman on June 29, 1937, and divorced him on Dec. 5, 1938. Futterman was a clothing manufacturer from New Orleans, much older than JW. JW biographical file, HER.

153   **I gathered that**   See p. 40. For more on the mutual attraction between RR and JW, see Quirk, *Jane Wyman,* 42.

154   **Marrying Ronnie**   Unidentified clipping, ca. 1943, SHSW.

154   **Ours was a generation**   Louise Brooks, one of the most sexually liberated stars of the Twenties and Thirties, cautioned presentist biographers to be aware of this discretion. "Up to 1940 when I left Hollywood *no* man swore before women, and Lombard was the only woman who ever got away with it." Qu. by Tom Dardis, *Vanity Fair,* Apr. 1998.

154   **We exercised hard**   EM Diary, Sept.–Dec. 1938, *passim;* Lyle Talbot interview, Aug. 27, 1987. See also Errol Flynn, "Young Man About Hollywood" in Tony Thomas, ed., *From a Life of Adventure: The Writings of Errol Flynn* (Secaucus, N.J., 1980), and Jean Howard, *Jean Howard's Hollywood: A Photo Memoir* (New York, 1989).

154   **"Make that good-*looking*"**   Leonora Hornblow interview, Jan. 25, 1989.

154   **Perhaps not. He**   Unidentified news clipping, 1940, in LAW (RR's statistics were given as height, 6 ft. 1 in., weight 180 pounds, waist 32 in., chest 44 in.; Gloria Hébert interview, Aug. 17, 1986; Jeanne Campbell interview, Apr. 18, 1988; Pee Wee Williams interview, Aug. 31, 1987.

156   *Brother Rat* **was**   Filmography in Quirk, *Jane Wyman,* 207–11. Wayne Morris and Leonora Schinasi were married on Jan. 8, 1939. They divorced eighteen months later.

156   **Watching** *Brother Rat*   RR was on the set of *Brother Rat* from July 5 to Aug. 11, 1938.

156   **Jane was so**   The word *gorgeous* is that of Hal Wallis, Warner Bros.'s production chief. After viewing JW's wardrobe tests, he commented that she was too "terrifically attractive" to be allowed any vestige of elegance in the movie. Unless her part was designed down, "I am very much afraid that it is going to throw our whole story out of key." Hal Wallis to Robert Lord and William Keighley, June 28, 1938, WBC. EM Notes, Apr. 14, 1990.

PAGE

156 **Yet there was one** *Brother Rat,* print copy, LC.

156 **Bubbles now says** Leonora Hornblow interview, Jan. 25, 1989; Irv Kaplan interview, Aug. 23, 1988; Edwards, *Early Reagan,* 197.

157 **Dutch, meanwhile** "Reagan Most Entertaining Fellow on the Warner Set," *Girls on Probation* publicity file, WBC; Lawrence Williams in Westport *News,* Oct. 31, 1930, qu. in Edwards, *Early Reagan,* 170–71; Wayne Morris, qu. in Chicago *American,* Aug. 24, 1938. Leonora Hornblow recalls being drawn to RR at age eighteen because of her own passionate interest in politics. "He was my political mentor. It was unusual to have a Hollywood actor so politically inclined then, and even more unusual for a girl." Interview, Jan. 25, 1989.

157 ASTOR HALL The following dialogue is taken from EM Diary, Nov. 8, 1990.

158 **Got a memoir** Howard Fast, *Being Red* (New York, 1991). Fast's other writing credits include *Citizen Tom Paine* (1943), *Spartacus* (1952), and *The Art of Zen Meditation* (1977).

159 **Dutch a Red** Howard Fast repeated this story a few weeks later on *Nightwatch* (CBS) and was so amazed by the lack of public response that he published it in the New York *Observer* (Apr. 5, 1991), still without stirring any interest. "One would think that a one-time decision of the man who would be President to join the Communist Party would be a matter of importance," he grouched, "if only for the historical record."

159 **Cy Gomberg turned** Cy Gomberg interview (telephone), Feb. 10, 1991; Eddie Albert interview, Feb. 27, 1991, Barbara Poe Levee interview, Feb. 15, 1991.

159 **The Red Question** The author heard from Jascha Kessler, another close friend of Margo Albert, that after RR became President, she confirmed her role in dissuading him from joining the CP, and expressed mock regret. "What a mistake that was! He said he wanted to get a card, but we talked him out of it. I said, 'Better that you don't. Better you work outside the Party.' If he had joined—can you *imagine?*" Qu. in Jascha Kessler interview, Oct. 15, 1998.

159 **"Good Lord, no."** RR interview, June 27, 1989.

159 **the ash heap** This famous RR phrase (see p. 461) actually derives from Trotsky.

159 **So what if** Albert Maltz finely articulates this message in Victor Navasky, *Naming Names* (New York, 1980, 1991), 296ff.

159 **Moreover, SAG** RR, *Where's the Rest of Me?,* 20, 132–33; Jack Dales in *The Screen Actor,* 21.3; Wills, *Reagan's America,* 221, 227. RR joined as a class A member on June 30, 1937, just after SAG and the IA, acting in concert, had won a closed-shop contract for the actors. RR membership file, SAGA. For an excellent compact history of SAG before RR joined it, see Wills, *Reagan's America,* Ch. 23.

160 **One of my first** Philip Dunne Oral History, HER.

161 *The Enemy Within* Renamed *Murder in the Air* and released in July 1940. See below, next chapter, and Stephen Vaughn, "Spies, National Security, and the 'Inertia Projector': The Secret Service Films of Ronald Reagan," *American Quarterly,* 39 (fall 1987). For Hollywood's skittish at-

titude toward movies about the Spanish Civil War, see Colin Schindler, *Hollywood Goes to War* (London, 1979), 3–4.

161   **Crossing the ramp**   The "rubes" were the members of RR's old barber-shop quartet from Cy's Moonlight Inn in Des Moines, now transposed to Los Angeles. They had taken RR up on an invitation to join him in Southern California. In 1937 and 1938 they were his regular companions on Santa Monica beach, with JW as a feminine fifth. One of the group said to RR on this occasion, "Don't worry, when your time is up, it's up." RR replied, "Yeah, but what if it's the *pilot's* time that's up?" Glen Claussen and Pee Wee Williams interview, Aug. 31, 1987.

161   **"They just got engaged"**   Los Angeles *Examiner*, Nov. 1, 1939.

161   **"Well, he's moved"**   "We all knew he was living with her." Leonora Hornblow interview, Jan. 25, 1989. RR's first established Los Angeles address was in the Montecito Apartments at 6650 Franklin Avenue, Hollywood. Sometime in late 1938 he moved to 1128 Cory Avenue, Beverly Hills, and thence in the spring of 1939 to JW's building at 1326 Londonderry View. RR personnel file, WBC.

161   **Phil approved of**   Philip Dunne, *Take Two* (New York, 1980), 120–23; Ronald Brownstein, *The Power and the Glitter: The Hollywood-Washington Connection* (New York, 1990), 61–64.

161   **A few days later**   Louella Parsons, *The Gay Illiterate* (Garden City, N.Y., 1944), 158; Annette Dowling Morris to author, Nov. 14, 1939, AC. Hedda Hopper, qu. in *Los Angeles Times,* Oct. 3, 1948, remembers her in 1938 as "a little, loud, brassy blonde."

162   **PATIO RESTAURANT**   NR interview, June 28, 1989.

162   **When I told**   Joy Hodges interview, Aug. 8, 1989; Douglas Bell interview, Oct. 3, 1992; Eddie Albert interview, Feb. 27, 1991. Miss Hodges admitted to the author that she herself had made a play for RR about a year previously. When she suggested they would make a good team, he had interrupted her by tenderly taking her hand in both of his and saying: "Why, honey, I'm in love with Jane Wyman."

162   **At eighty-four**   Sam Marx interview, July 13, 1989; Edwards, *Early Reagan,* 197–98; A. Alleborn to T. C. Wright, Oct. 4, 1939, WBC. The book mentioned is Sam Marx and Joyce Vanderveen, *Deadly Illusions: Jean Harlow and the Murder of Paul Bern* (New York, 1990).

163   **"There was a young"**   Fred Kline (FBI investigative agent) interview, Sept. 29, 1992.

163   **"Because as I"**   Sam Marx interview, July 13, 1989. Hollywood being Hollywood, there are of course several romanticized versions of RR's and JW's decision to marry, but the flavor of protective publicity is strong. See, e.g., Ruth Waterbury, "Wanted—One Honeymoon," *Movie Mirror,* Mar. 1940; Quirk, *Jane Wyman,* 93; Doug McClelland, *Hollywood on Ronald Reagan* (Winchester, Mass., 1983), 22.

163   **Louella Parsons used**   Los Angeles *Examiner,* Nov. 1 and 8, 1939. Miss Parsons had predicted the engagement several times in recent weeks but hinted at bilateral difficulties. "You never can tell in Hollywood." Ibid., Oct. 18, 1939.

163   **It was Ronald Reagan's**   Louella Parsons in Los Angeles *Examiner,*

PAGE

Nov. 21, 1932. For a modern reassessment of Miss Parsons, see A. F. Collins, "Idol Gossips," *Vanity Fair,* Apr. 1997.

163   **opening in San Francisco** *Brother Rat and a Baby* production file, Nov. 1, 1939, WBC. For a review of the opening night ("Ronald Reagan is very personable, deft, and obviously at home on a stage"), see *Variety,* Nov. 22, 1939.

164   **"I hope my Ronald"** Nelle Reagan to Mrs. Kennedy, ca. Nov. 10, 1939, qu. in Helen Lawson interview, Sept. 5, 1986.

164   **I am not sure** Glen Claussen and Pee Wee Williams interview, Aug. 31, 1987; Edwards, *Early Reagan,* 199–200.

164   **He was more pleasantly** The following account of the Parsons personal-appearance tour, Oct. 1939–Jan. 1940, is taken primarily from the Louella O. Parsons Scrapbooks, HER. Supplemental details come from Claussen and Williams interview, Aug. 31, 1987, and from Joy Hodges interview, May 30, 1989. In Pittsburgh, where the show played from Nov. 29 through Dec. 7, Parsons advertised for the return of two pairs of RR's socks "because Jane Wyman knitted them." Although such demonstrations were trivial in comparison with the hysteria that a Gable or a Cooper evoked, they were significant in view of the fact that RR was still an obscure junior actor. Parsons was quick to notice this and in three separate columns predicted stardom for him in 1940. Louella O. Parsons Scrapbooks, HER.

164   **Onstage and off** The cast had a week off in Manhattan before opening at the Loew's State Theater on Dec. 21. S. Trilling memo, Dec. 30, 1939, WBC.

164   **Dutch is emcee** PR to EM, Dec. 24, 1939, AC; *The New York Times,* Dec. 23, 1939; stage photographs in Joy Hodges collection.

165   **On December 27** Louella Parsons in Los Angeles *Examiner,* Dec. 28, 1939. On Nov. 30, 1939, the Soviet Union had invaded Finland with half a million troops, only to be humiliated—at least through the early winter months—by heroic and canny Finnish resistance.

165   **If Jane had ever** JW biographical file, HER; Louella Parsons in Los Angeles *Examiner,* Dec. 31, 1939; Joy Hodges interview, Aug. 8, 1989.

165   **After their long** Louella Parsons in Los Angeles *Examiner,* Jan. 26, 1940. *An Angel from Texas* was adapted from George S. Kaufman's 1925 hit, *The Butter and Egg Man.*

166   **Paul Rae was** A news release typed up by Twentieth Century–Fox during the shooting of JW's loaner *Tail Spin* in Oct. 1938 has her "in a state of near collapse" over the looming interment of "her father, Ernest F. Wyman" at Forest Lawn. The deceased was in fact her former father-in-law. Ernest F. Wyman death certificate, Los Angeles City Hall.

166   **"It was *awful*"** Leonora Hornblow interview, Jan. 25, 1989; Los Angeles *Examiner,* Jan. 19 and 27, 1940.

166   **When the newlyweds** Pee Wee Williams interview, Aug. 31, 1987. "And when we saw the damn movie, sure enough it popped out again."

166   **Actually, he was** RR interview, Nov. 4, 1987; *Daily Variety,* Jan. 17 and Feb. 5, 1940.

167   **[Teammates]** Biographical notes (based on interviews with Mrs. Rockne) in *Knute Rockne, All-American* production file, WBC.

PAGE

167   **It was inconceivable** RR to Tony di Marco, Oct. 3, 1986, RRL/pp/hw; RR interview, Nov. 4, 1987.

167   **Foy shrugged** RR interview, Nov. 4, 1987; Pat O'Brien, *The Wind at My Back* (New York, 1964), 240; RR, *Where's the Rest of Me?*, 91; *Knute Rockne* production file, WBC. Other actors rejected early in the casting process were John Wayne, Robert Young, Robert Cummings, and William Holden.

12: A Lonely Impulse of Delight

168   **the only tongue** EM Diary, May 19, 1940. A full transcript of Churchill's speech, his first radio address as Prime Minister, appeared in the *Los Angeles Times* the following morning.

168   **President Roosevelt's** John Rae, *Climb to Greatness: The American Aircraft Industry 1920–1960* (Cambridge, Mass., 1966), 113–15; Lloyd Morris and Kendall Smith, *Ceiling Unlimited: The Story of American Aviation from Kitty Hawk to Supersonics* (New York, 1953), 337. Lindbergh's reaction to Roosevelt's "hysterical" call was featured in the same issue of the *Los Angeles Times* that quoted Churchill (May 20, 1940). For changing American attitudes in the spring of 1940, see Kenneth S. Davis, *FDR: Into the Storm, 1937–1940* (New York, 1993), 548–49, and Richard M. Ketchum, *The Borrowed Years, 1938–1941: America on the Way to War* (New York, 1989), 354.

168   ***Gawain, that didst*** Simon Ruddmer, *Sir Gawain Seeks the Grail* (London, 1840), 143.

168   **Dutch, whose location** *Knute Rockne* production file, WBC; RR "201" file, NRPC.

169   **Warner Bros., itself** RR, *Where's the Rest of Me?*, 95.

169   **In mid-July** Philip Dunne to EM, July 8, 1940. A copy of the release is preserved in WBC.

169   **We went to see** This paragraph is based closely on Vaughn, "Spies, National Security, and the 'Inertia Projector.' " The author's perception of the Inertia Projector of 1939 as a progenitor of the SDI of 1983 owes much to Vaughn's scholarly essay. See in addition Vaughn, *Ronald Reagan in Hollywood,* 77–80.

169   **U.S. neutrality restraints** There was also the inhibition of not wanting to endanger Hollywood's overseas distribution market, which importantly included Germany and Austria. See Clayton Koppes and Gregory D. Black, *Hollywood Goes to War: How Politics, Profits, and Propaganda Shaped World War II Movies* (New York, 1987), Ch. 2.

169   **"Ronald Reagan, Chief"** See facsimile card in Vaughn, *Ronald Reagan in Hollywood,* 144–45.

170   **Dutch's previous fly-spy** The other Brass Bancroft movies, all exhibited in 1939, were *Secret Service of the Air, Code of the Secret Service,* and *Smashing the Money Ring.* The series is discussed in the works by Vaughn cited above. Warners publicists stated frankly that its intent was "to install patriotism" by "glorifying the United States Secret Service."

RR was "ideal for the part, for he is, both in appearance, and personality, the representative of all that is admirable in young American manhood." *Secret Service of the Air,* advance publicity file, WBC. For Warner Bros.'s sudden change in 1940 from an isolationist to interventionist stance, see John Davis, "Notes on Warner Brothers Foreign Policy," *The Velvet Light Trap* 4 (May 1972).

170   **At least one boy**   Jerry Parr interview, May 28, 1999; *Code of the Secret Service,* advance publicity file, WBC.

170   **FLYERS' UNIT AIDS**   Ts. copy for Barry Trivers in *International Squadron* production file, WBC. The definitive history of the Eagle Squadrons is Philip D. Caine, *American Pilots in the RAF: The WWII Eagle Squadrons* (Washington, D.C., 1993).

170   **The cinematic potential**   R. Taplinger to Jack Warner, Jan. 6, 1941, *International Squadron* file, WBC; memo Mar. 15, 1941, to "Mr. Mace," WBC; RR, *Where's the Rest of Me?,* 102. Hoffman and Lucas started on *Flight Patrol* Oct. 26, 1940; Trivers was on it from Dec. 21, 1940, to Mar. 1, 1941. Production file, WBC.

170   **In Los Angeles**   Rae, *Climb to Greatness,* 105, 111; Ingells, *Tin Goose,* 56–57; Philip Dunne Oral History, HER.

171   **Shortly before Christmas**   Ingells, *Tin Goose,* 59; *Los Angeles Times,* Dec. 17 and 22, 1941.

171   *Nor law, nor duty*   Yeats, "An Irish Airman Foresees His Death," *Collected Poems* (New York, 1963), 133.

172   **Ronald Reagan ranked**   *Daily Variety,* Dec. 18, 1940, and Jan. 15, 1941. "The whole country is getting Reagan conscious." Louella Parsons, Los Angeles *Examiner,* Dec. 21, 1940.

172   **His stardom only**   Owen Crump to EM, Jan. 15, 1941.

172   **"Gee!" he complained**   Qu. by Nelle Reagan to Mary Emmert, Jan. 5, 1941, privately held.

172   **The birth notice**   Copy, AC.

173   **Written by Barry**   *Flight Patrol,* first draft, Jan. 21, 1941, WBC. This "original" script of what eventually became *International Squadron* was actually based on the play *Ceiling Zero* by Frank Wead, itself the source of a 1935 movie by that name.

173   **Owen persuaded**   Another reason for the rewrite was that Jimmy Grant's womanizing as written in the original script was not approved by the Hays Office. Vaughn, *Ronald Reagan in Hollywood,* 103. Although the author was not a member of the Writers Guild, it was possible in 1940 to get freelance studio work in exchange for cash under the table—tax free, but also credit free. Malvin Wald interview, July 28, 1994.

174   *RAF recruiters are in town*   This was literally true in Feb. 1941, as a covert committee operating out of the Hollywood Roosevelt Hotel helped assemble two more Eagle squadrons. See Caine, *American Pilots,* Ch. 2.

174   **Ronald Reagan was duly**   *Flight Patrol* production file, WBC. Stephenson died a few days after completing his performance. Three Los Angeles area fields were used as locations in the movie: Alhambra (home base to a motley fleet of twenty "Spitfires"—actually doctored Ryan

trainers—and seven Electra 14 bombers painted to look like Hudsons), Lockheed Terminal (hangar with a genuine Hudson), and Metropolitan Airport, Van Nuys (night arrivals and departures). In addition, Glendale's Grand Central Airport was used for a brief establishing shot in the final print. Dixon *Evening Telegraph,* Sept. 15, 1941.

175   **"There's something"**   EM Diary, Mar. 24, 1941; advance publicity, *Code of the Secret Service; Flight Patrol* production file, *passim,* WBC.

175   *Million Dollar Baby*   In this improbable production, RR was the despair of Max Rabinowitz, head of Warners' music department. After his first attempt to coach RR at a dumb keyboard, Rabinowitz complained, "The man is without any musical feeling and sense." His unmusicality was such that he could not even go through the motions. RR took up the challenge, training daily in imitation of a real pianist. "For a while there, I almost convinced myself I could play." But the director, Curtis Bernhardt, found his Chopin unconvincing, and took full advantage of the grand piano's screening properties whenever RR launched into a cadenza. Bernhardt to David Lewis, Dec. 3, 1940, WBC; RR, *Where's the Rest of Me?,* 99–100.

175   **Even as he zipped**   T. C. Wright memos, Apr. 9 and 21, 1941, WBC; Warner Bros. casting memo, Feb. 10, 1941. RR was not, however, a favorite for either role. For a full discussion of the casting of *Kings Row,* see Edwards, *Early Reagan,* 239–41.

175   **Not having been**   *Flight Patrol* production file and publicity material, WBC; print of *International Squadron* in LC.

176   **Yet he had the gift**   Flynn complained about his own sweat quotient in *My Wicked, Wicked Ways* (New York, 1959), 375.

176   **There were countless**   Lou Baum to T. C. Wright, Apr. 4, 8, and 10, 1941; Wright to E. Grainger, Apr. 28, 1941; Lewis Seiler to Jack Warner, May 6, 1941, all in WBC. Perhaps as a sign of executive displeasure, Lothar Mendes received credit for the final picture.

176   **On May 1, because**   *Flight Patrol* production file, WBC. The following account is based on an item in *Daily Variety,* May 7, 1941; RR interview, Oct. 27, 1982; and *Flight Patrol* publicity material, WBC.

177   **Just twelve days**   Neil Reagan interviews, Mar. 7, 1987, and Jan. 31, 1990; JR death certificate, Los Angeles County Registrar's Office.

177   **Dutch happened to be**   Neil Reagan interviews, May 7, 1987, and Jan. 31, 1990; R. Taplinger to Obringer, May 13, 1941, WBC ("I rushed back to California": RR, *An American Life,* 94); *Daily Variety,* May 21, 1941; Maureen Reagan, *First Father,* 60. See p. 120.

177   **Morally, as far**   RR, *Where's the Rest of Me?,* 7–8; Maureen Reagan, *First Father,* 61; Ron Reagan interview, Jan. 31, 1990, qu. RR. See also RR, *An American Life,* 93–94.

177   **As a final chore**   Warner Bros./Lockheed agreement, Mar. 17, 1941, WBC. The Electra was lent at a token rate of seventy-five dollars per day, on condition that its markings were washed off before return.

177   **He could fly under**   Frank Tallman, *Flying the Old Planes* (Garden City, N.Y., 1973), 156–57.

179   **and nothing brought**   The allusion is to Shakespeare's *Timon of Athens,*

5.1: "My long sickness / Of health and living now begins to mend, / And nothing brings me all things."

13: The End of the Beginning

180   **An exhausted Reagan**   *Flight Patrol* production file, May–June 1941, WBC; Edwards, *Early Reagan,* 236; Los Angeles *Examiner,* June 7, 1941; *Kings Row* production file, June 18, 1941. RR got some excellent reviews for his performance in *Nine Lives*: "Ronald Reagan continues his march forward, turning an exuberant performance that fairly sparkles" (*Hollywood Reporter,* Aug. 13, 1941).

181   **an exasperated aide**   Robert MacFarlane.

181   **Yet here, jammed**   Edmund Morris, "Desperate Journey: Wartime Correspondence Concerning Ronald Reagan, June 15, 1941–Nov. 21, 1942," ts., RRL.

182   **"Looks like Reagan"**   See Jack Warner to Hal Wallis, May 23, 1941, WBC.

182   **Drake! Drake!**   Henry Bellamann, *Kings Row* (New York, 1940), 465.

183   **Miss Pee**   Louella Parsons, PR's competitor and *bête noire.* See p. 164 for the origin of this cruel nickname.

183   **Reagan just sold**   Actually, on Sept. 12, 1940.

183   **"I'm sure the good"**   RR interview, Mar. 22, 1985.

183   *Dixon, Ill., Sept. 15*   For other accounts of RR's return to Dixon in the fall of 1941, see Dixon *Evening Telegraph,* Sept. 15, 1941, and Myrtle Walgreen, *Never a Dull Day* (Washington, D.C., 1963).

184   **Such is the power**   The size of the crowd was estimated at thirty-five thousand (Dixon *Evening Telegraph,* Sept. 15, 1941); Edwards, *Early Reagan,* 18.

184   **present him a clock**   This clock is now in the possession of JW. Maureen Reagan interview, Feb. 23, 1991.

184   **"I Knew Them Better"**   See Dixon *Evening Telegraph,* Sept. 12 and 15, 1941.

184   *Mr. Nice Guy*   RR, self-portrait in *Photoplay,* Aug. 1942; "History of Ronald Reagan's Contracts with Warner Bros. Pictures, Inc.," ts., Sept. 24, 1951, WBC; Parsons, *Gay Illiterate,* 161. RR's second seven-year contract, cannily negotiated by his new agent, Lew Wasserman, to take advantage of his rise to star billing, displaced his first, which had more than two years left to run. It guaranteed him $1,650 a week for the next three years, $3,000 for the next three, and $5,000 for the last. War service was to shortchange this munificent deal.

185   **Reagan is six feet**   The following portrait of RR in 1941 is compiled from a profile in the Dixon *Evening Telegraph,* Sept. 15, 1941, the *International Squadron* publicity file, WBC, and from the author's conversations with RR.

185   **the Screen Actors Guild**   Strictly speaking, RR was only an alternate director in 1941, sitting in for other officers when they were out of town. But from Aug. 11, when he deputized for Heather Angel, he was manifestly a

coming man at the union. SAG Board Minutes, Aug. 11 and Sept. 21, 1941.

185   **Is a fan**   RR in *Photoplay,* Aug. 1942; JW and RR to Jack Warner, Sept. 5, 1941, WBC; Edwards, *Early Reagan,* 230–31.

185   **That pesky problem**   RR was first threatened with the call to active duty in late Aug. A pleading telegram from R. J. Obringer to the Adjutant General in Washington, D.C., Aug. 29, 1941, stated that RR was expensively involved in *Kings Row,* and requested deferment through the end of production. He was deferred until Oct. 10.

186   **You asked about**   Owen Crump to EM, Oct. 4, 1941, AC; Jack Warner to Harry Warner, May 23, 1941, WBC; Harry Warner to David Lewis, Sept. 4, 1941, WBC. Sam Wood was the director of *Kings Row.*

186   **Feel sympathetic toward**   U.S. War Department to R. J. Obringer, Sept. 16, 1942, WBC; Los Angeles *Examiner,* Oct. 1 and 19, 1941; R. J. Obringer to Jack Warner, Oct. 20, 1941, WBC. *Jook Girl* (original spelling) was restyled *Juke Girl.* RR's latest deferment, obtained after frantic wire-pulling by the studio, was until Jan. 1, 1942. FDR had announced an "unlimited state of national emergency."

186   **nearly $1 million**   Crump is making a reasonable estimate here, although the total value of the new contracts (seven-year for RR, three-year for JW) was $746,000. For each of the next three years RR was projected to earn $66,000 (working a minimum of forty weeks per year) while JW overtook him, earning $60,000, $80,000, and $100,000 respectively. His income would then be $120,000 for two years, and $200,000 for the last. Bearing in mind that JW would be free to contract again in 1944, and that they might both work more than the annual minimums, their total expectations up to the fall of 1944 came nearer to a million dollars.

187   **a definite lack of warmth**   Vern Haugland, *The Eagle Squadrons: Yanks in the RAF, 1940–1942* (New York, 1979), 103.

187   **Audience laughter**   *Motion Picture Guide,* vol. 4, 1395. The Churchill title reads [*sic*]: "Never before in the field of human conflict have so many, owed so much, to so few."

187   *That bravery without*   *The Times* (London), Nov. 3, 1941.

187   **written for laughs**   Sample sound-track wit: "Where are you from, Omaha?" "Walla Walla, Washington." "Walla Walla, Washington? I thought you were from Omaha."

188   *I balanced all*   Yeats, "An Irish Airman."

188   **Paul Rae sent**   PR to EM, Oct. 4, 1941, AC.

188   ***SatEvePost***   PR to EM, Dec. 10, 1941, AC; RR, *Where's the Rest of Me?,* 105; Lew Wasserman interview, Mar. 6, 1987; Dunne, *Take Two,* 146.

189   **"a first-rate actor"**   *Los Angeles Times,* Oct. 31, 1941. RR indeed shot his second RAF movie (retitled *Desperate Journey,* and co-starring Errol Flynn) in the early weeks of 1942.

189   **A few weeks into**   PR to EM, Feb. 10, 1942, AC. *Kings Row* succeeded despite a fine flurry of negative adjectives by Bosley Crowther in *The New York Times* ("thoroughly muddled and miserably pretentious . . . utterly depressing and artistically sour"). Crowther echoed PR's percep-

tion of superficiality, saying that RR "made only casual acquaintance with the character" (Feb. 8, 1942). Many other critics thought *Kings Row* gloomy, but RR good. He was "breezily at ease," "excellent," "living, laughing, natural," and "remarkably effective." *New York Post,* New York *Herald Tribune,* and *P.M.,* Feb. 3; *The Philadelphia Inquirer,* Feb. 6.

189   **Legless or not** Louella Parsons, Los Angeles *Examiner,* Mar. 23, 1942; *Hollywood Reporter,* Jan. 5, 1942. RR was rumored to be prepping the role of Victor Laszlo (it ultimately went to Paul Henreid). His "casting" in *Casablanca* was probably little more than a publicity ploy; Warner Bros. was well aware that he would soon have to go into the Army. Yet this remains one of the most intriguing "what ifs?" of RR's career. Tony Thomas, *The Films of Ronald Reagan* (Secaucus, N.J., 1980), 182.

189   **You wouldn't recognize** Philip Dunne Oral History, HER.

190   **Dutch's disqualification** RR, final orders, Mar. 24, 1942, WBC. He reported in San Francisco on Apr. 20. RR "201" file. Unidentified newsclip, Mar. 23, 1942, Hearst Collection, USC.

190   **"Button Nose" is** Claudette Colbert was with the Reagans when RR brought news of his special order. "She [JW] was furious with him . . . said he'd gone behind her back to sign up [for limited service]." Claudette Colbert interview, Dec. 23, 1985.

190   **Ronnie's the *first*** *Variety,* Apr. 8, 1942. RR, qu. in Quirk, *Jane Wyman,* 63. The move took place on approximately Apr. 1. RR's new contract was suspended effective Apr. 20, 1942. As a consolation to RR, Jack Warner agreed to pay Nelle Reagan seventy-five dollars per week to handle RR's fan mail, on condition he reimburse the studio after the war. This typically hard-nosed favor became a real one when the mounting debt was canceled on Nov. 15, 1944. "History of Ronald Reagan's Contracts," WBC. Nelle became an expert forger of her son's handwriting and even handled some of JW's mail. Herman M. Darvick in *Pen and Quill,* 18.1 (Jan./Feb. 1942).

191   **After lunch I** No. 121 Squadron Operations Record Book, Apr. 24, 1942; A. C. Ward, *A Literary Journey Through Wartime Britain* (New York, 1943), 23.

191   **Mike Duff** Sir Michael Duff Assheton-Smith, No. 121 Squadron Intelligence Officer. Caine, *American Pilots,* 187.

191   **Just what branch** Aircheck, KMH, Apr. 30, 1942 (overseas-forces broadcast), RRL/oh.

191   **"tired of being used"** George O'Malley interviewed by Marion Elizabeth Rodgers, Feb. 4, 1988.

191   **At least that's** Ibid; PR to EM, May 28, 1942.

192   **effective Jul. 15** "History of the First Motion Picture Unit [FMPU]," ts., 1945, BOL. Owen Crump to Jack Warner, June 25, 1943, recalls that the Unit was activated on June 26, 1942 (JLWP).

192   **Last Feb. 24** "Suggested Plan of Operation," Apr. 24, 1942, JLWP; Owen Crump to Jack Warner, June 25, 1943, JLWP; "History of the FMPU," 6; Owen Crump interview, Aug. 20, 1987.

192   **Surprise: Ronnie Reagan** War Department Assignment Action Sheet, June 3, 1942; RR "201" file; Owen Crump interview, Aug. 20, 1987. M.G.'s = machine gunners. Owen Crump produced *Rear Gunner.* Strictly

speaking, it and *Winning Your Wings* were Warner Bros. productions tabbed to the USAAF Public Relations Division, since the FMPU was still being organized in June–July 1942. RR's transfer was to this division's "station" in the Burbank studio.

193   **I've gotten**   "History of the FMPU"; Malvin Wald interview, Feb. 12, 1991.

193   **Funny how events**   General Ira Eaker's negotiators were able to offer USAAF commissions to all serving Eagles by the late summer of 1942.

193   **Guinevere**   The author's Miles Master monoplane.

193   **The combat lasts**   Persons interested in hearing a live recording of a dogfight over the English Channel should visit the little Battle of Britain Museum at Hawkinge.

193   **Eight weeks later**   Owen Crump to EM, Oct. 3, 1942, AC.

194   **Please consider this**   Ibid.; Owen Crump interviews, Aug. 20, 1987, and Aug. 28, 1988; "History of the FMPU"; RR, qu. in Don Dwiggins, *Hollywood Pilot: A Biography of Paul Mantz* (New York, 1967), 157. The move took place on Oct. 1, 1942. Crump obtained permission from General Arnold to recruit industry personnel directly into the unit, without the normal six-month training period.

194   **After a spell**   USAAFHQ Routing and Record Sheet, Oct. 3, 1942; FMPU Personnel Sheet, Sept. 28, 1942, in Jay Schlein Papers, HER. RR was also assigned to public-relations duty. Promotion recommendation, Nov. 4, 1943, RR "201" file. In a follow-up recommendation, Dec. 15, 1942, signed by Major Mantz, RR was also listed as "Detachment Commander" and graded "Excellent Plus" in his discharge of duties.

194   **Owen added**   Owen Crump to EM, Oct. 3, 1942, AC; "History of the FMPU," 30. Mantz had been acting C.O. since Sept. 22, 1942.

195   **Prime Minister's announcement**   *Daily Mirror* (London), Nov. 10, 1942.

195   **crabbed**   flew low.

195   **enormous tintinnabulation**   *Kentish Gazette and Canterbury Press,* Nov. 14 and 21, 1942; Paul Pollak to EM, Feb. 20, 1991, AC.

14: Celluloid Commandos

196   **What with Christmas**   General Arnold issued a blanket authorization (via Jack Warner) to transfer all non-essential motion-picture personnel to the FMPU, without going through the normal basic-training process. Malvin Wald to author, Mar. 9, 1993; Jay Schlein to an unidentified correspondent, ca. Oct. 21, 1942, Jay Schlein Papers, HER.

196   **When I drove**   EM War Diary, Jan. 20, 1943; Notes, Sept. 1992.

197   **The MP at the**   Lyle Talbot interview, Aug. 27, 1987.

197   **I parked in**   Visual and atmospheric details in the following paragraphs from EM War Diary, Jan. 20–23, 1943, supplemented by photographs in Jay Schlein Papers, HER.

197   **They were bright silver**   RR, *Where's the Rest of Me?*, 116–17. The outsize bars were a gift from enlisted men at the base, RR's long second lieutenancy having become something of a joke. He was provisionally

promoted to first lieutenant on Jan. 14, 1943, but the official order did not arrive from Washington, D.C., until Monday, Jan. 18. RR "201" file, NRPC. RR reverted to normal bars the following day.

198   **He returned the**   Elvin Crawford interview, Sept. 26, 1992.

198   **Half a lifetime**   RR interview, Mar. 24, 1987. Q. "I guess they made it easier for you as an actor?" A. "No. I never wore 'em when I acted. They gave me, uh, sort of a pop-eyed look." RR could not remember exactly when he began wearing contacts, but told a reunion of the FMPU in 1989 that he failed his first Army medical exam because "there were no contact lenses then" (Nov. 1941). He was certainly wearing them by Feb. 1943: Jules Levy in an interview, Sept. 29, 1992, recalls RR putting contacts in "with a little red plunger" before playing basketball. See also *Modern Screen,* Apr. 1943: "[RR] wears contacts over his eyes when he plays." Illustration (p. 64) shows the staring quality of RR's gaze.

198   **"This is really"**   Apparently this was RR's standard speech of welcome to the FMPU. Jules Levy interview, Sept. 24, 1992; Richard Webb interview, qu. RR to William Holden, Sept. 20, 1992.

198   **Dutch wrote**   Copy in AC. Also in R. G. Elliott Papers, privately held.

199   **Captain Gable might**   Clark Gable was on furlough from overseas service in Great Britain, where (as a combat cameraman) he shot *Combat America.*

199   **Had Major Mantz**   See p. 177. USAAF regulations required that all unit commanders be flying men. Hence Major Mantz's "seniority" over Major Crump.

200   **After lunch he**   Max Wilk in *Variety,* Jan. 14, 1981; John Leverence, *Irving Wallace: A Writer's Profile* (Bowling Green, Ohio, 1974), 62–63 and *passim.*

200   **Forty-nine years**   NR interview, 1992.

200   **Writer-director**   See Geoffrey Brown, "Vorhaus: A Director Rediscovered," *Sight & Sound,* Winter 1986–87.

201   **This morning I find**   The following text has been checked and revised by Malvin Wald.

201   **'Look, son, I don't'**   Malvin Wald interview, Mar. 9, 1993. The short was *Fighter Bomber Against Mechanized Targets* (1943).

201   **This top-priority**   FMPU no. 1024 (Dec. 15, 1942–Apr. 9, 1943). FMPU Production log, Jay Schlein Papers, HER.

201   **Vorhaus managed**   "FMPU Information Sheet," 4, AC; Irving Wallace, "The Zero's Hour," *Contact,* Nov. 20, 1942; FMPU no. 1609 (Oct.–Nov. 1943). There is a copy of *Recognition of the Japanese Zero* in NA.

202   **Owen Crump decided**   The five basic types of film created by the FMPU were (1) mechanical maintenance inspection; (2) aircraft recognition; (3) tactics; (4) personnel training; (5) specialized subjects (meteorology, escape, survival, etc.). The unit produced no entertainment-type pictures, although it won worldwide fame with its color documentary *Memphis Belle* (1944). "FMPU Production Progress Report," Oct. 15, 1943; Alex Greenberg and Malvin Wald, "Report to the Stockholders," *Hollywood Quarterly,* July 1946. A sixty-five-minute instructional "starring" Corporal Arthur Kennedy, *Resisting Enemy Interrogation,* was compelling

PAGE

enough to be released nationally as a "spy thriller" in Aug. 1944 (see *Time,* Aug. 14, 1944). It was nominated for an Academy Award the following year. For an excellent short history of the FMPU on video, see Gregory Orr, *Hollywood Commandos,* A&E documentary, 1997.

202   **Dutch has discovered**   Irving Wallace complains about having to endure RR's monologues in the *Los Angeles Times,* Aug. 17, 1980. Yet he remembers him in 1942 as having "a kind of sweet quality . . . an absolutely adorable guy."

203   **It's 1938**   Arnold Laven interview, Sept. 26, 1992.

203   **The first time I**   *Skyreel* (FMPU newsletter), Mar. 1943; photographs in Jay Schlein Papers, HER.

203   **That night the Officers**   *Contact* (FMPU monthly magazine), Mar. 1943; *Modern Screen,* Apr. 1943; Jules Levy interview, Sept. 29, 1992. "He loved handling balls—passing 'em, throwing 'em—and the *idea* of handling 'em still more. He seemed to fantasize himself as an athlete." Ibid.; photographs in Jay Schlein Papers, HER.

205   **The word from**   Edwards, *Early Reagan,* 273; Robert William interview, Feb. 15, 1991; RR, *Where's the Rest of Me?,* 139; George Murphy, *Say . . . Didn't You Used to Be George Murphy?* (New York, 1970), 280. Murphy supported Willkie in 1940 and Dewey in 1944. Twenty years later, RR wrote: "I owe a great deal to this cool, dapper guy who had to deal with me in my early white-eyed liberal daze. There were some of [my] associates, I'm sure, who believed I was as red as Moscow, but Murph never wavered in his defense of me, even though I ranted and raved at him as an arch-reactionary." RR, *Where's the Rest of Me?,* 179.

205   **In my opinion**   "Hollywood Democratic Committee Background," Hollywood Democratic Committee [HDC] Papers, SHSW; Nancy Lynn Schwartz, *The Hollywood Writers' Wars* (New York, 1982), 213–14; Larry Ceplair and Steven Englund, *The Inquisition in Hollywood: Politics in the Film Community, 1930–1960* (Berkeley, Calif., 1979, 1983), 226. *Casablanca* screenwriter Howard Koch recalls RR as "a divisive element" at HDC meetings, in that whenever a resolution was drawn up condemning Nazism, he would insist on a condemnation of Communism, too. "This created a split in the membership that was no doubt a factor in the club's dissolution." Koch, qu. in McClelland, *Hollywood on Ronald Reagan,* 180. The HDC did not so much dissolve as merge with other liberal groups to form (after World War II) HICCASP, described in the next chapter. When RR testified under oath on July 1, 1955 (*Jeffers v. Screen Extras Guild,* 3397) that he was a member of the latter organization "during some of the war years," he was obviously referring to the HDC.

205   **I was not aware**   Dunne, *Take Two,* 109; Walter Doniger interview, Feb. 10, 1993.

205   **Dutch and Bernie**   Forty-three years later, Bernard Vorhaus still held this opinion. See David Meeker, "Bernard Vorhaus," in Edinburgh Festival Vorhaus Retrospective brochure, 1986.

206   **By April 1943**   "History of the FMPU," 44–45; Dwiggins, *Hollywood Pilot,* 159.

206   **The genius of**   By Nov. 1, 1943, the number of production-unit heads

had risen to ten, and the FMPU's output soon outstripped that of the commercial studios, for a wartime total of 228 productions totaling 78½ hours of running time. FMPU directory in Jay Schlein Papers, HER; "History of the FMPU," 42; Greenberg and Wald, "Report to the Stockholders."

206 **Owen told me**   Owen Crump interview, Sept. 26, 1992.

206 **First anniversary**   Program and photographs in Jay Schlein Papers, HER; Owen Crump to Jack Warner, Oct. 25, 1943, WBC; Jack Klock interview by Jim Beaver, Feb. 1983; Malvin Wald interview, Feb. 10, 1993; Owen Crump interview, Aug. 20, 1987.

207 **That midsummer**   RR bet Lieutenant Edwin Gilbert twenty-five dollars that the war would be over by Labor Day, and lost out. Dwiggins, *Hollywood Pilot,* 157. Even FDR calculated despondently, around the end of 1942, that if advances in the Pacific did not quicken, the U.S. would need two thousand years to reach Japan. Eric Larrabee, *Commander in Chief: Franklin Delano Roosevelt, His Lieutenants, and Their War* (New York, 1987), 340.

207 **Professional doggedness**   Owen Crump interview, Aug. 20, 1987; Larrabee, *Commander in Chief,* 240–51 (the Ploesti raid); Los Angeles *Examiner,* July 18, 1943. RR's promotion became official on July 27, 1943. RR "201" file. His lecture with Vorhaus was entitled "America's Growing Air Power: Its Role in the War and the Coming Peace."

207 **Our work sheets**   Wesley Craven and James L. Cate, *The Army Air Forces in World War II* (Chicago, 1948–1958), vol. 5, 570; Larrabee, *Commander in Chief,* 589, 594. "Black Thursday" raid of Oct. 14, 1943, was a particular disaster in terms of B-17 casualties and plummeting morale (ibid., 597–98).

207 **a "blue discharge"**   Fred Kline interview, Sept. 29, 1992; Owen Crump interview, Aug. 20, 1987. For full details of this affair, in which Mantz was found more careless than venal, see Dwiggins, *Hollywood Pilot,* 177ff.

208 **Crump continued**   Colonel Jones had been a balloonist in World War I. RR became Adjutant effective Dec. 15, 1943. RR "201" file, NPRC.

208 **One might have**   RR told the FBI that he became "highly incensed," to the point of physical violence, by the suggestion that "Jews involved in shipping were glad of the sinkings of Allied vessels by German submarines because they profited thereby through an insurance racket." An eyewitness also reported that his interlocutor maligned Winston Churchill, predicted an Axis victory, and complained that "the Jews have ruined this country." RR also got into a heated argument with Edward G. Robinson that night. "Memo to Mr. Nichols," RR FBI file, Nov. 18, 1943, and May 23, 1951, SAGA.

208 **"Ronnie's kinda sensitive"**   William Orr interview, Sept. 29, 1992. Lakeside was the most exclusive WASP golf club in Hollywood. Edwards, *Early Reagan,* 203, has a thirdhand version of this story, attributed to Jack Warner. Orr is not only a firsthand witness, but a member of the Warner family.

209 **The record shows**   See Neal Gabler, *An Empire of Their Own: How the Jews Invented Hollywood* (New York, 1988), 275–76, for Hillcrest.

209   **Not all his behavior** Bernard Vorhaus interview, Aug. 12, 1993. Vorhaus's wife, Hetty, also remarked on RR's smutty tendencies to an interviewer in 1986. Obituary, *The Guardian* (U.K.), Oct. 10, 1997.

209   **One day in** The MP's name was Leon Skorupski. His photograph was reproduced in the Bloomfield *Independent Press* ca. 1980 (loose news clipping in RRL/pp). There is a copy of *For God and Country* in NA.

209   **Thanks to the** *Box Office Records 1942–1943,* 10. RR scored 195 percent, Cagney 186 percent. Other brand-name stars were Bing Crosby at 176 percent, Clark Gable at 171 percent, and Cary Grant at 169 percent. The author is indebted to Gloria Hébert for bringing this historic ratings list to his attention.

209   **Which might explain** RR, after twenty-seven years as an actor, eight years as Governor of California, and eight years as President of the United States, is probably the most photographed man in history. Yet he never ceased to feel uncomfortable before the still camera, explaining to the author that film permitted him to perform, rather than merely pose. His print images almost invariably show a characteristic tenseness of thumbs against fingers, a stiff throwing back of the shoulders, and a set smile.

210   **Maybe I'm reading** Eddie Albert interview, Feb. 27, 1991. Tarawa, in which more than one thousand Marines died and two thousand fell wounded in the space of three days, was the first World War II battle whose horror was visited on the American people without sentimental varnishing. See Paul Fussell, *Wartime: Understanding and Behavior in the Second World War* (New York, 1989), 12–13.

210   **When I asked** RR, qu. in John Hutton interview, Jan. 25, 1993; John Hutton Diary, Aug. 24, 1987, privately held; RR, *Where's the Rest of Me?,* 117. "SWPB" to AGO Promotion Section, July 17, 1945, RR "201" file, NPRC. A qualitative review of RR's wartime sevice is appropriate here. Three months after activation, he was cited by Lieutenant Colonel Warner for "outstanding performance of duty" and recommended for promotion to First Lieutenant. The Air Force P.R. Officer apologetically blocked the recommendation, saying there was some sensitivity at headquarters in Washington "with respect to 'name' personalities" (P.R. Officer to Jack Warner, Aug. 22, 1942). Major Mantz was more successful with another request for RR's promotion on Nov. 4, 1942, describing him as "excellent plus." Eight months later, Mantz again rated him as "excellent" and recommended his promotion to Captain (Paul Mantz to Commanding General, Nov. 4, 1942, and July 14, 1943). Sixteen months later, Colonel J. K. McDuffie, Officer Commanding, Eighteenth AAF Base, awarded RR the top rating of "superior," and on a scale of 1 to 7 graded him 6 for "Intelligence, Attention to Duty, Cooperation, Ability to Obtain Results, Judgment, and Common Sense." For "Physical Activity and Endurance, Stability Under Pressure, Initiative, Force, and Leadership," RR scored 5, still in the higher category of excellence. He was cited in addition for his "most pleasing personality" (J. K. McDuffie memo, Dec. 31, 1944). Four months later, Major General James P.

Hodges, Assistant Chief of Air Staff (Intelligence), recommended RR for promotion to Major. "Captain Reagan has proven himself to be an officer of exceptional ability, demonstrating unusual initiative." RR's overall efficiency (AAF Qualification) record shows that after being rated "Excellent" for his first three six-month spells as an officer, he was consistently "Superior" for the rest of the war. Colonel McDuffie's final report raised RR's intelligence grade to the maximum level of 7 (J. K. McDuffie memo, June 30, 1945; RR "201" file).

210   **First, he would**   Woody Mark interview, Sept. 26, 1992.

211   **Of all the**   The following paragraphs are based on Gene Bennett, Jules Levy, Bob Creamer, and Fred Kline interviews, Sept. 1992, fiftieth reunion of the FMPU, Los Angeles; Jack Glass interview, Feb. 10, 1993. Supplemental details from photographs in Owen Crump collection, privately held; and Orr, *Hollywood Commandos.*

211   **Our first indication**   FMPU Daily Log of Activities, Aug. 27, 1944, NRPC; Jack Glass interview, Feb. 10, 1993.

211   **He had been asked**   HqAAF order papers, Aug. 1944, in possession of Jack Glass.

212   **Dutch clearly looked**   General order, Aug. 15, 1944, Schlein Papers, HER. The following description of Project 152 is based on EM War Diary, Sept.–Dec. 1944, and group interviews at the FMPU 50th Reunion, Los Angeles, Sept. 26, 1992. See also articles in *New York Herald-Tribune,* Sept. 21, 1945; *Air Force,* Nov. 1945; and *International Photographer,* Nov. 1945.

213   **I can still hear**   RR interview, Aug. 18, 1988.

214   **narrated himself hoarse**   His Army medical file shows almost daily throat treatments throughout the spring of 1945. RR "201" file. See also the FMPU's official documentary, *Target Tokyo* (1945), narrated by RR. Copy in NA.

214   **more lethal than Hiroshima**   Craven and Cate, *Army Air Forces,* vol. 5; 573; Curtis E. LeMay, *Mission with LeMay* (Garden City, N.Y., 1965), 10, 352–53; Larrabee, *Commander in Chief,* 617–19. Eighty-four thousand Japanese were killed on the night of March 9–10, 1945, and 267,171 buildings annihilated over an area of sixteen square miles. Convection from the incendiaries tossed some of the B-29s two thousand feet above their approach altitude. General Arnold's high-altitude ("precision bombing") strategy was scaled down in consequence, but it kept Project 152 staff busy through V-J Day.

214   HEAVENLY HQ   RR adoption announcement memo, Mar. 18, 1945. Copy in AC. See also California State Welfare Department, Case No. LA 8510 AD; Louella Parsons, "This is the Truth about Jane & Ronnie," *Photoplay,* Jan. 1945; Michael Reagan, *On the Outside Looking In* (New York, 1988).

215   **That weekend I**   Elvin Crawford interview, Sept. 26, 1992.

215   **In the projection**   Malvin Wald to EM, ca. Apr. 24, 1944, and Sept. 1, 1993, AC; also interview, Feb. 13, 1991.

216   **Graf subsequently**   In late Apr. 1985, RR separately impressed George Shultz, Elie Wiesel, and Hugh Sidey with the sharpness and sympathy of

his memories of that first FMPU screening. "It was unbelievable to sit there," he told Sidey, "and see that film of not only the dead and the ranks of the dead, but the condition of the living. I remember one shot— I can never forget. There was a building that looked like a warehouse. The floor was entirely carpeted with bodies . . . while we were look-ing . . . out in the middle of all those bodies, suddenly, slowly one body moved and raised up, a man on his elbow, and tried with his other hand to gesture. He was alone, alive with the dead." *Time,* May 13, 1985. See also George Shultz, *Turmoil and Triumph: My Years as Secretary of State* (New York, 1993), 550–51. On Feb. 27, 1991, RR told the author that he discovered, when packing up to leave the FMPU in late Aug. 1945, that there were extra copies of the concentration-camp footage in the duplicating room. "So I took one with me to show doubters and skeptics in the future. Things like, Jews who had tried to make an escape and just got mowed down. . . . The camera just panned along the fence, showed their hands still clutching at the wire off the ground."

216   **"Can't figure why"**   Malvin Wald to EM, Aug. 23, 1945, and Sept. 1, 1993, AC.

216   **By the end of**   RR's release was approved Aug. 24, 1945. He was ordered discharged from Fort MacArthur, Sept. 8; three months leave granted Sept. 11, 1945. RR "201" file.

15: The Regeneration of the World

218   **Lake Arrowhead glimmers**   WPA, *Los Angeles,* 293; John W. Robinson, *The San Bernardinos* (Arcadia, Calif., 1989); June Lockhart interview, Dec. 13, 1993; EM Notes, Aug. 29, 1993; RR interview, Aug. 18, 1988.

218   **"Just relax"**   Jack Warner, qu. by RR, Los Angeles *Examiner,* Dec. 3, 1945. The contract, exercised on Sept. 12, 1945, had been cannily pre-negotiated by Lew Wasserman almost a year before on Nov. 11, 1944, when RR's recent rise to the top of the Hollywood box-office draw list still redounded to his dollar value. Terms were for seven years straight, at $3,500 per week for a minimum of forty-three weeks, averaging five pic-tures a year. "History of Ronald Reagan's Contracts," ts., Sept. 24, 1951, WBC; Lew Wasserman interview, Apr. 15, 1987.

219   **I went up there**   EM, War Diary, Sept. 23, 1945; Robinson, *The San Bernardinos,* 128. Lake Arrowhead went into receivership in 1946.

219   **At thirty-four**   RR, *Where's the Rest of Me?,* 140, 138; RR "201" file, medical examinations, NPRC. A spring 1945 poll showed RR to be sixth in popularity among male Hollywood stars.

219   **Those of us**   Richard Severo and Lewis Milford, *The Wages of War: When America's Soldiers Came Home* (New York, 1989), 284.

219   **swelling, truculent unions**   The 1945 post-war strike wave began on Sept. 17, when a walkout of oil workers halted refinery production in twenty states. For an eloquent expression of contemporary *angst,* see Carey McWilliams's speech to the executive council of HICCASP, Sept. 28, 1945, HDC Papers, SHSW.

220   **Creative intellects sensed** Although Pollock's "drip" technique did not emerge as his primary style until 1947, he was already experimenting with it in 1946, a year that marked "a critical juncture" between his past and future art. Deborah Solomon, *Jackson Pollock: A Biography* (New York, 1987), 169.

220   **What finally did** *New York Herald-Tribune,* Sept. 21, 1945; Bob Creamer interview, Oct. 1, 1992.

220   **The soothing busyness** RR interview, Aug. 18, 1988. See also RR, *Where's the Rest of Me?,* 140.

220   **He had plenty** *Variety,* Sept. 24, 28, and Dec. 18, 1945; *Hollywood Reporter,* Sept. 28 and Oct. 2, 1945.

220   **Jane, moreover** JW was in her twenty-ninth year.

220   **He told me** RR interview, June 27, 1989; Quirk, *Jane Wyman,* 86–87. See also Maureen Reagan, *First Father,* 44: "She lived through every role to such an extent that it was hard to recognize her when she came home. My recollections of her during this time are of many different people." JW appears to have had depressive tendencies. RR told NR in the 1950s that sometimes JW would be unable to speak from despair. NR interview, July 3, 1998.

221   **"All I wanted"** RR, *Where's the Rest of Me?,* 138.

221   **At the time** Ibid., 139–40; AVC membership circular, Sept. 15, 1945; Malvin Wald Scrapbook, privately held.

221   **I still have** AVC subscription flyer, 1945; Malvin Wald Scrapbook, privately held. The full text of this statement, plus a useful account of the genesis of the AVC, is given in Oren Root, *Persons and Persuasions* (New York, 1964), Ch. 3. See also Charles Bolté, *The New Veteran* (New York, 1945) 97ff., and Severo and Milford, *Wages of War,* 309–13.

221   **"Let me tell"** Gilbert Harrison interview, Jan. 18, 1987; Gilbert Harrison, *The Enthusiast: A Life of Thornton Wilder* (New York, 1983). RR was elected to the board of the AVC's Hollywood chapter as chairman of the Membership Committee on Aug. 25 (AVC memo, Sept. 15, 1945, Malvin Wald Scrapbook, privately held).

221   **The support, once** Gilbert Harrison interview, Jan. 18, 1987; Bolté, *New Veteran,* 4, 40–43, 169, 191. In *AVC Bulletin,* Apr. 1, 1946, RR is praised for "doing a marvelous recruiting for AVC in LA." By year's end the Hollywood chapter was the second biggest in the nation, with nearly two thousand members. Ibid., Dec. 15, 1946.

222   **Reagan was personally** In 1986, Mauldin told the author that despite RR's urgent importunings he declined. "I was young and famous and had my own political agenda. Or so I thought. Later on I changed my mind and ended up national chairman of the AVC. What I want to know is, how did Reagan know I was that kind of idealist long before *I* knew it?" Bill Mauldin interview, May 23, 1986; RR to Mauldin, June 27, 1945, and Mauldin to RR, Aug. 1, 1945, Mauldin Papers, LC. For the immediate post-war veterans'-affairs scene, see Mauldin's *Back Home* (1947), a classic document of American liberalism.

222   **He was talking** For background to this strike, and the involvement of the CPUSA, see Ceplair and Englund, *Inquisition in Hollywood,* 216–19.

222   **He was just back**   Philip Dunne was a division chief in the OWI from 1942 through its sudden folding, Aug. 31, 1945. Dunne, *Take Two,* 165–82.

223   **a lapel badge**   *Screen Writer,* Oct. 1945.

223   **"Not to mention"**   Dunne, *Take Two,* 212; Philip Dunne to EM, Jan. 11, 1987. For "the bad old days" of IATSE, see Wills, *Reagan's America,* 227.

223   **"hammer it good"**   Philip Dunne quoted accurately. Herbert Sorrell confirms the order in his Oral History, UCLA.

223   **"I'm afraid what"**   The weekend of Oct. 5–7, 1945, marked an early climax in the wave of strikes that followed V-J Day. President Truman had just (Thursday, Oct. 4) ordered the U.S. Navy to take over and operate refineries in twenty states struck by the Oil Workers International. On Oct. 6, the *Los Angeles Times* noted that well over half a million union members were idle nationwide, including coal miners, auto workers, longshoremen, and bus drivers. A further twenty thousand long-distance telephone operators were set to strike. "This was the beginning of [a] twelve-month series of labor-management conflicts unmatched for their 'scope and intensity' in any comparable period in American history." Philip Taft, *Organized Labor in American History* (New York, 1964), 567.

223   **We swung north**   Ceplair and Englund, *Inquisition in Hollywood,* 217; Schwartz, *Hollywood Writers' Wars,* 222. For an analysis of the power play between these two AFL union groups, see Wills, *Reagan's America,* Ch. 24.

224   **Hollywood's block of**   George H. Dunne, *Hollywood Labor Dispute: A Study in Immorality* (Los Angeles, 1952), 25.

224   **"Jack's a very"**   Philip Dunne interview, Mar. 13, 1987. For Sorrell's alleged Party membership, see "Un-American Activities in California, 1947," Third Report of the State Fact-Finding Committee to the Fifty-seventh California Legislature, 1947, 169–72.

224   **"Warners is way"**   *Hollywood Reporter,* Oct. 8, 1945; George Dunne Oral History, UCLA, 18; John Strickland interview, Oct. 21, 1993. According to Herbert Sorrell, the CSU's motives were also photo-opportunistic. "Warner Brothers was a big studio with . . . one employment gate. We could put a mass demonstration on it and it would look great." U.S. House of Representatives, 80th Congress, 1 session, "Jurisdictional Disputes in the Motion Picture Industry," *Hearings Before the Special Subcommittee on Education and Labor* (Washington, D.C., 1948), Mar. 4, 1948, 1920. Hereafter "Jurisdictional Disputes."

224   **I had lived**   The following account of disturbances outside Warner Bros. on the morning of Oct. 5, 1945, is based on participant interviews with Arthur and Meta Wilde, Sept. 24, 1992, and John Strickland interview, Oct. 21, 1993; newsreel footage in Southern California Library of Social Studies, Los Angeles; photographs and news clippings in Burbank Historical Society; news clippings in the Hearst Collection, USC, and JLWP; the "Hollywood Strike file" and Herbert Sorrell Scrapbooks, UCLA; Kearns Committee testimony of Herbert Sorrell, 1920–21; Bur-

bank *Evening Review,* Oct. 5; *Los Angeles Times,* Oct. 6; *Daily Variety,* Oct. 10; and *People's Daily World,* Oct. 9, 1945.

225   **Suddenly, two**   Sorrell Oral History, 153; photographs in UCLA Strike file and Burbank Historical Society; *Los Angeles Times,* Oct. 6, 1945. One demonstrator got his ribs caved in, and another lost his hearing as a result of the water pressure. Scrapbooks, JLWP.

225   **A big man**   *People's Daily World,* Oct. 9, 1945; Herbert Sorrell in "Jurisdictional Disputes," 1921.

226   **"Herb, don't cry"**   Qu. by ibid.

226   **Then something**   *People's Daily World,* Oct. 9, 1945.

226   **Burbank's Black Friday**   Oct. 8 soon eclipsed it as "Bloody Monday." The violence, lasting through Oct. 24, is amply documented in the Strike Scrapbooks of Herbert Sorrell and Jack L. Warner, UCLA and JLWP.

226   **What I heard**   RR, *Where's the Rest of Me?,* 138–39.

227   **The results of**   Ibid., 139–40; Schwartz, *Hollywood Writers' Wars,* 239.

227   **They lay dead**   RR's models of USS *America* and *Liberty* are now on display at RRL.

227   **Ronald Reagan used to**   RR, *Where's the Rest of Me?,* 141.

228   **The occasion was**   For sample incidents, see Mauldin, *Back Home,* 162–70, and Bolté, *The New Veteran,* 78.

228   **Ranked about**   June Masuda Goto interview, Aug. 31, 1993; Santa Ana *Register,* Dec. 10, 1945; Santa Ana *Register,* Dec. 10, 1945. RR was officially discharged from the USAAF the following day, having served three years, seven months, and twenty days of active duty. His reserve commission lasted until Apr. 1, 1953. Army Separation Record in RR "201" file, NPRC.

228   **The general spoke**   Mrs. Goto, reading her memo of the occasion to the author, Aug. 31, 1993; *Los Angeles Times,* Dec. 9, 1945; Santa Ana *Register,* Dec. 10, 1945. RR repeated his speech, with minor word changes, at the White House on Aug. 10, 1988. See also *Los Angeles Times,* Apr. 22, 1988. See also RR to Bill Shaffer, Aug. 10, 1946: "Now we have the job of keeping another war from ever breaking out again, we've got to educate the people against race hatreds." RAA.

228   **On January 17**   *Variety,* Dec. 21, 1945, and Jan. 18, 1946. *Stallion Road* went into production on Apr. 2, 1946. Michael Paul Rogin, *Ronald Reagan, "the Movie": and Other Episodes in Political Demonology* (Berkeley, Calif., 1987), 25, notes perceptively: "The characters RR played after the war were invaded by illness and women."

228   **Gracious as always**   *Variety,* Oct. 15, 1945; leave memo, Dec. 31, 1945, WBC.

229   **To begin with**   RR, "Fascist Ideas Are Still Alive in U.S.," *AVC Bulletin,* Feb. 15, 1946.

229   **Ronald Reagan thus**   From platform adopted at the first AVC Convention, Des Moines, June 14–16, 1946 (*AVC Bulletin,* July 1, 1946).

229   **Not content with**   *People's Daily World,* Feb. 26, 1946. Joining RR as Committee sponsors were, among others, Edward Dmytryk, Carey McWilliams, Artie Shaw, and Gregory Peck. RR FBI file, SAGA.

229   **Beady eyes took**   The first report in ibid. is dated Mar. 13, 1946. An-

PAGE

other, Apr. 11, 1946, notes that RR and his fellow Far East Committee sponsors "all . . . have records of Communist activity and sympathies." J. Edgar Hoover scrawls at bottom: "It is outrageous that House Un-American Activities Committee got 'cold feet' and dropped Hollywood Investigation." Memo to "Mr. Nichols" in ibid., May 23, 1951, notes FBI interest in RR as a potential informer as early as Sept. 1941.

230   **It was during**   Clarke to Chicago Bar Association, June 21, 1946, qu. by Schwartz, *Hollywood Writers' Wars,* 239. There is no doubt that American Communists were displaying a new aggression in the spring of 1946, under direct orders from Comintern. Richard Gid Powers, *Not Without Honor: The History of American Anticommunism* (New York, 1995), Ch. 8.

230   **Not until April**   RR to Charles Bolté, May 11, 1946, Gilbert Harrison Papers, privately held.

230   **He confessed**   Ibid.

230   **The word *still***   RR, *Where's the Rest of Me?,* 165; RR FBI file, May 23, 1951, SAGA; Michael Straight, *After Long Silence* (New York, 1983), 235. Straight says that the New York area council was also controlled by the Communist Party.

231   **Bolté urged Reagan**   For accounts of this highly dramatic convention, see *AVC Bulletin,* July 1, 1946; Root, *Persons and Persuasions,* 90–93; Straight, *After Long Silence,* 235ff. RR did not quit the AVC as immediately as he implies in his anti-Communist memoirs. He was still listed as a member of its finance committee in Nov. 1946, and on July 1, 1955, he confirmed, "I am still a member of the national organization." RR FBI file, Apr. 29, 1947, SAGA; RR testimony in *Jeffers v. Screen Extras Guild,* 3400.

231   **"the slow awakening"**   RR, *Where's the Rest of Me?,* 139–40.

231   ***Modern Screen* noticed**   *Modern Screen,* July 1946. Edwards, *Early Reagan,* 294, qu. Los Angeles *Daily News,* "a few days" after JW interview, ibid., June 18, 1946 ("He's very politically minded. I'm not").

231   **"My personal conversion"**   RR to Charles Bolté, May 11, 1946, Gilbert Harrison Papers, privately held.

232   **Then, on July 2**   At Alice Hunter's house, 9481 Readcrest Drive, Beverly Hills. HICCASP Executive Council minutes state that the meeting occurred on "Tuesday July 3." But Tuesday was the second—a date confirmed by Harry Grobstein to True Boardman, July 3, 1946, HDC Papers, SHSW.

232   **He joked that**   RR, *Where's the Rest of Me?,* 166. Nancy Lynn Schwartz credits Orson Welles as the original namer of HICCASP. *Hollywood Writers' Wars,* 213. It was formed on June 6, 1945, but like the AVC did not achieve critical mass for a year. For its early history and background, see Ceplair and Englund, *The Inquisition in Hollywood,* 227–29 and Vaughn, *Ronald Reagan in Hollywood,* 123–24.

232   **"Lots of people"**   RR, *Where's the Rest of Me?,* 166–67; RR qu. by Charles E. Davis in Los Angeles *Examiner,* Sept. 14, 1958, RR Scrapbook, RRL/pp; HICCASP Executive Council minutes, July 2, 1946, HDC Papers, SHSW. Trumbo's constipation in the summer of 1946 is

self-documented, with a wealth of detail that belies his cautionary re-mark, "One tends to be reserved about his anus." Dalton Trumbo to Philip Berg, Sept. 7, 1946, Trumbo Papers, SHSW.

232   **Cromwell presented**   HICCASP Executive Council minutes, July 2, 1946, HDC Papers, SHSW. RR's after-the-fact accounts of his few meet-ings as a HICCASP officer, beginning in Apr. 1947, are vivid but some-times confused as to chronology and content. The author bases his account on contemporary accounts in HDC and HICCASP Papers, SHSW, with the Reaganesque details reorganized accordingly.

232   **The room at**   RR testimony in *Jeffers v. Screen Extras Guild*, 3398–99; RR, *Where's the Rest of Me?*, 166–67; RR to Hugh Hefner, July 4, 1960, *Playboy* Archives, Los Angeles; RR interview, Charles E. Davis, Los An-geles *Examiner*, Sept. 14, 1958.

233   **Olivia de Havilland**   RR, *Where's the Rest of Me?*, 167–68. A copy of the resolution is included in Minutes, HDC Papers, SHSW. According to RR's later recollection, Lawson finally declared, pounding the table, "This committee never will adopt a statement of policy which repudiates Communism or endorses private enterprise as an economic system." RR interview, Charles E. Davis, Los Angeles *Examiner*, Sept. 14, 1958.

233   **In the sour**   Minutes, HDC Papers, SHSW. The committee's other mem-bers were Don Hartman and True Boardman, both politically moderate writers. Ceplair and Englund, *Inquisition in Hollywood*, 238. For a sam-ple admonition to them not to declare "an attack on the Soviet Union, and foster hatred against it," see Harry Grobstein to True Boardman, July 3, 1946, HDC Papers, SHSW.

233   **Three nights later**   "SAC" to J. Edgar Hoover, Apr. 18, 1947; RR, testi-mony in *Jeffers v. Screen Extras Guild*, 3398, 3411; Vaughn, *Ronald Rea-gan in Hollywood*, 130–31; RR, testimony in *Jeffers v. Screen Extras Guild*, 3411; RR, *Where's the Rest of Me?*, 168. The latter source derides Lawson's words as "not sophisticated enough." See also Vaughn, *Ronald Reagan in Hollywood*, 130–31.

234   **A consensus was**   HICCASP Minutes, July 10, 1946, HDC Papers, SHSW.

234   **Reagan did not**   Roosevelt resigned on grounds of ill health (James Roo-sevelt to Jo Davidson, July 9, 1946, and to John Cromwell, telegram, ca. July 22, 1946, SHSW). Although the Executive Council approved the policy committee's statement of principles on July 10, HICCASP's gov-erning Executive Council began to radicalize it almost immediately. Trumbo and Lawson were just as active, and even more influential, at this higher level. RR did not sit on the Council, but de Havilland did, and in a last-ditch defense of democracy she attempted to insert an anti-Communist resolution. When her effort failed, she resigned, on or around July 23, along with several other disillusioned liberals. HICCASP Executive Council minutes, July 10, 23, and 30, 1946, HDC Papers, SHSW; Vaughn, *Ronald Reagan in Hollywood*, 131–32. For RR's reac-tion, see below.

234   **But he did not**   RR testimony in *Jeffers v. Screen Extras Guild*, 3399; Ce-plair and Englund, *Inquisition in Hollywood*, 238; RR, *Where's the Rest*

of Me?, 169; Executive Council memo, Aug. 27, 1946, HDC Papers, SHSW. For critical reaction to the radicalization of HICCASP at this time, see Arthur M. Schlesinger, Jr., in *Life,* July 29; also *Time,* Sept. 29, 1946. The defection of other anti-Marxists caused HICCASP to reformulate itself as the Hollywood Arts, Sciences, and Professions Council, which Jack Tenney's committee identified in 1951 as "the most potent Communist-controlled cultural front in California today." California Legislature, *Sixth Report of the Senate Fact-Finding Committee on Un-American Activities,* 1951, 268.

234   **Reagan remained at HICCASP**   De Havilland qu. on "The Real Life of Ronald Reagan," *Frontline,* PBS, 1989, transcript, 9. "He always seemed to be observing. And then I learned much later . . . he was with the FBI."

16: Star Power

235   **I came across a letter**   Copy in AC. Original in *Playboy* Archives, Los Angeles.

235   **early one evening**   The night in question was that of Dec. 19, 1986. Atmospheric details from EM Diary, Dec. 18–20, 1986. Dialogue edited in collaboration with Philip Dunne.

236   *a number of others*   Ring Lardner, Jr., and Herbert Biberman.

236   **"Bathtub Communist"**   See Bruce Cook, *Dalton Trumbo* (New York, 1977).

237   **"something happened"**   Joseph Heller, *Something Happened* (New York, 1974).

237   *the "Unfriendly 10"*   Notwithstanding his disdain for Trumbo, who had publicly called him a "turncoat" in the liberal/Communist split of Mar. 1940, Dunne acted as the blacklisted screenwriter's character witness in 1948. See Dunne, *Take Two,* 113, 200, 219–20.

237   **"Well, there was"**   Leonora Hornblow interview, Jan. 25, 1989.

237   **"He received"**   At Point Mugu. *Night unto Night* production file, WBC. According to RR's co-star in *Night,* the call came "on the fourth day" of shooting—i.e., Sept. 24. Viveca Lindfors, *Viveka-Viveca* (New York, 1981), 153.

237   **"Gets called to"**   Lindfors, *Viveka-Viveca,* 153; RR, *Where's the Rest of Me?,* 189–90. Lindfors recalls overhearing a studio police officer ordering one of his men, "Take Reagan home and stay [there] on patrol all night. . . . We don't want to take any chances."

237   **"Even so, he didn't"**   RR testimony in *Jeffers v. Screen Extras Guild,* 3395; RR, *Where's the Rest of Me?,* 174. Edwards, *Early Reagan,* 321, quotes JW as saying that she would sometimes wake to see RR bolt upright in bed, gun in hand, listening for noises in the house. On Apr. 5, 1955, his friend the labor columnist Victor Riesel was blinded in just such an acid attack.

237   **"No. He's convinced"**   RR interview, Mar. 22, 1985.

238   **"Herb thought he had"**   For the almost impossibly complicated story of the CSU strikes of 1946–1947, see RR, *Where's the Rest of Me?,*

Chs. 9–10; Ceplair and Englund, *Inquisition in Hollywood,* Ch. 7; Vaughn, *Ronald Reagan in Hollywood,* Ch. 11; and Wills, *Reagan's America,* Ch. 24.

238   **"What he remembers"**   "Jurisdictional Disputes," 223.

239   **"By then Reagan"**   RR was re-elected to the SAG board as an alternate, and attended his first board meeting on Apr. 1, 1946.

239   **"It *tried* to clarify"**   George Dunne, *Hollywood Labor Dispute,* 28; Vaughn, *Ronald Reagan in Hollywood,* 135.

239   **"Well, the Wise Men"**   George Dunne, *Hollywood Labor Dispute,* 29; RR, *Where's the Rest of Me?,* 146–47.

239   **"on September 11"**   Pat Casey, minutes of producers' meetings, Sept. 11–24, 1946, in House Special Subcommittee, "Jurisdictional Disputes," 910; George Dunne Oral History, UCLA; Wills, *Reagan's America,* 234–36.

239   **"The producers," I told**   RR, *Where's the Rest of Me?,* 140.

240   **"Yes, he was up"**   Ibid., 147; *Hollywood Reporter,* Aug. 20 and 22, 1946; Strike Scrapbooks, 1946, JLWP; Wills, *Reagan's America,* 233–34; "Jurisdictional Disputes," 910; *Los Angeles Examiner,* Sept. 14, 1946. Owen Crump's production of *Night unto Night* began on Sept. 20, 1946. The first week of shooting was on location at Point Mugu. Production file, WBC.

240   **"We stayed clear"**   A Lester Cole motion calling for screenwriters to meet and vote on the lockout issue, *à la* the actors, was rejected by a nervous SWG board (including Philip Dunne) on Sept. 20, 1946. Ceplair and Englund, *Inquisition in Hollywood,* 223. See ibid., 221, for the emergence of Trumbo as SWG's *enfant terrible* in 1945.

240   **"All he will admit"**   Vaughn, *Ronald Reagan in Hollywood,* 142; RR to Republican conservatives, Sept. 22, 1987, EM Notes. This was probably the bus at 4251 Beverly Blvd. described by the *Hollywood Citizen-News* as "engulfed in flames" on Nov. 13, 1946.

241   **"He took great trouble"**   RR, *Where's the Rest of Me?,* 171–72. He specifically dates the patio meeting as "two nights" before the SAG mass meeting, i.e., Sept. 30, 1946, and the acid threat as the following day, Oct. 1. Ida Lupino confirms this anecdote of RR's in "What 18 Smart Women Think of Ronald Reagan," *Good Housekeeping,* Jan. 1968. She says she was not the hostess but had merely lent her patio to the radicals. See also Wills, *Reagan's America,* 117–18.

241   **"Yes. Only this"**   Adolphe Menjou, qu. in FBI report, "Screen Actors Guild," ca. Apr. 10, 1947, SHSW; Franchot Tone spoke next and declared that as far as SAG was concerned, this was a jurisdictional dispute between two fellow AFL members—something only the AFL could pass final judgment on. Pending that, it was in the best interests of actors that the studios be kept open. *The Screen Actor,* Oct. 1946.

241   **After I made**   RR interview, Nov. 4, 1987.

242   **"Well, he goes on"**   According to former Equity President Ralph Bellamy (Oral History, SAGA), this technique of shouts from four equidistant points of a room gave the impression that audience reaction was unanimous. It worked especially well during voice votes.

242   **You know, Bob Cummings**   According to the *New York Post,* Sept. 1, 1981, the actor Jean-Pierre Aumont said to him about this time, "You

know, one of these days you're going to end up as President of the United States." RR reportedly replied with no apparent emotion, "Yes."

243   **"More for Robert"**   *The Screen Actor,* Oct. 1946.

243   **"Most astronomers these"**   See David Hughes, *The Star of Bethlehem: An Astronomer's Confirmation* (New York, 1979), 84.

243   **"this very night"**   The sky map for Dec. 19, 1986 (Dec. 20, Universal Time) shows Mars and Jupiter in Aquarius, within half a degree of each other.

244   **"Really the whole thing"**   The trip occurred on Oct. 7–8, 1946. Board minutes, Oct. 7, 1946, SAGA; RR, *Where's the Rest of Me?,* 148. Dick Powell also attended. George Montgomery, president of SAG, and Pat Somerset were in Chicago officially as 4 A's delegates to the AFL Convention. Eddie Arnold acted as chief "negotiator."

244   **"the Wise Men admitted"**   RR, *Where's the Rest of Me?,* 148–49.

244   **"But they didn't"**   Herbert Sorrell Oral History, UCLA; RR, *Where's the Rest of Me?,* 154.

245   *"I am no longer"*   Vaughn, *Ronald Reagan in Hollywood,* 142.

245   **"Throughout his speech"**   Robert Stack interview; RR testimony in *Jeffers v. Screen Extras Guild;* Alexander Knox qu. by Schwartz, *Hollywood Writers' Wars,* 249–50.

245   **"I'm not sure"**   Jack Dales interview, Feb. 23, 1986. See also Vaughn, *Ronald Reagan in Hollywood,* 143.

246   **"Reagan's phrase is"**   *Where's the Rest of Me?,* 157. A measure of SAG's power in 1946–1947 is that the much more liberal Writers Guild, which tended to sympathize with the CSU, was forced to go along with the policy of nonpartisanship.

248   **"a black hole"**   See p. 616.

17: Down the Divide

249   **Reaganesque figures**   RR, *Where's the Rest of Me?,* 194–95.

250   *This short documentary*   RR, *Where's the Rest of Me?,* 194. Except where otherwise cited, this scenario closely follows the text of ibid., 194–96.

250   *She reports that*   Frank Mattison to R. J. Obringer, June 18, 1947, JLWP.

250   *We see the face*   According to Michael Reagan, *On the Outside,* 18, JW had been told after Maureen's eight-and-a-half-hour birth that she "could not have any more children."

250   *Dissolve to a hazy*   RR told Louella Parsons on June 26 that JW was a constant presence beside him until her own hospitalization the day before. Louella Parsons, Los Angeles *Examiner,* June 27, 1947.

251   *He is harking back*   Probably the attack of bronchial pneumonia described above on p. 25.

251   *"Big Casino, bet"*   RR, *Where's the Rest of Me?,* 195.

251   *Crosscut to*   F. Mattison to R. J. Obringer, June 18, 19, 1947, JLWP; Christine Reagan death certificate, Los Angeles County Clerk's Office, copy in AC.

251   *Dissolve to the*   RR, *Where's the Rest of Me?,* 195.

PAGE

252   *And no music*   Michael Reagan, *On the Outside,* 18, states that Christine Reagan is still mentioned in JW's will.

252   *Again, no music*   Robert Raison interview, Jan. 30, 1990; Irv Kaplan interview, Aug. 23, 1988.

252   *He has been president*   Board minutes, Mar. 10, 1947, SAGA. On May 8 and 9, 1947, Committee chairman J. Parnell Thomas and three other HUAC officials secretly quizzed Hollywood executives, including a nervous Jack Warner, about the Communist "menace" in Hollywood. Warner named some names, to the disgust of John Huston. Warner also advised Thomas that RR would make an excellent public witness. Gabler, *An Empire of Their Own,* 361–66; Edwards, *Early Reagan,* 340. Thom Andersen suggests that subliminal Communist propaganda in Hollywood movies of this period remains a subject worthy of serious study and should not be affected by HUAC's low historical reputation. "Red Hollywood," *Literature and the Visual Arts in Contemporary Society,* Susan Ferguson and Barbara Groseclose, eds. (Columbus, Ohio, 1985), 179ff.

252   *The work fascinates*   RR to Lorraine Makler, Jan. 5, 1947, RAA ("Too many late strike meetings at night. I think I can sleep standing up."); Jack Dales interview, Feb. 23, 1986. The building (no longer occupied by SAG) can still be seen at no. 7750.

252   *(His election coincided)*   On Mar. 12, 1947, President Truman sent to Congress his message stating that the United States must henceforth be the protector of "free people who are resisting attempted subjugation by armed minorities or by outside pressures."

252   *There was a time*   Herman Hover, in the *Los Angeles Times,* Oct. 3, 1948, recalls seeing JW trying to escape RR's harangues at parties: "You'd walk away from him and he'd follow you, talking." See also Quirk, *Jane Wyman,* 76, 109; Otto Friedrich, *City of Nets: A Portrait of Hollywood in the 1940's* (New York, 1986), 327; Cannon, *Reagan,* 65.

253   *Director: I suggest*   JW, qu. by Edward Anhalt interview, Oct. 2, 1992.

253   *Camera holds on*   RR, qu. in *Chicago Tribune,* May 19, 1947.

253   *Outside, the pool*   Photographs in RR Scrapbook, RRL/pp.

253   **When the August**   "Jurisdictional Disputes," 194, 223.

254   *WYMAN, her ears*   JW interview by Hedda Hopper, Oct. 4, 1948, Hopper Papers, HER; Quirk, *Jane Wyman,* 100–101.

254   *When REAGAN comes*   Quirk, *Jane Wyman,* 100–101. Maureen Reagan interview, Feb. 23, 1991. Maureen went so far as to learn a few deaf-mute signs in order to communicate with her mother.

254   *I'm tempted to*   Robert William interview, Feb. 15, 1991.

254   *Our scenario now*   These rushes also disturbed Jack Warner, who thought Negulesco was destroying the glamorous image of one of his dependable cupcakes. Owen Crump interview, Oct. 1, 1992.

254   *We see REAGAN*   Owen Crump interview, Oct. 1, 1992.

254   *Between takes, he*   Robert William interview, Feb. 15, 1991; Arno Johanson, "The True Love Story of Jane Wyman," *Movieland* clipping, ca. Feb. 1949, in JW biographical file, HER; Jean Negulesco, *Things I Did . . . and Things I Think I Did* (New York, 1984), 127.

254   *"Oh, no!"*   The scene was cut. This paragraph is a near-verbatim transcript of RR, *Where's the Rest of Me?,* 194. For a detailed description of

That Hagen Girl, see Harry Medved, *The Fifty Worst Films of All Time* (New York, 1978), 244–50.

255   **We are still**   Vaughn, *Ronald Reagan in Hollywood,* 147; and Ceplair and Englund, *Inquisition in Hollywood,* 279–80.

255   **Today's roster**   Hearst newsreel clips, UCLA; quotations from House Committee on Un-American Activities, *Hearings Regarding the Communist Infiltration of the Motion Picture Industry,* 80th Cong., 1st sess., Oct. 1947, 94ff. None of the actors who appeared before HUAC on this occasion named names.

255   **REAGAN's tall body**   *The Washington Post,* Oct. 24, 1947; Hearst newsreel clips, UCLA.

256   **The investigative report**   Confidential FBI report, May 23, 1951, reflecting information received from RR on Feb. 10, 1948. RR FBI file, SAGA.

257   **"Anne Revere" would fit**   See below, pp. 290–91.

257   **"a fine statement"**   Dunne, *Take Two,* 206. RR's testimony may be heard in the audiobook version of this biography (New York, 1999).

257   **I believe that**   For a more extended statement of RR's principles regarding the legality of the Communist Party, see "Mr. Reagan Airs His Views," *Chicago Tribune,* May 19, 1947.

258   **Hold on his Indian**   RR's testimony was reported widely. He won praise for being intellectually superior to "his better-known colleagues" and for being a "decidedly creditable" witness. Vaughn, *Ronald Reagan in Hollywood,* 148.

258   **a thunderclap, no less**   Los Angeles *Examiner,* Dec. 5, 1947; M. Friedman to Jack Warner, Nov. 10, 1947, WBC; Louella Parsons, Los Angeles *Examiner,* Dec. 5, 1947. On Dec. 15, Jerry Wald was still hopeful that JW would play Mary to RR's John, but by the end of the year it was obvious that they would never be able to act together again. Patricia Neal, a twenty-one-year-old ingenue, replaced JW. She was the witness of the patio incident at the end of this scenario.

258   **Now the screen**   Joy Hodges interview, May 30, 1989. (The adverb *furiously* is Miss Hodges's. She and her husband were hosts to JW on this trip to New York.) RR to Louella Parsons, Los Angeles *Examiner* clipping, ca. Dec. 15, 1947, Hearst Collection, USC. See also Quirk, *Jane Wyman,* 113.

259   **"I love Jane"**   RR, qu. in Hedda Hopper, *Modern Screen,* Mar. 1948. Privately, he described JW as being "a pretty sick girl in mind," but was sure that she would love him again when recovered from her "nervousness." RR to Lorraine Makler, Jan. 8, 1948, RAA.

259   **Camera is passing**   Patricia Neal interview, July 6, 1987; Los Angeles *Examiner,* Jan. 8, 1948. See also Patricia Neal, *As I Am* (New York, 1988), 90.

18: Red or Palest Pink

260   **My dear Jacob**   On Oct. 1, 1948, the author's former school friend Alaric Jacob wrote to the author that he was back in London after four years representing the *Daily Express* in Moscow. He announced that he

was writing "a sort of anti-memoir," contrasting the respective social and political systems of East and West, and was curious as to whether Hollywood's current blacklist was official or not (AC).

260   **She died last year** On Nov. 8, 1947. For an appreciation of Annette "Bess" Dowling, see James Lockhart, "The Kentish Skylark," *Vocalise,* 48 (winter 1947–1948), 112–33.

260   **I had no idea** For Jacob's radicalizing experiences in Stalinist USSR, see his brilliant *Scenes from a Bourgeois Life* (London, 1949). "I have embarked on the S.S. *Sozialisticheskie Revoluzie.*"

260   **Now as to** *Ça vous amuse, la vie?* Roughly translatable as, "It's a fun life, isn't it?" Quite apart from the developing Red Scare, the Hollywood movie industry was in a severe slump, largely due to the collapse of its European market. In the late summer of 1947, over two thirds of the screenwriters in Hollywood were out of work. *The New Masses,* Aug. 26, 1947.

261   **Hence, am by no** *Variety,* Nov. 26, 1947; Navasky, *Naming Names,* 83–84. The much-maligned "Waldorf Conference" in New York on Nov. 24, 1947, at least had the effect of keeping HUAC out of Hollywood for the next three years. Historians of the left and right predictably differ as to whether a private blacklist, conducted by executives answerable to their own industry, such as Louis B. Mayer, is preferable to a public blacklist conducted by members of Congress, such as Senator Joseph McCarthy. Most historians agree that, given the climate of the times, a blacklist of some kind was inevitable.

261   **And he grilled** Vaughn, *Ronald Reagan in Hollywood,* 153–54.

261   **Reagan doesn't sound** Ibid., 155. At Mayer's request, RR agreed to serve on "a committee . . . for the purpose of purging the motion picture industry." He did so with misgivings, feeling it would be hampered by Congress's failure to ban the Communist Party outright. FBI report, May 23, 1951, RR FBI file, SAGA. The committee eventually became the Motion Picture Industry Council of 1949, which RR chaired.

261   **"Hollywood for Harry"** *Variety,* Oct. 6, 1948. RR's co-campaign manager was the fanatical anti-Communist Roy Brewer.

262   **Reason I'm telling** *Variety,* Oct. 20, 1948. On Jan. 28, 1947, Warner Bros. and the Associated British Picture Corporation announced a two-year co-production deal that would help refurbish the Elstree studio facility—and Britain's trade balance. *The Times* (London), Jan. 29, 1947.

262   **Watch out for** Quirk, *Jane Wyman,* 102–3. RR sarcastically remarked, "I think I'll name *Johnny Belinda* as co-respondent." Curiously, RR, who had always signed himself as "Ronald" when writing to the president of his fan club, switched to "Dutch" after JW's testimony in *Reagan v. Reagan.* This lasted until the new year of 1952, when he became "Ronnie." RR to Lorraine Makler, *passim,* RAA.

262   **"on the verge of"** Sam Marx interviews, Aug. 17, 1987, and Feb. 19, 1989. RR was due to leave Los Angeles for New York by train on Nov. 15, embarking immediately. But a dock strike diverted him to the Canadian port of Halifax, whence he sailed on Nov. 20 for Liverpool aboard the *Britannic.* RR to Lorraine Makler, Nov. 13, 1948, RAA; typed itinerary, WBC. See also RR, *Where's the Rest of Me?,* 206–7.

PAGE

262   **JW accused him** The divorce suit stated that RR had inflicted "grievous mental suffering" upon JW with his incessant harangues about politics. Los Angeles *Examiner,* June 5, 1948.

19: This Dismal Wilderness

263   **Ronald Reagan strode** RR, *Where's the Rest of Me?,* 208; Liverpool *Daily News,* Nov. 29, 1948. Other fog-related details in the paragraphs that follow are taken from *The Times* (London), the *Daily Telegraph,* and the *Daily Mail,* Nov. 29 and 30, 1949. Descriptive passages throughout this chapter not directly attributed to RR are based on the author's researches in contemporary issues of *Picture Post, Illustrated London News,* and the *Daily Mirror,* Nov. 1948–Feb. 1949.

264   **all breathed *foreign*** RR to Jack Warner, n.d. [ca. Dec. 1948], WBC; RR, *Where's the Rest of Me?,* 208–9.

264   **He was clear of** RR itinerary, Nov. 15–28, 1948, WBC.

264   **Reagan's sensitive sinuses** "Fearing an explosion of this gaseous stuff I ordered, 'no smoking.' Better I should have ordered,—'no breathing.' " RR to Jack Warner, nd. [ca. Dec. 1948], WBC. See also RR, *Where's the Rest of Me?,* 209.

264   **He was surprised** RR, *Where's the Rest of Me?,* 209. See p. 18.

264   **He awoke the next** Neal, *As I Am,* 110; *Daily Telegraph,* Nov. 29, 1949; Savoy Hotel guest book, Nov. 28, 1948.

264   **He was not, however** RR, *Where's the Rest of Me?,* 209; Patricia Neal interview, July 6, 1987; Neal, *As I Am,* 109; Marvin Liebman interview, Aug. 2, 1987.

265   **"What's rationing?"** RR qu. in Richard Todd interview, May 16, 1987; *Daily Mail, Daily Telegraph, Daily Express,* Nov. 29, 1948.

265   **The only positive** *Daily Express,* Nov. 29, 1948; Richard Todd interview, May 16, 1987. Later in life, RR changed his mind: "Today we have known 40 or more years of peace & one time enemies are the closest of friends and allies as a result of the Marshall Plan." RR insert in pre-Venice summit address, June 1, 1987, RRL/pp/hw.

266   **During the next week** Publicity material in *The Hasty Heart* production file, WBC; Patricia Neal interview, July 6, 1987; *Daily Telegraph* and *Daily Mail,* Nov. 30, 1948; *Variety,* Dec. 1 and 22, 1948.

266   **Dutch tried to kiss** Patricia Neal interview, July 6, 1987; Joy Hodges interview, May 30, 1989.

266   **"For what?"** RR interview, June 27, 1989.

267   **The fact that he** Edie Wasserman interview, Apr. 15, 1987; RR interview, June 27, 1989.

267   **At 7:00 A.M.** An unidentified illustrated article (*Photoplay*?), Aug. 1949, RR scrapbook, RRL, takes RR through a typical day's work on *The Hasty Heart.*

267   **Elstree—a dark** Patricia Warren, *Elstree: The British Hollywood* (London, 1983).

267   **Aside from Pat** Publicity material in *The Hasty Heart* production file, WBC; RR, *Where's the Rest of Me?,* 210.

PAGE

267   **The thickest accent**   RR, *Where's the Rest of Me?,* 210. RR was still brooding about "playing second lead to Todd" when his relations with Warner Bros. went sour in 1950. R. J. Obringer to Jack Warner, Feb. 17, 1950.

268   **Incapable of jealousy**   Richard Todd interview, May 16, 1987. See also Richard Todd, *Caught in the Act: The Story of My Life* (London, 1986): "He was the sweetest, most patient and kindly of men, from whom I never heard a sharp or irritable word" (233).

268   **"Ronnie couldn't have"**   Richard Todd interview, May 16, 1987; publicity brief, Dec. 28, 1948, *The Hasty Heart* production file, WBC.

268   **Like Eddie Albert**   Todd had been the first main-force paratrooper to land behind enemy lines on D-Day. Todd, *Caught in the Act,* 167–68.

268   **"I have never met"**   Ibid., 233, 235–36.

268   **"He told me"**   Patricia Neal interview, July 6, 1987.

269   **Old, crippled**   Ibid.

269   **In Miss Neal's**   Ibid.; Neal, *As I Am,* 113.

269   **It was both**   Photocopy, AC. Original in possession of Hamish Thomson.

269   **One glance at**   William Steig, *The Lonely Ones* (New York, 1942), 42.

269   **A much less cryptic**   RR to Jack Warner, n.d. [ca. Dec. 1948], WBC; *The Hasty Heart* production file, WBC. An unverifiable report in ibid. has RR spending Christmas with "a British family."

270   **the "Frozen Dollar"**   An allusion to the Attlee government's post-war freeze on movie box-office receipts, forcing U.S. studios to spend them on cooperative productions shot in Britain.

270   **On the first shooting**   Sound track, *The Hasty Heart,* LC print (recorded Feb. 3, 1949).

271   **He had to repeat**   *The Hasty Heart* production file, WBC; RR, *Where's the Rest of Me?,* 210; RR interview, June 12, 1986.

271   **Reagan, who took**   Todd, *Caught in the Act,* 234; RR, *Where's the Rest of Me?,* 210; Marvin Liebman interview, Aug. 2, 1987.

271   **He vented some**   Vincent Sherman interview, May 21, 1987; Richard Todd interview, May 16, 1987.

271   **Both men were**   Richard Todd interview, May 16, 1987; Vincent Sherman, qu. in McClelland, *Hollywood on Ronald Reagan,* 160; RR to "Ben," ca. 1976, RRL/pp.

272   **Wet week followed**   RR, *Where's the Rest of Me?,* 210; RR interview, June 12, 1986; Marvin Liebman interview, Aug. 2, 1987; Patricia Neal interview, July 6, 1987.

272   **"Reagan does not look"**   Jack Warner, Jr., to S. Trilling, Feb. 23, 1949, WBC. A few days before, RR had been the subject of another report, from an unidentified executive, presumably with Warners (U.K.), to the studio head office in New York. "Ronnie Reagan last night did just about the finest Public Relations job . . . in years for the American Film Industry in this country." He had addressed an audience of one hundred British female writers, reporters, and critics on the current political situation in Hollywood. Rebecca West, author of *The Meaning of Treason,* had been the chair. "We figured Ronnie would talk for twenty minutes. Instead his time was doubled, then we had a no-holds-barred session in

which he was to answer any question they put to him. He did it in such grand shape that the BBC Recording Unit, which came expecting to cut about five discs . . . finished up with sixteen discs covering seventy minutes [for] national broadcast next Thursday week. . . . This morning they have asked us for permission to use it throughout the world." To Mort Blumenstock, Feb. 17, 1949, RRL/pp.

272   **Arthur Abeles**   Arthur Abeles interview, July 28, 1986.

272   **Abeles was**   Ibid; Savoy Hotel guest book, Mar. 17–22, 1949; RR interview, June 12, 1986. See also RR, *Where's the Rest of Me?*, 211–12.

273   **The rest of their**   Arthur Abeles interview, July 28, 1986. "I look back on those days with great warmth. He was so . . . nice." *Poids Lourds* (heavy weight) is a traffic sign, common in France, directing trucks into roads bypassing villages.

273   **On March 23**   *The Hasty Heart* production file, WBC; Savoy Hotel guest book, Mar. 24, 1948; Arthur Abeles interview, July 28, 1986. The following year, Mr. and Mrs. Abeles were divorced.

20: And Then Along Came Nancy

277   **God seemed to agree**   The accident occurred on June 19, 1949, when RR, playing for the Tragedians against the Comedians, tried to beat out a bunt, got blocked off first base, and shattered his femur into six separate pieces. He remained in traction until Aug. 16. It would be years before he could ride a horse again, and for the rest of his life he would walk with a slight, flowing limp. RR to Tressie Kozelka, Sept. 22, 1949, WAL; Los Angeles *Examiner,* June 20, 1949; photographs in RR Scrapbook, RRL; *Daily Variety,* Aug. 17, 1949; RR, *Where's the Rest of Me?*, 213–14.

277   **preview of his latest**   "Am sorry you could not make it," an aggrieved Jack Warner wrote him the next day. Oct. 12, 1949, WBC. For RR's physical incapacitation, see a chilling photograph in *Movie Life,* Dec. 6, 1949.

278   **Who's going to carry?**   Sound track, *The Hasty Heart,* LC print.

278   **he moved in with Nelle**   From this time until he remarried, RR made a habit of visiting Nelle every Sunday morning for brunch. She served once more as mother, cook, and comforter, and allowed him the supreme luxury of being able to dunk his doughnuts. Nelle Reagan to Helen Lawton, n.d. [ca. 1949], LAW. For this period of RR's life, see also Maureen Reagan, *First Father,* 18, 55; *Silver Screen,* Nov. 1949; RR, *Where's the Rest of Me?*, 214; Michael Reagan, *On the Outside,* 25–26.

278   **Motion Picture Industry Council**   Proposed originally by Roy Brewer, RR, and Louis B. Mayer in the immediate aftermath of the 1947 HUAC hearings, the MPIC remained largely quiescent until Feb. 1, 1949, when Brewer and Cecil B. DeMille reorganized it as a complex of all the major Hollywood trade organizations. The SWG alone remained wary of its stated purpose to "purge" (RR's own word) the movie industry of unrepentant Communists. DeMille became chairman under a rule that switched the office every six months between representatives of management and labor. He was succeeded by RR in late July, but the latter's in-

capacitation again caused the MPIC to lose momentum. *The New York Times,* Feb. 6 and July 24, 1949.

278   **Now, if ever**   RR to Lorraine Makler, Sep. 21, 1949, RAA; "History of Reagan's Contracts with Warner Bros. Pictures, Inc.," ts., Sept. 24, 1951, WBC. For the deterioration of RR's relationship with Jack Warner, 1949–1950, see Edwards, *Early Reagan,* Ch. 19.

278   **Like Charles Ryder**   Evelyn Waugh, *Brideshead Revisited* (New York, 1945, 1979), epilogue; Bellamann, *Kings Row,* 486.

279   **Over the years,**   The emasculating symbolism of Drake's double amputation (from the hip) is quite clear in the novel, although, of course, much muted in the film version. That it got through to RR nonetheless is suggested by his own word-associations in the opening pages of *Where's the Rest of Me?* He characterizes Drake McHugh as "the gay blade who cut quite a swath among the ladies," then segues into a self-description of himself as "only half a man" before he became politically aware and moved out of "the monastery of movies into the world" (4, 6, 7). See also Wills, *Reagan's America,* 176.

279   **fresh from the shower**   RR's fondness for post-ablutionary sex is detailed by Viveca Lindfors in *Viveka-Viveca,* 154.

279   **Jerry Wald wanted him**   For an account of the filming of *Storm Warning* (late Nov.–Dec. 1949), see Edwards, *Early Reagan,* 396–400. By mid-Dec., RR was able to dispense with his canes but still walked with difficulty. Nelle Reagan to Helen Lawton, Dec. 14, 1949, LAW.

279   **"I just can't"**   Doris Lilly, "All for the Love of Ronnie," *Quest,* ca. Oct. 1988. Lilly (best known as the author of *How to Marry a Millionaire*) had noticed that RR never wrote "Love, Ronnie" in letters to her. "Such an honest man. He wouldn't put that unless he meant it." Interviewed by Marion Elizabeth Rodgers, Oct. 17, 1988.

280   **"along came Nancy"**   See p. xv.

280   **The name "Nancy"**   Kitty Kelley, *Nancy Reagan: An Unauthorized Biography* (New York, 1991), 78; Sam Marx interviews, Aug. 12, 1987, and Feb. 19, 1989, NR interview, Sept. 12, 1992. The phrase "bleeding-heart briefs" is RR's (*Where's the Rest of Me?,* 235).

280   **How she engineered**   RR, *An American Life,* 121–22; Jill Robinson interview (telephone), Oct. 13, 1987. For more about RR's first date with NR, see pp. 628–29.

281   **So there she stood**   Louella Parsons in *Motion Picture,* May 1954; Lilly, "All for the Love of Ronnie"; Irving "Swifty" Lazar interview, Apr. 16, 1987.

281   **But Dutch, blind**   RR, *Where's the Rest of Me?,* 235.

281   **"It was just"**   Ibid. They went on to dinner at LaRue's before attending Sophie Tucker's midnight show at Ciro's. Miss Tucker sang, *If I had my life to live over, I'd still fall in love with you.* RR's lameness notwithstanding, they shuffled around the dance floor until three. RR and Nancy Reagan interview, Nov. 15, 1987; lyrics and program, Sophie Tucker Scrapbooks, NYPL/pa.

281   **The traditional privilege**   RR, *Where's the Rest of Me?,* 203; Errol Flynn, qu. in Lilly, "All for the Love of Ronnie."

PAGE

281   **A "girl" Nancy**   Kelley, *Nancy Reagan,* 76–77. Unlike JW, who has consistently added two years to her real age, NR (b. Anne Frances Robbins, July 6, 1921) has always subtracted two.

281   **My research cards**   The phrase "celestial view" is Doris Day's. *Doris Day: Her Own Story* (New York, 1976), 121. See also McClelland, *Hollywood on Ronald Reagan,* 94–104; Piper Laurie interview, *People,* Apr. 30, 1990. For a more detailed discussion of RR's sex life, 1948–1952, see Kelley, *Nancy Reagan.*

282   **He did admit**   Michael Deaver interview, May 18, 1989.

282   **Dutch's "cocker spaniels"**   Ibid.; Doris Lilly interview, Oct. 17, 1988; McClelland, *Hollywood on Ronald Reagan,* 94, 130, qu. Doris Day.

282   **Since childhood, she**   Kelley, *Nancy Reagan,* Ch. 2 (an excellent sketch of Nancy Reagan's background); Sam Marx interview, Aug. 12, 1987; LC presentation anthology of Nancy Davis film appearances, May 5, 1993.

282   **Nancy's chief charm**   RR, *Where's the Rest of Me?,* 236; Edwin Meese III interview, Aug. 6, 1988; Malvin Wald interview, Feb. 12, 1991.

283   **In all the repetitive**   Kelley, *Nancy Reagan,* 538–39.

21: The Unexplored Mystery of Ploughed Ground

284   **Dutch's bullying brother**   After following RR to California in 1939, Neil Reagan worked successively as sports announcer, news editor, and production manager at KFWB, producer at KWX, and program director at CBS (1947). He joined McCann as manager in 1948 and remained in control of that agency for the next thirty years. An efficient if uninspired radio and TV producer, he later devoted much of his professional time to political campaigns, including his brother's.

285   **a little stud farm**   The ranch was an eight-acre property in Northridge, bought for breeding purposes in the fall of 1946. RR, *Where's the Rest of Me?,* 187–88.

285   **It was impossible**   *Daily Variety,* Feb. 9 and 15, 1950; Louella Parsons, Los Angeles *Examiner,* Feb. 11, 1950; unidentified news clippings in Constance McCormick Collection, USC.

285   **The word *television***   *Daily Variety,* Feb. 15, 1950. For details of the bitter SAG/TVA negotiations, which lasted through Sept. 10, 1952, see RR, *Where's the Rest of Me?,* 221–31.

285   **"The only difference"**   Mrs. Luce, qu. in Sylvia Jukes Morris, "In Search of Clare Boothe Luce," *The New York Times Magazine,* Jan. 31, 1988; Thom Andersen, "Red Hollywood"; Lary May, *Recasting America: Culture and Politics in the Age of the Cold War* (Chicago, 1989). The last-named book contains (125–53) an excellent short study of SAG during RR's rise to Board power: "Movie Star Politics: The Screen Actor's Guild, Cultural Conversion, and the Hollywood Red Scare."

286   **Committee on the**   Not to be confused with the second Committee on the Present Danger, formed by other nervous Brahmins twenty-six years later. John Newhouse, *War and Peace in the Nuclear Age* (New York, 1989), 292.

PAGE

286   **A flock of geese**   Diary of *Time* editor John Billings, Jan. 10, 1951, copy
in AC. For extended treatment of the subjects alluded to in this para-
graph, see James G. Hershberg, *James B. Conant: Harvard to Hiroshima
and the Making of the Nuclear Age* (New York, 1994); Sam Tanenhaus,
Whittaker Chambers (New York, 1997); Vance Packard, *The Hidden Per-
suaders* (New York, 1957); Lewis A. Erenberg, "Things to Come: Swing
Bands, Bebop, and the Rise of a Postwar Jazz Scene," and Clifford E.
Clark, Jr., "Ranch-House Suburbia: Ideals and Realities," both in May,
Recasting America, 221–45, 171–91; and Richard Rhodes, *Dark Sun:
The Making of the Hydrogen Bomb* (New York, 1995).

286   **The onset of**   Powers, *Not Without Honor,* 235ff.

287   **both of them conservative**   RR was also active in the even more conservative Motion Picture Alliance for the Preservation of American Ideals.
Garry Wills argues cogently that, contrary to the received view that RR
became a conservative in the late 1950s, "his world and his views were
conservative, business-oriented and actively anti-Communist from 1947
on." *Reagan's America,* 257.

287   **"He's playing right into"**   Nixon defeated Mrs. Douglas. Edwards, *Early
Reagan,* 417–18, has RR secretly switching his allegiance to Nixon
halfway through the campaign. This is based on a remark made by
Robert Cummings in 1982, qu. in McClelland, *Hollywood on Ronald
Reagan,* 229. It is clear, however, that Cummings is remembering RR's
later conversion to the Republican Party. All authoritative sources confirm that RR supported Douglas in 1950. See, e.g., William E. Leucht-
enburg, *In the Shadow of FDR: From Harry Truman to Ronald Reagan*
(Ithaca, N.Y., 1983), 209–17.

287   **Now in his fourth**   Lyle Talbot interview, Aug. 27, 1987; RR, "How Do
You Fight Communism?" *Fortnight,* Jan. 22, 1951.

288   **after his re-election**   Aug. 25, 1985.

288   **His behavior was**   Powers, *Not Without Honor,* is the best overall study
of American anti-Communism. But it reverently neglects to mention
RR's years as "T-10."

288   **In 1943**   "Memo to Mr. Nichols," Nov. 18, 1943, RR FBI file, SAGA
(see p. 208); RR, *Where's the Rest of Me?,* 169–70; FBI report, "Screen
Actors Guild," ca. Apr. 10, 1947, SHSW; FBI report, May 23, 1951, RR
FBI file, SAGA. See also Wills, *Reagan's America,* 245–47.

288   **I remember very**   RR interview, Jan. 30, 1987.

289   **those blotted-out names**   On Oct. 27, 1997, the fiftieth anniversary of
the creation of the blacklist, SAG formally apologized for participating
in it. *The Washington Post,* Nov. 23, 1997.

289   **Let just three**   Gale Sondergaard to SAG Board of Directors, Mar. 13,
1951, SAGA.

289   **Miss Sondergaard's letter**   *Daily Variety,* Mar. 16, 1951.

289   **One might have**   RR, "How Do You Fight Communism?"; Vaughn,
Ronald Reagan in Hollywood, 211. RR was not above political maneu-
vering himself, since he waited at least five days after receipt of Sondergaard's letter before calling the emergency meeting on Mar. 19. This
short-notice summons produced only a few directors, who happened to
be predisposed to his view of the situation.

290   **Or her. John**   John Dales interview, Feb. 23, 1986; Gale Sondergaard interview, *Screen Actor,* 21.3 (summer 1979), 14.

290   **"You know," he**   Anne Revere interview, *Screen Actor,* 21.3 (summer 1979), 17.

291   *Listen, my children*   Clipping, ca. Oct. 1951, AC.

291   **Dutch hated the idea**   The 1947 Taft-Hartley Act, a *locus classicus* of governmental groupthink, required all union officers to sign affidavits confirming that they were not Communists. Liberals on the SAG board, notably Treasurer Anne Revere, felt (as did many AFL leaders) that the Act, passed over President Truman's veto, was anti-democratic. RR's attitude toward Taft-Hartley set the tone of his cautiously conservative guild presidency. He endorsed a loyalty oath so long as it was voluntary, and suggested a rider allowing signers to pledge active involvement in patriotic programs. He also endorsed the affidavits and got a reluctant board majority in favor. Miss Revere refused to sign hers and resigned as Treasurer. See Vaughn, *Ronald Reagan in Hollywood,* 161–62, and Edwards, *Early Reagan,* 333–35.

291   **They would volunteer**   Ceplair and Englund, *Inquisition in Hollywood,* 359; RR, *Where's the Rest of Me?,* 163–64; Vaughn, *Ronald Reagan in Hollywood,* 215. RR always insisted that there was "no blacklist" in Hollywood, while taking credit, often in the same sentence, for getting Hollywood names "off the list." Insofar as these conflicting claims can be resolved at all, his reasoning seems to have been that the blacklist was an evil thing that HUAC sought to impose on Hollywood ("I was never a fan of that Committee"), in contrast to the motion picture industry's own list, which could not be "black" because it was benign. That is to say, it was a private list, democratically compiled ("Producers were getting word from the theatres saying, 'We don't want to run a picture that has so-and-so in it' ")—which gave listees the opportunity to volunteer evidence that would clear them of suspicion. The beauty of the scheme, he felt, was that no dyed-in-the-wool Communists would risk such scrutiny. By not coming forward, they would finger themselves just as effectively as the FBI could, and producers would be justified in boycotting them. RR interview, Jan. 30, 1987.

291   **Dutch had personally**   Philip Dunne interview, Apr. 15, 1987; Vaughn, *Ronald Reagan in Hollywood,* 212–13; Ceplair and Englund, *Inquisition in Hollywood,* 367, 392–93; *The New York Times,* July 19, 1951. Vaughn tells the full story of the Patriotic Services Committee in his Ch. 17, "Loyalty."

291   **"There seems to be"**   RR, qu. in Vaughn, *Ronald Reagan in Hollywood,* 217.

291   **Nancy Davis, meanwhile**   *Variety,* June 21, 1950; Nancy Reagan, *My Turn: The Memoirs of Nancy Reagan* (New York, 1989), 91; PR, "Picture Parade," AP syndicated column, June 23, 1950. (Shakespeare, *King Lear,* 5.3: "Her voice was ever soft,/Gentle, and Low, an excellent thing in woman."

292   **Commentators who like**   An old New York beau and lifelong friend of NR remarked in 1980 that on the contrary RR had a transforming effect

on her. "She seemed to be almost apolitical to me. After she met Ronald Reagan, she seemed so happy. And then suddenly she became rather proper. . . . She became like a Chinese wife, walking five paces behind." Ron Fletcher, qu. in Ellen Farley and William Knoedelseder, "Ronald Reagan in Hollywood: The Making of a Saga," *Los Angeles Times,* Aug. 17, 1980. The old vaudevillian Ken Murray, who knew both women well, defined the difference between them: JW "had a theatrical girlishness, sort of *Oh, poopidoo. . . .* Jane was a girl, primarily. Nancy was a woman." Ken Murray interview, Aug. 28, 1988.

292   ***Reagan v. Reagan***   Laurence Beilenson interview, June 12, 1987. JW, indeed, actually called RR at one point and suggested they should "get back together for the sake of the kids." According to NR, JW also exacted a strange promise from him that he would not remarry before she did. When circumstances obliged him to break this vow, she was enraged and promptly married the bandleader Freddy Karger (NR interview, Sept. 12, 1992). JW's later career and final fame as the Matriarch of *Falcon Crest* is covered amply in Quirk, *Jane Wyman,* but also see Dominick Dunne's portrait of her in *Vanity Fair,* Nov. 1989.

292   **On March 4, 1952**   The two witnesses to RR's wedding were William and Ardis Holden. A strange sense of guilt pervades RR's account of it in *Where's the Rest of Me?,* 239–40. The ceremony was furtive—even his mother and children were excluded—and the dark brown church as dismal as any in Des Moines. Patti was born on Oct. 21, 1952. For a grotesquely amusing account of this event, see Patti Davis, *The Way I See It* (New York, 1992), 24–25.

292   **Pray as I am**   RR to Sam Harrod, Jr., ca. Dec. 1952, privately held.

293   **By the new year**   RR, *Where's the Rest of Me?,* 246; Brownstein, *The Power and the Glitter,* 220. RR was deeply hurt by Wasserman's loss of interest in him. "They didn't reconcile until Ronnie became President." NR interview, Sept. 12, 1992. After wrapping his last Warner Bros. picture, *The Winning Team,* on Jan. 28, 1952, RR did not work again for fourteen months. He sacrificed $150,000 by rejecting two of the five roles Universal had agreed to offer him, so that the studio foreshortened his contract for noncompliance on Jan. 15, 1952. RR's other Universal pictures were *Louisa* (1950), *Bedtime for Bonzo* (1951), and *Law and Order* (1953). As a freelancer, he also made *The Last Outpost* (Paramount, 1951), *Hong Kong* (Paramount, 1951), *Tropic Zone* (Paramount, 1953), *Prisoner of War* (MGM, 1954), *Cattle Queen of Montana* (RKO, 1954), *Tennessee's Partner* (RKO, 1955), and (with co-star Nancy Davis) *Hellcats of the Navy* (Columbia, 1957). His last movie, *The Killers* (Universal, 1964), was made for television, but released as a feature film.

293   **"His *mother?*"**   George Putnam interview, Aug. 28, 1987. RR, in an interview on Sept. 23, 1987, remembered this visit, and allowed that his mother "had strong views." But he denied that she had been trying to get him a job in television.

293   **The foregoing article**   "Yearling Row," holograph ms., ca. spring 1954, RRL/pp.

294   **If I had known**   Like many servicemen, RR had deferred his taxes dur-

ing World War II, not anticipating the punitive schedules imposed on high-income earners in the post-war period. He found himself now in the 91 percent bracket, while carrying heavy mortgages on his ranch and a new house at 1258 Amalfi Drive, in Pacific Palisades. By the end of 1952, he was eighteen thousand dollars in debt. Even after signing up with *General Electric Theater* in 1954, he remained for a while "really hard up." Earl Dunckel Oral History, 3, RRL.

294   **There followed a**   "Yearling Row" ms., RRL/pp. The property lay on the south side of Mulholland Highway, just west of Malibu Canyon. RR bought most of it at $293 an acre in 1951, using his Northridge ranch as a deposit. Dan E. Moldea, *Dark Victory: Ronald Reagan, MCA, and the Mob* (New York, 1986), 106. It is now part of the Santa Monica Mountains National Seashore, and the ranch house, much altered, serves as a ranger outpost.

295   **a variety act in Vegas**   The most detailed account of this engagement is Terry Mulgannon, "When Ronnie Played Vegas . . . ," *Los Angeles,* Apr. 1983. See also RR, *Where's the Rest of Me?,* 248–51. According to Herman Hover interview, Feb. 15, 1986, RR earned $5,500 a week, far less than he implies in his memoir.

22: Remember Old Ma Reagan

298   **She has already**   This chapter is based entirely on a tape recording of Nelle Reagan's appearance, Mar. 12, 1954, on an unidentified Los Angeles radio station, RRL/av.

300   *Three years after*   Nelle Reagan to two friends [unidentified] in Dixon, July 10, 1957, NIC; NR interview, Apr. 10, 1992; RR to William Thompson, Sept. 28, 1982, RRL/pp/hw. When the author asked RR if Nelle had had Alzheimer's disease, he looked stricken and said, "Yes." RR interview, Jan. 31, 1990.

301   *If so, Nelle's*   *Los Angeles Times,* July 26, 1962; news clipping, n.d., RR Scrapbooks, RRL/pp. Nelle Reagan's room is described by Patti Davis in *The Way I See It,* 22. The detail about the lack of headstones was ventured by NR, who informed the author with an air of casual surprise in 1992 that her son Ron had only just discovered that both graves are unmarked. NR interview, Apr. 10, 1992.

23: Ladies and Gentlemen of the California Fertilizer Association

302   **(Blacklisted Bernie)**   Bernard Vorhaus interview, Aug. 12, 1993.

302   *Fein Liebchen*   Franz Schubert and Wilhelm Müller, *Winterreise* (1828), I. Sydney Ann Morris died of heart failure and was buried in Hillside Cemetery, Redlands. Her close friend Michael Mann (son of Thomas Mann) of the Pittsburgh Symphony Orchestra played the viola at her funeral. An NBC aircheck of her performing Bach and Hindemith in the

late 1930s was issued privately as a memorial. She left no other recordings.

303   **And again and again**   RR had been hired by General Electric in the spring of 1954 to act as host ("Program Supervisor") and occasional actor in CBS's *General Electric Theater,* debuting on Sept. 26 of that year. The initial stage of his contract, negotiated by MCA/Revue with GE's advertising agency, BBD&O, called for thirteen half-hour dramas. With RR as host, the program proved instantly popular, topping *I Love Lucy* as early as November. A copy of its pioneering color "Christmas Special" on Dec. 19 shows RR not yet entirely comfortable in his role as MC, with a hand-washing habit reminiscent of Mr. Jaggers. RR, *Where's the Rest of Me?,* 251; *Variety,* Apr. 4, 28, Sept. 22, and Nov. 3, 1954; *General Electric Theater* film clip, Dec. 19, 1954, RRL/av.

303   **Gavin's adolescent *angst***   In the fall of 1956, GM became a boarder at the Judson School in Arizona, an institution later attended by RR's son Michael. The author did not relocate to New York until 1968.

303   **Dutch, who has**   He had thoughtfully sized up the new medium during his weeks of almost total immobilization in hospital in 1949. A few examples of RR's "subconscious sense of the future": his silhouette self-portraits drawn at age sixteen; his short story "Rock Redux," prefiguring *Knute Rockne, All-American* by eight years; his enlistment in the Cavalry Reserve when America's pre-war isolationism was at its height; his enlistment of the shattered Goldwater forces in late 1964 and cultivation of Young Americans for Freedom at the height of Sixties student liberalism; his welfare reforms as Governor of California; his rejection of détente and embrace of the notion of strategic defense in the late 1970s; his absolute confidence in the fragility of Soviet power when that power reached its maximum at the beginning of the 1980s; and his turn-on-a-dime willingness to negotiate nuclear disarmament with Mikhail Gorbachev in 1985.

303   **his small-screen debut**   In *The Disappearance of Mrs. Gordon* took place on Dec. 7, 1950. James R. Parish, *Actors' Television Credits, 1950–1972* (Metuchen, N.J., 1973), 696. RR ultimately acted in more television dramas than cinema features: some fifty different roles (exclusive of his many miscellaneous appearances as show host and MC) in the fifteen years 1950–1965. Wayne Federman to EM, Mar. 11, 1999. Already, four million American homes had television. By 1954, the number of TV households had risen more than sixfold, to twenty-six million. R. D. Heldenfels, *Television's Greatest Year: 1954* (New York, 1994), 19.

303   **Then, on July 23**   The most informed discussion of the blanket waiver, harshly critical of RR, is Wills, *Reagan's America,* Ch. 28. For the defensive statements of RR and his executive secretary at SAG, see Edwards, *Early Reagan,* 435–40.

303   **"Ron and Lew"**   Copy in AC.

303   **"Lew, did you ever"**   Lew Wasserman interview, Mar. 6, 1987; RR interview, Mar. 24, 1987. See Dennis McDougal, *The Last Mogul: Lew Wasserman, MCA, and the Hidden History of Hollywood* (New York, 1999).

303   **Despite the burrowings**   Moldea, *Dark Victory,* 100–104; RR, *Where's the Rest of Me?,* 253; Lew Wasserman interview, Mar. 6, 1987.

304   **It was this**   Lew Wasserman interview, Mar. 6, 1987; RR in Moldea, *Dark Victory,* 182; *Variety,* Apr. 18, 1984.

304   **So Kit Carson**   Ironically, all of RR's own early performances on *General Electric Theater* were "live." Dunckel Oral History, 13, RRL.

305   **BBD&O paid him**   RR never directly touted GE products. Garry Wills argues that "Reagan was always by temperament a company man" and cites his "successful" and "harmonious" relations with all his employers, *Reagan's America,* 281–83. But RR was fired by B. J. Palmer within weeks of joining WOC (albeit rehired later), quarreled angrily with Jack Warner in 1949 (souring mutual relations for the next three years), and was eventually fired by GE for preaching aggressive politics at odds with the company line. It is more accurate to say that RR's general affability and lack of vanity made company men think he was one of them, just as political groups as various as HICCASP and the John Birch Society found him unclaimable and obstinate in his personal beliefs.

305   **Even so, the**   *Variety,* Aug. 24, 1955; RR, "Here We Go Again," *Journal of the Screen Producers Guild* 9.12 (June 1962); RR, *Where's the Rest of Me?,* 257.

305   **And he succeeded**   RR to Richard Nixon, July 15, 1960, RNL ("Invariably the result [of my speech] is a standing ovation—not for me, but for the views expressed."); RR to George Ward, Apr. 29, 1937, RRL/pp.

306   **He started off**   All speech quotations in this chapter are transcribed from the author's own recording. A copy is on file in RRL/av.

307   *Crapmeisters crack*   EM Notes, "CFA Convention, Nov. 10, 1958," AC.

308   **the force that**   Dylan Thomas, *Collected Poems* (New York, 1957), 10.

308   **"Freedom," Dutch declaimed**   This line was to become one of RR's favorite platform epigrams.

309   **There followed a**   Persons interested in this sentence will find it, according to RR, on p. 8 of the 1040 instruction booklet for 1958, under the heading "Additional Charge for Underpayment of Estimated Tax."

310   **History has long**   Edward Langley, a GE public-relations officer who sometimes accompanied RR on his tours, remembered, "At one time I pressured him into giving 25 talks in a single day. . . . Doctors, lady coil-winders, welders, people from box-pack-and-ship accosted him by the minute. . . . I can think of no politician in our history—not even William Jennings Bryan—who has been so dunked in Middle America." Letter to *The New York Times,* n.d. [ca. July 1983], AC. For a harshly critical analysis of RR's speeches in this period, see Mary E. Stuckey, *Getting into the Game: The Pre-Presidential Rhetoric of Ronald Reagan* (New York, 1989).

310   **By all accounts**   RR to Richard Nixon, June 27, 1959, RNL. On July 6, Nixon, clearly courting RR as a potential campaign speaker for 1960, wrote: "You have the ability of putting complicated technical ideas into words everyone can understand," RNL. The exchange precipitated a polite but wary correspondence that lasted through the presidencies of both men.

310   **it was the *Urtext***   RR's CFA speech was an almost word-for-word repetition of his May 2, 1958, address to the Chicago Executives Club,

"whose speakers," he noted proudly, "have included Presidents and visiting heads of state." *Chicago Executives' Club News* 34.30 (May 9, 1958); RR, *Where's the Rest of Me?,* 267. See ibid., 257–61, for his exultant self-discovery as a "barnstorming politician" during these years on the industrial lecture circuit. "I enjoyed every whizzing moment of it."

24: Dark Days

311   **"As you know"**   EM to GM, Jan. 13, 1959, AC.

312   *excreta tauri vincit omnia*   Latin for "bullshit conquers all."

312   **P.S. Read Mills**   C. Wright Mills, *The Power Elite* (New York, 1956, 1959).

312   **What seized my**   Mills, *The Power Elite,* 4.

312   **famous for being famous**   Daniel J. Boorstin is commonly credited with this sociological *aperçu* in *The Image: Or, What Happened to the American Dream* (New York, 1962), 60–61. But Mills said it first: "They are celebrated because they are displayed as celebrities. . . . Often they seem to have celebrity and nothing else. Rather than being celebrated because they occupy positions of prestige, they occupy positions of prestige because they are celebrated," *The Power Elite,* 74–75.

312   **In 1929, the chairman**   Mills, *Power Elite,* 86.

313   **[Celebrity] is carried**   Ibid., 74, 91–93.

313   **I'd heard on**   Arthur Park (RR's MCA agent) interview, Apr. 15, 1987; Elizabeth Brower (widow of BBD&O president Charles Brower) interview, June 3, 1987. RR, *Where's the Rest of Me?,* 208. The text of RR's speech, including his attack on the TVA, is reprinted as an appendix to ibid., 302–12.

313   **"Call off Ronald Reagan"**   Arthur Park interview, Apr. 15, 1987; RR, *Where's the Rest of Me?,* 268–69.

314   **a substantial increase**   Moldea, *Dark Victory,* 193. RR was to become an employee of MCA/Revue and a co-producer with a 25 percent stake in all future productions of *General Electric Theater.* He was to continue to be paid an annual salary (currently $169,000, plus generous expenses), but this was in effect increased by more than 10 percent, because he would no longer owe MCA's talent division an agency fee. And his new status as co-producer meant that he could claim investment deductions for a substantial part of his income. Due to circumstances RR could not foresee, this munificent arrangement in fact lasted only three years. He negotiated it himself. Ibid., 108–9, 189–96.

314   **The full irony**   Dales Oral History, RRL. The initial invitation for RR to run again for president of SAG came from the executive board in Oct. 1959. "We knew that [getting residuals] was going to be a battle. . . . We wanted a strong leader, and everybody's mind turned back to Ronnie Reagan," ibid. RR claims to have accepted the draft with extreme reluctance, in view of his other commitments, RR, *Where's the Rest of Me?,* 276.

314   **Whether he did**   For some reason the producers' strike of Mar.–Apr. 1960 has been frequently misdated. RR himself says that it "lasted six

months," an error that Anne Edwards repeats, while Garry Wills states that it lasted "seven weeks." RR, *Where's the Rest of Me?*, 278; Edwards, *Early Reagan*, 472; Wills, *Reagan's America*, 276. The actual dates were Mar. 7–Apr. 18, 1960. For full details of the negotiations, including two accounts by RR himself, see *Screen Actor*, Mar.–June 1960. See also Will Tusher, "Reagan and the Missing Minutes," *Variety*, Oct. 30, 1980.

314   **Bitterness over the deal**   On Dec. 12, 1981, the Guild's liberal directorate overrode a majority vote of the membership to confer the Bronze Mask Award upon RR. Kim Fellner, "spokeswoman" for SAG president Ed Asner, announced that to honor Reagan would be "a slap in the face to the rest of the labor movement." Charlton Heston interview, Sept. 1, 1987; *San Francisco Chronicle*, Dec. 19, 1981.

314   **I will only**   The ovation and the vote came despite RR's frank warning, at the beginning of his speech, that he had "bad news" regarding residuals. He justified the concession on the grounds that the studios were themselves hurting badly from a decade of declining production. "There are . . . things that, as negotiations go on, you find yourself forced to give up." Actors gained, however, in base salaries and pension percentages over and above the initial two million dollar funding of their welfare plan. They ratified the approval vote 5,362 to 207, an approval percentage of over 96 percent. RR to SAG membership, Apr. 18, 1960, qu. in *Variety*, Oct. 30, 1980; SAG Board Minutes, Apr. 18, 1960, SAGA; *Screen Actor*, Apr.–May and Aug.–Sept. 1960.

315   *la tristesse au fond de tout*   The sadness at the bottom of everything.

315   **For Ronald Reagan**   JFK had impatiently dismissed the sedentary complacency of the Eisenhower years, qu. Lloyd George's remark that "a tired nation is a Tory nation." He made many other transatlantic and classical allusions in a speech with a witty, cerebral, Boston-accented tone that was guaranteed to madden white-shoe conservatives such as RR.

315   **"Unfortunately he is"**   RR to Richard Nixon, July 15, 1960, RNL.

316   **It is strange**   Cannon, *Ronnie and Jesse*, 69; RR interview, Mar. 29, 1988; EM Diary, Sept. 26, 1960. The author was unaware, as were most Americans, that JFK's unlined, not to say bulging, boyishness was the result of daily cortisone shots for Addison's disease and that Nixon was also in medical distress, although much the healthier man of the two. See Jonathan Aitken, *Nixon: A Life* (Washington, D.C., 1993), 276–79.

316   ***"For I have thought"***   Shakespeare, Sonnet 147. The correct quotation is: *For I have sworn thee fair, and thought thee bright, / Who art as black as hell, as dark as night.*

316   **"A sweet, sibilant"**   GM to EM, Oct. 24, 1960, AC. Baldwin's Oct. 22 lecture was part of an annual *Esquire* symposium, "The Role of the Writer in America."

316   **a subsequent book**   James Baldwin, "Notes for a Hypothetical Novel," in *Nobody Knows My Name: More Notes of a Native Son* (New York, 1961, 1963), 117–18.

317   **It seems to me**   Ibid., 125–26.

317   **Now *there* was**   Baldwin, short of money and not yet well known, spent

the late fall and winter of 1960–1961 with William Styron, who mentions his transforming racial rage. "Jimmy in the House," *The New York Times Book Review,* Dec. 20, 1987.

317   **Besides his Cadillac**   Photographs in AC and Reagan family scrapbooks, RRL/pp. The House of the Future was featured on a *General Electric Theater* infomercial. RR and NR draw particular attention to a battery of twelve recessed ceiling lights encircling a dining-room chandelier, "like a necklace of jewels." Video copy, n.d. [ca. 1958] in SLA. William Styron, "Jimmy," remembers Baldwin assuring an incredulous white questioner, "Baby, yes baby, I mean *burn.* We will *burn your cities down.*"

318   **Dutch had to think**   RR and his brother were also still supporting Nelle Reagan, who had a year and a half to live.

318   **However, he did not**   Maureen, a big, brainy girl, had already begun her lifelong run of bad luck. Her pretty face and mimetic abilities won her a gold medal in drama in high school, but her size militated against any hope of a stage or screen career. In 1960, she desperately entered the Miss Washington, D.C., beauty contest. Eliminated in the semifinals, she took what comfort she could licking envelopes for Richard Nixon, discovering in the process that she had a passion for politics. Kennedy's win put paid to any hopes of a Republican appointment. At the time of the 1961 inaugural she was on the verge of entering what proved to be an abusive marriage with a D.C. policeman. Maureen Reagan, *First Father,* 111–21; Maureen Reagan interview, Feb. 23, 1991.

318   **I was real proud**   Michael Reagan interview, June 27, 1989. Michael, repeating this story in his *On the Outside,* 96, prints RR's reaction: "Oh, I didn't recognize you."

    See also Davis, *The Way I See It*: "Often, I'd come into a room and he'd look up from his notecards as though he wasn't sure who I was. Ron would race up to him, small and brimming with a child's enthusiasm, and I'd see the same bewildered look in my father's eyes, like he had to remind himself who Ron was" (97–98).

318   **Paul Rae cherished**   See p. 319. For a color version, see Chris Wallace, *First Lady: A Portrait of Nancy Reagan* (New York, 1986), 5.

320   **As "Karl Marx"**   RR, "Encroaching Controls," an address first given before the Phoenix Chamber of Commerce, Mar. 30, 1961, and repeated across the country, with variations, throughout the year. Recording and transcripts in RRL.

320   **All this was**   RR, "The Danger of Losing Our Freedom by Installments," Pasadena *Independent Star-News,* Jan. 7, 1962. This very long speech is notable for rhythmic use of the word *liberal,* which was to take on such obscene force in conservative rhetoric over the next three decades. The Soviet bomb had a one-hundred-megaton capability and gave the USSR a technical advantage over the United States that lasted through RR's presidency. Paul Nitze, *From Hiroshima to Glasnost* (New York, 1989), 150.

320   **It was the TVA**   See "The Incredible Electrical Conspiracy," *Fortune,* Apr.–May 1961; Sissela Bok, *Lying* (New York, 1978), 245–46. "Robert Kennedy is behind this attack on me," Patti Davis remembers RR saying

angrily over dinner. "Because I'm speaking out against the Kennedy Administration and the road they're trying to lead us down." Davis, *The Way I See It,* 67.

321 **only former President Eisenhower** Holmes Tuttle interview, Feb. 24, 1986.

321 **He did so** Transcript of RR testimony in Moldea, *Dark Victory,* 167–201; PR, "Picture Parade," AP syndicated column, Mar. 18, 1962; Larry J. Giancanos, *TV Drama Series Programming: A Comprehensive Chronicle, 1959–1975,* 83.

321 **"Reagan has become"** EM to GM, Mar. 3, 1962. AC. Earl Dunckel confirms that by this time the "antipathy" of "liberals" within GE (presumably those executives who had the most interest in Kennedy Administration goodwill) was "very, very strong." Dunckel Oral History, 23–25, RRL.

321 **A quarter of** Elizabeth Brower interview, June 3, 1987.

321 **"The President says"** Cordiner did not retire as chairman and CEO until Dec. 1963. Cannon, *Reagan,* 97. He subsequently became finance chairman of the Goldwater campaign. Stephen Shadegg, *What Happened to Goldwater?* (New York, 1965), 178.

321 **"He cried."** Elizabeth Brower interview, June 3, 1987. RR strenuously denied the story, although in *Where's the Rest of Me?* he does admit to a "strange" call from "an executive of an advertising agency" who wanted him to tone down the political content of his speeches. "I told this gentleman that if the speeches were an issue I could see no solution short of severing our relationship. . . . Twenty-four hours later *General Electric Theater* was canceled" (272–73). Charles H. Brower's two sons both confirm his desperate trip to New York. Judge Charles Brower interview, Apr. 2, 1987; Brock Brower interview, Aug. 16, 1987.

322 **The Reagans spent** Mae Tally interview, Oct. 18, 1989; RR interview, Mar. 24, 1987; RR to Hedda Hopper, May 6, 1965, interview transcript, HER. He finished the book around Nov. 1963. His collaborator was Richard G. Hubler, a sometime scenarist who once served on the editorial board of *The Screen Writer* with Philip Dunne.

322 **There was also politics** Cannon, *Ronnie and Jesse,* 70; Stephen Ambrose, *Nixon: The Triumph of a Politician, 1962–1972* (New York, 1989), 656–57.

322 **The strangeness of** RR interview, Mar. 29, 1988.

322 **"Like any actor"** RR in *Sunshine Magazine,* Oct. 1961.

322 **"I think I offended"** The occasion was a Fourth of July party (1962) given by Sydney and Francy Lasker Brodie. "Ronnie got turkey red. I could see I'd gone too far." Philip Dunne interview, Apr. 15, 1987.

323 **get out of the talent business** MCA did so on Sept. 18, 1962. See Edwards, *Early Reagan,* 478.

323 **"You've been around"** Lew Wasserman interview, Feb. 18, 1987; NR interview, Feb. 18, 1987 ("Ronnie was devastated—devastated"); Arthur Park interview, Apr. 16, 1987. Wasserman vehemently denied to the author that RR's right-wing politics had anything to do with his failure to find RR a film role in 1962. "I must confess, though, I was disappointed

he went that way." For more on the political relationship between
Wasserman and RR, see Brownstein, *The Power and the Glitter,* 219–21.

323   **"It was a real"**   RR interview, Mar. 24, 1987.

324   ***Dad, hi—***   GM to author, Aug. 8, 1962, AC. For a detailed account of
the drafting and debating of the Port Huron Statement, see James Miller,
Democracy Is in the Streets: From Port Huron to the Siege of Chicago
(New York, 1987), Ch. 6.

324   **His enclosure**   Copy in AC, one of twenty thousand run off as the first
mimeograph edition, Aug. 1962.

324   **We are people**   Miller, *Democracy Is in the Streets,* 329–77, reprints the
entire Port Huron Statement as an appendix.

325   SUMMARY FOR   GM paraphrases, AC. Italics represent phrases in original. See Miller, *Democracy Is in the Streets,* 330–36.

325   **We commit to**   Ibid., 331–65, 335.

326   **There were periodic**   Ibid., 120–21, 351, 363. There was a pro-
Communist pressure group at Port Huron, bitterly contested by Harrington. Ibid., 111–15.

326   **Perhaps I should**   Ibid., 353, 347.

326   *If we appear*   Ibid., 374.

326   **For Ronald Reagan, too**   RR, *An American Life,* 97; Wills, *Reagan's
America,* 286–87; Curt Gentry, *The Last Days of the Late, Great State of
California* (New York, 1968), 47; "Ronald Reagan, Extremist Collaborator: An Exposé," Democratic State Central Committee of California
pamphlet, Aug. 15, 1966; Edwards, *Early Reagan,* 479. Loyd Wright had
also been a Bircher. Ibid.

326   **"I'm glad you think"**   The first "free" Algerian government of Ahmed
Ben Bella and Houari Boumedienne had just taken power, and was busy
slaughtering moderate Moslems. See Paul Johnson, *Modern Times: The
World from the Twenties to the Eighties* (New York, 1983), 504–5.

327   **"No one's paid *me*"**   RR statewide political address, Nov. 4, 1992, transcript in RNL.

327   **For twenty-eight**   President Kennedy had just issued an appeal to Congress for expanded welfare services, the first such appeal since Franklin
Roosevelt's Social Security Message of 1935. See below, p. 368.

327   **The assassination of**   For the less-than-anguished reaction of the Reagans to JFK's death, see Davis, *The Way I See It,* 81–83.

328   **"You know that feeling"**   GM to EM, Oct. 1, 1964, AC. For a detailed,
participant account of the disturbances at Berkeley in 1964–65, see
David Lance Goines, *The Free Speech Movement: Coming of Age in the
1960s* (Berkeley, 1993).

328   **"Here," I gathered**   EM Diary, Oct. 3, 1964, AC; "The Berkeley Free
Speech Controversy: Preliminary Report by a Fact-finding Committee
of Graduate Political Scientists at UCB," part 1: Chronology of Events,
ts., SCLSS (hereafter "Chronology"), 2; Goines, *Free Speech Movement,*
116–17.

328   **"We set up ten more"**   GM to EM, Oct. 1, 1964, AC; Goines, *Free
Speech Movement,* 120–26, 149–50; "Chronology," 2–3.

328   **About a quarter**   GM to EM, Oct. 1, 1964, AC. See illustrations in

Goines, *Free Speech Movement,* 162–64. Weinberg was a recent graduate of UCB, a civil-rights organizer, and author of the famous phrase "You can't trust anybody over thirty." William O'Neill, *Coming Apart* (Chicago, 1971), 279.

328   **CORE**   Congress of Racial Equality.

328   **The wave builds**   GM to EM, Oct. 1, 1964, AC. See also Goines, *Free Speech Movement,* 165–72; Rorabaugh, *Berkeley at War,* 21–22; Karlyn Baker, "Rebel with a Cause," *The Washington Post,* Nov. 8, 1996. For Savio's own account of his politicization in 1964, see Goines, *Free Speech Movement,* 93–99.

328   **When Mario's hot**   Savio's father was a machinist. Rorabaugh, *Berkeley at War,* 22. This source makes a rather strained attempt to interpret Savio's oratory sexually. A student cartoon reproduced between pp. 50 and 51 more graphically evokes the FSM concept of "The American University." Three plump, dollar-faced regents (one military) sit on a high pedestal. Below them stands President Kerr, noosed around the neck, and dangling from his fingers are two stringed puppets, Vice Chancellor Sherriffs (as Hitler) and Dean of Students Towle (as prude). They all overlook a data-processing machine into which students march, and are spat out as perforated IBM cards.

329   **"a small bald"**   GM to author, Oct. 3, 1964, AC. The settlement, an interim one pending further negotiations, freed Weinberg and ended the sit-in, while committees of faculty and students framed guidelines for on-campus politicking. *Free Speech Movement Newsletter,* Oct. 3, 1964, SCLSS.

329   **Kerr, not Savio**   Clark Kerr, *The Uses of the University* (Cambridge, Mass., 1963). The term *multiversity,* first coined by Kerr, connotes a massively funded research institution working hand in hand with government and industry to advance the power of the "state"—more precisely the established power-complex of public and private institutions—at cost to individual student education. For the long-term consequences of this statist concept, see Charles J. Sykes, *Profscam: Professors and the Demise of Higher Education* (Washington, D.C., 1988).

329   **If the "wave"**   RR, in *An American Life,* 139–43, is at his usual pains to depict himself as being coerced into political action in the fall of 1964. The circumstances in which he recorded his famous speech for Goldwater are discussed below in the text, but note should be made of Garry Wills's reading of all the self-positionings RR went through long before he became California co-chairman of the Goldwater campaign. Wills lays particular emphasis on *Where's the Rest of Me?* (written 1962–1963) as "a political campaign waiting to happen." Wills, *Reagan's America,* 288.

329   **So, at least, Gavin**   EM Diary, Oct. 29, 1964, AC.

329   **"Including bakery ladies"**   See, e.g., Faith Stewart to Hedda Hopper, Nov. 1, 1964, Hopper Papers, HER.

330   **"What he does"**   Lou Cannon, *Reagan* (New York, 1982), 98–100.

330   **A few days after**   RR's Oct. 27, 1964, speech ("The Speech") is entitled "A Time for Choosing." In 1989 an uncut video version of the original

kinescope tape was reissued under that name by Edmonds Associates, Washington, D.C.

331 **Paul's attached note**   PR to EM, Nov. 18, 1964, AC.

331 **A GOP elder**   See *Oakland Tribune,* Oct. 30, 1964; RR, qu. in Los Angeles *Herald-Examiner,* Nov. 25, 1964; Frank Jordan, qu. in *San Francisco Chronicle,* Nov. 5, 1964. On Nov. 3, 1964, at least one California resident, Dr. Neil Smithwick of Sunnydale, awarded him his first write-in vote for President. RR to Smithwick, Mar. 18, 1986, RRL/pp/hw.

331 **Calif. Citizens for Goldwater**   For an acutely observed description of RR at the 1964 GOP convention, see Gore Vidal, *United States: Essays, 1952–1992* (New York, 1993), 980–94. "He was slumped in a folding chair . . . totally concentrated on Eisenhower. . . . I do remember being struck by the intensity . . . of [that] concentration. . . . I said to myself: Mr. Reagan is planning to go into politics" (981–82).

331 **Delivered speech at**   Other versions of RR's enlistment by his future "Kitchen Cabinet" are available in RR, *An American Life,* 139–43; Shadegg, *What Happened to Goldwater?,* 252–53; Wills, *Reagan's America,* 290–91; and Russ Walton Oral History, 11–14, RRL. The author has also interviewed RR (June 27, 1987), Holmes Tuttle (Feb. 24, 1986), and William French Smith (Aug. 25, 1988).

331 *room full of students*   RR's deliberate cultivation of conservative youth, an important element of his future political strength, can be traced back as early as May 29, 1962, when he issued a fund-raising appeal for Young Americans for Freedom. "In these historically tragic days, this generation—mature beyond their years—are our best and only true hope for the future" (RRL/pp/hw). At the 1964 Republican Convention, delegate Holmes Tuttle noticed how RR made a daily point of cultivating "about a hundred screaming kids." Holmes Tuttle interview, Feb. 24, 1986.

331 **The rest is history**   For analysis and comment on "A Time for Choosing," see David Broder and Stephen Hess, *The Republican Establishment* (New York, 1967), 253–54 ("The most successful national political debut since William Jennings Bryan electrified the 1896 Democratic Convention with the 'Cross of Gold' speech"), Paul D. Erickson, *Reagan Speaks: The Making of an American Myth* (New York, 1985), 12–30, and Kurt W. Ritter, "Ronald Reagan's 1964 TV Speech for Goldwater: Millennial Themes in American Political Rhetoric," in *Rhetorical Dimensions in Media,* ed. Martin J. Medhurst (Dubuque, Iowa, 1991), 568–72. The speech has been reprinted many times, most recently in Kurt Ritter and David Henry, *Ronald Reagan: The Great Communicator* (Westport, Conn., 1992), 135–43, which is the most exhaustive study of RR's oratory to date.

331 **On December 2, 1964**   "Chronology," 8; Rorabaugh, *Berkeley at War,* 23. See ibid., 24–31, for the complicated negotiations of Oct. and Dec.

332 **There's a time**   Savio qu. in Gentry, *Last Days,* 93–94. Goines, *Free Speech Movement,* 361–62, shows that the imagery of this speech owes much to Thoreau.

332 **If so, Savio**   Rorabaugh, *Berkeley at War,* 32–33; Goines, *Free Speech Movement,* 361–85; "Chronology," 8. An editorial article to which GM

contributed, "Golly Gee, California Is a Strange State!" *Ramparts,* Oct. 1966, has a glimpse of RR's future Attorney General, highly excited, on the phone to Brown at 2 A.M. on Dec. 3: "They're busting up the place. We have to go in." Brown approved police action on the spot.

332   **President Kerr convened**   Goines, *Free Speech Movement,* 423–27; Kitchel, *Berkeley in the Sixties;* Rorabaugh, *Berkeley at War,* 36.

333   *Piper, pipe that song*   The quotation is from William Blake's *Songs of Innocence.*

333   **But Ronald Reagan was**   Davis, *The Way I See It:* "Politics was his passion, and it was becoming stronger all the time" (84).

333   **"If only I"**   To Sheilah Graham, *San Francisco Chronicle,* Dec. 2, 1964.

334   **Holmes Tuttle thought**   Holmes Tuttle interview, Feb. 28, 1988; William French Smith interview, Aug. 25, 1988. RR has never confirmed that Tuttle, Rubel, or Salvatori told him in 1965 that they already had the Presidency in mind. But Tuttle assured the author that this was indeed the case. He told the same story to Martin Anderson (Anderson interview, Aug. 8, 1989). And Armand Deutsch, a close friend, recalls NR putting down the phone shortly after Goldwater's defeat and saying in a dazed voice, "They want Ronnie to be President." Armand Deutsch interview, Aug. 22, 1988.

334   **The dispatch of**   Nitze, *From Hiroshima to Glasnost,* 281. A sour joke circulated among American conservatives, "They warned me that if I voted for Goldwater, we'd get into a war. Well, I did, and we have." Lee Edwards, "The Other Sixties: A Flag-Waver's Memoir," *Policy Review,* fall 1988.

334   **Assistant Secretary of Labor**   Daniel P. Moynihan, *Family and Nation* (New York, 1986), 3–39; Todd Gitlin, *The Sixties: Years of Hope, Days of Rage* (New York, 1987, 1993), 168.

334   **"Heady wine," indeed!**   See above, p. 74. On the eve of RR's appearance, a poll of delegates found him to be their favorite choice for Governor. *San Francisco Chronicle,* May 27 and 28, 1964.

335   **far and away**   Vidal, *United States,* 981.

335   **Jane Wyman would**   Holmes Tuttle interview, Feb. 24, 1986; Gentry, *Last Days,* 80–82; Cannon, *Ronnie and Jesse,* 73.

335   **From Reagan's opening**   RR, *Where's the Rest of Me?,* 3, 300.

335   **Since the book**   The author is indebted to Gentry, *Last Days,* 100, for this anecdote. Another pre-emptive move by Spencer-Roberts was to tell Maureen Reagan, now living in Anaheim and a passionately enthusiastic minor GOP functionary, that she was "not to be involved in any way in the campaign," on the grounds that conservative voters would not like to be reminded of RR's divorce. Maureen Reagan, *First Father,* 146–47.

336   **I dined once**   Gerald Blakely interview, May 15, 1986.

336   **In asking so many**   Cannon, *Reagan,* 113; RR to Comstock Club, Sacramento, Aug. 3, 1965.

336   **What he heard**   RR interview, Oct. 11, 1988; Cannon, *Ronnie and Jesse,* 82–83; Gentry, *Last Days,* 100.

337   **"I never had"**   Edmund G. Brown interview, Aug. 26, 1988.

337   **"Serious is the word"**   Ibid.

PAGE

337   **There was nothing** "Golly Gee!" *Ramparts,* Oct. 1966; Jack B. Tenney Oral History, UCLA; Pat Brown, qu. in Michael Deaver interview, Feb. 27, 1989; James R. Miller Oral History, RRL/oh. Another famous Brown gaffe was his remark apropos of catastrophic floods in Northern California: "This is the worst disaster since I was elected Governor." Qu. in Gentry, *Last Days,* 49. For a contrary view of Brown as a candidate, see ibid., 82–84.

337   **hubris on the Governor's** Cannon remarks on Brown's chronic "inner defeatism" in *Ronnie and Jesse,* 77.

338   **Every cop beaten** GM to EM, Sept. 4, 1965, AC. Elsewhere in this letter, GM, an indefatigable collector of juxtapositional data, noted that RR and Brown were exactly the same weight (185 lbs.), had both switched allegiances from one party to the other, and represented the two regional halves of California politics, "the Governor being as Northern in temperament as Reagan is Southern." For a discussion of these extremes, see Edmund G. (Pat) Brown, *Reagan and Reality: The Two Californias* (New York, 1970), 6–7.

338   ***Definition Yahoo*** For a discussion of RR's anti-intellectualism and essentially moralistic attitude toward teaching, see Erickson, *Reagan Speaks,* 60–71.

338   **On January 4, 1966** Within days, the "First Republicans for Ronald Reagan," Owosso, Mich., reported, "Our P.O. Box '1968' is already filling up with donations." Robert M. Smith to RR, Jan. 26, 1966, in RRL/pp.

338   **a published author** Sylvia Jukes Morris, *Edith Kermit Roosevelt: Portrait of a First Lady* (New York, 1980); and *Rage for Fame: The Ascent of Clare Boothe Luce* (New York, 1997).

338   **"Watch out for"** EM Diary, Feb. 24, 1966.

338   **If your reason** Philip Dunne to EM, May 15, 1966, AC. For a more extended version of this story, see Dunne, *Take Two,* 328–30.

339   **In recent weeks** Stanley Plog Oral History, RRL/oh; RR to Western Wood Production Association, qu. in Cannon, *Reagan,* 115 (this was the speech that has been extensively misquoted as "If you've seen one redwood you've seen them all"); *San Francisco Chronicle,* Mar. 7 and 5, 1966. RR's remark about Christopher was reportedly "I'll get that SOB." *Los Angeles Times,* Mar. 7, 1966. He issued an angry statement saying, "There is no single thing I detest more in others than bigotry, and to have this charge directed at me was more than I could take," ibid. For an eyewitness account, see Lyn Nofziger, *Nofziger* (Washington, D.C., 1992), 38–39.

339   **Primary day** The official Republican vote tally was 1,417,623 to 675,683. Cannon, *Ronnie and Jesse,* 84–85.

339   **Gavin's reaction to** Gentry, *Last Days,* 176; Pat Brown press-conference transcript, June 23, 1966, SAL; Cannon, *Ronnie and Jesse,* 77, 79–81.

340   **"the morality gap"** See RR's speech of like title, May 12, 1966, t.s. in RRH; Also Herbert L. Phillips, *Big Wayward Girl: An Informal Political History of California* (New York, 1968), 258.

340   **Dad, this is urgent**   GM to EM, June 10, 1966, AC. See Gentry, *Last Days,* 121, for more on RR's alleged "*sub rosa* dialogue" with conservative audiences.

340   **Dutch's call for**   RR, "The Morality Gap at Berkeley.

340   **protest mail from Berkeley**   GM to EM, Aug. 9, 1966, AC. See Moldea, *Dark Victory,* 203, for grand-jury leaks to MCA—PR's likely source of transcripts. *Variety* eventually broke this story on Apr. 18, 1984 ("New Info on Reagan, MCA Waiver Probe").

340   **Dutch once told me**   RR interview, Nov. 4, 1987.

340   **I think he was always**   Wills, *Reagan's America,* 296; Lyn Nofziger Oral History, Miller Center for Public Affairs, University of Virginia; "Ronald for Real," *Time,* Oct. 7, 1966.

340   **But he proceeded**   Copy of "Ronald Reagan, Extremist Collaborator," AC; Cannon, *Ronnie and Jesse,* 80–81, 86. Brown's wisecrack was worsened by the fact that he was seen delivering it to an integrated classroom. Twenty-two years later, he still believed it to have been "hilariously funny." Pat Brown interview, Aug. 26, 1988.

341   **"Whatever you think"**   EM to GM, Oct. 9, 1966, AC; GM to EM, Oct. 16, 1966, AC. See also Gentry, *Last Days,* 274–76, and Wills, *Reagan's America,* 294–98.

342   **What Reagan wrote**   RR, *Where's the Rest of Me?,* 12. See p. 27.

342   **To that extent**   RR's personal and campaign papers in RRH and RRL/pp bulge with manuscript speeches, which he wrote out in full before codifying them on cards. Even in the White House, when he reluctantly allowed a team of young professionals to write for him, he continued to card his more important speeches. A stenographer had to be specially trained to interpret and type out the President's cryptographs. For a detailed account of RR's card technique, see Martin Anderson, *Revolution: The Reagan Legacy* (Stanford, Calif., 1990), Ch. 6.

342   **"Remember, this is"**   Stanley Plog Oral History, RRL. Henry Salvatori had been so distressed by RR's loss of control at the black businessmen's convention in Mar. that he had threatened to switch support to former Governor Goodwin Knight. RR and his press secretary, Lyn Nofziger, were reduced to begging him not to do so. Nofziger, *Nofziger,* 41–42.

342   **Their counsel was**   Stanley Plog Oral History, RRL. Pat Brown interview, Aug. 26, 1988; Stanley Plog interview, *Frontline,* Jan. 18, 1989.

342   **Like many later**   Stanley Plog Oral History, RRL. This interview was recorded in 1981.

342   **When, one damp**   *Time,* Oct. 7, 1966.

343   **How could anybody**   According to Nofziger, *Nofziger,* 65–66, a plot to run RR for President in 1968 began less than a month after his election to the governorship in 1966. RR made no effort either to encourage it or to stop it.

343   **On November 8**   Cannon's description of the Democratic vote cannot be bettered: "Brown carried only his home county of San Francisco plus Alameda County (Oakland-Berkeley) and sparsely settled Plumas County." *Ronnie and Jesse,* 86–87. See also Phillips, *Big Wayward Girl,* Ch. 36, for an extended analysis. Nationwide, the elections of 1966 rep-

resented a cyclical comeback for the Republican Party, with solid gains at every level, including forty-seven new seats in the House, three in the Senate, and eight governorships. As Governor-elect of the nation's most populous state, RR became overnight a leading power player in GOP convention politics.

343   **"In all the sound"**   RR qu. in *Los Angeles Times,* Dec. 3, 1966.

343   **He was referring**   Rorabaugh, *Berkeley at War,* 108–9. The most detailed study of this period is F. Alex Crowley, "The Transition from Pat Brown to Governor Reagan," Ph.D. diss., Princeton University, 1968.

344   **"No one is compelled"**   RR qu. in *Los Angeles Times,* Dec. 3, 1966.

25: Reagan Country

345   **"Well, George"**   Cannon, *Ronnie and Jesse,* 130–31. Both Maureen Reagan and Patti Davis remark in their respective memoirs how transfigured, even "radiant," RR looked at the inaugural ceremony.

345   *upward into the rotunda*   The author was intrigued to learn, during a recent tour of the Capitol, that the rotunda's inner gilt decorations are cast from "Dutch Metal."

346   *It has seen thirty-two*   RR never quite became a Sacramentan. Throughout his Governorship, he spent every available weekend, holiday, and legislative recess at home in Pacific Palisades.

346   *Now tilt the*   Loraine B. Donnelly and Evelyn T. Cray, *California's Historic Capitol* (Davis, Calif., 1985). California Office of Architecture and Construction, *Seismic Study: West Wing, California State Capitol* (Sacramento, Calif., 1972), 43–47; Peter Hannaford, *The Reagans: A Political Portrait* (New York, 1983), 31.

346   *Since the Governor*   NR interview, Apr. 10, 1992; "Golly Gee!" *Ramparts;* Caspar Weinberger, "The First 100 Days: A GOP Appraisal," *Los Angeles Times West Magazine,* Apr. 23, 1967; Maureen Reagan, *First Father,* 156.

347   **Chief of these**   The following descriptive details are based on Cannon, *Ronnie and Jesse,* 131–33, a profile of Battaglia in the Riverside *Press-Enterprise,* Aug. 7, 1966, and interviews with Nofziger and Clark. See also Helene von Damm, *At Reagan's Side* (New York, 1989), 46–56, and Gary G. Hamilton and Nicole Woolsey Biggart, *Governor Reagan, Governor Brown: A Sociology of Executive Power* (New York, 1984), 25, 19.

347   **That superlative**   Hamilton and Biggart, *Governor Reagan,* 182–83.

347   **Their comforts**   Gentry, *Last Days,* 11–14; Davis, *The Way I See It,* 51–52. According to Ms. Davis, who is something of an expert on the subject of pills, NR's other drug of choice in the Fifties and Sixties was the downer Seconal: "For years, every night, she would lay out two Seconals and one Miltown." During the day, she would take "three or four" Miltowns, and be subject to such alarming mood swings that both RR and Loyal Davis feared for her life. "Over the years, the name of the drug would change, but the behavior wouldn't." Ibid., 53–54, 56.

348   **He had a bronze**   Cannon, *Ronnie and Jesse,* 228.

348   **So much for**   Nofziger, *Nofziger,* 61; GM to EM, Jan. 15, 1967, AC.

348   **What interested me**   Rorabaugh, *Berkeley at War,* 81. As Attorney General of the United States, Meese had a hobby of listening in to cop conversations on his CB radio. His home boasted a collection of toy pigs and squad cars.

348   **Clark Kerr's dismissal**   President Nathan Pusey of Harvard called it "an affront to higher education." Phillips, *Big Wayward Girl,* 260.

349   **"I simply was"**   RR interview, Oct. 11, 1988; Minutes of an Adjourned Session of the Regents of the University of California, Jan. 20, 1967, copy in AC. According to these minutes, Regent Theodore R. Meyer, not RR, was in the chair. The vote was precipitated by Kerr, who "stated . . . that he could not carry on effectively under existing conditions," and demanded an immediate decision as to his future, "one way or the other." Meyer and RR expressed concern about the timing of this request and asked if "he would be willing to resign." Kerr replied that he would not and left the meeting. "The Board then discussed the matter at length. It was moved by Regent Kennedy, seconded by Regent Forbes, that President Kerr's services be terminated, effective immediately." RR voted with the majority to dismiss. Kerr afterward insisted, with fine equivocation, that he had not been asking for a vote of confidence, only a "confirmation" of his authority before plunging into four or five months of negotiations against the Governor's "almost incredible budget cut." Clark Kerr, interviewed by Ralph Keyes, ca. Feb. 22, 1967, KEY.

349   **One document**   Collection of Arthur Van Court.

349   **Clark Kerr probably**   Weinberger, "First 100 Days"; Cannon, *Ronnie and Jesse,* 232–33. The deficit, first mentioned by Brown's outgoing finance director on Nov. 28, was projected for the first half of 1968—i.e., the second half of RR's initial fiscal year. It had been caused by a preelection decision to not raise taxes and a creative accounting ploy wherein "accruals"—tax payments earned but not yet paid—were counted as real income. Ibid., 133–34; Weinberger, "First 100 Days."

349   **The idea of giving**   "I will tell you right now," RR said at his first press conference, "that it is my own personal view that there is no such thing as 'free education.' There is *costly* education, and the question is, how do you share the cost." Transcript, Jan. 10, 1967, RRH.

349   **This did not mean**   Phillips, *Big Wayward Girl,* 277; Weinberger, "First 100 Days."

350   **Executive authority**   Cannon, *Ronnie and Jesse,* 14–17.

350   **There was such**   The most detailed account of the mental-hygiene controversy is in Cannon, *Ronnie and Jesse,* 144–48.

350   **When Meese communicated**   *Los Angeles Times,* Apr. 11, 1967.

351   ***After the first death***   Dylan Thomas, "A Refusal to Mourn the Death by Fire of a Child in London," *Collected Poems* (London, 1952), 112; *Los Angeles Times,* Apr. 13, 1967.

351   **Dutch assured me**   RR interview, May 10, 1988; *Los Angeles Times,* Apr. 13, 1967. Pat Brown always supported RR's decision, even though he himself became a foe of capital punishment. "[Mitchell] was a cop-

killer, and cops protect society." Interview, Aug. 26, 1988. Cannon notes that opposition to the death penalty would have been RR's only reason for clemency in the Mitchell case, his legal obligation being otherwise clear. In a later case, involving a young, black baby-killer, RR noted the convict's history of brain damage and spared him. *Ronnie and Jesse,* 179–80.

352   **Reagan had to admit**   RR press-conference transcript, May 9, 1967, SAL.

352   **he got five weeks**   "The nervous system is intact and functioning in 'total pattern response' by the sixth week of intrauterine life." William J. Hogan, M.D., letter to *The Washington Post,* Feb. 1, 1984.

352   **"Bill, I've got to"**   William P. Clark, Jr., interview, Dec. 20, 1993. RR also secretly received Cardinal McIntyre of Los Angeles, and was subject to considerable pressure from his former campaign managers at Spencer-Roberts, whom the Archdiocese had retained to lobby against the Act. Cannon remarks that RR's repeated denials of any talks with these emissaries, at a press conference on June 13, were the first lies of his public career. *Ronnie and Jesse,* 181. The author, knowing RR to be consciously an honest man, would describe these "lies" more in terms of RR's reverse will: a determination always to command the past in terms of his present interest.

352   **The very word "Therapeutic"**   "The term 'mental health' . . . means mental illness to the extent that the woman is dangerous to herself or to the person *or property* of others *or is in need of supervision or restraint."* California State Health and Safety Code No. 25950-4 (Therapeutic Abortion Act of 1967), in Zad Leavy and Alan F. Charles, "California's New Therapeutic Abortion Act: An Analysis and Legal Guide to Medical and Legal Procedure," *UCLA Law Review* 15 (Dec. 1967).

352   **the feelings of fathers**   David W. Louisell and Charles Carroll, "The Father as Non-Parent," *The Catholic World,* Dec. 1969. This article compares ironically the old Roman legal doctrine of *patria potestas* (a father's right to slaughter his own offspring) to that of "the modern *materfamilias* [*sic*] of the permissive abortion laws." It notes that whereas the California Health and Safety Code denied any father the right to be consulted "or even notified" of the abortion of his child, the state's Penal Code held him responsible for its welfare as long as it remained in the womb. See also Jane Lang McGrew, "To Be or Not to Be: The Constitutional Question of the California Abortion Law," *University of Pennsylvania Law Review* 118.643 (Feb. 1970).

352   **Reagan was left**   Nofziger, *Nofziger,* 243; RR interview, Mar. 27, 1987; RR to Milton Ammel, Jan. 8, 1979, RRL/pp; "NR" to "Mrs. Smith," ca. Dec. 1967, copy in Nancy Clark Reynolds Papers, privately held; E. W. Jackson, M. Tashiro, and G. C. Cunningham, "Therapeutic Abortions in California," *California Medicine* 115.1 (July 1971). The Smith document, in RR's own hand, is a three-page draft of a letter to be signed by his wife as an expression of her own abortion views. It survives in early contradiction of the fallacy that NR shaped RR's social policies. Indeed, she tried to moderate his opposition to abortion when it became a polit-

ical issue for him as President and found him absolutely inflexible. For a commentary on RR's "Abortion and the Conscience of the Nation" (1983), see Edmund Morris, "In Memoriam Christine Reagan," *American Spectator,* Aug. 1993.

352   **The lesser figure**   Pat Gayman interview, Aug. 12, 1988; photographs in the possession of RR's former security agent, Arthur Van Court, Sacramento.

354   **I now trace**   Frantz Fanon, *Les Damnés de la terre* (Paris, 1961), trans. Constance Farrington as *The Wretched of the Earth* (New York, 1968).

354   **Four years of Labour**   Johnson, *Modern Times,* 602–3; EM Diary, Jan.–Mar. 1968. Writing to Richard Nixon on Mar. 12, RR described his "touchy position" *vis-à-vis* the GOP nomination campaign: "maintaining a neutral stand while running as California's Favorite Son" (RRH).

355   **He and Tom**   Reed had resigned as RR's appointments secretary, so as not to embarrass the Governor with his preparations for 1968. The full, ugly story of Battaglia's dismissal is told in Nofziger, *Nofziger,* 75–82. Kemp was evidently an innocent party in the matter. See *San Francisco Chronicle,* Aug. 21, 1996.

355   **Funds had been**   Nofziger, *Nofziger,* 65–69; Paul Haerle Oral History, RRL.

355   **All that was**   *San Francisco Chronicle,* May 5, 1968; Nofziger, *Nofziger,* 70.

355   **Reagan dutifully**   Lyn Nofziger reminiscing at Gubernatorial Review Conference, ca. Dec. 1974, transcript in RRH. See also Nofziger, *Nofziger,* 70.

356   **About half an hour**   Ibid., 70–71; Arthur Van Court interview, Aug. 11, 1988. RR was also accompanied by his Washington representative, Ed Gillenwaters.

356   **Or, depending on**   Nofziger, *Nofziger,* 71; RR interview, June 12, 1986.

356   ***"Big things happening"***   Lacouture, *De Gaulle,* 529–30.

356   **So it was**   Miller, *Democracy Is in the Streets,* 290–92; Charles Kaiser, *1968 in America: Music, Politics, Chaos, Counterculture, and the Shaping of a Generation* (New York, 1988), 150–54; Mitchell Goodman, ed., *The Movement Toward a New America* (New York, 1970), 356.

357   **With Johnson headed**   RR speech script, June 13, 1968, RRL/pp. This passionate handwritten document, addressed to an unnamed Republican audience, gave vent to RR's feelings after the assassination of Robert Kennedy.

357   **Visiting IBM's Austin**   The following account is based on EM Diary, Aug. 3–5, 1968, AC.

358   **They were right**   Cannon, *Ronnie and Jesse,* 273–75.

358   **Ever afterward**   The author learned not to mention 1968 to RR in interviews, for fear of an immediate monologue of obscuration.

359   **At a biographical**   Tom Wolfe interview, Aug. 19, 1990; James Q. Wilson, "A Guide to Reagan Country: The Political Culture of Southern California," *Commentary,* May 1967.

359   **"We must, I"**   Wilson, "A Guide to Reagan Country."

360   **Reagan, their oracle**   RR, open letter to the Regents of the University of California, June 7, 1968, RRH.

PAGE

360   **Gavin remained**   See Gitlin, *The Sixties,* 315–16; GM to EM, May 28, 1968. SDS, under siege for most of 1967 by Marxist/Maoist doctrinaires, was increasingly torn by ideological dissension in 1968. See Miller, *Democracy Is in the Streets,* 282–86, for its pre-Chicago strategy.

360   **de Gaulle's government**   May 27, 1968. Lacouture, *De Gaulle,* 540.

360   ***Fuck you Jew***   Richard J. Daley, qu. in Miller, *Democracy Is in the Streets,* 21.

360   **"Listen, you queer"**   John Judis, *William F. Buckley: Patron Saint of Conservatives* (New York, 1988), 292.

361   ***Dear Parentals***   GM to EM, Dec. 1, 1968, AC. See Seymour Chatman, *Antonioni: Or the Surface of the World* (Berkeley, Calif., 1985), 159–68.

362   **On February 5**   *Daily Californian,* Jan. 29, 1969; RR press-conference transcript, RRH.

362   **When a preliminary**   Minutes of Executive Session of the Regents, Feb. 21, 1969, RRH.

363   **"Who the hell?"**   Art Goldberg, qu. by RR to Commonwealth Club, June 13, 1969, transcript, RRH; Rorabaugh, *Berkeley at War,* 156.

363   **"We have been presented"**   Heyns to faculty of UCB, May 13, 1969, transcript, RRH.

364   ***Les tyrannies***   Albert Camus, "L'Artiste et son temps," in *Actuelles II: Chroniques 1948–1953* (Paris, 1953), 174. English trans. by GM, AC.

365   **a yellowish spray**   The gas, technically known as CS, is an irritant far more panic-inducing than tear gas. Its "extremely sobering effects" include "burning sensations" and feelings of asphyxiation. Advertisement reproduced in Goodman, *The Movement,* 559.

26: A Sixty-Year-Old Smiling Public Man

366   **The Governor had**   Details from *Los Angeles Times,* Sacramento *Union,* Berkeley *Daily Gazette,* Jan. 5, 1971; photographs in RRL/pp.

366   **In just over**   "I've already lived 10 yrs. longer than my life expectancy when I was born." RR to Laurie Rothe and Jeffrey Trauberman, ca. Mar. 16, 1971, RRL/pp. "Last Friday I had my hair cut and the barber told me it's getting pretty speckled on top." RR to Mrs. Linquist, n.d. [ca. 1971], RRL/pp.

367   **a bruising little book**   Brown, *Reagan and Reality.* This book's chapter titles, strung together, convey its message: "A State of Diversity—A Style of Simplicity—Two-dimensional Politics—Amateur Governor—The Ax Falls—The Fastest Gun in the West—A Black and White Issue—War on the Campus—War on Education—The Politics of Life—Reagan the Reactionary Radical."

367   **a decisive, if reduced, majority**   3,439,664 votes to Unruh's 2,938,607, or 53 percent to 45 percent. Cannon, *Reagan,* 175.

367   **Blame and recriminations**   The mood among GOP governors and governors-elect (including RR) was so bitter at a post-election conference held at Sun Valley, Idaho, that some attendees suggested it should have been held in Death Valley. *The New York Times,* Dec. 15, 1970.

367   **Inflation was rampant**   Michael Barone, *Our Country: The Shaping of*

America from Roosevelt to Reagan (New York, 1990), 487; *San Francisco Examiner,* Nov. 8, 1970. Kossen was the paper's political editor. See also "Hottest Candidate in Either Party," *Life,* Oct. 30, 1970. After Kent State, a powerful body of liberal opinion held that Nixon had triggered the massacre by denouncing campus anti-war protesters as "bums" (Aitken, *Nixon,* 370, 402–3). That presidential epithet, coinciding with the invasion of Cambodia, erased memories of Reagan's own, much more inflammatory call for a campus "bloodbath" less than a month before. On ca. June 28, 1970, Senator Mark Hatfield predicted that unless the Vietnam War ended and the economy improved, the GOP might well turn to RR over Nixon. *The New York Times,* June 29, 1970. See Cannon, *President Reagan,* 75–76, for anecdotes about Nixon's nervous resentment of RR in the early 1970s.

367   **"They're like mosquitoes"**   Berkeley *Daily Gazette,* Jan. 5, 1971.

368   **The Governor's words**   Qu. by the *Los Angeles Times,* Jan. 5, 1971.

368   **exploding welfare system**   California's AFDC caseload at the time of RR's first inauguration was 769,000; at the time of his second it had more than doubled, to 1,566,000. The state's total welfare roll in the spring of 1971 was 2.4 million, and was increasing at a rate of 37 percent. With 10 percent of all Americans living in California, it was home to 16 percent of the nation's welfare recipients. RR to National Press Club, Jan. 25, 1971, LC; RR in *The New York Times,* Apr. 1, 1971; Cannon, *Reagan,* 176.

368   **Relief money**   *Los Angeles Times,* Jan. 5, 1971. In 1971, welfare for the first time exceeded defense as the largest item in the federal budget.

368   **"Here in California"**   Johnson, *Modern Times,* 639.

368   **He had been wanting**   RR, "Welfare Reform" memo, Aug. 4, 1970, qu. by Cannon, *Reagan,* 166; Vincent J. and Vee Burke, *Nixon's Good Deed: Welfare Reform* (New York, 1974), 8–9; Edwin Meese interview, Sept. 18, 1985.

368   **For a generation**   Jon Jeter, "Who Are the Deserving Poor?" *The Washington Post,* Jan. 8, 1997; RR to National Press Club, Jan. 25, 1971; Robert Carleson Oral History, 35, RRL; Burke and Burke, *Nixon's Good Deed,* 11, 175; Charles Murray, *Losing Ground: American Social Policy, 1950–1980* (New York, 1984), 162.

369   **"They go out"**   RR in Cabinet Notes, Nov. 6, 1967, CLA.

369   **The Governor's prejudice**   Burke and Burke, *Nixon's Good Deed,* 10; *The New York Times,* Apr. 28, 1971. RR, Basic Speech, ms., ca. Feb. 1976, RRL/pp.

369   **"I want to know"**   Conversational and other details based on the author's group interview with RR associates George Steffes, K. Hall, William Bagley, James Jenkins, *et al.,* Aug. 12, 1988. See also Staff Historical Conference, late 1974, transcript, 87, RRH. On Jan. 21, 1971, RR announced a reorganization of his executive staff, with Executive Secretary Edwin Meese III becoming Executive Assistant to the Governor and Michael Deaver becoming Director of Administration.

369   **more than a ton**   The special glass had been installed after Black Panthers invaded the Capitol in May 1967.

369   **Before him lay**   Staff Historical Conference, 87–89, RRH. Meese now

claims to have been in favor of welfare reform in 1971 (interview, Sept. 18, 1995).

369   **Robert "Macho Bob"**   Robert Moretti Oral History, RRL. Failing help from Washington, Moretti would move to raise state taxes. *Los Angeles Times,* Mar. 4, 1971.

369   **There he could**   For an elegant, if self-serving, account of the genesis of the FAP, see Moynihan, *Family and Nation,* Ch. 1. See also Burke and Burke, *Nixon's Good Deed,* 110, 112. Nixon's original welfare-reform proposals had been spelled out in a message to Congress on Aug. 11, 1969. They included a guaranteed income for a family of four, requirements that states place a similar floor under the aged, blind, and disabled, and a limited "workfare" scheme for able-bodied men. RR expressed support for the last idea only, and he was not charmed by Nixon's subsequent addition to the FAP bill of a provision compelling states to take over the entire cost of AFDC benefits. Ibid., 115.

370   **Reagan gazed**   Group interview, Aug. 12, 1988; Staff Historical Conference, 87, RRH; Robert B. Carleson, "The Reagan Welfare Reforms," *Journal of the Institute for Socioeconomic Studies,* Winter 1980. RR flatly refused to cover the state's expected rise in welfare costs (from $750m. to $3.3b. in 1972, without reform) with a tax increase. His state budget for 1971–1972 balanced at a record $6.1 billion, but as he told reporters, its equilibrium depended on $700 million in welfare cuts and savings—the exact negative value of his reform package. *New York Times,* Feb. 3, 1971.

370   **Nixon's 1971**   *The New York Times,* Jan. 22, 1971.

370   **His first caller**   H. R. Haldeman, *The Haldeman Diaries: Inside the Nixon White House* (New York, 1994), 208; *Los Angeles Times,* Jan. 24, 1971.

371   **But Nixon in turn**   Kevin Phillips in *Sacramento Union,* Feb. 17, 1971; Haldeman, *Diaries,* Jan. 23, 1971, 238.

371   **Reagan coyly told**   Tape recording in LC. From now on RR's control of the California GOP was complete.

371   **Reagan and Nixon proceeded**   *The New York Times,* Feb. 11, 1971, RRH; J. R. Mills to RR, Feb. 25, 1971, RR. Mills's letter reflected fear among Democratic leaders that RR's rhetorical powers would weaken their new majority. *Los Angeles Times,* Feb. 26, 1971.

371   **Nixon sent a**   *The New York Times,* Feb. 25 and 26, Mar. 2, 1971; RR, *Meeting the Challenge: A Responsible Program for Welfare and Medi-Cal Reform, Transmitted to the Legislature March 3, 1971* (Sacramento, CA, 1971); Edmund G. ("Pat") Brown and Bill Brown, *Reagan the Political Chameleon* (New York, 1976), 126. RR was by no means the first governor to write such a message. As Lou Cannon, *Reagan,* 178, notes, Kansas, New Jersey, and Nevada were already pursuing the welfare bogey, much more stringently.

372   **The Governor did not**   Robert B. Carleson to EM, May 10, 1998.

372   **Reading *Meeting***   For detailed discussions, pro and con, of *Meeting the Challenge* and its effects, see Carleson, "The Reagan Welfare Reforms," *passim,* and Frank Levy, *M.I.T. Studies in American Politics and Public Policy,* vol. 4 (Cambridge, Mass., 1978), Ch. 14.

PAGE

372   **There was a lot**   Ibid., 14, 119, 89–90.

372   **On March 27**   *Los Angeles Times,* May 3, 1971; *The New York Times*
Apr. 3 and 1, 1971. Nixon also told RR he would like to send him to
Japan and possibly to Vietnam in the fall as a special representative of
the President. *The New York Times,* Mar. 30, 1971.

373   **But Reagan struck**   RR's article amounted to a condensation of *Meeting the Challenge.* Richard Nathan, Deputy Undersecretary for Welfare
Reform at HEW, announced in 1972 that H.R. 1's welfare-reform provisions alone would cause the agency's personnel to swell by 75 percent.
Burke and Burke, *Nixon's Good Deed,* 180.

373   **The delicacy with**   Nixon, recognizing RR to be a threat as early as
1969, made careful and clever use of Weinberger as an emissary. James
Schlesinger interview, Aug. 6, 1988.

373   **The sound of**   Joan Hoff-Wilson, *Nixon Reconsidered* (New York,
1994), 129; *The New York Times,* Apr. 7, 1971; *The New York Times,* Apr.
11, 1971; Burke and Burke, *Nixon's Good Deed,* 174.

374   **Alarm of a**   *The New York Times,* Apr. 12, 1971; Burke and Burke,
Nixon's Good Deed, 164.

374   **Having added**   *The New York Times,* Apr. 20, 1971.

374   **About this time**   *The New York Times,* May 9, 1971.

374   **Reagan felt his**   *The New York Times,* May 20, 1971; RR to Ron Dock-
sai, May 21, 1971, RRL/pp. See Haldeman, *Diaries,* 291, for Nixon's
concerns about RR and Young Americans for Freedom (YAF).

374   **The Governor's nervousness**   RR to "Mr. Schultz," handwritten draft,
RRL/pp; *The New York Times,* May 9 and 12, 1971.

375   **It also unfortunately**   *The New York Times,* May 25 and June 13, 1971;
RR to William F. Buckley, Jr., ca. June 14, 1971, RRL/pp. MCA, of
course, owed much of its current prodigious wealth to the "blanket
waiver" of 1952, negotiated by RR as president of SAG. See p. 303.

375   **Irish luck saved him**   On ca. June 20, 1971, Buckley had written to A. M.
Rosenthal, editor of the *Times,* protesting innuendos in the article. RR
supplied a rationale for his deductions, obviously hoping that Buckley
would pass it on: "Let me spoil his martini with a fact or two." The Reagan brand expired on Jan. 1, 1970.

375   **Since March, Director**   These decreases, brought about by eligibility au-
diting and other streamlining procedures, reversed ten years of welfare
growth. Carleson, "The Reagan Welfare Reforms." H.R. 1 passed the
House, with the FAP intact, on June 22 but with fewer votes than in 1970
and ominous prospects in the Senate. By now Moretti had also accepted
that Assembly Democrats would not be able to commandeer the welfare-
reform issue without a tax increase. *Los Angeles Times,* Mar. 4, 1971; RR
to Rev. Benjamin H. Cleaver, May 1971, qu. in von Damm, *Sincerely,* 43.

375   **"Governor, I don't"**   Robert Moretti Oral History, RRL.

375   **As a veteran**   RR interview, Mar. 22, 1985.

375   **Moretti was, as**   Edwin Meese interview, Sept. 13, 1994; Robert
Moretti, Earl Brian, and Robert Carlson Oral Histories, 172; Robert
Carleson, "The Enduring Myth of Ronald Reagan's Second Term as
Governor," unpublished ms., AC.

PAGE

376 **"I think he really"** Moretti, qu. by Brown, *Reagan the Political Chameleon,* 67. Brown himself had not raised benefits by so much as a dime in his eight years of office. Cannon, *Reagan,* 176.

376 **The California Welfare** *The New York Times,* Aug. 12, 1971; Jeter, "Who Are the Deserving Poor?"; *The New York Times,* Aug. 12, 1971; Cannon, *Reagan,* 182–83; RR to National Press Club, Jan. 25, 1971, LC.

376 **"we reduced the rolls"** RR, Basic Speech, ms., ca. 1975, RRL/pp; Carleson, "The Reagan Welfare Reforms."

377 **What was more** "RR sent me to Washington in 1973, first to carry his reforms to other states, second to stop efforts to [centralize] all welfare decisions . . . and third to replace AFDC with finite block grants. All three goals have been accomplished. The third and most important . . . had to wait until we got a Ronald Reagan Congress that forced Bill Clinton to sign Ronald Reagan's welfare reform." Robert B. Carleson to EM, May 10, 1998.

377 **Moretti's reward** News clipping photograph in RRL/pp, attached to Bob Martinet to RR, Aug. 18, 1971.

377 **The ink on** Technically speaking, he postponed by one year H.R. 1's effective date—meaning no revenue sharing until at least 1973.

377 **He managed to** *The New York Times,* July 16, 1971. David Swoap Oral History, RRL; Hoff-Wilson, *Nixon Reconsidered,* 132.

377 **And so the strange** For more on the RR-Nixon canon, see *The New York Times,* Aug. 15, 1971, and *Newsweek,* Dec. 20, 1971.

378 **"[The President] has"** Speech draft for YAF Convention, Houston, RRL/pp.

378 **Chiang Kai-shek received him** The following eyewitness account of RR's Taiwan mission derives from an interview with Michael Deaver, June 5, 1988. See also Deaver, *Behind the Scenes,* 65–66.

378 **Flying home** *Firing Line,* Jan. 5, 1972. As President, RR never catered to China's neurosis about the "crucial and fundamental issue" of Taiwan. He remained a strong supporter of Taiwanese independence against the accommodationist arguments of his first Secretary of State. Alexander M. Haig, Jr., *Caveat: Realism, Reagan, and Foreign Policy* (New York, 1984), 195–201.

379 **On the morning of** Gerald S. and Deborah H. Strober, *Nixon: An Oral History of His Presidency* (New York, 1994), 312–13.

380 **"This can't be"** RR qu. in von Damm, *Sincerely, RR,* 17. The Yeats phrase is from "Among School Children," *The Collected Poems of W. B. Yeats* (New York, 1956), 213. There were two other foreign missions during RR's governorship: a trip to the Philippines in 1969, and one to Australia and Indonesia in 1973.

380 *Remember me as* Undated t.s., 1972, in RRL/pp.

382 **"leavings of a life"** D. H. Lawrence, "Shadows," *Last Poems,* ed. W. E. Williams (London, 1965), 133.

382 **"Politics is the refuge"** Clare Boothe Luce, qu. in Morris, "In Search of Clare Boothe Luce."

382 **It was a fiscal** Sacramento *Union,* Nov. 4 and 8, 1973. The vote was 54 percent to 46 percent. Proposition One's chances were not helped when

RR confessed, on the eve of the election, that he did not understand it himself. *Los Angeles Times,* Nov. 2, 1973.

383   **policy at Wing Fat's**   Frank Fat interview, Aug. 12, 1988.

383   **A folder labeled**   Rose Gotner to RR, n.d., 1973, RRL/pp.

383   **Throughout his**   John McCain interview, Mar. 21, 1995.

383   **A military couple**   Howard E. Rutledge to RR, June 9, 1973, RRL/pp.

383   **Hadn't I registered**   Meese functioned as RR's gubernatorial chief of staff for the last six years in Sacramento. For an admiring analysis of his managerial style, see Hamilton and Biggart, *Governor Reagan,* 188–90.

384   **I leafed through**   RR Executive Schedule, Jan. 2, 1975, RRL.

384   **"Governor, you're"**   George N. Zenovich Oral History, RRL.

384   **"As a human"**   Brown, *Reagan and Reality,* 32.

384   *Time*   *Tendril* 12 (winter 1982).

27: The Ripple Effect

387   **Politely turning**   Cannon, *Reagan,* 195; Hannaford, *The Reagans,* 55; RR, *An American Life,* 192–94; RR interview at Rancho del Cielo, Aug. 18, 1988.

387   **Yet he raised**   Hannaford, *The Reagans,* 57–58; von Damm, *At Reagan's Side,* 78. The contracts Deaver and Hannaford arranged were highly lucrative. RR accepted about ten platform engagements a month at an average fee of $5,000—about $20,000 in today's money. Mark Hertsgaard, *On Bended Knee: The Press and the Reagan Presidency* (New York, 1988), 12.

388   **One hundred radio**   Hannaford, *The Reagans,* 59; Copley News Service announcement, *Editor and Publisher,* Jan. 11, 1975. RR's 1975 income, swelled by other freelance fees, was estimated at over $800,000. Cannon, *Reagan,* 196.

388   **Stunningly sooner**   Michael Deaver interviews, June 5, 1989, and Mar. 3, 1995; Michael Deaver, *Behind the Scenes* (New York, 1987), 63–64. The latter source misdates the airline encounter as "Jan. 1976." RR's first rhetorical attack on President Ford came in mid-Feb. *Los Angeles Times,* Feb. 15, 1975.

389   **"Not in Arkansas"**   PR to EM, Mar. 27, 1975; see also John C. Moon of Copley Newspapers to Peter Hannaford, Mar. 31, 1975, RRL/pp.

390   **This may have**   Nofziger, *Nofziger,* 166; Hannaford, *The Reagans,* 58; "Viewpoint" radio disc, n.d. [ca. spring 1975], RRL/av.

390   **"You don't understand"**   Nancy Clark Reynolds interview, Nov. 18, 1986.

390   **Indeed they did**   Hannaford, *The Reagans,* 59; Elizabeth Drew, *American Journal: The Events of 1976* (New York, 1977), 55; EM Diary, Nov. 17, 1975; "Viewpoint" radio disc, RRL/av.

390   **"cool intensity"**   Brown, *Reagan and Reality,* 50.

390   **"the hero of"**   "Inside Story," 235. See above, p. 142.

391   **President Ford, suspicious**   Peter J. Wallison interview, Dec. 3, 1987; Hannaford, *The Reagans,* 63. RR attended only half of the Intelligence

Commission's twenty-two sessions, and impressed fellow members mainly with his reluctance to countenance any criticism of FBI Director J. Edgar Hoover. Lane Kirkland interview, Feb. 18, 1987; James Schlesinger to author, Aug. 6, 1988.

391   **When I asked**   RR interview, Jan. 9, 1989. See also RR press conference, Sept. 10, 1968, RRH.

391   **Dutch was fundamentally**   As early as 1968, RR had spelled his attitude out. For the mutual dislike of Ford and RR, see Robert T. Hartman, *Palace Politics: An Inside Account of the Ford Years* (New York, 1980), 334–36.

391   **When Young Americans**   Marlene M. Pomper, ed., *The Election of 1976; Reports and Interpretations* (New York, 1977); RR to Jerry Norton, ca. Feb. 24, 1975, RRL/pp. RR was at pains around this time to play down serious talk, among conservatives, of a third-party Reagan campaign for the Presidency. Jules Witcover, *Marathon: The Pursuit of the Presidency 1972–1976* (New York, 1977), 46.

391   **"Ron has wanted"**   James Cannon, *Time and Chance: Gerald Ford's Appointment with History* (New York, 1994), 406.

391   **Early in April**   *The Times* (London), Apr. 8, 1975; Hugo Young, *The Iron Lady: A Biography of Margaret Thatcher* (New York, 1989), 84–85. Ibid., 250, notes that RR had been a focus of Tory interest since at least 1970.

392   **"Status quo"**   Hannaford, *The Reagans,* 64.

392   **The resultant**   Speech text with RR annotations, Apr. 7, 1975, RRL/pp; *The Times* (London), Apr. 8, 1975.

392   **Before leaving**   Young, *The Iron Lady,* 78–80, 92–101; RR interview, Aug. 18, 1988; RR interviewed by David Brinkley, ABC, Dec. 22, 1988; Margaret Thatcher interview, June 24, 1995.

392   **He shook his head**   EM Notes, Aug. 18, 1988. Margaret Thatcher's former aides privately confirm her healthy interest in hunks.

393   **"no longer at war"**   Ford proclamation, May 7, 1975; Witcover, *Marathon,* 48.

393   **And indeed, on**   Witcover, *Marathon,* 49. Ford's approval rating rose from 35 to 50 percent, then dropped in mid-July to a level seven points below Senator Edward Kennedy's. Barone, *Our Country,* 541, 748.

393   **by *seeming* reluctant**   RR assured Laxalt in confidence that the reverse was true. In the meantime, he wanted to build up his personal income, depleted by eight years of government service. After declaring his candidacy he would have to waive all fees. Paul Laxalt interview, Feb. 10, 1988; Nofziger, *Nofziger,* 170.

393   **For most of**   RR's campaign team, chaired by Laxalt and led by John Sears, otherwise consisted of Michael Deaver (PR, liaison with the Reagans), Peter Hannaford (PR, writing), Lyn Nofziger (press, finances), James Lake (press), and Jack Courtemanche (fund-raising). Two later important recruits were the Stanford economist Martin Anderson (general policy adviser) and Edwin Meese (domestic policy/law and order).

394   **"Every time I"**   Peter Hannaford interview, Feb. 1, 1988, qu. Donald Livingston, RR's chief program planner.

394   **Exhaustive research**   Frank Ford to Roy Howard, May 26, 1959; Roy

Howard to Frank Ford, June 4, 1959, Roy Howard Papers, LC; Pavel Palazchenko interview, Oct. 3, 1995. Another one of RR's spurious Lenin quotes, lovingly enunciated and ineradicably fixed in memory, was: "The last bastion of capitalism will not have to be taken: it will fall into our outstretched hands like an overripe fruit."

394   **"It's terrible"**   Michael Deaver interview, May 27, 1989. For another version of this story, see Deaver, *Behind the Scenes,* 52–53.

394   **Apparently, you**   RR interview, Oct. 11, 1988. The author's supposition was in any case a *non sequitur.* Nixon did consider RR in 1973, and decided against him because he feared the selection would have split the party. Tip O'Neill and William Novak, *Man of the House: The Life and Political Memoirs of Speaker Tip O'Neill* (New York, 1987), 259.

395   **One set of**   Cannon, *Reagan,* 203; Witcover, *Marathon,* 373–77. The Ford strategist was Stuart Spencer of Spencer-Roberts, architects of RR's first gubernatorial campaign.

395   **Reagan finally decided**   Maureen Reagan, *First Father,* 226–29.

395   **Not until son**   Ron Reagan interview, Feb. 22, 1991.

396   *Dear E:*   Paul Rae to EM, Nov. 15, 1976, AC. RR himself notes the parallels between the first two of these four women in *An American Life,* 40.

396   **completely changed their**   Not entirely true. Sarah Jane Mayfield at least retained her second name through life. Anne Frances Robbins became Nancy Davis.

397   **When I went**   *The New York Times,* Jan. 6, 1976; Witcover, *Marathon,* 390.

397   **I remember that reporters**   Cannon, *Reagan,* 204; EM Diary, Feb. 12, 1976.

397   **Ford won**   The vote totals were Ford 54,824, RR 53,507. EM Diary, Jan. 6, 1976; *The Washington Post,* Jan. 6, 1976; Witcover, *Marathon,* 395–96. RR afterward maintained that "actually . . . I won N.H. as far as the number of votes received. I lost by less than 1500 but 6000 of my votes were thrown out because [party members] voted for all 19 of the Reagan delegates on the ballot. They were supposed to vote for only 16." RR to Margaret Warner, ca. July 1980, RRL/pp.

397   **Campaign specialists**   Witcover, *Marathon,* 388–89; Drew, *American Journal,* 51. The "welfare queen" turned out to have had only four aliases. Ibid., 52.

398   **"I've been told"**   RR, qu. in the Sacramento *Bee,* June 3, 1976; Morton Mintz interview, Mar. 14, 1991.

398   **The candidate said**   Wills, *Reagan's America,* 165–66; Severo and Milford, *Wages of War,* 298–99. Doris "Dorie" Miller was killed in action in 1945, and had a destroyer named after him in the early 1970s. See Severo and Milton, *Wages of War,* for the effect of his case on military desegregation.

398   **Dutch's surprise recovery**   See Anderson, *Revolution,* 44–45.

399   **A colleague of mine**   Alaric Jacob to EM, July 22, 1976, AC.

400   **Actually Reagan's**   Witcover, *Marathon,* 438–39. Sears was also working on a devious plan to force Ford to name his own running mate before balloting began. It was the defeat of this plan (which would have re-

quired a change in convention rules) that ultimately quashed RR's hopes of being nominated. Ibid., Ch. 32.

400   **Kansas City—Now**   The winning margin was seventy votes (RR, 1,070; Ford, 1,187). Cannon, *Reagan,* 224–25, does not share the author's view that RR would probably have been elected in 1976. He argues that RR's right-wing views on issues such as the Panama Canal and abortion were repellent to a prohibitive number of moderate to liberal voters. However, as the election turned out, RR would not have had to do much better than Ford to win: the President attracted 26.1 percent of all voting-age Americans, Carter only 27.2 percent.

400   **Few political punters**   Witcover, *Marathon,* 150. "I'm gonna run in every single primary in every one of the goddamn states, right through to the end," RR assured his despondent advisers on Mar. 23, 1976. Martin Anderson interview, Aug. 8, 1989. For fuller treatment of this low point in the campaign, see Anderson, *Revolution,* Ch. 5, and Nofziger, *Nofziger,* 178–80.

401   **His "final service"**   In the small hours of nomination day, Thursday, Aug. 19, 1976, Holmes Tuttle, Justin Dart, and William French Smith urged RR to accept the Vice Presidency, if Ford could be persuaded to offer it. Their reasoning was that his political career was over anyway, and by doing so he would reunify the GOP. Accounts diverge as to RR's reaction. Ford made the question moot by visiting RR's suite at 1:30 A.M. to ask his opinion of six possible running mates. RR recommended Dole, and a few hours later Ford called to confirm that the Senator had been chosen. RR interview, Apr. 15, 1986; Holmes Tuttle interview, Feb. 24, 1986; William French Smith interview, Aug. 25, 1988; Hannaford, *The Reagans,* 135.

401   **"Don't give up"**   RR farewell address to campaign staff, Aug. 18, 1976, videotape in Vanderbilt University Archives, Tenn.

401   **It was a striking**   RR himself has said he thought he was quoting Governor John Winthrop's declaration, "We must consider that we shall be a City upon a Hill." But there is no luminosity in that image, or in the biblical phrase, "A city that is set on a hill cannot be hid." The author believes that RR was unconsciously recalling the Celestial City invoked at the end of Part One of *The Pilgrim's Progress.* Bunyan's evangelical epic was one of Nelle Reagan's favorite books, and no doubt she read it to RR as a boy. Bunyan's city, set "upon a mighty hill, [was constructed of] pearls and precious stones, also the streets thereof were paved with gold; so that by reason of the natural glory of the City, and the reflection of the sunbeams upon it, Christian with desire fell sick . . . Behold the City shone like the sun."

401   **All that remained**   The following description of RR's address to the 1976 GOP Convention is based on interviews with RR, NR, Maureen and Ron Reagan, Michael Deaver, and video clips preserved in RRL. Parts of it may be heard in the audiobook version of this biography.

404   **The roar**   The speech was at least partially memorized. A senior aide recalls RR musing and muttering its lines at least two days before delivery. Edwin Meese interview, Sept. 18, 1995.

PAGE

404   **Just as the**   Drew, *American Journal,* 405, 410–11; Richard Wirthlin in-
      terview, Apr. 12, 1987. Pomper, *The Election of 1976,* 18, points out that
      Ford won with only 52.5 percent of the delegates. "An explanation is
      needed . . . not of Ford's success, but of Reagan's virtual victory."

404   **"My fellow Americans"**   James Cannon, *Time and Chance,* 348–49.

405   **At sixty-five**   Even RR's closest aides, Michael Deaver and Lyn
      Nofziger, were convinced that he would not and could not run again.
      Nofziger, *Nofziger,* 215.

405   **So we are unlikely**   The above article, accepted but not printed by Jacob,
      was eventually adapted by the author for publication in *Time* (Aug. 19,
      1996).

405   **"stage a crusade"**   *The New York Times,* Aug. 20, 1976. RR privately
      wrote a pair of loyalists after the convention, "The way everything
      turned out, I'm sure the Lord has something in mind" (RR to Elwood
      and Lorraine Wagner, ca. Aug. 1976, RRL/pp). NR informed the author
      that RR was already plotting a run in 1980 on their flight back home
      from Kansas City. NR interview, July 9, 1993.

405   **But with Jimmy Carter**   RR's private opinion of the Democratic candi-
      date was, for him, unusually harsh. "I have a deep-seated feeling that he
      is a real phony." To Sandy Wagner, Oct. 26, 1976, RAA.

405   **Early in September**   Nofziger, *Nofziger,* 215–16; Richard Wirthlin inter-
      view, Apr. 12, 1987.

406   **"Without question"**   EM Diary, Mar. 17, 1981. Carter chose instead to
      open his book with an account of his very last hours in power. Jimmy
      Carter, *Keeping Faith: Memoir of a President* (New York, 1982).

406   **"I've seen"**   EM Notes, Mar. 17, 1981.

407   **"I suppose"**   Ibid., Apr. 16, 1980.

408   **at the very hour**   EM Diary, Apr. 24, 1980; Carter, *Keeping Faith,*
      516–17.

408   **So Dutch won**   Cannon, *Reagan,* 298–303.

408   **From that moment**   Richard Wirthlin interview, Apr. 12, 1987; EM to
      Philip Dunne, Sept. 20, 1980.

409   **one sublime riff**   For a detailed account of this speech, at Steubenville,
      Ohio, on Oct. 8, 1980, see Cannon, *Reagan,* 287–89.

409   **Dutch's charm**   Nofziger, *Nofziger,* 262–63.

409   **An announcer at**   RR interviewed by Lindsay Davis, WSDR, Nov. 4,
      1980, transcript in AC.

28: I, Ronald Wilson Reagan

410   **Reagan adjusted**   Michael Reagan, *On the Outside,* 188.

410   **And so he was**   Max Lerner, *Wounded Titans: American Presidents and
      the Perils of Power,* ed. Robert J. Schmuhl (New York, 1996), 403; An-
      derson, *Revolution,* 205; RR, *An American Life,* 227.

411   **He spoke of his**   The following extracts from RR's inaugural are taken
      from Erickson, *Reagan Speaks,* 139–45. Supplementary details from
      WHCA videotapes, RRL/av.

411   **It was evident**   For an account of the composition of RR's First Inaugural, see Cannon, *President Reagan,* 96–100. Khachigian had been RR's traveling speechwriter during the 1980 campaign, and earlier (with Diane Sawyer) had assisted Nixon in the composition of his memoirs.

411   **runaway living costs**   Inflation had risen 13 percent in each of the two years preceding RR's inauguration, and the latest interest rate, posted in December 1980, had been a record 21.5 percent. Unemployment was nearly 8 percent.

411   **One was a populism**   See Richard Reeves, *The Reagan Detour* (New York, 1985), Ch. 4 for an acute analysis of how RR "redefined populism" *vis-à-vis* big government.

412   **Whatever the cadence of**   "To strive, to seek, to find, and not to yield." Alfred, Lord Tennyson, "Ulysses."

412   **A man just about**   See also Susan Jeffords's agitated study, *Hard Bodies: Hollywood Masculinity in the Reagan Era* (New Brunswick, N.J., 1989). Hardness: Michael Reagan, *On the Outside,* 169. Hair: EM Notes, *passim.* For authoritative denials that RR used hair dye, see Anderson, *Revolution,* 193; Deaver, *Behind the Scenes,* 98, and RR's many patient letters on the subject. They date back as early as Oct. 24, 1972: "Honestly & cross my heart, my hair isn't dyed an 'unreal brown' or any other color. A close look will reveal some gray ones sneaking in . . . like the ad says, it's just 'a little dab of Brylcreem' " (to Theodore Loeffler, RRL/pp). Oral hygiene: Patti Davis, *Angels Don't Die: My Father's Gift of Faith,* (New York, 1985), 80 ("I noticed how sweet his breath was"); Dr. John Hutton Diary, July 15, 1987, quoting a White House dentist: "Even his saliva—so very clear—like a child's," JHP. Nails, complexion: EM Notes, May 27, 1992, and Nov. 15, 1987. RR, whose public humor was carefully sedate, loved robust male jokes, as long as they were not blasphemous.

413   **Earlier today, for example**   RR's speech began at 12:01, 32 minutes before the first hostage transport was permitted to take off [12:33 P.M. EST]. The second plane followed at 12:42 P.M. RR was advised of this as he went into lunch with Congressional leaders. About twenty minutes into the lunch, Michael Deaver informed him that the hostages had left Iranian airspace. This enabled RR, with his usual delight in good timing, to announce the news when he rose to toast his hosts. Meanwhile, Carter was en route to a drizzly homecoming in Georgia. Mark and Antoinette Hatfield interview, Jan. 7, 1986; Carter, *Keeping Faith,* 13; Jordan, *Crisis,* 403–4; Maureen Reagan, *First Father,* 17.

413   **Even his rare**   See page 394; Cannon, *Ronnie and Jesse,* 165; Anderson, *Revolution,* 286–87. Ron Reagan interview, Feb. 22, 1991.

413   **And even fewer**   Doris Day remembered RR as "the only man I ever knew who really liked to dance." *Parade,* Aug. 6, 1986.

414   **Inserting the story**   Cannon, *President Reagan,* 98–100.

414   **The world that**   These stated beliefs of RR all predate his 1981 Inauguration. RR interview, EM Notes, Aug. 18, 1988; RR qu. in *Chicago Tribune,* May 10, 1980; Detroit *Free Press,* Mar. 23, 1980.

414   **Reagan's world**   Morton Mintz, *Quotations from President Ron* (New

York, 1986), 41; Mark Green and Gail MacColl, *Ronald Reagan's Reign of Error: The Instant Nostalgia Edition* (New York, 1983, 1987), 98–99; Brian Mulroney interview, Dec. 8, 1993; Washington *Star,* Nov. 12, 1979; Mintz, *Quotations,* 15, 25, 10; Green and MacColl, *Reagan's Reign,* 32, 153, 39, 111. The definitive history of RR's *petits moments d'embarras* as President is Paul Slansky, *The Clothes Have No Emperor* (New York, 1989).

414 **What horrifies, though** In 1975, for example, RR treated General Lyman Lemnitzer, a fellow member of the Rockefeller Commission, to his theory that the Cold War was caused by the West's cowardly failure to retake Berlin during the Soviet blockade of 1948–1949. Our forces, he complained, should have slammed right through those of "the Reds," and driven them back to Russia. Instead, we had instituted the Berlin Airlift, thereby proving to Stalin that we were scared of him. General Lemnitzer turned out to be the wrong person to have told this story to; he had been on the Airlift's planning committee at the time. "Governor, in the first place I suggest you look at a map. You'll find that Berlin lies not on, but inside the East German border—one hundred miles inside—and the only way to get an army there is along a single road surrounded by forty of the toughest divisions in the Red Army. We had exactly eight divisions in our half of Germany, and not very well trained ones, either. If you think we were going to take Berlin with them, you're out of your mind." Lane Kirkland, head of the AFL-CIO, was a witness to this tongue-lashing. Five years later, Kirkland listened in stupefaction as the President-elect repeated exactly the same story at a dinner party in the house of George Will. Lane and Irina Kirkland interview, Feb. 21, 1987.

415 **When he expresses** Patti Davis, *The Way I See It,* 203; RR press conferences, Feb. 29 and May 11, 1972, SAL; RR to Rev. W. R. Vaiden, n.d. [ca. Sept. 1975], RRL/pp; RR to Editor, Eureka *Pegasus,* Mar. 18, 1971, RRL/pp. In his handwritten letter to Rev. Vaiden, RR also states that he believes homosexuality to be "a neurotic sickness." Yet in 1978 he strenuously opposed a California proposition that sought to ban homosexual schoolteachers. He believed that if they did not openly advertise "an alternate lifestyle," they should not be persecuted.

415 **passivity in matters** David Stockman, *The Triumph of Politics: How the Reagan Revolution Failed* (New York, 1986), 74–76; Geoffrey Kemp, in Deborah Hart Strober and Gerald S. Strober, *Reagan: The Man and His Presidency* (Boston, 1998), 109.

415 *My Dear First Lady* RR to NR, Christmas 1971, Nancy Reagan Papers, privately held. NR shared several of her husband's love letters from the 1950s through the 1980s with the author, and they are repetitively similar in ardor and expression. It might be noted here that RR had a way of addressing his children to express further adoration of his wife, much to her pleasure but hardly to theirs. Thus, to Patti as a little girl: "Maybe it's a good thing to be apart now and then. Not that I have to be away from your Mommie to know how much I love her but a thirst now and then makes you know and remember how really sweet the water is"

[from Browning, Mont., ca. 1957, privately held]. And to Michael Reagan on the occasion of his marriage: "There is no greater happiness for a man than approaching a door at the end of a day knowing someone on the other side of that door is waiting for the sound of his footsteps." The latter sentence, written in June 1973, duplicates the paean to NR at the end of *Where's the Rest of Me?* (1965). Until then, Michael, twenty-six years old, had never received a letter from his father.

416   **To her credit**   NR frankly states, in *My Turn,* 106, that RR lives behind an invisible wall. "There are times when even I feel that barrier."

416   **"I have his hands"**   NR interview, May 20, 1988.

417   **But on returning**   Michael Reagan, *On the Outside,* 158. The first time RR saw Ron dance, he had difficulty recognizing him onstage, but on the second occasion, in Washington, he wrote in his diary, "[Ron] was darn good. He has a grace that is remindful of Fred Astaire—a little extra flair that makes it all look easy." RR Diary, May 18, 1981, RRP.

417   **There is double**   Not to mention the quadruple irony that NR had herself adopted the name Davis in youth. She nevertheless resolutely refused to acknowledge her daughter's right to use it. Patti is indexed as "Patti Reagan Grilley" in *My Turn,* and the entries thereunder amount to a concise summary of NR's attitude toward her: "birth of—as child of celebrities—leniency with—Nancy's problems with—novel by—politics hated by." For an alternative take on the word *leniency,* see Davis, *As I See It,* pp. 10–335.

417   **She has not yet**   By 1998, Patti Davis had become the author of six memoirs and novels, *Deadfall, Home Front, A House of Secrets, The Way I See It, Bondage,* and *Angels Don't Die.* These books have been vilified for vanity and a whining animus toward her parents. However, the author confesses he finds Ms. Davis a lucid stylist, with a good ear for dialogue and pleasantly sardonic sense of humor. *The Way I See It* has been neglected by Reagan scholars, but it is an important document that shows the dark side of RR's cool moon. Its portrait of an abusive, domineering NR is far more damaging than Kitty Kelley's *Nancy Reagan* because the material is primary. *Angels Don't Die* is a pallid little religious meditation redeemed by some moving scenes of reconciliation with her father. Of the other Reagan family memoirs, Michael's *On the Outside Looking In* is self-pitying but crudely powerful, Maureen's *First Father, First Daughter* difficult to read because of its forced, little-girl sentimentality, and NR's *My Turn* so guarded and stiff as to lend force to Patti's remark, "My mother is a woman who needs to control everything around her. Yet inside, she doubts her ability to do so." *The Way I See It,* 90.

417   **Michael is the most**   Michael Reagan, *On the Outside,* 117; RR Diary, Nov. 19, 26, and 29, 1984, RRP. Michael's molestations took place when he was eight. He describes them in chapter 3 of his autobiography. Such revelations apart, *On the Outside* is remarkable for its involuntary exposure of RR as a coldly distant father, and of JW as a generous and compassionate mother, behind her mask of stern religiosity.

418   **They communicate best**   For "Sonny Boy's" participatory attitude to his

father's fame, see Larry Speakes, *Speaking Out: The Reagan Presidency from Inside the White House* (New York, 1988), 99.

418 **"I've never really"**   Maureen Reagan interview, Feb. 23, 1991.

418 **The only grandchild**   The importance the senior Reagans attached to Cameron can be gauged from their failure to stop by the hospital the day he was born, May 30, 1978, even though he lay in a hospital minutes from the freeway they were taking to Rancho del Cielo. Michaél dryly notes that they "sent a plant." JW, in contrast, showed up at once, full of avid interest in the baby, and insisted on paying for two weeks of private nursing. RR did not manage to see his grandson until July 1980, when the boy was more than two. Michael Reagan, *On the Outside,* 165–66, 175–76.

418 **a house so beautiful**   Patti Davis was the guest who noted the narcissus. *The Way I See It,* 262.

419 **Through the small**   For a terse description of RR's new élite ("They are philistine and unphilanthropic. But they are not evil"), see Sir Nicholas Henderson, *Mandarin: The Diaries of an Ambassador, 1969–1982* (London, 1994), 378–79.

419 **"The inaugural"**   RR Diary, Jan. 20, 1981, RRP.

419 **January 21, 1981**   RR Diary, *passim.* RR's Cabinet consisted, besides himself *ex officio,* of thirteen departmental members: Secretary of State Alexander M. Haig, Jr. (57); Secretary of the Treasury Donald T. Regan (62); Secretary of Defense Caspar W. Weinberger (64); Attorney General William French Smith (64); Secretary of the Interior James G. Watt (43); Secretary of Agriculture John R. Block (46); Secretary of Commerce Malcolm Baldrige (59); Secretary of Labor Raymond J. Donovan (51); Secretary of Health and Human Services Richard S. Schweiker (55); Secretary of Housing and Urban Development Samuel R. Pierce, Jr. (59); Secretary of Transportation Andrew L. "Drew" Lewis, Jr. (50); Secretary of Energy James B. Edwards (54); and Secretary of Education Terrel H. Bell (60). Other Cabinet-rank officers were UN Ambassador Jeane Kirkpatrick, U.S. Trade Representative William Brock III, Director of Central Intelligence William Casey, and Edwin Meese III. See Ronald Brownstein and Nina Easton, *Reagan's Ruling Class: Portraits of the President's Top One Hundred Officials* (New York, 1983).

419 **Fortunately, the Reagan**   Richard Darman, *Who's in Control? Polar Politics and the Sensible Center* (New York, 1996), 40; von Damm, *At Reagan's Side,* 132, 127; Cannon, *President Reagan,* 72–73. Ms. von Damm was assistant chief of personnel during the transition. For a notes-based record of RR's participation in a Cabinet appointments meeting, with examples of his elliptical executive style, see pp. 135–39 of *At Reagan's Side.*

419 **One appointment**   Except where otherwise indicated, the following portraits are based on the author's personal observations and conversations with private individuals. They should be balanced against the self-portraits in *My Turn,* Edwin Meese III, *With Reagan* (Washington, D.C., 1992); Deaver, *Behind the Scenes;* and Stockman, *Triumph of Politics.* See also the chapter-length biographical studies in Laurence I. Barrett,

Gambling with History: Reagan in the White House (updated paperback ed., New York, 1984).

420 **For these reasons** Cannon, *President Reagan,* 69–70, shows that the prime agent of Meese's downfall was RR. "Ed cannot be chief of staff," the President-elect said. "He's not organized." See Barrett, *Gambling with History,* Ch. 6, and Deaver, *Behind the Scenes,* 131–32.

420 **Reagan, who could** Hedrick Smith, *The Power Game: How Washington Works* (New York, 1988), 315. See also Anderson, *Revolution,* 288, on RR's "unique" ability to be "warmly ruthless."

420 **It also meant** In addition to serving Bush in 1980, Baker had been a delegate hunter for Ford in 1976. However, RR made clear to Baker as early as the fall of 1976 that he considered him an ideological soul mate. See Barrett, *Gambling with History,* 384, and Ch. 21, *passim.*

421 **"You know, I am"** Anderson, *Revolution,* 215, 216–18. After the assassination attempt on RR, Deaver told his wife, "Carolyn, I'll never be the same." Qu. in Wallace, *First Lady,* 125.

421 **Deaver's casual** Anderson, *Revolution,* 213–14; Deaver, *Behind the Scenes,* 165–66. See Deaver, Ch. 12 for his self-confessed (and successfully conquered) alcoholism.

422 **David A. Stockman** Barrett, *Gambling with History,* 126–34, offers the best brief summary of the economic crisis that brought Stockman to control RR's initial budgetary policy in the new year of 1981. See also Stockman, *Triumph,* Ch. 2. (He spells out the equation and its inherent anomaly on p. 91.) Strictly speaking, the recession of 1981 did not begin until August, but inflation and high interest rates early in the year almost guaranteed it.

422 **His platitudes** *The New York Times,* Feb. 18 and 19, 1981; Stockman, *Triumph,* 79–80; Cannon, *President Reagan,* 118. After RR's appeal to Congressmen to make the Program *"our* plan," their applause made it difficult for him to continue speaking. Barrett, *Gambling with History,* 149.

423 **Neglected, somehow** Stockman, *Triumph,* 87, 91; Darman, *Who's in Control?,* 75.

423 **These announcements** See Stockman, *Triumph,* 81–84, on the importance of speed in budgetary reform.

423 **"Everywhere we look"** RR, handwritten insert on Conservative PAC speech draft, Mar. 18, 1981, RRL/hw; RR Diary, Feb. 26, 1981, RRP.

424 **Capitalizing to the full** According to Cannon, *Reagan,* 333, in RR's first one hundred days of power, he met with 467 Senators and Congressmen on sixty-nine different occasions. Some or them later commented that they had seen more of him in four months than they had of Jimmy Carter in four years.

424 **Like many aging** The following paragraphs describing RR's typical schedule in 1981 are based on "Access to the President," an unsigned twenty-five-page memorandum of Presidential procedure in RRL, probably the work of Richard Darman's office. Supplementary details from Richard Darman interview, Mar. 18, 1987, and Helene von Damm interview, July 11, 1987.

425   **Then, according to**   RR attached great importance to the NSC, which met about 150 times during his first Administration, as opposed to 45 in Jimmy Carter's. Constantine Menges in Strober and Strober, *Reagan,* 102.

425   **Except for**   Von Damm, *At Reagan's Side,* 184. Much to RR's pleasure, his desserts grew more voluptuous during the second Administration, so much so that he would skip his main course in order to indulge them without guilt. The slightest increase in his weight was immediately compensated for by extra exercise and dieting.

426   **his well-known need**   Michael Deaver recounts that at 9 A.M. on Jan. 20, 1981, he found RR fast asleep in a pitch-dark bedroom at Blair House. "Governor . . . you're going to be inaugurated in two hours." Deaver, *Behind the Scenes,* 98–99.

426   **But the journalists**   "Access to the President"; Richard Darman interview, Mar. 18, 1987 ("It's psychologically necessary for him to clear his desk"). See also Darman, *Who's in Control?,* 39–40, and Caspar W. Weinberger, *Fighting for Peace: Seven Critical Years in the Pentagon* (New York, 1990), 176–77.

426   **Entertainment remained**   RR Diary, *passim,* RRP.

427   **His diaries avoided**   Ibid., Mar. 21, 1981, RRP.

427   **On March 30**   Ibid., Mar. 30 [written on Apr. 11], 1981, RRP.

427   **Helene von Damm saw**   Von Damm, *At Reagan's Side,* 192. That same morning, Press Secretary James Brady told his staff that they would be briefed at 4 P.M. on security procedures if "there ever was a crisis." Mollie Dickenson, *Thumbs Up: The Life and Courageous Comeback of White House Press Secretary James Brady* (New York, 1987), 41, 44.

427   **Reagan's speech at**   Deaver, *Behind the Scenes,* 16; Herbert L. Abrams, *"The President Has Been Shot": Confusion, Disability, and the 25th Amendment in the Aftermath of the Attempted Assassination of Ronald Reagan* (New York, 1992), 51.

428   **What was not usual**   RR, *An American Life,* 259; Abrams, *"The President,"* 54; Dickenson, *Thumbs Up,* 66. RR specifically described his glimpse of Hinckley to Dickenson, but she notes that he had previously told Laurence Barrett, "I never saw the man with the gun."

428   **Now it was**   Dickenson, *Thumbs Up,* 72. See p. 170; Jerry Parr interview, May 18, 1999. After seeing *Code of the Secret Service* in 1940, young Parr had had repeated daydreams of "being on a rooftop and monitoring the progress of a presidential motorcade."

428   **"Jerry, get off"**   RR, *An American Life,* 259; Dickenson, *Thumbs Up,* 66; Abrams, *"The President,"* 303. See p. 170 of this biography.

428   **"Rawhide not hurt"**   Mari Maseng interview, Jan. 12, 1989; Abrams, *"The President,"* 56–57, 303–4; John Hutton interview, Aug. 26, 1998.

429   **Reagan, ashen-faced**   John Pekkanen, "The Saving of the President," *Washingtonian,* Aug. 1991. The E.R. admission sheet recording RR's arrival deserves immortality: "*Name* Ronald Reagan. *Occupation* President of the United States. *Insurance* Self-pay. *Chief complaint* Nosebleed." Dr. Wesley Price, qu. in ibid. Pekkanen's article is the most exhaustive chronicle of the events of Mar. 30–Apr. 11, 1981, and is the

main basis of the following paragraphs. Other essential sources are Abrams, *"The President"*; Benjamin L. Aaron, "The Attempted Assassination of President Ronald Reagan," *Journal of the American Medical Association* 272. 21 (Dec. 9, 1994); Jeffrey Donahoe, "Head for George Washington," *GW Medicine,* spring 1991; and Oliver H. Beahrs, "The Medical History of President Ronald Reagan," *Journal of the American College of Surgeons* 178 (Jan. 1994). For the separate ordeals of James Brady and John Hinckley, see Dickenson, *Thumbs Up,* and Aaron Latham, "The Dark Side of the American Dream," *Rolling Stone,* Aug. 5, 1982.

429   **He remained**   Deaver, *Behind the Scenes,* 18; Abrams, *"The President,"* 61. Due to the haste of trauma therapy on RR, there is a considerable divergence of opinion on just how low his blood pressure (normally 140/80) sank. Aaron and Beahrs have it at 80 systolic, Abrams at 78, Donahue at between 50 and 60. Dr. Joseph Giordano, head of the E.R., described him at one point having a diastolic reading of 0. Without drastic reperfusion, RR would have died in less than ten minutes.

429   **By now it was**   Pekkanen, "The Saving"; John Hutton interview, Jan. 27, 1993. One member of the trauma unit actually squeezed the blood packs to increase the rate of inflow. When Dr. Hutton tried to take blood samples from the President in 1988, "I had difficulty finding a vein in his left arm that I could needle—most of them had been used up after the assassination attempt." During his subsequent operation alone, RR received 5¼ units of packed red blood. Beahrs, "Medical History."

429   **Only when a nurse**   Dickenson, *Thumbs Up,* 75–76. Dr. Wesley Price, who arrived later, claims to have been the discoverer of the bullet hole. Pekkanen, "The Saving."

429   **She remembered**   It is clear from RR's own accounts in *An American Life,* 261, and his diary, Mar. 30, 1981, that he realized in the E.R. that he had been shot.

429   **I focused**   RR Diary, Mar. 30, 1981, RRP. See also RR, *An American Life,* 260–61. At first, doctors working on RR in the trauma unit tried to keep NR away. "They don't know how it is with us," she pleaded to Deaver. "He has to know I'm here!" NR, *My Turn,* 4.

429   **Earlier, when the white**   Pekkanen, "The Saving"; Donahoe, "Head for George Washington," 12.

430   **All of this urgency**   As is inevitable in multiple accounts of an emergency, discrepancies abound among those concerning the events of Mar. 30, 1981. The author has generally relied on primary memory; NR, *My Turn,* 9; Dickenson, *Thumbs Up,* 75; Abrams, *"The President,"* 86; Darman, *Who's in Control?,* 49; and von Damm, *At Reagan's Side,* 193. The White House officially confirmed the news that RR had been shot at 3:18 P.M. For a critical view of the Reagan Administration's "lack of contingency planning" and deliberate disregard of the Twenty-fifth Amendment, see Abrams, *"The President,"* Ch. 4.

430   **Most chilling**   Two of RR's attending physicians described him as being "on the brink" of death at around 2:40 P.M. Pekkanen, "The Saving." It is clear, in retrospect, that he was saved by four things: Jerry Parr's deci-

sion to divert the motorcade; flawlessly synchronized trauma procedures; NR's presence at his side; and Dr. Aaron's decision for an immediate thoracotomy. See Beahrs, "Medical History."

430 **We had no idea** Aaron, "Attempted Assassination." RR received eight units of packed red blood cells, three of fresh frozen plasma, and one pack of platelets. See also Abrams, *"The President,"* 42, 137–38, and Ch. 6, *passim.* Larry Speakes's notes, reflecting private hospital briefings, state unequivocally, "Doctors believe bleeding to death. . . . Touch and go." Speakes, *Speaking Out,* 6.

430 **Joseph Giordano, head** Pekkanen, "The Saving"; Abrams, *"The President,"* 60–61. Donahoe, "Head for George Washington," 12; Benjamin Aaron interview, Jan. 11, 1989. The damaged vessel turned out to be a small artery adjacent to the main pulmonary artery. Beahrs, "Medical History." Meanwhile, upstairs, the Troika was considering whether to invoke the Twenty-fifth Amendment, empowering Vice President Bush (then in Austin, Texas, waiting for Air Force Two to refuel for an emergency flight back to Washington) to take over temporarily the functions of Chief Executive. Michael Deaver reports that at approximately 3:30 P.M., after a telephone call from White House Physician Dr. Daniel Ruge confirming that RR's condition was "stable" (surgery had not yet begun), "the three of us looked at each other and nodded." That gesture was mutually understood to be a decision not to invoke. Deaver, *Behind the Scenes,* 22. See also Abrams, *"The President,"* 94–95. In the Situation Room at the White House, a less controlled crisis was unfolding. Secretary of State Haig, assuming charge of an *ad hoc* "crisis team," took it upon himself to race upstairs to the press room at 4:14 and announce to startled reporters, "As of now, I am in control here at the White House." His trembling voice and beaded brow, not to mention his misreading of the Constitutional line of succession ("You have the President, the Vice President, and the Secretary of State, in that order") hardly reassured television viewers. In fairness, it should be noted that Haig's first statement was accurate: he had been appointed Situation Room manager by James Baker, since Vice President Bush (normally the first person to direct an emergency involving the President) was out of town. Haig was, moreover, trying to correct a disastrous briefing by White House Deputy Press Secretary Larry Speakes, who had implied that senior staff members were unsure what to do if RR died on the operating table. Unfortunately, the stairs Haig had to run up were steep, and the lights he had to face were hot. His political career never recovered. Haig, *Caveat,* 158–66; Darman, *Who's in Control?,* 49–52; Weinberger, *Fighting for Peace,* 86–97.

431 **Notwithstanding his** Nothing so indicates the essentially creative nature of RR's psyche than his compulsion to change trauma into humor or drama. According to Dr. Aaron, "he continued with his jokes as the anesthesiologist was trying to put him to sleep. He was even talking through the mask!" Interview, Jan. 11, 1989. And see Dr. Price, below.

431 **The operation, beginning** Deaver, *Behind the Scenes,* 23; Dr. Aaron interview, Jan. 11, 1989. For detailed accounts of RR's surgery, see Pekka-

PAGE

nen, "The Saving," and Abrams, *"The President,"* 62–64. At 5:20 P.M.
Baker called from the hospital to state that the operation on the President had been a success, and that invoking the Twenty-fifth Amendment
was no longer so urgent an option. Abrams, *"The President,"* 97–98. For
a critical review of this decision, see Arthur S. Link and James F. Toole,
"Presidential Disability and the Twenty-fifth Amendment," *Journal of
the American Medical Association* 272. 21 (Dec. 9, 1994).

431   **the hospital announced** The first claim, at least, was misleading. According to Pekkanen, "The Saving," RR was worryingly deoxygenated
after the operation, and his lower left lung lobe was collapsed. These
conditions corrected themselves overnight, with the help of a respirator.

431   **Regaining consciousness** Pekkanen, "The Saving"; NR, *My Turn,*
11–12; Deaver, *Behind the Scenes,* 23. RR was informed the following afternoon that his press secretary had been wounded in the head, and at
once asked if Brady's brain was damaged. Michael Deaver reports that
his eyes filled on hearing the affirmative. "My God, that means four bullets landed." Deaver, *Behind the Scenes,* 25.

431   **He was able** Deaver, *Behind the Scenes,* 24; Pekkanen, "The Saving";
Abrams, *"The President,"* 67–71. Michael Deaver was so distraught at
RR's appearance when the fever took him that "I came home at night
and just totally broke down." Qu. in Strober and Strober, *Reagan,* 122.
Aaron, "Attempted Assassination," reports casually that three of RR's
blood-transfusion bags tested as "suspicious" for hepatitis B.

432   **He proceeded** Deaver, *Behind the Scenes,* 24.

432   **"I know it's"** RR Diary, Apr. 11, 1981, RRP.

432   **I wrote a letter** *The New York Times,* Apr. 5, 1981.

433   ***Dear Mr. President Duch*** Marianna S. Mundstock to RR, Apr. 2,
1981, RRL/pp.

29: Back into the Iron Vest

434   **Aides conditioned** Hospital blood is unavoidably loaded with broken-
down cells, and, because it is stored in refrigerators, often lowers the
(already low) temperature of patients. According to Dr. Benjamin
Aaron, the President's massive transfusion had been "at the virtual top
of insults to the body—number 10 magnitude, worse than a prolonged
beating." Benjamin Aaron interview, Jan. 11, 1989. According to Louis
A. Gottschalk *et al.,* "Presidential Candidates and Cognitive Impairment
Measure from Behavior in Campaign Debates," *Public Administration
Review,* Mar./Apr. 1988, "President Reagan's cognitive impairment
scores taken over time [1980–1984] showed a significant increase."

434   **His face seemed** Weinberger, *Fighting for Peace,* 98; Darman, *Who's in
Control?,* 60–61; Patti Davis interview, Feb. 10, 1991; Abrams, *"The
President,"* 72–73, 148–49.

434   **On Good Friday** Deaver, *Behind the Scenes,* 26.

435   **The upshot** Ibid.; RR Diary, Apr. 17, 1981, RRL. A shaky superscript
on a speech draft dated July 31, 1985, reads: "As I learned of some of the

near miracles that just seemed to fall into place in my favor, I decided that whatever time was left to me belonged to someone else." RR was at that time recovering from cancer surgery. RRL/pp/hw.

435 **Demonstrably, since** For a dramatic indication of the CIA's depth of information regarding pre-martial law Poland, see Benjamin Weiser, "A Question of Loyalty," *The Washington Post Magazine,* Dec. 13, 1992.

435 **Ronald Reagan had** RR qu. in Brown, *Reagan and Reality,* 34; San Jose *News,* July 24, 1968; Anderson, *Revolution,* 74; RR qu. in *U.S. News and World Report,* May 31, 1976; Michael Reagan interview, June 27, 1989; Powers, *Not Without Honor,* 362, 392–93. See also RR, *An American Life,* Ch. 43.

436 **So far, détente's** Qu. in Cannon, *President Reagan,* 281–82.

436 **"How is he"** Anatoly Dobrynin, *In Confidence: Moscow's Ambassador to America's Six Cold War Presidents, 1962–1986* (New York, 1995), 484; Haig, *Caveat,* 103. According to Dobrynin, the Politburo met on Feb. 11 for a formal review of RR's press conference, and unanimously condemned it. "It was a catastrophe in personal relations at the highest level," the Ambassador wrote years later, adding that in his long career he had never seen such united prejudice toward an American President (p. 486).

436 **That exchange** RR, *An American Life,* 268.

436 **Now it was spring** Ibid., 269; Wallace, *First Lady,* 23. This was not, of course, RR's first critical apprehension of MAD. He was disillusioned with détente as early as 1976. Anderson, *Revolution,* 72–73. Kenneth Adelman dryly notes that in Soviet MAD terminology, a four-hundred-ton nuclear counterstrike was defined as "One McNamara." Kenneth Adelman, *The Great Universal Embrace* (New York, 1989), 305.

436 **He wondered** Stephen White, *Gorbachev and After* (New York, 1991), 3; RR, *An American Life,* 269–70; RR Diary, Apr. 18, 1981, RRP. The date of RR's meeting with Brezhnev was June 27, 1973.

437 **With that, he resigned** RR Diary, Apr. 21–22, 1981, and *passim,* RRP; RR, *An American Life,* 255–56, 270–71.

437 *Mr. President . . .* RR to Leonid Brezhnev, Apr. 24, 1981, qu. in RR, *An American Life,* 272–73. Cannon, *President Reagan,* 298, misdates RR's original draft. The presidential diary makes clear that it was composed on Apr. 18, given to State on the twenty-first, and returned, heavily edited, the next day. See also Michael Deaver, *Behind the Scenes,* 262–63.

438 **It seemed to the** Haig's attitude toward the grain embargo is spelled out in *Caveat,* 110–16. See also Barrett, *Gambling with History,* 32–33.

438 **Reagan heard him** RR interviewed by Hugh Sidey, *Time,* Aug. 23, 1982; RR, *An American Life,* 271–72. Ambassador Dobrynin concedes in his memoirs that Brezhnev's reply to this letter, while not as "icy" as RR recalls, "underestimated the psychological aspects" of Reagan's original desire to write. The Soviet leadership should have recognized that the President's letter, however "naïve," justified more than a "standard polemical" response. Dobrynin, *In Confidence,* 492–93.

438 **The strange device** Abrams, *"The President,"* 148–49. The rumors were probably spread by the normally unflappable Richard Darman, who had

seen the device on April 12 and, assuming it was a respirator, was badly frightened by it. Darman, *Who's in Control?*, 60–61. In Bob Woodward's later book on William Casey, the Respirex mushroomed into an inhalator, "a large masklike breathing device" that administered oxygen "with a wheezing sound." *Veil: The Secret Wars of the CIA* (New York, 1987), 122.

438   **"I walked in"**   RR Diary, Apr. 28, 1981, RRP; Ritter and Henry, *Reagan: The Great Communicator*, 161–65, prints the live text of RR's speech. A later Speaker of the House, Jim Wright, noted how ingenuously RR arranged for this appearance. Waiting until Speaker Tip O'Neill was out of the country, the President put in a long-distance call and asked for an opportunity to thank the American people for their good wishes during his convalescence. He said that he might add "a word or two about economic matters." Jim Wright, *Balance of Power: Presidents and Congress from the Era of McCarthy to the Age of Gingrich* (Atlanta, 1996), 352.

439   **Not forty**   Barrett, *Gambling with History*, 154. By now, the Reagan budget had become a bipartisan plan, and was known, in typically ungainly Congressional nomenclature, as "the Gramm-Latta resolution." It had been formally submitted by the Administration on March 10, with an adjustment of February's proposed spending cuts to $48.6 billion (reduced by the Senate Budget Committee to $36.4 billion). Overcoming the frenzied competition of a Democratic substitute measure in April, it was adopted by the House on May 7 as a $689 billion provisional budget, including a token deficit, for fiscal 1982.

439   **The Administration, overconfident**   Barrett, *Gambling with History*, 401–7; Stockman, *Triumph*, 229; Wright, *Balance of Power*, 358–61. Barrett notes (15) that on June 11, at the height of the White House's budgetary battle with Congress, Wright admitted in his diary to "awe" at RR's political skill. "I am not sure that I have seen its equal."

439   **I tend to remember**   This account of the 1981 gathering of the American Academy of Achievement is taken from EM Diary, June 26–27, 1981, AC.

439   **I cannot say**   The original manuscript of David Stockman's *The Triumph of Politics* was translated into English by Christopher Buckley. For a lucid, short account of the negotiation of RR's spending and tax-reduction bills, Jan.–Aug. 1981, see Darman, *Who's in Control?*, Ch. 3–5.

440   **Go from me**   Lionel Johnson, "Mystic and Cavalier," (1895) qu. in Louis Untermeyer, *Modern British Poetry* (New York, 1936), 217.

440   **Was it mere**   EM Diary, May 17, 1981, AC.

441   **Lunch with Lucky**   Ibid., July 15, 1981, AC.

442   **Mrs. Thatcher tactfully**   Cannon, *President Reagan*, 466. The Jesuit priest referred to in the following anecdote is George H. Dunne. RR had a short, angry brush with him in February 1947. There is no evidence that Fr. Dunne was ever a Communist or Soviet agent. See *King's Pawn: The Memoirs of George H. Dunne, S.J.* (Chicago, 1990), 111–17, 152–56, 215–18; RR, *Where's the Rest of Me?*, 181–82; Jacques Attali, *Verbatim I: Chronique des Années 1981–1986* (Paris, 1993), 59.

PAGE

442   **"You don't think"**   Qu. in Attali, *Verbatim I,* 59–60. Attali, a writer and economist, served as Mitterrand's in-house intellectual from 1981 to 1991. His marvelous memoirs, half journal, half documentary scrapbook (including many direct transcriptions of top-level meetings), are not available in English. All translations in this book are by the author.

442   **The following afternoon**   Persons able to read French should check the much funnier original: Attali, *Verbatim I,* 63. See also Pierre Elliott Trudeau, *Memoirs* (Toronto, 1993), 329–32.

443   **"This is a man"**   Qu. in Attali, *Verbatim I,* 104. It is difficult to figure quite what Mitterrand meant by *libéral,* since he used the word critically: perhaps "libertarian" in the American sense.

443   **For all that**   Cannon, *President Reagan,* 467–68.

443   **The President, buoyed**   The final budget vote on July 29, 1981, had been 238 to 195 in the House, and a staggering 89 to 11 in the Senate. RR allowed himself a rare moment of self-congratulation in his diary: "This . . . is the greatest pol. win in half a century." RRP. See also RR qu. in *Newsweek,* Aug. 17, 1981.

443   **The taxi driver**   EM Diary, Aug. 5, 1981, AC.

443   **Years later**   Weinberger, *Fighting for Peace,* 176–77; RR Diary, Aug. 5, 1981, RRP.

444   **That evening, we approached**   The following account of the Sadat state dinner is based on EM Diary, Aug. 5, 1981, AC.

445   **President Sadat, I know** [facsimile]   Speech draft, Aug. 5, 1981, RRL. Note RR's emendations: (First sentence) Elimination of dull introductory link—a joke has to begin arrestingly; change of person from third to second, compelling butt of joke to listen and respond; avoidance of awkward inner rhyme *playing—creating.* (Second sentence) Colloquial lead-in; second-person construction continues; punch line changed from flat statement to pointed question. RR's sense of appropriateness caused him also to delete a punning follow-up, courtesy of the speechwriting department, about being "shot" as an actor and shot again as President. He was not averse to mordant humor in the right surroundings, but knew such a joke would not work in the brittle atmosphere of a state dinner.

446   **Sadat laughed**   In a few days, RR was to announce the resumption of warplane sales to Israel. Barrett, *Gambling with History,* 331–32. Anwar el-Sadat was assassinated on Oct. 6, 1981.

446   **The next day, Reagan**   Darman, *Who's in Control?,* 69, 94. The 1982 deficit actually totaled $113 billion. Stockman, *Triumph,* 396.

446   **There was no doubt**   Darman, *Who's in Control?,* 70. The tax cut had been negotiated down to 25 percent from his original demand for 30 percent over three years, but the superlative still applied.

446   **Stockman was now saying**   Stockman, *Triumph,* 8–9.

446   **Among all the millions**   Ibid., 271.

447   **There the two**   Darman, *Who's in Control?,* 68–70.

448   **That, as the Sovietologist**   Speaker Tip O'Neill, who visited Moscow after the PATCO strike, was struck by how seriously RR was taken by Soviet leaders as a result of his firm action. According to an O'Neill aide,

the Kremlin detected "something new in presidential policy: steel that showed." Chris Matthews interview, Jan. 7, 1988.

448   **Had the KGB**   Summaries of Congressional mail, prepared for the President by the White House Office of Legislative Affairs, Aug. 13–Sept. 10, 1981, RRL/pp/hw. Organized labor never quite forgave RR for his action in the strike. On Feb. 16, he noted in his diary, "Funny—I'm the 1st Pres. *never* invited to the AFL-CIO conventions & I'm the only Pres. who is a life time member of an AFL-CIO union." RRP.

448   **"Magnificent" though**   Weinberger, *Fighting for Peace,* 177; Barrett, *Gambling with History,* 212.

449   **Secretary Weinberger continued**   News of the continuing flights over the Gulf of Sidra did not leak to the press. Weinberger coolly mentioned them in 1990 (*Fighting for Peace,* 179). Had the press known about them in 1981, criticism of Meese would doubtless have been even stronger.

449   **Nobody seemed to remember**   Nitze, *From Hiroshima to Glasnost,* 216; EM Diary, Aug. 26, 1981, AC. *Hellcats of the Navy* (1952) was the only movie in which RR and NR co-starred.

449   **"How do we"**   RR superscript on Keith Stager to RR, Sept. 23, 1981, RRL/pp/hw.

449   **The Budget Director**   Stockman, *Triumph,* 271.

450   **Reagan agreed**   Ibid., 283, 274. An early casualty of all this brave intent was the MX-MPS (multiple protective shelter) missile system, which RR and Weinberger had always been ambivalent about because it was perceived to be a Carter program. Because of their combined prejudice, and one of RR's most embarrassing displays of public ignorance on a defense program (press conference, Oct. 2, 1981), the MX survived only as a grotesquely adapted, strategically weakened, and hugely overpriced system, a monument to partisan prejudice. See Cannon, *President Reagan,* Ch. 9.

450   **Given this determination**   Stockman, *Triumph,* 274.

450   **"Why don't you"**   Ibid., 293.

450   **Staffers ranged along**   Joseph R. Wright, Jr., interview, Nov. 20, 1995.

451   **One of the Budget**   Stockman, *Triumph,* 282; *Theodore Roosevelt Association Journal,* Vol. XI, no. 1 (Winter 1983), 2–14.

451   **Separately and together**   Darman, *Who's in Control?,* 102. Privately, RR vowed, "I will not give in and raise taxes." RR Diary, Oct. 17, 1981, RRP.

452   **Then, at 7:02**   Darman, *Who's in Control?,* 103.

452   **Late workers**   This sentence closely follows the account in von Damm, *At Reagan's Side,* 222.

452   **"He's outta here"**   Ibid., 223.

452   **"Dave," Reagan said**   Stockman, *Triumph,* 1. See ibid., 4–5, for an account of the tongue-lashing by James Baker that preceded this lunch.

452   **Their respective**   RR Diary, Nov. 12, 1981, RRP; Darman, *Who's in Control?,* 107–8; Stockman, *Triumph,* 1–3, 396.

453   **Even before Weinberger**   RR Diary, Sept. 28, 1981, RRP. NSDD-13 was signed on Oct. 2.

453   **a small plastic card**   There had been a frenzied search for the card by Secret Service agents when RR's suit was cut from him in the emergency

room after the assassination attempt. The following description of the SIOP (Single Integrated Operational Plan) is based on the reporting of David B. Ottoway and Steve Coll in "Trying to Unplug the War Machine," *The Washington Post*, Apr. 12, 1995.

453   **Now Reagan had** Nitze, *From Hiroshima to Glasnost,* 369–71. The other acronyms in this paragraph stand for Basic National Security Policy, Mutually Assured Destruction, Intercontinental Ballistic Missiles, Multiple Independently Targeted Reentry Vehicle, Sea-Launched Ballistic Missiles, and Short Range Attack Missiles.

453   **Apparently these** Ibid., 367–70. At the Ottawa economic summit in July, Reagan had tried to reassure President Mitterrand that he did not discount European feelings of vulnerability under the barrels of the Soviet arsenal. He had told the expressionless Frenchman one of his favorite stories, about the man who was convinced he was a grain of corn. "He went to a psychiatrist to be treated for delusion, and after a coupla months he seemed to be cured and the doctor discharged him. But when he goes out into the parking lot he sees a chicken, and runs back inside screaming with terror. The psychiatrist says, 'I thought you knew you're not a grain of corn any more.' The man says, 'Right, but does the *chicken* know?' " Mitterrand was reportedly charmed. Ty Cobb interview, Nov. 19, 1985.

453   **That was Reagan's** Barrett, *Gambling with History,* 203; RR Diary, May 5, 1981, RRP. Haig had shown copies of RR's handwritten letter to Brezhnev around the European diplomatic circuit, and seen how its peaceable tone impressed previous skeptics.

454   **With some misgivings** Haig, *Caveat,* 228–29. The White House Communications Office saw to it that the speech got maximum exposure, by linking the National Press Club stage to an estimated worldwide audience of two hundred million. Extraordinarily elaborate security measures added an extra note of drama, and sharp-eyed reporters perceived that the President was looking unusually broad about the chest. "Funny, I was talking peace but wearing a bullet proof vest," Reagan noted that night. "It seems Kadaffi [*sic*] put a contract on me & some person named Jack was going to try for me at the speech." RR Diary, Nov. 18, 1981, RRP. The NSC took extremely serious notice of intelligence from Libya that RR and other high-level U.S. officials were in danger. On December 8, it authorized a "secret or private warning" to Qaddafi from RR that any attack upon him or his staff would be considered "an act of war." A few days later, RR's helicopter to Camp David was diverted because of advice that a Libyan hit squad had crossed the border from Canada, and was pursuing him with hand-fired, heat-seeking missiles. RR Diary, Dec. 8 and 11, 1981, RRP.

454   **His sober speech** RR Diary, Nov. 21, 1981, RRP. RR's speech was praised by *The New York Times* and *The Washington Post*. Similar enthusiastic reactions were voiced in Western Europe. For a contextual analysis, see Whittle Johnson, "The Reagan Revolution and German Democracy," in Carl Hodge and Cathan Nolan, eds., *Shepherd of Democracy? America and Germany in the Twentieth Century* (Westport,

Conn., 1992). RR proposed the dismantling of 250 Russian SS-20 medium-range missiles, plus 350 SS-5s and SS-4s, in exchange for non-deployment of 108 U.S. Pershing II and 464 cruise missiles. In terms of actual warheads deliverable by these two forces, the Soviets would lose 1,100, the NATO countries 572. *Time,* Nov. 30, 1981. It could be argued that RR, by announcing such a drastic arms-control initiative so flamboyantly, was playing into Weinberger's hands after all, because Brezhnev could not agree to zero-zero without giving the impression of being bullied. Russia, being on the opposite side of the strategic mirror, saw Pershings as American missiles capable of hitting "targets almost everywhere in the European part of the Soviet Union," whereas SS-20s could not hit any part of the United States. Dobrynin, *In Confidence,* 430.

454   **On December 13** "Our intelligence is that it was engineered and ordered by the Soviet [Union]." RR Diary, Dec. 12–13, 1981, RRP. The reports were correct. See Christopher Andrew and Oleg Gordievsky, *KGB: The Inside Story of Its Foreign Operations from Lenin to Gorbachev* (New York, 1990), 581–82.

454   **By the time** Dobrynin, *In Confidence,* 482, 495, 504.

454   **Reagan did not seem** RR Diary, Dec. 21, 1981; Jan. 5, 26, 29, 1982, RRP.

455   **"a fucking"** Haig qu. Michael Deaver interview, June 5, 1989.

455   **Unlike Haig** Barrett, *Gambling with History,* 328; Anderson, *Revolution,* 96–97.

455   **When Reagan snuck** Another frequent guest was Commerce Secretary Malcolm Baldrige, a champion rodeo roper who had been out riding when RR called to appoint him. "That's my kind of man," the President-elect said approvingly. Von Damm, *At Reagan's Side,* 140.

455   **The relationship went** Paul Haerle Oral History, RRH; author's group interview with RR gubernatorial associates, Aug. 12, 1988; Robert Moretti Oral History, RRL. Laurence Barrett indulges a witty fantasy of RR making his movie comeback in "a film biography of Bill Clark" in *Gambling with History,* 326. For an extended portrait of Clark, see Barrett, Ch. 18.

456   **"You can't just** *walk*" Lyn Nofziger interview, July 13, 1991.

456   **Instead of boring** Clark, qu. in Cannon, *President Reagan,* 157; William P. Clark, Jr., interview, Dec. 20, 1993 ("I knew from Sacramento days that he liked celluloid"); Woodward, *Veil,* 248–49.

457   **yet on April 10** Mikhail Gorbachev, *Memoirs* (New York, 1996), 126. According to Andrew and Gordievsky, *KGB,* 582, Andropov had been instrumental in encouraging Brezhnev to impose martial law in Poland.

457   **This made him** Barrett, *Gambling with History,* 314, has an amusing footnote regarding the original coinage of START. But see also Anderson, *Revolution,* 72.

457   **(we may as well)** John Hutton interview, May 8, 1991; John Hutton Diary, Dec. 29, 1985, JHP; RR interview, May 29, 1987.

458   **I think people** RR interview, May 29, 1987.

458   **"And when we sit"** Qu. Barrett, *Gambling with History,* 320.

458   **The speech** John Newhouse, *War and Peace,* 345–46; Dobrynin, *In*

Confidence, 502–3. Andropov had been convinced since at least May 1981 that the Reagan Administration was intent on nuclear war with the Soviet Union. Andrew and Gordievsky, *KGB,* 584.

459   **He instructed his**   The term *one-sided* was used by Brezhnev in his formal letter to RR accepting the idea of resumed strategic-arms talks in Geneva. He went on to accuse RR of wanting to upset "the existing balance of forces" worldwide. "He means 'imbalance,'" RR wrote in the margin, and, farther down, "He's a barrel of laughs." RR, *An American Life,* 553–54.

459   **Clark, meanwhile**   Georgetown University Center for Strategic and International Studies, May 21, 1982; Ilya Zemtsov, *Andropov: Policy Dilemmas and the Struggle for Power* (Jerusalem, 1983), iii.

459   **The United States, Clark**   TASS wire report, May 22, 1982, CLA.

459   **The statistics of decline were**   Gorbachev, *Memoirs,* 117–18, 135; Murray Feshbach and Alfred Friendly, Jr., *Ecocide in the USSR* (New York, 1992), Ch. 3–5. The latter work is a definitive survey of the physical degradation of the Soviet Union in its last years.

460   **Three days after**   Gorbachev, *Memoirs,* 127, 133.

460   **"Poland is not"**   Dobrynin, *In Confidence,* 500.

460   **So Reagan**   Carl Bernstein, "The Holy Alliance," *Time,* Feb. 24, 1992. This important article was written with help from William Clark. It was later expanded into a political biography of Pope John Paul II, *His Holiness* (New York, 1996), that makes much of slim evidence that the Vatican and the Reagan Administration were engaged in a massive plot to bring about Polish independence. See Garry Wills, "All the Pope's Men," *The New Yorker,* Dec. 2, 1996.

460   **Early in June**   RR Diary, May 24, 1982, RRP.

460   **His principal statement**   RR, *An American Life,* 555; Margaret Thatcher, *The Downing Street Years* (New York, 1993), 233, 258; RR Westminster Address speech file, RRL; Cannon, *President Reagan,* 314–17.

461   **Two days later**   Michael Deaver interview, Aug. 6, 1990; RR interview, Mar. 22, 1985; perspective drawing of Berlin Wall checkpoint, RRL/pp; Barrett, *Gambling with History,* 254.

461   **On midsummer days**   RR column in Des Moines *Dispatch,* ca. June 21, 1936, Nelle Reagan Scrapbook, RRL/pp.

462   **He had known**   RR Diary, June 7, 1981, RRP. According to ibid., June 16, President Carter had approved such an attack in advance, but neglected to inform him. RR accordingly accepted Begin's explanation that the reactor was on the verge of producing anti-Israel weapons. He wasted no sympathy on the Iraqi leader, whom he despised. "Saddam Hussein is a 'no good nut.' . . . He has called for the destruction of Israel & he want to be the leader of the Arab world—that's why he invaded Iran." Ibid., June 11.

462   **Meanwhile, American-built**   Weinberger, *Fighting for Peace,* 142.

462   **Israel's declaration**   William P. Clark, Jr., interview, Dec. 20, 1993; Haig, *Caveat,* 312. For some unpleasant examples of "the hazing of Al Haig," see Speakes, *Speaking Out,* 77.

PAGE

462   **"It's amazing"**   RR Diary, June 14, 1982, RRP.

462   **Clark's first choice**   William P. Clark, Jr., interview, Dec. 20, 1993; Cannon, *President Reagan,* 347–49.

463   **Clark asked what**   William P. Clark, Jr., interview, Dec. 20, 1993.

463   **Reagan did not**   William P. Clark, Jr., interview, Dec. 20, 1993; Haig, *Caveat,* 314. Since the Inauguration, Shultz had visited the White House regularly as chairman of RR's Economic Policy Advisory Board. This group, whose membership included Milton Friedman and Alan Greenspan, was influential in support of RR's tax and spending cuts in 1981. Martin Anderson interview, Sept. 5, 1998.

463   **Haig spent**   William P. Clark interview, Dec. 20, 1993; Haig, *Caveat,* 315.

463   **He opposed it**   Robert C. McFarlane, *Special Trust* (New York, 1994); Weinberger, *Fighting for Peace,* 143–45. For the genesis of the peace initiative, see Shultz, *Turmoil and Triumph,* 85–96.

464   **What Weinberger**   Weinberger, *Fighting for Peace,* 152–53. McFarlane, *Special Trust,* 210, makes a bitter accusation that Weinberger was "criminally irresponsible" for ordering U.S. Marines to leave Lebanon on Sept. 14, after the roving U.S. Ambassador, Philip Habib, had pledged they would stay "up to thirty days" after the departure of the PLO. Weinberger defines the understanding as "after ten quiet days" (150). The last remnants of the PLO were gone by Sept. 1. McFarlane does not allow for the fact that the Phalangist killing squad might simply have delayed its massacre in the event of a later withdrawal of Marines.

464   **Its ostensible purpose**   Shultz, *Turmoil and Triumph,* 104–11; Grace Halsell, *Prophecy and Politics: Militant Evangelists on the Road to Nuclear War* (Westport, Conn., 1986), 76; Weinberger, *Fighting for Peace,* 150–53.

464   **Ronald Reagan's was biblical**   William Clark felt that RR's attitude toward Israel had been permanently affected by his exposure to raw concentration-camp footage in April 1945. (See pp. 215–16) "I've always felt that he overreacted to the Holocaust—its horrors left such a mark on him that he let his emotions flow into almost any issue involving Israel—almost as if he were compensating." Interview, Dec. 30, 1993.

464   **which had divers**   Ezekiel 17:3. For the pro-invasion influence upon RR of the combined Moral Majority/Israel lobbies in 1982–83, see Halsell, *Prophecy and Politics,* 74–77.

465   **"I've always felt"**   Interview, Dec. 30, 1993.

465   **I told him**   RR Diary, Aug. 12, 1982, RRP.

465   **Robert McFarlane, listening**   Ibid. This anecdote has been subjected to the vagaries of memory. Michael Deaver, who was also present (at the President's morning national-security briefing, Aug. 12, 1982), claims to have initiated the call by threatening to resign if RR did not do something about the continuing bombardment. McFarlane writes that RR "surprised us by picking up the telephone" in the midst of a harangue on the horrors of the previous night's TV news (209). However, RR's diary states that what upset him was a "desperate" call from Philip Habib, describing the carnage. Deaver, *Behind the Scenes,* 166; McFarlane, *Special Trust,* 208–9.

PAGE

465   **Reagan has been** Cannon, *President Reagan,* 486–89; Michael Korda, *Another Life* (New York, 1999), 472. Cannon errs only in saying that the images RR remembers were those shown in U.S. theaters: the FMPU footage (shot by Owen Crump's combat camera crew in early April) was processed and cut for private showing to Pentagon officials, and RR was responsible for its dispatch to Washington. William Graf and Owen Crump interviews, Oct. 1, 1992; Shultz, *Turmoil and Triumph,* 550–51.

465   **What matters, surely** RR was seventy-eight, and thirty-four floors above the Avenue of the Stars in Century City, when he revisited Ohrdruf. Korda, *Another Life,* 470–71.

466   **All the above discussion** Teller was talking about the "miniature" nuclear explosions needed in exo-atmospheric space to precipitate an aimable X-ray laser. RR Diary, Sept. 14, 1982, RRP; Edward Teller, interviewed by Donald R. Baucom, Nov. 11, 1987, RRL/oh. See Anderson, *Revolution,* 90–95, for background.

466   **"Just tell"** Cannon, *President Reagan,* 311; Nitze, *From Hiroshima to Glasnost,* 388–89. The openings derived from Nitze's famous "walk in the woods" with his Soviet counterpart, Yuli Kvitsinskiy, on July 16, 1982. See Nitze, 376ff.

466   **At home** Darman, *Who's in Control?,* 113; Bill Adler, ed., *Kids' Letters to President Reagan* (New York, 1982), 16. According to Milton Friedman, RR was seduced into his 1982 tax increase by a promise of a three-dollar-to-one return in revenues. Friedman interview, Aug. 11, 1989.

466   **Even the free-market** Darman, *Who's in Control?,* 113.

466   **Michael Deaver came** Michael Deaver interview, Aug. 6, 1990.

466   **He was dressed** The following account is taken from EM Diary, Oct. 27, 1982, AC.

467   **When he stood** RR speech script, TRA lunch, Oct. 27, 1982, RRL/pp/hw.

467   **Six nights later** See Barrett, *Gambling with History,* 1–5, for an eyewitness account of RR's subdued reaction to the election results. RR memo (with attachment) to Secretary of Agriculture, ca. Nov. 30, 1982, RRL/pp/hw.

467   **In public, the President** Barrett, *Gambling with History,* 8. The advisers who tried in vain to persuade RR to attend Brezhnev's funeral included Robert McFarlane and George Shultz.

467   **"We had rabbits"** RR Diary, Dec. 7, 1982, RRP.

468   **The accession** Gorbachev, *Memoirs;* RR Diary, Nov. 16, 1982, RRP; Shultz, *Turmoil and Triumph,* 126–27.

468   **Reagan had to ponder** Martin Anderson interview, Aug. 8, 1989; Anderson, *Revolution,* 97.

468   **The National Security Adviser** Anderson, *Revolution,* 97; McFarlane, *Special Trust,* 226–27. These two sources conflict over who authorized whom in the early stages of SDI policy initiation. Anderson meticulously lists several meetings, between Sept. 14, 1981, and Jan. 8, 1982, when a group of non-governmental consultants, including Edward Teller and members of RR's Californian "Kitchen Cabinet," pressed the philosophy of missile defense on senior presidential aides. RR himself dropped by the last of these meetings, and took a "lively" interest in the

proceedings for as long as he stayed. McFarlane's account betrays a bureaucratic reluctance to acknowledge the influence of lobbyists on policy. He does not mention Teller's key visit to the Oval Office on Sept. 14, 1982, and claims to have reawakened RR's interest in strategic defense some three months later. His book *in toto* is so querulous (an appendix reproduces many testimonial letters and commissions in facsimile) as to arouse doubts about its objectivity.

468   **"Act as if"** Gorbachev, *Memoirs,* 146.

30: Huge Cloudy Symbols of a High Romance

469   **At first, in** For an eyewitness account of RR's speech, see Darman, *Who's in Control?,* 115–18.

470   **Only those** Michael Deaver interview, Jan. 6, 1995; Darman, *Who's in Control?,* 119. The latter wittily compares Moynihan's orchestration of the ovation to the "Marseillaise" scene in *Casablanca.*

470   **On February 11** RR to Robert Dick, June 1988, RRL/pp/hw; RR, *An American Life,* 550; Cannon, *President Reagan,* 320; Donald Baucom, *The Origins of SDI, 1944–1983* (Lawrence, Kans., 1992), 15–16.

470   **What Reagan meant** RR, *An American Life,* 548; Don Oberdorfer, *The Turn: From the Cold War to a New Era—The U.S. and the Soviet Union, 1983–1990* (New York, 1991), 26–27; Kenneth Adelman interview, Nov. 9, 1998; George A. Keyworth II, oral history interview with Donald R. Baucom, Sept. 28, 1987 [hereafter Keyworth/Baucom interview], RRL/oh.

470   **So much for** Edward Teller interviewed by Donald R. Baucom, Nov. 11, 1987, RRL/oh; Anderson, *Revolution,* 82–83. See ibid., Ch. 9, and Baucom, *Origins of SDI,* for detailed accounts of RR's pre-SDI defense education.

471   **At that time** RR schedule and briefing papers, Feb. 11, 1983, RRL. See also Lord (Solly) Zuckerman, *Star Wars in a Nuclear World* (New York, 1987), 134–35.

471   **a million Hiroshimas** Twenty-four countries shared these weapons, or the technology to produce them quickly and cheaply. The United States alone had more than ten thousand strategic nuclear weapons (i.e., warheads deliverable to Soviet territory by missiles or bombers), and the Soviet Union eight thousand—which conflicts with Teller's notion of Kremlin "superiority." Oberdorfer, *The Turn,* 32.

471   **"We should protect"** Smith, *Power Game,* 607; Keyworth/Baucom interview, RRL/oh; Weinberger, *Fighting for Peace,* 304. RR's diary entry ran as follows: "So far the only policy worldwide on nuclear weapons is to have a deterrent. What if we were to tell the world that we want to protect our people not avenge them; that we are going to embark on a program of research to come up with a defensive weapon that could make nuclear weapons obsolete?" Feb. 11, 1983, RRP.

471   **He asked the Chiefs** Smith, *Power Game,* 609; Keyworth/Baucom interview, RRL/oh.

471   **"None of us"** Robert McFarlane interview, Feb. 28, 1994; EM Diary,

Feb. 14, 1983, AC. "I want to remove the threat of war in our relations," RR told Anatoly Dobrynin in an extraordinary private audience the following day. "I want a positive turn." Neither Dobrynin nor George Shultz, sitting in, understood what the President was talking about, but both noticed his unusual animation. Dobrynin, *In Confidence,* 517–20; Shultz, *Turmoil and Triumph,* 164–65.

471 **Yet, even as** The Catholic bishops had greatly annoyed RR in 1982 by endorsing the Soviet-inspired freeze movement in Europe, thereby encouraging its spread to the United States. Dolan had been an undergraduate at Yale when Reagan visited the campus as a Chubb Fellow in December 1967, and had ideologically fallen in love with him then and there. He won his Pulitzer for investigative reporting in 1978. The best and most eccentric of RR's writers, Dolan wrote the 1982 Westminster Address and the 1988 speech to Moscow University students, as well as the speech under discussion. Anthony R. Dolan interview by Marion Elizabeth Rodgers, Dec. 20, 1988.

472 **However, two foreigners** Transcript of Solzhenitsyn speech, June 30, 1975, in George Meany Memorial Archives, Silver Spring, Md.; Alexandre de Maranches, *The Evil Empire: The Third World War Now* (London, 1988), 102; Arnaud de Borchgrave interview, July 1, 1995.

472 **"You are the American"** Alexandre de Maranches to RR, Dec. 15, 1980, qu. in Arnaud de Borchgrave, the *Washington Times,* June 18, 1995.

472 **Ironically, for an** The complete text of RR's "Evil Empire" speech is available in Erickson, *Reagan Speaks,* 155–66.

473 **The reaction to Reagan's** Qu. in *Historic Documents of 1983* (Washington, D.C., 1984), 270.

473 **The consensus of critics** See Robert Ivie, "Speaking 'Common Sense' about the Soviet Threat: Reagan's Rhetorical Threat," *Western Journal of Speech Communications* 48 (1984): 39–40.

473 **In an official** Qu. TASS, Mar. 9, 1983; Andrew and Gordievsky, *KGB,* 590; Feshbach and Friendly, *Ecocide in the USSR,* 61–66; James Billington interview, May 4, 1993; Robert Conquest, *The Great Terror: A Reassessment* (New York, 1989); L. H. Gann and Peter Duigan, *World War II and the Beginning of the Cold War* (Stanford, Calif., 1996), 7.

474 **Western travelers who** Max Kampelman interview, Nov. 21, 1994. For a ten-year retrospective on the Evil Empire speech by its author, see Anthony R. Dolan, "Premeditated Prose: Reagan's Evil Empire," *The American Enterprise,* Mar./Apr. 1993.

474 **Let me share** *Historic Documents of 1983,* 315–16 (emphasis added).

475 **Shultz's rage** Keyworth/Baucom interview, RRL/oh; President's Remarks, 6:15 P.M., Mar. 23, 1983, RRL/pp/hw.

475 **Dr. George A. "Jay"** George Keyworth interview, Dec. 31, 1985; Smith, *Power Game,* 610 ("Keyworth told others Teller was his intellectual 'father' ").

475 **Even he had been** George Keyworth interview, Dec. 31, 1985. According to McFarlane, *Special Trust,* 230, RR specifically charged him with

executing the first draft. "I want you to keep this tightly under wraps." Shultz's first sight of it was on the afternoon of Mar. 21, 1983. William P. Clark, Jr., interview, Feb. 6, 1994; Shultz, *Turmoil and Triumph,* 246–50.

475   **The Secretary of State**   EM Diary, Apr. 6, 1983, and EM Notes, 1985–1989; confidential source, May 27, 1987. Persons interested to know what Shultz looked like on a bad day should consult Balthus's famous portrait of André Derain, or p. 78 of William Steig, *The Lonely Ones* (New York, 1942). The latter work is incidentally a prescient gallery of future Reagan Era familiars. See its uncanny representations of James Baker as a man of glass (12), Alexander Haig (14), Nancy Reagan (20), Raymond Donovan hung out to dry (22), Richard Darman (24), shuttle diplomat Robert McFarlane (26), Jeane Kirkpatrick (30), Admiral John Poindexter (34), Lyn Nofziger (46), Edwin Meese (50), George Bush (52), Patti Davis (58), Jimmy Carter on Inauguration Eve, 1981 (68), Caspar Weinberger (68), Shultz on a good day (72), Michael Deaver *agonistes* (74), Ringmaster Donald Regan (76), James Watt (88), David Stockman (92), and First Daughter Maureen Reagan (102).

475   **A veteran of**   Alexander Haig described Shultz to Anatoly Dobrynin as "alien to fantasy and hasty improvisation" and "something of a slow coach." Dobrynin, *In Confidence,* 507. For an example of Shultz's native caution, note how carefully he disclaims responsibility for, while expressing after-the-fact agreement with, the "Evil Empire" speech: "How conscious of the implications of their words the president and his speechwriters were, I do not know. Whether or not he was wise to use this phrase to describe the Soviet Union, it was in fact an Evil Empire and evil abounded." Shultz, *Turmoil and Triumph,* 266–67.

475   **He particularly mistrusted**   Defense Secretary Weinberger was in Lisbon on Mar. 22 and 23. Although surprised by the timing of the SDI announcement, he knew it was coming, and fully supported it. Weinberger, *Fighting for Peace,* 305–6.

476   **As described by**   The following description of the SDI is taken from the best analysis of the system in its prime: John A. Adam and Mark Fischetti, "SDI: The Grand Experiment," *IEEE Spectrum,* Sept. 1985. George Shultz is sure he saw the phrase "evil empire" in the speech draft transmitted to him on Mar. 22, 1983. Shultz, *Turmoil and Triumph,* 251.

476   **The whole concept**   Adam and Fischetti, "SDI"; Fred Iklé, RR's Undersecretary of Defense for Policy, has suggested that RR seized on the SDI as an imaginative response to the unimaginableness of MAD: "a metaphor to combat that illegitimate situation." "The Cold War: Ten Years Later," RRL, conference transcript, Nov. 13, 1995.

476   **In which case**   Sonnet, "When I Have Fears," Jan. 31, 1818, *The Poetical Works of John Keats* (London, 1910), 303.

476   **To the more**   Keyworth/Baucom interview, RRL/oh; Shultz, *Turmoil and Triumph,* 250; Smith, *Power Game,* 614. For RR's last-minute notification of his European allies, see Attali, *Verbatim I,* 400–401, but note that Attali misplaces the letter under "22 February." It should be transposed with the one reproduced on p. 416 under "23 March."

PAGE

476   **Each Party**   ABM Treaty, Article 5.1, qu. in Nitze, *From Hiroshima to Glasnost,* 476 (emphasis added). For a comprehensive analysis of Reagan Administration arms-control policy *vis-à-vis* the Treaty, see ibid., 467–74.

477   **"I can see"**   Shultz, *Turmoil and Triumph,* 252–53.

477   **As Martin Anderson once**   Anderson, qu. in Jaquelin Hume interview by Donald Baucom, Oct. 28, 1987, RRL/oh; Shultz, *Turmoil and Triumph,* 255.

477   **I call upon**   RR handwritten insert on speech draft, Mar. 22, 1983, RRL/pp/hw. Both Keyworth and McFarlane tried in vain to get RR to delete the last three words. Smith, *Power Game,* 610–12.

477   **After the television**   RR Diary, Mar. 23, 1983, RRP.

477   **So it was**   Adam and Fischetti, "SDI." Teller had been honest enough to use the adjective *nuclear* in describing his laser experiments to Reagan, but presumably he avoided the more graphic qualifier *bomb-based.* For a concise summary of negative scientific criticism of the SDI, see Zuckerman, *Star Wars,* Ch. 4.

478   **This hardly assuaged**   RR Diary, Dec. 6, 1982, RRP. His daughter had enraged him by inveigling him into a confrontation with Helen Caldicott ("a round the clock anti-nuke lecturer and writer"). See Patti Davis, *The Way I See It,* 294–97.

478   **Yuri Andropov came**   Andropov, qu. by TASS in *The New York Times,* Mar. 27, 1983; Gorbachev, *Memoirs,* 215. The Soviet figure might have been slightly lower in March 1983, but this was the *status quo ante* General Secretary Gorbachev inherited in March 1983. He reported that military R&D consumed twenty of the twenty-five billion roubles allotted to science, and assessed defense spending at 20 percent of GNP.

478   **During all the**   EM Diary, Feb. 15, 1983, AC.

478   **Ronald Reagan was not**   Cannon, *Reagan,* 151; Arnold Kramish in *The Washington Post,* Mar. 31, 1983, replying to McGeorge Bundy's criticism of the SDI in ibid., Mar. 28, 1983.

479   **Reagan followed his**   Weinberger, *Fighting for Peace,* 310–11.

479   **The President signed**   Richard Darman to RR, Mar. 26, 1983, RRL/pp/hw. The article was subsequently republished under RR's name, along with afterwords by C. Everett Koop and Malcolm Muggeridge, as *Abortion and the Conscience of the Nation* (Nashville, Tenn., 1983). For another view of RR's anti-abortion philosophy, see Morris, "In Memoriam Christine Reagan."

480   **The person most**   Dobrynin, *In Confidence,* 529.

480   **A sudden disaster**   Woodward, *Veil,* 246; RR Diary, Apr. 18–19, 1983.

480   **At Andrews Air**   RR Diary, Apr. 23, 1983.

481   **TODAY . . .**   RR speech draft, ca. Apr. 22, 1983, RRL/pp/hw.

481   **This was a juncture**   The agreement, signed on May 17, 1983, was negotiated only between Israel and Lebanon. Shultz, making his first major attempt at a diplomatic negotiation, assumed that Syria would approve it as a *fait accompli.* This President Hafez al-Assad declined to do. McFarlane, *Special Trust,* 240–41; Cannon, *President Reagan,* 411–14; Shultz, *Turmoil and Triumph,* Ch. 14; Weinberger, *Fighting for Peace,* 155–56.

481   **By then Reagan**   McFarlane, *Special Trust,* 244ff.

482   **Reagan liked the last**   William P. Clark, Jr., interview, Feb. 6, 1994.

482   **Neither of these**   Shultz, *Turmoil and Triumph,* 292–97; William P. Clark, Jr., interview, Feb. 6, 1994.

482   **On the other**   Peter Kornbluh and Malcolm Byrne, eds., *The Iran-Contra Scandal: The Declassified History* (New York, 1993), 11 (document facsimile); Cannon, *President Reagan,* 355.

482   **"all of Central America"**   RR Diary, Jan. 26, 1983, RRP.

482   **Congressional opinion**   *Report of the Congressional Committees Investigating the Iran-Contra Affair,* 100th Cong., 1st sess., 1987, 32–33.

483   **"Congress," Reagan fumed**   RR Diary, Apr. 26, 1983, RRP.

483   **As was his habit**   RR speech draft, ca. Apr. 25, 1983, RRL/pp/hw.

483   **"The tiny island"**   RR mentioned here the recent impoundment of some Nicaragua-bound Libyan cargo planes while refueling in Brazil. Their consignment of "medical supplies" had turned out to be munitions. Had Grenada's air base been ready, "those planes could have refueled there & completed their journey." Ibid. See also Steven Emerson, *Secret Warriors: Inside the Covert Military Operations of the Reagan Era* (New York, 1988), 122–23.

483   **Reagan permitted**   RR speech draft, ca. Apr. 25, 1983, RRL/pp/hw; James Monroe message to Congress, Dec. 23, 1923, qu. in Daniel J. Boorstin, ed., *An American Primer,* vol. 1 (Chicago, 1966), 257.

484   **Baker, Deaver, and Meese**   For a good example of troika interaction, see the various drafts of RR's speech in boxes 31–32, RRL/pp/hw. There are copious marginalia contributed by RR, Meese, and Deaver. The absence of such by Baker are equally revealing. As William Clark remarked to the author, "Jim's action was always like a cat's—no print, no marks." Interview, Dec. 20, 1993.

484   **Their colleagues**   Cannon, *President Reagan,* 359–60.

484   **A feeling of declining**   RR Diary, May 10 and 16, 1983, RRP; von Damm, *At Reagan's Side,* vii–x. Ambassador von Damm proved to be an energetic and innovative diplomat, but these attributes never quite overcame local prejudices, let alone NR's constant pressure to have her recalled. She sealed her own fate by falling in love with Peter Gürtler, a member of the Sacher Hotel dynasty, and not bothering to conceal the fact that they were cohabiting. When she divorced her third husband to marry Gürtler, the Austrian Prime Minister allegedly informed the White House that "she was no longer a credible representative of America." Shultz demanded her resignation on June 8, 1985. Shultz, *Turmoil and Triumph,* 562–63. See also von Damm, *At Reagan's Side,* 299–303.

485   **On May 27**   RR Diary, May 26, 1983, RRP; Cannon, *President Reagan,* 56–57.

485   **The subsequent proceedings**   Thatcher, *Downing Street Years,* 301; RR, *An American Life,* 351.

486   **Reagan ranged**   RR, *An American Life,* 351; RR Diary, May 27–31, 1983, RRP; Thatcher, *Downing Street Years,* 300.

486   **Neither François Mitterrand**   RR Diary, May 27–31, 1983, RRP; Thatcher, *Downing Street Years,* 300; Attali, *Verbatim I,* 453–55. "If I

don't stop this text," Mitterrand whispered to his aide, "France will be without nuclear weapons in ten years."

486   **For the first**   RR Diary, May 27–31, 1983, RRP; Attali, *Verbatim I,* 456. *La gloire de la France* was preserved by means of occasionally substituting the phrase *some of us* for the word *we.*

486   **"Except,"**   Thatcher, *Downing Street Years,* 300.

486   **he had plainly**   Ibid., 300–301. By refusing to let the summit be directed by a prearranged communiqué, as was customary, RR was able to bring Japan into the Western security alliance for the first time, and greatly strengthen the United States's negotiatory hand at the INF talks in Geneva. See Shultz, *Turmoil and Triumph,* 354–57, and *The Washington Post,* June 1, 1983: "Mr. Reagan personally acted very much the leader of the alliance. . . . [He] will take political credit for his performance, and has every right to."

487   **On the same**   Michael Petit, *Peacekeepers at War* (Boston, 1986), 46–47, 161.

487   **The failure**   Weinberger, *Fighting for Peace,* 156–58.

487   **The Secretary of Defense argued**   Ibid. According to Shultz, *Turmoil and Triumph,* 221, the shells from the Chouf Mountains were fired by Druse militia at the behest of Syria, to increase pressure on the United States to withdraw.

487   **"We're losing"**   RR Diary, June 26, 1983, RRP.

487   **At this moment**   Ibid., July 6, 1983, RRP. Andropov had just been appointed chairman of the Soviet Defense Council and chairman of the Presidium of the Supreme Soviet, making his titles constitutionally equivalent to RR's as President and Commander in Chief.

487   **It was, of all**   Oberdorfer, *The Turn,* 37–38.

488   **Defense experts**   Ibid., 38–39. RR's final handwritten text is reproduced in Shultz, *Turmoil and Triumph,* 359.

488   **On July 25**   RR Diary, July 25, 1983, RRP; Shultz, *Turmoil and Triumph,* 312–13; McFarlane, *Special Trust,* 237–44. See also Cannon, *President Reagan,* 416–17.

488   **"There is no"**   Shultz, *Turmoil and Triumph,* 313; William Clark, Jr., interview, Dec. 20, 1993.

488   **The President listened**   RR Diary, May 10, July 13 and 25, 1983, RRP; William Clark, Jr., interview, Dec. 20, 1993.

489   **Reagan, looking**   Shultz, *Turmoil and Triumph,* 313.

489   **Shultz's self-confidence**   *Time,* Aug. 8, 1983. See also "The Influence of William Clark," *The New York Times Magazine,* Aug. 14, 1983.

489   **The worst of these**   Ibid. The vote (228–195) had been prompted by RR's announcement, on July 20, of a six-month program of U.S./Honduran military maneuvers, set to begin in August along three of Nicaragua's four borders.

490   **Shultz did not**   Shultz, *Turmoil and Triumph,* 317.

490   **August came**   *The Washington Post,* Aug. 8–9, 1983. By the end of August, statistics showed that the month had been the hottest one in history for the country as a whole, with average temperatures in many areas running eight degrees above normal. The bizarre weather affecting much of

the planet, with dry areas getting drier and wet areas succumbing to floods and tidal waves, was ascribed to El Niño.

491   **One's sense**   McFarlane, *Special Trust,* 244–48. At one point McFarlane's own stone-faced stiffness cracked, and he ended up in what one observer called "a barracks-room diatribe" against Israeli negotiators. Shultz, *Turmoil and Triumph,* 318–19.

491   **Feelings of paralysis**   *The Washington Post,* Aug. 20, 1983. Andropov's announcement was made to a delegation of nine U.S. Senators.

492   **For whatever reason**   The best recent account of the 1983 Korean Air Lines tragedy is Murray Sayle, "Closing the File on Flight 007." *The New Yorker,* Dec. 13, 1993. Seymour M. Hersh, *"The Target Is Destroyed": What Really Happened to Flight 007 and What America Knew About It* (New York, 1986), 24–29, is detailed but dated, due to release of new information summarized by Sayle.

492   **KE007 left the peninsula**   Tokyo time for the attack was 3:26 A.M. It is difficult to get a narrative sense of the unfolding of the KE007 incident, due the wide range of latitudes between the Far East and Washington, local variations on standard time, and the confusing interposition of the International Date Line. The following table shows how the main events related to RR's time frame in California (right-hand column).

TIME ZONE	DATE	EVENT	PACIFIC COAST TIME
4:00 A.M. Alaska time	Aug. 31	007 leaves Anchorage	6:00 A.M. Aug. 31
2:33 A.M. Tokyo time	Sept. 1	007 enters Soviet radarscope	10:33 A.M. Aug. 31
3:26 A.M. Tokyo time	Sept. 1	007 fired on	11:26 A.M. Aug. 31
3:38 A.M. Tokyo time	Sept. 1	007 hits water	11:38 A.M. Aug. 31
7:10 P.M. EST	Aug. 31	First CRITIC alert	4:10 P.M. Aug. 31
9:05 P.M. EST	Aug. 31	Second CRITIC alert	6:05 P.M. Aug. 31
	Aug. 31	Clark, in Calif., tells RR 007 missing	7:30 P.M. Aug. 31
	Aug. 31	Clark, second call; Soviets suspected	10:30 P.M. Aug. 31
1:53 A.M. EST	Sept. 1	CIA deduces Soviet responsibility	10:53 P.M. Aug. 31
6:30 A.M. EST	Sept. 1	Shultz, in D.C., informed of shootdown	3:30 A.M. Sept. 1
8:22 A.M. EST	Sept. 1	Shultz briefs Clark by phone	5:22 A.M. Sept. 1
	Sept. 1	Meese briefs RR at ranch	7:05 A.M. Sept. 1
10:45 A.M. EST	Sept. 1	Shultz announces shootdown	7:45 A.M. Sept. 1

492   **The first CRITIC**   Hersh, *"The Target,"* 66; Oberdorfer, *The Turn,* 52.

492   **Not until he was**   RR, *An American Life,* 582–83; Andrew and Gordievsky, *KGB,* 596. *Yolki palki,* according to Andrew and Gordievsky, may be roughly translated as "Holy shit!" When the recording was played to the UN General Assembly later by Ambassador Jeane Kirkpatrick, this expletive was prudishly rendered as "Fiddlesticks!"

492   **Edwin Meese came**   Speaker Tip O'Neill and many press reports tried to foment the impression that RR had again been allowed to sleep

through a crisis, as in August 1981. This time, however, he was in full possession of the known facts before he elected to go to bed and not "overreact." He was certainly better briefed than George Shultz, who learned nothing of the crisis until 6:30 A.M., EST, the following day. Oberdorfer, *The Turn,* 52; Shultz, *Turmoil and Triumph,* 361–62.

493   **Reagan allowed**   RR Diary, Sept. 2, 1983, RRP; RR, qu. in Shultz, *Turmoil and Triumph,* 366. Larry Speakes, the White House Deputy Press Secretary, was so nonplussed by the President's silence that weekend that he actually fabricated some wrathful Reagan quotations. They had little effect except to destroy Speakes's own reputation when, years later, he boasted about what he had done. Speakes, *Speaking Out,* 121.

493   **Not until Monday**   RR Diary, Sept. 5, 1983, RRP; RR speech draft, Sept. 5, 1983, RRL/hw. RR proudly quoted this passage himself in *An American Life,* 583–84. Part of his speech, and the Soviet aircheck quoted above, can be heard in the audiobook version of this biography.

494   **This apparent weakness**   Oberdorfer, *The Turn,* 59; *Time,* Sept. 19, 1993; Drew, *American Journal,* 141; RR to John A. Lindon, ca. Sept. 10, 1983, RRL/pp/hw.

494   **We now know**   Sayle, "Closing the File." This article is based on "Secret of the Korean Boeing 747," a long series of investigative reports by Andrei Illesh, published by the official Soviet newspaper *Izvestiya* in 1991, importantly supplemented by the Andropov documents, which came to light a year later and were released to the International Civil Aviation Organization, by order of President Boris Yeltsin, in 1993. Although Andropov did not actually write Article 36 of the Law of the State Border, it was, as Illesh notes, "adopted with [his] direct participation" on May 11, 1983. General Ivan M. Tretyak was subsequently promoted to commander of all Soviet Air Defense Forces.

494   **Reagan, then**   According to Dobrynin, *In Confidence,* 537, Andropov privately acknowledged that the shootdown had been a "gross blunder" on the part of his Defense Ministry. He nevertheless shared a general Politburo conviction that KE007 had been engaged in espionage, a conviction that lasted until long after the last piece of child's clothing had been fished from the crash site.

494   **No number**   Qu. in Sayle, "Closing the File." Ogarkov was the Soviet Chief of Staff. In 1993, Aleksandr Zuyer, a defecting, high-level Russian pilot, reported on U.S. television that the failure to identify KE007 properly was the result of a panic on Sakhalin Island. Apparently, local radars had been leveled in a freak storm two weeks before and were not yet fixed, despite orders from Moscow to do so at once. The passage of a giant intruder over the island compelled local officials to react violently, or face the consequences of their dereliction. *60 Minutes,* Jan. 4, 1993; *The New York Times,* Jan. 3, 1993. Anatoly Dobrynin confirms this story, with some variations of detail. *In Confidence,* 536–38.

494   **"This is not"**   RR to John A. Lindon, ca. Sept. 10, 1983, RRL/pp/hw. For international outrage at the KE007 shootdown, exceeding even that which had followed the invasion of Afghanistan, see *Time,* Sept. 19, 1983.

PAGE

495   **home & Mother**   RR Diary, May 25, 1983, RRP.

495   **mantra against insomnia**   RR, *An American Life,* 31, 354.

495   **For what was**   The draconian Article 36 of the Law on the State Border of the USSR was enacted on Nov. 24, 1982, two weeks after the death of Brezhnev and three days after RR's call for a dense-pack MX capability. The Soviet Air Code was strengthened on May 11, 1983, following RR's "Evil Empire" and SDI speeches.

495   **"We have to show"**   RR Diary, Sept. 7 and 10, 1983, RRP.

497   **Here were George**   For the dramatic, but diplomatically unproductive meeting of Shultz and Gromyko on Sept. 8, 1983, see Oberdorfer, *The Turn,* 57–61, and Shultz, *Turmoil and Triumph,* 368–70.

497   **On Friday**   RR Diary, Sept. 16, 1983, RRP; Kornbluh and Byrne, *Iran-Contra Scandal,* 12–14 (document facsimile). RR signed the document on Sept. 12.

498   **"I think we're"**   RR Diary, Sept. 18, 1983, RRP.

498   **As fall approached**   Drew, *American Journal,* 144; Andropov, qu. in Andrew and Gordievsky, *KGB,* 598. See also Michael Mandelbaum and Strobe Talbott, *Reagan and Gorbachev* (New York, 1987), 35–37.

498   **Reagan's cheerful opinion**   Thatcher, *Downing Street Years,* 322–24; RR Diary, Oct. 4, 1983, RRP ("Chalk up another 1st in my experience in Washington").

498   **Even his optimism**   RR Diary, Oct. 10, 1983, RRP.

498   **a strange greeting card**   Sent on to RR by Jeane Kirkpatrick, Feb. 16, 1983, RRL/pp/hw.

498   **Now Bishop**   Shultz, *Turmoil and Triumph,* 324–27. See also Bob Shacochis, "Yesterday's Revolution: Grenada, Mr. Reagan, and the Hangman," *Harper's Magazine,* Oct. 1984.

499   **It was triggered**   "We have every kind of mix you can have," Watt had boasted, in praise of an Interior Department commission. "I have a black, I have a woman, two Jews, and a cripple." As Lou Cannon commented, "Never had a public official offended as many constituencies in so few words." *President Reagan,* 428.

499   **Reagan distractedly**   RR Diary, Oct. 14, 1983, RRP.

499   **"I've got your successor"**   Smith, *Power Game,* 323.

499   **Clark, who**   Michael Deaver interview, Feb. 27, 1987; Cannon, *President Reagan,* 429–32; Shultz, *Turmoil and Triumph,* 319–20. According to Cannon, Clark persuaded the President not to announce the reassignments of Baker and Deaver at the NSPG meeting.

499   **"Mike," Reagan said**   Michael Deaver interview, Feb. 27, 1987.

499   **Deaver was bruised**   Smith, *Power Game,* 324, has Deaver yelling, "You don't have enough confidence in me to make me Chief of Staff!"

500   **By Sunday**   RR Diary, Oct. 15–16, 1983, RRP; Woodward, *Veil,* 284–85. In 1981, RR had telegraphed his opinion of a turf battle between Mrs. Kirkpatrick and Alexander Haig by silently and affectionately kissing her at the beginning of a Cabinet meeting. William P. Clark, Jr., interview. Dec. 20, 1993; Jeane Kirkpatrick interview, May 7, 1998.

500   **The appointment**   Michael Deaver interview, Feb. 27, 1987.

500   **Radio Free Grenada**   Shultz, *Turmoil and Triumph,* 325; Weinberger, *Fighting for Peace,* 106–8.

500   **At least through**   Woodward, *Veil,* 289.

500   **It was North**   Woodward, *Veil,* 289–92.

501   **Reagan, asleep**   McFarlane recalls the emergency call (from George Bush in Washington) as coming at shortly after 3 A.M., and RR, in his diary, thought he was awoken around 4 A.M. The author goes by Shultz's timekeeping, which is characteristically exact.

501   **He joined them**   Shultz, *Turmoil and Triumph,* 329; McFarlane, *Special Trust,* 262; RR Diary, Oct. 21, 1983, RRP; RR, *An American Life,* 449–50.

501   **He delegated**   Ibid. (all), plus George Shultz interview, Aug. 15, 1989.

501   **Much later on**   RR, *An American Life,* 452; Shultz, *Turmoil and Triumph,* 330; McFarlane, *Special Trust,* 262. RR actually got through to the gunman ("Hello, this is Ronald Reagan") but failed to engage him in conversation.

502   **If so, there was**   RR Diary, Oct. 23, 1983, RRP; Petit, *Peacekeepers,* 3; McFarlane, *Special Trust,* 262–63.

502   **The President looked**   McFarlane, *Special Trust,* 263. About the same time that the President asked, "How can this happen?" a young Marine at the bomb site was wailing exactly the same question. Petit, *Peacekeepers,* 167.

502   **The next few days**   RR Diary, Oct. 23–27 and Nov. 4, 1983, RRP.

502   **Mitterrand had already**   Attali, *Verbatim I,* 526–28. "Morland" had been Mitterrand's *nom de guerre* as a Resistance fighter in World War II.

503   **"There is no"**   Ibid., 528–29.

503   **Reagan said nothing**   Weinberger, *Fighting for Peace,* 119; Thatcher, *Downing Street Years,* 331. McFarlane, *Special Trust,* 265, has RR "occasionally holding the receiver a couple of inches from his ear." The first planeloads of Rangers left for Grenada at 8:36 P.M., EST.

503   **The invasion was**   Weinberger, *Fighting for Peace,* 117–19; O'Neill and Novak, *Man of the House,* 364–67.

504   **Of course it was**   Lou Cannon meticulously refutes O'Neill's aspersion in *President Reagan,* 446–47.

504   **"Operation Urgent Fury"**   *Frontline,* PBS, Feb. 2, 1988; *The New Republic,* Sept. 30, 1991; RR, *An American Life,* 456; *Selected Letters of Philip Larkin, 1940–1985* (New York, 1993), 703.

504   **A scrawl on a wall**   EM Diary, Nov. 29, 1983. One of the most eloquent—and historic—pro-INF speeches in the Bundestag was given by a guest orator, François Mitterrand. Nitze, *From Hiroshima to Glasnost,* 399, notes the speed with which the European freeze movement collapsed "about two weeks" after deployment.

504   **Yuri Andropov issued**   Gorbachev, *Memoirs,* 181–82; Dobrynin, *In Confidence,* 542.

504   **In Lebanon, world**   This point was first made by Albert E. Pierce in a *Washington Post* Op-Ed column, June 22, 1995, responding to one by Mrs. Kirkpatrick on June 9.

505   **Two days before**   Cannon, *President Reagan,* 451–53; Oberdorfer, *The Turn,* 98. The United States withdrew from Lebanon on Feb. 27, 1984.

505   **Or as the**   RR to William F. Buckley, Jr., ca. Christmas 1983, RRL/pp/hw.

PAGE

505   **Nineteen eighty-four**   See Yegor Ligachev, *Inside Gorbachev's Kremlin: The Memoirs of Yegor Ligachev* (New York, 1993), 29–31, and Gorbachev, *Memoirs,* 153–56, for the succession of intrigues surrounding Andropov's illness and death.

506   **Isn't our choice**   Handwritten insert in RR, Independence Day Address, July 3, 1984, RRL/pp/hw.

506   **"He can't lose"**   EM Diary, July 4, 1984, AC.

506   **Poor decent, dull**   Drew, *American Journal,* 705–8; EM Diary, Oct. 21, 1984, AC. For a discussion of the aftereffects of RR's disastrous first debate against Mondale, see Darman, *Who's in Control?,* 125–42.

507   **Such at least**   Oct. 27, 1984, was the 126th anniversary of Theodore Roosevelt's birth. Newport News officials said they did not "think" the launching had any added relevance to the upcoming election. *The Washington Post,* Oct. 28, 1984. EM Diary, Oct. 27, 1984, AC. See also "The Launch of the USS Theodore Roosevelt," *Theodore Roosevelt Association Journal,* 11.1 (winter, 1985).

31: Physicians of Memory

508   **Snow—polar snow**   WHCA video, Jan. 20, 1985, RRL/av; *Los Angeles Times, The Washington Post,* Jan. 21 and 22, 1985.

508   **Inside the vestibule**   See Souza, *Unguarded Moments,* frontispiece. A WHTV video of the proceedings is in RRL/av.

508   **The Twentieth**   The hour was of particular interest to NR, too. She instructed Michael Deaver to note the exact time (11:57 A.M.) her husband began to utter the oath, so that she could inform her astrologer and thus be able to predict when the next member of her family would die. Carolyn Deaver Diary, Jan. 20, 1985, DEA.

509   **laid his free hand**   "I like to think maybe she's still giving me a hand now and then." RR to Mrs. Hugh Harris, Jan. 9, 1985, RRL/pp/hw.

509   **When, moments afterward**   WHCA video, RRL/av; *Los Angeles Times,* Jan. 21, 1985.

509   **Later, it grew**   *Los Angeles Times,* Jan. 22, 1985.

509   **When an overnight**   *The Washington Post,* Jan. 22, 1985.

509   **When told, Reagan**   The "kids" were consoled with a hastily rigged Inaugural Event, held indoors the following afternoon at Maryland's Capital Center. RR and NR attended. *The Washington Post,* Jan. 22, 1985.

510   **The cold spread**   Ibid.; EM Notes, Jan. 21, 1985.

510   **Inauguration Day**   *Los Angeles Times,* Jan. 22, 1985; Courtland Milloy, "Inaugural Blue," *The Washington Post,* Jan. 22, 1985.

510   **The walruses were**   President's Inaugural Schedule, RRL; WHTV video, RRL/av.

510   **I got to the steps**   WHCA video, RRL/av; EM Diary, Jan. 21, 1985.

511   **Reagan's Second**   "I told everybody months ago that while you might take a few words or concepts from the drafts, you were going to write your own Inaugural which is just what happened." Anthony R. Dolan, speechwriter, to RR, Jan. 23, 1985, RRL. Carolyn Deaver Diary, Jan. 21, 1985, DEA.

PAGE

511   **Four years ago**   All quotes from *The New York Times* transcript, Jan. 22, 1985.

511   **After a couple**   A few days previous, he had frankly told his returning delegation, "I don't have any euphoria." WHTV tape 218, RRL/av. Privately, however, he was much encouraged by the agreement they had won. RR Diary, Jan. 7 and 8, 1985, RRP. For accounts of the Shultz-Gromyko negotiations, see Adelman, *The Great Universal Embrace,* 89–120; Nitze, *From Hiroshima to Glasnost,* 403–6; Shultz, *Turmoil and Triumph,* 500–519; McFarlane, *Special Trust,* 304–5.

512   **We're not just**   Italics supplied.

512   **the very item**   See Oberdorfer, *The Turn,* 83–100, for Soviet attempts to renew a dialogue with the U.S. in 1984.

512   **Over sole mousse**   RR Diary, Jan. 21, 1985, RRP; Tip O'Neill, qu. himself to *The Washington Post,* Jan. 23, 1985. He might have added that for the first time in that same half-century, voters favoring the Republican party outnumbered their Democratic opposites, 47 to 41 percent. Smith, *The Power Game,* 676. RR's job-approval rating was 70 percent.

512   **Had the Speaker**   Mondale won Minnesota (his home state) by only 3,761, less than a percentage point. RR scored an overall popular majority of 59 percent, with 152 electoral votes to Mondale's 10. This majority was not quite as large as those amassed by Franklin D. Roosevelt in 1936, Lyndon B. Johnson in 1964, and Richard Nixon in 1972, but it was still, as Michael Barone remarks, "devoid of any ambiguity." *Our Country,* 645. Nationwide, RR won over the support of every occupational category except the unemployed, and one-quarter of all registered Democrats. Cannon, *President Reagan,* 492.

513   **Mitch Snyder, the street**   *The Washington Post,* Jan. 22, 1985.

513   **That evening**   RR to Rudolph Hines (pen pal), Jan. 25, 1985, RRL/pp/hw; RR Diary, Jan. 21, 1985, RRP; *The New York Times,* Jan. 22, 1985.

513   **Around the curve**   William J. Eaton, "A Fine Winter!" *Los Angeles Times,* Jan. 21, 1985. See Ligachev, *Inside Gorbachev's Kremlin,* 58–63, for that winter's nation-cracking hundred days of snow. *The New York Times,* Jan. 8, 1985. *Los Angeles Times,* Jan. 22, 1985.

513   **There is something**   The author is indebted to Judith Miller, *One by One* (New York, 1990), 44, for the splendid word *Schlusstrich.* RR Diary, Nov. 30, 1984, RRP; Shultz, *Turmoil and Triumph,* 540–41; Cannon, *President Reagan,* 573; Ronald Lehman interview, Oct. 5, 1997. Although the Berlin Wall could not have gone up without Soviet approval, the executive body that authorized and built it was East Germany's *Volkskammer.*

513   **The Chancellor's idea**   RR Diary, Nov. 30, 1984, RRP; Kenneth Khachigian, notes of meeting with RR, Apr. 26, 1985, AC.

514   **The proposal was**   RR Diary, Apr. 4–14, 1985, RRP; RR, *An American Life,* 376–77. See also Smith, *Power Game,* 374–76. *Federal Broadcast Information Service* 7 (Apr. 17, 1985), qu. Kohl to RR, Apr. 15, 1985; Shultz, *Turmoil and Triumph,* 541–42.

PAGE

514   **At least one** *Der Spiegel,* Jan. 19, 1985; Shultz, *Turmoil and Triumph,* 541, Smith, *Power Game,* 374; RR interview, Mar. 22, 1985; Shultz, *Turmoil and Triumph,* 767–68. Axel Springer reminded RR on Feb. 14, 1985, of "Lenin's dictum: 'Whoever controls Berlin, controls Germany; and whoever controls Germany is the master of Europe.'" RRL/pp/hw.

514   **The President's State** *The Washington Post,* Feb. 7, 1985. Both houses of Congress joined in singing "Happy Birthday." Domestically, RR called for reduced and simplified personal taxes, fewer regulatory restraints on American productivity, special opportunity zones for young entrepreneurs, empowerment of minorities, protection of the unborn ("unless it can be proven that an unborn child is not a living human being" (RR, handwritten insert), reduced subsidies for farms and Amtrak, and a Constitutional amendment permitting Presidential line-item veto of the federal budget. In foreign policy, he emphasized the urgency of Congressional support for SDI research, as well as for the MX missile and "all facets of our assistance to Central America." He also urged, in vague but potent terms, that Americans "not break faith with those who are risking their lives—on every continent, from Afghanistan to Nicaragua—to defy Soviet-supported aggression and secure rights which have been ours from birth." The columnist Charles Krauthammer took this to be the birth of what he called "the Reagan Doctrine" of covert support for anti-Communist insurrections, and the phrase stuck. Speech draft and final cards, RRL/pp/hw; Stephen F. Knott, "Reagan's Critics," *The National Interest* (summer 1996).

514   **One was young** *The New York Times,* Feb. 7, 1985, and Dec. 20, 1992. The former was Cadet Jean Nguyen, the latter Mrs. Clara Hale of Harlem. RR had to be persuaded not to use the phrase "American heroine," as per his amended speech draft, RRL/pp/hw. Senator Moynihan, while confirming Mrs. Hale's "quite splendid" achievement, wittily demonstrates the hollowness of RR's tribute to her in *Family and Nation,* 105–8.

515   **Watching on CBS** Shakespeare, Sonnet 97. RR was pleased to receive another grudging compliment from Speaker Tip O'Neill, and wrote Dwight Morrow, "Introducing my two guests really blew his safety valve." Feb. 11, 1985, RRL/pp/hw.

515   **A changing roster** Donald Regan, *For the Record: From Wall Street to Washington* (New York, 1988), 223–29. RR's only comment on the Regan/Baker job switch in his diary was, "I'm agreed. . . . I think it will resolve a lot of problems." (Jan. 7, 1985, RRP.)

515   **On television** *The Washington Post,* Feb. 7, 1985.

515   **Michael Deaver had** *Ehrefriedhof* = honor cemetery. According to *Frankfurter Allgemeine Zeitung,* Feb. 20, 1985, Tuesday, Feb. 19, was the climax of one of the coldest spells in recent memory, with rivers and canals freezing all over Germany. Heavy snowfalls on Saturday and Monday blocked roads and runways in the Frankfurt area.

515   **"You think maybe"** Michael Deaver interview, Nov. 16, 1989. See also

Deaver, *Behind the Scenes,* 180. Another member of Deaver's party, Peter Somer, asked a similar question and was assured by the Germans, "There are no painful surprises here." Shultz, *Turmoil and Triumph,* 544.

515   **That evening in** Michael Deaver interview, Nov. 16, 1989; Helmut Kohl, qu. by William McWhirter, *Time,* May 6, 1985; Michael Deaver cable to the Secret Service, Feb. 20, 1985, DEA.

516   **A veteran advance** James Hooley interview, Apr. 29, 1991; Deaver, *Behind the Scenes,* 180.

516   **Somebody remarked** James Hooley interview, Apr. 29, 1991. The detail about bones comes from Kathy A. Smith, who was a member of Gerald Ford's party.

516   **On Friday March 8** RR Diary, Mar. 8, 1985, RRP. Kampelman was personally responsible for space and defense talks. Other members were Maynard Glitman (INF) and former Senator John Tower (START). Shultz, *Turmoil and Triumph,* 521. Paul Nitze remained in Washington as arms-control adviser to Secretary Shultz.

516   **"I think he'll go"** RR Diary, Mar. 7, 1985, RRP. Shcherbitsky went home railing that "neo-Nazi tendencies in the U.S. and W. Germany 'remind world society of . . . the fascist coalition on the eve of the War.' " Qu. by John W. Parker, *Kremlin in Transition* (Boston, 1991), vol. 2, 31, 35; Ligachev, *Inside Gorbachev's Kremlin,* 69.

516   **Shcherbitsky's aggression** Chernenko's speech, published in *Pravda* on Feb. 23, contained some fairly impassioned freeze rhetoric. RR found it "very interesting" but vague. "All they have to do is indicate how fast they are willing to go in destroying weapons." RRL/pp/hw. Donald Regan interview, Nov. 18, 1985.

516   **Reagan, in contrast** Beahrs, "The Medical History," 91; John Hutton Diary, Mar. 8, 1985, JHP. Actually and ironically, in view of later developments, the sigmoidoscope examined only the lower portion of RR's large intestine.

516   **He did not know** RR Diary, May 8, 1985, RRP. The President's jiggly handwriting indicates that this entry was written on Marine One.

517   **on the Eifel** Weather details from Antony Beaumont to EM, Apr. 5, 1994, AC.

517   **Years later, in** EM Notes, May 19, 1990, AC.

517   **There came to me** Philip Larkin, "Thaw" (1946), *Collected Poems* (New York, 1989), 19.

517   **The President returned** RR Diary, Mar. 11, 1985, RRP; Gorbachev, *Memoirs,* 168; Peter Robinson and Clark Judge interview.

517   **He agreed, however** RR, qu. in Don Regan interview, Dec. 27, 1985; RR Diary, Mar. 11, 1985, RRP. When he arrived to sign the condolence book, he reminded Soviet Ambassador Anatoly Dobrynin that he had done the same thing twice before already and added pointedly, "I hope to come to the embassy next time on a happier occasion." This hint that he was willing to negotiate with the new Soviet leader was confirmed by Secretary Shultz and transmitted excitedly to Gorbachev. Dobrynin, *In Confidence,* 567.

517   **This story shared** John Hutton Diary, Mar. 8 and 12, 1985, JHP. Dr.

Smith proceeded to brief the White House press office on Monday without further reference to the President, and his excessive candor about stool specimens and cancer diets enraged NR. Ibid., Mar. 12, 1985.

517 **The growth seemed** In view of the apparent benignity of RR's polyp, his doctors decided, not without dissension, to delay an operation to remove it until it suited his political schedule (see below). John Hutton Diary, Mar. 11 and July 9, 1985, JHP.

518 **The real pathophobia** "Manifesto for Socialist Renewal," a secret document made available by Acting Secretariat Chairman Gorbachev to Dwayne Andreas, the American agribusiness tycoon, in December 1984. Copy in AC. Since Gorbachev was by then clearly the next leader of the CPSU (Chernenko, dying, had just made his final public appearance), and since Andreas was known to be an old friend of RR, delivery of such an astonishingly self-condemnatory document can only be interpreted as a private *cri de coeur,* a plea to the West for technological aid and relief from crippling military expenditures.

518 **Unlike any previous** Jeane Kirkpatrick interview, May 7, 1998; Dwayne Andreas interview, Mar. 8, 1985.

518 **Yet Reagan, watching** Martin Anderson interview, Aug. 15, 1989. Ligachev, *Inside Gorbachev's Kremlin,* 54, describes Mrs. Chernenko as "a modest and kind woman . . . unquestionably, a courageous one."

519 **He became obsessed** Robert McFarlane interview, Feb. 28, 1995; Brian Mulroney interview, Dec. 8, 1993; Allan Gotlieb interview, Jan. 29, 1994. George Shultz brought back a confrontational image of Gorbachev saying to him and Vice President Bush, right after the funeral, that any "new breakthroughs resulting from the scientific and technological revolution," especially "shifting the arms race to space," could cause spiraling hostilities between the US and USSR. Shultz, *Turmoil and Triumph,* 529–30. There was, however, a notable absence of military brass atop the Lenin Mausoleum during the funeral parade. Parker, *Kremlin in Transition,* vol. 2, 13.

519 **Addressing the White** RR's invitation was delivered personally by Vice President Bush. Several days later a letter from Gorbachev (Mar. 24, 1985) arrived, guardedly expressing a "positive attitude to 'the idea' of a summit meeting." See RR, *An American Life,* 613–14.

519 **Mr. President** *The Washington Post,* Apr. 22, 1985. In an interview with three *Post* reporters on Apr. 1, RR said that a concentration-camp visit would "take advantage" of Kohl's hospitality.

519 **The following evening** EM Diary, Mar. 22, 1985, AC. See pp. 4–5.

519 *Il se trouvait* Qu. by Brian Mulroney, interview, Dec. 8, 1993. A possible contribution to RR's glow: he had that morning been briefed by the Joint Chiefs of Staff on the state of the U.S. military after four Reagan years. They informed him that in "readiness, quality of manpower, weaponry, and reserves," all services were at a peacetime peak. "I came out of the cabinet room feeling 10 ft. tall." RR Diary, Mar. 22, 1985, RRP.

519 **"My blood pressure"** John Hutton Diary, Mar. 11, 1985, confirms it was down from 140/78 to 130/74. JHP.

519 **sh-shimmering glory** In the later days of the Reagan Administration Bill Griffith's sublime Zipster grew so distraught over the looming loss of

RR's hair ("*Sniff*... Maybe it could stay on in an *honorary* capacity") that his sidekick, Griffy, surprised him with a gift of the entire tonsure, mounted on a plinth. "You had it *bronzed!!!*" Zippy ejaculated with delight. "It wasn't easy," Griffy advised. "I had to pull a few strings with Jane Wyman." *Washington Post* comics pages, Oct. 18, 1988.

519   **"I always take"**   EM Diary, Mar. 22, 1985, AC.

520   **I tried to get**   Ibid; Sylvia Jukes Morris, memo, "Dining with the President," Mar. 23, 1985, AC. The other guest at the dinner party was a mutual friend, Nancy Clark Reynolds.

520   **"My favorite view"**   See also RR to Patrick Mulvey, June 20, 1983, RRL/pp.

521   **It happened to be**   The first two and last two days of Passover outside of Israel are Yomim Tovim (holy days), as opposed to intermediate semi-holidays (Hol-ha-Moed). Sunrise on the twentieth of Nisan ushers in a solemn forty-eight hours; the faithful are expected to attend synagogue both before and after dark, and to say Kaddish before the celebratory repast.

521   **For a tormented**   Elie Wiesel in *The New York Times,* Apr. 14, 1985.

521   **Now chairman**   Elie Wiesel in *The New York Times* and *The Washington Post,* Apr. 13, 1985.

521   **As I browsed**   Passover 1985 began on Good Friday, Apr. 5. Originally, the Council of Nicaea made special provisions to ensure that Easter and Passover did not coincide—ordaining that the latter be postponed a week when necessary. The growing schism between Christianity and Judaism put an end to this sensible policy.

521   **To Dutch, Easter**   See p. 53.

522   **But as the**   The ecumenical movement referred to was that of the Quartodecimans, who believed with the Jews that Easter should be observed on the fourteenth day of Nisan.

522   **It wishfully seemed**   *The Works of Theodore Roosevelt,* Memorial Edition (New York, 1923), vol. 1, 309–10. See Matthews, *The Grail,* 41, 71, for Parzival's half-comprehending vision of old law (Synagoga) and new law (Ecclesia).

522   **White House staffers**   RR Diary, Apr. 4 and 14, 1985, RRP.

522   **The ethical parallels**   Elie Wiesel on *This Week with David Brinkley,* ABC, May 5, 1985; Geoffrey Hartman, ed., *Bitburg in Moral and Political Perspective* (Bloomington, Ind., 1986), xiv. This book contains the most distinguished group of essays yet devoted to the Reagan presidency. It should be read in conjunction with Midge Decter, "Bitburg: Who Forgot What?" *Commentary,* Aug. 1985.

523   **They reckoned**   RR Diary, Apr. 15, 1985, RRP; Shultz, *Turmoil and Triumph,* 545–46.

523   **Reagan was both**   RR Diary, Apr. 15, 1985, RRP.

523   **"Dear Mr. President"**   Qu. by *The New York Times,* Jan. 17, 1993.

523   **"I think that"**   Qu. by Shultz, *Turmoil and Triumph,* 546.

524   **the wound of Memory**   According to *Newsweek,* Apr. 29, 1985, a recent survey showed West Germany to be the most pessimistic of seventeen nations. "Many Germans believe the country's inability to shrug off the past is eroding its confidence."

524   ***Nun endet Sorg'***   From the *Parzival* of Wolfram von Eschenbach (Leipzig, 1943), 119. The full quotation is *Nun endet Sorg' und Leid! / Wie uns des Grales Zeichen lehrt, / kommt er, nach dem wir stets begehrt, / seit uns umstricht des Jammers Seil.* "Now endeth care and wailing sound! / To us there comes in Grail-light shining / He for whom we have been pining / Since corded sorrow roped us round" (author's translation).

524   **"The press . . . really"**   RR Diary, Apr. 18, 1985, RRP.

524   **In another ironic**   Wiesel had been up since 4 A.M. rewriting his acceptance speech after hearing RR's remarks the day before on a car radio. "I couldn't believe it." Even after requesting and reviewing a transcript, "I still couldn't believe it." *The New York Times,* Apr. 19, 1985.

524   **Outside in the**   RR Diary, Apr. 19, 1995, RRP; WHTV video, RRL/av. The following dialogue is taken entirely from WHTV's sound track.

525   **Reagan, uninterested**   The video makes it obvious that RR thought Kohl had personally toured and vetted the Bitburg cemetery.

525   **In any case**   Situation Room memo, Apr. 12, 1985, RRL/pp/hw.

525   **During the ceremony**   RR speech cards, RRL/pp/hw. The following account is based on WHCA and WHTV video coverage in RRL/av, and "Bitburg," a compilation of contemporary television coverage, Apr.–May 1985, by Paul Slansky, SLA. See also *The New York Times,* Apr. 20, 1985. Extracts from Wiesel's speech can be heard on the audiobook version of this biography.

526   **It was the first**   Slansky, "Bitburg."

526   **If the President**   The phrase "morally right" appears again and again in RR's diary and letters for this period, along with condemnations of his critics, e.g., "Well d--n their hides I think it is morally right to go and I'm going" (RR Diary, Apr. 24, 1985, RRP). Both Richard Nixon and Henry Kissinger telephoned RR to urge him to hold to his resolve.

526   **Forty years ago**   See RR, interviewed by Hugh Sidey, *Time,* May 13, 1985. This may be an appropriate place to discuss recurrent allegations that RR, both during his Presidency and after, informed incredulous auditors that he had personally participated in liberation of the camps in April 1945. (See, e.g., Cannon, *President Reagan,* 486–90; Korda, *Another Life,* 472.) The author can only say that he never heard this story from RR, in the course of several discussions of the Holocaust. But he nevertheless believes that both Cannon and Korda are reporting accurately, for the simple reason that to RR, raw film and raw experience were the same. It is a matter of fact that RR, as base intelligence officer at Fort Roach in April 1945, had to sit through hours of intolerably graphic color footage from Ohrdruf and Buchenwald, and that he kept copies of some of it to show to his children and friends in later years. (See pp. 215–16.) Cannon errs only in saying that the images he remembers were those shown in U.S. theaters: the FMPU footage (shot by Owen Crump's combat camera crew in early April) was processed and cut for private showing to Pentagon officials, and the Adjutant was responsible for its dispatch to Washington. To the extent that what he saw was "real" in his mind (where RR, a highly imaginative person, in effect lived), he "really" *was* there when the wire went down at Ohrdruf. The

age of the computer will determine whether such "virtual" perception is authentic, or not. William Graf and Owen Crump interviews, Oct. 1, 1992; Shultz, *Turmoil and Triumph,* 550–51.

527   **a plenum of the Central**   Ligachev, *Inside Gorbachev's Kremlin,* 48.

527   **Just how incendiary**   Gorbachev, *Memoirs,* 174; Henry Brandon interview, July 14, 1990; Mandelbaum and Talbott, *Reagan and Gorbachev,* 70–72; Ligachev, *Inside Gorbachev's Kremlin,* 45–48; "Manifesto for Socialist Renewal," AC. See also Stephen White, *Gorbachev and After* (New York, 1991), 103.

527   **It was not**   Oberdorfer, *The Turn,* 114–15.

527   **Reagan got the**   RR, *An American Life,* 615–16; Shultz, *Turmoil and Triumph,* 533–34. On Apr. 26, the White House ordered the expulsion of a Soviet military *attaché,* Oleg M. Sokolov, in view of the Kremlin's "unacceptable" attitude. *The New York Times,* Apr. 27, 1985.

528   **Once it became**   RR Diary, Apr. 22, 1985, RRP; Kenneth Khachigian interview, Aug. 31, 1987; *The Times* (London), Apr. 26, 1985.

528   **The saturnine**   Kenneth Khachigian interviews, Aug. 31 and Mar. 8, 1987.

528   **He stressed**   Kenneth Khachigian, transcript of Presidential remarks, Apr. 26, 1985, AC.

528   **"Out of these ashes"**   Ibid.

529   **For twenty-five minutes**   Kenneth Khachigian interviews, Mar. 8 and Aug. 31, 1987.

529   **"Chancellor Kohl"**   Representatives of the Jewish community and synagogue boycotted the ceremony because of RR's intent to go on afterward to Bitburg. *The New York Times,* May 6, 1985. The following account of the Bergen-Belsen speech is based on Kenneth Khachigian's final draft, Apr. 29, 1985, amended by RR in delivery, May 5, 1985; CNN, NBC, and ABC footage in Slansky, "Bitburg"; EM Notes, May 5, 1985, and May 19, 1990.

530   **Khachigian had written**   Kenneth Khachigian to Marion Elizabeth Rodgers, Sept. 2, 1987, AC.

532   **Tom Shales**   *The Washington Post,* May 6, 1985. For a critique of the Bergen-Belsen eulogy, see Decter, "Bitburg: Who Forgot What?"

532   **Two hours after**   Slansky, "Bitburg." For the story behind General Ridgway's appearance at Bitburg ("It appears to me that my Commander-in-Chief is in trouble and I would like to help"), see Deaver, *Behind the Scenes,* 185.

532   **That evening**   WHTV video, RRL/av; ABC News, May 5, 1985, in Slansky, "Bitburg."

532   **While Reagan accepted**   *The New York Times,* May 6, 1985. RR and Gorbachev did, however, exchange icily formal messages acknowledging the anniversary. *Los Angeles Times,* May 9, 1985. See also President von Weizsäcker's historic address of this date to the European Parliament, in Richard von Weizsäcker, *A Voice from Germany* (London, 1987).

532   **His speech**   *The New York Times,* May 9, 1985. RR congratulated Western Europe on resisting "the call of new tyrants" after World War II "and the lure of their seductive ideologies." He directly accused the So-

viet Union of global "adventurism," destabilization, bureaucratic corruption, and "murder" of Major Nicholson. RR speech cards, RRL/pp/hw.

533   **"What's new?"** *The New York Times,* May 11, 1985.

533   **"What about the"** Shultz, *Turmoil and Triumph,* 563–64. See also Nitze, *From Hiroshima to Glasnost,* 409–10.

534   **Shultz returned** Shultz, *Turmoil and Triumph,* 566; RR Diary, May 17 and 22, 1985, RRP. Shultz does not mention his resignation request in *Turmoil and Triumph,* 566. Writing for publication years later in *An American Life,* RR emphasizes his desire to have Shultz stay. The diary gives the reverse impression.

534   **June 1985 taxed** RR Diary, May 28, June 1 and 29, 1985, RRP. The latest hostage was David Jacobsen.

534   **Reagan tried** RR Diary, June 3, 1985, RRP; RR, *An American Life,* 620. Another consideration was that "narrow" observance would almost immediately require the Navy to start dismantling its Poseidon submarine fleet in order to make way for missile-firing Tridents.

534   **"We will continue"** RR Diary, May 6, 1985, RRP. Senator Dale Bumpers (D., Ark.) praised RR's SALT II decision as "the most statesmanlike act of his presidency." *The Washington Post,* June 11, 1985. The seventh hostage, kidnapped on June 9, was Thomas Sutherland.

535   **Mikhail Gorbachev was** Gorbachev to RR, June 12, 1985, qu. in RR, *An American Life,* 621–22.

535   **The Middle East reverted** Shultz, *Turmoil and Triumph,* 657; Speakes, *Speaking Out,* 167–68. The latter notes that when the crisis was resolved, NBC flew hostages' family members to a reunion in Frankfurt on condition that they granted no interviews to the network's rivals.

536   **"This of course"** RR Diary, June 17, 1985, RRP.

536   **So wrote** Ibid. For a detailed account of the TWA hijacking crisis, see Shultz, *Turmoil and Triumph,* 653–68.

536   **The unlikely rescuers** Shultz, *Turmoil and Triumph,* 665, 667; Jane Mayer and Doyle McManus, *Landslide: The Unmaking of the President, 1984–1985* (Boston, 1988), 124–25; Cannon, *President Reagan,* 607.

536   **"Both the President"** Michael Deaver interview, Oct. 24, 1990; EM Diary, May 27, 1985.

537   **on Friday, July 10** *The Washington Post,* July 11, 1985; John Hutton Diary, Mar. 11 and July 9–11, 1985, JHP. Shortly before this press conference, Dr. Hutton took it upon himself to explain to George Bush exactly what was to happen during the upcoming surgery. "I was amazed at how little he had been told about what might be in store for the President." John Hutton drew diagrams to illustrate the colonoscopy and warned that RR would be "profoundly sleepy" with the sedative effects of Valium and Demerol for "more than a few hours." Meanwhile, White House counsel Fred Fielding took steps to prepare for a partial delegation of power under the Twenty-fifth Amendment. Ibid., July 11, 1985. Inexplicably, the Vice President was permitted to proceed to Kennebunkport, Maine, for the weekend. *The New York Times,* July 13, 1985.

537   **I sensed this** RR Diary, July 3 and 10, 1985, RRP.

537   **At lunchtime**   EM Diary, July 12, 1985; John Hutton Diary, July 12, 1985, JHP.

537   **The room darkened**   The following description of RR's colonoscopy is based on John Hutton interviews, Dec. 29, 1992, and Jan. 11, 1995. Supplementary details from John Hutton Diary, July 12–13, 1985, and his preliminary map of the expedition, July 10, 1985, JHP.

538   **"Carcinoma. Unmistakable."**   The consensus of surgical opinion was that the tumor had been lurking in RR's cecum "for several years." Ibid.

538   **"I stood there"**   In the event, it was Mrs. Reagan who told her husband, "Honey, the doctors have found a polyp that is too large to be removed the way the other ones were. The only way they can get it out is to do it surgically." The President's eyes grew round as he listened to her. "As long as we're here, why don't we do it tomorrow and get it over with?" By now RR's eyes were popping in mock horror. "Does this mean I won't be getting dinner tonight, either?" NR, *My Turn,* 273; John Hutton interview, Dec. 29, 1992.

538   **Block headlines**   *The Washington Post,* July 13, 1985; John Hutton interview, Dec. 29, 1992. Neil Reagan's tumor, however, was circumferential, as opposed to RR's large lump.

539   **"physicians of memory"**   The quote is used without attribution by Geoffrey Hartman in Hartman, *Bitburg,* 2.

539   **On the way out**   EM Diary, July 13, 1985.

32: Almost Air Force One

540   **memorizing the wisecrack**   Which indeed he did. "Met with Edmund Morris, who is going to do my official biography. I'm pleased—his book on Teddy Roosevelt was wonderful. Of course I can't charge up San Juan hill." RR Diary, Nov. 5, 1985, RRP.

540   **The patina on**   EM Notes, Nov. 5, 1985. Before becoming President, RR obstinately refused to throw away a pair of ancient, brown, high-tongued alligator pumps. "Do you realize what I *paid* for these thirty years ago?" Nancy Clark Reynolds interview, Aug. 20, 1986.

540   **successful colonectomy**   Dr. John Hutton described RR's operation to the author with a surgeon's relish. "We cut him open from pubis to breastbone, slicing slightly to one side, and all three surgeons palpitated the mass. It was as hard as putty. We tied it off north and south, and I passed my hand over the rest of his insides. They were like those of a twenty-year-old man. I was amazed at the lack of fatty deposits. No calcium in the major blood vessels. No adhesions—everything pliable and soft. A beautiful liver. Then we cut off two feet of colon, and half a foot from the smaller intestine." Interview, Dec. 29, 1992.

541   **As far as *he***   A more detailed letter to Joseph Gold of the Syracuse Cancer Research Institute illustrates how RR, Janus-like, could look both at and past facts: "The impression has been given that I was suffering from cancer and surgery removed the cancerous tumor. A more accurate account is that in a routine physical examination a polyp of the

type that can become cancer was discovered. It was still within the colon and self-contained. . . . I told them to remove it. It had already developed a few cancer cells we discovered, but that was the extent of it." Jan. 24, 1986, RRL/pp/hw.

541   **"I look like"**   John Hutton interview, Dec. 29, 1992.

541   **"Like the fella"**   WHTV video, Nov. 5, 1985, RRL/av.

541   **"It tends to settle"**   EM to NR, Apr. 25, 1985, AC.

542   **He began to read**   EM Notes, Nov. 5, 1985. RR expressed similar sentiments in *Time,* May 17, 1976, and *The New York Times,* Aug. 17, 1980, and Dec. 23, 1981. See Green and MacColl, *Reagan's Reign of Error,* 95.

542   **I congratulated Dutch**   EM Notes, Nov. 5, 1985. Rev. Weir was released on Sept. 15, 1985, the first beneficiary of the Reagan Administration's secret Iran Initiative.

542   **If he was concerned**   RR's diary makes plain that he had already heard from Shultz on the scramble phone: "Apparently not much progress." The meeting had been difficult for Shultz, whom Gorbachev treated as a conduit of messages regarding what agenda he would and would not tolerate at Geneva. RR Diary, Nov. 5, 1985, RRP; Shultz, *Turmoil and Triumph,* 589ff.

542   **"Somebody in the"**   EM Notes, Nov. 5, 1985.

543   **"See you in Geneva"**   Ibid; EM to RR, Nov. 6, 1985.

543   **I believe Gorbachev**   RR memorandum, ca. Nov. 1985, RRL/pp/hw. This turns out to have been a fair assessment of Gorbachev at the time of writing. The *gensek*'s three major statements of domestic policy so far, while sowing the seeds of *perestroika,* had been on the whole more remarkable for caution and conservatism. White, *Gorbachev and After,* 214–17.

544   **The President's Foreign**   Clare Boothe Luce interview, Dec. 3, 1985; RR memorandum, ca. Nov. 1985, RRL/pp/hw. In April, Col. Aleksander Sazhin, Soviet military attaché in London, had told a meeting of KGB personnel that the Kremlin believed the SDI would result in a 90 percent effective anti-ballistic shield over the USA. He saw "little chance" of Soviet ABM technology "keeping pace with that of the United States." Qu. in Christopher Andrew and Oleg Gordievsky, *Comrade Kryuchkov's Instructions: Top Secret Files on KGB Foreign Operations* (Stanford, Cal., 1991), 107.

544   **Gorbachev, in his**   RR memorandum, ca. Nov. 1985, RRL/pp/hw.

544   **Two days later**   The following account is taken from EM Notes, Nov. 5, 1985.

545   **only four percent**   In his published account of the Kremlin meeting, McFarlane raises this figure to 6 percent. McFarlane, *Special Trust,* 315.

545   **"Bud needs secrecy"**   Clare Boothe Luce interview, Jan. 10, 1986.

546   **"Air Force One?"**   EM Diary, Nov. 8, 1985.

546   **"The dollar I can afford"**   Ibid., Nov. 16, 1985.

547   **"I hope they never do."**   They never have.

547   **"permafrost of the soul"**   Varlam Shalamov, *Kolyma Tales,* translated by John Glad (New York, 1982), 48. A slight misquotation, at least of Glad's rendering. The latter reads: "If bones could freeze, then the brain

could also be dulled and the soul could freeze over. And the soul shuddered and froze—perhaps to remain frozen forever."

547   **Quoted it in**   EM to NR, Nov. 8, 1985.

547   **Gorbachev may be**   McFarlane, *Special Trust,* 315, NR to EM, Nov. 14, 1985, qu. Dr. Richard Davis, AC.

547   **What might happen**   RR interview, Nov. 5, 1985. He repeats this almost word for word in his diary for that night. RRP.

548   **My young companion**   Kimberly Timmons was a researcher in the speechwriting department of the White House, 1985–1986.

548   *lues Boswelliana*   The disease of admiration.

548   **that blind belief**   See p. 42. The author would have been less apprehensive if he had seen an alteration RR made to the draft of his pre-summit address to the American people (Nov. 14, 1985). Instead of reading, "It is with your prayers, and God's guidance, that I hope to succeed," he changed the word *guidance* to *help.* This shows the workings of a devout, yet fiercely proud mind. RRL/pp/hw.

548   **that Russian folk character**   A perennial figure in Russian children's folklore, Mr. Bear-Squash-You-All-Flat was introduced to the West in a ballet of that name by Constant Lambert (1924).

548   *Höhenlust*   Mark Helprin, "The Schreuderspitze," *Ellis Island and Other Stories* (New York, 1976); Jean Laloy, *Yalta: Yesterday, Today, Tomorrow* (New York, 1990), 104.

549   *10:25 PM*   The ground temperature was freezing. WHTV commentary, Nov. 17, 1985, RRL/av.

33: One on One

551   **Around ten o'clock**   EM Diary, Nov. 17, 1985; Franz Liszt to George Sand, Nov. 23, 1835, qu. by Charles Suttoni, *An Artist's Journey: Lettres d'un Bachelier ès Musique, 1835–1841* (Chicago, 1989), 4.

551   **"obliterated grandeurs"**   Ibid., 8.

551   **The President, meanwhile**   RR Diary, Nov. 17, 1985, and RR, *An American Life,* 635; Donald Regan Notes, LC, and EM Notes, Nov. 17, 1985.

551   **Nancy, equally by**   During this walk, there was a "photo opportunity" that permitted a reporter to ask RR whether he intended to fire Defense Secretary Weinberger for allegedly leaking a letter urging confrontational tactics at the summit. "Do you want one word or two?" the President asked, then gave them: "Hell no" (WHTV, RRL/av). Weinberger's letter, published in full on the eve of the summit, had been sensationalized as a sour-grapes reaction to his exclusion from the U.S. delegation. Its arguments for a broad interpretation of the ABM Treaty and against trading away the SDI were provoked by Soviet arms-control violations, which Weinberger itemized in an attached report. Text in *The Washington Post,* Nov. 17, 1985. RR chose not to add to his comment the fact that he had personally asked for the letter. In his diary that night he wrote, "I agree with Cap" (RRP).

552   **"Why, Mr. Gorbachev!"**   Donald Regan Notes, Nov. 17, 1985, LC.

552   **The President, still**   RR Diary, Nov. 18, 1985, RRP.

553   **Gorbachev had scored**   Through Foreign Minister Shevardnadze, who had visited the Oval Office on Sept. 27. Gorbachev's proposal, tailored more for newspaper headlines than for the serious consideration of arms-control experts (Dobrynin, *In Confidence,* 579–80), sought to neutralize U.S. carrier and bomber superiority. George Shultz estimated that it would leave 70 percent of the Soviet Union's ICBM force intact. Shultz, *Turmoil and Triumph,* 576–77.

553   **Nothing would delight**   EM Notes. See also Nitze, *From Hiroshima to Glasnost,* 388–89.

553   **Reagan stirred**   EM Notes, Nov. 18, 1985.

554   **"Lord," he wrote**   RR Diary, Nov. 18, 1985.

554   **like old pewter**   EM Notes, Nov. 19, 1985. The author was intrigued to note that RR used this same image in *An American Life,* 11.

554   **Reagan was closeted**   EM Notes, Nov. 19, 1989.

555   **Shortly before ten**   Ibid; Donald Regan interview, Dec. 7, 1985.

555   **The forty-eight**   EM Notes, WHTV video, Nov. 19, 1985, RRL/av.

556   **Many years later**   EM Diary, Oct. 3, 1995; Mikhail Gorbachev interview, Oct. 3, 1995. The interpreter was Pavel Palazchenko.

557   **Inside Fleur d'Eau**   WHTV video, Nov. 19, 1985, RRL/av; Ron Reagan, "While the Summit Slept," *Playboy,* Mar. 1986. Howard Baker told the author that it was his impression, when the President and his son were together in the same room, "that Ron was stronger." Howard Baker interview, July 13, 1987.

557   **He listened with**   WHTV video, RRL/av; EM Notes, Nov. 19, 1985.

558   **"Should I go in?"**   Shultz in "The Cold War," RRL conference transcript, Nov. 13, 1995. See also Shultz, *Turmoil and Triumph,* 600.

558   **If we choose**   Bertrand Russell, *The ABC of Relativity* (New York, 1925, 1959), 215.

558   **When I asked**   RR interview, Nov. 19, 1985; Donald Regan Notes, Nov. 19, 1985, LC; RR, *An American Life,* 13.

558   **He followed by**   Gorbachev interview, Oct. 3, 1995.

559   **For the rest**   Donald Regan Notes, Nov. 19, 1985, memo after limousine conversation with RR, ca. 12:15 P.M., LC.

559   **The General Secretary certainly**   Ibid.

559   **Reagan, oscillating**   RR interview, Dec. 12, 1985; Adelman, *Great Universal Embrace,* 123; Donald Regan Notes, Nov. 19, 1985, LC.

559   **The only proposal**   Donald Regan Notes, Nov. 19, 1985, LC.

559   **Gorbachev replied**   Gorbachev, *Memoirs,* 406; Adelman, *Great Universal Embrace,* 124; Donald Regan Notes, Nov. 19, 1985, LC.

560   **Finally they came**   EM Notes, Nov. 19, 1985; WHTV video, Nov. 19, 1985; Mikhail Gorbachev interview, Oct. 3, 1995. All timings from Donald Regan Notes, Nov. 19, 1985, LC.

561   **The General Secretary started**   Donald Regan Notes, Nov. 19, 1985, LC.

561   **"You want to reduce"**   Ibid.

561   **"Let me tell you"**   "As I reread the minutes, I am amazed at the ex-

tremely ideological stands taken by both partners." Gorbachev, *Memoirs,* 405.

562   **Reagan accused**   Donald Regan Notes, Nov. 19, 1985, LC.

562   **"It's not a weapon"**   Ibid.

563   **"This man is"**   Mikhail Gorbachev interview, Oct. 3, 1995. See also Gorbachev, *Memoirs,* 407.

563   **At lunch in**   Adelman, *Great Universal Embrace,* 124–25.

563   **The big Zil**   EM Notes, Nov. 19, 1985.

564   **"Spy dust!"**   An allusion to the contemporary "spy dust" scare at the U.S. Embassy in Moscow, where certain objects had been found to be impregnated with a powder supposedly capable of transmitting sound waves to KGB receivers. Oberdorfer, *The Turn,* 220.

564   **Rachmaninoff's Cello Sonata**   Preserved on Sony Classical SM2K 46743(117). The author presented a cassette of this performance to Gorbachev in 1995, "as a souvenir of how you sounded at Geneva." Gorbachev allowed that he would prefer to be compared to Tchaikovsky. Interestingly, he later stated that the music *he* felt best expressed the essential melancholy of the Russian people was the slow movement of Mahler's Fifth Symphony.

564   **Gorbachev's voice**   EM Notes, Nov. 19, 1985. *Mir* = peace, *voennyi* = military.

564   **"He's going on"**   Ibid. According to Gorbachev, *Memoirs,* 407, he was saying: "SDI is the continuation of the arms race into a different, more dangerous sphere . . . I think you should know that we have already developed a response. It will be effective and far less expensive than your project, and be ready for use in less time."

565   **Weinberger says**   Donald Regan Notes, Nov. 19, 1985, LC.

565   **I crouched**   EM Notes, Nov. 19, 1985. "Isn't it true," RR wrote a friend, "that someone once said, 'Scratch a Russian and you will find a tragedian?' " RR to Barney Oldfield, Feb. 25, 1985, RRL/pp.

566   **"It looks like"**   Gorbachev, *Memoirs,* 408.

566   **"At this point"**   The following account is based on EM Diary, Nov. 19, 1985.

567   **a flying coal**   Terry Arthur (photographer) interview, Apr. 19, 1987.

567   **The proposals**   Also included in pool-house proposals: an INF agreement, pending total elimination by treaty. Oberdorfer, *The Turn,* 145–46, and Nitze, *From Hiroshima to Glasnost,* 411–19.

567   **For the next fifty-five**   EM Diary and Notes, Nov. 19, 1985. Gorbachev's laughter was caused by a joke RR had just told him about a Russian and an American who argued about free speech. The American declared, "In my country, I can go into the White House, pound on the President's desk, and say, 'I don't like Ronald Reagan.' " The Russian replied, "It's the same in my country. I can go into the Kremlin, pound on Gorbachev's desk, and say, 'I don't like Ronald Reagan.' "

568   **"Well, Mr. General Secretary"**   EM Notes, Nov. 19, 1985 ("very close, face to face"). RR had been strongly cautioned not to raise the question of another summit. Oberdorfer, *The Turn,* 147.

568   **Gorbachev went quite pale**   In his memoirs, he writes: "I suddenly felt

very cold—maybe in contrast to the warmth by the fireside or our heated discussion." Although the antagonisms of the day had not faded, "I think there [were] two factors at work—responsibility and intuition" (408).

568 **They locked hands**   EM Notes, Nov. 19, 1985. Ten years later, in a letter addressed to the RR Presidential Foundation, which was hosting a Geneva Summit commemorative conference, Gorbachev recalled "that spark of mutual trust which ignited between us, like a voltaic arc between two electric poles." Copy in AC.

568 **Debriefing the President**   Oberdorfer, *The Turn,* 146–48; Donald Regan Notes, Nov. 19, 1985, LC; McFarlane, *Special Trust,* 319–20.

569 **Reagan repeated**   "I'm *sure* this man believes in God," RR told President von Wiezsäcker of West Germany in 1987. "If I could only get him alone, I'm *sure* I could talk to him about these things." Richard Burt interview, Oct. 7, 1987; Donald Regan Notes, Nov. 19, 1985, LC.

569 **He listened to**   Kornienko had been stationed at the Poltava base during World War II. See Shultz, *Turmoil and Triumph,* 600. EM Notes, Nov. 19, 1985; Donald Regan Notes, Nov. 19, 1985, LC.

569 **And turn Gorbachev**   Shultz, *Turmoil and Triumph,* 602–3, WHTV video, RRL/av; Donald Regan Notes, Nov. 20, 1985, LC.

570 **They were back**   Oberdorfer, *The Turn,* 148; McFarlane, *Special Trust,* 317; Donald Regan Notes, Nov. 20, 1985, LC.

570 **As they got**   Donald Regan Notes, Nov. 20, 1985, LC; Robert McFarlane interview, Feb. 28, 1995. See Oberdorfer, *The Turn,* 149, and McFarlane, *Special Trust,* 318, for slight variants in this dialogue.

570 **This the President**   Donald Regan Notes, Nov. 20, 1985, LC.

570 **At this they**   Ibid.; George Shultz at "Retrospective on the End of the Cold War" conference, Woodrow Wilson School, Princeton University, Feb. 25–27, 1993. Oberdorfer, *The Turn,* 149–50, describes this morning's events in different sequence but similar content. Shultz, *Turmoil and Triumph,* 603, has the silence following a Gorbachev ultimatum: "SDI has to come to an end."

571 **There was a brief explosion**   Ca. 10:40 P.M. Donald Regan Notes, Nov. 20, 1985, LC.

571 **What is it**   The clutching and gaze-locking continued for the rest of the summit. RR told the author that when he took his final leave of Gorbachev, and recited a sentimental Irish valedictory, "that hand tightened on mine—it was really crushing it." Interview, Nov. 7, 1987.

573 **We've come to**   RR's toast may be heard in the audiobook version of this biography.

573 **"We have it"**   See p. 387.

575 **After the joint**   Adelman, *Great Universal Embrace,* 156–57, John Hutton interview, Oct. 29, 1996; William Henkel interview, Jan. 16, 1986.

575 **Dear Friends**   RR to Hussain Aga Khan, Nov. 21, 1985, copy courtesy NR. RR enclosed a presidential portrait inscribed "From your 'fish nanny.' "

575   **The workday begun**   In his diary that night he wrote, "I haven't gotten such a reception since I was shot." RR, *An American Life,* 641.

575   **Next morning he**   RR Diary, Nov. 22, 1985, RRP.

34: Explosions

576   **If there was any**   July 4, 1986. Except where otherwise indicated, the following account of Liberty Weekend is based on EM Diary, July 3–4, 1986, and EM Notes, same dates, AC, supplemented by (official program), AC, and The Schedule of President Ronald Reagan, July 3–5, 1986, RRL.

576   **"That's two thousand"**   EM Notes, July 3, 1986.

577   **Oldest of Presidents**   See Lance Morrow, "Why Is This Man So Popular?," *Time* cover story, July 7, 1986. RR's fame overseas was also burgeoning. Two examples: the declaration by Marguerite Duras, doyenne of French literary intellectuals: "I am a Reaganite. . . . He is the incarnation of a kind of primal, almost archaic power." *Harper's,* Aug. 1986.

577   **prostate problems**   RR had had "several episodes of prostatitis" and "long-standing urinary hesitancy" since his transurethral prostate resection of 1967. By July 1986, the urinary problem became acute, with hematuria occurring before the end of the month. The White House then announced that RR would undergo "a urological evaluation" at Bethesda Naval Hospital, Aug. 9, 1986. See text below, and Beahrs, "Medical History."

577   **"Mr. President, how was"**   EM Diary, July 3, 1986, AC. RR's own record of the working lunch is somewhat more informative: "Our meeting had to do with East-West relations. I tried to give the Pres. all the info. I could about our dealings with the Gen Sec. on arms reductions, so that he would know our side if he was subjected to any propaganda. It was a good meeting although Pres. Mitterrand can be very unpredictable." RR Diary, July 3, 1986, RRP.

577   **Napoleon's long halts**   Vincent Cronin, *Napoleon Bonaparte: An Intimate Biography* (New York, 1978), 180.

578   **I detached myself**   The Liberty Weekend Opening Ceremonies, "executive-produced" by the Reagans' friend David Wolper, reached such a pitch of vulgarity that Tom Shales was moved to ask despairingly, "Is good taste incompatible with love of country?" *The Washington Post,* July 4, 1986.

578   **Or so the literature**   "Liberty Weekend," official program, AC.

578   **It was not that Dutch**   Handwritten insert, RR speech draft, Alfafa Club Dinner, Jan. 21, 1986, RRL/pp/hw.

579   **For seven months**   Gramm-Rudman was a popular bill, sponsored by Senators Phil Gramm of Texas and Warren Rudman of New Hampshire, that compelled cuts in spending if the federal deficit did not decline at an agreed-on rate.

579   **he would, smile, shrug**   See also Attali, *Verbatim I,* 238. The tone of RR's diary in Feb. 1986 is noticeably perfunctory and bored.

579   **In Tokyo, on**   RR interview, June 12, 1986.

580   **Peter J. Wallison**   Notwithstanding his inflexibility in office, Wallison afterward generously offered his White House diary to the author as a historical source. It contains the following passage, dated Sept. 17, 1986: "I met with the Pres. about Edmund Morris. . . . [He] expressed some impatience, saying he was already three minutes late for his next appointment [with the author]. I . . . told the Pres. that there was a potential conflict of interest between Edmund Morris's biography and the President's own memoirs, and that he might consider not answering some of the questions that Morris poses about his state of mind at the time he makes decisions. I said this was material that should go in his own memoirs, and that if it is given to Morris the memoirs may have less value and may in fact be contradicted by what Morris has been told. I mentioned that I had already talked to Mrs. R. about this subject, and she had agreed. During this time the Pres. was staring at me very directly, not saying anything and with no expression on his face. Perhaps it was the light, but the pupils of his eyes seemed to be bright points—somewhat disconcerting. . . . I don't think he was persuaded, but [Don] Regan thought he would be more careful with Morris in future." Copy in AC.

580   **I recollect a Cabinet**   For another use of the presidential wink, see Morrow, "Why Is This Man?," 12.

581   **He also deleted**   RR to Joseph Gold, Jan. 24, 1986, RRL/pp/hw; RR interview, May 10, 1988.

582   **It hung before me**   See Henry James, *The Ambassadors* (1903; New York, 1963), 57. See also photographs in *Time,* July 7, 1986.

582   **On the first**   EM Diary, Dec. 14, 1985, AC.

582   **He had recently**   EM Diary, Dec. 14, 1985, AC. McFarlane dates his resignation as Dec. 4, 1985 (*Special Trust,* 330–31). But RR Diary, Nov. 30, 1985, RRP, makes plain that it was tendered and accepted five days earlier. ("I believe that his successor should be John Poindexter.")

582   **McFarlane was polite**   McFarlane's resignation was rendered even more personally painful by rumors, encouraged by mutual enemies, that he was having an affair with a female White House correspondent. See McFarlane, *Special Trust,* 328–29; Mayer and McManus, *Landslide,* 165–66.

583   **The other expression**   EM Notes, June 3, 1986.

583   **Liberty Weekend's**   EM Diary, July 3, 1986, AC. RR lifted off from Governors Island at 11:23 P.M.

583   **Had I been permitted**   Jacques Attali, *Verbatim II: Chronique des années 1986–1988* (Paris, 1995; pocket edition), 134.

584   **A bugle blowing**   EM Notes, July 4, 1986.

584   **Donald Regan's chairman**   *The New York Times,* July 6, 1986.

584   **Mr. J. E. Reagan**   See p. 31.

585   **He had gotten**   RR in *Parade,* June 29, 1986.

585   **Dutch had articulated**   RR speech cards, Jan. 28, 1986, RRL/pp/hw.

585   **Nobody watching**   Jan. 29, 1986; Lou Cannon in *The Washington Post,* Feb. 3, 1986. See O'Neill and Novak, *Man of the House,* 362–63, for the full text of his furious exchange with RR. According to Michael Deaver,

RR was not so moved by the shuttle tragedy as to see why the State of the Union address had to be postponed. George Bush had to telephone Deaver, in London, to beg him to make the President understand the consequences of insensitivity. Michael Deaver interview, May 18, 1989. For an acerbic interpretation of RR's speech as "silvery platitudes" designed to wish the tragedy away, see Howard Nemerov's poem "On an Occasion of National Mourning," in *Trying Conclusions: New and Selected Poems, 1961–1991* (Chicago, 1991), 124.

586   **Two U.S. citizens**   RR Diary, Apr. 6, 7, 9, 1986, RRP; Shultz, *Turmoil and Triumph,* 677; Woodward, *Veil,* 444–45. For an example of Qaddafi's psychotic detestation of RR ("the new Hitler of the world"), see his letter to François Mitterrand, qu. in Attali, *Verbatim I,* 530–31.

586   **With no help**   Attali, *Verbatim II,* 26. "It will unify the Arab world behind Qaddafi," Mitterrand exclaimed. This source makes plain that the United States intended to strike Libya as early as March 21, 1986, before the Berlin bombing. See Woodward, *Veil,* 440–43.

586   **When I**   RR interview, Apr. 15, 1986.

586   **The raid**   Shultz, *Turmoil and Triumph,* 686–88.

586   **I wish**   Donald Regan Notes, Apr. 28–29, 1986; Shultz, *Turmoil and Triumph,* 714–15; Gorbachev, *Memoirs,* 189 ("We simply did not know the whole truth yet").

587   **"Chernobyl means"**   EM Notes, July 8, 1986; Grigori Medvedev, *The Truth about Chernobyl* (New York, 1991), 79; Roy Medvedev and Giulietto Chiesa, *Time of Change: An Insider's View of Russia's Transformation* (New York, 1989), 41.

587   **Dutch's theological**   Cannon, *President Reagan,* 757, notes that RR once misrepresented this as "Wedgwood."

587   **When Gorbachev finally**   Medvedev and Chiesa, *Time of Change,* 6; Gorbachev, *Memoirs,* 192.

587   **It was the catalyst**   Medvedev, *The Truth about Chernobyl,* 70; Medvedev and Chiesa, *Time of Change,* 7. On Dec. 11, 1991, members of the Ukrainian Parliament voted to prosecute Gorbachev for attempting to conceal the extent of the Chernobyl disaster. *The New York Times,* Dec. 12, 1991.

35: The Beginning of the End

589   ***The withness of the body***   Used as the epigraph to Delmore Schwartz's "The Heavy Bear Who Goes with Me," qu. in Cleanth Brooks and Robert Penn Warren, *Understanding Poetry* (New York, 1938, 1959), 558.

589   **"A delayed step"**   RR Diary, July 27 and 28, 1986, RRP.

589   **["Dr. Smith]"**   Ibid., July 28, 1986, RRP. White House Physician T. Burton Smith was a urological specialist.

589   **He had been distracted**   Ibid., July 18, 1985, and July 31, Aug. 8–9, 1986, RRP; John Hutton Diary, July 31, 1986, JHP; Kornbluh and Byrne, *Iran-Contra Scandal,* 237–39, 250. For Robert McFarlane's first hints of a hostage-release "plan," see text later in this chapter.

589   **Nancy Reagan swung**   John Hutton Diary, Aug. 1, 1986, JHP.

590   **The results of**   Beahrs, "Medical History"; EM Diary, Aug. 12 and 15, 1986, AC.

590   **It was a typically**   RR Diary, Aug. 20 and 27, 1986, RRP; John Hutton Diary, Aug. 21–22, 1986, JHP; RR Diary, Aug. 26, 1986, RRP.

590   **Blood or no blood**   White House Physician Dr. Burton Smith dissented, saying that RR was "living with a situation he has had for years." John Hutton Diary, Sept. 9, 1986, JHP.

590   **A tetchy Soviet-American**   RR Diary, Sept. 19, 1986, RRP ("I enjoyed being angry"); Regan, *For the Record,* 338–39; Shultz, *Turmoil and Triumph,* 742–43.

590   **The letter, when**   Adelman, *Great Universal Embrace,* 24.

591   **An idea has come**   Mikhail Gorbachev to RR, Sept. 15, 1986, copy in REG.

591   **"I opt for Iceland."**   RR Diary, Sept. 19, 1986, RRP.

591   **The "spies"**   EM Diary, Sept. 30, 1986, AC; *The New York Times,* Oct. 1, 1986.

592   **An exhausted**   Steingrimur Hermannsson interview, Sept. 1, 1995 ("I hold Ronald Reagan in great esteem, but I was very disappointed and surprised").

592   **Gorbachev, whom Hermannsson**   Ibid.

592   **Night fell over**   "Iceland was something of a different world," RR wrote his pen pal Rudolph Hines, noting its oppressive late-afternoon darkness. Nov. 6, 1986, RRL/pp/hw. Gorbachev also found it to be "an unknown world." Gorbachev, *Memoirs,* 416.

593   **At least, that was**   Dobrynin, *In Confidence,* 621; RR to Kenneth Adelman, qu. in Adelman, *Great Universal Embrace,* 74 ("Hell, he doesn't want to set up a summit. He wants to have a summit. Right here"). Whether or not Reykjavík was "a trap," as Adelman has suggested, the fact remains that RR had less than two weeks to prepare for it, whereas Gorbachev had been doing so since at least the late summer. Gorbachev, *Memoirs,* 414.

593   **The two men faced**   Souza, *Unguarded Moments,* 128; EM Notes, Sept. 2, 1995.

594   **He noticed at once**   Serge Tarasenko, Soviet note taker, interview [in English], Nov. 13, 1995.

594   **A six-on-six**   Pavel Palazchenko, *My Years with Gorbachev and Shevardnadze: The Memoir of a Soviet Interpreter* (University Park, Pa., 1997), 55; RR, *An American Life,* 676; George Shultz interview, Aug. 15, 1989. See also Gorbachev, *Memoirs,* 417: "He appeared confused."

594   **Shultz, too, was**   Gorbachev, *Memoirs,* 417–18; Shultz, *Turmoil and Triumph,* 758–59.

594   **"What it really"**   Qu. in Shultz, *Turmoil and Triumph,* 759. In Administration parlance, this was the "zero-zero" option. See p. 454.

594   **This was not true**   Oberdorfer, *The Turn,* 156, 159–60, 165–67; Mikhail Gorbachev interview, Oct. 3, 1995; Gorbachev, *Memoirs,* 184–85, 412–14. Oberdorfer shows (169–74) that the Administration did make a bold attempt to respond to Gorbachev's zero-option proposal, at least in

regard to ballistic missiles, in the early summer of 1986. But the bureaucratic NSC of Admiral John Poindexter "experted" this counterproposal into a letter from RR, July 25, 1986, which Kenneth Adelman describes as "nearly unintelligible." Adelman, *Great Universal Embrace,* 29–30.

595   **Disillusionment—Gorbachev's** Serge Tarasenko interview, Nov. 13, 1995; Gorbachev, *Memoirs,* 417.

595   **Still talking** Shultz, *Turmoil and Triumph,* 759 (emphasis added).

595   **This was a major** Serge Tarasenko interview, Nov. 13, 1995; Shultz, *Turmoil and Triumph,* 760.

595   **"This is the best"** Shultz, *Turmoil and Triumph,* 760.

596   **Suddenly he flare** Serge Tarasenko interview, Nov. 13, 1995.

596   **A more prosaic** Adelman, *Great Universal Embrace,* 47; RR interview, Nov. 18, 1986.

596   **"When you tag"** RR interview, Nov. 18, 1986.

596   **"You will take"** Shultz, *Turmoil and Triumph,* 761. At another point Gorbachev grudgingly conceded, "I may believe you, Mr. President, but would your successors repeat the offer?" Palazchenko, *My Years,* 56.

597   **I was not a** The U.S. delegation to Reykjavík consisted of 267, rather than the usual summit contingent of 1,000. In addition to RR, Gorbachev, Shultz, Tarasenko, and Hermannsson, the author interviewed Donald Regan, Paul Nitze, Kenneth Adelman, Pete Souza, Pavel Palazchenko, and Ingvi-Hrafn Jonsson, anchor of Iceland TV's twenty-four-hour coverage of the summit. He found (as with the Geneva summit) wide discrepancies of memory as to who said what, and when, at Reykjavík. This account is based primarily on RR's own fairly fresh recollections to the author on Nov. 18, 1986, and on George Shultz's well-documented narrative in *Turmoil and Triumph,* Ch. 36. Other important sources are cited *passim.* Extra details come from WHTV footage in RRL/av and from the author's own visit to summit sites in Aug.–Sept. 1995. See Edmund Morris, "Push and Shove in a Cold Climate," *Forbes FYI* (summer 1996).

597   **Sergei Akhromeyev** Marshal Akhromeyev was then chief of the Soviet Armed Forces. A man of unimpeachable integrity, revered by both sides, he hanged himself after the fall of the Soviet Union.

597   **I tried to imagine** Nitze, *From Hiroshima to Glasnost,* 432; Shultz, *Turmoil and Triumph,* 765. For details of the overnight negotiation, see Nitze, 429–32; Oberdorfer, *The Turn,* 193–95; and especially Adelman, *Great Universal Embrace,* Ch. 1, still the most clear-eyed analysis of Reykjavík.

597   **"Wait a minute"** RR interview, Nov. 18, 1986.

597   **Reagan shot** Ibid. See also Oberdorfer's longer, Shultz-flavored version of this exchange in *The Turn,* 202. Oberdorfer writes (201) that RR "never seemed to fully appreciate the important difference" between missiles and weapons. RR's quotations in interview show that on the contrary he understood it perfectly. See Shultz, *Turmoil and Triumph,* 770–71, for the text to which Gorbachev and RR were referring.

598   **The tension** Pavel Palazchenko told the author that Gorbachev had difficulty controlling his contempt for RR's patient, word-for-word repeti-

tiveness, including multiple repetitions of the phrase *doveryai non proveryai* ("trust, but verify"). "I had to explain to the General Secretary that it's a cultural thing. Americans are not embarrassed to repeat themselves. In our culture, we constantly try to rephrase." Interview, Nov. 15, 1995.

598   **Reagan thought to**   RR, *An American Life,* 677. Gorbachev also offered to cut the Soviets' INF arsenal in Central Asia to one hundred SS-20s. Nitze, *From Hiroshima to Glasnost,* 432.

598   **Reagan had been**   RR, *An American Life,* 677; Oberdorfer, *The Turn,* 191; Shultz, *Turmoil and Triumph,* 769. According to Adelman, *Great Universal Embrace,* 71, the laboratory clause would have cut SDI research by as much as 70 percent, in effect neutralizing it.

598   **"I've said again"**   RR, *An American Life,* 678. For a similar version of this exchange (reflecting what RR told Donald Regan afterward), see Regan, *For the Record,* 350–51.

598   **Gorbachev kept smiling**   RR interview, Nov. 18, 1986; Regan, *For the Record,* 351; Shultz, *Turmoil and Triumph,* 771. Gorbachev, *Memoirs,* 418, admits that their final haggle was "bizarre."

599   **"It's 'laboratory' "**   Shultz, *Turmoil and Triumph,* 773. RR, in a postsummit conversation with leaders of Congress, confirmed under hostile questioning that it was Gorbachev who first reached for his briefcase. EM Notes, Oct. 14, 1986.

599   **There was a long**   Shultz, *Turmoil and Triumph,* 773. See also Regan, *For the Record,* 352; RR interview, Nov. 18, 1986; RR, *An American Life,* 679.

599   **Gorbachev—incredibly**   RR Diary, Oct. 12, 1986; Adelman, *Great Universal Embrace,* 75; Gorbachev, *Memoirs,* 419; Regan, *For the Record,* 351 (earwitness account).

599   **"Mr. President,"**   This exchange, unreported elsewhere, was interpreted by Anatoly Dobrynin. Dobrynin, *In Confidence,* 621.

599   **"I don't know"**   Souza, *Unguarded Moments,* 130. Souza, snapping close by, was the original overhearer of these much-quoted words.

599   **"Goddammit"**   Donald Regan interview, July 14, 1999. Inevitably, given the haste with which the summit concluded (RR's car pulled away two minutes after he ended the discussion), there are discrepancies in remembered scraps of dialogue. The author has quoted only those exchanges that are confirmable by earwitnesses, and by visual evidence as to where people were, and when. For example, Gorbachev (writing in 1994) recalls his invitation to return to the table as occurring outside, by RR's car, but Regan (writing in 1987) could have overheard it only in the hall.

599   **When Steingrimur**   Steingrimur Hermannsson interview, Sept. 1, 1995. In March 1987, Gorbachev repeated these remarks to Hermannsson in Moscow. Transcript, AC. See also Shultz in *Washington Post Book World,* Mar. 13, 1994: "Years later . . . I asked [Gorbachev] what he considered the turning point in U.S.-Soviet relations during his tenure in office. He answered without hesitation, 'Reykjavík.' "

600   **continuing cacophony**   The following montage of Reykjavík comment is derived, sequentially, from these sources: RR qu. in Regan, *For the Record,* 350–51; Adelman, *Great Universal Embrace,* 37; Thatcher to

Mitterrand, qu. in Attali, *Verbatim II,* 222; Shultz, *Turmoil and Triumph,* 774; Shultz qu. in *The New York Times,* Oct. 13, 1986; RR, qu. in Don Regan interview, Oct. 18, 1986; O'Neill to Shultz, Dole to RR, White House Congressional briefing, Oct. 14, 1986, EM Notes; Shultz, *Turmoil and Triumph,* 775; Poindexter, qu. in Speakes, *Speaking Out,* 144; Haig, qu. in *The Washington Post,* Jan. 25, 1987; Wallop to RR, Oct. 15, 1986, RRP/pp; Adelman, *Great Universal Embrace,* 40; Robert Karl Manoff, *The New York Times,* Op-Ed, Oct. 15, 1986; Regan qu. in *The Washington Post,* Oct. 13, 1986; Kenneth Adelman interview, Dec. 26, 1988; RR Address to the Nation on Iceland Meeting, Oct. 13, 1986 (ms. and teletype script), RRL/pp/hw; Crowe, qu. in Adelman, *Great Universal Embrace,* 86; Wallop to RR, Oct. 15, 1986, RRL/pp; O'Neill and RR at Congressional briefing, Oct. 14, 1986; EM Notes; Barney Oldfield to RR, Oct. 28, 1986, RRL/pp; Akhromeyev, qu. in Oberdorfer, *The Turn,* 209; Gorbachev, qu. in *The New York Times,* Oct. 15, 1986; James Billington interview, Feb. 11, 1994; RR, qu. in William F. Buckley, Jr., interview, Sept. 15, 1995; McNamara, qu. by Jacob Heilbrun in *National Review,* Mar. 22, 1993; French voice, qu. in *The Washington Post,* Oct. 27, 1986; *The New York Times*/CBS News poll, Oct. 19, 1986.

601   **Everybody's got it wrong!**   Kenneth Adelman interview, Dec. 26, 1986. Adelman notes in *Great Universal Embrace,* 81, that "not one of the top five Soviet or American participants [RR, Gorbachev, Shultz, Regan, Aleksandr Bessmertnykh] . . . accurately described the U.S. offer." This is true of their public statements, although RR's handwritten draft of his Oct. 13, 1986, television speech confirms that the total-ban suggestion was made by Gorbachev (RRP/pp/hw). RR was still quite clear about the specifics of each side's proposal on Nov. 12, when he "sharply" reprimanded Poindexter, in front of other senior staff, for the suggestion that he could profit politically by trumpeting a disarmament proposal that he had not in fact put forward. Peter Wallison Diary, Nov. 12, 1986, copy in AC. The author found RR equally clear in an interview on Nov. 18, while documents reproduced in Shultz, *Turmoil and Triumph,* 769–71, bear out the truth of Adelman's assertion. At least two presidential speech drafts (Oct. 12 and 13, 1986, RRL/pp/hw) show evidence of NSC alterations of RR's story. See Attali, *Verbatim II,* 233, for evidence that the White House was, for whatever reason, trying to mislead allies about what really happened at Reykjavík. RR, *An American Life,* 676, and Gorbachev, *Memoirs,* 418, are both carefully circumspect.

602   **On October 22**   RR Diary, Oct. 22, 1986, RRP.

603   **"To most Americans"**   *The Washington Post,* Oct. 19, 1986.

603   **He campaigned across**   Benjamin Weir had been released on Sept. 15, 1985; William Buckley died after torture at about the same time; Fr. Lawrence Jenco was released on July 26, 1986, and David Jacobsen on Nov. 2, 1986. Meanwhile, two more hostages, Frank H. Reed and Edward A. Tracy, had been taken in Sept. and Oct. 1986, joining Thomas Sutherland, Terry A. Anderson, and Joseph J. Cicippio in captivity.

603   **By late evening**   Cannon, *President Reagan,* 671–75; Speakes, *Speaking Out,* 279–82. The first report of this story hit the White House at the

daily operations meeting. Deputy National Security Adviser Alton G. Keel, Jr., speaking for Poindexter, assured senior staff that it was "nonsense." Peter Wallison Diary, Nov. 4, 1986, AC. McFarlane is "absolutely convinced" that the *Al-Shiraa* story was planted by either the KGB or the East German agency GRU in order to affect the U.S. elections. Strober and Strober, *Reagan,* 471.

603   **In due course** McFarlane, *Special Trust,* 89; Theodore Draper, *A Very Thin Line: The Iran-contra Affairs* (New York, 1991), Ch. 15. The chronology of the Iran Initiative, and the official statements of the Reagan Administration, have become so much a matter of public record that the author will dispense with obvious documentation. He expresses his considerable debt to Kornbluh and Byrne, *Iran-Contra Scandal,* which reprints many documents in facsimile. All items in the text reflecting less public sources are cited as usual.

604   **As with Bitburg** Cannon, *President Reagan,* 676; Kornbluh and Byrne, *Iran-Contra Scandal,* 405.

604   **But what was *it*?** Kornbluh and Byrne, *Iran-Contra Scandal,* 405.

604   **The "Iran Initiative"** McFarlane was still arguing in 1994, when he published his memoir, that to have neglected the chance of an "opening" to Iran in July 1985 would have been as gravely irresponsible "as ignoring Chinese overtures to re-establish relations in the 1970s" (*Special Trust,* p. 17). The author follows Draper's conscientious distinction between the Iran Initiative and the Contra Diversion. The two affairs "were . . . quite different operations and dealt with very different problems," despite their occasional intersections and some common participants. As Draper remarks, the catchphrase "Iran-*contra*" gives a misleading chronological impression. The Reagan Administration's search for alternate funding of the *contras* began long before its arms-for-hostage negotiations. Draper, *A Very Thin Line,* 3.

604   **What a morning** RR Diary, July 18, 1986, RRP.

605   **Let us in fairness** John Hutton interview, Dec. 29, 1992. Dr. Hutton's notes, July 16–18, 1985, show the President obsessing about his old movies, and at other times absently staring out of the window. Other medical distractions on the eighteenth: RR felt weak in the shower, and had a small, probably post-anesthetic, patch on his right lower lung. Ibid.

605   **Even Donald Regan** Regan, *For the Record,* 19–20. See ibid., 6–18, for McFarlane's urgent attempts to see RR from the first day of his hospitalization. Regan remarks on the disconnect between this urgency and the seeming inconsequence of the message McFarlane delivered when NR finally permitted a visit. Nor does it appear that RR was being circumspect in his diary entry for the eighteenth: he was always quick to note any new chance of freeing a hostage, and took a boyish pleasure in mentioning when he had been enjoined to secrecy. It would seem that McFarlane just wanted *carte blanche* to proceed with his vague "initiative."

605   **He hears only** Regan, *For the Record,* 21, notes that at least half of

McFarlane's twenty-three-minute visit was devoted to the Geneva arms talks. "It hardly seems likely that an entirely new [Iran] policy . . . could have been decided on in such a brief encounter."

605 **Dr. Steven Rosenberg**   Chief of surgery at the National Cancer Institute and member of the team operating on RR.

605 **Reagan's July 18**   See Draper, *A Very Thin Line,* 145–49, for a sample cross-section of these versions.

606 **Did McFarlane indeed**   McFarlane to George Shultz, July 13, 1985, qu. in *Testimony at Joint Hearings Before the House Select Committee to Investigate Covert Arms Transactions with Iran and the Senate Select Committee on Secret Military Assistance to Iran and the Nicaraguan Opposition* (Washington, D.C., 1987), vol. 100–9, 494–95. July 13 was the day of RR's operation, and this long letter represented the sum of what McFarlane urgently wanted to tell the President. As Draper (132–33) remarks, the letter contains the whole Iran Initiative in embryo: "dialogue with the West, political change in Iran, hostages, missiles."

606 **One can almost**   Draper, *A Very Thin Line,* 116; McFarlane, *Special Trust,* 26–27.

606 **"There is nothing in my notes"**   Regan, *For the Record,* 21. See also McFarlane's suggestion, in another interview, that it was RR who suggested the idea of weapons as "the currency of doing that" in the Middle East. Draper, *A Very Thin Line,* 146.

607 **Here, again, we have**   McFarlane, *Special Trust,* 23, 26; Draper, *A Very Thin Line,* 146; Regan, *For the Record,* 20, 11–19.

607 **fifty thousand pages**   See Draper, *A Very Thin Line,* introduction.

607 **Reagan had decided**   Don Regan notes, Nov. 10, 1986, qu. Kornbluh and Byrne, *Iran-Contra Scandal,* 405. On Nov. 13, RR informed the nation in a television address, "We did not—repeat not—trade weapons or anything else for hostages."

607 **Attorney General Meese insisted**   Peter Wallison Diary, Nov. 18–20, 1986, AC.

607 **Robert McFarlane, enjoying**   McFarlane had been hankering for a return to public life from the moment of his resignation in Dec. 1985. McFarlane to RR, Oct. 17, 1986, RRL/pp; McFarlane, *Special Trust,* 332–33, 94; Draper, *A Very Thin Line,* 291.

608 **CONVERSATION IN THE OVAL OFFICE**   The following conversation has been only lightly edited of longueurs. It is reproduced at length as an example of the author's thirty-nine interviews with RR, and of the President's mental and emotional state before his disastrous press conference of Nov. 19, 1986.

612 **I attended the former**   Peter Wallison Diary, Nov. 19, 1986, AC. "He still did not know the answers to many very basic questions. . . . Things were bad enough: Edmund Morris was there in the briefing room to witness this performance for his biography of Reagan."

612 **It would have to have**   *Report of the Congressional Committees Investigating the Iran-Contra Affair,* 100th Cong., 1st sess., 1987, 280–81.

612 **He did better**   EM Notes, Nov. 19, 1986. On Nov. 12, Wallison had found the arms sales to Iran to be in contravention of the AECA, and advised against a paragraph in RR's Nov. 13 address draft that stated that

no laws had been broken. Due to determined obfuscation by NSC and Justice Department officials, who insisted that the sale represented the President's will, Wallison had to back down. "I expressed particular disgust that the President had been put out in front on this matter, apparently in order to [give] credibility to the mistakes of his national security advisers." Peter Wallison Diary, Nov. 14 and 19, 1986, AC. See David Hoffman, "Reagan's Worst Speech," *The Washington Post,* July 20, 1987.

612   **The atmosphere in**   EM Notes, Nov. 19, 1986. According to Wallison, RR's performance at the first pre-brief, the day before, had been even worse—"frighteningly bad." Diary, Nov. 18, 1986.

613   **Predictably, he**   See Mayer and McManus, *Landslide,* 313–15.

613   **"I done good"**   RR Diary, Nov. 19, 1986, RRP. RR had emphatically *not* done well. According to the *Los Angeles Times,* only 14 percent of Americans believed him when he said he had not, "repeat not," traded arms for hostages. Regan, *For the Record,* 32.

613   *en déshabillé*   Peter Wallison Diary, Oct. 14, 1986, AC.

613 ·   **he made clear at Reykjavík**   On Oct. 10, RR was overheard saying to a television image of Gorbachev arriving in Iceland: "When you stop trying to take over the world, then maybe we can do some business." Adelman, *Great Universal Embrace,* 44.

614.   **Regan was another**   Regan, *For the Record,* 73–74. Why NR was so circumspect about her "Friend's" identity is a mystery, because Joan Quigley was by no means averse to the spotlight when reporters discovered her after the publication of *For the Record.* Her influence upon world events in the 1980s ("I wanted to pick the longest, and most prominent, time for Bergen-Belsen") is self-documented in Strober and Strober, *Reagan.*

614   **Michael Deaver had**   Regan, *For the Record,* 73–74; EM Notes, Feb. 27, 1987.

614   **Regan, an impatient**   Strober and Strober, *Reagan,* 313, 346–47; Regan, *For the Record,* 359. Regan misdates the year as 1987, although it is clear from the context that he means 1986.

614   **I knew something**   EM Notes, 3 P.M., Nov. 24, 1986. Peter Wallison Diary, Nov. 24, 1986, confirms that nothing substantive was said at the issues lunch.

615   **If we are to believe**   Regan, *For the Record,* 39. RR Diary, Nov. 24, 1986, RRP.

615   **"North didn't tell"**   RR Diary, Nov. 4, 1986, RRP.

615   **even Poindexter had never**   Peter Wallison Diary, Nov. 14, 1986, AC.

616   **eyes-only, unquotable**   C. Boyden Gray interview, Apr. 23, 1998. According to Gray, who was White House counsel to George Bush both as Vice President and President, the Boland Amendments (strictly speaking, about half a dozen different statutes) were specifically and secretly weakened by this "classified annex," in effect an outlet clause for RR to give whatever secret intelligence he deemed necessary to aid the *contras.* "Not even Tip O'Neill wanted to prevent Reagan from acting quickly, if the *contras* were indeed to run out of funds. Tip didn't want Communists in Nicaragua any more than the President did." The annex is in the Intelligence Authority Act of 1986, "which qualifies as a Boland Amend-

ment." Gray notes further that Boland II was not a criminal statute; it did not even contain enforceable civil penalties. It was deliberately left toothless, "while absolving Congress of any ultimate responsibility for a *contra* disaster." Ibid.

616   **Six years before**   Attali, *Verbatim I,* 66 (June 26, 1981). Author's translation.

616   **Now he felt**   EM Notes, Nov.–Dec. 1986; Mayer and McManus, *Landslide,* 362; RR Diary, Nov. 30, 1986, RRP. Shultz's pique diminished when RR assured him he would not engage in Iran-type adventures again. RR Diary, Dec. 3, 1986, RRP.

36: Album Leaves, 1987–1988

617   **Nancy (privately)**   NR, qu. in John Hutton interview, Dec. 17, 1986.

618   **Also—what she**   EM Notes, Jan. 4, 1987; Nancy Clark Reynolds interview, Dec. 2, 1986.

618   **Nancy & her**   Mayer and McManus, *Landslide,* 361–62; RR Diary, Dec. 17, 1986, RRP; Michael Deaver interview, May 18, 1989.

618   **The prostate surgery**   During the operation, RR, anesthetized from the waist down, was heard to say, "Where's the rest of me?" John Hutton Diary, Jan. 5, 1987, JHP. See p. 279.

619   **Bill Casey—the**   John Hutton Diary, Jan. 15 and 21, 1987, JHP.

619   **Mr. President, I just have**   Michael Deaver interview, Feb. 28, 1987. Deaver did not see RR again as President. They reconciled in 1992.

619   **Nadir—so far**   John Hutton Diary, Jan. 28 and Feb. 24, 1987, JHP; Adelman, *Great Universal Embrace,* 316; Donald Reagan interview, Feb. 11, 1987; Deaver, *Behind the Scenes,* 254–55; Nancy Clark Reynolds interview, Feb. 17, 1987; Mayer and McManus, *Landslide,* 372.

620   **Suggested title**   See Regan, *For the Record,* 88–89.

620   **Howard is looking**   RR was wrong about Baker's enthusiasm for the job. The Senator later told his old friend Sol Linowitz that he had been poised to announce his own presidential candidacy in three days. But RR was "literally begging," and he knew he could not refuse.

621   **The NSC system**   *Report of the President's Special Review Board* (Washington, D.C., Feb. 1987), IV-10.

622   **James Cannon, the**   James Cannon interview, Mar. 3, 1987. See also Mayer and McManus, *Landslide,* viii–x.

622   **his precipitous resignation**   Regan had intended, as he advised RR, to resign on Monday, March 2, but an early news leak of his demise (which he blamed on NR's "East Wing" operation) caused him to storm out three days early. Donald Regan interview, Apr. 8, 1987; Regan, *For the Record,* 372.

622   **Before lunch in**   EM Notes, Mar. 1, 1987; James Cannon interview, Dec. 1, 1987. See also Mayer and McManus, *Landslide,* x.

623   **[*A spring afternoon*]**   EM Diary, Apr. 19, 1987.

623   **"There is a lot of rage"**   Gore Vidal, *United States,* 481.

623   **Muffie [Brandon]**   Mabel H. Brandon, former White House social secretary, to NR.

PAGE

624   **"Issues lunch"**   EM Notes, May 4, 1987; Cannon, *President Reagan,* 816.

624   **What a rhetorical**   Robert Frost, "Mending Wall," *North of Boston* (New York, 1914); Edna St. Vincent Millay, *Aria da Capo* (see above, p. 82). The author underestimated the impact of RR's speech, written by Peter Robinson, on the very audience it was aimed at—those invisible millions, official and otherwise, living in totalitarian misery east of the Brandenburg Gate. The phrase "Tear down this wall!" (cravenly opposed by State Department accommodationists) embedded itself in the Communist consciousness as much as "Evil Empire" had five years before. See Robinson's tenth-anniversary review, "Tearing Down That Wall," in *The Weekly Standard,* June 23, 1987.

626   **Dear Edmund**   RR to EM, Sept. 26, 1987, AC. These two poems, as anyone who has heard RR recite them can attest, total 126 extremely long lines.

627   **NR has breast cancer**   Supplementary details from John Hutton interview, Nov. 12, 1993.

628   **NR's spirits**   EM Diary, EM Notes, Nov. 7–15, 1987.

628   **literati in formal dress**   Gay Talese (*The Kingdom and the Power* and *Thy Neighbor's Wife*); Nan A. Talese, editor in chief of Houghton Mifflin; Robert K. Massie (*Nicholas and Alexandra; Peter the Great*); Anthony Haden-Guest (*The Paradise Program; Bad Dreams*); Marion Elizabeth Rodgers (*Mencken and Sara: A Life in Letters*); Kenneth S. Lynn (*Mark Twain and Southwestern Humor; Hemingway*); Valerie Lynn, a psychologist; Phyllis Rose (*Parallel Lives: Five Victorian Marriages*).

628   **"Well, Mr. President"**   Item found in the Sophie Tucker Scrapbooks, NYPL/pa. The author felt it best not to quote further from this same issue of the *Hollywood Reporter,* "LEW AYRES and JANE WYMAN keep ga-ga with each other at the Beverly Hills Hotel."

629   **As Senator Hatfield did**   Copies in AC.

630   **Gorbachev arrives**   This section reflects interviews with RR, George Shultz, Colin Powell, Howard Baker, and Frank Carlucci, Dec. 14, 17, 21, 23, 1987.

631   **[Wednesday Dec. 9]**   RR Diary, Dec. 9, 1987; Frank Carlucci interview, Dec. 22, 1987.

631   **In the long, long**   Robert Service, "The Cremation of Sam McGee," *The Spell of the Yukon* (Philadelphia, 1907). For a detailed account of the 1987 Washington summit, see Oberdorfer, *The Turn,* 257–71.

632   **Neither of them has**   Michael Deaver interview, May 18, 1989.

632   **his Armageddon complex**   Michael P. Saba and Evan Hendricks, eds., *The Armageddon Network* (Brattleboro, Vt., 1984).

632   **"When it comes"**   See Ezekiel (RR's favorite book of prophecy), 38. His reference to *Meshech* connotes *Mushku,* the ancient Phyrigian kingdom in Anatolia, from whence the name *Moscow* might possibly be derived. For a study of RR's Armageddonophobia, see Halsell, *Prophecy and Politics.*

633   **[Sunday, May 29]**   Howard Baker interview, June 21, 1988; Frank Carlucci interview, July 5, 1988; Colin Powell interview, June 22, 1988. RR did recover enough memory to write in his diary that night: "I introduced my favorite pitch—why he should give his people religious freedom." RRP.

633   **"Few . . . are not"**   R. F. Christian, ed., *Tolstoy's Diaries* (New York, 1995), vol. 2, 405.

634   **[*Monday, May 30*]**   Dwayne Andreas interview, Mar. 8, 1995.

634   **Jim Billington [Librarian]**   Original text of Author's Diary, characterizing this as an "appalling gaffe," altered after a corrective letter from Dr. Billington, Oct. 2, 1999. RR's statement was no gaffe, but considered political rhetoric. Billington confirms that many members of the hierarchy were "visibly livid."

634   **Endless speeches**   According to Roy Medvedev, who attended, one of the speakers invoked an extraordinary trinity whereby "God created the world and Reagan and Gorbachev have saved it." No such words appear in the author's notes, but if such a hyperbole was indulged, it would seem to have been in line with the Christian imagery Gorbachev used to woo RR. Medvedev and Chiesa, *Time of Change,* pp. 273ff. For a detailed account of the 1988 Moscow summit, see Oberdorfer, *The Turn,* Ch. 7.

638   **We go to dine**   A silver-framed photograph prominently displayed on the table behind the President's desk in the Oval Office showed RR and Eisenhower, clad in golfing clothes, grinning together at their first meeting in 1965. The photograph's slightly crooked composition betrayed the fact that Holmes Tuttle, who introduced them, had been cropped out.

639   **"Reagan never even came"**   RR made good on this dereliction two and a half years later. See Prologue. Notwithstanding the author's pessimism in 1988, the Birthplace is once again (1999) a flourishing museum under local management.

37: The Shining City

641   **It was the eve**   EM Notes, Jan. 8, 1989.

641   **Dupuytren's contracture**   The involuntary inward curvature of RR's left fourth finger was first remarked by Dr. John Hutton in Mar. 1985. That night in front of the fire at Camp David, RR observed that "he could no longer twirl his revolver before holstering it." John Hutton Diary, Mar. 11, 1985, JHP. Edwards, *Early Reagan,* 177, reports that RR's father developed a similiar contracture in 1937.

642   **"Mr. President"**   The following dialogue is based on a tape recording by the author, AC, and EM Notes, Jan. 9, 1989.

644   **If circumstances should**   David Cecil, *Melbourne* (London, 1955), 156.

645   **"What about the homeless?"**   In 1994, a draft report by the Clinton Administration estimated that up to seven million Americans were homeless at the end of the Reagan era. *The New York Times,* Feb. 17, 1994.

646   **That printer of Udell's**   See p. 41.

646   **A few minutes later**   EM Notes, Jan. 8, 1989.

647   **his eyes, like Jeeves's**   P. G. Wodehouse, "Jeeves and the Impending Doom," *The Most of P. G. Wodehouse* (New York, 1969), 513.

647   **Does he glimpse**   See p. 80.

649   **And so, goodbye**   The text of RR's farewell speech is reproduced in Ritter and Henry, *Ronald Reagan: The Great Communicator,* 179–84.

649   **Thursday the nineteenth**   EM Notes, Jan. 19, 1989.

650   **His voice husked**   Ibid.

650   **At 4:15**   Ibid.

651   **Inauguration Day dawned**   Ibid., Jan. 20, 1989.

652   **there was a large crowd**   Ibid. The secretary's name was Kathy Reid.

Epilogue

655   **Four years**   The following account is taken entirely from EM Diary, Jan. 13, 1993.

656   **our trip to Tampico**   On May 10, 1992. See above, Prologue.

656   **Yet the following**   EM Diary, Jan. 14, 1993.

656   **Less than a month**   EM Diary, Feb. 7, 1993; EM to Kathy Osborne, Mar. 9, 1993, AC.

656   **After that, I visited**   John Hutton interview, Nov. 6, 1993; EM Diary, Apr. 2 and 3, 1993.

657   **It showed the five**   This famous photograph has been much reproduced. For other details about the dedication exercises at RRL, and a general description of the Library, see Edmund Morris, "A Celebration of Reagan," *The New Yorker,* Feb. 16, 1998.

657   **At five the next**   EM Diary and Notes, Apr. 3, 1993, AC.

657   **At the end of**   The proceedings of this conclave have been published: Eric J. Schmertz *et al., President Reagan and the World* (Westport, Conn., 1997). The following paragraphs are based on the author's informal report to RR, Apr. 28, 1993 (copy in AC).

658   *Let me tell*   Donald Regan Notes, Nov. 19, 1985, LC.

659   **Computers, not "imaginary lasers"**   This was a crack at the author, who had opined in his earlier speech that it was RR's belief in heaven-filling technology, no matter how impracticable, that made him such a tough negotiator at Geneva and Reykjavík.

661   **"I was the one"**   Brian Mulroney in interview, May 30, 1993. President Mitterrand's comment is roughly translatable as "He is in his own mind the God-appointed ruler of a priestly kingdom." A definition of *theocrat* in the Oxford English Dictionary would seem to apply to RR: "one who is ruled in civil affairs directly by God."

661   **It takes a secular**   Anyone doubting Mitterrand's sensuality should read Michael Paterniti's extraordinary account of his last meal in *Esquire* vol. 129, no. 5, May 1998.

662   **This comment**   See p. 635. The reference is to RR's favorite comic strip, the soap opera "Mary Worth."

662   **Oddly enough**   RR's willingness to let others take credit was amusingly demonstrated when Richard Darman claimed to have persuaded him to start keeping a diary some time after he took office in 1981. Actually, RR began the document of his own accord on Inauguration Day, but he never contested Darman's proud claim. Richard Darman interview, March 18, 1987; Martin Anderson interview, Aug. 8, 1989. See also *Nofziger,* 269–70.

662   **One further fact**   The author suggested, on the 1997 PBS documentary *Reagan,* that two RR diary entries, Sept. 26 and 27, 1987, show a "scary" detachment from reality. While the entries seem to speak for themselves in

recording, in different inks on two consecutive days, the arrival of NR's brother and his wife to stay, some family members point out that either or both could have been written up much later, when the President's memory was not fresh.

662 **On December 20, 1993**   The following section is taken entirely from EM Diary, this date.

663 **"cool intensity"**   Brown, *Reagan and Reality,* 50.

663 **When Richard Nixon**   EM Diary, Apr. 22 and 26–27, 1994.

664 **That summer**   John Hutton interview, July 8, 1998.

664 **Discussing the news**   EM Diary, Nov. 6, 1994. See also Appendix, no. 3.

664 **Dutch delayed**   Frederick J. Ryan interview, Dec. 9, 1994; John Hutton interview, Feb. 24, 1995.

666 **The letter was**   EM Diary, Nov. 6, 1994. RR's letter is now on permanent exhibit at RRL.

666 **Later, I called**   Max Kampelman interview, Nov. 21, 1994; EM Diary, Nov. 22, 1994. The award was presented to a largely uncomprehending RR on Dec. 15, 1994.

667 **In Los Angeles**   The author published a slightly different version of this section as "This Living Hand," *The New Yorker,* Jan. 16, 1995. Extra details from EM Diary, Dec. 9, 1994.

667 **a pleasant riverside watercolor**   See p. 655. This painting, by Fran Swarbrick of Dixon, Ill., now hangs in the VIP suite at RRL.

668 **The sky was neither**   EM Notes, May 19, 1990, and Apr. 4, 1995; RR Diary, May 5, 1985; Slansky, "Bitburg," SLA; RR, qu. in *The New York Times,* May 6, 1965. See also pp. 517, 532

669 *What's gone before*   Conclusion of Part Two of Goethe's *Faust,* translated by the author. *(Alles Vergängliche / Ist nur ein Gleichnis; / Das Unzulängliche / Hier wird's Ereignis; / Das Unbeschreibliche / Hier ist's getan; / Das Ewig-Weibliche / Zieht uns hinan.)*

670 **At the time of writing**   Patti Davis interview, July 7, 1993; John Hutton interviews, Feb. 24 and Nov. 8, 1995; Sept. 10, 1996; July 7, 1997; and July 8, 1998. Since RR's Alzheimer's diagnosis, the former White House physician has periodically, and at his own expense, relieved NR while she takes restorative vacations.

670 **My second pilgrimage**   The following account is based on EM Notes, Aug. 3, 1998.

672 *You're just another*   RR interview, Jan. 27, 1991.

672 **"breastward out of peril."**   Joseph L. Grucci, "Pittsburgh Memoir," Pennsylvania State University *Liberal Arts Alumni Review* 1.2, Winter 1984, 6.

Appendix

673 ***These Leaves Your Lips***   Written after a Moviola replay of RR's first movie, *Love Is on the Air,* fifty years after its first release.

674 ***Old Moon***   Written for the Alzheimer's Association of Greater Washington, Oct. 5, 1995.

ILLUSTRATIONS

The small illustrations above each chapter heading are represented in italics.

INDEX